Advertising & Marketing Law: Cases and Materials

Fifth Edition • Summer 2020

Rebecca Tushnet
Harvard Law
&
Eric Goldman
Santa Clara University School of Law

Table of Contents

CHAPTER 4: DECEPTION

CHAPTER 8: CONSUMER CLASS ACTIONS

CHAPTER 9: FALSE ADVERTISING PRACTICE AND REMEDIES

CHAPTER 10: OTHER BUSINESS TORTS

CHAPTER 11: COPYRIGHTS

CHAPTER 13: COMPETITIVE RESTRICTIONS

CHAPTER 19: CASE STUDIES IN HOUSING AND POLITICAL ADVERTISING
ONLINE ONLY

PREFACE TO THE FIFTH EDITION

Portions © 2012–2020 Rebecca Tushnet and Eric Goldman

To make this book as accessible and easy-to-use for readers as possible, we have deliberately priced this casebook low and provided a DRM-free e-book. If you think your friends and colleagues would like their own copies, we'd appreciate it if you encouraged them to buy their own low-cost copies rather than sharing your copy with them.

About the Authors

Eric Goldman is a professor of law and co-director of the High Tech Law Institute at Santa Clara University School of Law. Before he became a full-time academic in 2002, he practiced Internet law for eight years in the Silicon Valley. His research and teaching focuses on Internet, intellectual property and advertising law topics, and he blogs on those topics at the Technology & Marketing Law Blog, http://blog.ericgoldman.org. Email: egoldman@gmail.com.

Rebecca Tushnet is a professor of law at Harvard Law School. She clerked for Associate Justice David H. Souter and worked on intellectual property and advertising litigation before beginning teaching. Her academic work focuses on copyright, trademark and advertising law. Her blog is at http://tushnet.blogspot.com. Email: rtushnet@law.harvard.edu.

A Note to Professors

If you are adopting this book for your course, please email us. We can provide you with a variety of support materials, including our course notes and PowerPoint slide decks as well as access to a database of case-related props. We are also working on a teacher's manual.

A Note to Students

If you are interested in more information, consider the following resources:

- Professor Tushnet's blog at http://tushnet.blogspot.com or Twitter account at http://twitter.com/rtushnet.
- Professor Goldman's blog at http://blog.ericgoldman.org or Twitter account at http://twitter.com/ericgoldman.
- The ABA Antitrust Section's Advertising Disputes & Litigation Committee (at http://www.abanet.org/dch/committee.cfm?com=AT311570) has a number of useful resources as well, including an email list. It also puts on teleconferences about careers in advertising law.

You may also want to check out Professor Goldman's blog post on Pursuing a Career in Advertising Law, http://blog.ericgoldman.org/personal/archives/2012/07/careers_in_adve.html. The post includes course recommendations, too.

We are slowly developing a complementary website for the book. Check out our in-process efforts at http://www.advertisinglawbook.com/.

Please email us with your corrections to this casebook and any suggestions for improvement!

If You Bought a Hard Copy of the Book

If you bought a hard copy of this book: While we've done our best to make the hard copy version of the book useful to you, the hard copy is missing some features, such as color images, clickable links and keyword searching. You may find a PDF version of the book helpful to complement your hard copy version. Please email Professor Goldman (**egoldman@gmail.com**) your purchase receipt (showing which edition you bought), and he will happily email you a PDF at no extra cost.

A Note about International Advertising Law

On occasion, this book discusses international advertising laws and perspectives; however, we have deliberately chosen to focus on U.S. law. International advertising laws differ from U.S. law in many important ways, so it would be hard to address all of these major differences sufficiently. For more information about legal issues in international advertising, please consider the resources at http://www.galalaw.com/.

Editing Practices

Some notes about our editing practices:

- Textual omissions are noted with ellipses.
- Omitted footnotes are not indicated, but all footnote numbers are original.
- In-text citations are omitted without indication (including parenthetical explanations and some parallel citations).
- Although we usually preserved the original formatting (such as italics, bold and block quotes), some of this formatting may have changed or been lost in the conversion.

To improve readability, we have aggressively stripped out case citations and parenthetical explanations (more so than most casebooks). If you are interested in the case's/author's full text or if you intend to quote or cite any republished materials in the book, we *strongly* recommend that you obtain and reference a copy of the original materials.

To make the book more functional for you, we've liberally provided hyperlinks to underlying source materials throughout the book. You'll see these as blue text in the PDF. Not all sources are linked and, of course, links are likely to rot. Still, we hope you find them helpful.

Acknowledgements

Thanks are due to many people, including students in Professor Goldman's and Professor Tushnet's respective classes who provided feedback on drafts. Tamara Piety of the University of Tulsa organized a 2011 conference on the casebook, and participants were thoughtful and generous in their responses. Special thanks to James Grimmelmann, Sam Halabi and Brant Harrell for their comments. The authors also would like to extend special thanks to Susanna McCrea, Georgetown Law's manuscript editor, for her work.

1.   Why Study Advertising Law?

You've made an excellent choice to study advertising and marketing law! Some reasons why:

A Horizontal Course

Many of the courses you study in law school examine a single legal doctrine in some depth, such as contracts or criminal law. This course is structured differently. Instead of a deep "vertical" look at one legal doctrine, this course will survey a lot of disparate topics "horizontally." This course addresses material that may overlap in part with other law school courses—contracts, trademarks, copyrights, an intellectual property survey course, Internet law, constitutional law, consumer law, professional responsibility (especially with respect to attorney advertising), business torts/advanced torts, entertainment/sports law and many others.

Horizontal evaluation of legal issues is a skill most lawyers use daily, and this course will give you a sense of how to do it. Because of its realism, students often find this doctrinal heterogeneity liberating; however, if you've never taken a horizontal course before, it will require some adjustment on your part. We'll cover a lot of doctrines relatively superficially. You should not expect to master the nuances of each doctrine covered in this course. Instead, you should focus on how the various legal doctrines interact with each other.

An Industry-specific Course

This course focuses on a single industry: the advertising and marketing industry. You will get to know that industry in depth, including the business practices and lingo used by industry insiders.

Relevance to Your Practice

Advertising legal issues are ubiquitous. Every for-profit business needs to generate consumer demand, and even nonprofits advertise. Your clients will be engaging in advertising and marketing from the moment they launch their enterprises—and they will need legal help doing so. If you become an in-house attorney, it is even more likely that legal questions on advertising and marketing will hit your desk. You will have to consider law as well as ethics: What kinds of businesses are you willing to represent? What kinds of claims are you willing to approve?

Unlike consumer law courses, this course also covers lawsuits by competitors, rather than just consumer lawsuits and concomitant regulation. Nonetheless, consumer lawsuits are an important part of the enforcement puzzle and create substantial demand for both plaintiff and defense attorneys in this area.

Fun

Because you've been exposed to advertising all of your life, you already have first-hand experience with many of the issues we explore in this course. In fact, you may have seen or heard some of the ads spawning the litigation covered in this book. Even if not, advertising is an integral part of pop culture, and this is a rare course where enjoying television or the radio can improve your understanding of the course material—but only if you *don't* skip the ads!

Jobs?!

One report estimated that over a half-million employees work in the advertising industry. *Economic Impact of Advertising in the United States*, IHS.com, March 2015. You might join them, or you might find work providing legal support to them.

2.   A Few Words About the History of Advertising

Advertising is as old as commerce. For as long as vendors have sought to sell goods and services, they have needed to inform and persuade consumers to transact with them.

Advertisers' ability to reach consumer audiences has been inextricably linked to prevailing technologies. Before printing was widely available, businesses principally relied on advertising techniques that could only reach local audiences, such as criers in the town square and signage. A retailer's location also played a key role in generating consumer demand. Numerous 19th century "unfair competition" cases involved a new entrant that opened a store physically proximate to an existing well-known business and used ambiguous or confusing signage to siphon some consumers looking for the competitor's location.

Many manufacturers branded their goods with unique identifiers such as symbols. These symbols acted as signals of quality to future buyers—after all, manufacturers depended on their reputation for quality, and poor-quality goods would degrade that reputation. The symbol also acted simultaneously as a form of advertising. Consumers who encountered the goods after they had been purchased by someone else could learn where to procure goods of a similar quality. Manufacturers' use of identifiers on their goods gave rise to trademark law and the law of geographic indications of origin.

Technological innovations have created new ways to reach consumers, which have spurred changes in advertising. For example, proliferation of the printing press allowed advertisers to cost-effectively print handbills to give to consumers. The printing press led to print periodicals such as newspapers and magazines, and periodicals started running print advertising in the early 1700s. Ben Franklin was an important early innovator in print advertising, along with his other contributions to society.

The second half of the 1800s saw several interrelated technological innovations that spawned the modern advertising industry. First, industrialization improved manufacturing economies of scale, allowing manufacturers to cost-effectively produce mass identical copies of their goods. Manufacturers producing a high volume of goods concomitantly needed to reach increasingly larger markets. Second, railroads reduced manufacturers' distribution costs, enabling them to spread their mass-produced goods to new markets; however, this broadened geographic reach meant that manufacturers could not rely solely on local advertising to build consumer awareness of their goods. Manufacturers needed efficient ways to reach larger consumer audiences, and this fueled demand for mass-media advertising—first print, then postal mail, radio and TV advertising, and more recently Internet advertising.

Iconic Ad Campaigns

Occasionally, an advertising campaign transcends into popular culture. In many cases, iconic ads are generation-specific because the ad campaigns only run for a limited period of time and are therefore unknown to people who weren't around or were too young to remember them. The 1970s and 1980s produced many iconic ads because of media concentration—a small number of media outlets could reach large segments of consumers—which meant that many consumers saw the same ads.

In 1999, *Advertising Age* identified the Marlboro Man as the top icon of the 20th century.

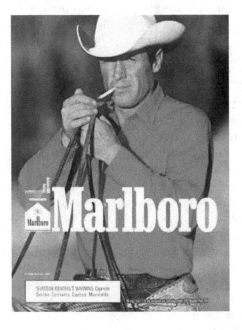

Advertising Age also ranked the top 100 advertising campaigns. How many of the top ten do you recognize?

#10: Avis, "We try harder" (1963)
#9: Clairol, "Does she . . . or doesn't she?" (1957)
#8: Miller Lite beer, "Tastes great, less filling" (1974)
#7: Absolut Vodka, the Absolut Bottle (1981)
#6: DeBeers, "A diamond is forever" (1948)
#5: McDonald's, "You deserve a break today" (1971)
#4: Nike, "Just do it" (1988)
#3: Marlboro, the Marlboro Man (1955)
#2: Coca-Cola, "The pause that refreshes" (1929)
#1: Volkswagen, "Think Small" (1959)

Sometimes, specific ads become iconic. For example, the line "Where's the Beef?" from a Wendy's TV advertisement spawned countless parodies and played a key role in the 1984 presidential campaign, when Walter Mondale ridiculed his Democratic primary opponent Gary Hart by asking "Where's the beef?" in response to Gary Hart's promise of "new ideas." The Old Spice Guy launched an acting career on the basis of his confident delivery and sculpted body shown in an ad, claiming to be "the man your man could smell like."

Over the past three decades, reaching a majority of consumers in a single ad campaign has become increasingly challenging. Consumers have more ways to consume media, and the proliferation of options has fragmented consumer audiences. Further, technology that makes it easier to skip or bypass ads, such as digital video recorders and streaming video, has reduced the odds that numerous consumers will see any given TV ad. Meanwhile, marketers are producing more specialized products targeted for ever-smaller consumer niches, so many advertisers no longer feel the need to reach large groups of consumers.

Even so, a truly fresh ad concept can still achieve wide recognition among most consumers. A more recent example is the 2018 Super Bowl "It's a Tide Ad" campaign, featuring David Harbour from the Netflix TV show "Stranger Things." The ads parodied traditional TV ads before switching to reveal that they were really ads for the laundry detergent Tide. This parody-and-interruption approach spawned many memes and copycats. Late 2019's Peloton ad also sparked a widespread conversation, not all of it complimentary.

3.   **Advertising Pervasiveness**

According to one estimate, advertisers spent well over $350 billion a year in the US on advertising in 2019, and they were projected (before the novel coronavirus) to spend over $390 billion in 2020. Erik Oster, *U.S. Advertising and Marketing Spend to Grow to Nearly $390 Billion in 2020,* Adweek, Jan. 17, 2020. Historically, advertising has constituted 2% or more of the United States' gross domestic product (GDP).* These amounts only include the

---

* A different study estimated that "US advertisers will spend nearly $565 on paid media, on average, to reach each consumer in the country in 2014." eMarketer, *Global Ad Spending Growth to Double This Year*, July 9, 2014, http://www.emarketer.com/Article/Global-Ad-Spending-Growth-Double-This-Year/1010997.

out-of-pocket expenditures of advertisers; they don't include the salary costs of marketing employees and may not include other costs of preparing ad copy, such as licensing intellectual property or retaining freelancers. As a result, the total economic scope of the advertising and marketing industry is likely even higher.

Here's one breakdown of how the total advertising dollars were allocated by medium in 2009 (on the left) and 2019 (on the right):

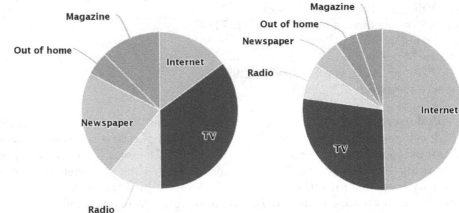

Source: Publicis Groupe's Zenith (Advertising Expenditure Forecasts, December 2019). Note: "Out of home" advertising includes billboards and cinema.

These charts show the growing dominance of Internet advertising and the concomitant decline of print advertising. Billboards are one of the few other sectors not declining. *See* Zachary Crockett, *The Hottest Advertising Trend of 2018? Billboards.*, THE HUSTLE, Nov. 30, 2018.

Advertising-Saturated Society

Wherever people go, advertisements will find them. There are ads on eggs, subway turnstiles, motion sickness bags on airplanes, bins in airport security lines, and other non-traditional advertising media. *See* Louise Story, *Anywhere the Eye Can See, It's Likely to See an Ad*, N.Y. TIMES, Jan. 15, 2007. Ads can be tattooed onto people (sometimes called "skinvertising"), placed on panhandler signs (sometimes called "bumvertising"), and placed in men's urinals. What's the most striking place you've ever seen an ad?

Collectively, we are exposed to a huge number of ads every day. No one knows exactly how many, and this quantity is often subject to hyperbole. David Shenk, author of the book *Data Smog* (1997), estimated that the average American encountered 560 daily advertising messages in 1971 and over 3,000 messages per day in 1997. Other estimates from around the same time were that the average American was exposed to 245 commercial messages each day. Even at the lower estimate, the average person would still encounter over 15 commercial messages every waking hour.

4.   Consumers Often Dislike Advertising

We all have examples of advertising we like: ads that saved us money or time. Ads that made us laugh out loud. Ads that evoke a special time in our lives or made us nostalgic. Ads that even moved us to tears. Sometimes, we go out of our way to seek out advertising—some folks arrive early at movie theaters to catch the previews. Some of us search Google to find advertisements.

Yet, if you are considering a career in advertising law, you need to accept a simple truth: Most consumers dislike most advertising most of the time. This general anti-ad sentiment holds true in every historical period, demographic segment, geography, and culture. This means that consumers try to avoid advertising in general, regardless of whether they'd like a particular ad if they saw it.

Thus, with respect to any particular advertisement, the odds are very high that most people will dislike that ad. Many advertisers—even those who understand the broad consumer antipathy towards ads—believe that *their* ads are the exception. They are almost always mistaken.

Eric Goldman, A Coasean Analysis of Marketing, 2006 Wis. L. Rev. 1151 (excerpt)

> Consumers hate spam. They hate pop-up ads, junk faxes, and telemarketing. Pick any marketing method, and consumers probably say they hate it. In extreme cases, unwanted marketing can cause consumers to experience "spam rage."
>
> There are many reasons for consumers' deep antipathy toward marketing, but a principal cause is that consumers get too much of it. According to a 2004 Yankelovich study, "61% feel the amount of marketing and advertising is out of control; and 65% feel constantly bombarded with too much marketing and advertising."
>
> Worse, the volume of marketing probably will increase as technology continues to lower marketing distribution costs and marketers seek out new ways to reach consumers. As one commentator has said, "marketers all over the world soak up every square inch of space, every extra second of time . . . . Every idle moment you possess is seen by some business somewhere as an opportunity to interrupt you and demand more of your attention." Because human attention is a scarce and largely fixed resource, continued growth in marketing volume creates a seemingly unavoidable crisis. Eventually, consumers may experience information overload, where their attention will be overrun by too much marketing. Some might feel that they have reached this point already.

NOTES AND QUESTIONS

The Medium is the Message. Consumers' antipathy towards ads varies with the delivery medium. Empirical studies repeatedly show that consumers overwhelmingly hate telemarketing more than any other form of advertising (door-to-door sales also garner massive consumer antipathy, but the practice is now rare). Spam is also heavily reviled, but the efficacy of anti-spam technologies has softened this attitude a bit. In contrast, while consumers dislike broadcast advertising, far fewer hate those ads compared to telemarketing. So consider this: The exact same ad copy could be broadcast on radio and used in telemarketing, yet it would produce a much stronger negative reaction in the latter form. Why does consumer response vary based on the advertising medium? *See* Eric Goldman, *Where's the Beef? Dissecting Spam's Purported Harms*, 22 J. MARSHALL J. COMPUTER & INFO. L. 13 (2003).

Why do consumers dislike advertising in general so much? Do *you* dislike most ads? Try a thought experiment: Imagine a world where advertising simply did not exist. Would you prefer that world over our current situation? What, if anything, would be lost? *See generally* Eric Goldman, *Fantasize About A World Without Advertising? Try Cuba*, FORBES TERTIUM QUID, Aug. 22, 2013. If you had a magic wand and could eliminate some or all ads, what kinds of ads would you allow, and in which media would you allow advertising? One legal scholar has argued that the rise of Internet search engines that allow consumers to find out factual information about products and services, if and when they want to know, removes the typical justifications for allowing persuasive, nonfactual advertising like the iconic campaigns listed above, which he contends should generally be banned as anticompetitive. Ramsi A. Woodcock, *The Obsolescence of Advertising in the Information Age*, 127 Yale L.J. 2204 (2018).

Advertising as a Negative Externality. Critics often characterize advertising as a negative externality similar to pollution. They argue that advertisers create uninternalized social costs—such as consumer annoyance—by "overproducing" ads (i.e., exceeding socially optimal levels of advertising). Based on this premise, critics sometimes argue that advertising should be regulated like an environmental pollutant. *See, e.g.*, Dennis Hirsch, *Protecting the Inner Environment: What Privacy Regulation Can Learn from Environmental Law*, 41 GA. L. REV. 1 (2006). Are advertisers properly analogized to smoke-belching factories? Why or why not? *See* Eric Goldman, *A Coasean Analysis of Marketing*, 2006 WIS. L. REV. 1151.

Advertising as the "Cost" of Content. Many publishers distribute valuable editorial content to consumers with the financial support of advertising, saving consumers from having to pay cash to obtain the content. Often, the ads are presented as what marketing guru Seth Godin has called "interruption marketing," i.e., the ads are intermixed with the editorial content in a way that interrupts consumers' consumption of the content.

Publishers sometimes characterize advertisements as the "price" consumers must pay for the free editorial content. For example, Jamie Kellner, the CEO and chairman of Turner Broadcasting, responded in 2002 to the proliferation of DVRs (and the ability to fast-forward through TV ads) by saying: "It's theft. Your contract with the network when you get the show is you're going to watch the [ad] spots. Otherwise you couldn't get the show on an ad-supported basis. Any time you skip a commercial … you're actually stealing the programming." He did acknowledge that "there's a certain amount of tolerance for going to the bathroom." Do you agree with Kellner's characterizations?

If advertising is a "cost" to consumers, naturally consumers will try to reduce their "costs" by avoiding the ads. This manifests itself in a variety of ways: the impulse to switch radio stations when ads come on; the development of "banner ad blindness," where consumers instinctively ignore banner advertisements on web pages; and skipping television ads by fast-forwarding through them or multi-tasking (getting a snack or going to the bathroom) during the commercial breaks. Sometimes, if technology, law, and business models allow, consumers may enlist outside assistance: using an ad blocker on a web browser, or paying extra to a video service for an ad-free experience. What steps do you take to ignore advertising? When do you pay attention to the ads? How did you learn these coping mechanisms?

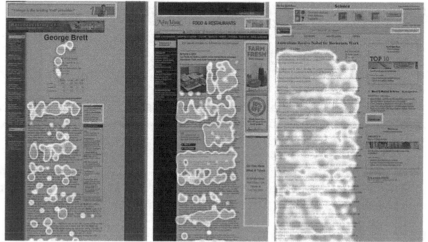

[Figure: three eye-tracking studies showing that web visitors ignore banner ads (shown in the yellow highlighted boxes). Used with permission of Jakob Nielsen, http://www.useit.com.]

When advertisers treat ads as a "cost," they condition consumers to avoid ads—a net loss for the entire advertising community. It would be much better if consumers were conditioned to expect that the ads they receive are helpful and relevant, in which case consumers would *want* those ads. Unfortunately, achieving this degree of advertising relevancy has proven exceptionally hard in practice. *See generally* Daniel G. Goldstein et al, *The Economic and Cognitive Costs of Annoying Display Advertisements*, 51 J. MKTG. RES. 742 (2014).

Consumer Distrust. Consumers say that they distrust advertising and rank it as generally not believable. *See* Dakota Shane, *96 Percent of Consumers Don't Trust Ads*, INC., May 31, 2019. At the same, most people know that advertising changes consumer behavior. And consumers do enjoy particular ad campaigns, even turning them into cultural touchstones, as Section 2 indicated. Do you have any thoughts about how we might reconcile this apparent paradox? Consider this as you read the first few sections of Chapter 2.

Despite the Distrust, Does Advertising Actually Work? The eye-tracking images showing "banner blindness" aren't unique to online advertising. A well-known quote, attributed to retail mogul John Wanamaker, says: "Half the money I spend on advertising is wasted; the trouble is I don't know which half." Even highly informational banner ads, presented to consumers searching for specific terms, may not have much effect, at least for brands that are already well known. *See* Tom Blake et al., *Consumer Heterogeneity and Paid Search Effectiveness: A Large Scale Field Experiment*, 83 ECONOMETRICA 155 (2015).

Consumer behavior is so erratic that it is hard to say what works even when a marketer has massive amounts of data at its disposal. *See* Randall A. Lewis & Justin M. Rao, *The Unfavorable Economics of Measuring the Returns to Advertising* (Sept. 19, 2014) (research by Google and Yahoo! data scientists). *But see* Randall A. Lewis & David H. Reiley, *Does Retail Advertising Work? Measuring the Effects of Advertising on Sales via a Controlled Experiment on Yahoo!* (June 8, 2011) (research by data scientists at Google finding that display ads on Yahoo! led to more purchases in stores).

Even if advertising doesn't directly translate to sales, it may still indirectly boost sales. Maybe most advertising by major advertisers is really brand advertising, familiarizing the audience—sometimes against its will—with the advertiser so that it seems familiar and reliable. See Tim Ambler & E. Ann Hollier, *The Waste in Advertising is the Part That Works*, J. ADVERTISING RES., Dec. 2004, at 375. As Internet evangelist Doc Searls has written:

> In terms of direct effects (what direct response marketing wants . . .), 99.x% of advertising is wasted. In terms of indirect effects (which old fashioned brand advertising wants), 100% might be effective.
>
> . . . Brand advertising doesn't want to get personal. That would be too expensive, might creep people out, and isn't the idea anyway, because brand advertising isn't looking for a direct response. All it wants is to make an impression. Not a sale.
>
> . . . [W]hen [I] replace my busted subwoofer, I am far more likely to be attracted to brands I know than to be swayed by advertising targeted at me because robots that follow me suspect I'm looking for a subwoofer at this moment in time.

Doc Searls, *Rethinking John Wanamaker*, Jan 20, 2016. What do you think of this argument?

5. Some Key Issues

Throughout the semester, keep your eyes on the following key issues:

The Advertising/Non-Advertising Divide

This book is specifically about advertising as a discrete subset of information in our society. In theory, then, we should be able to confidently and accurately classify information into "advertising" and "not advertising." In practice, those categorizations are messy. First, the term "advertising" doesn't have one universally accepted definition. Second, advertisers and publishers are constantly developing new ways of delivering their advertising messages. These ongoing innovations put stress on legal doctrines. Lawyers need to recognize when their clients are advertising and what issues might arise.

Telling the Truth

The top-line objective of false advertising law is simple: Advertisers must tell consumers the truth. But as you've surely learned in school, determining what's "true" or "false" is rarely simple. Typically, false advertising law is interested in how consumers perceive an advertiser's claims. But groups of consumers may evaluate or understand claims differently, and we have to consider both the express claims advanced by the advertiser as well as any implied claims that consumers might derive from the information they receive. So complying with the basic tenet of advertising law—tell the truth—turns out to be more nuanced than you might anticipate.

As Jean Wegman Burns has written:

> Most areas of life lack the precision of mathematics, and the search for a single, unchanging, and ascertainable "truth" is a near impossible quest. To choose just one example, a court has determined that it is misleading to label a vegetable-based food product as "gelatin," despite the fact that the general public has no clear idea of whether gelatin is an animal- or vegetable-derived product. Compounding the problem of discerning the "truth" of an advertising claim, courts are often faced with advertising claims based on highly technical areas of science, medicine, or engineering in which they have no expertise. In addition . . . courts must often determine the truth or falsity of advertising jargon written in "catchy" phrases containing broad claims that do not lend themselves to precise analysis.

Jean Wegman Burns, *Confused Jurisprudence: False Advertising Under the Lanham Act*, 79 B.U.L. REV. 807 (1999).

Because truth isn't binary, advertising lawyers constantly encounter ethical challenges. Even if an advertisement is "truthful" (or, at least, truthful enough) in the legal sense, when should advertising lawyers still object to it as unethical? As you read about the ads at issue in this book, ask yourself whether you would have approved the advertisement in question if you had been the advertiser's lawyer. If not, why not? And do you think you could explain your position well enough to overcome the pressure of marketing folks who really, *really* want to make the claim?

You might also self-reflect whether your internal ethical standards towards advertising become more (or less) flexible as you study the materials this semester. After seeing so many egregious examples of advertisements, will you become more tolerant of ads that merely stretch the truth? If you're an advertising lawyer dealing with clients who, every day, are asking you to approve ads filled with puffery and not-exactly-deceptive-but-not-exactly-truthful claims, will you become desensitized to the grey areas between truthful and deceptive?

Who Regulates Advertising?

Advertising is subject to a complex mosaic of regulators and regulations, including federal, state and local requirements. There are also many self-regulatory efforts, both across all industries (such as the National Advertising Division, "NAD," discussed in Chapter 3) and within individual industries.

Advertisers face numerous potential plaintiffs, including:

- *Government agencies*, especially consumer protection agencies such as the Federal Trade Commission and state analogues. Other agencies may have enforcement powers against advertisers in specific media or specific fields, such as the Federal Communications Commission and the Food and Drug Administration. Indeed, most major federal agencies have some advertising-related regulations in their regulatory domain.
- *Competitors*. Government agencies tend to focus on the most severe or pervasive advertising abuses. For everything else, we rely heavily on businesses to monitor and contest the errors of their competitors.
- *Consumers*. Individual consumers can and do sue advertisers, but most consumer lawsuits against advertisers involve aggregated claims in the form of class action lawsuits. Because class action lawsuits are a key part of advertising regulation, developments in class action procedures and practices may have significant implications for advertising law.
- *Rightsowners*, including copyright owners, trademark owners and individuals asserting their personality rights.

Partially reflecting this array of plaintiffs, this book divides into four major parts and a coda:

- Chapters 1 and 2 provide an overview and define the key terms.
- Chapters 3 through 9 explore false advertising claims, including claims by government agencies, competitors and consumers.
- Chapters 10 through 15 discuss legal restrictions on advertising other than regulations of truth/falsity, including intellectual property rights, privacy, and antitrust law; similarly, Chapters 16 and 17 address recurring issues that apply across advertising and marketing campaigns, often but not always intersecting with truth/falsity issues.
- Chapter 18 explores a sampling of the regulations applicable to marketing of food, drugs, and related products, while Chapter 19 (available only online) looks at two special advertising issues: discrimination in advertising and political advertising.

As you go through, you should ask yourself who is the *best* enforcer to stop advertiser misstatements or misdeeds. Each option has pros and cons. As you review the material in this book, consider if you can conceive of a more effective regulatory scheme.

Who Is Liable for a Problematic Ad?

As you review this casebook's materials, take note of the defendants' identity. Typically the advertiser is responsible for its choices, but a variety of other players are potentially liable as well, including company executives, ad agencies, publishers and more. Think about how that legal exposure affects the behavior of these secondary actors.

What is advertising? In many cases, we know it when we see it; however, those instincts do not always translate into precise or predictable legal conclusions.

Advertising is more heavily regulated than other types of speech and receives reduced constitutional protection. Yet, we sometimes struggle to explain why we regulate advertising differently than other means of human communication. This chapter will attempt to define advertising for purposes of legal regulation and explore some justifications for developing advertising-specific regulations.

1.   Definitions

Before we address the legal definitions of advertising in section 3 of this chapter, we'll survey some key terminology and concepts.

Advertising vs. Marketing vs. Sales

Advertising. Communications scholars often characterize "advertising" as paid persuasive communication that has an identified sponsor and occurs via mass media. These can include "marketing communications"/"commercial persuasion," special events, stealth marketing (where sponsorship isn't disclosed), public relations, and corporate communications that might appear in news stories.

Legal definitions of advertising do not track these theorists' definitions. In particular, this book does not restrict advertising to mass media because the legal regulation of promotional communication extends beyond that—but how far beyond is often uncertain.

Marketing. Marketing experts often refer to the "Four Ps of Marketing": product, place, price and promotion. *Product* refers to designing commercial offerings based on consumer preferences. *Place* stands for the distribution channels used to deliver the offering to consumers. *Price* is price-setting, such as using a low price to beat the competition or a high price to position the product as a luxury good. *Promotion* includes advertising, press relations, product placement, sports event sponsorships, partnerships with other organizations, and sales.

Each "P" offers options for sellers to differentiate themselves from their competition. For example, some sellers compete principally based on price; others compete by developing non-traditional distribution channels (e.g., selling products via in-home parties instead of retail stores). Advertising and sales are other ways for competitors to differentiate themselves.

Advertising v. Sales. Although both are considered "promotion," advertising is often distinguished from sales both in content and in the personnel responsible for carrying it out.

Typically, advertising stimulates general consumer interest in the advertiser's offerings. *See, e.g.,* the Merriam-Webster dictionary definition of advertising ("the action of calling something to the attention of the public especially by paid announcements"). Some types of transactions are complicated enough that buyers benefit from individual counseling about their purchase. "Sales" refers to this individual counseling by salespeople.

Consider how the process can work in automobile transactions. Auto manufacturers advertise to get consumers to consider their models. Auto retailers ("dealers") advertise to get consumers to choose them over other dealers. Even in the relatively rare cases where the advertising efforts "make the sale" (i.e., convince consumers to purchase a car without any further persuasion), many consumers need individual counseling to decide about specific models, customizable options, financing, trade-ins, etc. Thus, typically, good auto advertising gets consumers interested enough to show up at the dealer; the salesperson takes over from there to close the deal.

The Different Purposes of Advertising

To make things more complicated, advertising can have different objectives. Advertising by for-profit enterprises (as opposed to cause advertising and political advertising) can be organized into at least four categories:

- *Direct Response Advertising* (sometimes called "direct marketing"): This type of advertising seeks to get an immediate response (such as a sale) from consumers. Examples include telemarketing and infomercials imploring viewers to "CALL NOW!"

- *Brand or Image Advertising*: Brand advertising has the opposite intent from direct response advertising. Instead of trying to get consumers to act now, brand advertising seeks to define and reinforce the brand in consumers' minds as a way of affecting future consumer decisions. Successful brand advertising establishes and increases consumer loyalty for future transactions. Examples include Nike's television advertising and the advertising for most luxury goods. The slogan "GE brings good things to life" is an example of "image" advertising designed to enhance consumer perceptions of the GE brand.

- *Informational Advertising*: Another type of advertising is designed to get the facts—product specifications, product availability, price—out to consumers. An example: standard grocery store circulars showing products and prices.

- *Ideological or Issue Advertising*: Advertising can also have political or public service objectives, and publishers regularly accept payment for such ads (or "donate" time and space for them). Philip Morris ads touting freedom of choice are examples of issue advertising. (Philip Morris sells tobacco products.)

2. Why Does Advertising Exist?

Advertising plays several roles in our society. This part highlights three complementary explanations for the existence of advertisers: (1) advertising helps vendors maximize profits; (2) advertising improves competition; and (3) advertising influences consumer behavior. We'll begin to discuss some of the socially disadvantageous consequences associated with these motivating forces.

A. Advertising and Profit Maximization

If consumers were omniscient, advertising would not be necessary; consumers would know all of the competitive offerings and each vendor's trustworthiness, so there would not be any educational or informational benefits from ads. In contrast to that theoretical ideal, the real world has many information deficiencies. It takes time for consumers to research product availability, pricing information and vendor trustworthiness. Advertising can fill these information gaps for consumers. (Some critics complain that advertising hurts consumers' information management rather than helping; we'll address those complaints later).

From an advertiser's standpoint, advertising is a necessary cost of doing business. Although some commercial offerings become successful solely by word-of-mouth or based on other factors like customer foot traffic from a prime physical location, many advertisers need to inform consumers of their availability and competitive superiority.

When advertisers decide how much to spend on advertising, the answer is theoretically simple: Advertisers should keep buying advertising until it stops being profitable. In economic terms, the advertiser should advertise until the marginal dollar of advertising (the marginal cost) produces only one dollar of incremental profit (the marginal benefit).

You can see how an advertiser might maximize profits through a highly stylized example involving search engine advertisers. Search engines pit companies against each other in a bidding war over keywords. Assume that when users enter a keyword into the search engine, the highest bidder's advertisement is prominently displayed at the top of the page; lower bidders go below, and predictably get fewer consumer clicks (in fact, search ad sorting algorithms consider the consumers' likelihood of clicking on the advertiser's ads, not just advertisers' bids). Further assume that for every 100 clicks on the advertisement, the advertiser makes one sale with an average gross profit of $10 (meaning that each click has an expected gross profit of $0.10).* Further assume that for the keyword, the advertiser anticipates the following results:

Bid Per Click	Anticipated Clicks	Gross Profit	Click Costs	Net Profit
$0.10	1,200	$120	$120	$0
$0.09	1,000	$100	$90	$10
$0.08	800	$80	$64	$16
$0.07	600	$60	$42	$18
$0.06	400	$40	$24	$16
$0.05	200	$20	$10	$10
$0	0	$0	$0	$0

You can visualize net profits in this diagram:

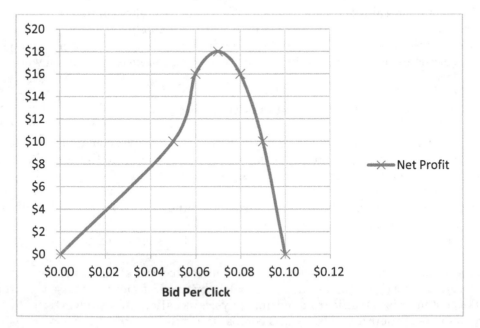

---

* Special note for economics geeks: In a perfectly competitive market, advertisers should not make any "profit" at all after internalizing the cost of capital. If so, the $10 "profit" represents the return on capital.

As the diagram shows, bidding 7 cents per click delivers the highest total amount of net profit, so that's the optimal bid for the advertiser. Bidding 8 or 9 cents will increase the number of anticipated clicks and gross profit, but those extra clicks cost more than the revenue they generate, so the extra expenditures reduce net profit.

Note: Google tells advertisers how many clicks they can anticipate based on different bid prices, but its estimates aren't reliable. Thus, the above example assumes away the advertiser's significant challenge of accurately estimating the numbers. Many advertisers—even large advertisers you might assume are fairly sophisticated—do not know such basic details as their profits and losses from product sales or how to attribute sales to any particular advertising source. This is true even in contexts such as keyword advertising, where in theory profits-per-click are computable. The advertiser's lack of data often makes such decisions more like guess-work. And many ads, such as brand advertisements, aren't meant to lead directly to sales at all, making it virtually impossible to calculate their profitability.

B.   Advertising, Competition and Persuasion

The legal literature on advertising regulation has tilted toward economic analyses of advertising. This section draws heavily on some key law-and-economics articles and responses thereto: Howard Beales et al., *The Efficient Regulation of Consumer Information*, 24 J. L. & ECON. 491 (1981); Lillian R. BeVier, *Competitor Suits for False Advertising under Section 43(a) of the Lanham Act: A Puzzle in the Law of Deception*, 78 VA. L. REV. 1 (1992); Fred S. McChesney, *Deception, Trademark Infringement and the Lanham Act: A Property-Rights Reconciliation*, 78 VA. L. REV. 49 (1992); Roger E. Schechter, *Additional Pieces of the Deception Puzzle: Some Reactions to Professor Bevier*, 78 VA. L. REV. 57 (1992); and Lee Goldman, *The World's Best Article on Competitor Suits for False Advertising*, 45 FLA. L. REV. 487 (1993).

The Economists' Perspectives

In theory, advertising can make markets more competitive. To make good decisions, consumers require sufficient information about products and services. Advertising can educate consumers about price, quality, safety, and other product attributes, helping consumers choose the options that best meet their preferences. Furthermore, producers have incentives to improve their products across the attributes desired by consumers, because consumers should recognize those improvements and allocate their dollars accordingly. Thus, in theory, advertising encourages new entrants and makes markets more competitive because a company with a superior or lower-cost offering can explain to consumers why they should switch.

There is empirical evidence to support these theoretical arguments.

In a classic study, for example, Lee Benham showed that eyeglass consumers paid higher prices in markets with restrictions on advertising eyeglass prices than in markets where such price advertising was permitted. Lee Benham, *The Effect of Advertising on the Price of*

Eyeglasses, 15 J. L. & ECON. 337 (1972). Subsequently, Benham and his coauthor reported that the benefits of advertising were strongest for the least educated consumers. Lee Benham & Alexandra Benham, *Regulating through the Professions: A Perspective on Information Control*, 18 J.L. & ECON. 421 (1975).

Benham's studies focused on ads that disclosed prices; however, these pro-competitive effects do not necessarily extend to other types of advertising. A comprehensive study of legal fees and attorney advertising found that advertising appeared to drive down the price of wills, personal bankruptcies, and uncontested divorces, but lawyers who advertised personal injury legal services charged higher prices than their non-advertising counterparts. WILLIAM W. JACOBS ET AL., CLEVELAND REG'L OFFICE & BUREAU OF ECON., FTC, IMPROVING CONSUMER ACCESS TO LEGAL SERVICES: THE CASE FOR REMOVING RESTRICTIONS ON TRUTHFUL ADVERTISING (Nov. 1984). Consider possible explanations for this result: contingent fees may complicate consumers' ability to compare prices; personal injury lawyers may be able to increase demand for their services via advertising more than divorce lawyers can; the personal injury lawyers' ad copy didn't mention price; etc.

Another study found that Quebec's ban on television advertising to children raised the price of children's cereals in Quebec compared to other provinces, while prices for other cereals, which were still allowed to advertise, were no higher in Quebec. C. Robert Clark, *Advertising Restrictions and Competition in the Children's Breakfast Cereal Industry*, 50 J.L & ECON. 757, 759-60 (2007). This result is particularly interesting given that such ads rarely include price information—yet advertising still apparently lowered children's cereal prices, perhaps by increasing competition.

Advertising is sometimes criticized as creating or highlighting artificial distinctions between vendors that do not actually improve consumer welfare. However, economists generally view brand preferences as neutral or even positive. If people feel better about buying Tide than the store's generic detergent, then they may be better off paying a brand premium—even if both products perform equally well. In those cases, brand loyalty reflects satisfaction, not deception. Further, advertising can educate consumers why a particular offering is superior to substitutes/alternatives, which can prompt consumers to spend their dollars on the best option (in economic terms, advertising can change the cross-elasticity of demand between rival offerings).

Some Responses to the Economists' Perspectives

Economists talk about advertising as a means of conveying information, whereas psychologists and marketers are more likely to talk in terms of persuasion. (Robert Cialdini's *Influence: The Psychology of Persuasion* provides an excellent overview from the psychological/marketing side.) This means that the academic disciplines will often talk past each other. The economists worry about false or misleading information, which can distort consumer choice. In contrast, psychologists worry about misleading or unfair persuasion of consumers, even when predicated on truthful or non-false information.

The dichotomy between "bad" information and "bad" persuasion can illustrate how advertising can enhance competition and yet harm consumers in other ways.

For example, advertising may persuade consumers to spend money on things they don't need and do not necessarily "want." Cigarettes are a prime example of pernicious consumer behavior driven by decades of advertising. *See* Allan M. Brandt, *The Cigarette Century: The Rise, Fall, and Deadly Persistence of the Product that Defined America* (2007). Advertising law generally tolerates advertising's ability to reshape consumer preferences—arguably, the opposite of consumer "autonomy"—to make objectively harmful choices. Still, as a policy matter, we try to stop consumers from deciding that the risk of a horrible smoking-related death is less important to them than the cool image of smoking and the temporary high it provides.

Advertising can also manufacture consumer demand for offerings where none would have otherwise existed. For example, Listerine coined the "disease" of "chronic halitosis" (basically, the non-medical condition of having bad breath) and then advertised Listerine as a cure for the new disease. Consumers demanded Listerine because Listerine defined the problem and then offered itself as a solution. *See* Gary Cross, *An All-Consuming Century: Why Commercialism Won in Modern America* 35 (2000); *see also* Susan Strasser, *Satisfaction Guaranteed: The Making of the American Mass Market* (1989) (providing a historical overview); Carl Elliott, *How to Brand a Disease—and Sell a Cure*, CNN.com, Oct. 11, 2010 (pharmaceutical marketers make consumers aware of diseases; consumer demand for drugs to cure those diseases follows). Economists respond that if consumers perceive new needs—even if advertising sparked that realization—then ads help consumers satisfy those new preferences.

Furthermore, in an advertising-saturated society, consumers are constantly reminded that they have unmet needs and told that buying more consumer products is the cure-all solution. This can make consumer feel perpetually inadequate and that they need to spend more money—money they often don't have—in a Sisyphean quest to fix those inadequacies. *See* Barry Schwartz, *The Paradox of Choice* (2004).

Advertisers regularly create these feelings among consumers. Most "image" advertising/brand advertising help consumers envision an aspirational lifestyle, which consumers then hope to achieve by buying the product. Also, advertisers in fashion-driven industries must find ways to distinguish themselves from their peers. At its most insidious, advertising subtly changes consumers' subconscious thinking—the antithesis of free will/informed consumer choices. There is little evidence that classic "subliminal" advertising directly triggers purchases, but there is substantial evidence that simply repeating exposure to brands can increase preferences for those brands even though consumers (1) don't understand that this has occurred and (2) offer alternate explanations for their preferences when asked.

We'll revisit the implications of persuasion and deception in Chapters 4 and 5.

3.   Legal Definitions of Advertising

We now turn to the legal question: What kinds of information is legally defined as "advertising," and how is that information regulated?

We acknowledge the high risk that you will be disappointed after reading this section. You are hoping to get a nice, precise, predictable legal standard that makes it easy to classify information as advertising or not. You are not going to get that, at least with respect to a sizable range of border cases. The Constitutional tests are designed to prevent the government from regulating almost all speech on the dubious premise that virtually every speaker has some arguably economic interest in being heard. This translates into common sense classifications in many situations; but it leaves many nonstandard situations where the outcome, and the logic, may be hard to follow.

Introduction to the Central Hudson Case

Typically, courts apply one of three levels of scrutiny when determining whether a legal regulation of speech comports with the First Amendment: strict scrutiny, intermediate scrutiny and rational basis scrutiny.

Presumptively, government restrictions on speech are subject to strict scrutiny, which (almost) invariably means courts will find the restriction violates the First Amendment.

Some categories of speech do, however, get lower levels of judicial scrutiny that make the government regulations more likely to survive Constitutional review. For example, "content-neutral" speech restrictions, such as "time/place/manner" restrictions, are typically subject to intermediate scrutiny.

Certain categories of harmful speech, including obscenity, imminent threats of violence and (importantly for our purposes) false advertising, are not protected by the First Amendment at all. Government restrictions of those speech categories are effectively subject to rational basis review, which means they are rarely if ever found to violate the First Amendment.

The following case established that regulations of truthful commercial speech are subject to an intermediate level of First Amendment scrutiny. It has become a seminal citation for a reduced, but not zero, level of judicial scrutiny of advertising regulations.

CENTRAL HUDSON GAS & ELEC. CORP. V. PUBLIC SERVICE COMMISSION OF NEW YORK, 447 U.S. 557 (1980)

POWELL, J., delivered the opinion of the Court.

This case presents the question whether a regulation of the Public Service Commission of the State of New York violates the First and Fourteenth Amendments because it completely bans promotional advertising by an electrical utility.

I.

In December 1973, the Commission, appellee here, ordered electric utilities in New York State to cease all advertising that "promot[es] the use of electricity." The order was based on the Commission's finding that "the interconnected utility system in New York State does not have sufficient fuel stocks or sources of supply to continue furnishing all customer demands for the 1973–1974 winter."*

Three years later, when the fuel shortage had eased, . . . the Commission extended the prohibition in a Policy Statement issued on February 25, 1977.

. . . The Commission declared all promotional advertising contrary to the national policy of conserving energy. It acknowledged that the ban is not a perfect vehicle for conserving energy. . . . [S]ince oil dealers are not under the Commission's jurisdiction and thus remain free to advertise, it was recognized that the ban can achieve only "piecemeal conservationism." Still, the Commission adopted the restriction because it was deemed likely to "result in some dampening of unnecessary growth" in energy consumption.

The Commission's order explicitly permitted "informational" advertising designed to encourage "*shifts* of consumption" from peak demand times to periods of low electricity demand. (emphasis in original). . . .

When it rejected requests for rehearing on the Policy Statement, the Commission supplemented its rationale for the advertising ban. The agency observed that additional electricity probably would be more expensive to produce than existing output. . . . This additional electricity would be subsidized by all consumers through generally higher rates. The state agency also thought that promotional advertising would give "misleading signals" to the public by appearing to encourage energy consumption at a time when conservation is needed. . . .

II.

The Commission's order restricts only commercial speech, that is, expression related solely to the economic interests of the speaker and its audience. The First Amendment, as applied to the States through the Fourteenth Amendment, protects commercial speech from unwarranted governmental regulation. Commercial expression not only serves the economic interest of the speaker, but also assists consumers and furthers the societal interest in the fullest possible dissemination of information. In applying the First Amendment to this area, we have rejected the "highly paternalistic" view that government has complete power to suppress or regulate commercial speech. "[P]eople will perceive their own best interests if only they are well enough informed, and . . . the best means to that end is to open the channels of communication rather than to close them. . . ." Even when advertising communicates only an incomplete version of the relevant facts, the First Amendment presumes that some accurate information is better than no information at all.

---

* [Editor's note: In 1973, OPEC (a cartel of oil-producing countries) embargoed oil sales to the United States as punishment for the United States' military assistance to Israel in the Yom Kippur War. The resulting oil undersupply contributed to a brief but severe economic crisis. OPEC lifted the embargo in March 1974.]

Nevertheless, our decisions have recognized "the 'commonsense' distinction between speech proposing a commercial transaction, which occurs in an area traditionally subject to government regulation, and other varieties of speech."[5] The Constitution therefore accords a lesser protection to commercial speech than to other constitutionally guaranteed expression. The protection available for particular commercial expression turns on the nature both of the expression and of the governmental interests served by its regulation.

The First Amendment's concern for commercial speech is based on the informational function of advertising. Consequently, there can be no constitutional objection to the suppression of commercial messages that do not accurately inform the public about lawful activity. The government may ban forms of communication more likely to deceive the public than to inform it, or commercial speech related to illegal activity.[6] . . .

In commercial speech cases, then, a four-part analysis has developed. At the outset, we must determine whether the expression is protected by the First Amendment. For commercial speech to come within that provision, it at least must concern lawful activity and not be misleading. Next, we ask whether the asserted governmental interest is substantial. If both inquiries yield positive answers, we must determine whether the regulation directly advances the governmental interest asserted, and whether it is not more extensive than is necessary to serve that interest.

III.

We now apply this four-step analysis for commercial speech to the Commission's arguments in support of its ban on promotional advertising. . . .

B.

The Commission offers two state interests as justifications for the ban on promotional advertising. The first concerns energy conservation. Any increase in demand for electricity—during peak or off-peak periods—means greater consumption of energy. The Commission argues, and the New York court agreed, that the State's interest in conserving energy is sufficient to support suppression of advertising designed to increase consumption of electricity. In view of our country's dependence on energy resources beyond our control, no one can doubt the importance of energy conservation. Plainly, therefore, the state interest asserted is substantial.

---

[5] . . . This Court's decisions on commercial expression have rested on the premise that such speech, although meriting some protection, is of less constitutional moment than other forms of speech. As we stated in *Ohralik*, the failure to distinguish between commercial and noncommercial speech "could invite dilution, simply by a leveling process, of the force of the [First] Amendment's guarantee with respect to the latter kind of speech."

[6] In most other contexts, the First Amendment prohibits regulation based on the content of the message. Two features of commercial speech permit regulation of its content. First, commercial speakers have extensive knowledge of both the market and their products. Thus, they are well situated to evaluate the accuracy of their messages and the lawfulness of the underlying activity. In addition, commercial speech, the offspring of economic self-interest, is a hardy breed of expression that is not "particularly susceptible to being crushed by overbroad regulation."

The Commission also argues that promotional advertising will aggravate inequities caused by the failure to base the utilities' rates on marginal cost. . . . If peak demand were to rise, . . . the extra costs would be borne by all consumers through higher overall rates. Without promotional advertising, the Commission stated, this inequitable turn of events would be less likely to occur. The choice among rate structures involves difficult and important questions of economic supply and distributional fairness. The State's concern that rates be fair and efficient represents a clear and substantial governmental interest.

C.

Next, we focus on the relationship between the State's interests and the advertising ban. Under this criterion, the Commission's laudable concern over the equity and efficiency of appellant's rates does not provide a constitutionally adequate reason for restricting protected speech. The link between the advertising prohibition and appellant's rate structure is, at most, tenuous. The impact of promotional advertising on the equity of appellant's rates is highly speculative. Advertising to increase off-peak usage would have to increase peak usage, while other factors that directly affect the fairness and efficiency of appellant's rates remained constant. Such conditional and remote eventualities simply cannot justify silencing appellant's promotional advertising.

In contrast, the State's interest in energy conservation is directly advanced by the Commission order at issue here. There is an immediate connection between advertising and demand for electricity. Central Hudson would not contest the advertising ban unless it believed that promotion would increase its sales. Thus, we find a direct link between the state interest in conservation and the Commission's order.

D.

We come finally to the critical inquiry in this case: whether the Commission's complete suppression of speech ordinarily protected by the First Amendment is no more extensive than necessary to further the State's interest in energy conservation. The Commission's order reaches all promotional advertising, regardless of the impact of the touted service on overall energy use. But the energy conservation rationale, as important as it is, cannot justify suppressing information about electric devices or services that would cause no net increase in total energy use. In addition, no showing has been made that a more limited restriction on the content of promotional advertising would not serve adequately the State's interests.

Appellant insists that but for the ban, it would advertise products and services that use energy efficiently. These include the "heat pump," which both parties acknowledge to be a major improvement in electric heating, and the use of electric heat as a "backup" to solar and other heat sources. . . . In the absence of authoritative findings to the contrary, we must credit as within the realm of possibility the claim that electric heat can be an efficient alternative in some circumstances.

. . . . To the extent that the Commission's order suppresses speech that in no way impairs the State's interest in energy conservation, the Commission's order violates the First and Fourteenth Amendments and must be invalidated.

The Commission also has not demonstrated that its interest in conservation cannot be protected adequately by more limited regulation of appellant's commercial expression. To further its policy of conservation, the Commission could attempt to restrict the format and content of Central Hudson's advertising. It might, for example, require that the advertisements include information about the relative efficiency and expense of the offered service, both under current conditions and for the foreseeable future.[13] In the absence of a showing that more limited speech regulation would be ineffective, we cannot approve the complete suppression of Central Hudson's advertising. . . .

[Justices Brennan's and Blackmun's concurrences in the judgment, and Justice Rehnquist's dissent, omitted]

JUSTICE STEVENS, concurring in the judgment.

Because "commercial speech" is afforded less constitutional protection than other forms of speech, it is important that the commercial speech concept not be defined too broadly lest speech deserving of greater constitutional protection be inadvertently suppressed. The issue in this case is whether New York's prohibition on the promotion of the use of electricity through advertising is a ban on nothing but commercial speech.

In my judgment one of the two definitions the Court uses in addressing that issue is too broad and the other may be somewhat too narrow. The Court first describes commercial speech as "expression related solely to the economic interests of the speaker and its audience." Although it is not entirely clear whether this definition uses the subject matter of the speech or the motivation of the speaker as the limiting factor, it seems clear to me that it encompasses speech that is entitled to the maximum protection afforded by the First Amendment. Neither a labor leader's exhortation to strike, nor an economist's dissertation on the money supply, should receive any lesser protection because the subject matter concerns only the economic interests of the audience. Nor should the economic motivation of a speaker qualify his constitutional protection; even Shakespeare may have been motivated by the prospect of pecuniary reward. Thus, the Court's first definition of commercial speech is unquestionably too broad.

The Court's second definition refers to "'speech proposing a commercial transaction.'" A salesman's solicitation, a broker's offer, and a manufacturer's publication of a price list or the terms of his standard warranty would unquestionably fit within this concept. Presumably, the definition is intended to encompass advertising that advises possible buyers of the availability of specific products at specific prices and describes the advantages of purchasing such items. Perhaps it also extends to other communications that do little more than make

---

[13] The Commission also might consider a system of previewing advertising campaigns to insure that they will not defeat conservation policy. It has instituted such a program for approving "informational" advertising under the Policy Statement challenged in this case. We have observed that commercial speech is such a sturdy brand of expression that traditional prior restraint doctrine may not apply to it. . . .

the name of a product or a service more familiar to the general public. Whatever the precise contours of the concept, and perhaps it is too early to enunciate an exact formulation, I am persuaded that it should not include the entire range of communication that is embraced within the term "promotional advertising."

This case involves a governmental regulation that completely bans promotional advertising by an electric utility. This ban encompasses a great deal more than mere proposals to engage in certain kinds of commercial transactions. It prohibits all advocacy of the immediate or future use of electricity. . . . The breadth of the ban thus exceeds the boundaries of the commercial speech concept, however that concept may be defined.

The justification for the regulation is nothing more than the expressed fear that the audience may find the utility's message persuasive. Without the aid of any coercion, deception, or misinformation, truthful communication may persuade some citizens to consume more electricity than they otherwise would. I assume that such a consequence would be undesirable and that government may therefore prohibit and punish the unnecessary or excessive use of electricity. But if the perceived harm associated with greater electrical usage is not sufficiently serious to justify direct regulation, surely it does not constitute the kind of clear and present danger that can justify the suppression of speech. . . .

In sum, I concur in the result because I do not consider this to be a "commercial speech" case.
. . .

NOTES AND QUESTIONS

Advertising as a Social Good. As we discussed in Chapter 1, most people view advertising as bad. Here, the court is dealing with advertising that may prompt socially beneficial behavior, such as increasing awareness of heat pumps or encouraging conservation. If this advertising benefits society, should the government undertake the consumer education function itself rather than relying on a profit-maximizing private company to do it?

For the majority, advertising's informational function provides the basis for First Amendment protection for advertising. But even heavily-regulated utilities may run non-informational advertising. See, e.g., this advertisement for a Belgian electric company: https://www.youtube.com/watch?v=HXy0a-nGMEs (featuring adorable puppies).

Relatedly, an advertiser's promotion of its offerings can spur consumer demand for that item from any source, not just the advertiser. For example, when POM Wonderful educates consumers about the purported health benefits of pomegranate juice, it can increase consumer demand for pomegranate juice from any source—in which case the advertiser doesn't capture all of the financial benefits attributable to its advertising. The advertiser may be comfortable with this consequence when it has substantial market share (or, in the case of a utility, effectively 100% market share). For example, when de Beers dominated the diamond industry (up to 90% market share in the 1980s), it ran ads promoting the benefits of diamonds, knowing they were likely get any interested consumer's money. Otherwise, the advertiser will want to highlight real or perceived differences from its competitors, so that any increased consumer demand only accrues to its purportedly unique offering.

Alternatively, industry participants may pool their resources (subject to antitrust limits) to support advertising that builds demand for the entire industry. You've likely seen ads touting the benefits of milk ("Got Milk?"), meats (including beef ("It's What's For Dinner") and pork ("the other white meat"), and other foods, which are the results of such industry-wide advertising initiatives.

What is Commercial Speech? The opinion refers to "commercial speech" as a possible synonym for "advertising." This proliferation of terms introduces ambiguity. Are "advertising" and "commercial speech" co-extensive? If not, how do they differ?

Much of the confusion in the constitutional rules governing regulation of advertisers derives from this semantic ambiguity. As Justice Stevens indicates in his *Central Hudson* concurrence, the court articulated multiple definitions of "commercial speech," which have different First Amendment implications.

Frequently, commercial speech is defined as "speech that proposes a commercial transaction." However, another definition of commercial speech is "expression related solely to the economic interests of the speaker and its audience." Justice Stevens fears this broader definition could allow the restriction of speech that deserves the highest level of First Amendment scrutiny (*i.e.*, strict scrutiny). Consider whether subsequent cases validate his concern, or whether courts have basically gotten it right as new forms of advertising have emerged.

The Four-Factor Test. With respect to information that qualifies as "commercial speech," *Central Hudson* established a four-factor test to scrutinize government restrictions of such speech (the four factors are essentially a recapitulation of the court's typical intermediate scrutiny analysis, but rearticulated for commercial speech):

(1) the First Amendment protects non-misleading commercial speech about lawful activity. If the commercial speech is protected and the government seeks to regulate it, then:
(2) the asserted governmental interest must be substantial,
(3) the regulation must directly advance the governmental interest asserted, and
(4) the regulation must not be more extensive than is necessary to serve that interest.

Notice the possible inherent tension between factors three and four: A regulation that directly advances the government's interest (by going after most or all of the speech that causes harm) is likely to be fairly broad, while a narrow regulation may be unlikely to do much to advance the asserted interest.

Subsequent Case Law. The Supreme Court has generally been hostile to the regulation of truthful commercial speech in recent years, regularly finding that a given regulation fails to satisfy one of the last three *Central Hudson* factors.

Citizens United v. Federal Election Commission, 558 U.S. 50 (2010), made it nearly impossible to regulate corporation-funded political speech. However, the ruling did not itself purport to change *Central Hudson*'s legal test as applied to conventional product/service advertising.

Sorrell v. IMS Health Inc., 564 U.S. 552 (2011), suggested that regulation of commercial speech was content-based and subject to heightened scrutiny, though the majority did not revisit the first *Central Hudson* factor, which takes as a given that false and misleading commercial speech receives *no* First Amendment protection. As a result, some courts now treat *Sorrell* as having superseded *Central Hudson*'s four-factor test for the regulation of truthful, nonmisleading commercial speech. *See, e.g.*, Retail Digital Network, LLC v. Appelsmith, 810 F.3d 638 (9th Cir. 2016) (holding that strict scrutiny applies to content- or speaker-based restrictions on nonmisleading commercial speech regarding lawful goods or services); United States v. Caronia, 703 F.3d 149 (2d Cir. 2012) (same).

The Eighth Circuit, taking a slightly different approach, held that *Sorrell* "devised a new two-part test for assessing restrictions on commercial speech." 1-800-411-Pain Referral Serv., LLC v. Otto, 744 F.3d 1045, 1054 (8th Cir. 2014). According to the Eighth Circuit, because *Sorrell* "did not define what 'heightened scrutiny' means, ... [t]he upshot is that when a court determines commercial speech restrictions are content- or speaker-based, it should then assess their constitutionality under *Central Hudson*." *Id.* at 1055. *See also* King v. Governor of the State of N.J., 767 F.3d 216, 236 (3d Cir. 2014) (suggesting that strict scrutiny might apply to some commercial speech regulations but declining to apply strict scrutiny to the challenged content- and speaker-based restriction on "professional speech" because the court found that the law did not "discriminat[e] on the basis of content [or speaker] in an impermissible manner"). How could any regulation targeting commercial speech not be content-based?

United States v. Alvarez, 567 U.S. 709 (2012), invalidated a statute criminalizing false claims of military honors. The Court indicated that the First Amendment can protect false speech if the speech didn't cause any specific harm. Per the first factor of the *Central Hudson* test, false commercial speech receives no First Amendment protection, but the *Alvarez* court's protection of noncommercial false speech could raise questions about whether that rule is still categorically true.

4.   Distinguishing Between Advertising and Editorial Content

If regulations could precisely and accurately categorize advertising and editorial content, the First Amendment implications of regulating advertising might be less troubling. Instead, a number of edge cases demonstrate the overlap in the Venn diagrams of advertising and editorial content. Thus, regulations of advertising pose some risk of covering—and chilling—editorial content that ought to receive the highest level of First Amendment protection.

A.   Kasky v. Nike, Inc., 27 Cal. 4th 939 (Cal. 2002)

Introduction to the Case

Kasky v. Nike is a flagship case involving commercial speech regulation, but it produced such a complicated and long-winded set of opinions that (based on strong student feedback) we have chosen to summarize it rather than present it in full. If you are still confused about particular issues after reading to the end of our notes on the case, you may wish to review the full opinion.

The case involves what we might call "corporate speech": speech that doesn't directly propose any commercial transaction but still might financially benefit the speaker. Furthermore, the plaintiff wasn't Nike's competitor or consumer, but was an activist seeking to use false advertising laws to attack a social issue. The interplay between false advertising law and political discourse often flummoxes judges, and balancing the competing interests caused the judges on the California Supreme Court to fracture.

As you read the case summary, focus on two key issues:

1) Under the court's holding, is information disseminated by a for-profit company always "commercial" speech?

2) What makes commercial speech more appropriate to regulate than noncommercial speech?

Case Summary

In 1997, Nike reported $9.2 billion of revenues from selling shoes and sports apparel, and it spent about $1 billion on advertising and marketing. Most of Nike's products were manufactured in China, Vietnam and Indonesia by subcontractors. The subcontractors' labor practices were the subject of substantial public scrutiny. Activists repeatedly charged that Nike's subcontractors violated local labor and safety laws and provided unacceptable working conditions.

Nike publicly responded to the criticism in several ways, including full-page ads in newspapers. An example:

> *"It is my sincere belief that Nike is doing a good job... but Nike can and should do better."*
>
> Ambassador Andrew Young
> GoodWorks International, LLC
>
> *After six months of investigation, visiting twelve Asian factories and interviewing hundreds of workers in Indonesia, China, and Vietnam about Nike's overseas labor practices, this was how Andrew Young concluded his independent 75-page report, released yesterday.*
>
> *Nike agrees. Good isn't good enough in anything we do. We can and will do better.*
>
> *For details on exactly how — and for a complete copy of Ambassador Young's report and recommendations — please call 1-800-501-6295, go to www.nike.com/report, or go directly to GoodWorks at www.digitalrelease.com and enter the keyword: GoodWorks*

Nike also sent a letter to many university administrators claiming its innocence for the working conditions of its subcontractors' employees:*

June 18, 1996

Dear President and Director of Athletes,

As most of you have probably read, heard or seen, NIKE Inc. has recently come under attack from the Made in the USA Foundation, and other labor organizers, who claim that child labor is used in the production of its goods. While you may also be aware that NIKE has gone on the record to categorically deny these allegations as completely false and irresponsible, I would like to extend the courtesy of providing you with many of the facts that have been absent from the media discourse on this issue. I hope you will find this information useful in discussions with faculty and students who may be equally disturbed by these charges.

First and foremost, wherever NIKE operates around the globe, it is guided by principles set forth in a code of conduct that binds its production subcontractors to a signed Memorandum of Understanding. The Memorandum strictly prohibits child labor, and certifies compliance with

---

* [Text retyped for clarity].

applicable government regulations regarding minimum wage and overtime, as well as occupational health and safety, environmental regulations, worker insurance and equal opportunity provinces.

NIKE enforces its standards through daily observation by staff members who are responsible for monitoring adherence to the Memorandum. NIKE currently employs approximately 100 staff members in Asia alone to oversee operations. Every NIKE subcontractor knows that the enforcement of the Memorandum includes systematic, evaluation by third-party auditors. These thorough reviews include interviews with workers, examination of safety equipment and procedures, review of free health-care facilities, investigation of worker grievances and audits of payroll records.

Furthermore, over the past 20 years we have established long-term relationships with select subcontractors, and we believe that our sense of corporate responsibility has influenced the way they conduct their business. After all, it is incumbent upon leaders like NIKE to ensure that these violations do not occur in our subcontractor's factories.

We have found over the years that, given the vast area of our operations and the difficulty of policing such a network, some violations occur. However, we have been proud that in all material respects the code of conduct is complied with. The code is not just word. We live by it. NIKE is proud of its contribution in helping to build economies, provide skills, and create a brighter future for millions of workers around the world.

As a former Director of Athletes, and currently the Director of Sports Marketing at NIKE, I am indeed sensitive to these issues. I would be more than happy to make myself available to either discuss these issues and/or receive any opinions or insights you may have. We are committed to the world of sports and all that it stands for. I remain at your disposal.

Kindest regards,

Steve Miller
Director
NIKE Sports Marketing

SM:en

cc: Philip H. Knight
        Donna Gibbs
        Kit Morris
        Erin Patton

The plaintiff asserted that Nike's public communications were false and therefore violated California's false advertising and unfair competition laws.

JUSTICE KENNARD wrote the majority opinion, joined by three other judges. The majority opinion summarized its conclusion:

Because the messages in question were directed by a commercial speaker to a commercial audience, and because they made representations of fact about the speaker's own business operations for the purpose of promoting sales of its products, we conclude that these messages are commercial speech for purposes of applying state laws barring false and misleading commercial messages.

Summarizing U.S. Supreme Court precedent, the majority opinion identified three reasons for denying First Amendment protection for false advertising:

(1) the speaker can more easily verify the accuracy of commercial speech,

(2) commercial speech is "hardier" than noncommercial speech because the speaker wants to make a profit, and

(3) the regulation of commercial speech may be intertwined with the government's authority to regulate the underlying commercial transaction.

The majority wrote:

> The United States Supreme Court has not adopted an all-purpose test to distinguish commercial from noncommercial speech under the First Amendment, nor has this court adopted such a test under the state Constitution, nor do we propose to do so here.

The majority examined the U.S. Supreme Court's ruling in *Bolger v. Youngs Drug Products Corp.*, 463 U.S. 60 (1983), which involved the dissemination of educational pamphlets about contraceptives. The *Bolger* opinion identified three attributes that can help gauge if speech is commercial: the message's "advertising format, product references, and economic motivation." *Bolger* did not provide any bright lines. The court found that the presence of all three factors at the same time isn't *necessary* for speech to be commercial, but the combination of all three factors might render some speech commercial even in circumstances in which the presence of only one or two factors wouldn't be sufficient. The *Kasky* opinion explained that *Bolger* held that:

> [S]tatements may properly be categorized as commercial "notwithstanding the fact that they contain discussions of important public issues," and that "advertising which 'links a product to a current public debate' is not thereby entitled to the constitutional protection afforded noncommercial speech," explaining further that "[a]dvertisers should not be permitted to immunize false or misleading product information from government regulation simply by including references to public issues."

The *Kasky* majority identified a different set of three attributes to distinguish commercial from noncommercial speech:

> [C]ategorizing a particular statement as commercial or noncommercial speech requires consideration of three elements: the speaker, the intended audience, and the content of the message.

The majority explained the "speaker" and "intended audience" factors:

> [T]he speaker is likely to be someone engaged in commerce—that is, generally, the production, distribution, or sale of goods or services—or someone acting on behalf of a person so engaged, and the intended audience is likely to be actual or potential buyers or customers of the speaker's goods or services, or persons acting for actual or potential buyers or customers, or persons (such as reporters or reviewers) likely to repeat the message to or otherwise influence actual or potential buyers or customers.

(In dissent, Justice Brown objected to changing the status of speech based on the speaker's identity, saying that speaker-neutrality is "a fundamental tenet of First Amendment jurisprudence.")

The majority also defined the "message content":

> [Commercial] speech consists of representations of fact about the business operations, products, or services of the speaker (or the individual or company that the speaker represents), made for the purpose of promoting sales of, or other commercial transactions in, the speaker's products or services.

The majority then applied those factors to Nike's public messages about its labor practices, as follows:

Factor One (Commercial Speaker): Nike was a commercial speaker because it is "engaged in commerce."

Factor Two (Intended Audience of Purchasers / People Who Would Act for or Communicate to Purchasers). University administrators were a commercial audience for Nike's letters because they buy large amounts of shoes and athletic apparel. Nike's press releases and letters to the editor, even though not communicated directly to consumers, were nevertheless intended to influence the buying public; and Nike desired "to maintain and/or increase its sales and profits."

Factor Three (Factual Content Promoting Sales). Nike made factual representations about the labor conditions in its subcontracting manufacturers' facilities, and "Nike was in a position to readily verify the truth of any factual assertions it made on these topics." The majority continued:

> Nike engaged in speech that is particularly hardy or durable. Because Nike's purpose in making these statements, at least as alleged in the first amended complaint, was to maintain its sales and profits, regulation aimed at preventing false and actually or inherently misleading speech is unlikely to deter Nike from speaking truthfully or at all about the conditions in its factories. To the extent that application of these laws may make Nike more cautious, and cause it to make greater efforts to verify the truth of its statements, these laws will serve the purpose of commercial speech protection by "insuring that the stream of commercial information flow[s] cleanly as well as freely."

The majority categorically rejected Nike's argument that its speech wasn't commercial because it addressed an issue "of intense public interest."

In dissent, Justice Brown argued that "Nike's commercial statements about its labor practices cannot be separated from its noncommercial statements about a public issue, because its labor practices are the public issue." Plainly, if globalization leads to children being abused in factories, one might feel differently about globalization than if it improves those children's lives. So, the dissents contended, chilling Nike's factual claims would make its broader argument harder or impossible to convey. (Previous Supreme Court cases had applied strict scrutiny where commercial elements were "inextricably intertwined" with noncommercial speech, such as fundraising for nonprofits by paid fundraisers.)

The majority responded that commercial speech regularly addresses matters of public interest, even if it is "inextricably intertwined" with noncommercial speech. To take the speech at issue in *Bolger* as an example, condom ads inherently relate to political debates about contraception, but they're still ads.

The majority also wasn't concerned about foregone commercial speech because of its hardiness and verifiability. The majority did, however, concede:

> To the extent Nike's press releases and letters discuss policy questions such as the degree to which domestic companies should be responsible for working conditions in factories located in other countries, or what standards domestic companies ought to observe in such factories, or the merits and effects of economic "globalization" generally, Nike's statements are noncommercial speech. Any content-based regulation of these noncommercial messages would be subject to the strict scrutiny test for fully protected speech.

Nike argued that the false advertising laws constituted a viewpoint-based restriction (which would be subject to strict scrutiny) because they favored the speech of Nike's critics over Nike's own speech. The majority responded that the laws simply restrict false factual claims.

JUSTICES CHIN and BROWN, in their dissents, objected to holding Nike to the equivalent of strict liability for any false statements it made about its labor practices, while Nike's activist critics—disseminating noncommercial speech when criticizing Nike—typically would be liable for factual errors only if they had "actual malice" about those errors. The majority said this doctrinal asymmetry was the logical consequence of the Supreme Court's jurisprudence and was defensible because of the hardiness and verifiability of commercial speech.

In dissent, Justice Brown objected:

> The majority . . . creates an overbroad test that, taken to its logical conclusion, renders all corporate speech commercial speech. As defined, the test makes any public representation of fact by a speaker engaged in commerce about that speaker's products made for the purpose of promoting that speaker's products commercial speech. . . . Because all corporate speech about a public issue reflects on the corporate

image and therefore affects the corporation's business goodwill and sale value, the majority's test makes all such speech commercial notwithstanding the majority's assertions to the contrary. . . .

By subjecting all corporate speech about business operations, products and services to the strict liability provisions of [California's false advertising and unfair competition laws], the majority's limited-purpose test unconstitutionally chills a corporation's ability to participate in the debate over matters of public concern.

Justice Brown's dissent argued that the Supreme Court should revisit *Central Hudson* and give full constitutional protection to much commercial speech. She suggested that some, but not all, false advertising regulation would survive higher scrutiny: For efficacy, quality, value, or safety, "the governmental interest in protecting consumers from fraud is especially strong because these representations address the fundamental questions asked by every consumer when he or she makes a buying decision." But "the governmental interest in protecting against consumer fraud is less strong if the [advertiser's] representations are unrelated to the characteristics of the product or service," as they were here. Do you agree? If the advertiser chooses to tell consumers about the conditions under which their products are made, what does that communicate about the importance of that information?

NOTES AND QUESTIONS

Subsequent Proceedings. In response to the California Supreme Court ruling, the U.S. Supreme Court granted certiorari in this case, but later dismissed the grant as improvidently granted. Nike, Inc. v. Kasky, 539 U.S. 654 (2003). Three justices dissented from the dismissal. Shortly after the Supreme Court's non-ruling, the parties settled the case, with Nike paying $1.5 million to a non-profit organization. *See* Adam Liptak, *Nike Move Ends Case Over Firms' Free Speech*, N.Y. TIMES, Sept. 13, 2003.

In 2004, California voters enacted Proposition 64, which requires that a plaintiff suffer an injury in fact and have "lost money or property" to bring a claim under California's unfair competition law and false advertising laws (the provisions at issue in *Kasky*). Prop. 64 doesn't change the case's holding about the characterization of corporate speech, but it prevents similar lawsuits from labor activists like Kasky because they have not lost money or property due to Nike's labor practices.

Distinguishing Commercial from Noncommercial Speech. In the *Bolger* case, the U.S. Supreme Court indicated that commercial and noncommercial speech could be distinguished by considering the "advertising format, product references, and economic motivation." The majority's opinion uses different factors, finding that courts should consider "the speaker, the intended audience, and the content of the message" to determine if speech is commercial or noncommercial. Which (if either) set of factors do you find more convincing?

While *Kasky* may provide helpful considerations, you should not rely on *Kasky*'s factors too heavily. The *Kasky* opinion remains the governing law in California, but courts routinely use various tests and factors.

Can you think of any ways to better distinguish between commercial and noncommercial speech than those offered by the majority or JUSTICE BROWN? Or is this a situation where border cases always will be confounding?

Is Justice Brown correct that all corporate speech is commercial speech under the majority's test? *Cf.* Citizens United v. FEC, 558 U.S. 310 (2010) (protecting speech by a corporation as core First Amendment-protected political speech). As long as only factual statements in commercial speech can be challenged in court, and political advocacy claims like "globalization is a good idea" remain protected speech, would such a result be undesirable? (Return to this question once you've learned what kinds of claims are factual rather than puffery or opinion.)

Consider the following example: A "counseling organization" represented that it could "cure" homosexuality—for a fee, of course. Former clients sued the organization for false advertising, claiming that the organization falsely advertised that homosexuality was a mental illness or disorder and that its therapy program was effective in changing the sexual orientation of clients. Commercial speech? *See* Ferguson v. JONAH (Jews Offering New Alternatives for Healing F/K/A Jews Offering New Alternatives to Homosexuality), No. HUD-L-5473-12 (N.J. Super. Ct. Feb. 5, 2015) (New Jersey Consumer Fraud Act claim).

Justifying Differential Treatment of Commercial Speech. The majority opinion lays out three reasons for allowing the government more freedom to regulate commercial speech than it has to regulate noncommercial speech:

1) The disseminator can more easily verify the commercial speech's veracity because the disseminator knows its products better than anyone else.

2) Commercial speech is "hardier" than much other speech because the profit motive helps trump any chilling effects from regulation.

3) The government's power to prevent commercial harms extends to speech that is "linked inextricably" to those harms.

How persuasive do you find these rationales? Would they apply to noncommercial speech as well?

In their article, *Who's Afraid of Commercial Speech?*, 76 VA. L. REV. 627 (1990), Alex Kozinski and Stuart Banner have several rejoinders to these rationales. First, they note that the words of the First Amendment ("Congress shall make no law . . . abridging the freedom of speech, or of the press") do not distinguish between commercial and noncommercial speech. Then, they show how the various arguments in support of the commercial speech doctrine are both under- and over-inclusive. For example, much commercial speech, just like noncommercial speech, is not easily objectively verifiable; and much editorial content, such as newspapers, is produced with a profit motive, just like commercial speech. Finally, as illustrated by cases like *Kasky*, they show that efforts to define commercial speech are also under- and over-inclusive.

Focusing on this case in particular, do you think that the speech at issue—Nike's responses to criticisms about its labor practices—is "hardy"? As JUSTICE CHIN'S dissent explains, the First Amendment will likely excuse most errors made by Nike's non-competitor critics because they will be liable for defamation only if their errors are made with actual malice. In contrast, due to the reduced First Amendment protection for commercial speech, Nike can be liable for its errors on the same topics with a lower level of scienter. As Nike's counsel, knowing your potential liability exposure, what would you advise your client to say if you are less than 100% certain about the facts?

Can you imagine circumstances where you, as Nike's counsel, might authorize factual claims despite the liability exposure? Would the market provide adequate incentives for companies to produce this information despite potential liability? As an analogy, note that vendors still produce goods and services in the face of tort liability (sometimes even strict liability) for those offerings.

Note that legislatures may have the option of compelling companies to produce information about their practices. For example, the California Transparency in Supply Chains Act requires some companies to disclose their efforts to prevent human trafficking themselves and by their suppliers. As we will discuss in Chapter 6, however, this power depends on the lesser First Amendment protection given to commercial speech.

Conflicting Norms. It's easy to see why this case vexed the judges. On the one hand, for the market to function properly, companies must publish accurate content. Nike was effectively litigating for the right to publish inaccurate claims—an awkward position. *See* Tamara R. Piety, *Grounding Nike: Exposing Nike's Quest for a Constitutional Right to Lie*, 78 TEMPLE L. REV. 151 (2005) (discussing specific statements, such as a press release claiming that Nike's policy "guarantee[s] a living wage for all workers" and a contrasting statement Nike made more privately that "[w]e simply cannot ask our contractors to raise wages to that level"). Furthermore, Nike had a profit incentive to misstate the facts. If Nike's labor practices were dissuading potential customers from buying Nike's products, then providing more favorable characterizations of its labor practices should help boost/preserve sales.

On the other hand, labor practices are a major social issue. Nike's practices related to broader public debates about offshoring U.S. jobs to less costly labor markets and the ethical implications of companies taking advantage of foreign laws that provide less protection to employees than U.S. labor laws. Further, United States-based Nike executives may have trouble confirming the accuracy of reports coming from Nike's foreign offices. Finally, a ruling against Nike could prompt Nike to emphasize (more than it already does) ads that do not disseminate any factual information, engaging consumers' emotions instead of their reason. If Nike prioritized more image advertising as a response to this ruling, are consumers really better off?

One Final Wrinkle: "Misleading" Speech May Not Mean What You Think. In the constitutional arena—but not elsewhere—the courts have made a distinction between "inherently" or "actually" misleading speech, which may simply be banned under *Central*

Hudson, and speech that is merely "potentially" misleading. *In re R.M.J.*, 455 U.S. 191 (1982), an attorney advertising case, introduced the terminology:

> Truthful advertising related to lawful activities is entitled to the protections of the First Amendment. But when the particular content or method of the advertising suggests that it is inherently misleading or when experience has proved that in fact such advertising is subject to abuse, the States may impose appropriate restrictions. Misleading advertising may be prohibited entirely. But the States may not place an absolute prohibition on certain types of potentially misleading information ... if the information also may be presented in a way that is not deceptive.

Thus, the government apparently must at least first try to require a corrective disclosure rather than a ban if the speech is only "potentially" misleading. As you will see in Chapter 6, the fact that many disclosures don't work well could complicate this scheme. And the definition of "potentially" misleading can be contested. It seems to contrast with "inherently" or "actually" misleading—but how do we know what falls in those categories?

The *R.M.J.* case referred to "experience," but courts may be dubious about deferring to regulators' judgments of what experience shows. In *Express Oil Change, L.L.C v. Mississippi Board of Licensure for Professional Engineers & Surveyors*, 916 F.3d 483 (5th Cir. 2019), a survey showed that roughly 55% of potential consumers were deceived by the name "Tire Engineers" into thinking that the company had tire engineers on staff; tire engineer is a generally recognized term for engineers who have expertise in the manufacture, selection, and repair of tires. However, the court of appeals ruled that the survey showed only "potential" deception, and the state provided no testimony from an actually deceived consumer. (In private law false advertising cases, by contrast, 55% deception would be considered an extremely high level, and testimony from a single deceived consumer would not generally suffice to show that confusion was likely.) Since the term "tire engineer" was not "devoid of intrinsic meaning," the court of appeals held, it wasn't inherently misleading.

What Would Advertising Regulation Look Like Without the First Amendment? We will occasionally contrast U.S. regulation with the regimes of other countries. In the U.K., for example, the Advertising Standards Authority (ASA) oversees all sorts of advertising, including what we would call political or issue advertising. The ASA regulates far more than truthfulness. For example, the ASA ordered one advertiser to stop advertising labial plastic surgery which offered "a more natural appearance" and claimed to be appropriate for "enlarged labia." The ad encouraged women to be dissatisfied with their bodies and wrongly implied that any part of a person's body was not natural in appearance. It thus violated the ASA's requirement that advertising be socially responsible. This kind of advertising, by contrast, would be considered nonmisleading in the United States and any restrictions of it would be subject to intermediate scrutiny and almost certainly invalid.

A few other examples: The ASA ordered that this ad not be repeated because the player depicted was twenty four years old, and it was socially irresponsible to feature a person under twenty five in a gambling ad, as it might encourage other young people to gamble.

This ad was condemned for showing a child in an unsafe position:

This ad was irresponsibly sexualized:

Other repeat topics at the ASA in recent years have included disputes over what part of Jerusalem can be attributed to Israel; disputes over what people for and against wind farms in Scotland can say; and disputes over what people advocating for a planned airport expansion can say.

The First Amendment leads U.S. regulation down a different path. Regulators cannot restrict truthful advertising for lawful goods based on moral norms or other considerations about how society should function, and some of the ASA's examples involve obvious political speech that would be fully protected by the First Amendment. Is the ASA's, or the First Amendment's, approach to advertising regulation better?

B.   Other Examples

Commercial speech regulation manifests itself in so many ways that the considerations relevant in one situation may be less helpful in others. Does *Nike* help in determining whether commercial speech is involved in the following cases?

Signage Regulation. Wag More Dogs, LLC v. Artman, 795 F. Supp. 2d 377 (E.D. Va. 2011), *aff'd*, 680 F.3d 359 (4th Cir. 2012), involved a county zoning ordinance that restricted "business signs" to 60 square feet total. Wag More Dogs was a local store providing services to pets. The store's building faced a local park popular with dog owners, so on the park-side exterior, the business commissioned a large mural (16 feet x 60 feet, or nearly 1,000 square feet) (image from the Institute for Justice, which represented the store owner):

This mural is both an artistic expression and brand advertising for the store's offerings. The store admitted as much, saying that the mural was commissioned, in part, to "create goodwill with the people who frequented the dog park, many of whom were potential Wag More Dogs customers." Furthermore, the dogs depicted in the mural resembled the dogs in the store's logo:

The county zoning enforcement authorities deemed the mural an illegal business sign. The court upheld the business sign restrictions against the store's constitutional challenge, holding that the zoning regulation was content-neutral and should be evaluated using intermediate scrutiny. The court said that a mural depicting "generic images of waterfalls, meadows, flowers, or some other object or scenery wholly unrelated to" the store's business wouldn't violate the zoning restriction, nor would "a County informational mural that included images of dogs but said 'Welcome to Shirlington Park's Community Canine Area.'" Later, the court upheld the zoning enforcer's position that the business signs restriction applies to any mural whose subject had "any relationship" to the store's business. Does it seem odd that the zoning restriction restricts a dog-themed mural in a dog park, but only when paid for by a pet-oriented business? If the result of this zoning requirement is that the wall never gets painted, is that a net win for consumers?

Blog Posts. A litigator writes a blog, mostly about his cases (though only about the ones he's won). The blog is part of his firm's website and contains information about how to hire him; it does not allow comments, but it has a "contact us" link. The litigator says his motivation is partly marketing, partly educational—to make the point that not everyone who's arrested is guilty. The state bar attempts to sanction him for advertising without the associated legally required disclaimers that all cases are unique and that past results don't guarantee future successes. Is his blog commercial speech? *See* Va. State Bar *ex rel.* Third Dist. Comm., 744 S.E.2d 611 (Va. 2013) (the majority says yes; the dissent would have characterized posts about the criminal justice system, even those discussing specific cases, as political speech because the attorney "uses the outcome of his cases to illustrate his views of the system"); *cf.* State Bar of California Standing Committee on Professional Responsibility and Conduct Formal Opinion No. 2016-196 (categorizing several examples of attorney blogging).

Company Press Releases. As the *Nike* ruling did, cases often treat companies' press releases as advertising, even when the press releases do not expressly promote a commercial offering. *See, e.g.*, Yeager v. Cingular Wireless LLC, 673 F. Supp. 2d 1089 (E.D. Cal. 2009) (determining that a Cingular press release touting its disaster preparedness equipment, called MACH 1 and MACH 2, and invoking legendary pilot Chuck Yeager's accomplishment of flying at Mach 1 speed, made a commercial use of Yeager's identity); Tamara R. Piety, *Free Advertising: The Case for Public Relations as Commercial Speech*, 10 Lewis & Clark L. Rev. 367 (2006).

Corporate Newsletters. Many companies publish newsletters filled only with editorial content as a way of building relationships with customers. For example, many law firms publish "news alerts" about recent legal developments. Not infrequently, the clear implication is that the new development requires the reader to find an expert who can help the reader with his/her specific situation; but in many cases that sales pitch is only by implication. Nevertheless, courts are likely to treat these corporate-published editorial newsletters as advertising.

For example, in *Holtzman v. Turza*, 08 C 2014 (N.D. Ill. Oct. 19, 2010), *aff'd*, 728 F.3d 682 (7th Cir. 2013), an attorney sent repeated unsolicited one-page junk faxes, of which about 75% was a single editorial article and the remainder of the page had various ways to identify and contact the attorney. The court concluded that the newsletter was an "advertisement" for purposes of the federal anti-junk-fax law. The court said it was clear the attorney's goal was to "generate awareness of defendant's services and build his client base. . . . [There were] no facts to show that his genuine, primary motivation . . . was to educate CPAs and his business contacts on various industry-related topics rather than to build brand recognition and solicit business referrals for his law practice." It also didn't help that the attorney didn't write the editorial content himself; instead, the marketer who also delivered junk faxes wrote the content.

Other Corporate Statements. What about companies' public remarks of other kinds, such as statements to an interviewer for a magazine, or edits made to a company's Wikipedia page by one of the company's agents? *See* Scott v. Citizen Watch Co., 2018 WL 1626773 (N.D. Cal. Apr. 4, 2018) (suggesting that Wikipedia edits by a company about its products might be commercial use of mentioned person's identity).

Article Reprints. Courts have held that a newspaper or magazine article—which starts out as "editorial" content—can become commercial speech when distributed verbatim by a company with an economic interest in the article's contents. *See* Gordon & Breach Sci. Publishers S.A. v. Am. Inst. of Physics, 859 F. Supp. 1521 (S.D.N.Y. 1994); *United Fabricare Supply, Inc. v. 3Hanger Supply Co., Inc.*, No. CV 12-03755-MWF (C.D. Cal. 2012). Is this consistent with the First Amendment?

C.   Advertising Masquerading as Editorial Content

Consumers frequently treat advertising as less credible than editorial content. In one study, consumers were shown multiple sets of Internet search results, some of which were labeled as advertising. Study participants rated 52% of the organic results as "relevant," but identical results labeled as advertising were only rated "relevant" 42% of the time. *See* Bernard J. Jansen & Marc Resnick, *Examining Searcher Perceptions of and Interactions with Sponsored Results*, June 2005. In other words, the label "advertising," by itself, caused consumers to deem the information less relevant.

To avoid this negative consumer response, advertisers have incentives to make ads look like editorial content, sometimes by mimicking a publication's font and layout. Some call these ads "advertorials." An advertorial example:

41

Some print publishers have internal policies that limit ad mimicry and label the ad as "advertising" when the mimicry is too close. These rules often trace back to the Post Office Appropriation Act of 1912, which gave cheaper postal rates to periodical publishers that labeled editorial-like advertising. *See* Lewis Publ'g Co. v. Morgan, 229 U.S. 288 (1913) (upholding the statute).

"Video news releases," or VNRs, are another example of ads mimicking editorial content. *See* Ellen P. Goodman, *Stealth Marketing and Editorial Integrity*, 85 TEX. L. REV. 83 (2006). VNRs are short videos that promote a product or service, but they are designed to look like regular news reports, often including canned interviews into which shots of the local reporter can be inserted so it looks like he or she is asking the questions. The television station makes the ultimate decision to run a VNR, and it is not paid for doing so (but saves on costs of production). Are VNRs commercial speech? *See* Annie Palmer, *Local TV stations air Amazon PR piece on worker safety as if it were a real news story*, CNBC.com, May 26, 2020.

"Native advertisements" are an advertorial variation where the advertiser pays to publish promotional content that looks like editorial content. In some cases, a publication's editorial staff writers prepare the content rather than the advertiser's marketing team or ad agency, ensuring the content reflects the publication's editorial voice. *See, e.g.*, Michael Sebastian, *Native Ad Production Values Keep Growing With 'Orange is the New Black' Promo*, AD. AGE, June 13, 2014 (Netflix promoted the TV series *Orange Is the New Black* by hiring a New York Times native ad team to publish a story about women in prison).

A case brought by the NAD (a self-regulatory body we will consider in more detail in Chapter 3) concerned a story in *Shape* magazine and on the *Shape* website. The article bore the caption "News," discussed the importance of staying hydrated, and recommended SHAPE Water Boosters: "The obvious solution is to stick with water, but about 20 percent of Americans reportedly don't like the taste. If that sounds like you, check out the new SHAPE Water Boosters . . . Just a single squeeze . . . adds delicious flavor—but not calories—along with a concentrated punch of nutrients that offer some important bonus benefits."

The NAD "was concerned that consumers may give more credence to the advertiser's objective claims about the product's attributes because of the context in which the claims appeared." Unlike standard product placement (see below), the ad made specific and objective claims about the product. It might be true that the connection between the content and the magazine was obvious to consumers, but the NAD noted that "consumers can reasonably attach different weight to recommendations made in an editorial context than recommendations made in an advertising context. Put another way, consumers may reasonably believe that editorial recommendations in *SHAPE* magazine are independent of the influence of a sponsoring advertiser." American Media, Inc. (Shape Water Boosters), NAD Case #5665 (Dec. 18, 2013).

One study found that many common forms of disclosure to consumers that the material was sponsored or "native" advertising were ineffective. Only one form—disclosure within the content itself—resulted in more than half of readers recognizing that the content was an ad. *See* Ricardo Bilton, *Which Native Ad Disclosed Itself Best?*, DIGIDAY, Sept. 17, 2014 (discussing a study by Nudge, an analytics company).

How often do you encounter native advertising? How do you know?

Ads Intermixed with Editorial Content. In *Stewart v. Rolling Stone LLC,* 181 Cal. App. 4th 664 (Cal. Ct. App. 2010), *Rolling Stone* magazine had run an editorial feature, called "Indie Rock Universe," on pages that folded out of the magazine. The editorial feature referenced numerous band names and musicians presented in a cartoonish manner. Foldout pages at the beginning and end of the feature included music-themed ads for Camel Cigarettes drawn in a similar (but not identical) cartoonish style. One of the ads said "COMMITTED TO SUPPORTING & PROMOTING INDEPENDENT RECORD LABELS" and contained the text:

> The world of independent music is constantly changing. New styles and sounds emerge daily. That's why we're bringing you The FARM. A collaboration between Camel and independent artists and record labels. It's our way of supporting these innovators as they rise up to bring their sounds to the surface. We give them more opportunities to be heard through online music and countless events across the nation.
>
> Visit THEFARMROCKS.COM
>
> Free shows, great bands and more!

[Beginning of the feature]

[The Camel ad spanning the editorial feature. Each page folds open.]

[The feature's 4 interior pages]

[Ad on the back page of the feature.]

Some musicians named in the feature article sued *Rolling Stone* for publicity rights violations and related claims. As discussed more in Chapter 14, publicity rights limit the commercial use of a person's name, so the dispositive question was whether *Rolling Stone* made a commercial use of the musicians' names included in the editorial feature. The court explained:

> Plaintiffs claim "It is hard to tell where, if at all, the Camel cigarettes advertisement begins and ends." We have examined the pages at issue and do not perceive . . . the distinction between the ad and the Feature to be as close as plaintiffs allege. The graphic designs of the ad and the Feature are quite different, one being based on hand-drawn cartoons and the other being based on collages of photographs. The background of the Feature is white college-ruled paper, not a grassy rural landscape. It is undisputed that, standing alone, the Feature itself is completely devoid of any commercial message. In fact, the only nexus between the ad and the Feature is the mutual references to independent music. None of the band names in the Feature appear in the Camel ad, and none of the language or elements of the Camel ad appear in the Feature. . . . [P]laintiffs have not cited us to a case, and our research has disclosed none, in which a magazine's editorial content has been deemed transformed into commercial speech merely because of its proximity to advertisements touching on the same subject matter. . . .

The court also noted that "the cigarette company had no role in the design of the Feature itself." As a result, the court said that the editorial feature was noncommercial speech (and the musicians' publicity rights claim failed).

Later in the opinion, the *Stewart* court observes:

> We also note that the November 15, 2007 issue of *Rolling Stone* magazine is replete with full-page advertisements, many of which appear to target the magazine's

readership. These ads are primarily for alcoholic beverages, automobiles, personal grooming devices, fashion items, and cellular telephones. Out of the magazine's 215 pages, including the cover pages, no fewer than 108 pages are devoted to full-page advertisements, including several multipage ads. Thus, all of the editorial content of the magazine is, in a sense, "embedded" with advertising. It is true that the gatefold layout may intensify the readers' exposure to the ads because the pages run more or less contiguously and because the format requires readers to lift the advertising pages to the left and to the right, instead of just mindlessly turning them. But we see no principled legal distinction between a page of editorial content that is preceded and followed by full-page ads, and the gatefold format, in which the ads appear only on the reverse side of a feature's pages.

Would it matter if the *Rolling Stone* graphic designers knew that R.J. Reynolds had bought the advertising spots around the feature and knew what the R.J. Reynolds ad looked like?

Product Placement. Product placement is the paid inclusion of products in editorial content, such as TV or movie characters using a branded product or a product reference in song lyrics. A famous early product placement was the inclusion of Reese's Pieces in the movie *E.T.*, which contributed to a huge sales growth for the candy. *See Did M&Ms Turn Down 'E.T.'?*, SNOPES, July 24, 2001.

Product placement may be most familiar in TV shows and movies, but many other media have taken advantage of the phenomenon. In one initiative, DC Comics featured six different Pontiacs on its comic covers, and used a storyline about a man who had become one with his Pontiac.

Even novelists engage in product placement. For example, Amazon sponsored a Kindle-only novella by Stephen King focusing on the company's e-reader. *See generally* Zahr K. Said, *Mandated Disclosure in Literary Hybrid Speech*, 88 WASH. L. REV. 419 (2013). Another example: Artificial sweetener Sweet 'N Low invested $400,000 in an e-book romance novel whose heroine loves Sweet 'N Low. In one scene, a friend asks her "isn't it bad for you?" The heroine "replies that she has researched the claims online and found studies showing that the product is safe: 'They fed lab rats twenty-five hundred packets of Sweet 'N' Low a day ... And still the F.D.A. or E.P.A., or whatevs agency, couldn't connect the dots from any kind of cancer in humans to my party in a packet.'" "To help shape the scene," the sponsor showed the author some of the research the heroine cites. Alexandra Alter, *E-Book Mingles Love and Product Placement*, N.Y. TIMES, Nov. 2, 2014. What legal issues might you, as counsel to the company, have considered? What about legal issues for the author?

It was anticipated that advertisers would spend over $11 billion on product placements in the U.S. in 2019. There are good reasons for the popularity of product placements. Product placements can take advantage of the higher cognitive credit that consumers assign to editorial content instead of advertising. Consumers may implicitly assume that the publishers editorially chose to include the product because it is the most popular, the "best," or the most noteworthy. In this sense, consumers may interpret a product's inclusion as an implicit product endorsement by the publisher.

The endorsement effect may be magnified when the characters extol the product's attributes. For example, contestants on the TV show *Survivor* responded joyously when they received branded food items as part of a product placement deal. The contestants were so hungry that they would have been overjoyed to get any food, but their response makes the placed product seem even more attractive and desirable. Similarly, when TV show hosts like Oprah or Ellen gave away freebies to their audience, audience members inevitably responded with glee about getting a freebie.

In addition, consumers cannot "skip" the product placement advertising because it is embedded in the editorial content. In this sense, product placements are "DVR-proof" and "stream-proof" from consumers bypassing the commercials. Therefore, some television advertisers—fearful that no one is watching TV ads anymore—are shifting their ad dollars to product placements.

Regulators have struggled with developing sensible policies toward product placements. By definition, product placements are integrated into editorial content, so regulators have a tough time isolating the "ad" for special regulatory treatment without also regulating the editorial content, which may trigger strict scrutiny of the regulation.

How should product placement be treated under the First Amendment? Does it matter how much editorial control the sponsor exerts over the artists—for example, whether the artists are required to describe the product in favorable terms, or barred from associating it with villainous characters or poor performance?

We're also seeing "reverse" product placement, where fictional products depicted in fictional materials are turned into real products that consumers can buy. Examples include the Bubba Gump Shrimp Restaurants inspired by the movie *Forrest Gump*, Wonka Candy inspired by the movie *Willy Wonka and the Chocolate Factory*, Buzz Cola inspired by the TV show *The Simpsons*, and Dunder Mifflin copy paper inspired by the TV show *The Office*. *See* Stuart Elliott, *Expanding Line of Dunder Mifflin Products Shows Success in Reverse Product Placement*, N.Y. TIMES, Nov. 23, 2012.

"*Astroturfing*." Astroturfing occurs when an advertiser publishes online content, such as a blog, designed to look like a consumer's genuine opinion. For example, a website in 2006 called "All I Want for Xmas is a PSP" featured "amateur" videos and a "fansite" blog raving about the PSP. The content, in fact, was created by an ad agency of Sony Computer Entertainment America (makers of PSP). Although there are no specific anti-astroturfing laws, it is difficult or impossible for the advertiser to deny that such content is, in fact, advertising; and the failure to disclose the advertiser's role in creating the content can support both private claims as well as government enforcement actions such as, for example, enforcement pursuant to the FTC's endorsement and testimonials guidelines. *See In re* Reverb Communic., F.T.C. No. 092-3199 (settlement announced Aug. 26, 2010). We will discuss disclosure issues surrounding endorsements in greater detail in subsequent chapters.

Advertising Hyperlinks in Editorial Content. Some major newspapers, such as the *Los Angeles Times* and the *Chicago Tribune*, have displayed key phrases in their editorial articles as paid hypertext link ads. *See* Kate Kaye, *LA Times Follows Chicago Tribune's Paid Link Lead*, CLICKZ NEWS, April 28, 2010. An example is depicted in the screenshot below.

[Screenshot taken on August 8, 2010. The words *Sigur Ros* and *"Go"* are green-colored, hyperlinked ads (you can see the alt text "Click to Shop" when the word *"Go"* is moused over). Both links went to topically relevant pages on Amazon.com.]

Without the link ads, the articles are almost certainly noncommercial content that receives the highest level of First Amendment protection. With the text ads, does the content's character morph into commercial speech? Does it make a difference if the online newspaper sometimes embeds links in articles as an editorial decision (*i.e.*, without being compensated)?

Several screens below the top, the blog has the following disclosure in its right hand navigation list:

> Affiliate links disclaimer:
>
> Clicking on the green links will direct you to a third-party Web site. Bloggers and staff writers are in no way affiliated with these links that are placed by an e-commerce specialist only after stories and posts have been published.

Does adequate disclosure of the paid nature of the links to readers, whatever "adequate" means, ameliorate any of your concerns? Do you consider this adequate disclosure?

Does the purported wall between editorial and the e-commerce specialist change your feelings about the practice?

In a factually similar situation, the NAD concluded that BuzzFeed shopping guides did not become "advertising" due to the post-authoring addition of affiliate links by a separate department. *See* NAD 6210: Shopping Guides – St. Ives Renewing Collagen & Elastin Moisturizer, Sept. 18, 2018. However, the NAD identified a number of minor factual changes that could have reversed the outcome.

Content as Advertising. Just like advertising, "pure" editorial content can call attention to commercial offerings and create a demand for them. For example:

- Despite the impressive box office revenue for the *Star Wars* movie franchise, the gross revenues from *Star Wars*–themed merchandise dwarfs the box office returns. In effect, the movies (the "editorial content") create and drive demand for the merchandise.
- Talk show interviews with recent book authors—a standard feature of an author's "book tour"—can help drive demand for the author's books. For example, former President Bill Clinton's interview with Oprah, timed with the release of his memoirs, helped the book achieve sales records. Similarly, television show performances (such as on *Saturday Night Live*) increase bands' sales of their recorded music and live performances.

Due to the ability of editorial content to create consumer demand, some advertisers would gladly pay for inclusion in editorial content. Product placement is only one example.

Another example is payola. In the 1950s "payola scandal," some record companies paid radio DJs money to play their songs, which boosted the popularity of the songs and increased sales of those songs. In response, Congress enacted anti-payola laws requiring "sponsorship identification"—if the publisher (in this case, the radio station) accepts payment for publishing content (in this case, playing songs on the radio), then the publisher is required to disclose this fact to consumers. This concept has been extended to television broadcasts as well. To this day, the FCC occasionally fines broadcasters for violating these rules.

Sponsorship identification laws address one sort of problem: consumers' preference to know when content is advertising. *See* Ellen Goodman, *Stealth Marketing and Editorial Integrity*, 85 TEX. L. REV. 83 (2006); *see also* Eric Goldman, *Stealth Risks of Regulating Stealth Marketing*, 85 TEX. L. REV. 11 (2006) (critiquing this rationale). But can regulatory distinctions between "content" and "advertising" survive if editorial content drives consumer behavior just like advertising?

This chapter provides an overview of the various laws and institutions that regulate truth in advertising. Broadly speaking, there is a tripartite regulatory structure: (1) government regulators at the federal, state and local levels, acting as enforcers of the public interest; (2) competitors, who pursue their own interests against unfair competition and, we hope, thereby protect the public from the same; and (3) consumers, often in class actions based on state consumer protection law, asserting that they have been deceived or harmed by advertising. All three regulatory systems interact. Each tends to have its own emphasis, and an advertiser must take each into account. We will get into the substantive rules of false advertising in Chapters 4 and 5.

1.   The Federal Trade Commission (FTC)

A.   Statutory Background

The FTC is an independent agency created in 1914 that administers a wide variety of consumer protection laws. In early years, courts often confined the FTC's power to antitrust, requiring the FTC to prove injury to competitors; injury to consumers was insufficient. Over time, the FTC's mission broadened. In 1938, an amendment to the FTC Act (FTCA) added the prohibition of "unfair or deceptive acts or practices" to the FTC's mandate. 15 U.S.C. § 45. The House Report explained that the purpose of the new language was to "prevent such acts or practices which injuriously affect the general public as well as those which are unfair to competitors." 9 H.R. Rep. No. 1613, 75th Cong., 1st Sess. (1937). The amendment also specifically prohibited false advertising in the areas of food, drugs, medical devices and cosmetics.

There are a number of highly specialized laws regulating specific industries and behaviors under which the FTC has the authority to regulate everything from collectible coins and political items (Hobby Protection Act, 15 U.S.C. §§ 2101–2106) to petroleum marketing (Petroleum Marketing Practices Act, 15 U.S.C. §§ 2801–2841) to "dolphin-safe" tuna labeling (Dolphin Protection Consumer Information Act, 15 U.S.C. § 1385).

The relatively young Consumer Financial Protection Bureau (CFPB) is changing the regulatory landscape, though the FTC works closely with it. For example, the FTC retains the ability to enforce rules the Truth in Lending Act, 15 U.S.C. §§ 1601–1667f, which governs widespread credit practices, but now shares that enforcement power with the CFPB, which has inherited rulemaking authority for that law.

Section 45 is at the core of the FTC's consumer protection powers. Unfair or deceptive methods, acts or practices "in or affecting commerce" are within the scope of the law, and courts have interpreted this broadly.*

The FTC is the exclusive enforcer of the FTCA. The FTCA does not provide for a private cause of action. *See, e.g.*, Carlson v. Coca-Cola Co., 483 F.2d 279 (9th Cir. 1973).

Deceptiveness

Under 15 U.S.C. § 45(a), "deceptive acts or practices in or affecting commerce" are unlawful. The FTCA also has special provisions for food, drug, medical device, service, and cosmetic advertising, reflecting the traditional division in responsibility between the FTC and the Food and Drug Administration in responsibility for regulating such things. 15 U.S.C. § 52. The language of the FTCA is often quite broad, with much room for interpretation.**

Unfairness

Although the FTC primarily relies upon its authority to enforce against deceptive trade acts, the FTCA also provides the FTC with the authority to enforce against "unfair" trade acts.

After a variety of controversies during the 1970s, many politicians felt that the FTC was trying to regulate too much of the economy, e.g., by sharply restricting advertising to children. "Unfair" had not previously been defined in the FTCA, and Congress codified a definition designed to limit the FTC's authority: Unfairness requires that "the act or practice causes or is likely to cause substantial injury to consumers [that] is not reasonably avoidable by consumers themselves and not outweighed by countervailing benefits to consumers or to competition." Section 45(n). Public policy cannot serve as a primary basis for a determination of unfairness. For the next three decades, the FTC rarely relied on its unfairness jurisdiction in the absence of an element of deception.

Increased attention to privacy and changing technologies have reinvigorated the FTC's interest in using its unfairness jurisdiction. For a detailed history of the FTC and its regulatory context and future, with special attention to privacy, *see* CHRIS JAY HOOFNAGLE, FEDERAL TRADE COMMISSION PRIVACY LAW AND POLICY (2016). We will discuss privacy in greater detail in Chapter 15, but by way of example, the FTC has successfully pursued a commercial site that posted sexually explicit pictures of women without their consent (e.g., "revenge porn") for unfairness.

Another unfairness enforcement action targeted Apple's policy of allowing in-app purchases, which were particularly popular in apps often used by children, such as "Tiny Zoo Friends." For an extended period, Apple treated a single authorization (e.g., a parent entering her

---

* Certain institutions are exempt from the FTC's regulation, usually because some other industry-specific regulatory agency or enforcement scheme exists. Banks, savings and loan institutions, and federal credit unions are probably the most significant. Common carriers, air carriers, and businesses that are subject to the Packers and Stockyards Act of 1921 are some other examples.

** Not everything is delegated to the FTC's discretion. Section 55(a)(2), for example, is a highly specific provision prohibiting producers of margarine from indicating in any way in ads that margarine is a dairy product. This reflects lobbying by dairy producers to gain advantages over competitors.

password to download an app) as valid for fifteen minutes. This period allowed many children to incur charges that they didn't understand and that were a surprise to their parents. Some of these charges were quite large, from $500 to $2,600. The FTC alleged it was unfair to bill parents and other iTunes account holders for children's activities in apps that are likely to be used by children without obtaining the account holders' express informed consent. Apple agreed to provide full refunds of at least $32.5 million. *In re* Apple Inc., FTC File No. 112-3108 (Jan. 15, 2014).

However, some cases have pushed back on the FTC's use of unfairness to deal with problems such as data breaches due to allegedly poor security. Even if companies mishandled consumer data, the FTC may not be able to show actual harm to consumers. *See, e.g.*, LabMD v. FTC, 678 Fed.Appx. 816 (11th Cir. 2016) (staying FTC order against defendant where exposure of consumer information had not been shown to be likely to cause harm), *upheld on other grounds*, 891 F.3d 1286 (11th Cir. 2018); FTC v. D-Link Sys. Inc., No. 3:17-cv-00039 (N.D. Cal. Sept. 19, 2017) (dismissing unfairness claim because, despite alleged cybersecurity vulnerabilities, the FTC failed to allege that harm to consumers was likely as opposed to possible), *consent settlement filed* (Jul. 2, 2019).

Unfairness gives the FTC an extra tool (beyond its authority over deception) to combat bad behavior by advertisers, as long as it falls within the statutory definition. *See, e.g.*, FTC v. Roca Labs, Inc., No. 15-cv-02231 (M.D. Fla. Oct. 29, 2015) (enjoining a contractual prohibition on truthful and nondefamatory but "disparaging" reviews as unfair, and barring defendant from seeking to collect extra money from those who published such reviews). Does the statutory definition of unfairness leave the FTC with too much discretion?

Structure of the Commission

The president appoints, with Senate confirmation, five commissioners to manage the FTC's activities. Appointments are for seven-year terms. No more than three commissioners may be members of the president's political party. Within the FTC, the Bureau of Competition administers antitrust law, the Bureau of Economics provides economic analysis and supports investigations and rulemakings, and the Bureau of Consumer Protection enforces the laws and rules on which we will focus.

The FTC has a number of avenues for exercising its broad regulatory mandate:

- Federal court litigation against a specific advertiser;
- Adversarial administrative proceedings to require a specific advertiser to cease and desist unfair or deceptive practices, resulting in consent decrees or opinions pursuant to a final cease-and-desist order;
- Rulemaking and public statements of enforcement policies to guide advertisers as a group; and
- Formal and informal advisory opinions for specific advertisers.

This section will look more closely at each of these options.

B. Enforcement of FTC Advertising Regulations

There are two pillars of truth in advertising according to the FTC: First, advertising must be truthful and not misleading. Second, advertisers must have adequate substantiation for all product claims before disseminating their advertising. Advertising Substantiation Policy Statement, 49 Fed. Reg. 30999, Aug. 2, 1984.

The FTC does not, of course, pursue every instance of misleading advertising. The factors that guide its enforcement discretion include:

- *Purchase Frequency and Price.* When a product is relatively inexpensive and purchased often, *and* the characteristic at issue is relatively easy for consumers to evaluate, the FTC assumes that sellers have little incentive to misrepresent themselves. Consumers can stop buying a product if they're unhappy with it, and the market can be trusted. As we'll discuss in Chapters 4 and 5, there are reasons why the market might not correct problems of this sort, given consumers' vulnerability to certain kinds of manipulations. Nonetheless, the FTC usually follows this rule.

- *Deterrence of Widespread Deceptive Conduct.* The FTC is more interested in national and regional advertising than purely local matters, in order to protect the maximum number of consumers. The rise of the Internet, however, has made this distinction less meaningful because more small businesses can now reach national audiences. The FTC is also interested in objective claims that are difficult for consumers to evaluate, such as scientific claims about product performance.

- *Risk of Physical or Economic Injury.* Health and safety claims are, for obvious reasons, traditional areas of FTC interest. Diet schemes and health supplements have been repeated targets over the past decade. Economic injury also matters: With economic downturns, the FTC focuses more attention on business opportunity and credit repair schemes targeting consumers who are already at financial risk.

In the 1970s and early 1980s, the FTC was especially willing to act against inexpensive products making health claims: Kraft Singles claiming to have more calcium than imitation cheese slices; Listerine claiming to prevent colds; various headache medicines claiming various kinds of superiority. These claims are difficult for consumers to verify, even though the products are inexpensive. The FTC continues to take similar actions against mainstream advertisers, such as Kellogg for claims that its Frosted Mini-Wheats were "clinically shown to improve kids' attentiveness by nearly 20%" (as compared to an empty stomach, it turned out—and Kellogg cherry-picked the evidence even for that claim) and that its Rice Krispies "now helps support your child's immunity."

The FTC also accepts consumer complaints and may act on them. In calendar year 2019, the FTC received 3.2 million consumer complaints—53% related to fraud and 20% related to identity theft. FEDERAL TRADE COMMISSION, CONSUMER SENTINEL NETWORK DATA BOOK 2019: EXECUTIVE SUMMARY (2020).

Competitors also may submit complaints to the FTC, but they are reluctant to do so. Once the FTC starts investigating a matter, the FTC might broaden its inquiry—potentially to include the complaining competitor's practices. As a result, a competitor must be confident that its own affairs are in order before complaining to the FTC. Competitors often prefer suing a competitor directly or initiating a proceeding with the National Advertising Division of the Better Business Bureau.

Once it has decided to act, whether in response to a third-party complaint or on its own initiative, the FTC can pursue individual companies or the entire industry. If a deceptive practice is widespread, an industry-wide investigation may lead to multiple actions against companies, and that will educate other companies in the same field. In "Operation Waistline," for example, the FTC brought multiple actions against the providers of an entire spectrum of weight loss devices, products and programs—including supplements, diet programs and shoe inserts that promised to burn calories for the wearer. The FTC also runs Internet sweeps and "surf days," targeting websites that offer products and services that are often associated with fraud, such as jewelry, healthcare, auctions, scholarship services and get-rich-quick schemes.

The FTC can issue civil investigative demands (CIDs) to investigate potential deception or unfairness. A CID, like a subpoena, can compel document production or oral testimony. The FTC may require the recipient to file written reports or responses to questions.

In the Undertaking Spam, Spyware, and Fraud Enforcement with Enforcers beyond Borders Act of 2006 (US SAFE WEB Act of 2006 or SAFE WEB), Congress further broadened the FTC's investigation and enforcement powers. SAFE WEB allows the FTC to share information with foreign agencies tasked with consumer protection; to use its civil investigative demand power to obtain information for a foreign consumer protection agency; and to share data with any foreign agency "vested with law enforcement or investigative authority in civil, criminal, or administrative matters" as long as the matter being investigated is "substantially similar" to practices prohibited by the FTC Act or other laws administered by the FTC.

Administrative Trials

Once a specific target has been identified, the FTC may use internal administrative trials to obtain cease-and-desist orders, which can then be enforced in federal court. 15 U.S.C. § 45(b). When the FTC first files an administrative complaint, the respondent may sign a consent agreement consenting to the entry of a final order. If the FTC accepts the agreement, it will post the order in the Federal Register for public comment before making the order final.

If the respondent instead contests the charges, FTC staff will argue the case before an independent administrative law judge ("ALJ"). The FTC staff acts as complaint counsel. The FTC's rules govern the proceedings, but those rules are derived from the Federal Rules of Civil Procedure and the Federal Rules of Evidence, and the FTC has stated that the federal rules, and interpretations of them, can be consulted for guidance on the FTC's rules of practice. Discovery is allowed at the discretion and under the control of the ALJ. 16 C.F.R. § 3.43(b). The proponent of a factual assertion bears the burden of proof, and the findings and order must be based on competent and substantial evidence in order to be upheld in court in any subsequent appeal. 5 U.S.C. § 706(2)(E).

The ALJ holds a hearing and issues a decision that sets forth findings of fact and conclusions of law and recommends either a cease-and-desist order or dismissal. Either the complaint counsel or respondent (or both) may appeal the ALJ's decision to the full commission (the five FTC Commissioners). The Commissioners will hear the appeal, also in a trial-type proceeding with briefing, oral argument and ultimately a final decision and order. A final decision is appealable by any respondent against whom it is issued, in any court of appeals within whose jurisdiction respondent "resides or carries on business or where the challenged practice was employed." A party dissatisfied with a court of appeals ruling may, as in other cases, petition for certiorari to the Supreme Court.

Federal Court Litigation

The FTC goes to federal court in two classes of cases. The first type is enforcement of an FTC order. A respondent who violates a final order may be sued in federal district court. The penalty can range up to $11,000 per violation, along with injunctive relief and "other further equitable relief" as the court deems appropriate. 15 U.S.C. § 45(l).

The second type of FTC proceeding in federal court is direct action against unfair and deceptive practices. Under Section 13(b)(1) of the FTCA, the FTC is authorized to seek preliminary injunctive relief in court where the FTC has reason to believe that a defendant "is violating, or is about to violate," a law enforced by the FTC. Section 13(b)(2) provides that the FTC may seek a permanent injunction "in proper cases." While courts increasingly hold competitor and consumer plaintiffs to Rule 9(b)'s rigorous standards for pleading with particularity in false advertising cases on the theory that false advertising is the same as fraud, they have been more forgiving with the FTC. *See* FTC v. AFD Advisors, LLC, No. 13 CV 6420, 2014 WL 274097 (N.D. Ill. Jan. 24, 2014) (fraud and mistake are not elements of an FTC Act claim, so Rule 9(b) did not apply).

The FTC can ask for an injunction against the allegedly unlawful conduct while the FTC investigation is pending. 15 U.S.C. § 53(b) (also known as § 13(b) of the FTC Act). This provision, added in the 1970s, expanded the FTC's power to go to federal court, which previously only existed in cases involving false advertising for food, drugs, medical devices or cosmetics. The initial intent of § 53(b) was to expand antitrust enforcement authority, but the FTC began to use injunctions to challenge false advertising in the 1980s. The FTC has obtained other relief in federal courts as well, such as asset freezes. *See, e.g.*, FTC v. Southwest Sunsites, Inc., 665 F.2d 711 (5th Cir. 1982) (freezing assets and sending notifications to potentially injured consumers); FTC v. Equinox Int'l Corp., 1999 WL 1425373 (D. Nev. Sept. 14, 1999) (appointing receiver).

However, a court recently clipped the FTC's ability to get an injunction if the defendant has ceased its allegedly false advertising. In *FTC v. Shire ViroPharma, Inc.*, 917 F.3d 147 (3d Cir. 2019), the court held the FTC could get a permanent injunction only if it alleged sufficient facts to demonstrate that the defendant was "violating, or is about to violate," the law, which the FTC had not done in that case.

If the FTC successfully obtains redress for consumer injury and disgorgement of ill-gotten gains, the FTC will disburse money to harmed consumers. The FTC may decide to forego restitution and disgorgement, however, if it believes that private actions or criminal proceedings will bring complete relief for consumers. In recent years, the FTC has taken an increased interest in private class-action lawsuits, occasionally intervening to ensure that settlements are large enough to make deceived consumers whole.

The FTC often has a choice of venue because it can sue in either its internal administrative proceeding or in federal court. There are pros and cons of each venue. From the FTC's standpoint, starting with federal court has typically been more efficient because injunctive and monetary relief are often available together, though in several circuits this is no longer true. When the FTC wins an administrative proceeding, it must still bring a later federal court action to get consumer redress. Moreover, an administrative cease-and-desist order is not final and effective until sixty days have passed, unlike an injunction.

So why would the FTC choose the administrative route? When it starts in federal court, the FTC must prove the facts as any plaintiff must. A federal court reviewing an FTC administrative action, however, must affirm the commission's findings of fact if they are supported by "substantial evidence," and must give "substantial deference" to the FTC's constructions of the FTC Act as articulated in both adjudication and rulemaking. *See* 15 U.S.C. § 45(c) ("if supported by evidence, [FTC findings of fact] shall be conclusive"); Hospital Corp. of Am. v. FTC, 807 F.2d 1381 (7th Cir. 1986) ("Our only function is to determine whether the Commission's analysis of the [evidence] is so implausible, so feebly supported by the record, that it flunks even the deferential test of substantial evidence."). A court may, however, examine the FTC's findings more closely where they differ from those of the ALJ. Thiret v. FTC, 512 F.2d 176 (10th Cir. 1975). The FTC receives some deference as to its informed judgment that a particular commercial practice violates the FTC Act, but courts resolve issues of law on their own merits. *See* FTC v. Ind. Fed'n of Dentists, 476 U.S. 447 (1986).

Reviewing the years 1978–1988, Ross D. Petty found 125 FTC administrative proceedings and thirteen federal district court actions related to false advertising. Sixty percent settled by consent order during investigation, and nearly half of those litigated also settled. The FTC won almost every remaining case, losing only one ALJ trial and one of twelve cases appealed to a court of appeals. Ross D. Petty, *FTC Advertising Regulation: Survivor or Casualty of the Reagan Revolution?*, 30 AMER. BUS. L.J. 1 (1992); see also Maureen K. Ohlhausen, *Administrative Litigation at the FTC: Effective Tool for Developing the Law or Rubber Stamp?*, 12 J. COMPETITION L. & ECON. 623 (2016) ("[T]he FTC has found liability in almost every Part 3 case in the last decade. But the appellate record suggests that those matters had merit, meaning that the law and facts likely warranted liability. Indeed, the federal courts have affirmed 100 percent of the FTC administrative final orders issued in the last decade and challenged on appeal").

As you can see, the number of actions filed in 2019 is rather low, but the balance has shifted to federal court, and the amounts involved in each case can be rather large:

CONSUMER PROTECTION

⚖ ACTIONS FILED

Administrative	27
Federal	41
Civil Penalty	8

⚒ ORDERS OBTAINED

Administrative	19
Redress, Disgorgement & Permanent Injunction	97
Civil Penalty	10

📋 POLICY INITIATIVES

Workshops, Conferences & Hearings	14
Rulemakings Completed	1
Reports	14

CONSUMER REPORTS

- Identity Theft 650,572 (20.33%)
- Imposter Scams 647,472 (20.23%)
- Telephone & Mobile Services 186,475 (5.83%)
- Online Shopping & Negative Reviews 173,785 (5.43%)
- Credit Bureaus, Info Furnishers & Report Users 165,831 (5.46%)
- Banks & Lenders 149,457 (4.67%)
- Debt Collection 135,147 (4.22%)
- Prizes, Sweepstakes & Lotteries 124,841 (3.90%)
- Auto Related 115,109 (3.60%)
- Internet Services 78,848 (2.46%)
- Other Categories* 375,074 (11.72%)

3,200,329 TOTAL REPORTS⁺

*Does not include Do Not Call reports. "Other Categories" does not include Unspecified or Miscellaneous reports.

MONETARY RELIEF

💲 TOP 5 REDRESS, DISGORGEMENT AND CIVIL CONTEMPT JUDGMENTS

Equifax*	$425 million
University of Phoenix	$190.97 million
AdvoCare International, L.P.	$150.1 million
AT&T Mobility	$60 million
OMICS Group	$50.13 million

⚖ TOP 5 CIVIL PENALTY CASES**

Google LLC & YouTube LLC***	$136 million
Musical.ly (TikTok)	$5.7 million
NetDotSolutions (James Christiano)	$1.35 million
Jasjit Gotra (Alliance Security)	$300,000
Media Mix 365	$264,000

*Equifax will also pay an additional $175 million in civil penalties to 48 states, the District of Columbia and Puerto Rico, as well as $100 million to the CFPB

**This does not include the Facebook settlement, which would require the company to pay $5 billion in civil penalties, because the final order and judgment has not yet been entered by the court.

***Google and YouTube paid an additional $34 million to the state of New York

1.92 MILLION consumers received **$136 MILLION** in redress directly from the FTC

ADDITIONAL REDRESS ADMINISTERED BY OTHERS	$95.86 million
NEW REDRESS, DISGORGEMENT AND CIVIL CONTEMPT AWARDS	$1.17 billion
CIVIL PENALTIES AWARDED**	$143.76 million

FEDERAL TRADE COMMISSION, STATS & DATA 2019.

Older studies have found that FTC deceptive advertising complaints are correlated with the targeted companies suffering stock market losses. Alan Mathios & Mark Plummer, *The Regulation of Advertising by the FTC: Capital Market Effects*, 12 RES. L. & ECON. 77 (1989); Sam Peltzman, *The Effects of FTC Advertising Regulation*, 24 J.L & ECON. 403 (1981) ("[T]he overall message of the results is that the salary of the copywriter or lawyer who avoids entanglement with the FTC in the first place is a bargain."). Some critics of the FTC's pursuit of monetary remedies have used these results to suggest that additional FTC financial penalties are unnecessary to deter major, publicly traded companies from making false claims, especially given the likelihood that an FTC complaint will trigger a follow-on class action asserting the same claims on behalf of consumers. *But see* Michael A. Wiles et al., *Stock Market Response to Regulatory Reports of Deceptive Advertising: The Moderating Effect of Omission Bias and Firm Reputation*, 29 MKTG. SCI. 828 (2010) (finding that stock market returns decrease less than 1% as a result of regulatory action against deceptive advertising). Others defend consumer redress measures as important ways to protect consumers who have suffered losses, especially given the increasing barriers to successful consumer class actions that we will discuss in Chapters 8 and 9.

Non-litigation Activity

The FTC engages in substantial consumer and business education efforts, most of which are available on its website. Its activities for children provide a useful introduction to the types of consumer education the FTC has offered in recent years. Business guidance focuses on advice intelligible to non-lawyers. *See, e.g.*, FEDERAL TRADE COMM'N, ADVERTISING FAQ'S: A GUIDE FOR SMALL BUSINESS.

The FTC may also offer formal and informal advisory opinions. Parties may "request advice from the Commission with respect to a course of action which the requesting party proposes to pursue." 16 C.F.R. § 1.1(a). Although the FTC is under no obligation to answer an inquiry, it will consider the inquiry and issue an advisory opinion "where practicable," when (1) the matter involves a substantial or novel question of fact or law and there is no clear FTC or court precedent; and (2) the subject matter of the request and consequent publication of FTC advice is of significant public interest. 16 C.F.R. §§ 1.1(a)(1)–(2).

The FTC will not consider hypothetical questions and will generally decline to consider requests that are already the subject of rulemaking, industry guidelines or enforcement proceedings against other parties. Advisory opinions are not binding, and the FTC expressly reserves the right to reconsider the question and rescind its opinion. However, good faith reliance on a commission opinion will preclude an enforcement action if all the relevant facts and circumstances were disclosed. The FTC's informal advice also is not binding. The FTC reserves the right not only to rescind informal advice, but also to commence an enforcement proceeding "where appropriate."

In addition, the FTC has rulemaking authority to deal with persistent problems, but its authority is extremely limited compared to that of most federal agencies. It cannot make rules according to the notice-and-comment procedure that is governed by the Administrative

Procedure Act.[1] Instead, it must go through a significantly more complex and burdensome process—another consequence of the perception in the late 1970s and early 1980s that the FTC was trying to exercise too much control over the economy.

Rulemaking must begin with a determination that the practice at issue is "prevalent." 15 U.S.C. § 57a(b)(3). It therefore often follows a series of individual actions against specific advertisers. The FTC staff engages in a preliminary investigation, after which the Federal Register publishes an advanced notice of proposed rulemaking. Interested parties are invited to comment on whether a rulemaking should occur. If the FTC decides to initiate formal rulemaking, the Federal Register publishes a notice of the proposed rule and the FTC holds public hearings. Interested parties have limited rights of cross-examination. After a period for rebuttal comments, the staff publishes a recommended decision and invites further public comment. At that point, the full commission decides whether or not to promulgate the rule. The rule, if any, is subject to appeal. Knowingly violating FTC rules may result in a civil penalty of up to $11,000.

Given how challenging this process is, an investigation often results in some other action, such as a staff report, a policy statement or a report to Congress. These are not legally binding, but advertisers should pay attention to them. The FTC's policy statements and guides are often good indicators of what activity will trigger FTC action.

One common form of FTC policy is the "Industry Guide," a statement of enforcement policy with respect to a practice common to many industries or to specific practices of a particular industry. Some industry guides are sector-specific, targeting sellers of automobiles, jewelry, leather and tires, among others. Other guides apply to specific types of advertising, including "free" offers, endorsements by third parties, price comparisons and warranties. If the FTC alleges a violation of a guide, the respondent may still argue that its conduct does not violate the FTC Act, and it is entitled to a full adjudicatory hearing on the matter. *See* FTC v. Mary Carter Paint Co., 382 U.S. 46 (1965). Nevertheless, the guides provide helpful insights into how the FTC views the law. As a result, advertisers have strong incentives to honor the industry guides to reduce the risks of an FTC investigation.

NOTES AND QUESTIONS

Degree of Judicial Deference to FTC Pronouncements. Given that guides and policy statements don't have the force of formally enacted rules, what sort of deference should a reviewing court give them? In a case involving enforcement of a cease-and-desist order against one dental organization's policy designed to give member dentists leverage in dealing with insurers, the Supreme Court stated that "courts are to give some deference to the Commission's informed judgment that a particular commercial practice is to be condemned as 'unfair.'" FTC v. Ind. Fed'n of Dentists, 476 U.S. 447 (1986).

If the FTC is entitled to deference in particular cases, do the same rationales apply to its general guidelines? In *Miller v. Herman*, 600 F.3d 726 (7th Cir. 2010), the court noted that

---

[1] With respect to "Made in the USA" and similar claims, the FTC can use ordinary notice and comment rulemaking. 15 U.S.C. § 45a. In June 2020, nearly 26 years after this authority was granted to it, the FTC announced that it intended to promulgate such a rule.

FTC actions not rising to the level of substantive rules are not entitled to the deference given to government agencies under *Chevron U.S.A., Inc. v. Natural Resources Defense Council, Inc.*, 467 U.S. 837 (1984), which upholds agency determinations if they are based on a permissible construction of the governing statute. However, it continued, an agency interpretation may be entitled to some deference "whatever its form, given the specialized experience and broader investigations and information available to the agency, and given the value of uniformity in its administrative and judicial understandings of what a national law requires." The amount of deference given depends on factors such as the thoroughness with which the FTC developed the policy, the agency's expertise in the area, the persuasiveness of its reasoning and its consistency with other FTC pronouncements.

Due to FTC's role as a primary consumer watchdog, courts often defer to the FTC's position even if not legally required to do so.

What role should FTC policy statements play in cases that are not brought by the FTC? In other words, if a court finds that a defendant has engaged in conduct that a Guide declares deceptive, should that suffice to show that the defendant has, in fact, engaged in deceptive conduct? What if the defendant's conduct matches an example a Guide approves as nondeceptive? Should the plaintiff necessarily lose? *See* B. Sanfield, Inc. v. Finlay Fine Jewelry Corp., 168 F.3d 967 (7th Cir. 1999) (finding in a Lanham Act case about deceptive pricing that the FTC Guides Against Deceptive Pricing "should serve as the starting, if not the ending, point of the court's analysis," in the context of finding no false advertising); Casper Sleep, Inc. v. Mitcham, 204 F. Supp. 3d 632 (S.D.N.Y. 2016) (citing cases holding that a plaintiff "may and should rely on FTC guidelines as a basis for asserting false advertising under the Lanham Act").

The FTC can use its rules to create legal standards that make enforcement actions easier—most prominently by establishing procedural requirements like record-keeping and substantiation to complement substantive anti-deception rules. For example, *Federal Trade Commission v. Tashman*, 318 F.3d 1273 (11th Cir. 2003), involved the FTC's Franchise Rules, which regulate advertising for certain types of business opportunities. The appeals court ruled that the franchisor didn't comply with the Franchise Rule's requirement that the franchisor have a documented and disclosed "reasonable basis" for its predictions about franchisees' revenues or profits. The enforcement action succeeded because the FTC showed the franchisor's procedural failure; although the FTC also showed deceptiveness under Section 5, it was not required to show that the violations of the Franchise Rule were deceptive to consumers.

Rulemaking vs. Other Enforcement Methods. POM Wonderful, facing an enforcement action before an ALJ, argued that the FTC had unlawfully required a new, higher level of substantiation for health claims than mandated by the existing rules. The FTC was allegedly imposing this new standard by requiring all consent orders involving health claims to include an agreement to make only claims that would satisfy the FDA's stringent requirements (two well-controlled double-blinded clinical studies supporting the claims). POM Wonderful alleged that this new standard had been imposed both in violation of the Administrative Procedure Act and the Constitution. After the full Commission upheld a finding that POM Wonderful had violated the FTCA, the D.C. Circuit affirmed POM

Wonderful's liability. POM Wonderful LLC v. FTC, 777 F.3d 478 (D.C. Cir. 2015). The court of appeals stated that it "is well settled that an agency 'is not precluded from announcing new principles in an adjudicative proceeding,'" and that "'the choice between rulemaking and adjudication lies in the first instance within the agency's discretion.'"

Individual Liability. The FTC can, and often does, sue corporate officers and executives personally. *See* Paul D. Rubin & Smitha G. Stansbury, *FTC Enforcement Against Individuals*, Patton Boggs LLP, April 2011. Individuals can be liable when they "participated directly in the practices or acts [that violate the FTC Act] or had the authority to control them." *See* FTC v. Amy Travel Serv., Inc., 875 F.2d 564 (7th Cir. 1989). In this respect, the FTC is not constrained by traditional limits on piercing the corporate veil.

The FTC also can pursue "relief defendants" who did not violate the FTC Act themselves but nevertheless possess ill-gotten gains, such as a spouse of an individual who violated the FTC Act.

The Consumer Financial Protection Bureau. Banks and other financial institutions (aside from debt collectors) were statutorily excluded from the FTC's authority. For a long time, there was no entity specifically charged with protecting consumers from deceptive and unfair conduct by banks, mortgage lenders and the like. The CFPB was created to fill that regulatory gap. The agency has rulemaking, supervision, and enforcement authority over "an extremely broad swath of the consumer financial services industry." Adam J. Levitin, *The Consumer Financial Protection Bureau: An Introduction*, 32 REV. BANKING & FIN. L. 321 (2013) (providing an overview of the CFPB's powers and limitations).

The CFPB's first public enforcement action was a major settlement with Capital One over charges of deceptive marketing of credit card "add-on" products, such as payment protection and credit monitoring. Capital One agreed to pay a total of between $140 million and $150 million in restitution to two million customers, along with $60 million in penalties. CFPB Probe into Capital One Credit Card Marketing Results in $140 Million Consumer Refund, July 18, 2012. Other big-dollar settlements have followed. *See* Brian Wolfman, *CFPB Obtains Massive Credit-Card Deception Consent Order from Bank of America*, CONSUMER L. & POL'Y BLOG (Apr. 9, 2014) (discussing settlement involving $727 million in consumer refunds and $20 million penalty based on deceptive marketing of credit card-protection services and unfair billing practices). The CFPB has also issued numerous rules, mostly on various aspects of mortgage lending. CFPB, *Regulations*.

While both the CFPB and the FTC have authority to stop unfair and deceptive conduct, the CFPB can also regulate "abusive" conduct. An "abusive" practice is one that:

> (1) materially interferes with the ability of a consumer to understand a term or condition of a consumer financial product or service; or
> (2) takes unreasonable advantage of—
>> (A) a lack of understanding on the part of the consumer of the material risks, costs, or conditions of the product or service;
>> (B) the inability of the consumer to protect the interests of the consumer in selecting or using a consumer financial product or service; or

(C) the reasonable reliance by the consumer on a covered person to act in the interests of the consumer.

Consumer Financial Protection Act § 1031(d)(2). Is there "abusive" conduct that wouldn't also be "unfair" or "deceptive?" One writer has suggested that conduct is abusive when it "exploit[s] certain predictable consumer behaviors, even when those behaviors are not economically rational." Benedict J. Schweigert, *The CFPB's "Abusiveness" Standard and Consumer Irrationality* (2012). That is, the CFPB has authority to act on the insights of behavioral economics, which identify systematic and predictable cognitive errors made by many people, such as overestimating their future ability to pay when borrowing or underestimating how often they will overdraft their accounts. "Unlike the 'unfair' and 'deceptive' standards, this provision places the burden of reasonableness on the lender and employs an empirical model of consumer behavior." Schweigert argues that, by contrast, the FTC has focused on injury to consumers acting rationally. (Recall that the definition of "unfair" conduct is conduct that causes "substantial injury to consumers which is not reasonably avoidable by consumers themselves and not outweighed by countervailing benefits to consumers or to competition." Consumer Financial Protection Act § 45(n).) Is abusiveness a good additional legal standard for government enforcement agencies?

How Other Countries Do It. Consumer protection agencies exist worldwide. Japan's consumer protection law, for example, was adopted in 1968. In the United Kingdom, comprehensive fair-trading legislation supplemented more-targeted consumer protection measures in 1973, creating the Office of Fair Trading. *See* IAIN RAMSEY, CONSUMER LAW AND POLICY: TEXT AND MATERIALS ON REGULATING CONSUMER MARKETS (2007). Canada's consumer protection regime has the same basic provisions as the FTCA, imposing both a nonmisleadingness and a substantiation requirement. Section 74.01(1)(a) of the Canadian Competition Act (R.S.C. 1985, c. C-34) prohibits any "representation to the public that is false or misleading in a material respect," while section 74.01(1)(b) prohibits any "representation to the public . . . of the performance, efficacy, or length of life of the product that is not based on an adequate and proper test thereof." Among other remedies, the law authorizes administrative penalties of up to $10 million for the first violation and $15 million per violation thereafter.

Some jurisdictions, including the United States, United Kingdom and Australia, combine consumer protection and competition (antitrust) regulation into the same agencies. Others separate the two functions. The Nordic countries have separate consumer ombudsmen. *See* Kjersti Graver, *A Study of the Consumer Ombudsman Institution in Norway with Some References to the Other Nordic Countries I: Background and Description*, 9 J. CONSUMER POL'Y 1 (1986). How do you think housing antitrust and consumer protection objectives within a single agency affects regulators' views of what helps consumers? From a business point of view, is there any downside to having regulation concentrated in a single agency?

In the European Community, Directive 2005/29/EC Article 2(e) (the Directive on Unfair Commercial Practices) prohibits misleading practices—defined as practices that are likely to mislead the average consumer—and misleading omissions—defined as omissions of material information that the average consumer needs—when the misleading acts or omissions are likely to cause the consumer to take a transactional decision he or she would not have taken otherwise. This rule applies even if the information provided to the consumer is misleading, even if it is literally true. To promote the free movement of goods and services, Member States can't implement stricter—or looser—substantive rules.

However, the Directive doesn't specify enforcement tools, and nations can choose from public or private enforcement as well as from civil, administrative or criminal penalties. Many choose combinations of the options. Nongovernmental organizations commonly help enforce consumer protection law. In the United Kingdom, for example, designated consumer bodies can file complaints with the competition authority and other regulators. By law, the regulators must respond expediently. *See* Colin Scott, *Enforcing Consumer Protection Laws*, in HANDBOOK OF RESEARCH ON INTERNATIONAL CONSUMER LAW (Howells et al. eds., 2010).

Other private parties can sometimes take action on their own. The Australian Trade Practices Act 1974, for example, allows consumers, competitors and consumer organizations to enforce the prohibition on misleading and deceptive practices. Most other countries, however, do not allow class action suits or embrace the American norms that make class actions so significant in the United States.

2.   Competitors: The Lanham Act and Self-Regulation

Although false advertising lawsuits between competitors regularly involve claims under state law, including common law unfair competition and statutory consumer protection violations, the main law used by competitors is the federal Lanham Act, which covers both trademark and false advertising. The major alternative to litigation for national advertisers is voluntary arbitration by the National Advertising Division (NAD) of the Better Business Bureau. Choosing between a lawsuit and a NAD proceeding can be complicated, as we will see.

A.   The Lanham Act

This overview is brief because the next few chapters will review the various elements of a Lanham Act false advertising claim in detail. For now, it will be useful to survey the broad contours of a Lanham Act claim to help contextualize the other legal mechanisms available to challenge advertising.

History

The initial version of Section 43(a) of the Lanham Act, as enacted in 1946, provided that:

> [a]ny person who shall . . . use in connection with any goods or services . . . any false description or representation, including words or other symbols tending falsely to describe or represent the same, and shall cause such goods or services to enter into commerce, . . . shall be liable to a civil action by any person . . . who believes that he is or is likely to be damaged by the use of any such false description or representation.

At first, because the Lanham Act was primarily considered a trademark statute, courts required something akin to trademark infringement, also known as "passing off" or "palming off"—misleading consumers into thinking that the defendant's goods came from the plaintiff. Over time, courts allowed plaintiffs to sue when defendants were making other false claims about their products. This transition was eased by cases that involved facts similar to "passing off." So, when a retailer advertised a picture of plaintiff's dress—which was not protected by any intellectual property rights and was thus free for copying—but actually sold an "inferior" and "notably different" dress, the facts supported a Section 43(a) claim. L'Aiglon Apparel, Inc. v. Lana Lobell, Inc., 214 F.2d 649 (3d Cir. 1954).

However, a significant minority of courts held that the Lanham Act only covered false advertising claims for a defendant's statements about its own products or services, not those made about the plaintiff's competing products or services. *See, e.g.*, Clamp-All Corp. v. Cast Iron Soil Pipe Inst., 851 F.2d 478 (1st Cir. 1988) (declining to disturb older law that Section 43(a) covered only source confusion).

Other cases required falsity about an "inherent quality or characteristic" of the advertised good or service, even if the defendant's false claims could influence consumers' decisions. For example, an ad for imitation fur claimed that it spared the lives of tigers and leopards. The claim was false; federal law already banned using tiger and leopard fur for clothing. The court, however, dismissed the claim because the advertiser didn't say anything false about the imitation furs themselves. *See* Fur Info. & Fashion Council, Inc. v. E.F. Timme & Son, Inc., 501 F.2d 1048 (2d Cir. 1974). The doctrine requiring misrepresentation about an "inherent quality" of the product or service enabled courts to dismiss claims when the relevant consumers cared about features that the court didn't think were really part of the advertised product. So, in *Hertz Corp. v. Avis, Inc.*, 725 F. Supp. 170 (S.D.N.Y. 1989), the court found that a car rental company's ad targeting travel agencies, which focused on the speed with which commissions were paid, did not pertain to an inherent quality of car rentals. Now, courts are likely to find that an "inherent quality" is any quality likely to influence consumer decisions.

Present Form

The Trademark Law Revision Act of 1988 ("TLRA"), which became effective in November 1989, split Section 43(a) (15 U.S.C. § 1125(a)) into two parts. Section 43(a)(1)(A) deals with source/origin claims and in essence confers federal jurisdiction for trademark infringement claims when the plaintiff lacks a federally registered trademark. Section 43(a)(1)(B) now bars the "use in commerce" of:

> any word, term, name, symbol, or device, or any combination thereof, or any false designation of origin, false or misleading description of fact, or false or misleading representation of fact, which . . . in commercial advertising or promotion, misrepresents the nature, characteristics, qualities, or geographic origin of his or her or another person's goods, services, or commercial activities.

This language codifies the older majority rule that Section 43(a) prohibits false advertising, whether the falsity concerns the plaintiff's products and services or the defendant's. Because false claims about anyone's products are actionable, false advertising claims under the Lanham Act substitute for or complement common law causes of action for commercial defamation, commercial disparagement or trade libel. The TLRA also broadened the Lanham Act language to clarify that virtually any type of false advertising or promotional claim may be actionable.

According to the statute, "any person who believes that he or she is or is likely to be damaged by" false advertising may sue in federal court. Nevertheless, consumers may not bring Lanham Act claims. Chapter 7 will explain.

Otherwise, courts often give broad effect to Section 43(a)'s sweeping language. For example, because the law prohibits misrepresentations about "commercial activities" as well as "goods" and "services," falsehoods about the general way in which a plaintiff conducts business are actionable. Proctor & Gamble, Co. v. Haugen, 222 F.3d 1262 (10th Cir. 2000) (statements that plaintiff's profits were used to fund a Satanic cult were actionable); *see also* Fuente Cigar, Ltd. v. Opus One, 985 F. Supp. 1448 (M.D. Fla. 1997) (statements made by competitor in trade publication interview that cigar manufacturer was trying to "trade on" reputation of winemaker and had "effectively appropriated" winemaker's mark were statements about manufacturer's commercial activities). For convenience, we generally refer only to goods and services, but keep in mind that commercial activities are also covered.

Today, many courts use a six-factor inquiry to determine a Lanham Act violation. A plaintiff will prevail when there is:

1) a false or misleading statement of fact;
2) in interstate commerce (this element is almost always satisfied and rarely contested);
3) in connection with commercial advertising or promotion;
4) that actually deceives or has the tendency to deceive an appreciable number of consumers in the intended audience;
5) that is material; and
6) that is likely to cause injury to the plaintiff.

A key point, on which we will elaborate in the next chapter and Chapter 7, is that the Lanham Act case law distinguishes between *false messages*—claims that are simply untrue on their face—and *misleading messages*—claims that are technically or literally true but whose ambiguities lead reasonable consumers to draw mistaken inferences. A Lanham Act plaintiff has a substantially easier time prevailing against a false statement than a misleading one, in large part because courts require evidence that consumers are actually deceived by misleading statements, usually with a consumer survey.

Critics of the Lanham Act's expansion of false advertising law argue that false advertising cases brought by competitors are more wasteful than most litigation. They often require judges to decide highly technical claims in which they have no background. The parties are often wealthy companies that can afford to litigate every aspect of the case to death. The claims often are more likely to change market share allocation (i.e., reallocate consumer dollars between competitors) than improve consumer welfare (i.e., drive consumers to alternative products or stop shopping altogether). *See* Lillian R. BeVier, *Competitor Suits for*

False Advertising Under Section 43(a) of the Lanham Act: A Puzzle in the Law of Deception, 78 VA. L. REV. 1 (1992).

NOTES AND QUESTIONS

Even if courts aren't perfect at determining the truth, how should we evaluate the risks of false positives (wrongly enjoining true claims) and false negatives (wrongly failing to enjoin false claims)? Are competitors likely to be worse advocates for the truth than other potential challengers such as consumers, the FTC or state attorneys general? As it happens, critics of competitor suits often dislike consumer class actions and government lawsuits as well.

Remedies. Both monetary and equitable remedies are available in Lanham Act cases. Damages (but not punitive damages) are available, though most courts require a plaintiff to show actual consumer confusion or intentional deception before awarding them. Damages may be trebled if needed to compensate the plaintiff if the harm "can neither be dismissed as speculative nor precisely calculated." ALPO Petfoods, Inc. v. Ralston-Purina Co., 997 F.2d 949 (D.C. Cir. 1993).

Possible equitable remedies include a temporary restraining order, a preliminary injunction and a permanent injunction against continuing false advertising. In extraordinary cases, the court may order product recall, destruction of advertising materials or corrective advertising, but such outcomes are extremely rare. In exceptional cases, courts can also award attorneys' fees. Chapter 9 discusses remedies in further detail.

B.   BBB/ASRC/NAD

The Advertising Self-Regulatory Council (ASRC), part of the Better Business Bureau (BBB), oversees the National Advertising Division (NAD) and other divisions focusing on children's advertising and direct-response advertising. The NAD provides a venue to adjudicate competitor disputes as an alternative to Lanham Act lawsuits in court.

The NAD was founded in 1971, and it has grown substantially in popularity as Lanham Act litigation became more expensive and court dockets more crowded. The deregulatory impulses of the 1980s and 1990s also meant that the FTC was more hesitant to challenge advertising except in extreme circumstances, increasing demand for self regulation.

As a self-regulatory body, the NAD can be both more aggressive in its inquiries and more limited in its powers than a court proceeding. Like the FTC and state attorneys general, the NAD monitors advertising, accepts consumer complaints and engages in its own investigations. Competitors can also bring challenges, which make up the bulk of the NAD's activities. A competitor challenge is less likely to occur in industries that have industry-wide substantiation difficulties, such as claims made by diet or vitamin supplement companies. In such cases, the NAD may act on its own initiative when it becomes aware of troublesome claims. The NAD handles about 150 cases per year.

Because NAD's staff attorneys have substantial experience reviewing advertising, advertisers tend to take their rulings seriously. Like the FTC and unlike the Lanham Act, the NAD requires substantiation from advertisers. Moreover, like the FTC, NAD staff attorneys often rely on their own expertise to determine that an ad is likely to deceive consumers; consumer surveys are not required, and discovery is not available. Thus, the NAD can be substantially cheaper and quicker than litigation in federal court.

As a national body, the NAD also attempts to create uniform nationwide precedents. Federal and state courts can't do the same, at least in the absence of a ruling from the Supreme Court (a rarity in advertising law-related matters). The NAD publishes its decisions, creating a "jurisprudence" that is relatively coherent and reliable.

Unlike the FTC or a court, the NAD cannot compel anyone to participate in its adjudicative process or comply with its decisions. If an advertiser declines to participate, or refuses to change its advertising after an adverse decision, the NAD simply closes the case. The challenger then must seek redress elsewhere, often by filing a lawsuit. The NAD, however, notifies the FTC when a business refuses to participate in its proceedings, and the FTC pays close attention to such referrals.

Thus, advertisers ignore NAD proceedings at their peril. One such NAD referral resulted in an $83 million FTC judgment against a weight-loss company. *See* Seth Stevenson, *How New Is "New"? How Improved Is "Improved"? The People Who Keep Advertisers Honest*, SLATE, July 13, 2009. In another case, the maker of "Cholestaway," a chewable tablet that promised a variety of health benefits, refused to comply with the NAD's findings that its claims were largely unsubstantiated. Bogdana Corp., NAD Case No. 3215 (closed 7/10/95). After the matter was referred to the FTC, the advertiser and its advertising agency were ultimately subject to a consent decree barring the claims, requiring adequate substantiation in the future and mandating regular compliance reports to the FTC. FTC Press Release, *Dietary Supplement Advertiser Settles FTC Charges of Deceptive Health Claims*, May 12, 1998 ("[A]s this case illustrates, when self-regulation fails, we are prepared to take action."). In 2017–18, the FTC took action in fifteen of the ninetten matters NAD referred to FTC. Lawrence Weinstein, *FTC Statistics Confirm Risks to Advertisers of Refusing to Participate in NAD Proceedings*, PROSKAUER ON ADVERTISING, Mar. 21, 2019.

Companies and/or competitors who make challenges must pay the BBB to offset some of the costs of the process. As of 2020, these charges range from $10,000 to $35,000.

The NAD will only evaluate "national" advertising, i.e., "if it is disseminated nationally or to a substantial portion of the United States, or is test-market advertising prepared for national campaigns." ADVERTISING SELF-REGULATORY COUNCIL, THE ADVERTISING INDUSTRY'S PROCESS OF VOLUNTARY SELF-REGULATION, § 1.1(A). Local campaigns, no matter how misleading, are not within its jurisdiction. The NAD advises: "If a complaint involves local advertising or local business practices, including order fulfillment or refund issues, delivery delays or 'bait and switch' tactics, please file a complaint with the Better Business Bureau."

In general, the NAD defines "advertising" broadly. It also evaluates challenges even when an advertiser argues that some federal agency already regulates the claim at issue: the NAD does not recognize a general "preemption" principle. *See* Intervet, Inc., NAD Case No. 3625 (closed Feb. 25, 2000) ("The fact that a government agency regulates a particular industry does not relieve NAD of its responsibility to ensure the truthfulness and accuracy of the advertising claims made by members of that industry. To avoid inconsistency, however, NAD strives to harmonize its analysis and decisions with any related regulations.").

NAD participants cannot issue press releases about bringing or winning challenges. If they do, the NAD will terminate their challenges. The idea is to avoid bringing the NAD into public relations wars. In addition, the NAD will not act while litigation between the parties is pending (see below for more on the interaction between the NAD and the courts).

If the NAD decides to evaluate a matter, the challenge is forwarded to the advertiser, who has fifteen business days to respond with evidence and its argument. Submissions are not released to the public, and the advertiser has the right to submit confidential materials (such as product tests) without sharing them with the opponent. Proceedings may or may not involve an in-person hearing.

The NAD produces a written decision. The advertiser may add an Advertiser's Statement to the decision, indicating whether the advertiser will comply with the decision or appeal to the National Advertising Review Board (NARB). Because the NAD has no enforcement power, it can only find advertising substantiated or recommend that it be changed.

In a typical successful challenge, (1) the NAD will recommend that the advertiser change some or all of the challenged claims, and (2) the advertiser will attach a statement that it disagrees with the NAD's decision but, because the ad campaign at issue has run its course, it is discontinuing the claims at issue. The final decision, including the Advertiser's Statement, is then published, along with a press release, on the NAD's website. Decisions ideally take only a few months, but as the caseload has increased at the NAD, some resolution times have stretched further.

For an appeal, each NARB panel consists of five members—three who work in national advertising, one from an advertising agency and one from the "public" (academics and former members of the public sector). Panel hearings include representatives of the NAD, the advertiser and the complainant. The NARB's review is on the record, without new evidence, and it rarely reverses NAD determinations.

The NAD claims a compliance rate of 90–95% (including compliance after an appeal).

It can be complex to decide between filing a NAD challenge and going to court. If the advertising at issue has sufficiently high stakes, the advertiser may need faster relief from a court than the NAD can provide—such as a temporary restraining order (TRO)— and it may also need to do public relations during the dispute pendency, which the NAD does not allow. For example, Jenny Craig began an advertising campaign in early January 2010—New Year's resolution time—claiming that a major clinical trial had found that Jenny Craig clients lost on average over twice as much weight as lost via the leading competitor, Weight Watchers. Weight Watchers immediately sought a TRO, and it was able to announce the TRO on television on January 20, the day the order was granted. The need for discovery, the likelihood that the advertiser won't comply with the NAD or the prospect of substantial damages from a favorable verdict can also counsel in favor of proceeding in court.

In order to resolve some claims faster, the NAD recently enacted a new program, Fast-Track SWIFT (Single Well-Defined Issue Fast Track), for reviewing "the prominence and/or sufficiency of disclosures in influencer marketing and native advertising as well as other advertising truth and transparency issues that do not require complex claim substantiation." This program promises a decision in twenty business days and is intended to cover issues on which the NAD already has expertise, such as misleading pricing and sales claims and other issues that don't turn on clinical testing or consumer perception evidence.

NOTES AND QUESTIONS

Self-Regulation v. Government Regulation. Angela Campbell has summarized the arguments for and against industry self-regulation as compared to government regulation. *See* Angela J. Campbell, *Self-Regulation and the Media*, 51 FED. COMM. L.J. 711 (1999).

In favor of self-regulation: (1) efficiency, especially in terms of industry participants' superior knowledge about how advertising works on consumers and substantiation of particular claims; (2) flexibility to recognize when change is necessary (e.g., when new claims like "carbon neutral" become popular) and adopt new standards swiftly compared to staid government rulemaking; (3) better compliance because industry participants perceive self-regulation as more reasonable and less intrusive; (4) lower costs to government; and (5) fewer constitutional constraints, such as First Amendment limits on government controls of advertising.

Against self-regulation: (1) expertise may be used to benefit industry rather than the public by approving tactics that sell products but that don't help consumers; (2) self-regulation often results in under-regulation because industries may not invest sufficient resources in the self-regulatory body or give it any bite, which in turn makes the self-regulatory body more cautious in finding violations for fear of triggering open defiance; (3) bad actors can easily ignore industry self-regulation; (4) on the other side, enforcement might be biased, and discretionary decisions might be hard to review; and (5) relatedly, self-regulation might be anticompetitive when it supports the aims of established companies against upstarts who might be using unusual or aggressive tactics to attract consumers' attention.

Does the NAD demonstrate these pros and cons?

Relationship Between the NAD and the Courts. As mentioned above, the NAD will stop a proceeding if either party sues in court. In *Russian Standard Vodka (USA), Inc. v. Allied Domecq Spirits & Wine USA, Inc.*, 523 F. Supp. 2d 376 (S.D.N.Y. 2007), the NAD respondents initiated a lawsuit after a NAD proceeding had already started. The court granted a thirty-day stay to allow the NAD to complete its proceeding because "allowing the NAD, a highly reputable institution, to provide its expert view on Stoli's authenticity as a Russian vodka would be extremely useful in resolving remaining claims in the complaint."

Other courts have reached a different conclusion. *See* Expedia, Inc. v. Priceline.com Inc., 2009 WL 4110851 (W.D. Wash. Nov. 23, 2009) (no stay in part because it wasn't clear that a final NAD decision would be admissible evidence); Rexall Sundown, Inc. v. Perrigo Co., 651 F. Supp. 2d 9 (E.D.N.Y. 2009) (NAD findings are "inadmissible hearsay.").

A competitor who brings a NAD proceeding before suing is less likely to be denied a preliminary injunction for delaying the lawsuit. *See* Millennium Imp. Co. v. Sidney Frank Importing Co., 2004 WL 1447915 (D. Minn. Jun. 11, 2004). Given that injunctive relief often contemplates further disputes between the parties, it may also be tempting to order them to resolve their differences in a NAD proceeding instead of going back to court. *See* Bracco Diagnostics, Inc. v. Amersham Health, Inc., 627 F. Supp. 2d 384 (D.N.J. 2009) (ordering that the parties must submit disputes about future advertising to an arbitrator such as the NAD; the defendant would bear the costs of arbitration if the ads were found to be false, and the plaintiff would do so if the ads were not found to be false, which is not the usual rule in NAD proceedings).

Other Self-Regulatory Bodies. There are numerous trade associations that may also issue guidance or even resolve specific complaints about advertising. Given antitrust concerns, their ability to self-regulate advertising may be limited, but they have a freer hand when targeting false or misleading advertising. *See* California Dental Assn. v. FTC, 526 U.S. 756 (1999). What about targeting "irresponsible" ads? In 2020, the Distilled Spirits Council of the United States (DISCUS) told Aviation Gin to pull a video ad that had gone viral because it starred a woman who had previously acted in a controversial Peloton ad. The Aviation gin ad showed her, possibly distressed because of the end of the relationship shown in the Peloton ad, gulping down a full martini and quickly receiving a new drink from a friend who said, "This is going to be a fun night." DISCUS concluded that the video violated its *Code of Responsible Practices for Beverage Alcohol Advertising and Marketing*, which says that ads should not "depict situations where beverage alcohol is being consumed excessively or in an irresponsible manner."

In Canada, Ad Standards is a similar industry self-regulatory body that enforces the Canadian Code of Advertising Standards. Like NAD, Ad Standards accepts consumer complaints; disputes by competing advertisers are confidential.

3.   State Law: Consumers (and Occasionally Others)

A.   Common Law Claims

Contracts (a Historical Perspective)

From a consumer's perspective, a false ad is a broken promise. The advertiser has offered one thing, but has delivered something else, and the difference is significant to the consumer.

A breach of contract is also a broken promise. Sometimes, a broken promise can support both a false advertising claim and a breach of contract claim; in other cases, it can support only one of the two claims—and sometimes neither.

To sort through the interactions between contracts and false advertising, we start with the classic Carbolic Smoke Ball case, an early example of how courts used contract law to redress a false advertisement.

CARLILL V. CARBOLIC SMOKE BALL COMPANY [1892] EWCA CIV 1 (ENGLISH COURT OF APPEAL)

LORD JUSTICE LINDLEY: . . . We are dealing with an express promise to pay £100 in certain events. Read the advertisement how you will, and twist it about as you will, here is a distinct promise expressed in language which is perfectly unmistakable—

> £100 reward will be paid by the Carbolic Smoke Ball Company to any person who contracts the influenza after having used the ball three times daily for two weeks according to the printed directions supplied with each ball.

We must first consider whether this was intended to be a promise at all, or whether it was a mere puff which meant nothing. Was it a mere puff? My answer to that question is No, and I base my answer upon this passage:

> £1000 is deposited with the Alliance Bank, shewing our sincerity in the matter.

Now, for what was that money deposited or that statement made except to negative the suggestion that this was a mere puff and meant nothing at all? The deposit is called in aid by the advertiser as proof of his sincerity in the matter—that is, the sincerity of his promise to pay this £100 in the event which he has specified. . . .

It appears to me, therefore, that the defendants must perform their promise, and, if they have been so unwary as to expose themselves to a great many actions, so much the worse for them.

LORD JUSTICE BOWEN: I am of the same opinion. . . .

[T]he main point seems to be that the vagueness of the document shews that no contract whatever was intended. It seems to me that in order to arrive at a right conclusion we must read this advertisement in its plain meaning, as the public would understand it. It was intended to be issued to the public and to be read by the public. How would an ordinary person reading this document construe it?

. . . . And it seems to me that the way in which the public would read it would be this, that if anybody, after the advertisement was published, used three times daily for two weeks the carbolic smoke ball, and then caught cold, he would be entitled to the reward. Then again it was said:

How long is this protection to endure? Is it to go on for ever, or for what limit of time?

. . . I think . . . it means that the smoke ball will be a protection while it is in use. That seems to me the way in which an ordinary person would understand an advertisement about medicine, and about a specific against influenza. It could not be supposed that after you have left off using it you are still to be protected for ever, as if there was to be a stamp set upon your forehead that you were never to catch influenza because you had once used the carbolic smoke ball. I think the immunity is to last during the use of the ball. . . .

But it was said there was no check on the part of the persons who issued the advertisement, and that it would be an insensate thing to promise £100 to a person who used the smoke ball unless you could check or superintend his manner of using it. The answer to that argument seems to me to be that if a person chooses to make extravagant promises of this kind he probably does so because it pays him to make them, and, if he has made them, the extravagance of the promises is no reason in law why he should not be bound by them.

It was also said that the contract is made with all the world—that is, with everybody; and that you cannot contract with everybody. It is not a contract made with all the world. There is the fallacy of the argument. It is an offer made to all the world; and why should not an offer be made to all the world which is to ripen into a contract with anybody who comes forward and performs the condition? . . . It is not like cases in which you offer to negotiate, or you issue advertisements that you have got a stock of books to sell, or houses to let, in which case there is no offer to be bound by any contract. Such advertisements are offers to negotiate—offers to receive offers . . . . If this is an offer to be bound, then it is a contract the moment the person fulfils the condition.

. . . If I advertise to the world that my dog is lost, and that anybody who brings the dog to a particular place will be paid some money, are all the police or other persons whose business it is to find lost dogs to be expected to sit down and write me a note saying that they have accepted my proposal? Why, of course, they at once look after the dog, and as soon as they find the dog they have performed the condition. The essence of the transaction is that the dog should be found, and it is not necessary under such circumstances, as it seems to me, that in order to make the contract binding there should be any notification of acceptance. It follows from the nature of the thing that the performance of the condition is sufficient acceptance without the notification of it, and a person who makes an offer in an advertisement of that kind makes an offer which must be read by the light of that common sense reflection. He does, therefore, in his offer impliedly indicate that he does not require notification of the acceptance of the offer. . . .

[The opinion of Lord Justice A.L. Smith, who agrees with the others, is omitted.]

NOTES AND QUESTIONS

Carbolic acid (phenol) is caustic and can affect the human nervous system. The Nazis used it to execute people. Basically, it's a poison.

At the time of the influenza pandemic of 1889–90, when the Carbolic Smoke Ball Company was advertising, no one knew what the flu was or how to prevent or cure it. The makers of the smoke ball, like many sellers of useless remedies, advertised heavily and successfully.

After the case, the company's founder formed a new company and started advertising again. In a new ad, the new Carbolic Smoke Ball Co., Ltd., described the previous ad and then claimed,

> Many thousand Carbolic Smoke Balls were sold on these advertisements, but only three people claimed the reward of £100, thus proving conclusively that this invaluable remedy will prevent and cure the above mentioned diseases. The CARBOLIC SMOKE BALL COMPANY LTD. now offer £200 REWARD to the person who purchases a Carbolic Smoke Ball and afterwards contracts any of the following diseases. . .

The fine print had some restrictive conditions, allowing three months to use the ball and present a claim.

Now, a number of statutory remedies would be available for a false advertisement of this type in the United Kingdom. *See* Consumer Protection from Unfair Trading Regulations 2008/1277 at § 5 (a commercial practice is misleading "if it contains false information and is therefore untruthful . . . or if it or its overall presentation in any way deceives or is likely to deceive the average consumer . . . even if the information is factually correct."). The modern regulatory response would likely focus on the fact that the carbolic smoke ball did not work, rather than on the reward.

Ads as Contract Offers Today. Consider the following case. Shell service stations displayed this ad:

After buying ten gallons of fuel, a customer got a voucher with the receipt. But the voucher was a two-for-one coupon and couldn't be exchanged for a free lift ticket. The consumer could only get a free ticket by buying another at full price, and there were various other restrictions. (This promotion appears to violate FTC and similar state rules about "free" offers.)

In response to a breach of contract claim, defendant Equilon argued that its ad lacked sufficient specificity to be an offer and therefore there could be no acceptance or meeting of the minds. How would you evaluate this argument? *See* Kearney v. Equilon Enters., LLC, 65 F. Supp. 3d 1033 (D. Or. 2014).

Recall Lord Justice Bowen's statement: "[W]e must read this advertisement in its plain meaning, as the public would understand it. It was intended to be issued to the public and to be read by the public. How would an ordinary person reading this document construe it?" If we take this idea as the foundation of advertising law, does the addition of the legal concepts of offer, acceptance, and consideration advance the analysis at all?"

Warranties. Modern consumer protection class actions often add a breach of warranty count. State law requirements for breach of warranty claims vary; in *Sandoval v. PharmaCare US, Inc.*, 145 F. Supp. 3d 986 (S.D. Cal. 2015), for example, the consumer plaintiff adequately pled breach of express warranty by identifying specific statements on a supplement product's packaging that promised increased sexual performance from consumption; alleging reasonable reliance on those statements; and alleging harm because the product didn't and couldn't provide its promised benefits. *Sandoval*, like many consumer cases asserting warranty claims, also claimed for breach of the implied warranty of merchantability, which in California "is breached when the goods do not conform to the promises or affirmations contained on the container or label or are not fit for the ordinary purposes for which the goods are used." Given the allegations that the product didn't work, the *Sandoval* plaintiff stated a claim under the former theory. Despite the plaintiff's survival of a motion to dismiss in *Sandoval*, breach of warranty claims can be difficult to win.

Finally, some plaintiffs may be able to bring Magnuson–Moss Warranty Act (MMWA) claims. The MMWA regulates warranties on consumer goods. It applies to written warranties, which are defined as a written affirmation that "relates to the nature of the material or workmanship and affirms or promises that such material or workmanship is defect free or will meet a specific level of performance over a specific period of time." 15 U.S.C. § 2301(6)(A). Separately, it borrows state-law causes of action for breach of warranty and makes them enforceable in federal court.

One way to look at things is that, under modern consumer protection law, there is a space for liability between a promise serious enough to count as an offer or a warranty and promise-like assertions that no reasonable consumer would take seriously. The space in between— where a reasonable consumer would believe the claim but a court would not find an offer, warranty or other actionable promise under contract law—is now the province of consumer protection law. Of course, a false or misleading offer or warranty might *also* violate a consumer protection statute.

Common-Law Fraud or Deceit. A common-law fraud or deceit action generally requires a plaintiff to show the following elements: (1) a false and material representation, (2) knowledge or recklessness by defendant of its falsity with an intent to deceive and (3) justifiable reliance by the purchaser upon the misrepresentation. Consider the following case, involving a sympathetic but deluded plaintiff. As you read, try to imagine how the plaintiff Audrey Vokes initially understood her relationship to the dance studio (and perhaps to individual instructors), and also try to imagine how the studios' employees thought about her.

VOKES V. ARTHUR MURRAY, INC., 212 SO. 2D 906 (FLA. CT. APP. 1968)

Defendant Arthur Murray, Inc., a corporation, authorizes the operation throughout the nation of dancing schools under the name of 'Arthur Murray School of Dancing' through local franchised operators, one of whom was defendant J. P. Davenport whose dancing establishment was in Clearwater.

Plaintiff Mrs. Audrey E. Vokes, a widow of 51 years and without family, had a yen to be 'an accomplished dancer' with the hopes of finding 'new interest in life'. So, on February 10, 1961, a dubious fate, with the assist of a motivated acquaintance, procured her to attend a 'dance party' at Davenport's 'School of Dancing' where she whiled away the pleasant hours, sometimes in a private room, absorbing his accomplished sales technique, during which her grace and poise were elaborated upon and her rosy future as 'an excellent dancer' was painted for her in vivid and glowing colors. As an incident to this interlude, he sold her eight 1/2-hour dance lessons to be utilized within one calendar month therefrom, for the sum of $14.50 cash in hand paid, obviously a baited 'comeon'.

Thus she embarked upon an almost endless pursuit of the terpsichorean art during which, over a period of less than sixteen months, she was sold fourteen 'dance courses' totalling in the aggregate 2302 hours of dancing lessons for a total cash outlay of $31,090.45, all at Davenport's dance emporium [sic] . . . .

These dance lesson contracts and the monetary consideration therefor of over $31,000 were procured from her by means and methods of Davenport and his associates which went beyond the unsavory, yet legally permissible, perimeter of 'sales puffing' and intruded well into the forbidden area of undue influence, the suggestion of falsehood, the suppression of truth, and the free exercise of rational judgment, if what plaintiff alleged in her complaint was true. From the time of her first contact with the dancing school in February, 1961, she was influenced unwittingly by a constant and continuous barrage of flattery, false praise, excessive compliments, and panegyric encomiums, to such extent that it would be not only inequitable, but unconscionable, for a Court exercising inherent chancery power to allow such contracts to stand.

She was incessantly subjected to overreaching blandishment and cajolery. She was assured she had 'grace and poise'; that she was 'rapidly improving and developing in her dancing skill'; that the additional lessons would 'make her a beautiful dancer, capable of dancing with the most accomplished dancers'; that she was 'rapidly progressing in the development of her dancing skill and gracefulness', etc., etc. She was given 'dance aptitude tests' for the ostensible purpose of 'determining' the number of remaining hours' instructions needed by her from time to time.

At one point she was sold 545 additional hours of dancing lessons to be entitled to award of the 'Bronze Medal' signifying that she had reached 'the Bronze Standard', a supposed designation of dance achievement by students of Arthur Murray, Inc.

Later she was sold an additional 926 hours in order to gain the 'Silver Medal', indicating she had reached 'the Silver Standard', at a cost of $12,501.35.

At one point, while she still had to her credit about 900 unused hours of instructions, she was induced to purchase an additional 24 hours of lessons to participate in a trip to Miami at her own expense, where she would be 'given the opportunity to dance with members of the Miami Studio'.

She was induced at another point to purchase an additional 123 hours of lessons in order to be not only eligible for the Miami trip but also to become 'a life member of the Arthur Murray Studio', carrying with it certain dubious emoluments, at a further cost of $1,752.30.

At another point, while she still had over 1,000 unused hours of instruction she was induced to buy 151 additional hours at a cost of $2,049.00 to be eligible for a 'Student Trip to Trinidad', at her own expense as she later learned.

Also, when she still had 1100 unused hours to her credit, she was prevailed upon to purchase an additional 347 hours at a cost of $4,235.74, to qualify her to receive a 'Gold Medal' for achievement, indicating she had advanced to 'the Gold Standard'.

On another occasion, while she still had over 1200 unused hours, she was induced to buy an additional 175 hours of instruction at a cost of $2,472.75 to be eligible 'to take a trip to Mexico'.

Finally, sandwiched in between other lesser sales promotions, she was influenced to buy an additional 481 hours of instruction at a cost of $6,523.81 in order to 'be classified as a Gold Bar Member, the ultimate achievement of the dancing studio'.

All the foregoing sales promotions, illustrative of the entire fourteen separate contracts, were procured by defendant Davenport and Arthur Murray, Inc., by false representations to her that she was improving in her dancing ability, that she had excellent potential, that she was responding to instructions in dancing grace, and that they were developing her into a beautiful dancer, whereas in truth and in fact she did not develop in her dancing ability, she had no 'dance aptitude', and in fact had difficulty in 'hearing that musical beat'. The complaint alleged that such representations to her 'were in fact false and known by the defendant to be false and contrary to the plaintiff's true ability, the truth of plaintiff's ability being fully known to the defendants, but withheld from the plaintiff for the sole and specific intent to deceive and defraud the plaintiff and to induce her in the purchasing of additional hours of dance lessons'. It was averred that the lessons were sold to her 'in total disregard to the true physical, rhythm, and mental ability of the plaintiff'. In other words, while she first exulted that she was entering the 'spring of her life', she finally was awakened to the fact there was 'spring' neither in her life nor in her feet. . . .

Defendants contend that contracts can only be rescinded for fraud or misrepresentation when the alleged misrepresentation is as to a material fact, rather than an opinion, prediction or expectation, and that the statements and representations set forth at length in the complaint were in the category of 'trade puffing', within its legal orbit.

It is true that 'generally a misrepresentation, to be actionable, must be one of fact rather than of opinion'. But this rule has significant qualifications, applicable here. It does not apply where there is a fiduciary relationship between the parties, or where there has been some artifice or trick employed by the representor, or where the parties do not in general deal at 'arm's length' as we understand the phrase, or where the representee does not have equal opportunity to become apprised of the truth or falsity of the fact represented. As stated by Judge Allen of this Court in *Ramel v. Chasebrook Construction Company*, Fla. App. 1961, 135 So.2d 876:

> . . . A statement of a party having . . . superior knowledge may be regarded as a statement of fact although it would be considered as opinion if the parties were dealing on equal terms.

It could be reasonably supposed here that defendants had 'superior knowledge' as to whether plaintiff had 'dance potential' and as to whether she was noticeably improving in the art of terpsichore. And it would be a reasonable inference from the undenied averments of the complaint that the flowery eulogiums heaped upon her by defendants as a prelude to her contracting for 1944 additional hours of instruction in order to attain the rank of the Bronze Standard, thence to the bracket of the Silver Standard, thence to the class of the Gold Bar Standard, and finally to the crowning plateau of a Life Member of the Studio, proceeded as much or more from the urge to 'ring the cash register' as from any honest or realistic appraisal of her dancing prowess or a factual representation of her progress.

Even in contractual situations where a party to a transaction owes no duty to disclose facts within his knowledge or to answer inquiries respecting such facts, the law is if he undertakes to do so he must disclose the whole truth. From the face of the complaint, it should have been reasonably apparent to defendants that her vast outlay of cash for the many hundreds of additional hours of instruction was not justified by her slow and awkward progress, which she would have been made well aware of if they had spoken the 'whole truth.'

. . . We repeat that where parties are dealing on a contractual basis at arm's length with no inequities or inherently unfair practices employed, the Courts will in general 'leave the parties where they find themselves.' But in the case sub judice, from the allegations of the unanswered complaint, we cannot say that enough of the accompanying ingredients, as mentioned in the foregoing authorities, were not present which otherwise would have barred the equitable arm of the Court to her. In our view, from the showing made in her complaint, plaintiff is entitled to her day in Court.

NOTES AND QUESTIONS

Vokes purchased over 2,300 hours of training. If she did dance training for 40 hours a week (a remarkable physical endurance feat for anyone), it would take her about 14 straight months to use up her purchased hours. If she trained 7 hours a week—an hour a day, every day—it would take her over 6 years to use up her hours. Obviously, at some point, she was accumulating training hours that she was unlikely to use—ever.

Then again, the "hours" arguably functioned more like a loyalty program or a metric for studio engagement, and the studio provided rewards such as medals for more "loyal" customers. If the "hours" really measured something other than actual hours of dance lessons, would that change your perspective about the court's analysis?

As to Vokes' dancing potential, do you agree that it was reasonable for Vokes to rely on the defendants' claimed expertise? Shouldn't she have been able to assess her progress for herself? If you think she was fooling herself with the eager assistance of the defendants, might you still think the defendants behaved actionably?

The idea that people with special knowledge may have special duties is a common one. If a health professional falsely told Vokes that her treatment for cancer was going well, would we expect Vokes to be able to discern the truth? When one's own senses are not necessarily reliable, reliance on an apparent expert may be more reasonable.

Consider the role of gender stereotypes in the court's decision: Was the court influenced by the idea that women, especially older single women, need special protection? In a time when women were routinely denied financial education and experience, was the court acting appropriately in assessing Vokes' capacities according to her pleadings? *See* Debora L. Threedy, *Dancing Around Gender: Lessons from Arthur Murray on Gender and Contracts*, 45 WAKE FOREST L. REV. 749 (2010). What would a gender-neutral standard of reasonability look like, and how would that differ from a standard of reasonability that uses an unimpaired adult male as the model "reasonable person"?

The result in *Vokes* is not particularly common today. In fraud cases, the courts are often less solicitous of consumers who have let themselves be duped when they could have protected themselves. In many states, various doctrines require "reasonable" consumers to behave like suspicious lawyers, reading for ambiguity and disbelieving promises that aren't contained in a binding contract, even when a salesperson explicitly promises that the fine print is just meaningless legalese. *See* Debra Pogrund Stark & Jessica M. Choplin, *A License To Deceive: Enforcing Contractual Myths Despite Consumer Psychological Realities*, 5 N.Y.U. J. L. & BUS. 617 (2009).

In recent years, the trend has been to tighten reliance requirements, which allows sellers to disavow promises made by salespeople or in ads through contracts that consumers don't read or understand. Research, however, shows that people often fail to read written contracts that contradict oral promises, even when the contradictory terms are (1) highlighted in red, (2) in a larger font than other terms, (3) require the consumer to initial the terms *and* (4) part of a single-page document. Even when people do read the contracts, they often accept the oral representations instead because of social norms about trusting conversation partners. *See* Jessica M. Choplin et al., *A Psychological Investigation of Consumer Vulnerability to Fraud: Legal and Policy Implications*, 35 L. & PSYCH. REV. 61 (2011).

Under the modern Federal Rules of Civil Procedure, plaintiffs must plead fraud claims with particularity, which requires far more detail than other claims do. Consumer-plaintiffs often struggle to fulfill the heightened pleading requirements for a fraud claim and prove the scienter element. *See* Bell Atlantic Corp. v. Twombly, 550 U.S. 544 (2007) (raising the pleading standard in general).

Not every "lie" counts as "fraud," depending on what the defendant might have known or believed. Thus, consumer plaintiffs tend to emphasize statutory causes of action, though they may plead fraud in the alternative. The remainder of this chapter explains how state consumer protection laws operate, both for consumer-plaintiffs and for state attorneys general, who enforce the laws on behalf of their states' populations.

B. Consumer-Protection Laws

Overview

Every state has a consumer protection law that protects its own consumers. State consumer protection litigation is a growth field, and it's growing faster in federal than state courts (a cumulative average growth rate of 6.1%and 3.4%, respectively, from 2000–2013). James C. Cooper & Joanna Shepherd, State Unfair and Deceptive Trade Practices Laws: An Economic And Empirical Analysis.

Many state consumer protection laws were enacted in the 1960s out of concern that the FTC and other agencies were under-enforcing the law. *See generally* RICHARD ALDERMAN & MARY DEE PRIDGEN, CONSUMER PROTECTION AND THE LAW § 2:10 (2008). Lawmakers were also concerned that traditional fraud causes of action imposed burdens too high for deceived plaintiffs to meet, and that even when a case could be made, the remedies didn't deter deception. Traditional fraud doctrine, for example, presumed a one-on-one transaction, not a repeated campaign, and made prospective injunctive relief difficult to secure. The requirement of proving fraudulent intent also defeated many claims even when consumers had been deceived and harmed. And without awards of statutory damages or attorneys' fees, most losses due to deception were simply too small to litigate. The solution was new laws protecting consumers from false advertising and deceptive business techniques.

State consumer protection laws mirror the FTC Act's prohibition of *"unfair or deceptive acts or practices* in or affecting commerce," 15 U.S.C. § 45(a)(1), and they are often called UDAP or "Little FTC" statutes. A critical difference between the FTCA and most UDAP statutes, however, is that state laws allow private enforcement by consumer-plaintiffs.

Consumers—or at least their lawyers—have taken advantage of that opportunity. According to one study of over 17,000 reported federal district and state appellate decisions, "[b]etween 2000 and 2007 the number of CPA [consumer protection act] decisions reported in federal district and state appellate courts increased by 119%. This large increase in CPA litigation far exceeds increases in tort litigation as well as overall litigation during the same period." Searle Civil Justice Institute, *State Consumer Protection Acts: An Empirical Investigation of Private Litigation Preliminary Report* (Dec. 2009).

There is a sometimes-bewildering amount of variety in state UDAP laws. For example, statutes of limitation range from one year in Arizona to six years in Maine. But that is far from the most important difference. This section sketches out generalities and indicates points of variation that are often significant.

Some UDAP statutes are based on the Uniform Deceptive Trade Practices Act (UDTPA), drafted in 1964 and rewritten in 1966. The UDTPA enumerates twelve specific deceptive practices, covering misleading trade identification (including passing off and trademark infringement), false advertising, deceptive advertising and a final catch-all ban on "any other conduct which similarly creates a likelihood of confusion or misunderstanding."* As the inclusion of trademark infringement and similar conduct indicates, the UDTPA prioritized competitive concerns.

Other state laws are based on the Model Unfair Trade Practices and Consumer Protection Law (UTPCPL), which was developed by the FTC, published in 1967 and amended in 1969 and 1970. *See* Unfair Trade Practices and Consumer Protection Law (Council of State Gov'ts 1970).

---

* The list: (1) passing off goods or services as those of another; (2) causing likelihood of confusion or of misunderstanding as to the source, sponsorship, approval, or certification of goods or services; (3) causing likelihood of confusion or of misunderstanding as to affiliation, connection, or association with, or certification by, another; (4) using deceptive representations or designations of geographic origin in connection with goods or services; (5) representing that goods or services have sponsorship, approval, characteristics, ingredients, uses, benefits, or qualities that they do not have or that a person has a sponsorship, approval, status, affiliation, or connection that he does not have; (6) representing that goods are original or new if they are deteriorated, altered, reconditioned, reclaimed, used, or secondhand; (7) representing that goods or services are of a particular standard, quality, or grade, or that goods are of a particular style or model, if they are of another; (8) disparaging the goods, services, or business of another by false or misleading representation of fact; (9) advertising goods or services with intent not to sell them as advertised; (10) advertising goods or services with intent not to supply reasonably expectable public demand, unless the advertisement discloses a limitation of quantity; (11) making false or misleading statements of fact concerning the reasons for, existence of, or amounts of price reductions; (12) engaging in any other conduct which similarly creates a likelihood of confusion or of misunderstanding.

The UTPCPL: (1) tracks the FTCA almost verbatim and bars unfair methods of competition or unfair or deceptive acts in trade or commerce; (2) prohibits false, misleading or deceptive acts or practices like the FTCA, but does not use a separate definition of "unfair" as the FTCA does to distinguish unfairness from deceptiveness; and (3) enumerates prohibited activities, including the "laundry list" from the UDTPA, including a prohibition on acts or practices that are "unfair or deceptive to the consumer." Unlike the UDTPA, the UTPCPL has a consumer-directed orientation.

Today, most of the states using a list of prohibited practices also have a catch-all provision covering deceptive practices. Some states—such as Hawaii, Georgia and Illinois—have adopted both the UTPCPL and the UDTPA. Moreover, the items on the basic laundry list vary substantially in specificity. This raises the statutory drafting question of why the laws include specific enumerated verboten practices as a supplement to the general catch-all prohibitions on false and misleading ads.

Many states, including California and New York, also allow claims for unfair trade practices based on the advertiser's violation of another governing law (including federal law). *See, e.g.,* People v. Ford Motor Co., 74 N.Y.2d 495 (1989). This may sound redundant, but it can be extremely important for creating causes of action based on laws that don't otherwise permit private enforcement.

Some state laws explicitly include or exclude certain industries, such as real estate, franchising, insurance or industries regulated by some other agency. States often exempt conduct specifically approved by a regulatory agency, though an agency's failure to regulate (yet) does not constitute approval of the practice.

UDAP laws also exclude suits over ordinary breach-of-contract claims and employment disputes. However, UDAP laws cover deceptive practices designed to induce a consumer to *enter into* a standard contract.

States vary somewhat in the degree that their laws draw upon the FTCA's jurisprudence. Twenty-five state statutes explicitly instruct courts to draw on FTC decisions in deciding cases. The degree of deference due to the federal standard varies widely, from requiring that state courts give it "consideration" or "due consideration and great weight," to requirements that courts be "guided" by or "consistent" with federal decisions. Additional states direct that state enforcement policies, rules and regulations be "consistent" with their federal counterparts. Many state laws also direct courts to harmonize their decisions with those of other states.

It's worth elaborating further on the difference between consumer protection statutes and the common law. The absence of a reliance requirement can be important in situations where, for example, the fine print of a contract contradicts the message the consumer took away from the advertiser's claims. Under many state consumer-protection laws, the consumer has a cause of action even if the parol evidence rule would defeat her fraud claim. *See* Salisbury v. Chapman Realty, 465 N.E.2d 127 (Ill. App. Ct. 1984); Victor E. Schwartz & Cary Silverman, *Common-Sense Construction of Consumer Protection Acts*, 54 KAN. L. REV. 1 (2005). . Other traditional barriers to success in fraud cases, such as the Statute of Frauds, warranty disclaimers, the common-law merger doctrine and contractual limitations on liability or remedies—ways in which a seller can use a written contract to argue that the plaintiff agreed to accept what she got even though that may not have been what she was originally promised or what she thought she was getting—are also less likely to defeat consumer protection claims. *See* Hinrichs v. DOW Chemical Company, 937 N.W.2d 37 (Wisc. 2020) (economic-loss doctrine doesn't apply to Wisconsin statutory consumer protection claims).

Nonetheless, there are substantial state-by-state variations in how far the consumer protection law deviates from the common law. The current trend is to tighten causation requirements, so that even without an explicit reliance element, a false or misleading representation must be directly connected to a plaintiff's harm, which is often the same thing as reliance (though not necessarily the same as *reasonable* reliance). California achieved this result by amending its consumer protection laws to require actual injury.

Statutes may impose limits on lawsuits by non-consumers. Massachusetts allows claims by people engaged in "trade or commerce" but specifically requires courts in such cases to be guided by antitrust principles, a requirement absent from the portion of the law allowing consumers to sue. MASS. GEN. LAWS, Chapter 93A § 11. In addition, Massachusetts requires that such claims can only be brought if the unfair or deceptive acts or practices "occurred primarily and substantially within" the state, whereas consumer suits are not subject to this requirement. Why make this distinction?

State Attorneys General

In virtually every state, the attorney general (AG) can enforce consumer-protection laws on behalf of the public. Acting as a public representative, the attorney general in practice often receives greater deference from courts than private plaintiffs do. And, when a public enforcer brings a claim, the defendant may not be entitled to a jury trial, even when the enforcer seeks civil penalties, if the state at issue considers the claim fundamentally equitable in nature. Nationwide Biweekly Administration Inc. v. Superior Court of Alameda County, 2020 WL 2107914, – P.3d – (Cal. 2020).

Attorneys generals have the authority to issue Civil Investigative Demands (CIDs) requesting documents or testimony from targets. Some attorneys generals also promulgate rules and guidance, similar to the FTC. AGs may issue cease-and-desist orders; enter into consent decrees or voluntary assurances of compliance, which if breached may result in contempt charges; or file lawsuits on behalf of consumers, seeking prospective injunctive relief, restitution for deceived consumers and/or disgorgement of unlawfully acquired profits. Restitution goes directly to affected customers when they can be readily identified, though a number of states have shown a preference for seeking monetary awards that can be used by the state for its own purposes. Both civil and criminal penalties are generally available to attorneys general. In some larger cities, the state attorney or district attorney may also have a consumer-protection division enforcing state and local law.

The National Association of Attorneys General (NAAG) coordinates activity by individual attorneys general, so multistate attorney-general actions are common. Generally, one attorney general or a small group will take the lead, with the aim of obtaining a comprehensive nationwide resolution of the claims. *See* Dee Pridgen, *The Dynamic Duo of Consumer Protection: State and Private Enforcement of Unfair and Deceptive Trade Practices Laws*, 81 ANTITRUST L.J. 911 (2017) (discussing various multimillion-dollar settlements; though the states and the FTC brought roughly the same number of cases against national advertisers during the period, "the states challenged bigger-name advertisers and imposed larger and more-frequent monetary penalties" and concluding that "state UDAP enforcement can serve as a check on federal agencies that may be 'captured' by their regulatory 'clients'"). *But see* PAUL NOLETTE, FEDERALISM ON TRIAL: STATE ATTORNEYS GENERAL AND NATIONAL POLICY MAKING IN CONTEMPORARY AMERICA (2015) (arguing that state-AG enforcement can disrupt federal policymaking).

A study of every UDAP matter resolved by state and federal enforcers in 2014 indicated that the states have different enforcement approaches. Some attorneys general go after only small, largely local fraudsters; some go after only "big fish;" some against both; and some against neither. Despite California's size and extensive consumer protection laws, California's attorney general is one of the less-active enforcers, while Vermont (49th largest state), Iowa (30th largest state) and Colorado (22nd largest state) disproportionately target larger entities and exercise leadership in multistate attorney general coalitions. Also, three states rely heavily on outside counsel to sue very large companies for sizeable awards of money that can be used for anything the states want, rather than for consumer redress— litigation over the harms of cigarettes is a prominent example. Prentiss Cox et al, *Strategies of Public UDAP Enforcement*, 55 HARV. J. LEGIS. 37 (2018).

State attorneys general may also assert "unfairness" violations where statutorily authorized. In one Massachusetts case, *Commonwealth of Massachusetts v. Fremont Investment and Loan & Fremont General Corporation*, 123 Mass. L. Rep. 567 (2008), the state attorney general obtained a preliminary injunction requiring a lender to submit its pending Massachusetts subprime mortgage foreclosures to the attorney general for prior review and approval because the mortgages were unfairly structured and likely to drive borrowers into foreclosure. Unfairness jurisdiction was superior to deceptiveness jurisdiction for this purpose because there was no need to prove individual-borrower injury or a deceptive pattern or practice—the attorney general could move for injunctive relief before too many consumers were injured and was able to obtain loan modification as a remedy. LARRY KIRSCH, THE STATE ATTORNEY GENERAL AS CONSUMER ADVOCATE: A RECENT EFFORT TO TAME UNFAIR SUBPRIME LENDING (2010).

Attorneys' general consumer-protection divisions generally view themselves as experts, able to tell whether it's likely to deceive consumers just by looking at it. In Lanham Act cases, plaintiffs alleging that an ad is misleading must present extrinsic evidence of consumer deception, usually through survey evidence. Despite many defendants' attempts to argue for a similar requirement under state UDAP laws, courts generally (but not always) reject the analogy between UDAP laws and the Lanham Act. Extrinsic evidence is useful but not required. As with the FTC, courts will often defer to the attorney's general expertise.

As we proceed, consider the merits and costs of requiring extrinsic evidence of likely consumer deception and whether expertise in the area can substitute for such evidence. Just because a lawyer works in the consumer-protection field, does that mean that she knows how consumers are likely to react to a particular claim?

Consumer Lawsuits

Unlike the FTCA, most state statutes let consumers sue. The private right evolved over time: The model UDTPA, for example, only allowed private parties to obtain injunctive relief. As amended in 1966, the UDTPA authorized reasonable attorneys' fees for plaintiffs if the defendant's conduct was willful and knowing, and most UDTPA statutes ultimately amended their consumer-protection laws to allow monetary relief to consumers. All state consumer-protection laws now allow private parties to sue to enforce them, but Arkansas limits its private right of action to elderly and disabled persons. ARK. CODE § 4-88-204.

Class Actions

Lawsuits under state consumer-protection/UDAP laws are often brought as class actions, which can substantially increase the size of potential damages awards compared to individual claims.

In response to concerns about abuses of class actions, Congress, in the Class Action Fairness Act (CAFA), and the courts have made it harder to maintain many class actions. Chapter 8 discusses class actions in greater detail.

Most prominently, differences between various state laws can hinder multistate class actions. To get around this, plaintiffs in large consumer class-action lawsuits may create state-specific subclasses, at least for the more-populous states. Questions about individual reliance on deceptive statements can additionally make it difficult to maintain a class action at all, if each plaintiff will be required to show that she saw and relied on the deceptive statements at issue to prevail.

For a chart comparing the major differences among different states' laws, see National Consumer Law Center, Consumer Protection in the States: A 50-State Evaluation of Unfair and Deceptive Practices Laws (March 2018).

Case Study: Law School Advertising

The following two cases involved consumer class actions about a topic that you may find personally relevant. As you read the descriptions, pay attention to the pleading standard as applied to the elements of the cause of action.

In *Gomez-Jimenez v. New York Law School*, 943 N.Y.S.2d 834 (Sup. Ct. 2012), nine graduates of NYLS alleged that data published by their school about the school's graduates' employment and salaries were misleading; that they relied on this misleading information to make their decision to attend NYLS, which charged nearly $48,000 per year; and that they found themselves in disadvantaged employment positions as a result. They sought damages equal to the difference between the alleged inflated tuition they paid because of the allegedly misleading statements and the "true value" of a NYLS degree.

Many graduates who worked in the legal sector held part-time or temporary employment, which paid much less. This created two related problems.

First, while NYLS reported that approximately 90–92% of NYLS graduates secured employment within nine months of graduation, it did not report the percentage of graduates employed in part-time or temporary positions. "According to plaintiffs, a graduate could be working part-time as a barista in Starbucks—or toiling away in any job—and be deemed employed in business, although such employment is temporary and does not require a law degree. A contract attorney, without permanent employment, working in document-review projects in a law firm, would be deemed employed in private-law practice under the NYLS profile."

Second, when NYLS reported average salaries of full-time graduates working in the legal sector, it allegedly inflated them by reporting "based on a small, deliberately selected, intensely solicited, subset of graduates." The employment and salary data reported by NYLS (the former in the 90% range) were allegedly at odds with national legal employment statistics reported by the National Association for Law Placement (NALP) and with the reality of NYLS's relatively lower ranking by the U.S. News & World Report (U.S. News).

Plaintiffs asserted violations of N.Y. General Business Law (GBL) 349 as well as common-law fraud/negligent misrepresentation. A cause of action under GBL 349 requires that the defendant's conduct was: (1) consumer oriented; (2) deceptive or misleading in a material way; and (3) that plaintiff suffered injury as a result. It does not require a showing of justifiable reliance or intentional deception, but the deceptive acts or practices must have "resulted in actual injury to the plaintiff." New York applies "an objective definition of deceptive acts and practices": actionable representations or omissions are "limited to those likely to mislead a reasonable consumer acting reasonably under the circumstances."

Plaintiffs alleged that reasonable consumers would infer that NYLS's employment numbers referred to full-time, permanent employment for which a law degree was required or preferred. The court disagreed: NYLS never said that. "[R]easonable consumers—college graduates—seriously considering law schools are a sophisticated subset of education consumers, capable of sifting through data and weighing alternatives before making a decision regarding their post-college options, such as applying for professional school." Reasonable consumers should have compared NALP's employment reports, or other sources, showing that the percentage of law school graduates who found full-time legal employment on a national level was around 40 percent at the time. Reasonable consumers, armed with NYLS's U.S. News ranking, would have incorporated that into their estimates of their own chances of securing full-time legal employment. The court took "judicial notice" that U.S. News "has published a plethora of information ranking law schools, including NYLS, in a number of job-related categories including: 'Whose graduates are the most and least likely to land a job?,' 'Whose graduates earn the most? The Least?,' 'Where do graduates work?,' 'Who's the priciest? Who's the cheapest?,' 'Whose graduates have the most debt? The Least?.'" Prospective law students "cannot claim that it was reasonable to confine their research and reliance solely on what amounts to just two sentences in NYLS's marketing materials."

As for the salary data, the court found that "the relatively small percentage of responding students was disclosed whenever the salary data included the average salary statistic," and NYLS's materials also cautioned that the highest reported salary for those years "is not the typical salary for most law school graduates—in New York City and nationwide." NYLS never stated that the sample of the reported salaries was in any way representative of the salaries earned by all its employed graduates. "[T]here can be no [GBL 349] claim when the allegedly deceptive practice was fully disclosed."

Furthermore, NYLS's website made clear that not all graduates practiced law, despite paying a significant sum for a law degree. "The widely held perception that a law degree from a respectable, accredited institution opens innumerable career paths beyond solely the practice of law, and leads to advancement in other fields is thus also an integral part of defendant's marketing materials." This made it implausible that NYLS deceptively represented that all jobs reported were full-time law jobs for which a law degree is required or preferred.

The court also pointed to the impact of the "2008 Great Recession": given "the obvious, dramatic changes in the economy as they began to impact the legal profession," NYLS's website couldn't have misled reasonable consumers.

Separately, the court rejected the GBL 349 claim for failure to plead actual injury. Plaintiffs claimed that the value of a NYLS degree had been misleadingly inflated. But the court did not believe that it was possible to measure the difference between the pecuniary value of "a degree where you have a 40 percent or 30 percent chance of getting a job," and the value of "a degree where you have a 90 percent chance of a job," and the plaintiffs didn't allege that there was any method for doing so. Additionally, the impact of the Great Recession made any such damages speculative. "In these new and troubling times, the reasonable consumer of legal education must realize that these omnipresent realities of the market obviously trump any allegedly overly optimistic claims in their law school's marketing materials." The common-law fraud and misrepresentation claims failed for the same reason.

In *Harnish v. Widener University School of Law*, 931 F. Supp. 2d 641 (D.N.J. 2013), by contrast, the court of appeals denied a motion to dismiss based on similar allegations, pointing out that the New Jersey Consumer Fraud Act (NJCFA) "was intended to be one of the strongest in the country" and "should be construed liberally." (It reached the same result under the Delaware Consumer Fraud Act.)

The NJCFA covers "any unconscionable commercial practice, deception, fraud, false pretense, false promise, misrepresentation, or the knowing, concealment, suppression, or omission of any material fact with intent that others rely upon such concealment, suppression or omission, in connection with the sale or advertisement of any merchandise or real estate, or with the subsequent performance of such person as aforesaid, whether or not any person has in fact been misled, deceived or damaged thereby . . . ." N.J. Stat. Ann. § 56:8-2. New Jersey law requires (1) unlawful conduct; (2) an ascertainable loss; and (3) a causal relationship between the unlawful conduct and the ascertainable loss. (Does this differ from the requirements of NY GBL § 349?)

The allegations of deceptive representations were similar to those in *Gomez-Jimenez*. For example, Widener's website stated that "Graduates of the Class of 2004 had a 90% employment rate within nine months of graduation," but didn't disclose that this included part-time and nonlegal employment. The court noted that "the fact that the [advertisements are] literally true does not mean they cannot be misleading to the average consumer." The court pointed to the juxtaposition of various claims:

> Perception is often affected by location of the object. Here, we have data displayed above the category of "Full Time Legal Employers." Why should a reasonable student looking to go to law school consider that data to include non law-related and part-time employment? Should that student think that going to Widener Law School would open employment as a public school teacher, full or part-time, or an administrative assistant, or a sales clerk, or a medical assistant?

> . . . The employment rate was disseminated to third-party evaluators to establish Widener's standing among law schools. Within this context, it is not implausible that a prospective law student making the choice of whether or which law school to attend would believe that the employment rate referred to law related employment. *See* Hallock v. University of San Francisco, No. CGC-12-517861, at *2 (Cal. Super. Ct. July 19, 2012) ("[T]here is nothing before me to suggest that any of the plaintiffs were not reasonable consumers of a law school education. Moreover, the statements attributed to defendant were allegedly made in a context (i.e., in materials designed to attract and retain law students to defendant's law school) where a reasonable prospective or current law student could reasonably believe that the statements pertained only to jobs for which a law school education is a requirement or preference and did not include jobs for which a law school education is irrelevant or of minimal utility. This issue . . . must await factual development by the parties.").

Despite information available from other sources such as NALP, "[u]nlike other states that require plaintiff to prove reliance under their consumer protection statutes, the proof requirements that the New Jersey statute places on its claimants is less burdensome." Instead of reliance, "consumer fraud requires only proof of a causal nexus between the concealment of the material fact and the loss." The court emphasized that the NJCFA is "aimed at more than the stereotypic con man." It was intended to "promote the disclosure of relevant information to enable the consumer to make intelligent decisions." Indeed, "[a] practice can be unlawful even if no person was in fact misled or deceived thereby."

Although "the thread of plausibility may be slight, it is still a thread," and was sufficient at the motion to dismiss stage.

The court reasoned similarly with respect to plaintiffs' deceptive omission claims, which required that Widener (1) knowingly concealed (2) a material fact (3) with the intention that plaintiff rely upon the concealment. "What makes the posted and disseminated employment rate misleading is the failure to include notice that the employment rate refers to all types of employment, that it is not specifically referring to law-related employment, and that the rate may have been inflated by selectively disregarding employment data (as example, failure to count the graduate if she responded 'not seeking work')." These were plausibly material omissions.

The *Widener* court also found that plaintiffs had pled an ascertainable loss. Under the NJCFA, "to demonstrate a loss, a victim must simply supply an estimate of damages, calculated within a reasonable degree of certainty." The complaint sought damages based on "the difference between the inflated tuition paid by Class members based on the material representations that approximately 90–95 percent of graduates are employed within nine months of graduation and the true value of a [Widener] degree." The plaintiffs alleged that they wouldn't have paid as much as they did (over $30,000 per year in tuition alone) if they'd known the truth. That was enough to establish ascertainable loss. (The court cited *Miller v. American Family Publishers*, 663 A.2d 643 (N.J. Super. Ct. Ch. Div.1995) ("[F]or their money, they received something less than, and different from, what they reasonably expected in view of defendant's presentations. That is all that is required to establish 'ascertainable loss'."); and *Talalai v. Cooper Tire & Rubber Co.*, 823 A.2d 888 (N.J. Super. Ct. Law Div.2001) ("[O]ne has suffered an ascertainable loss under the New Jersey Consumer Fraud Act where that loss is measurable—even though the precise amount is not known.").) The court pointed out that the alleged harm stemmed from the influence of the allegedly misleading statements on plaintiffs' decisions to pay so much for a legal education, not on whether they ultimately got full-time legal jobs.

NOTES AND QUESTIONS

Which case is more persuasive? (How does your own educational experience affect your determination of plausibility?)

Macdonald v. Thomas M. Cooley Law School, 724 F.3d 654 (6th Cir. 2013), reached a similar result as *Gomez-Jimenez* on fraud and misrepresentation claims. Michigan's Consumer Protection Act (CPA) doesn't cover purchases for business or commercial purposes. Because the complaint alleged that the graduates attended law school in order to obtain full-time legal employment, they weren't covered by the statute.

Traditional Fraud Claims. What benefits did NY GBL Section 349 and the NJCFA offer plaintiffs that traditional fraud claims did not? These laws, like other state consumer-protection laws, were designed to offer broader relief for consumers than the common law. Are the changes from common-law fraud sufficient? Too much?

Buyer Sophistication. Do the courts treat these buyers as naïve, completely capable of protecting their interests or somewhere in between? How does each court justify the level of sophistication it attributes to the buyers?

Procedural Considerations. Generally, in evaluating a motion to dismiss, courts may consider concededly authentic documents integral to a complaint without waiting until summary judgment. This is an important rule in advertising cases, because on a motion to dismiss, courts can evaluate any tangible advertising materials that the plaintiff complains about.

Iqbal and *Twombly* pose special challenges for advertising cases. Defendants typically want to dismiss advertising cases before expensive discovery. *Iqbal* and *Twombly* required facially plausible allegations of liability. How much can a judge rely on his or her own reaction to an ad in assessing the plausibility of a claim that consumers were deceived by that ad?

In *Wright v. General Mills, Inc.*, 2009 WL 3247148 (S.D. Cal. 2009), the complaint at issue challenged the "100% Natural" label on Nature Valley cereal and cereal bars as false and misleading because the products actually were made with high fructose corn syrup, a substance that was allegedly not "natural." To the court, this complaint contained little more than conclusory and speculative allegations. For example, it was insufficient simply to allege that members of the public were likely to have been deceived and to have made purchases because they believed that a "100% natural" product would not have high fructose corn syrup.

Does your assessment of plausibility differ from that of the *Wright* court's? Does it matter that different people often have different ideas of what counts as "common sense"? *See* Dan M. Kahan et al, *Whose Eyes Are You Going to Believe? Scott v. Harris and the Perils of Cognitive Illiberalism*, 122 HARV. L. REV. 838 (2009) (reporting on a study showing that demographic variables profoundly affected the interpretation of videotape evidence, even though a majority of Supreme Court justices determined that the tape could bear only one reasonable interpretation); Terry A. Maroney, *Emotional Common Sense as Constitutional Law*, 62 VAND. L. REV. 851 (2009). What about when "common sense" is the same thing as a stereotype about how people—women, low-income consumers, elderly people or even Americans in general—think and behave? *See* Linda Hamilton Krieger & Susan T. Fiske, *Behavioral Realism in Employment Discrimination Law: Implicit Bias and Disparate Treatment*, 94 CAL. L. REV. 997 (2006).

Choice of Law. The Lanham Act is a federal statute and applies nationwide (though circuits may differ in some details). In contrast, state consumer protection laws vary enough that they often present a conflict between state laws. If a putative class-action plaintiff cannot succeed in convincing a court that the law of one state (usually, but not always, the defendant's home state) covers all claims, it may be impossible to maintain the class action. Chapter 8 will revisit this topic.

The Private Lawsuit and Public Purposes of the Law. Some argue that litigation under state consumer-protection acts leads to overenforcement because private plaintiffs bring lawsuits that the FTC would not. *See* Henry N. Butler & Joshua D. Wright, *Are State Consumer Protection Acts Really Little-FTC Acts?*, 63 FLA. L. REV. 163 (2011). What do you think plaintiffs' attorneys would say in response to this criticism? Are there reasons the FTC might underenforce the prohibition on deceptive advertising? Why would a legislature have decided to provide for class actions while also relaxing the standards for relief compared to the common law of fraud? How hard *should* it be to recover in court against advertising that a factfinder, whether judge or jury, determines to be false or misleading?

4.   Comparing the Types of Regulation

The relationship between the FTC, the Lanham Act and state-law actions is complicated. *See generally* Arthur Best, *Controlling False Advertising: A Comparative Study of Public Regulation, Industry Self-Policing, and Private Litigation*, 20 GA. L. REV. 1 (1985). The FTC is a political agency and will generally move in the direction of the political position of the executive branch. For example, FTC activism waned in the Reagan years and ramped up in the Obama years. States may have different political orientations. New York, for example, is known for its aggressive consumer-protection positions (and not incidentally, perhaps, the political ambitions of its enforcers), taking action against everything from the financial sector to restrictive contracts that purport to prohibit software buyers from writing critical reviews about that software.

The FTC, like most other institutions, wants to win the cases that it brings, especially when, by virtue of its status as a major federal agency, it can expect publicity about its outcomes. A few representative cases may change the behavior of major national advertisers, whose lawyers and ad agencies pay attention to FTC activities. The FTC takes positions that structurally tilt in its own favor, such as who has the burden of providing substantiation (the advertiser) and whether the FTC needs to conduct a consumer survey to show deception (it does not). The FTC does not design its principles with the idea that they'll be enforced by multiple plaintiffs.

Moreover, due to resource constraints, the FTC can only pursue a limited number of cases. Private plaintiffs, both competitors and consumers, have different incentives. This could lead to overenforcement of the law by private plaintiffs seizing on minor and irrelevant inaccuracies to correction of the inevitable underenforcement that comes from a resource-constrained government, or both. "Overenforcement" critics point to the incentives for competitors to shut down legitimate competition and for class-action lawyers to seek easy settlements with large fee awards. "Underenforcement" critics note that the number of FTC employees has not kept pace with the economy's expansion. The FTC's $250 million budget is a small fraction of the dollar value of U.S. advertising.

Competitors are likely to police some kinds of claims much more carefully than the FTC or other regulators can. For one thing, competitors may be well-placed to evaluate highly technical claims. They are likely to routinely test both their own products and their competition's, and they may detect falsity or misleadingness invisible to non-experts. Because competitors can and do sue, the FTC and attorneys general can give lower priority to false comparative claims and false claims in fields like shaving, antacids and analgesics, where false representations can affect the market share of major producers. The FTC's tendency to avoid intervening in markets for cheap, repeat-purchase goods may make sense in part because competitor suits exist to police falsity and protect consumers in such markets.

Competitors may not sue when it's in every competitor's interest to make a certain set of false claims, such as cigarette companies' toleration for claims about the health effects of particular brands of cigarettes. Similar patterns exist in the supplement and weight-loss industries, where extravagant claims are common and competition is so intense that most advertisers benefit more from being able to make shaky claims of their own than from suppressing any one competitor's shaky claims. In industries with many small players making outsized claims, no single competitor will want to incur the costs to bring an enforcement action that will benefit other competitors. In situations like that, only the government may have the necessary motivation, resources and perseverance to discipline fraudsters.

Consumer plaintiffs may be motivated to go after larger players, especially national advertisers, whose deep pockets may make settlement more attractive even with a relatively weak case. As many critics of the plaintiffs' bar have argued, this dynamic is encouraged by the fact that consumer protection cases often involve large fees for the lawyers and minimal recovery for individual plaintiffs. Defenders of class actions, however, respond that this pattern is precisely what the class action is for: joining claims that are too small to justify litigation on their own but, in the aggregate, represent substantial social harm despite small individual recoveries.

Sometimes, competitors are more likely to succeed than consumers. Consider a mass-market ad campaign for a common product. Consumers are often unlikely to remember which ads they saw or keep records about what they bought. Even if the relevant UDAP laws don't require reliance, they will usually be interpreted to require some sort of causation linking the false ads to purchases, and this may be hard to establish, especially in a class action. Courts increasingly reject class actions that require an individualized showing of deception or harm for each class member. Thus, a competitor—which need only show that a substantial percentage of consumers are likely to be deceived to prevail—can succeed with a probabilistic showing of harm, while a consumer class action predicated on the exact same deception might fail. In such cases, the competitor acts as a stand-in for consumers whose injury is hard to show.

Private plaintiffs face more evidentiary problems than the government, providing a potential constraint. Even if a private lawyer is willing to fund a lawsuit's initial stages (which can be essential for consumer class actions), that lawyer needs a willing plaintiff and adequate evidence—some of which may not be functionally available until after discovery—but the lawsuit might be foreclosed by *Twombly/Iqbal*. In contrast, government entities can open investigations that will lead to CIDs or voluntary disclosures by the investigatory target, even if the government actor lacks enough evidence initially to survive a *Twombly/Iqbal* motion to dismiss.

Private lawsuits may move faster than government investigations, which generally have multiple layers of procedural constraints, including requirements that a high-level official approve any resulting lawsuit. If a competitor is willing to spend the money to prepare a case, it can seek a temporary restraining order (TRO) a few days after an ad starts to run. Government agencies, by contrast, are much more likely to rely on the general deterrent effect of large penalties, imposed long after the fact. The FTC and the attorneys general generally wish to send messages to entire industries in their enforcement actions, whereas an advertiser who sues under the Lanham Act is much more likely to want one specific ad to stop (and in fact may prefer a certain freedom to operate in its own advertising).

If the problem is industry-wide (as with cigarettes, alcohol or other products with substantial negative externalities), and if consumers can't win and competitors won't sue, then a regulatory response is the only alternative.

The following chart, though far from comprehensive, offers a few comparisons:

	FTC	AG	Competitor	Consumer
Source of Authority	FTCA	State law	Lanham Act; some state laws; NAD (voluntary)	State law (both common & statutory)
Legal Standard	Unfair or deceptive/ misleading; burden on advertiser to substantiate	Various; burden usually on AG to show deception (but in some states, e.g. California, advertiser must substantiate)	False or deceptive (Lanham Act); burden on competitor to show falsity/deception (but NAD requires substantiation)	Various; burden on consumer to show violation of law
Key Constraints	Resources; politics	Resources; politics	Time; resources; interest in preserving own freedom to make claims	Low recovery usually means only class actions are sustainable; barriers to class actions
Key Remedies	Full range, including consumer redress	Full range, including consumer redress	Injunction usually a priority; damages possible	Damages; fees for counsel in class actions

Another way to compare and contrast the various options is from a policy standpoint:

	Pros	Cons
FTC	* Broad authority * Broad remedies * Enhanced discovery powers	* Small agency + national scope = selective enforcement * Political
State AGs	* Similar to FTC	* Power restricted to state * Not uniform * Political
Competitor—NAD	* Quick (but slower than TRO) * High expertise * Cheap (no discovery) * Confidential submissions * Uniform rules nationally * Rules can evolve flexibly	* "Voluntary" * Only for national campaigns * Limited remedies
Competitor—Court	* Incentive to call out competitive overclaims * Don't need to prove consumer reliance	* Litigation over market allocation, not consumer interest * Enforcement is public good * Won't sue over bad industry practices * Judges lack expertise * Expensive * Litigation duration > ad campaign
Consumer Litigation	* Can challenge industry-wide practices * Can overcome the public goods problem	* Expensive * Self-interested attorneys * *Twombly/Iqbal* lead to quick dismissals

It is very easy to say that the law requires truth, and much harder to say when something is true or false. This chapter covers key elements of the law of falsity.

We start with an overview of the ways false advertising harms consumers and society. We then turn to the boundary question: What kinds of statements can be considered true or false? Though a legal regime could require advertisers to make only claims that they can prove to be truthful, the United States instead generally regulates only falsity. Thus, non-falsifiable claims, often categorized as mere opinion or puffery, are outside the scope of false advertising law.

After laying those foundations, the chapter turns to claims that are concededly factual and examines how decision makers deem them truthful or false. We consider the substantiation requirement imposed by the Federal Trade Commission (and the Better Business Bureau in its voluntary arbitration program), as well as various subtypes of factual claims, including claims that might only be "true" based on the placebo effect and the difference between explicit and implicit falsity, a distinction that is of great importance in private Lanham Act claims.

1.   The Harms of False Advertising*

Truthful informational advertising is generally considered socially beneficial. Conversely, false advertising is generally considered to be unequivocally bad for society. It causes consumers to misallocate their dollars, and consumers can suffer irreparable harm because of it—such as a consumer who takes medicine falsely advertised to help her medical condition and who foregoes other treatments that might have helped.

False advertising can also cause economic loss to society if consumers spend money on a product that doesn't work. As Professor Lee Goldman explains, "[I]f Excedrin does not relieve headache pain fast, not only will there be many cranky consumers, but too much capital and labor will be employed to produce a worthless product rather than a more-effective pain reliever or some other socially useful good."

Many people additionally believe that it is morally wrong to deceive consumers, even if they suffer no identifiable physical or economic harm as a result. False advertising also harms competitors, both through sales they don't get and by undermining the general trustworthiness of advertising, a point we take up in greater detail in the next section.

---

* [Note: consult Chapter 2 for citations to several of the sources discussed in these first two parts.]

Deception: An Introduction

Information can be deceptive if it makes a false claim about something that consumers care about—a material fact. But because people make inferences, we can't confine the definition of deception to claims that are explicitly false. Beales et al. use the example of a product that truthfully but misleadingly claims that "no product is more effective" in curing an incurable condition. This claim is deceptive because it *implies* effectiveness.

We could try again: Perhaps a claim is deceptive if it produces in consumers a false belief about a material fact. But omitting information can also be deceptive—for example, failing to disclose that a book is an abridged version or failing to disclose that a used product isn't new. So failing to correct a preexisting belief may be deceptive under some circumstances. As Beales et al. note, consumers have standard expectations for things that are advertised as "books," as products *not* marked as used, and so on. Failure to disclose implies compliance with those expectations. These expectations are so standard that consumers probably don't even think about them consciously unless prompted to do so. This can lead to deception by omission.

Taking these expectations into account, we could say that an ad is deceptive if it fails to disclose material information (i.e., information that would change consumers' behavior). But that's clearly unworkable, because most ads can't disclose all material information, and if they did, consumers wouldn't read them (consider the overwhelmingly long disclosures in ads for prescription drugs or car leases). Information is costly to provide and to process, so perfect information will never be possible. We could say that an ad is deceptive if it fails to disclose the optimal amount of information—but the devil is in the details.

A Note on Implicature

Much advertising relies not on the strict logical meanings of the words, images and sound it uses, but on the contextual meaning of the information actually presented. Philosopher Paul Grice attempted to explain how conversation generally works with his cooperative principle, which states that contributions to a conversation must be guided by the accepted purpose or direction of that conversation. PAUL GRICE, LOGIC AND CONVERSATION, SYNTAX AND SEMANTICS, 3: SPEECH ACTS (P. Cole & J. Morgan ed. 1975).

People have to cooperate in order to have a conversation. Grice proposed four "maxims of conversation" that people generally assume are being followed by other people. The maxims are:

(1) *Relevance*: What you say should have something to do with the topic of the conversation.

(2) *Quantity*: Say neither more nor less than required: enough to get your meaning across, but not so much information that meaning is lost.

(3) *Manner*: Be brief and orderly; avoid ambiguity and obscurity. In particular, don't be so vague that the other person can't figure out why you're saying something. If you say "Paul is

either in Los Angeles or Boston," you actually should be uncertain where Paul is. If you know that Paul is in Los Angeles, you have violated the maxim of manner.

(4) *Quality*: Do not lie; do not make unsupported claims.

Because of the cooperative principle, when someone obviously violates one of these maxims, we ordinarily presume that he or she is doing it for a reason, and we try to relate the statement to the conversation. This is known as *implicature*. For example, when someone asks her dinner companion, "Could you pass the salt?," he's unlikely to interpret this as a literal inquiry into whether he's physically able to pass the salt. Using the maxim of relevance, he infers that she wants the salt, and he passes it.

Another example from personal relationships would be this exchange: Q: "What's Doug like? Is he nice?" A: "He's very tall." The answer here violates the maxim of quantity, failing to say enough to answer the questions. We infer that the speaker has done so for some reason, and it's probably because he thinks Doug is not nice at all.

Grice's maxims are not the only tool for parsing grammatical constructions, but they can provide a helpful metric for understanding the ways that advertisers can sway, and possibly manipulate, consumers.

For example, when an advertiser prominently claims some feature for its product, we are likely to assume that the feature is relevant and desirable. The advertiser is using the cooperative principle of relevance to *imply* these things without stating them directly. The only direct statement is that the feature exists. Researchers have studied irrelevant claims used to tout brands, such as claims that instant coffee has flaked crystals. When some consumers saw ads featuring relevant attributes and others saw ads featuring irrelevant attributes, the latter group preferred the product more. Even when the researchers told consumers which attributes were irrelevant in advance, consumers still preferred the product more when shown ads using the irrelevant attribute. *See* Gregory S. Carpenter et al., *Meaningful Brands From Meaningless Differentiation: The Dependence on Irrelevant Attributes*, 31 J. MKTG. RES. 339 (1994).

The maxims are not separate. While it might seem that the maxim of quality (don't lie) is the basic foundation of truth in advertising, distracting or overwhelming a consumer with too much information or with irrelevant information—violating the maxim of quantity—can also fool the consumer. And devices common in advertising, such as humor, may play with several maxims at once. Human communication ordinarily presupposes cooperation in making and interpreting meaning, and advertisers can exploit this cooperation.

The law often recognizes implicature. If a prospectus advertises that a piece of property is five miles from the waterfront, readers will have good cause to cry foul if the five miles are measured as the crow flies, while the driving distance is actually fifteen to forty miles. *See* Lustiger v. United States, 386 F.2d 132 (9th Cir. 1967). The statement "five miles from the waterfront" in a real estate prospectus ordinarily implies that humans could reach the water by traveling that distance. Otherwise, the information is irrelevant and unhelpful.

Similarly, if Kraft advertises that its cheese slices are made with five ounces of milk, an ordinary consumer may infer that the benefits of those five ounces—especially the calcium, milk's best-known nutrient—are retained in the slices, not dissipated in the processing. Otherwise, the information about the *number* of ounces involved is irrelevant to an ordinary purchasing decision. *See* Kraft, Inc. v. FTC, 970 F.2d 311 (7th Cir. 1992) (affirming the decision that Kraft's ads made a misleading and material claim); Richard Craswell, *Taking Information Seriously: Misrepresentation and Nondisclosure in Contract Law and Elsewhere*, 92 VA. L. REV. 565 (2006).

Are reasonable consumers entitled to assume that advertisers are following the maxims? Are they entitled to do so under some circumstances—such as when the advertiser makes a claim that could be scientifically proven—but not others?

How Much Information?

If publishing information were costless, sellers would have an incentive to disclose it all. The better products on the market would benefit from full disclosure, and incomplete disclosure would signal some relative defect. But publishing information is not costless, so advertisers don't always disclose optimally.

Moreover, information is a public good. It can benefit people who don't pay for it. For example, consider how pomegranate products gained popularity after POM Wonderful invested millions of dollars in research on the benefits of pomegranates and more millions on ads promoting that research. Competitors' ability to piggyback on the new consumer demand decreases the advertiser's incentive to provide positive information—though obviously not enough to destroy it altogether. Still, an advertiser like POM Wonderful wants consumers to believe that it delivers more pomegranate-related benefits than its piggybacking competitors. This is only one of many roadblocks to the development and dissemination of complete market information.

When Can Law Help?

To answer the question "when should law intervene to govern ads?," we can start by evaluating consumers' disparate information sources.

Consumers can examine some products or product characteristics for themselves ("search" characteristics, like the color of a car). They can rely on their own prior experience ("experience" characteristics, like the taste of a soda or the quality of a cable company's service). They can get information from other sources—friends, product reviews on the Internet or from *Consumer Reports*, home inspectors and so on. They can even get information from industry competitors—though competitors typically only make claims that highlight their own advantages. For example, e-cigarette manufacturers may advertise superiority to traditional tobacco products, but they will rarely voluntarily mention the health risks of nicotine posed by their competitors' (and thus their own) products. To the extent that consumers are relying on expert claims such as "studies prove that this drug effectively treats high blood pressure"—whether from third parties or from the advertisers themselves—they are relying on "credence" claims, since consumers cannot themselves verify whether a drug works better than a placebo or whether a car model has a better overall performance record than a different model.

Categorizing advertising into search, experience or credence characteristics can help identify where advertisers are most likely to deceive consumers. Advertisers are, in theory, unlikely to misrepresent search characteristics. After all, a consumer can easily determine whether or not a car is red and can punish the seller for a misrepresentation by publicizing an instance of obvious deception—especially in the Internet age. Thus, we could argue that regulators shouldn't worry too much about claims relating to search characteristics. *See* Gary T. Ford et al., *Consumer Skepticism of Advertising Claims: Testing Hypotheses from Economics of Information*, 16 J. CONSUMER RES. 433 (1990). As Lillian BeVier writes, consumers "should be understood as capable of punishing false advertisers both by spreading the word about the offending product and by not repurchasing it." Indeed, you've probably publicly shared your opinions about marketplace offerings by telling your friends or posting on Yelp.

Despite the possibility of punishment in the market, advertisers can and do misrepresent search characteristics. Counterfeiting brand names is one example. A consumer looking for, say, actual Eveready batteries can be deceived by counterfeits because the "search" characteristic—the brand name—acts as a proxy for other quality features.

Sellers also may misrepresent search characteristics if they're engaging in bait-and-switch tactics, such as claiming to have a particular product in stock but then trying to sell consumers something more expensive once the consumers show up. Will dissatisfied consumers adequately punish sellers for bait-and-switch tactics? Perhaps—but only if the business intends to remain in business in the same place or under the same name for a long time.

Bait and switch can benefit even long-term market participants. For example, a buyer is promised a low car payment, but just before the contract is signed, the seller reveals that the price is actually substantially higher. The buyer often feels committed and willing to pay more to be able to drive off the lot with "her" car. *See* Philip Reed, *Confessions of an Auto Finance Manager*, Edmunds.com, updated Sept. 4, 2013. Even if some buyers walk away in disgust, the ones who stay may be profitable enough to more than cover the loss. "One large scale study suggests that the bait-and-switch practice may have a substantial (negative) impact on consumers. Moreover, consumers are drawn in to promotions and where the item is out of stock, they predominantly switch to another item within the same store, due to lowered search intentions." GORKAN AHMETOGLU ET AL., PRICING PRACTICES: THEIR EFFECTS ON CONSUMER BEHAVIOUR AND WELFARE (Mar. 2010). Older consumers are particularly likely to stick with earlier decisions and thus may be particularly vulnerable.

What about false claims about experience characteristics, such as "our frozen pizza tastes freshly made"? Advertisers can succeed with those claims even if they are untrue, especially if consumers' negative experiences take time to accumulate.

False claims about credence qualities are even more likely to be effective (if consumers believe them) because consumers may never know they've been fooled—and may even go on to provide testimonials to other consumers. For example, if a consumer takes an ineffective

97

headache relief remedy and then his headache goes away, as it naturally would have done no matter what he did, then he may falsely believe that the remedy worked.

One view, articulated well by Lillian BeVier, is that because experience and credence claims can deceive consumers, rational consumers will know better than to trust such claims, and rational advertisers will therefore avoid making such claims. BeVier says, "[t]he rational advertisers' reaction to consumer skepticism, moreover, will be not to waste resources making direct, inherently unbelievable quality claims at all—either true or false. Such a reaction further protects consumers." Indeed, consumers routinely say they don't trust ad claims very much.

Still, think back to the ads you've seen recently: Did they make experience or credence claims? BeVier acknowledges that, in practice, there are plenty of credence claims in the market. Drawing on work by Philip Nelson, however, BeVier argues that advertising is not primarily about specific factual claims. Instead, advertising signals to consumers—regardless of the ad copy—that the advertiser is investing in its brand. Consumers can infer that an advertiser intends to reap the returns from advertising over time, which will happen only if the advertiser delivers quality goods that actually satisfy consumer preferences. Thus, advertising can improve consumers' trust in the advertiser's intentions. *See* Phillip Nelson, *Advertising as Information*, 82 J. POL. ECON. 729 (1974); Phillip Nelson, *The Economic Consequences of Advertising*, 48 J. BUS. L. 213 (1975). According to this theory, ads offer a general quality signal rather than a specific claim, no matter what claims the ads *seem* to make. Is that what you think ads are doing?

Trust and Rationality: Do Consumers Follow the Search-Experience-Credence Model?

BeVier's argument does not satisfactorily resolve the problem of generalized mistrust, also known as the "market for lemons" problem. Assume consumers understand that credence claims are unverifiable and therefore disbelieve or discount them. If so, a producer who has a product that really does what it says—e.g., cures headaches faster—can't reap the full benefits of its investment in creating and advertising that product. The level of investment in products that really cure headaches will drop, and consumers will lose out. In this account, regulations that promote the flow of truthful information—such as subjecting credence claims to verification by the Food & Drug Administration or other authority—prevent a destructive cycle of consumer cynicism and lower investment in truthful claims. *See* George A. Akerlof, *The Market for 'Lemons': Quality Uncertainty and the Market Mechanism*, 84 Q. J. ECON. 488 (1970).

Advertisers can also try to overcome consumer cynicism by offering warranties and money-back guarantees to consumers. But Beales et al. point out that these trust-enhancing moves pose significant information and enforcement problems of their own. Especially for low-cost products where pre-purchase research or post-purchase enforcement aren't cost-justified, consumers may end up unable to take advantage of such guarantees as a practical matter, and thus consumers will either ignore them (rendering them incapable of performing their desired function of making claims credible) or be deceived by them. (Recall the Carbolic Smoke Ball from Chapter 3.)

Certification by nongovernmental third-party entities can also combat consumers' distrust of experience or credence claims, but the consumer still needs to trust that the certifier is really independent and actually certified the advertiser's product.

Furthermore, consumers may rely on observable attributes (like price) or potential signals of quality (like celebrity endorsements) more than on quality itself. As Beales et al. write, "[i]f consumers cannot easily obtain information about a product's safety (but can easily observe its price), price competition may reward those who cut price by offering a less-safe product." In markets where quality information is hard to come by, consumers may use low price as a signal of low quality, even though price isn't a reliable signal. *See* Donald R. Lichtenstein & Scot Burton, *The Relationship Between Perceived and Objective Price-Quality*, 26 J. MKTG. RES. 429 (1989); Freddy S. Lee, *Wine and the Consumer Price-Perceived Quality Heuristics*, 4 INT'L J. MKTG. STUD. 31 (2012).

As Beales et al. also point out, consumers might not know why they need to know more; or they might make errors of judgment or submit to sales pressure to buy now without finding out more. They might take a chance that the claim is true and then stick to the brand out of habit. Thus, advertisers may make a false claim hoping that consumers will not discount it enough. Consider shopping for funeral homes—bereaved consumers may not have enough time or energy to do full research, and prices may be needlessly high and quality needlessly low. Indeed, the FTC and state regulators specifically regulate funeral and casket providers to prevent them from exploiting consumers' relative inability to do comparison shopping.

Lee Goldman also notes how consumers may fail to test claims that are testable in theory. Suppose a competitor falsely claims superiority to another competitor and consumers buy the first product. If they are satisfied, even if they would have been happier with the competing product, they may stick with what they know (especially given widespread habits of brand inertia). If they're dissatisfied, they may well assume that the competitor is no better, given the initial superiority claim.

In empirical research, Ford et al. tested the prediction that "consumers will be most skeptical of advertising claims they can never verify and least skeptical of claims they can easily and inexpensively verify prior to purchase," as well as the prediction that consumers are more likely to believe experience claims about cheap goods than about expensive ones. Their results were only somewhat consistent with the predictions made by the search-experience-credence model. Consumers were relatively less skeptical of search claims, trusting them because they were easily verified, but they were not more skeptical of credence claims than of experience claims. They were not more skeptical of experience claims for high-priced goods than of experience claims for low-priced goods. In other words, they were skeptical of claims that the Nelson model said they ought to trust (experience claims for low-priced goods), and not especially skeptical of credence claims that the model predicted they ought to distrust. As Roger Schechter explains, "[a]s long as consumers put at least some stock in credence claims, advertisers have an incentive to make such claims, and ultimately, to exaggerate them."

Consumers may also believe that there is some government regulation of advertising claims, such that a producer would not be allowed to make such a claim if it weren't true. For example, research has shown that consumers believe that the FDA is actively evaluating claims for nutritional supplements. Does that belief itself justify government intervention to protect consumers?

Do you believe some ad claims more readily than others? When was the last time you consciously relied on a search quality of a good or service you were considering buying? Did you trust the advertiser's claims or did you verify the quality yourself, and how hard was it to do so? When was the last time you relied on an experience claim in choosing a good or service? When was the last time you consciously relied on a credence claim in choosing a good or service? When you consider friends' recommendations or reviews, what kinds of information do they offer, and why do you trust or distrust them?

Recall that one part of Nelson's argument, taken up by BeVier, is that advertising is about signaling general quality (ability to invest in advertising, which implies that the seller has a product in whose quality the seller is confident and for which consumers have proven willing to pay) rather than about making specific claims. But advertisers may overinvest in the signal and compete until they destroy its information value. For example, "lead generation" companies have outspent traditional locksmiths in Internet advertising. Local locksmiths generally have more expertise and may often cost consumers less, but because they can't take advantage of economies of scale in advertising, consumers can't find them among advertisers who falsely claim to operate locally and who spend their resources on "search optimization." *See* David Segal, *Picking the Lock of Google's Search*, N.Y. TIMES, July 9, 2011.

Roger Allan Ford summarizes a more pro-regulatory position when he discusses the effectiveness of advertising claims as a matter of consumer and claim variation:

> First, a set of studies finds that advertising has the greatest effect on consumers who have not made recent purchases in the advertised category; otherwise, prior experience and loyalty or inertia plays a much greater role in dictating consumer behavior. This suggests both that advertising has its greatest effect on the consumers most in need of information and that it can do only so much to shape consumer demand. Second, another set of studies shows that advertising can be especially effective when it introduces new products or new features of an existing product, informing consumers about those new products or features. Third, a set of studies shows that consumers respond to specific information content in advertising. When producers of fiber-containing cereals promoted claims that the cereals helped prevent cancer, for instance, sales of those cereals spiked out of proportion to the simple quantity of advertising.

Roger Allan Ford, *Data Scams*, 57 HOUS. L. REV. 111 (2019). Ford's distinctions suggest that search/experience/credence is not the only spectrum along which credibility or effectiveness might be classified.

No Free Lunch: When Is Intervention Worth Its Costs?

Ultimately, the classical law-and-economics approach discourages regulatory intervention in the market for advertising. Just as strict product liability raises the cost of production, strict liability for deceptive advertising may limit the production of truthful information. If, as

BeVier argues, consumers can cheaply protect themselves from deception, legal intervention may be more trouble than it's worth. Or, at least, the law should focus on instances in which it is difficult for consumers to protect themselves.

BeVier argues that courts should be particularly cautious because consumers may receive multiple messages from ads, only some of which are deceptive. She gives an example of an ad for a shampoo that claimed that 900 women like the model in the ad preferred the shampoo to three major competitors. One of those competitors sued, successfully arguing that the survey on which this claim was based was so flawed as to be unreliable. But, BeVier argues, many consumers probably got only truthful messages from the ad—that the shampoo was available for purchase, that it competed with the leading brands, that the model in the ad liked the shampoo, that the shampoo would produce similar results for the consumer as for the model and so on. Only a small fraction might have paid attention to the specifics of the survey claim, and an even smaller fraction would have believed and relied on that claim. And, if they tried the shampoo and didn't like it, they could quickly punish the advertiser. Therefore, allowing the competitor to sue was wasteful at best and suppressed all these true messages at worst.

But couldn't the advertiser have communicated the truthful messages BeVier identified without communicating the false claims about the survey? If so, wouldn't it be better to require the advertiser to use that ad instead?

2.   The Psychology of Advertising

Advertising's Powerful Effects on Factual Beliefs

Though consumers don't like to believe that ads influence them, and though some ads plainly don't work, advertising works in ways that don't fit well with the model of the perfectly rational consumer.

For example, ads can distort memory and perception, even when consumers have direct experience with a product. Researchers showed people a false claim of "no bitterness" in coffee and then had them taste coffee made bitter by deliberate over-brewing. Consumers who'd seen the ad and tasted the coffee rated the coffee as less bitter than consumers who had only tasted the coffee. Even though the tasting had some effect on the first group's opinions, they still ended up being affected by the ad in the face of directly contradictory experience. Jerry C. Olson & Philip A. Dover, *Cognitive Effects of Deceptive Advertising*, 15 J. MKTG. RES. 29 (1978). This result—that ads can change memories, even memories of direct experiences—has been confirmed in numerous other contexts by other researchers. *See, e.g.,* Kathryn A. Braun, *Postexperience Advertising Effects on Consumer Memory*, 25 J. CONSUMER RES. 319 (1999) (finding that advertising can induce consumers to change taste judgments from negative to positive). As one researcher comments, "[f]rom an advertising and marketing perspective, this is a major breakthrough: [T]he work showed that exposure to advertising can transform 'objective' sensory information, such as taste, in a consumer's memory, prior to the judgment process, and after the consumer [has] tasted the product." Bruce F. Hall, *A New Model for Measuring Advertising Effectiveness*, 42 J. ADVERT. RES. 25

(Mar. 2002). These results provide evidence of a confirmation bias. People do not want to feel like a dupe who believed an untrue claim.

Simple repetition of advertising also improves its credibility. *See, e.g.*, Scott A. Hawkins et al., *Low-Involvement Learning: Repetition and Coherence in Familiarity and Belief*, 11 J. CONSUMER PSYCHOL. 1 (2001). As Sarah Haan has explained, the "truth effect" means that the more familiar a claim appears to a consumer, the more likely the consumer is to believe that the claim is true. Thus, repeated advertising can wear down consumers' skepticism. *See* Sarah C. Haan, Note, *The "Persuasion Route" of the Law: Advertising and Legal Persuasion*, 100 COLUM. L. REV. 1281 (2000).

The effects of repeated exposures occur even when consumers initially rate the claim as low in credibility. Ian Skurnik et al. elaborate:

> [S]uppose the claim "shark cartilage will help your arthritis" feels familiar to consumers because they have encountered it recently. They might trust it less if they remember reading it in a tabloid headline than if they remember hearing it as advice from their physician. A weakness of this strategy is that memory for prior exposure to a claim is often much better than, and can be wholly independent of, memory for the context in which the claim appeared. And, when people find a claim familiar because of prior exposure but do not recall the original context or source of the claim, they tend to think that the claim is true.

Ian Skurnik et al., *How Warnings about False Claims Become Recommendations*, 31 J. CONSUMER RES. 713 (2005).

Skurnik et al. also found that warnings that claims are false can be counterproductive. Their research showed that "after 3 days had passed, the more times older adults had been warned that a claim was false, the more likely they were to misremember the claim as true," and that "trying to discredit claims after making them familiar to older adults backfired and increased their tendency to call those claims true." As a result, "merely identifying a given claim as unsubstantiated or false" may actually increase belief in the claim.

Other psychological evidence suggests that consumers tend to default to assuming that statements are true. It can be very hard to resist advertising claims, especially when consumers don't have a lot of time to devote to consciously debunking them. The ads are, after all, designed to persuade. *See* DAVID M. BOUSH, DECEPTION IN THE MARKETPLACE: THE PSYCHOLOGY OF DECEPTIVE PERSUASION AND CONSUMER SELF-PROTECTION 17 (2009) ("Deception self-protection among high school friends or in everyday work environments is not the same as effective self-protection against professional marketers' ploys."). And, unfortunately, falsity-detection skills we learn in one context may not transfer easily to new contexts, even new advertising media.

What lessons does this empirical evidence suggest for advertising regulation? Do the results about repetition and counter-speech provide justification for banning certain claims entirely? Could simple repetition cross the line into deception?

The Example of Price as a Signal of Other Characteristics

Research by Baba Shiv et al. found that pricing can actually change the physical effects of products. Apparently, price triggers unconscious expectations about efficacy. Researchers told some study participants that the researchers had bought the energy drink being studied at a steep discount and told other participants that the researchers had paid the regular price. The first group rated their workouts as less intense and rated themselves as more fatigued than the second group. The participants didn't, however, *believe* that price had influenced their perceptions.

In another study, consumers who paid a discounted price for an energy drink that they were told was supposed to increase mental acuity were able to solve fewer puzzles compared to consumers who paid the regular price—and even compared to consumers who didn't drink anything. And the detrimental effect was worsened by greater expectations for the product. However, study participants who bought the drink at its regular price and heard strong advertising claims about the drink's effectiveness solved more puzzles than those in the control condition. In other words, the price affected not just the perceived quality of the product, but its objective effectiveness. Baba Shiv et al., *Placebo Effects of Marketing Actions: Consumers May Get What They Pay For*, 42 J. MKTG. RES. 383 (2005); *see also* Emir Kamenica et al., *Advertisements Impact the Physiological Efficacy of a Branded Drug*, PROC. OF THE NATI'L ACAD. OF SCIENTISTS (June 6, 2013) (finding that ads for Zyrtec decreased the physiological effect of Claritin by over 90% for subjects not familiar with antihistamines; subjects familiar with antihistamines didn't differ in their responses).

These results are consistent with earlier research finding that consumers often believe and judge lower-priced items to be of lower quality, even when objective testing finds no quality differences or advantages for the lower-priced versions. In one case, an advertiser carefully priced its instant coffee sold in single-serving pods just below the price of brand-name Keurig ground coffee, which contributed to consumers' beliefs that the advertiser's product couldn't be instant coffee. "This had the dual benefit of reaping a high profit and forestalling consumer suspicions. As one executive admitted candidly, 'If you actually got the price too low, people would perceive it as poor quality.'" Suchanek v. Sturm Foods, Inc., 764 F.3d 750 (7th Cir. 2014).

Price effects may be an instance of framing effects, in which how a product is presented affects how consumers evaluate it. For example, meat labeled "25% fat" tastes better than the same meat that is labeled "75% fat free." I.P. Levin & J.G. Gaeth, *How Consumers Are Affected by the Framing of Attribute Information Before and After Consuming the Product*, 15 J. CONSUMER RES. 374 (1988); *see also, e.g.*, Dirkjan Joor et al., *The Emperor's Clothes in High Resolution: An Experimental Study of the Framing Effect and the Diffusion of HDTV*, 7 ACM COMPUTERS IN ENT., No. 3, Article 40 (September 2009) (telling consumers that they were watching HDTV led them to report that the picture quality was higher).

Is deliberate framing of this sort deceptive? The practice undeniably induces people to choose products for reasons they don't understand and couldn't accurately explain, but does that differ from ordinary persuasion? Does it matter if consumers hold false *conscious* beliefs, instead of unconscious ones?

Price can be used to manipulate choices in other ways. What if an advertiser claims that it's offering a new, lower price? If it actually charges the "new" price, would it matter that there was never an old, higher price? As one group of researchers explains,

> [t]here is a large body of evidence to show that the presence of an advertised *reference price* increases consumers' valuations of a deal and purchase intentions, and can lower their search intentions. Reference prices can have a significant impact *even* when these are disproportionally large and when consumers are skeptical of their truthfulness. The effects of reference prices are stronger when consumers are not readily able to compare them to an industry price, such as with unbranded, or retailers' "own brand" goods, and with less frequently purchased and more expensive items.

GORKAN AHMETOGLU ET AL., PRICING PRACTICES: THEIR EFFECTS ON CONSUMER BEHAVIOUR AND WELFARE (2010).

California—like many states—specifically bans false claims of discounts. The defendants argued that, nonetheless, the consumer hadn't suffered any actionable harm, since he received the product at the advertised price. Hinojos v. Kohl's Corp., 718 F.3d 1098 (9th Cir. 2013), rejected this argument, citing Dhruv Grewal & Larry D. Compeau, *Comparative Price Advertising: Informative or Deceptive?*, 11 J. PUB. POL'Y & MKTG. 52 (1992) ("By creating an impression of savings, the presence of a higher reference price enhances subjects' perceived value and willingness to buy the product. . . . [E]mpirical studies indicate that as discount size increases, consumers' perceptions of value and their willingness to buy the product increase, while their intention to search for a lower price decreases."). As the court pointed out, the "what a great bargain!" effect is exactly why retailers have an incentive to falsely advertise sales and exactly why the California legislature barred the practice.

Images and Words

Advertising regulation focuses a lot on claims communicated via words. However, advertisers make heavy use of images as well, and images don't always work the same way as words do. To what extent, if any, should the law treat images (or other nonverbal forms of advertising) differently?

Edward F. McQuarrie and Barbara J. Phillips point out that "[i]t is rare to find a magazine ad that makes a straightforward claim like 'Tide gets clothes clean.' Instead, detergent ads claim to make your clothes 'as fresh and clean as sunshine,' or show a picture of a measuring cup filled with blue sky." They argue that using images as metaphors makes consumers more likely to pay attention to an ad, encouraging them to use their imaginations to interpret the image, which is more fun than just getting explicit information.

One benefit for advertisers is that this process is more convincing: "Consumers are less likely to argue against associations they came up with themselves, and more likely to remember and act on them." But depending on how consumers use their imaginations, they might draw truthful or misleading conclusions. McQuarrie and Phillips found in their empirical research that when comparing ads using straightforward claims, verbal metaphors or visual metaphors, all three ads communicated the same basic message. Nonetheless, the metaphors left consumers with more positive thoughts toward the product—they even reported receiving factual claims not explicitly present in the ad—and visual metaphors did better than verbal metaphors. Moreover, the visual metaphors worked immediately, whereas verbal metaphors required further prompting.

These researchers conclude that:

> [L]egal protections may need to evolve beyond a focus on whether a claim made in words is true or false. . . . [I]t is not reasonable to infer from a picture of a cleaning product next to a grenade that this brand is more powerful than others. Nonetheless, based on the evidence of this study, it is an empirical fact that such thoughts do occur when consumers are exposed to visual metaphors.

Edward F. McQuarrie & Barbara J. Phillips, *Indirect Persuasion in Advertising: How Consumers Process Metaphors Presented in Pictures and Words*, 34 J. ADVERT. 7 (2005).

Persuasion happens in other subtle ways. Putting an antiperspirant in a box, for example, may lead people to think it's stronger than an identical unboxed version. *See* Jack Neff, *Wanting Less But Buying More*, ADVERT. AGE, March 3, 2008. More generally, packaging sends a variety of powerful messages that affect consumers' choices. In one experiment, researchers sent subjects an identical deodorant in three differently colored packages and asked them to rate the three. With one color scheme, subjects "praised its pleasant yet unobtrusive fragrance and its ability to stop wetness and odor for as many as twelve hours." The second color scheme "was found to have a strong aroma, but not really very much effectiveness." The third "was downright threatening. Several users developed skin rashes after using it, and three had severe enough problems to consult dermatologists." THOMAS HINE, THE TOTAL PACKAGE: THE SECRET HISTORY AND HIDDEN MEANINGS OF BOXES, BOTTLES, CANS, AND OTHER PERSUASIVE CONTAINERS (1997).

Drinks and food in thin bottles and packages are perceived to have fewer calories than those in wide packages. Jieun Koo & Kwanho Suk, *The Effect of Package Shape on Calorie Estimation*, 33 INT'L J. RES. MKTG. 856 (2016). A thin container with an indented "waist" (a concave shape) seems healthier, especially to women who have a high body mass index. Nadine Yarar et al., *Shaping Up: How Package Shape and Consumer Body Conspire to Affect Food Healthiness Evaluation*, 75 FOOD QUALITY & PREFERENCE 209 (2019). And people perceived a candy bar with a green calorie label as healthier than the same bar with the same information on a red label. J.P. Schuldt, *Does Green Mean Healthy? Nutrition Label Color Affects Perceptions of Healthfulness*, 28 HEALTH COMM. 814 (2013).

Trademark law recognizes the communicative power of packaging by providing trademark rights for distinctive packaging (what it calls "trade dress"). Should advertising law generally regulate product shapes? If antiperspirant in a box isn't actually stronger, should we deem the practice of putting it in the box misleading? Does it matter that extra packaging creates additional social costs, like manufacturing and disposing of the packaging?

3.   Facts and Non-facts: Puffery and Related Doctrines

No matter who the challenger is and no matter what the forum, the basic target of false advertising law is the same: deception that tends to make consumers more likely to buy what the advertiser is selling or less likely to buy the competitors' products or services.

But U.S. law has also determined that, as a rule, only false statements of *fact* are actionable. We know that nonfactual atmospherics in an ad, such as the presence of attractive people, drive sales. Nonetheless, we have chosen not to regulate such atmospherics. The FTC or states with unfair practices laws can find particular nonfactual sales techniques to be *unfair* because of their effects on consumers' reasoning. However, as a matter of doctrine, only ad elements that convey (or obscure) factual claims can be *false or misleading*.

As you read the materials in this section, consider whether this result is sound as a matter of policy. Even if consumers are affected by nonfactual claims, perhaps the fact that they're open to all competitors is sufficient to justify a hands-off approach, especially given the costs of litigation. Without a specific factual claim that can be falsified, it may simply be too hard to determine which ads take persuasion too far. Or does our tolerance for puffery reflect an unwarranted confidence in consumers' ability to apply careful logic to every ad claim they see?

Fact vs. Opinion

Courts in advertising cases sometimes use the construct "fact v. opinion" instead of "fact v. puffery," depending on the parties' arguments and the particular statements at issue. An ad that quotes a third-party review, such as "*Toaster Magazine* raves: 'This is the best toaster on the market!'" could be deemed Toaster Magazine's opinion about toasters, though "best" is also considered puffery (note that the ad makes a separate fact claim that Toaster Magazine actually said those words). In general, think of opinion and puffery as two similar but distinct ways for courts to say that the statements aren't factual enough to be actionable.

A statement of fact is a "specific and measurable claim, capable of being proved false or of being reasonably interpreted as a statement of objective fact." Coastal Abstract Serv. Inc. v. First Am. Title Ins. Co., 173 F.3d 725 (9th Cir. 1999). By contrast, when a statement is "obviously a statement of opinion," it cannot "reasonably be seen as stating or implying provable facts." Groden v. Random House, 61 F.3d 1045 (2d Cir. 1995). The fact/opinion divide grows out of defamation law—only facts can be defamatory, not opinions in themselves.

Consistent with the rule in defamation law, simply couching an advertisement in terms of the advertiser's opinion will not insulate it from challenge if the statement is one that is, in fact, verifiable. In *National Commission on Egg Nutrition v. Federal Trade Commission*, 570 F.2d 157 (7th Cir. 1977), the Commission on Egg Nutrition argued that its statement that there was "no scientific evidence" that eating eggs increased the risk of heart and circulatory disease was merely an expression of opinion. The Seventh Circuit agreed with the FTC that the phrase "is also, and perhaps more reasonably[,] subject to the interpretation" that no such reliable scientific evidence existed. If a claim can be confirmed or disconfirmed, the claim will be treated as factual.

Relatedly, an opinion can be actionable if consumers would understand it to be based on particular facts, but the facts are different than the opinion suggests. Thus, some states' consumer protection laws will cover opinions that are accompanied by failure to disclose facts that would lead a reasonable person to question the opinion. *See, e.g.*, Canady v. Mann, 419 S.E.2d 597 (N.C. Ct. App. 1992) (upholding claim based on agent's statement that properties were good investments and suitable for building where agent knew or had reason to know that representations were false because wetlands precluded development), *review dismissed*, 429 S.E.2d 348 (N.C. 1993). More generally, the *Restatement (Third) of Unfair Competition* points out that "[i]n many circumstances prospective purchasers may reasonably understand a statement of opinion to be more than a mere assertion as to the seller's state of mind. Some representations of opinion may imply the existence of facts that justify the opinion, or at least that there are no facts known to the speaker that are substantially incompatible with the stated opinion." § 3 cmt. d (1995); see also PhotoMedex, Inc. v. Irwin, 601 F.3d 919 (9th Cir. 2010) (while "[a]n honest or sincere statement of belief about a future event is not actionable, . . . a statement known at that time by the speaker to be false, or a statement by a speaker who lacks a good faith belief in the truth of the statement, may constitute an actionable misrepresentation."). (Compare this with the *Vokes* fraud case from Chapter 3.)

Thus, statements in the form of opinions may be actionable when it would be reasonable for a consumer, under the circumstances, to treat the opinion as a factual representation, e.g., when the speaker purportedly possesses special expertise unavailable to the consumer. FTC Policy Statement on Deception, § III (Oct. 14, 1983) ("Claims phrased as opinions are actionable . . . if they are not honestly held, if they misrepresent the qualifications of the holder or the basis of his opinion or if the recipient reasonably interprets them as implied statements of fact. . . . [R]epresentations of expert opinions will generally be regarded as representations of fact."); FTC v. Sec. Rare Coin & Bullion Corp., 931 F.2d 1312 (9th Cir. 1991) (upholding injunction against representations that coins were good investment vehicles with high profit potential and low risk). This rule is similar to the rule for defamation law, which also holds that statements with the semantic form of opinion may assert defamatory facts or imply the existence of undisclosed defamatory facts. Milkovich v. Lorain Journal Co., 497 U.S. 1 (1990).

In the ordinary case, however, where reasonable consumers should understand that a statement is no more than a prediction and might not be accurate, there can be no liability. *See, e.g.*, Ameritox, Ltd. v. Millennium Labs., Inc., 2014 WL 1456347 (M.D. Fla. 2014) (layperson's claims about the legality of a billing practice under federal statutes and rules were non-actionable opinion, because no court or agency had yet found the billing practice to be unlawful; a clear and unambiguous judicial or agency holding is required for falsity of statements about law); Koagel v. Ryan Homes, Inc., 562 N.Y.S.2d 312 (N.Y. App. Div. 1990) (defendant not liable for statement regarding property taxes because statement was merely estimate and tax rates and assessments are volatile); Opsahl v. Pinehurst, Inc., 380 S.E.2d 796 (N.C. Ct. App. 1989), *review dismissed*, 385 S.E.2d 400 (N.C. 1987) (defendant not liable for statement that utilities would be available to rural lot by a certain date because it is common knowledge that projected completion dates in construction industry are frequently missed). As the case law indicates, courts are more likely to use the language of "opinion" when dealing with individualized or specialized sales pitches than with the more blanket statements made in general advertising—though such statements may still be non-actionable puffery.

Courts may find that a statement is opinion even when the defendant explicitly tries to get people to rely on it. In *ZL Technologies, Inc. v. Gartner, Inc.*, 2009 WL 3706821 (N.D. Cal. 2009), the defendant sold its research reports on business software, claiming to have the "combined brainpower of 1,200 research analysts and consultants who advise executives in 80 countries every day," "tens of thousands of pages of original research annually," "highly discerning research that is objective, defensible, and credible to help [customers] do their job better," "relevant experience and institutional knowledge [that] prevent[s] costly and avoidable errors" and an ability to "show you how to buy, what to buy, and how to get the best return on your technology investment." The court found that all the challenged statements were not factually verifiable, despite the use of words such as "objective." Gartner's "sophisticated readers"—corporate and government executives and professionals—would not infer that Gartner's rankings were anything other than opinion. But if all of these statements were opinion, why did Gartner try so hard to convince customers that it was using accurate, objective and reliable criteria?

When should the question of whether a statement is fact or opinion be left to a finder of fact? This determination is highly dependent on the circumstances, and it can be difficult to predict. Courts sometimes send the matter to the jury if they aren't sure whether a statement is fact or opinion, but they also routinely make a determination as a matter of law.

Science

Is a scientific conclusion a fact? You might think that the answer is yes, and most false advertising cases accept that result without hesitation. The following case explores why a court might refuse to treat a scientific conclusion as a fact for purposes of false advertising law.

ONY, INC. V. CORNERSTONE THERAPEUTICS, INC., 720 F.3D 490 (2D CIR. 2013)

This case asks us to decide when a statement in a scientific article reporting research results can give rise to claims of false advertising under the Lanham Act, deceptive practices under New York General Business Law § 349, and the common-law torts of injurious falsehood and interference with prospective economic advantage. We conclude that, as a matter of law, statements of scientific conclusions about unsettled matters of scientific debate cannot give rise to liability for damages sounding in defamation. We further conclude that the secondary distribution of excerpts of such an article cannot give rise to liability, so long as the excerpts do not mislead a reader about the conclusions of the article.

BACKGROUND

. . . Plaintiff ONY, Inc. ("ONY") and defendant Chiesi Farmaceutici, S.p.A. ("Chiesi") are two of the biggest producers of surfactants, biological substances that line the surface of human lungs. Surfactants are critical to lung function: they facilitate the transfer of oxygen from inhaled air into the blood stream. Although the human body naturally produces surfactants, prematurely born infants often produce inadequate surfactant levels. Infants with such a deficiency are at a higher risk for lung collapse and Respiratory Distress Syndrome ("RDS"), a condition that can result in respiratory failure and death. The non-human surfactants produced and sold by, among others, ONY and Chiesi are the primary treatment for RDS. . . . ONY produces one derived from bovine lung surfactant that bears the trade name "Infasurf." Chiesi produces a competing surfactant derived from porcine lung mince that goes by "Curosurf." Chiesi, an Italian pharmaceutical firm, contracts with its co-defendant Cornerstone Therapeutics, Inc. ("Cornerstone") to distribute and market Curosurf in the United States.

. . . . The parties agree that two variables are particularly relevant to this comparison: mortality rate and length of stay. Mortality rate means the percentage of infants treated with a particular surfactant who do not survive. Length of stay refers to the amount of time an infant remains in the hospital for treatment. These two variables are not entirely independent: in some cases the length of stay is shortened by death, which is reflected in the mortality rate. Put differently, some of the same causes of increased mortality rate (low birth weight, shorter gestational period) also cause shorter lengths of stay. Conversely, infants with shorter hospitalization might have had less serious medical conditions from the beginning, independent of treatment variables. At the same time, a particularly effective drug may both reduce mortality rate and shorten length of stay.

In 2006, as part of its effort to promote and sell Curosurf, Chiesi hired defendant Premier, Inc. ("Premier") to build a database and conduct a study of the relative effectiveness of the different surfactants. . . . Chiesi then hired several medical doctors, including defendants Rangasamy Ramanathan, Jatinder J. Bhatia, and Krishnamurthy Sekar (the "physician defendants"), to present findings based on Premier's database at various medical conferences. . . .

In 2011, the physician defendants [along with a Chiesi employee] eventually decided to publish some of the findings from the same data set in a peer-reviewed journal. They submitted their article to the *Journal of Perinatology*, the leading journal in the field of neonatology, which is the study of newborn infants. The article was published in the September 1, 2011 volume of the journal after being peer reviewed by two anonymous referees.

According to ONY, the article contains five distinct incorrect statements of fact about the relative effectiveness of Curosurf versus Infasurf: (1) that Infasurf "was associated with a 49.6% greater likelihood of death than" Curosurf; (2) that Curosurf "treatment for RDS was associated with a significantly reduced likelihood of death when compared with" Infasurf; (3) that the authors' "model found [Infasurf] to be associated with a significantly greater likelihood of death than" Curosurf; (4) that the authors' study showed "a significant greater likelihood of death with" Infasurf than Curosurf; and (5) the summary concluding sentence:

> In conclusion, this large retrospective study of preterm infants with RDS found lower mortality among infants who received [Curosurf], compared with infants who

received either [Infasurf] or [a third competitor's product], even after adjusting for patient characteristics such as gestational age and [birth weight], and after accounting for hospital characteristics and center effects.

Plaintiff also alleges that the circumstances surrounding the article's publication were unusual: Bhatia is an Associate Editor, and Sekar is a member of the editorial board of the *Journal of Perinatology*. Plaintiff alleged in its complaint that one of the two peer reviewers objected to its publication, but the other peer reviewer recommended the article for publication, and the Editor-in-Chief broke the tie. Plaintiff does not allege, however, that the publication of the article based on the affirmative opinions of one reviewer and the Editor-in-Chief was a departure from accepted or customary procedure. Further, the article was published in an "open access" format, which allows it to be viewed electronically by the general public without paying the typically applicable fee or ordering a subscription; the fees associated with such publication were paid by Chiesi and Cornerstone.

The article's conclusions were not unqualified. The authors considered the objection that the retrospective nature of the study might cause a disparity between the groups included in the study. More specifically, the authors noted that the article's finding may "most likely . . . be due to different surfactant doses administered to the infants included in the database," because Curosurf was, on average, prescribed in higher doses than its competitors. Finally, the authors disclosed that the study was sponsored by Chiesi, that Ernst was an employee of Premier, that Chiesi hired Premier to conduct the study, and that all three physician defendants had served as consultants to Chiesi.

Plaintiff's primary objection to the substance of the article's scientific methodology is that the authors omitted any mention of the length-of-stay data . . . . Because an important determinant of mortality rate is the pre-treatment health of the infants in the sample, plaintiff contends that the omission of length-of-stay data was intentional and designed to mask the fact that the neonatal infants treated with Curosurf had a greater ex ante chance of survival than did the group treated with Infasurf. If the length-of-stay data had been included, plaintiff alleges, "it would be obvious to readers that the differences in the results were a result of differences in the groups of patients treated, not of any differences in the effect of the particular lung surfactant administered." Plaintiff also objects to the authors' failure to cite articles with different primary conclusions, although such contradictory authority was known to them, and to the use of retrospective data, which was allegedly improper because it rendered the data subject to "selective distortion." Finally, plaintiff contends that Chiesi and Cornerstone paid Premier to collect data that supported their own product's effectiveness.

After the article's publication, Chiesi and Cornerstone issued a press release touting its conclusions and distributed promotional materials that cited the article's findings. Since the article's publication, meanwhile, plaintiff has, through its corporate officers—themselves pediatricians—written letters to the *Journal of Perinatology* rebutting the article's conclusions, objecting to its methods, and asking that it be retracted. We take judicial notice of the fact that several of those letters were eventually published by the journal, although they did not appear in print until after the district court dismissed the complaint. The authors were given, and took, the opportunity to respond to those letters. . . .

DISCUSSION

... The Lanham Act generally prohibits false advertising. In particular, it provides a civil cause of action against "any person" who, in interstate commerce, "uses ... any ... false or misleading description of fact, or false or misleading representation of fact." 15 U.S.C. § 1125(a)(1). Because the Act proscribes conduct that, but for its false or misleading character, would be protected by the First Amendment, free speech principles inform our interpretation of the Act. Indeed, "we have been careful not to permit overextension of the Lanham Act to intrude on First Amendment values." We have been especially careful when applying defamation and related causes of action to academic works, because academic freedom is "a special concern of the First Amendment."

Generally, statements of pure opinion—that is, statements incapable of being proven false—are protected under the First Amendment. Milkovich v. Lorain Journal Co., 497 U.S. 1, 19-20 (1990). But the line between fact and opinion is not always a clear one. In *Milkovich*, the Supreme Court declined to carve out an absolute privilege for statements of opinion and reaffirmed that the test for whether a statement is actionable does not simply boil down to whether a statement is falsifiable. To illustrate the difficulty, the Court provided the example of a statement of fact phrased as a statement of opinion: stating that "in my opinion John Jones is a liar" is no different from merely asserting that John Jones is a liar. Thus, the question of whether a statement is actionable admits of few easy distinctions.

... Scientific academic discourse poses several problems for the fact-opinion paradigm of First Amendment jurisprudence. Most conclusions contained in a scientific journal article are, in principle, "capable of verification or refutation by means of objective proof." Indeed, it is the very premise of the scientific enterprise that it engages with empirically verifiable facts about the universe. At the same time, however, it is the essence of the scientific method that the conclusions of empirical research are tentative and subject to revision, because they represent inferences about the nature of reality based on the results of experimentation and observation. Importantly, those conclusions are presented in publications directed to the relevant scientific community, ideally in peer-reviewed academic journals that warrant that research approved for publication demonstrates at least some degree of basic scientific competence. These conclusions are then available to other scientists who may respond by attempting to replicate the described experiments, conducting their own experiments, or analyzing or refuting the soundness of the experimental design or the validity of the inferences drawn from the results. In a sufficiently novel area of research, propositions of empirical "fact" advanced in the literature may be highly controversial and subject to rigorous debate by qualified experts. Needless to say, courts are ill-equipped to undertake to referee such controversies. Instead, the trial of ideas plays out in the pages of peer-reviewed journals, and the scientific public sits as the jury.

... The Seventh Circuit has also declined to allow suits based on claims of false conclusions in matters of scientific controversy to proceed. *See* Underwager v. Salter, 22 F.3d 730, 736 (7th Cir.1994) ("Scientific controversies must be settled by the methods of science rather than by the methods of litigation. ... More papers, more discussion, better data, and more satisfactory models—not larger awards of damages—mark the path toward superior understanding of the world around us."). . . . *cf.* Padnes v. Scios Nova Inc., 1996 WL 539711 (N.D. Cal. 1996) ("Medical researchers may well differ with respect to what constitutes acceptable testing procedures, as well as how best to interpret data garnered under various protocols. The securities laws do not impose a requirement that companies report only information from optimal studies, even if scientists could agree on what is optimal." (internal citation omitted)).

Where, as here, a statement is made as part of an ongoing scientific discourse about which there is considerable disagreement, the traditional dividing line between fact and opinion is not entirely helpful. It is clear to us, however, that while statements about contested and contestable scientific hypotheses constitute assertions about the world that are in principle matters of verifiable "fact," for purposes of the First Amendment and the laws relating to fair competition and defamation, they are more closely akin to matters of opinion, and are so understood by the relevant scientific communities. In that regard, it is relevant that plaintiff does not allege that the data presented in the article were fabricated or fraudulently created. If the data were falsified, the fraud would not be easily detectable by even the most informed members of the relevant scientific community. Rather, plaintiff alleges that the inferences drawn from those data were the wrong ones, and that competent scientists would have included variables that were available to the defendant authors but that were not taken into account in their analysis. But when the conclusions reached by experiments are presented alongside an accurate description of the data taken into account and the methods used, the validity of the authors' conclusions may be assessed on their face by other members of the relevant discipline or specialty.

We therefore conclude that, to the extent a speaker or author draws conclusions from non-fraudulent data, based on accurate descriptions of the data and methodology underlying those conclusions, on subjects about which there is legitimate ongoing scientific disagreement, those statements are not grounds for a claim of false advertising under the Lanham Act [or under state law]. Here, ONY has alleged false advertising not because any of the data presented were incorrect but because the way they were presented and the conclusions drawn from them were allegedly misleading. Even if the conclusions authors draw from the results of their data could be actionable, such claims would be weakest when, as here, the authors readily disclosed the potential shortcomings of their methodology and their potential conflicts of interest. . . .

NOTES AND QUESTIONS

Taken seriously, *ONY* would seem to prohibit most of what the Food and Drug Administration (FDA) does with respect to pharmaceuticals: The FDA evaluates scientific studies and determines whether they support the health-related claims the manufacturer wishes to make for the drug. If the FDA finds the study insufficient, the claim may not legally be made on the drug's label, no matter what the manufacturer believes or is willing to disclose about the study's limitations. Is this materially distinguishable from what the *ONY* court said the government—in the form of a court—could not do? (Some pharmaceutical companies are beginning to make precisely this type of argument as to off-label claims, and the Second Circuit has proven highly receptive.)

Should we let the claim "this paint will last up to twenty years even in tough weather conditions" be "settled by the methods of science rather than by the methods of litigation"? In fact, most cases, even in the Second Circuit, treat scientific claims as falsifiable, even if the actual facts are hard to discern because the science is complicated.

In *Eastman Chemical Co. v. Plastipure, Inc.*, 775 F.3d 230 (5th Cir. 2014), the Fifth Circuit explicitly rejected the argument that *ONY* required it to remain agnostic on a disputed question of scientific proof. Eastman alleged that Plastipure disparaged Eastman's plastic resin by falsely stating that it could leach chemicals capable of harming humans. A jury found in Eastman's favor. Defendants sought to overturn the verdict, arguing that they didn't make empirically falsifiable factual statements, but rather participated in a scientific debate protected by the First Amendment.

The *Plastipure* court reasoned that the *ONY* plaintiff sought to enjoin statements "within the academic literature and directed at the scientific community." Here, Eastman didn't sue Plastipure for publishing in a scientific journal, but for ads directed at nonscientist customers without the full scientific context, including a description of the data, the methodology, conflicts of interest and divergences between raw data and the experimenter's conclusions. "In this commercial context, the First Amendment is no obstacle to enforcement of the Lanham Act":

> Advertisements do not become immune from Lanham Act scrutiny simply because their claims are open to scientific or public debate. Otherwise, the Lanham Act would hardly ever be enforceable—"many, if not most, products may be tied to public concerns with the environment, energy, economic policy, or individual health and safety." [*Central Hudson*.] . . . The First Amendment ensures a robust discourse in the pages of academic journals, but it does not immunize false or misleading commercial claims.

Does the court succeed in distinguishing *ONY*? Why couldn't a jury have resolved the battle of the experts in that case as well? Wasn't the defendant in *ONY* using the scientific paper to tout itself to the relevant consumers as well, who just happened to be doctors who read journals? (As you can see, the concept of the reasonable consumer, to be discussed in Chapter 5, may inform the concept of what is falsifiable.)

What about a business that advertised that it could "cure" gay men and lesbians and turn them heterosexual? Should such claims be subject to false advertising laws, given the consensus of counselors and healthcare professionals that such therapies are ineffective and harmful? *See* Ferguson v. JONAH, No. L-5473-12 (N.J. Super. Ct. July 19, 2013) (denying "cure" organization's motion to dismiss New Jersey false advertising claims).

4. Puffery

Some advertising is just bluster. Vague superlatives such as "best," "finest," "brightest," "most delicious," and the like are so common that reasonable consumers are presumed to treat them as unverifiable, unquantifiable, subjective and unreliable. This conclusion is normative—it is about how consumers should behave, not about what advertisers should say. As Learned Hand wrote in *Vulcan Metals Co. v. Simmons Mfg. Co.*, 248 F. 853 (2d Cir. 1918), "There are some kinds of talk which no sensible man takes seriously, and if he does he suffers from his own credulity." The result is that an advertiser has a privilege "to lie his head off, so long as he says nothing specific." W. Page Keeton et al., *Prosser & Keeton on The Law of Torts* § 109 (5th ed. 1984). Thus, the slogan "You're in good hands with Allstate" was puffery, as was a claim that the advertiser's baby food was the "most nutritious." The law treats these claims as meaningless sales patter.

Puffery generally constitutes claims about the advertiser's own product. However, courts have also held that vague derogatory claims can be puffery. *See, e.g.*, U.S. Healthcare, Inc. v. Blue Cross, 898 F.2d 914 (3d Cir. 1990) ("Better than HMO. So good, it's Blue Cross and Blue Shield" tag line was "the most innocuous kind of 'puffing'"). *Compare* Tempur Seal Int'l, Inc. v. Wondergel, LLC, 2016 WL 1305155 (E.D. Ky. Apr. 1, 2016) (statement "Looking for some shoulder pain? Try a hard mattress. It may feel like a rock and put pressure on your hips, but it's the perfect way to tell your partner: 'Hey baby, want some arthritis?'" wasn't puffery, "as these statements regarding potential negative health effects clearly cross the line beyond what is permissible advertising."). Non-U.S. jurisdictions are more likely to consider negative puffing to be unfair and even misleading, even if it is vague.

A.   Verifiable or Merely Puff?

What is puffery? Students often find the concept challenging, and the cases are scattered and arguably highly inconsistent—even chaotic. The cases involve widely diverging factual situations, with no clear patterns distinguishing different states or circuits, and you may find yourself dissatisfied by the gap between the general principles stated in the cases and the highly specific claims found to be puffery or fact. In reviewing these materials, you should aim to train your judgment and to be able to liken new claims to previous cases, even though certainty may be impossible.

First, we will present an influential case that tries to define puffery, as many courts have before it. After you read it but before you read the notes, consider whether you think you have a grasp on puffery. Then read the notes.

PIZZA HUT, INC. v. PAPA JOHN'S INT'L, INC., 227 F.3D 489 (5TH CIR. 2000)

This appeal presents a false advertising claim under Section 43(a) of the Lanham Act, resulting in a jury verdict for the plaintiff, Pizza Hut. At the center of this appeal is Papa John's four-word slogan "Better Ingredients. Better Pizza."

. . . We conclude that (1) the slogan, standing alone, is not an [objectively verifiable] statement of fact upon which consumers would be justified in relying, and thus not actionable under Section 43(a); and (2) . . . the slogan, when utilized in connection with some of the post–May 1997 comparative advertising—specifically, the sauce and dough campaigns—conveyed objectifiable and misleading facts . . .

I.

. . . Since 1995, Papa John's has invested over $300 million building customer goodwill in its trademark "Better Ingredients. Better Pizza." The slogan has appeared on millions of signs, shirts, menus, pizza boxes, napkins and other items, and has regularly appeared as the "tag line" at the end of Papa John's radio and television ads, or with the company logo in printed advertising.

. . . In early May 1997, Papa John's launched its first national ad campaign. The campaign was directed towards Pizza Hut, and its "Totally New Pizza" campaign. . . . The ad campaign was remarkably successful. During May 1997, Papa John's sales increased 11.7 percent over May 1996 sales, while Pizza Hut's sales were down 8 percent.

. . . Papa John's ran a series of ads comparing specific ingredients used in its pizzas with those used by its "competitors." During the course of these ads, Papa John's touted the superiority of its sauce and its dough. During the sauce campaign, Papa John's asserted that its sauce was made from "fresh, vine-ripened tomatoes," which were canned through a process called "fresh pack," while its competitors—including Pizza Hut—make their sauce from remanufactured tomato paste. During the dough campaign, Papa John's stated that it used "clear filtered water" to make its pizza dough, while the "biggest chain" uses "whatever comes out of the tap." Additionally, Papa John's asserted that it gives its yeast "several days to work its magic," while "some folks" use "frozen dough or dough made the same day." At or near the close of each of these ads, Papa John's punctuated its ingredient comparisons with the slogan "Better Ingredients. Better Pizza." [Pizza Hut sued.] . . . .

On November 17, 1999, the jury returned its responses to the special issues finding that Papa John's slogan, and its "sauce claims" and "dough claims" were false or misleading and deceptive or likely to deceive consumers.

The court concluded that the "Better Ingredients. Better Pizza." slogan was "consistent with the legal definition of non-actionable puffery" from its introduction in 1995 until May 1997. However, the slogan "became tainted . . . in light of the entirety of Papa John's post–May 1997 advertising." Based on this conclusion, the magistrate judge permanently enjoined Papa John's from "using any slogan in the future that constitutes a recognizable variation of the phrase 'Better Ingredients. Better Pizza.' or which uses the adjective 'Better' to modify the terms 'ingredients' and/or 'pizza'." . . .

Essential to any claim under Section 43(a) of the Lanham Act is a determination of whether the challenged statement is one of fact—actionable under Section 43(a)—or one of general opinion—not actionable under Section 43(a). Bald assertions of superiority or general statements of opinion cannot form the basis of Lanham Act liability. Rather the statements at issue must be a "specific and measurable claim, capable of being proved false or of being reasonably interpreted as a statement of objective fact." . . .

(b) . . . Drawing guidance from the writings of our sister circuits and the leading commentators, we think that non-actionable "puffery" comes in at least two possible forms: (1) an exaggerated, blustering, and boasting statement upon which no reasonable buyer would be justified in relying; or (2) a general claim of superiority over comparable products that is so vague that it can be understood as nothing more than a mere expression of opinion. . . .

Bisecting the slogan "Better Ingredients. Better Pizza.," it is clear that the assertion by Papa John's that it makes a "Better Pizza." is a general statement of opinion regarding the superiority of its product over all others. This simple statement, "Better Pizza.," epitomizes the exaggerated advertising, blustering, and boasting by a manufacturer upon which no consumer would reasonably rely. Consequently, it appears indisputable that Papa John's assertion "Better Pizza." is non-actionable puffery.[8]

Moving next to consider separately the phrase "Better Ingredients.," the same conclusion holds true. Like "Better Pizza.," it is typical puffery. The word "better," when used in this context is unquantifiable. What makes one food ingredient "better" than another comparable ingredient, without further description, is wholly a matter of individual taste or preference not subject to scientific quantification. Indeed, it is difficult to think of any product, or any component of any product, to which the term "better," without more, is quantifiable. As our court stated in *Presidio*:

> The law recognizes that a vendor is allowed some latitude in claiming merits of his wares by way of an opinion rather than an absolute guarantee, so long as he hews to the line of rectitude in matters of fact. Opinions are not only the lifestyle of democracy, they are the brag in advertising that has made for the wide dissemination of products that otherwise would never have reached the households of our citizens. If we were to accept the thesis set forth by the appellees, [that all statements by advertisers were statements of fact actionable under the Lanham Act,] the advertising industry would have to be liquidated in short order.

. . . . Finally, turning to the combination of the two non-actionable phrases as the slogan "Better Ingredients. Better Pizza.," we fail to see how the mere joining of these two statements of opinion could create an actionable statement of fact. . . .

. . . [T]here is sufficient evidence to support the jury's conclusion that the sauce and dough ads were misleading statements of fact actionable under the Lanham Act. [The court reviews and accepts Pizza Hut's evidence that there are no "demonstrable" or "quantifiable" differences between the parties' sauces and doughs.]

---

[8] It should be noted that Pizza Hut uses the slogan "The Best Pizza Under One Roof." Similarly, other nationwide pizza chains employ slogans touting their pizza as the "best": (1) Domino's Pizza uses the slogan "Nobody Delivers Better."; (2) Danato's uses the slogan "Best Pizza on the Block."; (3) Mr. Gatti's uses the slogan "Best Pizza in Town: Honest!"; and (4) Pizza Inn uses the slogans "Best Pizza Ever." and "The Best Tasting Pizza."

. . . Consequently, the district court was correct in concluding that: "Without any scientific support or properly conducted taste preference test, by the written and/or oral negative connotations conveyed that pizza made from tomato paste concentrate is inferior to the 'fresh pack' method used by Papa John's, its sauce advertisements conveyed an impression which is misleading. . . ." . . .

(3) . . . . In support of the district court's conclusion that the slogan was transformed, Pizza Hut argues that "in construing any advertising statement, the statement must be considered in the overall context in which it appears." . . .

We agree that the message communicated by the slogan "Better Ingredients. Better Pizza." is expanded and given additional meaning when it is used as the tag line in the misleading sauce and dough ads. . . . [A] reasonable consumer would understand the slogan, when considered in the context of the comparison ads, as conveying the following message: Papa John's uses "better ingredients," which produces a "better pizza" because Papa John's uses "fresh-pack" tomatoes, fresh dough, and filtered water. In short, Papa John's has given definition to the word "better." Thus, when the slogan is used in this context, it is no longer mere opinion, but rather takes on the characteristics of a statement of fact. When used in the context of the sauce and dough ads, the slogan is misleading for the same reasons we have earlier discussed in connection with the sauce and dough ads.[11]

NOTES AND QUESTIONS

Do you have a working definition of puffery now?

The Fifth Circuit's statement that "non-actionable 'puffery' comes in at least two possible forms: (1) an exaggerated, blustering, and boasting statement upon which no reasonable buyer would be justified in relying; or (2) a general claim of superiority over comparable products that is so vague that it can be understood as nothing more than a mere expression of opinion" resembles the FTC's take. C&H Sugar Co., 119 F.T.C. 39, 44 (1995) ("The term 'puffery' as used by the Commission here generally includes representations that ordinary consumers do not take literally, expressions of opinion not made as a representation of fact, subjective claims (taste, feel, appearance, smell) and hyperbole that are not capable of objective measurement.").

---

[11] . . . . Our review of the record convinces us that there is simply no evidence to support the district court's conclusion that the slogan was irreparably tainted as a result of its use in the misleading comparison sauce and dough ads. At issue in this case were some 249 print ads and 29 television commercials. After a thorough review of the record, we liberally construe eight print ads to be sauce ads, six print ads to be dough ads, and six print ads to be both sauce and dough ads. Further, we liberally construe nine television commercials to be sauce ads and two television commercials to be dough ads. Consequently, out of a total of 278 print and television ads, the slogan appeared in only 31 ads that could be liberally construed to be misleading sauce or dough ads.

We find simply no evidence, survey or otherwise, to support the district court's conclusion that the advertisements that the jury found misleading—ads that constituted only a small fraction of Papa John's use of the slogan—somehow had become encoded in the minds of consumers such that the mention of the slogan reflectively brought to mind the misleading statements conveyed by the sauce and dough ads. Thus, based on the record before us, Pizza Hut has failed to offer sufficient evidence to support the district court's conclusion that the slogan had become forever "tainted" by its use as the tag line in the handful of misleading comparison ads.

Now we will examine some specific factual situations; consider whether your working definition of puffery survives contact with the case law.

Vagueness. Sometimes the vagueness of a claim precludes it from being verifiable. *See, e.g.,* Silver v. BA Sports Nutrition, LLC, 2020 WL 2992873 (N.D. Cal. Jun. 4, 2020) ("Superior Hydration" and "More Natural Better Hydration" were puffery); Yetter v. Ford Motor Co., 428 F. Supp. 3d 210 (N.D. Cal. 2019) ("superior gas mileage and performance to previous Ford models" and a "better truck with better performance" were puffery); Oestreicher v. Alienware Corp., 544 F. Supp. 2d 964 (N.D. Cal. 2008) ("faster, more powerful, and more innovative than competing machines," "higher performance," "longer battery life," "richer multimedia experience," "faster access to data" and "ensure optimum performance" were puffery); Apodaca v. Whirlpool Corp., 2013 WL 6477821 (C.D. Cal. Nov. 8, 2013) ("statements about dependability and superiority ('built to last,' 'dependable,' 'unequaled tradition of quality production,' 'unrivaled performance') are too vague to be actionable."); Imagine Medispa, LLC v. Transformations, Inc., 999 F. Supp. 2d 873 (S.D. W. Va. 2014) ("West Virginia's Lowest Price Weight Loss and Skin Care Clinic" and "Lowest Prices in WV!" didn't refer to any specific services or products, and drew no direct comparisons but instead were "broad, vague exaggerations or boasts on which no reasonable consumer would rely.").

What about claims to have won awards, where the nature of the award isn't specified? See General Steel Domestic Sales, LLC v. Chumley, 129 F. Supp. 3d 1158 (D. Colo. 2015) (a boast, "Awarded Best in the Industry," was puffery, "as no reasonable consumer would rely on such an assertion without first inquiring further into the nature and credibility of the entity granting the award."); Hackett v. Feeney, 2011 WL 4007531 (D. Nev. 2011) (a boast that a particular theatrical performance was "Voted #1 Best Show in Vegas," when no such "vote" ever occurred, was puffery).

But arguably very similar, nonspecific claims have been deemed verifiable. *See, e.g.,* Southland Sod Farms v. Stover Seed Co., 108 F.3d 1134 (9th Cir. 1997) (claim that one type of grass required "50% less mowing"); Castrol Inc. v. Pennzoil Co., 987 F.2d 939, 945 (3d Cir. 1993) (claim that a motor oil provided "longer engine life and better engine protection"); U.S. Healthcare, Inc. v. Blue Cross, 898 F.2d 914 (3d Cir. 1990 (the statement that "The hospital my HMO sent me to just wasn't enough" combined with an image of an empty hospital bed); EP Henry Corp. v. Cambridge Pavers, Inc., 383 F. Supp. 3d 343 (D.N.J. 2019) (claims that "EP Henry developed our state-of-the art Durafacing technology, allowing us to create pavers of unrivaled beauty and durability;" "Durafacing process produces pavers with a smother surface texture and richer color;" and similar claims related to allegedly superior manufacturing process that "only EP Henry" could provide); Analysts Intern. v. Recycled Paper Prods., 1988 WL 17626 (N.D. Ill. 1988) (claims that the advertiser employs "seasoned professionals who have experience in all types of hardware and software environments," and that "it is highly unlikely for us to be presented with an application or problem to which we have had no exposure").

The context of the product or service must be taken into account to determine whether there is a verifiable claim being made. DIRECTV Satellite Television Service (Charter Communications, Inc. v. DIRECTV, Inc.), NAD Case No. 6157 (Feb. 7, 2018) (finding that TV provider's claim to offer "99% worry-free signal reliability" was different from "99% signal reliability," and that provider failed to substantiate that consumers wouldn't worry about their signals, where challenger showed that a significant number of provider's customers identified loss of service as the aspect of service that they liked the least, and consumers often used the service for many hours each day).

When performance on the advertised attribute is bad enough, even vague claims can be false. The FTC prevailed against a defendant who advertised the opportunity to buy "good condition" cars at "hot prices" as low as $100, where the evidence established that the cars were usually in poor condition and, when they weren't, they sold for market price. F.T.C. v. US Sales Corp., 785 F.Supp. 737 (N.D. Ill. 1992). Likewise, advertising for a cruise ship touting "a very special kind of luxury" with "impeccable taste, in the design and furnishings of the beautifully appointed lounges, dining room and cabins," combined with pictures and other representations that the cabins would be "beautiful" and "luxurious," supported a consumer fraud claim where the plaintiffs' cabin was actually dirty and furnished with broken, damaged and outworn furniture. Vallery v. Bermuda Star Line, Inc., 532 N.Y.S.2d 965 (City Civ. Ct. 1988); *see also* Vigil v. General Nutrition Corp., 2015 WL 2338982, (S.D. Cal. May 13, 2015) (where over-the-counter supplement was allegedly useless, statements such as "formulated with premium ingredients to provide maximum potency," "[t]his premium formula combines the best herbs with guaranteed potencies to support vitality and enhance performance," and "scientifically formulated to provide maximum potency" could falsely represent that the product was capable of producing "some effect."); *In re* Countrywide Financial Corp. Secs. Litig., 588 F. Supp. 2d 1132 (C.D. Cal. 2008) ("[T]he [complaint] adequately alleges that [the defendant's] practices so departed from its public statements that even 'high quality' became materially false or misleading; and that to apply the puffery rule to such allegations would deny that 'high quality' has any meaning."). *But see* Intertape Polymer Corp. v. Inspired Techs., Inc., 725 F. Supp. 2d 1319 (M.D. Fla. 2010) (finding vague superiority claims to be puffery despite internal testing evidence suggesting that the advertiser knew that its product performed worse than that of the challenger).

Context. In the absence of extremely poor quality, what causes a claim to cross the line to verifiability? Context always matters, whether that's the context of the ad or the larger competitive context. For an example of a larger regulatory context, consider *Bruton v. Gerber Products Co.*, 961 F. Supp. 2d 1062 (N.D. Cal. 2013). Bruton challenged Gerber's "As Healthy As Fresh" tagline for its baby food. Gerber defended this as puffery, but the word "healthy" is regulated by the FDA when used on food products. Unlike ordinary puffery cases, "the products at issue here are covered by federal regulations which impose specific labeling requirements and which appear to assume that consumers in fact do rely on health-related claims on labels." Even if they didn't originally do so, consumers might now rely on the fact that "healthy" can only be used on foods that meet certain standards. *See also* Animal Legal Defense Fund v. HVFG LLC, 939 F. Supp. 2d 992 (N.D. Cal. 2013) (advertising slogan promoting foie gras as "the humane choice" was not puffery where plaintiffs alleged foie gras was produced by force-feeding ducks resulting in significant illness and injuries and, "in some contexts, including the treatment of food animals, Congress has found that 'humane' is susceptible of definition . . . .").

Government definition of terms isn't necessary to provide relevant context. When an insurer told its clients that the replacement parts it used in car repairs were of "like kind or quality" as the original parts, and that the parts would restore insured clients' cars to their "pre-loss condition," an Illinois court rejected a puffery defense, upholding most of a $1.18 billion judgment. The court concluded that a reasonable policyholder would have interpreted the representations as factual. Avery v. State Farm Mut. Auto. Ins. Co., 746 N.E.2d 1242 (Ill. Ct. App. 2001) (unpublished portion). Other cases involving "like new" claims had found such statements to be puffery. But the *Avery* plaintiffs established that industry standards existed for replacement parts, that the defendant's parts were inferior by any reasonable measure and that the defendant knew this. Thus, subjective knowledge might do more than make the defendant look bad; it might indicate that the matter at issue is factual enough for reasonable people to consider it true or false.

Other parts of an ad can also give specific meaning to otherwise vague words. Thus, a claim that a product was "economical," which standing alone has been found too general to support a false advertising claim, was false because of its context: The advertiser claimed that its de-icing product was economical because users need only use half as much as a competitor's, but the prices made the advertiser's product four times more expensive per unit of coverage. *See* Performance Indus. Inc v. Koos Inc., 18 U.S.P.Q.2d 1767 (E.D. Pa. 1990). Though "the world's best aspirin" was puffery standing alone, it was false when it appeared "in a context which invites the viewer to conclude that Bayer is therapeutically superior to any other aspirin." Sterling Drug Inc., 102 F.T.C. 395 (1983); *see also* U.S. Bank Nat'l Ass'n v. PHL Variable Ins. Co., 2013 WL 791462 (S.D.N.Y. March 5, 2013) (holding that statements that insurance policies were "flexible" and allowed lower payments, while not absolute or "measurable," described such fundamental characteristics of the policies that they weren't necessarily puffery when taken in context of other claims).

What is the appropriate role of context in evaluating puffery? Should statements like "best" simply be removed from consideration and any more specific claims be evaluated on their own terms? What else—besides specific claims made in the same ad—counts as relevant "context" when determining what is mere puffery? Courts have mentioned consumer understanding and industry norms;: how would you provide evidence of those in court?

Extrinsic Evidence? The FTC generally does not seek empirical evidence of consumer reaction before calling a claim puffery. In private plaintiff cases, the courts are not in agreement on whether puffery is a matter of law or a factual question that can be answered by showing that a claim is in fact material to consumers. Sometimes, courts decide for themselves. *See, e.g.*, Perkiss & Liehe v. Northern Cal. Collection Serv., Inc., 911 F.2d 242 (9th Cir. 1990) (puffery determinations are for court as matter of law); *In re* Century 21–RE/MAX Real Estate Advert. Claims Litig., 882 F. Supp. 915 (C.D. Cal. 1994) (refusing to consider plaintiff's evidence that public could be misled by claim because statement was puffery as matter of law).

But in *Federal Express Corporation v. United States Postal Service*, 40 F. Supp. 2d 943 (W.D. Tenn. 1999), the court reached a different result. FedEx alleged that the USPS violated the Lanham Act by falsely advertising itself as a private commercial entity that offers delivery service "around the world." The USPS argued that calling itself a "company" and claiming delivery around the world was puffery.

On a motion to dismiss, the court ruled that the use of "company" was not an example of "exaggerated advertising, blustering and boasting" or "claims of general superiority." Nor was it so vague and exaggerated that no reasonable person could have relied upon it. The USPS argued that common sense knowledge about the Postal Service and its governmental nature would prevent any reasonable reliance on the implication that a "company" is private. The court rejected this argument:

> [I]t would not be appropriate for this court to rely upon such ambiguous concepts as "common sense" or its own intuitive notions of how an advertising statement should have been interpreted to conclude that Defendant's statement is not actionable because no one could have relied upon it. The relevant barometer is the opinion of the consumer, not that of a court.

Whether "around the world" had a specific enough meaning, in the context of mail delivery, to be falsifiable was also incapable of resolution on a motion to dismiss.

When, if ever, *should* a court seek consumer perception evidence before determining that a claim is or is not puffery? The issue is that puffery may give consumers a favorable image of a product or service—otherwise it is hard to understand why advertisers would bother to puff—but it does not actually give consumers a specific reason to act. Thus, such claims may be effective in influencing purchases without being either provable or falsifiable. And it may be beyond the desirable reach of the law to combat advertising that changes consumers' preferences for no good reason. Thus, a determination that a claim is pure puffery should arguably trump evidence that it actually influences consumers.

On the other hand, an essential justification for excusing puffery is that reasonable consumers are unlikely to rely on it. If a significant number of consumers actually *would* rely on a claim, then that justification has been shown to be inapplicable. This may explain why some courts consider the advertiser's intent in evaluating puffery defenses. *See, e.g.,* People v. Maclean Hunter Pub. Corp., 457 N.E.2d 480 (Ill. Ct. App. 1983) ("It is true that a bare and naked statement as to value is ordinarily deemed the opinion of the party making the representation . . . [but] such statement may be a positive affirmation of a fact, intended as such by the party making it, and reasonably regarded as such by the party to whom it is made. When it is such, it is like any other representation of fact . . . .").

Applying the Standard. Consider the following case. In *Procter & Gamble Co. v. Kimberly-Clark Corp.*, 569 F. Supp. 2d 796 (E.D. Wis. 2008), P&G challenged the advertising of Huggies Natural Fit diapers, whose sides were contoured toward the center. Kimberly-Clark ads suggested that other diapers would fit bricks well, but not babies:

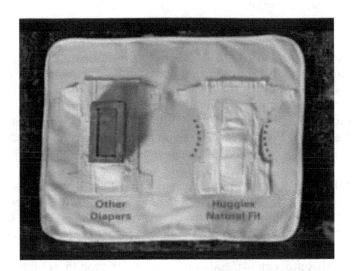

The ads claimed that Huggies were designed for "babies of the human variety" and that a Huggies diaper "fits more naturally." Huggies' own study concluded that the ad was very persuasive.

The court found that "natural fit" and "fits more naturally" were puffery, "so vague and subjective that they are neither provable nor disprovable." Neither of the parties were able to identify "a fixed set of criteria" for what "fit more naturally" might mean. The court asked: "which garment fits a woman more 'naturally'—a tailored English business suit, a Japanese kimono, or an Indian sari?" Indeed, testimony before the court suggested that consumers' standards for measuring fit vary widely because fit is subjective and even depends on the diapers' appearance.

As the court pointed out, despite extensive testing, P&G still doesn't know how consumers decide that a given product "fits naturally." In fact, P&G's designers were once convinced, after using quantifiable measures, that a particular diaper would be an excellent fit, but consumers disagreed. Given that the benchmark concept is incapable of concrete definition, the court continued, "fits more naturally" and "natural fit" could neither be proved nor disproved, and thus they could not be falsified. In fact, even if we could all agree on what it meant for a diaper to "fit more naturally," our individual conclusions on which diaper did so "would be based on purely subjective judgments." Such "opinion puffery" can't be proved.

The court concluded that even if consumer testing provides companies with useful market information, that doesn't make it a legitimate way of assessing truth or falsity for Lanham Act purposes. The court held that, just as it's impossible to prove which pizza is better (as in *Pizza Hut*), it's impossible to demonstrate "conclusively" whether one diaper "fits more naturally." "[A]n assertion whose truth depends solely on consumer opinion is an inactionable one." Thus, taste tests showing that Pizza Hut was preferred by 75% of consumers over Papa John's still wouldn't have disproved the "Better Pizza" claim.

Do you agree that taste tests could not have disproved "Better Ingredients. Better Pizza."?

B. The Advertiser's Special Knowledge and Puffery

The amount of authority possessed by the advertiser can indicate that claims are merely subjective. For example, one court found that disparaging oral statements by salespeople to individual customers were claims that "an ordinary listener would recognize as personal opinion as opposed to representations of hard definable facts, such as product descriptions." Licata & Co. v. Goldberg, 812 F. Supp. 403 (S.D.N.Y. 1993). What if the statement were contained in a published ad? Would consumers be more likely to believe that the statement had been made by a more-authoritative source, vetted and verified?

Not all individual salespersons' statements are subjective puffery. Drug sales representatives are supposed to be well-trained, and courts have held drug manufacturers liable for individual statements when the representatives' training encouraged (or failed to discourage) false or unsubstantiated claims. If individual salespeople are supposed to be experts on their products or services compared to consumers, then their statements are less likely to be taken as opinion. (Consider this statement: "Sales people are like toddlers by pools; you never leave them unattended because trouble often follows. They begin spouting puffery about earning potential of properties, regardless of their sincere promises not to do so. It's inherent in the sales personality." Marianne M. Jennings, *From the Courts*, 38 REAL EST. L.J. 66 (2009). If their statements are puffery, is it a problem? If it's a problem, then are they spouting puffery?)

There are other important limitations to the principle that subjective claims are mere puffery. If the source of the subjective statement presents his or her experience as typical when in fact it is not, then the fact that the statement describes a subjective state will not prevent it from being labeled false advertising. As an application of that principle, taste tests may be subjective as to each individual taster, but—contrary to the Huggies case above—some cases indicate that a superiority or equivalence claim based on taste tests may be falsifiable.

Ivan Preston, whose views are discussed in more detail in the next section, argues that, in the modern economy, consumers are likely to see advertisers as experts with special access to the facts, including facts about competing products. Moreover, if the advertiser is communicating in a mass medium, consumers are likely to believe that its claims are valid across a large group of consumers. As a result, he argues, consumers will give greater deference to their statements—treating them as inherently less subjective and more verifiable—than they would to the statements of a single individual.

Some courts, however, have reasoned to the contrary: Broad advertising is more likely to be puffery. *See, e.g.*, Guidance Endodontics, LLC v. Dentsply Int'l, Inc., 708 F. Supp. 2d 1209 (D. N.M. 2010) ("[T]he larger the audience, the more likely it is that the statement is puffery"; in marketing materials, "a seller is expected to cast his wares in the best possible light to tempt consumers to buy his product rather than any other."). Is this more plausible? When would an individualized pitch be more credible than a mass advertising campaign, and when would it be less so? If a salesperson says, "This mortgage is the best fit for you," should we accept a puffery defense, given that "best mortgage for you" would ordinarily be puffery in a newspaper ad? Consider how the generalized/individualized comparison relates to the difference between fact and opinion discussed above. Should it matter if the salesperson and the prospective customer have one or more social connections beyond the vendor-vendee relationship? For example, if they have occasionally dined together in social settings, or if a person hosts a party at their house to sell to his or her friends?

C.   What If Puffery Works?

The powerful effect of puffery, as well as the law's refusal to regulate it, can be seen in the FTC's response to requests to modify consent orders against advertisers. Firestone had been ordered not to make unsubstantiated safety claims. *See* Firestone Tire & Rubber Co., 81 F.T.C. 398 (1972). It successfully asked the FTC to exclude "generalized safety claims." Thus, Firestone could, without substantiation, make claims such as "quality you can trust." *See* Clarification of Three Provisions of a 1972 Order Concerning Safety Claims for its Tires, 112 F.T.C. 609 (1989) (advisory opinion). A dissent argued that such claims were capable of being substantiated.

Similarly, C&H Sugar was ordered in 1977 not to call its brand "superior" to or otherwise different from other granulated sugars without substantiation. *See* C&H Sugar Co., 119 F.T.C. 39 (1995) (rehearing), *rev'g* 89 F.T.C. 15 (1977). In 1995, it claimed that it was barred from using ads such as "I love C&H the best" or "C&H tastes best," which harmed it because its competition was free to make similar unsubstantiated claims. The FTC granted the modification, because competing ad campaigns were able to "take advantage of C&H's inability to counter claims that either constitute puffery or relate to the source or origin of the product . . . ." The underlying problem was that:

> [t]he homogeneous nature of the product means that there are few truthful, nondeceptive comparisons that can be made among competing products. In order to promote their brands, sugar refiners must rely on . . . subjective endorsement claims . . . or objective product source and origin claims which are precisely the kinds of claims prohibited by the existing order. . . . The order against C&H was intended to protect consumers from misleading claims about the alleged superiority or difference of C&H sugar, not to stifle the respondent's ability to participate in healthy competition on the basis of truthful, nondeceptive advertising. We are persuaded, therefore, that modification to permit puffery is warranted.

The FTC, however, then suggested that "I love C&H the best" or "C&H tastes best" are capable of being substantiated. (In light of the *Pizza Hut* case, do you agree? How would you disprove the statement?) But then it went on to say that claims not relating to "health, safety, nutritional quality, or purity . . . will not be deemed to contain an implied comparison under this order." Thus, taste claims would be allowed.

Ivan Preston argues that this conclusion is both paradoxical—the better taste claim is concededly capable of being substantiated—and wrong. Ivan L. Preston, *Puffery and Other "Loophole" Claims: How The Law's "Don't Ask, Don't Tell" Policy Condones Fraudulent Falsity in Advertising*, 18 J.L. & COM. 49 (1998). C&H is only at a competitive disadvantage if puffery *works*: that is, if consumers are influenced by puffery to think that competitors' products are better than C&H's. But if that is so, what happened to the definition of puffery as vague and unverifiable claims on which reasonable consumers wouldn't rely? Doesn't this decision show that it's a mistake to have a category of puffery distinct from actual consumer reaction? As Preston points out, the president of the American Advertising Federation said that without puffery, advertisers "would, in effect, be denied the ability to compete on anything other than factual grounds. Thousands of products do not compete on factual grounds because they are essentially the same." Is that a justification, or a damning critique, of the puffery doctrine?

Preston argues that current puffery doctrine is a mistaken evolution from nineteenth-century cases involving individual buyers and sellers that held that buyers couldn't sue for fraud based on statements that they could easily have verified or disproved themselves. When buyers were unable to verify the claims, however, the law provided them redress. But as the puffery doctrine developed, it turned into a rule that consumers treated certain claims as meaningless and therefore rejected them at the outset.

In fact, Preston argues, marketing research demonstrates that, with many claims that the law calls puffery, consumers receive messages containing factual, verifiable, and reliable claims, so failure to regulate puffery exposes consumers to a substantial risk of deception. He argues that courts and regulators should ask what messages consumers actually receive rather than presuming that puffery is meaningless.

Preston points to consumer research asking respondents whether ad claims were "completely true," "partly true," or "not true at all." Twenty-two percent said that "State Farm is all you need to know about life insurance" was completely true, and 36% said it was partly true. Even higher percentages found Pan Am's claim to be "the world's most experienced airline" completely or partly true; Texaco's "you can trust your car to the man who wears the star" obtained similar levels of agreement. Preston claims that, if consumers were responding to puffery in the way the law presumes, they would have answered "not true at all." Do you agree? Does it matter that the researchers didn't give consumers the option of responding "neither true nor false"?

In another study cited by Preston, a researcher used different versions of a car ad, one using facts such as "27 miles per gallon" and the other using puffery such as "truly excellent gas mileage." Consumers rated the importance and credibility of these claims essentially the same, though courts would usually call the latter claim puffery. *See* Morris B. Holbrook, *Beyond Attitude Structure: Toward the Informational Determinants of Attitude*, 15 J. MKTG. RES. 545 (1978). More generally, Preston argues, while one can criticize various aspects of these studies, there is no empirical evidence supporting the law's assumption that consumers typically see puffery as meaningless. (What about consumers' general skepticism about ads, discussed in the first section of this chapter? Does that have any bearing on puffery?)

Preston concludes that, since puffs generally imply facts, and since advertisers could benefit even more from adding explicit truthful statements if they could do so, a puff without an accompanying fact claim is likely to be fraudulent. That is, an advertiser who has safety tests (or some other tests) showing its tires to be the best should logically advertise that it has conducted such tests rather than simply claim to be the best. If it makes only the weaker puff, then it is trying to fool people into thinking that some kind of superiority exists. Do you agree? What about the risk of overwhelming consumers with detail?

Consider *Daugherty v. Sony Electronics, Inc.*, 2006 WL 197090 (Tenn. Ct. App. 2006), allowing a Tennessee Consumer Protection Act claim to survive on appeal. The complaint named several Sony ads touting Sony's product quality, including statements that "the company has earned a solid reputation for quality, reliability, innovation and stylish design." As to DVD players specifically, Sony's ads claimed that its DVD players "set[] the standard" and were "superior." The court decided to leave the issue of puffery to the jury: The key issue was whether the buyer reasonably understood that he or she was getting some kind of assurance about specific facts. Echoing Preston's reasoning, the court refused to find as a matter of law that, "notwithstanding the amount of money that Sony spends on advertising its DVD players, Sony never intended for Plaintiff or any consumer actually to rely on so much as even one of these advertisements and, if there was such reliance by a consumer, it was altogether unjustified." Do you agree with the result?

Other Countries' Approaches. By contrast to the U.S. approach, China bans superlative claims, an important class of puffery in the United States. Grace Guo, *Watch Out: Superlative Words Still Targeted Frequently by Administrative Authorities*, LEXOLOGY, Mar. 14, 2017 (describing false advertising cases deemed typical by the Shanghai Administration for Industry and Commerce, including claims for "the best option for real estate investment, "Ranked No. 1 in Australia," "the highest caliber," and "the first and foremost CAD/CAM brand in the world," all found to violate the law). PRC *Advertising Law* Article 9 includes a prohibition on using words such as "highest -grade," "the newest science," "the most advanced process," "the most recent technology," or "best." The law provides for fines from RMB 200,000 (around $28,000 in 2020) to RMB 1,000,000 (around $142,000 in 2020) for violations. Do you foresee any trouble enforcing this law fairly?

While Australia recognizes puffery as a defense, it may be more restrictive in its definition. When an Expedia-owned company promised that Australian consumers could "book with confidence," this overrode disclaimers in the fine print and allowed one disgruntled consumer to recover when his Hawaiian rental lacked the promised beach view and was "dilapidated." Jordan Hayne, *Wotif Forced to Refund Holidaymaker Given 'Basement' After Tribunal Finds Misleading Conduct*, ABC NEWS, Dec. 17, 2018.

D.   Are Incomprehensible Claims Puffery?

In *Date v. Sony Electronics Inc.*, 2009 WL 435289 (E.D. Mich. 2009), Sony advertised its television as offering "Full HDTV," the "World's Greatest High Definition Television," "new display technology . . . to meet and exceed the demands of a High Definition Image at its full 1080 line resolution," and the ability to display digitally transmitted high-definition signals without interlacing. Sony also stated in the specifications sheet that the televisions' native video resolution was "1080p" (the best available technology). The TVs, however, could not display a 1080p signal. Instead, at best they could display an upconverted 1080i (interlaced) signal from a 1080p device. The upconversion process resulted in undesirable visual artifacts that make the viewing experience worse.

Sony argued that its claims were puffery, based on a prior similar case. In *Johnson v. Mitsubishi Digital Electronics America, Inc.*, 578 F. Supp. 2d 1229 (C.D. Cal. 2008), the court concluded that, although Mitsubishi designated its television set as a 1080p television set, the phrase 1080p "does not convey a specific claim that is recognizable to the targeted customer." The *Johnson* court thought 1080p only had meaning for engineering professionals and that all that the plaintiff wanted was a top-of-the-line set. Because he didn't understand what 1080p meant, the claim was puffery to him.

The *Date* court found that at least some plaintiffs had an idea of what 1080p meant and pointed out that Sony put the term on its specification sheet addressed to consumers, suggesting that it wasn't puffery. Which court's reasoning makes more sense? Does a consumer have to be able to define the term in order for us to conclude that she received a specific message? That is, if a consumer receives a message that she thinks is factual, credible and material, is anything more needed?

That information is of marginal value to the buying public does not make it false. In *OPA (Overseas Publishing Association) Amsterdam BV v. American Inst. of Physics*, 973 F. Supp. 414 (S.D.N.Y. 1997), a federal district court dismissed claims that a publisher of physics journals engaged in false advertising when it touted its journals as more "cost-effective" than others, even though cost-effectiveness might be a bad measure for academic journals. Similarly, another court found that an idiosyncratic "formula" concocted by a vacuum cleaner manufacturer to measure the cleaning power of its vacuum cleaners was not very useful, but not false in that all the components of the rating were accurate. Royal Appliance Mfg. Co. v. Hoover Co., 845 F. Supp. 469 (N.D. Ohio 1994).

E. Humor and Parody

An ad may be humorous and yet still make believable claims, in which case those claims will be tested using the same standards as those applied to any other claims. However, humor can make clear to reasonable consumers that an exaggerated claim is not meant to be believed. As a result, humor can take a claim or representation out of the realm of falsifiable fact—but it might not do so.

S.C. JOHNSON & SON, INC. V. CLOROX CO., 241 F.3D 232 (2D CIR. 2001)

This case involves a Lanham Act challenge to the truthfulness of a television commercial and print advertisement depicting the plight of an animated goldfish in a Ziploc Slide-Loc bag that is being held upside down and is leaking water. Plaintiff-appellee S.C. Johnson & Son manufactures the Ziploc bags targeted by the advertisements. In an Order dated April 6, 2000, the United States District Court for the Southern District of New York (Griesa, J.) permanently enjoined the defendant-appellant, The Clorox Company, manufacturer of Ziploc's rival Glad-Lock resealable storage bags, from using these advertisements. We conclude that the district court did not abuse its discretion in entering this injunction and accordingly affirm.

BACKGROUND

In August 1999, Clorox introduced a 15-second and a 30-second television commercial ("Goldfish I"), each depicting an S.C. Johnson Ziploc Slide-Loc resealable storage bag side-by-side with a Clorox Glad-Lock bag. The bags are identified in the commercials by brand name. Both commercials show an animated, talking goldfish in water inside each of the bags. In the commercials, the bags are turned upside-down, and the Slide-Loc bag leaks rapidly while the Glad-Lock bag does not leak at all. In both the 15- and 30-second Goldfish I commercials, the Slide-Loc goldfish says, in clear distress, "My Ziploc Slider is dripping. Wait a minute!," while the Slide Loc bag is shown leaking at a rate of approximately one drop per one to two seconds. In the 30-second Goldfish I commercial only, the Slide-Loc bag is shown leaking while the Slide-Loc goldfish says, "Excuse me, a little help here," and then, "Oh, dripping, dripping." At the end of both commercials, the Slide Loc goldfish exclaims, "Can I borrow a cup of water!!!"

On November 4, 1999, S.C. Johnson brought an action against Clorox under Section 43(a) of the Lanham Act, 15 U.S.C. § 1125(a), for false advertising in the Goldfish I commercials. . . .

Dr. Phillip DeLassus, an outside expert retained by S.C. Johnson, conducted "torture testing," in which Slide-Loc bags were filled with water, rotated for 10 seconds, and held upside-down for an additional 20 seconds. He testified about the results of the tests he performed, emphasizing that 37 percent of all Slide-Loc bags tested did not leak at all. Of the remaining 63 percent that did leak, only a small percentage leaked at the rate depicted in the Goldfish I television commercials. The vast majority leaked at a rate between two and twenty times slower than that depicted in the Goldfish I commercials.

On January 7, 2000, the district court entered findings of fact and conclusions of law on the record in support of an Order permanently enjoining Clorox from disseminating the Goldfish I television commercials. . . .

The court found that "the commercial impermissibly exaggerates the facts in respect to the flow of water or the leaking of water out of a Slide-Loc bag." The court further found that:

> [t]he commercial shows drops of water coming out of the bag at what appears to be a rapid rate. In fact, the rate is about one fairly large drop per second. Moreover, there is a depiction of the water level in the bag undergoing a substantial and rapid decline. Finally, there is an image of bubbles going through the water.

The district court found that "the overall depiction in the commercial itself is of a rapid and substantial leakage and flow of water out of the Slide-Loc bag." The court noted that "[t]his is rendered even more graphic by the fact that there is a goldfish depicted in the bag which is shown to be in jeopardy because the water is running out at such a rate."

The district court found "that when these bags are subjected to the same kind of quality control test as used by Clorox for the Glad bags, there is some leakage in about two-thirds of the cases." However, the court found "that the great majority of those leaks are very small and at a very slow rate." The court found that "[o]nly in about 10 percent of these bags is there leakage at the rate shown in the commercial, that is, one drop per second." The district court further found that "[t]he problem with the commercial is that there is no depiction in the visual images to indicate anything else than the fact that the type of fairly rapid and substantial leakage shown in the commercial is simply characteristic of that kind of bag." . . .

In February 2000, Clorox released a modified version of the Goldfish I television commercials as well as a related print advertisement ("Goldfish II"). In the 15 second Goldfish II television commercial, a Ziploc Slide-Loc bag and Glad-Lock bag are again shown side-by-side, filled with water and containing an animated, talking goldfish. The bags are then rotated, and a drop is shown forming and dropping in about a second from the Slide-Loc bag. During the approximately additional two seconds that it is shown, the Slide-Loc goldfish says, "My Ziploc slider is dripping. Wait a minute." The two bags are then off-screen for approximately eight seconds before the Slide-Loc bag is again shown, with a drop forming and falling in approximately one second. During this latter depiction of the Slide-Loc bag, the Slide-Loc goldfish says, "Hey, I'm gonna need a little help here." Both bags are identified by brand name, and the Glad-Lock bag does not leak at all. The second-to-last frame shows three puddles on an orange background that includes the phrase "Don't Get Mad."

In the print advertisement, a large drop is shown forming and about to fall from an upside-down Slide-Loc bag in which a goldfish is partially out of the water. Bubbles are shown rising from the point of the leak in the Slide-Loc bag. Next to the Slide-Loc bag is a Glad-Lock bag that is not leaking and contains a goldfish that is completely submerged. Under the Slide-Loc bag appears: "Yikes! My Ziploc® Slide-Loc™ is dripping!" Under the Glad-Lock bag is printed: "My Glad is tight, tight, tight." On a third panel, three puddles and the words "Don't Get Mad" are depicted on a red background. In a fourth panel, the advertisement recites: "Only Glad has the Double-Lock™ green seal. That's why you'll be glad you got Glad. Especially if you're a goldfish."

After these advertisements appeared, S.C. Johnson moved to enlarge the January 7 injunction to enjoin the airing and distribution of the Goldfish II advertisements. On April 6, 2000, after hearing oral argument, the district court entered another order on the record, setting forth further findings of fact and conclusions of law in support of an Order permanently enjoining the distribution of the Goldfish II television commercial and print advertisement. . . .

The court then addressed the Goldfish II print advertisement, which, it found "is, if anything, worse," because "[i]t has a single image of a Slide-Loc bag with a large drop about to fall away and a goldfish in danger of suffocating because the water is as portrayed disappearing from the bag." The district court concluded that the Goldfish II print advertisement "is literally false." The court also found that the inability of a Ziploc Slide-Loc bag to prevent leakage is portrayed as an inherent quality or characteristic of that product. Accordingly, the court found that the Goldfish II television commercial and print advertisement "portray[ ] the leakage as simply an ever-present characteristic of the Slide-Loc bags."

. . . Clorox now appeals from this April 6, 2000 Order permanently enjoining the use of the Goldfish II television commercial and print advertisement.

DISCUSSION

. . . "[T]he district judge's determination of the meaning of the advertisement [is] a finding of fact that 'shall not be set aside unless clearly erroneous.' "

. . . In considering a false advertising claim, "[f]undamental to any task of interpretation is the principle that text must yield to context."

> Thus, we have emphasized that in reviewing FTC actions prohibiting unfair advertising practices under the Federal Trade Commission Act a court must "consider the advertisement in its entirety and not . . . engage in disputatious dissection. The entire mosaic should be viewed rather than each tile separately." . . .

I. The district court's findings of fact are not clearly erroneous.

Clorox argues that the district court committed clear error in finding that its Goldfish II television commercial and print advertisement contain literal falsehoods. We find no clear error in the district court's findings of fact in support of its conclusion that the Goldfish II television commercial and print advertisement are literally false as a factual matter. We note that the court made its finding of literal falsity after a seven-day bench trial. The evidence presented at trial clearly indicates that, as the court found, only slightly more than one out of ten Slide-Loc bags tested dripped at a rate of one drop per second or faster, while more than one-third of the Slide-Loc bags tested leaked at a rate of less than one drop per five seconds. Over half of the Slide-Loc bags tested either did not leak at all or leaked at a rate no faster than one drop per 20 seconds. Moreover, less than two-thirds, or 63 percent, of Slide-Loc bags tested showed any leakage at all when subjected to the testing on which Clorox based its Goldfish I and II advertisements.

The only Slide-Loc bag depicted in each of the two Goldfish II advertisements, on the other hand, is shown leaking and, when shown, is always leaking. Moreover, each time the Slide-Loc bag is on-screen, the Goldfish II television commercial shows a drop forming immediately and then falling from the Slide-Loc bag, all over a period of approximately two seconds. Accordingly, the commercial falsely depicts the risk of leakage for the vast majority of Slide-Loc bags tested.

Clorox argues that, because approximately eight seconds pass between the images of the drops forming and falling in the Goldfish II television commercial, the commercial depicts an accurate rate of leakage. However, the commercial does not continuously show the condition of the Slide-Loc bag because the Slide-Loc bag is off-screen for eight seconds. Likewise, the print ad does not depict any rate of leakage at all, other than to indicate that the Slide-Loc bag is "dripping." . . .

II. The district court committed no error of law.

. . . [T]he Goldfish II advertisement depicts a literal falsity . . . : that Slide-Loc bags always leak when filled with water and held upside down. . . .
. . . [I]f Clorox wants to portray water leakage from Slide-Loc bags, it must portray the rate of leakage accurately and indicate that only a certain percentage of bags leak, even when subjected to an extreme water "torture" test.

NOTES AND QUESTIONS

Why doesn't the court directly address the humor of the ads? Is the humor irrelevant to the falsity at issue, or did the court ignore an important aspect of the case? Could you make an argument that the offending image should be deemed puffery?

Why doesn't it matter that, as far as the record shows, Clorox's bags outperform Johnson's when it comes to leakage? How easy will it be to create a good ad that is more precise about the extent of Clorox's comparative advantage?

What happens if reasonable consumers would believe that the claim is exaggerated, but also believe that the claim is true to some degree, and they mistake the degree? Should this be actionable false advertising? Consider the famous Wendy's "Where's the Beef?" commercial. If a Wendy's burger is 5% bigger than a McDonald's burger, but a substantial number of consumers take away the message that the Wendy's burger is at least 25% bigger, then isn't the ad both funny and deceptive?

In *SmithKline Beecham Consumer Healthcare, L.P. v. Johnson & Johnson-Merck Consumer Pharmaceuticals Co.*, 19 Fed. Appx. 17 (2d Cir. 2001), SmithKline sued J&J for an ad comparing J&J's Pepcid Complete to Tums as heartburn treatments. Pepcid Complete, an acid blocker, decreases the production of acid in the stomach and can last for nine hours, while Tums, an antacid, neutralizes acid in the stomach and leaves the stomach in an hour or two. Many people receive complete relief from this because their acid production is time-limited, but some sufferers need to re-dose, and for them Pepcid Complete can provide superior relief.

The Pepcid Complete ad depicted:

> a rumpled, slobby man vacuuming out his car. His car dashboard is littered with
> Tums tablets, food and other debris. The man picks up an old slice of pizza from
> among the trash and begins to eat it. The announcer asks, "Ever notice how many
> Tums you have around because your heartburn keeps coming back?" There is a pause
> in the vacuuming as the man looks quizzically down the vacuum hose, at which point
> the vacuum explodes, coating the man and the car with white powder. The
> Commercial then cuts to a shot of the Pepcid complete box, with the words "fast" and
> "seven times longer" superimposed on top. The announcer states, "There's a neater
> idea. New Pepcid Complete. It works as fast as Tums, but lasts seven times longer all
> in a chewable tablet." The Commercial returns to the slobby man, shown sitting in
> the front seat of his car, covered in white powder and attempting to vacuum himself.
> It closes with the announcer saying, "New Pepcid Complete. Just one and heartburn's
> done."

SmithKline argued that only a small percentage of Tums users actually needed to re-dose,
and argued that the *S.C. Johnson* case supported its claim of literal falsity through
exaggeration. The court of appeals disagreed, because the Leaky Goldfish ad:

> targeted all consumers interested in the product by showcasing a flaw found only in a
> small percentage of the product. Here, the Commercial targets a small segment of
> consumers who may suffer continuing heartburn symptoms as a result of a
> characteristic common to all antacids: they work for less time than acid blockers do.
> There is no showcasing of a product flaw, as both parties agree the effect of antacids
> lasts for only an hour or two. That all consumers may not need the extended period of
> protection offered by acid blockers does not render the Commercial literally false.

Is the court's distinction between the facts of this case and those of *S.C. Johnson* sensible?
Are consumers more likely to know whether they fall into the class that needs to re-dose
than they are to know whether Slide-Loc bags are risky for them? Could a reasonable
consumer who was presently satisfied with Tums have been affected by the ad?

In another case, the NAD rejected the idea that consumer familiarity with reality could save
the ad. The advertiser touted its wood-fired grills with an ad stating: "[t]he problem with
propane is that when you cook with gas, your food tastes like gas"; the phrase "tastes like
gas" was spoken so quickly that it sounded like the actors were saying that gas-grilled food
"tastes like ass." NAD rejected Traeger's argument that, because almost every adult has
eaten food from a propane-fueled grill, they would understand that the claim was untrue and
therefore funny. Rather, NAD stated, "no amount of humor . . . can rectify an expressly false
claim." Traeger Pellet Grills LLC Traeger Grills, Report #6327, NAD/CARU Case Reports
(December 2019).

Other Exaggeration Cases. The law sometimes presumes that consumers are unlikely to
accept vague or hyperbolic claims at face value. *See* Hansen Beverage Co. v. Vital Pharm.,
Inc., 2010 WL 1734960 (S.D. Cal. 2010) (the claim that an energy beverage "will leave you
'amped' to the max in minutes, ready to tear apart the weights and wear out the treadmill

like a tiger released from its cage!" was puffery); Blue Cross v. Corcoran, 558 N.Y.S.2d 404 (App. Div. 1990) ("Remember, if you don't have Blue Cross, you're not covered" so obviously false that it was neither intended nor likely to be taken literally by people of average education and intelligence). Where an ad for a dry shaver portrayed wet shavers as snakes biting, bees stinging, and flamethrowers burning, a court concluded that these derogatory exaggerations were based on colloquialisms used to describe the actual pain of wet shaving, and that it was not deceptive to exaggerate their underlying meaning "beyond the point of believability, in order to ensure that that underlying message is conveyed." *See* Gillette Co. v. Norelco Consumer Prods. Co., 946 F. Supp. 115 (D. Mass. 1996). What makes the claims in *Clorox* any different from the exaggerated representations of the pain of wet shaving?

Are Images Special? In *Time Warner Cable, Inc. v. DirecTV, Inc.*, 497 F.3d 144 (2d Cir. 2007), Time Warner offered both analog and digital signals, but its competitor DirecTV had only digital service. Both offered high-definition (HD) service on a limited number of channels. The parties agreed that the HD services were equivalent in picture quality. For non-HD channels, digital is generally better than analog because it resists interference. But Time Warner's analog service met FCC requirements for a signal that provides "enjoyable viewing with barely perceptible impairments."

DirecTV began an ad campaign to educate consumers that, even with an HD TV set, one must also receive HD programming from the TV service provider in order to enjoy an HD picture. Among other things, it ran Internet ads showing unwatchable TV images contrasted to sharp and clear images, labeled "Other TV" and "DirecTV," and inviting consumers to "Find out why DirecTV's picture beats Cable."

The district court agreed with Time Warner that DirecTV's own rationale for running the ads—that consumers were highly confused about HD technology and needed to be educated that both digital equipment and digital signals were required to experience HD quality—was reason to think that consumers might rely on the ads.

The court of appeals observed that prior puffery cases didn't offer good principles for evaluating images. "Unlike words, images cannot be vague or broad." While one standard definition of puffery—general claims of superiority that are so vague as to be meaningless—fits images badly, the other—"an exaggerated, blustering, and boasting statement upon which no reasonable buyer would be justified in relying," could be applied.

The court of appeals found that the district court clearly erred in accepting Time Warner's argument about consumer uncertainty. The "other TV" images in the Internet ads were extremely bad—"unwatchably blurry, distorted, and pixelated, and . . . nothing like the images a customer would ordinarily see using Time Warner Cable's cable service," according to Time Warner's senior network engineer. Indeed, the pixelation was "not the type of disruption[] that could naturally happen to an analog or non-HD digital cable picture." Thus, the ads were not even remotely realistic, and the court found it difficult to imagine that any consumer, no matter how unsophisticated, could be fooled into thinking cable's picture quality would be that bad. The court accepted DirecTV's argument that even a person who didn't know anything about cable would know that Time Warner couldn't supply an unwatchable signal and still survive in the market. The comparison of DirecTV picture quality to basic cable picture quality was so "obviously hyperbolic" that no reasonable buyer would be justified in relying on it.

Do you agree that it was clearly erroneous to accept Time Warner's argument about the transitioning market? A new HD customer might know that "ordinarily" her cable wouldn't be anything near that bad. But would she have been confident about what cable would look like when she attached an analog cable feed to her new HDTV?

Should courts treat negative puffery differently than positive puffery, or are the justifications for discounting both equally persuasive?

With the *Time Warner* case in mind, consider the following images from McDonald's and Burger King ads paired with pictures of actual burgers. Do you think the ads are puffery because everyone knows fast food burgers don't look like that? Or actionable because it is possible for burgers to look like that, but these companies' burgers don't? (Credit Dario D.) Similar to these burger ads, which of the tricks used in this video, illustrating common tricks used by advertisers for photography and video ads, might be permitted by law?

[Burger King Whopper]

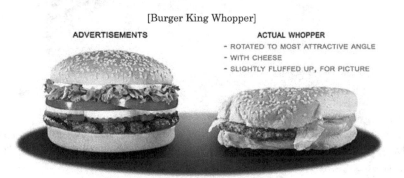

[McDonald's Angus Deluxe Third Pounder]

One court of appeals actually used burger ads as an analogy to explain why other images were also puffery. The plaintiff, Wysong, had challenged pet food packages with images such as the following, alleging that they misleadingly indicated that the pet food was made with premium cuts of meat and not meat by-products:

Wysong Corp. v. APN, Inc. 889 F.3d 267 (6th Cir. 2018). The court of appeals reasoned that, just as reasonable consumers at a fast-food drive-through don't expect that their hamburgers will look just like the one pictured on the menu, without more facts, "it is not plausible that reasonable consumers believe most of the (cheap) dog food they encounter in the pet-food aisle is in fact made of the same sumptuous (and more costly) ingredients they find a few aisles over in the people-food sections." Should it matter that some pet foods, such as the plaintiff's, do contain premium cuts of meat?

Finally, consider that very subtle tweaks in ads may have profound effects. Could they still be puffery? When researchers tested the images below, 60% of consumers thought that a paid spokesperson was a medical expert when she was shown with a background image of blue products versus 23% when she was shown with a white background. Is the background misleading? *See* Chris Jay Hoofnagle & Eduard Meleshinsky, *Native Advertising and Endorsement: Schema, Source-Based Misleadingness, and Omission of Material Facts*, TECH. SCI., Dec. 15, 2015.

5.   Falsity

We arrive now at the core of advertising regulation: falsity. A basic tenet of modern advertising law is that falsity and misleadingness are actionable, even if the advertiser did not intend to deceive. In that sense, there is strict liability for false advertising. Bad intent may be relevant to trigger various presumptions or increase damages, but it is not required. Here, American law is consistent with that of most other countries, including the European Union. *See* CHS Tour Serv. GmbH v. Team4 Travel GmbH, Case C-435/11 (E.C.J. 2013) (holding that the advertiser's exercise of due diligence didn't protect against a determination that a claim was false or misleading).

But how do we know what claims are false? Context—both general social knowledge and other information conveyed by the ad—is often vital, as is the substantiation possessed by the advertiser for its claims. As we will discuss, certain types of factual claims pose particular challenges for the law. For example, we will consider whether claims based on the placebo effect—real, but created solely by the claim itself—can be true.

A.   Advertising Claims in the Context of the Ad

"Fundamental to any task of interpretation is the principle that text must yield to context, and that a court must view the 'entire mosaic' of the advertisement rather than 'each tile separately.'" Avis Rent-A-Car Sys., Inc. v. Hertz Corp., 782 F.2d 381 (2d Cir. 1986). The context of the ad may modify the explicit message of the ad as a whole (as is the case with a sufficiently prominent and effective disclaimer, see Chapter 6), or it may change the implicit message.

In the context of an ad for a headache remedy, then, the claim that "nothing is better than Advil" does not mean that (1) Advil is better than everything else in the world, or (2) it is better to use nothing than to use Advil. Rather, it means that nothing beats Advil at treating headaches.* The fact that the ad is about headaches provides interpretive guidance, as in contract law. Likewise, when Avis challenged the statement that "Hertz has more new cars than Avis has cars," Avis initially won an injunction when it was able to show that it *owned* as many cars as Hertz did, if cars in its corporate fleet and cars it had put up for sale were counted. But on appeal, the Second Circuit reversed: In context, the ad was a claim about the number of new cars *available for rental*. The ad was targeted to potential renters, rather than car buyers or financial analysts; it showed a rental lot; and the text three times referred to rentals. *Avis, supra.*

Avis is an example of truth in context. But context can also show falsity. When an international pharmacy advertised "FDA guidelines let you import drugs for your personal

---

* One of the casebook's authors suggested rewording this statement as "Advil is the best way to treat headaches." Note the success of the advertiser's implication even with this highly ad-savvy and careful lawyer: the *formal* logical meaning of "nothing beats Advil" is not that Advil is the best, but that it has no superior. Other methods of treatment could be equal, and the explicit claim would still be true. However, the advertiser wants the audience to believe that Advil is the *best*—and seems to have succeeded! If other treatments are in fact equal, then the explicit claim is true but that implicit message is false. Recall this example when we consider implication.

use. . . . If a drug you use is on our list, order today," the first statement was true standing alone but false combined with the second statement because the FDA did not in fact allow importation of certain drugs on the pharmacy's list. Syntex (U.S.A.), Inc. v. Interpharm, Inc., 1993 WL 643372 (N.D. Ga. 1993).

Proximity of claims to each other can often affect whether the claims are false. For example, ads for Anacin appeared to claim that it had a unique pain-killing formula that was proven superior to all other over-the-counter analgesics. If "read with sedulous attention," however, the challenged advertising actually claimed only that Anacin was (1) **as** effective as the leading prescription analgesic and (2) had more pain reliever than other over-the-counter analgesics. Am. Home Prod. Corp. v. FTC, 695 F.2d 681 (3d Cir. 1982). The court of appeals declined to parse the claims with lawyerly precision. Instead, it noted that the ad was "designed to resemble a clipping from a medical journal" that gave the impression of clinical accuracy, and that, by claiming equivalence to prescription medicine, the ad appeared to claim superiority to other over-the-counter medicines.

A magistrate judge reached a similar conclusion with the juxtaposition of two claims on the following package:

The "#1 Most Powerful Steam*" claim in the upper right was qualified by additional information about the models to which the advertiser was comparing its product, while "More Powerful Steam vs. Rowenta*† at half the price" in the lower right was qualified by *different* additional information comparing different Rowenta models. This juxtaposition was literally false. Moreover, the court used the definition of "power" set forth in the packaging's footnote, because "[w]hen a product's packaging includes an advertising claim and unambiguously defines a claim term, the packaging's definition of the claim term applies to the claim's explicit message." Grpe. SEB USA, Inc. v. Euro-Pro Operating LLC, 774 F.3d 192 (3d Cir. 2014). As you will see in Chapter 6, fine print can't redefine a term that is misleading on its own, but the problem here was different: The defendant made a claim based on a particular kind of evidence, and then when its evidence was proven false, said that it didn't mean to rely on that kind of evidence.

B.   Literally False Claims, Also Known as Explicitly False Claims

Explicitly or literally false statements violate the Lanham Act without further proof of consumer deception: Courts presume that consumers receive the false message. In many circuits, showing that a claim is literally false also entitles a plaintiff to various other presumptions in its favor. But the biggest advantage for a Lanham Act plaintiff in arguing literal falsity is the avoidance of an expensive, and no doubt hotly contested, consumer survey showing what consumers actually perceive the message of the ad to be. For this reason, Lanham Act cases focus intensely on the difference between literally false and implicitly false (misleading) claims. Chapter 7 will explore this distinction further. For other types of cases, the distinction is less vital; the FTC, state attorneys general and the NAD all determine misleadingness without consumer reaction evidence, and consumer class actions have also generally not focused on the distinction. Still, the more expressly a false claim is made, the less likely a court is to be sympathetic to the advertiser, so even in non–Lanham Act cases the distinction is worth keeping in mind.

Express claims are stated literally in an ad. They may be verbal or visual. An example of a visually deceptive ad featured images of two identical gas pumps or airline tickets with varying prices accompanied by the slogan "Which one would you choose?" This was literally false because it made a claim that, like the gas and the tickets, the advertised drug was completely equivalent to the competitor. Rhone-Poulenc Rorer Pharms., Inc. v. Marion Merrell Dow, Inc., 93 F.3d 511 (8th Cir. 1996). In another case, an ad showing an orange being squeezed directly into a carton was literally false because the juice was actually made from pasteurized, and occasionally frozen, oranges. Coca Cola Co. v. Tropicana Prods., Inc., 690 F.2d 312 (2d Cir. 1982). How good do you think courts are at translating images into express word claims? Do you agree that showing two tickets is a claim of complete equivalence, or that consumers would perceive the juice ad as a representation that the oranges didn't undergo any processing?

Literally false claims come in many flavors; scientific testing (or its absence) isn't always required to establish falsity. *See, e.g.*, JR Tobacco of America, Inc. v. Davidoff of Geneva (CT), Inc., 957 F.Supp. 426 (S.D.N.Y. 1997) (claims to offer the "same," "identical," and "duplicate" cigars as more-expensive makers, where the defendant made no attempt to duplicate the origin or regional conditions of the tobacco used); Guggenheimer v. Ginzburg, 372 N.E.2d 17 (N.Y. 1977) (claim that a dictionary was "The Authentic Webster's").

Suppose the defendant advertises its dog kibble as "personalized" with "unique blends" based on "expert advice," but in fact just mixes different kibbles (using one of three protein sources, and with or without soy or grains) without any scientific justification for which type of dog gets which mix. Is this false? Is it puffery?

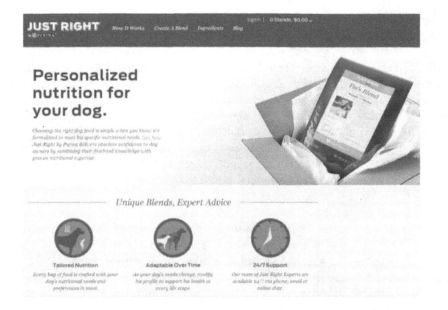

See Blue Buffalo Co. v. Nestle Purina PetCare Co., 2015 WL 3645262 (E.D. Mo. 2015) (dog owners were required to identify their pet's breed, age, weight, level of activity, coat quality and stool consistency to get a recommended mix).

Individual Words. In *Kraft General Foods, Inc. v. Del Monte Corp.*, 28 U.S.P.Q.2d 1457 (S.D.N.Y. 1993), the court found the use of the word "gelatin" literally false to describe snacks made from carageenan, a substance derived from seaweed, reserving use of the term to traditional animal-based "gelatin." Another court found the name BreathAsure literally false for a capsule that did nothing to produce or sustain fresh breath. Warner-Lambert Co. v. BreathAsure, Inc., 204 F.3d 87 (3d Cir. 2000).

Exaggerations. Some exaggerations have been treated as expressly false, perhaps because the context makes exaggeration seem real. This occurred in the *S.C. Johnson* "leaky goldfish" case, excerpted above, where the court interpreted the defendant's ads to claim that the competitor's bags would "always leak," rather than leak 63% of the time. Similarly, the First Circuit found that a claim that "whiter is not possible" than the results achieved with "Ace con Blanqueador" detergent might be literally false if, as the plaintiff alleged, tests proved that chlorine bleach produced better results. Clorox Co. Puerto Rico v. Proctor & Gamble Commercial Co., 228 F.3d 24 (1st Cir. 2000). But exaggeration may also be puffery, or perhaps at most implicit falsehood. The concreteness of the claims, and the likelihood that reasonable consumers would perceive the exaggeration to be truthful, help distinguish between an unacceptable exaggeration and one that may survive scrutiny.

Overgeneralizations. An advertisement claiming that one manufacturer's tractors had "approximately three times as many failures" as the advertiser's was literally false because the language was "overinclusive, drawing no distinction between mowing and garden tractors, and offering no specificity as to the kinds of tractors that [defendant's] engineers tested." Garden Way Inc. v. The Home Depot Inc., 94 F. Supp. 2d 276 (N.D.N.Y. 2000). The advertiser tested only three units of a single model. Vastly overclaiming the scope of its test constituted falsity.

Slight qualifications, however, unrelated to the core advertising claim, are unlikely to make an advertisement literally false. For example, a computer manufacturer alleged that a competing advertiser's claims to be "100% compatible" and "fully compatible" with the manufacturer's products were false, because the advertiser's products would give pre-failure warnings at different times than the manufacturer's products and were slightly different physically. The court determined that "compatibility" meant that the products would work or function with the manufacturer's products, and dismissed the manufacturer's claims because they did not refute the core advertising promise. *See* Compaq Computer Corp. v. Procom Tech., Inc., 908 F. Supp. 1409 (S.D. Tex. 1995).

Situations of this sort may also be handled under the heading of puffery or materiality (whether it would make a difference to consumers, addressed later in this chapter). If a court finds a claim to be puffery, it will not accept evidence of consumer confusion. If the court instead thinks that the qualification means that the claim is not literally false but still potentially misleading, then extrinsic evidence of confusion becomes relevant and even required in a Lanham Act case. One court found that a claim that a miter saw offered "4,000 RPM" was not false because, although a test found the actual speed to be 3,650 RPM, this was "an acceptable variance speed." Black & Decker (U.S.) Inc. v. Pro-Tech Power Inc., 26 F. Supp. 2d 834, 863 (E.D. Va. 1998). How should the fact finder determine what sort of variance is "acceptable?"

For an example that may hit closer to home, consider the results of empirical testing finding that, in fact, Double Stuf Oreos only contain roughly 1.9 times the "stuf" of regular Oreos. Dan Anderson, *Oreo Verification*, Aug. 20, 2013. Is "Double Stuf" a literally false claim? Starbucks has been sued for false advertising based on its Doubleshot prepared drinks by plaintiffs alleging that the caffeine content of a two-shot Starbucks Doppio (150mg) exceeds that of four varieties of Doubleshot drinks. Naimi v. Starbucks Corp., No. 17-cv-06484 (C.D. Cal. filed Sept. 1, 2017).

Unavoidable Falsity. Strict liability means that unavoidable falsity is still falsity. In *Playtex Prods., LLC v. Munchkin, Inc.*, 2016 WL 1276450 (S.D.N.Y. Mar. 29, 2016), Munchkin made bags that it advertised as suitable for use with Playtex's diaper pail, the Diaper Genie. When it redesigned the Diaper Genie, Playtex informed Munchkin that its refills wouldn't fit the redesigned products. The redesigned products launched on March 1, 2014. On March 17, 2014, Munchkin put an orange sticker on its refills that said that the refills were guaranteed to fit all Diaper Genie pails bought before March 1, 2014.

The court found that, between March 1 and March 17, 2014, Munchkin's fit claims were literally false because they failed to disclose that the refills wouldn't fit the newly released redesigned Diaper Genies. The fit claims were also material and caused harm to Playtex, so Playtex won summary judgment as to Munchkin's liability for this period. What, if anything, could Munchkin have done to avoid this result on liability? Pulled the product entirely? Pre-stickered with an open-ended date, which might be more confusing? Limited its guarantee to pails sold before 2014, even though it could indeed guarantee fit for pails sold in the first three months of 2014?

C.   Constraining the Boundaries of Literal Falsity?

Sometimes courts just don't think one side deserves to win. In *Schering-Plough Healthcare Products, Inc. v. Schwarz Pharma, Inc.*, 586 F.3d 500 (7th Cir. 2009), plaintiff Schering had FDA approval to sell a laxative over the counter (OTC). Defendant Schwarz sold a generic version of the same laxative, but only had approval to sell it as a prescription drug. This created a problem under FDA rules, which require generics to have the exact same labels as the original drug. The label on Schwarz's version of the laxative differed from Schering's label in two ways: It contained the prescription-only warning, and it omitted a warning to "use [for] no more than 7 days" that the FDA had required as part of the Schering's OTC approval.

Under FDA rules, it seemed that Schwarz was both required to use an identical label and barred from doing so (since its product was still prescription-only and the additional warning was not approved for its label). The FDA was looking into the matter, but Schering decided to litigate under the Lanham Act, perhaps because the FDA was likely to take a long time to act. Schering argued that Schwarz's labels were false because the drug was not "prescription only" and because patients wouldn't realize that, if their conditions changed and they didn't need to use the drug for more than seven days, they could buy the OTC version.

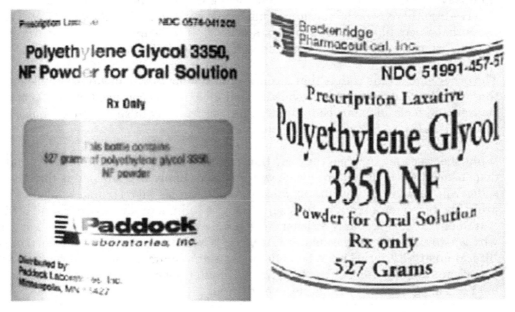

[defendants' labels]

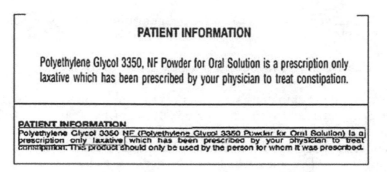

PATIENT INFORMATION

Polyethylene Glycol 3350, NF Powder for Oral Solution is a prescription only laxative which has been prescribed by your physician to treat constipation.

PATIENT INFORMATION
Polyethylene Glycol 3350 NF (Polyethylene Glycol 3350 Powder for Oral Solution) is a prescription only laxative which has been prescribed by your physician to treat constipation. This product should only be used by the person for whom it was prescribed.

[defendants' patient information inserts]

Writing for the court of appeals, Judge Posner ruled that Schering was mistaken to argue that all it needed to show was "literal falsity":

> The purpose of the false-advertising provisions of the Lanham Act is to protect sellers from having their customers lured away from them by deceptive ads (or labels, or other promotional materials). Many literally false statements are not deceptive. When the Soviet Union in the 1930s declared that "2 + 2 = 5," it was not deceiving anyone; it was announcing a slogan designed to spur workers to complete the Five-Year Plan in four years. If one opened the *New York Times* "literally" at random one might find an ad that calls Graff Diamonds "The Most Fabulous Jewels in the World." That is literally false because the jewels sold by Graff are no more fabulous than, say, the Crown Jewels of England, or the Hope Diamond. But no one is deceived, so there is no injury, and a suit by a competitor of Graff would fail. The cases that reject liability do so in the name of "puffery"—meaningless superlatives— but the principle cuts deeper; if no one is or could be fooled, no one is or could be hurt.

> The other side of this coin is that a representation may be so obviously misleading that there is no need to gather evidence that anyone was confused. And it is often clearer that a claim is misleading than that it is literally false, because what is "literally" false is often a semantic question.

> What the cases mean when they say that proof of literal falsity allows the plaintiff to dispense with evidence that anyone was misled or likely to be misled is that the seller who places an indisputably false statement in his advertising or labeling probably did so for a malign purpose, namely to sell his product by lies, and if the statement is false probably at least some people were misled, and since it was a lie why waste time on costly consumer surveys? When this is stated as the doctrine of "literal falsity," "literal" must be understood in the common colloquial sense in which Americans . . . say things like "I am literally out of my mind." A "literal" falsehood is bald-faced, egregious, undeniable, over the top.

> We know this is what the cases are driving at because they add to "literal falsity" such qualifiers as that the meaning of the alleged literal falsehood must be considered in context and with reference to the audience to which the statement is addressed. That is how one obtains an understanding of the real meaning of "2 + 2 = 5" in Soviet propaganda.

The proper domain of "literal falsity" as a doctrine that dispenses with proof that anyone was misled or likely to be misled is the patently false statement that means what it says to any linguistically competent person, unlike the examples we have given. So suppose the labels on the defendants' products stated: "All polyethylene glycol 3350, by whomever made, can be sold only by prescription; there is no over-the-counter version of this drug." That would be false and misleading per se; there would be no need to consider context or audience.

But that is not what the labels say. There is no statement in the ordinary sense, because there is no verb. There is the manufacturer's name at the top, the name of the active ingredient, the symbol "Rx only," and some other information. Obviously this product, the product of the named manufacturer, is prescription only, but it is not obvious . . . that every other product containing polyethylene glycol 3350 is prescription only. Schering cannot just intone "literal falsity" and by doing so prove a violation of the Lanham Act. . . .

Does the opinion import a fault requirement into the Lanham Act? Are many of the literal falsehoods described in this chapter "bald-faced, egregious, undeniable, [or] over the top"? Is it enough that they are, on the weight of the evidence, wrong? Consider the line of cases, to be discussed below, about claims that "tests prove" that a product works. If the tests on which the advertiser relies don't actually prove that the product works, because the plaintiff shows the tests to be unreliable or insufficient even if reliable, the defendant loses. How would Judge Posner analyze such cases?

Similarly, should a false ad require a "statement in the ordinary sense," including a verb? Could "55 MPG" be a false representation on a car ad? How would Posner deal with an allegedly false image, such as two identical gas pumps used to indicate that two drugs were equivalent?

Another example of creative reinterpretation of the concept of "literal falsity" came from *In re GNC Corp.*, 789 F.3d 505 (4th Cir. 2015), in which the court held that "marketing statements that accurately describe the findings of duly qualified and reasonable scientific experts are not literally false," and that a plaintiff must plead that *no* reasonable scientist would agree with defendant's claims in order to plead literal falsity. This was a class action case purporting to borrow Lanham Act standards, though you should be able to see that it was in fact a serious reinterpretation (not to say misreading) of them. *See* Sonner v. Schwabe North America, Inc., 911 F.3d 989 (9th Cir. 2018) (rejecting *GNC*: "We are unpersuaded by the notion that a plaintiff must not only produce affirmative evidence, but also fatally undermine the defendant's evidence, in order to proceed to trial. . . .If the plaintiff's evidence suggests that the products do not work as advertised and the defendant's evidence suggests the opposite, there is a genuine dispute of material fact for the fact-finder to decide.").

D.   Substantiation

FTC Substantiation Policy. The FTC takes the position that advertisers are "required to have substantiation not just for express statements but for all reasonable interpretations of their advertisements" in order to avoid an FTCA violation, and courts have agreed. See Fed. Trade Comm'n v. Lights of Am., Inc., No. 10-1333 (C.D. Cal. Sept. 17, 2013). Here, the FTC explains its general thinking on substantiation.

FTC POLICY STATEMENT REGARDING ADVERTISING SUBSTANTIATION, APPENDED TO THOMPSON MEDICAL CO., 104 F.T.C. 648, 839 (1984), AFF'D, 791 F.2D 189 (D.C. CIR. 1986)

. . . The Reasonable Basis Requirement

First, we reaffirm our commitment to the underlying legal requirement of advertising substantiation—that advertisers and ad agencies have a reasonable basis for advertising claims before they are disseminated.

The Commission intends to continue vigorous enforcement of this existing legal requirement that advertisers substantiate express and implied claims, however conveyed, that make objective assertions about the item or service advertised. Objective claims for products or services represent explicitly or by implication that the advertiser has a reasonable basis supporting these claims. These representations of substantiation are material to consumers. That is, consumers would be less likely to rely on claims for products and services if they knew the advertiser did not have a reasonable basis for believing them to be true.[2] Therefore, a firm's failure to possess and rely upon a reasonable basis for objective claims constitutes an unfair and deceptive act or practice in violation of Section 5 of the Federal Trade Commission Act.

Standards for Prior Substantiation

Many ads contain express or implied statements regarding the amount of support the advertiser has for the product claim. When the substantiation claim is express (e.g., "tests prove", "doctors recommend", and "studies show"), the Commission expects the firm to have at least the advertised level of substantiation. Of course, an ad may imply more substantiation than it expressly claims or may imply to consumers that the firm has a certain type of support; in such cases, the advertiser must possess the amount and type of substantiation the ad actually communicates to consumers.

Absent an express or implied reference to a certain level of support, and absent other evidence indicating what consumer expectations would be, the Commission assumes that consumers expect a "reasonable basis" for claims. The Commission's determination of what constitutes a reasonable basis depends, as it does in an unfairness analysis, on a number of factors relevant to the benefits and costs of substantiating a particular claim. These factors include: the type of claim, the product, the consequences of a false claim, the benefits of a truthful claim, the cost of developing substantiation for the claim, and the amount of substantiation experts in the field believe is reasonable. Extrinsic evidence, such as expert testimony or consumer surveys, is useful to determine what level of substantiation consumers expect to support a particular product claim and the adequacy of evidence an advertiser possesses.

---

[2] Nor presumably would an advertiser have made such claims unless the advertiser thought they would be material to consumers.

One issue the Commission examined was substantiation for implied claims. Although firms are unlikely to possess substantiation for implied claims they do not believe the ad makes, they should generally be aware of reasonable interpretations and will be expected to have prior substantiation for such claims. The Commission will take care to assure that it only challenges reasonable interpretations of advertising claims. . . .

NOTES AND QUESTIONS

Ex Post and Ex Ante Regulations. The substantiation requirement is broader than the no-falsity rule in a variety of ways. How will advertisers' behavior differ when substantiation is added to the no-falsity rule? For an economic model suggesting that, even setting aside enforcement cost issues, a substantiation requirement will improve the quality of information in the marketplace by encouraging marketers to invest in testing and to reveal information about their products, *see* Kenneth S. Cortsa, *Prohibitions on False and Unsubstantiated Claims: Inducing the Acquisition and Revelation of Information Through Competition Policy*, 56 J.L. & ECON. 453 (2013). A study by John Samuel Healey found mixed results: The substantiation policy reduced ambiguous statements where the consumer was expected to fill in the details and led instead to claims that "were either 'pure pap' or very factual in nature." Healy found that advertisers made fewer claims after the substantiation policy came into effect, but not that the studied products were advertised in a more informative way overall. John Samuel Healey, The Federal Trade Commission Advertising Substantiation Program and Changes in the Content of Advertising in Selected Industries (1978) (Ph.D. dissertation, University of California, Los Angeles, CA). A more-recent study supports the FTC's standard, finding that consumers find specific factual claims more credible, and increase their purchase intentions, compared to their reactions when they're exposed to similar ads that just promote positive emotions. Sungho Cho &Yongjae Kim, *Empirical Rationalization of Prior Substantiation Doctrine:* Federal Trade Commission v. Reebok & Sketchers, 29 LOY. CONSUMER L. REV. 55 (2016).

Canada also requires that advertisers possess substantiation for their claims, and interprets that requirement in similar ways. The Canadian Competition Act, Section 74.01 (1), bars advertising about "the performance, efficacy or length of life of a product that is not based on an adequate and proper test thereof, the proof of which lies on the person making the misrepresentation." In *R v Bristol-Myers Ltd.*, ((1979), 45 CPR (2d) 228), for example, the court concluded that the claim "Fleecy in the rinse softens right through the wash for three times more softness than any dryer product" was unsubstantiated. Bristol-Myers relied on panels of consumers who reported that fabrics washed with the recommended amount of the FLEECY fabric softener were softer than fabrics treated with three times the recommended amount of competing fabric softeners. Although qualitative consumer testing was the only means of measuring softness and could have supported a "feels softer" claim, it could not be used to support a quantitative "three times softer" claim. In Canada (Commissioner of Competition) v Chatr Wireless Inc., 2014 ONSC 1146, the court imposed a C$500,000 fine where, even though the advertiser's claim of fewer dropped calls than competitors' wireless services turned out to be true, it was unsubstantiated when made—Chatr tested only in a few cities and only against some competitors before making the claim—and thus consumers were exposed to the risk of falsity. (Although the FTC's official position is that post-claim

146

substantiation is insufficient, a fine for a claim that turns out to be true is practically unlikely in the United States.)

New Zealand is another example of a country requiring substantiation for advertising claims: Traders must have "reasonable grounds" to support claims before disseminating them to the public, unless the claim is one "that a reasonable person would not expect to be substantiated" (puffery). Fair Trading Act 1986, pt 1 s 12A (NZ).

Example: Made in the USA. The repeated disputes over "Made in the USA" claims illustrate how, in order to determine the required substantiation, one must first determine the claim being made. The FTC's current policy statement on "Made in the USA" states that users of the phrase should be able to substantiate that "all or virtually all" of the product is made in the United States. The FTC may consider several different factors, including the proportion of the product's total manufacturing costs attributable to U.S. parts and processing, how far removed any foreign content is from the finished product, and the importance of the foreign content or processing to the overall function of the product. FTC, *Issuance of Enforcement Policy Statement on "Made in USA" and Other U.S. Origin Claims*, 62 FR 63756, 63766 (Dec. 2, 1997). One recent study cited by the FTC found that 57% of consumers agreed that "Made in America" means that all parts of a product, including any natural resources it contains, originated in the United States, and 33% percent of consumers think that 100% percent of a product must originate in a country for that product to be called "Made" in that country. Fed. Trade Comm'n, Staff Report of the Bureau of Consumer Protection, *Made in the USA: An FTC Workshop* (Jun. 19, 2020). Given these findings, why do you think the FTC allows a showing that "virtually all" of a product originates in the United States to constitute adequate substantiation for a "Made in the USA" claim?

Substantiation of Scientific Claims—What Is the Appropriate Standard? The FTC and courts have been willing to require a significant amount of evidence for some claims. For example, "[w]here an advertiser makes claims using specific figures or facts, a high level of substantiation, such as scientific or engineering tests, is required." Fed. Trade Comm'n v. Lights of Am., Inc., No. 10-1333 (C.D. Cal. Sept. 17, 2013).

In several consent decrees for advertisers who had made insufficiently substantiated health claims for their products, such as claims that drinking "probiotic" yogurt would reduce the chances of getting a cold or the flu, the FTC articulated a high substantiation standard for future health claims. *See* Fed. Trade Comm'n, File No. 082 3158, The Dannon Company, Inc.; Analysis of Proposed Consent Order to Aid Public Comment, Federal Register/Vol. 75, No. 244, December 21, 2010.

In the probiotic yogurt case, Dannon was prohibited from claiming that yogurt products identified in the order "reduce[] the likelihood of getting a cold or the flu unless the FDA has issued a regulation authorizing the claim based on a finding that there is significant scientific agreement among experts qualified by scientific training and experience to evaluate such claims, considering the totality of publicly available scientific evidence."

Dannon *could* make a claim "characterizing limited scientific evidence supporting the relationship between a covered product and a reduced likelihood of getting a cold or the flu."

But Dannon did so at substantial risk: "[I]f the net impression of that advertising is that the covered product reduces the likelihood of getting a cold or the flu, and not merely that there is limited scientific evidence supporting the claim," the advertisement would violate the consent decree. Thus, if consumers interpreted limited claims as making broader claims, Dannon could suffer potentially severe sanctions.

The day after the FTC settlement was publicly announced, a Dannon spokesperson emphasized that Dannon admitted no wrongdoing in connection with the settlement, and noted that only $1 million had been claimed out of a potential fund of $35 million that was established in a 2009 class-action settlement (the remainder of the fund would be remitted to charities). However, Dannon also entered into a $21 million settlement with thirty-nine states, which added a periodic compliance monitoring requirement. What factors might have convinced Dannon to enter into the FTC and state settlements?

As Dannon's lawyer, how would you work to ensure compliance? Aside from the scientific evidence, would you also require copy testing to make sure consumers understand the limitations of the claims before authorizing a large-scale ad campaign? Given the costs of these tests, would you expect your client to make many health claims?

The FTC also attempted to give more precision to the substantiation requirement in an administrative proceeding against POM Wonderful (POM), which had long made aggressive claims about the health benefits of its pomegranate products, with ads like this one:

"Cheat Death," this ad promised, with "the world's most powerful antioxidant," which "can help prevent premature aging, heart disease, stroke, Alzheimer's, even cancer." With respect to a number of POM ads, the FTC found that reasonable consumers would receive an implied claim that the POM products treated, prevented, or reduced the risk of heart disease, prostate cancer, or erectile dysfunction, and some of the ads falsely conveyed the further message that these effects were clinically proven. The ads' references to studies to which they referred as "promising," "initial" or "preliminary," in context, were insufficient to neutralize the otherwise unequivocally positive claims of specific results. As the FTC held, the "use of one or two adjectives does not alter the net impression," especially "when the chosen adjectives" (such as "promising") "provide a positive spin on the studies rather than a substantive disclaimer."

In general, in order to determine the appropriate level of substantiation required for a claim, the FTC considers (1) the amount of substantiation experts in the field would consider to be sufficient, (2) the products involved, (3) the type of claim, (4) the benefits of a truthful claim, (5) the ease of developing substantiation for the claim, and (6) the consequences of a false claim. In POM, the Commission reasoned, although POM's product was a well-known food generally known to be safe, it was making a health claim, which justified a high standard. With or without explicit "clinically proven" language, POM's claims weren't sufficiently substantiated, since experts in the relevant scientific communities would require the same level of substantiation for the claim in either form. The economic injury was also significant, since consuming pomegranate products at the level suggested by POM would cost a consumer hundreds of dollars per year.

The FTC complaint counsel argued that two double-blind, placebo-controlled, randomized clinical trials—the kind of evidence required by the FDA before approving a prescription drug—were required to substantiate health claims of the sort made by POM. A majority of the commissioners agreed, but the D.C. Circuit modified the relief ordered. Under *Central Hudson*, a requirement that POM have at least one well-conducted randomized clinical trial supporting any health claim that it made was justified, but not a two-trial requirement. POM Wonderful, LLC v. Fed. Trade Comm'n, 777 F.3d 478 (D.C. Cir. 2015). A single trial that was good enough, and supported by other evidence, might justify a disease-related claim. The court noted that two-trial requirements had been upheld in the past, but found them limited to specific situations where experts agreed that replication was necessary given the limitations of the data.

POM argued that randomized clinical trials are expensive, which is true, but the Court of Appeals emphasized that POM could choose to specify a lower level of substantiation with an effective disclaimer.

Tradeoffs in Scientific Substantiation Requirements. If consumers do in fact receive disease prevention/treatment messages from health claims made by food or supplement producers, why *not* require those claims to meet the same standards as would be required if a drug manufacturer made the exact same claims about a drug? Otherwise, drug manufacturers are at a perhaps unwarranted competitive disadvantage to food producers, just because the food has other characteristics than a claimed health benefit. We discuss the laws specific to drugs and supplements in Chapter 18.

Requiring advertisers to meet FDA standards in order to make certain claims may in practice deter them from making such claims at all. This may prevent consumers from getting potentially useful information, and may encourage advertisers to use more puffery, or make claims that are more easily substantiated but less valuable to consumers. Are consumers better off if producers differentiate their products using, say, celebrity endorsers instead of potentially but not definitely true health claims? What if producers instead make their products taste better at the expense of nutrition because it's too hard—for them *and* for the competition that would otherwise keep them in check—to make nutrition claims? Is there any way to avoid disincentivizing truthful health claims while also maintaining a high standard of substantiation? Can you draft a disclaimer that, as the D.C. Circuit suggested, explains a lesser level of substantiation? (*See* Chapter 6.)

One reason for the FTC's attempt to define acceptable substantiation more precisely is to avoid disputes over whether particular evidence suffices as substantiation. *See* F.T.C. v. Garden of Life, Inc., 516 Fed. Appx. 852 (11th Cir. 2013) (where consent decree only required advertiser to have "competent and reliable scientific evidence substantiating its claims," the court of appeals largely upheld district court's refusal to find a violation of the consent decree based on a "battle of the experts").

Claims Must Be Relevant, Even if Substantiated. If the advertiser substantiates a claim about an extreme or irrelevant situation, it may still be unable to substantiate the implicit claim it's also making that the extreme or irrelevant situation is relevant to ordinary consumers. In one case, an auto parts maker had made strong safety claims:

The print ad, which was echoed by TV ads, said: "Wagner OE brake pads can stop your truck, SUV, or crossover up to 50 feet sooner than other leading pads. It can mean 50 feet saved when you need it most. And when you family's safety is on the line, isn't that what really matters?" Though the advertiser hired an independent testing firm, it didn't test stopping distance by measuring how consumers usually use their brakes in emergency situations: by stomping on them, instead of applying slow, even pressure. And the firm tested brakes in hotter-than-normal conditions, which further exaggerated the results. *In re* Federal-Mogul Motorparts LLC, No. C-172-3102 (proposed order Mar. 25, 2020). *See also* BP Lubricants USA, Inc. (Castrol EDGE), NAD Report No. 5674 (Jan. 14, 2014) (ad showed a "torture test" of motor oil with two cars running at seventy-five miles per hour on a 7% grade, fully loaded with 1600 pounds; on day five of the test, the engine using the competitor's motor oil failed while the advertiser's engine continued to run; while ad accurately depicted the test conditions, no real consumer's vehicle would ever be subjected to these conditions; the NAD determined that torture tests can only be used to support product claims when they represent conditions with real-world relevance).

If the situation is properly described and the extreme or unusual circumstances are important to consumers, however, such statements may not be misleading. Thus, when an advertisement for residential heat detectors promoted the products as useful additions to smoke detectors for home fire safety, the FTC did not find the advertisement deceptive even though heat detectors would rarely improve safety. Figgie Int'l, Inc., 107 F.T.C. 313 (1986). "Even a very small amount of additional protection from death or serious injury caused by fire would no doubt be considered significant by some consumers."

A Recurring Issue in Substantiation: Testimonials. The FTC has more-specific statements about certain types of substantiation. Repeatedly, advertisers have tried to substantiate their claims by recounting an individual's actual experience with a product, but one that was not necessarily average or typical. At one time, the FTC took the position that, while all ads needed to be assessed on their own merits, it would generally regard a clear "results not typical" disclaimer as sufficient when the advertiser was touting a testimonial by a consumer who'd achieved spectacular results. Research accumulated that this disclaimer simply did not work, however, and the FTC issued a revised guide in 2009.

FTC GUIDES CONCERNING THE USE OF ENDORSEMENTS AND TESTIMONIALS IN ADVERTISING, § 255.2 CONSUMER ENDORSEMENTS

(a) An advertisement employing endorsements by one or more consumers about the performance of an advertised product or service will be interpreted as representing that the product or service is effective for the purpose depicted in the advertisement. Therefore, the advertiser must possess and rely upon adequate substantiation, including, when appropriate, competent and reliable scientific evidence, to support such claims made through endorsements in the same manner the advertiser would be required to do if it had made the representation directly, i.e., without using endorsements. Consumer endorsements themselves are not competent and reliable scientific evidence.

(b) An advertisement containing an endorsement relating the experience of one or more consumers on a central or key attribute of the product or service also will likely be interpreted as representing that the endorser's experience is representative of what consumers will generally achieve with the advertised product or service in actual, albeit variable, conditions of use. Therefore, an advertiser should possess and rely upon adequate substantiation for this representation. If the advertiser does not have substantiation that the endorser's experience is representative of what consumers will generally achieve, the advertisement should clearly and conspicuously disclose the generally expected performance in the depicted circumstances, and the advertiser must possess and rely on adequate substantiation for that representation.[1] . . .

Example 1: A brochure for a baldness treatment consists entirely of testimonials from satisfied customers who say that after using the product, they had amazing hair growth and their hair is as thick and strong as it was when they were teenagers. The advertiser must have competent and reliable scientific evidence that its product is effective in producing new hair growth.

The ad will also likely communicate that the endorsers' experiences are representative of what new users of the product can generally expect. Therefore, even if the advertiser includes a disclaimer such as, "Notice: These testimonials do not prove our product works. You should not expect to have similar results," the ad is likely to be deceptive unless the advertiser has adequate substantiation that new users typically will experience results similar to those experienced by the testimonialists.

Example 2: An advertisement disseminated by a company that sells heat pumps presents endorsements from three individuals who state that after installing the company's heat pump in their homes, their monthly utility bills went down by $100, $125 and $150, respectively. The ad will likely be interpreted as conveying that such savings are representative of what consumers who buy the company's heat pump can generally expect. The advertiser does not have substantiation for that representation because, in fact, fewer than 20% of purchasers will save $100 or more. A disclosure such as, "Results not typical" or, "These testimonials are based on the experiences of a few people, and you are not likely to have similar results" is insufficient to prevent this ad from being deceptive because consumers will still interpret the ad as conveying that the specified savings are representative of what consumers can generally expect. The ad is less likely to be deceptive if it clearly and conspicuously discloses the generally expected savings and the advertiser has adequate substantiation that homeowners can achieve those results. There are multiple ways that such a disclosure could be phrased, e.g., "the average homeowner saves $35 per month," "the typical family saves $50 per month during cold months and $20 per month in warm months," or "most families save 10% on their utility bills." . . .

Example 7: An advertisement for a recently released motion picture shows three individuals coming out of a theater, each of whom gives a positive statement about the movie. These individuals are actual consumers expressing their personal views about the movie. The advertiser does not need to have substantiation that their views are representative of the opinions that most consumers will have about the movie. Because the consumers' statements

---

[1] The Commission tested the communication of advertisements containing testimonials that clearly and prominently disclosed either "Results not typical" or the stronger "These testimonials are based on the experiences of a few people and you are not likely to have similar results." Neither disclosure adequately reduced the communication that the experiences depicted are generally representative. Based upon this research, the Commission believes that similar disclaimers regarding the limited applicability of an endorser's experience to what consumers may generally expect to achieve are unlikely to be effective.

Nonetheless, the Commission cannot rule out the possibility that a strong disclaimer of typicality could be effective in the context of a particular advertisement. Although the Commission would have the burden of proof in a law enforcement action, the Commission notes that an advertiser possessing reliable empirical testing demonstrating that the net impression of its advertisement with such a disclaimer is non-deceptive will avoid the risk of the initiation of such an action in the first instance.

would be understood to be the subjective opinions of only three people, this advertisement is not likely to convey a typicality message.

NOTES AND QUESTIONS

Typicality and Opinions. The FTC exempts atypically positive opinions from this guidance. But experiments indicate that consumers often believe that an advertised opinion is the typical consumer opinion, and that disclosure of the typical consumer opinion would cause consumers to greatly discount advertised atypical opinions. Ahmed E. Taha & John V. Petrocelli, Advertising Opinions (unpublished manuscript). Should the FTC require substantiation that a testimonalist's opinion is typical?

FTC Guidance. Given the two documents above, suppose your client wanted to advertise a new sneaker with the claim, "The construction is built for support and enhanced agility in your workout, on the track or off." What kinds of claims are being made? Is the client making a representation about performance? About the risk of injury? What sort of substantiation would you ask for? How, if at all, would the concept of puffery fit into your analysis? What kind of substantiation would you ask for if the client wanted to run a TV ad showing an athlete wearing the sneakers outside, who says, "These sneakers give me great support, and I've never had an easier workout!" A lawyer reviewing an ad should always think about ethical and attractive alternatives; your job is not simply to say yes or no, but to assist in developing a truthful message. This can require you to discuss alternative possible claims with your clients.

Substantiation and Private Claims. The FTC and the states require advertisers to possess substantiation for their factual claims; unsubstantiated claims are treated like false claims. (Is this consistent with the First Amendment?) The NAD also applies a substantiation requirement.

In a private action, however, the burden is on the plaintiff—whether a competitor or a consumer—to show that the defendant's statements were false or misleading. The Third Circuit has recognized an exception to this rule in Lanham Act cases, however: Where an advertiser makes a claim with no reason to believe that it is true—pulls the claim out of a hat, essentially—that utter lack of substantiation violates the Lanham Act. *See* Novartis Consumer Health, Inc. v. Johnson & Johnson-Merck Consumer Pharms. Co., 290 F.3d 578 (3d Cir. 2002) (antacid's claim of nighttime superiority made with no evidence of such superiority was literally false). Should all courts adopt this rule for private plaintiff actions? Should we put at least the burden of production on an advertiser whose factual claim is challenged in court, even if we leave the burden of proof with the plaintiff? *See* Grpe. SEB USA, Inc v. Euro-Pro Operating LLC, 2014 WL 2002126 (W.D. Pa. May 15, 2014) (applying *Novartis* where defendant claimed superiority to plaintiff's steam iron "based on independent comparative steam burst testing" but did not produce such testing to the court or to its expert).

6.   False Establishment Claims

An establishment claim conveys an explicit or implicit message that "tests prove that X cleans better," "studies show that Y lasts longer" or some similar message indicating to the consumer that scientific or experimental evidence supports an advertising claim. Establishment claims are not limited to claims about laboratory tests; a claim about consumer preferences ("surveys show . . .") or another kind of quantitative claim can be an establishment claim. Establishment claims can be implicit as well as explicit. The impression that scientific studies lie behind a claim can be created by an actor in a lab coat, by pictures of scientific reports or by showing graphs or diagrams. *See* Sterling Drug, Inc. v. F.T.C., 741 F.2d 1146 (9th Cir. 1984) (establishment claim made because of visual aspects of ad, including "pictures of medical and scientific reports from which consumers could infer that Bayer's effectiveness had been objectively evaluated" and "serious tone" and "scientific aura" of ads).

As in *POM Wonderful*, sufficiently scientific language may inherently make an establishment claim. Smithkline Beecham Consumer Healthcare, L.P. v. Merck Consumer Pharms. Co., 906 F. Supp. 178 (S.D.N.Y. 1995) (treating the claim "based on pH data of stomach acidity" as an establishment claim); W.L. Gore & Assoc., Inc. v. Totes Inc., 788 F. Supp. 800 (D. Del. 1992) (finding that the statement that advertiser's golf suit allowed "seven times more air and sweat vapor" to pass through than competitor's product falsely indicated that advertiser had run independent tests when no such tests existed). These results may be an application of the "necessary implication" doctrine, discussed in Chapter 7, where implications that would be understood by any reasonable consumer are considered as if they'd been explicitly stated.

Establishment claims may be more persuasive, but that also means that advertising law subjects them to special scrutiny:

> We live in [a] society that values quantification. You can read about the 100 "top" colleges in *U.S. News & World Report* or the ten "best" cars in *Consumer Reports*. But comparative advertising confers on advertisers a serious responsibility to the public and competitors. If Defendants wish to secure the undoubted advantage of numerical comparisons, then they should get them right.

Garden Way Inc. v. The Home Depot Inc., 94 F. Supp. 2d 276 (N.D.N.Y. 2000). In other contexts, courts have in recent years expressed concerns over "junk science" used to convince juries that products are dangerous when they aren't. But junk science can be found everywhere, including advertisers with incentives to claim superiority.

Courts applying the Lanham Act have developed the rule that an establishment claim may be proven false by showing that the studies on which the ad relies are not sufficiently reliable to support with reasonable certainty the claim made by the ad. This may be shown by demonstrating either (1) that the tests, even if valid, do not establish the claim actually made by an ad or (2) that the tests are invalid and objectively unreliable. Similarly, the NAD has stated that when tests or surveys are cited in advertising as support for a claim, the advertising is false if the test or survey is "inadequate to support the claim." *In re* Visa U.S.A., Inc. NAD Case No. 3426 (closed 11/6/97).

Courts consider "all relevant circumstances, including the state of the testing art, the existence and feasibility of superior procedures, the objectivity and skill of the persons conducting the tests, the accuracy of their reports, and the results of other pertinent tests." Proctor & Gamble Co. v. Chesebrough-Pond's, Inc., 747 F.2d 114 (2d Cir. 1984). One court has suggested in dicta that, where the relevant consumers are sophisticated and the advertiser provides them with abstracts of the tests on which a claim is founded, the consumers are in a position to decide for themselves whether the tests are sufficiently reliable. *See* Pfizer, Inc. v. Miles, Inc., 868 F. Supp. 437 (D. Conn. 1994); *cf. ONY, supra.*

Any flaws in the supporting test must be substantial to trigger this rule. In general, "[t]o ensure vigorous competition and to protect legitimate commercial speech, courts applying [the sufficient reliability] standard should give advertisers a fair amount of leeway, at least in the absence of a clear intent to deceive or substantial consumer confusion." Rhone-Poulenc Rorer Pharms., Inc. v. Marion Merrell Dow, Inc., 93 F.3d 511 (8th Cir. 1996). As a result, two competing advertisers may be able to make contradictory establishment claims, if each relies on weak but not worthless tests. *See* Proctor & Gamble Co. v. Chesebrough-Pond's, Inc., 747 F.2d 114 (2d Cir. 1984) (allowing competing lotions to make diametrically opposed claims because neither party's tests could be proven scientifically invalid). Likewise, if the defendant's tests were, at the time they were conducted, the best-known way to measure the tested characteristic, later developments, and even doubts about the reliability of the conclusions on the part of the defendant's own employees, do not show that the tests were not reasonably reliable. See Omega Eng'g, Inc. v. Eastman Kodak Co., 30 F. Supp. 2d 226 (D. Conn. 1998).

Nevertheless, advertisers should make establishment claims carefully. An establishment claim that significantly overstates the amount of superiority shown by the supporting tests may be found false. In addition, in context, consumers may attribute a "tests prove" claim about one aspect of the product to other, related claims, resulting in liability when the tests do not prove those other claims. *See* Porter & Dietsch, Inc. v. F.T.C., 605 F.2d 294 (7th Cir. 1979) (where ad generally created impression that most users of diet pill would lose significant amounts of weight, claims that pill was "clinic tested" [sic] and "medically recognized" were treated as establishment claims that users would lose significant weight).

The burden of challenging a non-establishment claim has sometimes been labeled "greater" than the burden of challenging an establishment claim because, in establishment cases, a plaintiff need only show that the underlying statement about the product lacks support from the evidence on which the defendant relies, not that it is affirmatively untrue. However, a plaintiff's demonstration that "tests *don't* show X" disproves the defendant's "tests show X" claim. In other words, the burden of showing falsity is the same, but the claim at issue is different: It is the "tests prove" claim that the plaintiff alleges is false and not the substantive claim that the "tests" supposedly "prove" to be true. Is such a falsehood as likely to be important to consumers as the underlying factual claim? See the discussion of materiality *infra.*

If an ad simply asserts a fact without stating (or implying) that tests back up the claim, then it generally is not enough for a Lanham Act plaintiff to show that the claim was unsubstantiated. *See, e.g.,* C.B. Fleet Co. v. SmithKline Beecham Consumer Healthcare, L.P., 131 F.3d 430 (4th Cir. 1997). Moreover, even if an advertisement is based on tests, if it makes no establishment claims, it is not subject to establishment claim standards.

But what should happen if a competitor shows with credible evidence that consumers expect that a particular claim is only made because it is substantiated? Logically, the claim should be treated as an implicit establishment claim, like a claim made while showing a chart or graph. *See* C.B. Fleet Co. v. SmithKline Beecham Consumer Healthcare, L.P., 131 F.3d 430 (4th Cir. 1997) (whether claim implies a basis in surveys or tests is question of fact); Sandoz Pharms. Corp. v. Richardson-Vicks, Inc., 902 F.2d 222 (3d Cir. 1990) ("[A] plaintiff must produce consumer surveys or some surrogate therefore to prove whether consumers expect an advertising claim to be substantiated and whether they expect the level of substantiation to be greater than that which the defendant has performed.").

The FTC has adopted the view that scientific substantiation is required for certain classes of products, such as drugs. American Home Prods. Corp. v. F.T.C., 695 F.2d 681 (3d Cir. 1982) (approving FTC's reasoning that consumers are likely to believe that statements about drug efficacy are supported by scientific evidence, though the existence of such evidence is neither stated nor otherwise implied); *In re* Pfizer, Inc., 81 F.T.C. 23 (1972) ("[T]here may be some types of claims for some types of products for which the only reasonable basis, in fairness and in the expectations of consumers, would be a valid scientific or medical basis.").

Should courts deciding cases brought by private plaintiffs accept the FTC's reasoning? *See* Glaxo-Warner Lambert OTC G.P. v. Johnson & Johnson-Merck Consumer Pharms. Co., 935 F. Supp. 327 (S.D.N.Y. 1996) (rejecting the argument that statements about the equivalency of two over-the-counter drugs inherently suggested that tests supported the claims).

The Placebo Effect

What happens when a product only "works" because consumers believe it helps them? Is it misleading to advertise that the product will help them? The following case uses economic reasoning, but is it ultimately enforcing a moral distaste?

FEDERAL TRADE COMMISSION V. QT, INC., 512 F.3D 858 (7TH CIR. 2008)

WIRED Magazine recently put the Q-Ray Ionized Bracelet on its list of the top ten Snake-Oil Gadgets.

[the "Gold Deluxe" Q-Ray Ionized Bracelet]

The Federal Trade Commission has an even less-honorable title for the bracelet's promotional campaign: fraud. In this action under 15 U.S.C. §§ 45(a), 52, 53, a magistrate judge, presiding by the parties' consent, concluded after a bench trial that the bracelet's promotion has been thoroughly dishonest. The court enjoined the promotional claims and required defendants to disgorge some $16 million (plus interest) for the FTC to distribute to consumers who have been taken in.

According to the district court's findings, almost everything that defendants have said about the bracelet is false. Here are some highlights:

- Defendants promoted the bracelet as a miraculous cure for chronic pain, but it has no therapeutic effect.
- Defendants told consumers that claims of "immediate, significant or complete pain relief" had been "test-proven"; they hadn't.
- The bracelet does not emit "Q-Rays" (there are no such things) and is not ionized (the bracelet is an electric conductor, and any net charge dissipates swiftly). The bracelet's chief promoter chose these labels because they are simple and easily remembered—and because Polaroid Corp. blocked him from calling the bangle "polarized".
- The bracelet is touted as "enhancing the flow of bio-energy" or "balancing the flow of positive and negative energies"; these empty phrases have no connection to any medical or scientific effect. Every other claim made about the mechanism of the bracelet's therapeutic effect likewise is techno-babble.
- Defendants represented that the therapeutic effect wears off in a year or two, despite knowing that the bracelet's properties do not change. This assertion is designed to lead customers to buy new bracelets. Likewise the false statement that the bracelet has a "memory cycle specific to each individual wearer" so that only the bracelet's original wearer can experience pain relief is designed to increase sales by eliminating the second-hand market and "explaining" the otherwise-embarrassing fact that the buyer's friends and neighbors can't perceive any effect.
- Even statements about the bracelet's physical composition are false. It is sold in "gold" and "silver" varieties but is made of brass.

The magistrate judge did not commit a clear error, or abuse his discretion, in concluding that the defendants set out to bilk unsophisticated persons who found themselves in pain from arthritis and other chronic conditions.

Defendants maintain that the magistrate judge subjected their statements to an excessively rigorous standard of proof. Some passages in the opinion could be read to imply that any statement about a product's therapeutic effects must be deemed false unless the claim has been verified in a placebo-controlled, double-blind study: that is, a study in which some persons are given the product whose effects are being investigated while others are given a placebo (with the allocation made at random), and neither the person who distributes the product nor the person who measures the effects knows which received the real product. Such studies are expensive, not only because of the need for placebos and keeping the experimenters in the dark, but also because they require large numbers of participants to achieve statistically significant results. Defendants observe that requiring vendors to bear such heavy costs may keep useful products off the market (this has been a problem for drugs that are subject to the FDA's testing protocols) and prevent vendors from making truthful statements that will help consumers locate products that will do them good.

Nothing in the Federal Trade Commission Act, the foundation of this litigation, requires placebo-controlled, double-blind studies. The Act forbids false and misleading statements, and a statement that is plausible but has not been tested in the most reliable way cannot be condemned out of hand. The burden is on the Commission to prove that the statements are false. (This is one way in which the Federal Trade Commission Act differs from the Food and Drug Act.) Think about the seller of an adhesive bandage treated with a disinfectant such as iodine. The seller does not need to conduct tests before asserting that this product reduces the risk of infection from cuts. The bandage keeps foreign materials out of the cuts and kills some bacteria. It may be debatable how much the risk of infection falls, but the direction of the effect would be known, and the claim could not be condemned as false. Placebo-controlled, double-blind testing is not a legal requirement for consumer products.

But how could this conclusion assist defendants? In our example the therapeutic claim is based on scientific principles. For the Q-Ray Ionized Bracelet, by contrast, all statements about how the product works—Q-Rays, ionization, enhancing the flow of bio-energy, and the like—are blather. Defendants might as well have said: "Beneficent creatures from the 17th Dimension use this bracelet as a beacon to locate people who need pain relief, and whisk them off to their homeworld every night to provide help in ways unknown to our science."

Although it is true, as Arthur C. Clarke said, that "[a]ny sufficiently advanced technology is indistinguishable from magic" by those who don't understand its principles, a person who promotes a product that contemporary technology does not understand must establish that this "magic" actually works. Proof is what separates an effect new to science from a swindle. Defendants themselves told customers that the bracelet's efficacy had been "test-proven"; that statement was misleading unless a reliable test had been used and statistically significant results achieved. A placebo-controlled, double-blind study is the best test; something less may do (for there is no point in spending $1 million to verify a claim worth only $10,000 if true); but defendants have no proof of the Q-Ray Ionized Bracelet's efficacy. The "tests" on which they relied were bunk. (We need not repeat the magistrate judge's exhaustive evaluation of this subject.) What remain are testimonials, which are not a form of proof because most testimonials represent a logical fallacy: post hoc ergo propter hoc. (A person who experiences a reduction in pain after donning the bracelet may have enjoyed the same reduction without it. That's why the "testimonial" of someone who keeps elephants off the streets of a large city by snapping his fingers is the basis of a joke rather than proof of cause and effect.)

To this defendants respond that one study shows that the Q-Ray Ionized Bracelet does reduce pain. This study, which the district court's opinion describes in detail, compared the effects of "active" and "inactive" bracelets (defendants told the experimenter which was which), with the "inactive" bracelet serving as a control. The study found that both "active" and "inactive" bracelets had a modest—and identical—effect on patients' reported levels of pain. In other words, the Q-Ray Ionized Bracelet exhibits the placebo effect. Like a sugar pill, it alleviates symptoms even though there is no apparent medical reason. The placebo effect is well established. Defendants insist that the placebo effect vindicates their claims, even though they are false-indeed, especially because they are false, as the placebo effect depends on deceit. Tell the patient that the pill contains nothing but sugar, and there is no pain relief; tell him (falsely) that it contains a powerful analgesic, and the perceived level of pain falls. A product that confers this benefit cannot be excluded from the market, defendants insist, just because they told the lies necessary to bring the effect about.

Yet the Federal Trade Commission Act condemns material falsehoods in promoting consumer products; the statute lacks an exception for "beneficial deceit." We appreciate the possibility that a vague claim—along the lines of "this bracelet will reduce your pain without the side effects of drugs"—could be rendered true by the placebo effect. To this extent we are skeptical about language in *FTC v. Pantron I Corp.*, 33 F.3d 1088 (9th Cir. 1994), suggesting that placebo effects always are worthless to consumers. But our defendants advanced claims beyond those that could be supported by a placebo effect. They made statements about Q-Rays, ionization, and bio-energy that they knew to be poppycock; they stated that the bracelet remembers its first owner and won't work for anyone else; the list is extensive.

One important reason for requiring truth is so that competition in the market will lead to appropriate prices. Selling brass as gold harms consumers independent of any effect on pain. Since the placebo effect can be obtained from sugar pills, charging $200 for a device that is represented as a miracle cure but works no better than a dummy pill is a form of fraud. That's not all. A placebo is necessary when scientists are searching for the marginal effect of a new drug or device, but once the study is over a reputable professional will recommend whatever works best.

Medicine aims to do better than the placebo effect, which any medieval physician could achieve by draining off a little of the patient's blood. If no one knows how to cure or ameliorate a given condition, then a placebo is the best thing going. Far better a placebo that causes no harm (the Q-Ray Ionized Bracelet is inert) than the sort of nostrums peddled from the back of a wagon 100 years ago and based on alcohol, opium, and wormwood. But if a condition responds to treatment, then selling a placebo as if it had therapeutic effect directly injures the consumer.

Physicians know how to treat pain. Why pay $200 for a Q-Ray Ionized Bracelet when you can get relief from an aspirin tablet that costs 1¢? Some painful conditions do not respond to analgesics (or the stronger drugs in the pharmacopeia) or to surgery, but it does not follow that a placebo at any price is better. Deceit such as the tall tales that defendants told about the Q-Ray Ionized Bracelet will lead some consumers to avoid treatments that cost less and do more; the lies will lead others to pay too much for pain relief or otherwise interfere with the matching of remedies to medical conditions. That's why the placebo effect cannot justify fraud in promoting a product. . . .

NOTES AND QUESTIONS

A double-blinded, placebo-controlled test failed to find any benefit from these bracelets. *See* Stewart J. Richmond et al., *Copper Bracelets and Magnetic Wrist Straps for Rheumatoid Arthritis—Analgesic and Anti-Inflammatory Effects: A Randomised Double-Blind Placebo Controlled Crossover Trial*, PLoS ONE (2013), doi:10.1371/journal.pone.0071529.

Some courts are more willing to consider the potential of the placebo effect to make claims "truthful." *See* Allen v. Hylands, Inc., 773 Fed. Appx. 870 (9th Cir. 2019) (affirming jury verdict in favor of homeopathic producer; trial court did not abuse discretion in declining to give proposed instruction that the jury "may not take into consideration the placebo effect in determining whether [Hyland's] products provided relief," since California law hasn't adopted the FTC's rejection of the placebo effect as a way a product could "work").

A False Distinction? Judge Easterbrook says that the $200 bracelet and a one-cent aspirin tablet will yield the same result. What if the defendant could show that by spending the extra money, at least some buyers experienced a more pronounced placebo effect? What if the difference is statistically significant but small (such that, for example, one out of thirty sufferers will benefit from the enhanced pain relief, while the other twenty-nine will not)?

Why do people buy worthless products? Are health (or weight-loss or beauty) claims areas where hope beats out experience? Do consumers really know, deep down, that they're buying snake oil, and, if so, why protect them against such claims?

7.   False Demonstrations and Dramatizations

Even if an advertiser possesses substantiation that a product or service is capable of achieving a certain result, it is false to advertise it by using a rigged demonstration. A famous case involves a shaving cream that actually could "shave" sandpaper. On TV, however, real sandpaper looked like nothing but colored paper. The advertiser, therefore, rigged a demonstration using simulated "sandpaper" made of plexiglass covered with sand. The Supreme Court upheld the FTC's order barring the ad. FTC v. Colgate-Palmolive Co., 380 U.S. 374 (1965). The Court agreed with the FTC's conclusion that "even if an advertiser has himself conducted a test, experiment or demonstration which he honestly believes will prove a certain product claim, he may not convey to television viewers the false impression that they are seeing the test, experiment or demonstration for themselves, when they are not because of the undisclosed use of mock-ups."

In another case, a commercial advertising the strength of a Volvo automobile showed a "monster truck" crushing a row of conventional cars, leaving the Volvo unharmed. The Volvo, unlike the other cars, had been reinforced to make it stronger. The FTC found that this dramatization was false and fined the company $150,000. *See In re* Volvo North America Corp., F.T.C. File No. 912-3032 (June 12, 1991).

Recently, the U.K. advertising regulator has challenged post-production editing on ads for beauty products, leading major companies to withdraw some ads. Competitors in the beauty market have not challenged each others' use of such editing techniques, even when they make the advertised products look more effective than they are.

Likewise, the NAD opened an investigation on its own initiative into Procter & Gamble's ads for CoverGirl mascara, suggesting that the ads could convey the implied messages that consumers who use the product would get lashes like those depicted and that the lashes depicted were achieved solely by using the CoverGirl product, even though the ads bore the legend "lashes enhanced in post-production." The NAD has also examined similar mascara ads where there was an explicit disclosure that the model was "styled with lash inserts," which make the lash fringe look thicker. Makeup ads are not exempt from the general rules about false demonstrations and dramatizations, even though makeup sells a fantasy more blatantly than some other products. The advertiser presented a consumer survey that it claimed indicated that consumers did not expect their lashes to look like the model's even if they used the mascara. The NAD reasoned that, even if consumers didn't take away the message that they'd achieve the *same* results as the model, the false demonstration nonetheless enhanced the credibility of the key claim that the mascara would make the user's lashes thicker and lusher. But because the photo didn't depict the volume that could be achieved using the mascara alone, even on an unusually beautiful woman, it was literally false. *See* L'Oréal U.S.A., Inc., NAD Case No. 5628 (Sept. 6, 2013). On appeal, NARB found that a sufficiently clear and conspicuous disclaimer (see Chapter 6) that inserts were used could keep the ad from being literally false. L'Oréal U.S.A., Inc. (NARB Jan. 23, 2014).

Is there good reason for regulatory intervention into this market? Suzanne Grayson, a beauty consultant, offered one perspective: "'Everybody does it,' said Ms. Grayson, . . . adding that retouching of lashes in mascara advertising has become particularly aggressive in recent years. 'It's been more aggressive by manufacturers, because they see what other people are getting away with, and it becomes, "Can you top this?"' Ms. Grayson said." Jack Neff, *National Ad Division Goes After Retouching of Beauty Ads*, ADAGE, Dec. 15, 2011.

Demonstrations and dramatizations may be legitimate if they sufficiently replicate all the significant aspects of the testing environment and carry a sufficient disclaimer, as discussed in Chapter 6. In addition, using undisclosed props is not necessarily false. Falsity arises when consumers are told to rely on their own perceptions to verify the advertiser's claim. The Supreme Court gave the example of a scoop of mashed potatoes used to stand in for ice cream under hot studio lights. If the potatoes are not used to prove a product claim, there is no problem. But if "the focus of the commercial becomes the undisclosed potato prop and the viewer is invited, explicitly or by implication, to see for himself the truth of the claims about the ice cream's rich texture and full color, and perhaps compare it to a 'rival product,'" it would become false.

As you read the following case, recall the drowning goldfish from the *S.C. Johnson* case, *supra*. Consider when dramatizations count as "factual"—how would you direct an ad agency to animate the claim at issue?

SCHICK MANUFACTURING, INC. V. GILLETTE COMPANY, 372 F. SUPP. 2D 273 (D. CONN. 2005)

The plaintiff, Schick Manufacturing Company ("Schick"), seeks a preliminary injunction enjoining the defendant, The Gillette Company ("Gillette"), from making certain claims about its M3 Power razor system ("M3 Power"). Schick contends that Gillette has made various false claims in violation of Section 43(a) of the Lanham Act, 15 U.S.C. § 1125(a), and the Connecticut Unfair Trade Practices Act ("CUTPA"), Conn. Gen. Stat. § 42-110a, *et seq.*

. . . Gillette's original advertising for the M3 Power centered on the claim that "micropulses raise hair up and away from skin," thus allowing a consumer to achieve a closer shave. This "hair-raising" or hair extension claim was advertised in various media, including the internet, television, print media, point of sale materials, and product packaging. . . . Of Gillette's expenditures on advertising, 85% is spent on television advertising. At the time of the launch, the television advertising stated, "turn on the first micro-power shaving system from Gillette and turn on the amazing new power-glide blades. Micro-pulses raise the hair, so you shave closer in one power stroke." The advertisement also included a 1.8 second-long animated dramatization of hairs growing. In the animated cartoon, the oscillation produced by the M3 Power is shown as green waves moving over hairs. In response, the hairs shown extended in length in the direction of growth and changed angle towards a more vertical position.

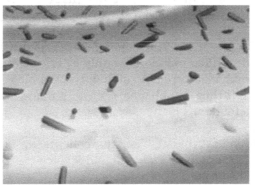

[screenshot from first ad]

. . . In late January of 2005, Gillette revised its television commercials for the M3 Power in the United States. . . . The animated product demonstration in the television commercials was revised so that the hairs in the demonstration no longer changed angle, and some of the hairs are shown to remain static. The voice-over was changed to say, "Turn it on and micropulses raise the hair so the blades can shave closer." The product demonstration in the revised advertisements depicts the oscillations to lengthen many hairs significantly. The depiction in the revised advertisements of how much the hair lengthens—the magnitude of the extension—is not consistent with Gillette's own studies regarding the effect of micropulses on hair. The animated product demonstration depicts many hairs extending, in many instances, multiple times the original length. . . .

Gillette conceded during the hearing that the M3 Power's oscillations do not cause hair to change angle on the face. Its original advertisements depicting such an angle change are both unsubstantiated and inaccurate. Gillette also concedes that the animated portion of its television advertisement is not physiologically exact insofar as the hairs and skin do not appear as they would at such a level of magnification and the hair extension effect is "somewhat exaggerated." The court finds that the hair "extension" in the commercial is greatly exaggerated. Gillette does contend, however, that the M3 Power's oscillations cause beard hairs to be raised out of the skin. Gillette contends that the animated product demonstration showing hair extension in its revised commercials is predicated on its testing showing that oscillations cause "trapped" facial hairs to lengthen from the follicle so that more of these hairs' length is exposed. . . .

[Gillette's theory of why the razor would raise hairs was unsupported by scientific evidence; the parties both submitted studies that were small, uncontrolled, and otherwise unreliable.]

The flaws in testing conducted by both parties prevent the court from concluding whether, as a matter of fact, the M3 Power raises beard hairs.

II. ANALYSIS

. . . B. False Advertising

. . . Where, . . . as here, the accused advertising does not allege that tests or clinical studies have proven a particular fact, the plaintiff's burden to come forward with affirmative evidence of falsity is qualitatively different. "To prove that an advertising claim is literally false, a plaintiff must do more than show that the tests supporting the challenged claim are unpersuasive." The plaintiff must prove falsity by a preponderance of the evidence, either using its own scientific testing or that of the defendant. If a plaintiff is to prevail by relying on the defendant's own studies, it cannot do so simply by criticizing the defendant's studies. It must prove either that "such tests 'are not sufficiently reliable to permit one to conclude with reasonable certainty that they established' the claim made" or that the defendant's studies establish that the defendant's claims are false.

The challenged advertising consists of two basic components: an animated representation of the effect of the M3 Power razor on hair and skin and a voice-over that describes that effect. . . . Schick asserts that this M3 Power advertising is false in three ways: first, it asserts the razor changes the angle of beard hairs; second, it portrays a false amount of extension; and third, it asserts that the razor raises or extends the beard hair.

With regard to the first claim of falsity, if the voiceover means that the razor changes the angle of hairs on the face, the claim is false. . . .

With regard to the second asserted basis of falsity, the animation, Gillette concedes that the animation exaggerates the effect that the razor's vibration has on hair. Its own tests show hairs extending approximately 10% on average, when the animation shows a significantly greater extension. The animation is not even a "reasonable approximation," which Gillette claims is the legal standard for non-falsity. Here, Schick can point to Gillette's own studies to prove that the animation is false.

Gillette argues that such exaggeration does not constitute falsity. However, case law in this circuit indicates that a defendant cannot argue that a television advertisement is "approximately" correct or, alternatively, simply a representation in order to excuse a television ad or segment thereof that is literally false. Indeed, "[the Court of Appeals has] explicitly looked to the visual images in a commercial to assess whether it is literally false."

. . . . Clearly, a cartoon will not exactly depict a real-life situation, here, *e.g.*, the actual uneven surface of a hair or the details of a hair plug. However, a party may not distort an inherent quality of its product in either graphics or animation. Gillette acknowledges that the magnitude of beard hair extension in the animation is false. The court finds, therefore, that any claims with respect to changes in angle and the animated portion of Gillette's current advertisement are literally false.

The court does not make such a finding with respect to Schick's third falsity ground, Gillette's hair extension theory generally. Gillette claims that the razor's vibrations raise some hairs trapped under the skin to come out of the skin. While its own studies are insufficient to establish the truth of this claim, the burden is on Schick to prove falsity. Neither Schick's nor Gillette's testing can support a finding of falsity.

While there can be no finding of literal falsity with respect to Gillette's hair extension claim at this stage in the instant litigation, the court expresses doubt about that claim. . . .

Nevertheless, putting forth credible evidence that there is no known biological mechanism to support Gillette's contention that the M3 Power raises hairs is insufficient to meet Schick's burden. Such evidence is not affirmative evidence of falsity. . . . [H]ere Gillette's own tests do not prove hair extension does not occur. Schick merely proved that Gillette's testing is inadequate to prove it does occur.

NOTES AND QUESTIONS

Schick sued Gillette for false advertising around the world. Courts in France, Belgium and the Netherlands refused to enjoin the disputed advertising, but courts in Germany and Australia, along with the district court whose opinion is excerpted here, issued preliminary injunctions. After extensive U.S. discovery, Gillette and Schick reached a worldwide settlement. But class-action litigation followed in several states and Canadian jurisdictions. All the state cases were removed and all the federal cases were transferred to the Massachusetts district court and consolidated. The district court gave preliminary approval to a proposed settlement, discussed in Chapters 8 and 9. *In re* M3 Power Razor Sys. Mktg. & Sales Practice Litig., 270 F.R.D. 45 (D. Mass. 2010).

8. False Implied Claims

A claim that is literally true but nonetheless deceives or misleads consumers by its implications also constitutes false advertising. Otherwise, "clever use of innuendo, indirect intimations, and ambiguous suggestions could shield the advertisement from scrutiny precisely when protection against such sophisticated deception is most needed." Am. Home Prods. Corp. v. Johnson & Johnson, 577 F.2d 160 (2d Cir. 1978).

In Lanham Act cases, plaintiffs usually need consumer surveys indicating that a not insubstantial number of consumers understood the implied message, a requirement we explore in detail in Chapter 7. However, some circuits have ruled that survey evidence of consumer deception may not be necessary if a plaintiff can show that the defendant intended to deceive consumers with the implicit message, though this rule is rarely applied in a plaintiff's favor. *See, e.g.*, Cashmere & Camel Hair Mfrs. Inst. v. Saks Fifth Ave., 284 F.3d 302 (1st Cir. 2002). The general rule: Without a survey, plaintiff loses.

By contrast, both the FTC and the NAD have sufficient advertising expertise to judge an ad's implied claims for themselves regardless of intent, and survey evidence is unnecessary (though potentially helpful) in FTC and NAD proceedings. Indeed, courts often give the FTC substantial deference. FTC v. Lights of Am., Inc., No. 10-1333 (C.D. Cal. Sept. 17, 2013) ("The FTC is not required to show that every reasonable consumer would have been, or in fact was, misled," and ads "that are capable of being interpreted in a misleading way should be construed against the advertiser"). This flexibility increases the FTC's freedom to act and allows it to invest fewer resources in proving each case.

In the following case, the Seventh Circuit rejected Kraft's argument that the FTC should be required to follow an explicit/implicit distinction in determining what claims Kraft had made about the superiority of its processed cheese slices to imitation cheese slices.

KRAFT, INC. V. FEDERAL TRADE COMMISSION, 970 F.2D 311 (7TH CIR. 1992)

. . . In determining what claims are conveyed by a challenged advertisement, the Commission relies on two sources of information: its own viewing of the ad and extrinsic evidence. Its practice is to view the ad first and, if it is unable on its own to determine with confidence what claims are conveyed in a challenged ad, to turn to extrinsic evidence. The most convincing extrinsic evidence is a survey "of what consumers thought upon reading the advertisement in question," but the Commission also relies on other forms of extrinsic evidence including consumer testimony, expert opinion, and copy tests of ads.

Kraft has no quarrel with this approach when it comes to determining whether an ad conveys express claims, but contends that the FTC should be required, as a matter of law, to rely on extrinsic evidence rather than its own subjective analysis in all cases involving allegedly implied claims. The basis for this argument is that implied claims, by definition, are not self-evident from the face of an ad. This, combined with the fact that consumer perceptions are shaped by a host of external variables—including their social and educational backgrounds, the environment in which they view the ad, and prior experiences with the product advertised—makes review of implied claims by a five-member commission inherently unreliable. The Commissioners, Kraft argues, are simply incapable of determining what implicit messages consumers are likely to perceive in an ad. Making matters worse, Kraft asserts that the Commissioners are predisposed to find implied claims because the claims have been identified in the complaint, rendering it virtually impossible for them to reflect the perceptions of unbiased consumers. *See* Comment, *The Use and Reliability of Survey Evidence in Deceptive Advertising Cases*, 62 OR. L. REV. 561, 572 (1983) ("since the commissioners are highly trained attorneys with very specialized views of advertising, they lack the perspective to accurately identify the meaning given an advertisement by the general public").

Kraft buttresses its argument by pointing to the use of extrinsic evidence in an analogous context: cases brought under [Section] 43(a) of the Lanham Act. Courts hearing deceptive advertising claims under that Act, which provides a private right of action for deceptive advertising, generally require extrinsic proof that an advertisement conveys an implied claim. Were this a Lanham Act case, a reviewing court in all likelihood would have relied on extrinsic evidence of consumer perceptions. While this disparity is sometimes justified on grounds of advertising "expertise"—the FTC presumably possesses more of it than courts—Kraft maintains this justification is an illusory one in that the FTC has no special expertise in discerning consumer perceptions. Indeed, proof of the FTC's inexpertise abounds: false advertising cases makes up a small part of the Commission's workload, most commissioners have little prior experience in advertising, and the average tenure of commissioners is very brief. That evidence aside, no amount of expertise in Kraft's view can replace the myriad of external variables affecting consumer perceptions. Here, the Commission found implied claims based solely on its own intuitive reading of the ads (although it did reinforce that conclusion by examining the proffered extrinsic evidence). . . .

While Kraft's arguments may have some force as a matter of policy, they are unavailing as a matter of law. Courts, including the Supreme Court, have uniformly rejected imposing such a requirement on the FTC, and we decline to do so as well. We hold that the Commission may rely on its own reasoned analysis to determine what claims, including implied ones, are conveyed in a challenged advertisement, so long as those claims are reasonably clear from the face of the advertisement.

Kraft's case for a per se rule has two flaws. First, it rests on the faulty premise that implied claims are inescapably subjective and unpredictable. In fact, implied claims fall on a continuum, ranging from the obvious to the barely discernible. The Commission does not have license to go on a fishing expedition to pin liability on advertisers for barely imaginable claims falling at the end of this spectrum. However, when confronted with claims that are implied, yet conspicuous, extrinsic evidence is unnecessary because common sense and administrative experience provide the Commission with adequate tools to make[ ] its findings. . . .

Second, Kraft's reliance on Lanham Act decisions is misplaced. For one, not all courts applying the Lanham Act rely on extrinsic evidence when confronted with implied claims, but more importantly, when they do, it is because they are ill equipped—unlike the Commission—to detect deceptive advertising. And the Commission's expertise in deceptive advertising cases, Kraft's protestations notwithstanding, undoubtedly exceeds that of courts as a general matter. That false advertising cases constitute a small percentage of the FTC's overall workload does not negate the fact that significant resources are devoted to such cases in absolute terms, nor does it account for the institutional expertise the FTC gains through investigations, rulemakings, and consent orders. The Commissioners' personal experiences quite obviously affect their perceptions, but it does not follow that they are incapable of predicting whether a particular claim is likely to be perceived by a reasonable number of consumers.

. . . Kraft contends that by relying on its own subjective judgment that an ad, while literally true, implies a false message, the FTC chills nonmisleading, protected speech because advertisers are unable to predict whether the FTC will find a particular ad misleading. Advertisers can run sophisticated pre-dissemination consumer surveys and find no implied claims present, only to have the Commission determine in its own subjective view that consumers would perceive an implied claim. Indeed, Kraft maintains that is precisely what happened here. Even more troubling, Kraft maintains that the ads most vulnerable to this chilling effect are factual, comparative ads, . . . of greatest benefit to consumers. The net result of the Commission's subjective approach will be an influx of soft "feel good" ads designed to avoid unpredictable FTC decisions. The way to avoid this chilling effect, according to Kraft, is to require the Commission to rely on objective indicia of consumer perceptions in finding implied claims.

Kraft's [F]irst [A]mendment challenge is doomed by the Supreme Court's holding in *Zauderer*, which established that no [F]irst [A]mendment concerns are raised when facially apparent implied claims are found without resort to extrinsic evidence. In *Zauderer*, a lawyer advertised that clients who retained him on a contingent-fee basis would not have to pay legal fees if their lawsuits were unsuccessful, without disclosing that these clients would be charged for costs, even though these are terms of art unknown to most laypersons; thus, the ad implied that hiring this lawyer was a no-lose proposition to potential clients. The state sanctioned Zauderer for engaging in misleading advertising, and he challenged that sanction on [F]irst [A]mendment grounds. In approving the state's action, the Supreme Court declared, "When the possibility of deception is as self-evident as it is in this case, we need not require the State to 'conduct a survey of the . . . public before it [may] determine that the [advertisement] had a tendency to mislead.'"

Thus, *Zauderer* teaches that consumer surveys are not compelled by the [F]irst [A]mendment when the alleged deception although implied, is conspicuous. . .

Our holding does not diminish the force of Kraft's argument as a policy matter, and, indeed, the extensive body of commentary on the subject makes a compelling argument that reliance on extrinsic evidence should be the rule rather than the exception. . . .

NOTES AND QUESTIONS

A concurring opinion by Judge Manion emphasized that "neither this case nor *Zauderer* gives the FTC leave to ignore extrinsic evidence in every case." When, under *Kraft* (or under the First Amendment), should the FTC be required to submit consumer survey evidence?

The *Kraft* court leans heavily on precedent in upholding the FTC's ability to determine how consumers would respond to an implicit claim without a survey. If the court were writing on a blank slate, how should it decide? Kraft's arguments for requiring a survey are well articulated in the opinion; are there any countervailing considerations?

The Variety of Implicit Claims. Examples of false implicit claims are as numerous as there are products and services to advertise:

- The "extreme" situations discussed above with respect to substantiation, where the advertisers implicitly claimed that product performance in extreme situations was relevant to product performance in ordinary situations
- An ad portraying a broken, hard-to-find toy being replaced because the toy had been purchased with a particular credit card, when the credit card company did not replace broken goods but merely refunded the purchase price
- An advertisement for windshield wipers including an order form that asked for the make and model of the buyer's car, implying that the wipers were customized to fit certain cars when in fact the buyers had to alter them to fit their cars
- A claim that hospitals recommend "acetaminophen, the aspirin-free pain reliever in Anacin-3, more than any other pain reliever," when hospitals were actually recommending Tylenol (which contains acetaminophen), but consumers received the message that hospitals were recommending Anacin-3
- Claims that Geritol would cure tiredness caused by "iron deficiency anemia," when most tired people have no such deficiency

As that last example suggests, misleadingness can be a matter of failing to disclose material facts that change the import of the explicit claim.

Implication often arises out of context, such as the contrast between the words of an advertisement, which may be literally true, and the accompanying images. For instance, an advertisement for an allergy drug showed consumers of a competitor's product falling asleep in all sorts of unlikely situations, creating two misleading impressions: (1) that the competitor's drug caused irresistible drowsiness, and (2) that the advertiser's drug did not cause drowsiness. *See* Warner-Lambert Co. v. Schering-Plough Corp., 1991 WL 221107 (S.D.N.Y. 1991). In another case, the defendant claimed that its new anti-irritation strip was six times smoother than the rival razor's strip. The visuals in the commercial, however, focused on the smoothness of the resulting shave, and a survey revealed that 37% of consumers thought the commercial meant that the *shave* was smoother. As a result, the rival won an injunction and an award of damages. Gillette Co. v. Wilkinson Sword, Inc., 1992 WL 30938 (S.D.N.Y. 1992).

What about when consumers don't know the meaning of a word? *Suchanek v. Sturm Foods, Inc.*, 764 F.3d 750 (7th Cir. 2014), involved an advertiser who wished to make generic single-serving coffee pods for Keurig's expensive coffee brewing machine. However, for patent reasons it couldn't use a filter in the pods, and so it decided to use instant coffee instead— coffee crystals that dissolve in water. Sturm's consultants warned that "use of the word 'instant' is a real no-no" and should be avoided "if at all possible" in marketing the product to Keurig owners. The packaging displayed roasted coffee beans next to images of a pod, but stated in small font that it contained "naturally roasted soluble and microground Arabica coffee." Sturm did not use the better-known name for soluble coffee: instant coffee. The contents were over 95% instant coffee with only a tiny bit of microground coffee mixed in.

Other parts of the package offered a Coffee Lover's Bill of Rights promising "highest quality Arabica beans, roasted and ground to ensure peak flavor" and evoked the narrative of a neighborhood coffee shop.

In one survey, only 14% of participants who looked at the packages said the product contained instant coffee. Another survey found that essentially all consumers expected ground coffee in the pods, not instant coffee. Sturm's own expert found that only one in 151 test participants equated the term "soluble and microground" with the term "instant and microground." The district court ruled that no reasonable consumer could have been confused because the packages were clearly marked "soluble." As it pointed out, the lead plaintiff admitted that she understood the word "soluble" to mean that something is capable of dissolving.

In reversing, the court of appeals commented:

> But the fact that Suchanek correctly understood the definition of that English word is not enough to throw out her entire consumer-fraud claim. Did she know that soluble coffee is instant coffee? Did she understand that the [Sturm] product was over 95% instant? Suchanek says not. As she stated, "Keurig brews coffee. . . . If I was going to buy a k-cup of instant coffee, I would have used my hot water tap that has boiling water at the sink instead of buying an expensive Keurig machine." Taking all disputed facts in the light most favorable to Suchanek, a reasonable juror could conclude that Suchanek was deceived.

Here, consumers apparently failed to grasp the significance of the term "soluble" even though they knew what it meant in the abstract. Was the court of appeals correct to find sufficient evidence of misleadingness? Does Sturm's intent matter?

Ideally, and often in practice, the advertiser will be aware of the material claims implied by its ad. A lawyer reviewing an ad should begin by asking the advertiser what it intends to convey and what it expects reasonable consumers will take away from the ad. From there, for a sufficiently large campaign, consumer testing may further elucidate what the ad implies. In all cases, the advertiser must possess substantiation for claims reasonably implied by the ad. If the advertiser says that it can only substantiate the explicit claims but intends a broader implicit claim, a good lawyer will insist that the ad go back to the drawing board, rewriting the ad to ensure that the claims it makes are substantiated and (if these will cure the problem) providing consumers with better disclosures or a disclaimer (*see* Chapter 6). Where it's impossible to fix the unsupported/unsupportable implied claim, the lawyer may have to veto the ad altogether.

What happens when context creates implications? Researchers found that consumers visiting hospitals with McDonald's restaurants on-site believed that McDonald's food was healthier than consumers visiting hospitals without such restaurants. Hannah B. Sahud et al., *Marketing Fast Food: Impact of Fast Food Restaurants in Children's Hospitals*, 118 PEDIATRICS 2290 (2006). What kind of regulation, if any, is appropriate for implications such as this?

In another case, a court found that it couldn't be false advertising for Wal-Mart to market two headache remedies with identical ingredients, where one was in a box with a red background and was two to three times more expensive than the other, which was sold in a box with a green background. The consumer plaintiffs alleged that the differences deceived consumers into thinking that the more expensive product was stronger and more effective. They contended that "no reasonable consumer would pay more than $9 for Equate Migraine when he or she could pay less than $3 for Equate ES [Extra strength] unless he or she believed Equate Migraine was more effective than Equate ES." But the court ruled that Wal-Mart hadn't engaged in any relevant "act, statement, or omission" as required by the relevant consumer protection law and that a consumer's assumptions couldn't establish liability.

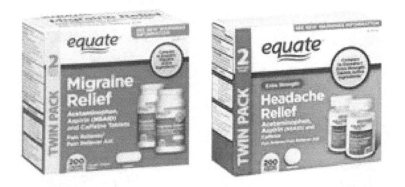

Boris v. Wal-Mart Stores, Inc., 35 F.Supp.3d 1163 (C.D. Cal. 2014). Why can't price and color be "acts" or even "statements" that imply comparative strength? Recall the discussion of price as a quality signal earlier in this chapter. Even if this packaging is legal, would you green-light it as the lawyer? *Cf.* Al Haj v. Pfizer Inc., 2019 WL 3202807 (N.D. Ill. Jul. 16, 2019) (Pfizer plausibly deceived consumers by charging more for "Maximum Strength" Robitussin cough syrup than for "Regular Strength" Robitussin even though the former had a lower concentration of active ingredients than the latter and a recommended dose of twenty milliliters compared to the recommended dose of ten milliliters for Regular Strength; "it is not reasonable to expect a consumer to cross-check a product's ingredient list against another product's list and then perform arithmetic to make sure she is comparing equivalent dosage volumes, all to ensure that the product she intends to purchase has the qualities it purports to have," and "a reasonable consumer would conclude that she was being charged more for a bottle of Maximum Strength Robitussin than she would have paid for a bottle of Regular Strength Robitussin because the former had more potency per volume than the latter").

If we are ultimately concerned with harm to consumers, or with the distorting effects on markets of deception, then we also need to examine how consumers process information and make decisions. In this Chapter, we consider how courts identify the reasonable target consumer for an ad and assess what kinds of responses to ads are expected or too unreasonable to matter. We then turn to a related, and increasingly important, component of the false advertising inquiry: materiality. Not every detail in an ad necessarily influences consumers. If a falsehood would not affect a reasonable consumer's purchasing decision, then judicial intervention to suppress that falsehood may not be justified.

1. The Target Consumer

Our discussion of falsity and misleadingness has focused on the meaning of the claim, but we must ask: the meaning of the claim *to whom*? As it turns out, the answer involves both normative and descriptive elements, operationalized in the idea of the reasonable consumer of the relevant goods or services. This section focuses on the concept of the reasonable consumer and its variations in specific contexts. The reasonable consumer doesn't believe everything—this principle is one source of the puffery doctrine discussed in Chapter 4. But neither is the reasonable consumer required to be a scientist and a lawyer in every transaction.

Indeed, it is possible that the standard for reasonability might be low, at least in some circumstances. Consumers have always been inattentive to the details of ads. In 1759, Samuel Johnson noted that "advertisements are now so numerous that they are very negligently perused." SAMUEL JOHNSON, THE WORKS OF SAMUEL JOHNSON, LL.D 159 (Luke Hansard & Sons 1810). Given that we know that this inattention will occur, what is required of consumers to protect themselves, and what obligations should advertisers have to predict consumer reaction?

A. Introductory Note on Misleadingness and Belief

The standard applied under all false advertising laws asks whether an advertisement is "likely to mislead" consumers. For FTC and most state law purposes, no proof of actual deception is required; even an unsuccessful advertisement may be prohibited. *See, e.g.*, Novartis Corp. v. FTC, 223 F.3d 783 (D.C. Cir. 2000). Similarly, under the Lanham Act, once a plaintiff shows that an ad contains an explicit or implicit falsehood, injunctive relief has traditionally been available without proof that the falsehood actually convinced consumers to buy the advertised product or service.

"Misleading" is not, however, the same as "confusing." If consumers do not understand what message is being conveyed, as when they are presented with a "rating" that means nothing to them, there is no deception. *See* Royal Appliance Mfg. Co. v. Hoover Co., 845 F. Supp. 469 (N.D. Ohio 1994) ("While one might independently question the wisdom and effectiveness of a marketing campaign that leaves consumers shaking their heads in confusion, the Lanham Act does not speak to masochism.").

Traditionally, though not with perfect consistency, courts have held that consumers do not need to accept the false message as true in order to qualify as deceived. All that is required is that they perceive the false message—that is, understand that the advertiser wants them to believe the message. *See* Castrol, Inc. v. Pennzoil Quaker State Co., 2000 WL 1556019 (D.N.J. 2000) (enjoining a radio advertisement that was "not only inane, but insult[ed] the intelligence of the average consumer."); Am. Home Prods. Corp. v. Abbott Labs., 522 F. Supp. 1035 (S.D.N.Y. 1981) (enjoining claim interpreted by consumers to have false meaning, though "most consumers appear to discount or disregard this intended meaning"; "skepticism . . . does not affect the meaning itself or the fact that the meaning was conveyed.").

If consumers instead understand something else—for example, that the advertiser is joking—then they haven't been deceived. In *Ebsco Industries, Inc. v. LMN Enterprises, Inc.*, 89 F. Supp. 2d 1248 (N.D. Ala. 2000), a manufacturer of fishing lures included on its packaging stories about "Boomer Wells," said to be a professional fisherman, including stories of his winning a trip to Finland and a trip to "the slammer" after winning a fishing tournament. Purchasers had stated "that they either love the funny stories about Boomer Wells, or wish the defendants' brand would be more serious." Under the circumstances, the court found no evidence of likely deception.

Why require only evidence of *reception* and not the extra step of evidence of *deception*? First, if an express claim is falsely made, the law presumes that consumers are likely to be deceived by it. Once it has been demonstrated that consumers receive a message, it is the same as if the message had been explicitly stated. Second, consumers may be better judges of what messages they receive from ads than of what ultimately influences their purchasing decisions. If a claim is false and is being received, there is no justification for allowing it to influence consumers, even subliminally. Third, even if many consumers apply an automatic discount to most advertising claims, the law can still keep advertisers from calculated exploitation of consumer cynicism. Otherwise, there would be a classic problem of the market for lemons. True claims would be indistinguishable from a welter of false claims. As a result, courts generally only require that consumers receive a false message, not that they believe it, before granting relief.

What should happen if a defendant provides a properly conducted, convincing survey demonstrating that consumers overwhelmingly don't believe the message they receive? Is that proof that the message is puffery, even if it has the form of fact?

B.   The Historical Role of the Credulous Consumer

When Charles of the Ritz advertised that Rejuvenescence skin cream would "restore natural moisture necessary for a live, healthy skin" and produce a skin that would "know no drought years," the FTC alleged that this was a deceptive promise that the cream would actually reverse the aging process. Charles of the Ritz responded that no reasonable person would believe such a thing, but the court of appeals found the "reasonable" person irrelevant. The "law was not made for the protection of experts, but for the public—that vast multitude which includes the ignorant, the unthinking and the credulous." Charles of the Ritz Dist. Corp. v. FTC, 143 F.2d 676 (2d Cir. 1944).

The FTC staff even brought a complaint against the maker of a bathing garment (to be worn under a bathing suit) advertised as "invisible." The commission dismissed the case, reasoning that:

> [a]n advertiser cannot be charged with liability in respect of every conceivable misconception, however outlandish, to which his representations might be subject among the foolish or feeble-minded. . . . Perhaps a few misguided souls believe, for example, that all "Danish pastry" is made in Denmark. Is it therefore an actionable deception to advertise "Danish pastry" when it is made in this country? Of course not.

Heinz W. Kirchner, 63 F.T.C. 1282 (1963).

Even though the FTC has abandoned this standard, the "credulous consumer" concept remains in some state consumer protection cases. See, e.g., Weinberg v. Sun Co., 740 A.2d 1152 (Pa. 1999) (Pennsylvania Unfair Trade Practices and Consumer Protection Law); Doe v. Boys Clubs, Inc., 907 S.W.2d 472 (Tex. 1995) (Texas Deceptive Trade Practices Act). Unless a state has recent precedent applying this standard, however, it may be unwise for a plaintiff to rely on it even if there is older case law using this language, given the modern trend. See, e.g., Freeman v. Time, Inc., 68 F.3d 285 (9th Cir. 1995) (interpreting California statutes to protect a person of ordinary intelligence, unless particularly gullible consumers are targeted).

The original formulation of the standard can be read as an empirical claim: The vast multitude of the public includes those who are ignorant, unthinking and/or credulous. If, as some tort cases hold, "[a] drunken man is as much entitled to a safe street as a sober one, and much more in need of it," Robinson v. Pioche, Bayerque & Co., 5 Cal. 460 (1855), then doesn't the same reasoning hold for advertising?

Or should we worry more about discouraging wariness? Do we want the ignorant, unthinking and credulous to take more care, and *can* we make them do so? In other words, would a few bad experiences with believing ad claims really encourage them to become more educated, thoughtful and skeptical? Marketers tend to identify certain groups as having a generally high or generally low skepticism about ads, suggesting that it might be hard for the legal regime to have significant effects on consumers' default level of wariness. See, e.g., Prendergast et al., *A Hong Kong Study of Advertising Credibility*, 26 J. CONSUMER MKTG. 320 (2009) (skeptical consumers tend to be older and more educated than credulous ones and to have more self-esteem).

Recall the facts of *Vokes v. Arthur Murray, Inc.*, 212 So. 2d 906 (Fla. Ct. App. 1968), from Chapter 3. Was Audrey Vokes a credulous consumer? An average consumer? What standard did the court use to protect her?

C.   The Reasonable Consumer

In 1983, in response to congressional directives to revisit its policies, the FTC issued a new Policy Statement. *See* FTC Policy Statement on Deception, Appended to Cliffdale Associates, Inc., 103 F.T.C. 110 (1984). First, the FTC took the position that a practice is deceptive if it is "likely to mislead," rather than having a "tendency to mislead." Second, the FTC would examine the practice from "the perspective of a consumer acting reasonably in the circumstances. If the representation or practice affects or is directed primarily to a particular group, the commission examines reasonableness from the perspective of that group." And finally, the practice would have to be material—"likely to affect the consumer's conduct or decision with regard to a product or service." Courts applying the Lanham Act also use these standards. In general, European regulators also use the concept of the average or reasonable consumer, though they are likely to be more concerned with vulnerable consumers in a mixed population.

If a practice is "likely to mislead" a substantial number of the relevant consumers, then is anything additional gained by asking if they are acting reasonably? Can you imagine a situation where a practice would be likely to mislead a substantial number of consumers who were not acting reasonably under the circumstances? In practice, regulators and courts are likely to interpret these two requirements in tandem *if*—and it is a big if—they have not already deemed the representation at issue to be puffery.

The reasonable consumer standard is flexible. Because the focus is on the relevant consumers, an ad targeted at children will be evaluated from their perspective. Children are presumed to have less experience sorting truth from untruth. *See, e.g.*, ITT Continental Baking Co. v. FTC, 532 F.2d 207 (upholding FTC's determination that advertising for Wonder Bread was deceptive as to children, who were targeted). Similarly, advertisements targeted at other vulnerable populations (e.g., people in search of magical charms or cures for serious illnesses) are evaluated from their perspectives. *See* Gottlieb v. Schaffer, 141 F. Supp. 7 (S.D.N.Y. 1956) (claims that "magical or necromantic articles" would produce good luck and romantic success constituted mail fraud; products were targeted "only to the ignorant, superstitious and credulous, who by reason of the representations might rely upon the worthless articles"); FTC Policy Statement on Deception § III ("[T]erminally ill consumers might be particularly susceptible to exaggerated cure claims.").

According to the FTC Policy Statement, "[t]o be considered reasonable, the interpretation or reaction does not have to be the only one. When a seller's representation conveys more than one meaning to reasonable consumers, one of which is false, the seller is liable for the misleading interpretation." In addition, if an advertiser intends a meaning, that interpretation will be presumed reasonable. And reasonability is not necessarily the same thing as rationality; predictable cognitive failures can be taken into account (as advertisers are surely doing when they run ads). *See* Porter & Dietsch, 90 F.T.C. 770 (1977) ("[M]any people who need or want to lose weight regard dieting as bitter medicine. To these corpulent consumers, the promises of weight loss without dieting are the Siren's call, and advertising that heralds unrestrained consumption while muting the inevitable need for temperance, if not abstinence, simply does not pass muster."), *aff'd*, 605 F.2d 294 (7th Cir. 1979).

Courts sometimes determine a reasonable consumer's understanding as a matter of law, even without evidence. *See* Oswego Laborers' Local 214 Pension Fund v. Marine Midland Bank, 647 N.E.2d 741 (N.Y. 1995). Depending on the situation, a reasonable consumer might have to consult other available information rather than relying solely on the advertiser's claims. (Recall the *New York Law School* case from Chapter 3.) Moreover, a reasonable consumer isn't necessarily entitled to rely on a slogan or catchphrase, especially where it should be clear that individual results may vary. A consumer who failed to amass "True Savings" as a result of a telephone company's "True Savings" slogan had no remedy under the "reasonable consumer" standard. Marcus v. AT&T Corp., 938 F. Supp. 1158 (S.D.N.Y. 1996). Another court held that a reasonable consumer would use common sense and would not expect a telephone company's billing to be calculated in seconds. Porr v. NYNEX Corp., 230 A.D.2d 564 (2d Dep't 1997). (Is the factual, commonsense basis for this conclusion still valid?)

In fact, the difference between the "reasonable" and "credulous" standards may not be that significant in the majority of cases. The "reasonable consumer" is an average target consumer. An ad violates the FTC Act if it misleads a substantial number of consumers, even if the majority are not misled. FTC Policy Statement on Deception, § III (Oct. 14, 1983) n. 20. Especially if an advertiser exploits the credulity of its target consumers, it can't rely on *caveat emptor*—the rule that the FTC Act and similar state laws were enacted precisely to reverse. *See* FTC v. Standard Educ. Soc., 302 U.S. 112 (1937) ("There is no duty resting upon a citizen to suspect the honesty of those with whom he transacts business. Laws are made to protect the trusting as well as the suspicious.").

The modern sales context also makes a difference. Given how many products and services are on the market, it would be impossible, and indeed unreasonable, for even the most prudent consumer to learn all the necessary information to evaluate them all. Thus, for example, an average consumer is not likely to know that 30% of the calcium in milk is lost in the process of making cheese. *See* Kraft, Inc. v. FTC, 970 F.2d 311 (7th Cir. 1992); *see also* Troncoso v. TGI Friday's Inc., 2020 WL 3051020 (S.D.N.Y. Jun. 8, 2020) ("A reasonable consumer would not understand that potato starch and potato flakes could not contain potato peels, and thus would not believe that the list of ingredients reversed the label's representation that the product contains potato peels.").

However, what is "reasonable" has limits. *See, e.g.*, Kang v. P.F. Chang's China Bistro, Inc., 2020 WL 2027596 (C.D. Cal. Jan. 9, 2020) (no reasonable consumer would think that food with "krab mix" contained actual crab meat); Pelayo v. Nestle USA, Inc., 989 F. Supp. 2d 973, 979 (C.D. Cal. 2013) (no reasonable consumer would be misled by the use of the words "All Natural" on pasta, where pasta contained two artificial ingredients); McKinnis v. Kellog USA, 2007 WL 4766060 (C.D. Cal. Sept. 19, 2007) (no reasonable consumer would be misled by the word "Froot" in "Froot Loops" into believing the product contained "Fruit"); Werbel v. Pepsico, Inc., 2010 WL 2673860 (N.D. Cal. July 2, 2010) (no reasonable consumer would be led to believe that "Cap'n Crunch's Crunch Berries" cereal contained real fruit berries despite the use of the word berries in the product); Welk v. Beam Suntory Import Co., 124 F. Supp.3d 1039 (S.D. Cal. 2015) (no reasonable consumer expects that "handmade" bourbon is made without machines). *But see, e.g.*, Dumont v. Reily Foods Co.,

934 F.3d 35 (1st Cir. 2019) (reasonable consumers could think "Hazelnut Crème" coffee contained hazelnuts).

Reasonable consumers take at least some factual claims at face value, even if they know that a certain percentage is unreliable. The costs of sorting the false from the true are too great. For smaller purchases, it's even reasonable not to think much about ad claims at all. *See* Sterling Drug, Inc. v. FTC, 741 F.2d 1146 (9th Cir. 1984) (approving FTC's reliance on testimony that "consumers did not devote mental energy to interpreting [analgesic] advertisements and would not 'rationally process advertising communications' " to show that "given a broad general representation of 'quality,' consumers would not attempt to analyze the components of quality.").

Even if the subject matter is expensive or important, reasonable consumers who lacks the specialized information necessary to evaluate a claim are allowed to rely on the advertiser's apparent authority because they have no practical alternative. Thus, for example, an average consumer acting reasonably won't know much about credit insurance. *See* Card v. Chase Manhattan Bank, 669 N.Y.S.2d 117 (Civil Ct., City of N.Y. 1996). Consumers may also reasonably rely on "the representations of an apparently reputable firm staffed by experts and specializing in" the relevant market, such as the market for rare and valuable coins. *See* FTC v. Sec. Rare Coin & Bullion Corp., 931 F.2d 1312 (9th Cir. 1991).

The European Community has also adopted what looks like a flexible standard for the consumer's reasonability. Unfair Commercial Practices Directive, 2005/29/EC (Preamble par. 18) ("[T]his Directive takes as a benchmark the average consumer, who is reasonably well-informed and reasonably observant and circumspect, taking into account social, cultural and linguistic factors, as interpreted by the Court of Justice, but also contains provisions aimed at preventing the exploitation of consumers whose characteristics make them particularly vulnerable to unfair commercial practices."); *see also id.* Art. 5 ("Commercial practices which are likely to materially distort the economic behaviour only of a clearly identifiable group of consumers who are particularly vulnerable to the practice or the underlying product because of their mental or physical infirmity, age or credulity in a way which the trader could reasonably be expected to foresee, shall be assessed from the perspective of the average member of that group. This is without prejudice to the common and legitimate advertising practice of making exaggerated statements or statements which are not meant to be taken literally.").

D.   The Sophisticated Consumer

The law generally presumes that a sophisticated audience—usually, one composed of people with experience in the topic at hand—is less likely to be fooled. This is especially true when the issue is misleadingness rather than pure falsity. Sophisticated groups include:

- advertising buyers, *see* San Juan Star v. Casiano Communic., Inc., 85 F. Supp. 2d 89 (D.P.R. 2000);
- doctors, *see* FTC Policy Statement § III; *cf. ONY, supra*;
- hospitals, *see* First Health Gp. Corp. v. United Payors & United Providers Inc., 95 F. Supp. 2d 845 (N.D. Ill. 2000);

- retailers, *see* Plough, Inc. v. Johnson & Johnson Baby Prods. Co., 532 F. Supp. 714 (D. Del. 1982); FASA Corp. v. Playmates Toys, Inc., 107 F.3d 140 (7th Cir. 1997); and
- veterinarians, *see* Pfizer, Inc. v. Merial, Ltd., 2000 WL 640669 (S.D.N.Y. 2000).

Buyer sophistication won't always translate into advertiser wins. Specialized training in medicine or another field, for example, may not confer special ability to ferret out linguistic ambiguities and uncertainties in advertising claims. *Cf.* CARL ELLIOTT, WHITE COAT, BLACK HAT: ADVENTURES ON THE DARK SIDE OF MEDICINE (2010) ("The best mark is often a person to whom the possibility of a con never occurs, simply because he thinks he is too smart to be tricked. . . . Many doctors know nothing about advertising, salesmanship, or public relations. They believe these are jobs for people who could not get into medical school. This is probably why doctors are so easily fooled."). Sophistication also can't protect against hard-to-verify false claims, such as misrepresentations about product ingredients. *See* Genderm Corp. v. Biozone Labs., 1992 WL 220638 (N.D. Ill. Sept. 3, 1992) (finding actionable misrepresentation of a drug's active ingredient to physicians and pharmacists).

In close cases, the principle that all audiences are entitled to truth in advertising may control. *See* JR Tobacco, Inc. v. Davidoff of Geneva (CT), Inc., 957 F. Supp. 426 (S.D.N.Y. 1997) ("Regardless of the sophistication JR attributes to its audience [of cigar buyers], purchasers are entitled to truthful statements. . . ."). So an advertiser who touted its legal directory as "official" gave it an "imprimatur of state authority," and, even though the audience of lawyers might have been unlikely to regard the directory as state-sponsored, the term was still found to be literally false. *See* Skinder-Strauss Assoc. v. Mass. Continuing Legal Educ., 914 F. Supp. 665 (D. Mass. 1995).

In addition, a statement that specialists would understand correctly may mislead a general audience. *See* Zauderer v. Office of Disciplinary Counsel of Supreme Court of Ohio, 471 U.S. 626 (1985) (lawyer's statements to public that clients would not have to pay "legal fees" if their lawsuits were unsuccessful were likely to deceive without disclosure that clients would have to pay costs of action; "it is a commonplace that members of the public are often unaware of the technical meanings of such terms as 'fees' and 'costs'—terms that, in ordinary usage, might well be virtually interchangeable.").

E. A "Not Insubstantial Number" of Consumers

An ad only violates the law if it's *likely* to deceive consumers. Minimal deception resulting from unusual carelessness or idiosyncratic interpretations is insufficient to show false advertising. Thus, to justify relief, a "not insubstantial number" (the general phrase used in Lanham Act cases) or a "substantial number" (the standard adopted by the FTC) of consumers must be likely to be deceived.

The different wording doesn't seem to make a difference in result. Recall that the FTC doesn't need to provide consumer surveys, so it will less often need to speak in percentage terms than Lanham Act plaintiffs. (The FTC and NAD will, however, consider consumer evidence when it's available and generally react similarly to surveys as courts applying the

Lanham Act do.) Even with the Lanham Act, if a statement is false on its face, courts won't require independent proof that a substantial number of consumers are actually deceived.

When numbers are present, the percentage considered "substantial" varies depending on the circumstances. Unsurprisingly, the FTC takes the position that, where deception is likely to cause very serious harm, the advertiser will be held to a very high standard, and Lanham Act courts have reasoned similarly when products involve human safety. *See, e.g.*, Firestone Tire & Rubber Co., 81 F.T.C. 429 (1972), *aff'd*, 481 F.2d 246 (6th Cir. 1973); Am. Home Prods. Corp. v. Johnson & Johnson, 654 F. Supp. 568 (S.D.N.Y. 1987).

But what litigants and courts really want to know is: What percentage of deceived consumers is sufficient to enjoin an ad? The case law here comes from the Lanham Act, and because false advertising sits side by side with trademark infringement in the Lanham Act, courts have drawn freely from both bodies of law in evaluating survey evidence, including the percentage of deception that will suffice to show likely deception/confusion.

We will consider surveys in more detail later, but a good rule of thumb is that a good, well-controlled survey that shows net 20% or greater deception will be highly persuasive for the plaintiff, and that one that shows 10% or less will be highly persuasive for the defendant. *Compare* McNeilab, Inc. v. Am. Home Prods. Corp., 675 F. Supp. 819 (S.D.N.Y. 1987), *aff'd*, 848 F.2d 34 (2d Cir. 1988) (21–34% was not insignificant); *and* R.J. Reynolds Tobacco Co. v. Loew's Theatres, Inc. 522 F. Supp. 867 (S.D.N.Y. 1980) (20–33% was not insignificant), *with In Re* Campbell Soup Co., NAD Case No. 3302 (closed May 21, 1996) (survey finding of slightly above 10% confusion "insufficient to warrant a finding that people are being misled."). For the substantial number of cases in which survey numbers fall in the middle of that range, other factors (specifically the court's own assessment of likely deception) will probably determine the outcome. *See* Johnson & Johnson v. Carter-Wallace, Inc., 487 F. Supp. 740 (S.D.N.Y. 1979) (15% was not insubstantial).

There are always outliers, however. One court found 27% confusion not to be substantial enough. Borden, Inc. v. Kraft, Inc., 224 U.S.P.Q. 811 (N.D. Ill. 1984). Lower percentages will be more persuasive when that still means a large absolute number of consumers. *See* James Burrough, Ltd. v. Sign of the Beefeater, Inc., 540 F.2d 266 (7th Cir. 1976) (court "cannot agree that 15% is 'small'' percentage of deception, given the size of the restaurant-going community); Humble Oil & Refining Co. v. Am. Oil Co., 405 F.2d 803 (8th Cir. 1969) ("11% of a [consumer population] figure in the millions is a high number.").

In cases where courts are dealing with a small minority of deceived or confused consumers, don't forget the super-majority of consumers who do not find the ads problematic—or maybe they even find the ads helpful. *Cf.* Michael Grynberg, *Trademark Litigation as Consumer Conflict*, 83 N.Y.U. L. REV. 60 (2008). How should courts consider the interests of these consumers, and who speaks for them?

2.   Materiality

Not all false claims actually change consumer behavior. To succeed, a plaintiff must show that the false claim is "material."

A.   Introduction (adapted from Rebecca Tushnet, Running the Gamut from A to B: Federal Trademark and False Advertising Law, 159 U. Penn. L. Rev. 1305 (2010))

To be actionable under Section 43(a)(1)(B), a falsehood must be material: It must be likely to affect a reasonable consumer's purchasing decision because not all deceptions affect consumer decisions. Materiality, among other concepts, allows courts to exonerate certain ad claims on their face as non-actionable puffery because consumers allegedly don't rely on general superiority claims or other puffing. Consumers are irrebuttably presumed not to rely on sufficiently vague or exaggerated claims.

Until the late twentieth century, the test for false advertising under the Lanham Act could be simply stated: A plaintiff only needed to show falsity plus harm to prevail. Materiality is intuitively part of harm because harm only comes when there is a causal link between the falsehood and consumers' behavior. Materiality is now generally split out into a separate requirement in the more elaborate modern multifactor test for false advertising. Some courts applying the Lanham Act have demanded a showing that an advertiser "misrepresented an 'inherent quality or characteristic'" of a product or service, but this requirement is essentially equivalent to materiality.

Given the variety of products and services on the market, the number of possible material claims is almost infinite. A few litigated examples: a mixer's speed and efficiency; a tax preparer's claim to offer instant "refunds" rather than instant loans against anticipated refunds; and a representation that a product was EPA-approved. Still, not every divergence between claim and reality is material: Courts have denied false advertising claims based on overstatements of the number of the defendant's real estate transactions by 4%; statements about technical aspects of a product when those aspects were not generally understood by and were not a significant concern of purchasers; statements that reimbursements would be "two and a half times faster" than competitors' reimbursements; statements that sports scores were updated "from the arena" when they actually were taken from simultaneous broadcasts; and a letter that warned of three lawsuits against a competitor's product when there were only two lawsuits.

In general, courts have evaluated materiality by inquiring whether, as a matter of common sense and the intended uses of the product or service, a claim is likely to be relevant to a purchasing decision. Cases have often taken materiality for granted, especially when a claim is central to an advertising campaign or relates to health or safety. Courts have also developed various doctrines allowing them to presume materiality in cases of outright falsity or bad intent.

In rare cases, courts have used materiality to express uncertainty about the effects of advertising writ large: One court thought that a cough syrup's claim to work instantly was not likely to be material because "[p]arents buy what their pediatrician or their own experience tells them is most effective." Sandoz Pharm. Corp. v. Richardson-Vicks, Inc., 735 F. Supp. 597 (D. Del. 1989).

Materiality can also help explain the "#1 Choice of Doctors" case, *Mead Johnson & Co. v. Abbott Labs.*, 201 F.3d 883, modified by 209 F.3d 1032 (7th Cir. 2000). In that case, the Seventh Circuit rejected the relevance of a survey showing that many consumers believed that "#1 Choice of Doctors" meant that most doctors preferred Abbott's infant formula, when in fact most doctors thought the products were all basically the same. Because Abbott's formula was the first choice *of the doctors who had a preference* (a not insignificant number, though not a majority), the court held that the claim was literally true and that survey evidence was inappropriate. The Seventh Circuit distinguished between claims that are "misleading" and claims that are merely "misunderstood" by consumers. Only the former, the court ruled, can be found to violate the Lanham Act. One way to read this is that the Lanham Act requires intentional falsity; *misleading* can imply a knowing misstatement, whereas a consumer might misunderstand an innocent, well-meant claim.

A better way to think about the difference between misunderstood and misleading claims is to focus on materiality. One may misunderstand a fact in the abstract: I could be wrong about how big a computer's hard drive is. If I am misled, however, I am *led*: induced, or at least potentially induced, to change my position by my misunderstanding, as when I am more likely to buy the computer because of my misunderstanding. It is the combination of misunderstanding and likelihood of action—materiality—that produces misleadingness. Understood in that way, *Mead Johnson*'s distinction makes some sense.

The Seventh Circuit's attempt to focus on materiality in this somewhat confusing way is consistent with a general judicial trend of greater attention to materiality, albeit without a standardized vocabulary. The case that triggered greater attention to materiality was *Pizza Hut v. Papa John's*, whose facts are introduced *supra*. In the following excerpt, the court of appeals reverses the jury finding of false advertising. Given what you've read in the introductory materials, why wouldn't "Better ingredients" and similar claims be presumptively material to consumers?

PIZZA HUT, INC. V. PAPA JOHN'S INT'L, INC., 227 F.3D 489 (5TH CIR. 2000)

[Review the facts from the Puffery section in Chapter 4.] . . . Concluding that when the slogan ["Better Ingredients. Better Pizza."] was used as the tag line in the sauce and dough ads it became misleading, we must now determine whether reasonable consumers would have a tendency to rely on this misleading statement of fact in making their purchasing decisions. We conclude that Pizza Hut has failed to adduce evidence establishing that the misleading statement of fact conveyed by the ads and the slogan was material to the consumers to which the slogan was directed. Consequently, because such evidence of materiality is necessary to establish liability under the Lanham Act, the district court erred in denying Papa John's motion for judgment as a matter of law.

As previously discussed, none of the underlying facts supporting Papa John's claims of ingredient superiority made in connection with the slogan were literally false. Consequently, in order to satisfy its prima facie case, Pizza Hut was required to submit evidence establishing that the impliedly false or misleading statements were material to, that is, they had a tendency to influence the purchasing decisions of, the consumers to which they were directed. *See* American Council, 185 F.3d at 614 (stating that "a plaintiff relying upon statements that are literally true yet misleading cannot obtain relief by arguing how consumers could react; it must show how consumers actually do react."). We conclude that the evidence proffered by Pizza Hut fails to make an adequate showing.

. . . . Although Papa John's 1998 Awareness, Usage & Attitude Tracking Study showed that 48% of the respondents believe that "Papa John's has better ingredients than other national pizza chains," the study failed to indicate whether the conclusions resulted from the advertisements at issue, or from personal eating experiences, or from a combination of both. Consequently, the results of this study are not reliable or probative to test whether the slogan was material. Further, Pizza Hut provides no precedent, and we are aware of none, that stands for the proposition that the subjective intent of the defendant's corporate executives to convey a particular message is evidence of the fact that consumers in fact relied on the message to make their purchases. Thus, this evidence does not address the ultimate issue of materiality.

NOTES AND QUESTIONS

How could Pizza Hut have proved materiality, especially if many people have in fact eaten at Papa John's and thus have personal experience? What is the relevance of the evidence that advertising can affect how people remember their own sensory experiences of a product, discussed in Chapter 4?

Although survey evidence of materiality is unlikely to be required in other cases, the *Pizza Hut* case, and others like it, shows an increased attention to particularized evidence of materiality, such as statements from consumers that they care about a specific product claim. Thus, in a case involving "100%" pomegranate juice that was, in fact, made mostly of other juices and added coloring, the court carefully went through evidence that consumers cared that a product whose name was "100% Pomegranate Juice" actually contained pomegranate juice. POM Wonderful LLC v. Purely Juice, Inc., 2008 WL 4222045 (C.D. Cal. Jul. 17, 2008). The common sense that consumers care about health, safety and/or explicit product claims that are the focus of advertising is no longer enough to guarantee a victory for a Lanham Act plaintiff, though it will often suffice if unchallenged.

Some courts presume that explicitly false claims are material. *See, e.g.*, Pizza Hut, Inc. v. Papa John's Int'l, Inc., 227 F.3d 489 (5th Cir. 2000); AECOM Energy & Constr., Inc. v. Ripley, 348 F. Supp. 3d 1038 (C.D. Cal. 2018); Bracco Diagnostics, Inc. v. Amersham Health, Inc., 627 F. Supp. 2d 384 (D.N.J. 2009). Other courts reject any such presumption. *See, e.g.*, Johnson & Johnson Vision Care. Inc. v. 1-800 Contacts. Inc., 299 F.3d 1242 (11th Cir. 2002); Cashmere & Camel Hair Mfrs. Institute v. Saks Fifth Ave, 284 F.3d 302 (1st Cir. 2002); S.C. Johnson & Son, Inc. v. Clorox Co., 241 F.3d 232 (2d Cir. 2001) ("The plaintiff must establish materiality even when a the court finds that the defendant's advertisement is literally false.").

Depending on the evidence, materiality may be a question of fact for a jury. *See* LivePerson, Inc. v. 24/7 Customer, Inc., 83 F. Supp. 3d 501 (S.D.N.Y. 2015) ("[M]ateriality is generally a question of fact."); Fed. Express Corp. v. USPS, 40 F. Supp. 2d 943 (W.D. Tenn. 1999) (finding that the question of whether claims to be a "company" and to offer "worldwide" service were material required further factual development regarding consumer perceptions); Oil Heat Inst. v. Nw. Nat'l Gas, 708 F. Supp. 1118 (D. Or. 1988) (holding that jury could reasonably conclude that claims regarding amount of maintenance required by natural gas equipment were material). What kind of evidence would be relevant for a jury making this determination?

The Puffery/Materiality Interface. As the introductory excerpt to this section suggested, puffery is in some ways the flip side of materiality. If the court is convinced that a statement is (or should be) immaterial, it may call that statement puffery. But to the extent that puffery is a legal fiction—as a matter of law, the claim at issue didn't change a substantial number of reasonable consumers' behavior—is it inherently incompatible with an empirical approach to materiality?

Materiality Doesn't Have to be Rational. Regardless of how it is shown, materiality remains a matter of subjective consumer preference. "The public is entitled to get what it chooses, though the choice may be dictated by caprice or by fashion or perhaps by ignorance." FTC v. Algoma Lumber Co., 291 U.S. 67 (1934) (Cardozo, J.). "[P]eople like to get what they think they are getting, and courts have steadfastly refused in this class of cases to demand justification for their preferences. Shoddy and petty motives may control those preferences; but if the buyers wish to be snobs, the law will protect them in their snobbery." Benton Announcements v. FTC, 130 F.2d 254 (1942) (per curiam).

Therefore, an affirmative misrepresentation of EPA approval was enjoined because consumers are likely to consider it significant. Performance Indust. Inc. v. Koos Inc., 18 U.S.P.Q.2d 1767 (E.D. Pa. 1990) ("In today's environmentally conscious world, [false claims regarding environmental safety] are serious misrepresentations. Consumers these days seem to favor products that are environmentally benign and to disdain those that are environmentally harsh. Middlemen merchants would tend to fill their inventories with the former. Thus, the potential economic impact is pronounced.").

The Supreme Court has embraced the idea that materiality depends on consumers' subjective preferences. A seller may regard consumers' preferences for new goods instead of reprocessed ones, or for verified product claims, as "an annoying or irrational habit," and may reason that "when the habit is broken the buyer will be satisfied with the performance of the product he receives." Nonetheless, misrepresentation may not be used to break such bad habits. FTC v. Colgate-Palmolive Co., 380 U.S. 374 (1965).

The Role of Contextual Factors in Judging Materiality. A statement's prominence (or lack thereof) in an advertisement may be relevant to its materiality. For example, statements that sports updates provided by a pager company came "from the arena" (they were actually taken from broadcasts) were immaterial "minutiae," "a reality demonstrated by their lack of prominence in the advertisement." The court reasoned that if the claim "Nationwide game updates from the arena" was instead "Nationwide game updates," "I find it difficult to envision (and NBA has not shown otherwise) that consumers suddenly would reassess their decisions to purchase [the pager]." NBA v. Sports Team Analysis & Tracking Sys., Inc., 939 F. Supp. 1071 (S.D.N.Y. 1996), *aff'd in relevant part sub nom.* National Basketball Ass'n v. Motorola, Inc., 105 F.3d 841 (2d Cir. 1997). Prominence in an ad is certainly relevant to the advertiser's belief in the importance of the statement, which is often a good guide to consumer reactions. *See* Pegasystems, Inc. v. Appian Corp., 2020 WL 2616280 (D. Mass. May 22, 2020) (changes to graph titles in presentation that was on screen for thirty seconds were not plausibly material to "the sophisticated consumers who purchase business process management software"; it was also implausible that "the precise number of currently certified professionals, as conveyed in passing on a presentation slide," would be material).

In *Schick Manufacturing, Inc. v. Gillette Co.*, 372 F. Supp. 2d 273 (D. Conn. 2005), whose facts are set forth in the section on explicit falsity, the court noted that "[b]ecause of the expense of television advertising, companies have a very short period of time in which to create a 'reason to believe' and are generally forced to pitch only the key qualities and characteristics of the product advertised." The court thus concluded:

> It is clear that whether the M3 Power raises hairs is material. Gillette's employees testified that television advertising time is too valuable to include things that are "unimportant." Furthermore, in this case, hair extension is the "reason to believe" that the M3 Power is a worthwhile product. The magnitude and frequency of that effect are also, therefore, material. Whether a material element of a product's performance happens very often and how often that element happens are, in themselves, material. . . .

Materiality and the NAD. The NAD takes the position that materiality is not relevant to NAD's inquiry, which is focused on determining whether the advertiser has provided a reasonable basis substantiating all messages reasonably conveyed by its advertising. Sprint Corp. (Sprint Wireless Services), NAD Case #5812 (2/18/15).

B.   Materiality and the FTC

The FTC applies a presumption of materiality to several types of claims: (1) express claims (since the advertiser's reason for making a claim is ordinarily that consumers would rely on it); (2) implied claims, where the seller intended to make the claim; (3) omissions, where the seller knew that an ordinary consumer would need the omitted information to evaluate the product or service; and (4) claims that significantly involve health, safety or other matters with which reasonable consumers would be concerned. This last category includes claims that concern the purpose, safety, healthfulness, efficacy or cost of the product or service; its durability, performance, warranties or quality; or findings by another agency regarding the product. FTC Policy Statement on Deception, 103 F.T.C. 174, appended to Cliffdale Assocs., 103 F.T.C. 110 (1984).

In one case, the advertiser offered an ad agency executive's opinion that consumers didn't care about aspirin content for rub-on pain relievers such as the company's Aspercreme. The FTC rejected this opinion, given research showing that a substantial percentage of consumers preferred aspirin over non-aspirin pain relievers. Thus, it was material that consumers believed that Aspercreme contained aspirin. Thompson Med. Co., 104 F.T.C. 648 (1984), *aff'd*, 791 F.2d 189 (D.C. Cir. 1986). In addition, a price premium charged for the misleading product compared to the prices of non-misleading products may be good extrinsic evidence that the misleading claim is material, since the advertiser expects consumers to be willing to pay extra for it. *See* Am. Home Prods., 98 F.T.C. 136 (1981), *aff'd*, 695 F.2d 681 (3d Cir. 1982). However, most FTC cases don't involve extrinsic evidence of materiality on either side. And, as the next case shows, an advertiser may face difficulty disavowing the materiality of a claim it has prominently made.

KRAFT, INC. V. FEDERAL TRADE COMMISSION, 970 F.2D 311 (7TH CIR. 1992)

Kraft, Inc. ("Kraft") asks us to review an order of the Federal Trade Commission ("FTC" or "Commission") finding that it violated [Sections] 5 and 12 of the Federal Trade Commission Act ("Act"). The FTC determined that Kraft, in an advertising campaign, had misrepresented information regarding the amount of calcium contained in Kraft Singles American Pasteurized Process Cheese Food ("Singles") relative to the calcium content in five ounces of milk and in imitation cheese slices. The FTC ordered Kraft to cease and desist from making these misrepresentations and Kraft filed this petition for review. We enforce the Commission's order.

I.

. . . Process cheese food slices, also known as "dairy slices," must contain at least 51% natural cheese by federal regulation. Imitation cheese slices, by contrast, contain little or no natural cheese and consist primarily of water, vegetable oil, flavoring agents, and fortifying agents. While imitation slices are as healthy as process cheese food slices in some nutrient categories, they are as a whole considered "nutritionally inferior" and must carry the label "imitation." . . .

Kraft Singles are process cheese food slices. In the early 1980s, Kraft began losing market share to an increasing number of imitation slices that were advertised as both less expens[ive] and equally nutritious as dairy slices like Singles. Kraft responded with a series of advertisements, collectively known as the "Five Ounces of Milk" campaign, designed to inform consumers that Kraft Singles cost more than imitation slices because they are made from five ounces of milk rather than less expensive ingredients. The ads also focused on the calcium content of Kraft Singles in an effort to capitalize on growing consumer interest in adequate calcium consumption.

The FTC filed a complaint against Kraft charging that this advertising campaign materially misrepresented the calcium content and relative calcium benefit of Kraft Singles. The FTC Act makes it unlawful to engage in unfair or deceptive commercial practices, 15 U.S.C. § 45, or to induce consumers to purchase certain products through advertising that is misleading in a material respect. Thus, an advertisement is deceptive under the Act if it is likely to mislead consumers, acting reasonably under the circumstances, in a material respect. In implementing this standard, the Commission examines the overall net impression of an ad and engages in a three-part inquiry: (1) what claims are conveyed in the ad; (2) are those claims false or misleading; and (3) are those claims material to prospective consumers.

Two facts are critical to understanding the allegations against Kraft. First, although Kraft does use five ounces of milk in making each Kraft Single, roughly 30% of the calcium contained in the milk is lost during processing. Second, the vast majority of imitation slices sold in the United States contain 15% of the U.S. Recommended Daily Allowance (RDA) of calcium per ounce, roughly the same amount contained in Kraft Singles. Specifically then, the FTC complaint alleged that the challenged advertisements made two implied claims, neither of which was true: (1) that a slice of Kraft Singles contains the same amount of calcium as five ounces of milk (the "milk equivalency" claim); and (2) that Kraft Singles contain more calcium than do most imitation cheese slices (the "imitation superiority" claim).

. . . The Skimp ads were designed to communicate the nutritional benefit of Kraft Singles by referring expressly to their milk and calcium content. The broadcast version of this ad on which the FTC focused contained the following audio copy:

> Lady (voice over): I admit it. I thought of skimping. Could you look into those big blue eyes and skimp on her? So I buy Kraft Singles. Imitation slices use hardly any milk. But Kraft has five ounces per slice. Five ounces. So her little bones get calcium they need to grow. No, she doesn't know what that big Kraft means. Good thing I do.

> Singers: Kraft Singles. More milk makes 'em . . . more milk makes 'em good.

> Lady (voice over): Skimp on her? No way.

The visual image corresponding to this copy shows, among other things, milk pouring into a glass until it reaches a mark on the glass denoted "five ounces." The commercial also shows milk pouring into a glass which bears the phrase "5 oz. milk slice" and which gradually becomes part of the label on a package of Singles. In January 1986, Kraft revised this ad, changing "Kraft has five ounces per slice" to "Kraft is made from five ounces per slice," and in March 1987, Kraft added the disclosure, "one 3/4 ounce slice has 70% of the calcium of five ounces of milk" as a subscript in the television commercial and as a footnote in the print ads.
. . .

After a lengthy trial, the Administrative Law Judge (ALJ) concluded that [the Skimp ad and another ad violated the FTCA. The FTC affirmed the ALJ's decision, finding that the ad conveyed a milk equivalency claim and an imitation superiority claim].

. . . The FTC next found that the claims were material to consumers. It concluded that the milk equivalency claim is a health-related claim that reasonable consumers would find important and that Kraft believed that the claim induced consumers to purchase Singles. The FTC presumed that the imitation superiority claim was material because it found that Kraft intended to make that claim. It also found that the materiality of that claim was demonstrated by evidence that the challenged ads led to increased sales despite a substantially higher price for Singles than for imitation slices. . . .

II.

Our standard for reviewing FTC findings has been traditionally limited to the highly deferential, substantial evidence test. . . . Accordingly, we decline to review de novo the FTC's findings and, with the substantial evidence test in mind, turn to the facts of this case.

III.

. . . A claim is considered material if it "involves information that is important to consumers and, hence, likely to affect their choice of, or conduct regarding a product." The Commission is entitled to apply, within reason, a presumption of materiality, and it does so with three types of claims: (1) express claims; (2) implied claims where there is evidence that the seller intended to make the claim; and (3) claims that significantly involve health, safety, or other areas with which reasonable consumers would be concerned. Absent one of these situations, the Commission examines the record and makes a finding of materiality or immateriality.

Here, the ALJ concluded that both claims were presumptively material because calcium is a significant health concern to consumers. The Commission upheld this conclusion, although it applied a presumption of materiality only to the imitation superiority claim. Kraft asserts the Commission's determination is not supported by substantial evidence. We disagree.

In determining that the milk equivalency claim was material to consumers, the FTC cited Kraft surveys showing that 71% of respondents rated calcium content an extremely or very important factor in their decision to buy Kraft Singles, and that 52% of female, and 40% of all respondents, reported significant personal concerns about adequate calcium consumption. The FTC further noted that the ads were targeted to female homemakers with children and that the 60 milligram difference between the calcium contained in five ounces of milk and that contained in a Kraft Single would make up for most of the RDA calcium deficiency shown in girls aged 9–11. Finally, the FTC found evidence in the record that Kraft designed the ads with the intent to capitalize on consumer calcium deficiency concerns.

Significantly, the FTC found further evidence of materiality in Kraft's conduct: [D]espite repeated warnings, Kraft persisted in running the challenged ads. Before the ads even ran, ABC television raised a red flag when it asked Kraft to substantiate the milk and calcium claims in the ads. Kraft's ad agency also warned Kraft in a legal memorandum to substantiate the claims before running the ads. Moreover, in October 1985, a consumer group warned Kraft that it believed the Skimp ads were potentially deceptive. Nonetheless, a high-level Kraft executive recommended that the ad copy remain unaltered because the "Singles business is growing for the first time in four years due in large part to the copy." Finally, the FTC and the California Attorney General's Office independently notified the company in early 1986 that investigations had been initiated to determine whether the ads conveyed the milk equivalency claims. Notwithstanding these warnings, Kraft continued to run the ads and even rejected proposed alternatives that would have allayed concerns over their deceptive nature. From this, the FTC inferred—we believe, reasonably—that Kraft thought the challenged milk equivalency claim induced consumers to purchase Singles and hence that the claim was material to consumers.

With regard to the imitation superiority claim, the Commission applied a presumption of materiality after finding evidence that Kraft intended the challenged ads to convey this message. It found this presumption buttressed by the fact that the challenged ad copy led to increased sales of Singles, even though they cost 40 percent more than imitation slices. Finally, the FTC determined that Kraft's consumer surveys were insufficient to rebut this inference and in particular criticized Kraft's survey methodology because it offered limited response options to consumers.

Kraft asserts that neither materiality finding is supported by substantial evidence. It contends that the survey evidence on which the Commission relied shows only that calcium, not milk equivalency, is important to consumers. Materiality, Kraft maintains, turns on whether the claim itself, rather than the subject matter of the claim, affects consumer decision-making; accordingly, the Commission had to show that consumers would have acted differently with knowledge that Singles contain 70% rather than 100% of the calcium in five ounces of milk. *See* FTC Policy Statement, 103 F.T.C. at 175 (claim is material if it is "likely to affect the consumer's conduct or decision with regard to a product"). With the inquiry defined in this manner, the only relevant evidence on point—a Kraft consumer survey showing that 1.7% of respondents would stop buying Singles if informed of the effect of processing on calcium content—definitively disproves materiality. With regard to its conduct, Kraft argues it persisted in running the ads because it thought the ads as a whole, not the milk equivalency claim per se, contributed to increased sales and that, in any event, it responded to warnings by making a good faith attempt to modify the ads. Kraft repeats these arguments in attacking the FTC's finding that imitation superiority claim was material to consumers, claiming the evidence adduced showed only that Kraft intended to use the ads to differentiate Singles from imitation slices based on milk content, and not on calcium content, and that sales increased as a result of this general theme; inferring that the imitation superiority claim contributed to increased sales is pure conjecture.

Kraft's arguments lack merit. The FTC found solid evidence that consumers placed great importance on calcium consumption and from this reasonably inferred that a claim quantifying the calcium in Kraft Singles would be material to consumers. It rationally concluded that a 30% exaggeration of calcium content was a nutritionally significant claim that would affect consumer purchasing decisions. This finding was supported by expert witnesses who agreed that consumers would prefer a slice of cheese with 100% of the calcium in five ounces of milk over one with only 70%. Likewise, the materiality presumption applied to the imitation superiority claim was supported by substantial evidence. This finding rested on internal company documents showing that Kraft designed the ads to deliver an imitation superiority message. Although Kraft produced a study refuting this finding, the Commission discounted that study after finding its methodology flawed. Kraft concedes that the Skimp ads increased sales of Singles, but contends that the Commission cannot carry its burden of demonstrating a linkage between the ads and the imitation superiority claim per se. However, this increase in sales corresponded directly with the ad campaign and indisputably reversed that sagging sales and market share of Kraft Singles that had been attributed to competition from imitation slices. Moreover, Kraft's increase in market share came at a time when Singles were priced roughly 40% higher than imitation slices. Thus, the Commission reasonably inferred that the imitation superiority message, as a central theme in the ads, contributed to increased sales and market share.

NOTES AND QUESTIONS

Which view of materiality is better: Kraft's contention that we should look specifically at the effect of *difference* between the truth and the misleading claim or the FTC's more general view? If there isn't much difference between the truth and the misleading claim, why did Kraft choose to advertise the misleading claim?

In *Novartis Corporation v. Federal Trade Commission*, 223 F.3d 783 (D.C. Cir. 2000), Novartis contested a materiality finding by arguing that the market share of its product (a back-pain remedy) had not increased during the period in which misleading advertising touted its superior efficacy. The court was unimpressed. "The FTC's definition of materiality . . . embraces any claim that is 'likely to mislead a reasonable consumer.' There is no requirement of actual deceit. If a claim is material because it is likely to deceive, it is not rendered otherwise simply because it is unsuccessfully advertised." How can something be both likely to affect a consumer's decision and unsuccessful? (If you're familiar with statistics, does Novartis have a correlation-causation problem?).

C.   Materiality in the Face of Consumer Reaction Evidence

Are there some claims so self-evidently material that evidence purporting to show the contrary should be disregarded, as happened to Kraft's evidence of immateriality? Consider the following case.

IDT TELECOM, INC. V. CVT PREPAID SOLUTIONS, INC., 2009 WL 5205968 (D.N.J. 2009)

Prepaid calling cards are sold in dollar denominations (e.g., $5, $10) and can be used to dial numerous destinations. The number of minutes available on a calling card is determined by the rate per minute of talk time to the destination called minus any fees and charges. Advertisements for prepaid phone cards focus solely on the number of minutes to the key destinations for that card. For example, a poster will emphasize that a card offers "250 minutes to the Dominican Republic."

[Defendants] used a system of fees and charges that could vary according to destination, length and duration of the call, and reduced the number of minutes available for talk time. . . . [P]osters informed consumers about the gross number of minutes of talk time. The posters also contained a disclaimer that addressed specific fees and charges as follows: "Application of surcharges and fees will have the effect of reducing total minutes actually received on the card from the minutes announced . . . . Prices and fees . . . are subject to change without notice." The same disclaimer was also included on the packaging that accompanied the calling cards.

. . . In addition to being false or misleading, the Plaintiffs must also prove that the Defendants' misrepresentation is "material, in that it is likely to confuse the purchasing decision." Defendants argue that the number of advertised minutes is completely immaterial to purchasers of prepaid calling cards. Defendants state that "[a]mong the most important factors for consumers are: (a) the number of minutes actually delivered by a card, rather than the advertised minutes; (b) the clarity of the connection; and (c) the connectivity of the card." Plaintiffs conducted a survey of potential prepaid calling card consumers. In this survey, they found that only 2 of 401 respondents indicated that Advertising/Posters/Flyers are how they "generally decide" which card to buy. The Johnson Report further states that only 3% of the consumers surveyed "look at the printed material in the store" to tell how many minutes are available on their cards. Defendants argue that these low numbers, on their own, prove that the advertisements are not material to the purchasing decisions of consumers. The Court is not convinced that low polling numbers in the Johnson report mean that the number of advertised minutes are, by law, immaterial to consumers. Because the advertisements go so clearly to the purpose of the product—the amount of minutes of talk time that they deliver—the statements are material as a matter of law. *See* S.C. Johnson & Son, Inc. v. Clorox Co., 241 F.3d 232, 238 (2d Cir. 2001) (lack of leakage is an inherent quality or characteristic of Ziploc storage bags such that a claim was clearly material). Thus, summary judgment with relation to the allegedly false and misleading posters is denied.

NOTES AND QUESTIONS

Didn't the court find materiality in the face of strong evidence that consumers ignore the claims at issue? Why? In *Boshnack v. Widow Jane Distilleries LLC*, 2020 WL 3000358, No. 19cv8812 (DLC) (S.D.N.Y. Jun. 4, 2020), the challenged statement was that the water used in making defendant's expensive whiskey came from a particular limestone mine in New York; when the defendant changed the label so that attributed the origin to the general area but not to the specific mine, it didn't change the price, and sales apparently didn't decrease. The court thought that continuity justified finding that the origin of the water was immaterial as a matter of law. Do you agree? Are *Boshnack* and *IDT* distinguishable?

In *LG Electronics v. Whirlpool Corp.*, 2010 WL 2921633 (N.D. Ill. 2010), LG's basic claim was that Whirlpool used the term "steam" in its ads and in the name of its Duet Steam Dryer but that the product didn't truly use steam; instead, it used a mist of cold water sprayed into a warm dryer drum. Whirlpool allegedly falsely advertised a misting dryer that competed with LG's true steam dryer. Whirlpool's expert conducted a survey on materiality and opined that "even if one assumes that a majority of the consumers were taking away a claim that the Whirlpool Dryer injects hot vapor onto clothes . . . , my survey shows no statistical difference in the intent to purchase as well as in product quality in comparison to a control ad that explicitly added the language stating that a mist of water is injected and is heated after it is sprayed into the dryer drum."

The court found that this testimony would be relevant and helpful as a rebuttal to LG's implied falsity theory. However, if LG ultimately won the argument that it was literally false to call Whirlpool's dryer a "steam" dryer under any reasonable definition of steam, then the testimony would not be relevant because literally false claims can be enjoined without further evidence of consumer reaction.

In another opinion in the same case, the court noted that materiality can be "self-evident" when a claim goes to the inherent quality of a product or a defining feature. Consumer complaints about their disappointment with the inability to rely on the claims at issue can also show materiality. It can also be reasonable to infer materiality from a marketing strategy highlighting the claimed feature. The court concluded, however, that even though surveys and expert testimony on materiality are not necessary, they can still be helpful.

Why was a materiality survey appropriate in the LG/Whirlpool case but not important in *IDT*? Is the claim in *IDT* more central to the product? *See also* Rexall Sundown, Inc. v. Perrigo Co., 651 F. Supp. 2d 9 (E.D.N.Y. 2009) (consumers who were shown a package making the challenged claim and consumers who were shown the same package from which the claim had been deleted showed no statistically significant difference in purchase interest; nonetheless, a jury could still find materiality: "Unlike on the issue of consumer confusion, materiality need not be proven by extrinsic evidence such as consumer surveys. Moreover, . . . materiality may be proven by showing that the misrepresentation related to an inherent characteristic of the product . . . . In the instant case, a reasonable jury could conclude that the [challenged claim] relates to an inherent characteristic or quality of the product— namely, its composition (in terms of the quantity of its active ingredient) and/or effectiveness—such that it would be material to any consumer.").

Is these courts' apparent willingness to presume materiality when a claim is central to a product rebuttable and, if so, by what evidence?

By contrast, one Lanham Act case has adopted the perspective urged by Kraft against the FTC, finding that a literally false claim of 35% savings in purchase of dental supplies was not material because the evidence showed that the true savings were 19%. The plaintiff didn't show that 19% wouldn't have been enough to make the same sales; in fact, testimony suggested that 5–10% would be enough to get dentists to switch suppliers. SourceOne Dental, Inc. v. Patterson Cos., 328 F.Supp.3d 53 (E.D.N.Y. 2018). Does assessing the materiality of the *gap* between the truth and the advertising make more sense than the "inherent characteristic" approach? Unlike the courts above that didn't require extrinsic evidence, the *SourceOne* court reasoned:

> [I]t is not sufficient for defendants to presume materiality simply on the basis that purchasers generally like to spend less instead of more. This is because price sensitivity turns on the marginal price difference and the nature of the product at issue. Purchasers who see a product that they have purchased advertised for 33% less, but who have received excellent customer service from their current seller, might be well inclined to take an "if it ain't broke, don't fix it," approach. On the other hand, the same or other customers might also decide that it would be worth switching to a new distributor for even a 10-15% savings.

> Perhaps there is some level where materiality can be found as a matter of law – e.g., where customers were promised 90% savings over a competing product. But in the absence of that kind of obvious disparity, defendants were required to introduce some form of evidence – usually, although not necessarily, survey evidence or expert testimony based on it – to raise a factual question as to whether the differential between advertised and actual prices was material in this market.

Are you convinced?

What about more-generalized evidence of materiality? Some research suggests that "Made in the USA" is material to consumers. *See* Fed. Trade Comm'n, Staff Report of the Bureau of Consumer Protection, *Made in the USA: An FTC Workshop* (Jun. 19, 2020) (citing surveys showing strong preferences, though questioning whether they reflected actual consumer behavior, and Kong & Rao study of actual consumer behavior on eBay revealing up to 28% price premium for goods made in the USA); Xinyao Kong & Anita Rao, *Do Made in USA Claims Matter?* (Oct. 24, 2019) (research also showed that, after the FTC determined that use of the label for four products was misleading and stopped its use, sales of one product fell by 2%, another fell by 6%, a third by nearly 20%, and the fourth experienced a "trend decline"). In litigation, what would the proper role of such evidence be? It isn't specific to the challenged ad but does say something about consumer beliefs—and might be more credible insofar as it comes from a source not associated with a defendant or a plaintiff.

D.   Endorsements and Other Stamps of Approval

Claims that appear to give a stamp of approval are generally material. For example, claims that numbers in a reference book were "Chilton times," the industry standard for determining automotive repair time, when the numbers were different from the original Chilton times, were material because consumers had relied on and trusted the original. Hearst Bus. Publ'g, Inc. v. W.G. Nichols, Inc., 76 F. Supp. 2d 459 (S.D.N.Y. 1999).

Even the statement "as seen on TV" has been found material, where the plaintiff's products actually have been advertised on television and the defendant's misrepresentation likely piggybacks on the plaintiff's television campaign. *See* Telebrands Corp. v. Wilton Indus., Inc., 983 F. Supp. 471 (S.D.N.Y. 1997). A misstatement about television advertising could be material even without potential source confusion: Consumers may be more likely to purchase a product that is advertised on television, in the belief that the advertiser has a successful product that justifies the substantial outlay of television advertising. This is an implication of Nelson's signaling theory of advertising, discussed in Chapter 4.

Does this mean that a celebrity endorsement is material? What about the mere presence of a celebrity's name or image in an ad? Even if the celebrity has no reason to know any more than a random person on the street about whether or not the product is good? The FTC has addressed many issues surrounding endorsements in its guide to endorsements and testimonials. What current doctrine cannot quite explain is why the FTC requires celebrity endorsements to reflect some actual experience with/opinion about the product, even when celebrities makes no factual claim other than their preferences—that is, make a claim that seems like classic puffery. We will return to this puzzle in Chapter 6.

E.   The Scope of Materiality/Bait and Switch

If the consumer learns the truth about a claim before making a purchase and then buys anyway, the advertiser may protest that the falsity didn't affect the consumer's decision. Courts have been unsympathetic to this defense, on the theory that consumers may have been sucked into the decision-making process on false pretenses. Once there, various cognitive habits may lead consumers to stick with their choices instead of walking out; consumers may also simply not have the energy to go through the search process again. At the very least, if leaving the transaction is harder than clicking the "back" button on a browser, courts are likely to find the falsity an actionable but-for cause of the consumer's decision to buy.

As the FTC says, "it is well established that it is unfair to make an initial contact or impression through a false or misleading representation, even though before purchase the consumer is provided with the true facts." Chrysler Corp., 87 F.T.C. 719 (1976), *modified on other grounds*, 90 F.T.C. 606 (1977). If a car is depicted in an ad with a certain price, the model depicted must be available at that price. If the model is instead substantially more expensive, even a disclaimer will not avoid liability. Federal Trade Commission Regulations, 16 C.F.R. § 238.0, et seq. The NAD reasons similarly. *See* BMW of North America LLC, NAD Case No. 4156 (Mar. 17, 2004) ("starting at" base price should reflect the automobile shown in advertisement).

More generally, once the advertiser has the consumer's attention, it may not discourage the purchase of the advertised product or service (which is usually a precursor of touting a more-expensive alternative, completing the "switch"). Under the FTC regulations, evidence of whether or not an offer is bona fide includes (a) the refusal to show, demonstrate or sell the product offered in accordance with the terms of the offer; (b) the disparagement of the advertised product or associated services; (c) the failure to have sufficient quantity of the advertised product to meet reasonably anticipated demands; (d) the refusal to take orders for timely delivery; (e) the showing of a product that is defective or inappropriate for the purpose advertised; or (f) a sales or incentive plan designed to prevent or discourage salespeople from selling the advertised product.

F.   Materiality in Class-Action Lawsuits

Class actions present a unique challenge for materiality: If a court requires evidence that a claim influenced each consumer, then class-action treatment is impossible. As a result, in some states, including California, a finding that a claim is deceptive leads to a presumption of materiality that can be invoked on a class-wide basis. Other states disagree, and many putative class actions have failed on materiality or causation grounds—courts conclude that the plaintiff hasn't shown that, but for the misrepresentations, the class wouldn't have bought the product or service at issue or would have paid less for it. At times, only competitors can bring viable claims when a significant percentage, but not all, of the relevant consumers would have been affected by a false claim.

G.   A Final Note on What Really Affects Consumer Decisions

As the materials at the beginning of Chapter 4 indicated, numerous factors influence consumer decision making. For example, advertisers exploit our urge for reciprocity: Free samples and other "gifts" trigger a feeling of responsibility, so that we buy more. Surprisingly, this tactic even works when we didn't want and didn't like the free "gift," if we were unable to avoid accepting it. Regulators have attempted to control abuses of this practice, such as the FTC's guides on the use of "free" and various statutory provisions regarding receipt of unsolicited merchandise. But free samples and other reciprocity-triggering tactics, which can be as small as complimentary candy at a car dealership, remain powerful and largely unregulated. *See* David A. Friedman, *Free Offers: A New Look*, 38 N.M. L. REV. 45 (2008).

So do other techniques. Modern advertising is not primarily, and sometimes not at all, directed at providing traditional information such as price. Research suggests that the amount of information per unit of advertising has declined substantially even as consumers' exposure to advertising has steadily increased and ads have become shorter. This is consistent with marketing researchers' conclusions that creation of positive effect is often the most-effective way of persuading consumers to buy, and that more information can be less persuasive. Especially when consumers are distracted or overwhelmed by all the ads competing for their attention, they respond much more readily to non-informational cues such as humor. *See* Sarah C. Haan, Note, *The "Persuasion Route" of the Law: Advertising and Legal Persuasion*, 100 COLUM. L. REV. 1281 (2000).

Haan cites research showing that the more we like something, the more we discount the problems or risks it poses. Advertisers can therefore get us to ignore products' downsides by appealing to positive emotions. As a result, we get pictures and animation, humor and cuteness, and this impels us to buy, even though we are convinced that we are unaffected.

Occasionally, awareness of these techniques has an impact on ad regulation. Opponents of tobacco advertising argued that the attractive cartoon mascot Joe Camel was intentionally designed to appeal to known cognitive weaknesses and to override factual messages of the dangers of tobacco. Joe Camel is no longer Camel's mascot, and the tobacco industry has agreed to avoid the use of cartoons entirely in the United States. *See* Jon D. Hanson & Douglas A. Kysar, *Taking Behaviorism Seriously: Some Evidence of Market Manipulation*, 112 HARV. L. REV. 1423 (1999).

But legal acknowledgement of the cognitive/behavioral background of marketing is in its infancy. And researchers are adding new nuances to our understanding of marketing all the time. For example, Marianne Bertrand et al. tested the effects of various marketing treatments on purchase decisions. A South African lender sent out over 53,000 letters to consumers who'd previously taken out loans with the lender, offering short-term loans at randomly chosen monthly interest rates ranging from 3.25% to 11.75%. The letters varied: Some had detailed descriptions of loan terms, others had promotional giveaways, and others had pictures of a smiling, attractive woman in the corner. The picture of the attractive woman produced an increased response rate for men equivalent to dropping the monthly interest rate by 4.5% (that is, about 25% of the rate). By contrast, a large selection of example loans decreased responses compared to a single example loan, consistent with other research suggesting that proliferation of options makes consumers more hesitant to pick any one (the so-called paradox of choice). Marianne Bertrand et al., *What's Advertising Content Worth? Evidence from a Consumer Credit Marketing Field Experiment*, 125 Q. J. ECON. 263 (2010).

A special rate for you.

Congratulations! As a valued client, you are now eligible for a special interest rate on your next cash loan from   This is a limited time offer, so please come in by 31 October 2003

You can use this cash to buy an appliance, or for anything else you want.

Enjoy low monthly repayments with this offer! For example:

	4 Months	6 Months	12 Months
R500	R149.95	R108.28	R66.62
R1000	R299.90	R216.57	R133.23
R2000	R599.80	R433.13	R266.47
R4000	R1199.60	R866.27	R532.93

LOAN AVAILABILITY SUBJECT TO TERMS & CONDITIONS

Loans available in other amounts. There are no hidden costs. What you see is what you pay.

If you borrow elsewhere you will pay R280.14 more in total on a R350.00, 4 month loan.

How to apply:

Bring your ID book and latest payslip to your usual branch, by **31 October 2003** and ask for

Names of clients, employees and Lender supressed to preserve confidentiality.

Customer Consultant

P.S. Unfortunately, if you have already taken a loan since the date this letter was issued, you do not qualify for this offer. Comparison based on a competitor's interest rate of 25%.

What do these results suggest about materiality? About the relationship between the "reasonable" consumer and the average consumer? More broadly: Given all this evidence that facts are at best a small part of what consumers respond to in ads, is the law's focus on facts a losing game? What are the alternatives?

No ad can provide all the information that might help a consumer's decision making. An advertiser's obligation to disclose material information often turns on what else the advertiser has affirmatively said, though there are also many sector-specific regulations requiring certain types of disclosures. When some disclosure is required, questions arise as to its presentation. Advertisers may wish to hide uncomfortable information; the FTC in particular has developed many guidelines to make sure any disclosures actually convey information to consumers. This chapter covers actionable omissions, formulation of required disclosures and the legal treatment of mandatory disclosures for specific categories of products, services and marketing techniques (specifically, endorsements).

1.   Omissions as False Claims

This section will explore situations in which failure to disclose could cause an advertisement to be misleading. The following section discusses how to effectively implement any required disclosures.

The Lanham Act and the NAD

In connection with the 1988 amendment of Section 43(a), Congress considered including a section that explicitly made failure to disclose actionable. The Senate Report explains that the section was ultimately not included "to respond to concerns that it could be misread to require that all facts material to a consumer's decision to purchase a product or service be contained in each advertisement. . . . The committee does not through the deletion indicate that it condones deceptive advertising, whether by affirmative misrepresentation or material omission, and leaves to the courts the task of further developing [and] applying this principle under section 43(a)."

As a result, the Lanham Act does not require advertisers to disclose all the information that consumers might find relevant to making a purchase decision. Advertisers can generally promote only their products' strengths without mentioning their weaknesses. An advertiser may therefore tout a tire as "better" than a cheaper tire because it has a better warranty without disclosing that in all physical respects the tires are the same. *See* Tire Kingdom, Inc. v. Morgan Tire & Auto, Inc., 915 F. Supp. 360 (S.D. Fla. 1996). A drug maker can advertise that "hospitals trust" its product and use ten times as much of it as the next four brands combined, without revealing that the reason is that the drug maker supplies it to hospitals at very low prices. Am. Home Prods. v. Johnson & Johnson, 654 F. Supp. 568 (S.D.N.Y. 1987).

Indeed, an advertiser may fail to correct a popular misconception unrelated to the claim it's actually advertising without fear of Lanham Act liability. *See, e.g.*, Avon Prods., Inc. v. S.C. Johnson & Son, Inc., 984 F. Supp. 768 (S.D.N.Y. 1997) (advertiser not liable for failing to state publicly that its skin lotion was not an insect repellent). *But see* Church & Dwight Co. v. SPD Swiss Precision Diagnostics, GMBH, 843 F.3d 48 (2d Cir. 2016) (taking advantage of well-known consumer lack of understanding about medical calculation of pregnancy duration was misleading).

The NAD follows similar rules: Disclosures are only required to avoid materially misleading consumers. The NAD does feel free to recommend additional disclosures where there is some uncertainty.

Typically, treating omissions as not actionable preserves advertisers' freedom and doesn't pose real threats to consumers. Consumers aren't likely to expect that an advertisement promising cheapness also promises highest quality. At some point, though, an omission may so change the message of an advertisement that the omission makes the overt claim false or misleading for Lanham Act purposes. *See, e.g.*, U-Haul Int'l, Inc. v. Jartran, Inc., 601 F. Supp. 1140 (D. Ariz. 1984) (failure to reveal that advertised prices were "special prices" or did not include drop-off charges violated Lanham Act), *aff'd in relevant part*, 793 F.2d 1034 (9th Cir. 1986). In other words, an omission becomes actionable if it leads consumers to draw erroneous conclusions about the meaning of the explicit claims.

Consider the *S.C. Johnson* "leaky goldfish" case from the puffery section of Chapter 4 in this light: Arguably, the affirmative representation of leakiness didn't disclose typical rates of leakage, which was so closely related to the affirmative representations in the ad that the overall ad was false. Similarly, the Second Circuit reasoned that eBay's failure to disclose that substantial amounts of counterfeit Tiffany jewelry were for sale on the auction site might make its ads misleading when they stated that Tiffany jewelry was available. *See* Tiffany v. eBay, 600 F.3d 93 (2d Cir. 2010) ("An online advertiser such as eBay need not cease its advertisements for a kind of goods only because it knows that not all of those goods are authentic. A disclaimer might suffice. But the law prohibits an advertisement that implies that all of the goods offered on a defendant's website are genuine when in fact, as here, a sizeable proportion of them are not.").

In NAD Case # 3879 (02/12/02), *Guinness UDV of North America, Inc. (Smirnoff Ice Malt Beverage)*, the NAD considered a complaint by Mike's Hard Lemonade against the Smirnoff Ice brand of citrus-flavored malt beverages. The complaint charged that the trade dress of Smirnoff Ice, which looked almost exactly like the trade dress of Smirnoff Vodka, misled consumers into thinking that Smirnoff vodka was a main ingredient and failed to make clear that the product did *not* contain vodka. The challenger submitted two surveys. The first found that, based on the label and packaging, 43% of respondents believed that Smirnoff Ice contained vodka. The second found that, based on Smirnoff Ice TV commercials, 25% of respondents believed that the product contained vodka. In both surveys, over 60% of respondents indicated that vodka content would be important to a purchase decision. Ultimately, however, Guinness declined to participate in the NAD proceeding, so all the NAD could do was refer the matter to the appropriate governmental agencies, which declined to act. What was the source of the alleged deception in the Smirnoff Ice advertising and labeling? Could any disclosure short of a name change have corrected this deception?

Often, false and misleading omissions arise in comparative advertising, where an advertiser selectively highlights its comparative advantages. This can be *literal falsity*: A claim that a product was "economical" compared to a competitor's product, backed up by a statement that consumers only needed a pound of the advertiser's product to match the effectiveness of two pounds of the competitor's product, was false because the advertiser neglected to disclose that its product was eight times more expensive per pound, and thus four times less "economical" than the competitor's product. *See* Performance Indus. Inc. v. Koos Inc., 18 U.S.P.Q.2d 1767 (E.D. Pa. 1990).

Omissions can also make a statement *misleading*, for example, a comparison of an advertiser's circulation with its competitor's, without revealing that the advertiser's newspaper circulated only weekly while the competitor's was daily. *See* San Juan Star v. Casiano Commc'ns, Inc., 85 F. Supp. 2d 89 (D.P.R. 2000). When a defendant advertised that its plastic building blocks connected to plaintiff's blocks, but the connection required the use of special adapter blocks, and a survey revealed that consumers were less likely to buy defendant's product knowing of the need for adapter blocks, the failure to disclose the need for adapter blocks was misleading. Tyco Indus., Inc. v. Lego Sys., Inc, 5 U.S.P.Q.2d 1023 (D.N.J. 1987).

Sometimes an omission converts what looks to the consumer like an apples-to-apples comparison into an apples-to-oranges comparison. So, if an advertiser notes the side effects of a competitor's medication but neglects to disclose its own medication's side effects, a consumer is likely to believe that only the competitor's medication has such side effects. The ad prevents the consumer from making a true comparison. E.R. Squibb & Sons, Inc. v. Stuart Pharm., 1990 WL 159909 (D.N.J. Oct. 1990).

How significant is the advertiser's knowledge of what its consumers are likely to consider important? In *Gillette Co. v. Norelco Consumer Products Co.*, 946 F. Supp. 115 (D. Mass. 1996), Gillette, a leading maker of razors and blades (wet-shaving), sued Norelco, a leading seller of electric razors (dry-shaving). Norelco launched an ad campaign to convince consumers that its Reflex Action was less irritating than wet-shaving. The problem was that Norelco's ads omitted "a material caveat—that the shaver is less irritating only after an acclimation period of at least twenty-one days." There was extensive evidence that Norelco was aware that the acclimation period was vital. The instructions devoted significant attention to acclimation, including the statement that "[a]t first you may not get as close a shave as you expect, or your face may even become slightly irritated. This is normal since your beard and skin will need time to adjust."

Norelco developed its ad campaign knowing that most consumers were not interested in a two- or three-week trial period to get used to an electric razor because Norelco had been unable to convince them that the ultimate results were worth the initial discomfort. The court found that Gillette was likely to succeed in showing that Norelco's ads were misleading. The court did not require survey evidence, because "[t]he fact that Norelco has expressly and impliedly acknowledged the importance of acclimation to the success of the Reflex Action as a lessirritating shaving system than wet shavers, but has withheld that information in some of its advertisements, is *in se* strong evidence that such advertisements are misleading." Gillette Co. v. Norelco Consumer Prods. Co., 946 F. Supp. 115 (D. Mass. 1996).

Example: Country of Origin Disclosures

Federal law requires labeling to mark goods as foreign-made. *See* 19 U.S.C. § 1304(a) (2000) ("[E]very article of foreign origin . . . imported into the United States shall be marked in a conspicuous place as legibly, indelibly, and permanently as the nature of the article . . . in such manner as to indicate to an ultimate purchaser in the United States . . . the country of origin of the article."). Failure to satisfy the country-of-origin labeling rule may be a *per se* material omission for Lanham Act purposes. Without labeling, a consumer will likely assume the goods are domestically produced and is therefore likely to be deceived. *See, e.g.,* Alto Prods. Corp. v. Tri Component Prods. Corp., 1994 WL 689418 (S.D.N.Y. Dec. 8, 1994). This legal construct is a variant of falsity by necessary implication (to be addressed in Chapter 7) because the mandatory labeling requirement sets the expectations of reasonable consumers.

The FTC and Omissions

The FTC Act prohibits omissions that are "material in the light of [affirmative] representations or material with respect to consequences which may result from the use of the commodity to which the advertisement relates under the conditions prescribed in said advertisement, or under such conditions as are customary or usual." 15 U.S.C. § 55(a)(1).

Interpreting this provision, the Ninth Circuit recognized that "no single advertisement could possibly include every fact relevant to the purchasing decision . . . . Advertisers need not disclose negative aspects of their product, other than material consequences of normal use. Otherwise, an advertisement is misleading only if it fails to disclose facts necessary to dissipate false assumptions likely to arise in light of the representations actually made." FTC v. Simeon Mgmt. Corp., 532 F.2d 708 (9th Cir. 1976). The court therefore held that a weight-loss program had no obligation to disclose that the program involved treatment with a drug not approved by the FDA for such use: "The FTC presented no evidence that those seeing the advertisements formed a belief either that HCG was not used or that, if used, HCG had been approved by the FDA. This would be a different case if the respondents had advertised their use of HCG; one could plausibly suggest that the public would then assume that the drug was effective or approved by the FDA." Does this distinction make sense? Does it encourage promoters of weight loss programs to provide less information to consumers?

As a result of these doctrines, the FTC Act and the Lanham Act similarly handle omissions that are material in light of affirmative representations. *See* MacMillan, Inc., 96 F.T.C. 208 (1980) (holding that failure to disclose the number of assignments in an educational course was deceptive because students needed to know the number of assignments to calculate their tuition obligations). Moreover, significant omissions relating to the ordinary uses or central qualities of the product are also prohibited if consumers are likely to be misled. For example, the Seventh Circuit sustained an FTC ruling that ads for diet pills were deceptive because they failed to disclose that the pills were not safe for all potential consumers. In fact, obese consumers, at whom the ads were directed, were particularly at risk for the side effects. *See* Porter & Dietsch v. FTC, 605 F.2d 294 (7th Cir. 1979). (Consider whether using Lanham Act jurisprudence would have produced the same result given cases such as *Tyco* and *Gilette*, *supra*.)

State Laws

Many state consumer-fraud laws prohibit omissions of material facts, usually requiring intent that consumers rely on the omission (or concealment or suppression).* *See, e.g.,* Casper Sleep, Inc. v. Mitcham, 204 F. Supp. 3d 632 (S.D.N.Y. 2016) (finding New York consumer protection law to be broader than the Lanham Act in requiring "clear and conspicuous" disclosures of speaker's economic relationships with producers of products it touted). While these provisions might seem broader than the Lanham Act, in practice they are often quite similar, except where some class of persons—such as realtors or those in the relationship of a trustee to the consumer—has a duty to disclose *every* material fact regardless of what the speaker affirmatively states. *See, e.g.,* Carter v. Gugliuzzi, 716 A.2d 17 (Vt. 1998) (finding violation of Vermont Consumer Fraud Act for real estate broker's failure to disclose material facts, relying upon statutory duty of brokers to disclose such facts). Moreover, California, the source of much significant consumer protection law, does not generally require disclosure of material information unless it relates to an affirmative statement by the advertiser or to product health and safety. *See* Hodsdon v. Mars, Inc., 891 F.3d 857 (9th Cir. 2018) ("[T]he manufacturers do not have a duty to disclose the labor practices in question, even though they are reprehensible, because they are not physical defects that affect the central function of the chocolate products."); *cf.* Otto v. Abbott Laboratories, Inc., 2013 WL 12131380 (C.D. Cal. Aug. 2, 2013) (finding that deception by omission was plausible because advertised supplement would help elderly people—targets of the ad—only if they had a sufficient blood level of vitamin D, and at least 60% of elderly adults did not; "it is reasonable to think that a person buying a product would find significant that it is more likely than not that the product will fail to deliver its promised benefits.").

A large and difficult-to-surmount knowledge gap between advertiser and consumer can justify a finding that an omission was material. *Compare* Oswego Laborers' Local 214 Pension Fund v. Marine Midland Bank, N.A., 647 N.E.2d 741 (N.Y. 1995) ("[The New York consumer protection] statute surely does not require businesses to ascertain consumers' individual needs and guarantee that each consumer has all relevant information specific to its situation. The scenario is quite different, however, where the business alone possesses material information that is relevant to the consumer and fails to provide this information."), *with* Super Glue Corp. v. Avis Rent A Car Sys., 557 N.Y.S.2d 959 (App. Div. 1990) (failure to tell car renters that renters' own automobile insurance might protect rental vehicles was not deceptive because renters were in better position to know the terms of their own insurance policies), *appeal denied*, 567 N.E.2d 980 (N.Y. 1991).

An advertiser's special expertise can therefore create heightened disclosure obligations, even when there's no fiduciary relationship and even when the consumer is relatively sophisticated (such as a business). For example, an insurance company violated the law by failing to disclose that health insurance might not provide adequate coverage for the

---

* The wording varies, though this is unlikely to affect outcomes. States prohibiting intentional omissions of material fact include Arizona and South Dakota. Delaware and Texas bar omissions of material fact with intent that others rely. Alaska, Illinois, Missouri, New Jersey and West Virginia additionally bar concealment or suppression of material facts with intent that others rely. Arkansas bars concealment of material facts. South Dakota bans intentional concealment, suppression or omissions of material fact. New York, like the FTCA, bars failure to reveal facts in light of affirmative representations, and Maryland, Michigan, New Mexico, Pennsylvania and Vermont generally bar deceptive omissions.

insured's employees because it failed to fully disclose its method for calculating rates, which obscured the fact that lower initial rates could result in future spikes. Woodworker's Supply, Inc. v. Principal Mut. Life Ins. Co., 170 F.3d 985 (10th Cir. 1999).

When the advertiser knows that the consumer would not make the purchase if he or she knew the omitted fact, that satisfies the requirement in many states that omissions must be made with intent that the consumer rely on the omission. *See, e.g.*, Mackinac v. Arcadia Nat'l Life Ins. Co., 648 N.E.2d 237 (Ill. Ct. App. 1995) (actionable omission does not require intent to deceive, but does require intent to induce reliance).

Consistent with this principle, although state laws may by their terms require only that the omitted information be "material," courts often require a fairly high standard of materiality when an omission is unrelated to an advertiser's affirmative statements. Courts will find liability only when it is likely that the advertiser knew that the omitted facts were important to many consumers and expected consumers to rely on the nondisclosure. *Compare* Haisch v. Allstate Ins. Co., 5 P.3d 940 (Ariz. Ct. App. 2000) (because consumers purchase insurance coverage for protection from calamity, failing to disclose that insurance did not provide for double recovery was not material omission under Arizona law), *with* Connick v. Suzuki Motor Co., 675 N.E.2d 584 (Ill. 1996) (allegation that car manufacturer omitted material fact that car posed safety hazard stated claim under Illinois law), *and* Salmeron v. Highlands Ford Sales, Inc., 271 F. Supp. 2d 1314 (D.N.M. 2003) (failure to disclose that a used car had been used as a rental car violated the law).

Thus, courts finding violations of state law often explain why a particular omission was so unreasonable that the advertiser must have known that consumers would rely on the omission, implicitly limiting the duty to disclose to facts glaringly in need of disclosure. *See* Williams-Ward v. Lorenzo Pitts, Inc., 908 F. Supp. 48 (D. Mass. 1995) (claim over a lease in which the defendant knew that the property contained lead paint). Conversely, where the omitted information is unlikely to make a difference to consumers, an advertiser may be able to show that it did not intend consumers to rely on the omission. *See* State *ex rel.* Brady v. 3-D Auto World, Inc., 2000 WL 140854 (Del. Super. Ct. 2000) (where car dealer misrepresented interest charge as "carrying charge," but buyers allegedly knew exact amount and payment schedule of charges, dealer could show that he did not intend consumers to rely on omission or concealment of fact that charge was actually "interest").

These principles can be applied to a common scenario: the absence of price terms in an ad. Though price is ordinarily material, states are unlikely to require its disclosure if advertising touts only non-price-related characteristics, unless some other law specifically requires price disclosure. An advertiser's intent to get consumers to care more about quality than about cost does not constitute an intent to induce consumers to rely on the absence of price information. Omitting price information does not deceive consumers into thinking the product or service is free; a reasonable consumer realizes there will be a price and can ask about it. By contrast, advertising that implies cheapness, playing on consumers' existing price preferences, could be deceptive for omitting price information.

Many actionable omissions under state law involve one-on-one sales, particularly sales of expensive goods such as homes or cars, where the advertiser knows something about the consumer's particular requirements. In such individualized situations, complete silence on an important topic can more readily imply that the offered alternatives suit the buyer's already-understood requirements. By contrast, in the usual case, it would be difficult to find that an advertiser intended a consumer to rely on an omission merely by touting its mass-marketed product's desirable features in general, non-personalized advertising, unless it also made a *related* affirmative statement or did something else wrong. *See* Commonwealth v. Bell Tel. Co., 551 A.2d 602 (Pa. Commw. Ct. 1988) (omission of material facts that made service less desirable was actionable in standardized sales pitch by telephone company, where pitch also included a number of falsehoods and high-pressure tactics that would enhance the deceptive effect of the material omissions).

2.   Disclosures/Disclaimers and Their Effectiveness

There are two key questions about disclaimers: First, absent the disclaimer, is the ad going to be materially incomplete or misleading? If the answer is "no," then the disclaimer is fine. The advertiser may even be using it for reasons having little to do with consumers. For example, fine print may signal to competitors or regulators that the advertiser possesses substantiation. Second, if the disclaimer is required to avoid misleadingness, does the disclaimer—as it is actually presented—correct the problem?

Space and time limitations, as well as creative imperatives, all limit the amount of factual information that advertising can effectively communicate. These limits are fairly obvious in common ad formats such as fifteen-second radio ads, thirty-second television commercials and even full-page newspaper ads. Advertisers try to overcome these limits by using disclaimers, usually in small type at the bottom of a print ad or rapid-fire narrative at the end of a radio or television commercial. Notwithstanding their prevalence, many disclaimers are ineffective at educating consumers—and, not coincidentally, are legally dubious.

To be effective, a disclaimer must be clearly written and prominent. Courts and the FTC accept that a clearly written footnote or a prominent on-screen super* can alert consumers to the availability of further information. Thus, disclaimers may be effective at clarifying an ad's claims (e.g., "shipping and handling not included"), providing additional information of interest to certain subgroups (e.g., "contains phenylalanine") or offering ways to find out more information.

The European Community reasons similarly: Not only does it bar misleading omissions, but it specifies that a violation occurs when a trader "hides or provides in an unclear, unintelligible, ambiguous or untimely manner [material information that needs to be disclosed] or fails to identify the commercial intent of the commercial practice if not already apparent from the context, and where, in either case, this causes or is likely to cause the average consumer to take a transactional decision that he would not have taken otherwise." Directive 2005/29/EC (Directive on Unfair Commercial Practices) art. 7(2). Likewise, in Argentina, Resolution 248/2019, issued by the Secretariat of Domestic Trade, specifies that an ad will be considered misleading when the information provided is incomprehensible by

---

* A "super" is information superimposed on TV ad copy, such as a disclaimer, logo or other information.

reason of the speed of spoken language, the size of lettering or any other aspect that blocks comprehension.

A.   Guidelines for Effective Disclosures and Disclaimers

According to the FTC Deception Statement, "[w]ritten disclosures or fine print may be insufficient to correct a misleading representation." Among other things, "[o]ther practices of the company may direct consumers' attention away from the qualifying disclosures," and "[a]ccurate information in the text may not remedy a false headline because reasonable consumers may glance only at the headline." In many circumstances, the solution is to rewrite the main claim. *See, e.g.*, FTC, *.Com Disclosures: How to Make Effective Disclosures in Digital Advertising* (March 2013) ("Often, disclosures consist of a word or phrase that may be easily incorporated into the text, along with the claim.").

Scholars have argued that many deceptive ads could be rewritten simply and easily. Preston and Richards tested ads that had been challenged by the FTC as misleading even though the falsity was not explicit, along with ads that had been rewritten to avoid the false implication. For example, the FTC charged that ads for Efficin pain reliever falsely implied that "Efficin is not associated with most of the side effects and contraindications with which aspirin is associated" by stating that Efficin "contains no aspirin." The resulting consent order allowed the advertiser to compare Efficin's safety to aspirin only if it clearly and prominently stated that Efficin "has side effects similar to aspirin." Adria Labs., Inc., 103 F.T.C. 512 (1984).

Preston and Richards tested the original ad as well as an ad written to the specifications of the consent order. Rewriting prevented the vast majority of subjects from being deceived. Subjects who saw the rewritten version were much more likely to report the true message as true and reject the false message, without decreasing their comprehension of the other, concededly nondeceptive, messages in the ad. *See* Ivan L. Preston & Jef I. Richards, *Consumer Miscomprehension and Deceptive Advertising: A Response to Professor Craswell*, 68 B.U. L. REV. 431 (1988).

The corollary of the principle that rewriting is often preferable is that a disclaimer cannot remove the deceptive effect of a literally false claim. *See, e.g.*, Cont'l Wax Corp. v. FTC, 330 F.2d 475 (2d Cir. 1964) ("[T]he effectiveness of qualifying language is usually limited to situations where the deception sought to be eliminated is created by an ambiguity. . . . [W]here, as here . . . the offending deception is caused by a clear and unambiguous false representation . . . and, because of this, the addition of a qualifying phrase denying the truth of that representation would lead to a confusing contradiction in terms, no remedy short of complete excision . . . will suffice."); WebMiles.com Corp., NAD Case No. 3749 (closed Apr. 20, 2001) (claim that airline travel program had "absolutely no restrictions" could not be made truthful by disclaimer that revealed actual restrictions).

In one NAD case, Citibank aired a commercial in which a woman searched all over town to buy a specific, nearly impossible-to-find toy. After she found one and bought it with her Citibank credit card, her son promptly broke it. The ad claimed that because she used Citibank, "They'll take care of it. It's that simple." A small disclaimer read: "Cardmembers are reimbursed for cost and repair or replacement." Citicorp Credit Services, Inc., NAD Case

No. 3235 (closed Sept. 14, 1995). Because the entire theme of the commercial was "the difficulty in obtaining the item that is broken as opposed to the cost of the item," however, the ad falsely communicated that Citibank would replace the broken toy, not simply give the woman the money to redo the hunt.

Advertisers also can't use disclaimers to change the ordinary meaning of an unambiguous statement. Advertising that a shopping website would "Pay Your Debt to Uncle Sam or Match Your Refund" for visitors before April 15 could not be effectively qualified by a footnote that limited the offer to five customers and the payment to "under $1000 each." DealTime.com, NAD Case No. 3673 (closed July 28, 2000). And a claim that one manufacturer's nicotine patch was the "only" one that could be worn for twenty-four hours could not be qualified by a footnote limiting the claim just to "non-prescription patches." SmithKline Beecham Consumer Healthcare, L.P., NAD Case No. 3436 (closed Jan. 1, 1998).

This principle is often coupled with the general distrust of small-print disclaimers for important qualifications. An oft-cited formulation is that a disclaimer that "purports to change the apparent meaning of the claims and render them literally truthful, but which is so inconspicuously located or in such fine print that readers tend to overlook it, . . . will not remedy the misleading nature of the claims." Am. Home Prods. Corp. v. Johnson & Johnson, 654 F. Supp. 568 (S.D.N.Y. 1987). In *DirecTV Inc. v. Comcast of Illinois III, Inc.*, 2007 WL 2808235 (N.D. Ill. 2007), DirecTV claimed that consumers preferred DirecTV's picture quality to that of cable, but the ad didn't disclose that they'd been comparing analog cable to a digital signal; failure to disclose this was "obviously" misleading. There was a disclaimer on the ad, but the court discounted it entirely. It was on the screen for four seconds, but "even if it were on the screen for 40 seconds, it wouldn't be legible enough or conspicuous enough for anyone to see it and to read it and to understand it."

Clear and Conspicuous

The key principle is that disclaimers must be "clear and conspicuous." "Small and inconspicuous portions of lengthy descriptions" generally do not protect consumers, particularly where advertisements are "models of clarity" in presenting those aspects of the claims designed to attract consumers but "models of obscurity" in presenting the unpleasant details in small type, buried where none but the most meticulous reader would read and understand them. Donaldson v. Read Magazine, Inc., 333 U.S. 178 (1948).

Clear disclosures must be readily understood and use language appropriate to the targeted consumers. Thus, advertisers contemplating disclaimers must take into account the relative sophistication of their audiences. In general, audiences shopping for more-expensive products are presumed to read claims carefully, understand fairly subtle distinctions, and therefore be more easily informed through the use of disclaimers. *See, e.g.*, Core-Vent Corp. v. Nobel Indus. Sweden A.B., 163 F.3d 605 (9th Cir. 1998) (promotional materials and newsletters sent to dental offices using study and stating study's limits were not false). By contrast, advertising directed at children requires more disclosures and disclaimers than advertising to adults, including making clear that an advertisement *is* an advertisement.

The FTC has broken down the elements of clear and conspicuous disclosures into Four Ps:

(1) Prominence: Is it big/loud/etc. enough for consumers to notice and read/hear?
(2) Presentation: Is the wording and format easy for consumers to understand both physically and conceptually and presented without distracting consumers' attention elsewhere?
(3) Placement: Is it in a place consumers will look and/or conveyed in a way consumers will hear?
(4) Proximity: Is it near the claim it qualifies?

Here is an example of problematic disclosure:

See Network Solutions, Inc., F.T.C. File No. 132 3084 (Apr. 7, 2015) (consent order). Network Solutions offered a "30 Day Money Back Guarantee," but did not adequately disclose that it imposed cancellation fee—up to 30 percent—on customers who cancelled. Consumers had to scroll to the bottom of the screen to find this statement in comparatively tiny print: "* See Terms and Conditions for . . . 30- Day Money Back Guarantee . . . ." The link sometimes appeared in blue on a black background and was usually sandwiched between other links. A consumer who did click on the link would see a pop-up in which Network Solutions began calling the offer a "30 -Day Limited Money Back Guarantee" and revealed details of the cancelation fee. This, the FTC concluded, was a classic "too little, too late" disclosure.

Proximity and Placement

Disclaimers must be legible, meaningful and of sufficient size, and (where appropriate) they must remain on screen long enough to allow viewers to easily read and understand them. Small print, by itself or combined with other features such as color, contrast and placement, is almost always deemed ineffective because consumers are unlikely to wade through a long paragraph of fine print in order to find significant information.

For online disclosures, the FTC has issued numerous types of guidance. For example, The FTC's Endorsement Guides: What People Are Asking addresses numerous practical disclosure issues, such as:

> **If I upload a video to YouTube and that video requires a disclosure, can I just put the disclosure in the description that I upload together with the video?**
>
> No, because it's easy for consumers to miss disclosures in the video description. Many people might watch the video without even seeing the description page, and those who do might not read the disclosure. The disclosure has the most chance of being effective if it is made clearly and prominently in the video itself. That's not to say that you couldn't have disclosures in both the video and the description.

Some statutes mandate different types of disclosures for different media. For warranties, the FTC mandates specific disclosures for video ads. 16 C.F.R. § 239.2(a) (mandating disclosure "simultaneously with or immediately following the warranty claim" in the audio portion or "on the screen for at least five seconds" in the video portion). Rules governing advertising for credit terms and leases distinguish between print and broadcast disclosure. 12 C.F.R. § 213.7(d) (print); § 213.7(f) (broadcast). The rules for prescription-drug advertising are also changing because of Internet advertising and use of short-form media such as Twitter. *See* Chapter 18. Some states also have specific regulations. New Jersey, for example, requires consumer contracts with terms that are invalid in New Jersey to specify exactly which terms don't apply to New Jersey residents, rather than simply having an additional general term that says that terms that are invalid in a given jurisdiction will not apply. Does this rule make sense as a consumer protection measure?

Disclosures generally have to be complete within their specific context. Where the product is particularly complex and consumers will naturally understand this, however, it may be acceptable to direct consumers to another source for more information. Thus, radio and TV ads for consumer leases are permitted to direct consumers to complete lease terms disclosed elsewhere in appropriate circumstances, and broadcast advertisements for prescription drugs must direct consumers to the package labeling. Even for these products, however, regulators may require significant disclosures in the ad copy.

Moreover, in an ordinary case, the FTC takes the position that if (1) a particular format makes disclosure impossible and (2) disclosure is necessary to avoid misleadingness, then the advertiser should not run ads in that format, since not every affected consumer will seek out more information. Thus, if a message becomes misleading when it's compressed into 280 characters, then Twitter isn't an appropriate ad medium for that message. *See* Caroline McCarthy, *Yes, New FTC Guidelines Extend to Facebook Fan Pages*, CNET NEWS.COM, Oct. 5, 2009 (quoting the associate director of the FTC's advertising division: "You may have to say a little bit of something else, but if you can't make the disclosure, you can't make the ad."). The NAD agrees. *See, e.g.*, Eggland's Best Eggs, Inc., NAD Case No. 3016 (June 1, 1993

("To rely on a total communications program to make up for any possible lack in the television commercials is unacceptable. Each piece of advertising must stand on its own."); *see also* F.T.C. v. Colgate-Palmolive Co., 380 U.S. 374 (1965) ("If, however, it becomes impossible or impractical to show simulated demonstrations on television in a truthful manner, this indicates that television is not a medium that lends itself to this type of commercial, not that the commercial must survive at all costs.").

This principle is an application of general proximity/prominence requirements. In the absence of more-specific mandates, the default rule is that a disclosure or disclaimer should be presented in the same space or time as the claim it modifies. In writing, clear and conspicuous disclosures are printed in type that is large enough for consumers to readily read it, with the same emphasis and contrast as the offer. Oral disclosures should be at normal speed and in the same tone and volume as the sales offer. *See, e.g.*, Federal Trade Commission, *Complying with the Telemarketing Sales Rule: What Does the Rule Require Sellers and Telemarketers To Do?*

Here is an example of what the FTC considers poor placement:

[Asterisk circled in red; arrow indicates placement of disclosure, "frozen yogurt and sorbet combinations"]

207

See Häagen-Dazs Co., 119 F.T.C. 762 (1995) (consent order).

The FTC's recommendations are supported by consumer research indicating that improving size and contrast of disclosures can increase consumers' recall. Bigger disclosures and disclosures that are more isolated from other material (rather than embedded in a paragraph of unrelated text) are more noticeable. By contrast, background noise and clutter reduce awareness of disclosures. "Peripheral cues" such as color, celebrities or music can distract consumers from a disclosure. Consumers are more likely to grasp a disclosure in the same mode (visual and/or audio) as the claim it qualifies. Regulators may point to the shortness of a disclosure and the presence of distractions to conclude that a disclosure is ineffective. *See, e.g.*, Kraft, Inc., 114 F.T.C. 40 (1991), *aff'd*, 970 F.2d 311 (7th Cir. 1992).

Despite this guidance, many disclaimers used over the years have failed these requirements. *See* Maria Grubbs Hoy & Michael J. Stankey, *Structural Characteristics of Televised Advertising Disclosures: A Comparison with the FTC Clear and Conspicuous Standard*, 22 J. ADVERT. 47 (1993) (none of 157 TV commercial disclosures studied met all of the FTC clear-and-conspicuous standards). Given this, it's perhaps unsurprising that non-traditional advertisers are also unlikely to comply fully. Jim Tobin, *Ignorance, Apathy Or Greed? Why Most Influencers Still Don't Comply With FTC Guidelines*, FORBES, Apr. 27, 2018 ("New research analyzing 800 Instagram influencers found that 71.5% attempted to disclose their relationships, but only 1 in 4 actually did it in a way that complies with FTC regulations."). Affiliate links, where the speaker makes money if audience members follow the link and make a purchase, were even less likely to be properly disclosed. *Id.* ("90% of [YouTube] videos and 93% of [Pinterest] pins [containing affiliate links] failed to disclose the 'material connection' as required.").

For audiovisual disclosures, time is also a factor. In the United States, the upper range of reading comprehension is about 300 words per minute (wpm) and the lower range is 100 wpm, with 150 considered the average. In the study cited above, the average presentation rate was 181.4 wpm, above the 180 wpm upper bound the FTC had allowed in warranty disclosure cases. TV disclosures regularly blast past even the upper ranges. In an ad for Brink's Home Security, for example, the audio portion stated: "For over 135 years, Brink's has been protecting people and their valuables around the world without the loss of one single dollar." One disclosure appeared for 2 seconds, requiring a reading speed of 1860 wpm. *See also* Keith B. Murray, *Broadcast Disclosures and Communication Effectiveness: Required Reading Comprehension Rate* (finding similar results).

Sometimes, however, courts will relax comprehension requirements. *Time Warner Cable, Inc. v. DirecTV, Inc.*, 2007 WL 1138879 (S.D.N.Y. 2007), was another round in litigation over DirecTV's comparative advertising for its high-definition services versus cable. The ad touted DirecTV's HD channels but used a graphic stating, "Starting at $29.99/mo. Everyday price." The small print stated that HD programming carried an additional fee on top of the quoted price. The court found the disclaimer sufficient because "starting at" indicated that higher prices were also part of the offer and "the existence of a disclaimer of some sort[] is clearly visible at the bottom of the screen." Given that the ad focused on HD channels, was this the right result? How much weight should a court give to "the existence of a disclaimer of some sort," where the consumer can't tell what the subject of the disclaimer is?

Time Warner is an outlier. More typically, an asterisk, dagger or other sign to direct readers to disclaimers located elsewhere simply won't work for important information, such as any disclosures that contradict or substantially change a claim's meaning.

In such cases, qualifications should appear in direct conjunction with the claim itself. In one NAD case, the advertiser offered insurance coverage for home appliances with language including "never pay for covered home repairs again. But there was a cap of $1,500 per system or appliance that, in the context of high-cost home appliances, was material to the ads' promise that consumers could save "thousands"; the information thus needed to be disclosed more clearly than in small font and with the weasel words "limitations apply." NAD No. #6341 (Choice Home Warranty) (2020).

The FTC rejects disclaimers that appear only when a consumer has already taken affirmative steps toward purchasing a product or service. This is part of the prohibition on bait-and-switch sales practices. Guides Against "Bait" Advertising, 16 C.F.R. § 238. Once consumers have determined to make a purchase or have made substantial progress toward that end, they are likely to discount or ignore disclosures.

Some courts even regard a hard-to-find disclaimer as evidence of the advertiser's intent to deceive consumers. *See* Miller v. Am. Family Publishers, 663 A.2d 643 (N.J. Sup. Ct. Ch. Div. 1995) ("If [the disclosure] is not designed expressly for the purpose of minimizing its visibility, the overall layout of the literature certainly enhances that likelihood.").

Online Disclosures

The FTC has provided guidance for disclosures in online interfaces. Disclosures should be near the triggering claim and, when possible, on the same screen (though advertisers should remember that screen sizes vary, especially for mobile devices). If that's not possible, text and visual cues should be labeled to clearly indicate that consumers should scroll or click to find out specific important information. "See below for details" is insufficient. Hyperlinks may be acceptable for lengthy disclosures or disclosures that need to be repeated, so long as they are properly labeled and clearly signaled as links, and so long as the click-through page presents the disclosure properly. Advertisers need to keep technical limitations in mind, and the FTC has recently emphasized that many consumers access the internet through mobile devices; disclosures must be visible on such devices. Advertisers cannot assume that consumers will read an entire web page. The FTC's recommendation is simply stated: "Don't be subtle." And since advertisers can easily collect data on click-through rates, the FTC recommends monitoring click-through on disclaimers and changing the form if the rate is low.

Duration and Repetition

Disclaimers that are stated only once or twice, when the associated claim is repeated, are ineffective. This rule is particularly applicable to lengthier advertising such as websites and infomercials. In one infomercial, Hair Club for Men offered "free hair" and a "free round-trip" airline ticket to those who signed up for a one-year membership. The disclosure that the one-year membership was a necessary part of the offer was not made at the same time as the offer. The NAD held that "consumers viewing only this segment of the infomercial . . . would not understand the true cost of the offer." Hair Club for Men, NAD Case No. 3457 (closed May 1, 1998).

Understandability

Consumers' ability levels (age, education, special product knowledge) will be considered in assessing a disclosure's effectiveness. Thus, for a toy advertised to children, a disclosure "some assembly required" is less helpful than "you have to put this together." Most consumers won't be able to do much math quickly. *See* Kraft, Inc., 114 F.T.C. 40 (holding that complicated superscript—"one ¾-ounce slice has 70% of the calcium of five ounces of milk"—did not cure deceptive calcium content claim for cheese slices), *aff'd*, 970 F.2d 311 (7th Cir. 1992).

In general, shorter disclosures are easier for consumers to comprehend than longer ones. On the other hand, overly general statements, such as "read the label" or "consult your doctor," tend not to be understood as well as more-specific information. Consumers may perceive these too-short phrases as further statements about product benefits rather than as cautions. This concern must, however, be balanced by length considerations. "Consult your doctor for important information about side effects and people who shouldn't use X" might improve understanding, but a full list of the side effects might cause consumers to tune out.

Non-English Speakers

What happens if the main language of the ad is in Spanish, but the disclosures are in English? The FTC has increasingly taken the position that if disclosures are required to avoid misleadingness, then disclosures in a language other than that of the main ad do not help. *See, e.g.,* 16 C.F.R. 14.9 ("clear and conspicuous" disclosure must be made in the language of the target audience); 16 C.F.R. 610.4(a)(3)(ii) (in marketing free credit reports, mandatory disclosures must be made in the same language as that principally used in the advertisement).

Final Note: When Does a Disclosure Avoid Literal Falsity and Create Ambiguity?

Occasionally, a disclaimer can cause an advertiser's claim to become ambiguous when it might have been explicitly false without the disclaimer. The result is that the plaintiff needs a consumer survey to prove that consumers didn't see the disclaimer (thus leaving the claim as unambiguously false) or failed to understand it. In *PBM Products, LLC v. Mead Johnson Nutrition Co.*, 2009 WL 1684471 (E.D. Va. 2009), for example, Mead Johnson's ad stated, "It may be tempting to try a less expensive store brand [of infant formula], but only Enfamil LIPIL is clinically proven to improve brain and eye development." The small-print disclaimer said that the comparison was old Enfamil versus new Enfamil, not Enfamil versus store brands. Similar comparisons were made several times, each time with small-print disclaimers.

The court rejected a preliminary injunction for failure to show literal falsity. The reference to clinical studies was not literally false. (Were the studies sufficiently reliable to establish the claim being made?) "Moreover, to the extent that a consumer could read the statement to mean that clinical studies have compared Mead Johnson's formula to other brands (which indubitably would be inaccurate), the Disclaimer clarifies the point . . . ." A subsequent jury verdict, however, found Mead Johnson liable for $13.5 million in damages based on this advertising. PBM Prods., LLC v. Mead Johnson & Co., 2010 WL 723739 (E.D. Va. 2010).

As *PBM* demonstrates, even when courts accept the argument that disclaimers avoid literal falsity, sufficient proof of actual deception will still justify relief. But it is important to note that a disclaimer may substantially change the litigation landscape, making it much harder for the plaintiff to prevail. *See* Merial, Inc. v. Zoetis, Inc., 2017 WL 4466471 (N.D. Ga. Jun. 6, 2017) (an on-screen disclosure in a TV ad was relevant to the literal falsity analysis because the claim at issue "primes the viewer to look to the Clarifying Text by stating, '[i]n a study, Simparica blocked Lyme disease transmission,'" and the disclosure explains how Simparica blocked Lyme disease; defendant also provided evidence that the disclosure met TV network standards for legibility and that it tested the disclosure with consumers).

3. Mandatory Disclosures and Their (Dis)contents

Instead of banning a troubling sales or commercial practice, policymakers often attempt to make it less appealing by requiring certain disclosures of the less-attractive features of the relevant product or service. The most-familiar example may be the warnings on cigarette packages and ads. Product- or service-specific regulations can make omission of required information unlawful without a separate showing of deceptiveness in any individual case. For example, the FTC has promulgated various rules and guides requiring specific disclosures for particular products and services or claims, including household appliances, textiles, jewelry and others, and states have their own rules, especially for contests and sweepstakes (as detailed in Chapter 16).

In general, when are such prophylactic disclosures justified?

A. Criticisms of Disclosure and Disclosure Creep

Many people think that more information is always better. Thus, it's tempting to think that mandatory disclosures can't hurt, even if they don't always help. Tess Wilkinson-Ryan has criticized this argument from a psychological perspective. She argues that the presence of unread fine print can lead others—including legal decision makers—to blame consumers for any bad consequences they experience from a transaction, even though no one reads the fine print. In that case, mandatory disclosures could backfire, leaving consumers worse off. Tess Wilkinson-Ryan, *A Psychological Account of Consent to Fine Print*, 99 IOWA L. REV. 1745 (2014). Mandatory disclosures can backfire in other ways, by causing consumers to reach untrue conclusions. Oren Bar-Gill et al., *Drawing False Inferences from Mandated Disclosures*, BEHAV. PUB. POL'Y, Feb. 15, 2018 (consumers' beliefs about product risk increase when they think that the disclosure mandate was motivated by new research or by a belief in consumers' "right to know," but not when they think that the mandate was driven by political pressure, in which case the disclosure results in a small but statistically significant decrease in perceived risk); Molly Mercer & Ahmed E. Taha, *Unintended Consequences: An Experimental Investigation of the (In)Effectiveness of Mandatory Disclosures*, 55 SANTA CLARA L. REV. 405 (2015) (disclosures telling consumers that most consumers don't actually redeem rebates, and that consumers overestimate their own probability of doing so, counterproductively *increase* consumers' willingness to buy products offering rebates and optimism about the consumer's own likelihood of actually redeeming the rebate); Yael Steinhart et al., *Warnings of Adverse Side Effects Can Backfire Over Time*, 24 PSYCHOL. SCI. 1842 (2013) (warnings about cigarettes, artificial sweeteners and medication increased consumption because they made the advertisers' messages more trustworthy overall); *see also* D. Murphy et al., *Generic Copy Test of Food Health Claims in Advertising*, Federal Trade Commission Staff Report, Nov. 1998 (disclaimers must be very carefully and strongly worded; if not, they may be counterproductive).

Furthermore, Omri Ben-Shahar and Carl E. Schneider argue that mandatory disclosures almost never work because of the flawed incentives of the regulators and of the advertisers required to implement the disclosures, combined with the cognitive limitations that justified the FTC's detailed disclosure requirements in the first place. *See* Omri Ben-Shahar and Carl E. Schneider, *The Failure of Mandated Disclosure*, 159 U. PENN. L. REV. 647 (2011); *see also* Kesten C. Green & J. Scott Armstrong, *Evidence on the Effects of Mandatory Disclaimers in Advertising*, 31 J. PUB. POL'Y & MKTG., 293 (2012) (reviewing studies and concluding that mandatory disclaimers are useless or even counterproductive). Advertiser sabotage can be fairly blatant. In a case involving multilevel marketing, the court noted that, "[i]n live presentations, when Vemma speakers include 'results not typical' disclaimers with income representations, they often follow the disclaimer with a statement such as, 'I hope you're not typical,' to weaken the disclaimer. As a result, the net impression is still that a Vemma Affiliate is likely to earn substantial income, which is deceptive under the FTC Act." F.T.C. v. Vemma Nutrition Co., No. 15-cv-01578 (D. Ariz. Sept. 18, 2015).

Ben-Shahar & Schneider argue that, even without deliberate sabotage, mandatory disclosures often hurt more than help—by crowding out useful information, creating anticompetitive burdens, crowding out other consumer protection measures (as noted above, an advertiser can claim that no protection other than full disclosure is warranted) and helping only those who are already wealthy and educated enough to use disclosures.

Evidence of Disclosure Failure

The key problem is that consumers regularly don't pay attention to, much less understand, disclosures. For example, Ben-Shahar & Schneider cite studies showing that 90% of consumers don't understand how annual percentage rates (disclosed under the Truth in Lending Act) relate to simple annual interest rates.* There are too many messages for to

---

* Unfortunately, many mandatory disclosures are wordy and hard to understand. The Consumer Financial Protection Bureau allows limited waivers of existing disclosure requirements for financial services to experiment with other ways of conveying disclosures, seeking empirical data on which measures were effective and encouraging disclosures written in clear, succinct language. *See* BUREAU OF CONSUMER FINANCIAL PROTECTION, POLICY TO ENCOURAGE TRIAL DISCLOSURE PROGRAMS; INFORMATION COLLECTION, 12 CFR Chapter X, 78 Fed. Reg. 64389 (Oct. 29, 2013).

which consumers must pay attention, even if any given disclosure might be a good idea in isolation. *See* Svetlana Bialkovaet al., *Standing Out in the Crowd: The Effect of Information Clutter on Consumer Attention for Front-of-Pack Nutrition Labels*, 41 FOOD POL'Y 65 (2013).

Even regulatory attempts to simplify disclosures may fail. In one study, simplification of terms and use of a short list of key features in a "Warning Label" helped only a little to inform consumers and didn't change their behavior, even when the "Warning Label" disclosed unpleasant privacy practices:

Omri Ben-Shahar & Adam Chilton, *Simplification of Privacy Disclosures: An Experimental Test*, 45 J. LEGAL STUD. 541 (2016).

Required calorie disclosures on fast-food menus illustrate the challenges of designing effective mandatory disclosures. So far, such disclosure obligations have survived First Amendment challenges. *See, e.g.*, New York State Restaurant Ass'n v. New York City Board of Health, 2008 WL 1752455 (S.D.N.Y. 2008). However, research suggests that they are basically ineffective. People, if asked, say they pay attention to the disclosures—then order almost exactly the same food. *See also* Nathaniel Good et al., *Stopping Spyware at the Gate: A User Study of Privacy, Notice and Spyware*, Symposium on Usable Privacy and Security (SOUPS) 2005 (even when orally told that P2P software contained unwanted adware bundled with it, users proceeded to download the bundle anyway). If these findings suggest that mandatory disclosures will not help consumers make good marketplace choices for themselves, what policy alternatives would do a better job?

The "results not typical" language discussed in Chapter 4 is another example of failed disclosure. When an advertiser touts a particularly successful user, consumers disregard the advertiser's bias in choosing an exemplar, even when consumers explicitly acknowledge that the advertiser probably chose its best examples. This is related to the fact that concrete, vivid and easily remembered examples are misperceived as more common. *See* Ahmed E. Taha, *Selling the Outlier*, 41 J. CORP. L. 459 (2015); Jonathan J. Koehler & Molly Mercer, *Selection Neglect in Mutual Fund Advertisements*, 55 MGMT. SCI. 1107, 1110 (2009). In one study using a testimonial advertisement for a dietary supplement, "despite the presence of strongly worded, highly prominent disclaimers of typicality, between 44.1% and 70.5%" of the participants believed that the supplement would benefit "at least half of the people who try it." Manoj Hastak & Michael Mazis, *Effects of Consumer Testimonials in Weight Loss, Dietary Supplement and Business Opportunity Advertisements* (2004).

Similarly, "up to" as a disclosure about savings doesn't work very well. Consumers interpreted a promise of 47% savings and a promise of "up to" 47% savings as the same thing. Even when a clear and conspicuous disclosure of average results was added, it had little effect. Manoj Hastak & Dennis Murphy, *Effects of a Bristol Windows Advertisement With an "Up To" Savings Claim on Consumer Take-Away and Beliefs* (2012). As you can see from this study, requiring a disclosure of typical results alongside a testimonial or extreme claim doesn't work very well either, in part because most consumers can't do math very well. Should we ban advertising of atypical testimonials and outlier results?

One study found that the calorie labels on soda bottles were only slightly more effective than no labels at all at increasing consumer knowledge about the health effects of sugar--sweetened beverages or discouraging parents from choosing them for their children. Without a warning label, 60% of parents chose a sugar-sweetened beverage for their child. With a calorie label, 53% of parents did; with various warning labels, 40% did. The warning label therefore reduced parents' choice of sugar-sweetened beverages by one-third, but that reduction was from 60% to 40%. Is this a success or a failure? Christina A. Roberto et al., *The Influence of Sugar-Sweetened Beverage Health Warning Labels on Parents' Choices*, PEDIATRICS (Jan. 2016).

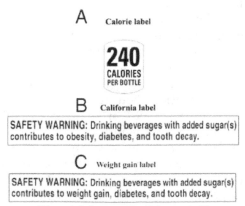

[Three labels tested by Roberto et al.]

214

Areas of Hope

There may be hope for properly formulated disclosures that focus on material attributes. Understanding why some disclosures fail can guide advertisers and regulators towards disclosures that succeed. For example, dieters who see a message focusing on the negative aspects of unhealthy food have an increased desire for and consumption of unhealthy foods, while dieters who see a two-sided message (focusing on both the negative and positive aspects of unhealthy food) are more likely to choose fewer unhealthy foods. Dieters interpret one-sided negative messages as a threat to their freedom, but two-sided messages such as "All dessert tastes good, but is bad for your health" provide more freedom of choice. Nguyen Pham et al., *Messages from the Food Police: How Food-Related Warnings Backfire among Dieters*, 1 J. ASSOC. CONSUMER RES. 175 (2016).

Some research suggests that visual disclosures or simple grading schemes may be more easily comprehended by a wider range of consumers than verbal disclosures. The FTC's research found, for example, that the health-claim disclaimers the FDA currently requires of dietary-supplement makers don't give ordinary consumers a good sense of the reliability of the underlying scientific evidence. However, a "report card" format with grades from A to D did better. *FTC Staff Comments on Assessing Consumer Perceptions of Health Claims*, Jan. 17, 2006. Traffic signal-style disclosures (red, yellow, green lights) have also proven effective for food. Christina A. Roberto et al., *Facts Up Front Versus Traffic Light Food Labels A Randomized Controlled Trial*, 43 AM. J. PREV. MED. 134 (2012); Tina Rosenberg, *Labeling the Danger in Soda*, N.Y. TIMES, Mar. 30, 2016 (in Ecuador, where traffic-light labeling for food is mandatory, consumers in 31% of households surveyed said they had stopped buying products because of the stoplight).

Other promising results come from a study in which a sign explained to purchasers how long they'd have to exercise to work off the calories in a bottle of soda or juice. The presence of the sign was associated with fewer purchases of caloric drinks and smaller bottles when there was a purchase, and the effect persisted even after the sign was removed. Sara N. Bleich et al., *Reducing Sugar-Sweetened Beverage Consumption by Providing Caloric Information: How Black Adolescents Alter Their Purchases and Whether the Effects Persist*, 104 AM. J. PUB. HEALTH 2417 (2014).

Likewise, Marianne Bertrand and Adair Morse studied payday loan borrowers and found that presenting certain information about the cost of payday borrowing—specifically information that made the long-term additive cost of payday loans salient—reduced the use of payday loans by about 10% for four months following exposure to the new information. The results were best with borrowers without a college education, those with higher self-control on self-reported measures and those with lower borrowing-to-income ratios, suggesting that they were using the increased information about total costs of borrowing to satisfy their true preferences. Their results were consistent with other research finding that people shopping for new cars were much more likely to use the miles per gallon (MPG) information if it was presented as the expected total cost of gas for a year, instead of just "miles per gallon" in the abstract. Bertrand and Morse concluded that targeted disclosure can be effective when done right, though context is vital: Disclosure at the point of on-the-spot decisions can serve to "debias" consumers away from typical mistakes. Marianne Bertrand & Adair Morse,

Information Disclosure, Cognitive Biases and Payday Borrowing, 66 J. FIN. 1865 (2011); *see also* J. Michael Collins, *Protecting Mortgage Borrowers through Risk Awareness: Evidence from Variations in State Laws*, 48 J. CONSUMER AFF. 124 (2014) (loan applicants in states that mandated enhanced warnings about foreclosures were more likely to reject high-cost refinance mortgage loan offers from a lender compared to applicants in other states).

Responding to Ben-Shahar and Schneider's general criticism of mandatory disclosure, Richard Craswell makes several points. Richard Craswell, *Static Versus Dynamic Disclosures, and How Not to Judge Their Success or Failure*, 88 WASH. L. REV. 333 (2013). Briefly summarized, he distinguishes between static disclosures, which try to help consumers choose from a fixed set of options, and dynamic disclosures, which try to change the market. A disclosure that looks like a failure from the static perspective may still have dynamic effects.

Consider the example of mandatory fat labeling on food labels. Before the Nutritional Labeling Education Act (NLEA), makers of low-fat salad dressings often disclosed their calories and fat content voluntarily as a selling point. But after the NLEA required all sellers to disclose, the market share of high-fat dressings declined. Alan Mathios, *The Impact of Mandatory Disclosure Laws on Product Choices: An Analysis of the Salad Dressing Market*, 43 J. L. & ECON. 651 (2000). Craswell notes that consumers don't need to understand technical terms, such as the meaning of "net carbohydrates" or how "miles per gallon" is calculated, as long as they can compare products: This is the dynamic effect of disclosures. Mandatory disclosure therefore supports the voluntary disclosures of some advertisers—those that have a product that's superior on the relevant attribute.

And making the disclosure mandatory can create a commonly accepted metric, such as MPG, that is easier for consumers to understand and trust than multiple competing metrics. The mandatory nature of the disclosure may also signal to some consumers that the topic is important enough to consider in their decision making.

But even from a static perspective, Craswell argues that it's a mistake to say that disclosures "fail" without carefully defining "success." Recall that no ad is understood by 100% of viewers. It would be shocking if a disclosure could do better. The question is whether a disclosure requirement's marginal benefits justify the marginal costs. A safety-related disclosure might be worthwhile even if it only helped 10% of consumers, whereas a disclosure about a less-important topic might not be. *Cf.* Joshua Mitts, *How Much Mandatory Disclosure is Effective?* (finding that prominent disclosures deterred 20–30% of study respondents from accepting unusual contract terms and increased understanding by 9–10%, though consumers tuned out if there were too many disclosures).

As an alternative, Lauren Willis has proposed performance-based measures: Rather than mandating any particular disclosures, advertisers should be prepared to prove that their ads leave consumers with a correct understanding of key terms. This, she suggests, is the only way to overcome the otherwise inevitable incentives of advertisers to chip away at the effectiveness of disclaimers and their nearly infinite creativity in doing so. For example, when AT&T added a mandatory arbitration clause to its contract, "it designed the envelope, cover letter, and amended contract through extensive *anti-marketing* market testing to ensure that most consumers would not open the envelope, or if they did open it, would not read beyond the cover letter." Lauren E. Willis, *The Consumer Financial Protection Bureau and the Quest for Consumer Comprehension, in* MICHAEL S. BARR, ED., FINANCIAL REFORM: PREVENTING THE NEXT CRISIS (2016). What do you think of this alternative to mandatory disclosures? How would performance be monitored?

A. Case Study: Distinguishing Ads from Editorial Content

The FTC's Campaign Against Undisclosed Ads

The FTC fights against surreptitious ads, such as advertising that looks like editorial content. In effect, the FTC treats the failure to disclose that the ad is an ad as a legally actionable omission.

For example, the FTC expects search engines to clearly distinguish between "organic" search results from their keyword ads. In 2013, it reminded major search-engine providers that it thinks paid keyword advertising is misleading if its nature as advertising was insufficiently disclosed. FTC, *Sample Letter to General Purpose Search Engines*, June 24, 2013. The FTC suggested use of prominent visual cues, including clear shading and borders, to distinguish ads, as well as text labels. How well does the search engine you use comply with the FTC's expectations?

Similarly, the FTC has fought against display ads that look like editorial content, sometimes called "advertorials" or "native ads." The FTC expects these advertisements to be accompanied by an effective disclosure, which may involve prominent placement—e.g., on video thumbnail images for video channels. FTC, Native Advertising: A Guide for Businesses. The evidence suggests that consumers are not very aware of such "native advertising"—and hard to educate about it. For example, in one study, ads labeled "brand voice" or "presented by" were seven times less likely to be identified as paid content than ads labeled "advertising" or "sponsored content." Only 40% of readers noticed a disclosure at the top of a page, while 90% noticed it if it appeared in an outlined box in the middle of the story, and 60% noticed it at the bottom. Only 18.3% of readers recognized the ad as an ad when the term "sponsored content" was used. Bartosz W. Wojdynski & Nathaniel J. Evans, *Going Native: Effects of Disclosure Position and Language on the Recognition and Evaluation of Online Native Advertising*, 45 J. ADVERT. 157 (2016). The FTC, which continues to prioritize this issue, has identified formatting interventions that help some consumers, but even with the fixes, many other consumers remained confused. FTC Staff Report, *Blurred Lines: An Exploration of Consumers' Advertising Recognition in the Contexts of Search Engines and Native Advertising* (Dec. 2017).

The FTC has expansive positions about what constitutes an "advertisement" and thus requires disclosure. In particular, as discussed further in Chapter 14, the FTC thinks that when an advertiser gives online bloggers and social-media influencers free product samples, any resulting blog or social media posts are advertisements that need to be disclosed as such.

Lord & Taylor's Paisley Dress

Lord & Taylor launched a new product line and decided to focus on one dress from that line. Lord & Taylor paid *Nylon*, an online fashion magazine, to run an article (and Instagram post) about the clothing featuring a photo of the dress. Lord & Taylor reviewed and approved the resulting article and Instagram post but didn't require *Nylon* to add a disclosure. In addition, Lord & Taylor recruited fifty "fashion influencers," who were paid to post photos of themselves in the dress on Instagram on one specified "product bomb" weekend, when the *Nylon* article appeared. Lord & Taylor preapproved each Instagram post to make sure the influencers included Lord & Taylor's chosen hashtags and edited some of what the influencers planned to say—but didn't require them to disclose that they were paid.

The Instagram campaign reached 11.4 million users and led to 328,000 "brand engagements" (likes, comments, reposts, etc.) using Lord & Taylor's Instagram handle. The paisley dress sold out. The FTC complaint alleged three violations of the FTCA: (1) Lord & Taylor falsely represented that the fifty Instagram images and captions reflected the independent statements of impartial fashion influencers; (2) Lord & Taylor failed to disclose the material fact that the influencers were the company's paid endorsers; and (3) Lord & Taylor falsely represented that the *Nylon* article and Instagram post reflected *Nylon*'s independent opinion about the Design Lab line, when they were really paid ads. *In re* Lord & Taylor, LLC, No. 152 3181 (F.T.C. Mar. 15, 2016).

The Lord & Taylor campaign attempted to leverage both traditional media and social media. Are disclosure obligations equally justified for these types of communications? Were the "influencers" making material representations by posting images of themselves in the paisley dress without a disclosure? Would it have made a difference if the people who posted images of themselves in the dress weren't "influencers," but were just fifty people to whom Lord & Taylor had given the dress in return for posting about it? (Do you rely on user reviews on Amazon, Yelp or other sites when you don't know the user leaving the review personally? Why or why not?)

As an exercise, can you draft a disclosure for an "influencer" that would have addressed the FTC's concerns? Can you fit it in a single tweet?

Policy Justifications for Telling Consumers When Content is Advertising

Does the FTC's efforts to squash undisclosed ads make sense? Consider these two perspectives:

REBECCA TUSHNET, *ATTENTION MUST BE PAID: COMMERCIAL SPEECH, USER-GENERATED ADS, AND THE CHALLENGE OF REGULATION*, 58 BUFFALO L. REV. 721 (2010) (EXCERPT)

[H]idden relationships may give advertisers excessive credibility by using apparently independent sources to confirm the advertiser's message.[81] Helen Norton summarizes:

> [E]vidence from cognitive psychology and related fields reveals that individuals often use a message's source as a mental shortcut, or heuristic, for evaluating its quality. Studies confirm that the more credible a speaker, the more likely her message will be effective, regardless of its content. Because speakers perceived as unpopular and/or unreliable will have more difficulty persuading listeners, they may be wise to seek the imprimatur of more trustworthy sources . . . . Moreover, the perception that a

---

[81] *See* Ellen Goodman, *Peer Promotions and False Advertising Law*, 58 S. CAR. L. REV. 683 (2007) ("Marketing theory predicts . . . that consumers will be more inclined to believe promotions when they are not clearly sourced by the brand owner. Marketing authorities instruct sponsors to keep a low profile in Web 2.0 promotions because speech that is or seems to be pure peer is more credible. If this is true, then peer promotions would seem to be highly credible and therefore potentially harmful if misrepresenting the facts. Even more so than traditional advertising, consumers would be at risk of 'uninformed acquiescence' to the advertiser's promotional scheme.") (footnotes omitted). . . .

message is endorsed by such sources can help dispel onlookers' suspicion of perspectives understood to be in the speaker's own interest.[82]

. . . Studies of Internet use in particular replicate this result. To take one significant example, consumers seek out and trust health information from other people (apparently) like them much more than they seek out and trust information from pharmaceutical companies.[84]

Advertisers can also take advantage of the phenomenon of social proof: People have a powerful tendency to put faith in the wisdom of crowds, which viral marketing can simulate.[85] Multiple sources endorsing the same product are more persuasive than a single source repeated multiple times.[86] Using apparently different sources is especially useful for strengthening initially less-plausible claims. Even better from the marketer's perspective, people don't understand why they find the repeated, multiple-source claim plausible. They attribute it to the inherent truth value of the claim rather than to the repetition, making them particularly vulnerable to manipulation of this type.[87]

With a wide swath of user-generated content, in the absence of disclosure, a consumer can't tell whether a reviewer was compensated for the review or was simply sharing her opinion because she believed everyone is entitled to it. . . . Given that companies exist to sell their products and services, the default expectation is that the money has flowed from consumer to seller by the consumer's choice and not the reverse. As a result, in the absence of disclosure,

---

[82] Helen Norton, *The Measure of Government Speech: Identifying Expression's Source*, 88 B.U. L. REV. 587, 592–93 (2008) (footnotes omitted); *see also* Shelly Chaiken & Durairaj Maheswaran, *Heuristic Processing Can Bias Systematic Processing: Effects of Source Credibility, Argument Ambiguity, and Task Importance on Attitude Judgment*, 66 J. PERSONALITY & SOC. PSYCHOL. 460, 464 (1994) (finding that, under many circumstances, product evaluations supposedly from *Consumer Reports* were more persuasive than the identical evaluations supposedly from a retailer); Roobina Ohanian, *The Impact of Celebrity Spokespersons' Perceived Image on Consumers' Intention to Purchase*, 31 J. ADVERT. RES. 46 (1991) (noting that friends are perceived as more trustworthy than sales personnel because of the potential conflict of interest and that "the audience does not associate a high level of trustworthiness with individuals [such as celebrity endorsers] who get paid handsomely to promote a product"); Elaine Walster et al., *On Increasing the Persuasiveness of a Low Prestige Communicator*, 2 J. EXPERIMENTAL SOC. PSYCHOL. 325 (1966) *available at* http://www2.hawaii.edu/~elaineh/14.pdf (stating that perceived self-interest decreases the credibility of a source, while perceived altruism increases it, whether the source is generally low in credibility (a criminal) or high in credibility (a prosecutor)).

[84] Noah Elkin, *How America Searches: Health and Wellness*, ICROSSING, Jan. 2008, *available at* http://www.icrossing.com/research/how-america-searches-health-and-wellness.php (showing substantial use of user-generated content and online social communities for health and wellness information); *id.* ("Consumers rank pharmaceutical companies and television as the two least trusted sources for information about health-related issues and questions, and place them in the bottom tier in terms of sources that influence their medication choices.").

[85] ROBERT B. CIALDINI, INFLUENCE: SCIENCE AND PRACTICE 99 (5th ed. Pearson 2009) (1985); Norton, *supra* ("Some onlookers also rely on the public's reaction to a message as a shortcut for evaluating its content, using widespread acceptance or audience enthusiasm to gauge a message's quality.").

[86] Anne L. Roggeveen & Gita Venkataramani Johar, *Perceived Source Variability Versus Familiarity: Testing Competing Explanations for the Truth Effect*, 12 J. CONSUMER PSYCHOL. 81 (2002) ("[B]elief in a claim is greater when it is perceived as coming from two different sources (vs. a single source).") . . . .

[87] *Id.* ("[T]he truth effect does occur for seemingly less plausible statements; however this occurs only under conditions where the multiple repetitions can be attributed to multiple sources. . . . [S]ubjects had no access to their use of number of sources in rating the truth value. Instead, subjects seized on the most likely explanation for their ratings—the plausibility of the claim. It appears that the use of source variability is an automatic process.").

consumers will not assume that an apparently independent endorsement is in fact sponsored.

Without regulation, a market for lemons will develop—a deterioration in the credibility of public discourse because audiences won't be able to trust that a stated opinion is independent and sincerely held. . . .

A final matter of significant theoretical interest is the question of what, exactly, is false or misleading about undisclosed endorsement relationships. In the U nited States, the law has rarely attempted to regulate "image" advertising—advertising that does not make factual representations but attempts to create a warm fuzzy glow or other feeling about a product or service. From a classic commercial speech perspective, regulation of image ads would be difficult to justify because such ads are not falsifiable and thus can't be false. In false advertising doctrine, such claims are considered non-actionable puffery, on which no reasonable consumer would rely. The law has, in other words, equated non-falsifiability with unreliability and irrebuttably presumed that consumers do not rely on that which is objectively unreliable.

But what about an endorser paid to puff? The regulatory theory is that an undisclosed sponsorship relationship could distort consumer decision making. Yet how could there be material deception if the endorser's positive but detail-free message was puffery? The endorsement guidelines implicitly recognize that, as advertising scholars have long maintained, image ads *do* affect consumer decisions—puffery *works*, which is why advertisers use it. Nonetheless, in the United States, we usually do not try to regulate puffery because of the falsifiability problem. It is only when there is an undisclosed financial relationship that we can identify a specific element of the message that's deceptive.

It is still important to recognize that in an undisclosed sponsorship case where the speaker simply puffs, the deception can only be material if vague, fact-free claims made by a sufficiently credible source affect purchase decisions. . . .

The cool kid who tells her friends that a product is really awesome can get them to buy it. The cool kid's endorsement might even be performative, in that the endorsement *makes* the product cool. This is related to the problem of the placebo effect, where claiming that a product produces certain effects leads consumers to believe in (and even experience) those effects. The law has had little trouble finding that products that only work because of the placebo effect are falsely advertised. Regardless of how coolness is produced, it matters whether the cool kid is telling her friends voluntarily or for pay. This conclusion requires us to take even non-falsifiable claims seriously as claims that can distort a consumer's decisions.

ERIC GOLDMAN, *STEALTH RISKS OF REGULATING STEALTH MARKETING: A COMMENT ON ELLEN GOODMAN'S STEALTH MARKETING AND EDITORIAL INTEGRITY*, 85 TEXAS L. REV. SEE ALSO 11 (2006) (EXCERPT)

[C]onsumer distrust toward marketing is so strong that consumers often disregard marketing without assessing its actual utility to them. The "advertising" label is a powerful disclosure; it can single-handedly cause consumers to overlook content they would have otherwise found meritorious. A 2005 study by Jansen and Resnick illustrates this risk. Consumers were shown multiple sets of Internet search results, some of which were labeled advertising. Although the search results substantively were the same, consumers rated the unlabeled search results as more relevant than the labeled results. In other words, the advertising label single-handedly degraded the consumers' relevancy assessment even though the search results had the same level of relevancy.

The risk of consumer overresponse to marketing labels poses an interesting policy conundrum. Superficially, the populist approach would be to give consumers what they want (to know when content is marketing). Yet, this approach has the risk of counterproductively and systematically increasing consumers' erroneous content assessments, which in turn may hurt consumers' ability to get content they would find useful. At minimum, any cost–benefit analysis of sponsorship disclosure laws should account for the costs of these errors.

. . . [M]any consumers already suffer from information overload. Yet, noisy disclosures consume more of their already-strapped attention. Some consumers will feel that the disclosed information is valuable enough that they will not mind the "cost" of having their attention consumed, but others will resent the imposition. For the latter consumers, the mandated disclosure becomes another form of spam (unwanted content).

Ironically, mandated sponsorship disclosures could create a negative externality analogous to the one that [Ellen Goodman's] article attributes to stealth marketing. The article argues that stealth marketing degrades consumer trust in otherwise-trustworthy content. Similarly, to the extent that consumers do not find mandated sponsorship disclosures valuable to them, they will tune them out. Further, if consumers routinely find mandated disclosures unhelpful, they may be inclined to adopt an across-the-board heuristic to tune out mandated disclosures, even if those disclosures are socially valuable. Thus, as disclosures generally become noisier, consumers may increasingly become disinterested in all of them—a different negative externality than the one identified by the article, but problematic nonetheless.

Second, as discussed above, noisier disclosures should increase the number of consumers who see the disclosure and use it to make erroneous categorization judgments about the marketing. Indeed, this effect may support a self-reinforcing feedback loop. By mandating sponsorship disclosures, the government communicates to consumers that they should care about the distinctions between editorial and marketing content. Thus, consumers may care about the editorial–marketing divide because the government has mandated disclosure, while the government may mandate disclosure because consumers say they care about the divide.

NOTES AND QUESTIONS

Aren't so many things material that if we treated each one like sponsorship, we'd drown consumers in theoretically relevant—but functionally useless—information? *See* Sarah C. Haan, Note, *The 'Persuasion Route' of the Law: Advertising and Legal Persuasion*, 100 COLUM. L. REV. 1281 (2000) (discussing research indicating that consumers prefer not to face more than a few bits of information per advertisement). In any event, how can undisclosed sponsorship be material in cases where the only message conveyed is puffery?

Disclosure as Panacea? Research on disclosure of conflicts of interest sounds a cautionary note. Recipients of advice don't discount advice from biased advisors after disclosure as much as they should. *See* Daylian M. Cain et al., *The Dirt on Coming Clean: Perverse Effects of Disclosing Conflicts of Interest*, 34 J. LEGAL STUD. 1 (2005). Disclosure of a conflict of interest may increase trust unwarrantedly by making the audience feel that the speaker is being scrupulously honest. This is especially troubling because, as Cain et al. show, disclosure can increase advisors' bias, perhaps because they feel "morally licensed" by disclosure to pursue their own self-interest, and also perhaps because self-interest leads them to persuade themselves that their biased advice is best. While disclosures did lead listeners to discount the advice they received, that wasn't enough to offset the increase in the bias of the recommendations. *But see* Genevieve Helleringer, *Trust Me, I Have a Conflict of Interest! Testing the Efficacy of Disclosure in Retail Investment Advice*, Oxford Legal Studies Research Paper No. 14/2016 (finding that disclosing that the disclosure is legally required, and clearly explaining the financial implications of the conflict of interest, could be effective when participants could compare advice and disclosures across multiple ads); Eva A. van Reijmersdal et al., *The Effects of Brand Placement Disclosures on Skepticism and Brand Memory*, 38 COMM. 127 (2013) (noting conflicting studies on whether disclosure about persuasion triggers skepticism and resistance).

How might this research apply to disclosure of endorsements? Is a blogger who follows the disclosure rules even more likely to give a positive review of a product she got for free? On the other side, will consumers be more or less trusting after disclosure?

B.   Legislative Definition of Terms

Closely related to the issue of mandatory disclosures is the question of when, if ever, the government can establish by fiat that a word or phrase has a particular meaning, so that an advertiser who uses the word or phrase differently is engaged in false advertising. The following case considers this issue against the backdrop of economic exploitation of Native Americans and the hope that Native American arts and crafts can provide economic benefits to Native American artisans. Being able to promise "authenticity," when non-Native artisans can't, is apparently valuable, so non-Native American artisans have incentives to suggest that they too are offering "real" Native American art. How far can the government go in combating this free-riding?

NATIVE AMERICAN ARTS, INC. V. WALDRON CORP., 399 F.3D 871 (7TH CIR. 2005)

The Indian Arts and Crafts Act, 25 U.S.C. §§ 305 et seq., forbids (so far as bears on this case) selling a good "in a manner that falsely suggests it is . . . an Indian product." The principal plaintiff, Native American Arts (NAA), is a seller of goods produced by Indians. It brought this suit for damages against a non-Indian manufacturer of Indian-style jewelry that is advertised under such names as "Navajo," "Crow," "Southwest Tribes," and "Zuni Bear" and sold with tags that give information about the tribe. The ads identify the designer of the jewelry as Trisha Waldron, who is not an Indian. Neither the tags nor the ads contain any disclaimer of authenticity. The case was tried to a jury, the verdict was for the defendants, and the plaintiffs appeal.

Although the Indian Arts and Crafts Act dates back to 1935, this is—amazingly—the first reported appellate case under it. Until 1990, the only sanction for violating the false-advertising provision was criminal; and there were no prosecutions—zero. In 1990, Congress authorized government and private civil suits, in which hefty damages can be awarded. There have been some suits under the amended statute, but none until this one that got beyond the district court level.

The plaintiffs' principal argument is that the district judge should not have held unconstitutional, and therefore refused to base an instruction to the jury on, a regulation that provides that "the unqualified use of the term 'Indian' or . . . of the name of an Indian tribe . . . in connection with an art or craft product is interpreted to mean . . . that the art or craft product is an Indian product." 25 C.F.R. § 309.24(a)(2). . . .

[The plaintiffs] challenge the soundness of Judge Der-Yeghiayan's ruling that the "unqualified use" regulation infringes freedom of speech and is also unconstitutionally vague and overbroad. He indeed was wrong. If he were right, trademark law would be unconstitutional. In effect the regulation makes "Indian" the trademark denoting products made by Indians, just as "Roquefort" denotes a cheese manufactured from sheep's milk cured in limestone caves in the Roquefort region of France. A non-Indian maker of jewelry designed to look like jewelry made by Indians is free to advertise the similarity but if he uses the word "Indian" he must qualify the usage so that consumers aren't confused and think they're buying not only the kind of jewelry that Indians make, but jewelry that Indians in fact made. There is no constitutional infirmity. But this conclusion does less for the plaintiffs than they hoped.

The regulation is the work of a small office in the Department of Interior called the Indian Arts and Crafts Board, and a more substantial question than the constitutional questions that bedazzled the district judge is whether a regulation that "interpret[s]" "the unqualified use of the term 'Indian' . . . or the unqualified use of the name of an Indian tribe" to denote "an Indian product" is authorized by the Indian Arts and Crafts Act, which so far as relates to this issue merely authorizes the Department of the Interior to define the term "Indian product." That is not an authorization to determine what representations convey the impression that a work is such a product. There is no indication that Congress delegated to the Department authority to determine what constitutes sufficient proof of false advertising. The meaning of "Indian product" is plausibly within the scope of knowledge of an Indian Arts and Crafts Board—but not the requisites for proving consumer confusion, especially when it is not Indians, but non-Indians, who are the principal consumers of faux Indian products, and especially since the Board's enforcement role is extremely limited. The Board cannot conduct or initiate remedial proceedings; all it can do is refer complaints to the FBI for investigation, and to the Department of Justice for prosecution or civil action.

Well, it can do a little more; it can indicate the circumstances in which it will make such a reference. . . . The Board is certainly free to announce the policy that will guide it in deciding whether to refer matters to the Department of Justice for possible action. The "qualified use" regulation should be understood in this light rather than as an attempt to tell the courts how to decide whether consumers are likely to be confused.

But suppose we are wrong and the regulation governs suits to enforce the Indian Arts and Crafts Act; the next question would be the meaning of "unqualified use" and the bearing of that meaning on jury instructions, the closing arguments, and the jury's verdict. Perhaps the most natural meaning of "unqualified use of the term 'Indian' " or of the name of an Indian tribe is using the word or the name to denote an Indian product without including a disclaimer, such as "Indian style," or, more emphatically, if rather off-putting, "not manufactured by Indians." A common dictionary definition of "unqualified" is "not modified by reservations or restrictions."

. . . [T]he required qualification of the use of the name could consist of any pertinent contextual elements, such as the picture of Trisha Waldron that appears in some of the advertising or the type of store in which her jewelry is sold. [The court found that plaintiffs' proposed instruction related to the Board's rule would have been unhelpful to the jury.]

In any event the regulation (always assuming, contrary to our earlier ruling, that the regulation governs in litigation) would be pertinent only in a case in which there was no context: a case for example in which Waldron sold an unadvertised product labeled simply "Navajo Bracelet," with no mention of the manufacturer or even identification of the outlets in which the bracelet was sold—with nothing but the name and the price. There was plenty of context in this case. The question the jury had to answer was not what the names of the various items of jewelry meant but what the entire sales package, including advertising, labeling, and place of sale, suggested to the average consumer. In such a case, asking whether the defendant falsely suggested that it was selling Indian products, and asking whether it failed to qualify its use of the names of Indian tribes, come to the same thing.

So there was no error in the instructions. . . .

NOTES AND QUESTIONS

Should Congress enact the Board's rule into law? If it did, would that be constitutional?

How could "the picture of Trisha Waldron that appears in some of the advertising or the type of store in which her jewelry is sold" educate consumers about the true origin of the jewelry? Is the court making warranted assumptions about what Native Americans look like or where they sell their goods? If consumers use pictures and types of stores as proxies for authenticity, are they buying into stereotypes, and if so, could explicit labeling do anything to help?

In 2019, the federal government secured a guilty plea for a criminal violation of IACA by a seller who admitted "selling Native American-style jewelry made by laborers in the Philippines; mixing Filipino-made jewelry with Native American-made jewelry without labeling the Filipino-made jewelry with the country of origin; intentionally stocking the Filipino-made jewelry in a manner that falsely suggested that it was Native-American made; providing lists for the employees to reference symbols and initials to falsely suggest the jewelry was Native American-made; and training employees to tell customers the jewelry was Native American-made." As an example of the false suggestion of Native American origin, the seller told an undercover agent that one set of jewelry was "Zuni" and that another was "Navajo." Dep't of Justice, U.S. Attorney's Office, D.N.M., *Owner of Old Town Albuquerque Jewelry Stores Sentenced to Six Months for Fraudulently Selling Filipino-Made Jewelry as Native American-Made*, Aug. 28, 2018.

C.   Disclosures and the First Amendment

The *Native American Arts* case involves a government attempt to define certain terms, but government control goes much farther. Sometimes, consumers might distinguish between products, but the government might want them to be labeled identically—or, contrariwise, the government might want to highlight differences about which consumers wouldn't otherwise know or care. Mandatory definitions and disclosures thus implicate important policy concerns—from what we should be consuming to how extensive commercial speakers' rights should be.

Consider the following case:

AM. MEAT INST. V. U.S. DEPT. OF AGRICULTURE, 760 F.3D 18 (D.C. CIR. 2014) (EN BANC)

WILLIAMS, Senior Circuit Judge:

Reviewing a regulation of the Secretary of Agriculture that mandates disclosure of country-of-origin information about meat products, a panel of this court rejected the plaintiffs' statutory and First Amendment challenges. The panel found the plaintiffs unlikely to succeed on the merits and affirmed the district court's denial of a preliminary injunction. On the First Amendment claim, the panel read *Zauderer v. Office of Disciplinary Counsel,* 471 U.S. 626, 651 (1985), to apply to disclosure mandates aimed at addressing problems other than deception (which the mandate at issue in *Zauderer* had been designed to remedy). . . . We now hold that *Zauderer* in fact does reach beyond problems of deception, sufficiently to encompass the disclosure mandates at issue here.

* * *

Congress has required country-of-origin labels on a variety of foods, including some meat products, and tasked the Secretary of Agriculture with implementation. . . . For meat cuts, at least, the amended statute defined country of origin based on where the animal has been born, raised, and slaughtered—the three major production steps.

The Secretary, whom we refer to interchangeably with his delegate the Agricultural Marketing Service ("AMS"), first promulgated rules in 2009. The rules did not demand explicit identification of the production step(s) occurring in each listed country, but called more simply for labeling with a phrase starting "Product of," followed by mention of one or more countries. The 2009 rule also made allowance for a production practice known as "commingling." This made the labeling of meat cuts from animals of different origins processed together on a single production day relatively simple; the label could just name all the countries of origin for the commingled animals.

After the 2009 rule's adoption, Canada and Mexico filed a complaint with the Dispute Settlement Body of the World Trade Organization. In due course the WTO's Appellate Body found the rule to be in violation of the WTO Agreement on Technical Barriers to Trade. The gravamen of the WTO's decision appears to have been an objection to the relative imprecision of the information required by the 2009 rule. In a different section of its opinion, the Appellate Body seemed to agree with the United States that country-of-origin labeling in general can serve a legitimate objective in informing consumers. A WTO arbitrator gave the United States a deadline to bring its requirements into compliance with the ruling.

The Secretary responded with a rule requiring more precise information—revealing the location of each production step. For example, meat derived from an animal born in Canada and raised and slaughtered in the United States, which formerly could have been labeled "Product of the United States and Canada," would now have to be labeled "Born in Canada, Raised and Slaughtered in the United States." In a matter of great concern to plaintiffs because of its cost implications, the 2013 rule also eliminated the flexibility allowed in labeling commingled animals.

The plaintiffs, a group of trade associations representing livestock producers, feedlot operators, and meat packers, whom we'll collectively call American Meat Institute ("AMI"), challenged the 2013 rule in district court as a violation of both the statute and the First Amendment. This led to the decisions summarized at the outset of this opinion.

AMI argues that the 2013 rule violates its First Amendment right to freedom of speech by requiring it to disclose country-of-origin information to retailers, who will ultimately provide the information to consumers. The question before us, framed in the order granting en banc review, is whether the test set forth in *Zauderer,* 471 U.S. at 651, applies to government interests beyond consumer deception. Instead, AMI says, we should apply the general test for commercial speech restrictions formulated in *Central Hudson,* 447 U.S. 557, 566, 100 S.Ct. 2343 (1980). . . .

* * *

The starting point common to both parties is that *Zauderer* applies to government mandates requiring disclosure of "purely factual and uncontroversial information" appropriate to prevent deception in the regulated party's commercial speech. The key question for us is whether the principles articulated in *Zauderer* apply more broadly to factual and uncontroversial disclosures required to serve other government interests. AMI also argues that even if *Zauderer* extends beyond correction of deception, the government has no interest in country-of-origin labeling substantial enough to sustain the challenged rules.

Zauderer itself does not give a clear answer. Some of its language suggests possible confinement to correcting deception. Having already described the disclosure mandated there as limited to "purely factual and uncontroversial information about the terms under which [the transaction was proposed]," the Court said, "we hold that an advertiser's rights are adequately protected as long as [such] disclosure requirements are reasonably related to the State's interest in preventing deception of consumers." 471 U.S. at 651. (It made no finding that the advertiser's message was "more likely to deceive the public than to inform it," which would constitutionally subject the message to an outright ban. *See Central Hudson,* 447 U.S. at 563.) The Court's own later application of *Zauderer* in *Milavetz, Gallop & Milavetz, P.A. v. United States,* 559 U.S. 229 (2010), also focused on remedying misleading advertisements, which was the sole interest invoked by the government. Given the subject of both cases, it was natural for the Court to express the rule in such terms. The language could have been simply descriptive of the circumstances to which the Court applied its new rule, or it could have aimed to preclude any application beyond those circumstances.

The language with which *Zauderer* justified its approach, however, sweeps far more broadly than the interest in remedying deception. After recounting the elements of *Central Hudson, Zauderer* rejected that test as unnecessary in light of the "material differences between disclosure requirements and outright prohibitions on speech." Later in the opinion, the Court observed that "the First Amendment interests implicated by disclosure requirements are substantially weaker than those at stake when speech is actually suppressed." After noting that the disclosure took the form of "purely factual and uncontroversial information about the terms under which [the] services will be available," the Court characterized the speaker's interest as "minimal": "Because the extension of First Amendment protection to commercial speech is justified principally by the value to consumers of the information such speech provides, appellant's constitutionally protected interest in *not* providing any particular factual information in his advertising is minimal." All told, *Zauderer*'s characterization of the speaker's interest in opposing forced disclosure of such information as "minimal" seems inherently applicable beyond the problem of deception, as other circuits have found. . . .

In applying *Zauderer,* we first must assess the adequacy of the interest motivating the country-of-origin labeling scheme. AMI argues that, even assuming *Zauderer* applies here, the government has utterly failed to show an adequate interest in making country-of-origin information available to consumers. AMI disparages the government's interest as simply being that of satisfying consumers' "idle curiosity." Counsel for AMI acknowledged during oral argument that her theory would as a logical matter doom the statute, "if the only justification that Congress has offered is the justification that it offered here. . . ."

Beyond the interest in correcting misleading or confusing commercial speech, *Zauderer* gives little indication of what type of interest might suffice. In particular, the Supreme Court has not made clear whether *Zauderer* would permit government reliance on interests that do not qualify as substantial under *Central Hudson*'s standard, a standard that itself seems elusive. But here we think several aspects of the government's interest in country-of-origin labeling for food combine to make the interest substantial: the context and long history of country-of-origin disclosures to enable consumers to choose American-made products; the demonstrated consumer interest in extending country-of-origin labeling to food products; and the individual health concerns and market impacts that can arise in the event of a food-borne illness outbreak. Because the interest motivating the 2013 rule is a substantial one, we need not decide whether a lesser interest could suffice under *Zauderer.*

Country-of-origin information has an historical pedigree that lifts it well above "idle curiosity." History can be telling. In *Burson v. Freeman,* 504 U.S. 191, 211 (1992) (plurality opinion), for example, the Court, applying strict scrutiny to rules banning electioneering within a 100–foot zone around polling places, found an adequate justification in a "long history, a substantial consensus, and simple common sense." And country-of-origin label mandates indeed have a "long history." Congress has been imposing similar mandates since 1890, giving such rules a run just short of 125 years.

The history relied on in *Burson* was (as here) purely of legislative action, not First Amendment rulings by the judiciary. But just as in *Burson,* where "[t]he majority of [the] laws were adopted originally in the 1890s," the "time-tested consensus" that consumers want to know the geographical origin of potential purchases has material weight in and of itself. The Congress that extended country-of-origin mandates to food did so against a historical backdrop that has made the value of this particular product information to consumers a matter of common sense.

Supporting members of Congress identified the statute's purpose as enabling customers to make informed choices based on characteristics of the products they wished to purchase, including United States supervision of the entire production process for health and hygiene. Some expressed a belief that with information about meat's national origin, many would choose American meat on the basis of a belief that it would in truth be better. Even though the production steps abroad for food imported into the United States are to a degree subject to U.S. government monitoring, it seems reasonable for Congress to anticipate that many consumers may prefer food that had been continuously under a particular government's direct scrutiny.

Some legislators also expressed the belief that people would have a special concern about the geographical origins of what they eat. This is manifest in anecdotes appearing in the legislative record, such as the collapse of the cantaloupe market when some imported cantaloupes proved to be contaminated and consumers were unable to determine whether the melons on the shelves had come from that country. Of course the anecdote more broadly suggests the utility of these disclosures in the event of any disease outbreak known to have a specific country of origin, foreign or domestic.

The record is further bolstered by surveys AMS reviewed, such as one indicating that 71–73 percent of consumers would be willing to pay for country-of-origin information about their food. The AMS quite properly noted the vulnerabilities in such data. Most obvious is the point that consumers tend to overstate their willingness to pay; after all, the data sound possibly useful, and giving a "Yes" answer on the survey doesn't cost a nickel. But such studies, combined with the many favorable comments the agency received during all of its rulemakings, reinforce the historical basis for treating such information as valuable. . . .

Finally, agency statements (from prior rulemakings) claiming that country-of-origin labeling serves no food safety interest are not inconsistent with any of the government's litigation positions here. Simply because the agency believes it has other, superior means to protect food safety doesn't delegitimize a congressional decision to empower consumers to take possible country-specific differences in safety practices into account. Nor does such an agency belief undercut the economy-wide benefits of confining the market impact of a disease outbreak.

Having determined that the interest served by the disclosure mandate is adequate, what remains is to assess the relationship between the government's identified means and its chosen ends. Under *Central Hudson,* we would determine whether "the regulatory technique [is] in proportion to [the] interest," an inquiry comprised of assessing whether the chosen means "directly advance[s] the state interest involved" and whether it is narrowly tailored to serve that end. *Zauderer* 's method of evaluating fit differs in wording, though perhaps not significantly in substance, at least on these facts.

When the Supreme Court has analyzed *Central Hudson*'s "directly advance" requirement, it has commonly required evidence of a measure's effectiveness. But as the Court recognized in *Zauderer,* such evidentiary parsing is hardly necessary when the government uses a disclosure mandate to achieve a goal of informing consumers about a particular product trait, assuming of course that the reason for informing consumers qualifies as an adequate interest. 471 U.S. at 650; *see also Milavetz,* 559 U.S. at 249 (referring to *Zauderer* as providing for "less exacting scrutiny"). *Zauderer,* like the doctrine of *res ipsa loquitur,* identifies specific circumstances where a party carries part of its evidentiary burden in a way different from the customary one. There, a plaintiff proves negligence by meeting the specified criteria (such as proving the defendant's exclusive control over the agency causing the injury); here, by acting only through a reasonably crafted disclosure mandate, the government meets its burden of showing that the mandate advances its interest in making the "purely factual and uncontroversial information" accessible to the recipients. Of course to match *Zauderer* logically, the disclosure mandated must relate to the good or service offered by the regulated party, a link that in *Zauderer* itself was inherent in the facts, as the disclosure mandate necessarily related to such goods or services. For purposes of this case, we need not decide on the precise scope or character of that relationship.

The self-evident tendency of a disclosure mandate to assure that recipients get the mandated information may in part explain why, where that is the goal, many such mandates have persisted for decades without anyone questioning their constitutionality. In this long-lived group have been not only country-of-origin labels but also many other routine disclosure mandates about product attributes, including, for instance, disclosures of fiber content, care instructions for clothing items, and listing of ingredients.

Notwithstanding the reference to "narrow tailoring," the Court has made clear that the government's burden on the final *Central Hudson* factor is to show a "reasonable fit," or a "reasonable proportion," between means and ends. To the extent that the government's interest is in assuring that consumers receive particular information (as it plainly is when mandating disclosures that correct deception), the means-end fit is self-evidently satisfied when the government acts only through a reasonably crafted mandate to disclose "purely factual and uncontroversial information" about attributes of the product or service being offered. In other words, this particular method of achieving a government interest will almost always demonstrate a reasonable means-ends relationship, absent a showing that the disclosure is "unduly burdensome" in a way that "chill[s] protected commercial speech."

Thus, to the extent that the pre-conditions to application of *Zauderer* warrant inferences that the mandate will "directly advance" the government's interest and show a "reasonable fit" between means and ends, one could think of *Zauderer* largely as "an *application* of *Central*

Hudson, where several of *Central Hudson's* elements have already been established."

In this case, the criteria triggering the application of *Zauderer* are either unchallenged or substantially unchallenged. The decision requires the disclosures to be of "purely factual and uncontroversial information" about the good or service being offered. AMI does not contest that country-of-origin labeling qualifies as factual, and the facts conveyed are directly informative of intrinsic characteristics of the product AMI is selling.

As to whether it is "controversial," AMI objected to the word "slaughter" in its reply brief. Though it seems a plain, blunt word for a plain, blunt action, we can understand a claim that "slaughter," used on a product of any origin, might convey a certain innuendo. But we need not address such a claim because the 2013 rule allows retailers to use the term "harvested" instead, and AMI has posed no objection to that. And AMI does not disagree with the truth of the facts required to be disclosed, so there is no claim that they are controversial in that sense.

We also do not understand country-of-origin labeling to be controversial in the sense that it communicates a message that is controversial for some reason other than dispute about simple factual accuracy. Leaving aside the possibility that some required factual disclosures could be so one-sided or incomplete that they would not qualify as "factual and uncontroversial," country-of-origin facts are not of that type. AMI does not suggest anything controversial about the message that its members are required to express.

Nor does the mandate run afoul of the Court's warning that *Zauderer* does not leave the state "free to require corporations to carry the messages of third parties, where the messages themselves are biased against or are expressly contrary to the corporation's views."

Finally, though it may be obvious, we note that *Zauderer* cannot justify a disclosure so burdensome that it essentially operates as a restriction on constitutionally protected speech, as in *Ibanez v. Florida Department of Business and Professional Regulation,* 512 U.S. 136, 146–47 (1994), where a required disclaimer was so detailed that it "effectively rule[d] out notation of the 'specialist' designation on a business card or letterhead, or in a yellow pages listing." Nor can it sustain mandates that "chill[ ] protected commercial speech." AMI has made no claim of either of these consequences.

Accordingly we answer affirmatively the general question of whether "government interests in addition to correcting deception," can be invoked to sustain a disclosure mandate under *Zauderer,* and specifically find the interests invoked here to be sufficient. . . .

So ordered.

[ROGERS, J., concurring in part, argued that *Central Hudson* and *Zauderer* were in fact separate standards and that thinking of *Zauderer* as a mere application of *Central Hudson* to the mandatory disclosure situation blurred the tests. Specifically, *Zauderer* does not put the burden on the government to show that a disclosure requirement directly advances its interest. Because commercial speakers have minimal interests in avoiding truthful, relevant disclosures, and such disclosures promote the free flow of truthful information, disclosure requirements need only be reasonably related to the State's interest in preventing deception of consumers. *Zauderer* explained that "disclosure requirements trench much more narrowly on an advertiser's interests than do flat prohibitions on speech," and Judge Rogers concluded that "the Court was not tracing a shortcut through *Central Hudson* but defining a category in which the interests at stake were less threatened."]

KAVANAUGH, Circuit Judge, concurring in the judgment:

May the U.S. Government require an imported Chinese-made product to be labeled "Made in China"? For many readers, the question probably answers itself: Yes. This case requires us to explain why that is so, in particular why such a requirement passes muster under the First Amendment. The precise First Amendment issue before us concerns a federal law that requires country-of-origin labels for meat and other food products. Country-of-origin labels are of course familiar to American consumers. Made in America. Made in Mexico. Made in China. And so on. For many decades, Congress has mandated such country-of-origin labels for a variety of products. I agree with the majority opinion that the First Amendment does not bar those longstanding and commonplace country-of-origin labeling requirements.

As a starting point, all agree that the First Amendment imposes stringent limits on the Government's authority to either restrict or compel speech by private citizens and organizations. This case involves commercial speech. The First Amendment protects commercial speech, and regulations of commercial speech are analyzed under the Supreme Court's *Central Hudson* framework. To justify laws regulating commercial speech, the Government must (i) identify a substantial governmental interest and (ii) demonstrate a sufficient fit between the law's requirements and that substantial governmental interest.

I will address in turn how those two basic *Central Hudson* requirements apply to this case.

First, under *Central Hudson,* the Government must identify a substantial governmental interest that is served by the law in question. Since its decision in *Central Hudson,* the Supreme Court has not stated that something less than a "substantial" governmental interest would justify either a restriction on commercial speech or a compelled commercial disclosure. And likewise, the majority opinion today does not say that a governmental interest that is less than substantial would suffice to justify a compelled commercial disclosure.

What interests qualify as sufficiently substantial to justify the infringement on the speaker's First Amendment autonomy that results from a compelled commercial disclosure? Here, as elsewhere in First Amendment free-speech law, history and tradition are reliable guides. ...

[T]he Government cannot advance a traditional anti-deception, health, or safety interest in this case because a country-of-origin disclosure requirement obviously does not serve those interests. Rather, the Government broadly contends that it has a substantial interest in "providing consumers with information." For *Central Hudson* purposes, however, it is plainly not enough for the Government to say simply that it has a substantial interest in giving consumers information. After all, that would be true of any and all disclosure requirements. That circular formulation would drain the *Central Hudson* test of any meaning in the context of compelled commercial disclosures. Not surprisingly, governments (federal, state, and local) would love to have such a free pass to spread their preferred messages on the backs of others. But as the Second Circuit has stated, "Were consumer interest alone sufficient, there is no end to the information that states could require manufacturers to disclose about their production methods." International Dairy Foods Association v. Amestoy, 92 F.3d 67, 74 (2d Cir.1996). Some consumers might want to know whether their U.S.-made product was made by U.S. citizens and not by illegal immigrants. Some consumers might want to know whether a doctor has ever performed an abortion. Some consumers might want to know the political affiliation of a business's owners. These are not far-fetched hypotheticals, particularly at the state or local level. Do such consumer desires suffice to justify compelled commercial disclosures of such information on a product or in an advertisement? I think not, and history and tradition provide no support for that kind of free-wheeling government power to mandate compelled commercial disclosures. . . .

Although the Government's broad argument is meritless, country-of-origin labeling is justified by the Government's historically rooted interest in supporting American manufacturers, farmers, and ranchers as they compete with foreign manufacturers, farmers, and ranchers. Since the early days of the Republic, numerous U.S. laws have sought to further that interest, sometimes overtly and sometimes subtly. Although economists debate whether various kinds of protectionist legislation help U.S. consumers and the overall U.S. economy, there is no doubt that Congress has long sought to support and promote various U.S. industries against their foreign competition. How is that interest implicated by country-of-origin labeling? Country-of-origin labeling, it is widely understood, causes many American consumers (for a variety of reasons) to buy a higher percentage of American-made products, which in turn helps American manufacturers, farmers, and ranchers as compared to foreign manufacturers, farmers, and ranchers. That is why Congress has long mandated country-of-origin disclosures for certain products. *See, e.g.,* United States v. Ury, 106 F.2d 28, 29 (2d Cir.1939) (purpose of early country-of-origin labeling requirements "was to apprise the public of the foreign origin and thus to confer an advantage on domestic producers of competing goods"). That historical pedigree is critical for First Amendment purposes and demonstrates that the Government's interest here is substantial. The majority opinion properly relies on the history of country-of-origin labeling laws as a basis for finding that the Government has a substantial interest in this case.

That said, one wrinkle in this case [is that] the Executive Branch has refrained during this litigation from expressly articulating its clear interest in supporting American farmers and ranchers in order to justify this law, apparently because of the international repercussions that might ensue. But the interest here is obvious, even if unarticulated by the Executive Branch for reasons of international comity. And more to the point for *Central Hudson* purposes, Members of Congress did articulate the interest in supporting American farmers and ranchers when Congress enacted this country-of-origin labeling law. And Congress's articulation of the interest suffices under *Central Hudson*.

In short, the Government has a substantial interest in this case in supporting American farmers and ranchers against their foreign competitors.

The second question under *Central Hudson* concerns the fit between the disclosure requirement and the Government's interest—as plaintiff AMI succinctly puts it, whether the disclosure requirement is "tailored in a reasonable manner."

As I read it, the Supreme Court's decision in *Zauderer* applied the *Central Hudson* "tailored in a reasonable manner" requirement to compelled commercial disclosures. ... In applying the teachings of *Central Hudson* to the state disclosure requirement, the *Zauderer* Court required that such mandatory disclosures be "purely factual," "uncontroversial," not "unduly burdensome," and "reasonably related to" the Government's interest. So *Zauderer* is best read simply as an application of *Central Hudson,* not a different test altogether. In other words, *Zauderer* tells us what *Central Hudson's* "tailored in a reasonable manner" standard means in the context of compelled commercial disclosures: The disclosure must be purely factual, uncontroversial, not unduly burdensome, and reasonably related to the Government's interest.

. . .*Zauderer* tightly limits mandatory disclosures to a very narrow class that meets the various *Zauderer* requirements. So to the extent that some courts, advocates, and commentators have portrayed a choice between the "tough *Central Hudson* standard" and the "lenient *Zauderer* standard," I see that as a false choice. . . .

In this case, as the majority opinion properly concludes, those stringent *Zauderer* fit requirements are met. . . .

[JUDGE HENDERSON's dissenting opinion is omitted.]

BROWN, Circuit Judge, dissenting:

. . .The court holds "*Zauderer* . . . reach[es] beyond problems of deception, sufficiently to encompass" factual and noncontroversial disclosure mandates aimed at providing more information to some consumers. As a result, the fundamental First Amendment right not to be coerced or compelled to say what one would not say voluntarily is now demoted to a mere tautology: "[B]y acting . . . through a reasonably crafted disclosure mandate, the government meets its burden of showing that the mandate advances its interest in making the 'purely factual and uncontroversial information' accessible to the recipients." In other words, a business owner no longer has a constitutionally protected right to refrain from speaking, as long as the government wants to use the company's product to convey "purely factual and uncontroversial" information.

In so finding, the court today ignores the plain words of *Zauderer*'s text and disregards its historical context; both the text and history of the case emphasize the government's unique interest in preventing commercial deception. . . .

In short, the state's option to require a curative disclosure cannot be disconnected from its right to entirely prohibit deceptive, fraudulent, or misleading commercial speech. Requiring an advertiser to provide "somewhat *more* information than they might otherwise be inclined to present," is thus constitutionally permissible when the government's available alternative is to completely ban that deceptive speech. Nowhere does *Zauderer* claim a commercial speaker can be *forced* to speak factual and noncontroversial information in the first instance. Instead, the text emphasizes the interests of advertisers, i.e., those who have already spoken.

Thus, even when the advertiser makes affirmative claims and the basis for a curative disclosure is self-evident, the advertiser still retains minimal First Amendment protections. Conversely, when the government is not curing deception, constitutional protections remain robust and undiminished. That the compelled information must be factual and noncontroversial is part of the government's burden. This characterization is not a trigger that transforms every seller's packaging into the government's billboard. . . .

. . .By holding the amorphous interests in today's case to be "substantial (and questioning whether any governmental interest could fail to be substantial, except those already found to be trivial, the court effectively absolves the government of any burden. Any interest that is not "trivial" will do. . . .

III.

This case is really not about country-of-origin labeling. It is not even about patriotism or protectionism. And it is certainly not about health and safety. What is apparent from the record and the briefing is that this is a case about seeking competitive advantage. One need only look at the parties and amici to recognize this rule benefits one group of American farmers and producers, while interfering with the practices and profits of other American businesses who rely on imported meat to serve their customers. Even the court's citation to the congressional record underscores this point. Such a disproportionate burden "stands in sharp conflict with the First Amendment's command that government regulation of speech must be measured in minimums, not maximums."

Of course the victors today will be the victims tomorrow, because the standard created by this case will virtually ensure the producers supporting this labeling regime will one day be saddled with objectionable disclosure requirements (perhaps to disclose cattle feed practices; how their cattle are raised; whether their cattle were medically treated and with what; the environmental effects of beef production; or even the union status or wage levels of their employees). Only the fertile imaginations of activists will limit what disclosures successful efforts from vegetarian, animal rights, environmental, consumer protection, or other as-yet-unknown lobbies may compel.

If patriotism or protectionism would sell products, producers and sellers would happily festoon their products with Made in the USA or Product of the USA labels. Thus, any consumer's desire to buy American could be easily satisfied by voluntary action. Yet today this court offers to facilitate blatant rent-seeking behavior. . . .

The scheme is not designed to inform consumers; it is designed to take away the price advantage enjoyed by one segment of a domestic industry. The government's alleged interest in providing information that some consumers may desire will actually result in higher prices. Forcing meat packers to pay a premium for domestic beef will raise costs for consumers. Query whether the protections of the First Amendment should be abrogated for some businesses in order to benefit other businesses. . . .

There can be no right *not* to speak when the government may compel its citizens to act as mouthpieces for whatever it deems factual and non-controversial and the determination of what is and what is not is left to the subjective and ad hoc whims of government bureaucrats or judges. In a world in which the existence of truth and objective reality are daily denied, and unverifiable hypotheses are deemed indisputable, what is claimed as fact may owe more to faith than science, and what is or is not controversial will lie in the eye of the beholder. . . .

NOTES AND QUESTIONS

Would any disclosure mandates be disallowed by the majority's analysis? Would any blanket mandatory disclosures (i.e., disclosures that are mandatory based on the product, not based on anything in the advertising for the product, such as cigarette and alcohol warnings) be allowed by Judge Brown's dissent?

Subsequently, Congress repealed the country-of-origin labeling requirements after another adverse ruling by a trade panel. The *AMI* decision, however, remains precedential.

Purely Factual. What does it mean for a disclosure requirement to be "purely factual," as described in *Zauderer* and *AMI*? Does it have to be the case that factual accuracy is undisputed (by reasonable people)? Where Kimberly-Clark maintained that its moistened wipes were flushable—capable of being flushed down a toilet—and the District of Columbia maintained that the wipes weren't flushable because they didn't reliably disintegrate in time to avoid clogging sewer systems, the court found that the District's attempt to require Kimberly-Clark to label its wipes as "not flushable" was not purely factual because of the underlying dispute. Thus, the mandatory disclosure was unconstitutional, absent further demonstrations that other alternatives wouldn't work. Kimberly-Clark Corp. v. District of Columbia, 286 F. Supp. 3d 128 (D.D.C. 2017). Assuming the District continues to believe that the wipes aren't flushable and are doing damage to its sewer system, what else could it do? The district court suggested a publicly funded education campaign as an alternative—how would that work? Could you draft a statutory ban on such wipes that doesn't depend on what the manufacturer says about the wipes? Would it be better to allow the thousands of state and local bodies with the power to enact laws and ordinances around the country to find facts of this nature? As the tort claims against wipe makers around the country go to trial, many juries will be charged with determining whether these wipes are in fact "flushable." *See, e.g.*, Kurtz v. Kimberly-Clark Corp., 321 F.R.D. 482 (E.D.N.Y. 2017) (certifying class for false advertising claims). Can a jury resolve this factual dispute without violating the First Amendment?

Images. Graphic warnings have been found to be highly effective at getting people to quit cigarettes and discouraging them from starting. David Hammond, *Health Warning Messages on Tobacco Products: AReview*, TOBACCO CONTROL 2011; Christine Jolls, *Product Warnings, Debiasing, and Free Speech: The Case of Tobacco Regulation*, 169 J. INST'L & THEORETICAL ECON. 53 (2013) (reporting study results that images improved consumers' factual perceptions of smoking risks).

However, the first set of graphic warnings proposed by the FDA were held unconstitutional because they were too emotional and not "purely factual and uncontroversial." The graphic warnings were not "purely" factual because "they [were] primarily intended to evoke an emotional response, or, at most, shock the viewer into retaining the information in the text warning"; they were "unabashed attempts to evoke emotion (and perhaps embarrassment) and browbeat consumers into quitting," and thus could not satisfy *Zauderer*. Two of the images—a woman crying and a man wearing an "I QUIT" shirt—weren't even "accurate," since they didn't convey "information" about cigarettes. And "the image of a man smoking through a tracheotomy hole might be misinterpreted as suggesting that such a procedure is a common consequence of smoking—a more logical interpretation than FDA's contention that it symbolizes 'the addictive nature of cigarettes,' which requires significant extrapolation on the part of the consumers." R.J. Reynolds Tobacco Co. v. Food & Drug Admin., 696 F.3d 1205 (D.C. Cir. 2012).

Here are the warnings. Do you agree?

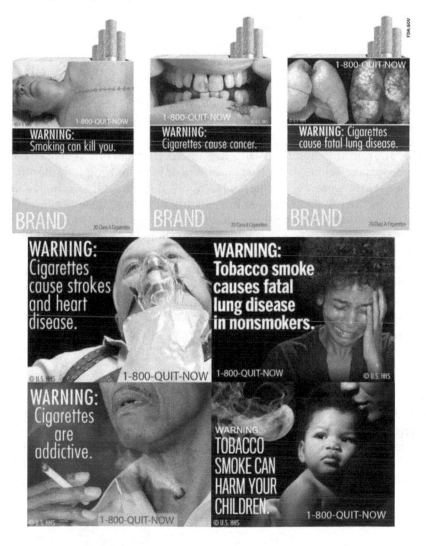

By contrast, the dissent accepted the FDA's argument that the emotions evoked by the images were appropriate because emotions assist people in making judgments, reasoning that "factually accurate, emotive, and persuasive" are not mutually exclusive descriptions. While comprehending the facts about smoking "is likely to provoke emotional reactions," that's a natural consequence of the reality that the facts are grim. To the dissent, the warning text put the images in context, which made them factual and truthful. For example, the image accompanying the text "[c]igarettes are addictive" depicted a man smoking through a tracheotomy opening in his throat. "Viewed with the accompanying text, this image conveys the tenacity of nicotine addiction: even after under undergoing surgery for cancer, one might be unable to abstain from smoking." In fact, 50% of neck- and head-cancer patients continue to smoke—this image didn't depict an extreme or unusual situation. Similarly, the dissent concluded, images of an autopsy effectively symbolized death, while images of a baby enveloped in smoke and of a woman crying depicted the significant harms of secondhand smoke.

If vivid images are easier to remember and to act upon, is that sufficient reason to use them, even if consumers don't consciously understand that's why they're responding to the images and not to warning text? After Australia adopted similar graphic warnings, some Australians even reported that exposure to graphic warning labels made their cigarettes taste worse. Matt Siegel, *Labels Leave a Bad Taste*, N.Y. TIMES, July 11, 2013. Does that suggest that images are wrongfully manipulative?

The FDA recently released its revised graphic warnings. Here are some of them:

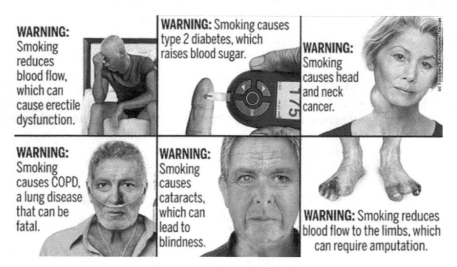

Philip Morris has challenged the warnings on First Amendment grounds. Philip Morris USA Inc. v. U.S. Food & Drug Admin., No. 20-cv-01181 (D.D.C. filed May 6, 2020). Are these images noticeably different from the previously rejected ones?

Frankenfoods? In the midst of significant consumer concern over genetically modified foods, the FDA intervened in the debate in a way highly favorable to producers of such foods. FDA Draft Guidance for Industry: Voluntary Labeling Indicating Whether Food Has or Has Not Been Derived From Genetically Engineered Atlantic Salmon (Nov. 2015); Guidance for Industry: Voluntary Labeling Indicating Whether Foods Have or Have Not Been Derived from Genetically Engineered Plants (Nov. 2015).

First, the FDA concluded that there was no evidence that bioengineered foods differ from other foods in any material way. Even though comments overwhelmingly requested mandatory disclosure of the fact that food was produced using bioengineered ingredients, the FDA found such disclosure unnecessary. The FDA cautioned that statements that a food or its ingredients were not developed using bioengineering could be misleading by implying, contrary to the FDA's determination, that the food was therefore safer or of higher quality. In addition, a claim that "None of the ingredients in this food are genetically engineered" when some of the ingredients, like salt, are incapable of being processed through genetic engineering, could be misleading.

In the FDA's view, if a producer made bioengineering-free claims, sufficient disclaimers would have to be added to ensure that no such health or safety message was conveyed. *See, e.g.,* Joanna Sax & Neal Doran, *Food Labeling and Consumer Associations with Health, Safety and Environment,* 44 J.L. MED. & ETHICS 630 (2016) (finding that consumers consistently believed that foods labeled "GMO" were less healthy, safe and environmentally friendly compared to all other labels). Given what you know about disclosures, how, if it all, could this be done? Under the FDA's guidance, a producer that wants to claim that it uses non-bioengineered ingredients as a selling point seems to face some serious risks. Is this deliberate shaping of the market legitimate? If it isn't, are other disclosure requirements any better?

If a state enacted the FDA's recommendations into law, would they violate the First Amendment?

Many consumer advocates believe that mandating the public production of information has a recursive effect on the production process (the dynamic effect of disclosures discussed by Richard Craswell, *supra*). Once manufacturers know what information they must publicly disclose, they will try to manage that information to make themselves look better in the eyes of consumers, so they won't have to disclose anything embarrassing. Intermediaries may also put pressure on manufacturers once disclosure is mandatory. If clear labeling for the presence of GMO ingredients were mandatory, for example, some retailers might decide not to carry any GMO produce, just as some retailers won't carry video games with high ratings. As a result, required disclosures are likely to change the underlying level of activity.

If different groups are likely to be misled by disclosure and by nondisclosure, whom should we favor? Does it matter that consumers who might not spend extra money on fruit produced in ways that protect traditional farms *would* spend extra money on fruit that is less dangerous to their children? Some have argued that GMO-free labels deceive poor consumers into misallocating their scarce resources, believing that they are protecting their children from harmful chemicals. What do you think of this argument?

After the FDA issued its guidance, Congress passed a law regulating the labeling of GMO foods. S. 764 (2016). The law defines "bioengineering," and any similar term, applied to food as meaning that the food "contains genetic material that has been modified through in vitro recombinant deoxyribonucleic acid (DNA) techniques; and for which the modification could not otherwise be obtained through conventional breeding or found in nature." The law directs the Secretary of Agriculture to establish a mandatory disclosure standard for bioengineered food and food that may be bioengineered. A food derived from an animal can't be considered bioengineered simply because the animal consumed bioengineered feed. The Secretary has authority to establish how much of a bioengineered substance has to appear in food for the food to be considered "bioengineered." (How will consumers learn these definitions?)

The food manufacturer can choose how to disclose—whether by text, symbol or digital or electronic link—though the Secretary can regulate the form of the disclosure. The law mandates that it is sufficient disclosure to provide a digital or electronic link that says only "Scan here for more food information," or equivalent language, or a phone number that says only "Call for more food information." Manufacturers using the digital link can't collect, analyze or sell information generated by consumers accessing the link. Restaurants aren't required to disclose. State disclosure requirements are preempted. (This might be the actual point of the law.)

The Secretary is also required to study the effects of digital disclosure. If the Secretary concludes that the study shows that "consumers, while shopping, would not have sufficient *access* to the bioengineering disclosure through electronic or digital disclosure methods" (emphasis added) then new options must be implemented. Consider how this study should proceed: What questions should it ask, to whom and in what contexts? Contrast the study's goal with Lauren Willis's idea, discussed *supra*, that disclosures should be tested for their performance in aiding consumer comprehension.

Given what you know about disclosures, how likely is "Scan here for more food information" to inform consumers about GMO content? Consider also how detailed the regulatory apparatus around the disclosure requirement is—suddenly privacy concerns are involved, as well as other design considerations. Is the game worth the candle?

Finally, the law provides that "[a] food may not be considered to be 'not bioengineered,' 'non-GMO,' or any other similar claim describing the absence of bioengineering in the food solely because the food is not required to bear a disclosure that the food is bioengineered under this subtitle." (However, organic certification is deemed sufficient as a matter of law to make a "non-GMO" claim; we take up organic certification in Chapter 18.) Does this make any sense? How do the FDA's earlier conclusions bear on this provision of the law? Does this part of the law pass First Amendment scrutiny? What about the rest of it?

For an excellent discussion of the issues arising from attempts to prohibit or limit disclosures about processes of production such as use of GMOs, *see* Douglas A. Kysar, *Preferences for Processes: The Process/Product Distinction and the Regulation of Consumer Choice*, 118 HARV. L. REV. 525 (2004). Kysar argues that consumer preferences are not stable and depend on what gets disclosed to them. Disclosure at the point of purchase makes conditions of production (child labor, GMOs, etc.) more salient and removes "moral wiggle room." As a result, we face a choice between a vision of a marketplace in which "consumers satisfy their personal interests unimpeded by concern for the welfare of others" and one in which consumers behave in accordance with more "altruistic" ideals promoted by activists who focus on particular conditions of production. These ideals may involve animal welfare, union labor, foreign production or something else. Kysar concludes that neither set of behaviors reveals "true" preferences. Rather, context and the ability to see how one's choices affect others will determine behavior, meaning that the choice of a disclosure regime is fundamentally normative.

Slave Labor and Human Trafficking. California's Transparency in Supply Chains Act requires retailers and manufactures to "develop, maintain, and implement a policy setting forth its efforts to comply with state and federal law regarding the eradication of slavery and human trafficking from its supply chain" and post the policy on companies' websites. Does this requirement violate the First Amendment? Does it bear out disclosure opponents' concern for an infinite number of burdensome disclosures being imposed by busybody legislatures?

Competitor lawsuits present a number of specific challenges. The federal law under which such suits are brought is the Lanham Act, 15 U.S.C. § 1125(a)(1)(B), also known as § 43(a)(1)(B):

> (a) Civil action
> (1) Any person who, on or in connection with any goods or services, or any container for goods, uses in commerce any word, term, name, symbol, or device, or any combination thereof, or any false designation of origin, false or misleading description of fact, or false or misleading representation of fact, which—
> . . .(B) in commercial advertising or promotion, misrepresents the nature, characteristics, qualities, or geographic origin of his or her or another person's goods, services, or commercial activities,
> shall be liable in a civil action by any person who believes that he or she is or is likely to be damaged by such act.

Courts have articulated the following elements for false advertising liability under the Lanham Act:

> (1) the defendant made a false or misleading description of fact or representation of fact in a commercial advertisement about his own or another's product; (2) the misrepresentation is material, in that it is likely to influence the purchasing decision; (3) the misrepresentation actually deceives or has the tendency to deceive a substantial segment of its audience; (4) the defendant placed the false or misleading statement in interstate commerce; and (5) the plaintiff has been or is likely to be injured as a result of the misrepresentation . . . .

Cashmere & Camel Hair Mfrs. Inst. v. Saks Fifth Ave., 284 F.3d 302 (1st Cir. 2002). The "interstate commerce" requirement is easily satisfied and rarely contested.

Lanham Act liability is strict; an advertiser's good-faith belief in the truth of its claims is no defense. In recent cases, courts have held that even a claim that was true when initially made can be rendered instantly false by a change in circumstances, such as a competitor's launch of a new product that makes a comparative claim false. Liability attaches at the moment the claim becomes false, without a grace period for the advertiser to remove the claim from the market. (This rule is mitigated by the fact that it might be extremely hard to prove damages based only on the period after the claim became false.) One court summarized as follows:

> The language of the statute is compulsory, and it includes no exceptions for cases in which a manufacturer undertakes good faith, commercially reasonable efforts to

remove a false claim from the marketplace upon learning of its falsity. Good faith is simply not a defense to a false advertising claim under the Lanham Act. Thus, the case law and the statute seem to appropriately establish that an advertiser that puts a claim into the marketplace bears all of the risk of the claim being false or becoming stale. An approach that allowed such an advertiser to continue to benefit from false or stale claims, so long as reasonably commercial efforts were undertaken to remove the advertising, would not adequately disincentivize the behavior prohibited by the Lanham Act or foster vigilance about the accuracy of advertising claims. Further, it would unfairly shift the cost of stale or inaccurate claims from the sponsor of such claims to its competitors, as long as the sponsor made reasonable efforts to remove those claims.

SharkNinja Operating LLC v. Dyson Inc., 200 F. Supp. 3d 281 (D. Mass. 2016). B*ut see* Ghostbed, Inc. v. Casper Sleep, Inc., 2018 WL 2213008 (S.D. Fla. May 3, 2018) ("While Plaintiffs do not have an obligation to monitor a competitor's offerings minute-to-minute to correct a comparison that may later become untrue, Plaintiffs do have an obligation not to make misleading statements in advertising. A fact finder could find that a substantial delay, if there was one, in correcting a statement that became untrue, was misleading.").

How does this work in practice? Competitors often sue over comparative statements, so first we will examine the law governing comparative claims, with representative examples.

We will then turn to a key Lanham Act issue: distinguishing between explicit and implicit falsity. This distinction is regularly outcome determinative, and it dictates the complexity, expense and length of the litigation. We will then cover surveys, which are almost always required to win an implied-falsity Lanham Act claim. Finally, we will consider the questions of standing in Lanham Act cases and what constitutes the "commercial advertising or promotion" covered by the statute.

1.   False Comparative Claims

Comparative claims are of two sorts: superiority claims and parity claims. Statements that consumers "prefer" a product or that it is "more effective" than its competitors are comparative superiority claims, which can be proven false by showing that the competitor's product is superior or equivalent to the advertiser's product on the relevant measure. A claim that consumers think that a product is "as good as" a competitor, or that "nothing is more effective," by contrast, are comparative parity (or equivalence) claims that can only be proven false by showing that the competitor's product is superior.

Preference claims must be based on an adequate study or survey of the relevant market. For example, ads claiming that VISA was the "preferred lodging card" were found to be false because VISA's evidence showed only that consumers *use* VISA more but did not prove that consumers *like* VISA more. *In re* Visa USA, Inc., 28 NAD Case Rep. #3506NFY (closed Dec. 7, 1998), *aff'd*, Panel No. 101 (NARB, May 1999).

Generally, comparative preference claims are more likely to be found false (or, where substantiation is required, inadequately substantiated) if they are based on "monadic" testing, in which one group rates one product and a second group rates another. Use of two separately conducted studies to substantiate comparative claims is even more questionable. With some exceptions, courts have largely accepted the argument that comparisons should be based on head-to-head testing, not on separate test cells or studies. Different studies may select differing populations, methodologies, endpoints and other factors that make comparison difficult if not inherently misleading.

Generally, advertising claims should compare apples to apples. Even without changes in the market that make an existing true ad false, testing a product against an outdated or unavailable version of a competitor's product can produce false claims. One court found that a defendant's comparative "This Week's Eyewear Price Check" ad using its competitor's prices from weeks, and even months, before could be literally false, even with a small print disclosure of the actual survey dates. *See* LensCrafters, Inc. v. Vision World, Inc., 943 F. Supp. 1481 (D. Minn. 1996).

In addition, the "apples-to-apples" principle requires fairness in definition. Though the advertiser is generally free to choose the terms of its comparison, once those terms are chosen, it must be consistent. In one case, a home pregnancy test claimed it was a "one-step" test, referring to the *chemical reaction* in the test. But the ad compared the test to competing products that allegedly required multiple manipulations by the user, counting the *number of manipulations* as "steps." Because the "one-step" test also required multiple manipulations by the user, the comparison was false. Tambrands Inc. v. Warner-Lambert Co., 673 F. Supp. 1190 (S.D.N.Y. 1987). Similarly, a bar chart that advertised "237 million prescriptions" for the advertiser's heartburn medications compared to a competitor's "36 million" was false because the former was spread out over eighteen years and the latter over only nine. *See* SmithKline Beecham Consumer Healthcare, L.P. v. Merck Consumer Pharms. Co., 906 F. Supp. 178 (S.D.N.Y. 1995).

One brand of bread claimed to have fewer calories than other brands, but the lower calorie content was achieved by making thinner slices out of loaves that had the same number of calories as other loaves. The comparison ignored significant nutritional differences, and consumers' consumption behaviors meant that slice-by-slice comparison was inappropriate. The FTC found that this comparison was therefore misleading. *See In re* Nat'l Bakers Servs., Inc., 62 F.T.C. 1115, *aff'd*, 329 F.2d 365 (7th Cir. 1964).

Visual claims must also be apples-to-apples. Consider the following image:

COVERAGE DOWN TO THE STORE LEVEL

Leading Competitor Coverage · ECRM Data Coverage

Top 50
Advertising DMA's

Over 65,000 Stores
100% Census Coverage

Over One Billion Ads | Over 1,000 Categories | Over 500 Retail Chains
Over 275K Different Brands | Over 14K Unique Manufacturers | 7 Distinct Media Types | 5 Year History

Here, the defendant, an ad tracking company, capped its competitor's markets at the top fifty but showed *all* of its own coverage. It also consolidated all stores in any given area covered by its competitor into a single dot (representing up to 1500 stores) but didn't do the same for itself. Because each dot was identically sized, the defendant conveyed the literally false message that its data covered 1300 times the geographic area as its competitor did. Mkt. Track, LLC v. Efficient Collaborative Retail Mktg., LLC, 2015 WL 3637740 (N.D. Ill. June 11, 2015).

Nonetheless, products need not be identical to be compared. If the basis of comparison is sensible in light of consumer uses of a product or service, then comparison is legitimate even though other types of comparisons are also possible. Thus, one advertiser compared two low-calorie breath mints on a per-mint basis. Its competitor claimed that the comparison should be by weight. The court found that there were no significant nutritional differences making a mint-by-mint comparison false and also no evidence that there was a standard serving size by weight or that actual consumption habits depended on weight rather than number of mints. *See* Ragold, Inc. v. Ferrero, U.S.A. Inc., 506 F. Supp. 117 (N.D. Ill. 1980). In other words, even if another comparison might be more useful to consumers, an advertisement's comparison is legitimate if it is truthful and non-misleading.

So what counts as a comparative ad? A claim may be comparative if the competitor's identity is readily inferred from the advertisement. References to "the leading motor oils" have been treated as comparative, even though the leading motor oils were not named. Similarly, an ad using a readily identifiable product silhouette is likely to be understood by consumers as comparative. A claim that "Only PEPCID AC has proven that it can prevent heartburn and acid indigestion" was a false exclusivity claim that necessarily targeted competitors, whereas "PEPCID AC can actually prevent heartburn" is non-comparative. *See* SmithKline Beecham Consumer Healthcare, L.P. v. Johnson & Johnson-Merck Consumer Pharms. Co., 1996 U.S. Dist. LEXIS 7257 (S.D.N.Y. 1996).

Yet not all advertising using terms such as "better" or "stronger" is comparative. A competitor must be reasonably identifiable. One court refused to find that an ad referring to "most spill proof cups," with a picture of a cup that did not have any recognizable distinctiveness, compared the advertiser's product with the leading competitor. *See* Playtex Prods., Inc. v. Gerber Prods. Co., 981 F. Supp. 827 (S.D.N.Y. 1997). Particularly in a field with many contenders, such as analgesics, broad references to "better" performance are unlikely to be deemed comparative without a more specific identification of the targeted competitor.

2.   Determining the Nature of the Claim

The line between implicitly false claims and explicitly or literally false claims can be difficult to draw. Nonetheless, the first step in a Lanham Act case must be to determine the literal claim being made by the advertisement. Only then can a fact finder decide whether the claim is explicitly false or implicitly false.

Courts have held that literally false claims are so likely to deceive consumers that no additional evidence of consumer reaction is required, unless no reasonable consumer would take them seriously (puffery, covered in Chapter 4). Claims that are not literally false, but which are potentially misleading, lead to liability if there is evidence that they do in fact deceive consumers (or, in some cases, if there is evidence of a deliberate intent to deceive). However, courts will sometimes dispense with the requirement of extrinsic evidence if the misleadingness is obvious enough—a doctrine called falsity by necessary implication, which we will cover in the next section. The following chart provides an overview:

	Consumers receive false message	**Consumers don't receive false message**
Explicitly/literally false message	Liability (courts presume reception of false message without extrinsic evidence)	Puffery (possibly as a matter of law, presumed without extrinsic evidence); no liability
Literally true message with allegedly false implication	Liability if consumer reception of false implication demonstrated (usually through survey); courts may use doctrine of necessary implication to presume reception	No liability

Whether a claim is explicitly or implicitly false affects many aspects of a case, including the cost of litigation and the choice of forum because the NAD does not require consumer surveys and may be a better venue for an implicit falsity claim if the NAD is otherwise acceptable. (However, the national advertisers who use NAD repeatedly may submit surveys to NAD anyway. From mid-2013 to late 2018, only 8% of NAD cases referred to a consumer perception survey; forty-two surveys were submitted in support of the challenger and ten were submitted by the advertiser. In 28% of cases that reached a decision, the NAD mentioned "the absence of consumer perception evidence," suggesting that it believes it would benefit from more such evidence. John E. Villafranco, *Consumer Perception Surveys in NAD Cases,* AD LAW ACCESS, Dec. 10, 2018.) Notably, the recently adopted SWIFT fast-track process at NAD, which promises decisions in twenty business days, does not cover implicit claims, so NAD makes the implicit/explicit distinction as well.

Courts may rely on their own logic and common sense to determine a claim's literal meaning. "The greater the degree to which a message relies upon the viewer or consumer to integrate its components and draw the apparent conclusion, . . . the less likely it is that a finding of literal falsity will be supported. Commercial claims that are implicit, attenuated, or merely suggestive usually cannot be characterized as literally false." United Indus. Corp. v. Clorox Co., 140 F.3d 1175 (8th Cir. 1998). Courts can also rely on advertisers' own definitions, when those definitions are not themselves misleading: When the advertiser of a steam iron chose to claim superior "power" to its main competition, and then defined how it measured "power" in fine print, the court found literal falsity when the competitor was actually superior according to that measurement. Grpe. SEB USA, Inc. v. Euro-Pro Operating LLC, 774 F.3d 192 (3d Cir. 2014) (finding this claim explicit and unambiguous, even if portions were in fine print).

Of course, all advertising requires consumers to apply their general beliefs, such as definitions of words and a basic understanding of society. For example, automobile advertising rarely explains why braking power is important. Courts thus increasingly invoke "ambiguity" in determining whether an ad is literally or implicitly false. If consumers could reasonably get either a false message or a truthful message from a particular ad, then the ad cannot be facially false and must be evaluated under the standards for implied falsity. On the other hand, if the only message a reasonable consumer in the target audience could get from the ad is false, then the ad is explicitly and facially false.

Thus, an advertisement that Maxxatrax roach bait "kills roaches in 24 hours" was not *literally* false because it was literally true in one sense—roaches who came into contact with Maxxatrax died within twenty-four hours. Any other claim perceived in the phrase—such as the *implied* claim that it rids the entire home of roaches in twenty-four hours—would need a consumer survey to prove. United Indus. Corp. v. Clorox Co., 140 F.3d 1175 (8th Cir. 1998). Similarly, claims that computer equipment was "fully compatible" and "100% compatible" might be understood to mean that it would perform in exactly the same way but might also mean something less. Actual consumer perception evidence was required in order to find the claim false. Compaq Computer Corp. v. Procom Tech., Inc., 908 F. Supp. 1409 (S.D. Tex. 1995).

There are at least two kinds of ambiguity. There are some claims, like "number one in the industry!" that might not have a specific meaning to consumers at all. In other words, they might be puffery. Other claims, such as "kills roaches in 24 hours," have a specific meaning, but a court might not be sure what that meaning is for large groups of consumers. In both cases, the plaintiff gets a chance to prove how consumers perceive the claim, though the difference might affect, among other things, how a survey should ask consumers about the claims they understand from the ads at issue.

Moreover, not every conceivable ambiguity removes a claim from the ambit of literal falsity. Rather, courts have found ambiguity sufficient to move a claim from explicit to implicit where an advertisement's claims are "equally open" to a true or a false interpretation, *Coors Brewing Co. v. Anheuser-Busch Cos., Inc.*, 802 F. Supp. 965 (S.D.N.Y. 1992), or are "so balanced between several plausible meanings that the claim made by the advertisement is too uncertain to serve as the basis of a literal falsity claim," *Clorox Co. Puerto Rico v. Proctor & Gamble Commercial Co.*, 228 F.3d 24 (1st Cir. 2000). If an advertiser's interpretation of a contested claim is strained, courts will ignore it. Thus, when an ad claimed that a competitor's product had experienced "catastrophic failure," the court accepted testimony that the phrase was generally understood in the relevant medical community to mean failure resulting in serious equipment damage or patient injury and rejected the advertiser's proposed broader definition. *Energy Four, Inc. v. Dornier Med. Sys., Inc.*, 765 F. Supp. 724 (N.D. Ga. 1991).

Context can also sweep away ambiguity: In one case, an advertiser claimed that its odor-absorbing product worked "five times better" than baking soda. The court examined the advertisements at issue, which showed visuals such as five puppies apparently urinating on a floor, reduced to three puppies, then to one, then to none, and also promoted the product "to keep your home smelling fresh and clean."

MAN SINGS: It's five times fresher.

ANNCR: New Glade Carpet Potpourri, in a new Pet Formula too,

for wet pet accidents.

AN SINGS: It's five times better

than baking soda.

ANNCR: Fresh from Glade, S.C. Johnson Wax. (MUSIC OUT)

The court had no difficulty determining that the meaning of "five times better" was that consumers would perceive a fivefold improvement, not that the product reduced "odor particles" in a laboratory five times better than baking soda, as the advertiser claimed. *Church & Dwight Co. v. S.C. Johnson & Son., Inc.*, 873 F. Supp. 893 (D.N.J. 1994).

But even an altered image may not create literal falsity. *Louisiana-Pacific Co. v. James Hardie Building Products, Inc.*, 928 F.3d 514 (6th Cir. 2019), held that digitally altered images and videos of a woodpecker perched in a hole in Louisiana-Pacific's wood siding were not literally false where the siding actually had that hole, which might well have been created by a woodpecker:

> The Lanham Act doesn't require advertisers to lie in wait, cameras in hand, for an actual woodpecker to drum away at a house's siding. Reasonable consumers know that marketing involves some level of exaggeration, and some amount of digital retouching to tell a story. Here, neither party contests that the photograph depicts a real hole in Louisiana-Pacific's siding. And no reasonable consumer would expect that [the photographer] caught a woodpecker in flagrante delicto. . . . Thus, though its digital enhancements might, colloquially speaking, render the image "false," they are not the sort of literal falsity the Lanham Act targets.

In close cases, a court may choose to let a jury determine whether a statement is literally false or literally true (and thus only actionable if there's further evidence of actual consumer deception). Where a product containing mineral seal oil was sold as "wax" for cars, a jury found the claim literally false, rejecting several experts' testimony that "wax" could be defined broadly, in favor of the plaintiff's expert testimony that mineral seal oil was plainly not "wax" because it lacked the basic characteristics of wax. *See* Hot Wax, Inc. v. S/S Car Care, 1999 WL 966094 (N.D. Ill. 1999).

3.   Implicit Falsity and a New Category: Falsity by Necessary Implication

A.   Introduction (adapted from Rebecca Tushnet, Running the Gamut from A to B: Federal Trademark and False Advertising Law, 159 U. Penn. L. Rev. 1305 (2010))

In Lanham Act cases, literally true statements must be shown by extrinsic evidence to mislead consumers. The concern is that consumers might not be receiving the same implication as the challenger takes from the ad, so the challenger must first show that a substantial number receive a false message. This requires a consumer survey, which usually adds six figures to the cost of a false advertising case, imposing a significant practical barrier to suit. An explicit claim, in other words, is much easier to challenge than an implicit claim, even when they are the same claim from the consumer's standpoint.

But there are numerous cases in which a claim, though technically implicit, is quite obviously as clearly stated as if it were explicit. This is a feature of ordinary human communication, which regularly relies on implicature (see Chapter 4). Implication is especially useful for advertisers because consumers end up with stronger beliefs when they do some of the persuading for themselves by following implications to their natural conclusions. *See, e.g.*, Alan G. Sawyer, *Can There Be Effective Advertising Without Explicit Conclusions? Decide for Yourself*, in NONVERBAL COMMUNICATION IN ADVERTISING 159–61 (Sidney Hecker & David W. Stewart eds., 1988).

Consumers routinely and automatically draw inferences from ads, because they expect ads, like all forms of communication, to contain implicit information. *See* Julie A. Edell, *Nonverbal Effects in Ads: A Review and Synthesis, in* NONVERBAL COMMUNICATION IN ADVERTISING 11 (Sidney Hecker & David W. Stewart eds., 1988) (finding that, "when asked to form beliefs about a brand, subjects take whatever data they have been given and make inferences about what those data could mean for that brand"—thus, tissue advertised with a picture of a kitten gets high ratings for softness, even higher than tissue advertised with the words "Brand I Facial Tissues Are Soft."). Consumers even remember implicit claims as if they'd been explicitly presented. *See, e.g.,* Richard J. Harris et al., *Memory for Implied Versus Directly Stated Advertising Claims*, 6 PSYCHOL. & MKTG. 87 (1989).

As a result, advertisers can arbitrage current Lanham Act doctrine, making implicit claims that they could not make explicitly, while still producing the same, or greater, effect on consumers. As Sawyer notes, the research "offers strong evidence that audience members will spontaneously strive to make inferences and conclusions under certain conditions. . . . [A]dvertising audiences are also very likely to 'complete' ambiguous advertising statements or claims. Under conditions [where consumers aren't paying very careful attention], . . . subjects tended to make false conclusions . . . which, if the advertiser could or should be considered as the cause of the incorrect conclusion, would be judged deceptive." Consumers may use ordinary rules of communication to interpret claims as factual that courts dismiss as puffery.

In recent years, courts have reacted to the doctrinal rigidity of the explicit/implicit divide, accepting that some misleading implications are better treated like literally false claims. The resulting doctrine is known as "falsity by necessary implication." The standard is as follows: "A claim is conveyed by necessary implication when, considering the advertisement in its entirety, the audience would recognize the claim as readily as if it had been explicitly stated." Clorox Co. P.R. v. Proctor & Gamble Commercial Co., 228 F.3d 24 (1st Cir. 2000). Thus, an advertisement claiming "longer engine life and better engine protection" without explicitly mentioning what competitors it was "longer" and "better" than, made a comparison to major competitors by necessary implication. Castrol, Inc. v. Pennzoil Co., 987 F.2d 939 (3d Cir. 1993).

The first false advertising case to use the term "necessary implication" involved a claim that a pregnancy test would provide results in "as fast as ten minutes." While some users would know they were pregnant in ten minutes, others wouldn't, and *all* users who weren't pregnant would have to wait half an hour to be sure. The necessary implication that the test was a "ten-minute" test was false. *See* Tambrands Inc. v. Warner-Lambert Co., 673 F. Supp. 1190 (S.D.N.Y. 1987). The ten-minute claim at issue can also be seen as a run-of-the-mill false claim that certain unusual results are typical. The necessary implication of a ten-minute claim in the context of a pregnancy test is that most users will get such results, just as the necessary implication of an ad focusing on an extremely successful user of another product or service may be that such results are typical or likely.

The Second Circuit adopted the doctrine of necessary implication in *Time Warner Cable, Inc. v. DirecTV, Inc.*, allowing liability without evidence of consumer reaction and without an explicitly false assertion "if the words or images, considered in context, necessarily and unambiguously imply a false message." 497 F.3d 144 (2d Cir. 2007). DirecTV ran an amusing ad featuring William Shatner as Captain Kirk, who praised the "amazing picture quality" of DirecTV and told viewers, "With what Starfleet just ponied up for this big screen TV, settling for cable would be illogical." Though there was no explicit claim that cable's HD picture quality was worse, in context "illogical" had to mean picture quality. Because cable's HD picture quality was in fact identical, the ads violated the Lanham Act.

. . . Necessary implication is fundamentally social. It depends on general expectations, not necessarily on what's within the four corners of an ad. In *Playskool, Inc. v. Product Development Group, Inc.*, 699 F. Supp. 1056 (E.D.N.Y. 1988), a toy manufacturer argued that a competitor's claim that its components for play structures "attach[ed]" to the manufacturer's components was false because a structure made from elements of both parties' products would be unstable and unsafe. The court found that the claim might be "literally true" in the sense that "defendant's pieces can in fact be joined or connected to plaintiff's pieces." Nonetheless, the "clear implication" of the claim was that the components would attach *safely*. "On a box of toys for preschool children the statement can have no other reasonable meaning." Background assumptions thus structure interpretation, even when they remain unstated. *Cf.* Mirza v. Ignite USA, LLC, 2020 WL 704791 (N.D. Ill. Feb. 12, 2020) ("One would expect products made for children, at the very least, to be free from defects that would pose a choking hazard given the frequency of choking incidents for this age group... The name ["Contigo Kids"] signals that the water bottles were made for children, and a necessary implication of products made for children is that they are safe for their use.").

The social construction of implied meaning creates difficult problems in certain product areas, such as the area of prescription drugs and supplements. Does the presence of a drug on the market imply that the FDA has found it safe and effective? *See* Mut. Pharm. Co. v. Watson Pharm., Inc., 2010 WL 446132 (D.N.J. 2010) (holding that plaintiff would be allowed a chance to prove this claim). Studies show that consumers expect the FDA to be looking out for them, approving only ads for the safest and most effective drugs, even though a number of drugs are grandfathered out of current safety and efficacy requirements. *See, e.g.*, S.W. Wolfe, *Direct-to-Consumer Advertising-Education or Emotion Promotion?* 346 NEJM 524 (2002).

Falsity by necessary implication is a way for courts to relieve plaintiffs of the burden of an expensive and hotly contested consumer survey, even when a false message in an ad, though obvious, is not stated in full syllogistic form.

B.   Putting the Concept of Falsity by Necessary Implication into Practice

Consider, as you read the following cases, whether the explicit/implicit division and the falsity by necessary implication doctrine are making the appropriate distinctions between types of claims. Would it be better for courts to trust their own judgment, or, given that judges are often from a particular segment of society (not to mention already overconfident of their interpretive prowess), should we perhaps move in the direction of *always* requiring extrinsic evidence of deception? Are there other alternatives?

In the following two cases, try to identify the assumptions the courts make about how consumers think about the relevant product category, which then affects what statements the court deems ambiguous or unambiguous.

AUSSIE NAD'S U.S. CORP. V. SIVAN, 41 FED. APPX. 977 (9TH CIR. 2002)

The district court entered a preliminary injunction prohibiting Aussie Nad's U.S. Corp. ("NADS/USA") from advertising its "No Heat Hair Removal Gel" with the representation that "No Preparation is Required," without a disclosure that the consumer's hair needs to be a minimum 1/8 to 1/4-inch long for the gel to be effective. NADS/USA appeals, contending that the district court erred in concluding that the advertisement is literally false unless reference is made to the minimum hair length. We . . . agree with NADS/USA.

. . . . To find an advertisement "literally false" by "necessary implication," as the district court did here, the claim must be analyzed in its entirety to determine whether "the audience would recognize the claim as readily as if it had been explicitly stated." Here, NADS/USA's claim that its "no heat" hair removal gel requires "no preparation" is at least ambiguous as to whether "no preparation" of the gel is required, as opposed to that required for other hair removal products (such as heating, for wax), or "no preparation" of the person is required. Given that ambiguity, the doctrine of literal falsity is inapplicable and thus cannot sustain the preliminary injunction. . . .

MILLENNIUM IMPORT COMPANY V. SIDNEY FRANK IMPORTING COMPANY, INC., 2004 WL 1447915 (D. MINN. 2004)

Millennium Import Company ("Millennium" or plaintiff), maker of the luxury vodka Belvedere, brought this lawsuit against Sidney Frank Importing Company ("Sidney" or defendant), maker of the luxury vodka, Grey Goose. Millennium accuses Sidney of false and misleading advertisement practices relating to a print advertisement ("print ad") and a "hang tag" advertisement, both of which reference a 1998 taste test in which Grey Goose outscored Belvedere. . . .

BACKGROUND

I. THE VODKAS

Belvedere, introduced in 1996, and Grey Goose, introduced about a year later, are part of a new and fast-growing category of "luxury imported vodka." According to the parties' representations, Belvedere and Grey Goose hold the vast majority of the market share for luxury vodkas. Both types of vodka seem to have done well in the market, though sales of Grey Goose have outpaced those of Belvedere.

II. THE TASTE TEST

In 1998 the privately run Beverage Testing Institute of Chicago ("BTI") conducted a taste test of over 40 vodkas. The BTI is an independent taste-testing organization, which conducts periodic taste tests of wine, beer, and distilled spirits, including vodka. For the 1998 vodka taste test, the BTI tested "luxury" vodkas, as well as the more run-of-the-mill variety. The vodkas were rated on a scale of 1 to 100, according to BTI's regular practices. Points were awarded based on smoothness, nose, and taste. Scores from 100–96 are "superlative;" from 95–90 are "exceptional;" 81–89 are either "recommended" or "highly recommended;" below 80 are "not recommended." Grey Goose came out on top, with a score of 96. Belvedere fared much worse, and scored 74. Although Millennium suggests the test was an anomaly, neither party complains that the 1998 BTI taste test at issue did not follow accepted procedure or was otherwise unreliable.

III. THE AD

Sidney took advantage of Grey Goose's top score, and began to run advertisements touting the 1998 BTI taste-test results. The at-issue print ad has appeared in multiple issues of numerous different magazines, and reads as follows:

> Rated The # 1 Vodka In The World [in large type]
>
> In 1998, the Beverage Testing Institute of Chicago conducted a blind taste test of more than 40 vodkas. They awarded points based on smoothness, nose, and most importantly, taste. Of all the vodkas, Grey Goose Vodka emerged victorious, receiving 96 points out of a possible 100.
>
> Founded in 1981, the Beverage Testing Institute conducts tests in a specially designed lab that minimizes external factors and maximizes panelists' concentration. The Institute selects judges based on their expertise, and its testing and scoring procedures are widely praised as the best in the industry." [two paragraphs are in a smaller type]

This print ad then lists 31 vodka brands, their countries of origin, and their scores from the 1998 test. In very small print, the ad states that the 31 vodkas are a "sampling" of the 40 vodkas tested. Millennium states that only three "luxury" vodkas are on the list. . . .

[the ad]

Millennium suggests that the 1998 taste test was an anomaly, and points out that in subsequent tests conducted by the BTI, Belvedere consistently has earned "Exceptional" ratings. Millennium reports that Belvedere has attained the following scores in BTI tests: 90 in 1999, 91 in 2001, and 92 in two separate tests in 2002. . . .

1. False by necessary implication

Plaintiff first argues that the ads are "literally false by necessary implication." Plaintiff does not claim that the test was wrong in 1998, or that defendant changed the results. Instead, this "literally false by necessary implication" argument hinges on looking at the overall message of the advertisement, and determining whether "the audience would recognize the claim as readily as if it had been explicitly stated."

. . . . Here, plaintiff's claim is that looking at the overall message of the advertisement, it is clear that Grey Goose is claiming that it is currently ranked the best tasting vodka in the world. Plaintiff also argues that the ad communicates the false message that Belvedere's rating of 74 is the current rating. Plaintiff suggests that even the qualifying words—noting that the tests were conducted in 1998, and the use of the past tense—do not render the ad true. Plaintiff argues that the later tests supersede and contradict the results of the 1998 test.

Defendant responds by arguing that the Grey Goose ad is not "false by necessary implication" because there simply is no implication in the ad. Defendant analogizes to a sporting event, and suggests that advertising a "win" in year one is not false, even if the ad fails to mention that the team "lost" in year two. Defendant also notes the past tense language, and points out that the year of the test is displayed prominently. As a slightly different argument, defendant emphasizes that consumers are accustomed to "taste tests" and understand that taste tests occur with some frequency, and that the results are somewhat subjective. Essentially, defendant argues that consumers know how to read this ad, and consumers are not reading it as putting forth current results of taste tests.

Plaintiff's likelihood of success on the false by necessary implication argument is bolstered somewhat by defendant's alleged violation of the Federal Trade Commission's (FTC) guidelines. Plaintiff argues that according to those guidelines, advertisers should not use outdated third-party endorsements. Some courts have granted FTC guidelines significant weight. . . . [C]ourts, however, also caution against "blur[ring] the distinctions between the FTC and a Lanham Act plaintiff" and note that the Lanham Act plaintiff must "show that the [advertisements] are literally false or misleading to the public," not merely that the advertisements violate FTC guidelines.

The print ad is not literally false, and despite the FTC guidelines, the Court is not persuaded by plaintiff's "false by necessary implication" argument. Given the sheer number of claims by adult beverage makers that theirs is "the best" or "the premier," it is unlikely that the plaintiff will be able to show (and plaintiff has not yet shown) that "the audience would recognize the claim"—that Grey Goose is currently rated the best vodka in the world—"as readily as if it had been explicitly stated."

Plaintiff has not yet persuaded the Court that consumers have no way of knowing that any taste test was ever conducted after 1998, or that it is reasonable to conclude that many consumers would think that the 1998 taste test is the last word on the tastiness of vodkas. The Court notes, however, that at some point, reliance on an outdated test could well render an ad "false by necessary implication" especially where the ad appears to report the most recent taste test results. . . .

NOTES AND QUESTIONS

The NAD Reaches a Different Result. Unlike the district court's decision, the NARB affirmed the NAD's finding that the ad was misleading and its recommendation that it be withdrawn. Report of NARB Panel #120, June 4, 2003, Appeal of NAD Final Decision Regarding Advertising for Grey Goose Vodka by Sidney Frank Importing Co., Inc. NARB considered the issue to be "straight forward": It was misleading to refer to the 1998 test when at least two subsequent tests gave Belvedere a significantly higher score.

The NARB noted that BTI asserted that its tests were objective and "repeatable," used detailed procedures designed to ensure consistency, and, on its own website, listed vodkas with side-by-side numerical scores from different taste tests conducted over a period of several years. The NARB concluded that, "[i]n the absence of consumer perception evidence, the panel must place itself in the shoes of a reasonable consumer in evaluating the message received from challenged advertising. The panel believes that the challenged advertisement can reasonably be perceived by consumers as reflecting BTI's current assessment of Belvedere Vodka."

The NARB also commented:

> The FTC Guides Concerning Use of Endorsements and Testimonials in Advertising provides some guidance here. . . . The FTC guides provide that an advertiser may use the endorsement of an expert "only as long as it has good reason to believe that the endorser continues to subscribe to the views presented." . . . There is no question that BTI's rating of Belvedere Vodka changed dramatically from 1998 (when BTI's score placed it in the "not recommended" category) to the present (with BTI's currently reported score placing it in the "exceptional" category).

Sidney Frank, however, rejected the NARB's ruling, arguing that BTI does not permit advertisers to make comparisons between different taste tests (and it certainly wasn't about to advertise the more-recent results for its own vodka). Since BTI was the expert, Sidney Frank concluded, it would not comply with the NARB.

Which opinion is more persuasive? How do BTI's own standards factor into your analysis?

Individual Words. All words have definitions. A court must therefore interpret the meaning of a word or phrase before it can determine whether that word or phrase is false. In the following case, who has the authority to define the key term?

CASHMERE & CAMEL HAIR MANUFACTURERS INSTITUTE V. SAKS FIFTH AVENUE, 284 F.3D 302 (1ST CIR. 2002)

. . . The Institute is a trade association of cashmere manufacturers dedicated to preserving the name and reputation of cashmere as a specialty fiber. . . .

In 1993, defendant-appellee Harvé Benard, Ltd. ("Harvé Benard") began manufacturing a line of women's blazers that were labeled as containing 70 percent wool, 20 percent nylon, and 10 percent cashmere. Its labels also portrayed the blazers as "A Luxurious Blend of Cashmere and Wool," "Cashmere and Wool," or "Wool and Cashmere." Harvé Benard sold large quantities of these cashmere-blend garments to retail customers, including defendants Saks Fifth Avenue ("Saks") and Filene's Basement.

In 1995, plaintiffs began purchasing random samples of the Harvé Benard garments and giving them to Professor Kenneth Langley and Dr. Franz-Josef Wortmann, experts in the field of cashmere identification and textile analysis. After conducting separate tests on the samples, the experts independently concluded that, despite Harvé Benard's labels to the contrary, the garments contained no cashmere. In addition, Dr. Wortmann found that approximately 10 to 20% of the fibers in the Harvé Benard garments were recycled—that is, reconstituted from the deconstructed and chemically-stripped remnants of previously used or woven garments.

Relying on their experts' findings, plaintiffs filed this suit in district court claiming that defendants falsely advertised their garments in violation of § 43(a) of the Lanham Act, the Massachusetts Unfair and Deceptive Trade Practices Act, Mass. Gen. Laws ch. 93A, and the common law of unfair competition. . . .

[Discussion of the allegations that the garments contained no cashmere at all is omitted.] Whether literal falsity is involved in plaintiffs' claim that defendants improperly labeled their goods as cashmere rather than recycled cashmere . . . is a contentious issue. Defendants argue that this claim is, by definition, one of implied falsity—that is, a representation that is literally true but in context becomes likely to mislead. As further support for their argument, defendants offer a simple syllogism: all suits based on implied messages are implied falsity claims; since plaintiffs assert that the term "cashmere" on the garments' labels implicitly conveys the false message that the garments contain virgin cashmere, their claim must be one of implicit falsity.

We agree with defendants that normally a claim like plaintiffs', in which the representation at issue is literally true (the garments do contain cashmere as the label states) but is misleading in context (defendants failed to disclose that the cashmere is recycled), is evaluated as an implied falsity claim. However, we disagree with defendants' assertion that all claims that rely on implied messages are necessarily implied falsity claims. . . .

After drawing all reasonable inferences in favor of the nonmoving party, a rational factfinder could conclude that plaintiffs' recycled cashmere claim is one of literal falsity. The Wool Products Labeling Act, requires recycled garments and fabrics, including cashmere, to be labeled as such. As a result, whenever a label represents that a garment contains the unqualified term "cashmere," the law requires that the garment contain only virgin cashmere. The Act, then, is essentially telling consumers that garments labeled "cashmere" can be presumed to be virgin cashmere "as if it had been explicitly stated." Plaintiffs also presented evidence demonstrating that experienced retailers, like Saks, were aware of the Act's requirements. Based on this evidence, we conclude that plaintiffs have presented sufficient evidence to demonstrate that consumers would view the term "virgin" as necessarily implicated when a garment was labeled "cashmere." . . .

NOTES AND QUESTIONS

Is the court using necessary implication as a shortcut to accept non-consumer survey evidence about how consumers would likely react to the claims at issue? That is, the court seems to accept testimony from those experienced in the field about the meaning of the otherwise ambiguous term "cashmere." But isn't that the role of consumer survey evidence, according to the formal doctrine? Why can't a plaintiff in an implicit falsity case *always* offer expert testimony about what a contested term means instead of providing a survey?

Images. What about non-verbal claims? An eco-tourism company displayed a picture of a suspension bridge and caves to which it had no right of access and to which other companies did. The court found false advertising. Though the pictures didn't explicitly say so, they necessarily implied that the bridges and caves were part of the defendant's tour. Veve v. Corporan, 977 F. Supp. 2d 93 (D.P.R., 2013). *See also* Schering-Plough Healthcare Prods,, Inc. v. Neutrogena Corp., 702 F. Supp. 2d 253 (D. Del. 2010) (overlaying the words "Neutrogena" and "28% propellant" on the bare chest of an athlete necessarily implied the literally false message that 28% of the sunscreen product applied to the body was propellant, rather than the truthful message that the sunscreen can contained 28% propellant by weight).

Will images often have necessary implications? What might they be (e.g., "this is what the product looks like")? Recall the attractive hamburgers from Chapter 4's puffery discussion.

C.   Putting It All Together in a Lanham Act Case

The following case involves claims of both literal and implied falsity. As you read, pay attention to (1) the role of scientific evidence in establishing underlying facts about the world and (2) the importance of definitions even given those facts. Whose definition of what it means to be "as effective as floss" does the court accept? You should see that the dictionary does not always provide easy answers.

McNEIL-PPC, INC. V. PFIZER INC., 351 F. SUPP. 2D 226 (S.D.N.Y. 2005)

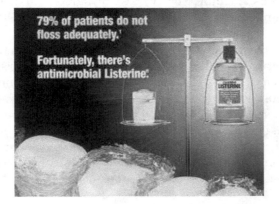

In June 2004, defendant Pfizer Inc. ("Pfizer") launched a consumer advertising campaign for its mouthwash, Listerine Antiseptic Mouthrinse. Print ads and hang tags featured an image of a Listerine bottle balanced on a scale against a white container of dental floss, as shown above.

The campaign also featured a television commercial called the "Big Bang." In its third version, which is still running, the commercial announces that "Listerine's as effective as floss at fighting plaque and gingivitis. Clinical studies prove it." Although the commercial cautions that "[t]here's no replacement for flossing," the commercial repeats two more times the message that Listerine is "as effective as flossing against plaque and gingivitis." . . .

In this case, plaintiff McNeil-PPC, Inc. ("PPC"), the market leader in sales of string dental floss and other interdental cleaning products, alleges that Pfizer has engaged in false advertising in violation of § 43(a) of the Lanham Act, and unfair competition in violation of state law. . . .

A. The Facts

[Plaintiff J&J was the market leader in dental floss.] . . .

2. Oral Hygiene and Oral Diseases

. . . . Plaque build-up may cause gingivitis, an inflammation of the superficial gum tissues surrounding the tooth. Gingivitis is common, affecting some two-thirds of the U.S. population. Its symptoms include red, inflamed, swollen, puffy, or bleeding gums. Periodontitis is inflammation that develops in deeper tissues . . . . Periodontitis is less common, affecting some 10–15% (more or less) of the population, although it becomes more prevalent with age. It is a major cause of tooth loss.

Gingivitis is generally considered an early form of or precursor to periodontitis. . . .

The ADA recognizes that "[p]laque is responsible for both tooth decay and gum disease."

. . . [F]or most people "toothbrushing alone cannot effectively control interproximal plaque," *i.e.*, the plaque in the hard-to-reach places between the teeth. As a consequence, removal of plaque from the interproximal areas by additional methods is particularly important, for it is in these areas between the teeth that plaque deposits appear early and become more prevalent. . . .

Flossing provides a number of benefits. . . . As part of a regular oral hygiene program, flossing helps reduce and prevent not only gingivitis but also periodontitis and caries.

Some 87% of consumers, however, floss either infrequently or not at all. Although dentists and dental hygienists regularly tell their patients to floss, many consumers do not floss or rarely floss because it is a difficult and time-consuming process. . . .

3. The Listerine Studies

Pfizer sponsored two clinical studies involving Listerine and floss. . . . These studies purported to compare the efficacy of Listerine against dental floss in controlling plaque and gingivitis in subjects with mild to moderate gingivitis. [The studies compared daily brushing plus rinsing with Listerine twice a day to daily brushing plus once-daily flossing and to daily brushing plus rinsing with a control. At-home use was unsupervised. The study concluded that both Listerine and flossing were significantly more effective than the control.]

. . . . In general, the Listerine results were better than the floss results.

The authors [of the first study] noted that their study "was designed to simulate actual conditions under which flossing instruction might be employed in dental practice." The results, according to the authors, "indicated" that Listerine was "at least as good as" flossing in reducing interproximal gingivitis and "significantly more effective" than flossing in reducing interproximal plaque over the six-month period.

The authors recognized, however, a potential issue as to compliance. The plaque reductions in the flossing group "appeared to be somewhat lower than would be expected," and there was greater improvement at three months than at six months, suggesting "a deterioration of flossing technique with increased time following instruction." As in real life, the subjects apparently flossed better immediately after they received instruction from a dental hygienist, but the quality of their flossing apparently diminished with the passage of time. . . .

[The second study was substantially identical, and produced consistent results. The authors concluded that Listerine was "at least as good as" dental floss in controlling interproximal gingivitis but concluded: "[W]e do not wish to suggest that the mouthrinse should be used instead of dental floss or any other interproximal cleaning device."] . . .

4. The ADA Approval for Professional Advertising

The ADA requires that all labeling and advertising bearing the ADA seal of acceptance be submitted to the ADA for review and approval prior to use. Listerine carries the ADA seal. . . . Pfizer acknowledged to the ADA that "[w]e recognize that any comparison v. flossing may send an *unintended* message to dental professionals that Listerine can replace flossing," and Pfizer assured the ADA that its advertising was "constructed" to "ensure that this does not happen."

Some consultants to the ADA expressed concerns about the Pfizer studies and the proposed professional advertising. One consultant noted:

> . . . . Because of floss' historically poor compliance record, a replacement for flossing [for] the regimen of daily plaque removal would be most welcome. However, in order for a substitute product to be "as good as" or "better" than flossing it must be compared against the data of a subject group who demonstrates they can and are flossing effectively, which the subjects in the flossing groups [in the two Pfizer studies] were not[,] based on the evidence presented.

. . . . By letter dated June 6, 2002, the ADA approved Pfizer's professional advertisements, as follows:

> . . . . The Council concurs with your request for the claim, "Now clinically proven as effective as flossing" for patients with mild to moderate gingivitis. Since study subjects with advanced gingivitis or periodontitis were not included in the studies, no claim can be made about such patients. . . .

The claims were approved for use only with professionals "because of the potential to mislead consumers that they no longer need to floss."

. . . . 6. The ADA Approval for Consumer Advertising

In January 2004, Pfizer sought approval from the ADA to expand its "as effective as flossing" advertising campaign to consumers. Pfizer emphasized in its submission that it had spent the prior eighteen months "educating dental professionals."[10]

. . . . [The ADA approved the following language]:

> "Rinsing with Listerine is as effective as floss at reducing plaque and gingivitis between teeth."
> "Ask your dentist."
> "Floss daily."

. . . . Prior to the launch of the consumer campaign, the ADA expressed concern about "the concept" that "if consumers don't have the time to floss, they can use Listerine instead." . . . .

---

[10] A number of individual dentists and hygienists complained directly to Pfizer that consumers would get the wrong message. (*See, e.g.*, PX 74 ("I was aghast to read your newsletter wherein you indicate that rinsing with 'Listerine is as effective as floss.' Rinsing with *water* will reduce interproximal plaque. But there is no substitute for flossing. . . . [M]alarkey like this can set back years of progress by the ethical dental profession in convincing patients that flossing is essential for their oral health." (emphasis in original)).

7. The Consumer Advertising Campaign

. . . . Pfizer attended a convention of the American Dental Hygienists' Association in Dallas in late June 2004. Its representatives observed:

> The hot topic of conversation was the new Listerine commercial. Many professionals voiced concern over the message conveyed. Approximately 85% of professionals said patients would "get the wrong idea" and stop flossing. . . .

8. The Surveys

[The plaintiff's survey concluded that 31% of consumers who saw the TV commercial and 26% of those who saw the label on the bottle's shoulder took away the message that Listerine can replace floss.] . . .

DISCUSSION

. . . To prevail on a Lanham Act false advertising claim, a plaintiff must demonstrate the falsity of the challenged advertisement, by proving that it is either (1) literally false, as a factual matter; or (2) implicitly false, *i.e.*, although literally true, still likely to mislead or confuse consumers.

. . . . In considering the issue of falsity, the court should " 'consider the advertisement in its entirety and not . . . engage in disputatious dissection. The entire mosaic should be viewed rather than each tile separately.' " "[T]ext must yield to context." Finally, the "visual images in a commercial" must also be considered in assessing falsity.

When the challenged statement is literally or explicitly false, the court may grant relief " 'without reference to the advertisement's impact on the buying public.' "

. . . . Where a plaintiff proceeds on a claim of implied falsehood, the plaintiff "must demonstrate, by extrinsic evidence, that the challenged commercials tend to mislead or confuse consumers." As the Second Circuit has explained, the inquiry is: "what does the public perceive the message to be?" The trial judge may not determine whether an advertisement is deceptive "based solely upon his or her own intuitive reaction." The trial judge must first determine "what message was actually conveyed to the viewing audience," and then it must determine the truth or falsity of the message.

Typically, an implied claim is proven through the use of a consumer survey that shows a substantial percentage of consumers are taking away the message that the plaintiff contends the advertising is conveying. Cases have held that 20% would constitute a substantial percentage of consumers. . . .

The plaintiff need not rely on consumer survey evidence to prove an implied falsity claim if the plaintiff " 'adequately demonstrates that a defendant has intentionally set out to deceive the public,' and the defendant's 'deliberate conduct' in this regard is of an 'egregious nature.' " In these circumstances, "a presumption arises 'that consumers are, in fact, being deceived.'"

. . . . 2. The Merits

I conclude that PPC has demonstrated a likelihood of success on both its literal falsity claim and on its implied falsity claim. I address each claim in turn.

a. Literal Falsity

Pfizer's advertisements make the explicit claim that "clinical studies prove that Listerine is as effective as floss against plaque and gingivitis." As Pfizer purports to rely on "clinical studies," this is an "establishment claim" and PPC need only prove that "the [studies] referred to . . . were not sufficiently reliable to permit one to conclude with reasonable certainty that they established the proposition for which they were cited." . . . .

First, [the court found the claim was overbroad, because the studies only covered individuals with mild to moderate gingivitis.] The advertisements do not specify that the "as effective as floss" claim is limited to individuals with mild to moderate gingivitis. Consequently, consumers who suffer from severe gingivitis or periodontitis (including mild periodontitis) may be misled by the ads into believing that Listerine is just as effective as floss in helping them fight plaque and gingivitis, when the studies simply do not stand for that proposition.

Second, the two studies were not sufficiently reliable to permit one to conclude with reasonable certainty that Listerine is as effective as floss in fighting plaque and gingivitis, even in individuals with mild to moderate gingivitis. What the two studies showed was that Listerine is as effective as floss when flossing is not done properly. . . .

Hence, the studies did not "prove" that Listerine is "as effective as floss." Rather, they proved only that Listerine is "as effective as improperly-used floss." . . .

Pfizer and its experts argue that the two studies are reliable, notwithstanding the indications that the participants in the flossing group did not floss properly, because these conditions reflect "real-world settings." But the ads do not say that "in the real world," where most people floss rarely or not at all and even those who do floss have difficulty flossing properly, Listerine is "as effective as floss." Rather, the ads make the blanket assertion that Listerine works just as well as floss, an assertion the two studies simply do not prove. Although it is important to determine how a product works in the real world, it is probably more important to first determine how a product will work when it is used properly. . . .

b. Implied Falsity

In considering the claim of implied falsity, in accordance with Second Circuit law, I determine first the message that consumers take away from the advertisements and second whether that message is false.

(i) The Implicit Message

Pfizer argues that its advertisements do not implicitly send the message that Listerine is a replacement for floss. I disagree. Rather, I find that Pfizer's advertisements do send the

264

message, implicitly, that Listerine is a replacement for floss—that the benefits of flossing may be obtained by rinsing with Listerine, and that, in particular, those consumers who do not have the time or desire to floss can switch to Listerine instead.

First, the words and images used in the advertisements confirm that this is the message being sent. The words ("as effective as floss") and images (a stream of blue liquid tracking floss as it is removed from a floss container and then swirling between and around teeth; a bottle of Listerine balanced equally on a scale against a container of floss) convey the impression that Listerine is the equal to floss.

Second, the [plaintiff's] survey is convincing and was conducted in a generally objective and fair manner. . . .

Fourth, Pfizer's own documents, . . . internal reports of feedback from the dental community (including the overwhelming reactions at the two dental conventions), and internal documents showing that Pfizer anticipated and prepared responses to deal with complaints that it was sending a message that consumers could rinse instead of floss, further confirm that consumers were and are taking away a replacement message.

Pfizer argues that the ads contained cautionary language and disclaimers telling consumers to "floss daily," urging them to consult their dentists, and noting that "[t]here's no replacement for flossing." . . . Notwithstanding the disclaimer language, Pfizer's ads are clearly suggesting to consumers, through its overall words and images, that if they do not have the time or desire to floss, they can rinse with Listerine instead, for Listerine is just "as effective as floss." The few words of disclaimer are lost when the ads are considered as a whole. After all, the point of an implied falsity claim is that even though an advertisement "is literally true it is nevertheless likely to mislead or confuse consumers."[22]

Accordingly, I conclude that the Pfizer ads send an implicit message that Listerine is a replacement for floss. . . .

NOTES AND QUESTIONS

Why did the court believe that the proper comparison was to flossing "correctly," when everyone agreed that over 80% of consumers don't floss correctly? Did this litigation suppress useful information that might have helped some consumers' teeth, even if it also made them even less likely to floss correctly? What would Grice's Maxims have had to say about the relationship of these ad claims to ordinary conversational implicature?

Did the distinction between explicit and implicit messages make a difference in this case? Given all the other evidence, if the floss replacement message was false, should PPC really have had to spend a substantial amount of time and money proving that consumers received such a message?

---

[22] Moreover, when consumers see the words "as effective as floss in fighting plaque and gingivitis," they are not likely to appreciate the distinction between "plaque and gingivitis" and "tooth decay and periodontitis."

Exercise: Pfizer comes to you with the following ad text, to be read by an actor: "Every time I go to the dentist, she tells me I need to floss more. And every time I promise to try. I'm still trying, but I know I'm not perfect. For people who don't floss properly, Listerine is as effective as floss at reducing plaque and gingivitis between the teeth. You should floss—but flossing correctly is hard. Listerine can help."

Would you approve this ad? Would you suggest changes? What would they be? (Keep in mind that your client will not want to have an ad that can't fit in a thirty-second TV or Internet spot.)

4.   Surveys

A.   Survey Evidence

At one time, survey evidence was regarded as hearsay. It is now routinely admitted, generally in conjunction with an expert's opinion. Survey use has substantially increased in scope and importance in false advertising cases over the past two decades.

Properly done surveys are endorsed by the Judicial Conference of the United States. *See* MANUAL FOR COMPLEX LITIGATION § 21.493 (3d ed. 1995); Shari Seidman Diamond, *Reference Guide on Survey Research*, in FEDERAL JUDICIAL CENTER, REFERENCE MANUAL ON SCIENTIFIC EVIDENCE (2d ed. 2000). Nevertheless, courts may turn skeptical when they are confronted with necessarily imperfect surveys or surveys that don't comport with judicial intuitions.

In Lanham Act cases, surveys are generally needed to show that an impliedly false message is actually communicated to some practically significant portion of the commercial audience. Surveys can also form the basis for substantiating certain types of preference claims. And they can be used to demonstrate or disprove materiality.

As a practical matter, a survey can be vital to a false advertising case. Evidence of actual confusion is rare, especially for cheap products where consumers are unlikely to complain or when the claims are hard for consumers to evaluate. One court concluded that "proof of actual confusion is almost impossible to obtain." Bristol-Myers Squibb Co. v. McNeil-P.P.C., Inc., 786 F. Supp. 182 (E.D.N.Y. 1992), *aff'd in part, vacated in part*, 973 F.2d 1033 (2d Cir. 1992). Also, competitors need to react very quickly to competitive threats to secure a preliminary injunction, since courts have found that even short delays may undermine claims of irreparable harm (see Chapter 9 on Remedies).

Thus, survey evidence stands in for actual consumers confused in the marketplace. A surveyor shows the accused ad to a representative sample of likely consumers—and usually shows another representative sample a control ad not alleged to be deceptive—and asks questions designed to measure whether the ad deceived them. Courts have deemed this process superior to the alternatives. It's impractical to get a significant number of the relevant consumers to testify directly. And even direct testimony from selected consumers, or expert testimony about them, is less persuasive than "the justifiable inferences from a scientific survey." Zippo Mfg. Co. v. Rogers Imps., Inc., 216 F. Supp. 670 (S.D.N.Y. 1963) (trademark case).[*]

Surveys may be necessary, but presenting a successful one isn't necessarily easy. Opponents will attack any survey, and courts have disregarded numerous surveys not conducted to their satisfaction. Improperly conducted surveys can be regarded as "junk science." *See, e.g.,* Indianapolis Colts, Inc. v. Metro. Balt. Football Club Ltd. P'ship, 34 F.3d 410 (7th Cir. 1994) (disparaging the "survey researcher's black arts"); L&F Prods. v. Proctor & Gamble, 845 F. Supp. 984 (S.D.N.Y. 1994) ("[Courts are] familiar with the subtle ways surveys are structured. Those who believe they can manipulate the structure of consumer surveys to gain a tactical advantage in the courtroom may actually harm their client's strategic position before the finder of fact."), *aff'd* 45 F.3d 709 (2d Cir. 1995).

To introduce some of the issues that may arise, we will first look at a case involving a hotly contested survey. While you read about the survey, consider how you might criticize it, then compare your criticisms to the defendant's. After this introduction, we will review more general principles courts have developed to evaluate surveys and bring in other examples of contested surveys.

ROCKY BRANDS, INC. V. RED WING SHOE CO., 2009 WL 5125475 (S.D. OHIO 2009)

Plaintiffs assert claims of false advertising and false designation of origin under § 43(a)(1) of the Lanham Act, 15 U.S.C. § 1125(a)(1), and the Ohio Deceptive Trade Practices Act ("ODTPA"). Plaintiffs allege, inter alia, that defendants market and advertise their boots in a manner that falsely suggests the boots are made in the United States, when in fact some lines of defendants' boots are manufactured wholly or partially overseas.

Defendants move to exclude the testimony and survey evidence of plaintiffs' expert The Mantis Group, Inc., arguing that the methodology of the survey is so flawed that the survey lacks any probative value. Plaintiffs contend that the survey's alleged flaws go to the weight of the evidence, not its admissibility. For the reasons that follow, the Court denies defendants' motion to exclude the survey evidence.

I. Background

[The parties compete to sell hunting and work boots. Plaintiff Rocky makes its boots overseas. Defendant Red Wing makes boots in the U.S. and overseas. Sometimes its components are made overseas and then assembled in the U.S.]

B.   The Mantis survey

Rocky's expert, George Mantis . . . states that the purpose of his survey in this case was "to determine whether and if so, to what extent relevant consumers believe that the Irish Setter brand and the Red Wing and Worx brands of footwear are made in the United States." The survey was also "designed to determine consumer choice between two boots that are identical

---

[*] Because the issues in trademark and false advertising surveys are often similar and courts cite them both without distinction, this section will discuss many trademark survey cases.

in all respects except country of origin; one made in the USA or one made in another country."

The Mantis survey was conducted at four knife and gun shows in Pennsylvania and Tennessee from July 2007 to October 2007 using three different questionnaires. Respondents were limited to individuals eighteen years old or older who had purchased hunting boots for Questionnaire Version 1 ("V1") and Questionnaire Version 2 ("V2"), or hunting or work boots for Questionnaire Version 3 ("V3") or those who were likely to do so in the next twelve months for all three versions. The survey included responses from 383 individuals.

Mantis's survey was conducted by way of face-to-face interviews. For V1, the respondents were shown an Irish Setter boot with labels and tags stating "made in the USA with imported materials." The respondents were then asked, "Where do you think this product is made?" As follow up respondents were asked, "Why do you say that?" and "Anything else?"

For V2, the respondents were shown the same boot as in V1, but with references to "with imported materials" removed from the boot's labels and tags. The respondents were then asked the same questions as in V1.

For V3, the respondents were shown a page from one of Red Wing's catalogs that contained the words "Red Wing Shoe Company, Inc.," "Red Wing Shoes Since 1905," and "WORX by Red Wing Shoes." Respondents were then asked, "Where do you think shoes from this company are made?" Respondents were also asked the same follow-up questions as in V1 and V2: "Why do you say that?" and "Anything else?"

For all three versions, the respondents were asked a third question ("Q3"). Q3 asked respondents to assume that there were two brands of hunting boots (or hunting or work boots for V3) that were the same in every respect except that one was made in the USA and the other was made in another country. Respondents were then shown a card with four statements and asked to select the statement that described the boot they would purchase:

> Statement 1: "I would purchase the boot made in the USA."

> Statement 2: "I would purchase the boot made in another country."

> Statement 3: "I have no preference and would purchase either boot."

> Statement 4: "I don't know and have no opinion."

II. Standard of review

To be admissible, a survey should generally satisfy the following requirements:

> (1) the "universe" was properly defined, (2) a representative sample of that universe was selected, (3) the questions to be asked of interviewees were framed in a clear, precise and non-leading manner, (4) sound interview procedures were followed by competent interviewers who had no knowledge of the litigation or the purpose for

which the survey was conducted, (5) the data gathered was accurately reported, (6) the data was analyzed in accordance with accepted statistical principles, and (7) objectivity of the process was assured.

"'Because almost all surveys are subject to some sort of criticism, courts generally hold that flaws in survey methodology go to the evidentiary weight of the survey rather than its admissibility.'" "'There are limits, however. The court need not and should not respond reflexively to every criticism by saying it merely "goes to the weight" of the survey rather than to its admissibility. If the flaws in the proposed survey are too great, the court may find that the probative value of the survey is substantially outweighed by the prejudice, waste of time, and confusion it will cause at trial.'"

As the proponent of the evidence, Rocky bears the burden of demonstrating admissibility . . .

III. Discussion

. . .

A.   Alleged flaws

  . . . 1.   Survey's universe

Red Wing argues that the survey's universe is overinclusive because it included respondents who were not potential purchasers. . . .

In trademark infringement cases, it is well-established that for a consumer confusion survey, the universe must consist only of potential purchasers, not past purchasers. Although there is a dearth of case law on the subject, it appears the same rule may not always apply in a false advertising case.

More importantly, Red Wing will have the opportunity to cross-examine Mantis on the issue of alleged overinclusiveness. Red Wing's expert, Dr. Itmar Simonson, may also address the issue. To the extent the survey's universe is overinclusive as a result of including past purchasers, such overinclusiveness goes to the weight of the evidence rather than its admissibility.

Red Wing also contends that the survey's universe is underinclusive because it was conducted only at gun and knife shows in two states. Red Wing argues that gun and knife show patrons represent only a narrow segment of the relevant market. In addition, Red Wing suggests the survey should have been conducted in states such as California, Florida, Texas, or New York which have larger, more diverse populations. Rocky maintains that Red Wing's arguments go to the weight of the survey evidence, and not its admissibility.

Red Wing's criticisms amount to second-guessing. Red Wing presents no evidence to demonstrate that gun and knife show patrons do not adequately represent likely purchasers of Red Wing's boots. The same is true with the suggestion that the survey should have been conducted in other states. Moreover, to the extent Mantis's choice of venue was deficient, it goes to the weight of the evidence, not its admissibility. . . .

2. Relevance

. . . Red Wing also contends that the V2 stimuli is irrelevant because it uses a "defaced" product that the respondents would never encounter in the marketplace. The V2 boot is the same as V1 except that any reference to "with imported materials" was removed from the boot's tags and labels. As noted above, comparing the results of V1 with V2 measures the effect of the words "with imported materials" on consumers' perceptions of the country of origin. Hence, V2 is relevant because it measures the difference in response, if any, between shoes labeled "made in USA with imported materials" and "made in USA."

Red Wing argues the stimuli used in V3 is irrelevant because it contains no designation of manufacturing origin and does no more than test the respondents' assumptions about Red Wing and/or WORX. Rocky explains that the purpose of using the catalog page as stimuli for V3 was simply to place before respondents the language "Red Wing Shoe Company, Inc.," "Red Wing Shoes Since 1905," and "WORX by Red Wing Shoes."

V3 tests whether consumers believe that Red Wing and WORX brands of footwear are made in the United States. This issue is "of consequence to the determination of the action." Fed. R. Civ. P. 401. V3 is, therefore, relevant.

Red Wing further asserts that Q3 is irrelevant because it does not test an allegedly false statement and assumes what it seeks to prove—that country of origin is material. . . . [T]he design of Q3 does not force respondents to conclude that country of origin is material because it provides the choices of "no preference" and "no opinion." Whether consumers prefer boots made in the United States over boots made overseas is a central issue in this case. Q3 is relevant. . . .

3. Market conditions

Red Wing also faults the Mantis survey because it was not conducted in a retail setting, such as a shopping mall. Red Wing suggests the survey should have used a pair of boots, and that respondents should have been given the opportunity to try them on. It maintains that other footwear should have been on hand for comparison, and that a sales staff should have been present to answer questions. . . .

Rocky points out that in V1 and V2 the boot was located on a table. Rocky also notes that respondents were allowed to pick up and examine the boot, and were afforded as much time as they needed to do so. Rocky asserts that the survey therefore adequately approximated market conditions.

. . . Given the purposes for which it was designed, the Mantis survey satisfactorily replicates marketplace conditions. In the alternative, to the extent it does not, the flaw goes to the weight to be given the survey evidence rather than its admissibility.

4. Leading, ambiguous, and suggestive questions

Red Wing argues that the questions asked in V1 and V2 are both leading and suggestive because the respondents were shown boots with tags that included the words "made in USA." In this sense, Red Wing contends V1 and V2 shows only that a respondent can read English. . . .

The questions in V1 and V2 are not leading. Nonetheless, the Court agrees with Red Wing that the answer to the first question in V1 and V2 ("Q1") is suggested by the text on the labels and tags of the stimuli boot. Q1 asks the respondent, "Where do you think this product is made?" A boot which is marked "made in USA with imported materials" or "made in USA" suggests that the correct answer to Q1 is the United States. Accordingly, the Court finds that V1 and V2 are suggestive. . . .

Red Wing further asserts that the entire survey is ambiguous because Mantis failed to define the word "made." Rocky argues that the word "made" is not ambiguous because the FTC has determined that "made in USA" means that all or virtually all of a product is made in the United States.

The Court has not yet decided whether it will instruct the jury on the FTC's "all or virtually all" standard for "made in USA." It strikes the Court that the FTC standard is not so much a legal definition as it is a measurement of what the FTC determined consumers believed "made in USA" meant when the FTC conducted its research more than a decade ago. Furthermore, the Court has already determined that the FTC standard is not binding on the Court or the jury. Thus, for purposes of the trial, the FTC standard is simply evidence of a federal commission's opinion on the subject, which the jury may give whatever weight, if any, it deems appropriate in light of all of the other evidence in the case. . . .

Nevertheless, Red Wing's argument concerning the lack of a definition for the word "made" misses the mark. Undoubtedly, if the Mantis survey had attempted to define "made," Red Wing would have asserted the definition was incorrect, since Red Wing has argued from the beginning that the term "made in USA" is subject to varying interpretations. The Mantis survey did not ask respondents what "made in USA" meant to them, so the survey does not provide an answer to that question. That does not, however, render the survey unreliable or inadmissible. The survey is still probative at least to show the difference, if any, between consumers' perceptions of "made in USA" and "made in USA of imported materials."

Lastly, Red Wing argues that Q3 is leading and suffers from demand effects and order bias. Rocky contends that Red Wing's argument improperly suggests that Q3 forced respondents to choose between a boot "made in the United States" and one "made in another country." It points out that Q3 also includes the alternatives "I have no preference and would purchase either boot," and "I don't know and have no opinion."

Given that the first answer to Q3 is "I would purchase the boot made in the USA," the Court tends to agree that Q3 exhibits some degree of order bias. The Court does not view this as a particularly serious flaw, however, and does not render Q3 unreliable. Thus, the flaw goes to the weight of the evidence as opposed to its admissibility. . . .

B.   Admissibility

. . . *Leelanau* [a trademark case] is illustrative. There, the court found three significant flaws in the survey. First, the court found that the survey's universe was substantially overbroad. In addition, the court concluded that the survey failed to approximate actual market conditions, and was "little more than a memory test." Lastly, the court held that "the entire survey was suggestive." Stating that the case was "close," the court in *Leelanau* ruled that despite "substantial flaws," "the better course is to admit the survey. . . ."

. . . In light of [the court's rulings above], in contrast to *Leelanau*, this is not a close case. . . . The actual flaws are few, and do not so undermine reliability as to render the survey evidence inadmissible. Rather, as Rocky suggests, the flaws go to the weight of the evidence, not its admissibility. Indeed, the Mantis survey's methodology appears to be significantly more reliable than that of the substantially flawed survey admitted into evidence in *Leelanau*. Accordingly, the Court finds that the survey evidence is sufficiently reliable to meet the requirements of Fed. R. Evid. 702 and 703. . . .

NOTES AND QUESTIONS

The court disagreed that the questions were leading, though they were suggestive given the labels and tags. What's wrong with a suggestive question if it's not leading? Is it that it focuses respondents' attention on particular messages?

B.   **Reliable Survey Design**

While no survey is perfect, there are well-recognized flaws that may make a survey entirely unhelpful. Surveys, like other evidence, must be both relevant and reliable. The current standards developed from *Daubert v. Merrill Dow Pharmaceuticals, Inc.*, 509 U.S. 579 (1993), and *Kumho Tire Co., Ltd. v. Carmichael*, 526 U.S. 137 (1999). A survey expert must show "in the courtroom the same level of intellectual rigor that characterizes the practice of an expert in the relevant field." *Kumho*, 526 U.S..

Federal Rule of Evidence 702, which is mirrored by similar rules in many state courts, says a testifying expert must:

> (1) assist the trier of fact to understand the evidence or determine a fact issue;
> (2) base the testimony on sufficient facts or data;
> (3) use reliable principles and methods; and
> (4) apply those principles and methods reliably to the facts of the case.

The *Rocky Brands* case recites the accepted principle that, applied to surveys, an expert should show that a survey is trustworthy and probative because: (1) the population (universe) was properly chosen and defined; (2) the sample chosen was representative of that population; (3) the questions asked were clear and not leading; (4) the survey was conducted by qualified persons following proper interview procedures; (5) the data gathered were accurately reported; (6) the data gathered were analyzed in accordance with accepted statistical principles; and (7) the process was conducted so as to ensure objectivity (which may be lacking if, for example, the survey was conducted by persons who were connected with the parties or counsel or aware of its purpose in the litigation). MANUAL FOR COMPLEX LITIGATION § 21.493 (3d ed. 1995); *see also* Diamond, *supra.*

The Surveyed Population

Actual or Prospective Purchasers? The relevant survey universe typically includes prospective purchasers of the *defendant's* product. Surveying the plaintiff's customers ordinarily makes little sense unless they're likely to consider the defendant's goods or services in the future. But how do we know who's a prospective purchaser? Depending on the relevant market, and on circuit precedent, courts have defined prospective purchasers as (1) past purchasers of the defendant's products, Church & Dwight Co., Inc. v. S.C. Johnson & Son, Inc., 873 F. Supp. 893 (D.N.J. 1994) ("past purchasers' behavior provides the most accurate forecast of future behavior"), (2) current users of the product at issue; or, most commonly, (3) people who indicate that they are *likely* to purchase the product in the future.

Current antacid users were a proper universe to test an antacid ad "because the primary objective . . . is to convince current users to change brands, not to persuade nonusers to try over-the-counter antacid[s]." Johnson & Johnson-Merck Consumer Pharms. Co. v. Rhone-Poulenc Rorer Pharms., Inc., 19 F.3d 125 (3d Cir. 1994). But current wearers of jeans were not an acceptable universe for a jeans survey because the survey "did not inquire as to whether those participants intended to purchase jeans in the future." Jordache Enters., Inc. v. Levi Strauss & Co., 841 F. Supp. 506 (S.D.N.Y. 1993). Other courts have rejected surveys of people who already had the video game at issue, Universal City Studios, Inc. v. Nintendo Co. Ltd., 746 F.2d 112 (2d Cir. 1984); who owned hiking boots but "did not necessarily have any present purchase interest" in them, Am. Footware Corp. v. Gen. Footware Co., Ltd., 609 F.2d 655 (2d Cir. 1979); or who were current subscribers of a magazine, Inc. Publ'g Corp. v. Manhattan Magazine, Inc., 616 F. Supp. 370 (S.D.N.Y. 1985), *aff'd*, 788 F.2d 3 (2d Cir. 1986). Is the key difference here about how often the product is purchased, or is there anything special about "switch" ads?

Note that courts and marketing experts do not necessarily agree on the proper universe. Many experts point out that stated intentions are often an extremely poor guide to actual purchasing behavior, so that surveying people who identify themselves as potential purchasers might target the wrong population. *See* DAVID H. BERNSTEIN & BRUCE P. KELLER, THE LAW OF ADVERTISING, MARKETING AND PROMOTIONS § 5.02[1] (2011). Nonetheless, where the science and the precedent diverge, lawyers typically rely on the precedent.

Under- and Over-Inclusivity. A survey universe must look specifically at prospective *purchasers*, not just users, when those two groups differ. For instance, a survey of safety-razor buyers was found "not reliable" for failing to include women in its universe because market research showed that many women were likely to purchase the advertised razors as gifts for men. Gillette Co. v. Norelco Consumer Prods. Co., 69 F. Supp. 2d 246 (D. Mass. 1999); *see also* Dannon Co., NAD No. 3129 (July 1, 1994) (a survey universe composed entirely of women is flawed when men account for 27% of all yogurt consumption).

More generally, surveying an underinclusive universe is a potentially fatal defect because there is no way of knowing if the unrepresented members would have responded the same way as those who were represented. In one case, the court discounted surveys from both plaintiff Domino's Sugar and defendant Domino's Pizza for selecting underinclusive universes. Domino's Sugar interviewed mainly suburban women shoppers, entirely ignoring "single, male college students," who were likely to be the pizza's primary purchasers. Domino's Pizza interviewed only walk-in customers at its stores, ignoring customers who order by phone. Amstar Corp. v. Domino's Pizza, Inc., 615 F.2d 252 (5th Cir. 1980).

Over-inclusivity can also doom a survey. A survey of the general consumer population may be acceptable for general consumer goods. Light bulbs, lamps, batteries and flashlights, for example, are products "almost anyone would be likely to have." Union Carbide Corp. v. Ever-Ready Inc., 531 F.2d 366 (7th Cir. 1976). By contrast, courts have found general population surveys unreliable when the relevant groups were regular restaurant-goers, Frisch's Rest., Inc. v. Elby's Big Boy of Steubenville, Inc., 661 F. Supp. 971 (S.D. Ohio 1987), aff'd, 849 F.2d 1012 (6th Cir. 1988); convenience-and-gasoline store shoppers, Sears, Roebuck & Co. v. Sears Realty Co., Inc., 1990 WL 198712 (N.D.N.Y. 1990); and buyers of financial services, Franklin Res., Inc. v. Franklin Credit Mgmt. Corp., 1997 WL 543086 (S.D.N.Y. 1997). Likewise, the universe of frozen-food purchasers was overinclusive for a survey about frozen diet foods. Weight Watchers Int'l, Inc. v. Stouffer Corp., 744 F. Supp. 1259 (S.D.N.Y. 1990).

A good advertising lawyer needs some numerical literacy (not just for surveys—substantiation will also often involve being able to understand a chart!). The statistics of surveys may seem intimidating, but the principles are important and well worth learning.

Sampling Techniques

When the pool of potential purchasers is in the millions, only a sample can be feasibly surveyed. If the sample is representative, one can fairly project the results from the survey to the entire universe. One way to get a representative sample is to take a "probability sample" by selecting the sample randomly from the entire universe. This technique is often used with telephone surveys, where the numbers can be drawn randomly from a complete list or, for surveys of the general population, randomly generated.[*]

"Mall intercept" surveys, in which consumers are randomly selected at various shopping malls, are not, strictly speaking, probability surveys because they require that a subject first go to the mall, and some categories of consumers are more likely to go to the mall than others. Furthermore, interviewers, unless instructed otherwise, may be likely to choose friendly looking people or more-frequent shoppers. Shari Diamond, *Reference Guide on Survey Research*, in FEDERAL JUDICIAL CENTER, REFERENCE MANUAL ON SCIENTIFIC EVIDENCE 246 (2d ed. 2000). (Can you offer reasons why that might matter?)

Notwithstanding these technical criticisms, courts routinely admit properly conducted mall intercept surveys as evidence. Courts generally recognize that mall sampling often is "used

---

[*] Even then, lack of randomness creeps into telephone surveys because some categories of consumers may be more likely to answer the telephone from an unknown phone number and engage a telephone surveyor than others. The rise of mobile phones and do-not-call lists further muddies the picture.

by major American companies in making decisions of considerable consequence," and, when properly conducted, is probative of responses to be expected from the relevant consumers. Nat'l Football League Props, Inc. v. N.J. Giants, Inc., 637 F. Supp. 507 (D.N.J. 1986).

Another typically acceptable approach is to ensure that one or two categories of demographics of the sample population closely approximate those of the universe. For example, if one knows the general age and gender demographics for the product or services at issue, as sophisticated marketers often do, the survey researcher can use quotas in a mall intercept (or Internet) survey to ensure that the same demographics are reflected in the survey pool.

Sample size can be a tricky issue. Jacob Jacoby, Amy Handlin and Alex Simonson argue that most contemporary political polls do a good predictive job by sampling 600–2,500 representative voters. *See* Jacob Jacoby, Amy H. Handlin, & Alex Simonson, *Survey Evidence in Deceptive Advertising Cases Under the Lanham Act: An Historical Review of Comments From the Bench*, 84 TRADEMARK REP. 541 (1994). Indeed, they note that the sampling distributions achieve "reasonable stability" with a sample size around thirty. A larger sample size doesn't necessarily increase accuracy. It does, however, permit the surveyor to reduce the size of the confidence interval surrounding the estimate.

The confidence interval is an indication of how sure we are that a sampled result reflects the underlying reality of the universe. (Technically, it only applies to probability samples, but it is used with reference to non-probability samples such as mall-intercept surveys as well.) It is largest around an estimate of 50%, and decreases as the estimate moves in either direction.

Jacoby et al. illustrate the role of the confidence interval with three sample sizes producing the same estimate of the number of confused consumers, 57.14%:

Sample size	Percentage confused	+/- with 95% confidence*	Range at this confidence level
35	57.14%	16.57%	40.57%–73.71%
350	57.14%	5.24%	51.90%–62.38
3,500	57.14%	1.66%	55.48%–58.80%

In each case, we are 95% confident that the "true" level of deception is somewhere within the range. Nonetheless, in each of the three samples, the estimate is 57.14% deception. Jacoby et al. picked an extreme example, where even the lower bound of the thirty-five-person sample showed significant deception. If a survey instead showed 22% likely deception, reducing the range of the confidence interval might be vital to convincing a court that the true level of deception was high enough to be actionable. As Jacoby et al. conclude, "[w]hen likely deception levels are expected to be in the 15 percent to 25 percent range, the use of larger samples (say, in the order of 300 to 500) not only sounds better, but reduces the size of the confidence interval around the estimate, thereby giving the court more reason for accepting

---

* The 95% confidence interval is often accepted as the standard for reliability.

the findings." They recommend using at least 200–300 respondents in each test group, and at least fifty per sub-group when sub-groups of consumers are at issue.

Courts strongly prefer larger samples, regardless of the magnitude of deception found in a survey. In *Ragold, Inc. v. Ferrero U.S.A., Inc.*, 506 F. Supp. 117 (N.D. Ill. 1980), the court found that a thirty-person sample was so small as to "cast[] into doubt the general applicability of the results." Accepting a 149-person sample, however, another court reasoned that a small sample size "merely means that the results cannot be treated as a relatively precise numerical determination which can be reliably extrapolated to the target universe, but only as an indication whether the commercials have the tendency to mislead." McNeilab, Inc. v. Am. Home Prods. Corp., 675 F. Supp. 819 (S.D.N.Y.1987).

Survey Questions, Controls and Procedures

Even with the right group, surveys have to ask the right questions in the right way. Survey questions should be clear and relevant, not leading. Stimuli should be displayed, where possible, in the survey as they would be in the marketplace. Neither interviewers nor consumers should know the survey's sponsor or the proposition the survey is designed to test; this is known as double-blinding. *See* Pharmacia Corp. v. Alcon Labs., Inc., 201 F. Supp. 2d 335 (D.N.J. 2002) (responses elicited from interviewer who became aware of the lawsuit should have been discarded). Results must be accurately coded and understandably reported. A poorly designed survey can even backfire and enhance the court's suspicions about the sponsoring party's case. *See* Sterling Drug Inc. v. Bayer AG, 792 F. Supp. 1357 (S.D.N.Y. 1992) (defendant's survey, although "designed to obfuscate the relevant issues," actually proved that confusion was likely), *aff'd in part*, 14 F.3d 733 (2d Cir. 1994).

Questions

Where appropriate, the order of questions or advertisements ("stimuli") should be rotated among respondents to reduce "order bias." Respondents to written questions, for instance, are more likely to pick the first choice offered, while telephone respondents tend to pick the last. Shari Diamond, *Reference Guide on Survey Research*, in FEDERAL JUDICIAL CENTER, REFERENCE MANUAL ON SCIENTIFIC EVIDENCE 255 (2d ed. 2000). A consumer is more likely to examine closely the first jacket handed to her than a second one that closely resembles it. *See* Winning Ways, Inc. v. Holloway Sportswear, Inc., 913 F. Supp. 1454 (D. Kan. 1996). Rotation among different respondents corrects for this bias.

Suggestive or leading questions are one of the most-common targets for criticism. One survey seeking to show that defendant's "Donkey Kong" mark for video games infringed the plaintiff's rights in the "King Kong" mark, asked: "To the best of your knowledge, was the Donkey Kong game made with the approval or under the authority of the people who produce the King Kong movies?" Universal City Studios, Inc. v. Nintendo Co., Ltd., 746 F.2d 112 (2d Cir. 1984). The court rejected the question: "The above-mentioned inquiry was an obvious leading question in that it suggested its own answer. The participants were presented with the Donkey Kong–King Kong connection rather than permitted to make their own associations."

One way to avoid suggestive questions is to ask open-ended questions. An open-ended question is not multiple choice and does not require "yes or no" or "true or false" answers. Merial Ltd., NAD No. 3844 (Dec. 18, 2001) ("Open-ended questions are better indicators of how consumers interpret a commercial message because respondents' answers are not colored by the suggestions contained in the questions themselves."). For that reason, surveys often use open-ended questions, such as "What is the main message communicated by the labeling on this product?"

But open-ended questions are more difficult to administer. Interviewers may be unable to ask appropriate follow-up questions. Consumers may have taken many messages away from an ad, and only one of them may be relevant to the case. Without a closed-ended follow-up question ("Did the ad say anything about *X*?"), it may be impossible to determine whether consumers received the relevant message if it isn't the first thing that comes to their minds. When a response to an open-ended question is ambiguous or incomplete, it is appropriate to instruct the interviewer to probe for a more-complete answer. Common probes include asking "Anything else?" or "Can you explain that a little more?"

Relatedly, open-ended questions may result in so many different responses that they are difficult to code and analyze. And even open-ended questions may be leading if they probe too much (e.g., "anything else?" too many times), prompting the respondent to eventually give the "right" answer. One survey asked three times what people thought of aluminum as an antacid ingredient until the third question yielded 45% of people who thought that aluminum was bad for them. The court gave the survey little weight. Johnson & Johnson-Merck Consumer Pharms. Co. v. SmithKline Beecham Corp., 960 F.2d 294 (2d Cir. 1992).

Moreover, precisely because they're so much less likely to elicit a particular message, a defense survey asking only open-ended questions may be criticized as unlikely to identify deception that is in fact present, and an open-ended question can be badly worded or leading in its own way. In *Johnson & Johnson v. Carter-Wallace*, 487 F. Supp. 740 (S.D.N.Y. 1979), *rev'd on other grounds*, 631 F.2d 186 (2d Cir. 1980), the parties disputed whether Carter-Wallace's ads falsely implied that the baby oil in its depilatory smoothed and softened consumers' legs. The key survey question was "What, if anything, is good about having baby oil in the product?" and the court concluded that the question "asks the consumer to speculate as to what benefits, not limited to those claimed in the advertisement, could be attributed to baby oil."

In *American Home Products Corp. v. Abbott Laboratories*, 522 F. Supp. 1035 (S.D.N.Y. 1981), Abbott's ads falsely suggested that its hemorrhoid medication was new. Its survey purported to show that few consumers placed importance on newness. The court was unconvinced because of expert testimony that "consumers cannot, without prompting by specific questions, respond to more than one or two ideas as the most important conveyed by a commercial. Thus, ideas other than those identified as the most important are likely to be perceived and to be given weight by consumers." The court found further support in the "aided-response" portion of the survey, where consumers were asked more-specific questions. "No question asked directly about newness; yet, in connection with a question asking whether the defendant's product would live up to its claim that it would stop pain immediately, several respondents stated that they believed the claim because the product was new."

Given all the potential vulnerabilities of surveys, survey experts routinely use questions that are similar to those already approved in other cases to minimize (though never eliminate) admissibility concerns. This is a conventional format:

> [A] well-designed consumer survey first asks 'communication' questions to see what messages the viewer got and to 'filter' or separate those viewers who received certain messages from those who did not. In the next step, the survey asks those who received a particular message . . . "comprehension" questions to determine what the viewers thought the message meant.

Johnson & Johnson-Merck Consumer Pharms. Co. v. Rhone-Poulenc Rorer Pharms., Inc., 19 F.3d 125 (3d Cir. 1994).

The closed-ended question, "Did the ad communicate anything to you about *X*?" is often considered effective. Another accepted quasi-filter is a clear indication that "I don't know" is an acceptable answer. In fact, courts and the NAD are generally troubled by the absence of a "don't know" option, regardless of whether other filters are present. However, some survey researchers argue that providing "don't know" options produces less-accurate results because they allow people who do indeed have relevant opinions to skate quickly through a survey— but given existing precedents favoring "don't know" options, a court would have to be convinced that this cost was worth avoiding. *See* Bernstein & Keller, *supra*, § 5.02[3] at 5–24.

Filter questions can address fears of leading questions. In testing whether an analgesic ad conveyed a message about speedy relief, it might be best to ask first, "Did or didn't the commercial say or suggest anything to you about [various attributes, including 'how fast the product works,' and also an attribute not included in the commercial to serve as a control]?" Then, looking at those people who answered "yes" to the "how fast" question but "no" to the control/s, the surveyor can follow up with "What if anything, did the commercial say or suggest about how fast this product works?" *See* Alex Simonson, *Survey Design in False Advertising Cases*, 1207 PLI/Corp. 309 (2000).

However, this raises another issue: What is the appropriate denominator to calculate the percentage of deceived consumers? It's intuitive that someone who slept through the ad and therefore wasn't confused shouldn't really count as "exposed to the ad" or "not confused by the ad." But what about people who aren't asleep but still aren't really getting the point? In the example under discussion, suppose 30% of the sample responded "yes" to the "how fast" question, and 60% of those received a (false) superiority message. As Simonson points out, it's intuitive to say that likely deception is 18% (.30 x .60). Simonson argues that 60% might be more important. Upon noticing the claim, consumers readily perceived it as a superiority claim.

Courts have generally focused on overall "take away" from ads, but Simonson argues that this wrongly privileges level of attention over comprehension. Compare a different scenario, in which 60% of consumers notice a claim, and 30% of them interpret it as a superiority claim. The total is again 18%. But, Simonson asks, which variable—attention or comprehension—is more likely to vary between the test setting and the real world? Since attention is based on numerous external factors, he contends, it would be more likely to vary in an artificial survey setting—perhaps in the direction of greater attention because of the lack of distractions or in the direction of less attention because the respondent isn't actually making a purchasing decision. Either way, given that attention varies, comprehension is what we can be most confident about. The result would be a conclusion that 60% of relevant respondents in the former example, and only 30% in the latter, were deceived by the claim. Is this argument persuasive?

Controls

A control group is not shown the allegedly misleading ad (and is usually shown some other ad) but is asked the same questions as the group shown the ad. This can help eliminate "noise" by indicating whether respondents are (1) reacting to the actual ad or (2) merely guessing, being led by the survey questions or replaying their own preconceptions. In order to determine "net" confusion—confusion caused by the challenged ad and not by other causes—researchers subtract the percentage of the control group whose answers indicated confusion from the percentage reported by the test group. The importance of a control group has increased substantially over time, and courts are increasingly likely to exclude surveys without controls.*

In general, a proper control keeps everything constant except for the aspect or aspects of the ad being challenged. If the control changes too much or too little, it won't be testing the right question. For example, one case rejected a survey where the challenged ad was comparative but the test ad wasn't. The allegedly false message was that the defendant's nicotine patch produced superior quitting efficacy to the plaintiff's. The control ad just called the defendant's patch the "#1 Doctor Recommended Patch" without mentioning any other patch. The court accepted defendant's expert's testimony that consumers believe that comparative ads make superior efficacy claims by default, and that this preexisting bias must be controlled for in a survey. Pharmacia Corp. v. GlaxoSmithKline Consumer Healthcare, L.P., 292 F. Supp. 2d 594 (D.N.J. 2003). (If consumers believe that comparative ads make superior efficacy claims by default, though, why not require a comparative advertiser to disclaim superior efficacy?)

How should a proper control ad be identified? Among the alternatives might be no ad at all; a "tombstone" ad with just the name of the product; an edited version of the challenged ad with the allegedly deceptive claim taken out; the challenged ad plus a disclaimer; or another ad for the same product. Because the design of the control ad can affect the percentage of consumers who report a false claim, and because the control results will be subtracted from the results of the test cell, the control may determine whether the survey results fall above or

---

* A survey without a control group might have some weight if it has control questions—usually questions asking about a message clearly not in the ad. Respondents who say that the message is in the ad can be discounted as simply "yea-saying" or agreeing to anything in front of them. A very high level of confusion may also save a survey without a control. Gillette Co. (Venus ProSkin Moisture Rich Razor), NAD #5473 (2012) ("In cases where the percentage of confusion is closer to the threshold of approximately 20% the failure to adequately control might be more troublesome to a claim that there is consumer confusion. In this case, however, 45.3% of consumers perceived [the challenged claim], far above the 20% threshold.").

below the threshold for liability. Thus, courts may reject surveys with inappropriate controls. *See, e.g.*, Weight Watchers Int'l, Inc. v. Stouffer Corp., 744 F. Supp. 1259 (S.D.N.Y. 1994).

Richard Craswell looked at a study by Cornelia Pechmann, *Do Consumers Overgeneralize One-Sided Comparative Price Claims, and Are More Stringent Regulations Needed?*, 3 J. MKTG. RES. 150 (1996), which tested an actual print ad for United Parcel Services (UPS). The ad stated that the UPS rate for delivering a letter by 10:30 the next morning was $3 less than the Federal Express rate. This was true, but UPS's rate for the class of service used by many customers—delivery by any time before 5:00 pm the next afternoon—was actually higher than Federal Express's rate. Thirty-seven percent of respondents, however, received the false message that UPS had the lowest rates overall—a fairly high percentage of deception. Pechmann tested a control group exposed to no ad at all and found that only 16% of respondents believed that UPS had the lowest rates overall. If that had been the control, the net deception would be 21%—likely enough to be actionable. Pechmann also tested a control group with an ad that contained a disclaimer warning consumers that the same rates would not apply to deliveries after 10:30 a.m. Using that ad, 29% of consumers believed that UPS had the lowest rates overall. If that's the proper control, the net deception caused by the original ad is 8%—likely not enough to be actionable. (Was this a good control, or a bad disclaimer? Craswell points out that 29% deceptiveness is probably enough to make the *control* misleading under existing precedent. Richard Craswell, *"Compared to What?": The Use of Control Ads in Deceptive Advertising Litigation*, 65 ANTITRUST L.J. 757 (1997).)

As Craswell concluded, while any control will help with technical issues—leading questions, yea-saying biases, guessing and so on—defendants would prefer a control ad that produces a small difference between test and control, and plaintiffs would prefer the opposite. The choice of an appropriate control, then, is really a policy issue. While we might initially think that we want the control to reduce deception, we need to take into account truthful information that might be lost as well. To see Craswell's point, imagine a control ad that is merely the product name. Unless the product name itself is the problem, this is likely to avoid deception but at the potential cost of avoiding useful information as well. Given that in Lanham Act cases, surveys will only be relevant when the ad's facial claim is literally true, there is always the risk of suppressing literally truthful information that is useful to some consumers.

In fact, when Pechmann tested the ad with a disclaimer, it turned out to reduce comprehension of the truthful claim that UPS had lower rates for morning delivery from 47% to 33%—so the disclaimer reduced the number of deceived consumers by 8% while reducing the number of correctly informed consumers by 14%—probably not a good tradeoff. This result is not unique. More-effective disclaimers often reduce comprehension of truthful claims compared to less-effective disclaimers. *See* Richard Craswell, *Regulating Deceptive Advertising: The Role of Cost–Benefit Analysis*, 64 S. CAL. L. REV. 549 (1991).

A good control ad therefore should do its best to strip out the bad and not the good. If that can't be done, that may be good reason to conclude that the accused ad should not be suppressed unless the deception is much more harmful than the truthful information. Craswell proposes that a challenged ad should be illegal if it is sufficiently worse than whichever control ad has the best balance between decreasing deception and preserving truthful information. How easy do you think this will be for surveyors to implement? Should they test multiple control ads in every case?

Presentation

How should stimuli be presented? Ideally, they'd be shown as close as reasonably possible to their marketplace reality. Consumer surveys may not be relevant if they test only a certain claim in isolation without showing consumers the rest of the advertising at issue. *See* Scott's Co. v. United Indus. Corp., 315 F.3d 264 (4th Cir. 2002) (rejecting survey that showed respondents only an isolated portion of the product packaging because "the relevant issue in a false advertising case is the consumer's reaction to the advertisement as a whole and in context.").

Courts have taken different positions on whether an ad or other stimulus should be left in front of consumers during questioning. One strand of cases condemns such procedures as mere reading tests, reasoning that consumers don't study ads that way in real life. *See, e.g.,* Am. Home Prods. Corp. v. Proctor & Gamble Co., 871 F. Supp. 739 (D.N.J. 1994). But other courts dislike removing the stimulus because it turns the survey into a memory test and might not reflect market conditions. *See, e.g.,* Starter Corp. v. Converse, Inc., 170 F.3d 286 (2d Cir. 1999) (survey where stimulus was covered with cloth after respondents briefly examined it was "little more than a memory test"). The best rule is probably that the surveyor should make a reasoned decision about whether keeping or removing the stimulus reflects the particular market conditions at issue. Would it be appropriate to allow a survey respondent to replay a video ad that is normally delivered to viewers on YouTube?

Data Reporting and Analysis

Correct recording of responses and proper coding is the next essential step. Surveys have failed where they aggregated the answers to several questions, or otherwise manipulated the data, to inflate the results. L&F Prods. v. Proctor & Gamble Co., 845 F. Supp. 984 (S.D.N.Y. 1998). In connection with one survey, the expert concluded that a commercial for Maxwell House coffee claiming that "the coffee perking in this pot is America's best-loved coffee" communicated to a substantial percentage of consumers that Maxwell House was the "best-selling" brand of coffee in America. But reference to the underlying responses showed that most consumers understood the claim to be only that Maxwell House was "popular" or a "favorite." Kraft Foods, Inc., NAD No. 3201 (April 24, 1995).

Coding errors or other problems with the underlying survey answers can significantly reduce the weight of a survey. Pharmacia Corp. v. Alcon Labs., Inc., 201 F. Supp. 2d 335 (D.N.J. 2002) (according survey little weight because of, inter alia, flaws in the execution of the survey resulting in anomalous results from one survey interviewer).

Objectivity

As a general rule, surveys should be conducted by an independent outside party, not the advertiser's market research department. *See* Aurora Foods, Inc., NAD No. 3658 (June 1, 2000). Relatedly, courts have repeatedly rejected focus group evidence (from informal discussion sessions among small groups of consumers generally led by marketers) in place of surveys. *See, e.g.*, Scotts Co. v. United Indus. Corp., 315 F.3d 264 (4th Cir. 2002). Focus group moderators are not objective interviewers.

The lawyer must give the expert leeway to design the survey. Lawyer-shaped surveys can seem inadmissibly biased and may open the surveyor up for discovery and destructive cross-examination. *See, e.g.*, Greenpoint Financial Corp. v. Sperry & Hutchinson Co., 116 F. Supp. 2d 405 (S.D.N.Y. 2000) (expressing "serious doubts" about the validity of survey because of undue influence by the lawyers). As one federal judge complained:

> It is difficult to believe that it was a mere coincidence that when each party retained a supposedly independent and objective survey organization, it ended up with survey questions which were virtually certain to produce the particular results it sought. This strongly suggests that those who drafted the survey questions were more likely knaves than fools. If they were indeed the former, they must have assumed that judges are the latter.

Am. Home Prods. Corp. v. Johnson & Johnson, 654 F. Supp. 568 (S.D.N.Y. 1987).

Sometimes, an expert will conduct a pilot study—a cheaper survey of fifty to 100 people that can show the likely results of a full-scale survey. A pilot study may also help reveal flaws in the universe or the questions that can be corrected in the final survey. Though designed by the expert, a pilot study may be conducted by counsel, and if it turns out to be flawed, it may be protected from discovery as lawyer work product. *See* Jewel Cos., Inc. v. Granjewel Jewelers & Distribs., Inc., 185 U.S.P.Q. (BNA) 504 (M.D. Fla. 1975). Federal Rules 26(b)(4)(B) and (C) provide that most communications between the attorney and a testifying expert will be covered by the work-product privilege and will not be subject to broad discovery rights. Parties won't have to disclose a pilot study unless it counts as facts or data the expert considered in forming her opinion. If the advertiser chooses to rely on it, a pilot study might even be useful in obtaining preliminary relief, though it would be unlikely to be sufficient at trial or on summary judgment.

C.   Admitting Surveys as Evidence

Some courts admit surveys under the state-of-mind exception to the hearsay rule, Fed. R. Evid. 803(3), or under the related exception for contemporaneous statements describing or explaining an event or condition, Fed. R. Evid. 803(1). The Second Circuit explained that the great majority of surveys are admitted as Rule 803(3) exceptions because they poll individuals about their presently existing states of mind to establish facts about the respondents' mental impressions. This is particularly appropriate in the false advertising context because "[p]laintiffs alleging an implied falsehood are claiming that a statement, whatever its literal truth, has left an impression on the [consumer] that conflicts with reality. This . . . invites a comparison of the impression, rather than the statement, with the truth." Schering Corp. v. Pfizer, Inc., 189 F.3d 218 (2d Cir. 1999). Survey evidence has also been admitted under the present-sense exception as the basis of expert testimony under Rule 703 and under the residual hearsay exception, Rule 807.

As indicated by the *Red Wing* case, absent truly spectacular flaws, courts typically admit surveys and discount them according to their deficiencies. *See, e.g.*, KIS, S.A. v. FOTO Fantasy, Inc., 204 F. Supp. 2d 968 (N.D. Texas 2001) (admitting non-representative sample that failed to replicate market conditions). Jacob Jacoby, Amy Handlin and Alex Simonson studied the treatment of Lanham Act false advertising surveys in 1994. Of the surveys admitted in the cases they reviewed, 55% were accorded "considerable weight," 22% a "moderate amount" of weight and 23% "little or no weight." Jacob Jacoby et al., *Survey Evidence in Deceptive Advertising Cases under the Lanham Act: An Historical Review of Comments from the Bench*, 84 TRADEMARK REP. 541 (1994).

Courts also recognize that "[i]t is relatively easy for one expert to criticize a survey done by another." U-Haul Int'l v. Jartran, Inc., 522 F. Supp. 1238 (D. Ariz. 1981), *aff'd*, 681 F.2d 1159 (9th Cir. 1982). Litigants who attack an opponent's survey, but don't provide their own, will often receive little judicial sympathy. *See* Gucci v. Gucci Shops, Inc., 688 F. Supp. 916 (S.D.N.Y. 1988).

Internet Surveys

Internet surveys are becoming more common, perhaps close to standard. Internet surveys can be substantially cheaper and faster than conventional phone or mall-intercept surveys, especially if the survey concerns a general consumer product. A fast mall-intercept survey takes weeks; a fast Internet survey can be done in ten days. Controls are also cheaper and easier to create and modify on the Internet, where the magic of photo manipulation substitutes for generating physical samples.

Questions of proper universe are quite salient with Internet surveys. College graduates, persons with incomes above $75,000 and persons between the ages of eighteen and fifty-four are high Internet users. Non-college graduates, people with incomes below $50,000 and people fifty-five and older are less likely to use the Internet. Thus, it's important to be sure that the survey can sample relevant and representative consumers. Internet surveys can have trouble obtaining sufficient numbers of respondents in cases involving goods or services restricted geographically, by age or by income. Some survey vendors do try to create a probability sample but with increased expense and time.

Courts are also concerned with whether an Internet survey can adequately replicate the marketplace and purchase experience. If a consumer would typically be able to pick up or examine the product, an Internet survey will be trickier. Where products or services are sold with brochures and other written information, as insurance often is, they might make good candidates for Internet surveys.

Internet-specific concerns include frequent survey takers who are compensated for participation. Though a competent survey company will exclude people who've taken a certain number of surveys within a certain time period from being further surveyed, a careful survey expert will investigate the details. If the target consumers make up only a small percentage of the general population, but 70% of the survey respondents passed the initial screening by answering the questions as if they were target consumers, further inquiry is required. Relatedly, Internet surveys have fewer checks on the identity of survey respondents. An interviewer's in-person judgments are far from perfect, but in their absence, some other sort of validation of identity or qualification is required, such as following up with the respondent later on and cross-checking answers.

Survey responses are also different on the Internet, without an interviewer present to ask clarifying questions. A human interviewer can keep a respondent motivated to answer questions and bring a wandering one back on track. Respondents to web surveys can get lazy answering open-ended questions and tend to write very short, even unintelligible responses. A survey expert reported that one Internet survey showed no confusion among respondents who answered a question with fewer than ten words but substantial confusion among respondents who did the work. This is a problem that has not entirely been worked out, but keeping the survey as short as possible probably helps. Some experts suggest adding an algorithm that will pop up a request for a further explanation if a respondent enters an answer below a certain number of characters. But if the survey does this too often, it will likely trigger profane rants from some respondents!

Another difference is that respondents take very different amounts of time to get through Internet surveys; some blaze through in seconds (and perhaps their answers should be discarded) while others take hours (which means that they walk away and return later and perhaps also should be excluded). This reinforces the point that information about underlying responses, and not just aggregate numbers, is key to evaluating a survey. To identify respondents who may not be taking the survey seriously, the survey designer can insert fake questions or other clues that the respondent isn't taking enough care reading the survey and also record the time it took to complete the survey.

One expert concluded, based on sample surveys, that properly designed and conducted Internet surveys can be as reliable as the more-traditional telephone and mall-intercept surveys. *See* Hal Poret, *A Comparative Empirical Analysis of Online Versus Mall and Phone Methodologies for Trademark Surveys*, 100 TRADEMARK REP. 756 (2010). Poret concluded that Internet surveys can achieve similar if not better response rates and representative samples in terms of age, gender, geographic location and product/service use. "Negligible" numbers of respondents had trouble viewing the test stimuli, gave nonsense answers or took the survey extremely fast or extremely slowly. They expressed "no opinion" at about the same rate as respondents in phone and mall surveys. Validation attempts largely bore out the respondents' identity claims. Perhaps of greatest interest, the substantive results of surveys were statistically equivalent across different survey modes.

The most-important disadvantage of Internet surveys was that respondents provided shorter answers to open-ended questions. This could be troublesome for a plaintiff attempting to show that consumers received certain messages but conversely helpful for a defendant who'd rather be able to show that consumers *didn't* receive those messages. (Of course, opposing parties can be expected to be aware of these effects and criticize the choice of a survey method likely to produce favorable results.)

Internet surveys may even have advantages when answers may be sensitive (respondents are more likely to be honest about their use of potentially embarrassing or intimate personal products when they don't have to confront a human interviewer) or when respondents may need time to process the questions at their own paces. *See* Roger Tourangeau & Shari Seidman Diamond, *Internet Surveys for Evaluating Trademark Infringement and Deceptive Advertising*, 287, in TRADEMARK AND DECEPTIVE ADVERTISING SURVEYS: LAW, SCIENCE, AND DESIGN (ed. Shari Seidman Diamond & Jerre B. Swann, 2012).

How Carefully Should Courts Parse Survey Language?

In *PBM Products, LLC v. Mead Johnson & Co.*, 2010 WL 723750 (E.D. Va. 2010), Mead Johnson, which makes Enfamil infant formula, claimed that PBM was falsely advertising the equivalence of its store-brand infant formula with a label such as "Compare to Enfamil Lipil." Mead Johnson argued that the "compare to" message falsely implied that the products' performance had been tested and that the formulas were "identical." Mead Johnson's survey asked a close-ended question, "Based on [the "compare to"] phrase, which of the following do you believe?" The potential answer choices were (1) the formulas had the same ingredients; (2) the formulas had different ingredients; or (3) don't know or none of the above.

The court rejected Mead Johnson's reliance on the survey because the survey never defined "same." The evidence showed that the ingredients of the formulas were very similar, though not identical. In this context:

> [T]he critical question is whether consumers understand the 'compare to' language to make the claim that the formulas are indeed "identical," not whether the ingredients are nearly the same, substantially the same, or any other gradation one could create. Despite that focus, [the] surveys never used the word "identical" nor did the surveys probe what respondents may have meant when they said the products were the "same." Instead, [the expert] assumed that respondents who believed the parties' products had all of the same ingredients would have selected "the same," while respondents who believed the products had some or even most of the same ingredients would have selected "different." . . .

Is this a fair criticism? What if the ingredients had been substantially different—would the survey have been acceptable then?

Ambiguity in questions has doomed other surveys as well. *See* Scotts Co. v. United Indus. Corp., 315 F.3d 264 (4th Cir. 2002) (where false message was allegedly that defendant's product would kill mature crabgrass, asking respondents whether, based on the ad, they believed that the product would "prevent" crabgrass was fatally ambiguous; problem was worsened by lack of a "not sure" option).

Surveys to Disprove Prior Agency Findings

In *Sanderson Farms, Inc. v. Tyson Foods, Inc.*, 547 F. Supp. 2d 491 (D. Md. 2008), plaintiffs Sanderson and Perdue alleged that Tyson's "Raised Without Antibiotics"/"Raised Without Antibiotics that impact antibiotic resistance in humans" (RWA and qualified RWA) claims constituted false advertising. Tyson used ionophores in its chicken feed, and ionophores are antibiotics. People fear that the rise of antibiotic resistance will create "superbugs." But ionophores are not used in human drugs, so their use for chickens presents only a tiny threat—it is "as close to scientific certainty as possible" that ionophores won't lead to antibiotic resistance in humans. However, experts used to think that fluoroquinolones had no impact on human antibiotic resistance; they were removed from the market by the FDA when it turned out that they did.

Tyson also injected antibiotics into its eggs two-to-three days before hatching. Tyson defined "Raised Without Antibiotics" to mean "from hatch until slaughter," a definition it didn't provide to the public (or the USDA).

Plaintiff's Harvestland chickens were truthfully advertised with the slogan "No Antibiotics Ever." Harvestland chickens were more expensive to produce because Perdue had to use costly alternative measures to prevent disease. This cost translated to higher retail prices, which some consumers were willing to pay for antibiotic-free chicken. Tyson executives acknowledged that the RWA claims allowed them to raise the price of RWA chicken without losing sales.

The USDA, which has authority over the labels on the chicken itself, approved the "Raised Without Antibiotics that impact antibiotic resistance in humans" label on the grounds that this disclosure truthfully disclosed the limits of the claim. Tyson used both qualified and unqualified RWA claims in a multimillion-dollar nationwide ad campaign.

The court found plaintiffs' survey compelling as to the deceptiveness of both qualified and unqualified RWA claims. Four cells, each of about 150 shopping mall visitors who were likely chicken purchasers, were shown an unqualified RWA ad, a qualified RWA ad using the USDA-approved language, or a control touting "chicken with great taste, high quality and unmatched variety." Participants were asked "[w]hat is the main idea that the advertisement is trying to communicate?" Respondents who indicated that the advertisement communicated something about Tyson's chicken and antibiotics were then asked, "What does the advertisement imply or state about Tyson and antibiotics?"

The results showed that consumers largely responded to unqualified and qualified RWA claims the same way, and they understood both claims to imply that Tyson's chicken was safer and healthier than competitors' chicken. In the unqualified RWA cells, 71.4% and 85.1% reported a "no antibiotics" claim, whereas 63.4% did so in the qualified RWA cell. The net belief that the ads were claiming superior safety and health ranged from 21.9% to 35.7%.

The qualification, to the extent consumers perceived it, generally meant to them that resistance was a *reason* to avoid antibiotics, not an explanation of *which* antibiotics Tyson's chickens didn't get:

> Quite significant to this Court is the fact that only 4.6% of respondents understood the claim to mean what the experts at the USDA understood it to mean—i.e., that Tyson uses antibiotics, but that the antibiotics it uses do not cause antibiotic resistance in humans. . . . [P]articipants appeared to break down the qualified "Raised Without Antibiotics" into two distinct parts. The first part, "Raised Without Antibiotics," was taken literally by participants to mean that Tyson's chicken was not given antibiotics, which is not accurate. The second part of the qualified claim, "that

impact antibiotic resistance in humans," was taken by participants to mean that Tyson's chicken does not impact antibiotic resistance in humans because Tyson's chicken has no antibiotics, which is also inaccurate. . . . [T]his Court finds that the qualifying language may actually serve to reinforce the false impression that Tyson's chicken is antibiotic-free.

The percentage of consumers who reported an unqualified "no antibiotics" message after exposure to the qualified RWA claim was much higher than the 15% or so that is usually sufficient to show likely deception. Plaintiffs received an injunction.

Should the court have deferred to USDA's determination that the qualified RWA claim was true and not misleading? If not, then when, if ever, should agency approval of a claim preclude a private party from arguing misleadingness? We will return to this issue when we discuss preemption under the FDA in Chapter 18.

D.   Distrust of Surveys and Alternatives

Professor McCarthy has suggested that the credence a judge places in a given survey reflects the judge's own assessment of the evidence more than a survey's statistical accuracy. *See* 4 J. THOMAS MCCARTHY, TRADEMARKS AND UNFAIR COMPETITION § 32:196 (identifying two categories of survey cases: "[A] survey is accepted and relied upon when the judge already has his or her mind made up in favor of the survey results; and a survey is rejected and torn apart when the judge subjectively disagrees with the survey results.") (citation omitted).

Consider McCarthy's interpretation in light of the following sequence of opinions. Here, it is important to understand the evidence as the district court saw it before you can grasp the full meaning of the court of appeals ruling. What *exactly* do the plaintiff's surveys show in this case?

MEAD JOHNSON & CO. V. ABBOTT LABORATORIES, 41 F. SUPP. 2D 879 (S.D. IND. 1999)

Defendant Abbott Laboratories advertises its Similac line of infant formulas under the banner "1st Choice of Doctors." Abbott's chief competitor in the infant formula market is plaintiff Mead Johnson & Company. Mead Johnson contends that the "1st Choice of Doctors" claim is false and/or misleading and thus violates Section 43(a)(1) of the Lanham Act, 15 U.S.C. § 1125(a)(1). Mead Johnson contends the claim is misleading because consumers interpret it to mean that most doctors believe Abbott's product is medically superior to Mead Johnson's product, when in fact most doctors do not have a preference between the two leading brands and there is no evidence that one product is medically superior to the other.

[An example of the product packaging at issue]

. . . As explained below, the court finds that Mead Johnson has shown a substantial likelihood of prevailing on its claim that "1st Choice of Doctors" misleads consumers with respect to Similac in two independent ways. The market research on doctors' views of the competing brands is not consistent with consumers' actual and reasonable interpretations of the "1st Choice of Doctors" claim in two ways. First, consumers reasonably interpret the claim to mean that a majority of doctors choose Abbott products over Mead Johnson products. A fair reading of the many doctor surveys in question shows that Abbott products consistently gain the support of only a plurality of doctors. Second, consumers reasonably interpret the "1st Choice of Doctors" claim to mean that doctors base their choices on professional judgments about the relative quality of the products. The surveys that Abbott offers in support of the claim were not designed to elicit a doctor's exercise of professional judgment as distinct from a "top of the head" product or advertising recall. . . .

Mead Johnson has not tried to frame its case in terms of "literal falsity." As explained in detail below, the claim "1st Choice of Doctors" is deeply—and almost ingeniously—ambiguous. As a result, Mead Johnson must prove first what messages consumers actually receive when they are exposed to the "1st Choice of Doctors" claim. In the advertising business, these received messages are often called the "takeaway." Mead Johnson must prove next that the messages are false or misleading. . . .

Abbott correctly concedes that its "1st Choice of Doctors" claim implies the existence of market research to support the claim. . . . The "1st Choice of Doctors" claim plainly implies the existence of supporting survey data. . . .

1. Infant Formulas: The Market and the Products

. . . [Plaintiff Mead Johnson makes Enfamil; defendant Abbott makes Similac and Isomil.] All witnesses in this case agree that both parties' products are high quality and provide excellent nutrition for infants. . . .

Abbott makes no claim to medical superiority because it could not support such a claim with scientific evidence. There is no scientific evidence showing a clinically significant difference between these products, whether in terms of long-term or short-term health, growth, and development of infants.

. . . . For marketers of each company, proof of such a difference would be professionally equivalent to the discovery of the Holy Grail or the coming of the Apocalypse, depending on which product turned out to be better. Well-financed research teams for both Abbott and Mead Johnson have been trying for years to prove that one product is clinically better than the other. Neither has succeeded to date.

2. The Marketing of Infant Formulas and the Role of Doctors in Marketing

. . . . Abbott and Mead Johnson agree that doctors have significant influence over their patients' brand selections of infant formula. *See, e.g.*, I Tr. 50–51 (doctor recommendation is the strongest advertising message in the market and sells more product than any other message). The infant formulas are treated like medical products, and especially first-time mothers may not be confident that they know enough to make a good decision for their babies. Both Mead Johnson and Abbott view new mothers as emotionally vulnerable, especially with the birth of their first children. *See* III Tr. 85 (doctor's ratification of brand choice relieves consumer of worrying about choice).

. . . In the past, doctors often made specific brand recommendations to their patients. In recent years, however, fewer and fewer doctors have been recommending one particular brand with a high degree of frequency. Most doctors perceive both Abbott and Mead Johnson products as high quality and suitable for infants, which is consistent with the available medical evidence summarized above. Those doctors generally either make no brand recommendation or recommend two or more brands. Mead Johnson and Abbott agree that doctors have become less willing to direct their patients to one specific brand of infant formula. As doctors have become more passive in brand selection, mothers have become more active in the product choice, so both companies have increased their advertising aimed directly at new mothers.

3. Abbott's Use of the "1st Choice of Doctors" Claim

Abbott features the "1st Choice of Doctors" claim prominently in its advertising, marketing, and packaging. Abbott places a blue flag with the words "1st Choice of Doctors" on all its infant formula product labels. That specific phrasing first appeared late in 1995. . . . The uncontradicted testimony of Mead Johnson's McCabe shows that Abbott recently has been increasing the amount of money it spends to promote the "1st Choice of Doctors" claim. . . .

Exhibit 22 is a March 1998 report to Abbott on a test of consumer reactions to several informational advertising pamphlets on Similac. Among six pamphlets, the one stressing the "1st Choice of Doctors" claim scored highest in terms of consumers' likelihood of purchase. The report concluded: "Doctor recommendations and the 'science' behind the formula appeared to drive purchase interest for this concept, as well as the other concepts tested," and use of similar pieces emphasizing the claim was "highly recommended." The advertisement scored very high in terms of convincing consumers that Similac "is the formula doctors prefer."

That market research led to the development and use of Exhibit 39, Abbott's direct consumer advertising piece that leads with the "1st Choice of Doctors" claim. The piece then links the "1st Choice of Doctors" claim directly to a mother's desire for "only the best for your baby," and then emphasizes that "doctors know the science of good nutrition." The message and linkage between doctor preference and superior quality are plain. . . .

4. Consumer Perception of the "1st Choice of Doctors" Claim

. . . (a) Abbott's Evidence on the Message Conveyed

. . . The court does not agree that the meaning of the "1st Choice of Doctors" claim is straightforward or self-evident. . . . How, if at all, does the claim take into account the possibility that many doctors have no "choice" or preference among the top brands? At a more fundamental level, what does the claim mean by "choice?" Does it refer to a doctor's exercise of her professional judgment on behalf of patients, or does it refer to a more superficial brand recognition or top-of-the-head impression about brands?

. . . Why should consumers perceive "trust and confidence" from the "1st Choice of Doctors" claim? Abbott agrees that the claim is one of the most powerful it could use in marketing infant formulas. Why should that be so? One possible answer is that consumers expect doctors to have used their professional judgment in making any "choices" among competing brands. As Dr. McDonald testified, the claim "says to consumers that a professional who is knowledgeable has ratified it [the choice of brand] and, therefore, allows a consumer not to think any more about it." Also, unlike a blander, non-comparative claim such as "trusted by doctors", Abbott's claim to be "1st Choice of Doctors" is an inherently comparative (actually, a superlative) claim. Abbott's assertion that it seeks to communicate trust and confidence simply overlooks the comparative or superlative nature of its claim. . . .

(b) Dr. Ross Survey of Consumers

. . . Dr. Ross supervised a survey of consumers through face-to-face interviews at shopping malls in 16 cities across the United States. Participants were screened so as to be women between the ages of 18 and 44 who either had purchased infant formula in the last three months or intended to purchase infant formula within the next 12 months for one or more of their own children. . . .

For the first question to each participant, the interviewer pointed to the blue flag on the label claiming "1st Choice of Doctors" and then asked: "Please tell me what you understand this part of the label to communicate to you." The interviewer recorded the response verbatim, then continued to probe: "Anything else that communicates to you?" The interviewer was instructed to probe, that is, to repeat the "anything else" question, until the response was "unproductive," meaning the respondent said "no," or "nothing else." Some respondents were asked that question several times. If the respondent answered by essentially repeating or "playing back" the words "first choice," the interviewer was then instructed to ask "what do you mean by that?" or words to that effect.

The second question was a further follow-up: "Although you may already have mentioned this, what do you understand the wording 'first choice' to communicate to you?" The interviewer was again instructed to probe until the response was "unproductive."

The third question asked: "And although you may already have mentioned this, if you have an opinion, what reason or reasons do you think this product was 'first choice of doctors'?" The interviewer was again instructed to probe for additional reasons until the response was "unproductive." The interviewer then asked "why do you say that?" and probed the response once with: "Any other reasons you say that?" The fourth question asked the participants about the types of doctors referred to in the "1st Choice of Doctors" claim.

The survey then probed a central problem posed by doctors' approaches to these competing brands—the fact that a substantial proportion of doctors have no significant preference between them. The fifth question asked: "Now, suppose that a survey of doctors had been conducted by the company which makes this product and that they were relying on the results of that survey to make the statement you see here ["1st Choice of Doctors"]. If you have an opinion, in order for this statement ["1st Choice of Doctors"] to be true, what percent of those doctors would have had to say this product was their first choice?" Interviewers were instructed to probe once: "And why do you say that." Responses were recorded verbatim.

The sixth question went a step farther. The interviewer handed the participant a card showing:

> QUESTION: What brand of infant formula, if any, is your first choice?
> RESULTS: 50% — Said they had no first choice
> 30% — Said Similac was their first choice
> 20% — Said another brand was their first choice
> ———
> 100% — Total doctors surveyed

The interviewer then asked: ". . . If those were the results of the survey, would you say that this statement ["1st Choice of Doctors"] is accurate or would you say that this statement is not accurate, or don't you have an opinion about that one way or the other?"[3] Interviewers probed with "why do you say that?"

. . . In response to the first question about what the claim "1st Choice of Doctors" communicated, 52.6 percent of respondents gave answers that Dr. Ross and his associate coded as a reflection of qualitative superiority: superior, better, best, etc. Abbott's market research expert criticized this calculation because Dr. Ross included answers referring only to doctors' "preferences." The criticism was valid because a consumer perception of doctor "preference" does not necessarily show that the consumer perceived the preference in terms of a view of product quality. In response to the criticism, Dr. Ross did a new calculation

---

[3] To avoid possible bias resulting from the order of the choices, the questions to half the participants posed "accurate" as the first option and half posed "not accurate" as the first option.

showing that if the answers referring only to doctors' "preferences" are subtracted, as they properly should have been, the relevant figure is that 41.3 percent understood the claim as making some claim of superiority.

In response to questions about doctors' reasons for choosing Similac, Dr. Ross found that 54.9 percent of participants responded in terms of the quality of the product and/or superiority to other products. The Ross survey did not differentiate between claims of long-term medical superiority defined by clinically proven results, which is the standard Mead Johnson contends is relevant, and less dramatic claims of short-term convenience and tolerance effects.

In response to the fifth question about how many doctors would need to have identified Similac as their "first choice" for the statement to be true, 84 percent of the respondents said it would have to be more than 50 percent of doctors. Only 1.4 percent of respondents gave answers of less than 50 percent as supporting the claim.

The sixth question introduced the hypothetical survey in which 50 percent of doctors had no preference, 30 percent preferred Similac, and 20 percent preferred another brand. That question therefore introduced to participants the problem posed by those doctors having no preference and the possibility of a plurality of doctors preferring Similac. In response to the sixth question, 64.8 percent of respondents said those results would make the "1st Choice of Doctors" statement not accurate, while 19.8 percent said the statement would be accurate, and 15.4 percent had no opinion.

Dr. Ross concluded from the results of his study that more than 80 percent of the consumers understood the "1st Choice of Doctors" claim to convey that a majority of doctors choose or prefer Similac. He also concluded that more than 40 percent understood the claim as making some claim of product superiority. With respect to the issue of doctors' reasons for choosing or preferring Similac, more than half attributed doctors' reasons to the doctors' views of the quality or superiority of the product. More than 90 percent of those respondents who expressed any opinion about doctors' likely reasons for their choices thought that the doctors' opinions would be based on product quality or performance.

Abbott criticizes the Ross consumer survey on several major grounds. Abbott contends that the Ross survey used excessive probing, which can introduce biases into a study by forcing responses from a person who has no meaningful response to give. Second, Abbott criticizes the attempt to ask consumers to speculate about why doctors might choose Similac over other brands. Third, Abbott criticizes the attempt to have consumers quantify the proportion of doctors who would have to choose Similac for the "1st Choice of Doctors" claim to be true. The court is not persuaded by these criticisms.

First, probing was appropriate here because of the ambiguity of the "1st Choice of Doctors" claim. In market surveys probing can be a powerful tool, but it can also introduce biases and produce artificial responses from a participant who has run out of meaningful ideas on a subject. *Compare* L & F Prods. v. Procter & Gamble Co., 845 F. Supp. 984, 996 (S.D.N.Y.1994) (repeating questions "also serves the purpose of clarifying otherwise-ambiguous first responses by probing the implications of previous answers"), *aff'd*, 45 F.3d

709 (2d Cir.1995), *with* Am. Home Prods. Corp. v. Procter & Gamble Co., 871 F. Supp. 739, 748 (D.N.J.1994) (excessive probing undermined credibility of survey evaluating arguably implicit messages). Mead Johnson has the burden of showing what consumers understand that claim to mean. A more directive approach would no doubt have been criticized as introducing other biases into the study. Repeated probing was a fair means of determining the "takeaway" from the claim.

Also, Abbott's criticism of the probing rings a little hollow. An advertiser is responsible for both explicit messages in advertising and implicit messages communicated to a reasonable proportion of the audience. Abbott itself has not undertaken any study of the message or "takeaway" that consumers draw from the "1st Choice of Doctors" claim. . . . Abbott's criticism on this score might have more force if Abbott had offered some conflicting evidence tending to show consumers do not infer something about product quality from the "1st Choice of Doctors" claim. It has offered no such evidence.

Abbott's second criticism—that Dr. Ross invited consumers to speculate about why doctors might prefer Similac—is also unpersuasive. Some doctors may have brand preferences for reasons that have nothing to do with product quality. Perhaps they prefer the service from one brand's sales representative, perhaps they like one company's support for medical research, or perhaps they have any of a variety of other reasons for their preferences. *See, e.g.*, Ex. 456 at PAR00216 (good service and rapport with representative cited by doctors more often than other reasons for preferring Similac).

In the court's view, however, it is perfectly obvious to all the marketing and market research witnesses who testified that the reason the "1st Choice of Doctors" claim is so powerful is that many *consumers* assume that such preferences are based on doctors' professional judgments about product quality. The NAD similarly recognizes that professional recommendations of health-care products are powerful because consumers interpret them as based on professional assessments of product quality. Dr. Ross's questions on the perceived reasons for doctors' choices were less an invitation to speculate than a means of confirming what is common wisdom among those in the business. The strength of that wisdom is confirmed by the fact that, among consumers who offered an opinion on the subject, more than 90 percent answered in terms of product quality or superiority.

Abbott's third principal criticism of Dr. Ross's consumer survey is aimed at the questions about the proportion of doctors who would have to have preferred Similac to support the claim. Abbott argues the questions were "grossly unfair" because they ask lay people difficult problems about statistics and patterns of preferences. As Dr. McDonald observed, the consumers who were surveyed probably do not spend a lot of time thinking about "the base" and the difference between a majority and a plurality.

The court would not hold Abbott to a standard of 90 percent preference simply because one-third or so of the respondents thought that is what "first choice" meant, at least initially, before they were asked about the hypothetical survey of doctors. *See* Ex. 1 at F-13 (total of 32.8% answered 90% or more). The critical difference between a majority and a plurality, however, is well-recognized in the advertising business. When that difference was introduced expressly in the survey, an overwhelming proportion of respondents believed the "1st Choice of Doctors" claim would not be accurate if it were supported by only a plurality. The court agrees with that overwhelming majority.

. . . Thus, the weight of the evidence presented thus far shows that the "1st Choice of Doctors" claim communicates two key messages to consumers: (1) a majority of doctors choose Similac or other Abbott brands over Enfamil and other competitors; and (2) the doctors' choices are the result of the exercise of the doctors' professional judgment about the quality of the products. . . .

5. The Evidence on the Market Research Among Doctors

The central facts affecting all the market research and advertising in dispute in this case are these: surveys of doctors (especially pediatricians) show consistently (a) that a substantial proportion of doctors do not have a professional preference between Mead Johnson's Enfamil brand and Abbott's Similac brand, but (b) that among doctors who do have a brand preference, more favor Abbott's Similac over Mead Johnson's Enfamil brand. . . .

Based on the evidence of consumers' perceptions of the claim, the court reasons that the "1st Choice of Doctors" claim could legitimately be supported only by evidence that a majority, not a plurality, of doctors express a professional "choice" or "preference" for Abbott's products over competitors' products. To be fair and not deceptive or misleading, the base against which the majority is measured must include doctors who do not have a choice or preference for a single brand. *See* Gillette Co. v. Norelco Consumer Prods. Co., 946 F. Supp. 115, 124–125 & n. 7 (D. Mass. 1996) (in evaluating claim of superiority based on consumer test, responses favorable to competitor and "no preference" responses must be combined because all are responses contrary to claim of advertiser's superiority). . . .

Thus, in light of all the evidence presented thus far, the court finds that Mead Johnson has shown a substantial likelihood of prevailing on its claim that Abbott's use of the "1st Choice of Doctors" claim in its advertising is misleading consumers in two independent respects in violation of the Lanham Act. The claim is misleading first in that consumers reasonably understand it to express the choices of a majority of doctors rather than a mere plurality, and second in that consumers reasonably understand it to express doctors' preferences based on the exercise of their professional judgments rather than superficial or "top of the head" brand familiarity. . . .

MEAD JOHNSON & CO. V. ABBOTT LABORATORIES, 201 F.3D 883 (7TH CIR. 2000)

"1st Choice of Doctors", in a blue ribbon on a product's packaging, conveys the message that more physicians prefer this product than any of its rivals. Does (must?) this phrase mean something more—for example, that a majority of all physicians prefer the product, or that the preference is strong or based on particular grounds? The phrase appears on the packaging of Similac®, an infant formula made by the Ross Pediatrics division of Abbott Laboratories. More than a score of surveys show that pediatricians prefer Similac over Enfamil®, the second-place formula (made by Mead Johnson), with all other competitors far behind. Many of these surveys show that Similac attracts majority support; most show that two physicians prefer Similac for every one who chooses Enfamil. But the district court nonetheless held that "1st Choice of Doctors" violates § 43(a)(1) of the Lanham Act, because it implies to consumers that a majority of physicians strongly prefer the product for strictly professional reasons. All of the surveys that show majority support are inadequate, the judge concluded, because they were designed to elicit either weak preferences or those based on grounds other than medical judgment about quality. Other surveys, designed to eliminate slight or non-medical preferences, show that Similac enjoys only plurality support among physicians. A regular 2-to-1 margin is not enough to permit Abbott to make the "1st Choice" claim, the court held, and issued a preliminary injunction. In politics this would be a landslide: Bill Clinton was the "1st Choice of Voters" at the 1992 and 1996 Presidential elections even though he received less than half of the popular vote (43% in 1992, 49% in 1996). But in marketing, according to the district court, a product must have majority support to be "first."

In English, "first" is ordinal. It denotes rank in a series. A runner who crosses the finish line ahead of all others is "first" even if the race is slow and ends in a photo finish. A TV series ranks first in its time slot if it has a larger audience than any other series, even though there are so many networks, independent stations, and cable channels that no sitcom or drama attracts an absolute majority of viewers. A political candidate who receives more votes than the next-most-popular candidate finishes first, and for most offices a first-place finish is enough for election. Similac therefore is the "1st Choice of Doctors" according to ordinary usage. Perhaps a truthful claim of this kind could be misleading, and therefore actionable under § 43(a)(1), if both absolute and relative levels of preference were small. Suppose 1.1% of pediatricians preferred Similac, 1% preferred Enfamil, 0.9% preferred some other formula, and 97% thought that all of the infant formulas were functionally identical. But absolute and relative preferences for Similac are substantial. Even if, like the district court, we throw out the surveys finding that a majority of medical professionals recommend Similac, the remaining surveys find that between 25% and 48% of those questioned rank Similac first, while Enfamil is the preference of between 10% and 40% of the respondents and never beats Similac. Surveys designed to elicit weaker preferences show that Similac receives between 51% and 64% support and Enfamil from 29% to 37%, so the roughly two-to-one ratio is not sensitive to methodology. Pediatricians may believe (as Abbott contends) that Similac is better tolerated by infants (*i.e.*, less likely to induce unpleasant side effects such as gas, fussiness, and loose stools) and therefore is better in practice, even though clinical tests do not find nutritional differences and experts agree that both products are of high quality. No matter. When the absolute level of preference for the leading product is high, and the difference in support from the medical profession substantial, it is all but impossible to call the claim of "first choice" misleading.

Unless the meaning of language is itself a question of fact, to be determined by survey evidence. And this is what the district court concluded after a three-day hearing on the request for interlocutory relief. . . .

Everything in the district court's analysis depends on the survey of consumers about their understanding of the phrase "1st Choice of Doctors." It is a problematic exercise, for the survey assumes that "first" is a cardinal number—that is, a count such as "246" or "55" or a ratio of two such numbers, rather than a place in a series. Only if "first" is a ratio of cardinal numbers does it make sense to ask whether its meaning is 90% or 51% or a plurality.

Respondents in survey research are suggestible; the form of a question implies an answer, or at least the range of proper answers, and this survey ensured that the answers would be numbers rather than places in a series. Having told the respondents to treat "first" as cardinal, the survey was bound to produce a misleading if not meaningless answer. "First" does not mean 51%, or 90%, or any other ratio, so it is not surprising that the responses were all over the lot. The survey's opening set of questions is less troublesome, but it is hard to get from there to a conclusion that surveys of physicians must attempt to limit the grounds of choice. Many a medical choice depends on ease of use rather than therapeutic effect; think of the enduring debate between champions of oral versus injected polio vaccine. If consumers took away from "1st Choice of Doctors" the implication that Similac is a high-quality product, as the author of the survey concluded, then they were not deceived (this Mead Johnson concedes); we doubt that it is proper to draw more from this survey.

There is a deeper problem: the use of a survey in the first place. Surveys are accepted ways to probe for things such as confusion about the source of goods, for confusion depends on the effect of a phrase or trade dress on the consumer. So far as we can tell, however, never before has survey research been used to determine the meaning of words, or to set the standard to which objectively verifiable claims must be held. Dictionaries themselves are a form of survey; lexicographers determine how words have been used in both scholarly and popular texts. But philologists and others who contribute to dictionaries devote their lives to discovering usage and interpreting nuance. It would be a bad idea to replace the work of these professionals with the first impressions of people on the street, especially because consumers' sketchy understanding of science means that survey results are apt to present firms with unrealistic demands for verification.

Suppose a tube of toothpaste bears this phrase in large type: "SODIUM FLUORIDE ANTICAVITY TOOTHPASTE" immediately above a box with the words "ADA Accepted." These claims could be verified by showing that the American Dental Association had authorized the use of its name and that the dentifrice had "anticavity" effects. To a dentist, the word "anticavity" means that the toothpaste reduces the number of cavities compared with some benchmark (perhaps toothpaste without fluoride, perhaps no toothpaste at all) by a statistically significant amount. Perhaps a group of 1,000 persons using the toothpaste with fluoride for two years had 1,000 cavities, while a control group suffered 1,200 cavities. If the difference satisfies normal tests of significance—meaning that the difference is replicable, rather than the effect of chance—then the claim is true and properly may be made to distinguish this toothpaste from others that are less effective at controlling cavities. It is valuable information to consumers. Imagine, however, a survey administered to shoppers in the toothpaste aisles of drugstores. First the questioner asks consumers "what you understand 'ADA Accepted' to communicate to you." Many are likely to respond that this means that the toothpaste is the best on the market, solves (or at least addresses) all dental problems, or some variation—even though the ADA's rules permit multiple products in the same classification to be "Accepted" if each is medically useful, and the phrase "ADA Accepted" may be applied to a toothpaste that does not have any therapeutic effect against gum disease. *See* AMERICAN DENTAL ASSOCIATION ACCEPTANCE PROGRAM GUIDELINES FOR FLUORIDE-CONTAINING DENTIFRICES (May 1998). Perhaps the survey would continue with a question about what "anticavity" means to the shoppers: does it prevent, say, 90% of all cavities?, a majority of cavities?, and so on. Suppose most of those surveyed thought that "anticavity" means that its use will cut cavities in half. Combining that survey result with the district court's approach to verification would mean that the product could not carry the words "anticavity" or "ADA Accepted" even though these representations help shoppers distinguish toothpaste according to effects that they value. Consumers can't be made better off by removing these words from the product, because then buyers who understand their significance will be deprived of information. The market share of the toothpastes that are most effective in reducing cavities will fall, and the number of cavities will rise.

Section 43(a)(1) forbids misleading as well as false claims, but interpreting "misleading" to include factual propositions that are susceptible to misunderstanding would make consumers as a whole worse off by suppressing truthful statements that will help many of them find superior products. *A "misunderstood" statement is not the same as one designed to mislead.* [Editors' Note: Italics added. See following NOTES AND QUESTIONS for more about this italicized sentence.] Reducing ads and packaging to meaningless puffery can't be the objective of the Lanham Act—though it is a logical (and likely) outcome of Mead Johnson's approach, given the normal level of confusion and misunderstanding reflected in consumer surveys. Asked at oral argument whether a seller of aspirin could label that drug as an anti-inflammatory useful for arthritis (a medically established property of aspirin) if a survey showed that consumers confused palliation of symptoms with a cure for the disease, counsel for Mead Johnson replied that the claim of anti-inflammatory properties would be misleading for the same reason "1st Choice of Doctors" is misleading. This consequence of Mead Johnson's view is so counterproductive that the basic position cannot be accepted. We are not comforted by Mead Johnson's assurance that a seller could overcome consumer misunderstanding and make the claim about anti-inflammatory (or anticavity) benefits if it delivered additional details about the nature and extent of these effects. Requirements along the lines of a package insert with medical details are the province of regulations issued by the Food and Drug Administration, not of litigation under the Lanham Act. What is more, adding details could be so costly and burdensome that sellers might choose to omit all of the information. Anyway, if consumers did not read (or understand) the medical details they would be none the wiser, and on Mead Johnson's view the claim should be enjoined anyway.

By using Mead Johnson's survey to define the meaning of the phrase "1st Choice of Doctors" and then insisting that verification meet the standards thus established, the district court committed a legal error. . . .

MEAD JOHNSON & CO. V. ABBOTT LABORATORIES, 209 F.3D 1032 (7TH CIR. 2000)

Mead Johnson . . . has filed a petition for rehearing. In response to that petition, the panel amends its opinion by replacing the paragraph at slip op. 7–8 with this language:

> Section 43(a)(1) forbids misleading as well as false claims, but interpreting "misleading" to include factual propositions that are susceptible to misunderstanding would make consumers as a whole worse off by suppressing truthful statements that will help many of them find superior products. *A statement is misleading when, although literally true, it implies something that is false. "Misleading" is not a synonym for "misunderstood," and this record does not support a conclusion that Abbott's statements implied falsehoods about Similac.* [The "designed to mislead"

297

sentence is omitted, and the balance of the paragraph is the same; the court then adds the following new paragraph:]

None of this calls into question the understanding, expressed by many decisions, that whether a claim is either "false" or "misleading" is an issue of fact rather than law. Our fundamental conclusion is that a producer cannot make a factual issue just by conducting surveys about how science is done (or, worse, about how surveys should be conducted). The sort of survey evidence Mead Johnson gathered would not support a conclusion by a reasonable person that Abbott's claim either was false or implied a falsehood.

NOTES AND QUESTIONS

What concerns could have prompted the panel to amend its opinion? Does the amended language fully address those concerns?

Are there some claims that are so straightforward that it just shouldn't matter if consumers misunderstand them? Consider the "halo effect," where claims about good performance on one attribute leads audiences to believe that the product's performance on other attributes is also good. For example, one study has shown that consumers believe that "fair trade" chocolate is lower in calories than chocolate produced by mistreated laborers. Jonathon P. Schuldt et al., *The "Fair Trade" Effect: Health Halos From Social Ethics Claims*, SOC. PSYCHOL. & PERSONALITY SCI., Jan. 2012. Should producers of fair-trade chocolate be responsible for this erroneous belief? What are the regulatory options—leaving the misunderstanding alone, requiring disclosures or something else? Does it matter how easy it would be to correct the misunderstanding? *See* Pernod Ricard USA, LLC v. Bacardi U.S.A., Inc., 653 F.3d 241 (3d Cir. 2011) (rejecting survey evidence that 18% of consumers thought "Havana Club" rum came from Cuba when the label prominently stated that it was "Puerto Rican Rum"); *cf.* Molson Coors Beverage Co. USA v. Anheuser-Busch Cos., 957 F.3d 837 (7th Cir. 2020) (advertising that plaintiff's beer was made using corn syrup was not actionable even if it implied that the final product contained corn syrup, when the plaintiff itself listed corn syrup as an "ingredient").

When should courts look to the relevant consumers' definitions of terms used in advertising? In *Energy Four, Inc. v. Dornier Medical Systems, Inc.*, 765 F. Supp. 724 (N.D. Ga. 1991), mentioned *supra*, the defendant's advertisement claimed that the competitor's product was subject to "catastrophic failure." The plaintiff showed that the relevant medical community generally understood catastrophic failure to mean "a failure resulting in serious equipment damage or patient injury." The defendant countered with the definition of catastrophic failure found in an engineering dictionary: a sudden failure not associated with typical wear. The court rejected the dictionary definition because there was "no evidence that the dictionary definition reflected a common understanding among targeted consumers" and found literal falsity. Is this line of reasoning acceptable under *Mead Johnson*? Under *Mead Johnson*, what would it have taken to show that the ad was "misleading" rather than "misunderstood?"

Consider this excerpt from the Listerine/floss case, introduced *supra*, in light of *Mead Johnson*:

MCNEIL-PPC, INC. V. PFIZER INC., 351 F. SUPP. 2D 226 (S.D.N.Y. 2005)
[review facts from implicit falsity materials]

. . . . In the first survey, consumers were shown the third version of Big Bang twice and then asked a series of questions about the ideas that were communicated to them by the commercial. The survey found that 50% of the respondents took away the message that "you can replace floss with Listerine." . . .

In the third survey, a control survey, consumers were asked their "pre-existing beliefs" regarding Listerine and floss; the intent was to determine the number of people who did not recall seeing the commercials but who still believed that Listerine could be used instead of floss. A minority of those surveyed did not recall seeing Big Bang, and of those 19% stated the opinion that Listerine could be used in place of floss. . . .

The surveyors then took the three surveys together, subtracted the 19% figure from the 50% . . . figures, . . . and concluded that 31% of those who saw the commercial . . . took away a replacement message. . . .

[The court rejects technical criticisms of McNeil's surveys.]

. . . . Finally, Pfizer relies heavily on the Seventh Circuit's decision in *Mead Johnson & Co. v. Abbott Labs.*, 201 F.3d 883 (7th Cir. 2000). There, Judge Easterbrook wrote that:

> interpreting "misleading" [in § 43(a)(1) of the Lanham Act] to include factual propositions that are susceptible to misunderstanding would make consumers as a whole worse off by suppressing truthful statements that will help many of them find superior products. A "misunderstood" statement is not the same as one designed to mislead.

The *Mead Johnson* decision, however, is of little assistance in this case. The issue there was whether the statement "1st Choice of Doctors" on infant formula containers was misleading and constituted false advertisement. The plaintiff argued that "1st" meant more than 50% and that a simple plurality would not suffice.

Understandably, the Seventh Circuit rejected the argument. Here, the advertised claim is much less nebulous—it is a claim based on purported proof provided by "clinical tests." Moreover, the court in *Mead Johnson* was concerned that surveys were being used in that case "to determine the meaning of words." . . . In this case, the Ridgway surveys were used in the manner in which surveys are traditionally used in false advertisement cases. The *Mead Johnson* decision does not dictate a different result here.

NOTES AND QUESTIONS

The *Pfizer* court quotes the unamended version of *Mead Johnson*, using language the Seventh Circuit ultimately removed from the opinion. Courts interpreting *Mead Johnson* have done this several times.

Were you convinced by the distinctions the *Pfizer* court made between the survey it confronted and the survey in *Mead Johnson*? The court in *Clorox Co. Puerto Rico v. Proctor & Gamble Commercial Co.*, 228 F.3d 24 (1st Cir. 2000), also declined to extend the *Mead Johnson* holding from printed labels to television commercials. The court held that the claim before it, that people using its detergent would find that "whiter is not possible" for clothes, was "an integral part of a television commercial with substantial text and images. There is a fundamental difference between a slogan on a can label that communicates its meaning to consumers solely through the printed text and a tagline shown on the screen at the end of a television commercial that communicates its message to consumers through a combination of audio-visual and textual media." Does this distinction make sense?

Solvay Pharmaceuticals, Inc. v. Global Pharmaceuticals, 419 F. Supp. 2d 1133 (D. Minn. 2006), involved a lawsuit between two makers of pancreatic enzyme supplements. Defendant Global marketed a (purported) generic alternative to Solvay's supplements, which are used to treat cystic fibrosis patients and others who don't produce the proper enzymes to digest food. Solvay argued that manufacturing differences in formulation, blending and coating of supplements can lead to different enzyme activity and release rates, resulting in different effects on patients, even if they are truthfully labeled as containing the same enzyme content.

Global worked to have major drug information databases characterize its product Lipram-CR as a generic substitute for Solvay's Creon. Global also told pharmacists that Lipram was "equivalent" to, a "pharmaceutical alternative" to, a "true alternative to," and "the generic form" of Creon. Global argued that it never advertised Lipram as an FDA-approved generic, bioequivalent, "therapeutically equivalent" or "pharmaceutically equivalent" to Creon—all of these terms require extremely stringent standards of equivalence under FDA rules. However, Solvay's surveys of retail pharmacists indicated that 89% of pharmacists agreed that a generic substitute must be therapeutically equivalent to the name-brand product and 93% agreed that the generic must be bioequivalent to the name-brand product. The court denied Global's motion for summary judgment on literal falsity.

Should the surveys be accepted as evidence of what the terms mean? Is this result consistent with *Mead Johnson*? If you were the plaintiff, how would you distinguish *Mead Johnson*?

Getting Rid of a Survey Requirement? Lee Goldman argues that the survey requirement in cases of allegedly misleading advertising should be abandoned. *See* Lee Goldman, *The World's Best Article on Competitor Suits for False Advertising*, 45 FLA. L. REV. 487 (1993). Surveys are expensive, hotly contested and often not of high quality. In many instances, a judge or jury can determine whether an ad makes the allegedly false implied claim. Goldman gives the example of an ad claiming that Extra Strength Maalox Plus was "the strongest antacid there is." This allegedly falsely implied that Maalox was the most-effective product on the market. Goldman contends that it's difficult to see why the advertiser would make this strength claim if not to claim superior effectiveness. Because of the current state of Lanham Act doctrine, however, the challenger was required to submit a survey. Because the survey it submitted was flawed, the challenger lost. *See* Johnson & Johnson-Merck Consumer Pharm. Co. v. Rhone-Poulenc Rorer Pharms., Inc., 19 F.3d 125 (3d Cir. 1994). So, Goldman argues, the survey requirement is inefficient and leads to questionable results. The problem is worsened because of the short timeframe before preliminary relief hearings, which makes it harder to conduct a good survey. Mistaken rulings at the preliminary injunction stage are often irreversible because many if not most Lanham Act false advertising cases don't proceed past that stage.

Goldman suggests that (properly conducted) surveys should be considered probative, not mandatory, as they are in the related area of trademark law. He contends that the survey requirement, while defended by some as a way to make advertising law more predictable and avoid chilling advertisers' speech, doesn't in fact make the law more predictable or accurate. Judges should be considered competent to interpret ads, as they are competent to interpret other uses of language such as contracts, and juries should be able to evaluate how reasonable consumers would understand ad claims even without surveys. Since we do not live in an ideal world of perfect, cost-free surveys, he argues, the survey requirement should be made optional, as it is in trademark cases under the Lanham Act. Given the cases we've read, do you agree?

5.   Standing under the Lanham Act

15 U.S.C. § 1125(a) states the following:

> (1) Any person who, on or in connection with any goods or services, or any container for goods, uses in commerce . . . any false designation of origin, false or misleading description of fact, or false or misleading representation of fact, which—
>
> (B) in commercial advertising or promotion, misrepresents the nature, characteristics, qualities, or geographic origin of his or her or another person's goods, services, or commercial activities, shall be liable in a civil action by *any person who believes that he or she is or is likely to be damaged by such act.* [emphasis added]

Courts have construed standing expansively with respect to the trademark portions of the Lanham Act—all that is required to bring a federal trademark claim is ownership of a valid trademark. In some cases, this merely requires that the plaintiff show it has a commercial interest to be protected, as opposed to a noncommercial interest (such as a purely private individual's interest in her reputation for charitable or creative activities). *See* Stayart v. Yahoo! Inc., 623 F.3d 436 (7th Cir. 2010). When it comes to false advertising, however, courts apply different standards. The Supreme Court has resolved one conflict over who can be a Lanham Act plaintiff, but, as you will see, others remain.

LEXMARK INTERN., INC. V. STATIC CONTROL COMPONENTS, INC., 572 U.S. 118 (2014)

Scalia, J.

This case requires us to decide whether respondent, Static Control Components, Inc., may sue petitioner, Lexmark International, Inc., for false advertising under the Lanham Act, 15 U.S.C. § 1125(a).

I. Background

Lexmark manufactures and sells laser printers. It also sells toner cartridges for those printers (toner being the powdery ink that laser printers use to create images on paper). Lexmark designs its printers to work only with its own style of cartridges, and it therefore dominates the market for cartridges compatible with its printers. That market, however, is not devoid of competitors. Other businesses, called "remanufacturers," acquire used Lexmark toner cartridges, refurbish them, and sell them in competition with new and refurbished cartridges sold by Lexmark.

Lexmark would prefer that its customers return their empty cartridges to it for refurbishment and resale, rather than sell those cartridges to a remanufacturer. So Lexmark introduced what it called a "Prebate" program, which enabled customers to purchase new toner cartridges at a 20-percent discount if they would agree to return the cartridge to Lexmark once it was empty. Those terms were communicated to consumers through notices printed on the toner-cartridge boxes, which advised the consumer that opening the box would indicate assent to the terms—a practice commonly known as "shrinkwrap licensing." To enforce the Prebate terms, Lexmark included a microchip in each Prebate cartridge that would disable the cartridge after it ran out of toner; for the cartridge to be used again, the microchip would have to be replaced by Lexmark.

Static Control is not itself a manufacturer or remanufacturer of toner cartridges. It is, rather, "the market leader [in] making and selling the components necessary to remanufacture Lexmark cartridges." In addition to supplying remanufacturers with toner and various replacement parts, Static Control developed a microchip that could mimic the microchip in Lexmark's Prebate cartridges. By purchasing Static Control's microchips and using them to replace the Lexmark microchip, remanufacturers were able to refurbish and resell used Prebate cartridges.

Lexmark did not take kindly to that development. In 2002, it sued Static Control, alleging that Static Control's microchips violated both the Copyright Act of 1976, 17 U.S.C. § 101 et seq., and the Digital Millennium Copyright Act, 17 U.S.C. § 1201 et seq. Static Control counterclaimed, alleging, among other things, violations of § 43(a) of the Lanham Act, 60 Stat. 441, codified at 15 U.S.C. § 1125(a). Section 1125(a) provides:

> (1) Any person who, on or in connection with any goods or services, or any container for goods, uses in commerce any word, term, name, symbol, or device, or any combination thereof, or any false designation of origin, false or misleading description of fact, or false or misleading representation of fact, which—

(A) is likely to cause confusion, or to cause mistake, or to deceive as to the affiliation, connection, or association of such person with another person, or as to the origin, sponsorship, or approval of his or her goods, services, or commercial activities by another person, or

(B) in commercial advertising or promotion, misrepresents the nature, characteristics, qualities, or geographic origin of his or her or another person's goods, services, or commercial activities,

shall be liable in a civil action by any person who believes that he or she is or is likely to be damaged by such act.

Section 1125(a) thus creates two distinct bases of liability: false association, § 1125(a)(1)(A), and false advertising, § 1125(a)(1)(B). Static Control alleged only false advertising.

As relevant to its Lanham Act claim, Static Control alleged two types of false or misleading conduct by Lexmark. First, it alleged that through its Prebate program Lexmark "purposefully misleads end-users" to believe that they are legally bound by the Prebate terms and are thus required to return the Prebate-labeled cartridge to Lexmark after a single use. Second, it alleged that upon introducing the Prebate program, Lexmark "sent letters to most of the companies in the toner cartridge remanufacturing business" falsely advising those companies that it was illegal to sell refurbished Prebate cartridges and, in particular, that it was illegal to use Static Control's products to refurbish those cartridges. Static Control asserted that by those statements, Lexmark had materially misrepresented "the nature, characteristics, and qualities" of both its own products and Static Control's products. It further maintained that Lexmark's misrepresentations had "proximately caused and [we]re likely to cause injury to [Static Control] by diverting sales from [Static Control] to Lexmark," and had "substantially injured [its] business reputation" by "leading consumers and others in the trade to believe that [Static Control] is engaged in illegal conduct." Static Control sought treble damages, attorney's fees and costs, and injunctive relief.[2]

The District Court granted Lexmark's motion to dismiss Static Control's Lanham Act claim. It held that Static Control lacked "prudential standing" to bring that claim, relying on a multifactor balancing test it attributed to *Associated Gen. Contractors of Cal., Inc. v. Carpenters*, 459 U.S. 519 (1983). The court emphasized that there were "more direct plaintiffs in the form of remanufacturers of Lexmark's cartridges"; that Static Control's injury was "remot[e]" because it was a mere "byproduct of the supposed manipulation of consumers' relationships with remanufacturers"; and that Lexmark's "alleged intent [was] to dry up spent cartridge supplies at the remanufacturing level, rather than at [Static Control]'s supply level, making remanufacturers Lexmark's alleged intended target."

The Sixth Circuit reversed the dismissal of Static Control's Lanham Act claim. . . . The Sixth Circuit applied the Second Circuit's reasonable-interest test and concluded that Static

---

[2] Lexmark contends that Static Control's allegations failed to describe "commercial advertising or promotion" within the meaning of 15 U.S.C. § 1125(a)(1)(B). That question is not before us, and we express no view on it. We assume without deciding that the communications alleged by Static Control qualify as commercial advertising or promotion.

Control had standing because it "alleged a cognizable interest in its business reputation and sales to remanufacturers and sufficiently alleged that th[o]se interests were harmed by Lexmark's statements to the remanufacturers that Static Control was engaging in illegal conduct."

We granted certiorari to decide "the appropriate analytical framework for determining a party's standing to maintain an action for false advertising under the Lanham Act."

II. "Prudential Standing" . . .

In sum, the question this case presents is whether Static Control falls within the class of plaintiffs whom Congress has authorized to sue under § 1125(a). In other words, we ask whether Static Control has a cause of action under the statute. That question requires us to determine the meaning of the congressionally enacted provision creating a cause of action. In doing so, we apply traditional principles of statutory interpretation. We do not ask whether in our judgment Congress should have authorized Static Control's suit, but whether Congress in fact did so. Just as a court cannot apply its independent policy judgment to recognize a cause of action that Congress has denied, it cannot limit a cause of action that Congress has created merely because "prudence" dictates.

III. Static Control's Right To Sue Under § 1125(a)

Thus, this case presents a straightforward question of statutory interpretation: Does the cause of action in § 1125(a) extend to plaintiffs like Static Control? The statute authorizes suit by "any person who believes that he or she is likely to be damaged" by a defendant's false advertising. Read literally, that broad language might suggest that an action is available to anyone who can satisfy the minimum requirements of Article III. No party makes that argument, however, and the "unlikelihood that Congress meant to allow all factually injured plaintiffs to recover persuades us that [§ 1125(a)] should not get such an expansive reading." We reach that conclusion in light of two relevant background principles already mentioned: zone of interests and proximate causality.

A. Zone of Interests

First, we presume that a statutory cause of action extends only to plaintiffs whose interests "fall within the zone of interests protected by the law invoked." . . .

Identifying the interests protected by the Lanham Act . . . requires no guesswork, since the Act includes an "unusual, and extraordinarily helpful," detailed statement of the statute's purposes. Section 45 of the Act, codified at 15 U.S.C. § 1127, provides:

> The intent of this chapter is to regulate commerce within the control of Congress by making actionable the deceptive and misleading use of marks in such commerce; to protect registered marks used in such commerce from interference by State, or territorial legislation; to protect persons engaged in such commerce against unfair competition; to prevent fraud and deception in such commerce by the use of reproductions, copies, counterfeits, or colorable imitations of registered marks; and to

provide rights and remedies stipulated by treaties and conventions respecting trademarks, trade names, and unfair competition entered into between the United States and foreign nations.

Most of the enumerated purposes are relevant to false-association cases; a typical false-advertising case will implicate only the Act's goal of "protect[ing] persons engaged in [commerce within the control of Congress] against unfair competition." Although "unfair competition" was a "plastic" concept at common law, it was understood to be concerned with injuries to business reputation and present and future sales.

We thus hold that to come within the zone of interests in a suit for false advertising under § 1125(a), a plaintiff must allege an injury to a commercial interest in reputation or sales. A consumer who is hoodwinked into purchasing a disappointing product may well have an injury-in-fact cognizable under Article III, but he cannot invoke the protection of the Lanham Act—a conclusion reached by every Circuit to consider the question. Even a business misled by a supplier into purchasing an inferior product is, like consumers generally, not under the Act's aegis.

B. Proximate Cause

Second, we generally presume that a statutory cause of action is limited to plaintiffs whose injuries are proximately caused by violations of the statute. For centuries, it has been "a well-established principle of [the common] law, that in all cases of loss, we are to attribute it to the proximate cause, and not to any remote cause." That venerable principle reflects the reality that "the judicial remedy cannot encompass every conceivable harm that can be traced to alleged wrongdoing." Congress, we assume, is familiar with the common-law rule and does not mean to displace it sub silentio. We have thus construed federal causes of action in a variety of contexts to incorporate a requirement of proximate causation. No party disputes that it is proper to read § 1125(a) as containing such a requirement, its broad language notwithstanding.

The proximate-cause inquiry is not easy to define, and over the years it has taken various forms; but courts have a great deal of experience applying it, and there is a wealth of precedent for them to draw upon in doing so. Proximate-cause analysis is controlled by the nature of the statutory cause of action. The question it presents is whether the harm alleged has a sufficiently close connection to the conduct the statute prohibits.

Put differently, the proximate-cause requirement generally bars suits for alleged harm that is "too remote" from the defendant's unlawful conduct. That is ordinarily the case if the harm is purely derivative of "misfortunes visited upon a third person by the defendant's acts." In a sense, of course, all commercial injuries from false advertising are derivative of those suffered by consumers who are deceived by the advertising; but since the Lanham Act authorizes suit only for commercial injuries, the intervening step of consumer deception is not fatal to the showing of proximate causation required by the statute. That is consistent with our recognition that under common-law principles, a plaintiff can be directly injured by a misrepresentation even where "a third party, and not the plaintiff, . . . relied on" it.

We thus hold that a plaintiff suing under § 1125(a) ordinarily must show economic or reputational injury flowing directly from the deception wrought by the defendant's advertising; and that that occurs when deception of consumers causes them to withhold trade from the plaintiff. That showing is generally not made when the deception produces injuries to a fellow commercial actor that in turn affect the plaintiff. For example, while a competitor who is forced out of business by a defendant's false advertising generally will be able to sue for its losses, the same is not true of the competitor's landlord, its electric company, and other commercial parties who suffer merely as a result of the competitor's "inability to meet [its] financial obligations."

C. Proposed Tests

… [In response to arguments in favor of adopting a multifactor balancing test, the Court concluded that] potential difficulty in ascertaining and apportioning damages is not … an independent basis for denying standing where it is adequately alleged that a defendant's conduct has proximately injured an interest of the plaintiff's that the statute protects. Even when a plaintiff cannot quantify its losses with sufficient certainty to recover damages, it may still be entitled to injunctive relief under § 1116(a) (assuming it can prove a likelihood of future injury) or disgorgement of the defendant's ill-gotten profits under § 1117(a). Finally, experience has shown that [open-ended balancing tests] can yield unpredictable and at times arbitrary results. *See, e.g.*, Tushnet, *Running the Gamut from A to B: Federal Trademark and False Advertising Law*, 159 U. PA. L. REV. 1305, 1376–1379 (2011).

In contrast to the multifactor balancing approach, the direct-competitor test provides a bright-line rule; but it does so at the expense of distorting the statutory language. To be sure, a plaintiff who does not compete with the defendant will often have a harder time establishing proximate causation. But a rule categorically prohibiting all suits by noncompetitors would read too much into the Act's reference to "unfair competition" in § 1127. By the time the Lanham Act was adopted, the common-law tort of unfair competition was understood not to be limited to actions between competitors. One leading authority in the field wrote that "there need be no competition in unfair competition," just as "[t]here is no soda in soda water, no grapes in grape fruit, no bread in bread fruit, and a clothes horse is not a horse but is good enough to hang things on." It is thus a mistake to infer that because the Lanham Act treats false advertising as a form of unfair competition, it can protect only the false-advertiser's direct competitors. . . .

IV. Application

Applying those principles to Static Control's false-advertising claim, we conclude that Static Control comes within the class of plaintiffs whom Congress authorized to sue under § 1125(a).

To begin, Static Control's alleged injuries—lost sales and damage to its business reputation—are injuries to precisely the sorts of commercial interests the Act protects. Static Control is suing not as a deceived consumer, but as a "perso[n] engaged in" "commerce within the control of Congress" whose position in the marketplace has been damaged by Lexmark's false advertising. There is no doubt that it is within the zone of interests protected by the statute.

Static Control also sufficiently alleged that its injuries were proximately caused by Lexmark's misrepresentations. This case, it is true, does not present the "classic Lanham Act false-advertising claim" in which "one competito[r] directly injur[es] another by making false statements about his own goods [or the competitor's goods] and thus inducing customers to switch." But although diversion of sales to a direct competitor may be the paradigmatic direct injury from false advertising, it is not the only type of injury cognizable under § 1125(a). For at least two reasons, Static Control's allegations satisfy the requirement of proximate causation.

First, Static Control alleged that Lexmark disparaged its business and products by asserting that Static Control's business was illegal. When a defendant harms a plaintiff's reputation by casting aspersions on its business, the plaintiff's injury flows directly from the audience's belief in the disparaging statements. Courts have therefore afforded relief under § 1125(a) not only where a defendant denigrates a plaintiff's product by name, but also where the defendant damages the product's reputation by, for example, equating it with an inferior product. Traditional proximate-causation principles support those results: As we have observed, a defendant who "seeks to promote his own interests by telling a known falsehood to or about the plaintiff or his product" may be said to have proximately caused the plaintiff's harm.

The District Court emphasized that Lexmark and Static Control are not direct competitors. But when a party claims reputational injury from disparagement, competition is not required for proximate cause; and that is true even if the defendant's aim was to harm its immediate competitors, and the plaintiff merely suffered collateral damage. Consider two rival carmakers who purchase airbags for their cars from different third-party manufacturers. If the first carmaker, hoping to divert sales from the second, falsely proclaims that the airbags used by the second carmaker are defective, both the second carmaker and its airbag supplier may suffer reputational injury, and their sales may decline as a result. In those circumstances, there is no reason to regard either party's injury as derivative of the other's; each is directly and independently harmed by the attack on its merchandise.

In addition, Static Control adequately alleged proximate causation by alleging that it designed, manufactured, and sold microchips that both (1) were necessary for, and (2) had no other use than, refurbishing Lexmark toner cartridges. It follows from that allegation that any false advertising that reduced the remanufacturers' business necessarily injured Static Control as well. Taking Static Control's assertions at face value, there is likely to be something very close to a 1:1 relationship between the number of refurbished Prebate cartridges sold (or not sold) by the remanufacturers and the number of Prebate microchips sold (or not sold) by Static Control. "Where the injury alleged is so integral an aspect of the [violation] alleged, there can be no question" that proximate cause is satisfied.

To be sure, on this view, the causal chain linking Static Control's injuries to consumer confusion is not direct, but includes the intervening link of injury to the remanufacturers. Static Control's allegations therefore might not support standing under a strict application of

307

the "general tendency" not to stretch proximate causation "beyond the first step." But the reason for that general tendency is that there ordinarily is a "discontinuity" between the injury to the direct victim and the injury to the indirect victim, so that the latter is not surely attributable to the former (and thus also to the defendant's conduct), but might instead have resulted from "any number of [other] reasons." That is not the case here. Static Control's allegations suggest that if the remanufacturers sold 10,000 fewer refurbished cartridges because of Lexmark's false advertising, then it would follow more or less automatically that Static Control sold 10,000 fewer microchips for the same reason, without the need for any "speculative . . . proceedings" or "intricate, uncertain inquiries." In these relatively unique circumstances, the remanufacturers are not "more immediate victim[s]" than Static Control.

Although we conclude that Static Control has alleged an adequate basis to proceed under § 1125(a), it cannot obtain relief without evidence of injury proximately caused by Lexmark's alleged misrepresentations. We hold only that Static Control is entitled to a chance to prove its case.

* * *

To invoke the Lanham Act's cause of action for false advertising, a plaintiff must plead (and ultimately prove) an injury to a commercial interest in sales or business reputation proximately caused by the defendant's misrepresentations. Static Control has adequately pleaded both elements. The judgment of the Court of Appeals is affirmed.

NOTES AND QUESTIONS

Why not let consumers have standing? The statutory language clearly indicates an intent to protect consumers from "fraud and deception." Some courts inferred from the overall context of the Lanham Act that Congress intended Section 43(a)(1) primarily to protect competitors. Others reasoned that competitors would be better plaintiffs than consumers because of their greater resources, and that competitors would be good proxies for consumer interests. In addition, courts pointed to state laws providing consumers with remedies for false advertising and the FTC's jurisdiction to protect consumers as alternatives, showing that consumer standing under the Lanham Act was unnecessary.

Some courts have made explicit the key underlying reason: They don't want a flood of consumer plaintiffs in the federal courts. Jean Wegman Burns has argued that this rule conflicts with the broad language of the statute and invites precisely the wrong plaintiffs: competitors who may be more interested in stifling legitimate competition than in redressing true consumer injury. *See* Jean Wegman Burns, *Confused Jurisprudence: False Advertising under the Lanham Act*, 79 B.U.L. REV. 807 (1999); Jean Wegman Burns, *The Paradox of Antitrust and Lanham Act Standing*, 42 UCLA L. REV. 47 (1994).

After *Lexmark*, is pure disparagement actionable under the Lanham Act? Suppose the defendant is a law firm that, in the course of seeking clients for a personal injury lawsuit against a bank, says that the bank engaged in mortgage fraud, causing the bank to lose sales. Should this suffice for Lanham Act standing? *See* First Mariner Bank v. Resolution Law Grp., P.C., 2014 WL 1652550 (D. Md. 2014) (finding that such a claim "fits snugly within the *Lexmark* framework"). What if, instead, the defendant is a for-profit newspaper that ran a story in its science section about the supposed dangers of the drugs? What if the defendant is a former customer that wrote about its bad experience with the seller? *See* Buckeye Int'l, Inc. v. Schmidt Custom Floors, Inc., 2018 WL 1960115 (W.D. Wis. Apr. 26, 2018).

Suppose a landlord is entitled to a percentage of its commercial tenant's sales. One of the tenant's competitors disparages the tenant, and the tenant's sales fall. Under *Lexmark*, does the landlord have standing? Suppose a manufacturer sells to the trade; can it sue both its direct competitor and its competitor's customers for claims they make about the product? *See* Frompovicz v. Niagara Bottling, LLC, 313 F. Supp. 3d 603 (E.D. Pa. 2018).

What would suffice to plead proximate causation? Suppose the plaintiff is one of four dominant competitors in the market, each with roughly equal market shares. If a new market entrant starts advertising falsely, should we just assume that it will take market share from each of the dominant competitors? *See* Blue Star Press, LLC v. Blasko, 2018 WL 1904835 (W.D. Tex. Mar. 6, 2018).

6.   Commercial Advertising or Promotion

In order for a claim to be actionable under the Lanham Act, it must also be made in "commercial advertising or promotion." § 43(a)(1)(B). "Commercial advertising or promotion" is not a standing requirement, though it may fulfill some of the same functions. It's about what the defendant has done and (after *Lexmark*) not so much about the plaintiff's relationship to the speech.

Over the years, courts settled upon a test to define this phrase. The test incorporates concerns for limiting the scope of the law and currently has three elements: (1) commercial speech; (2) for the purpose of influencing consumers to buy the defendant's goods or services; (3) that is disseminated sufficiently to the relevant purchasing public to constitute advertising or promotion within that industry. Gordon & Breach Sci. Publishers v. Am. Inst. of Physics, 859 F. Supp. 1521 (S.D.N.Y. 1994) (also articulating a fourth prong, competition with the plaintiff, which has generally though not universally been recognized as abrogated by *Lexmark*); *see, e.g.* Grubbs v. Sheakley Gp., Inc., 807 F.3d 785 (6th Cir. 2015) (adopting a definition requiring (1) commercial speech; (2) for the purpose of influencing customers to buy the defendant's goods or services; (3) that is disseminated either widely enough to the relevant purchasing public to constitute advertising or promotion within that industry or to a substantial portion of the plaintiff's or defendant's existing customer or client base).

The second element, that the speech has a purpose of influencing purchases from the defendant, rarely has independent significance. After *Lexmark*, it may provide a hook for certain speech-protective holdings that used to be framed as applications of the "competition" element. *See, e.g.*, Huntingdon Life Scis., Inc. v. Rokke, 978 F. Supp. 662 (E.D. Va. 1997) (rejecting animal-testing laboratory's contention that People for the Ethical Treatment of Animals (PETA) was a competitor even though PETA was actively involved in promoting to laboratory's customers methods of testing that did not involve animals; PETA did not itself test any consumer products).

Finally, the amount of dissemination sufficient to constitute "advertising or promotion" depends on the size of the underlying market. A statement by a single salesperson to one of thousands of customers will not qualify. But if the relevant market is very small and specialized, a sales pitch to only a few—or even one—potential customer might suffice. *See* Champion Labs v. Parker-Hannifin Corp., 616 F. Supp. 2d 684 (E.D. Mich. 2009) (where parties occupied a niche market for fuel filters intended for a particular engine manufactured by General Motors, representations made to General Motors were in "commercial advertising and promotion" for purposes of avoiding summary judgment).

7. Competitor Suits under State Laws

Many state Unfair and Deceptive Acts and Practices ("UDAP") statutes can be applied to false advertising disputes between business entities. In some states, such as Massachusetts and Texas, businesses are expressly authorized as plaintiffs. In other states, such as Connecticut and North Carolina, the statute affords any "person" or "aggrieved party" a private right of action, and these terms have often been interpreted to grant standing to one business competitor aggrieved by the deceptive conduct of another. *See, e.g.*, POM Wonderful LLC v. Coca-Cola Co., 679 F.3d 1170 (9th Cir. 2012) (allowing competitor standing under state Unfair Competition Law when competitor is harmed by false advertising).

Several states, including New York, require a "public interest" element. This generally involves a pattern of conduct, a potential for repetition, or other factors suggesting a broader societal interest in the transaction at issue, as opposed to simple private injuries. In these "public interest" states, a business plaintiff asserting that it was harmed by deception of its potential consumers must show that the harm was more than simple private loss—ordinary trademark infringement, for example, harms the trademark owner, but unless the infringing product poses health or safety risks, it doesn't implicate a sufficient public interest under the state's false advertising law.

Further, whether or not they allow competitors to sue, many state consumer-fraud laws limit their scope to transactions involving "consumers," defined as those purchasing for personal, family or household use. Cases involving specialized products purchased only by businesses can therefore not be brought under state law, whether brought by the direct victim or by the false advertiser's competitors. In addition, these consumer-oriented rules exclude claims based on negotiation for personalized products or unique contracts and claims by retailers who bought goods for resale. *See, e.g.*, Abraham v. Penn Mut. Life Ins. Co., 2000 WL 1051848 (S.D.N.Y. 2000) (listing as possible sources of consumer-oriented injury that an insurance policy was sold to the public at large or that the insurer treated an entire class of policies or other policyholders similarly).

Some states choose to limit the reach of the law on the defendant/*seller's* side, covering only practices in the course of a person's business, vocation or occupation. How should a court in a state with a seller-side limitation evaluate whether a person who sells fifteen items a year on eBay is engaged in "business"? *Cf.* Real v. Radir Wheels, Inc., 969 A.2d 1069, 1079 (N.J. 2009) ("[t]here is no doubt that" an individual eBay seller "himself satisfies the statutory definition of 'person'" such that he may be held liable under the NJCFA's general antifraud provision); William J. Diggs, Comment, *Consumer Protection in an eBay Marketplace: An Analysis of the Supreme Court of New Jersey's* Radir Wheels *Decision to Extend Liability under the New Jersey Consumer Fraud Act to Individual eBay Sellers*, 40 SETON HALL L. REV. 811(2010) ("Notably, eighty-four percent of Internet-auction fraud is committed by a seller who is not engaged in the trade or business of making sales of the type of which he made on eBay . . . ; only the remaining sixteen percent is committed by a seller who is engaged in the trade or business of making sales of the type of which he made on eBay . . . . ") (citation omitted).

Class actions, in which a small number of class representatives bring a claim in the name of a much larger group, alleging common injuries and demanding shared remedies, merit a course of their own. This form of litigation makes lawyers passionate—both on the defense and plaintiff sides. In part, this is because there is a well-defined defense bar (representing advertisers) and a plaintiff's bar (representing consumers) with very few common members. In contrast, in Lanham Act lawsuits, competitors often flip between plaintiff (challenging their rivals) and defense (being challenged), so litigators representing those clients are less likely to view themselves as plaintiff- or defense-oriented.

This chapter attempts to give a sense of the issues that recur specifically in consumer-protection class-action cases, which make up a large and apparently growing fraction of class actions, as well as of civil litigation more generally. While research suggests that most consumer-protection cases are ultimately unsuccessful, that hasn't stopped their growth; for the practicing lawyer, there is plenty of legal work to do between filing and dismissal or settlement. James C. Cooper & Joanna Shepherd, *State Unfair and Deceptive Trade Practices Laws: An Economic and Empirical Analysis*, 81 ANTITRUST L.J. (2018) (finding that 16% of federal cases ultimately settle; defendants win over 95% of cases in which a federal court ultimately rules, with over half dismissed, defendants winning almost six out of seven times at the summary judgment stage, and winning more than half of trials).* This chapter covers key issues in certification, such as choice of law (multi-state or single-state); whether individualized issues of reliance and damages preclude class treatment; and special considerations relating to settlement classes.

No matter how many obstacles courts and defense counsel put up, a few class actions do survive. Whether this pattern continues indefinitely remains to be seen. As you read through this section, keep an eye on the ever-growing checklist of prerequisites to successfully achieving class certification, especially in a contested case (as opposed to approving a class for settlement purposes only).

For further reading, the National Association of Consumer Advocates has a useful volume that covers important elements of consumer class-action practice from both descriptive and normative standpoints. NATIONAL ASSOCIATION OF CONSUMER ADVOCATES, STANDARDS AND GUIDELINES FOR LITIGATING AND SETTLING CLASS ACTIONS (3d ed. 2014). A number of courts have referred to the Guidelines in their own decisions. *See, e.g.*, Figueroa v. Sharper Image Corp., 517 F. Supp. 2d 1292 (S.D. Fla. 2007).

---

* This research also indicated that, in federal cases, the average settlement was $5.3 million, with a median of $3.1 million, and average attorneys' fees were $1.46 million, with a median of $280,000, perhaps explaining the persistence of such suits.

1.   Overview: Special Features of the Class Action

A.   The Class Action: Villain or Avenger?

Critics often point to class actions claiming harms that seem small or even nonexistent, making litigation over them frivolous or even harmful to consumers. *See, e.g.,* Sway v. Benjamin Moore & Co., No. 2:11-cv-02343 (D.N.J. 2011) (class action brought against Benjamin Moore paint for "low-odor" paint that still smells like paint; dismissed); Johnson v. MFA Petroleum Co., 10 F. Supp. 3d 982 (W.D. Mo. 2014) (class action because a consumer who buys higher octane fuel from a single-hose gas pump incidentally receives a residual amount of lower-octane fuel lingering in the hose from prior fueling); Farley v. Subway Sandwich Shops Inc., No. 000185-2013 (N.J. Super. Ct. 2013) (class action brought against Subway because occasionally a "footlong" sandwich falls short of twelve inches; settled). Some contend that broad consumer-protection laws harm consumers by raising prices and deterring innovative advertising. Henry N. Butler & Jason S. Johnston, *Reforming State Consumer Protection Liability: An Economic Approach*, 2010 COLUM. BUS. L. REV. 1 (2010); Searle Civil Justice Inst., *State Consumer Protection Acts and Consumer Welfare, State Consumer Protection Acts and Costs to Consumers: The Impact of State Consumer Acts on Automobile Insurance Premiums* (Preliminary Report) 4 (2011).

Yet, class actions also address pervasive fraudulent or damaging schemes whose harms are small enough to make litigation too expensive for any individual. *See, e.g.,* Gutierrez v. Wells Fargo Bank, NA, 589 Fed. Appx. 824 (9th Cir. 2014) (a bank's misrepresentations cost a class of California consumers, who were disproportionately poor, $203 million collectively in unwarranted overdraft fees); Paul Bland, *Major Victory in Oregon Vindicates Class Actions*, PUB. JUSTICE, Jul. 16, 2019 (over two million customers were charged unadvertised thirty-five-cent fee on debit card gas purchases; fee was charged 13,000 times a day until trial ended; settlement provided at least $185 to each of 1.7 million people, based on jury verdict in favor of plaintiffs and statutory penalties of $200 per violation).

Although class actions are often associated with political liberals in the United States, there is an argument that the common-law oversight that can be provided by the class action is better, from a small-government perspective, than ex ante regulation. *See* BRIAN T. FITZPATRICK, THE CONSERVATIVE CASE FOR CLASS ACTIONS (2019).

Judge Posner provided an overview of the core dilemma of the class action in *Eubank v. Pella Corp.*, 753 F.3d 718 (7th Cir. 2014):

> The class action is an ingenious procedural innovation that enables persons who have suffered a wrongful injury, but are too numerous for joinder of their claims alleging the same wrong committed by the same defendant or defendants to be feasible, to obtain relief as a group, a class as it is called. The device is especially important when each claim is too small to justify the expense of a separate suit, so that without a class action there would be no relief, however meritorious the claims. Normally only a few of the claimants are named as plaintiffs . . . . The named plaintiffs are the representatives of the class—fiduciaries of its members—and therefore charged with monitoring the lawyers who prosecute the case on behalf of the class (class counsel).

They receive modest compensation, in addition to their damages as class members, for their normally quite limited services—often little more than sitting for a deposition—as class representatives. Invariably they are selected by class counsel, who as a practical matter control the litigation by the class. The selection of the class representatives by class counsel inevitably dilutes their fiduciary commitment.

The class action is a worthwhile supplement to conventional litigation procedure, but it is controversial and embattled, in part because it is frequently abused. The control of the class over its lawyers usually is attenuated, often to the point of nonexistence. Except for the named plaintiffs, the members of the class are more like beneficiaries than like parties; for although they are authorized to appeal from an adverse judgment, they have no control over class counsel. . . . Class actions are the brainchildren of the lawyers who specialize in prosecuting such actions, and in picking class representatives they have no incentive to select persons capable or desirous of monitoring the lawyers' conduct of the litigation.

A high percentage of lawsuits is settled—but a study of certified class actions in federal court in a two-year period (2005 to 2007) found that all 30 such actions had been settled. The reasons that class actions invariably are settled are twofold. Aggregating a great many claims (sometimes tens or even hundreds of thousands—occasionally millions) often creates a potential liability so great that the defendant is unwilling to bear the risk, even if it is only a small probability, of an adverse judgment. At the same time, class counsel, ungoverned as a practical matter by either the named plaintiffs or the other members of the class, have an opportunity to maximize their attorneys' fees—which (besides other expenses) are all they can get from the class action—at the expense of the class. The defendant cares only about the size of the settlement, not how it is divided between attorneys' fees and compensation for the class. From the selfish standpoint of class counsel and the defendant, therefore, the optimal settlement is one modest in overall amount but heavily tilted toward attorneys' fees. . . .

Fortunately the settlement, including the amount of attorneys' fees to award to class counsel, must be approved by the district judge presiding over the case; unfortunately American judges are accustomed to presiding over adversary proceedings. They expect the clash of the adversaries to generate the information that the judge needs to decide the case. And so when a judge is being urged by both adversaries to approve the class-action settlement that they've negotiated, he's at a disadvantage in evaluating the fairness of the settlement to the class.

Judge Posner goes on to explain that objectors, "[m]embers of the class who smell a rat," can object, and the judge must evaluate those objections. If the objectors succeed and a more-favorable settlement is ultimately approved, they receive a cash award. This dynamic—potentially great risk for defendants, low reward for any given class member, potentially great reward for class attorneys—affects every part of the class action proceeding, not just settlement. Keep these issues in mind as you read the materials that follow.

B.   Increasing Barriers of Many Kinds to Class Actions

Companies can avoid class-action litigation by directing consumer litigation into arbitration. Contractual arbitration clauses can contain "no-class-adjudication provisions" that can expressly say that class actions can't be heard in arbitration.

AT&T Mobility v. Concepcion, 563 U.S. 321 (2011), represented the death knell for many consumer class actions. AT&T's contract provided for mandatory arbitration of any disputes and prohibited class-wide arbitration (that is, an arbitration on behalf of a class; arbitration could only proceed on an individual-by-individual basis). California followed a rule that a contractual ban on class actions in consumer contracts is inherently unconscionable and thus unenforceable. The Supreme Court reversed, holding that the Federal Arbitration Act preempted this rule as applied to arbitration contracts.

Since *Concepcion*, courts are increasingly upholding mandatory arbitration clauses, including those that block class formation. Companies are also expanding their use of mandatory arbitration clauses. As a result, Myriam Gilles & Gary Friedman, *After Class: Aggregate Litigation in the Wake of* AT&T Mobility v. Concepcion, 79 U. CHI. L. REV. 623 (2012), have argued that "many—indeed, most—of the companies that touch consumers' day-to-day lives can and will now place themselves beyond the reach of aggregate litigation, including telephone companies, Internet service providers, credit card issuers, payday lenders, mortgage lenders, health clubs, nursing homes, retail banks, investment banks, mutual funds and the sellers of all manner of goods and services."

Because mass-market retailers rarely attempt to impose contract terms on their customers, the vast majority of current consumer class actions are for simple products purchased in stores, which generally don't have class action waivers attached—yet. But if retailers and consumer products manufacturers could figure out how to impose class-action waivers, they almost certainly would. For example, in 2014, major food manufacturer General Mills attempted to impose a class action waiver that consumers purportedly triggered by using General Mills coupons downloaded online, using its websites, or "liking" its Facebook page but soon retreated in the face of consumer backlash. *See* John Aziz, *General Mills Backed Down from Its Controversial Lawsuit Policy. But the Problem Isn't Over*, THEWEEK.COM, Apr. 22, 2014. Additional, and presumably more subtle or clever, attempts by advertisers to induce consumers to contractually agree to arbitration are surely coming. *See, e.g.*, Himber v. Live Nation Worldwide, Inc., 2018 WL 2304770 (E.D.N.Y. May 21, 2018) (visiting website with arbitration in its terms of use, then later purchasing offline, bound consumers to arbitration).

Even without *Concepcion*, the Class Action Fairness Act of 2005 ("CAFA"), 28 U.S.C. §§ 1332(d), 1453, and 1711–15, expanded federal jurisdiction (allowing removal from state courts) to include class actions in which the amount in controversy exceeds $5 million and in which any of the members of a class of plaintiffs is a citizen of a state different from any defendant, unless at least two-thirds or more of the members of all proposed plaintiff classes in the aggregate and the primary defendants are citizens of the state in which the action was originally filed. CAFA also directed greater scrutiny of class-action settlements.

CAFA's aim was to rein in a perceived explosion of class actions against businesses, particularly in certain allegedly overly plaintiff-friendly state courts. As a result, a substantial amount of class action practice shifted to federal courts. Still, some plaintiffs may be so determined to stay in state court that they plead their cases differently, such as seeking under $5 million in damages.

Consumer-protection class actions are a key subset of class actions and thus profoundly affected by CAFA. A study by the Federal Judicial Center found a post-CAFA increase in the number of class actions filed in or removed to federal courts based on diversity jurisdiction, due primarily to increases in consumer class actions. Many plaintiffs' attorneys are consciously attempting to satisfy the requirements of CAFA, perhaps to avoid a lengthy and expensive fight over removal. *See* Emery G. Lee et al., *The Impact of the Class Action Fairness Act of 2005 on the Federal Courts*, Federal Judicial Center (April 2008).

For the class action to succeed, a judge must certify the class. Certification under the rule most applicable to consumer class actions, FRCP Rule 23(b)(3), requires a judicial finding that "questions of law or fact common to class members predominate over any questions affecting only individual members, and that a class action is superior to other available methods for fairly and efficiently adjudicating the controversy." Courts break this down into requirements of "commonality," "predominance" and "superiority."

Courts have imposed increasing barriers to certification of class actions, rejecting certification of most non-federal question class actions. *See* Joel S. Feldman, *Class Certification Issues for Non-Federal Question Class Actions—Defense Perspective*, 728 PLI/Lit 221 (2005). The key issue is predominance, both legal and factual. Though federal courts have taken the lead in this reasoning, many state courts have followed suit, as their class action rules generally mimic the federal rules.

The Supreme Court's defendant-favorable decision in *Wal-Mart Stores, Inc. v. Dukes*, 564 U.S. 338 (2011), concerned an employment-discrimination class action and a provision of Rule 23 under which consumer class actions are rarely certified. However, it signaled the Court's discomfort with class actions that put defendants at risk of large damage awards, even when that risk exists simply because many people were affected. For arguments that the empirical evidence doesn't support the courts' fear of coercive and unjustified class actions, see Joanna C. Schwartz, *The Cost of Suing Business*, 65 DEPAUL L. REV. 655 (2016) ("One would expect that, were defendants accepting blackmail settlements, they would do so immediately after certification to avoid the costs of discovery. Instead, it appears that defendants do not generally settle soon after certification and often proceed through discovery. Moreover, settlement and trial rates in class actions are comparable to rates in non-class cases, suggesting that class actions, on the whole, are no more coercive to defendants than any other kind of litigation.").

Multi-state consumer class actions may fail to achieve class certification due to variations among state laws. Defendants identify different standards of proof, different elements for the cause of action, different statutes of limitation, different definitions of who can sue, different intent requirements and so on. When legal differences are sufficient, common legal issues don't predominate, and also a class action would be unmanageable—it would be impossible to instruct a jury on all the different laws. *See, e.g.,* Castano v. Am. Tobacco Co., 84 F.3d 734 (5th Cir. 1996).

Some courts even consider the extra pressure a class action puts on defendants as a reason that a class action is not superior to individualized adjudications; the theory is that by raising the stakes for defendants, class actions encourage them to settle even unmeritorious claims—legalized blackmail. Should courts also consider the extra leverage class actions provide to plaintiffs whose individual claims are too small to justify litigation but whose aggregate losses are large? How should a court determine which consideration is more important in any given case?

Factual variation is another reason to deny class certification. Where reliance or a reliance-type analysis (such as causation or damages) is at issue, some courts hold that individualized proof would be required for each plaintiff. Thus, common factual issues don't predominate. Factual variation means that even a single-state class may be negated. *See, e.g.,* Peltier Enter., Inc. v. Hilton, 51 S.W.3d 616 (Tex. Ct. App. 2000) (claim under Texas law requires individualized proof because reliance is an essential element).

Other states presume reliance, materiality or causation based on deceptive acts or practices, allowing a class action to proceed, but state-by-state analysis is essential. *Compare, e.g.,* Sikes v. Teleline, Inc., 281 F.3d 1350 (11th Cir. 2002) (refusing to presume reliance on misrepresentations because presumptions should benefit parties who don't control evidence on an issue, and individual plaintiffs best know the facts of their own reliance), *with, e.g.,* Varacallo v. Mass. Mut. Life Ins. Co., 752 A.2d 807 (N.J. Super. Ct. App. Div. 2000) (ordering certification of a class consisting of all New Jersey residents who purchased certain life insurance policies from defendant during the class period; presuming reliance and fraud where claim was based on insurer's omission of material information with intent that consumers rely on the omission).

Some courts have held that the class-action rules contain an implicit requirement of "ascertainability," under which courts in consumer cases have refused to certify classes in the absence of reliable proof of purchase or a knowable list of injured plaintiffs. *See* Carrera v. Bayer Corp., 727 F.3d 300 (3d Cir. 2013) (holding that certification when neither class members nor defendants would have purchase records risks due process violations); *cf., e.g.,* Karhu v. Vital Pharms., Inc., 2014 WL 815253 (S.D. Fla. 2014) (class action against dietary-supplement maker failed because membership could not be verified without central purchase records or proof of purchase). This requirement, Gilles & Friedman argue, "has sounded a death knell for many (if not most) cases arising from small retail purchases." Cases involving peanut butter, cough medicine, pineapples, cookware and aspirin have all been dismissed on ascertainability grounds.

Other courts hold that ascertainability merely requires an objective definition of the class, even if class members don't retain receipts. *See* Forcellati v. Hyland's, Inc., 2014 WL 1410264 (C.D. Cal. Apr. 9, 2014) (redressing small consumer claims is "[t]he policy at the very core of the class action mechanism"). There is an active circuit split on the issue. *See, e.g.,* Briseno v. ConAgra Foods, Inc. 844 F. 3d 1121 (9th Cir. 2017) (federal rules do not require demonstrating an administratively feasible way to identify class members as a prerequisite to class certification; joining Sixth, Seventh and Eighth Circuits).

In other variants, some courts find that the class isn't ascertainable if the representation at issue was made in an ad instead of the product package or label, since not every purchaser might have seen the ads. (This can also be characterized as a commonality problem.) *See In re* POM Wonderful LLC, 2014 WL 1225184 (C.D. Cal. 2014) (decertifying a class for this reason, among others).

Or class certification might be impossible because there's no appropriate way to compensate individual class members. If class-action plaintiffs aren't each entitled to a statutory damages award—and in many states they aren't—there needs to be some way of figuring out what they lost (restitution) or what defendants gained (disgorgement). If the product or service at issue wasn't completely worthless, how do we know how much of the price should be attributed to the misrepresentation? What if different people bought for different reasons, and some would have paid just as much without the misrepresentation—are they all entitled to an award regardless? Plaintiffs increasingly allege that a misrepresentation allowed defendants to charge a price premium. While this allegation may survive a motion to dismiss, it does not necessarily support certification. *See id.* (rejecting a price premium model because it depended on a "fraud on the market" theory; plaintiffs failed to establish why POM's higher price resulted from its misrepresentations, so damages couldn't be shown on a class-wide basis).

Plaintiffs have tried various workarounds to these problems. Federal courts often reject attempts to apply the law of the defendant's state to a nationwide consumer class. The theory is that choice-of-law principles and constitutional due process usually require analyzing claims based on plaintiffs' domicile, thus meaning that multiple jurisdictions' laws are implicated. *See* Lyon v. Caterpillar, Inc., 194 F.R.D. 206 (E.D. Pa. 2000) ("All of the relevant jurisdictions have an interest in utilizing the state statute crafted by their state's legislature to protect their consumers and/or residents . . . .").

The Ninth Circuit, where many consumer protection class actions are litigated, has made it almost impossible to certify a contested nationwide class. *See, e.g.*, Mazza v. Am. Honda Motor Co., 666 F.3d 581 (9th Cir. 2012). A few nationwide classes using a single state's law have, however, been certified. *See, e.g.*, Forcellati v. Hyland's, Inc., 2014 WL 1410264 (C.D. Cal. 2014) (even after *Mazza*, defendants must identify relevant differences in state law; where California-based defendants' homeopathic product was allegedly completely useless and where defendants failed to engage in detailed state-by-state analysis, nationwide class was appropriate). Should it matter if defendants can identify another state's laws that are more protective of consumers, if defendants may not face suit in that jurisdiction? *See* Barry A. Weprin, *Plaintiffs' Perspective on Recent Developments in Class Certification of Sales Practice Claims: The Focus Shifts to State Consumer Statutes*, ALI-ABA Conference on Life and Health Insurance Litigation, May 1–2, 2003 ("Courts should treat with healthy skepticism defendant's purported concerns for a consumer's right to litigate under the laws of his or her own state. What such defendants really seek, of course, is to defeat certification so that they need never face the merits of the class claims.").

An alternative is subclassing: dividing state laws into types, much as our overview in Chapter 3 did, for issues such as whether reliance is required. Courts have generally rejected subclassing as well, both because it's hard to find exact correspondences between different states' laws and because it's difficult to instruct a jury on multiple subclasses.

Still another alternative is partial certification: class treatment for liability or causation, for example, with an individual stage for damages. This too has not proved popular, even though Rule 23(c)(4)(A) specifically provides that "[w]hen appropriate . . . an action may be brought or maintained as a class action with respect to particular issues."

The most successful strategy has been single-state classes, usually filed in large-population states (California, Illinois, Massachusetts and New York are common). In states willing to presume class-wide reliance and deception, a single-state class has some chance of certification.

Amchem Products, Inc. v. Windsor, 521 U.S. 591 (1997), varied the analysis somewhat for a "settlement class," where both parties ask the court for certification so they can settle a claim comprehensively. Manageability isn't an issue for a settlement class; factual and legal variation therefore are less-significant problems. *See, e.g.*, O'Keefe v. Mercedes-Benz USA, LLC, 214 F.R.D. 266 (E.D. Pa. 2003) (certifying settlement class based on state consumer-fraud statutes). As a result, defendants can decide if they want to defeat class certification based on state-level legal variations, or if they would rather accept class certification to enable settlement—and thereby "buy" national resolution of a problem.

Amchem does, however, require that the other portions of Rule 23 designed to protect absentees "demand undiluted, even heightened, attention in the settlement context," so that settlements aren't overbroad or under-compensatory. Courts may conditionally certify a settlement class: If the settlement dissolves, certification must be relitigated. No certification, whether for a litigation class or a settlement class, is final until the court enters judgment approving the settlement after a Rule 23(e) fairness hearing.

C. Special Rules for California

California has historically had broad consumer-protection laws—generally known as the UCL (Unfair Competition Law), FAL (False Advertising Law) and CLRA (Consumer Legal Remedies Act)—and its courts are willing to entertain consumer claims. Combined with the fact that California's economy is, on its own, one of the largest in the world, California is therefore a magnet for consumer class actions. Even a California-only class has the potential to make a defendant nervous, and, as noted above, California courts occasionally entertain nationwide class actions under California law where the defendant's conduct occurred in California. Though California has cut back, both legislatively and judicially, on the scope of its laws, it remains a vital source of consumer-protection law. The UCL Practitioner blog covers California UCL, FAL and related cases.

After *Kasky v. Nike*, discussed in Chapter 2, California residents voted for Proposition 64, a measure that imposed an injury requirement on private plaintiffs: They must have suffered injury-in-fact and have lost money or property as a result of the unfair practice at issue. The

California Supreme Court interpreted Proposition 64 in *In re Tobacco II Cases*, 46 Cal. 4th 298 (Cal. 2009). The court emphasized that California's UCL differed from common-law fraud, which requires knowing falsity and reasonable reliance by the victim. Injunctive relief under the UCL requires neither because it focuses on defendant's conduct, rather than plaintiff's damages, in service of larger consumer protection goals.

The trial court had granted defendants' motion for decertification in *Tobacco II*, a case about cigarette marketing, because it reasoned that absent class members each had to show that they met Proposition 64's standing requirements, and individualized reliance determinations are inconsistent with class actions.

The California Supreme Court reversed. Only the representative plaintiff needed to satisfy the injury-in-fact/lost-money-or-property requirement. To effectuate the law's purposes, including the ability to grant injunctive relief and to award restitution to those who have been harmed, relief for false advertising under the UCL is available without individualized proof of deception, reliance and injury.

Given that Proposition 64 was clearly designed to impose limits on private claims under the UCL, it did impose an actual reliance requirement on private plaintiffs suing under the UCL's fraud prong. However, a plaintiff can prove reliance by showing that the defendant's misrepresentation or nondisclosure was an "immediate cause" of her injury; and this can be done by showing that, without the misrepresentation or nondisclosure, the plaintiff "in all reasonable probability" wouldn't have engaged in the injury-producing conduct. She need not show that the misrepresentation was the only cause of the injury-producing conduct, or even the predominant or decisive factor, as long as it played a substantial part in influencing her decision.

Moreover, "a presumption, or at least an inference, of reliance arises wherever there is a showing that a misrepresentation was material." Where a plaintiff alleges exposure to a long-term advertising campaign, "the plaintiff is not required to plead with an unrealistic degree of specificity that the plaintiff relied on particular advertisements or statements." As a California appellate court explained, "Plaintiffs may satisfy their burden of showing causation as to each by showing materiality as to all." *In re* Vioxx Class Cases, 180 Cal. App. 4th 116 (Cal. Ct. App. 2009).

The upshot of *Tobacco II* is that while the named class representatives must meet the new standing requirements, including reliance when the claim involves "fraudulent" conduct, the showing required for unnamed class members has not changed, and individualized proof of deception, reliance and injury are not required for them. The focus of the inquiry is on the reasonable consumer who is a member of the target population.

In *Kwikset Corporation v. The Superior Court of Orange County*, 51 Cal.4th 310 (Cal. 2011), the California Supreme Court further emphasized that "plaintiffs who can truthfully allege they were deceived by a product's label into spending money to purchase the product, and would not have purchased it otherwise, have 'lost money or property' within the meaning of Proposition 64 and have standing to sue." Thus, plausible allegations that, were it not for defendants' misrepresentations, plaintiffs would not have bought a product are sufficient to survive a motion to dismiss, even if the product worked fine and was no more expensive than competing products. (What kind of damages would be appropriate in such a case?) Despite these limiting constructions, Proposition 64 has curbed some consumer-protection claims. Joshua D. Wright, *Economic Report on the Fiscal and Consumer Impact of H.F. No. 84/S.F. No. 140*, Report for the International Center for Law and Economics (2010) (finding a roughly 17% decrease in such claims as a result).

D.   Securities Class Actions

Although we will not discuss securities law, advertisements may form the foundation of securities law class-action claims. Investors may allege that false statements in advertising constituted material misrepresentations for purposes of 10(b) claims under the Securities Exchange Act of 1934. *See, e.g.*, *In re* Carter-Wallace, Inc. Securities Litig., 150 F.3d 153 (2d Cir. 1998) (ads can be statements made "in connection with" a securities transaction); *see also* Jura Liaukonyte & Alminas Zaldokas, *Background Noise? TV Advertising Affects Real Time Investor Behavior* (2020) (finding that television ads affect investors' stock purchases; products with names that matched or were similar to the name of the company caused larger changes, and the most influential ads were longer, aired first during ad breaks and came from new, rather than long-running, campaigns).

2.   Examples of Consumer-Protection Class Actions

We will now examine two cases with opposing results. Together, they provide a survey of many of the most-common arguments in consumer-protection class actions. A defendant-favorable ruling often finds multiple issues blocking certification; when you read *Algarin*, keep track of how many of these issues were resolved against the plaintiff as a matter of law and how many were rejected on the facts as alleged. You will see that there are a large number of class-action legal issues that divide district courts, without significant guidance yet from the Supreme Court (or indeed from most federal appellate courts).

ALGARIN V. MAYBELLINE, LLC, 300 F.R.D. 444 (N.D. CAL. 2014)

This action arises out of the allegedly deceptive nature [in which] Defendant Maybelline, LLC, labels and advertises its Superstay 24HR product line. Plaintiffs . . . bring this putative class action pursuant to California's Unfair Competition Law ("UCL") and California's Legal Remedies Act ("CLRA") seeking both monetary and injunctive relief. Presently before the Court is Plaintiffs' motion for class certification. . . . For the following reasons, Plaintiffs' motion is DENIED.

I.   BACKGROUND

A. Factual Background

Maybelline manufactures, markets, sells and distributes SuperStay 24HR Lipcolor, a line of lipcolors, and SuperStay 24HR Makeup, a line of skin foundations (collectively the "Class Products"). The Lipcolor features the label "SuperStay 24," "Micro-Flex Formula," "No

Transfer," and "Up to 24HR Wear." The Makeup features the Label "SuperStay Makeup 24HR," "Micro-Flex Formula," "ZeroTransfer," and "24HR Wear." . . .

Plaintiff Algarin purchased the SuperStay Lipcolor for $10.00 in reliance on the claimed 24-hour staying power. Plaintiff Murdock purchased the SuperStay Makeup for $12.00 also in reliance on the claimed 24-hour coverage. Both Plaintiffs gave full credence to the claimed 24-hour duration and were thus willing to pay a premium for that purported benefit. Both Plaintiffs used the products as directed and needless to say, were decidedly unimpressed. Plaintiffs were exasperated that the products failed to live up to the representations as "neither the lipcolor nor the foundation lasted 24 hours, or anywhere near 24 hours. . . ." Had the two Plaintiffs known the "truth" about the "premium priced" Class Products, they would have purchased less expensive options. . . .

Maybelline allows dissatisfied consumers to make their complaints known to the company, and in some circumstances will issue a refund, through its Refund Program. . . . Between the Products' launch dates and mid-2013, approximately 2,700 consumers contacted Maybelline regarding the lipcolor and 700 regarding the makeup. Of these communications, 604 were performance complaints about the lipcolor and 97 about the makeup. The median compensation for the lipcolor is $10.00 and for the makeup is $11.00.

. . . Because of the Class Product's deceptive labels and advertisements, Maybelline is able to charge a "hefty price premium." The Lipcolor retails for approximately $10.00–$12.00, which is $1.00–$1.50 higher than other Maybelline products. The Makeup retails for approximately $11.00–$12.00, which is $1.00–$3.00 higher than other Maybelline foundations. Plaintiffs attribute this price premium solely to the alleged misrepresentations. . . .

II. LEGAL STANDARD

A. Class Certification

Federal Rule of Civil Procedure governs class actions. The party seeking certification must provide facts sufficient to satisfy the requirements of Rule 23(a) and (b). "Before certifying a class, the trial court must conduct a 'rigorous analysis' to determine whether the party seeking certification has met the prerequisites of [Rule] 23." Rule 23(a) requires that plaintiffs demonstrate numerosity, commonality, typicality and adequacy of representation in order to maintain a class. If the court finds the action meets the requirements of Rule 23(a), the court then considers whether the class is maintainable under Rule 23(b). In the instant matter, Plaintiffs seek certification under both 23(b)(2) and 23(b)(3).

Rule 23(b)(2) applies when "the party opposing the class has acted or refused to act on grounds that apply generally to the class, so that final injunctive relief or corresponding declaratory relief is appropriate respecting the class as a whole." Claims for monetary relief may not be certified under Rule 23(b)(2), at least where the monetary relief is not incidental to the requested injunctive or declaratory relief. Instead, individualized monetary claims belong in Rule 23(b)(3), "with its procedural protections of predominance, superiority, mandatory notice, and the right to opt out." Rule 23(b)(3) requires the court to find that questions of law or fact common to class members predominate over any questions affecting only individual members, and that a class action is superior to other available methods for fairly and efficiently adjudicating the controversy.

The merits of class members' substantive claims are highly relevant when determining whether to certify a class. It is not correct to say a district court may consider the merits to the extent that they overlap with certification issues; rather, "a district court must consider the merits if they overlap with the Rule 23(a) requirements." Nevertheless, the district court does not conduct a mini-trial to determine if the class "could actually prevail on their claims." . . .

III. DISCUSSION . . .

Of great importance to the matters in this class certification is the fact Maybelline has introduced unrefuted evidence of who the reasonable consumer in the target audience is and what drives her in making purchasing decisions. As Maybelline contends, the Court does not need to look to the hypothetical reasonable consumer. Similarly, the Court does not need to infer reliance given the evidence presented.

C. Maybelline's Expert Report

Maybelline's expert, Dr. Eli Seggev, is an expert in the field of marketing. After a thorough review of the Seggev report, the Court finds him qualified, and his opinion to be based on reliable methodologies, relevant to the issues at hand, and useful to the trier of fact. . . .

Dr. Seggev reports that repeat purchasing is a behavioral indicator of customer satisfaction and it follows that repeat purchasers are fully informed as to the duration claims and realities when they decided to purchase the Class Products again. Indeed, with cosmetics such as the ones at issue here, customers can readily discern how well they work and whether they lived up to the claimed representations. Accordingly, repeat purchasers cannot be considered injured in the manner proposed by Plaintiffs. As to the SuperStay lipcolor, Dr. Seggev's Report indicates that: (1) 45% of purchasers were satisfied with the product based on repeat purchases; (2) duration was not the only motivating factor in making the purchases; (3) over half of purchasers could not recall duration expectations or were satisfied with the duration of the product; (4) 4% of the total sample expected the specific 24-hour duration showing duration expectations varied among purchasers; and (5) only 9% of the total sample were one-time purchasers who expected the product to last 24-hours and thus are "injured" in the manner alleged by Plaintiffs. [The numbers for the makeup were similar though slightly less favorable to Maybelline.] . . .

D. Ascertainable Class

Though not explicitly stated in Rule 23, courts have held that the class must be adequately defined and clearly ascertainable before a class action may proceed. A class is sufficiently defined and ascertainable if it is "administratively feasible for the court to determine whether a particular individual is a member." . . . "[A]n identifiable class exists if its members can be ascertained by reference to objective criteria, but not if membership is contingent on a prospective member's state of mind."

Maybelline argues the proposed class fails to meet the ascertainability requirement based on two grounds. First, the proposed class is overly broad as it includes uninjured purchasers. Second, membership of the class cannot be readily determined.

Maybelline's first argument is essentially a challenge on the proposed class members' standing. Maybelline presents evidence, in the form of Dr. Seggev's survey and report as well as Maybelline's Early Trier Study, to show the proposed class includes: (1) a large percentage of the potential class of SuperStay purchasers are repeat purchasers who cannot be considered to be misled by the duration representation identified by Plaintiffs and (2) one-time purchases of the Class Products who had no duration expectations and whose purchasing decisions were made without regard to product duration. Because the proposed class includes these "uninjured" purchasers, the class is impermissibly overbroad and thus unascertainable.

As to these arguments regarding the inability of proposed members to show injury, the Court finds them more suitable for analysis under the Rule 23 rubric given the facts of this case. Though it may be true that many purchasers of the Class Products did not rely on the duration claims or were satisfied with the products, and thus "uninjured," these issues would not affect the Court's analysis of ascertainability based on the facts in the instant case.

Consumer action classes that have been found to be overbroad generally include members who were never exposed to the alleged misrepresentations at all. In the instant case, Plaintiffs have alleged a widespread advertising campaign promoting the alleged misrepresentations as well as uniform labeling for each of the Class Products. That the proposed class may include purchasers who did not rely on the misrepresentations and/or were satisfied with the products does not render the class "overbroad" where Maybelline has failed to demonstrate a lack of exposure as to some class members.

Maybelline further argues that because the class does not exclude purchasers who have already received refunds through Maybelline's Refund program, it is overbroad and not ascertainable. The Court agrees. As the UCL only permits recovery or restitution/disgorgement, for purchasers who have already received refunds, they have already been compensated well over any potential disgorgement. These purchasers have no claims. However, exclusion of these purchasers from the class definition would still not render certification appropriate.

The Court is satisfied that Plaintiffs' class definition is ascertainable in the sense that class membership can be determined based on an objective criterion. In the instant matter, that criterion will be whether members purchased either the SuperStay lipcolor or the SuperStay makeup. However, the Court is concerned that Plaintiffs have failed to provide a reliable method of determining who the actual members of the class are, indeed as Maybelline contends, such a task may be impossible.

Though the class may be ascertainable in the sense that there are objective criteria for determining who its members are, it is not in the sense that members could actually ever be determined. Plaintiffs have failed to show how it is "administratively feasible to determine whether a particular person is a class member." This inquiry overlaps with the "manageability" prong of Rule 23(b)(3) (D), in which a court assesses whether a class action is superior to other available methods of fairly and efficiently adjudicating the controversy.

Maybelline argues purchasers are unlikely to have documentary proof of purchase and Maybelline does not maintain a purchaser list or other identifying method. In such a situation, the Court and the parties would necessarily rely on class members to self-identify. The Court shares Maybelline's concerns. Indeed there are a number of cases that stand for the proposition that where a court has no way to verify if a purchaser is actually a class member, class certification may be improper.

Cases where self-identification alone has been deemed sufficient generally involve situations where consumers are likely to retain receipts, where the relevant purchase was a memorable "big ticket" item; or where defendant would have access to a master list of consumers or retailers. None of these factors exist in the instant case. The Class Products are small-ticket items that cost between $10.00 to $13.00, it is extremely unlikely the average purchaser would retain receipts and perhaps even remember she purchased the specific SuperStay products versus other similar Maybelline or competitor products. According to deposition testimony taken from named Plaintiffs, even they themselves did not retain receipts and had difficulty recalling many details about their purchases. . . .

However, a lack of ascertainability alone will not defeat class certification. As long as the class definition is sufficiently definite to identify putative class members, "the challenges entailed in the administration of this class are not so burdensome as to defeat certification." Thus, the Court continues to analyze whether the requirements of Rule 23(a) and 23(b) are met.

E. Rule 23(a)

Rule 23(a) provides a class action may proceed only where: (1) the class members are so numerous that joinder is impracticable; (2) common questions of law or fact exist; (3) the claims or defenses of the representative parties are typical of the class; and (4) the representative parties will fairly and adequately protect the interests of the class. Fed.R.Civ.P. 23(a).

1. Numerosity and Adequacy

Maybelline does not dispute that the proposed class meets the numerosity requirement nor do they dispute whether named Plaintiffs and counsel meet the adequacy requirement. Accordingly, the Court . . . finds these two requirements satisfied.

2. Commonality

The commonality factor "requires the plaintiff to demonstrate that the class members have suffered the same injury, which does not mean merely that they have all suffered a violation of the same provision of law." The "claims must depend on a common contention" and "that common contention . . . must be of such a nature that it is capable of class-wide resolution." The existence of shared legal issues with divergent factual predicates is sufficient, as is a common core of salient facts coupled with disparate legal remedies within the class." . . . [F]or purposes of Rule 23(a)(2), even a single common question will suffice.

Plaintiffs have identified several questions of law or fact common to the class: (1) whether the 24-hour/no transfer representation is true, or is misleading, or objectively reasonably likely to receive; (2) whether Maybelline engaged in false or misleading advertising; (3) whether Maybelline's alleged conduct violates public policy; (4) whether Maybelline's alleged conduct constitutes violations of the laws asserted; (5) the proper measure of the loss suffered by Plaintiffs and Class members; and (6) whether Plaintiffs and Class members are entitled to other appropriate remedies, including corrective advertising and injunctive relief. . . .

In light of the objective evidence showing that there was a substantial number of class members who were not misled by the 24-hour claim, whether Maybelline's conduct was false or misleading or likely to deceive is not subject to common proof on a class-wide basis. According to survey results, purchasers had a variety of duration expectations. Indeed, more purchasers expected the product to last less than 24 hours or had no specific duration expectations. Moreover, given the persuasive evidence presented on consumer expectations, the varying factors that influence purchasing decision, and consumer satisfaction, the Court finds that Plaintiffs have also failed to demonstrate that the elements of materiality and reliance are subject to common proof.

Expert evidence shows that materiality and reliance varies from consumer to consumer. Accordingly, the Court finds that these elements are not an issue subject to common proof.

Finally, the existence of economic injury is also not a common question as many purchasers were satisfied with the Class Products. [E.g.,] reviews say "This is the best lipcolor ever . . . I will be back for more," "I love this [lipcolor] . . . I will order more in the future," and "I am so happy I tried this foundation . . . this is my new foundation."
As for the other questions of law and fact posed, it is arguable that they may support a finding of commonality under the permissive standards governing this inquiry. As noted above, commonality can be established by the presence of a single significant common issue. However, Plaintiffs meet their downfall with the typicality requirement.

3. Typicality

Typicality requires a determination as to whether the named plaintiffs' claims are typical of those of the class members they seek to represent. "[R]epresentative claims are 'typical' if they are reasonably co-extensive with those of absent class members; they need not be substantially identical." Typicality, like commonality, is a "permissive standard[ ]." . . . To assess whether or not named Plaintiffs' claims are typical, the Court examines "whether other members have the same or similar injury." In other words, the inquiry is whether other members have the same or similar injury, whether the action is based on conduct which is not unique to named plaintiffs, and whether other class members have been injured by the same course of conduct.

The Court's analysis of the commonality requirement also informs the analysis for typicality. Based upon the evidence presented, the named Plaintiffs' reliance on the alleged misrepresentations was not typical of other class members.

. . . The Court further concludes that class certification under either 23(b)(2) or 23(b)(3) is improper.

F.   Rule 23(b)(2)

A class is proper under 23(b)(2) where the party opposing the class has acted or refused to act on grounds that apply generally to the class, so that final injunctive relief or corresponding declaratory relief is appropriate respecting the class as a whole. Class certification under Rule 23(b) (2) is appropriate only where the primary relief sought is declaratory or injunctive." For classes certified pursuant to Rule 23(b)(2), monetary damages must be "merely incidental to the primary claim for injunctive relief."

. . . [T]he restitution and disgorgement sought are not "incidental." Named Plaintiffs cannot possibly benefit from injunctive relief as they are now (or at least should be) fully knowledgeable that the Class Products do not last 24 hours. Thus monetary relief is necessarily their "primary concern." Rule 23(b)(2) "does not authorize class certification where each class member would be entitled to an individualized award of monetary damages." . . . Certification is improper where, as here, the request for injunctive and/or declaratory relief is merely a foundational step towards a damages award which requires follow-on individual inquiries to determine each class member's entitlement to damages.

G.   Rule 23(b)(3)

Certification pursuant to Rule 23(b)(3) requires Plaintiffs to establish that "the questions of law or fact common to the members of the class predominate over any questions affecting only individual members and that a class action is superior to other available methods for the fair and efficient adjudication of the controversy."

1.   Common Questions do not Predominate over Individual Inquiries

Rule 23(b) (3) predominance requires the class to be sufficiently cohesive to warrant adjudication by representation. This inquiry is more stringent than the commonality requirement of Rule 23(a)(2). . . .

The Court's analysis with regard to commonality under Rule 23(a) is fully applicable in the analysis of predominance. Given the number of individual purchasing inquiries as well as the evidence showing materiality and reliance varies consumer to consumer, it is evident that common issues do not predominate. Additionally, and of great importance, is the fact that Plaintiffs have failed to demonstrate sufficient evidence showing that any damages claimed to stem from the alleged misconduct.

. . . [A] party seeking certification must offer a class-wide means for calculating damages.

. . . While a court of equity "may exercise its full range of powers in order to accomplish complete justice between the parties," the restitution awarded must be a "quantifiable sum" and must be supported by substantial evidence. The restitution awarded "must correspond to a measurable amount representing the money that the defendant has acquired from each class member by virtue of its unlawful conduct."

Plaintiffs propose the "price premium" method of determining class-wide damage . . . . As Plaintiffs have stated, Maybelline charges $1.00–$3.00 more for the Class Products than its comparable products that do not bear the 24-hour/no transfer claims.

As an initial matter, it is not intuitively obvious at all that the 24-hour/no transfer claim commands a premium of $1.00–$3.00. Indeed, it is pure speculation on the part of Plaintiffs. The Court can fathom a number of reasons why the Class Products may be priced as they are. For example, perhaps it is due to a higher quality of ingredients, perhaps it is because of the selection of colors offered, or perhaps it reflects the costs Maybelline expended in the research and development of the products. Plaintiffs' method of using comparable products is inconsistent with the law. To establish that any difference in price is attributed solely to the alleged misrepresentation, the Court must use a product, exactly the same but without the 24-hour claim. As Maybelline stated, the Court would have to control and neutralize all other product differences. Such a task is nearly impossible as no two products are completely identical.

. . . Plaintiffs have failed to produce any expert testimony that demonstrate[s] a gap between the market price of the SuperStay 24 HR products and the price they purportedly should have sold at without the 24-hour/no transfer representations. . . .

Moreover, Maybelline contends that the proposed price premium method is inappropriate given the substantial variability in retail prices among the Class Products and competing products. The Court shares this concern. Maybelline does not sell retail and does not set retail prices. Establishing a higher price for a comparable product would be difficult where prices in the retail market differ and are affected by the nature and location of the outlet in which they are sold and/or the use of promotions and coupons. . . .

2.   The Class is Not Superior

Rule 23(b)(3) requires courts to find class litigation is superior to other methods of adjudication before certifying the class. Maybelline argues that its out-of-court Refund Program is a superior alternative. The Court questions the appropriateness of comparing such a private method of resolution.

Based on the language of Rule 23(b)(3) which requires a class action to be "superior to other available methods for . . . adjudicating the controversy," this determination involves a comparison of the class action as a procedural mechanism to available alternatives. In other words, Rule 23(b)(3) asks a court to compare the class action to other types of court action. Although the Court is mindful of cases which have considered whether the class action is superior to other "non judicial" methods of handling the controversy,[3] the Court is wary of stepping outside the text of Rule 23(b)(3).

However, included in the superiority analysis is whether the proposed class action would be manageable. "Courts are 'reluctant to permit action to proceed' where there are 'formidable . . . difficulties of distributing any ultimate recovery to the class members,' because such actions 'are not likely to benefit anyone but the lawyers who bring them.'" The Court has already concluded that the class is unmanageable and that common issues do not predominate, accordingly the class action is not a superior method of adjudicating the controversy. . . .

NOTES AND QUESTIONS

Consider the court's customer satisfaction rationale. How does it match up with the general prohibition on bait-and-switch advertising? *See* FTC v. Colgate-Palmolive Co., 380 U.S. 374, 389 (1965):

> [A]ll of the above cases, like the present case, deal with methods designed to get a consumer to purchase a product, not with whether the product, when purchased, will perform up to expectations. We find an especially strong similarity between the present case and those cases in which a seller induces the public to purchase an arguably good product by misrepresenting his line of business, by concealing the fact that the product is reprocessed, or by misappropriating another's trademark. In each the seller has used a misrepresentation to break down what he regards to be an annoying or irrational habit of the buying public—the preference for particular manufacturers or known brands regardless of a product's actual qualities, the prejudice against reprocessed goods, and the desire for verification of a product claim. In each case the seller reasons that when the habit is broken the buyer will be satisfied with the performance of the product he receives. Yet, a misrepresentation has been used to break the habit and . . . a misrepresentation for such an end is not permitted.

How would the *Maybelline* court address the following arguments: False claims interfere with consumers' autonomy, which is a harm in itself; they distort the market and make competition harder for producers who can deliver the promised value; and the consumer satisfaction rationale ignores many quirks of human psychology—among other things, once we've made a purchase, we like it more, so as to defend the soundness of our own judgment.

If these arguments are persuasive, should the result in *Maybelline* have been different, or were there still too many fatal problems with the class?

What about the relevance of survey evidence? Surveys are regularly required in Lanham Act cases; should consumer plaintiffs need to provide them in cases of implied falsity? In *Beardsall v. CVS Pharmacy, Inc.*, 953 F.3d 969 (2d Cir. 2020), plaintiffs' theory was that no reasonable consumer would buy aloe vera products with low concentrations of a key ingredient. The Second Circuit held that the plaintiffs could not proceed without "extrinsic"

---

[3] Indeed, these private methods of resolution have a number of appealing attributes, such as affording class members better remedies than a class action and not having to divert a substantial amount of the recovery to line the pockets of attorneys.

evidence that consumers were materially misled. It explained: "This is not to say that extrinsic evidence in the form of consumer surveys or market research is always needed for a plaintiff to survive summary judgment or judgment as a matter of law on a deceptive advertising claim. But such evidence is necessary where the advertising is not clearly misleading on its face and materiality is in doubt."

Superiority. Although usually the alternative to a class action is no lawsuit at all, courts have occasionally considered arguments that other forms of relief would be superior. In *Belfiore v. Procter & Gamble Co.*, 311 F.R.D. 29 (E.D.N.Y. 2015), the court found that the FTC was actively investigating the issue at bar—whether defendant's wipes had been falsely advertised as "flushable" when in fact they clogged sewer systems—and stayed six related class actions on the theory that the FTC could probably protect consumers more effectively. Given the risk of inconsistent results on a state-by-state basis, the FTC was better suited to protect consumers nationally by formulating a uniform definition of "flushable." Although the court merely stayed the cases, it indicated that this reasoning would likely lead it to find a lack of superiority for a damages class if forced to do so. Suppose the FTC closes the investigation without defining "flushable." Should the court certify a damages class?

The following case certifies a class. What's different?

McCRARY V. ELATIONS CO., LLC, 2014 WL 1779243 (C.D. CAL. 2014)

[McCrary sued for violation of the CLRA, FAL, and UCL—the usual California statutory consumer protection claims.] Defendant markets, distributes, and sells the Elations dietary joint supplement beverage and promotes it as "clinically proven" to have joint health benefits. However, Plaintiff contends that Elations is not clinically proven to have any impact on joints, and Elations' label was therefore false.

Plaintiff McCrary suffers from arthritic joint pain. While shopping at CVS in August 2011, Plaintiff alleges he reviewed the packaging of Elations which included the claims that Elations contains a "clinically-proven formula" and a "clinically-proven combination" of ingredients. In reliance on these claims, he purchased Defendant's product, followed all of the instructions, and used it as directed, but he did not receive the advertised benefits. Plaintiff claims that he would never have purchased the product had he known of its ineffectiveness. . . .

The decision to grant or deny a motion for class certification is committed to the trial court's broad discretion. However, a party seeking class certification must affirmatively demonstrate compliance with Rule 23—that is, the party must be prepared to prove that there are in fact sufficiently numerous parties and common questions of law or fact. This requires a district court to conduct a "rigorous analysis" that frequently "will entail some overlap with the merits of the plaintiff's underlying claim." . . .

B. Class Certification

Plaintiff moves to certify a class pursuant to Rules 23(a) and 23(b)(3) of "all persons residing in the state of California who purchased Elations, since January 28, 2009, for personal use and not for resale, when the following claims were on the packaging and/or labeling of Elations: 'clinically-proven combination' and/or 'clinically-proven formula.'" Plaintiff bears the burden of demonstrating that class certification is proper.

    1. Rule 23(a)
       a. Ascertainability

A class is ascertainable if it is "administratively feasible for the court to determine whether a particular individual is a member" using objective criteria. Plaintiff contends that the class definition objectively depicts who is bound and proposes that class members self-identify their inclusion via affidavits.

Defendant contends that the class is not ascertainable because there is no objective way to identify the individual members of the class, as it does not have any records identifying consumers of Elations—an over-the-counter supplement sold in retailers throughout the state. Defendant further contends that allowing class members to self-identify violates its due process right to raise individual challenges to class members.

Essentially, Defendant's concern is that class members do not have actual proof that they belong in the class. If Defendant's argument were correct, "there would be no such thing as a consumer class action." The class definition is sufficiently definite so that it is administratively feasible to determine whether a particular person is a class member. "Indeed, the proposed class definition simply identifies purchasers of Defendant's products that included the allegedly material misrepresentations. Because the alleged misrepresentations appeared on the actual packages of the products purchased, there is no concern that the class includes individuals who were not exposed to the misrepresentation."

Defendant's concern that it will be deprived of its due process right to defend against claims of class membership, such as by challenging a class member's actual purchase of the product or their failure to remember the Elations' label, is equally unavailing. . . . In this Circuit, it is enough that the class definition describes "a set of common characteristics sufficient to allow" a prospective plaintiff to "identify himself or herself as having a right to recover based on the description." . . . A prospective plaintiff would have sufficient information to determine whether he or she was an Elations customer who viewed the specified label during the stated time period. "[T]o the extent [Defendant] has individualized defenses, it is free to try those defenses against individual claimants."

Moreover, the fact that particular persons may make false claims of membership does not invalidate the objective criteria used to determine inclusion. Defendant points to the testimony of former Plaintiff Doucette who testified that he purchased Elations, but after further questioning at deposition, it was revealed he purchased another product. Defendant points to Doucette to argue that class members may not remember whether they purchased the product at issue, and the joint supplement market is crowded which may further confuse potential class members. Courts in this district have rejected this argument on the grounds that sufficient notice can cure confusion and these issues may be addressed later in the litigation. . . . [H]ere, Defendant can identify the retailers who sold its product. . . . [O]nce Defendant's "records establish which retailers sold [Elations] during the class period, class notice will further help reveal the class members." In addition, Defendant's contentions regarding a crowded market appear overstated. Defendant's Marketing Director stated that many of the joint supplements which likely competed with Elations were sold "in a pill form," and of the beverage options, many "vary by the additional factor of flavor." The product involved in this action was not available in pill form, nor has it ever been sold or manufactured in flavors. Accordingly, proper notice regarding the form of the product and its characteristics may help reduce consumer confusion regarding class membership.

In addition, Defendant argues that there is no precise time period when all class members purchased Elations with the "clinically-proven" labels. Although the challenged language was on the Elations label from January 28, 2009, through August 26, 2010, Defendant did not recall or re-label existing products once the label change was made. The fact that the allegedly false representation was not on every available product during the class period does not defeat ascertainability. However . . . Elations has a "two year shelf life from the date of bottling," therefore any remaining product should have been removed due to expiration. Accordingly, the Court finds it is necessary to limit the class definition to include purchasers of Elations between May 28, 2009, and December 26, 2012. With this limitation on the class period, the Court finds the class is ascertainable.

b. Numerosity

Rule 23(a)(1) requires the class to be so numerous that joinder of individual class members is impracticable. Here, the proposed California class is sufficiently numerous. During the unamended class period, Defendant shipped 615,623 units of Elations to locations in California. Thus, it is reasonable to estimate that there are thousands of potential class members in California. Defendant does not challenge Plaintiff's calculations, and the unrefuted evidence demonstrates that the numerosity requirement is satisfied.

c. Commonality

"Commonality requires the plaintiff to demonstrate that the class members 'have suffered the same injury,'" which "does not mean merely that they have all suffered a violation of the same provision of law." The "claims must depend on a common contention" and "[t]hat common contention . . . must be of such a nature that it is capable of class-wide resolution—which means that determination of its truth or falsity will resolve an issue that is central to the validity of each one of the claims in one stroke." Commonality is satisfied by "the existence of shared legal issues with divergent factual predicates" or a "common core of salient facts coupled with disparate legal remedies within the class."

Plaintiff has identified legal issues common to the putative class claims, namely whether the claims on Elations' packaging that it contains a "clinically-proven combination" and/or a "clinically-proven formula" are material and false. By definition, class members were exposed to these labeling claims, creating a "common core of salient facts." Defendant does not challenge the commonality requirement under Rule 23(a)(2), and "[c]ourts routinely find commonality in false advertising cases that are materially indistinguishable from this matter."

The Court therefore finds Plaintiff satisfied the commonality requirement under Rule 23(a)(2).

     d. Typicality

"The purpose of the typicality requirement is to assure that the interest of the named representative aligns with the interests of the class." "The test of typicality 'is whether other members have the same or similar injury, whether the action is based on conduct which is not unique to the named plaintiffs, and whether other class members have been injured by the same course of conduct.'" Thus, typicality is satisfied if the plaintiff's claims are "reasonably co-extensive with those of absent class members; they need not be substantially identical."

Plaintiff contends his claims are typical of those of the class because he purchased Elations believing it was proven to reduce his joint pain. If Plaintiff had known that Elations was not clinically proven to help with his joint pain, he would not have purchased it. These factual circumstances demonstrate that Plaintiff's claims are "reasonably co-extensive" with unnamed class members. Further, Plaintiff alleges to have suffered the same type of economic injury and seeks the same type of damages as the putative class members, namely a refund of the purchase price. As such, Plaintiff's interests "align[ ] with the interests of the class."

Defendant argues Plaintiff is not typical because he is subject to a unique defense based on his medical history. Specifically, Defendant points out that Plaintiff took Vicodin while he took Elations, which may have interfered with Elations' effectiveness in improving his joints. . . . "In determining whether typicality is met, the focus should be 'on the defendants' conduct and plaintiff's legal theory,' not the injury caused to the plaintiff." Thus, the central focus of the typicality analysis is that Plaintiff and the putative class claim Defendant labeled Elations with a claim of clinical proof knowing it was false. Moreover, the defense raised against Plaintiff is not "[a]typical of the defenses which may be raised against other members of the proposed class," as it is likely many other Elations' users took other medications and/or suffer from other illnesses. Accordingly, this potentially common defense does not render Plaintiff atypical.

In footnotes, Defendant raises the argument that customers who bought Elations online must be excluded from the proposed class. The Court agrees, but for reasons other than those offered. First, the proposed class definition requires that the putative member be exposed to the "packaging and/or labeling of Elations." Most, if not all, online consumers would not have seen the packaging or labeling on the product prior to purchase. This is particularly likely here where the "clinically-proven" claims were printed on "shrink wrap packaging" surrounding the Elations bottles. Thus, online consumers would not share a common injury with members of the class. Even if the websites offering Elations presented similar clinical proof claims in their marketing or description of the product, this would be insufficient because Plaintiff did not view any claims made on the website, nor did he purchase the product online. Therefore, Plaintiff is not typical of putative class members who purchased Elations online. . . .

With the exclusion of online consumers, the typicality requirement is satisfied.

e. Adequacy . . .

[T]he Court concludes that the class representative and class counsel are adequate.

2. Rule 23(b)(3)

Of the three possible bases for certification under Rule 23(b), Plaintiff seeks certification under Rule 23(b)(3) which requires that "the questions of law or fact common to the members of the class predominate over any questions affecting individual members, and that a class action is superior to other available methods for the fair and efficient adjudication of the controversy."

a. Predominance

Plaintiff moves to certify the class based on Defendant's liability under the UCL, FAL, and CLRA. . . . Class certification under Rule 23(b)(3) is proper when common questions present a significant portion of the case and can be resolved for all members of the class in a single adjudication. Defendant argues certification is improper because individual issues predominate over any common issues.

i. Standing, Materiality, and Reliance

Defendant makes several arguments contending that unnamed class members may lack standing or fail to satisfy elements of the UCL, FAL, or CLRA. Defendant contends that the Court must make individual determinations of whether each member actually viewed the "clinically proven" claim, that such statements were material to the class members' purchase of Elations, and that the consumers actually believed the product was ineffective and caused them damage.

As discussed above, the class definition presupposes exposure to the clinical proof claims. Any person who did not view the claims is not a class member and cannot raise any individualized issues. Moreover, a presumption of exposure is inferred where, as here, the alleged misrepresentations were on the outside of the packaging of every unit for an extended period. The fact that some of the packaging after August 2010 may not have included the clinical proof claims does not alter the presumption of exposure. The case Defendant cites to support its argument that Plaintiff must prove each class member had individualized exposure is distinguishable. In *Mazza v. Am. Honda Motor Co., Inc.*, 666 F.3d 581 (9th Cir. 2012), the Ninth Circuit held that a "presumption of reliance does not arise when class members 'were exposed to quite disparate information from various representatives of the defendant.'" In that case, plaintiff alleged misrepresentations in a brochure and television ads touting the benefits of a technology package available on certain

Honda models to which few class members could have been exposed. The Ninth Circuit reasoned that "the limited scope of that advertising makes it unreasonable to assume that all class members viewed it." Defendant does not argue, nor could it, that its clinical proof claims were of limited scope, since it placed them on the packaging of every unit of Elations sold over an 18-month period. The factual dissimilarity of *Mazza* renders it inapplicable.

In the Ninth Circuit, "standing is satisfied [under the UCL and FAL] if at least one named plaintiff meets the requirements. . . . Thus, we consider only whether at least one named plaintiff satisfies the standing requirements." Here, Defendant does not challenge Plaintiff's standing, and thus the Court need not examine whether each putative class member has standing.

Contrary to Defendant's assertion, at the class certification stage Plaintiff need not prove that the clinical proof claims were material to all consumers of Elations or that they relied on those claims. "[A] presumption, or at least an inference, of reliance arises [under the UCL and FAL] whenever there is a showing that a misrepresentation was material." Similarly, for a CLRA claim, "[i]f the trial court finds that material misrepresentations have been made to the entire class, an inference of reliance arises as to the class." The materiality determination under the FAL, UCL, and CLRA requires an objective test where plaintiff must "show that members of the public are likely to be deceived" by the alleged misrepresentations. Therefore, the determination of materiality, and thus reliance, is determined using objective criteria that apply to the entire class and do not require individualized determination.

Defendant contends that such an inference of reliance is unwarranted here because no evidence supports it. Defendant argues that many consumers purchase Elations based on the recommendation of a doctor or friend or for reasons other than the information printed on the label. However, Plaintiff points to evidence from Defendant's consumer survey showing that over 75 percent of Elations purchasers believed that "proven levels" of the active ingredients were worth paying for. Moreover, Plaintiff's claims of falsity concern the efficacy of the product and thus go to the heart of a customer's purchasing decision. Defendant cannot reasonably argue that a putative class member would purchase a product that does not work, regardless of who recommended it. Thus, Plaintiff has presented a sufficient factual basis to warrant an inference of reliance among the putative class of Elations purchasers.

Moreover, Defendant's concern that some putative class members were happy with Elations and thus were uninjured is unpersuasive. "[The requirement of concrete injury is satisfied when the Plaintiffs and class members in UCL and FAL actions suffer an economic loss caused by the defendant, namely the purchase of defendant's product containing misrepresentations." "The focus of the UCL and FAL is on the actions of the defendants, not on the subjective state of mind of the class members. All of the proposed class members would have purchased the product bearing the alleged misrepresentations. Such a showing of concrete injury under the UCL and FAL is sufficient to establish Article III standing." Accordingly, the Court need not examine whether each putative class member was unsatisfied with the product in order to find that common issues predominate.

In sum, the Court agrees with Plaintiff that common questions predominate over individual questions. Specifically, the predominating common issues include whether Defendant misrepresented that Elations is a "clinically-proven formula" or "clinically-proven combination," and whether the misrepresentations were likely to deceive a reasonable consumer.

ii. Damages

Defendant also contends that Plaintiff fails to present a viable damages model.

Plaintiff seeks full restitution of the retail price or disgorgement of Elations' net profits. Plaintiff contends that he will be able to prove the proper amount of restitution by relying on documents produced by Defendant relating to net sales, profits, costs, and the retail price of Elations. Defendant counters that return of the full purchase price violates restitutionary principles because Elations provided some value to consumers and that value must be deducted from the price putative members paid. Courts agree with Defendant and hold that "[w]hile Plaintiffs, should they prevail, are likely not entitled to a full refund of the purchase price, having obtained some benefit from the products purchased even if they were not as advertised, Plaintiffs may seek some amount representing the disparity between their expected and received value." This reduction in allowable damages, however, is not fatal to class certification. At this stage, the Court does not require Plaintiff to identify a comparable "clinically-proven" product which could serve to offset damages.

Next, Defendant contends that individual questions of damage would overwhelm the common questions of fact and law. However, "the amount of damages, even if it is an individual question, does not defeat class certification." . . .

Since Plaintiff seeks no remedy that would require an award of damages unique to any particular class member, the Court determines that the potential recovery is not an impediment to the requirement of predominance.

b. Superiority

Rule 23(b)(3) requires the Court to find "a class action is superior to other available methods for fairly and efficiently adjudicating the controversy." Fed.R.Civ.P. 23(b)(3). Considerations pertinent to this finding include:

> (A) the class members' interests in individually controlling the prosecution or defense of separate actions;
> (B) the extent and nature of any litigation concerning the controversy already begun by or against class members;
> (C) the desirability or undesirability of concentrating the litigation of the claims in the particular forum; and
> (D) the likely difficulties in managing a class action."
> Fed.R.Civ.P. 23(b)(3)(A)–(D).

The superiority requirement tests whether "class-wide litigation of common issues will reduce litigation costs and promote greater efficiency."

Here, the damages suffered by each putative class member are not large, favoring a class proceeding. It is more efficient to resolve the common questions regarding materiality and scientific substantiation in a single proceeding rather than to have individual courts separately hear these cases. There are no other cases challenging Defendant's advertising claims under California's consumer protection statutes, and the proposed class involves only California purchasers, making this forum desirable for the class. Finally, there is no evidence that this consumer class action will be difficult to manage.

Defendant does not oppose the superiority of a class action for resolving the putative class's claims. Given the large number of potential class members and small amount of the claims, the Court concludes that a class action is a superior method of resolving this case. . . .

NOTES AND QUESTIONS

What is your final count of divergent analyses between the *Maybelline* and *Elations* courts? Does it matter that one accused product is cosmetics and the other is a nutritional supplement?

3. The Special Case of Settlement Classes

The following case differs from the previous two in two key ways: (1) It examines many of the key issues for *multistate* consumer class actions, (2) in the context of a settlement. Pay attention to the issues that give the court the most pause: Numerosity is handled quickly, while predominance requires more detailed analysis. Crucially, because this is a settlement class, both sides want to convince the court to approve it. A contested certification would proceed very differently.

IN RE M3 POWER RAZOR SYSTEM MARKETING & SALES PRACTICE LITIGATION, 270 F.R.D. 45 (D. MASS. 2010)

This consolidated consumer litigation alleges misrepresentation by the defendant Gillette Company in the marketing of shaving devices. A motion seeking preliminary review and authorization of notice regarding a North American class action settlement raised the challenging question whether and, if so, how class action certification should be made when the governing substantive law is drawn from various North American jurisdictions. . . .

Ultimately, I have been satisfied that where, as here, all the plaintiffs "share[ ] a single, common claim that g[ives] rise to an identical right to recovery under a single state statute for every member of the class," class certification is appropriate in the absence of "variations in state laws . . . so significant as to defeat commonality and predominance, even in a settlement class." Finding no significant variations in other state laws sufficient to defeat the commonality and predominance evident in this case, where all class members have advanced a claim under the Massachusetts Unfair and Deceptive Practices Act, Mass. Gen. Laws ch.

93A, "on the ground that the allegedly deceptive communications originated from [Gillette's Massachusetts-based] headquarters," I certified a single settlement class and authorized publication of the class notice.

I. BACKGROUND . . .

A. Factual Background

[The facts are the same as those recounted in the *Schick v. Gillette* litigation in Chapter 4: Gillette advertised that the M3P could raise hair up and away from the skin with micropulses, allowing a closer shave than other razors.] Plaintiffs allege that the advertising claims were deceptive and materially misleading because Gillette was aware that the M3P did not actually raise facial hair "up and away" from the skin. All of the Representative Plaintiffs claim to have based a decision to purchase the razor on the misleading M3P advertising campaign.

B. Procedural History

. . . Following the issuance of the preliminary injunction in [*Schick v. Gillette*], plaintiffs filed consumer class actions based on the same underlying facts in several United States and Canadian jurisdictions. All actions filed in state courts in the United States were removed to federal court, and all the federal cases in other districts were transferred by the [Joint Panel on Multidistrict Litigation] to this Court. I consolidated the cases and resolved contentious disputes among the several plaintiffs' counsel regarding the appointment of Co-Lead and Liaison counsel.

The parties thereafter commenced formal discovery. . . . [The parties agreed to a settlement, and the court allowed a preliminary notice of settlement, but California Plaintiff Carlos Corrales objected.]

. . . I felt obligated to survey the relevant law on a jurisdiction-by-jurisdiction basis to determine whether material differences, as applied to the proposed settlement, might yield unfair and disproportionate advantages or disadvantages for class members from certain jurisdictions. . . .

II. THE PROPOSED SETTLEMENT

A. Settlement Terms

[Editors' note: The settlement, in brief, provided the option of a $15 refund (including postage and handling) for those class members who chose to return the razor to Gillette or a rebate of up to $10 for Gillette purchases for class members who could produce package codes or receipts from their purchases. If the settlement fund was not exhausted by these claims at the end of the initial claim period, each class member who submitted an approved claim would receive a new Gillette razor, and if that didn't exhaust the settlement fund, each class member who certified that he or she purchased or otherwise obtained an M3P razor during the class period would receive a new Gillette razor. Any leftover funds would be used to distribute free Gillette razors to the general population.]

III. CLASS CERTIFICATION

Federal Rule of Civil Procedure 23 governs class certification in the federal courts. Before certifying a class, "[a] district court must conduct a rigorous analysis of the prerequisites established by Rule 23 . . . " To obtain class certification, plaintiffs must establish each of the four elements of Rule 23(a)—numerosity, commonality, typicality, and adequacy of representation—and one of the elements in Rule 23(b). The fact that class certification is requested only for the purpose of settlement is no barrier to certification. However, considerations stemming from structural concerns about potential collusion and reverse auctions in settlement class actions make it "incumbent on the district court to give heightened scrutiny to the requirements of Rule 23 in order to protect absent class members."

A. Rule 23(a)

Rule 23(a) imposes four prerequisites to class certification:

> (1) the class is so numerous that joinder of all members is impracticable, (2) there are questions of law or fact common to the class, (3) the claims or defenses of the representative parties are typical of the claims or defenses of the class, and (4) the representative parties will fairly and adequately protect the interests of the class.

Fed. R. Civ. P. 23(a). The plaintiffs must demonstrate that each Rule 23(a) requirement is satisfied for class certification to be appropriate.

1. Numerosity

The numerosity requirement is easily satisfied in this case because Gillette sold over ten million M3P razors across the United States and Canada in the pertinent time periods. No purchaser records were maintained, so there is no possibility of locating, much less joining individually as plaintiffs, all of the potential class members. Given the large number of potential class members, and the relatively small claim each one has for damages, individual lawsuits are clearly impracticable, and Rule 23(a)(1) is satisfied.

2. Commonality

The threshold for commonality under Rule 23(a)(2) is not high. Because the Rule 23(a)(2) analysis is "[a]imed in part at 'determining whether there is a need for combined treatment and a benefit to be derived therefrom,' the rule requires only that resolution of the common questions affect all or a substantial number of the class members."

Although variations existed in the legal requirements of various state law claims and in the facts necessary to prove such claims, it is beyond dispute that common core questions lie at the heart of this litigation. Stated in their highest degree of generalities, these include:

whether Gillette misrepresented the capabilities of the M3P razor to the potential class, whether the potential class members sustained ascertainable damages from such conduct, and, if so, in what amount. These common issues of fact and law are sufficient to meet the threshold of Rule 23(a)(2), and indicate that class certification could be beneficial to the expeditious resolution of this dispute.

3. Typicality

To establish typicality, the plaintiffs need only demonstrate that "the claims or defenses of the class and the class representative arise from the same event or pattern or practice and are based on the same legal theory." Here, it is clear that the claims of the Representative Plaintiffs are based on the same event (purchase of an M3P razor based on misleading advertisements) as the potential class members. The legal theories of recovery for the Representative Plaintiffs are typical of those of the class as a whole. As reflected in the Amended Consolidated Class Action Complaint, most counts are based on common law causes of action (negligent misrepresentation, intentional misrepresentation, breach of express warranty, breach of implied warranty of fitness of purpose, and unjust enrichment), which will be substantially uniform across the class. The Amended Complaint also alleges violation of various state consumer protection statutes. Although the Representative Plaintiffs are not residents of each of the covered states, the consumer protection statutes in the states in which they reside (Florida, New York, California, Massachusetts, Illinois, Georgia and Canada) appear to be typical of, and generally even more consumer-friendly than, consumer protection laws in the range of jurisdictions that they represent. Consequently, the Representative Plaintiffs satisfy the typicality requirement of Rule 23(a)(3).

4. Adequate Representation

Rule 23(a)(4) requires that the proposed class representatives "fairly and adequately protect the interests of the class." This requirement has two parts. The plaintiffs "must show first that the interests of the representative party will not conflict with the interests of any of the class members, and second, that counsel chosen by the representative party is qualified, experienced and able to vigorously conduct the proposed litigation."

As to the former, the Representative Plaintiffs' interests generally align with the class as a whole, because all parties, named and unnamed, are seeking redress from what is essentially the same injury, the purchase of an M3P razor based on misleading advertisements. Indeed, all members of the class share a claim under Chapter 93A of the Massachusetts General Laws. Although some variations exist between potential remedies, depending on the state of residence, these differences do not create the type of intra-class conflicts that often appear in the mass tort context. The problem of differing remedies will be discussed in greater detail below. At this point, it is sufficient to note that the interests of the Representative Plaintiffs and the absent class members are not generally in conflict, and that counsel is adequate. . . .

B.   Rule 23(b)

In addition to satisfying the four elements of Rule 23(a), plaintiffs must demonstrate that at least one subsection of Rule 23(b) applies. I find Rule 23(b)(3) directly applicable, as this subsection allows for class certification if "the court finds that the questions of law or fact common to class members predominate over any questions affecting only individual members, and that a class action is superior to other available methods for fairly and efficiently adjudicating the controversy." Fed. R. Civ. P. 23(b)(3). In short, plaintiffs must demonstrate predominance and superiority.

1.   Predominance

The predominance inquiry overlaps with the commonality requirement of Rule 23(a)(2), but is more demanding. "The Rule 23(b)(3) predominance inquiry tests whether proposed classes are sufficiently cohesive to warrant adjudication by representation." The pertinent legal and factual questions are those that "qualify each class member's case as a genuine controversy," but do not include the fairness or desirability of the proposed settlement in a settlement class action. The predominance standard can be met even if some individual issues arise in the course of litigation, because "Rule 23(b)(3) requires merely that common issues predominate, not that all issues be common to the class." In this connection, some types of cases are uniquely well-suited to class adjudication, and "[p]redominance is a test readily met in certain cases alleging consumer or securities fraud or violations of the antitrust laws."

In this case, it is clear that the issues common to the class predominate over those that are personal to individual class members. The dominant common questions include whether Gillette's advertising was false or misleading, whether the company's conduct violated the statutory and/or common law causes of action delineated in the Amended Complaint, and whether the class members suffered damages as a result of this conduct. Even if state consumer statutes or other state causes of action differ in arguably material ways, common questions, not individual issues, predominate among and within each state's legal regimes. . . . I will address the problem of differences in legal theories in Section III.B.3, *infra*. For now, I note my finding that the predominance requirement of Rule 23(b)(3) appears to be satisfied.

2.   Superiority

Rule 23(b)(3) requires that a class action be "superior to other available methods for fairly and efficiently adjudicating the controversy." Courts must consider:

> (A) the class members' interests in individually controlling the prosecution or defense of separate actions; (B) the extent and nature of any litigation concerning the controversy already begun by or against class members; (C) the desirability or undesirability of concentrating the litigation of the claims in the particular forum; and (D) the likely difficulties in managing a class action.

The predominance and superiority requirements are inherently interrelated, and were added "to cover cases 'in which a class action would achieve economies of time, effort, and expense, and promote . . . uniformity of decision as to persons similarly situated, without sacrificing procedural fairness or bringing about other undesirable results.'" "Rule 23 has to be read to authorize class action in some set of cases where seriatim litigation would promise such modest recoveries as to be economically impracticable."

In this case, involving millions of potential plaintiffs with small individual claims, a class action is the only feasible mechanism for resolving the dispute efficiently. Absent class certification, it is highly unlikely that any individual aggrieved consumer will seek or obtain redress, because the transaction costs of filing and prosecuting a lawsuit individually far exceed the recoverable individual damages, even under the most generous state consumer protection statutes. In short, in the absence of class certification, there would be nothing for an individual class member to control because a separate action would not be prosecuted. . . . Under the circumstances, a class action pursued on a consolidated basis in the District of Massachusetts is superior to any other mechanism for adjudicating the case, and Rule 23(b)(3) is satisfied.

C. Subclassing

Objecting Plaintiff Corrales opposes certification of the class and authorizing notice of the settlement on the ground that the proposed settlement is insufficiently generous to potential California class members. Corrales argues that the consumer protection statutes in the state of California are so favorable to California consumers, particularly in terms of available remedies, that they should be treated differently from class members of other states. Assuming for the moment that Corrales' objections are valid, one potential mechanism for dealing with differential state remedies is to certify subclasses within the larger class. But this decision must not be made lightly because it inherently reduces the efficiency of the class action mechanism and increases transaction costs (particularly for notice).

Close analysis of a California subclass is a useful means to approach the problems presented by differences in legal theories among the several jurisdictions whose case law is involved by the consolidated complaint. I will consider three related questions to determine whether a California subclass is appropriate. First, what is the significance of variations in state law for purposes of certifying a nationwide class? Second, what is the content of California consumer protection law, and how does it compare to the common claim presented by Mass. Gen. Laws ch. 93A or otherwise differ from laws of other jurisdictions? Third, do any differences rise to a level that would necessitate the certification of a subclass? I will then address the problems more generally to determine what level of additional analysis is necessary given the common factual and legal issues shared by the plaintiff class members.

1. Variations in State Law

When nationwide class actions are based on state law claims, variations in state law create several potential challenges for certification under Rule 23, quite apart from the trial management issues that illustrate the challenges. State law differences signify "diverse legal standards and a related need for multiple [legal determinations]," and sometimes "multiply the individualized factual determinations" that a court must undertake. Legal variations also undermine the class's ability to satisfy the commonality requirement of Rule 23(a)(2). A related problem raised by state law variations is tension among the plaintiffs: conflicts of interest and allocation dilemmas can become evident and disabling during settlement or judgment. The Supreme Court has made it clear that before certifying a class—even in the settlement context—a court must closely examine potential conflicts of interest, as well as inequality in the strength of claims.

Circuits have required a rigorous analysis of state law variation must precede class certification. . . . Courts must remain sensitive, however, to the "common core" of issues among plaintiffs, even if coupled with "disparate legal remedies within the class."

One solution to the problems of state law variation in a nationwide class is to create a subclass of plaintiffs—a group of claimants from a state (or states) whose legal remedies differ substantially from those of other states. Certification of subclasses, however, must continue to facilitate the operation of the class action. [Klay v. Humana, Inc., 382 F.3d 1241, 1262 (11th Cir. 2004)] (warning that a court "must be careful not to certify too many groups," otherwise instructing the jury on—or otherwise applying—the relevant law would be an "impossible task").

2.   Consumer Protection Law as a Basis for Subclassing

Although the Consolidated Amended Complaint presents a multiplicity of causes of action (Negligent Misrepresentation, Intentional Misrepresentation, Express Warranty, Implied Warranty, Unjust Enrichment and Unfair Practices and Consumer Protection Statutes) from a multiplicity of North American jurisdictions, analysis of the relevant questions regarding class certification can be focused by discussion of the California Consumer Protection provisions relied upon by the California plaintiff objector and the Massachusetts claim under Chapter 93A common to all class members.

a.   California

. . . As a policy matter, the goal of the California consumer protection statutes is to return ill-gotten gains to consumers, with a secondary purpose of deterring future violations. The restitutionary remedy is not "intended as a punitive provision, though it may fortuitously have that sting when properly applied to restore a victim to wholeness." Before a court may award restitution, the appropriate amount of restitution must be shown by "substantial evidence." . . .

[T]he evidentiary standard for awarding restitution and actual damages is demanding in California state courts. The case before me has . . . valuation difficulties because Gillette has adduced evidence that consumers preferred the M3P razor, even if it did not perform exactly as advertised. The precise value of having one's hair raised "up and away" during a shave is inherently speculative. In this setting, it is not likely that a court applying California law in a California state class action would award restitution. The probability of a large monetary award in the form of restitution or actual damages is by no means the legal certainty Corrales suggests.

The CLRA also allows for punitive damages. . . . [I]t seems highly unlikely that a court applying California law would award such damages in the instant case, where courts around the world divided, at least on an interlocutory basis, over whether Gillette's conduct was even actionable.

It bears emphasizing that after a 2004 referendum, California's procedural and substantive consumer protection law became less consumer-friendly than it once may have been perceived to be. . . .

b.   Massachusetts

The protections for consumers provided by the Massachusetts Unfair and Deceptive Business Practices Act, Mass. Gen. Laws ch. 93A § 9, are quite robust and arguably more consumer-friendly than the California consumer protection regime. Unlike the California UCL cause of action, Chapter 93A does not require reliance, rather the applicable standard for determining whether an act is "deceptive" is whether "it possesses 'a tendency to deceive.'" The Massachusetts Supreme Judicial Court has emphasized that "[u]nlike a traditional common law action for fraud, consumers suing under c. 93A need not prove actual reliance on a false representation. . . . " Materiality and causation are established by a showing that the deceptive representation "could reasonably be found to have caused a person to act differently from the way he [or she] otherwise would have acted."

The consumer may recover compensatory damages under Chapter 93A for misrepresentation whether the misrepresentation is intentional or unintentional. . . . [T]he aggregate of actual damages afforded by a Chapter 93A consumer class action claim necessarily parallels the restitutionary remedy.

c.   Other Jurisdictions

After extended review of the various legal regimes, I find without reciting the details with particularity, that the Representative Plaintiffs have demonstrated that, although variations in state law exist, they do not overcome the common factual and legal issues shared by the potential class members. The only purported distinctions actually argued by an objector—those presented by California consumer protection law—are, to the extent they are significant at all, differences of degree, not of kind, and are not substantial and clear-cut enough to require a subclass.[10]

As is apparent from the text of this Memorandum, I have focused on consumer protection law as dispositive in this litigation. The various common law and commercial code counts alleged

---

[10] The similarity between state consumer protection laws was noted by the California Court of Appeals in a case relied upon by Corrales:

> [e]ven though there may be differences in consumer protection laws from state to state, this is not necessarily fatal to a finding that there is a predominance of common issues among a nationwide class. As the Ninth Circuit has observed, state consumer protection laws are relatively homogeneous: "the idiosyncratic differences between state consumer protection laws are not sufficiently substantive to predominate over the shared claims" and do not preclude certification of a nationwide settlement class.

[Editors' note: In *Mazza v. American Honda Motor Co.*, 666 F.3d 581 (9th Cir. 2012), the Ninth Circuit reached the opposite result with a contested nationwide class, holding that state law variations precluded certification over the defendant's opposition. However, the Ninth Circuit has reaffirmed that nationwide settlement classes are still allowed. In re Hyundai and Kia Fuel Economy Litigation, 926 F.3d 539 (9th Cir. 2019) (en banc).]

here do evidence significant differences among jurisdictions. Indeed, consumer protection statutes were developed principally to ease restrictions on consumer claims that were perceived to be embedded in common law and commercial law causes of action consumers might have otherwise deployed. And among consumer protection statutory schemes, the Massachusetts law under Chapter 93A appears to be in practice as generous as any available to class members in this litigation. . . .

NOTES AND QUESTIONS

Note the presence of a Canadian class. How should courts treat foreign citizens, whose overall legal systems may differ substantially from the American one even if the substantive right to be protected against false advertising looks similar?

How does this case differ from the contested cases above? Does it matter that Gillette had lost an earlier Lanham Act case and thus might have been estopped on certain issues if the case had gone to trial? What arguments against liability could it have made against the class that it could not have advanced against a competitor?

Suppose Gillette had decided to oppose certification. What arguments should it have made about legal and factual variation in plaintiffs' claims? Should it have prevailed? Does it make sense to relax the inquiry when the defendant wants to settle? Does that put too much power to control the litigation in the defendant's hands, or does it restore plaintiffs' leverage when without certification they'd likely have to litigate state-by-state, if they could litigate at all?

Should the presence of injunctive relief matter to the fairness of a settlement? How should it affect whether the class attorneys achieved a result good enough to justify their pay? *See, e.g.*, Swinton v. Squaretrade, Inc., 2020 WL 1862470, --- F.Supp.3d ---- (S.D. Iowa Apr. 30, 2020) ("As a general matter, injunctive relief is properly considered as part of a court's analysis of whether a settlement is fair, reasonable, and adequate."). *But see In re* Subway Footlong Sandwich Marketing & Sales Practices Litig., 869 F.3d 551 (7th Cir. 2017) (rejecting a settlement based on occasional variance in Subway "footlong" subs that left them less than twelve inches long; settlement should have been "dismissed out of hand" because it provided only "worthless benefits" to the class while "enrich[ing] only class counsel; injunctive relief was worthless because requiring Subway to warn consumers that "[d]ue to natural variations in the bread baking process, the size and shape of bread may vary" was already common sense).

4.   Alternatives to Class Actions?

As noted earlier, Myriam Gilles & Gary Friedman, *After Class: Aggregate Litigation in the Wake of* AT&T Mobility v. Concepcion, 79 U. CHI. L. REV. 623 (2012), argue that *Concepcion* allows most businesses to force consumers to waive their rights to class actions. The authors identify other barriers to consumer class actions that are also making them almost impossible to win if the defendant decides to fight.

Because consumer class actions are becoming impossible, but deceptive consumer practices are not, Gilles & Friedman recommend outsourcing AGs' consumer enforcement powers to private attorneys. Because the state has its own interests in protecting consumers, consumers' agreement to arbitration will not prevent attorneys general from suing to protect consumers. But attorneys general are traditionally underfunded, so Gilles & Friedman argue that states should make greater use of private lawyers with experience in consumer-protection cases. Attorney general supervision, they contend, will solve the "agency" problem of uncontrolled private lawyers suing over anything that might make them money in a settlement. However, they note that such partnerships "present especially rich political targets, making it imperative to institute transparent contracting processes and, probably, some measure of fee caps. . . . And attorneys general will have to be vigilant in their fundraising activities to avoid any element of 'pay-to-play' in the donations they accept from law firms or groups of lawyers."

Gilles & Friedman acknowledge the political risks involved:

> The poster child here is the tobacco litigation, where state AGs hired well-known plaintiffs' lawyers to sue the cigarette manufacturers on a subrogation theory. Although the private lawyers were able to wrest a $246 billion settlement from an industry that had enjoyed total success for decades in fending off any damages liability, critics balked at the $14 billion in aggregate fees paid to outside counsel under contingent fee agreements. Fierce lobbying and popular outcry drove some jurisdictions to place limits on the ability of AGs to hire outside counsel, and led President George W. Bush to ban the use of contingency fee agreements in federal contracts with outside counsel.

> But cooler heads have since prevailed. The Louisiana AG, Buddy Caldwell, recently sought permission from the state legislature to hire private attorneys to handle litigation against BP and others arising out of the Deep Water Horizon disaster. In Caldwell's press release, he noted "We just don't have enough money or enough knowledge to fight this fight as efficiently as the lawyers we want to hire. We think they're going to get the state of Louisiana a damned good settlement and force BP to pay up what it owes to the people it injured. And if we have to pay these lawyers to do that hard work and get us a good deal, I've got no problem with that . . . I think anyone who does have a problem with that just doesn't understand that the state's lawyers can't go up against the fancy firms that BP has hired the same way these private lawyers can." Other AGs have similarly turned to private outside counsel.

> In any event, AGs can easily protect themselves from a "tobacco problem" by negotiating to place some sort of limits on fees. Such capping arrangements—often couched as a fee of x% but not to exceed y times the ordinary hourly fees—are not unusual in private contracts, and they need not be particularly draconian to avoid the sort of "windfall" situation that is capable of drawing populist ire.

What do you think of this proposal? Can Gilles & Friedman really achieve the benefits AG-supervised private enforcement without suffering the current problems with class-action lawsuits or creating entirely new ones? See Daniel Aaron, *The Role of Attorneys General in the Opioid Litigation*, BILL OF HEALTH, Sept. 26, 2019 (pointing out that states that hired private lawyers want a quick settlement with Purdue Pharma for its involvement in creating the opioid crisis through aggressive and sometimes misleading marketing about its painkillers, while states whose attorneys general are pursuing the case themselves oppose the settlement and want more penalties).

Any lawsuit must begin with consideration of the plaintiff's desired outcome, which will profoundly shape the litigation strategy. This chapter covers the three major types of remedies for false advertising violations: injunctions, monetary damages or penalties, and criminal sanctions, though we reserve most of our attention for the first two, as they make up the vast majority of remedies issues.

1.   Injunctive Relief

In many competitor and regulator false advertising cases, the plaintiff's top priority is to stop the offending advertising before it causes more harm. As a result, injunctive relief is the remedy most often sought, and both the Lanham Act and the Federal Trade Commission Act grant courts broad authority to fashion appropriate injunctive relief. *See, e.g.*, Porter & Dietsch, Inc. v. FTC, 605 F.2d 294 (7th Cir. 1979) (setting forth standard of review of FTC orders: "[The FTC] has wide latitude for judgment and the courts will not interfere except where the remedy selected has no reasonable relation to the unlawful practices found to exist."). State attorneys general also may seek injunctive relief to prevent continuing harm to consumers.

Typically, because time is critical in advertising disputes, private competitor-plaintiffs seek provisional relief via a temporary restraining order (TRO) or preliminary injunction. If granted, provisional relief may be converted to permanent relief at the case's conclusion. Since evaluation of the application for a preliminary injunction requires the court to examine the case's merits, however, the resolution of that motion often gives the litigants enough information to resolve the case.

A.   Standard for a TRO or Preliminary Injunction

In cases brought by private litigants, courts traditionally consider four factors in determining whether to grant an application for preliminary relief:

(1) whether the movant has demonstrated a strong likelihood of success on the merits;
(2) whether the movant would suffer irreparable injury in the absence of injunctive relief;
(3) whether the issuance of the injunction would cause substantial harm to the defendant; and
(4) whether the public interest would be served by issuance of an injunction.

(Public enforcers generally do not have to show irreparable injury. *See* FTC v. Affordable Media, LLC, 179 F.3d 1228 (9th Cir. 1999); FTC v. Warner Commc'ns, Inc., 742 F.2d 1156 (9th Cir. 1984).)

In all jurisdictions, proof of irreparable harm to the private plaintiff and a likelihood of success on the merits are the key requirements. The various circuits analyze the four factors somewhat differently and give differing weight to each factor. Most significantly, the Second and Ninth Circuits have stated that preliminary injunctions may be appropriate if, instead of likely success on the merits, there is a "sufficiently serious" question going to the merits and a balance of hardships weighing "decidedly" in the plaintiff's favor, though it is not clear if this rule ever makes a difference in results. *See, e.g.*, Salinger v. Colting, 607 F.3d 68 (2d Cir. 2010).

Irreparable Harm

"Irreparable harm" refers to an injury that cannot be entirely remedied by a later payment of money damages. Such harm traditionally includes damage to a plaintiff's commercial reputation or a loss of goodwill caused by a competitor's false advertising, which will eventually lead to lost sales (but those lost sales will be difficult to measure).

In the past, irreparable harm was typically presumed if an advertisement was shown to be false, "based upon the judgment that it is virtually impossible to ascertain the precise economic consequences of intangible harms." Abbott Labs. v. Mead Johnson & Co., 971 F.2d 6 (7th Cir. 1992).

However, *eBay Inc. v. MercExchange*, L.L.C., 547 U.S. 388 (2006), undermined this presumption. *eBay* involved a permanent injunction against patent infringement. Prior to *eBay*, courts had developed a virtually irrebuttable presumption that an injunction was a more-appropriate remedy than damages in patent infringement cases. The Supreme Court rejected that presumption, concluding that injunctions in patent cases should be subject to the traditional four-factor test enumerated above. The Court's language indicated that blanket presumptions favoring injunctive relief were generally impermissible.

Some Lanham Act specialists argued that violations of the Lanham Act, with its consumer-protection objectives, deserved different treatment than property rights such as copyright and patent, so a presumption in favor of injunctive relief was still appropriate where a plaintiff showed likely success on the merits. *See* David H. Bernstein & Andrew Gilden, *No Trolls Barred: Trademark Injunctions after eBay*, 99 TRADEMARK REP. 1037 (2009).

Courts, however, have increasingly applied *eBay* to Lanham Act cases, and post-*eBay* precedent suggests that any presumptions in favor of injunctions are limited. For example, courts may still presume harm from literally false comparative advertising, or at least intentionally false comparative advertising. *See, e.g.*, Grpe. SEB USA, Inc. v. Euro-Pro Operating LLC, 774 F.3d 192 (3d Cir. 2014) (rejecting presumption of irreparable harm but accepting lost control of reputation and lost goodwill caused by false comparative advertising as irreparable harm); North American Medical Corp. v. Axiom Worldwide, Inc., 522 F.3d 1211 (11th Cir. 2008) (rejecting presumption of irreparable harm in non-comparative literal falsity case). Other cases stay agnostic on the effect of *eBay* but find case-specific evidence of irreparable harm from, for example, the seriousness of the statements in implicating the fundamental safety of the plaintiff's products. *See, e.g.*, Osmose, Inc. v. Viance, LLC, 612 F.3d 1298 (11th Cir. 2010).

Even if the applicable court isn't likely to embrace *eBay* as precedent, a plaintiff is well advised to submit evidence of actual irreparable harm, both to bolster the appropriateness of the presumption and, even more importantly, to educate the judge on why the equities strongly favor injunctive relief. What evidence would show irreparable harm as opposed to harm that could be redressed with money damages?

As you read the following case, consider what evidence you would want to show irreparable harm and how you would acquire that evidence.

IDT TELECOM, INC. V. CVT PREPAID SOLUTIONS, INC., 250 FED. APPX. 476 (3D CIR. 2007)
[review facts from Materiality section of Chapter 5]

. . . In their Complaint, the Appellants asserted claims for false advertising under the Lanham Act and violations of the consumer protection statutes of New Jersey, New York, California, Illinois, and Florida. All of the parties are engaged in the prepaid calling card business, and the dispute is centered around the advertising of the number of minutes a consumer receives when he or she purchases these calling cards.

Advertising posters and voice prompts are the main sources of information regarding the number of minutes on a particular calling card for calls to a particular destination. The Appellants discovered in 2006 that some of its competitors were offering a higher number of minutes for low-priced calling cards. After testing some of its competitors' calling cards, the Appellants allegedly learned that the cards were not actually providing the number of minutes promised, rather the cards provided fewer minutes than what was advertised. According to the Appellants, unlike their competitors, they provide one-hundred percent of the minutes advertised. The Appellants claim that this "false advertising" by their competitors caused them to lose consumers, which in turn caused distributors to reduce the number of the Appellants' prepaid calling cards they purchase. This loss, according to the Appellants, was a loss of market share, as the Appellees' sales increased during the same time period. They also claim that their distribution network, commercial relations and goodwill have been irreparably harmed.

. . . At the hearing on May 9, 2007, the District Court denied the Appellants' motion for a preliminary injunction. Although the District Court found that a public interest existed in accurate representations to consumers regarding the number of minutes they receive when they purchase a calling card, it determined that the Appellants did not meet their burden of demonstrating that they would suffer irreparable harm. It reached this conclusion because the Appellants failed to show that they would suffer any harm other than just a financial loss or a loss of market share. . . .

"We review the denial of a preliminary injunction for 'an abuse of discretion, an error of law, or a clear mistake in the consideration of proof.' " . . .

As the Appellants argue, we have held that a loss of market share can constitute irreparable harm. However, this does not change the fact that a preliminary injunction should not be granted if the injury suffered by the moving party can be recouped in monetary damages. At the preliminary injunction hearing the Appellants implicitly admitted that the alleged harm they suffered could be calculated in money damages. After explaining that some loss of market share was caused by factors other than the Appellees' alleged false advertising, counsel for the Appellants stated: "We're going to have a real hard time. I'm not saying we won't be able to put forward damage numbers, but our ability to fully capture the damages is going to be severely undermined by the fact that the [Appellees] are going to tell you there may be a number of other factors that may be causing this loss also." As the statement suggests, the Appellants believed that their market losses could be recouped through monetary damages. The only other evidence that IDT points to in support of a potential irreparable injury is its loss of reputation or goodwill. Although we have recognized that such losses may constitute irreparable harm, our case law also indicates that such harm is limited to "the special problem of confusion that exists in cases involving trademark infringement and unfair competition." As the harm claimed by the Appellants is not analogous to the harm caused by consumer confusion, the line of cases recognizing loss of goodwill or reputation as irreparable harm is not applicable. Based on the record we cannot say that the District Court abused its discretion in denying injunctive relief because the Appellants failed to meet their burden of proving irreparable harm. . . .

NOTES AND QUESTIONS

Why is the harm here not analogous to harm that the court has accepted as irreparable in the past? If the plaintiff had claimed its harms weren't quantifiable, would it have risked losing standing? (See Chapter 7.) What should plaintiff have argued, and what evidence would support its claims?

IDT is, historically, a bit of an outlier. Many courts that find likely success on the merits are likely to accept the argument that, though some measure of damages may ultimately be provable, the actual harm from false advertising is so hard to measure that a finding of irreparable harm is justified. *See, e.g.*, Eastman Chem. Co. v. Plastipure, Inc., 969 F. Supp. 2d 756 (W.D. Tex. 2013), *aff'd*, 775 F.3d 230 (5th Cir. 2014). But courts may be rethinking this idea in the digital age. *See, e.g.*, Carson Optical, Inc. v. Alista Corp., 800 Fed. Appx. 48 (Mem) (2d Cir. 2020) (online sales can be tracked perfectly, so financial harm from online false advertising is not irreparable).

Likelihood of Success on the Merits. The evaluation of the likelihood of a plaintiff's success on the merits essentially comes down to whether the plaintiff can show that the advertising claims, as understood by consumers, are false or misleading.

Balancing the Hardships. In evaluating this factor, the court compares the plaintiff's potential injury if an injunction is denied with the defendant's potential injury if an injunction is granted. An injunction that simply prevents the defendant from continuing to advertise falsely is generally not viewed by courts as a hardship for the defendant, as the defendant should be following that practice anyway.

A court may reject a proposed injunction if it would have too harsh an effect on the defendant—for example, if defendant is a small company or a company attempting to enter a new market. In *Abbott Laboratories v. Mead Johnson & Co.*, 971 F.2d 6 (7th Cir. 1992), for example, the parties marketed competing oral rehydration solutions for infants. The court held that the name of the defendant's product, Ricelyte, was misleading because, although it was derived from rice, it did not actually contain rice or rice carbohydrates. The court did not grant plaintiff its requested injunction requiring a recall of any product bearing the misleading labels. The court concluded that forcing the product off the market entirely—which would have been the effect of the proposed injunction—was too harsh a remedy. The Court of Appeals reversed. Although it agreed that a recall was too harsh, it directed the district court to fashion a less-drastic remedy, such as directing the defendant to cease propounding the false claims and to issue corrective advertising and brochures.

As this example illustrates, a plaintiff should be careful in framing its request for relief to avoid the appearance of overreaching. By the same token, if a defendant cannot defeat preliminary injunctive relief entirely, it may be able to narrow the relief granted by pointing to the hardships that would be imposed if the precise relief requested were granted or by offering less-drastic alternatives.

Public Interest. The public interest generally at issue is the public's right not to be deceived or confused by false advertising. This argument can be made by a plaintiff in virtually any case seeking to enjoin false advertising. The public interest factor, however, may be particularly compelling where public health and safety are at stake, especially that of children.

Defendants also can assert a First Amendment-backed public interest in the continued dissemination of advertising that provides consumers with accurate information and legitimate product choices. This factor may also help defendants if granting an injunction would deny the public access to a useful or innovative product. Abbott Labs. v. Mead Johnson & Co., 971 F.2d 6 (7th Cir. 1992) (recalling misleadingly named oral electrolyte solution "would disserve the public interest" because it "is a safe and effective product whose presence in the market has promoted the public welfare by focusing attention upon [oral electrolyte] products and increasing their use.").

B.   Permanent Injunctive Relief

The issues involved in permanent injunctive relief are similar to those attending a preliminary injunction, except that by definition, a violation of the law has been established—and that makes a big difference. Consider how the court treats the adjudicated false advertiser in the following case.

PBM PRODUCTS, LLC V. MEAD JOHNSON & CO., 2010 WL 957756 (E.D. VA. 2010)

. . . In April 2009, store-brand infant formula producer PBM Products, LLC and PBM Nutritionals, LLC (collectively "PBM") sued "name-brand" infant formula producer Mead Johnson & Co. over a Mead Johnson advertisement that PBM asserted violated the Lanham Act. During a seven day jury trial, held on November 2–10, 2009, the jury was asked to evaluate whether four specific claims made in the Mead Johnson mailer communicated certain false or misleading messages concerning store-brand infant formulas, such as PBM's. Two of the four claims were express claims—the Mailer stated that (1) "mothers who buy store brand infant formula to save baby expenses are cutting back on nutrition compared to

[Mead Johnson's] Enfamil" and (2) "only Enfamil has been clinically proven to improve infants' mental and visual development." Relying on consumer survey evidence, PBM contended that the Mailer also impliedly communicated two false and misleading claims: that (1) "Enfamil contains two important fatty acids, DHA and ARA, and that PBM's store brand infant formulas do not" and (2) "Enfamil has been clinically tested against and shown to be superior to PBM's formula with respect to brain and eye development in infants."

The Jury Verdict Sheet asked, "Has PBM established, by a preponderance of the evidence, that Mead Johnson engaged in false advertising in violation of the Lanham Act?" The jury answered in the affirmative and awarded PBM $13.5 million in damages.

On December 1, 2009, this Court granted the injunctive relief sought by PBM. The Order stated, in relevant part:

> (1) Mead Johnson is immediately enjoined and restrained, directly and indirectly, and whether alone or in concert with others, including any agent, employee, representative, subsidiary, or affiliate of Mead Johnson, from doing any of the following:
>
>> (A) publishing or circulating any advertisement, promotional material, or other literature that bears any designation, description, or representation concerning PBM's infant formula that is false, including that, "It may be tempting to try a less expensive store brand, but only Enfamil LIPIL is clinically proven to improve brain and eye development," or "There are plenty of other ways to save on baby expenses without cutting back on nutrition," or from implying the same.
>>
>> (B) making any false statement or representation concerning PBM's infant formula that is false, including that, "It may be tempting to try a less expensive store brand, but only Enfamil LIPIL is clinically proven to improve brain and eye development," or "There are plenty of other ways to save on baby expenses without cutting back on nutrition," or from implying the same.
>
> (2) Mead Johnson is DIRECTED to retrieve any and all advertisements, promotional materials or other literature containing the aforementioned assertions, claims, or allegations regarding PBM's store brand formula from the public forum.
>
> (3) This Order shall remain in full force until such time as this Court specifically orders otherwise.

Over the weeks since that injunction was issued, the parties have wrangled over the validity, scope, and effect of the injunction and have filed a number of motions now before the Court. . . .

II. DISCUSSION

Mead Johnson seeks to vacate and amend the injunction because (1) the Court failed to articulate the reasons for issuing the injunction, as is required by *eBay, Inc. v. MercExchange, LLC*, and (2) the scope of the injunction exceeds the bounds of the jury's verdict and the record. For its part, PBM has filed motions to modify and enforce the injunction. These motions create two issues the Court must now address: (1) whether an injunction should be entered at all and (2) if an injunction is entered, what should be its scope. Each issue is addressed below.

A. Propriety of Entering an Injunction

Federal courts have the power to enjoin behavior that is found to be false or misleading under the Lanham Act. 15 U.S.C. § 1116(a). Before an injunction may be issued, the party seeking the injunction must demonstrate that (1) it has suffered an irreparable injury; (2) remedies available at law are inadequate; (3) the balance of the hardships favors the party seeking the injunction; and (4) the public interest would not be disserved by the injunction. A decision to grant or deny a permanent injunction is reviewed for abuse of discretion. Here, each of the required elements favors PBM.

First, the Court observes that "the irreparable harm prong can be satisfied 'upon a demonstration that the competitor's advertising tends to mislead consumers.'" Consequently, the jury's verdict in favor of PBM presumptively satisfies the irreparable injury requirement. Moreover, trial testimony by representatives of both parties established that in addition to lost sales, false advertising also inflicts substantial harm on a company's reputation and goodwill.

Second, "[d]amages to reputation and goodwill are not items that are easily measured by a legal calculation of damages." Thus, while Mead Johnson is correct that it appears the jury awarded PBM some future damages, the Court disagrees with Mead Johnson's conclusion that an award of future damages indicates that monetary damages are an adequate and sufficient award in this case. The monetary judgment against Mead Johnson compensates PBM for harm that flowed from the Mailer, an injunction properly prevents Mead Johnson from infecting the marketplace with the same or similar claims in different advertisements in the future. Mead Johnson asserts, though, that the Mailer is no longer in circulation and it has not made any indication that it will continue to make those claims in future advertisements. It is that uncertainty, however, that makes an injunction all the more appropriate as preventing the necessity of multiple suits is a classic justification for finding common law remedies inadequate.

Third, when faced with the question of whether an injunction should be entered at all, an evaluation of the resulting hardships favors PBM. Mead Johnson simply has no equitable interest in perpetuating the false and misleading claims in the Mailer. Mead Johnson's main contentions concern the nature of injunctive relief, not whether that relief should be granted in the first instance, and therefore do not mandate a different conclusion.

Lastly, the public interest heavily favors injunctive relief in this case. It is self-evident that preventing false or misleading advertising is in the public interest in general. False or misleading messages concerning a matter of public health, such as the nutritional qualities of infant formula, makes that conclusion especially true in this case. Moreover, allowing false or misleading advertising to continue to seep into the public's discourse on the relative benefits of name brand versus store brand formula would undermine, rather than promote, the Lanham Act's goal of protecting consumers. Accordingly, the Court finds that the *eBay* factors each weigh in favor of PBM and therefore an injunction is appropriate in this case.

B. Scope of an Injunction

The parties also disagree over the scope of any available injunctive relief. Mead Johnson claims that because the general verdict entered by the jury did not specify which of the four statements in the Mailer the jury found false or misleading, the injunction must be limited to the entire Mailer or "other advertisements not colorably different from the Mailer." PBM responds by claiming that the Court should enjoin the two express as well as the two implied claims in the Mailer because such a ruling would be supported by the record and not inconsistent with the jury's general verdict.

Rule 65(d) of the Federal Rules of Civil Procedure requires that an injunction "state its terms specifically" and "describe in reasonable detail . . . the act or acts restrained or required." The type of injunctive relief granted "rests within the equitable discretion" of the district court. While that discretion is constrained by a jury's general verdict under the doctrine of collateral estoppel, district courts can nevertheless make factual findings to support equitable relief so long as those findings are not inconsistent with factual findings essential to the jury's verdict.

Based on the parties' arguments and a review of the pleadings and trial transcripts, the Court will enjoin Mead Johnson from distributing the Mailer or any advertisement not colorably different from the Mailer. Although PBM would like the Court to specifically enjoin the implied claims, the Court finds that an injunction applicable to the Mailer or anything similar sufficiently encompasses the implied claims made in the Mailer.

As was done in the original injunction, the Court will also specifically enjoin the two express claims made in the Mailer. Mead Johnson is correct that the general verdict did not specify if the jury concluded that the express claims that (1) store bought brands represent a cut back on nutrition and (2) only Enfamil is clinically proven to improve brain and eye development in infants are false or misleading. But the Court now concludes that the record supports an injunction including the express claims and that such an injunction would not be inconsistent with the jury's verdict. . . .

The original injunction also included a requirement that Mead Johnson retrieve the offending Mailer from the "public forum." PBM and Mead Johnson agree that the Mailer was sent to consumers' homes and thus such a requirement would be futile. PBM, however, requests that the injunction apply to the four claims made in the Mailer and that the retrieval requirement apply to any advertising or promotional material containing those claims. PBM adds that if retrieval is not possible, a sticker should be placed over the offending portions of any label. Mead Johnson has stated the Mailer is no longer distributed and that it is not making three of the claims in the Mailer at all, however, it has continued to make the "only Enfamil Lipil is clinically proven" claim. Mead Johnson, via an affidavit, also notes that this claim is on all of its labels and that retrieving them would cost millions of dollars and would disrupt the entire supply of infant formula in the United States. Placing a sticker, Mead Johnson states, would also cost millions of dollars. A retrieval or stickering requirement would significantly alter the balance of the hardships and thus the Court declines to impose those conditions on Mead Johnson. The injunction does apply, however, to all advertising or promotional material or statements going forward.

Lastly, PBM wants the Court to require Mead Johnson to send corrective advertising to all individuals in Mead Johnson's Enfamil Family Beginnings database stating that the four claims stated in the Mailer are false or misleading. Although the Court acknowledges the reputational harm that false messages can inflict, PBM is not entitled to an order requiring Mead Johnson to issue corrective advertising because it did not seek that remedy in its complaint and has not done any prospective corrective advertising of its own, suggesting that the desire for this remedy arose only after it obtained a favorable verdict. Moreover, the jury's award included damages for future harm from the Mailer, which encompasses the effect the Mailer had on those that received it. Thus, the request for corrective advertising is denied.

NOTES AND QUESTIONS

Why should the court care if it costs the defendant "too much" to remediate the harm it created? After all, those damages are proximately caused by the falsity. Wouldn't they serve as a good deterrent for other advertisers' wrongdoing?

Injunctions in Consumer Class Actions. Defendants sometimes argue that consumers can't get injunctive relief requiring ads to be changed because Article III requires plaintiffs to have standing for every type of relief sought, and a named plaintiff is by definition aware of the deception and can't be harmed again by the continuation of the false advertising in which she no longer believes. The Ninth Circuit has rejected this argument, at least as a categorical rule. *See* Davidson v. Kimberly–Clark Corp., 889 F.3d 956 (9th Cir. 2018) (holding that "a previously deceived consumer may have standing to seek an injunction against false advertising or labeling" because "the threat of future harm may be the consumer's plausible allegations that she will be unable to rely on the product's advertising or labeling in the future, and so will not purchase the product although she would like to."); *cf.* Morales v. Kimberly-Clark Corp., 2020 WL 2766050 (S.D.N.Y. May 27, 2020) (declining to apply *Davidson* where the allegedly misleading omission was that the product, a diaper, might cause rashes).

C.   Types of Injunctive Relief

As the *PBM* case suggests, the types of injunctive relief that may be obtained in a false advertising action fall into three broad categories: (1) prohibition of further dissemination of the false material; (2) a requirement that the offender engage in corrective advertising or consumer education to counter the false message presented; and (3) in extraordinary cases, recall or destruction of the product or advertising.

Prohibition on Further Dissemination

For obvious reasons, an order prohibiting further dissemination of the false advertising is the most commonly sought and granted form of injunctive relief. Such an order typically applies to the particular advertising at issue in all formats in which it appeared, such as television, radio and print, and requires that the defendant not make the contested claim in any other advertising.

However, in Lanham Act cases, any such injunction cannot limit a media company if enforcement would interfere with normal publication schedules. The Lanham Act prohibits the issuance of an injunction against the publisher "of a newspaper, magazine, or other similar periodical or an electronic communication containing infringing matter or violating matter" if such an injunction would "delay the delivery of such issue or transmission of such electronic communication after the regular time for such delivery or transmission." 15 U.S.C. § 1114(2)(c).

Fencing-in and Exclusion Orders

A fencing-in order—a remedy available to the FTC but not to private plaintiffs—restricts the defendant from future conduct that is broader than the defendant's present unlawful conduct. It may cover more claims and/or more products than at issue in the litigated case. An exclusion order goes further and bans the defendant from an industry entirely.

Such remedies are prophylactics to prevent future unlawful conduct. Violation of an FTC order can lead to swifter and greater penalties than violation of the FTC Act, even when the covered conduct is the same, which is why the FTC seeks such orders.

In *Telebrands Corp. v. Federal Trade Commission*, 457 F.3d 354 (4th Cir. 2006), the advertiser marketed a wide variety of products, all based on its strategy of free-riding on others' claims. Telebrands violated the FTC Act by advertising a device, the Ab Force; the ads referred to "those fantastic electronic ab belt infomercials on TV" and pointed out that the other belts "promis[e] to get our abs into great shape fast—without exercise." The ads also showed "[f]it, well-muscled models" using the Ab Force but made no other explicit claims. The ALJ found that Telebrands made unsubstantiated weight-loss and muscle-definition claims. As a remedy, the FTC sought an order governing all claims and products advertised by Telebrands.

The FTC's final order required that Telebrands, "in connection with the manufacturing, labeling, advertising, promotion, offering for sale, sale, or distribution of Ab Force, any other EMS device, or *any food, drug, dietary supplement, device, or any other product, service or program*, shall not make any representation, in any manner, expressly or by implication, about weight, inch, or fat loss, muscle definition, exercise benefits, *or the health benefits, safety, performance, or efficacy of any product, service, or program*, unless, at the time the representation is made, [Telebrands] possess[es] and rel[ies] upon competent and reliable evidence, which when appropriate must be competent and reliable scientific evidence, that substantiates the representation" (emphasis added).

The FTC and reviewing courts consider three factors in determining whether a final order reasonably relates to the violation it is intended to remedy: (1) the seriousness and deliberateness of the violation; (2) the ease with which the violative claim may be transferred to other products; and (3) whether the respondent has a history of prior violations. This is a sliding scale; not all three factors must be present to uphold a broad remedy.

In the *Telebrands* case, the violations of the FTC Act were serious, not merely overselling a product basically fit for its advertised purpose. Telebrands lacked any substantiation for the core claims at issue. It also mounted a major, successful, nationwide ad campaign, resulting in over $19 million of sales, an additional reason to find that the violation was serious. The violations were also deliberate. Telebrands wanted to capitalize on other ads claiming extensive benefits for abdominal belts. "Telebrands's assertion that, because it did not explicitly make those same claims in the Ab Force advertisements, it did not intend for consumers to believe that the Ab Force provided those same benefits strains credulity. In fact, Telebrands calculatedly fostered such beliefs through its choice of visual images for the television advertisements." These claims were misleading because, regardless of whether the other devices could deliver the promised benefits, Telebrands lacked substantiation for the Ab Force itself.

Moreover, Telebrands's conduct was easily transferable to other products, including many it already marketed. "Compare and save" was one of its standard marketing tools. "Telebrands deliberately selected a popular product category with frequently advertised comparative products. The product category became popular due, at least in part, to the claims that were subsequently the subject of FTC enforcement action." Telebrands controlled the degree of similarity between the Ab Force and the other devices on the market. "Only Telebrands's imagination and budget would limit its ability to use similar tactics in the future." The order didn't bar compare-and-save marketing, only using that approach to make unsubstantiated claims.

Because of the positive findings on the first two factors, the court found it unnecessary to consider Telebrands's history of prior violations.

Does a fencing-in order raise any First Amendment concerns? What about an exclusion order? *Cf.* POM Wonderful LLC v. FTC, 777 F.3d 478 (D.C. Cir. 2015) (finding that the First Amendment barred a requirement that advertiser possess two randomized clinical trials supporting health claims but allowing FTC to require at least one randomized clinical trial).

Recent precedent has suggested that the FTC's orders may sometimes be written too broadly, however. In *LabMD, Inc. v. Federal Trade Commission*, 894 F.3d 1221 (11th Cir. 2018), the court held that a cease-and-desist order directing LabMD to create and implement a variety of protective measures to improve its data security was too vague to be enforceable: The order required a "comprehensive information security program that is reasonably designed to protect the security, confidentiality, and integrity of personal information collected from or about consumers. . . . Such program . . . shall contain administrative, technical, and physical safeguards appropriate to respondent's size and complexity, the nature and scope of respondent's activities, and the sensitivity of the personal information collected from or about consumers. . . ."). Is "competent and reliable evidence," as required in *Telebrands* and other orders, less vague? Does the overall history of substantiation requirements provide guidance presently lacking for data security?

Corrective Advertising/Consumer Education by the Defendant

As indicated above, both courts and the Federal Trade Commission may order offending advertisers to disseminate advertising designed to correct any misperceptions created by the false advertisement. Corrective advertising is particularly appropriate where the offending advertising has contributed to a public perception of a product that is likely to linger in the public's mind even after the false advertising has ceased.

One famous example of corrective advertising ordered by the FTC involves the mouthwash Listerine. In extensive and repeated television commercials and print advertisements, Warner Lambert claimed that its Listerine mouthwash combatted sore throats and other symptoms of the common cold. The FTC determined that the advertisements, which had run in various forms since Listerine was first introduced in 1879, were false, and it ordered Listerine to cease the offending advertising. To help correct the misimpressions created in nearly a century's worth of false ads, the FTC also required Warner Lambert to include the statement "Listerine will not help prevent colds or sore throats or lessen their severity" in the next $10 million of advertising it ran. *See* Warner-Lambert Co. v. FTC, 562 F.2d 749 (D.C. Cir. 1977).

[Ad: Chicago Tribune, Aug. 26, 1979, w12]

The details of corrective advertising orders vary widely. Normally, such orders will set forth the disclosure required, either in specific wording or by general message and the time period during which the corrective advertising must run or, as an alternative, the minimum amount of money that must be spent on such advertising. *See, e.g.*, Novartis Corp. v. FTC, 223 F.3d 783 (D.C. Cir. 2000) (ordering that corrective advertising "continue for one year and until respondent has expended on Doan's advertising a sum equal to the average spent annually during the eight years of the challenged campaign"); Gillette Co. v. Norelco Consumer Prods. Co., 946 F. Supp. 115, 140 (D. Mass. 1996) (specifying content, type size and timing of corrective portion of advertising). Such specifications are designed to ensure that the corrective disclosures are as effective as possible and are not disseminated in such a way that obscures the intended message.

Orders requiring corrective advertising are less common in Lanham Act cases than in FTC cases; courts often expect Lanham Act plaintiffs to engage in counter-advertising to mitigate their own damages. *See, e.g.,* Eastman Chem. Co. v. Plastipure, Inc., 969 F. Supp. 2d 756 (W.D. Tex. 2013) (declining to order losing defendants to run plaintiff's proposed corrective advertising, given the significant investment plaintiff had already made in correcting the record; "it is unclear what additional effect a digital billboard written by [plaintiff] and posted on Defendants' website will have"), *aff'd,* 775 F.3d 230 (5th Cir. 2014); Irwin Indus. Tool Co. v. Worthington Cylinders Wis., LLC, 747 F. Supp. 2d 568 (W.D.N.C. 2010) (corrective advertising was inappropriate where there was no danger to public health or welfare; plaintiff succeeded on a theory of literal falsity rather than presenting evidence that consumers were actually confused, and the false ads at issue ran a total of four times in one professional publication over two years before trial. Plaintiff had already issued multiple press releases and letters to retail customers describing the lawsuit's outcome.). When a defendant was found liable for deliberate falsity, never attempted to retract any copies of the false video it made and continued to encourage its distributors to use the video, however, the court ordered it to send by first-class mail a copy of the jury's findings in the case to each of the vendors or distributors that received the video. *See* Nat'l Prods., Inc. v. Gamber-Johnson LLC, 734 F. Supp. 2d 1160 (W.D. Wash. 2010).

Orders requiring an advertiser to engage in corrective advertising can be challenged on First Amendment grounds, typically because such orders force it to disseminate statements that it would rather not make. In the case of commercial speech, though, courts have held that the First Amendment does not prohibit the government or the courts "from insuring that the stream of commercial information flow(s) cleanly as well as freely." *See, e.g.,* Castrol Inc. v. Pennzoil Co., 987 F.2d 939 (3d Cir. 1993). Thus, orders requiring corrective advertising have been upheld against constitutional challenge so long as the "restriction inherent in [the] order is no greater than necessary to serve the interest involved." *See, e.g.,* Novartis Corp. v. FTC, 223 F.3d 783 (2d Cir. 2000) (upholding order requiring corrective advertising as advancing a state interest and tailored to that interest).

Some courts sidestep this issue by adding the plaintiff's cost of responsive advertising to the defendant's damages obligation. This allows the plaintiff to control the content of corrective information, releases the defendant from the burden of unwanted speech and ensures that the plaintiff is compensated for advertising costs it would not otherwise have incurred. *See, e.g.,* ALPO Petfoods, Inc. v. Ralston Purina Co., 913 F.2d 958 (D.C. Cir. 1990). But is corrective advertising by the injured competitor, which will likely be seen as self-interested, likely to be as effective at educating consumers as corrective advertising by the false advertiser? Consider the likely burden of monitoring the corrective advertising and the advertiser's incentives to downplay the effects of the disclosure when comparing these two choices.

More generally, when an advertiser has caused the consuming public to believe false information, what are the best ways to fix that? Can you think of other options than the advertiser's corrective advertising or a competitor's counter-advertising? Consider the evidence from Chapter 6 about how hard it is to create an appropriate disclosure. Correcting existing misinformation may be even more challenging, since most people resist updating existing beliefs. *See* Stephan Lewandowsky et al., *Misinformation and Its Correction: Continued Influence and Successful Debiasing*, 13 PSYCHOL. SCI. PUB. INT. 106 (2012).

In the following case, the district court ordered a disclaimer, which is not exactly corrective advertising but has some similarities. Given what you know about disclosures and disclaimers, keep an eye on the reaction of the court of appeals—to what extent is the court of appeals making an empirical assessment, and on what evidence is it based?

TRAFFICSCHOOL.COM, INC. V. EDRIVER INC., 653 F.3D 820 (9TH CIR. 2011)

[Defendants operated a website at DMV.org offering drivers' education and related services. Many people falsely believed that it was an official DMV site, some going so far as to email sensitive personal information about traffic tickets, credit card numbers, and even Social Security numbers to the site. Even police officers were confused. The district court found both likely and actual confusion.]

. . . By way of a remedy, the district court ordered DMV.org to present every site visitor with a splash screen stating, "YOU ARE ABOUT TO ENTER A PRIVATELY OWNED WEBSITE THAT IS NOT OWNED OR OPERATED BY ANY STATE GOVERNMENT AGENCY." Visitors can't access DMV.org's content without clicking a "CONTINUE" button on the splash screen. Defendants argue that the district court abused its discretion by fashioning a "blanket injunction" that's overbroad—i.e., restrains conduct not at issue in plaintiffs' complaint—and violates the First Amendment.

Overbreadth. The district court reasoned that the splash screen was necessary to: (1) "remedy any confusion that consumers have already developed before visiting DMV.org for the first time," (2) "remedy the public interest concerns associated with [confused visitors'] transfer of sensitive information to Defendants," and (3) "prevent confusion among DMV.org's consumers." Defendants argue that the splash screen doesn't effectuate these stated goals. But their only evidence is a declaration from DMV.org's CEO stating that defendants tested several alternative disclaimers and found them to be more effective than the splash screen in preventing consumers from emailing DMV.org with sensitive personal information. To the extent we credit a self-serving declaration, defendants' evidence doesn't prove that the splash screen is ineffective in this respect, and says nothing about whether the alternative disclaimers serve the other two interests identified by the district court. Defendants haven't carried their "heavy burden" of showing that their alternative disclaimers reduce DMV.org's likelihood of confusing consumers. The scope of an injunction is within the broad discretion of the district court, and the district court here didn't abuse that discretion when it concluded that the splash screen was the optimal means of correcting defendants' false advertising.

First Amendment. Courts routinely grant permanent injunctions prohibiting deceptive advertising. Because false or misleading commercial statements aren't constitutionally protected, such injunctions rarely raise First Amendment concerns.

The permanent injunction here does raise such concerns because it erects a barrier to all content on the DMV.org website, not merely that which is deceptive. Some of the website's content is informational and thus fully protected, such as guides to applying for a driver's license, buying insurance and beating traffic tickets. The informational content is commingled with truthful commercial speech, which is entitled to significant First Amendment protection. The district court was required to tailor the injunction so as to burden no more protected speech than necessary.

The district court does not appear to have considered that its injunction would permanently and unnecessarily burden access to DMV.org's First Amendment-protected content. The splash screen forces potential visitors to take an additional navigational step, deterring some consumers from entering the website altogether. It also precludes defendants from tailoring DMV.org's landing page to make it welcoming to visitors, and interferes with the operation of search engines, making it more difficult for consumers to find the website and its protected content.[6] All of these burdens on protected speech are, under the current injunction, permanent.

The district court premised its injunction on its findings that defendants' "search engine marketing" and "non-sponsored natural listings, including the DMV.org domain name," caused consumers to be confused even before they viewed DMV.org's content [because defendants used terms associated with government entities]. The court also identified specific misleading statements on the website. The splash screen is justified to remedy the harm caused by such practices so long as they continue. But website content and advertising practices can and do change over time. Indeed, the court found that defendants had already "made some changes to DMV.org and how they marketed it."

The splash screen is also justified so long as it helps to remedy lingering confusion caused by defendants' past deception. But the splash screen will continue to burden DMV.org's protected content, even if all remaining harm has dissipated. At that point, the injunction will burden protected speech without justification, thus burdening more speech than necessary.

On remand, the district court shall reconsider the duration of the splash screen in light of any intervening changes in the website's content and marketing practices, as well as the dissipation of the deception resulting from past practices. If the district court continues to require the splash screen, it shall explain the continuing justification for burdening the website's protected content and what conditions defendants must satisfy in order to remove the splash screen in the future. In the alternative, or in addition, the court may permanently

---

[6] Defendants introduced unrebutted evidence that splash screens commonly interfere with the automated "spiders" that search engines deploy to "crawl" the Internet and compile the indexes of web pages they use to determine every page's search ranking. And splash screens themselves don't have high search rankings: Search engines commonly base these rankings on the web page's content and the number of other pages linking to it, and splash screens lack both content and links.

enjoin defendants from engaging in deceptive marketing or placing misleading statements on DMV.org.

NOTES AND QUESTIONS

Examine the splash screen:

How would this fare under the FTC's guidelines for online disclosures? Defendants used to put "Unofficial Guide to the DMV" in their license plate logo, but they removed it. Instead, the disclaimer runs at the very top, a couple of pixels away from the top of the browser window, in grey rather than black text, not near the invitation to click to continue and not near the DMV.org logo, both of which are far more prominent to the eye.

The district court found that the domain name played a key role in the deception. If the splash screen is justified "so long as [the deceptive practices]" continue, won't the splash screen be needed until there is a new domain name?

The remedy of a mandatory splash screen was, as far as your casebook authors are aware, unprecedented. A splash screen can hurt or destroy search engine indexing, substantially reducing the domain name's value. Therefore, even though the district court didn't award any damages (a ruling affirmed on appeal), the mandatory splash screen was potentially far more detrimental.

Should courts order disclaimers more often? When defendants propose them as alternatives to ceasing a type of advertising entirely, how should courts evaluate them? Despite its concern for the First Amendment, the *Edriver* court also emphasized the undesirability of forcing a successful plaintiff to relitigate every small change and thus the need to require the defendant to show that its proposed disclaimer would be effective.

Of course, the *court* didn't have to show that its own mandated disclaimer would actually help consumers. Should proof of effectiveness be required before granting any disclaimer remedy? Does it matter that the alternative is to suppress the speech entirely? One argument in favor of complete suppression: If consumers are truly being deceived, and if disclaimers often don't work, then the "compromise" of a disclaimer is likely to be no compromise at all.

Below is the DMV.org landing page as of June 2015. What do you think of this version?

Performance-Based Remedies? Lauren Willis has argued that affirmative remedies should be expected to get results, so that advertisers have the strongest incentives to fix the problems they've caused. Lauren Willis, *Performance-Based Remedies: Ordering Firms to Eradicate Their Own Fraud*, 80 L. & CONTEMP. PROBS. 7 (2017). Willis explains:

> For example, to resolve claims of false advertising, beverage seller Naked Juice Company agreed to hire an independent auditor to substantiate the non-GMO statements on its product labels. The class action settlement required the auditor to test samples of the company's raw materials and finished products and examine production sites and ingredient suppliers' supply chains for three years. If performed well, audits do two things. First, they better ensure that the defendant will obey the specific injunctive terms of the decree. Second, they internalize a substantial portion of the costs incurred due to defendant's violation of the law by having the defendant, rather than the taxpayer, bear monitoring costs. Given the opacity of internal firm practices and the limited resources and expertise of enforcement agencies, independent third-party audits are essential.

> To meet the challenge of twenty-first-century fraud, courts and enforcement agencies must adopt the same performance-based approaches firms now use to hone fair sales and fraud. Two are advocated here: confusion injunctions and consequences injunctions. Confusion injunctions prohibit firms that have unfairly, deceptively, or abusively exploited customer confusion from continuing to do so. Consequences injunctions prohibit firms from continuing to unfairly, deceptively, or abusively

inflict ill consequences on their customers. Defendants must demonstrate compliance with confusion and consequences injunctions through customer audits—random sample testing by independent third-party experts hired by the defendant firm to determine whether the firm's customers remain deceived about their transactions with the firm or are still suffering ill consequences from the firm's practices. Defendants must substantially eradicate the customer confusion and ill consequences wrought by their fraud or face penalties for violating a court order.

Moreover, substantial reductions in erroneous consumer beliefs are possible when a party with good access to the affected consumers is committed to addressing the problem. An example occurred when Consumer Reports released erroneous information about some children's car seats. The organization's subsequent effort to correct misimpressions among car seat purchasers was quite successful. [Uri Simonsohn, *Lessons From an Oops at Consumer Reports: Consumers Follow Experts and Ignore Invalid Information*, 48 J. MKTG. RES. 1 (2011).]

Do you foresee any objections to Willis's proposal?

Product Recall/Destruction. In extraordinary cases, courts may order the recall and destruction of the physical advertising materials. Such cases are rare, in part because of the remedy's drastic nature and the burden of complying with such an order. It can be appropriate, though, in cases of egregious misconduct or other unusual circumstances. *See* Playskool, Inc. v. Product Dev. Grp., Inc., 699 F. Supp. 1056 (E.D.N.Y. 1988) (toy recall ordered because misleading language on packaging created safety hazard for children).

To ensure that the recall is not overly drastic, some courts specifically allow the recalled materials to be preserved. For example, one court ordered a recall of advertising materials, including the tags used on garments on which the false claims were made, reasoning that, if the defendant were to succeed on the merits, it could reintroduce the recalled material. In that case, the court cited egregious actions by the defendant, noting that the defendant had no evidence to support the claims when it had made them and that the claims were "carelessly or irresponsibly made and that any 'prejudice' which accrues can be considered to be self-inflicted." W.L. Gore & Assoc., Inc. v. Totes, Inc., 788 F. Supp. 800 (D. Del. 1992). Another alternative where false claims are made on packaging is to place stickers over the false claims; while not cheap, it is less expensive than a full recall and may be easier for a court to order. *See* Grpe. SEB USA, Inc. v. Euro-Pro Operating LLC, 2014 WL 2002126 (W.D. Pa. May 15, 2014).

As a result of the First Amendment issues that can be implicated, recalls generally are not used when the false claims are made in published materials such as books and magazines.

D. Defenses to Injunctive Relief in Private Cases

The most-common equitable defenses to injunctive relief include delay or laches, acquiescence, mootness and unclean hands. Invariably, these defenses fail against a government enforcement action. *But cf.* FTC v. Lane Labs-USA, Inc., 624 F.3d 575 (3d Cir. 2010) (considering FTC's years-long delay in informing defendant that it considered defendant to be in violation of consent decree in evaluating whether defendant was entitled to a defense of substantial compliance, though noting that defendant could still be in violation, regardless of its good faith efforts, if the violations were more than technical or inadvertent).

Delay/Laches

Unreasonable delay by a private plaintiff in challenging a false advertisement, often called "laches," will almost always bar a preliminary injunction. It may also bar relief entirely. However, laches as a total defense is rarely favored because of the public interest in avoiding deception.

The Lanham Act itself contains no statute of limitations. As a result, courts typically consider the statute of limitations of analogous state law claims and hold that a claim is entirely barred by laches if the statute has run. *See* Jarrow Formulas, Inc. v. Nutrition Now, Inc., 304 F.3d 829 (9th Cir. 2002) (fifteen-year delay in challenging advertising was unreasonable where state false advertising law provided for three-year statute of limitations).

Laches may bar a claim for injunctive relief where the plaintiff has unreasonably delayed in pursuing a claim and the defendant suffered prejudice due to the delay. In such cases, courts have reasoned that "the 'failure to act sooner undercuts the sense of urgency that ordinarily accompanies a motion for preliminary relief and suggests that there is, in fact, no irreparable injury.'" Tough Traveler, Ltd. v. Outbound Prods., 60 F.3d 964 (2d Cir. 1995).

Even a short delay may be fatal to preliminary relief, especially where a relatively large company is the plaintiff. In *Hansen Beverage Co. v. Innovation Ventures, LLC*, 2008 WL 4492644 (S.D. Cal. 2008), Hansen claimed that 5-Hour Energy's name was false and misleading. Hansen's president indicated that he learned of the claims one month before filing suit. But Hansen's awareness of the energy shot market, in which 5-Hour Energy is a market leader, "must have" predated the lawsuit by "at least several months." This was too much delay.

Courts may, however, grant preliminary relief if a delay is attributable to plaintiff's efforts to investigate the offending activity or settlement negotiations between the parties. *See, e.g.*, W.L. Gore & Assoc., Inc. v. Totes, Inc., 788 F. Supp. 800 (D. Del. 1992) (four-month delay in filing from the discovery of the false claims was not unreasonable, where the plaintiff used that time to investigate the claims and try to negotiate with the defendant). Courts may excuse delay if the defendant made representations that lulled the plaintiff into a false sense of security. Similarly, if the defendant has changed its advertising campaign incrementally over time, a court may find that this "progressive encroachment" excuses the delay. For example, where a defendant incrementally changed its advertising over two years, the plaintiff lacked clear notice of when the line had been crossed, and laches did not bar a preliminary injunction. W.L. Gore, *supra*.

Plaintiffs may also avoid a laches defense by showing that their claims weren't complete earlier, for example, because harm hadn't yet materialized. *See* Star-Brite Distributing, Inc. v. Gold Eagle Co., 2016 WL 4470093 (S.D. Fla. Jan. 25, 2016).

A successful laches defense to a permanent injunction requires the defendant to show that "assertion [now] of a claim available some time ago would be 'inequitable' in light of the delay in bringing that claim" and that the defendant "has changed his position in a way that would not have occurred if the plaintiff had not delayed." One court thus rejected a false advertising claim brought against Turtle Wax—claiming that the product name was misleading because the product contained no wax—where the plaintiff had "permitted Turtle Wax's advertising and the development of its products to go unchecked for well over a ten- to twenty-year period." The court determined that Turtle Wax had suffered prejudice because, had plaintiff "pressed its claims in a timely manner, Turtle Wax certainly could have invested its time and money in other areas or simply renamed its products." Hot Wax, Inc. v. Turtle Wax, Inc., 191 F.3d 813 (7th Cir. 1999).

Since it is an equitable doctrine, a laches defense may not be available if the equities are against it. For example, if the defendant intentionally committed false advertising or if public health or safety concerns override considerations of equity, courts will be reluctant to bar an otherwise valid claim on laches grounds.

Acquiescence

A defendant may defeat a claim for injunctive relief, and Lanham Act damages, by showing that the plaintiff acquiesced in the advertising in question—that is, the plaintiff provided either an express or implied assurance that plaintiff would not object to the advertising—and those assurances prejudiced the defendant.

For example, where a music publisher expressly allowed the Walt Disney Company to represent to the public for many years in the context of film releases that the rendition of Stravinsky's "The Rite of Spring" in "Fantasia" was "full and accurate," the publisher could not challenge that representation when it was made in connection with release of a videotape of the film. *See* Boosey & Hawkes Music Publications v. Walt Disney Co., 145 F.3d 481 (2d Cir. 1998). Similarly, a court rejected a claim of false advertising where the plaintiff approved the advertisement in question in advance. L.S. Heath & Son, Inc. v. AT&T Information Systems, Inc., 9 F.3d 561 (7th Cir. 1993).

Mootness

When there's no reasonable expectation that the false advertising will resume, injunctive relief may be moot. *See* American Express Travel Related Servs. Co., Inc. v. Mastercard Int'l Inc., 776 F. Supp. 787 (S.D.N.Y. 1991).

Unclean Hands

An unclean hands defense has three elements: (1) the plaintiff intended to engage in inequitable conduct; (2) the plaintiff was engaged in inequitable conduct when it filed the suit; and (3) that plaintiff's inequitable conduct is substantially related to the issues in the litigation, such as plaintiff's own false advertising concerning a related claim. Substantial relation is often a barrier to success of an unclean hands defense. For example, the defense failed in a lawsuit over an ice cream advertisement suggesting that the product was from Sweden—but was actually domestically produced—where the challenger had engaged in similar advertising tactics because that wasn't sufficiently related to the advertiser's own allegedly false advertising. Häagen-Dazs, Inc. v. Frusen Glädjé Ltd., 493 F. Supp. 73 (S.D.N.Y. 1980).

Similarly, in *TrafficSchool.Com, Inc. v. Edriver, Inc.*, 653 F.3d 820 (9th Cir. 2011), discussed *supra*, the defendants argued that plaintiffs were guilty of unclean hands because they also registered domain names using "dmv," including dmvlicenserenewal.com. The district court found that those names were confusing in precisely the same way. Moreover, plaintiffs tried to advertise on DMV.org, running test ads on the site and negotiating with defendants for a partnership at precisely the same time as they were also internally planning a campaign of notifying DMVs that DMV.org was causing confusion. Thus, plaintiffs were complicit in the false advertising.

The district court nonetheless reasoned that unclean hands don't necessarily preclude injunctive relief. Injunctions protect the public, and it may be better to remedy one wrong than leave two wrongs unaddressed.

On appeal, the court of appeals held that the finding of unclean hands was clearly erroneous. Plaintiffs' registrations of DMV domain names and attempts to advertise on DMV.org were not the required "clear, convincing evidence" that "plaintiff[s'] conduct [wa]s inequitable" and "relate[d] to the subject matter of" their false advertising claims. First, registration of a domain name isn't unclean hands until there's a website that confuses consumers. And plaintiffs' ads on DMV.org ran for just six hours, a de minimis period of time. There was no evidence of actual deception caused by plaintiffs' advertising. Though an internal email from plaintiffs recommended an "[i]f you can't join 'em, shut 'em down approach" to DMV.org, bad intentions that weren't put into effect weren't unclean hands. "[U]sing litigation to shut down a competitor who uses unfair trade practices is precisely what the Lanham Act seeks to encourage."

This stringent requirement of a tight relationship between plaintiff's inequitable conduct and defendant's false advertising reinforces the idea that false advertising injunctions protect the public.

However, a court did allow an unclean hands defense to proceed where POM Wonderful (POM) sued Coca-Cola for selling a "Pomegranate Blueberry Flavored 100% Juice Blend" with very, very little pomegranate or blueberry juice in it. The court explained that "the relevant inquiry is 'not [whether] the plaintiff's hands are dirty, but [whether] [s]he dirtied them in acquiring the right [s]he now asserts, or [whether] the manner of dirtying renders inequitable the assertion of such rights against the defendants.'" POM's health claims allegedly created the demand for pomegranate juice. POM alleged that consumers were confused into thinking they were getting healthy pomegranate-blueberry juice when they were really mostly getting "less healthy" apple and grape juices. Coca-Cola responded that the health benefits were unsubstantiated, which violated the FTCA (a finding that had been recently affirmed by the D.C. Circuit). POM's unsubstantiated claims were directly related to the conduct POM alleged had harmed it, even though Coca-Cola wouldn't have been entitled to bring a claim under the FTCA. *See* POM Wonderful LLC v. Coca Cola Co., 166 F. Supp. 3d 1085 (C.D. Cal. 2016).

In another case, the plaintiff's own practice of manipulating review sites to make them seem unbiased constituted unclean hands as to the defendant's misrepresentation of its website's independence, but not as to the defendant's specific biased review of the plaintiff's addiction treatment services or the defendant's misrepresentations of how it wrote reviews; the plaintiff's own supposedly independent websites weren't sufficiently related to those misrepresentations. Even though the defendant willfully violated the law in misrepresenting that it was an independent third party, plaintiff's unclean hands precluded any monetary disgorgement for that violation. Grasshopper House, LLC v. Clean & Sober Media LLC, 394 F. Supp. 3d 1073 (C.D. Cal. 2019).

Lack of Standing in Consumer Claims

A number of courts have denied injunctive relief in consumer-protection class-action cases on the ground that a named plaintiff has no standing to seek injunctive relief, since by definition she now realizes she was fooled and she won't be fooled again. Article III standing must be assessed per remedy sought, and the named plaintiff must have that standing; it follows that injunctive relief claims must be dismissed. Recently, courts applying California law have modified this rule when the plaintiff plausibly alleges that she would like to buy a properly advertised product, but that her ongoing inability to trust the advertising inflicts an ongoing injury on her. Davidson v. Kimberly–Clark Corp., 889 F.3d 956 (9th Cir. 2018).

2. Money Awards

A. Monetary Remedies in FTC Actions

The FTC can seek redress for consumers or disgorgement of the defendant's ill-gotten gains, and it often does so when it finds a violation. (State attorneys general often proceed similarly). Given that the FTC targets the most-exploitative schemes, multimillion-dollar awards are not uncommon. In October 2016, the FTC received a $1.3 billion judgment, at the time the largest in its history, based on deceptive payday-lending schemes. In the same year, it received court approval for a settlement of up to over $11 billion with Volkswagen based on Volkswagen's sale of cars with secret "defeat devices" to evade emissions requirements. In 2019, Facebook agreed to a $5 billion penalty, based in part on violations of a previous consent order, related to its data-sharing/privacy practices and its misleading claims about those practices. *See United States v. Facebook, Inc.*, No. 19-cv-02184 (D.D.C. Jul. 24, 2019) (stipulated order and judgment). (Two dissenting Commissioners thought that Facebook unjustly bought freedom to do as it liked with our data and underpaid given the benefits it received from ignoring user privacy/falsely reassuring users about privacy.)

When the FTC litigates instead of obtaining a consent decree, it generally seeks monetary redress for consumers as part of a permanent injunction. *See* 15 U.S.C. § 53(b). To get the full amount due, it may pursue "relief defendants," people or entities who are in possession of money derived from the Section 5 violation, although they did not participate in it. Banks and spouses are the usual targets, though anyone to whom a gratuitous transfer has been made by a person who did engage in a Section 5 violation can be a relief defendant. *See* FTC v. LeadClick Media, LLC, 838 F.3d 158 (2d Cir. 2016) (payment of valid intercorporate debt was not a gratuitous transfer, so the corporate parent was not a valid relief defendant).

Seeking equitable monetary relief for consumers under Section 53(b) avoids Section 57(b), which explicitly authorizes consumer redress under the FTCA but only following both an administrative proceeding in which the FTC obtains a cease-and-desist order from an ALJ and a court case. Specifically, after such a proceeding, the FTC must go to federal court to either (1) seek penalties for any violation of the cease and desist order, 15 U.S.C. § 45(b), or (2) seek penalties or other equitable relief based on a showing that "the act or practice to which the cease and desist order relates is one which a reasonable man would have known under the circumstances was dishonest or fraudulent," 15 U.S.C. § 57b.

Given the utility of proceeding directly to federal court, the FTC defends its present practices. In the past, courts have given the FTC wide discretion in determining appropriate remedies, including consumer restitution (redress). *See, e.g.*, Federal Trade Commission v. Ross, 743 F.3d 886 (4th Cir. 2014) (explaining then-unanimity among circuits that Section 53(b) allows monetary redress).

However, recent court decisions have the potential to change the picture substantially in two key ways: the availability of federal courts to the FTC at all and the availability of restitution as a remedy for consumers. As to the first: *Federal Trade Commission v. Shire ViroPharma, Inc.*, 917 F.3d 147 (3d Cir. 2019), held that Section 53(b) was unavailable if the offending conduct has ended because the agency no longer has "reason to believe" that a defendant "is violating" or "is about to violate" any provision of law enforced by the FTC, as required by the statute; likely recurrence was not sufficient if the violation is not impending. *See also* Federal Trade Comm'n v. Nudge, 430 F. Supp. 3d 1230 (D. Utah 2019) (holding that, because one of the named parties was part of a common enterprise and continued to provide services to further the fraud, it was "about to violate" the law even if it had stopped its own marketing).

As to the second, *Federal Trade Commission v. Credit Bureau Center, LLC*, 937 F.3d 764 (7th Cir. 2019), rejected availability of restitution as an equitable remedy for consumers under Section 53(b). *See also* J. Howard Beales III & Timothy J. Muris, *Striking the Proper Balance: Redress under Section 13(b) of the FTC Act*, 79 ANTITRUST L.J. 1 (2013) (criticizing use of Section 53(b) to seek monetary relief). The FTC has received certiorari in the *Credit Bureau* case and another companion case. AMG Capital Management, LLC v. Federal Trade Comm'n, No. 19-508 (granted Jul. 9, 2020); Federal Trade Commission v. Credit Bureau Center, LLC, No. 19-825 (granted Jul. 9, 2020). The Supreme Court's recent decision in *Liu v. Securities & Exchange Commission*, No. 18–1501 (Jun. 22, 2020), resolved a similar question in favor of another agency with similar statutory powers albeit differing statutory wording. *Liu* held that a disgorgement award that does not exceed a wrongdoer's net profits and is awarded for victims constitutes "equitable" relief. *Liu* also indicated, however, that restitution may only be awarded to the extent that the specific defendant actually profited. Joint and several liability for restitution may thus be inappropriate unless the defendants acted as "partners" in wrongdoing, but the Court did not set out the full contours of any rule.

The FTC has suggested that Congress enact legislation granting it clear authority to seek permanent injunctions without the requirement that a defendant "is violating, or is about to violate" the law; express permission to seek monetary relief, including restitution and disgorgement; and a ten-year statute of limitations.

Because the FTC works from a premise of disgorgement/consumer redress, it can have an easier time than a private party would showing the damages it had suffered. In the following case, the defendants' gross receipts were much easier to establish than their net profits; defendants wanted the award to reflect significant deductions from gross receipts. The court was not impressed.

FEDERAL TRADE COMMISSION V. DIRECT MARKETING CONCEPTS, INC., 624 F.3D 1 (1ST CIR. 2010)

. . . Turning now to the issue of damages, the Defendants begin by arguing that damages for deceptive advertising are limited to actual profits, not gross receipts. If this were so, then at least part of the district court's damages award would be erroneous. However, the law allows for broad discretion in fashioning a remedy for deceptive advertising; many cases uphold rescission (effectively, restoring the parties to pre-sale status) or restitution (under these facts, the same) as appropriate remedies. Thus, consumer loss, as represented by the Defendants' gross receipts, would appear to be an appropriate measure of damages.

Nevertheless, the Defendants ask us to rely on *FTC v. Verity Int'l, Ltd.*, 443 F.3d 48 (2d Cir. 2006), for the proposition that the FTC's remedy is limited to the Defendants' profits rather than their gross receipts. *Verity*'s limited rule does not apply here.

In *Verity*, a series of unrelated, non-party middlemen partook of the proceeds from the defendants' scheme before the defendants themselves got a bite. The court found this payment structure highly relevant to the issue of damages, noting that "in many cases in which the FTC seeks restitution, the defendant's gain will be equal to the consumer's loss" but casting *Verity*'s facts as an exception limited to the situation "when some middleman not party to the lawsuit takes some of the consumer's money before it reaches a defendant's hands." Here, the Defendants seek to inflate *Verity*'s exception so that it overshadows the rule.

We are not persuaded. Because this set of facts lacks the non-party middleman that gave rise to the exception in *Verity*, we will follow the general rule. Here, the Defendants on appeal took in proceeds directly, except for roughly one year when fellow defendant (but non-appellant) Triad processed Coral Calcium orders. The FTC introduced ample evidence of the overall proceeds from Coral Calcium during this period; however, the parties' financial records were in such disarray that the actual split among the parties could not be determined.[12]

The Defendants on appeal now claim that Triad siphoned off the vast majority of the proceeds, leaving them holding an empty bag, but we cannot tell whether this is the case. Because every entity that had received consumer money was a defendant, the district court held that gross receipts were an appropriate measure of damages; because records were unclear as to how much consumer money each defendant received, the district court evenly split the total receipts between DMC and Triad for the time period when Triad acted as a middleman. This was consistent with *Verity* and within the bounds of the district court's discretion in fashioning an equitable remedy.

Thus, the district court committed no error in resting its damages determination on the Defendants' gross receipts rather than their net profits, and we will proceed to review the court's calculation of what those gross receipts actually were. To determine the appropriate amount of damages in deceptive advertising cases, courts apply a burden-shifting scheme. First, the FTC must provide the court with a reasonable approximation of damages.

Both gross receipts and net customer loss are appropriate measures. Once a reasonable approximation of damages has been provided, the defendant has an opportunity to demonstrate that the figures are inaccurate. Any fuzzy figures due to a defendant's uncertain bookkeeping cannot carry a defendant's burden to show inaccuracy. . . .

NOTES AND QUESTIONS

Is the allocation of burdens between the defendant and the FTC sensible? What are the alternatives? Does the risk of suppressing truthful speech matter at all once a court has determined that the defendant advertised falsely?

Should the defendant be able to deduct the value of the product or service it actually delivered, which will often (though not always) be above zero? Historically, courts have been far more generous to the FTC in awarding relief than to competitors or to consumers in class actions. For example, in *Federal Trade Commission v. National Urological Group*, 645 F. Supp. 2d 1167 (N.D. Ga. 2008), the FTC sued the defendants for falsely marketing weight-loss and erectile-performance dietary supplements. The court found injunctive relief and consumer redress appropriate. Defendants made over $15 million in sales. Defendants argued, among other things, that they should get to reduce this amount by sales to customers who reordered the product, who were obviously motivated by actual experience with it. The court disagreed. There was no evidence of what motivated reordering decisions, and the fact that the consumers' (presumably positive) experience may have contributed to the reorders didn't negate the problems with the ads. *See also* FTC v. Lights of Am., Inc., 2013 WL 5230681 (C.D. Cal. Sept. 17, 2013) (no damages offsets for purported benefits conferred by defendant's falsely advertised lamps; also rejecting argument that low rates of returns showed that there was no need for equitable relief).

---

[12] The FTC perhaps ought to have made more of an effort to nail down the details of the parties' finances during discovery. . . . but there is no question that the primary fault lies with the Defendants.

The *National Urological Group* defendants proposed to pay redress directly to purchasers, contacting customers and providing or offering a complete refund. The FTC wanted redress to be deposited into a fund in its name. After consumers were redressed, the FTC would use remaining funds for further equitable relief or pay them into the Treasury as disgorgement. The court had "ample discretion" to choose the FTC's proposal and saw no reason to charge "the purveyors of the deception" with competently and honestly reimbursing consumers. As a result, the court ordered the defendants to pay the entire $15+ million to the FTC.

However, in a contempt case based on claims made about defendant's calcium supplements in violation of a prior FTC consent order, the FTC sought $15 million in gross sales. But the FTC's own expert agreed that the product was a good form of calcium, and the defendant's conduct wasn't willful. The court therefore calculated damages based on the "price premium" commanded by the product. This premium was slightly over 20% of the price; the total price premium was slightly over $800,000, which was ordered refunded to consumers. F.T.C. v. Lane Labs-USA, Inc., 2014 WL 268642 (D.N.J. Jan. 23, 2014). Is this a better approach than full disgorgement?

State Attorneys General Also Seek Monetary Awards. Sometimes acting in concert with the FTC and sometimes on their own, state attorneys general regularly seek both penalties and consumer redress. *See, e.g.*, Jon Brodkin, *Comcast Broke Law 445,000 Times In Scheme To Inflate Bills, Judge Finds*, ARS TECHNICA, Jun. 7, 2019 (reporting on $9.1 million fine plus consumer refunds imposed by judge in Washington state attorney general action on deceptive marketing of service plans).

B.   Monetary Remedies in Private Actions

Since a decision on a preliminary injunction requires an evaluation of eventual likelihood of success on the merits, false advertising cases often settle after the initial decision granting preliminary relief. Thus, relatively few courts reach the issue of damages in private-competitor false advertising cases.

If the case does proceed beyond the preliminary relief stage, the Lanham Act specifically authorizes the award of "(1) defendant's profits, (2) any damages sustained by the plaintiff, and (3) the costs of the action" to a prevailing plaintiff. 15 U.S.C. § 1117(a). The award can in theory be cumulative but not duplicative—that is, for any given sale, the plaintiff can recover its losses or, in appropriate circumstances, the defendant's profits, but not both.

With respect to an award based on defendant's profits, if the court finds the award either inadequate or excessive, the court may in its discretion award an amount the court finds just. An award based on plaintiff's damages, by contrast, permits the court to increase the amount up to three times if needed to achieve a just result, but the court may not reduce the amount. Recovery must be compensatory and not a penalty. This provision confers broad discretion upon courts in assessing and awarding appropriate damages.

Many courts hold that, though literal falsity without evidence of consumer deception can justify an injunction, evidence of consumer deception is required before a damage award is allowed. *See, e.g.*, Bracco Diagnostics, Inc. v. Amersham Health, Inc., 627 F. Supp. 2d 384

(D.N.J. 2009) ("literal falsity, without more, is insufficient to support an award of money damages to compensate for marketplace injury."). Other courts allow presumptions to take the place of specific evidence under certain circumstances, especially willfully false comparative advertising. One court upheld a $19.25 million verdict based on false claims that the plaintiff was a Satanic corporation, using a presumption of actual confusion from the literal falsity of the claims; no further proof of actual confusion was required. Procter & Gamble Co. v. Haugen, 627 F. Supp. 2d 1287 (D. Utah 2008). *But see* Munchkin, Inc. v. Playtex Prods., LLC, 2012 WL 12886205 (C.D. Cal. Oct. 4, 2012) (presumption of harm is only appropriate where comparison is explicit or the market is essentially a binary one split between plaintiff and defendant).

In recent years, plaintiffs have achieved a small but noticeable number of multimillion-dollar verdicts. *See, e.g.*, Boltex Mfg. Co. v. Ulma Piping USA Corp., 2019 WL 5684201 (S.D. Tex. Nov. 1, 2019). Monetary awards thus represent a relatively low-probability but high-risk area for defendants.

Plaintiff's Damages

Courts may award actual damages sustained by the plaintiff. Recoverable damages may include any demonstrable damages suffered by plaintiff, including profits lost by the plaintiff on sales actually diverted to the false advertiser; profits lost by the plaintiff on sales made at prices reduced as a result of the false advertising; quantifiable harm to the plaintiff's goodwill; and amounts expended by plaintiff on corrective advertising designed to combat the false message disseminated by defendant. To receive compensation for expenditures for corrective advertising, the plaintiff must normally demonstrate that the corrective advertising was an actual and reasonable response to defendant's activities, which can be hard to do. *See* First Act Inc. v. Brook Mays Music Co., Inc., 429 F. Supp. 2d 429 (D. Mass. 2006).

Damages calculations rely on specialized testimony about the relevant markets, so it is hard to develop generalizable principles from those cases. In determining the amount of actual damages to award, a court may consider "the difficulty of proving an exact amount of damages from false advertising, as well as the maxim that 'the wrongdoer shall bear the risk of the uncertainty which his own wrong has created.'" ALPO Petfoods, Inc. v. Ralston Purina Co., 913 F.2d 958 (D.C. Cir. 1990).

As noted earlier, the Lanham Act further authorizes a court to "enter judgment, according to the circumstances of the case, for any sum above the amount found as actual damages, not exceeding three times such amount." 15 U.S.C. § 1117(a). These enhanced damages are meant to be compensatory: to ensure that the plaintiff is made whole even if it is difficult to prove all damages with specificity. Although enhanced damages are not supposed to be punitive in nature, some courts have required a showing of especially egregious conduct by defendant before enhancing damages awards. In one of the most-prominent cases involving treble damages, the *U-Haul* court awarded double actual damages based on the "publication of deliberately false comparative claims." As a general matter, however, courts rarely award treble damages.

Defendant's Profits

In addition to any damages sustained by the plaintiff, courts may also award the defendant's profits in appropriate cases. (There is a rule against double counting, however: Plaintiffs can't recover both defendants' profits and their own lost sales from the same sales.) An award of profits is generally justified on the grounds that it will deter similar illegal activity and deprive the defendant of the unjust enrichment obtained as a result of its false advertising. The standards for triggering profit disgorgement are usually higher than those for recovering plaintiff's damages because of the risk that some of defendant's profits were not attributable to plaintiff's losses, thus awarding the plaintiff a windfall (either at the expense of the defendant's legitimate sales or the lost sales of other competitors).

Once disgorgement of profits has been determined to be appropriate, awards can be quite high. In 2018, a jury awarded $16 million in disgorgement to Dyson after finding that competitor SharkNinja falsely advertised that its vacuum was better than Dyson's best-performing vacuum.

In a trademark case, the Supreme Court has interpreted the Lanham Act's provision for awarding defendant's profits "subject to the principles of equity," 15 U.S.C. § 1117(a), as not requiring the plaintiff to show willfulness, though willfulness is generally relevant to whether disgorgement of profits should be awarded. Romag Fasteners, Inc. v. Fossil, Inc., 140 S.Ct. 1492 (2020).

Even after *Romag*, courts may hesitate to award disgorgement where they are unconvinced that the defendant's profits are a good measure of the harm suffered by the plaintiff, especially if the defendant's false advertising might have taken sales from third parties instead of the plaintiff. The Second Circuit has said that relevant factors include: (1) the degree of certainty that the defendant benefited from the unlawful conduct; (2) availability and adequacy of other remedies; (3) the role of a particular defendant in effectuating the wrongful conduct; (4) plaintiff's laches; and (5) plaintiff's unclean hands. *See* Pedinol Pharmacal, Inc. v. Rising Pharms., Inc., 570 F. Supp. 2d 498 (E.D.N.Y. 2008) (when the jury found that both parties engaged in false advertising but awarded the plaintiff only $1 in nominal damages, the defendant/counter-plaintiff's own bad behavior didn't bar an award of profits to it; the plaintiff/counter-defendant was guilty of much-worse conduct); *cf.* Hipsaver Co., Inc. v. J.T. Posey Co., 497 F. Supp. 2d 96 (D. Mass. 2007) (profits may be awarded in Lanham Act cases not only as a rough measure of harm to the plaintiff, but also to avoid unjust enrichment and to deter a willful bad actor; though willfulness is not required, when the rationale for disgorgement is deterrence, and there is no evidence of actual harm, plaintiffs must show willfulness to recover profits).

Although these cases predate *Romag*, the flexibility allowed by "the principles of equity" suggests older cases will continue to be relevant, and willfulness will always assist a plaintiff's case. Planned deception and knowledge of significant consumer confusion will qualify as willfulness. TrafficSchool.com, Inc. v. Edriver Inc., 653 F.3d 820 (9th Cir. 2011). Likewise, a jury could reasonably find willfulness when, although the defendants based their statements on a published scientific paper, they didn't stick to the statements in the paper but rather redesigned a bar chart to denigrate a competitor and added in unsupported conclusions; there was evidence that the principal behind the claims had concluded what the results would be even before any tests were carried out; and one employee even testified that he didn't believe in the tests they used. Eastman Chem. Co. v. Plastipure, Inc., 969 F. Supp. 2d 756 (W.D. Tex. 2013), *aff'd*, 775 F.3d 230 (5th Cir. 2014).

When disgorgement is available, courts use a variety of methods to calculate profits. In the most commonly used method, courts calculate defendant's profits as "the sales defendant enjoyed as a result of its violations, less the costs and deductions attributable to those sales." Gillette Co. v. Wilkinson Sword, Inc., 1992 WL 30938 (S.D.N.Y. 1992). In such cases, the plaintiff is required to prove defendant's sales; the burden then shifts to defendant to prove any cost or deduction claimed. Although courts do not require mathematical precision in calculating profits, they will require a reasonable basis for the calculation, which may be difficult to produce without expert testimony.

In *National Products, Inc. v. Gamber-Johnson LLC*, 734 F. Supp. 2d 1160 (W.D. Wash. 2010), Gamber-Johnson lost a trial over its comparative advertising about the parties' emergency vehicle laptop-mounting systems. Though a jury awarded the plaintiff $10 million in defendant's profits, the court reduced the amount to fewer than $500,000. A jury verdict will be upheld if supported by substantial evidence, but the district court has discretionary power to modify monetary awards "subject to the principles of equity," 15 U.S.C. § 1117(a), and disgorgement is an equitable remedy.

NPI argued that its burden was simply to identify the pool of sales attributable or related to the false advertising and that it had done so by identifying the sales of the falsely advertised goods. The court disagreed. Only some of Gamber-Johnson's customers would have seen the false video. *Cf.* Rexall Sundown, Inc. v. Perrigo Co., 707 F. Supp. 2d 357 (E.D.N.Y. 2010) (in a case where the false advertising appeared on the product itself, the court ruled that the plaintiff must establish only the defendant's sales of the product at issue, while the defendant bears the burden of showing all costs and deductions, including any portion of sales that was not due to the allegedly false advertising); Trilink Saw Chain, LLC v. Blount, Inc., 583 F. Supp. 2d 1293 (N.D. Ga. 2008) (when a defendant "specifically disparages a market newcomer through deliberately false advertisements," the plaintiff's burden was only to show gross sales).[*] Note that, even though only some of Gamber-Johnson's customers would have seen the false video, the court's $500,000 award was not particularly tied to the number who did—it was produced by combining the defendant's estimate of its profits from sales diverted from plaintiff with the plaintiff's higher estimate of defendant's profit margins. This was classic equity: rough justice.

Costs

A prevailing plaintiff in a Lanham Act false advertising case also is entitled to an award of costs incurred in prosecuting the claim. 15 U.S.C. § 1117(a). "Costs," though, does not

---

[*] The Ninth Circuit has also calculated defendant's profits based on the cost of defendant's advertising on the theory that it is reasonable to assume that the defendant derives a benefit at least equal to the amount it spent. U-Haul Int'l, Inc. v. Jartran, Inc., 793 F.2d 1034 (9th Cir. 1986). But this approach is questionable and rarely used. *See* Harper House, Inc. v. Thomas Nelson, Inc., 889 F.2d 197 (9th Cir. 1989).

literally mean all costs of the action; rather, it generally refers to the kinds of statutory costs typically available for a prevailing plaintiff.

Costs typically include such items as printing briefs, court reporter fees for depositions actually used in the trial and filing fees, though the trial court retains discretion in determining what costs will be allowed. In one case, the plaintiff also attempted to recover as costs the expenses of conducting consumer surveys, but the court rejected that. Gillette Co. v. Wilkinson Sword, Inc., 1992 WL 30938 (S.D.N.Y. 1992). *Rimini Street, Inc. v. Oracle USA, Inc.*, 139 S.Ct. 873 (2019), reached a similar conclusion with respect to "costs" in the Copyright Act, plainly dooming any future claims for recovery of litigation expenses such as expert witnesses, e-discovery and jury consulting under the Lanham Act given the similarity of the relevant statutory language.

Unlike an award of attorneys' fees, willful or bad faith conduct is not necessary to get an award of costs.

Punitive Damages

The Lanham Act specifically prohibits recovery of punitive damages—a rule in some tension with the discretion it gives courts with respect to disgorgement of profits where disgorgement is justified on deterrence grounds. *See* 15 U.S.C. § 1117(a).

In contrast, most state statutes governing unfair competition and false advertising authorize such awards where the defendant's conduct was willful or malicious. This is one reason why many complaints for false advertising assert both federal and parallel state causes of action. In one prominent example, the *U-Haul* district court awarded $20 million in punitive damages under a parallel state claim as an alternative to its finding that damages were warranted under plaintiff's Lanham Act claim. Since the Ninth Circuit affirmed the district court's Lanham Act analysis, it did not reach the issue of punitive damages. This is consistent with most courts' requirement that a plaintiff elect either federal or state remedies, rather than being allowed to cumulate them.

Attorneys' Fees

The Lanham Act authorizes awards of attorneys' fees only in "exceptional cases," and even then, such awards are within the discretion of the court. 15 U.S.C. § 1117(a). *See* TrafficSchool.com, Inc. v. Edriver Inc., 653 F.3d 820 (9th Cir. 2011) (attorneys' fees may be available even if plaintiff received no damage award; "[i]t would be inequitable to force plaintiffs to bear the entire cost of enjoining defendants' willful deception when the injunction confers substantial benefits on the public."). Courts also may award attorneys' fees to a prevailing defendant.

One case granting attorneys' fees involved a challenge to tax preparer H&R Block's advertising in connection with its "Rapid Refund" program. In prior disputes, H&R Block had agreed in consent orders entered into with state attorneys general to represent a similar program as providing "loans" to consumers and not as "refunds." In addition, H&R Block had internal studies indicating that the difference between a "refund" and a "loan" was material to the public. Based on this prior history, the court viewed Block's new advertising as an attempt to circumvent consent orders into which it had previously entered and therefore awarded attorneys' fees. JTH Tax, Inc. v. H&R Block Eastern Tax Servs., 28 Fed. Appx. 207 (4th Cir. 2002).

The Supreme Court's decision in *Octane Fitness, LLC v. ICON Health & Fitness, Inc.*, 572 U.S. 545 (2014), which interpreted identically worded portions of the Patent Act, is likely to provide the rules going forward. *See, e.g.*, Sazerac Company, Inc. v. Fetzer Vineyards, Inc., 2017 WL 6059271 (N.D. Cal. Dec. 7, 2017) (adopting *Octane Fitness* standard for Lanham Act claims). Under *Octane Fitness:*

> [A]n "exceptional" case is simply one that stands out from the others with respect to the substantive strength of a party's litigating position (considering both the governing law and the facts of the case) or the unreasonable manner in which the case was litigated. District courts may determine whether a case is "exceptional" in the case-by-case exercise of their discretion, considering the totality of the circumstances [and without any] precise rule or formula for making these determinations.

Relatedly, *Highmark Inc. v. Allcare Health Management System, Inc.*, 572 U. S. 559 (2014), said that appellate courts can change fee awards only for abuse of discretion.

Sovereign Immunity

States and state agencies cannot be sued for false advertising unless they waive their sovereign immunity. College Sav. Bank v. Florida Prepaid Postsecondary Educ. Expense Fund, 527 U.S. 666 (1999).

Insurance Coverage

Standard commercial liability policies often include coverage for "advertising injury." *See generally* Kyle Lambrecht, Note, *The Evolution of the Advertising Injury Exclusion in the Insurance Service Office, Inc.'s Comprehensive General Liability Insurance Policy Forms*, 19 CONN. INS. L.J. 185 (2012). The advertiser's insurance coverage may determine the course of litigation, since the insurer is likely to have deeper pockets but also a greater willingness to settle if it takes over the defense.

Though insurance policies define advertising injury in various ways and often contain various exclusions, generally they provide insurance coverage for a non-publisher defendant who might allegedly disparage, invade the privacy of, "misappropriate . . . advertising ideas" of or otherwise harm someone else through advertising. (Publishers generally secure a separate "media" policy for the business of publishing). Standard exclusions include intentional acts and trademark infringement claims, but each policy must be read carefully.

Insurance law varies by state, but in general, an insurance policy is read broadly in favor of the insured, and the insurer has a duty to defend if the underlying complaint could be read to state a covered claim, even if the facts might ultimately not support that claim. The duty to defend thus is much broader than the duty to indemnify. This is important when, for example, the underlying complaint alleges a willful violation of the Lanham Act. Since the Lanham Act does not require intent, the exclusion for intentional acts does not excuse the insurer of its duty to defend (if the policy otherwise covers a claim), even though the insurer has no duty to indemnify if the advertiser is ultimately found liable for a willful violation.

Nonetheless, insurers routinely deny coverage and any duty to defend, so there is a fair amount of litigation about what constitutes "advertising injury." One issue that has come up repeatedly is whether allegedly false comparative advertising constitutes covered "disparagement." Usually, false positive things said about the advertiser's product will not be considered to have disparaged other parties by implication. *See, e.g.*, Skylink Tech. v. Assurance Co. of America, 400 F.3d 982 (7th Cir. 2005) (an insured's allegedly false claim that its garage-door openers are compatible with underlying plaintiff's garage-door openers was not covered "disparagement"). However, false advertising claims based on direct comparisons that claim superiority to a competitor may trigger advertising-injury coverage, even if the underlying complaint doesn't contain a cause of action styled "disparagement." *See, e.g.*, Winklevoss Consultants v. Fed. Ins. Co., 11 F. Supp. 2d 995 (N.D. Ill. 1998); *cf.* E.piphany v. St. Paul Fire & Marine Ins., 590 F. Supp. 2d 1244 (N.D. Cal. 2008) (disparagement can exist even without directly mentioning the underlying plaintiff negatively but instead through "clear implication," as when an ad claims that underlying defendant has the "only" product suitable for certain use).

Hyundai Motor America v. National Union Fire Insurance Co., 600 F.3d 1092 (9th Cir. 2010), found that "advertising injury" included a patent-infringement suit based on a patented method of advertising. Hyundai's "build your own" online tool let car buyers customize features like color, trim and model to see what the resulting car would look like. Hyundai prevailed against its insurer because the patents covered a marketing method, and thus the alleged patent infringement constituted covered "misappropriation of advertising ideas."

Monetary Remedies for Violations of State Consumer Protection Law

Some states provide for a set amount of statutory damages per violation; others allow recovery of actual damages. Attorneys' fees are also relatively standard.

California is a particularly plaintiff-favorable jurisdiction in some ways, but since it is such a large state and not unrepresentative of other states, it's worth examining how a California court imposes monetary remedies in an ordinary case.

PEOPLE V. SARPAS, 225 CAL. APP. 4TH 1539 (CAL. CT. APP. 2014)

Hakimullah Sarpas and Zulmai Nazarzai operated a scheme by which they promised customers they would obtain loan modifications from lenders and prevent foreclosure of the customers' homes. They operated this scheme through their jointly owned company, Statewide Financial Group, Inc. (SFGI), which did business as U.S. Homeowners Assistance (USHA). Sharon Fasela was, among other things, the office manager of USHA and came up with the key misrepresentation that USHA had a 97 percent success rate. Customers paid

USHA over $2 million but received no services in return. There was no credible evidence that USHA obtained a single loan modification, or provided anything of value, for its customers.

The Attorney General, on behalf of the People of the State of California, commenced this action in July 2009 by filing a complaint against SFGI, USHA, Sarpas, Nazarzai, and Fasela (collectively referred to as Defendants), seeking injunctive relief, restitution, and civil penalties under the California unfair competition law (UCL), Business and Professions Code section 17200 et seq., and the California False Advertising Law (FAL), section 17500 et seq. . . .

In July 2012, following a lengthy bench trial, the trial court issued a judgment and a 19-page statement of decision finding against Defendants. The court permanently enjoined USHA, Nazarzai, Sarpas, and Fasela, and ordered restitution be made to every eligible consumer requesting it, up to a maximum amount of $2,047,041.86. The court found USHA, Sarpas, and Nazarzai to be jointly and severally liable for the full amount of restitution, and Fasela to be jointly and severally liable with them for up to $147,869 in restitution. . . .

Sarpas was the 50-percent owner of SFGI, which did business as USHA. Nazarzai owned the other 50 percent. Sarpas and Nazarzai each received 50 percent of the company profits. From March 2008 to April 2009, Sarpas received $490,000 in profits from SFGI. Sarpas also served as operations manager of SFGI and oversaw the company's day-to-day operations.

Fasela worked as the office manager of SFGI for about one year, ending in July 2009. USHA paid Fasela $2,746 in 2007, $135,358 in 2008, and $11,611 in 2009.

. . . [Among other false claims,] USHA represented it had a 97-percent success rate [in modifying mortgages], that it had a success rate of "over 95 percent," or that USHA never had a case in which a loan modification was not approved. Fasela came up with the 97-percent success rate figure "in the beginning." One customer testified the sales representative guaranteed USHA would obtain a loan modification.

In addition, customers were told to stop making their mortgage payments because doing so would make obtaining a loan modification easier. As a result, customers often suffered ruined credit, additional fees, foreclosure proceedings, and even loss of the home USHA had promised to save.

No credible evidence was presented at trial that USHA ever obtained a loan modification, or did anything of value, for any customer. USHA made no refunds to customers, despite its promises, and despite customer demands. Not only did USHA not have a legal team, it had no attorneys whatsoever working on loan modifications.

Section 17203 authorizes an order of restitution as a remedy for violations of section 17200. In part, section 17203 reads: "The court may make such orders or judgments, . . . as may be necessary to restore to any person in interest any money or property, real or personal, which may have been acquired by means of such unfair competition." Section 17535 likewise authorizes an order of restitution for a violation of section 17500. "The restitutionary remedies of section 17203 and 17535 . . . are identical and are construed in the same manner." . . .

Restitution under the UCL and FAL may be ordered without individualized proof of harm. (In re Tobacco II Cases (2009) 46 Cal.4th 298, 326, 93 Cal.Rptr.3d 559, 207 P.3d 20 [" 'California courts have repeatedly held that relief under the UCL [(including restitution)] is available without individualized proof of deception, reliance and injury' "].)

Because individualized proof of harm was unnecessary, the Attorney General was not required to present testimony from each and every USHA customer for whom restitution and civil penalties were being sought. . . . The Attorney General presented evidence sufficient to support a reasonable inference of deception and harm as to all USHA customers, and, therefore, the restitution and civil penalties as to all USHA customers were lawful.

B. Restitution Is Not Limited to Direct Payment from Victims.

. . . Sarpas and Fasela argue they cannot be ordered to pay restitution absent evidence either one received money directly from USHA customers. Although the trial court found that USHA received over $2 million from customers, Sarpas and Fasela argue neither of them personally received money directly, and "[l]egally, under California law, a defendant who has violated the UCL, cannot be made to restore to a consumer that which he or she never directly received from the consumer." This argument is legally incorrect.

. . . Sarpas and Fasela received money indirectly from customers by having them pay USHA. The customers parted with property in which they had an ownership interest and are entitled to its return. The rule urged by Sarpas and Fasela would allow UCL and FAL violators to escape restitution by structuring their schemes to avoid receiving direct payment from their victims.

Sarpas and Fasela argue that, if Sarpas can be ordered to pay restitution, his share of restitution must be limited to the net profits he received from USHA. We disagree. "Where restitution is ordered as a means of redressing a statutory violation, the courts are not concerned with restoring the violator to the status quo ante. The focus instead is on the victim. 'The status quo ante to be achieved by the restitution order was to again place the victim in possession of that money.'" . . .

Sarpas and Nazarzai "drained substantial amounts of money from the corporation" and there was no evidence that either of them put funds into the corporation. Sarpas and Fasela do not challenge those findings. Based on those findings and the evidence presented at trial, the trial court could exercise its equitable discretion to conclude USHA, Sarpas, and Nazarzai acted as a single enterprise for the purpose of ordering restitution under the UCL and the FAL . . .

Pursuant to sections 17206 and 17536, the trial court imposed civil penalties against USHA, Sarpas, and Nazarzai, jointly and severally, in the amount of $2,047,041, and imposed additional civil penalties against Fasela, USHA, Sarpas, and Nazarzai, jointly and severally, in the amount of $360,540. In setting the amount of civil penalties, the court considered (1) the purpose of civil penalties to punish and deter; (2) Defendants' targeting of the elderly and the disabled; (3) the "enormous" number of UCL and FAL violations committed by Defendants; and (4) evidence establishing there were 1,259 "payors" checks deposited into USHA accounts.

Section 17206, subdivision (a) states in part that "[a]ny person who engages, has engaged, or proposes to engage in unfair competition shall be liable for a civil penalty not to exceed two thousand five hundred dollars ($2,500) for each violation." Section 17536, subdivision (a) states in part that "[a]ny person who violates any provision of this chapter shall be liable for a civil penalty not to exceed two thousand five hundred dollars ($2,500) for each violation." UCL penalties may be increased by up to $2,500 per violation if the victim is elderly or disabled. Under both section 17206, subdivision (b) and section 17536, subdivision (b), the court should consider, in assessing the amount of civil penalties, one or more of the following: "the nature and seriousness of the misconduct, the number of violations, the persistence of the misconduct, the length of time over which the misconduct occurred, the willfulness of the defendant's misconduct, and the defendant's assets, liabilities, and net worth." . . .

As we have emphasized, individualized proof of each and every UCL and FAL violation is not required; from the evidence presented at trial, the trial court could draw the reasonable inference Sarpas and Fasela committed hundreds, if not thousands, of UCL and FAL violations. In this regard, the trial court found: "Defendants made false and misleading statements to each and every consumer who entered into a contract with Defendants. . . . "

Sarpas and Fasela argue the amount of civil penalties is excessive in light of their respective financial situations. A court should consider a defendant's assets, liabilities, and net worth in calculating the amount of civil penalties. But, "evidence of a defendant's financial condition, although relevant, is not essential to the imposition of the statutory penalties, making the issue of a defendant's financial inability a matter for the defendant to raise in mitigation." Sarpas did not testify at trial. Fasela testified some about her financial situation, but she presented no documentary evidence in support, and the trial court found her testimony on the subject was not credible. As to Sarpas, all the civil penalties are affirmed.

. . . The trial court offered no explanation or computation for coming up with $360,540, despite requests from Fasela to make factual findings. . . . We therefore will strike the civil penalties awarded against Fasela only and remand with directions to recalculate the amount of civil penalties under sections 17206 and 17536.

NOTES AND QUESTIONS

Is it fair to order restitution for every consumer without individualized proof of harm? In fraud cases (like this one) where consumers received nothing of value, the answer seems easy: of course. But what if consumers had received a product or service worth less than they paid for it but still perhaps worth something? What if some of them were satisfied with the product or service? *See also* State v. Minn. School of Bus., Inc., 935 N.W.2d 124 (Minn. 2019) (ordering restitution for non-testifying consumers, who could be deemed to have been deceived in the same way as testifying consumers by misrepresentations about jobs for which for-profit school would qualify them).

In another case, a California trial court noted that "although the purchasers did not receive entirely what they bargained for . . . these Class members did benefit from the quality, usefulness, and safety of these multi-purpose tools [that were falsely advertised as made in the USA]," and it would be unfair to return to them the entire purchase price. Though its ultimate award was reversed on appeal, the court of appeals did not disagree with this reasoning. Colgan v. Leatherman Tool Grp., 135 Cal. App. 4th 663 (Cal. App. Ct. 2006).

By contrast to the case against Leatherman, *People v. Sarpas* was brought by the attorney general. Should statutory damages also be available to private plaintiffs? This is an area where states diverge.

Class-Action Settlements Under State Consumer-Protection Laws

As noted in previous chapters, class actions provide leverage against practices that would otherwise go unchallenged because of the minimal harm done to any individual consumer. This makes determination of appropriate remedies challenging, since the transaction costs of finding deceived consumers and redressing the harm can far outweigh any actual restitution. Concern over settlements that provide millions for the lawyers and virtually nothing for the consumers allegedly being protected have led to greater scrutiny of proposed settlements. The following case shows how a court analyzed a proposed settlement when it had already approved class treatment.

IN RE M3 POWER RAZOR SYSTEM MARKETING & SALES PRACTICE LITIGATION, 270 F.R.D. 45 (D. MASS. 2010)

. . . The revised proposed Settlement Agreement as Amended obligates Gillette to establish a Settlement Fund of $7.5 million for the distribution of cash and other benefits to class members. Up to $2.45 million of the Settlement Fund is available to provide notice to potential class members. Any notice costs over this amount, including the potential costs of providing additional notice if the settlement is not approved at the Final Fairness Hearing, will be borne solely by Gillette.

[Editors' note: Details of the settlement are discussed in Chapter 8. Recall the provision that any leftover funds would be used to distribute free Gillette razors to the general population. Was this provision appropriate, given its apparent distance from the harm Gillette allegedly caused and the potential for Gillette to build brand goodwill from this aspect of the settlement? Coupon settlements and other non-monetary redress provisions have been criticized on the grounds that they are marketing tools, not penalties.*]

The proposed Settlement Agreement contains no reverter clause, and the full $7.5 million, including up to $2.45 million for notice, will be distributed for the benefit of class members.

---

* For a particularly entertaining version of this criticism, see the objector's brief filed by William Chamberlain, then a Georgetown Law student, objecting to a proposed settlement of claims against Muscle Milk, where amounts remaining after distribution to class claimants would be distributed to charitable athletic events—in the form of free Muscle Milk for participants, valued for settlement purposes at retail value instead of the producer's cost. Chamberlain notes that this "remedy" has promotional value to the advertiser, and it's ironic given the underlying allegations that Muscle Milk was not a healthy product. *Objection To Proposed Settlement and Fee Request and Notice of Appearance*, Delacruz v. Cytosport Inc., No. 4:11-cv-03532 (N.D. Cal. filed Mar. 5, 2014).

Potential class members have the right to opt out, if written notice is postmarked at least 21 days prior to the date of the Final Fairness Hearing. In addition to the $7.5 million Settlement Fund, Gillette has agreed to pay up to $1,850,000, subject to Court approval, for attorneys' fees, costs, and expenses, as well as incentive awards to the Representative and named Plaintiffs in amounts of $500 (or the prevailing Canadian dollar equivalent) to $1,000 each.

IV. STANDARDS FOR CLASS ACTION SETTLEMENT APPROVAL

Federal Rule of Civil Procedure 23(e) requires judicial approval of all class action settlements. Before approving a class action settlement, I must find that it is "fair, reasonable, and adequate." When asked to review a class action settlement preliminarily, I examine the proposed settlement for obvious deficiencies before determining whether it is in the range of fair, reasonable, and adequate. . . . Ultimately, the more fully informed examination required for final approval will occur in connection with the Final Fairness Hearing, where arguments for and against the proposed settlement will be presented after notice and an opportunity to consider any response provided by the potential class members.

It is inherently difficult to determine the fairness and adequacy of a proposed settlement in the preliminary review context where the parties have advanced a settlement in lieu of litigation. Courts and commentators, nevertheless, have developed a presumption that the settlement is within the range of reasonableness when certain procedural guidelines have been followed. These guidelines include whether: "(1) the negotiations occurred at arm's length; (2) there was sufficient discovery; (3) the proponents of the settlement are experienced in similar litigation; and (4) only a small fraction of the class objected."

I am satisfied that the negotiations in this case occurred at arm's length, and that the revised proposed settlement is more favorable to the potential class members than was Gillette's original response to pre-suit demand letters under state consumer protection statutes. Gillette originally offered to provide a $12 refund, or the actual amount paid if documented to be higher, to any consumer who purchased an M3P razor on or before July 1, 2005 and wished to return the razor. Postage was to be reimbursed based on the actual postage cost, and participating consumers would receive a coupon for $1 off a future purchase. The offer was limited to two razors per household, and there was no minimum floor on recovery.

The revised and then amended Settlement Agreement has improved on the original offer in several ways. First, it establishes a minimum Settlement Fund of $7.5 million, and provides for notice with 80-percent reach to inform consumers of their rights as class members.[12] Second, the Settlement Class Period was extended from July 1, 2005 to either September 30 or October 31, 2005, depending on the class member's country of residence. Third, the refund amount was increased from $12 to $13, and the reimbursement for shipping and handling was increased from the actual cost of postage, which necessarily omitted any handling costs, to $2. Fourth, consumers are no longer required to return the M3P razor to obtain a benefit.

---

[12] Corrales argues that the original offer contained no ceiling either, but all parties recognize that consumer redemption rates in cases such as this are likely to be low, so it is highly unlikely that the request for refunds under the original offer would come close to the $7.5 million allocated to the proposed settlement.

Fifth, the Gillette shaving product available for rebate includes, as a result of the Amended Settlement Agreement, the newest offering in the Gillette product line. Sixth, the number of permitted claims per household was increased from two to three. Seventh, assuming money is left over from the Settlement Fund after the Initial Claim Period, members of the class will receive free Settlement Razors, along with coupons valued at $4.

The Objecting Plaintiff Corrales has not offered evidence that the negotiations were not at arm's length or were collusive in any way, and I see no reason to find otherwise. . . .

I am also satisfied that sufficient discovery has been undertaken to provide the parties with adequate information about their respective litigation positions. Gillette produced over 100,000 pages of documents from the District of Connecticut litigation against Schick, allowing the parties to acquire enough information rapidly to make serious settlement negotiations feasible. Gillette also produced pertinent financial information as part of confirmatory discovery, and Co-Lead counsel deposed a Gillette representative who was familiar with the relevant financial information. Having reviewed this information, I find it is sufficient to make an informed preliminary review of the fairness of the proposed settlement. Finally, the only practical way to ascertain the overall level of objection to the proposed settlement is for notice to go forward, and to see how many potential class members choose to opt out of the settlement class or object to its terms at the Final Fairness Hearing.

I do impose one additional requirement upon the Representative Plaintiffs as they proceed with the notice of the class action. In the notice to class members on the website created for this proposed settlement, the "Joint Submission by the Proponents of the Proposed Settlement Comparing the Relevant Laws of Applicable Jurisdiction for Settlement Class Certification" must be posted together with a copy of this Memorandum and Order alerting class members to the issues presented by the varying state law causes of action and remedies available to the class members. In this way, class members who may wish to learn more about those alternatives and consider their implications will have a foundation for doing so.

. . . On the present state of the record, I have found sufficient basis to permit notice of the proposed Settlement Agreement to go forward and to certify a class, without subclasses, solely for the purpose of settlement.

I believe this certification is consistent with the directions provided by the First Circuit, which has taken a practical and common sense approach toward class settlements. Recently, in *In re* Pharmaceutical Industry Average Wholesale Price Litigation, 588 F.3d 24 (1st Cir. 2009), the court observed that while Judge Saris, after detailed and rigorous analysis of the diverse legal regimes implicated, had originally excluded nine states from a nationwide litigation class, "since their consumer-protection statutes differed," she thereafter expanded the settlement class to reincorporate them. In affirming the settlement class order, the First Circuit explained that it was "perfectly clear why the district court expanded the settlement class . . . [The defendant] bargained for 'total peace' to resolve all remaining claims against it."

More recently, the First Circuit has observed that "[a]lthough in class actions there is a preference for individually proved damages," nevertheless, "it is well accepted that in some cases an approximation of damages or a uniform figure for the class is the best that can be done." After extended reflection, I am satisfied on the basis of the record before me, and subject to reconsideration or refinement in connection with the Final Fairness Hearing, that the proposed settlement represents an acceptable resolution of this dispute. . . .

NOTES AND QUESTIONS

An option in the settlement included a new Gillette razor, the product that allegedly deceived the class members to begin with. How is receiving another razor returning the ill-gotten gain to the consumer?

Concerns for protecting both class plaintiffs and defendants recur in consumer-protection class actions. While the concern for defendants essentially involves blackmail—the idea that defendants will make nuisance payments to lawyers to get a lawsuit to go away—the concern for plaintiffs is that those who are truly harmed will be ignored in low-value settlements. Where there are multiple plaintiffs' attorneys competing to represent a class, as is often the case when the claims are disseminated nationwide, the defendant can conduct a "reverse auction" among rival plaintiffs' groups. There is an incentive for the plaintiffs' lawyers to settle for low amounts, given that the lawyers who lose the auction usually get nothing because their compensation is on a contingency basis. As the *MP3 Power* decision suggests, courts are supposed to scrutinize a settlement for its fairness to both sides—in a situation where both litigants will be jointly urging the judge to approve the settlement.

Because claim rates in class actions are so low, when the defendant reserves a pool of money for settlement, it's usually the case that this pool is much larger than the actual total claims. But because of concerns over making sure that settlements serve some real deterrence function, and to avoid the manipulation of the nominal size of the pool in order to increase attorneys' fees, settling parties may provide that the defendant will pay some minimum amount of money. (The FTC does the same thing when it agrees on redress provisions.) But if the settlement money does not go to consumers who submit claims, then who gets it? The practice in false advertising cases had been to choose some uncontroversial charity related to the defendant's products or services, using a rationale drawn from trust law known as *cy pres* (Law French for "as close as possible"). The theory was that giving to the charity was as close as possible to compensating harmed consumers.

In *Dennis v. Kellogg Co.*, 697 F.3d 858 (9th Cir. 2012), the Ninth Circuit raised significant objections to a settlement heavily premised on *cy pres* payments. If we were serious about *cy pres*, the court reasoned, the residual amount in the pool wouldn't go to a product-related charity—in the Kellogg case, it was charities that provided food to hungry people. But "[t]his noble goal . . . has little or nothing to do with the purposes of the underlying lawsuit or the class of plaintiffs involved." Kellogg wasn't being sued for failing to feed people. It was being sued for deceiving people about how healthy its food was. To get "as close as possible" to benefiting consumers whose harm came from being deceived, some consumer protection-related charity would be far more appropriate as the residual charity.

While Kellogg likely has less philosophical objection to giving to a food bank than to Consumers Union or some other charity that often takes policy positions opposed to Kellogg, most large companies approach settlements rationally. Thus, on remand, the parties renegotiated, including by dropping plaintiffs' attorneys' fee request substantially in response to other concerns expressed by the Ninth Circuit. The final cash fund was $4 million, and Kellogg agreed to give the amount remaining after class members filed their claims to Consumers Union, Consumer Watchdog and the Center for Science in the Public Interest.

The district court approved the renegotiated settlement. Given the risks to both sides to pursuing the case through trial, and the nontrivial relief afforded to the class, in which claimants would receive at least $5 and up to $45, the court was satisfied that the settlement was fair, adequate and free of collusion. Dennis v. Kellogg Co., 2013 WL 6055326 (S.D. Cal. Sept. 10, 2013).

Why should we worry about the residual charity or about low consumer recoveries? Consider the following argument from Professor Brian Wolfman (formerly of Public Citizen):

> [I]n 2012, the Vermont Attorney General sued a company called Vermints under Vermont's consumer protection law alleging that Vermints had mislabeled its mints "*Vermont's* All-Natural Mints" (my emphasis). . . . According to the suit, the company is Massachusetts-based and the mints were manufactured in Canada, using mostly non-Vermont ingredients. . . . Vermints has settled the case by agreeing to remove the offending labels, paying Vermont $30,000, and giving $35,000 to the Vermont Foodbank, the state's largest anti-hunger organization. . . .
>
> If private lawyers (acting as so-called private attorneys general) had brought the suit on behalf of consumers of Vermints, the same settlement might have raised eyebrows. A class-action critic might have said the case bordered on the frivolous. Who cares about the label on a tin of mints? . . . In settling the suit [the AG] said:
>
>> Use of the term "Vermont" has great economic value, and many businesses go to the expense of sourcing their ingredients and processing within the state in order to market their products as Vermont products. We need to maintain a level playing field when it comes to claims of geographic origin, and to ensure that consumers who care about where their food comes from get accurate information in the marketplace.
>
> . . . [I]f the case had been filed by private plaintiffs, objectors might say that a cy pres award to the Foodbank was impermissible because of the lack of nexus between the underlying claim (misleading labeling of candy) and the mission of the cy pres recipient (alleviation of hunger in Vermont). They might even express concern that the plaintiffs themselves got no monetary relief. How can it be right to settle a case, they might say, where the lawyers and a charity, but not the class members, walk away with all the goodies?
>
> That concern makes little sense in many small-claims consumer cases, as the Vermont AG recognized in settling the Vermints case without providing a dime to consumers. It would have been economically irrational to provide money to a class of

people who had purchased mislabeled Vermints. Strictly speaking, some consumers may have been injured. But what would individualized relief look like? A buck for each class member who swore under oath on a claim form that she was duped by the faulty label into buying a tin of mints? Some class-action settlements actually seek to provide very small amounts of money to claiming class members. (I was once sent a three-cent class-action settlement check via first-class mail). But that's often a waste because most of the money the defendant has agreed to cough up goes for claims processing, check-writing, and postage. Generally, the best type of relief in small-harm cases is aggregated relief: injunctive-like benefits, such the label change the AG obtained, and lump-sum payments to help offset the costs of litigation and to promote deterrence, such as the payments to the state and to the Vermont Foodbank.

. . . [I[f a state's consumer protection laws authorize members of the public to act as private attorneys general, as most of them do to one degree or another, aren't private lawyers' suits, like AG suits, carrying out the legislature's intent—particularly given that consumer protection laws generally encourage suit by requiring the defendant to pay a successful plaintiff's attorney's fees? So, why shouldn't those suits be viewed as consistent with democratic ideals? After all, if a legislature decides it no longer likes private suits to enforce its consumer protection laws, because it thinks that private lawyers don't exercise the type of enforcement restraint that the political process imposes on AGs, it can amend those laws to eliminate or narrow private enforcement (as legislatures have done on occasion).

How might a critic of class actions respond to Professor Wolfman? Consider one study's findings: In fifteen lawsuits against large banks, between 1% and 70% of class members received compensation in these settlements, and the average payout ranged from $13 to $90, representing between 6% and 69% of average class-member damages as claimed. The high participation rates generally came when the parties were able to use information from the defendants to automatically deposit settlement proceeds into class members' accounts or mail checks to them. Many class members deposited checks mailed to them even when the checks were for under $5, sometimes as often as 80% of the time. Brian T. Fitzpatrick & Robert C. Gilbert, *An Empirical Look at Compensation in Consumer Class Actions*, 11 N.Y.U. J. L. & BUS. 767 (2015). But what are the implications of the fact that a substantial number of mailed checks were never deposited?

Another study of 149 consumer class-action settlements by the FTC found redemption rates of under 10% overall; mailed packets did the best, and email campaigns did the worst (3%). Check-cashing rates increased as the median amount increased; where a claims process was required (as opposed to a check automatically being sent out), the average check-cashing rate was 77%. The claims rate was higher in cases where the notices used visually prominent and "plain English" language to describe payment availability, but, perhaps surprisingly, documentation requirements didn't appear to diminish redemption rates. Federal Trade Comm'n, *Consumers and Class Actions: A Retrospective and Analysis of Settlement Campaigns*, Sept. 2019.

When the FTC tested different types of email notice, it found some other possibly unexpected results:

> Respondents had the highest stated opening rates for emails with subject lines that omitted any reference to a class action. In addition, omitting the amount of compensation from the subject line improved both comprehension and stated opening rates. Finally, using a long-format email with formal, legal writing improved the understanding of the nature of the email while a condensed form of the email improved the understanding of next steps. Respondents were also more suspicious of the condensed form email than the long form emails. Overall, less than half of respondents understood that the email pertains to a class action settlement or a refund rather than representing a promotional email, and less than half correctly understood the steps required to receive a refund.

By contrast, when the FTC has a list of eligible customers and mails consumer redress checks, 67% of eligible recipients cash their checks. When the FTC lacks sufficient information to do so, it sets up a notice process, and it generally receives claims from 5% to 20% of potential claimants (and about 95% of people who file a claim cash their checks). Does this range of response suggest any lessons for class actions?

3.   Criminal Liability

Criminal prosecutions for violations of the FTC Act or state consumer protection statutes are rare—but not unheard of.

The FTC Act provides that a violation committed with the intent to defraud or mislead is criminal. 15 U.S.C. § 54. The maximum penalty is a $10,000 fine or up to one year in prison. However, the FTC relies on the Department of Justice to prosecute criminal violations. The FTC has occasionally prosecuted criminal cases under CAN-SPAM, which, as its acronym indicates, governs deceptive commercial email schemes.

In addition, federal district court orders may be enforced through civil or criminal contempt actions filed in district court. In 1997, the FTC implemented Project Scofflaw, which involved both criminal and civil enforcement against violators of FTC-obtained district court orders. Results included a 125-month sentence for six counts of criminal contempt arising from violation of a court order barring violations of the FTC's Franchise Rule, United States v. Ferrara, 334 F.3d 774 (8th Cir. 2003), along with other prison sentences.

The FTC also established a Criminal Liaison Unit ("CLU") in 2003 to encourage criminal prosecution of consumer fraud by enhancing coordination with criminal law-enforcement authorities interested in pursuing such cases. The number of concurrent or subsequent criminal prosecutions in the past two decades is only in the dozens, but it remains a possibility for particularly egregious frauds. Multiple defendants may be indicted in a single fraud. *See* Frank Gorman, *How the FTC Can Help Local Prosecutors with Cases of Criminal Fraud*, THE PROSECUTOR, Oct./Nov./Dec. 2008.

The CLU works with state attorneys general or local prosecutors. State authority over consumer fraud is exclusively civil in some jurisdictions, but criminal sanctions are authorized in others, sometimes for specific types of fraud such as mortgage or insurance fraud. *See, e.g.*, Ohio Rev. Code Ann. § 1345.02(E)(3) (authorizing the Ohio attorney general to initiate criminal prosecutions for consumer-law violations if the local prosecuting attorney declines to prosecute or requests the attorney general to bring the case); Okla. Stat. tit. 15, § 762(B) (2001) (establishing that the Oklahoma attorney general has "powers of a district attorney to investigate and prosecute suspected violations of consumer laws"); *see also* Ga. Code Ann. § 16-8-104 (2007) (authorizing the Georgia attorney general and district attorneys to prosecute cases of residential mortgage fraud); Idaho Code Ann. § 41-213(3) (2010) (establishing that the Idaho attorney general has concurrent authority with county attorneys over insurance fraud). Some states, such as New Jersey, have units dedicated to prosecuting fraud, including consumer fraud.

Given the general scienter requirements of criminal law, criminal prosecutions for consumer protection violations require the prosecution to prove the defendant's knowledge of falsity, rather than mere falsity. For this and other reasons, such prosecutions are the least-common means of enforcing consumer-protection law. DEE PRIDGEN & RICHARD M. ALDERMAN, CONSUMER PROTECTION AND THE LAW § 7.22 (2009).

This chapter doesn't cover the full range of business torts. Instead, it focuses on those most closely connected to false advertising claims, primarily the common law claims of *defamation* and *disparagement*: saying nasty things about competitors or their goods or services. These claims implicate the First Amendment, and over time the jurisprudence has become more tolerant of critical remarks and comparative advertising.

The torts we'll consider in this chapter can be brought alongside Lanham Act and state consumer-protection claims or occasionally on their own when the plaintiff wouldn't have standing to bring those core claims. They mostly involve statements about competitors' products—not statements about an advertiser's own products. Tortious interference with existing or prospective economic advantage is a potential exception, though that is usually only alleged when there's some sort of comparative statement or solicitation being made.

1.   Defamation and Disparagement

Though the Lanham Act and state consumer-protection laws generally offer commercial plaintiffs greater prospects of success than defamation and product disparagement, the latter claims are still regularly pled and litigated. As you review the sometimes-bewildering variety of common-law claims, often with state-by-state variations in the way elements are described, keep in mind some core differences between the common-law causes of action in this chapter and statutory claims under the Lanham Act, the FTCA and state consumer-protection laws: (1) scienter (sufficient knowledge of falsity, usually called "malice" in disparagement cases), (2) intent to harm, and (3) circumstances in which harm to the plaintiff can be presumed for purposes of awarding damages.

The torts of defamation/disparagement cover all speech, not just commercial speech. Because the causes of action are available to anyone—not just government regulators, competitors or consumers—they are subject to higher standards with respect to awareness of falsity, intent to harm and proof of damages.

Thus, saying something mistaken and negative about a business doesn't automatically lead to liability. Consider, for example, a talk-show host who runs a story about the hidden dangers of apples or beef; without heightened standards for knowing falsity and intent to harm, sellers could deter speech about important health issues.

Given the more -ignificant First Amendment constraints on the common-law claims, it was only a matter of time before a plaintiff bringing both Lanham Act and defamation claims would face the argument that the First Amendment also barred liability without fault under the Lanham Act. As you read the following case, pay attention to the remaining differences between defamation (which targets the plaintiff) and disparagement (which targets the plaintiff's goods or services). Can you identify differences that will be important in practice?

U.S. Healthcare, Inc. v. Blue Cross of Greater Philadelphia, 898 F.2d 914 (3d Cir. 1990)

. . . Facts and Procedural History

These cross appeals arise from a comparative advertising war between giants of the health care industry in the Delaware Valley—U.S. Healthcare on the one side and Blue Cross/Blue Shield on the other. The thrust of these claims is that each side asserts the other's advertising misrepresented both parties' products.

For over fifty years, Blue Cross/Blue Shield operated as the largest health insurer in Southeastern Pennsylvania by offering "traditional" medical insurance coverage. Traditional insurance protects the subscriber from "major" medical expenses, with the insurer paying a negotiated amount based upon the services rendered, and the subscriber generally paying a deductible or some other amount. The subscriber has freedom in choosing hospitals and health care providers (i.e., doctors).

In the early 1970's, U.S. Healthcare began providing an alternative to traditional insurance in the form of a health maintenance organization, generically known as an "HMO." An HMO acts as both an insurer and a provider of specified services that are more comprehensive than those offered by traditional insurance. Generally, HMO subscribers choose a primary health care provider from the HMO network who coordinates their health care services and determines when hospital admission or treatment from a specialist is required. Usually, subscribers are not covered for services obtained without this permission or from providers outside this network. By 1986, U.S. Healthcare was the largest HMO in the area, claiming almost 600,000 members. During the same period, Blue Cross/Blue Shield experienced a loss in enrollment of over 1% per year, with a large number of those subscribers choosing HMO coverage over traditional insurance, and a majority of those defectors choosing a U.S. Healthcare company.

. . . In late 1985, in an admitted attempt to compete with HMO, Blue Cross/Blue Shield introduced a new product that it called "Personal Choice," known generically as a preferred provider organization or "PPO." PPO insurance provides subscribers with a "network" of health care providers and hospitals, and generally "covers" subscribers only for services obtained from the network providers and administered at the network hospitals. Subscribers must obtain permission to receive treatment from providers outside the network, and in such instances receive at most only partial coverage.

Thereafter, Blue Cross/Blue Shield consulted with two separate advertising agencies before arriving at a marketing strategy for its new product. In July 1986, Blue Cross/Blue Shield launched what it termed a deliberately "aggressive and provocative" comparative advertising campaign calculated "to introduce and increase the attractiveness of its products"—in particular, Personal Choice—at the expense of HMO products. Blue Cross/Blue Shield's campaign, which included direct mailings, as well as television, radio and print advertisements, ran for about six months at a total cost of approximately $2.175 million. According to a Blue Cross memorandum that purported to reflect the directions of Markson, the campaign was designed specifically to "reduce the attractiveness of [HMO]."

The Blue Cross/Blue Shield advertising campaign consisted of eight different advertisements for the print media, seven different advertisements for television, three different advertisements for radio, and a direct mailing including a folding brochure. . . . After describing HMO's referral procedure, . . . three of the eight print advertisements—as well as the brochure—say the following:

> You should also know that through a series of financial incentives, HMO encourages this doctor to handle as many patients as possible without referring to a specialist. When an HMO doctor does make a specialist referral, it could take money directly out of his pocket. Make too many referrals, and he could find himself in trouble with HMO.

One of the print advertisements and the brochure also feature a senior citizen under the banner heading "Your money or your life," juxtaposed with Blue Cross/Blue Shield's description of "The high cost of HMO Medicare."

Of the seven television advertisements run by Blue Cross/Blue Shield, four are innocuous, mentioning HMO only in the closing slogan common to all seven of the ads: "Personal Choice. Better than HMO. So good, it's Blue Cross and Blue Shield." The fifth features an indignant every man, who simply states "I resent having to ask my HMO doctor for permission to see a specialist," before a spokesperson extols the benefits of Personal Choice without reference to HMO until, again, the closing slogan. The sixth features a cab driver who says, "I don't like those HMO health plans. You get one doctor, no choice of hospitals," before a shopper tells him about the virtues of Personal Choice—again, without reference to HMO until the closing slogan. The seventh television advertisement used by Blue Cross/Blue Shield, while following the same general format, seems to us a dramatic departure from the others in that it appears consciously designed to play upon the fears of the consuming public. The commercial features a grief-stricken woman who says, "The hospital my HMO sent me to just wasn't enough. It's my fault." The implication of the advertisement is that some tragedy has befallen the woman because of her choice of health care.

. . . [U.S. Healthcare's] responsive advertising campaign, which began sometime after the Blue Cross/Blue Shield campaign and ran until late February 1987, cost $1.255 million. . . .

U.S. Healthcare's responsive campaign did not just highlight the positive characteristics in its own product, but also featured "anti-Blue Cross" advertisements. Of the three remaining print advertisements, one simply shows a comparative list of the features available under HMO and Personal Choice, with a banner heading that reads "It's your choice." The other two explain that under Personal Choice, the number of hospitals available to the subscriber is limited and, moreover, that many Personal Choice doctors do not have admitting privileges at even those few. One of these advertisements ran under a banner heading of "When it Comes to Being Admitted to a Hospital, There's Something Personal Choice May Not Be

Willing to Admit"; the other ran under a banner heading of "If You Really Look Into 'Personal Choice,' You Might Have a Better Name For It."

. . . The final television commercial was U.S. Healthcare's own attempt to play upon the fears of the consuming public. As solemn music plays, the narrator lists the shortcomings of Personal Choice while the camera pans from a Personal Choice brochure resting on the pillow of a hospital bed to distraught family members standing at bedside. The advertisement closes with a pair of hands pulling a sheet over the Personal Choice brochure.

. . . After a fourteen-day trial, followed by eight days of deliberations, the jury announced it was deadlocked on all issues of liability and damages. . . .

The [district] court held that because the objects of the advertisements are "public figures," and because the matters in the advertisements are "community health issues of public concern," heightened constitutional protections attach to this speech. [The district court then held that, under the First Amendment, the Lanham Act claims as well as the commercial disparagement, defamation and tortious interference claims required proof by clear and convincing evidence of knowledge or reckless disregard of falsity, and that neither party could satisfy that standard.] . . .

II. The Actionable Claims and Counterclaims under Applicable Substantive Federal and State Law . . .
    A. Applicable Federal and Pennsylvania Common Law.

       . . . 2. Defamation.

Under Pennsylvania law, a defamatory statement is one that "tends so to harm the reputation of another as to lower him in the estimation of the community or to deter third persons from associating or dealing with him." It is for the court to determine, in the first instance, whether the statement of which the plaintiff complained is capable of a defamatory meaning; if the court decides that it is capable of a defamatory meaning, then it is for the jury to decide if the statement was so understood by the reader or listener. To ascertain the meaning of an allegedly defamatory statement, the statement must be examined in context.

> The test is the effect the [statement] is fairly calculated to produce, the impression it would naturally engender, in the minds of the average persons among whom it is intended to circulate. The words must be given by judges and juries the same signification that other people are likely to attribute to them.

Opinion that fails to imply underlying defamatory facts cannot support the cause of action.

In an action for defamation, the plaintiff has the burden of proving 1) the defamatory character of the communication; 2) its publication by the defendant; 3) its application to the plaintiff; 4) an understanding by the reader or listener of its defamatory meaning; and 5) an understanding by the reader or listener of an intent by the defendant that the statement refer to the plaintiff. Additionally, in order to recover damages, the plaintiff must demonstrate that the statement results from fault, amounting at least to negligence, on the part of the defendant. Finally, the plaintiff has the burden of proving any special harm resulting from the statement. . . .

3. Commercial Disparagement.

A commercially disparaging statement—in contrast to a defamatory statement—is one "which is intended by its publisher to be understood or which is reasonably understood to cast doubt upon the existence or extent of another's property in land, chattels or intangible things, or upon their quality, . . . if the matter is so understood by its recipient." In order to maintain an action for disparagement, the plaintiff must prove 1) that the disparaging statement of fact is untrue or that the disparaging statement of opinion is incorrect; 2) that no privilege attaches to the statement; and 3) that the plaintiff suffered a direct pecuniary loss as the result of the disparagement.

The distinction between actions for defamation and disparagement turns on the harm towards which each is directed. An action for commercial disparagement is meant to compensate a vendor for pecuniary loss suffered because statements attacking the quality of his goods have reduced their marketability, while defamation is meant protect an entity's interest in character and reputation. . . .

Given the similar elements of the two torts, deciding which cause of action lies in a given situation can be difficult. The Court of Appeals for the Eighth Circuit gave the following time-honored explanation of when impugnation of the quality of goods crosses the line from disparagement of products to defamation of vendors:

> [W]here the publication on its face is directed against the goods or product of a corporate vendor or manufacturer, it will not be held libelous per se as to the corporation, unless by fair construction and without the aid of extrinsic evidence it imputes to the corporation fraud, deceit, dishonesty, or reprehensible conduct in its business in relation to said goods or product. . . .

B. The Actionable Construction of the Advertisements

. . . [W]e consider as a group the bulk of the advertisements, which either compare the competing health plans on one or more points, or simply criticize the competitor's health plan without detailed exposition of the advertiser's own competing plan. Because they may contain misrepresentations beyond puffing, a cause of action may lie under the Lanham Act, even for those advertisements that focus exclusively on the competitor's health plan. In addition, as these advertisements all make representations about the competitor's product, a cause of action may lie for commercial disparagement with respect to any of them. None of these, however, could be said to impute to the competitor by fair construction any "fraud, deceit, dishonesty, or reprehensible conduct." Consequently, no cause of action for defamation will lie with regard to these. . . .

We believe [certain] advertisements are capable of defamatory meaning. These include, first, the Blue Cross/Blue Shield advertisements that suggest HMO primary care physicians have a financial interest in not referring patients to specialists and, indeed, that HMO makes reprisals against those primary care physicians who make too many referrals. These advertisements imply that U.S. Healthcare, the people who run it, and the doctors who are employed by it, all place personal profit above adequate health care. Such an implication goes beyond the comparative quality of HMO health care to suggest reprehensible conduct by U.S. Healthcare and its employees in the conduct of their business.

Also capable of defamatory meaning is Blue Cross/Blue Shield's "Distraught Woman" advertisement. Her statement that "The hospital my HMO sent me to just wasn't enough," matched with her grief-stricken demeanor, suggests she has suffered some tragedy because of HMO's substandard care. The suggestion that U.S. Healthcare chose to send her to a hospital that could not adequately treat her problem goes beyond the product itself to impute reprehensible conduct to the corporation. Indeed, the scare tactic is the point of the commercial.

Finally, we find U.S. Healthcare's "Critical Condition" television commercial to be capable of a defamatory construction as well. As a dirge plays, the narrator lists the shortcomings of Personal Choice while the camera pans from a Personal Choice brochure resting on the pillow of a hospital bed to distraught family members standing around the bed. At the end of the advertisement, a pair of hands pulls a sheet over the Personal Choice brochure. We do not believe the depiction of a distressing death scene in a health insurance commercial is an uncalculated association. Again, we believe a scare tactic was the intent and, more to the point, a jury could find the commercial suggests Blue Cross/Blue Shield knowingly provides health care so substandard as to be dangerous.

As to this final group of advertisements, no action for commercial disparagement will lie because the statements are directed at the vendor, not his goods. Nonetheless, Lanham Act claims may lie. . . .

III. First Amendment Principles and the Standard of Proof in Claims Arising from a Comparative Advertising Campaign

Having determined that some of the advertisements may be actionable under federal and state law, we must now consider whether the First Amendment affects the standard of proof. . . . [The district court] rejected U.S. Healthcare's argument that the advertisements were commercial speech and thereby entitled to less constitutional protection. The district court viewed the comparative advertising campaign giving rise to this litigation as a "dispute . . . about how best to deal with spiraling medical costs," and concluded that, "[t]o characterize the advertisements in this case as mere commercial speech ignores the fact that, at their core, they are instruments in a debate between two providers of public health care 'intimately involved in the resolution of important public questions.'" . . .

A. Background

Distinguishing the Supreme Court's First Amendment jurisprudence is an express intention to "lay down broad rules of general application," rather than to allow balancing between competing values on a case-by-case basis, an approach that the Court fears would "lead to unpredictable results and uncertain expectations, and . . . render [its] duty to supervise the lower courts unmanageable." In delineating the limits placed on state authority by the First Amendment, the Court has articulated two distinct lines of cases, one involving defamation and the other involving government regulation of commercial speech. We have found no decision by the Court considering a defamation action involving expression properly characterized as commercial speech.

Despite its intention to enunciate general rules, the Court has implicitly recognized the need for balancing when a novel issue arises. Given the unique issue presented here, we believe it is necessary to evaluate the competing state and First Amendment interests. In taking this approach, we are mindful of the Supreme Court's admonition that nothing in *Gertz* "indicated that [the] same balance would be struck regardless of the type of speech involved."

Our approach will proceed in light of the analytical framework of the defamation cases. We have found no comparable case, and the parties cite none. In what we believe is a matter of first impression, we are presented with the unique circumstance of allegedly defamatory statements made in the context of a comparative advertising campaign.

B. Rules and Conceptual Framework

. . . In evaluating these competing interests, the Court has determined that the state has only a "limited" interest in compensating public persons for injury to reputation by defamatory statements, but has a "strong and legitimate" interest in compensating private persons for the same injury. The Court has provided a two-fold explanation for the discrepancy in the extent of the state interests. First, because public officials and public figures enjoy "greater access to the channels of effective communication and hence have a more realistic opportunity to counteract false statements than private individuals," the states have a greater interest in protecting private persons whose relative lack of "self-help" remedies render them "more vulnerable to injury." Second, the state has a stronger interest in protecting the reputations of private individuals because, unlike public persons, they have not voluntarily placed themselves in the public eye.

On the other side of the coin, the "type of speech involved" also affects the way in which the "balance is struck," by varying the weight of the First Amendment interest. "[S]peech on 'matters of public concern' . . . is 'at the heart of the First Amendment's protection.' " The Court has determined that "speech of private concern," such as a credit report for business, is of less First Amendment importance, in the same way that utterances labeled "commercial speech" are "less central to the interests of the First Amendment."

C. Application of the Rules and Conceptual Framework

. . . We next turn to assessing the relative weight of the First Amendment interests in this case. We recognize that traditional defamation analysis usually begins with an examination of the status of the plaintiff. Because of the facts presented, however, we shall first consider the content of the speech involved. Nor do we believe that such inverted analysis is improper.

Similarly, traditional defamation analysis would have us consider the public or private nature of the speech in assessing the weight of the First Amendment interests. We believe, however, that the novel facts here require a different approach. Our appraisal of these interests depends on whether the speech at issue can properly be characterized as commercial speech. "There is no longer any room to doubt that what has come to be known as 'commercial speech' is entitled to the protection of the First Amendment, albeit to protection somewhat less extensive than that afforded 'noncommercial speech.' " If the speech here is commercial speech, then it likely does not mandate heightened constitutional protection.

We recognize that the Supreme Court cases creating the commercial speech doctrine all involve some form of government regulation of speech and that none involve defamation actions. Further, the focus in the commercial speech cases is on First Amendment protection itself, not the heightened protection afforded by the actual malice standard. However, we believe the subordinate valuation of commercial speech is not confined to the government regulation line of cases.

In *Dun & Bradstreet*, the Court held that speech on matters of private concern, such as a credit report for business, receives less First Amendment protection than speech on matters of public concern. More significantly for our purposes, the Court justified its decision to allow less protection for speech of private concern by drawing an analogy to the reduced First Amendment protection afforded commercial speech:

> This Court on many occasions has recognized that certain kinds of speech are less central to the interests of the First Amendment than others. . . . In the area of protected speech, the most prominent example of reduced protection for certain kinds of speech concerns commercial speech. Such speech, we have noted, occupies a "subordinate position in the scale of First Amendment values." It also is more easily verifiable and less likely to be deterred by proper regulation. Accordingly, it may be regulated in ways that might be impermissible in the realm of noncommercial expression.

. . . [T]he statements here are commercial in nature. First, there is no question that they are advertisements; they were disseminated as part of an expensive, professionally run promotional campaign. Second, the speech specifically refers to a product; it touts the relative merits of Personal Choice (or U.S. Healthcare's HMO) over competing products. Third, the desire for revenue motivated the speech; the record contains abundant evidence that Blue Cross/Blue Shield launched the promotional campaign in order to recoup its share of the health insurance market. . . . Similarly, protection of its new market share motivated U.S. Healthcare's speech. In short, "common sense" informs us that the statements here propose a commercial transaction, and thus differ from other types of speech.

Even more importantly, we find it significant that the advertisements have all of the characteristics that the Supreme Court has identified in the commercial speech cases as making speech durable, not susceptible to "chill." Consequently, they do not require the heightened protection we extend to our most valuable forms of speech. Because the thrust of all of the advertisements is to convince the consuming public to bring its business to one of these health care giants rather than the other, there is no doubt that the advertisements were motivated by economic self-interest. Furthermore, given the size of the health care market in the Delaware Valley—Blue Shield virtually shouts about the hundreds of millions of dollars at stake—we believe it would have to be a cold day before these corporations would be chilled from speaking about the comparative merits of their products. *Cf. Dun & Bradstreet*, 472 U.S. at 762–63 (because credit report was solely motivated by profit "any incremental 'chilling' effect of libel suits would be of decreased significance").

In addition, these are advertisements for products and services in markets in which U.S. Healthcare and Blue Cross/Blue Shield deal—and, presumably, know more about than anyone else. The facts upon which the advertisements are based—comparative price, procedures, and services offered—are readily objectifiable. These advertisements were precisely calculated, developed over time and published only when the corporate speakers were ready. Consequently, the advertisements were unusually verifiable.

Finally, while the speech here does discuss costs and consequences of competing health insurance and health care delivery programs, some of the advertisements capable of defamatory meaning here add little information and even fewer ideas to the marketplace of health care thought.[26] The expression in these advertisements "differs markedly from ideological expression because it is confined to the promotion of specific . . . services." *Cf. Zauderer*, 471 U.S. at 637 & n. 77 (advertisement containing information that, in another context would be fully protected, nonetheless commercial speech, as it proposed commercial transaction in advertiser's self-interest). And to the extent that the advertisements are false statements of fact, of course, the speech has no constitutional value at all. . . .

Despite these conclusive indications that the speech here is commercial in nature, Blue Cross/Blue Shield argues that the speech should be accorded heightened constitutional protection. Relying on *Bigelow v. Virginia*, 421 U.S. 809 (1975), it argues that speech which does more than "simply propose a commercial transaction" constitutes something more than commercial speech. Furthermore, it maintains that the "*Bigelow* standard" is applicable when the products are not merely linked to a public debate but are themselves "at the center of the public debate."[27] Blue Cross/Blue Shield concludes that its own advertisements "educate[d] the public about the substantial differences among the[ ] available means for financing and delivering health care, thereby ensuring informed purchasing decisions" and rendering the advertisements non-commercial.

. . . [T]he *Central Hudson* decision, in which the Supreme Court expressly rejected such attempts to "blur further the line the Court has sought to draw in commercial speech cases," represents the proper approach. *Central Hudson* prevents an advertiser from immunizing, in

---

[26] We believe one such advertisement implicates important health care concerns. This advertisement suggests that HMO primary care physicians have a financial incentive to deny referrals to specialists. On the other hand, we believe the other advertisements capable of defamatory meaning make no such contribution. One portrays a woman grieving that the hospital to which HMO sent her was inadequate. The second, a "death" scene, shows a pair of hands pulling a hospital sheet over a personal choice brochure as a dirge plays. "There is simply no credible argument that this type of [advertisement] requires special protection to ensure that 'debate on public issues [will] be uninhibited, robust, and wide-open.' "

[27] In *Bigelow*, a newspaper editor published an abortion clinic's advertisement, which the state court determined violated a state criminal statute prohibiting dissemination of publications encouraging the processing of an abortion. The Supreme Court struck down the statute on First Amendment grounds, stating that the advertisement could not be regulated as commercial speech because, "[v]iewed in its entirety, [it] conveyed information of potential interest and value to a diverse audience—not only to readers possibly in need of the services offered . . . ."

effect, otherwise defamatory speech—behind the actual malice standard afforded to core speech by the First Amendment—simply by reference to an issue of public concern.

. . . Therefore, while the speech here is protected by the First Amendment, we hold that the First Amendment requires no higher standard of liability than that mandated by the substantive law for each claim. The heightened protection of the actual malice standard is not "necessary to give adequate 'breathing space' to the freedoms protected by the First Amendment."

. . . [T]raditional defamation analysis is not well suited to strike the proper balance between the state and federal interests and First Amendment values in the context of commercial speech.

In weighing the state interest, we must look to the status of the claimants. As we have noted, the Court has determined that the state has only a "limited" interest in compensating public persons for injury to reputation but has a "strong and legitimate" interest in compensating private persons for the same injury. Contending that the actual malice standard applies because a public figure is implicated, Blue Cross/Blue Shield argues that the following factors render U.S. Healthcare a "public figure": it has voluntarily exposed itself to public comment on the issues involved in this dispute; it is a contributor to the ongoing debate concerning health care insurance; it is among the nation's largest providers of HMO-type insurance coverage; it markets its products extensively and aggressively, and has a substantial annual advertising budget; and it frequently and consistently asserts the advantages of its method of health care financing and delivery, and has done so in advertisements, press releases, professional journals, newspapers, magazines and speeches before public assemblies. These activities, Blue Cross/Blue Shield submits, "constitute a voluntary effort to influence the consuming public." Similar statements can be made regarding Blue Cross/Blue Shield.

Gertz identified three classes of public figures: those who achieve such stature or notoriety that they are considered public figures in all contexts; those who become public figures involuntarily, but these are "exceedingly rare"; and those who are deemed public figures only within the context of a particular public dispute. The Court defined the last group, limited purpose public figures, as individuals who voluntarily "thrust themselves to the forefront of particular public controversies in order to influence the resolution of the issues involved."

. . . The first factor indicative of a claimant's status is his relative access to the media. Clearly, both parties have access to the media. Moreover, the magnitude of the advertising campaigns shows their ability to utilize it on a vast scale. While access to the media does not always make one a public figure for purposes of First Amendment analysis, the tremendous ability of these parties to advertise, indicating their lack of vulnerability, would support a finding that both are public figures.

The second factor is the manner in which the risk of defamation came upon them. Both companies, attempting to influence consumers' decisions, have thrust themselves into the controversy of who provides better value in health care delivery and insurance. Blue Cross/Blue Shield began the comparative advertising war with its pointed attacks on HMO.

U.S. Healthcare, even before responding with its own comparative advertising, had used advertising to help establish itself as a leading provider of health care in the Delaware Valley. Consequently, by inviting comment and assuming the risk of unfair comment, both claimants resemble public figures. *See* Steaks Unlimited, Inc. v. Deaner, 623 F.2d 264, 274 (3d Cir. 1980) ("In short, through its advertising blitz, [the plaintiff corporation] invited public attention, comment and criticism.").

Under traditional defamation analysis, the parties' considerable access to the media and their voluntary entry into a controversy are strong indicia that they are limited purpose public figures. Indeed, inflexible application of these factors would warrant a finding of public figure status and facilitate a finding of heightened constitutional protection. Nonetheless, we hold that these corporations are not public figures for the limited purpose of commenting on health care in this case.

As noted, *Gertz* defines the limited purpose public figure as one who has "thrust [himself] to the forefront of particular public controversies in order to influence the resolution of the issues involved." Although some of the advertisements touch on matters of public concern, their central thrust is commercial. Thus, the parties have acted primarily to generate revenue by influencing customers, not to resolve "the issues involved."

While discerning motivations of the speaker is often difficult, we have a more fundamental reason for declining to find limited purpose public figure status in this case. The express analysis in *Gertz* is not helpful in the context of a comparative advertising war. Most products can be linked to a public issue. And most advertisers—including both claimants here—seek out the media. Thus, it will always be true that such advertisers have voluntarily placed themselves in the public eye. It will be equally true that such advertisers have access to the media. Therefore, under the *Gertz* rationale, speech of public concern that implicates corporate advertisers—i.e., typical comparative advertising—will always be insulated behind the actual malice standard. We believe a corporation must do more than the claimants have done here to become a limited purpose public figure under *Gertz*.

In summary, we conclude that the speech at issue does not receive heightened protection under the First Amendment. Because this speech is chill-resistant, the *New York Times* standard is not, as we have noted, "necessary to give adequate 'breathing space' to the freedoms protected by the First Amendment." Therefore, the standard of proof needed to establish the substantive claims is that applicable under federal and state law. . . .

NOTES AND QUESTIONS

Revisiting Advertising Theory. Consider the search/experience/credence qualities framework from Chapter 4. The quality of medical services is a classic credence attribute. How might that affect consumer reactions to claims that a competitor's medical services are inferior?

Malice Is a Term of Art. A speaker acts with "malice" if it knows of the falsity of a statement or acts with reckless disregard toward its truth or falsity. Some states are also permit a malice finding if the defendant acts with ill will or intent to interfere with the plaintiff's economic interest in an unprivileged fashion. The Restatement (Second) of Torts takes no position on whether such a rule is appropriate, in part because the First Amendment implications of such a rule are unclear.

Kinetic Concepts, Inc. v. Bluesky Medical Corporation, 2005 WL 3068209 (W.D. Tex. 2005), found a genuine issue of material fact on malice when the defendant "described his marketing plan . . . as an effort to 'contract[ ] the market from $400 million per year to $40 million per year and therefore sow[ ] the seeds of chaos and contraction into the marketplace." The letter went on to state that the defendant wished to "reduce and change the profit vector of the competition from Black to a glowing deep red hue." That is, the defendant really wanted to harm the plaintiff. Does that indicate the defendant acted maliciously? Is it appropriate to find malice if the defendant was negligently mistaken but not reckless in its disregard for the truth? What if the defendant was not negligent, but simply mistaken—should its ill will or intent to interfere with the plaintiff's economic interest still count as malice? Recall that modern consumer-protection statutes often don't require negligence or any fault at all, nor does the Lanham Act.

Convergence in the Torts. As the *Blue Cross/Blue Shield* case indicates, First Amendment constraints on defamation have made it more similar to the product-disparagement tort. The differences between the classic causes of action for product disparagement, trade libel and defamation, though highly technical and subject to judicial nitpicking, are often not practically significant in the context of claims brought by commercial entities, especially when the claims are brought against other commercial entities.

In fact, the Restatement (Second) of Torts Section 623A subsumes the concept of trade libel within injurious falsehood, which is why we haven't used the term "trade libel" here, though some states still have a tort with that name. The Restatement says that "[o]ne who publishes a false statement harmful to the interests of another is subject to liability for pecuniary loss resulting to the other if (a) he intends for publication of the statement to result in harm to interests of the other having a pecuniary value, or either recognizes or should recognize that it is likely to do so, and (b) he knows that the statement is false or acts in reckless disregard of its truth or falsity." Then Section 626, Disparagement of Quality—Trade Libel, says that the injurious falsehood rules apply to statements "disparaging the quality of another's land, chattels or intangible things." "Trade libel" is simply the old term for this type of injurious falsehood.

Defamation law is aimed at protecting the personal reputation of the plaintiff, while the injurious falsehood tort is designed to protect economic interests. Before *New York Times v. Sullivan* (discussed in Chapter 17), the general rule was that damaging statements were presumed false in defamation cases, and liability for falsity was strict, neither of which were true for injurious falsehood. These differences between the torts have been swept away by modern First Amendment jurisprudence. Likewise, defamation used to allow presumptions of damage, while injurious falsehood always required proof. Presumptions of damage in defamation have been cut back substantially in many instances. However, the presumptions may still be significant in some cases, especially in allowing a claim to survive dismissal at the pleading stage, as we will discuss below.

The Line Between Defamation and Product Disparagement. The *Blue Cross/Blue Shield* court applied the rule that only ads that impute "fraud, deceit, dishonesty, or reprehensible conduct" to the other party could be defamatory, while product disparagement (or "commercial disparagement") covered a broader range of statements.

The remaining significance of this distinction involves pleading or presuming harm. Product disparagement requires proof of special damages—that is, specific harms such as specific lost customers. Courts often require plaintiffs to plead the names of lost customers or potential customers. Pleading only "lost sales" is insufficient to survive a motion to dismiss.

As a plaintiff's attorney, how would you find evidence of special damages for disparagement in the case of a large-scale, widely disseminated ad campaign? Is the special damages requirement an indication that the tort is not designed to govern large-scale advertising campaigns?

In defamation, by contrast, damages may generally be presumed if the statements are per se defamatory—if they're the kind of statements that naturally would be expected to injure a party's reputation.

In *Dorman Products, Inc. v. Dayco Products, LLC*, 749 F. Supp. 2d 630 (E.D. Mich. 2010), the court held that statements about the inferiority of Dorman's products weren't defamatory. Allegations of inferiority are "par for the course" and "the most innocuous kind of puffing," generally not capable of misleading the public. However, statements that arguably suggested that Dorman misrepresented product quality were actionable as defamation, not just as trade disparagement. The potentially actionable statements included suggestions that Dorman's products were defective and that Dorman misled the public into believing that its products conformed to industry standards. Asserting that Dorman infringed Dayco's trade dress, that the similarity was non-coincidental, and that Dorman misled consumers, "ha[d] the potential" to impute an intent to mislead to Dorman, which was enough to survive a motion to dismiss.

Given this result, when can an advertiser be confident that its negative statements about a competitor will be judged by trade disparagement standards and not defamation standards? *See also* Cohen v. Hansen, 2015 WL 3609689 (D. Nev. June 9, 2015) (statements alleging that executive had been convicted of fraud and the business was organized to perpetrate illegal activities constituted defamation per se, not business disparagement, so actual damages need not be proved).

Procter & Gamble Co. v. Haugen, 222 F. 3d 1262 (10th Cir. 2000), involved false claims by Amway distributors that P&G was a corporate agent of Satan.

horn

horn

Inverted 666!

The devil's two horns and Antichrist's number 666

[Procter & Gamble's old logo with critiques]

Though the court of appeals held that P & G alleged a violation of the Lanham Act's prohibition on false statements about "commercial activities," it affirmed dismissal of P&G's state-law defamation claims:

> With regard to summary judgment on P & G's state law claims, under Utah law the subject message would be actionable as slander per se if "the defamatory words fall into one of four categories: (1) charge of criminal conduct, (2) charge of a loathsome disease, (3) charge of conduct that is incompatible with the exercise of a lawful business, trade, profession or office; and (4) charge of the unchastity of a woman." Slander per se . . . permits a finding of liability without the need to prove special harm. On appeal, P & G challenges the district court's conclusion that the satanic rumor was "not incompatible with conducting a lawful business." It argues the representations that it "financially supports the Church of Satan and places the Devil's mark on its products are incompatible with P & G's lawful business of selling popular products for personal care and hygiene and for the home."

> The false statements contained in the subject message are not the kind of allegations that constitute slander per se. As P & G notes, the question is whether the alleged behavior is incompatible with its business of selling household consumer goods, not whether the alleged behavior is lawful. . . . P & G's business is clearly lawful. However, allegations that it directs a percentage of its profits to the church of Satan are not incompatible with that business in the manner necessary to be actionable as slander per se.

>> Disparaging words, to be actionable per se . . . must affect the plaintiff in some way that is peculiarly harmful to one engaged in [the plaintiff's] trade or profession. Disparagement of a general character, equally discreditable to

> all persons, is not enough unless the particular quality disparaged is of such a character that it is peculiarly valuable in the plaintiff's business or profession.
>
> For example, "charges against a clergyman of drunkenness and other moral misconduct affect his fitness for the performance of the duties of his profession, although the same charges against a business man or tradesman do not so affect him." Although offensive to many, an allegation of Devil worship, like drunkenness, is "[d]isparagement of a general character, equally discreditable to all persons" and does not pertain to a quality that is peculiarly valuable in plaintiffs' professional activities of manufacturing and selling household consumer goods. We therefore hold that the district court properly granted summary judgment as to this claim. . . .

Would a statement that a business was routinely late in paying its bills be "disparagement of a general character, equally discreditable to all persons"? Could an accusation that a company's products come from China, not from America, be defamatory? *See* AvePoint, Inc. v. Power Tools, Inc., 981 F. Supp. 2d 496 (W.D. Va. 2013) (party's allegedly false accusation that the other party's software was developed and maintained in China and India, not the United States as advertised, was appropriately the basis for a claim for defamation).

2.   Commercial Speech in an Age of Convergence

The Third Circuit's resolution of the First Amendment challenge to the Lanham Act assumed that ads were readily distinguishable from non-ads. But as advertising methods have changed and the lines between advertising and editorial content blur, can its distinction be preserved?

In *Edward B. Beharry & Co., Ltd. v. Bedessee Imports Inc.*, 95 U.S.P.Q.2d 1480 (E.D.N.Y. 2010), *The Caribbean New Yorker*, read by the parties' customer base, ran an article stating that Beharry's Special Madras Curry Powder posed a threat to the public, given that the FDA had rejected a June 2008 shipment because it was "filthy." "Contradicting Beharry's claim of pride in providing its customers with high quality products and services, its 'famous' Indi brand curry was denied entry to the United States." The article concluded that "[t]he West-Indian community must be made aware of repeated adverse FDA actions regarding Beharry's food products and any corollary health risks," and provided (broken) links to the FDA announcements.

Beharry sued for defamation, alleging that its competitor Bedessee "contributed to, authored, conceived, submitted and/or otherwise caused" the piece to be published. Beharry alleged that individual defendant Invor Bedessee circulated the full article by email to distributors and the customer base.

The court denied Bedessee's motion to dismiss. Bedessee's denial of any connection to the publication merely created a factual dispute. Beharry noted that the publication didn't contain a byline, and claimed that the piece was a paid ad rather than a news article.

What should the result be if Bedessee is "connected" to the article in the sense of convincing the magazine that it was a worthwhile story to run, but didn't pay for it to appear?

Beharry also claimed violation of the Lanham Act. Bedessee argued that the Lanham Act claim failed because the article wasn't commercial speech. The court agreed. "No named defendant appears anywhere in the publication, nor do any of defendants' products, prices, or business contacts. As the public would have no reason to associate the publication with defendants, it cannot possibly propose a commercial transaction between defendants and readers of *The Caribbean New Yorker*. Even if defendants paid to run the piece with a motivation toward indirectly influencing customers to buy their goods, such a motivation does not transform the piece into commercial speech."

Is attribution required for this article to be commercial speech? Is this holding consistent with its ruling on defamation?

Consider the following case of speech to an independent news organization. It was speech by a competitor, but not in a traditional advertising context. What standard should regulate it?

BOULÉ V. HUTTON, 328 F.3D 84 (2D CIR. 2003)

Plaintiffs-appellants René and Claude Boulé ("the Boulés") appeal from the decisions of the district court (1) granting partial summary judgment to defendants-appellees Ingrid Hutton ("Hutton"), the Leonard Hutton Galleries, Inc. ("the Gallery"), Mark Khidekel ("Mark") and Regina Khidekel ("Regina"), (2) finding for defendants on certain of plaintiffs' claims after a bench trial, and (3) denying plaintiffs' motion for relief from judgment under Fed. R. Civ. P. 60(b). For the reasons set forth below, we affirm in part, and vacate in part the decisions of the district court.

At its heart, this is a dispute about the authenticity of works of art (the "Paintings") owned by the Boulés. While the Boulés believe the Paintings to be early works of the Russian Suprematist artist Lazar Khidekel ("Lazar"), Lazar's son Mark and daughter-in-law Regina (collectively, "Khidekels") claim that they are not. The Khidekels are selling their own collection of Lazar's art through Hutton and her Gallery.

The Boulés brought suit under the Lanham Act and state law causes of action to recover for the damage to the value of the Paintings that they assert occurred because of statements made by the defendants. The Honorable Miriam Goldman Cedarbaum held, inter alia, that the Boulés had not carried their burden of showing that the Paintings were authentic, that is, painted by Lazar. On the other hand, she found that the Khidekels had falsely and in bad faith denied that Mark had given the Boulés certificates acknowledging that at least some of the Paintings were indeed his father's. Applying the special damage rules that pertain to the law of defamation, the district court awarded the Boulés nominal damages. Each of these rulings and others entered by Judge Cedarbaum in her three opinions have been challenged on appeal.

BACKGROUND

Lazar was born in 1904 in Vitebsk, Russia, and joined the Suprematist school of Russian avant-garde artists in the years following the Russian Revolution. In his youth, Lazar studied with two of the better-known artists of the period, Marc Chagall and Kazmir Malevich, and later in life became a prominent architect. The artworks in his possession upon his death in 1986 became the property of Mark and Regina.

The Boulés are Parisian art collectors who own a number of works from the Russian avant-garde period; in addition, Claude has published a scholarly work on Russian Constructivism. By the late 1980s, the Boulés had acquired 176 works attributed to Lazar. As it was both illegal and dangerous to acquire Russian avant-garde art prior to the fall of the Soviet Union, the majority of the Boulé's pieces were acquired through non-traditional channels.

The Boulés and the Khidekels first encountered each other in Paris in 1988. Over the next few years, the Khidekels and the Boulés developed a friendship, as the Khidekels were pleased to find admirers of Lazar's work in the West, and the Boulés were happy to show their collection to them. They made (ultimately unrealized) plans to pool their collections of Lazar's work for an exhibition in Canada, and, in 1991, in exchange for approximately $8,000, Mark signed certificates of authenticity in Paris for sixteen of the Paintings he selected from the Boulés' collection. The certificates stated: "I, Mark Khidekel, having examined the artwork shown to me . . . hereby confirm that it is the work of my father, Lazar Khidekel, and that it can be identified as a study."

During this period, although the Khidekels were surprised that a collection of Lazar's work existed in Paris, and told the Boulés that some of the pieces they owned were different from those of Lazar's works that the Khidekels possessed, Mark and Regina never expressed to the Boulés any reservations about the legitimacy of the collection. As the district court found at trial, "Mark noted some differences between the Boulés' collection and his collection, and commented that the bulk of the Boulés' collection was created when Lazar Khidekel was a very young student—possibly as early as 1920."

The Boulés exhibited the Paintings at the Joliette Museum of Art in Montreal, Canada in 1992, and galleries in Canada over the course of the months that followed. Although Mark expressed an interest in lecturing at the Joliette Museum in conjunction with the exhibition of the Paintings, the Khidekels ultimately did not participate.

The Khidekels began an association with Hutton in 1992, and moved to New York in 1993. Hutton is a prominent dealer of art of the Russian avant-garde, which has a small but global market. The Khidekels soon entered into a consignment agreement with Hutton to facilitate the sale of their collection of Lazar's work. In 1995, the Gallery exhibited works from the Khidekel's collection. The exhibition catalogue noted that it represented the first-ever display of Lazar's work, despite the earlier show at the Joliette Museum in Canada that had included works from the Boulés' collection. In late 1995 and early 1996, the Khidekels and Hutton sent a jointly-signed letter to at least twenty-five art galleries around the world (the "Repudiation Letter"), repudiating the Paintings that had been loaned by the Boulés and attributed to Lazar in the Canadian exhibition.

In 1996, after being approached by a reporter, Hutton arranged for the Khidekels to be interviewed for an article in *ARTnews*, a leading industry publication, entitled "The Betrayal of the Russian Avant-Garde." The article discussed the entry of "thousands" of fraudulent artworks into galleries, museums and private collections. The Khidekels were quoted in the article as stating that the Paintings were not Lazar's work, and as so advising the Boulés when they had initially viewed the Boulés' collection.[3] An article that appeared shortly thereafter in Le Devoir, a Montreal publication, contained a quotation from Regina specifically denying that she or Mark had ever authenticated any portion of the Boulés' collection.[4]

The Boulés brought suit in 1997, alleging that defendants' statements in the Gallery catalogue, the Repudiation Letter, *ARTnews*, and in *Le Devoir*, and other statements to art dealers and journalists violated the Lanham Act. They further alleged that the statements violated the New York General Business Law, and state law causes of action against disparagement, defamation, tortious interference with business relationships, unfair competition, unjust enrichment and breach of contract.

A. The summary judgment rulings

. . . . The district court found that the statements in the Repudiation Letter were not actionable because they could not be considered a "representation of fact" within the meaning of the Lanham Act. The claim pertaining to the statements to *ARTnews* was dismissed because the district court held that a response to an unsolicited inquiry from a reporter on a topic of public concern—fraud in the Russian avant-garde art market—was not a statement made "in commercial advertising or promotion."

B. The trial

. . . . Judge Cedarbaum did find for plaintiffs on part of their defamation claim. The district court found that the statements published in *Le Devoir* to the effect that Mark had never signed the certificates of authenticity, and in *ARTnews* representing that Mark and Regina had told the Boulés that the Paintings were not authentic, were false and defamatory, but that plaintiffs had not proved special damages. The district court found, however, that the *ARTnews* statements constituted libel per se with regard to Claude Boulé in her capacity as an art historian, but declined to award any more than nominal damages. The plaintiffs also received judgment on their breach of contract claim, as the district court found that Mark had breached the implied covenant of good faith and fair dealing by repudiating the

---

[3] The *ARTnews* article contained the following passages:

> [Lazar] never had a solo show during his lifetime, nor did he or his family ever sell or part with any of his works, according to his son and daughter-in-law, Mark and Regina Khidekel. On this point, they were adamant. . . .

> Mark and Regina say that they told the Boulés the works were not Khidekels. . . . What makes Mark and Regina most indignant is that the catalogue [for the Joliette Museum exhibition] gives the impression that they endorse the Boulé collection, which they most emphatically do not.

[4] In the February 23, 1996 *Le Devoir* article, Regina is quoted as saying that "neither she nor her husband ever 'authenticated' anything and the fake certificates were forged."

certificates. On this basis, plaintiffs were awarded restitution, but not expectation damages. The remaining state law causes of action were dismissed. . . .

DISCUSSION

[The court concluded that the plaintiffs could not bring Lanham Act claims based on the *ARTnews* statements because they were not commercial speech, and the Lanham Act covers only commercial speech.]

. . . ii. State law claims

The Boulés appeal from the denial at trial of their claims under Section 349 of New York's General Business Law and the New York common law of unfair competition by disparagement. The district court denied these claims based on its conclusion that the plaintiffs had failed to carry their burden to show that the Paintings were authentic. While most of the state law claims were based on statements about the authenticity of the Paintings, some were not. The *Le Devoir* and *ARTnews* statements addressed the certificates that Mark had provided to the Boulés and the conversations between the Boulés and Khidekels about the Paintings. As the district court held that plaintiffs proved by a preponderance of the evidence the falsity of the statements in *Le Devoir* and *ARTnews*, we remand for further proceedings to determine whether these false statements constitute a violation of Section 349 and the claim of unfair competition by disparagement. In addition, because Section 349 requires proof of a deceptive practice, and does not require proof that a statement is false, we remand for further proceedings on all of plaintiffs' claims under Section 349.

A few additional observations about these two causes of action may prove of assistance on remand. Section 349 prohibits "[d]eceptive acts or practices in the conduct of any business, trade or commerce." N.Y. Gen. Bus. Law. § 349(a). To establish a claim under Section 349, the plaintiff must show "a material deceptive act or practice directed to consumers that caused actual harm." We have not yet decided whether false statements are likely to be deceptive. "Deceptive acts" are defined objectively, as acts "likely to mislead a reasonable consumer acting reasonably under the circumstances." Further, a deceptive practice "need not reach the level of common-law fraud to be actionable under section 349."

The district court expressed reservations as to whether plaintiffs are within the class of persons, namely, consumers, for whose protection Section 349 was enacted. Section 349, however, allows recovery not only by consumers, but also by competitors if there is "some harm to the public at large." Although a Section 349 plaintiff is not required to show justifiable reliance by consumers, "[a]n act is deceptive within the meaning of the New York statute only if it is likely to mislead a reasonable consumer."

On appeal, the Boulés describe their claim of "unfair competition by disparagement" as a claim for defamation of another's business.[48] Where a statement impugns "the basic integrity" of a business, an action for defamation per se lies, and general damages are presumed. Nonetheless, actual damages must be proved with competent evidence of the injury. . . .

CALABRESI, Circuit Judge, concurring.

. . . . Congress did not wish to extend federal Lanham Act liability to speech that is subject to broader general First Amendment protection than is commercial speech. Such noncommercial speech, however, may well remain the grounds of recovery under state laws. In other words, as the opinion notes, even noncommercial speech may, in appropriate cases, be actionable. Today's holding means only that Congress chose not to make that kind of speech federally actionable under the Lanham Act. It is for these reasons that the opinion is able to remand the speech here discussed for consideration of whether it (a) violates section 349 of New York's General Business Law or (b) may be the basis for recovery under the New York common law of unfair competition by disparagement.

NOTES AND QUESTIONS

How far does New York's General Business Law go in making noncommercial speech actionable? As applied to commercial speech, the law clearly covers false speech even when made without fault, but how could it constitutionally apply the same rule to noncommercial speech? Should a court refuse to apply the GBL to such speech at all, or should it imply special constraints on a GBL cause of action against noncommercial speech in order to avoid First Amendment infirmity?

Opinion Versus Fact. Were the Khidekels' statements about authenticity statements of fact or statements of opinion? How can we tell?

Defamation law's treatment of opinion is roughly similar to false advertising law's approach. But because the kinds of things that can be defamatory are more limited than the infinite matters about which one might falsely advertise, judgmental language is more often crucial to defamation cases. In *Cuba's United Ready Mix, Inc. v. Bock Concrete Foundations, Inc.*, 785 S.W.2d 649 (Mo. Ct. App. 1990), the plaintiff sold concrete, and the defendant was a contractor that used concrete in construction. The defendant allegedly told many people that the plaintiff "was delivering inferior material and that he would not be a part of the fraud." The key question was whether this was a statement of fact or opinion. The court quoted the standard rule: "[A] defamatory communication may consist of a statement in the form of an opinion, but a statement of this nature is actionable only if it implies the allegation of undisclosed defamatory facts as the basis for the opinion." In this case, the defendant's statement implied that he had knowledge of undisclosed defamatory facts and could be defamatory.

---

[8] . . . On appeal, [the Boulés] press only the claim for defamation of their business presumably because of the difference in the standard for an award of damages. A claim for defamation of another's business is distinct from a claim for product disparagement. Among other things, special damages must be proven for a product disparagement claim. . . .

Consider: After *Lexmark*, could a Lanham Act claim have been brought against the defendant? A Lanham Act case involving *implied* defamatory facts would, as you recall, require extrinsic evidence of consumer deception, usually in the form of a survey, if they were not implied by necessary implication. However, no extrinsic evidence would be required under defamation law for a jury to find liability. (The stringent requirements for showing damage from defamation arguably perform the same function, however.)

Was it the defendant's position as a user of concrete that made it plausible to think that he had knowledge of undisclosed defamatory facts supporting his opinion? What if he'd posted the same statement as an anonymous comment on a blog about the plaintiff—would the statement still be potentially defamatory?

The *Bock* defendant's statements were of the kind one might expect an individual to make in the course of soliciting specific customers. Historically, the business torts developed to address that kind of situation. Consider how well these torts fit with a modern, mass-advertising campaign. (Hint: maybe not that well?).

In *Verizon Directories Corp. v. Yellow Book USA, Inc.*, 309 F. Supp. 2d 401 (E.D.N.Y 2004), Verizon sued Yellow Book over TV ads that used humor to suggest that Yellow Book was superior. According to Verizon, the ads falsely represented that more people used the Yellow Book than Verizon's offering; the number of users is relevant to the prices a directory can command from advertisers. One ad, for example, showed a "Senior Focus Group" in which everyone claimed to use the Yellow Book, and no one had heard of the alternative (Verizon). In another ad, a wind tunnel easily blew Verizon's directory away, while the Yellow Book proved more substantial because it had "the right stuff." Verizon alleged Lanham Act claims, violation of New York's statutory false advertising law (Sections 349–50, discussed *supra*) and product disparagement.

Yellow Book argued that its ads were merely puffery. The court, applying the same analysis to the Lanham Act claims as to the state-law claims, found that it could not determine puffery as a matter of law. Though the ads were literally "playful and absurd," in context, consumers might interpret the ads to mean that more people used the Yellow Book than the Verizon directory. The ads were "skillfully crafted and shown at great expense to subtly but firmly communicate an idea—that the Yellow Book is preferred by users to Verizon's book and that, more to the point, advertisers will reach more potential consumers if they put their names and money in the former rather than the latter." The judge's background was very different from ordinary viewers', and the judge declined to resolve the meaning of the ad to them, an issue requiring "surveys, expert testimony, and other evidence of what is happening in the real world of television watchers and advertisers in yellow pages."

In applying the Lanham Act puffery standards to the state law disparagement claims, was the *Verizon* court doing something different than what the court did in the *Bock* case with respect to the line between opinion and fact? Historically, defamation and product disparagement cases didn't involve expert testimony or consumer surveys—juries were left to their own interpretation of the accused materials. Is that still the right rule for a defamation/disparagement claim? Is there something different about mass-media campaigns that would justify different treatment?

3.   Why All These Negative Ads?: Public Policy and Comparative Advertising

Historically, comparative advertising was regarded with suspicion (and still is in the European Union; *see* Chapter 12). Over forty years ago, however, impelled by concerns that advertising restrictions were suppressing competition and raising prices, the FTC made a major push to encourage such advertising.

FEDERAL TRADE COMMISSION, STATEMENT OF POLICY REGARDING COMPARATIVE ADVERTISING, AUGUST 13, 1979

. . .(b) Policy Statement

The Federal Trade Commission has determined that it would be of benefit to advertisers, advertising agencies, broadcasters, and self-regulation entities to restate its current policy concerning comparative advertising.[5] Commission policy in the area of comparative advertising encourages the naming of, or reference to competitors, but requires clarity, and, if necessary, disclosure to avoid deception of the consumer. Additionally, the use of truthful comparative advertising should not be restrained by broadcasters or self-regulation entities.

(c) The Commission has supported the use of brand comparisons where the bases of comparison are clearly identified. Comparative advertising, when truthful and non-deceptive, is a source of important information to consumers and assists them in making rational purchase decisions. Comparative advertising encourages product improvement and innovation, and can lead to lower prices in the marketplace. For these reasons, the Commission will continue to scrutinize carefully restraints upon its use.

(1) Disparagement

Some industry codes which prohibit practices such as "disparagement," "disparagement of competitors," "improper disparagement," "unfairly attacking," "discrediting," may operate as a restriction on comparative advertising. The Commission has previously held that disparaging advertising is permissible so long as it is truthful and not deceptive. In *Carter Products, Inc.*, 323 F.2d 523 (5th Cir. 1963), the Commission narrowed an order recommended by the hearing examiner which would have prohibited respondents from disparaging competing products through the use of false or misleading pictures, depictions, or demonstrations, "or otherwise" disparaging such products. In explaining why it eliminated "or otherwise" from the final order, the Commission observed that the phrase would have prevented:

> respondents from making truthful and nondeceptive statements that a product has certain desirable properties or qualities which a competing product or products do not possess. Such a comparison may have the effect of disparaging the competing product, but we know of no rule of law which prevents a seller from honestly

---

[5] For purposes of this Policy Statement, comparative advertising is defined as advertising that compares alternative brands on objectively measurable attributes or price, and identifies the alternative brand by name, illustration or other distinctive information.

informing the public of the advantages of its products as opposed to those of competing products.

Industry codes which restrain comparative advertising in this manner are subject to challenge by the Federal Trade Commission.

(2) Substantiation

On occasion, a higher standard of substantiation by advertisers using comparative advertising has been required by self-regulation entities. . . . However, industry codes and interpretations that impose a higher standard of substantiation for comparative claims than for unilateral claims are inappropriate and should be revised.

Effect of the FTC Statement

The FTC's statement focused on consumer information and antitrust concerns: An agreement to refrain from saying nasty things about the competition could have anticompetitive effects. Comparative advertising became quite widespread in the United States. By some measures, one-third of U.S. ads are comparative, and comparative ads may be more persuasive and memorable than non-comparative ads. *See* Jenna D. Beller, Comment, *The Law of Comparative Advertising in the United States and Around the World: A Practical Guide for U.S. Lawyers and Their Clients*, 29 INT'L LAW. 917 (1995).

A separate question can be raised by comparative advertising: What happens when an ad doesn't name the competition? *Kinetic Concepts, Inc. v. Bluesky Medical Corporation*, 2005 WL 3068209 (W.D. Tex. 2005), applied the general defamation rule that "it is not necessary that the individual referred to be named if those who knew and were acquainted with the plaintiff understand from reading the publication that it referred to the plaintiff." The plaintiff in *Kinetic* conducted a study showing that 33.3% of physicians and 95% of nurses in its sample believed that the relevant ads were comparing the parties' products. This created a genuine issue of material fact on the element that a defamatory statement must be "of and concerning" the plaintiff to be actionable.

4.   A Final Business Tort: Tortious Interference

Tortious interference with contract or with prospective contractual relations is often alleged alongside various other advertising-related torts. There are substantial state-law variations in the elements of the tort, which we will not detail. It rarely succeeds in the advertising and marketing law context (or any others).

The following case against Google—which makes its money from advertisers who often bid against their competitors, even for their own trademarks—illustrates that the tort is not well-suited for a modern, large-scale advertising practice.

GOOGLE INC. V. AMERICAN BLIND & WALLPAPER FACTORY, INC., 74 U.S.P.Q.2D 1385 (N.D. CAL. 2005)

[This is a keyword advertising case, as described in Chapter 12: Google sells the plaintiff's trademark as keywords in its AdWords program so that competitors' ads appear as sponsored links in response to a search for "American Blind." The court refused to dismiss American Blind's trademark claims.]

. . . C. Tortious Interference with Prospective Business Advantage

Defendants move to dismiss American Blind's state law claim of tortious interference with prospective business advantage.[31] The elements of tortious interference with prospective business advantage are as follows: (1) an economic relationship between the plaintiff and some third party, with the probability of future economic benefit to the plaintiff, (2) the defendant's knowledge of the relationship, (3) intentional acts on the part of the defendant designed to disrupt the relationship, which acts are wrongful by some legal measure other than the fact of interference itself,[32] (4) actual disruption of the relationship, and (5) economic harm to the plaintiff proximately caused by the defendant's acts. Defendants argue that American Blind fails to allege an independently wrongful act, as required by the third element, or probability of future economic benefit from existing economic relationships, as required by the first element.

. . . . As American Blind's claims of trademark violations, unfair competition, false representation, and injury to business reputation will proceed past the motion-to-dismiss stage, so too can those claims serve, for present purposes, as allegations that satisfy the pleading requirements for the third element of tortious interference with prospective business advantage.

However, the Court agrees with Defendants that American Blind's allegations with respect to the first element of the claim are insufficient. The tort of interference with prospective business advantage applies to "interference with existing noncontractual relations which hold the promise of future economic advantage. In other words, it protects the expectation that the relationship eventually will yield the desired benefit, not necessarily the more speculative expectation that a potentially beneficial relationship will eventually arise." Allegations that amount to a mere "hope for an economic relationship and a desire for future benefit" are inadequate to satisfy the pleading requirements of the first element of the tort.

---

[31] American Blind alleges that (1) "[m]any" of its customers are "repeat customers" and "regularly" purchase products from its Web site, (2) it is probable that "such customers and others" will "continue to seek to visit" the Web site and purchase products and services "in the future," (3) Defendants were aware of American Blind's "reasonable expectation of future transactions" with its "returning customers," as well as with customers who "may be attracted" to its goods and services because of its goodwill, advertising, and promotion, (4) "[a]bsent Defendants' intentional and improper interference through their deceptive and manipulated search engine 'results,' it is reasonably certain that American Blind would realize additional sales from existing customers and/or new customers," (5) Defendants "intentionally and improperly interfered with American Blind's future and prospective sales," and (6) American Blind has suffered and will continue to suffer irreparable injury as a result of Defendants' actions.

[32] An act is independently wrongful if it is "unlawful, that is, if it is proscribed by some constitutional, statutory, regulatory, common law, or other determinable legal standard."

Even though American Blind has alleged relationships with "repeat customers" who "probabl[y]" will "continue to seek to visit" its Web site and purchase its goods and services, American Blind's alleged expectation of "future and prospective sales" to these customers, with which Defendants are alleged to have interfered, is too speculative to support this claim. It does not rise to the level of the requisite "promise of future economic advantage," instead expressing merely a "hope . . . and a desire" for unspecified future sales to unspecified returning customers, in the form of a legal conclusion. Moreover, it goes without saying that American Blind's even more speculative allegations regarding "new" customers with whom it cannot claim any past or present interactions, however insubstantial, also are inadequate to support this claim. American Blind has failed to point to any case law suggesting that its allegations regarding the probability of future economic benefit from its existing economic relationships with third parties are sufficient. Accordingly, Defendants' motions to dismiss American Blind's claim of tortious interference with prospective business advantage are GRANTED.

NOTES AND QUESTIONS

Can you think of any potential upside in asserting a tortious interference claim in a mass-market advertising case other than increasing defense costs?

Tortious Interference with Marketing. In *Monster Energy Co. v. Vital Pharmaceuticals, Inc.*, 2019 WL 3099711 (C.D. Cal. Jun. 17, 2019), Monster showed that its competitor Vital had a corporate policy of disrupting Monster's contracts, which were supposed to provide it with specific amounts of in-store shelf or cooler space in retail stores across the country. As a result, Vital's energy drink products were stocked in Monster's contracted-for space.

Vital's principal made Instagram posts demonstrating his knowledge of the existing agreements and further confirming tortious intent, such as one that showed an image of VPX products placed in front of Monster products accompanied by the text "When in doubt block them out. In life when they tell you there's no shelf space – make your own shelf space! When multibillion-dollar competitors pay for space[,] retaliate with a vengeance." The court commented: "In light of the extent of this practice, Plaintiff need not demonstrate specific knowledge of each contract in question in order to demonstrate a likelihood of success on the merits." However, Monster still struggled to show damages—there was no evidence that these practices fueled Vital's growth.

Copyright in the United States protects original works of authorship fixed in a tangible medium of expression, whether they are published or unpublished. Among other things, copyright protects most books, movies, music, software and art, as well as photographs, choreography and architectural works. Copyright does not protect facts, ideas, systems or methods of operation.

Copyright protection applies to a work even if there is no copyright notice on the work and even if the author has not filed a registration. Prompt registration (before infringement begins or within three months of publication), however, provides the owner with procedural benefits plus the possibility of receiving statutory damages and attorneys' fees in a successful infringement suit. Statutory damages can be significant—up to $150,000 per work infringed in the case of willful infringement. Registration, even if not done promptly, is a prerequisite for filing suit for infringement of a U.S. work.

Copyright owners' exclusive rights include the right to control reproduction, distribution, public performance (though there is no general public performance right for sound recordings) and derivative works. Derivative works are works that, while based on the original copyrighted work, transform, adapt, translate or otherwise rework the original's creative expression, such as a movie adapted from a novel. A claim for copyright infringement requires that the plaintiff prove two things: (1) its ownership of the copyright in a particular work and (2) that the defendant copied, or made another unauthorized use, of the work or a substantial and legally protectable portion of it.

1.   What is Protectable?

The U.S. Constitution specifically authorizes Congress to enact a copyright statute. *See* U.S. CONST., art. I, § 8, cl. 8. In the early years of copyright, it was unclear whether advertisements qualified for copyright protection. Ads were not "literary" works like books or articles, and advertisements do not clearly "promote the Progress of Science" as the Constitution contemplated. That uncertainty produced the following case.

BLEISTEIN V. DONALDSON LITHOGRAPHING COMPANY, 188 U.S. 239 (1903)

. . . The alleged infringements consisted in the copying in reduced form of three chromolithographs prepared by employees of the plaintiffs for advertisements of a circus owned by one Wallace. . . .The circuit court directed a verdict for the defendant on the ground that the chromolithographs were not within the protection of the copyright law, and this ruling was sustained by the circuit court of appeals.

417

. . . . [T]he plaintiff's case is not affected by the fact, if it be one, that the pictures represent actual groups—visible things. They seem from the testimony to have been composed from hints or description, not from sight of a performance. But even if they had been drawn from the life, that fact would not deprive them of protection. The opposite proposition would mean that a portrait by Velasquez or Whistler was common property because others might try their hand on the same face. Others are free to copy the original. They are not free to copy the copy. The copy is the personal reaction of an individual upon nature. Personality always contains something unique. It expresses its singularity even in handwriting, and a very modest grade of art has in it something irreducible which is one man's alone. That something he may copyright unless there is a restriction in the words of the act.

If there is a restriction, it is not to be found in the limited pretensions of these particular works. The least pretentious picture has more originality in it than directories and the like, which may be copyrighted. . . .

Certainly works are not the less connected with the fine arts because their pictorial quality attracts the crowd, and therefore gives them a real use—if use means to increase trade and to help to make money. A picture is nonetheless a picture, and nonetheless a subject of copyright, that it is used for an advertisement.

. . . It would be a dangerous undertaking for persons trained only to the law to constitute themselves final judges of the worth of pictorial illustrations, outside of the narrowest and most obvious limits. At the one extreme, some works of genius would be sure to miss appreciation. Their very novelty would make them repulsive until the public had learned the new language in which their author spoke. It may be more than doubted, for instance, whether the etchings of Goya or the paintings of Manet would have been sure of protection when seen for the first time. At the other end, copyright would be denied to pictures which appealed to a public less educated than the judge. Yet if they command the interest of any public, they have a commercial value—it would be bold to say that they have not an aesthetic and educational value—and the taste of any public is not to be treated with contempt. It is an ultimate fact for the moment, whatever may be our hopes for a change. That these pictures had their worth and their success is sufficiently shown by the desire to reproduce them without regard to the plaintiffs' rights. We are of opinion that there was evidence that the plaintiffs have rights entitled to the protection of the law. . . .

HARLAN, J., dissenting:

[Justice Harlan quoted the court of appeals]:

> What we hold is this: that if a chromo, lithograph, or other print, engraving, or picture has no other use than that of a mere advertisement, and no value aside from this function, it would not be promotive of the useful arts within the meaning of the constitutional provision, to protect the 'author' in the exclusive use thereof, and the copyright statute should not be construed as including such a publication if any other construction is admissible.

> . . . No evidence, aside from the deductions which are to be drawn from the prints themselves, was offered to show that these designs had any original artistic qualities. The jury could not reasonably have found merit or value aside from the purely business object of advertising a show, and the instruction to find for the defendant was not error. . . .

I entirely concur in these views, and therefore dissent from the opinion and judgment of this Court. The clause of the Constitution giving Congress power to promote the progress of science and useful arts, by securing for limited terms to authors and inventors the exclusive right to their respective works and discoveries, does not, as I think, embrace a mere advertisement of a circus.

NOTES AND QUESTIONS

Copyright's Non-Discrimination Principle. Bleistein is the leading case supporting copyright law's general nondiscrimination principle: Copyright protects all original creative works without judging their merit. Copyright equally protects major cultural contributions, pedestrian advertising and pornography.

Copyright law therefore protects works that would have been created without copyright's exclusion powers as an incentive to create them. For more on incentive arguments as applied to ads, *see* Lisa P. Ramsey, *Intellectual Property Rights in Advertising*, 12 MICH. TELECOMM. & TECH. L. REV. 189 (2006); Alfred C. Yen, *Commercial Speech Jurisprudence and Copyright in Commercial Information Works*, 58 S.C. L. REV. 665 (2007); Note, *Rethinking Copyright for Advertisements*, 119 HARV. L. REV. 2486 (2006).

Other countries may impose higher standards for copyrightability that can exclude advertising. *See, e.g.*, Euro Depot, S.A. v. Bricolaje Bricoman, S.L., No. 64/2017 (Feb. 2, 2017) (Spanish Copyright Act didn't protect a commercial brochure, and copying it wasn't unfair competition because imitation is allowed in the absence of exclusive rights). However, harmonization of E.U. law may have overridden this result in the European Union. See Cofemel — Sociedade de Vestuário SA v G-Star Raw CV (Case C-638/17) (holding that originality is the only requirement for copyright protection under E.U. law).

Functional Ad Copy. In *Webloyalty.com, Inc. v. Consumer Innovations, LLC*, 388 F. Supp. 2d 435 (D. Del. 2005), Webloyalty sued Consumer Innovations (CI) for copyright infringement. The parties competed in the market for membership discount programs. Webloyalty had registered copyrights in its "Sell Page" and "Special Offer Banner" that it used to entice consumers to subscribe to its programs when they visited websites with which Webloyalty had contracted. The Special Offer Banner read in part, "Click here to claim your Special Offer," and, if consumers clicked the Banner, they were directed to the Webloyalty Sell Page and could sign up for Webloyalty's program.

CI copied Webloyalty's Sell Page and Special Offer Banner with few changes, most related to the particular details of CI's rewards program, though CI's principal denied having done so under oath. This denial was not credible, in part because CI's draft sell page included Webloyalty's customer service phone number. CI also used a banner identical to the Webloyalty Banner except that "Reservation Rewards" was replaced by "Traveler Innovations."

The court set out the copyright infringement standard:

> In an action for copyright infringement under 17 U.S.C. § 501, the plaintiff must show by a preponderance of the evidence that its copyright registrations are valid and that the defendant copied the registered works. Copying is proven by showing that the defendant had access to the protected work and that there is a substantial similarity between the two works. The test for substantial similarity is subdivided into two considerations. The first consideration, actual copying, is established by showing the defendant's access to the copyrighted work coupled with "probative" similarity between the two works. The second consideration is whether the copying is actionable, which requires the fact finder to "determine whether a 'lay-observer' would believe that the copying was of protectable aspects of the copyrighted work."

CI challenged the validity of the copyrights on the ground that the material on the Sell Page and Special Offer Banner lacked sufficient originality.

To analyze this argument, the court needed to consider the copyright doctrines of "merger" and "*scènes à faire*." "Merger" applies when there is only one way, or are only a few ways, to express an unprotectable idea. In those circumstances, to keep the idea free for everyone to use, the expression can't be protected. The concept of *scènes à faire* is similar: When, because of the genre of the works at issue, certain elements would naturally be expected—a training montage in a sports film, a gruff lieutenant in a police drama and so on—similarity or even copying of those elements won't establish infringement.

The *Webloyalty* court rejected merger and *scènes à faire* as applied to the text. Other "sell pages" in the record established that there were other ways to express the same idea.

The court found infringement because an original visual arrangement of page elements, as well as other kinds of selection, coordination, and arrangement, can be copyrighted. Statutory damages were available because of the plaintiff's timely registration; the court awarded $25,000 per infringed work, twenty-five times CI's revenue from the infringing ads. The court also awarded attorneys' fees and costs of over $225,000 and an injunction.

If Webloyalty's ad copy did a better job than alternative ad copy at converting viewers into buyers than other ad copy, should the merger doctrine have barred copyright protection? Why did CI copy Webloyalty's ad copy instead of preparing its own text?

Copyright and Advertiser Poaching. Webloyalty applied the principle that copyright law can protect the ways in which unprotectable elements are organized. Publishers of ad compilations, like the "yellow pages" of phone books, have occasionally, though often unsuccessfully, invoked this rule to fight competing directories making copies of ads, even though the compilation publishers usually don't own the copyright to any of the individual ads appearing in their directories. *See, e.g.*, Bellsouth Advert. & Pub'g Corp. v. Donnelley Info. Pub'g, Inc., 999 F.2d 1436 (11th Cir. 1993). (The business directory information, like name, address and phone number, by contrast, are simply not copyrightable.) How should the doctrines of merger and *scènes à faire* apply to the selection, coordination and arrangement of ad compilations?

Product Shot Copyrights. Advertisers routinely want their ads to show consumers their products. Often, advertisers ask freelance photographers to create photos of the product. Who owns the resulting copyrights in the photos, and how far do those copyrights extend?

ETS-HOKIN V. SKYY SPIRITS, INC., 225 F.3D 1068 (9TH CIR. 2000)

This case requires us to apply copyright principles to stylized photographs of a vodka bottle. Specifically, we must decide whether professional photographer Joshua Ets-Hokin's commercial photographs, dubbed "product shots," of the Skyy Spirits vodka bottle merit copyright protection. Given the Copyright Act's low threshold for originality generally and the minimal amount of originality required to qualify a photograph in particular, we conclude that Ets-Hokin's photographs are entitled to copyright protection.

We also conclude that the district court erred in analyzing this case through the lens of derivative copyright. The photographs at issue cannot be derivative works because the vodka bottle—the alleged underlying work—is not itself subject to copyright protection. Accordingly, we reverse the grant of summary judgment for Skyy Spirits and remand for consideration of whether infringement has occurred.

BACKGROUND

I. THE STORY

. . . Ets-Hokin is a professional photographer who maintains a studio in San Francisco. Maurice Kanbar, the president of Skyy Spirits, Inc. ("Skyy"), and Daniel Dadalt, an employee of the company, visited his studio in the summer of 1993. During this visit, Kanbar and Dadalt reviewed Ets-Hokin's photograph portfolio and subsequently hired him to photograph Skyy's vodka bottle. Ets-Hokin then shot a series of photographs and ultimately produced and delivered three photographs of the bottle. In all three photos, the bottle appears in front of a plain white or yellow backdrop, with back lighting. The bottle seems to be illuminated from the left (from the viewer's perspective), such that the right side of the bottle is slightly shadowed. The angle from which the photos were taken appears to be perpendicular to the side of the bottle, with the label centered, such that the viewer has a "straight on" perspective. In two of the photographs, only the bottle is pictured; in the third, a martini sits next to the bottle.

[Two of the initial photos, courtesy of Wesley Kinnear.]

[Two of the challenged photos, taken by photographers other than Ets-Hokin. Photos courtesy of Wesley Kinnear]

Under the terms of a confirmation of engagement, signed by Dadalt on Skyy's behalf, Ets-Hokin retained all rights to the photos and licensed limited rights to Skyy. The parties dispute the scope of the license, including whether Skyy was licensed to use the photographs in advertising or in publications distributed to the public. After the confirmation was executed, Ets-Hokin applied to the U.S. Copyright Office for a certificate of registration for his series of photos, and a certificate was issued effective on March 10, 1995. . . .

Skyy claims that it found Ets-Hokin's photographs unsatisfactory and thus hired other photographers to photograph the bottle. In dealing with these photographers, Skyy sought to purchase all rights to the photographs of the bottle, as opposed to the license arrangement it had agreed to with Ets-Hokin. One photographer refused to sell his photograph outright, insisting on licensing. Two other photographers were apparently willing to sell all rights to their photographs.

Ets-Hokin brought suit against Skyy and three other defendants for copyright infringement, fraud, and negligent misrepresentation. He alleged that the company used his work in various advertisements, including in *Deneuve* magazine and the *San Francisco Examiner,* and on the side of a bus, without his permission and in violation of the limited license. He also alleged that Skyy used photographs taken by the other photographers that mimicked his own photos; specifically, he claimed that these photographers improperly used his photographs to produce virtually identical photos of the vodka bottle. . . .

II. VALIDITY OF THE COPYRIGHT

Skyy argues, in a nutshell, that the commercial photographs of its vodka bottle are not worthy of copyright protection. We disagree. The essence of copyrightability is originality of artistic, creative expression. Given the low threshold for originality under the Copyright Act, as well as the longstanding and consistent body of case law holding that photographs generally satisfy this minimal standard, we conclude that Ets-Hokin's product shots of the Skyy vodka bottle are original works of authorship entitled to copyright protection. The district court erred in analyzing copyright protection under the rubric of derivative works. . . .

A. History of Photography as Copyrightable Artistic Expression

It is well recognized that photography is a form of artistic expression, requiring numerous artistic judgments. As one photojournalist wrote,

> [u]p to and including the instant of exposure, the photographer is working in an undeniably subjective way. By his choice of technical approach (which is a tool of emotional control), by his selection of the subject matter to be held within the confines of his negative area, and by his decision as to the exact, climactic instant of exposure, he is blending the variables of interpretation into an emotional whole which will be a basis for the formation of opinions by the viewing public.

But these judgments are not the only ones. As the well-known photographer Edward Weston wrote,

> [b]y varying the position of his camera, his camera angle, or the focal length of his lens, the photographer can achieve an infinite number of varied compositions with a single, stationary subject. By changing the light on the subject, or by using a color filter, any or all of the values in the subject can be altered. By varying the length of exposure, the kind of emulsion, the method of developing, the photographer can vary

the registering of relative values in the negative. And the relative values as registered in the negative can be further modified by allowing more or less light to affect certain parts of the image in printing. Thus, within the limits of his medium, without resorting to any method of control that is not photographic (i.e., of an optical or chemical nature), the photographer can depart from literal recording to whatever extent he chooses.

. . . .

B. Contemporary Standards for Copyright Protection of Photographs

[The registration was prima facie evidence of validity. Defendants therefore had the burden of proving invalidity.] This they have failed to do, primarily because the degree of originality required for copyrightability is minimal.

. . . *Feist,* which involved listings in a telephone directory, described the requisite degree of creativity as "extremely low; even a slight amount will suffice. The vast majority of works make the grade quite easily, as they possess some creative spark, 'no matter how crude, humble or obvious' it might be." When this articulation of the minimal threshold for copyright protection is combined with the minimal standard of originality required for photographic works, the result is that even the slightest artistic touch will meet the originality test for a photograph.

In assessing the "creative spark" of a photograph, we are reminded of Judge Learned Hand's comment that "no photograph, however simple, can be unaffected by the personal influence of the author." This approach, according to a leading treatise in the copyright area, "has become the prevailing view," and as a result, "almost any[ ] photograph may claim the necessary originality to support a copyright merely by virtue of the photographer's personal choice of subject matter, angle of photograph, lighting, and determination of the precise time when the photograph is to be taken." . . .

In view of the low threshold for the creativity element, and given that the types of decisions Ets-Hokin made about lighting, shading, angle, background, and so forth have been recognized as sufficient to convey copyright protection, we have no difficulty in concluding that the defendants have not met their burden of showing the invalidity of Ets-Hokin's copyright, and that Ets-Hokin's product shots are sufficiently creative, and thus sufficiently original, to merit copyright protection. Finally, although Ets-Hokin took photos that undoubtedly resemble many other product shots of the bottle—straight-on, centered, with back lighting so that the word "Skyy" on the bottle is clear—the potential for such similarity does not strip his work of the modicum of originality necessary for copyrightability. Indeed, the fact that two original photographs of the same object may appear similar does not eviscerate their originality or negate their copyrightability.

Having concluded that Ets-Hokin's photos are entitled to copyright protection, we leave to the district court the scope of Ets-Hokin's copyright in the photographs vis-à-vis the claimed infringement.

C. Derivative Copyright . . .

2. The Bottle Is Not Copyrightable

. . . . The district court treated the bottle as a whole as the underlying, "preexisting work," even though the bottle as a whole is a utilitarian object that cannot be copyrighted. [Useful articles such as bottles are not copyrightable unless there are features that are "separable" from the utilitarian features of the articles. While the law here is complex, the court concluded that this was an easy case of lack of separability. As an aside, the court noted that "[a] claim to copyright cannot be registered in a print or label consisting solely of trademark subject matter and lacking copyrightable matter." 37 C.F.R. § 202.10(b). Although a label's "graphical illustrations" are normally copyrightable, "textual matter" is not—at least not unless the text "aid[s] or augment[s]" an accompanying graphical illustration.]

. . . Because Ets-Hokin's product shots are shots of the bottle as a whole—a useful article not subject to copyright protection—and not shots merely, or even mainly, of its label, we hold that the bottle does not qualify as a "preexisting work" within the meaning of the Copyright Act. As such, the photos Ets-Hokin took of the bottle cannot be derivative works. The district court erred in so concluding.

III. INFRINGEMENT

. . . Ets-Hokin claims infringement with regard to Skyy's use of his product shots and with regard to solicitation and use of shots produced by other photographers who, Ets-Hokin contends, unlawfully mimicked his work. This issue, which the district court did not reach in view of its holding that Ets-Hokin failed to establish the validity of his copyright, should be addressed in the first instance by that court.

NELSON, J., dissenting:

The majority opinion errs in reversing the district court's summary judgment order because there is no way that Ets-Hokin can prove infringement given the low standard of originality for photographs. I agree with the majority opinion that under this standard that Ets-Hokin's photographs are original. By the same token, however, so are the other allegedly infringing photographs of Skyy's vodka bottle. These subsequent photographs are based on slightly different angles, different shadows, and different highlights of the bottle's gold label. Thus, even if the district court had applied the proper standard of originality, Ets-Hokin's lawsuit would not have survived summary judgment because the subsequent photographs also possess originality. Furthermore, as a matter of law, legal defenses such as *scènes à faire* and the merger doctrine prevent Ets-Hokin from prevailing on his copyright infringement claims.
. . .

NOTES AND QUESTIONS

Thin Copyrights in Many Advertising Photos? The dissent proved prophetic. The case soon returned to the court of appeals, and the court held that the defendant's photos, which differed in terms of angle, lighting, shadow, reflection and background, did not infringe on the plaintiff's copyrights. Ets-Hokin v. Skyy Spirits, Inc., 323 F.3d 763 (9th Cir. 2003) (*Skyy*

II). Why? The only constant between the plaintiff's photographs and the defendant's photographs was the bottle itself, and an accurate portrayal of the unadorned bottle could not be infringing. Ets-Hokin had only a thin copyright offering protection perhaps only from verbatim reproduction of his photographs. His attempt to extend those copyrights to similar recreations of his work went too far, but it took a lot of courtroom time and attorneys' fees to reach that conclusion.

If the copyright in a basic photo of a product is so thin, what's the point of according it any protection at all? *Cf.* Pohl v. MH Sub I LLC, 770 Fed. Appx. 482 (11th Cir. 2019) (finding that before-and-after photos of dentist's patient were copyrightable, in infringement case involving alleged copying by other dentists). In *Pohl*, the photographer was not a professional photographer, but his choices were still deemed creative enough to sustain a copyright. Based on the images below, what choices did he make?

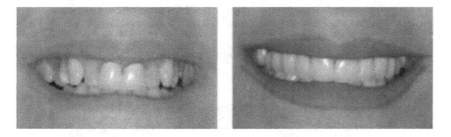

Consider this quote from *Feist*: "Assume that two poets, each ignorant of the other, compose identical poems. Neither work is novel, yet both are original and, hence, copyrightable." Is this a plausible scenario in the context of two ads showing the same product? Wouldn't the advertiser always have access to the first ad and thus have extreme difficulty showing independent creation? Maybe this is just a risk allocation issue: Under *Ets-Hokin* and similar cases, advertisers must ensure that their contracts are airtight about the disposition of subsequent photos if their relationship with the photographer/other independent contractor sours, or else the photographer may be able to control subsequent ads. Is this the right result? Recall that not all advertisers are multimillion-dollar companies.

Designers have developed norms, and some scientific evidence, about the most-effective ways to depict products in ads. *See, e.g.*, Joost Fromberg, *What's The Perfect Way to Show a Product in Advertisements?*, NEW NEURO MKTG., Dec. 17, 2015. Does this affect how the merger and *scènes à faire* doctrines apply to product shots?

Skyy involved a photo of a product that was not itself copyrightable according to the court. What happens when the underlying product *is* copyrightable? In *Schrock v. Learning Curve International, Inc.*, 586 F.3d 513 (7th Cir. 2009), the plaintiff photographer took pictures of "Thomas & Friends" trains, which had their own copyrights, for use on Learning Curve's packaging. After defendant Learning Curve stopped giving Schrock work, he registered his photos and sued for infringement.

The district court granted summary judgment for the defendants, holding that Schrock had no copyright in the photos. The court classified the photos as "derivative works" of the Thomas & Friends characters. Though Schrock had permission to *make* the photos, the district court (relying on earlier precedent) held that he also needed permission to *copyright* them, which he did not have.

The court of appeals reversed, reasoning that it did not need to decide whether the photos were derivative works, only whether they contained sufficient new expression to be copyrightable, and the photos had that:

> [T]he photographs are accurate depictions of the three-dimensional "Thomas & Friends" toys, but Schrock's artistic and technical choices combine to create a two-dimensional image that is subtly but nonetheless sufficiently his own. This is confirmed by Schrock's deposition testimony describing his creative process in depicting the toys. Schrock explained how he used various camera and lighting techniques to make the toys look more "life like," "personable," and "friendly." He explained how he tried to give the toys "a little bit of dimension" and that it was his goal to make the toys "a little bit better than what they look like when you actually see them on the shelf." The original expression in the representative sample is not

particularly great (it was not meant to be), but it is enough under the applicable standard to warrant the limited copyright protection accorded derivative works under § 103(b).

Copyright then arose by operation of law, not by permission: "As long as he was authorized to make the photos (he was), he owned the copyright in the photos to the extent of their incremental original expression." The appeals court reasoned that this would not let Schrock hold up the creation of subsequent photos of the toys, because Schrock's copyright protected only his own original contributions. Is this fact sufficient to protect against lawsuits from photographers who may perceive their own works as especially influential on later ads? How would you write a contract between an advertiser and a photographer in light of this decision?

The court of appeals remanded for examination of the agreements between the parties to determine whether they agreed to alter the default rule of ownership or whether Learning Curve had an implied license to continue to use Schrock's photos.

Schrock is far from unusual. Advertisers often distribute photographs beyond what the photographer contends is the scope of any license granted (or continue using them beyond the term of the license). *See* Latimer v. Roaring Toyz, Inc., 601 F.3d 1224 (11th Cir. 2010). Why do you think this fact pattern repeats itself so regularly, despite the significant risks to advertisers? We will examine ownership/license issues in Section 2 below.

Photos of Third-Party Products. May a retailer display photos of the goods it sells, including their copyrighted elements, without the photographer's permission?

Fragrancenet.com, Inc. v. Fragrancex.com, Inc., 679 F. Supp. 2d 312 (E.D.N.Y. 2010), involved hundreds of photos of products allegedly copied by a competing retailer. The court refused to dismiss the claim because the photos could be original, even if minimally so. However, "images of a third-party's intellectual property may receive less protection than a completely original work," protected only against "a precise re-creation or copying of the registrant's work." Given that the plaintiff asserted direct copying, it stated a claim despite the thinness of its copyright.

What about the issue that plaintiff's photos featured third parties' perfume bottles, which might themselves contain copyrightable elements? Here, unlike in *Ets-Hokin* and *Schrock*, there doesn't seem to have been any license to create the photo. However, the court held the photographer's copyright derives from the photographer's original choices in subject selection, lighting, angle and so on.

The court didn't mention the key reason that any copyright in the perfume bottles was irrelevant: In general, owning a copyrighted work doesn't give you the right to copy it, but 17 U.S.C. Section 113(c) allows retailers and others to create product shots of useful articles for advertisements and commentaries:

> In the case of a work lawfully reproduced in useful articles that have been offered for sale or other distribution to the public, copyright does not include any right to

prevent the making, distribution, or display of pictures or photographs of such articles in connection with advertisements or commentaries related to the distribution or display of such articles, or in connection with news reports.

Section 113(c) has some obvious limits. For example, books aren't useful articles, so they aren't covered by Section113(c). Are photos of book covers shown on Amazon.com or local bookstore websites infringing reproductions?

3D Models Are Not the Same as Photos. Compare this line of reasoning to *Skyy* to *Meshwerks, Inc. v. Toyota Motor Sales U.S.A., Inc.*, 528 F.3d 1258 (10th Cir. 2008), finding that digital wireframe models of Toyota vehicles, designed to be three-dimensional representations of the vehicles, were not copyrightable. Even though many decisions were required to figure out how best to create the 3D models, the court found that they lacked originality, since the whole point of all the decisions was to replicate the cars as well as possible. Is there anything other than the shift from three to two dimensions that made Ets-Hokins' decisions copyrightable?

Copying Advertising Concepts. When the copying at issue does not involve pure reproduction, courts require substantial similarity in protectable expression, not just similarity of ideas or tropes. For example, *Culver Franchising System, Inc. v. Steak N Shake Inc.*, 119 U.S.P.Q.2d 1808 (N.D. Ill. 2016), rejected similarities in television ads for fast food chains promoting their beef burgers:

> Culver identifies the following common elements: (1) the commercial opens with a butcher in a white uniform in a butcher shop; (2) then, the company logo appears; (3) the butcher describes the beef's quality; (4) three different cuts of beef are shown as the butcher identifies the cuts and describes how they are "well-marbled"; (5) patties are grilled and flattened with a spatula as the griller describes how the cuts "come[] together," using the words "sear" and "seal"; (6) the burger is stacked and topped with cheese; and (7) the commercial ends with a close-up of the completed burger before the company's logo again appears. Culver maintains that the unique "combination of dialogue, pacing, sequence, background, and other visual and expressive elements" in its ad deserves copyright protection.
>
> . . .[T]he commercials are not substantially similar as a matter of law. Several of the seven common elements identified by Culver lack the necessary modicum of creativity to give rise to copyright protection. Regarding the second and seventh elements, there is nothing unique about a company displaying its logo and product at the beginning and/or end of a commercial. The same is true for the sixth element; at least as early as the iconic 1975 "Two all-beef patties, special sauce, lettuce, cheese, pickles, onions on a sesame-seed bun" McDonald's Big Mac ad, burger commercials have regularly featured the grilling and/or assembling of a burger, followed by a view of the final product. The sequence of Culver's commercial is commonplace, as it would be nonsensical for a commercial to open with a cooked burger and then finish with a prolonged shot of a raw patty.

Regarding the fourth and fifth elements, pressing down on patties with a spatula and flipping them while they cook is standard grilling practice; adding cheese to a burger is not a stroke of originality; and it is common parlance to describe beef as "marbled," to speak of "searing" and "sealing" juices, and to discuss how flavors and ingredients "come together." . . .

As for the remaining common elements, both commercials take place in butcher shops and portray butchers wearing white aprons who show the three cuts of beef used to make the burgers in question. It is hardly original for an advertisement to describe the origins and quality of a meat product or to feature a butcher. The butchers function as stock characters—both don a white butcher coat and, unsurprisingly, work in a butcher shop. Indeed, Culver effectively concedes that the settings for the commercials are generic by describing each butcher shop as a "quintessential local butcher's shop." Because there is nothing distinctive about the expression of Culver's butcher, and because Culver cannot copyright the mere concept of a butcher talking about beef, Culver's butcher is not protected expression.

Moreover, the commercials differ in certain significant respects. While they both display images of raw beef, they do so differently; "Butcher-Quality Beef" displays the cuts simultaneously, while "The Original Steakburger" focuses on each cut individually. "ButcherQuality Beef" features a conversation between Craig Culver and Fritz, and twice uses a split screen to show three different images at once. In "The Original Steakburger," by contrast, an unnamed butcher speaks directly to the camera and the entire commercial consists of single images (i.e., it does not use split screens).

[From Culver's ad]

430

[From Steak n Shake's ad]

[From Culver's ad]

[From Steak N Shake's ad]

431

See also American Direct Marketing, Inc. v. Azad Int'l, Inc., 783 F. Supp. 84 (E.D.N.Y. 1992) (ads for competing tooth-whitening products not similar enough even though "the principal models are blond women; a girl with braces is one of the subsidiary models in both; a similar five-part list of the effects of plaque is used; a similar layout is used for a comparison with the advertisement of a more-expensive competitor. The organization of the commercials is similar. They move from simulations, to lists of product virtues, to price comparison with competitors, to request for telephone order"; similarities in content and organization resulted from the ads' genre, and five-part list was factual and unprotectable); *cf.* Betty, Inc. v. Pepsico, Inc., 420 F. Supp. 3d 208 (S.D.N.Y. 2019) (Pepsi didn't infringe ad agency's pitch for an ad that cycled through musical genres and associated costumes/backgrounds in historical order; "the overall concept, feel, setting, themes, characters, pace and sequence of Betty's written presentation are not substantially similar to Pepsi's halftime commercial). We will revisit ownership of ideas in Chapter 13.

Ads also sometimes emulate or draw inspiration from copyrighted artistic works. *See* Mia Fineman, *The Image Is Familiar; the Pitch Isn't*, N.Y. TIMES, July 13, 2008. For example, James Croak created a sculpture, "Pegasus, Some Loves Hurt More Than Others," a mixed-media, life-sized sculpture depicting "a winged, taxidermied horse that appears to be in the process of breaking through the roof of a sleek lowrider, as if about to take flight":

Toyota ran an ad campaign prominently featuring "a massive, pink stuffed animal—specifically, a hybrid of a unicorn and Pegasus—strapped to the roof of a Toyota RAV4." The voiceover narrates: "This is Lady. She's a unicorn. And a Pegasus. And why is she strapped to the roof of my RAV4? Well if you have kids, then you know why. Now the real question. Where's this going in the house? The RAV4. Toyota. Let's go places." The image also appeared in a print ad and a display featuring the stuffed animal at the 2015 Chicago Auto Show:

Is there substantial similarity between the Croak sculpture and the Toyota ads? *See* Croak v. Saatchi & Saatchi, North America, Inc., 174 F. Supp. 3d 829 (S.D.N.Y. 2016) (no).

## 2.	Who Owns Ad Copy?

When an advertiser creates an advertisement completely in-house using only its employees' labor, the advertiser will automatically own the copyright to the ad copy (unless it contracts with its employees otherwise).

In many cases, advertisers will rely on third-party help to prepare ad copy. It could be as simple as having a freelance designer help with ad layout or a photographer take photos of the advertised product. The advertiser might outsource the advertisement's development completely. For example, it may ask its ad agency to prepare the ad copy from scratch, subject only to the advertiser's approval.

Under default copyright law, independent third parties creating the copyrighted work own the copyright—even if the advertiser pays them to do custom work. This is counterintuitive. Advertisers unfamiliar with copyright law will assume, "I must own it because I paid for it!"

In theory, it's easy to avoid these unexpected outcomes or unwanted disputes: The parties' contract can spell out who owns what. The Copyright Act requires assignments or exclusive licenses of copyrighted works to be in writing, so *always get any copyright deals in writing*, and remember that *a deal involving the creation of ad content almost always involves the creation of copyrightable works*, even if the deal also serves other purposes.

Typically, advertisers prefer to specify that the third party's work is a "work for hire." In that case, copyright law automatically deems the commissioning party (here, the advertiser) the work's owner. When dealing with non-employees, however, a work for hire must be memorialized in writing and fit within one of nine content categories enumerated in the Copyright Act. The categories include motion pictures (which would include TV ads), compilations and contributions to a collective work. For example, a photo intended to be paired with ad copy might be a contribution to a collective work or a compilation. However, not all ads obviously fall into one of the relevant categories; e.g., a standalone billboard entirely created by the contractor.

Unfortunately for advertisers, not all independent contractors will sign work-for-hire agreements or other agreements transferring ownership or granting an expansive license. Worse, a substantial number of ads are created without any written contracts at all or with contracts that are silent about copyright ownership.

Ad Agencies

By default, the ad agency owns any ad copy the agency prepares for the advertiser, even if the advertiser paid for the work to be done. *See, e.g.*, Mkt. Masters-Legal, Inc. v. Parker Waichman Alonso LLP, 3:10-cv-40119-MAP (D. Mass. 2010) (ad agency got preliminary injunction against client law firm from using adcopy elements in other advertising). As a result, advertisers should address ownership issues in the ad agency contract.

Advertisers sometimes require ownership of materials that an ad agency prepares to pitch to acquire the advertiser's business, even before a full business relationship exists and the agency can be sure it will be paid. Not surprisingly, ad agencies don't like these requests. *See, e.g.*, Andrew McMains, *AutoZone Latest to Demand Ownership of Pitches*, ADWEEK, Oct. 31, 2010; American Association of Advertising Agencies, *Best Practice Guidance: Ownership of Agency Ideas, Plans And Work Developed During The New Business Process* (Dec. 2017). Then again, lawsuits over pitches are sometimes brought. *See, e.g.*, Betty, Inc. v. Pepsico, Inc., 420 F. Supp. 3d 208 (S.D.N.Y. 2019).

Website Designers

Similar issues arise over copyright ownership of an advertiser's website designed by an independent contractor. For example, in *108 Degrees, LLC v. Merrimack Golf Club, Inc.*, 2010 DNH 054 (D.N.H. 2010), 108 Degrees sued Merrimack for refusing to pay for a website it commissioned, and it added a copyright-infringement claim because Merrimack created a website that was nearly identical to the one 108 Degrees created.

Without a written contract specifying ownership or licensing terms, the website sponsor has to rely on an implied nonexclusive license to reuse the materials, which doesn't provide a lot of comfort. *See* Holtzbrinck Pub. Holdings, L.P. v. Vyne Commc'ns, Inc., 2000 WL 502860 (S.D.N.Y. 2000) (defendant, which created a website for plaintiff, granted at least an implied license to use its content, but that the license was in part revocable). *Holtzbrinck* also involved facts highlighting the vulnerability of a company to its website designer. When the dispute erupted between the parties, Vyne threatened to shut down the website in its entirety, obviously a great threat to any business (here, the magazine *Scientific American*). Copyright concerns may become secondary if a disgruntled business partner can cause the website files themselves to disappear.

Overlapping Publicity Rights

Even if the advertiser obtains all of the necessary copyright rights or permissions to include a copyrighted work in its advertising, the advertiser usually still needs separate permission to use the publicity/privacy rights of anyone depicted in the ad. (These issues are discussed more in later chapters.)

For example, Virgin Mobile downloaded a photo from the Internet for use in its ad campaign. The photo was distributed using a Creative Commons copyright license that allowed reuse in advertising. Nevertheless, the person in the photo sued the advertiser, alleging that she had been humiliated by the use. She also sued Creative Commons for allegedly failing to educate the photographer sufficiently about the license's scope. *See Lawsuit over Virgin Mobile's Use of Flickr Girl Blames Creative Commons*, OUT-LAW, Sept. 25, 2007.

A related issue involves reuse of television ads online. Most radio and TV actors are members of the relevant guilds (SAG/AFTRA), and their standard contracts provide for extra payments if an ad is used in new contexts or after a certain time. What happens if a third party who likes an ad puts it up on YouTube after the campaign ends? The actors would like to be paid, but the advertiser often likes the free publicity and disclaims any responsibility for the new use. What should happen in such cases?

3.   Other Copyright Risks

A.   Depicting Everyday Life in Ads: Davis v. The Gap

Given the low standard for copyrightability, creators of ads have to be careful about every element contained in the final ad copy. Posters in the background, images on T-shirts and anything else that might be copyrightable could potentially trigger a lawsuit.

In *Davis v. The Gap, Inc.*, 246 F.3d 152 (3d Cir. 2001), the plaintiff created Onoculii eyewear, "nonfunctional jewelry worn over the eyes in the manner of eyeglasses." As part of a campaign to show "people of all kinds" wearing Gap clothes, the Gap ran an ad described by the Court of Appeals as follows:

> [The ad] depicts a group of seven young people probably in their twenties, of Asian appearance, standing in a loose V formation staring at the camera with a sultry, pouty, provocative look. The group projects the image of funky intimates of a lively after-hours rock music club. They are dressed primarily in black, exhibiting bare arms and partly bare chests, goatees (accompanied in one case by bleached, streaked hair), large-brimmed, Western-style hats, and distinctive eye shades, worn either over their eyes, on their hats, or cocked over the top of their heads. The central figure, at the apex of the V formation, is wearing Davis's highly distinctive Onoculii eyewear; he peers over the metal disks directly into the camera lens.

[ad]

436

[closeup of Onoculii jewelry]

The people in the ad, who were not traditional models, were told to wear their own eyewear, wristwatches, earrings, nose-rings or other incidental items, thereby "permitting each person to project accurately his or her own personal image and appearance." Previous Onoculii designs had been seen on various entertainers, in runway shows and in fashion magazines, though there was no indication in the reported facts that anyone at TGap knew this. On one occasion, Davis received $50 from *Vibe* magazine for a photo showing the musician Sun Ra wearing an Onoculii piece.

The court first determined that The Gap's copying of the nonfunctional eyewear was not "de minimis," which covers unauthorized copying that is so trivial that the law refuses to impose liability. Here, "the infringing item is highly noticeable, in part because the design is "strikingly bizarre":

> [I]t is startling to see the wearer peering at us over his Onoculii. Because eyes are naturally a focal point of attention, and because the wearer is at the center of the group—the apex of the V formation—the viewer's gaze is powerfully drawn to Davis's creation. The impression created, furthermore, is that the models posing in the ad have been outfitted from top to bottom, including eyewear, with Gap merchandise. All this leads us to conclude that [T]he Gap's use of Davis's jewelry cannot be considered a de minimis act of copying to which the law attaches no consequence.

Likewise, the court rejected The Gap's fair use defense. Fair use is a flexible, case-by-case defense to infringement. The Copyright Act, Section 107, provides:

> [T]he fair use of a copyrighted work, including such use by reproduction in copies or phonorecords or by any other means specified by that section, for purposes such as criticism, comment, news reporting, teaching (including multiple copies for classroom use), scholarship, or research, is not an infringement of copyright. In determining

whether the use made of a work in any particular case is a fair use the factors to be considered shall include—

(1) the purpose and character of the use, including whether such use is of a commercial nature or is for nonprofit educational purposes;

(2) the nature of the copyrighted work;

(3) the amount and substantiality of the portion used in relation to the copyrighted work as a whole; and

(4) the effect of the use upon the potential market for or value of the copyrighted work.

The fact that a work is unpublished shall not itself bar a finding of fair use if such finding is made upon consideration of all the above factors.

Courts often emphasize the first factor and fourth factors. In the first factor, current doctrine favors "transformative" uses—that is, a use that has a different purpose or adds new expression, meaning or message, instead of substituting for the original.

The *Davis* court found nothing transformative about the Gap ad. "The ad shows Davis's Onoculii being worn as eye jewelry in the manner it was made to be worn—looking much like an ad Davis himself might have sponsored for his copyrighted design." In addition, The Gap's use was for an ad, which was the most extreme form of commerciality, weighing against fair use. *See* Campbell v. Acuff-Rose, Music, 510 U.S. 569 (1994) ("The use, for example, of a copyrighted work to advertise a product . . . will be entitled to less indulgence under the first factor . . . than the sale of [the new work] for its own sake.").

The second statutory factor, the nature of the copyrighted work, is rarely determinative. In theory, fair use should enable copying of factual works more freely than fictional/creative works, though empirical work does not confirm this. *See* Barton Beebe, *An Empirical Study of U.S. Copyright Fair Use Opinions, 1978–2005*, 156 U. PENN. L. REV. 549 (2008). In *Davis*, the court held that the plaintiff's work was an "artistic creation" close to the core of copyright's protective purpose.

The third factor, the "amount and substantiality of the portion used in relation to the copyrighted work as a whole," weighed against The Gap as well because the ad presented "a head-on full view of Davis's piece, centered and prominently featured."

The final factor, "the effect of the use upon the potential market for or value of the copyrighted work," asks whether the accused's work offers a market substitute for the original or harms its market through criticism or parody. Only the former kind of harm is cognizable in copyright. Here, The Gap's use was superseding. "By taking for free Davis's design for its ad, The Gap avoided paying 'the customary price' Davis was entitled to charge for the use of his design. Davis suffered market harm by losing the royalty revenue to which he was reasonably entitled in the circumstances, as well as through the diminution of his opportunity to license to others who might regard Davis's design as preempted by The Gap's ad."

Thus, all the fair use factors weighed in favor of Davis.

Because Davis didn't register until after the infringement began, he was only entitled to compensatory damages, which can include the infringer's profits from the infringement and the copyright owner's actual damages, but cannot provide a double recovery where the two overlap. In this case, however, it was impossible to figure out what percentage of The Gap's clothing sales was attributable to the appearance of Davis's jewelry in the Gap ad. Thus, there was no reasonable factual basis on which to award the infringer's profits. Davis also didn't show any lost sales. The court of appeals, however, held that Davis was entitled to a reasonable licensing fee for the use of his work in advertising.

NOTES AND QUESTIONS

Do you agree with the court's assessment of the prominence of Davis's design? Would the depiction have been excused if the wearer had been off-center?

The reasonable license fee Davis won was certainly less than his cost of litigating the case, so this ruling was almost certainly a financial loss for Davis,his lawyers or both. Was Davis' decision to litigate a good decision with a bad outcome, a bad decision with an expected bad outcome or something else entirely? If you had represented The Gap, how much would you have offered in settlement? Keep in mind that an appeal can easily cost several hundred thousand dollars in legal defense costs.

Davis probably achieved a financially dubious outcome, but Gap can't be too happy with it either. In addition to the many hassles of litigation, its legal defense costs alone reduced, and possibly exceeded, the overall profitability of the ad campaign.

So, how could The Gap have avoided this problem in the first place? Be honest: If you were doing clearance on this ad, would you have identified the "nonfunctional eyewear" as a copyright risk? How will you cope with potential risks like this when it's your responsibility?

Third-party copyrighted material can creep into visual ads in countless ways. Even graffiti captured in the background of ordinary street scenes may become a problem. *See, e.g.,* Anasagasti v. American Eagle Outfitters, Inc., 1:14-cv-05618-ALC (S.D.N.Y. complaint filed July 23, 2014) (copyright lawsuit over American Eagle's inclusion of "street art" in ad copy). You must scrutinize every visual element in every ad to consider its potential copyright risk.

B.   Characters and Parody

As you saw in *Davis*, verbatim copying is regularly considered infringing unless excused. But when less than the entire work is copied, the rules get more complicated. In the following case, the advertiser created its own ad but referenced a third party's copyrighted work for greater cultural relevance—to its peril.

METRO-GOLDWYN-MAYER, INC. V. AMERICAN HONDA MOTOR CO., INC., 900 F. SUPP. 1287 (C.D. CAL. 1995)

. . . This case arises out of Plaintiffs Metro-Goldwyn-Mayer's and Danjaq's claim that Defendants American Honda Motor Co. and its advertising agency Rubin Postaer and Associates, violated Plaintiffs' "copyrights to sixteen James Bond films and the exclusive intellectual property rights to the James Bond character and the James Bond films" through Defendants' recent commercial for its Honda del Sol automobile.

Premiering last October 1994, Defendants' "Escape" commercial features a young, well-dressed couple in a Honda del Sol being chased by a high-tech helicopter. A grotesque villain with metal-encased arms jumps out of the helicopter onto the car's roof, threatening harm. With a flirtatious turn to his companion, the male driver deftly releases the Honda's detachable roof (which Defendants claim is the main feature allegedly highlighted by the commercial), sending the villain into space and effecting the couple's speedy get-away. . . .

II.   FACTUAL BACKGROUND

In 1992, Honda's advertising agency Rubin Postaer came up with a new concept to sell the Honda del Sol convertible with its detachable rooftop. . . . As the concept evolved into the helicopter chase scene, it acquired various project names, one of which was "James Bob," which Yoshida understood to be a play on words for James Bond. In addition, David Spyra, Honda's National Advertising Manager, testified the same way, gingerly agreeing that he understood "James Bob to be a pun on the name James Bond."

. . . [W]hen casting began on the project in the summer of 1994, the casting director specifically sent requests to talent agencies for "James Bond"-type actors and actresses to star in what conceptually could be "the next James Bond film."

With the assistance of the same special effects team that worked on Arnold Schwarzenegger's "True Lies," Defendants proceeded to create a sixty-and thirty-second version of the Honda del Sol commercial at issue: a fast-paced helicopter chase scene featuring a suave hero and an attractive heroine, as well as a menacing and grotesque villain. . . .

On January 15, 1995, in an effort to accommodate Plaintiffs' demands without purportedly conceding liability, Defendants changed their commercial by: (1) altering the protagonists' accents from British to American; and (2) by changing the music to make it less like the horn-driven James Bond theme. This version of the commercial was shown during the Superbowl, allegedly the most widely viewed TV event of the year. . . .

III. LEGAL ANALYSIS . . .

b. What Elements Of Plaintiffs' Work Are Protectable Under Copyright Law

Plaintiffs contend that Defendants' commercial infringes in two independent ways: (1) by reflecting specific scenes from the 16 films; and (2) by the male protagonist's possessing James Bond's unique character traits as developed in the films.

Defendants respond that Plaintiffs are simply trying to gain a monopoly over the "action/spy/police hero" genre which is contrary to the purposes of copyright law. Specifically, Defendants argue that the allegedly infringed elements identified by Plaintiffs are not protectable because: (1) the helicopter chase scene in the Honda commercial is a common theme that naturally flows from most action genre films, and the woman and villain in the film are but stock characters that are not protectable; and (2) under the Ninth Circuit's *Sam Spade* decision, the James Bond character does not constitute the "story being told," but is rather an unprotected dramatic character.

(1) Whether Film Scenes Are Copyrightable

In their opening brief, Plaintiffs contend that each of their sixteen films contains distinctive scenes that together comprise the classic James Bond adventure: "a high-thrill chase of the ultra-cool British charmer and his beautiful and alarming sidekick by a grotesque villain in which the hero escapes through wit aided by high-tech gadgetry." Defendants argue that these elements are naturally found in any action film and are therefore unprotected "scènes à faire."

. . . Plaintiffs' experts describe in a fair amount of detail how James Bond films are the source of a genre rather than imitators of a broad "action/spy film" genre as Defendants contend. Specifically, film historian Casper explains how the James Bond films represented a fresh and novel approach because they "hybridize[d] the spy thriller with the genres of adventure, comedy (particularly, social satire and slapstick), and fantasy. This amalgam . . . was also a departure from the series' literary source, namely writer Ian Fleming's novels." Casper also states: "I also believe that this distinct mélange of genres, which was also seminal . . . created a protagonist, antagonist, sexual consort, type of mission, type of exotic setting, type of mood, type of dialogue, type of music, etc. that was not there in the subtype of the spy thriller films of that ilk hitherto." . . .

Based on Plaintiffs' experts' greater familiarity with the James Bond films, as well as a review of Plaintiffs' James Bond montage and defense expert Needham's video montage of the "action/spy" genre films, it is clear that James Bond films are unique in their expression of the spy thriller idea. A filmmaker could produce a helicopter chase scene in practically an indefinite number of ways, but only James Bond films bring the various elements Casper describes together in a unique and original way.

441

Thus, the Court believes that Plaintiffs will likely succeed on their claim that their expression of the action film sequences in the James Bond films is copyrightable as a matter of law.[8]

(2) Whether James Bond Character Is Copyrightable

. . .Like Rocky, Sherlock Holmes, Tarzan, and Superman, James Bond has certain character traits that have been developed over time through the sixteen films in which he appears. Contrary to Defendants' assertions, because many actors can play Bond is a testament to the fact that Bond is a unique character whose specific qualities remain constant despite the change in actors. . . . A James Bond film without James Bond is not a James Bond film. . . .

Accordingly, the Court concludes that Plaintiffs will probably succeed on their claim that James Bond is a copyrightable character ....

c. Defendants' Alleged Infringement

. . . Viewing Plaintiffs' and Defendants' videotapes and examining the experts' statements, Plaintiffs will likely prevail on this issue because there is substantial similarity between the specific protected elements of the James Bond films and the Honda commercial: (1) the theme, plot, and sequence both involve the idea of a handsome hero who, along with a beautiful woman, lead a grotesque villain on a high-speed chase, the male appears calm and unruffled, there are hints of romance between the male and female, and the protagonists escape with the aid of intelligence and gadgetry; (2) the settings both involve the idea of a high-speed chase with the villain in hot pursuit; (3) the mood and pace of both works are fast-paced and involve hi-tech effects, with loud, exciting horn music in the background; (4) both the James Bond and Honda commercial dialogues are laced with dry wit and subtle humor; (5) the characters of Bond and the Honda man are very similar in the way they look and act—both heroes are young, tuxedo-clad, British-looking men with beautiful women in tow and grotesque villains close at hand; moreover, both men exude uncanny calm under pressure, exhibit a dry sense of humor and wit, and are attracted to, and are attractive to, their female companions.

[8] Of course, these film sequences would be only "scènes à faire" without James Bond. It is Bond that makes a James Bond film as the following section bears out.

In addition, several specific aspects of the Honda commercial appear to have been lifted from the James Bond films:

(1) In "The Spy Who Loved Me," James Bond is in a white sports car, a beautiful woman passenger at his side, driving away down a deserted road from some almost deadly adventure, when he is suddenly attacked by a chasing helicopter whose bullets he narrowly avoids by skillfully weaving the car down the road at high speed. At the beginning of the Honda commercial, the Honda man turns to his companion and says, "That wasn't so bad"; to which the woman replies, "Well, I wouldn't congratulate yourself quite yet"—implying that they had just escaped some prior danger. Suddenly, a helicopter appears from out of nowhere and the adventure begins.

(2) In "Dr. No.," the villain has metal hands. In the Honda commercial, the villain uses his metal-encased hands to cling onto the roof of the car after he jumps onto it.

(3) In "Goldfinger," Bond's sports car has a roof which Bond can cause to detach with the flick of a lever. In the Honda commercial, the Honda del Sol has a detachable roof which the Honda man uses to eject the villain.

(4) In "Moonraker," the villainous henchman, Jaws, sporting a broad grin revealing metallic teeth and wearing a pair of oversized goggles, jumps out of an airplane. In the Honda commercial, the villain, wearing similar goggles and revealing metallic teeth, jumps out of a helicopter.

(5) In "The Spy Who Loved Me," Jaws assaults a vehicle in which Bond and his female sidekick are trying to make their escape. In the Honda commercial, the villain jumps onto the roof of the Honda del Sol and scrapes at the roof, attempting to hold on and possibly get inside the vehicle.

(6) In "You Only Live Twice," a chasing helicopter drops a magnetic line down to snag a speeding car. In the Honda commercial, the villain is dropped down to the moving car and is suspended from the helicopter by a cable.

In sum, the extrinsic ideas that are inherent parts of the James Bond films appear to be substantially similar to those in the Honda commercial. . . .

[The court rejected defendants' argument that the ad was independently created, and also rejected a fair use defense, focusing on its conclusions that the use was highly commercial and not transformative or commenting on the Bond films. In terms of the amount of the original taken, the court found that "the brevity of the infringing work when compared with the original does not excuse copying." As for market effect, the court accepted plaintiffs' argument that one of the most lucrative aspects of its copyrights was "their value as lending social cachet and upscale image to cars," and that association with a low-end Honda model would threaten the value of the franchise to future licensees.]

NOTES AND QUESTIONS

Honda argued that no character could be infringed in a thirty-second commercial. What do you think of the claim that the amount of detail conveyed in such a short time must almost necessarily be an abstract idea or scènes à faire, rather than protectable expression? Does the court give MGM a de facto monopoly over a certain genre of video?

MGM argued that the economic harm it suffered was the risk the Honda ad posed to future license agreements with upscale advertisers that would engage in cross-promotion (paying for placement in a movie, supporting the movie with coordinated advertising, etc.). Should copyright extend to that kind of value?

Courts regularly do not give advertisers the benefit of the doubt in similar attempts at parody. *See* Tin Pan Apple, Inc. v. Miller Brewing Co., 737 F. Supp. 826 (S.D.N.Y.1990) (beer commercial copying music video); D.C. Comics, Inc. v. Crazy Eddie, Inc., 205 U.S.P.Q. 1177 (S.D.N.Y. 1979) (commercial copying Superman).

C.   Defendants Don't Always Lose! A Successful Parody

EVEREADY BATTERY CO., INC. V. ADOLPH COORS CO., 765 F. SUPP. 440 (N.D. ILL. 1991)

This case arises from a recently made (and not yet aired) beer commercial by defendant Adolph Coors Company ("Coors") which spoofs a popular series of Eveready battery commercials featuring a pink mechanical toy bunny (the "Energizer Bunny"). . . .

After airing the initial Energizer Bunny commercial, Eveready hired a new ad agency, Chiat/Day/Mojo Inc. Advertising ("Chiat/Day"), which developed an ad campaign revolving around the Energizer Bunny. The series of television commercials created by Chiat/Day as part of this campaign use the Eveready Bunny in a "commercial within a commercial" format. Each spot begins with what at first appears to be a typical television advertisement (which the viewer later realizes is for a fictitious product or service). At some point during the spot, an off-camera drum beat appears to distract the actors in the bogus commercial while the Energizer Bunny—which virtually always appears in its characteristic beach thongs and sunglasses—strolls onto screen beating his bass drum. The actors of the bogus commercial stare incredulously as the intruding mechanical toy bunny nonchalantly propels across the screen, beating the drum and often knocking over props from the fictitious commercial's set. In many of these Energizer commercials, the bunny spins around once and twirls his drum mallets before proceeding to propel out of the picture. Each of the commercials ends with a voice-over which states: "Still going. Nothing outlasts the Energizer. They keep going and going . . . [voice fades out]."

In the past two years, Eveready has produced approximately twenty Energizer Bunny commercials with the interruptive "commercial within a commercial" motif. Although these commercials have cost Eveready approximately $55,000,000 over the past two years (apparently a very modest sum by current advertising standards), they have become among the most popular television commercials in the country and are deemed "break through" ads among those in the advertising industry. . . .

Eveready has also obtained federal copyright registration for two of its Energizer Bunny interruptive format commercials—one for a bogus product called "Tres Cafe," an instant coffee, and the other for "Chug-A-Cherry," a fictional cherry flavored soda.

In late 1990, . . . Foote, Cone and Belding Communications, Inc. ("FCB"), the advertising [agency] for Coors, was given the job of creating a humorous commercial involving Leslie Nielsen, a well-known actor who has been featured in previous Coors Light commercials. . . .

The Coors commercial begins with a background voice, speaking over a classical music score, heartily describing the attributes of an unidentified beer. As the voice speaks, the visual shows an extreme close-up of beer pouring into a glass. The voice and music then grind to a halt as a drum beat is heard and Mr. Nielsen appears walking across the visual. Mr. Nielsen wears a conservative, dark business suit, fake white rabbit ears, fuzzy white tail and rabbit feet (which look like rectangular pink slippers). He carries a life-sized bass drum imprinted with the COORS LIGHT logo. After beating the drum several times, Mr. Nielsen spins rapidly seven or so times and, after recovering somewhat from his apparent dizziness, resumes walking. He says "thank you" before exiting off the screen. As Mr. Nielsen exits, another background voice states: "Coors Light, the official beer of the nineties, is the fastest growing light beer in America. It keeps growing and growing and growing . . . [voice fades out]." At the end of the spot, a visual appears depicting Coors' "Silver Bullet" logo—a horizontal Coors Light can—streaking across the bottom of the screen, leaving in its wake the mark "Coors Light." . . .

_____

[6] Ed. note: Ad at https://www.youtube.com/watch?v=gvfMd7Ydx4c.

DISCUSSION

. . . Copyright Infringement

. . . In the present case, it is undisputed that the plaintiff has ownership of valid copyrights in its Energizer Bunny commercials. It is also undisputed that Coors had access to the Energizer spots and incorporated certain elements of those commercials into its commercial. In this sense, it is clear that Coors "copied" something from Eveready's commercials. Therefore, the court must determine whether the copied elements of the Energizer commercials constitute protectable original "expressions"—as opposed to unprotectable "ideas," *see* 17 U.S.C. § 102(b) (copyright protection does not extend to ideas underlying the author's expressions)[11]—and whether the extent of the copying was sufficient to constitute an improper appropriation.

. . . The court, however, finds it unnecessary to engage in a "substantial similarity" analysis here. Even assuming that Eveready can establish substantial similarity, it has not established a likelihood of success under the "fair use" provisions of the Copyright Act. . . .

Applying the statutory fair use factors to the Coors commercial, the court finds that Eveready cannot establish a likelihood of success on its position that the Nielsen commercial is an infringement of its copyrights. Although the first factor in the § 107 analysis—the purpose and character of Coors' use—weighs in Eveready's favor, none of the remaining three factors are similarly favorable.

The nature of the copyrighted work, like the character of the challenged work, is commercial. Indeed, the two works serve an identical purpose for their respective sponsors. Thus, Eveready cannot argue that its work is deserving of particularly strong protection. Thus, the second factor is at best neutral but certainly does not weigh in favor of Eveready.

Next, the court finds that the amount and substantiality of the portion used in relation to the copyrighted work as a whole is not sufficient to weigh in favor of Eveready. On this point, Eveready, quoting *Walt Disney Prods. v. Air Pirates*, 581 F.2d 751, 757 (9th Cir. 1978), asserts that: "One may lawfully parody copyrighted work *only* if he takes no more than is necessary to 'recall or conjure up the object of his satire.' " . . . This court, however, declines to adopt Eveready's rigid interpretation of the so called "conjure up" test. In *Fisher v. Dees*, the Ninth Circuit expressly stated that the "conjure up" test articulated in its *Air Pirates* opinion, was not meant to be interpreted rigidly "to limit the amount of permissible copying to that amount necessary to evoke only *initial* recognition" in the viewer. . . .

The court finds that the Coors spot did not borrow an impermissible amount of the Eveready commercials for the purposes of the fair use/parody analysis. As Coors points out, the Nielsen commercial is obviously not a verbatim copy of plaintiff's commercials. Rather, Coors' ad merely incorporates certain elements of those commercials necessary to conjure an image of

---

[11] It is established that the copyrightable expressions of a television commercial may include: "individual artistic choices such as particular montage style, camera angle, framing, hairstyle [of actors/actresses], jewelry, decor, makeup and background. These choices express the concept behind any given commercial and distinguish its images and sounds from the otherwise infinite universe of commercials which might have been made."

the Eveready spots for humorous effect. Its imitation of the Energizer Bunny is far from excessive. Mr. Nielsen is not a toy (mechanical or otherwise), does not run on batteries, is not fifteen inches tall, is not predominantly pink, does not wear sunglasses or beach thongs, and would probably make a better babysitter than a children's gift. Although Mr. Nielsen dons rabbit ears, tail, and feet (thus imitating certain bunny-like features), he by no means copies the majority of the Energizer Bunny's "look." Indeed, the dissimilarities between the two far outweigh the similarities. Unlike the Energizer Bunny, Mr. Nielsen speaks; he does not disrupt actors in a fictional commercial; and he does not disturb any props on the "fictional" commercial's set. Also notable is the fact that the Coors commercial does not imitate any particular one of the Energizer spots. Instead, it imitates a few identifiable features, exaggerates some, and leaves out most others. Thus, the court finds that the "amount and substantiality" prong of the fair use analysis weighs against Eveready.

The fourth prong of the statutory fair use test—the effect of the use upon the potential market for or value of the copyrighted work—also weighs against Eveready. This factor has been described as "undoubtedly the single most important element of fair use." In the *Fisher* case, the Ninth Circuit discussed the standard applicable this factor when the use at issue is a parody, stating:

> In assessing the economic effect of the parody, the parody's critical impact must be excluded. Through its critical function, a "parody may quite legitimately aim at garroting the original, destroying it commercially as well as artistically." Copyright law is not designed to stifle critics. . . . Accordingly, the economic effect of a parody with which we are concerned is not its potential to destroy or diminish the market for the original—any bad review can have that effect—but rather whether it *fulfills the demand* for the original. Biting criticism suppresses demand; copyright infringement usurps it. Thus, infringement occurs when a parody supplants the original in markets the original is aimed at, or in which the original is or has reasonable potential to become, commercially valuable.

. . . In the present case, there is no indication that the Coors commercial will supplant the market for the Eveready commercial. Viewers will not stop watching the Eveready commercials in order to watch the Coors commercial on another channel.[18] Thus, to the extent that the Coors commercial may have any effect on the market for the Energizer Bunny commercials, that effect would not be relevant to the copyright fair use analysis. For these reasons, the court finds that Eveready has not established a likelihood of success on its copyright claim. . . .

NOTES AND QUESTIONS

In *Leibovitz v. Paramount Pictures Corp.*, 137 F.3d 109 (2d Cir. 1998), the defendants' ad for the comic movie *Naked Gun 33 1/3: The Final Insult* copied Annie Leibovitz's famous photo of a pregnant, nude Demi Moore, except with star Leslie Nielsen's (again!) face on the body of a pregnant model:

---

[18] The court also notes that because the Coors commercial may only be aired for a maximum of six weeks, it would have little opportunity to "supplant" the Energizer ads in any event.

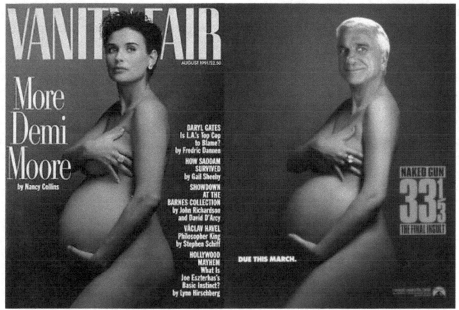

Unlike the *Eveready* case, the *Leibovitz* case came after the Supreme Court's 1994 decision in *Campbell v. Acuff-Rose*, in which the Supreme Court evinced special solicitude for parodies. Specifically, the Court favored "transformative" uses that "add[] something new, with a further purpose or different character, altering the first with new expression, meaning, or message." The Court also noted that commercial use is a factor weighing against fair use, and that the use of a copyrighted work to advertise a product is a context entitling the copying work to "less indulgence" than if it is marketed for its own worth. However, the Court also emphasized that each case must be decided on its own facts, and that commercial use is not fatal to fairness.

The critical question of transformativeness was whether the allegedly infringing use, at least in part, commented on the original's substance or style, though the Court warned against judging quality. The issue was "whether a parodic character may reasonably be perceived." When it comes to parodies, the "nature of the work" factor is not much help because parodies almost always copy expressive works (rather than factual ones). As to the amount copied, the Court required inquiry into both quantity and quality of what was taken but pointed out that a parody must be allowed to "conjure up" at least enough of the original to make its point. The amount taken must be assessed for reasonability in light of whether the overriding purpose is parody or substitution for the original. Finally, the Court rejected any presumption of market harm from copying "involving something beyond mere duplication for commercial purposes." Parodies and originals usually serve different markets, and harm to the original resulting from the critical sting of the parody is not cognizable harm. Only market substitution counts.

With this background, the *Leibovitz* court found that the ad could reasonably be perceived as commentary, at least in part, on the original photo. "Because the smirking face of Nielsen contrasts so strikingly with the serious expression on the face of Moore, the ad may reasonably be perceived as commenting on the seriousness, even the pretentiousness, of the original. The contrast achieves the effect of ridicule that the Court recognized in *Campbell* would serve as a sufficient 'comment' to tip the first factor in a parodist's favor." Though the court warned that differences aren't inevitably commentary on the original, this ad differed "in a way that may reasonably be perceived as commenting, through ridicule, on what a viewer might reasonably think is the undue self-importance conveyed by the subject of the Leibovitz photograph. A photographer posing a well-known actress in a manner that calls to mind a well-known painting must expect, or at least tolerate, a parodist's deflating ridicule." In addition, "the ad might also be reasonably perceived as interpreting the Leibovitz photograph to extol the beauty of the pregnant female body and, rather unchivalrously, to express disagreement with this message." In the end, "the strong parodic nature of the ad tips the first factor significantly toward fair use, even after making some discount for the fact that it promotes a commercial product."

Because Leibovitz's photo was significantly creative, the second factor favored her, but its weight was minimal.

In terms of the amount taken, a parodist may be allowed to take the heart of the original, because that is its usual target. "The copying of these elements, carried out to an extreme degree by the technique of digital computer enhancement, took more of the Leibovitz photograph than was minimally necessary to conjure it up, but *Campbell* instructs that a parodist's copying of more of an original than is necessary to conjure it up will not necessarily tip the third factor against fair use." The third factor had "little, if any" weight against fair use as long as the first and fourth factors favored the parodist.

Leibovitz could not realistically contend that the Paramount ad interfered with any potential market for her photo or for derivative works based on it. Her only argument was that Paramount deprived her of a licensing fee. But she was not entitled to a licensing fee for a work that otherwise qualifies as a fair use. Leibovitz was concerned with the effect of the parody on her "special relationships" with the celebrities she photographed. But "like market harm caused by a negative book review, any lost revenue Leibovitz might experience due to celebrities' reluctance to be photographed for fear of enduring parodies is not cognizable harm under the fourth fair use factor. The possibility of criticism or comment—whether or not parodic—is a risk artists and their subjects must accept."

Other Movie Ad Cases. In *Columbia Pictures Industries, Inc. v. Miramax Films Corp.*, 11 F. Supp. 2d 1179 (C.D. Cal. 1998), the court held that Miramax's ads for Michael Moore's *The Big One*, which targeted large corporations, were not fair uses of the ads for the science fiction movie *Men in Black*. Miramax's ads drew on *Men in Black*, imitating its advertising slogan ("Protecting the Earth from the scum of the universe" became "Protecting the Earth from the scum of corporate America"), as well as creating both posters and trailers that were similar to the *Men in Black* poster and trailer.

The court rejected the defense that the ads parodied *Men in Black* by putting an average, out-of-shape documentarian in the hero's role. Do you agree? Can this case be reconciled with *Leibovitz*?

What about the following images (Saul Steinberg's famous "New Yorker's—eye view of the world" cover for *The New Yorker*, made into a popular poster, and a detail from the poster for *Moscow on the Hudson*, starring Robin Williams)? Is the extent of copying the same as it was in the *Leibovitz* case? What exactly is being copied? Should there be copyright protection for artistic style? *See* Steinberg v. Columbia Pictures Indus., 663 F. Supp. 706 (S.D.N.Y. 1987) (*Moscow on the Hudson* poster was infringing).

Test Yourself: GoldieBlox. GoldieBlox makes engineering toys for girls. For an ad showing off girls' creative construction skills, it copied the music and structure of the Beastie Boys' song "Girls," but changed the lyrics:

Beastie Boys' original	GoldieBlox version
Girls—to do the dishes	Girls—to build the spaceship
Girls—to clean up my room	Girls—to code the new app
Girls—to do the laundry	Girls—to grow up knowing
Girls—and in the bathroom	That they can engineer that
Girls, that's all I really want is girls.	Girls. That's all we really need is girls.

GoldieBlox argued that this was a parody, criticizing the sexist attitudes expressed by the original as part of its mission to promote equality. It filed a declaratory judgment against the Beastie Boys, seeking a fair-use determination. The Beastie Boys responded that they didn't allow anyone to use their music in ads. *See* GoldieBlox, Inc. v. Island Def Jam Music Grp., No. 13-cv-05428 (N.D. Cal. complaint filed Nov. 21, 2013).

The case settled. GoldieBlox agreed to make annual payments of 1% of its gross revenue, until the total payments reached $1 million, to a charitable organization—chosen by the Beastie Boys and approved by GoldieBlox—that supports science, technology, engineering and/or mathematics education for girls. Beastie Boys v. Monster Energy Co., 983 F. Supp. 2d

369 (S.D.N.Y. 2014). If the litigation had continued, how should the court have ruled on fair use?

D.   Comparative Advertising

While advertising is quintessentially commercial and thus one part of the fair use test weighs against it, there is one situation where fair use defenses of advertising predictably succeed: where the challenged use aids comparative advertising.

In *Sony Computer Entertainment America, Inc. v. Bleem, LLC*, 214 F.3d 1022 (9th Cir. 2000), Bleem developed a software emulator that allowed consumers to play Sony PlayStation games on their computers. The emulator allowed consumers to skip purchasing a PlayStation console, which would have to be hooked up to a TV and to play games on higher-resolution computer monitors. (At the time, consumers were more likely to have high-resolution monitors than high-resolution TV screens.)

The emulator itself wasn't infringing. Sony nevertheless argued that displaying screenshots from Sony's copyrighted games on the emulator's packaging infringed its rights. The screenshots compared what a game looked like on a Sony console and with the emulator and a speed-enhancing graphics card on a computer screen.

The court found that screenshots are ubiquitous on videogame packages because it is important to consumers to see "exactly what the game will look like on a screen when it is played."

On the first factor, the court concluded that Bleem's use of the screenshots constituted comparative advertising, which favored a finding of fair use. The court quoted the FTC's position that truthful and nondeceptive comparative advertising "is a source of important information to consumers and assists them in making rational purchase decisions.

Comparative advertising encourages product improvement and innovation, and can lead to lower prices in the marketplace." The use here supported those goals:

> First, by seeing how the games' graphics look on a television when played on a console as compared to how they look on a computer screen when played with Bleem's emulator, consumers will be most able to make "rational purchase decisions." Sony argues that Bleem can advertise without the screen shots, which is certainly true, but no other way will allow for the clearest consumer decisionmaking. Indeed, Bleem's advertising in this fashion will almost certainly lead to product improvements as Sony responds to this competitive threat and as other emulator producers strive for even better performance.
>
> . . . Although Bleem is most certainly copying Sony's copyrighted material for the commercial purposes of increasing its own sales, such comparative advertising redounds greatly to the purchasing public's benefit with very little corresponding loss to the integrity of Sony's copyrighted material.

On the second factor, the nature of the work, the court reasoned that "although the copyrighted work is creative in nature generally, a screen shot is not necessarily. A screen shot is merely an inanimate sliver of the game," and the court found this factor generally worth "very little energy."

A screenshot, which was one of thirty frames per second, was temporally a small amount of the video game. Given that the games at issue had multi-hour plots, a screenshot was "of little substance to the overall copyrighted work."

Finally, on the fourth factor, which the court considered the most important, the relevant market was not the market for emulators or video games themselves because the emulator did not infringe. Sony argued that Bleem's use of screenshots "impinges upon Sony's ability to use the screen shots for promotional purposes in the market." The court disagreed: "Certainly screen shots are a standard device used in the industry to demonstrate video game graphics, but there is not a market for them, or at least not one in which Bleem may participate given Sony's refusal to license to it." Any market harm resulted from commercial competition with the underlying work, which was non-infringing. Thus, the court found fair use.

Fair Use of Competitors' Ads

Courts have also favored copying competitors' ads for the purpose of explicit comparison. Miller UK Ltd. v. Caterpillar Inc., 2015 WL 6407223 (N.D. Ill. Oct. 21, 2015) (annotated copy of competitor's brochure was fair use; "[T]he commercial value to Miller and any resulting decline in the commercial value of the original work resulted not from the value of the original, but from the Miller additions. Such uses are not considered substitutes for the original work and are encouraged by the fair use doctrine.").

But if truthful comparative advertising is favored by fair use, does the analysis change if the ad at issue is false? In *Ashley Furniture Industries, Inc. v. American Signature, Inc.*, 2014

WL 11320708 (S.D. Ohio June 25, 2014), the defendant copied the plaintiff's webpage to show it next to the defendant's furniture:

In other advertising, the defendant copied pictures of plaintiff's furniture in order to compare the parties' offerings; the plaintiff allegedly owned the copyright in the pictures:

The plaintiff, Ashley, argued that the comparisons were false and misleading for various reasons. The court rejected Ashley's argument that the falsity undermined fair use: "Very simply, copyright law protects Ashley's photographs, not Ashley's interest in selling the sofas depicted in the photos." Thus, "allegations that Value City's comparative advertisements did not disclose differences in the quality of the furniture, contained inaccuracies as to pricing, and led some consumers to believe that Value City was selling Ashley sofas are actionable, if at all, under the Lanham Act, not the Copyright Act." The copying was transformative fair use and didn't harm the (nonexistent) market for photos of Ashley's furniture.

4.   Adding Ads to Copyrighted Works

Ordinarily, a publisher displaying advertising adjacent to copyrighted material should not face copyright exposure because adjacencies don't implicate any of the exclusive rights of the copyright owner. For example, if newspapers want to show ads next to editorial content they license from others, newspapers don't need any separate permission to do so beyond the permission to publish the content. Similarly, movie theaters can show ads before a movie without requiring permission beyond the permission to exhibit the movie.

It would be great if we could categorically declare that placing ads around editorial content doesn't create copyright problems. Unfortunately, the case law is more equivocal.

A flagship case is *National Bank of Commerce v. Shaklee Corp.*, 503 F. Supp. 533 (W.D. Tex. 1980). The book at issue was called *All Around the House* by Heloise Bowles, author of a widely syndicated newspaper column called "Hints from Heloise." To boost her editorial integrity, Heloise never mentioned brand names in her column or endorsed any products.

Shaklee was a retailer of household goods sold via "independent distributors" typically via in-home sales (similar to Amway and Tupperware). Shaklee ordered 100,000 customized editions of the book that included Shaklee promotions on the front and rear covers and interspersed within the book's text.

[front and back covers]

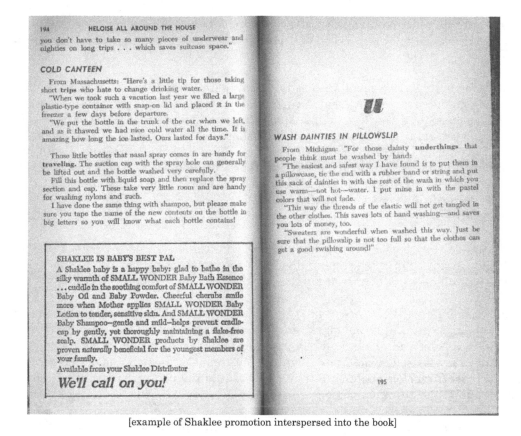

[example of Shaklee promotion interspersed into the book]

The court said Shaklee's additions were analogous to making unauthorized edits of a copyrighted work, so it held that the additions required the copyright owner's authorization, which hadn't been properly obtained.

Compare this to *Paramount Pictures Corp. v. Video Broadcasting Systems, Inc.*, 724 F. Supp. 808 (D. Kan. 1989). VBS added video advertisements (before the FBI warning) to cassettes rented or sold by video rental stores. Nevertheless, some VBS-inserted ads overlapped with the FBI warning or ads placed on the videocassettes by the copyright owner. With respect to its unauthorized editing, the court said:

> Paramount does not allege that defendants were granted certain rights in the motion pictures which they exceeded or abused. This is not a case where the substance of the protected work is significantly altered and its quality and integrity compromised by a licensee or grantee who oversteps his authority. This is not a case where the equities so obviously favor the copyright owner that the court must struggle with the notion of "moral rights." What . . . was applied in *Shaklee* . . . is the right to check distortion or truncation of a copyrighted work. This court is not satisfied that the result of defendants' addition is the distortion of plaintiff's motion picture.

The court said that "the mere addition of a commercial to the front of a videocassette" doesn't create a derivative work, and any distribution rights were exhausted by the cassette's first sale.

Can you reconcile these two results? Does the user's perception of whether the object at issue contains a single integrated work matter? (Note: Despite what the *Paramount* court said, the United States does not actually recognize "moral rights" in motion pictures or books distinct from copyright's derivative work right, although there are some limited moral rights in certain works of visual art. 17 U.S.C. Section 106A. Advertisements are specifically excluded from eligibility for moral rights protection, and reproducing a work in an advertisement could not violate the artist's moral rights because U.S. moral rights only apply to originals/limited editions, not to copies.)

NOTES AND QUESTIONS

Internet Issues. Because each browser makes a copy (or copies) of the webpage a user visits, copyright law might be invoked when individual users attempt to control the appearance of their own computers—or when third-party advertisers help them do so.

In *Wells Fargo & Co. v. WhenU.com, Inc.*, 293 F. Supp. 2d 734 (E.D. Mich. 2003), the defendant engaged in "contextual marketing." That is, WhenU supplied a program to consumers, SaveNow, that generated pop-up and pop-under ads based on data about the websites that they visited, sometimes meaning that competitors' pop-ups obscured the website (at least until the consumer minimized or closed the pop-up). Plaintiffs sued for trademark and copyright infringement.

The court described the typical Windows user's experience of the "desktop," which mimics an actual physical desktop in certain respects, giving the impression of a three-dimensional space in which items can be on top of and underneath each other. The Windows environment allows users to have multiple browser windows open simultaneously, each displaying a different web page, and web pages can overlap on the screen. The court thus held that SaveNow ads didn't appear "on" the plaintiffs' websites. There was no interference with or change in the contents of those sites. Nor did they "modify" plaintiffs' sites. The user's computer's copy of the HTML code associated with the webpage was saved into the computer's RAM (random access memory); SaveNow ads didn't interfere with the stored code.

Computers also maintain a temporary form of memory called video memory, with a pixel-by-pixel snapshot of the screen at any given instant. As a result, plaintiffs argued, a SaveNow ad altered the content of video memory while plaintiffs' web pages were being displayed.

The court held that WhenU did not violate plaintiffs' exclusive right to prepare derivative works. WhenU did not incorporate the plaintiffs' sites into a new work. They merely provided a software product to computer users. As the court pointed out, this could only be actionable under a theory of contributory liability. Defendants who substantially and knowingly contribute to infringement can be held liable as infringers. The problem for plaintiffs—and probably why they did not assert secondary liability theories—is that contributory liability requires someone else to be the primary infringer, and in this case the only candidate was the ordinary browsing consumer.

Thus, the court considered whether SaveNow users infringed the right to prepare derivative works and concluded that they did not alter plaintiffs' websites, even though they altered the display of their screens. "The WhenU Window has no physical relationship to plaintiffs' websites, and does not modify the content displayed in any other open window." The mere presence of an overlapping window, without generating a fixed transferable copy of a work or a public retransmission of an altered version, could not create a derivative work. "Plaintiffs do not have any property interest in the content of a user's pixels, much less a copyright interest."

Ad Subtraction. Most broadcast television channels, as well as many cable television channels, are ad-supported. When third parties help consumers skip ads, does that create an infringing derivative work?

Replay, an early digital video recorder, was sued in part for creating a thirty-second fast-forward button on its remote designed to allow easy ad skipping. This button is now available on various remotes, but Replay went out of business before the issue had been fully litigated. Under *Shaklee* and *Paramount Pictures*, what should the result have been? Does it matter that ads subsidize the production of creative broadcast works, and that ad skipping thus seems to attack the fundamental economic basis for offering free or cheap TV? *See* Fox Broad. Co. v. Dish Network LLC, 723 F.3d 1067 (9th Cir. 2013).

Brands are crucial business assets. According to a 2019 Brandz study, the top 100 global brands are worth a collective $4.7 trillion, and Amazon's brand is worth over $315 billion alone. Consumers can establish deep emotional responses to brands—favorite brands can lead to repeat patronage and good word-of-mouth, while disfavored brands can enter a death spiral.

Given these lofty stakes, it may not be surprising that companies look for ways to protect their brands against unwanted use. Trademark law is the principal legal tool for protecting brands.

Trademark protection is available for anything that signifies product source to consumers. This typically includes a company's brand names and logos. It can also include slogans, colors (e.g., the UPS's brown trucks), sounds (such as the trumpet fanfare preceding 20th Century Fox movies), unique product packaging and product features/attributes (the latter two are protected as "trade dress").

The contours of trademark law are notoriously amorphous for at least two structural reasons. First, trademark law attempts to govern consumers' cognitive associations. We still do not completely understand the psychology or physiology of these mental processes; and even if we did, trademark doctrine rarely considers or incorporates the scientific lessons from other disciplines. Instead, trademark doctrine reflects the guesses of a bunch of lawyers about consumers' thought processes, with occasional assistance from marketing experts paid by one side or another. Not surprisingly, the resulting legal doctrines are confusing.

Second, trademark law lacks a single theoretical justification. One common justification for trademark law is that it protects consumers by preventing them from being taken by imposter brands or having to invest in extra pre-purchase research to determine a product's quality. Instead, consumers can use the trademark as shorthand for at least some of the qualities of the product or service.

Another common justification for trademark law is that it rewards producers' investments in quality. Without trademark protection, competitive rivals would copy the branding of high-quality producers and offer lower-quality/cheaper knockoff products using the same brand. (This leads to the market for lemons, explored in Chapter 4.) The resulting price competition would negate the ability of producers to get an adequate return on their investments in producing high-quality products, discouraging those investments. Trademark law reverses that dynamic, encouraging those investments.

In some circumstances, such as undisclosed counterfeiting, these policy rationales (consumer protection and producer protection) align. When counterfeits fool consumers, consumers get unexpectedly inferior goods, and producers lose sales to competitors who do not make equivalent quality investments. In those situations, both consumers and producers benefit from suppressing counterfeits.

In other circumstances, producer interests and consumer interests diverge, exposing the lack of consensus about why we protect trademarks in the first place. For example, when a competitor buys online keyword advertising triggered by a third-party trademark, consumers may find the presentation of competitive alternatives useful, but producers often resent the consumer's "diversion" away from their offerings. If trademark law is about protecting consumers, competitive keyword advertising may not be a problem; if trademark law is about protecting producers, it may be.*

As you review this chapter, consider how the tensions between the consumer protection and producer protection justifications for trademark law affect the doctrine and specific case results. The first half of the chapter gives the general framework of trademark law that applies to all advertising. The second half considers Internet-specific problems, which represent an ever-increasing share of advertising issues. Although the technological specifics of online advertising are likely to change, the way courts have dealt with new technologies provides guidance for the next innovation.

1.   Brief Overview of Trademark Law

Unlike patents and copyrights, the Constitution doesn't expressly authorize Congress to provide trademark protection. Instead, Congress has enacted trademark legislation pursuant to its Commerce Clause authority.

Trademarks are protected under both federal and state law. The main federal trademark law is the Lanham Act, enacted in 1946 and modified many times since then. There is a federal registration system for trademarks at the U.S. Patent & Trademark Office (PTO). Unregistered trademarks also are protectable.

States concurrently offer trademark protection. Many states have adopted a version of the Model State Trademark Bill, although the state adoptions aren't especially uniform. States may have their own registration system for state trademarks. Although state laws may deviate from the Lanham Act, judges often interpret federal and state trademark claims identically, with minor exceptions for dilution, which we will discuss later in the chapter.

There are many other trademark-like laws at both the federal and state level. For example, Congress has enacted trademark-like protection for the Olympics and related marks, and those protections differ from the Lanham Act in subtle but crucial ways.

---

* Even knockoffs bought on street corners may satisfy consumers who are more interested in displaying the brand than in having the value of the product marked with the brand. In such cases, the trademark owner loses the cachet of exclusivity, and other consumers may suffer from that as well, which matters if we count the psychic benefits of being able to have something that other, less-wealthy people don't have as a social good, or if we think that anticopying/pro-exclusivity rules cut down on wasteful status competition. *See* DR. SEUSS, THE SNEETCHES AND OTHER STORIES (1953) (a parable of the waste that can occur when groups repeatedly seek distinction from other groups but the signals of distinction are easy to copy).

Private entities may offer their own systems for resolving trademark complaints. For example, Google and other search engines have voluntarily adopted internal trademark policies for when they will accept ads referencing third-party trademarks; Amazon has brand policies that help owners of federally registered trademarks control sales on its platform; and the domain name system has its own extra-judicial adjudication process for trademark disputes over domain names. In practice, these private policies may provide more recourse to trademark owners than actual "law."

Acquiring Trademark Rights

Trademark owners acquire their trademark rights principally by making a "use in commerce" of the trademark. The Federal Lanham Act (15 U.S.C. § 1127) defines "use in commerce" as "the bona fide use of a mark in the ordinary course of trade and not made merely to reserve a right in a mark." There are some picky details about the difference between goods and services, but in essence, a trademark owner starts accruing protectable trademark rights by offering products or services for sale with the trademark displayed on the product or in advertising for the trademark—so long as the offering is actually available. *See* Couture v. Playdom, Inc., 778 F.3d 1379 (Fed. Cir. 2015). (There are also provisions for acquiring rights via an application to register a trademark with a bona fide "intent to use" the trademark in commerce, known as an ITU application.[7]) Advertising also plays an important role in establishing rights for products: Advertising can strengthen consumers' recognition of the trademark, which can extend the geographic reach of the trademark rights or give the trademark owner extra leverage when evaluating consumer confusion (*see, e.g.,* the *Polaroid* factors discussed in the *MasterCard* case, to follow *infra*).

Even if a trademark owner doesn't file an ITU application before use, it will often seek a federal registration of its trademarks at some point, especially for word marks or specific devices (such as the Nike swoosh). Registration is not required to have enforceable trademark rights, but registration offers several advantages, including:

- The registration gives national priority to the trademark owner. Without this, a trademark owner's rights typically are limited only to the geographies where it has made a use in commerce, or where it is known to local consumers. So, for example, if the trademark owner has sold its products only regionally, a copyist might replicate

---

[7] In many cases, a trademark owner will file an ITU application in advance of a new product rollout. The ITU application establishes the trademark owner's "priority" as the application date rather than the date of first use in commerce. An ITU can be helpful when the vendor has selected a brand but has not begun using it; the ITU application reduces the fear that an interloper will emerge between product announcement and some subsequent date that qualifies as the first use in commerce.

An ITU application is merely a placeholder. The applicant must either make a use in commerce and convert the ITU to a use-based application or, if the application receives a "notice of allowance" from the PTO before that happens, must make a use in commerce and file a statement that it has done so. At that point, the allowed ITU converts into a normal trademark registration. The statutory period for showing use in commerce can, with the Trademark Office's permission, run up to three years after the notice of allowance; without a qualifying use in commerce during the specified period, the ITU expires. More than half of ITU applications never mature into valid trademarks. Barton Beebe, *Is the Trademark Office a Rubber Stamp?: Trademark Registration Rates at the PTO, 1981–2010*, 48 HOUS. L. REV. 752 (2012).

the trademark in a different region and obtain superior trademark rights in that region.

- The registration gives the trademark owner guaranteed access to federal courts and some procedural benefits in litigation, such as providing prima facie evidence of the trademark's validity, ownership and exclusive right to use the mark with associated goods.
- A federal registration provides eligibility for enhanced remedies in court, including potentially treble damages and attorneys' fees. As a practical matter, except when dealing with counterfeiters, the enhanced remedies are far less important than the registration's presumption of validity.

The stronger the trademark, the greater legal protection it gets. Trademark strength is also measured by a hierarchy of semantic distinctiveness (this focuses just on word marks; visual and sound marks are more complicated). From strongest to weakest:

- *Fanciful trademarks.* These are newly coined terms, such as Exxon and Oreo.
- *Arbitrary trademarks.* These are dictionary words being used for a novel meaning. For example, the word "Apple" had nothing to do with computers until Apple Inc. established that new meaning.
- *Suggestive trademarks.* These are dictionary words being used to suggest something about the associated product. For example, "Greyhound Bus" suggests something about the product's attributes (i.e., the bus service purports to be fast, like greyhound dogs are).
- *Descriptive trademarks.* These are dictionary words being used in a way that describes the product's attributes. For example, it does not require consumers to do much mental work to figure out what offerings they might find at a retailer named "Dress Barn." Personal names and geographic terms are treated like descriptive trademarks.
- *Generic words.* These are words used for their dictionary meaning, such as the term "apple" to describe the associated fruit or "aspirin" to describe acetylsalicylic acid.

Despite the relative clarity of this semantic hierarchy, bright minds often disagree about where a particular trademark belongs on it. Furthermore, while terms can start out as trademarkable, consumers may over time think of the term as the generic description for the class of goods, a phenomenon called "genericide." In that case, the trademark loses all protection no matter how hard the trademark owner tried to avoid that outcome. "Aspirin" is just one of many former trademarks that suffered genericide.

Fanciful, arbitrary and suggestive marks are called "inherently distinctive" trademarks. Inherently distinctive trademarks are eligible for trademark protection and registration immediately following their use in commerce. Generic terms are never protectable as trademarks. Descriptive trademarks (including personal names and geographic terms being

used as trademarks) can acquire distinctiveness and become protectable and registrable[*]
only after they achieve "secondary meaning."
Secondary meaning occurs when consumers believe the descriptive term refers to only one
producer in the marketplace. For example, the trademark "U-Haul" initially was descriptive,
but eventually consumers became so familiar with the brand that they associated the term
with one and only one marketplace participant. Once a sufficient number of consumers made
the same cognitive association, U-Haul achieved secondary meaning and became a
protectable trademark.

Although ordinarily a trademark owner needs to use the trademark in commerce itself to
generate protectable rights, occasionally consumers will coin a nickname for a product that
becomes so identified with the product that the trademark owner can enforce trademark
rights in the nickname too. *Compare* Volkswagenwerk Aktiengesellschaft v. Rickard, 492
F.2d 474 (5th Cir. 1974) (Volkswagen can protect the nickname "Bug" for its Beetle cars),
with Harley Davidson Inc. v. Grottanelli, 164 F.3d 806 (2d Cir. 1999) (Harley-Davidson
cannot protect the term "Hog" for its motorcycles because "hog" describes large motorcycles
generally). *See generally* Peter M. Brody, *What's in a Nickname? Or, Can Public Use Create
Private Rights?*, 95 TRADEMARK REP. 1123 (2005).

2.   Trademark Infringement

A trademark infringement claim typically has the following prima facie elements:

> (1) the plaintiff has valid and protectable trademark rights,
> (2) the plaintiff's use in commerce date (determined either through usage or the
> application date for a registered mark, if that is earlier) predates the defendant's,
> giving it "priority,"
> (3) the defendant has used the trademark in commerce (as discussed shortly, not
> everyone agrees that this factor is part of the prima facie case), and
> (4) the defendant's usage creates a likelihood of consumer confusion about the
> product's source, sponsorship or affiliation.

If the plaintiff establishes a prima facie case, the defendant can assert a number of possible
defenses, some of which we will discuss below.

A.   Consumer Confusion

Consumer confusion is at the core of trademark law. If there's no confusion, there's no
infringement (but dilution may still be possible). Likelihood of consumer confusion is
typically evaluated using a multi-factor test, as illustrated by the following case. As you read

---

[*] Descriptive trademarks are registrable on the principal registry only after they obtain secondary meaning. The
United States also allows registration of descriptive trademarks on a supplemental registry, even if they haven't
obtained secondary meaning. However, such registrations provide minimal rights for the registrant. The
supplemental registry is mainly used for U.S. trademark owners who wish to seek international trademark
registrations before they have achieved secondary meaning in the U.S. International standards for registering
descriptive trademarks are more relaxed than U.S. standards.

it, consider how the test for identifying likely consumer confusion in trademark cases differs from the test for identifying likely consumer deception in Lanham Act cases under Section 43(a)(1)(B).

MASTERCARD INTERNATIONAL INC. V. NADER 2000 PRIMARY COMMITTEE, INC., 2004 WL 434404 (S.D.N.Y. 2004)

THERE ARE SOME THINGS MONEY CAN'T BUY. FOR EVERYTHING ELSE THERE'S MASTERCARD. . . .

BACKGROUND

MasterCard, a Delaware corporation with its principal place of business in New York, is a large financial institution that engages in the interchange of funds by credit and debit payment cards through over 23,000 banks and other foreign and domestic member financial institutions. Since Fall of 1997, MasterCard has commissioned the authorship of a series of advertisements that have come to be known as the "Priceless Advertisements." These advertisements feature the names and images of several goods and services purchased by individuals which, with voice overs and visual displays, convey to the viewer the price of each of these items. At the end of each of the Priceless Advertisements a phrase identifying some priceless intangible that cannot be purchased (such as "a day where all you have to do is breathe") is followed by the words or voice over: "Priceless. There are some things money can't buy, for everything else there's MasterCard."

In August 2000, MasterCard became aware that Ralph Nader and his presidential committee were broadcasting an allegedly similar advertisement on television that promoted the presidential candidacy of Ralph Nader in the 2000 presidential election. That political ad included a sequential display of a series of items showing the price of each ("grilled tenderloin for fundraiser: $1,000 a plate;" "campaign ads filled with half-truths: $10 million;" "promises to special interest groups: over $100 billion"). The advertisement ends with a phrase identifying a priceless intangible that cannot be purchased ("finding out the truth: priceless. There are some things that money can't buy"). The resulting ad (the "Nader ad") was shown on television during a two-week period from August 6–17, during the 2000 presidential campaign, and also appeared on the defendants' web site throughout that campaign.* Plaintiff sent defendants a letter explaining its concern over the similarity of the commercials, and suggested that defendants broadcast a more "original" advertisement. When plaintiff contacted representatives of defendants a few days later, plaintiff MasterCard advised defendants to cease broadcasting their political advertisement due to its similarity with MasterCard's own commercial advertisement and resulting infringement liability. . . .

---

* [Editor's note: you can watch the ad on YouTube at http://www.youtube.com/watch?v=mJOuPZKAspQ.]

finding out the truth: priceless

DISCUSSION . . .

1. Trademark Infringement

MasterCard's first count is based on Section 43(a) of the Trademark Act, 15 U.S.C. Section 1125(a). Plaintiff claims that defendants have used two of MasterCard's service marks— "THERE ARE SOME THINGS MONEY CAN'T BUY. FOR EVERYTHING ELSE THERE'S MASTERCARD," and "PRICELESS" to misrepresent that the 2000 presidential candidacy of Ralph Nader for the office of President of the United States was endorsed by MasterCard. Plaintiff's second count also pleads a claim for trademark infringement due to defendants' use of the two federally registered trademarks, ("THERE ARE SOME THINGS MONEY CAN'T BUY. FOR EVERYTHING ELSE THERE'S MASTERCARD," and "PRICELESS"), pursuant to Section 32(1) of the Trademark Act, 15 U.S.C. Section 1114(1).

In trademark infringement cases, the Court must apply the undisputed facts to the balancing test outlined in *Polaroid Corp. v. Polarad Elecs., Corp.*, 287 F.2d 492, 495 (2d Cir.1961), and may grant summary judgment where it finds, as a matter of law, that there is no likelihood of confusion to the public. In determining whether there is a likelihood of confusion between MasterCard's Priceless Advertisements and Ralph Nader's Political Ad, the Court weighs eight factors, as articulated in *Polaroid*: (1) strength of the Plaintiff's mark; (2) degree of similarity between the two marks; (3) proximity of the products or services; (4) likelihood that the prior owner will "bridge the gap" into the newcomer's product or service line; (5) evidence of actual confusion between the marks; (6) whether the defendant adopted the mark in good faith; (7) the quality of defendants' products or services; and (8) sophistication of the parties' consumers.

In demonstrating the strength of the trademark, the plaintiff must establish either that the mark is inherently distinctive or alternatively, that the mark has acquired secondary meaning. MasterCard's marks, "PRICELESS" and "THERE ARE SOME THINGS MONEY CAN'T BUY,

FOR EVERYTHING ELSE THERE'S MASTERCARD," are registered. MasterCard asserts that their marks have attained secondary meaning. Defendants concede that MasterCard's Priceless Advertisements are strong enough to have become a part of present-day American popular culture. The strength of MasterCard's trademarks is indisputable.

In determining the second factor, the similarity of the marks in issue, a court must consider whether the marks create the same overall commercial impression when viewed separately. A court may rely upon its own visual inspection in making this determination. In this instance, it is not necessary for the Court to do so, because once again, defendants do not dispute that the Nader Ad employs the word "priceless" in the same manner used by MasterCard in its television advertisements. The Nader Ad also employs the phrase "there are some things money can't buy," which is part of a MasterCard trademark. Defendants do not dispute that they employ that phrase in the same look, sound and commercial impression as employed by MasterCard.

The third and fourth factors, the proximity of the products or services and the likelihood that the prior user will bridge the gap, respectively, weigh in favor of defendants. There is little similarity between MasterCard's credit and debit card business and Ralph Nader's political candidacy. There is little likelihood and no evidence that MasterCard, a financial services company, would have any direct involvement in supporting a candidate in a political presidential campaign. Similarly, neither Ralph Nader nor his political campaign committee have expressed any desire or intent to enter the credit card business or offer the public any direct financial services.

Evidence of actual confusion, the fifth factor, also weighs in favor of defendants. This factor is perhaps the most significant when considering the overall likelihood of confusion by the public. "The best evidence of likelihood of confusion is the occurrence of actual confusion and mistakes." While it is not essential for a finding of trademark infringement to demonstrate actual confusion, "there can be no more positive proof of likelihood of confusion than evidence of actual confusion." . . . As evident by the present record, out of 452 e-mails to MasterCard regarding the Nader Ad, only two are relied upon as possibly reflecting confusion. This is certainly not enough to show actual confusion or that such confusion inflicted commercial injury to MasterCard. In support of its argument that actual confusion exists, MasterCard also relies on the written transcript of a broadcast of CNN's Late Edition, during which Connecticut Senator Christopher Dodd stated that he thought the Nader Advertisement was a credit card ad. A viewing of a tape of that program shows Senator Dodd laughing at his own joke, while speaking the words on which MasterCard relies to establish actual confusion. It is little or no evidence of actual confusion. Even if Senator Dodd had actually been confused, a few isolated instances of actual confusion are not sufficient to defeat a motion for summary judgment. The plaintiff should be able to demonstrate a reasonable likelihood that reasonable people will be confused.

The sixth factor regarding good faith adoption of the mark also favors defendants. The relevant intent in this inquiry is whether the alleged infringer intended "to palm off his products as those of another." In the present case, there is no evidence that defendants intended to confuse the public. There is no basis to argue that the Ralph Nader political ad which has the clear intent to criticize other political candidates who accept money from wealthy contributors, at the same time, attempts or intends to imply that he is a political candidate endorsed by MasterCard. There is uncontradicted testimony that neither Ralph Nader, nor his committees, had any such intent.

The seventh factor, the quality of defendants' products or services, is of insignificant weight in this case. There is no reasonable comparison to be made between the quality of the products and services provided by MasterCard and the value of defendants' politics. MasterCard provides a quality of financial services which can readily be compared to its commercial competitors. However, it is purely the public's subjective opinion of the appeal and attractiveness of a political candidate's ideas and record which determines whether the public will buy the politics any candidate for office is selling.

The eighth and final factor to be weighed is the level of consumer sophistication in either of the relevant markets for credit card services or for political candidates. Unless otherwise demonstrated, it is reasonable to conclude that the general American public is sophisticated enough to distinguish a Political Ad from a commercial advertisement. Rarely, if ever, is there a realistic opportunity to confuse the two. Indeed, as previously discussed, out of the 452 e-mails received by MasterCard regarding Ralph Nader's Political Ad, only 2–3 questioned MasterCard's involvement with Ralph Nader's campaign. This sampling of American consumers, which is the only proof offered on the record, is a sufficient indication that consumers are generally sophisticated enough to decipher between MasterCard's commercial purposes and Ralph Nader's political agenda.

When balancing the eight *Polaroid* factors, no one factor can determine the ultimate issue of likelihood of confusion to the consumer. To properly weigh these factors requires the court to view each factor in light of the totality of the evidence. Thus, after balancing the *Polaroid* factors, this Court finds that there is no genuine issue of material fact with regard to any likelihood of confusion between MasterCard's Priceless Advertisements and Ralph Nader's Political Ad which could constitute a violation of the Trademark Act. Defendants' summary judgment motion to dismiss Counts One and Two of plaintiff's complaint is therefore granted.
. . .

NOTES AND QUESTIONS

Tests for Likelihood of Confusion. Most trademark-infringement claims turn on the likelihood of consumer confusion. To measure this likelihood, courts typically use a multi-factor test. Each federal appellate circuit has its own test, although most of the tests include the same or similar factors. This court used the Second Circuit *Polaroid* test, and the *Polaroid* factors are representative of the factors found in other circuits' tests. Compare the First Circuit's *Pignons* test discussed in the *Venture Tape* opinion and the Ninth Circuit's *Sleekcraft* test discussed in the *Network Automation* opinion below.

Copyright Claim. The court rejected MasterCard's claim that Nader's ad infringed MasterCard's copyright, concluding: "The Nader Ad is a non-infringing fair use parody of MasterCard's Priceless Advertisements."

A Humorless Legal System. If we take our legal hats off, it was entirely clear to everyone that Nader's ad was a joke. Yet, trademark law (and the legal system generally) doesn't handle jokes very well. Instead, trademark owners are rarely amused when they feel that someone takes advantage of an asset they built at great expense, and judges often will apply the legal tests seriously rather than breezily dismiss an effort to shut down an obvious joke. Compare the treatment of humor in false advertising cases, discussed in Chapters 4 and 5. For another example of a humorless trademark opinion, see the *Deere v. MTD* dilution case, *infra.*

Iconic Ad Campaigns. Occasionally, advertising campaigns such as the MasterCard "Priceless" campaign are so massively successful with consumers that they become culturally iconic. Should trademark law protect secondary references to these iconic campaigns more or less aggressively? On the one hand, Nader clearly was trying to invoke the consumers' knowledge of MasterCard's campaign to tell his own story. On the other hand, precisely *because* the MasterCard campaign was so successful, consumers were more likely to remember MasterCard's original campaign and be able to recognize that invocations of MasterCard's campaign are coming from a different source. If so, this could lead to the possibly counterintuitive result that trademarks generated through culturally iconic campaigns might be *less* enforceable against some secondary uses than trademarks generated through less-successful campaigns.

The Relationship Between Trademark Infringement and False Advertising. Assuming they qualify for both, plaintiffs will prefer to bring trademark-infringement claims over false advertising claims because trademark infringement applies to more activity than false advertising and has fewer doctrinal limits (such as the absence of a survey requirement for implicitly false claims and the absence of a materiality requirement). However, there may be reasons that a plaintiff can't bring a trademark claim—perhaps the term at issue is generic and not protectable as a trademark; perhaps the plaintiff is not using the mark at issue in commerce in the United States and thus can't claim rights of its own. Some courts will allow the plaintiff to bring a false advertising claim instead.

In *Belmora LLC v. Bayer Consumer Care AG*, 819 F.3d 697 (4th Cir. 2016), Bayer used the "FLANAX" mark in Mexico for analgesics.

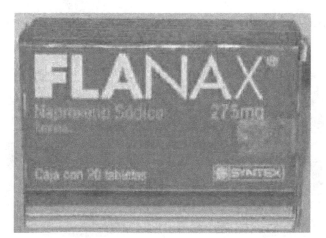

In the United States, Bayer used the brand name "Aleve" instead of FLANAX. Belmora registered FLANAX in the United States for analgesics and began selling the same type of analgesics under that mark in the United States Belmora's early packaging "closely mimicked" Bayer's Mexican FLANAX packaging in color scheme, font size and typeface.

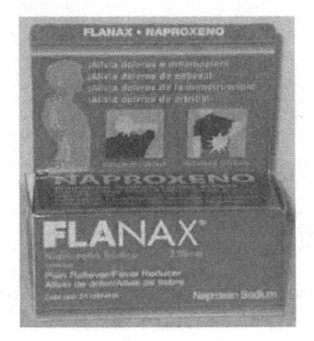

In addition, Belmora made statements to prospective distributors such as:

> For generations, Flanax has been a brand that Latinos have turned to for various common ailments. Now you too can profit from this highly recognized topselling brand among Latinos. Flanax is now made in the U.S. and continues to show record sales growth everywhere it is sold. Flanax acts as a powerful attraction for Latinos by providing them with products they know, trust and prefer.

Belmora ultimately revised the packaging, but there were still similarities to Mexican FLANAX.

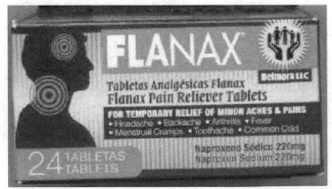

The Fourth Circuit allowed Bayer to proceed both on a claim under Section 43(a)(1)(A) for false association, based on its rights in Mexico, and on a false advertising claim under Section 43(a)(1)(B), based on its rights in Aleve in the United States. "If not for Belmora's statements that its FLANAX was the same one known and trusted in Mexico, some of its consumers could very well have instead purchased BHC's Aleve brand."

The court of appeals cautioned that Belmora owned Flanax as a mark in the United States. "But trademark rights do not include using the mark to deceive customers as a form of unfair competition, as is alleged here." An appropriate remedy might allow Belmora to use the mark, but with measures to avoid confusion. "[A]ny remedy should take into account traditional trademark principles relating to Belmora's ownership of the mark," such as altering the font and color of the packaging, attaching the manufacturer's name to the brand name, or using a disclaimer. What do you think of this resolution?

B.   Use in Commerce

We earlier suggested that the plaintiff's prima facie case may require it to show that the defendant used the plaintiff's trademark in commerce. This element is controversial for at least two reasons.

First, the federal statute defines the terms "commerce" and "use in commerce" in irreconcilable ways. The "use in commerce" definition suggests that plaintiffs must show that they used the plaintiff's trademark in ad copy or on product packaging as part of the plaintiff's prima facie case. The "commerce" definition conforms to the broader boundaries of the Commerce Clause. This poor drafting creates an unresolvable ambiguity in the statute that may ultimately require congressional fixing. *See* Rescuecom Corp. v. Google Inc., 562 F. 3d 123 (2d Cir. 2009) (especially the appendix).

Second, and perhaps more importantly, courts often gloss over this element when the defendant clearly made a use in commerce of the plaintiff's trademark. For example, referencing the plaintiff's trademark in ad copy almost always will qualify as the defendant's use in commerce of the trademark. In those cases, courts are not very careful to acknowledge this prima facie element. For example, the *MasterCard* court simply raced past this element—even though, as a political candidate, Nader did not make a traditional "use in commerce" of MasterCard's trademarks.

Sometimes, technological systems enable an advertiser to implicate a third-party trademark in a way that does not clearly constitute a use in commerce of the trademark. These circumstances force courts to tread more cautiously, and occasionally the defendant can win based on the absence of a use in commerce. We'll discuss two examples now and revisit this issue in the ambush marketing discussion later in this chapter.

Keyword Advertising Triggering

In *1-800 Contacts, Inc., v. WhenU.com, Inc.*, 414 F.3d 400 (2d Cir. 2005), WhenU operated "adware," software installed on users' computers that monitored their behavior and triggered "pop-up" advertisements when the software detected user behavior that matched one of the keywords purchased by advertisers. (We encountered the resulting copyright claim in Chapter 11.) Advertisers had purchased keywords such as "contact lenses," and WhenU programmed its databases so that those advertisers would show in pop-up ads when users accessed the 1-800 Contacts website. The Second Circuit held that WhenU's behind-the-scenes association of the 1-800 Contacts domain name with advertising categories such as "contact lenses" did not constitute a trademark use in commerce.

Although the Second Circuit has not expressly overturned the *1-800 Contacts* ruling, the 2009 *Rescuecom* opinion substantially limits the case's holding. *See* Rescuecom Corp. v. Google Inc., 562 F. 3d 123 (2d Cir. 2009). We revisit keyword advertising later in this chapter.

Billboards

In *Howard Johnson International, Inc. v. Vraj Brig, LLC*, 2010 WL 215381 (D. N.J. 2010), Tucci owned a hotel building that Vraj Brig operated as a franchised Howard Johnson's hotel. Tucci stopped operating the building as a hotel, but he left up a billboard bearing the "Howard Johnson's" name. Howard Johnson sued Tucci for trademark violations. The court ruled in Tucci's favor:

> Plaintiff has produced no evidence that Tucci ever did anything other than passively allow a preexisting billboard containing HJI's marks to remain standing on his property. Therefore, Tucci never "used" the protected marks within the meaning of that term as it appears in the Lanham Act. Furthermore, even if Tucci were held to have "used" HJI's marks, he never offered or provided any goods or services at the lodging facility in question. Therefore, his display of the marks does not satisfy the "in connection with goods or services" requirement either.

The court rejected Howard Johnson's argument even though the billboard might have frustrated consumers who exited the freeway looking for the hotel, only to be disappointed.

C.   Defense: Descriptive Fair Use

Descriptive fair use occurs when a defendant uses a descriptive term that is a plaintiff's trademark not as a trademark, but rather to describe the defendant's own product. 15 U.S.C. Section 1115(b)(4) provides a defense to trademark infringement when using "a term or device which is descriptive of and used fairly and in good faith only to describe the goods or services of such party." The descriptive fair use defense may only be invoked against when the defendant's use is descriptive. Using a term in an arbitrary, fanciful or suggestive way, or in a way that suggests that the defendant is trying to use the term as a trademark for its own goods or services, will not qualify.

In a classic example, a pump shoe manufacturer had a trademark in the slogan "Looks Like a Pump, Feels Like a Sneaker." A competitive shoe manufacturer nevertheless could advertise its own pump shoes with the following ad copy:

"Think Of It As A Sneaker With No Strings Attached." The text of the ad includes the phrase, "And when we say it feels like a sneaker, we're not just stringing you along."

U.S. Shoe Corp. v. Brown Grp., Inc., 740 F. Supp. 196 (S.D.N.Y. 1990). Although the phrase "feels like a sneaker" appears in both the original slogan and the competitor's ad, the court found a descriptive fair use:

> In this case, the defendant uses the phrase "feels like a sneaker" in a descriptive sense, claiming a virtue of the product. It essentially restates the key selling claim of defendant's product—that the Townwalker shoe was designed specifically to incorporate the comfort of athletic shoes.

Two other descriptive fair use examples:

- Sunmark, Inc. v. Ocean Spray Cranberries, Inc., 64 F.3d 1055 (7th Cir. 1995). Sunmark makes SweeTARTS, a classic sweet-and-sour sugar candy. Ocean Spray subsequently decided to advertise its cranberry juice as having a "sweet-tart" flavor. The court held that Ocean Spray's use of "sweet-tart" qualified as a descriptive fair use.
- Cosmetically Sealed Indus., Inc. v. Chesebrough-Pond's USA Co., 125 F.3d 28 (2d Cir. 1997). The plaintiff marketed lip gloss under the registered trademark "Sealed with a Kiss." Chesebrough subsequently offered long-lasting lipstick in a counter display that included free postcards and an encouragement to mark the postcards with a lip-print, which ended with the exhortation to "Seal it with a Kiss!!" ("it" referred to the postcard). The court held that this display constituted descriptive fair use.

D.   Defense: Comparative Advertising and Nominative Use

Advertisers often want to reference their competitors in ad copy to make comparative claims, e.g., "Acme is better than Bigco." If the comparative statements do not constitute false advertising, does trademark law nevertheless limit these comparative references?

That turns out to be an unexpectedly difficult question. Trademark law does not categorically permit the use of third-party trademarks in ad copy for comparative statements. Each ad copy reference must be independently analyzed under the applicable trademark doctrines.

The nominative-use doctrine facilitates some comparative references. Nominative use, sometimes called "nominative fair use," differs from descriptive fair use in how the defendant uses the plaintiff's trademark. In descriptive fair use, the defendant uses a word or symbol that is also a trademark to describe the *defendant's* product. In nominative use, the defendant uses the trademark to refer to the *plaintiff's* product. Unlike descriptive fair use, which only applies to terms that are descriptive for the defendant's products or services, the nominative use defense can be invoked to defend a use of any trademarks, even fanciful ones.

There are several different appellate-level definitions of nominative use. The Ninth Circuit has the best-developed standards for nominative use. It requires three elements for a successful defense:

1. The plaintiff's product is not readily identifiable without using the trademark.
2. The defendant uses the plaintiff's trademark only as reasonably necessary to identify the plaintiff's product.
3. The defendant's usage does not imply the plaintiff's sponsorship or endorsement.

These elements ought to permit many comparative advertising usages, but that doesn't mean comparative advertisers can confidently rely on the nominative-use defense. First, because it is a defense, nominative use may be difficult to win at the early stages of litigation, thus imposing substantial costs even when the defense is successful. Second, the implied sponsorship/endorsement factor depends on consumer perceptions, which sets up a factual dispute that may be hard to predict. Third, not every circuit has embraced the nominative-use defense. For example, the Sixth Circuit has questioned whether the nominative use defense should be recognized, and the Second Circuit has held that the nominative fair-use factors are simply to be added to the usual multifactor confusion test as additional considerations in appropriate cases, making nominative use very hard to resolve on a motion to dismiss.

The following case, a classic example of comparative advertising, was decided before the Ninth Circuit officially formulated its three-factor nominative-use test. Nevertheless, the case illustrates how the analysis *should* go.

SMITH V. CHANEL, INC., 402 F.2D 562 (9TH CIR. 1968)

Appellant R. G. Smith, doing business as Ta'Ron, Inc., advertised a fragrance called "Second Chance" as a duplicate of appellees' "Chanel No. 5," at a fraction of the latter's price. Appellees were granted a preliminary injunction prohibiting any reference to Chanel No. 5 in the promotion or sale of appellants' product. This appeal followed.

The action rests upon a single advertisement published in "Specialty Salesmen,' a trade journal directed to wholesale purchasers. The advertisement offered "The Ta'Ron Line of Perfumes" for sale. It gave the seller's address as "Ta'Ron Inc., 26 Harbor Cove, Mill Valley, Calif." It stated that the Ta'Ron perfumes "duplicate 100% Perfect the exact scent of the world's finest and most expensive perfumes and colognes at prices that will zoom sales to volumes you have never before experienced." It repeated the claim of exact duplication in a variety of forms.

The advertisement suggested that a "Blindfold Test" be used "on skeptical prospects," challenging them to detect any difference between a well known fragrance and the Ta'Ron "duplicate." One suggested challenge was, "We dare you to try to detect any difference between Chanel #5 (25.00) and Ta'Ron's 2nd Chance, $7.00."

In an order blank printed as part of the advertisement each Ta'Ron fragrance was listed with the name of the well known fragrance which it purportedly duplicated immediately beneath. Below "Second Chance" appeared "*(Chanel #5)." The asterisk referred to a statement at the bottom of the form reading "Registered Trade Name of Original Fragrance House."

[Editor's note: the ad, followed by a close-up of "The Blindfold Test" and the order form:]

ALL OF A SUDDEN—YOU'RE IN THE BUCKS

AND YOU STAY IN THE BUCKS BY REPRESENTING THE MOST FAMOUS "PERFUME DEVELOPMENT" IN ALL HISTORY!

The TA'RON Line of Perfumes

DUPLICATE 100% PERFECT the EXACT SCENT of the WORLD'S FINEST and MOST EXPENSIVE PERFUMES and COLOGNES at PRICES that will ZOOM SALES to VOLUMES YOU HAVE NEVER BEFORE EXPERIENCED! EXAMPLE: 1 oz. Patou Joy is $60.00. Ta'ron offers same scent for $7.00.

TA'RON INC., 26 Harbor Cove, Mill Valley, Calif.

The Blindfold Test

ARPEGE   TA'RON

WE DARE YOU—

WE DARE YOU to try to detect any difference between White Shoulders (18.50) and Ta'ron's Love Lure, $7.00.

WE DARE YOU to try to detect any difference between Christmas Night (35.00) and Ta'ron's Persuasive, $7.00.

WE DARE YOU to try to detect any difference between Chanel #5 (25.00) and Ta'ron's 2nd Chance, $7.00.

WE DARE YOU to try to detect any difference between Youth Dew (22.50) and Ta'ron's Temptacious, $7.00.

WE DARE YOU to try to detect any difference between Guerlain Shalimar (25.00) and Ta'ron's Tahisia, $7.00.

WE DARE YOU to try to detect any difference between Lanvin Arpege (27.00) and Ta'ron's Volarie, $7.00.

WE DARE YOU to try to detect any difference between My Sin (27.00) and Ta'ron's Sweet Love, $7.00.

WE DARE YOU to try to detect any difference between Patou Joy (60.00) and Ta'ron's Al Di La, $7.00.

USE THIS TEST ON SKEPTICAL PROSPECTS

474

"TA'RON LINE" EASY ORDER FORM

TA'RON, INC. Dept. S-5
Gentlemen
I sure do want to "get in the bucks all of a sudden." Please rush Prepaid the following for payment is enclosed. ☐ Please send C.O.D. $_____ enclosed covering 1/3 — Balance

FRAGRANCE	PERFUMES	PRICE	QTY	COLOGNES	PRICE
LOVE LURE *(White Shoulders)	½ oz. Princess	$3.00		2 oz. Princess Sprinkler	$2.75
	¾ oz. Spray	4.00		4 oz. Princess Sprinkler	4.00
	1 oz. Princess	7.00		4 oz. Gold Gift Set	7.00
PERSUASIVE *(Christmas Night)	½ oz. Princess	3.00		2 oz. Princess Sprinkler	2.75
	¾ oz. Spray	4.00		4 oz. Princess Sprinkler	4.00
	1 oz. Princess	7.00		4 oz. Gold Gift Set	7.00
2nd CHANCE *(Chanel #5)	½ oz. Princess	3.00		2 oz. Princess Sprinkler	2.75
	¾ oz. Spray	4.00		4 oz. Princess Sprinkler	4.00
	1 oz. Princess	7.00		4 oz. Gold Gift Set	7.00

[portions magnified so they are easier to read]

Appellees conceded below and concede here that appellants "have the right to copy, if they can, the unpatented formula of appellees' product." Moreover, for the purposes of these proceedings, appellees assume that "the products manufactured and advertised by (appellants) are in fact equivalents of those products manufactured by appellees." Finally, appellees disclaim any contention that the packaging or labeling of appellants' "Second Chance" is misleading or confusing.[4]

I.

The principal question presented on this record is whether one who has copied an unpatented product sold under a trademark may use the trademark in his advertising to identify the product he has copied. We hold that he may, and that such advertising may not be enjoined under either the Lanham Act, 15 U.S.C. § 1125(a) (1964), or the common law of unfair competition, so long as it does not contain misrepresentations or create a reasonable likelihood that purchasers will be confused as to the source, identity, or sponsorship of the advertiser's product. . . .

In *Saxlehner* [216 U.S. 375 (1910)] the copied product was a "bitter water" drawn from certain privately owned natural springs. The plaintiff sold the natural water under the name "Hunyadi Janos," a valid trademark. The defendant was enjoined from using plaintiff's trademark to designate defendant's "artificial" water, but was permitted to use it to identify plaintiff's natural water as the product which defendant was copying.

JUSTICE HOLMES wrote:

> We see no reason for disturbing the finding of the courts below that there was no unfair competition and no fraud. The real intent of the plaintiff's bill, it seems to us, is to extend the monopoly of such trademark or tradename as she may have to a monopoly of her type of bitter water, by preventing manufacturers from telling the

---

[4] Appellants' product was packaged differently from appellees', and the only words appearing on the outside of appellants' packages were "Second Chance Perfume by Ta'Ron." The same words appeared on the front of appellants' bottles; the words "'Ta'Ron' trademark by International Fragrances, Inc., of Dallas and New York" appeared on the back.

public in a way that will be understood, what they are copying and trying to sell. But the plaintiff has no patent for the water, and the defendants have a right to reproduce it as nearly as they can. They have a right to tell the public what they are doing, and to get whatever share they can in the popularity of the water by advertising that they are trying to make the same article, and think that they succeed. If they do not convey, but, on the contrary, exclude, the notion that they are selling the plaintiff's goods, it is a strong proposition that when the article has a well-known name they have not the right to explain by that name what they imitate. By doing so, they are not trying to get the good will of the name, but the good will of the goods. . . .

. . . [U]se of another's trademark to identify the trademark owner's product in comparative advertising is not prohibited by either statutory or common law, absent misrepresentation regarding the products or confusion as to their source or sponsorship . . . .

The rule rests upon the traditionally accepted premise that the only legally relevant function of a trademark is to impart information as to the source or sponsorship of the product. Appellees argue that protection should also be extended to the trademark's commercially more important function of embodying consumer good will created through extensive, skillful, and costly advertising. The courts, however, have generally confined legal protection to the trademark's source identification function for reasons grounded in the public policy favoring a free, competitive economy. . . .

Since appellees' perfume was unpatented, appellants had a right to copy it, as appellees concede. There was a strong public interest in their doing so, "for imitation is the life blood of competition. It is the unimpeded availability of substantially equivalent units that permits the normal operation of supply and demand to yield the fair price society must pay for a given commodity." But this public benefit might be lost if appellants could not tell potential purchasers that appellants' product was the equivalent of appellees' product. "A competitor's chief weapon is his ability to represent his product as being equivalent and cheaper . . . ." The most effective way (and, where complex chemical compositions sold under trade names are involved, often the only practical way) in which this can be done is to identify the copied article by its trademark or trade name. To prohibit use of a competitor's trademark for the sole purpose of identifying the competitor's product would bar effective communication of claims of equivalence. Assuming the equivalence of "Second Chance" and "Chanel No. 5," the public interest would not be served by a rule of law which would preclude sellers of "Second Chance" from advising consumers of the equivalence and thus effectively deprive consumers of knowledge that an identical product was being offered at one third the price.

As Justice Holmes wrote in *Saxlehner v. Wagner*, the practical effect of such a rule would be to extend the monopoly of the trademark to a monopoly of the product. The monopoly conferred by judicial protection of complete trademark exclusivity would not be preceded by examination and approval by a governmental body, as is the case with most other government-granted monopolies. Moreover, it would not be limited in time, but would be perpetual.

Against these considerations, two principal arguments are made for protection of trademark values other than source identification.

The first of these, as stated in the findings of the district court, is that the creation of the other values inherent in the trademark require "the expenditure of great effort, skill and ability," and that the competitor should not be permitted "to take a free ride" on the trademark owner's "widespread goodwill and reputation."

A large expenditure of money does not in itself create legally protectable rights. Appellees are not entitled to monopolize the public's desire for the unpatented product, even though they themselves created that desire at great effort and expense. As we have noted, the most effective way (and in some cases the only practical way) in which others may compete in satisfying the demand for the product is to produce it and tell the public they have done so, and if they could be barred from this effort appellees would have found a way to acquire a practical monopoly in the unpatented product to which they are not legally entitled.

Disapproval of the copyist's opportunism may be an understandable first reaction, "but this initial response to the problem has been curbed in deference to the greater public good." By taking his "free ride," the copyist, albeit unintentionally, serves an important public interest by offering comparable goods at lower prices. On the other hand, the trademark owner, perhaps equally without design, sacrifices public to personal interests by seeking immunity from the rigors of competition.

Moreover, appellees' reputation is not directly at stake. Appellants' advertisement makes it clear that the product they offer is their own. If it proves to be inferior, they, not appellees, will bear the burden of consumer disapproval.

The second major argument for extended trademark protection is that even in the absence of confusion as to source, use of the trademark of another "creates a serious threat to the uniqueness and distinctiveness" of the trademark, and "if continued would create a risk of making a generic or descriptive term of the words" of which the trademark is composed.

The contention has little weight in the context of this case. Appellants do not use appellees' trademark as a generic term. They employ it only to describe appellees' product, not to identify their own. They do not label their product "Ta'Ron's Chanel No. 5," as they might if appellees' trademark had come to be the common name for the product to which it is applied. Appellants' use does not challenge the distinctiveness of appellees' trademark, or appellees' exclusive right to employ that trademark to indicate source or sponsorship. For reasons already discussed, we think appellees are entitled to no more. The slight tendency to carry the mark into the common language which even this use may have is outweighed by the substantial value of such use in the maintenance of effective competition.

We are satisfied, therefore, that both authority and reason require a holding that in the absence of misrepresentation or confusion as to source or sponsorship a seller in promoting his own goods may use the trademark of another to identify the latter's goods. The district court's contrary conclusion cannot support the injunction. . . .

NOTES AND QUESTIONS

Fact-Specific Inquiries. Cases involving comparative advertising are often fact specific. Consider the ad on the left below. The Bailey's ad includes part of Newport's logo (the remainder is covered by the plant) and contains an upper right box saying "Compare Bailey's with our competitor Newport Cigarettes." The upper white box and "compare" text was added to the original ad after Newport complained. Does this revised ad infringe Newport's trademark rights? (To help your evaluation, the image below on the right is one of Newport's own ads).

Could Bailey's have made its point without showing half of Newport's logo? Does the location of the half-logo at the top left of the page matter? *See* Lorillard Tobacco Co. v. S&M Brands, Inc., 616 F. Supp. 2d 581 (E.D. Va. 2009) (preliminary injunction granted against initial ad without large top-right disclaimer, but denied against planned ad with disclaimer).

Mentioning Noncompetitors. Consumers Union, the publisher of *Consumer Reports*, engaged in a multi-year legal battle with Regina, a vacuum manufacturer, based on Regina's truthful quotes from a positive *Consumer Reports* review. *See* Consumers Union of United States, Inc. v. New Regina Corp., 664 F. Supp. 753 (S.D.N.Y. 1987). When Regina quoted *Consumer Reports*, at least some consumers perceived that *Consumer Reports* was affiliated with Regina, had been paid for the quote or for testing the Regina vacuum or authorized the use of its name in the ad. The court held that Regina could not avoid a trial on likely confusion. Should the nominative use defense have applied?

Should it change the result if Regina used the same quotes but attributed them in a different manner? Say, to "a leading independent testing organization" or "a leading consumer review publication."

Other Countries' Attitudes Toward Comparative Advertising. The European Union does not tolerate comparative advertising nearly as much as the United States does. In general, comparative advertising is virtually banned in the European Union. *See* Directive 2006/114/EC. Comparative advertising is permitted only if all of the following are true:

1. It is not misleading;
2. It compares goods or services meeting the same needs or intended for the same purpose;
3. It objectively compares one or more material, relevant, verifiable and representative features of those goods or services, which may include price;
4. It does not create confusion in the marketplace between the advertiser and a competitor;
5. It does not discredit or denigrate the trademarks, trade names or other distinguishing signs of a competitor;
6. For products with a designation of origin, it relates to products with the same designation;
7. It does not take unfair advantage of the trademark or other distinguishing sign of a competitor;
8. It does not present goods or services as imitations or replicas of goods or services bearing a protected trademark or trade name.

As a practical matter, comparative advertisements in the European Union require careful vetting. For example, the eighth requirement would preclude the ad at issue in the *Chanel* case.

India's approach resembles the European Union's more than the United States'. The Advertising Standards Council of India, a self-regulatory body, dictates that comparative ads must, among other things, make comparisons that are factual, accurate and capable of being backed by substantial facts and evidence and must not "make unjustifiable use" of the name or initials of any other entity, nor take unfair advantage of the goodwill attached to the trademark or symbol of another firm or its product or the goodwill acquired by its advertising campaign. In addition, a comparative ad must not be similar to another advertiser's ads in "general layout, copy, slogans, visual presentations, music or sound effects, so as to suggest plagiarism." Courts similarly require comparisons to be of material, relevant, verifiable and representative features, and as in the European Union, comparisons may not compare a product with one designation of origin to another with a different designation of origin (e.g., no comparing Parmesan to Camembert). Havells India Ltd & Anr vs Amritanshu Khaitan & Ors DelHC CS(OS) 107/2015. However, Indian courts have allowed comparative puffery, such as claiming to be the "best" or "better" than competitors, as long as the claim doesn't rise to the level of defamation or disparagement. Colgate Palmolive Company & Anr. vs. Hindustan Unilever Ltd., 2014 (57) PTC 47 [Del](DB); Dabur India Ltd. vs. Colortek Meghalaya Pvt. Ltd. & Anr., 167 (2010) DLT 278 (DB).

Contributory Trademark Infringement. In an omitted part of the opinion, Chanel unsuccessfully argued that Smith should be responsible for any unsanctioned misrepresentations made by retailers who bought the knockoff from Smith. The current standard for contributory trademark liability comes from *Inwood Laboratories, Inc. v. Ives Laboratories, Inc.*, 456 U.S. 844 (1982):

> [I]f a manufacturer or distributor intentionally induces another to infringe a trademark, or if it continues to supply its product to one whom it knows or has reason to know is engaging in trademark infringement, the manufacturer or distributor is contributorily responsible for any harm done as a result of the deceit.

The standard for contributory infringement may differ for service providers (in contrast to manufacturers/retailers of chattels). The Ninth Circuit ruled that a service provider can be contributorily liable when it has "direct control and monitoring of the instrumentality used by a third party to infringe the plaintiff's mark." Lockheed Martin Corp. v. Network Solutions, Inc., 194 F.3d 980 (9th Cir. 1999). For example, if a web host is providing hosting services to a trademark infringer, it may have the requisite control over the hosted website to face contributory liability. *See* Louis Vuitton Malletier, S.A. v. Akanoc Sols., Inc., 591 F. Supp. 2d 1098 (N.D. Cal. 2008), *aff'd*, 658 F.3d 936 (9th Cir. 2011). In contrast, a domain name registrar who merely associates a domain name with the customer-specified IP address lacks the requisite control (*see Lockheed*).

Furthermore, contributory infringement requires that the secondary defendant have an appropriate level of scienter. Thus, the Second Circuit concluded that eBay lacked the requisite scienter for contributory infringement even though it had generalized knowledge that eBay's vendors were auctioning counterfeit Tiffany goods on the site. Tiffany (NJ) Inc. v. eBay Inc., 600 F.3d 93 (2d Cir. 2010). However, the court also held that Tiffany retained a viable false advertising claim if eBay's ads offering "Tiffany" products would have fooled reasonable consumers about the genuineness of the "Tiffany" products available on the site.

The federal trademark statute limits the remedies against publishers who publish ads that infringe trademarks. 15 U.S.C. Section 1114(2)(B) states:

> Where the infringement or violation complained of is contained in or is part of paid advertising matter in a newspaper, magazine, or other similar periodical or in an electronic communication as defined in section 2510(12) of title 18, the remedies of the owner of the right infringed or person bringing the action under section 1125(a) of this title as against the publisher or distributor of such newspaper, magazine, or other similar periodical or electronic communication shall be limited to an injunction against the presentation of such advertising matter in future issues of such newspapers, magazines, or other similar periodicals or in future transmissions of such electronic communications. The limitations of this subparagraph shall apply only to innocent infringers and innocent violators.

We will revisit contributory liability principles in Chapter 17.

3. Trademark Dilution

Federal trademark law provides extra protection for "famous" marks, defined as trademarks that are "widely recognized by the general consuming public of the United States as a designation of source of the goods or services of the mark's owner." These famous marks are protected against "dilution," which can occur in one of two ways: by "blurring," a use that "impairs the distinctiveness of the famous mark," and by tarnishment, a use that "harms the reputation of the famous mark." 15 U.S.C. § 1125(c).

Trademark dilution does not require any consumer confusion about product source. The availability of remedies, even when no consumer suffered any harm, makes dilution a controversial doctrine.

Trademark dilution traces its origins to Frank Schecter's seminal 1927 *Harvard Law Review* article, "The Rational Basis of Trademark Protection." In response to that article, a number of states enacted trademark dilution statutes over the years. Congress enacted federal dilution protection in 1995. 15 U.S.C. §1125(c) (subsequently amended to clarify that it only protected marks that were famous among the general consuming public—household names— and that a plaintiff need only show likely, not actual, dilution to prevail). The following case illustrates a state dilution lawsuit prior to the federal statute's enactment. As you read it, consider how dilution may curb comparative advertising.

DEERE & CO. V. MTD PRODUCTS, INC., 41 F.3D 39 (2D CIR. 1994)

This appeal in a trademark case presents a rarely litigated issue likely to recur with increasing frequency in this era of head-to-head comparative advertising. The precise issue, arising under the New York anti-dilution statute is whether an advertiser may depict an altered form of a competitor's trademark to identify the competitor's product in a comparative ad. . . .

Although a number of dilution cases in this Circuit have involved use of a trademark by a competitor to identify a competitor's products in comparative advertising, as well as use by a noncompetitor in a humorous variation of a trademark, we have not yet considered whether the use of an altered version of a distinctive trademark to identify a competitor's product and achieve a humorous effect can constitute trademark dilution. Though we find MTD's animated version of Deere's deer amusing, we agree with Judge McKenna that the television commercial is a likely violation of the anti-dilution statute. We therefore affirm the preliminary injunction.

BACKGROUND

Deere, a Delaware corporation with its principal place of business in Illinois, is the world's largest supplier of agricultural equipment. For over one hundred years, Deere has used a deer design ("Deere Logo") as a trademark for identifying its products and services. Deere owns numerous trademark registrations for different versions of the Deere Logo. Although these versions vary slightly, all depict a static, two-dimensional silhouette of a leaping male deer in profile. The Deere Logo is widely recognizable and a valuable business asset.[3]

[Deere logo]

MTD, an Ohio company with its principal place of business in Ohio, manufactures and sells lawn tractors. In 1993, W.B. Doner & Company ("Doner"), MTD's advertising agency, decided to create and produce a commercial—the subject of this litigation—that would use the Deere Logo, without Deere's authorization, for the purpose of comparing Deere's line of lawn tractors to MTD's "Yard-Man" tractor. The intent was to identify Deere as the market leader and convey the message that Yard-Man was of comparable quality but less costly than a Deere lawn tractor.

Doner altered the Deere Logo in several respects. For example, as Judge McKenna found, the deer in the MTD version of the logo ("Commercial Logo") is "somewhat differently proportioned, particularly with respect to its width, than the deer in the Deere Logo." Doner also removed the name "John Deere" from the version of the logo used by Deere on the front of its lawn tractors, and made the logo frame more sharply rectangular.

More significantly, the deer in the Commercial Logo is animated and assumes various poses. Specifically, the MTD deer looks over its shoulder, jumps through the logo frame (which breaks into pieces and tumbles to the ground), hops to a pinging noise, and, as a two-dimensional cartoon, runs, in apparent fear, as it is pursued by the Yard-Man lawn tractor and a barking dog. Judge McKenna described the dog as "recognizable as a breed that is short in stature," and in the commercial the fleeing deer appears to be even smaller than the dog. Doner's interoffice documents reflect that the animated deer in the commercial was intended to appear "more playful and/or confused than distressed."

---

[3] Deere's net sales of equipment bearing the Deere Logo for the fiscal year 1993 exceeded $6.4 billion, and Deere contends that revenues from its financial services and insurance operations, which also utilize the Deere Logo, exceeded $1.1 billion. Deere has spent a substantial amount of money using the Deere Logo to advertise its products and services.

MTD submitted the commercial to ABC, NBC, and CBS for clearance prior to airing, together with substantiation of the various claims made regarding the Yard-Man lawn tractor's quality and cost relative to the corresponding Deere model. Each network ultimately approved the commercial, though ABC reserved the right to re-evaluate it "should there be [a] responsible complaint," and CBS demanded and received a letter of indemnity from Doner. The commercial ran from the week of March 7, 1994, through the week of May 23, 1994. . . .

On appeal, MTD argues that the anti-dilution statute does not prohibit commercial uses of a trademark that do not confuse consumers or result in a loss of the trademark's ability to identify a single manufacturer, or tarnish the trademark's positive connotations. Deere cross-appeals, contending that injunctive relief should not have been limited to New York State. We affirm both the finding of likely dilution and the scope of the injunction.

DISCUSSION

Section 368-d, which has counterparts in more than twenty states, reads as follows:

> Likelihood of injury to business reputation or of dilution of the distinctive quality of a mark or trade name shall be a ground for injunctive relief in cases of infringement of a mark registered or not registered or in cases of unfair competition, notwithstanding the absence of competition between the parties or the absence of confusion as to the source of goods or services.

The anti-dilution statute applies to competitors as well as noncompetitors, and explicitly does not require a plaintiff to demonstrate a likelihood of consumer confusion.

In order to prevail on a section 368-d dilution claim, a plaintiff must prove, first, that its trademark either is of truly distinctive quality or has acquired secondary meaning, and, second, that there is a "likelihood of dilution." A third consideration, the predatory intent of the defendant, may not be precisely an element of the violation, but, as we discuss below, is of significance, especially in a case such as this, which involves poking fun at a competitor's trademark.

MTD does not dispute that the Deere Logo is a distinctive trademark that is capable of dilution and has acquired the requisite secondary meaning in the marketplace. Therefore, the primary question on appeal is whether Deere can establish a likelihood of dilution of this distinctive mark under section 368-d.

Likelihood of Dilution. Traditionally, this Court has defined dilution under section 368-d "as either the blurring of a mark's product identification or the tarnishment of the affirmative associations a mark has come to convey."

In previous cases, "blurring" has typically involved "the whittling away of an established trademark's selling power through its unauthorized use by others upon dissimilar products" [including such] " 'hypothetical anomalies' as 'DuPont shoes, Buick aspirin tablets, Schlitz varnish, Kodak pianos, Bulova gowns, and so forth.' " Thus, dilution by "blurring" may occur

483

where the defendant uses or modifies the plaintiff's trademark to identify the defendant's goods and services, raising the possibility that the mark will lose its ability to serve as a unique identifier of the plaintiff's product.

"Tarnishment" generally arises when the plaintiff's trademark is linked to products of shoddy quality, or is portrayed in an unwholesome or unsavory context likely to evoke unflattering thoughts about the owner's product. In such situations, the trademark's reputation and commercial value might be diminished because the public will associate the lack of quality or lack of prestige in the defendant's goods with the plaintiff's unrelated goods, or because the defendant's use reduces the trademark's reputation and standing in the eyes of consumers as a wholesome identifier of the owner's products or services.

At the hearing on Deere's application for a temporary restraining order, the District Court initially suggested that there was neither blurring nor tarnishment as those terms have been used, and consequently no dilution of the Deere Logo. The Court observed that MTD's commercial "makes it clear that Deere is a distinct product coming from a different source than Yard-Man," and does not "bring the plaintiff's mark into disrepute." However, in its preliminary injunction ruling, the Court found that Deere would probably be able to establish a likelihood of dilution by blurring under section 368-d; tarnishment was not discussed.

The District Court noted that "the instant case [wa]s one of first impression" because it involved a defendant's use of a competitor's trademark to refer to the competitor's products rather than to identify the defendant's products. For this reason, the traditional six-factor test for determining whether there has been dilution through blurring of a trademark's product identification was not fully applicable. Focusing only on the alteration of the static Deere Logo resulting from MTD's animation, the Court concluded that MTD's version constituted dilution because it was likely to diminish the strength of identification between the original Deere symbol and Deere products, and to blur the distinction between the Deere Logo and other deer logos in the marketplace, including those in the insurance and financial markets. Although we agree with the District Court's finding of a likelihood of dilution, we believe that MTD's commercial does not fit within the concept of "blurring," but, as we explain below, nonetheless constitutes dilution.

The District Court's analysis endeavored to fit the MTD commercial into one of the two categories we have recognized for a section 368-d claim. However, the MTD commercial is not really a typical instance of blurring because it poses slight if any risk of impairing the identification of Deere's mark with its products. Nor is there tarnishment, which is usually found where a distinctive mark is depicted in a context of sexual activity, obscenity, or illegal activity. But the blurring/tarnishment dichotomy does not necessarily represent the full range of uses that can dilute a mark under New York law.

In giving content to dilution beyond the categories of blurring or tarnishment, however, we must be careful not to broaden section 368-d to prohibit all uses of a distinctive mark that the owner prefers not be made. Several different contexts may conveniently be identified. Sellers of commercial products may wish to use a competitor's mark to identify the competitor's product in comparative advertisements. As long as the mark is not altered, such use serves the beneficial purpose of imparting factual information about the relative merits of competing products and poses no risk of diluting the selling power of the competitor's mark. Satirists, selling no product other than the publication that contains their expression, may wish to parody a mark to make a point of social commentary, or perhaps both to comment and entertain. Such uses risk some dilution of the identifying or selling power of the mark, but that risk is generally tolerated in the interest of maintaining broad opportunities for expression.

Sellers of commercial products who wish to attract attention to their commercials or products and thereby increase sales by poking fun at widely recognized marks of noncompeting products risk diluting the selling power of the mark that is made fun of. When this occurs, not for worthy purposes of expression, but simply to sell products, that purpose can easily be achieved in other ways. The potentially diluting effect is even less deserving of protection when the object of the joke is the mark of a directly competing product. The line-drawing in this area becomes especially difficult when a mark is parodied for the dual purposes of making a satiric comment and selling a somewhat competing product.

Whether the use of the mark is to identify a competing product in an informative comparative ad, to make a comment, or to spoof the mark to enliven the advertisement for a noncompeting or a competing product, the scope of protection under a dilution statute must take into account the degree to which the mark is altered and the nature of the alteration. Not every alteration will constitute dilution, and more leeway for alterations is appropriate in the context of satiric expression and humorous ads for noncompeting products. But some alterations have the potential to so lessen the selling power of a distinctive mark that they are appropriately proscribed by a dilution statute. Dilution of this sort is more likely to be found when the alterations are made by a competitor with both an incentive to diminish the favorable attributes of the mark and an ample opportunity to promote its products in ways that make no significant alteration.

We need not attempt to predict how New York will delineate the scope of its dilution statute in all of the various contexts in which an accurate depiction of a distinctive mark might be used, nor need we decide how variations of such a mark should be treated in different contexts. Some variations might well be de minimis, and the context in which even substantial variations occur may well have such meritorious purposes that any diminution in the identifying and selling power of the mark need not be condemned as dilution.

Wherever New York will ultimately draw the line, we can be reasonably confident that the MTD commercial challenged in this case crosses it. The commercial takes a static image of a graceful, full-size deer—symbolizing Deere's substance and strength—and portrays, in an animated version, a deer that appears smaller than a small dog and scampers away from the dog and a lawn tractor, looking over its shoulder in apparent fear. Alterations of that sort, accomplished for the sole purpose of promoting a competing product, are properly found to be within New York's concept of dilution because they risk the possibility that consumers will come to attribute unfavorable characteristics to a mark and ultimately associate the mark with inferior goods and services.

Significantly, the District Court did not enjoin accurate reproduction of the Deere Logo to identify Deere products in comparative advertisements. MTD remains free to deliver its message of alleged product superiority without altering and thereby diluting Deere's trademarks. The Court's order imposes no restriction on truthful advertising properly comparing specific products and their "objectively measurable attributes." In view of this, the District Court's finding of a likelihood of dilution was entirely appropriate, notwithstanding the fact that MTD's humorous depiction of the deer occurred in the context of a comparative advertisement. . . .

NOTES AND QUESTIONS

Ad Redesign. How could you redesign the ad to avoid diluting Deere's trademark? How do you think the court would analyze an ad where the advertiser removes the competitor's product name but the competitive product nevertheless has a recognizable profile/trade dress? Revisit the Bailey's cigarette ad example discussed after *Smith v. Chanel*. How would the *Deere* court analyze that ad for dilution purposes?

Dilution and Nominative Use. Interpreting both the federal Lanham Act and New York state law, the Second Circuit reached a different result in *Tiffany (NJ) Inc. v. eBay Inc.*, 600 F.3d 93 (2d Cir. 2010). Tiffany sued eBay because eBay had advertised that consumers could buy Tiffany items on eBay—a partially true statement, as eBay's auctions contained both legitimate and counterfeit Tiffany items. The Second Circuit rejected the dilution claims. The court said that because eBay had made a nominative use of the Tiffany mark, "[t]here is no second mark or product at issue here to blur with or to tarnish 'Tiffany.'"

The Lanham Act expressly mentions nominative use and comparative advertising as defenses to dilution. Dilution defenses include:

> [a]ny fair use, including a nominative or descriptive fair use, or facilitation of such fair use, of a famous mark by another person other than as a designation of source for the person's own goods or services, including use in connection with—
>
> (i) advertising or promotion that permits consumers to compare goods or services; or
>
> (ii) identifying and parodying, criticizing, or commenting upon the famous mark owner or the goods or services of the famous mark owner.

For unexplained reasons, the Second Circuit did not rely on this defense in its *Tiffany* ruling, instead concluding that no blurring or tarnishment had occurred.

If these defenses had been available to MTD, would the *Deere* case have come out differently?

Test yourself: Does this law firm ad dilute the trademark of the nursing home?

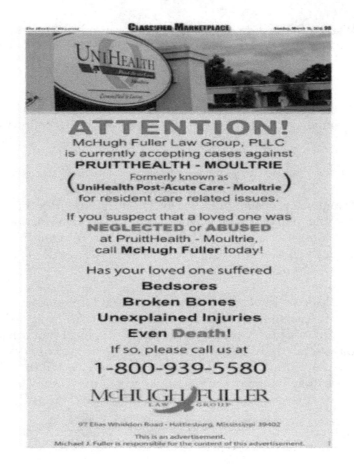

McHugh Fuller Law Group, PLLC v. PruittHealth, Inc., 300 Ga. 140 (Ga. Sup. Ct. 2016) (no dilution under Georgia's state trademark law).

MasterCard v. Nader. The court rejected MasterCard's dilution claim because Nader's use was political and not commercial and also because there was no evidence of any effect on the value of MasterCard's marks or on their capacity to distinguish MasterCard's services. Under current law, the trademark owner only needs to show "likely" dilution, though courts may consider the absence of evidence of an actual effect in their assessment of likelihood.

Evidence of Dilution. Apropos of the *Nader* case, what evidence persuasively demonstrates that dilution is occurring or likely to occur? Right now, no one has a clear understanding of how to prove—or disprove—dilution. *See* Barton Beebe et al, *Testing for Trademark Dilution in Court and the Lab*, 86 U. CHI. L. REV. 611 (2019).

Some courts make it easy on plaintiffs by excusing them from providing any rigorous evidence of dilution. In *Visa International Service Ass'n v. JSL Corp.*, 610 F.3d 1088 (9th Cir. 2010), Judge Kozinski said "a plaintiff seeking to establish a likelihood of dilution is not required to go to the expense of producing expert testimony or market surveys; it may rely entirely on the characteristics of the marks at issue." Courts appear to be particularly lax about evidentiary requirements in cases involving tarnishment by association with sex. *See*

V Secret Catalogue, Inc. v. Moseley, 605 F.3d 382 (6th Cir. 2010) (finding that tawdry Victor's Little Secret store, which sold lingerie and "adult toys," tarnished the classier Victoria's Secret mark).

Dilution and the First Amendment. In *L.L. Bean v. Drake Publishers*, 811 F.2d 26 (1st Cir. 1987), the court refused to allow dilution to suppress an article published in the adult magazine *High Society* called "L.L. Beam's Back-To-School-Sex-Catalog." The First Circuit ruled that the First Amendment did not allow anti-dilution protection "to encompass the unauthorized use of a trademark in a noncommercial setting such as an editorial or artistic context."

However, courts generally are reluctant to apply the First Amendment to trademark claims, and it may be especially hard to convince a court to find First Amendment protection for a trademark claim against an advertisement, even if the ad contains no false statements by ordinary Lanham Act standards.

Louis Vuitton Malletier, S.A. v. Hyundai Motor America, 2012 WL 1022247 (S.D.N.Y. 2012), illustrates this challenge. During the post-game show following the 2010 Super Bowl, Hyundai ran a thirty-second commercial that its counsel later described as "a humorous, socio-economic commentary on luxury defined by a premium price tag, rather than by the value to the consumer." Watch the ad at http://www.youtube.com/watch?v=O7I4v7NYHrY. It consisted of brief vignettes that show "policemen eating caviar in a patrol car; large yachts parked beside modest homes; blue-collar workers eating lobster during their lunch break; a four-second scene of an inner-city basketball game played on a lavish marble court with a gold hoop; and a ten-second scene of the Sonata driving down a street lined with chandeliers and red-carpet crosswalks." The basketball game scene included a one-second shot of a basketball decorated with a pattern resembling Louis Vuitton's toile monogram "LV" on a chestnut-brown background. The LV was changed to LZ, and the proportions of the other designs were slightly altered.

[image from ad]

The court granted summary judgment to Louis Vuitton on trademark dilution. It rejected Hyundai's parody argument because there was no direct commentary on Louis Vuitton specifically; Hyundai was at most commenting on the concept of "luxury" generally, and thus didn't qualify for the statutory exception for "identifying and parodying, criticizing, or commenting upon the famous mark owner or the goods or services of the famous mark owner." The court also rejected a First Amendment defense because any commentary was too "subtle," and the "broader social critique" didn't justify use of Louis Vuitton's marks.

How does this square with the commercial speech doctrine you encountered in Chapter 2? For an argument that dilution law unconstitutionally regulates commercial speech, *see* Rebecca Tushnet, *Gone in Sixty Milliseconds: Trademark Law and Cognitive Science*, 86 TEX. L. REV. 507 (2008).

At least one court expressly declined to follow *Hyundai*, though not explicitly on First Amendment grounds. Louis Vuitton Malletier, S.A. v. My Other Bag, Inc., 156 F. Supp. 3d 425 (S.D.N.Y. 2016), *aff'd*, 674 Fed. Appx. 16 (2d Cir. 2016).

4. Ambush Marketing

Some public events, such as major sporting events, are likely to attract substantial media hype and consumer interest. Think, for example, of the media coverage of the Olympics, the Super Bowl or the NCAA Men's Basketball tournament. The event organizers create and sell marketing opportunities to advertisers that allow them to capitalize on this media coverage and consumer interest, such as allowing the advertisers to call themselves "official sponsors" or to put up signage or other advertising displays at the event.

Advertising sponsorships might be "exclusive" among competitors, or sponsorship might be cost-prohibitive for some advertisers. For these and other reasons, advertisers have incentives to try to obtain the benefits of event sponsorship without paying the stated price. This is sometimes referred to as "ambush marketing." Examples of ambush marketing include running an advertising campaign while the Olympics are ongoing that shows athletes without explicit reference to the Olympics or finding unauthorized ways to get advertising incorporated into photos or broadcasts of the events. *See generally* Simon Chadwick & Nicholas Burton, *Ambushed!*, WALL ST. J., Jan. 25, 2010 (defining a taxonomy of different types of ambush marketing).

For example, during the World Cup 2010, a South African discount airline, Kulula, ran print advertisements in which it called itself the "Unofficial National Carrier of the You-Know-What," promoting airfares for flights that presumably soccer fans would want to take to attend games. To reinforce the soccer theme, the ad displayed stadiums, vuvuzelas (plastic trumpets used by South African soccer fans) and national flags. *See FIFA Orders South African Airline to Drop 'Ambush' Ad*, BBC NEWS, March 19, 2010.

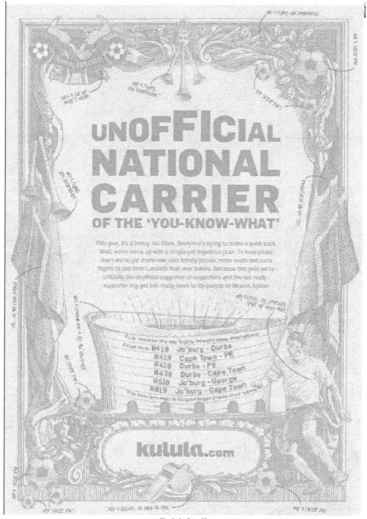

[initial ad]

FIFA, the organization that governs international soccer, objected to Kulula's ad as ambush marketing. As a result, Kulula created a second ad that had the same look and feel but replaced most soccer-related items with similar looking items. For example, the plastic trumpets were replaced with almost-identical-looking golf tees, and the soccer balls were replaced with other types of balls. *See* Herman Manson, *Kulula Answers FIFA with New Ad*, MARK LIVES, March 21, 2010.

[revised ad]

Ambush marketing is maddening to event organizers. It feels like the advertiser is free-riding on the event organizer's investments and intentionally drawing on consumers' goodwill towards the event, and it irritates the event organizer's customers (the sponsors) who pay huge sums only to see others obtain similar value for free.

Despite the tempting feeling that ambush marketers are "free riding," ambush marketing typically is not legally actionable in the United States (in contrast, some other nations have various laws designed to stop it). For example, an advertiser can freely run a sports- or athlete-themed ad during the Olympics so long as the ad copy does not reference any Olympic trademarks (which are protected by a special statute, 36 U.S.C. § 220506) or make an unauthorized use of personality rights. This is true even though we all know what is going on—that the advertiser is trying to invoke and associate itself in consumers' minds with the Olympics.

However, event organizers are not completely defenseless. Even if they cannot bring an intellectual property claim, they can proactively use contracts with broadcasters and athletes to restrict these tactics. As a result, major events now often involve an arms race of sorts: event organizers seek to maximize their revenue and protect their sponsors' investments by anticipating and squelching ambush-marketing efforts, and ambush marketers seek to get cheap advertising using innovative and unofficial techniques.

The next case is not a classic "ambush marketing" case, but it involves a situation where the advertiser tries to piggy-back on a competitor's marketing expenditures. Do you think the advertiser's actions are ethical or unethical? Why?

HEARTLAND RECREATIONAL VEHICLES, LLC. V. FOREST RIVER, INC., 2009 WL 418079 (N.D. IND. 2009)

. . . III. Factual Background

On October 22 and 23, 2008, Forest River hosted a private (by invitation only) trade show and more than 700 guests were invited to attend, representing approximately 350 RV dealerships from across North America and as far away as Australia. A theme of this trade show was "Pick Your Partner," referring to the business relationships that can develop between an RV manufacturer and an RV dealer. One of the purposes of this event was to encourage sales of various Forest River products to new and existing RV dealers. To provide overnight accommodations for its guests, Forest River reserved several hotels in Mishawaka, Indiana, including the Hyatt Place, Country Inn & Suites, Residence Inn, Courtyard Marriott, Springhill Suites, Holiday Inn Express, Hampton Inn, and Varsity Club. Forest River created an internal business document, called a "Master List," identifying each guest who would be attending the private trade show and identifying the hotel where each guest would be staying. Forest River paid for its guests' accommodations at these hotels.

On Wednesday, October 22, at approximately 3:30 p.m., while most of Forest River's guests were in attendance at the private trade show, several of Heartland's employees ("Heartland employees") entered the hotels reserved by Forest River. The Heartland employees were carrying stacks of envelopes, each labeled with the name of a Forest River guest and an identification of which hotel that guest was staying [sic]. The Heartland employees went to the front desks of the hotels and then falsely stated and represented to the hotel attendants that they were "from Forest River" and that they had "important" envelopes which needed to be delivered to the Forest River guests "for a Forest River dealer meeting the next day." The Heartland employees induced the hotel attendants to immediately deliver the envelopes to the rooms of each named guest in their respective hotels, such as by slipping the envelopes under the guests' room doors. Security video cameras monitoring the front desks in at least two of these hotels recorded this event and the Heartland employees doing it.

The envelopes contained documents advertising Heartland's travel trailers and documents comparing several Flagstaff models of Forest River products with certain North Trail models of Heartland products. The envelopes also contained a specific invitation to visit Heartland's place of business in Elkhart that same week, while the guests were in the area attending Forest River's private trade show, including a map showing how to get there. Several of Forest River's guests, who were RV dealers, were induced by the contents of those envelopes to visit Heartland's place of business that same week and placed orders for Heartland travel trailers, causing lost sales by Forest River, a direct competitor of Heartland. Those actions (hereinafter referred to as "the hotel action"), resulted in "disruption and confusion among several of Forest River's guests because of the incongruity and surprising manner in which the envelopes were delivered . . . [and] adversely affect[ed] Forest River's good will with its dealers and adversely affected Forest River's sales of its products."

IV. Discussion . . .

In general, passing off, or palming off, arises when a producer misrepresents his own goods or services as someone else's goods or services. As best stated by Forest River's counsel during oral argument, the hotel action may have occurred in connection with goods, in that Heartland would not have been in the hotels if it was not for the purpose of selling RV's for a commercial purpose and possibly confusing people in connection with those goods. While this Court questions, and indeed doubts, whether Forest River has adequately pled a passing off violation under the Lanham Act, that doubt, combined with our standards for federal pleading under Rule 8(a) and for dismissal under Rule 12(b)(6), does not permit dismissal of Forest River's counterclaim at this time where relief is plausible. . . .

As pled, Heartland's intentionally deceptive conduct in the hotel action plausibly had the natural and probable tendency and effect of which was to deceive the public so as to pass off its goods or business as for that of Forest River. Moreover, the Court will not condone Heartland's actions as simply healthy competition. "Though trade warfare may be waged ruthlessly to the bitter end, there are certain rules of combat which must be observed. The trader has not a free lance. Fight he may, but as a soldier, not as a guerilla." Forest River, having identified a plausible legal basis for its counterclaim, precludes the finding that no viable cause of action exists upon which relief can be granted. . . .

NOTES AND QUESTIONS

Fair vs. Unfair Competition. What exactly did Heartland do wrong, and why does the court conclude that Heartland's behavior was not "simply healthy competition"?

Was the problem just Heartland's misrepresentations to the hotel employees, or was Heartland's broader scheme condemnable? Could Heartland employees have approached the hotel staff and identified themselves as being from "a local RV manufacturer?" Could Heartland have run radio ads during the weekend encouraging visiting dealers to come to Heartland's facility? Could Heartland have put moving billboards right outside the targeted hotels encouraging visiting dealers to come to Heartland's facility? Prior to the weekend, could Heartland have sent direct mail or email to Forest River's dealers saying "if you're coming to Mishawaka, come visit us"? *See* Martha C. White, *The Convention Crashers*, N.Y TIMES, Feb. 15, 2010 (discussing trade show efforts to suppress "outboarders," defined as "vendors who set up shop in a hotel suite near a trade show site to promote their products").

If Heartland got unauthorized possession of Forest River's "master list," would that constitute trade secret misappropriation (see Chapter 13)? Could Heartland have deduced which Forest River dealers were in town and where they were staying without Forest River's master list?

Are Sponsorship Deals a Good Deal? In addition to the risk of ambush marketing, event sponsors face the constant risk that consumers will not give them full credit for their sponsorship. Consider the following chart showing who consumers thought sponsored Euro 2016, a major soccer event in Europe:

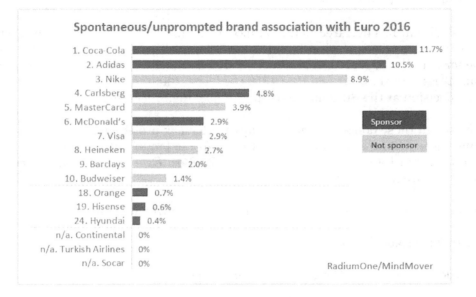

As you can see, consumers incorrectly assumed that several major consumer brands—including Nike, MasterCard, Visa and beer advertisers—were sponsors of Euro 2016. In other words, those brands got consumer goodwill for being event sponsors without paying a dime. How do you think the event sponsors feel about that? Is there anything the law can do? This chart is no anomaly. Because consumers expect big advertisers to sponsor events like sports competitions, a nontrivial number of consumers will always identify companies like Nike and Coca-Cola as sponsors of such events. See, e.g., Michel Tuan Pham & Gita Venkataramani Johar, Market Prominence Biases in Sponsor Identification: Processes and Consequentiality, 18 Psych. & Marketing 123 (2001).)

5.   Online Advertising Issues

Online advertising raises many of the same issues addressed throughout this book, but online advertising can also raise some novel complications. This section explores some of these.

A.   Domain Names

Every computer connected to the Internet has a unique numerical address associated with it, called an IP address. It can be hard to remember these long numerical strings. Instead, we typically identify Internet-connected computers by domain names, which function as mnemonics for the IP addresses.

Domain names have significant value independent of any trademark rights. We can see this from the lofty valuations attached to domain names that are unlikely to be eligible for trademark protection.

The Federal Circuit has declared that [noun].com domain names are generic, at least when the website offers goods or services having some relationship to the noun and are therefore ineligible for trademark registration. *See In re* Hotels.com, 573 F.3d 1300 (Fed. Cir. 2009); *In re* 1800mattress.com IP, LLC, 586 F.3d 1359 (Fed. Cir. 2009). As of May 2020, this issue is awaiting a decision at the Supreme Court in the Booking.com case.

Yet, even though these domain names lack any trademark protection, most of the domain names that have sold for a million dollars or more fit the [noun].com paradigm. *See* Jillian D'Onfro and Brandt Ranj, *Million-Dollar URLs: The Most Expensive Domain Names of All Time*, BUSINESS INSIDER, April 28, 2016.

To go further, we need to define terms. Consider the following domain name:

> http://news.google.com/nwshp

This is the domain name for Google News's home page. In this domain name:

1. .com is the "top level domain" (TLD)
2. google is the "second level domain" (SLD)
3. news is the "third level domain" which designates specific servers within the Google empire
4. nwshp is called the "post-domain path"

Domain names are typically sold through a two-level distribution chain. Each TLD is operated by a "registry," the rough equivalent of the domain name manufacturer. Registries ensure that only one person registers each domain name within the TLD. ICANN (Internet Corporation for Assigned Names and Numbers), a nongovernmental organization, licenses the registries of many well-known TLDs. Registries authorize "registrars," who function as retailers, to sell domain names to "registrants," the customers.

In the early 1990s, domain names were freely registrable by anyone just for asking. A 1994 *Wired* article, *Billions Registered*, described how the author, Josh Quittner, registered McDonalds.com. This article sparked a gold rush as everyone started grabbing unregistered domain names.

In some cases, the registrants grabbed domain names containing third-party trademarks with the intent of ransoming the name back to the trademark owner, a process we now call "cybersquatting." In 1995, Congress enacted federal dilution protection in part to curb cybersquatting, but the new dilution law caused courts to overextend dilution protection to trademarks that did not deserve such heavy protection, and it did little to squelch the speculative bubble. Congress cracked down more successfully with the 1999 Anti-Cybersquatting Consumer Protection Act, discussed in more detail *infra*.

In the 1990s, registrants believed that searchers might guess a domain name by adding ".com" to a generic word (i.e., pets.com) or a trademark (i.e., mercedes.com). Domain name owners call this "type-in traffic." Some domain name registrants even anticipate that searchers will make typographical errors when typing a domain name and register domain names containing logical typographical mistakes, a process sometimes called "typosquatting." While type-in traffic still exists, searchers rarely guess domain names anymore because search engines are so easy to use, and mistyped or expired domain names can lead to pop-up ads, unexpected porn or malware.

Meanwhile, many web browsers have eliminated an "address bar" altogether. Most popular browsers use an "omnibox" that triggers searches for many entries into the "address bar," including some domain names. Given how many users begin their web sessions with a search, many marketers value a top result in organic or paid search results much more than the best domain name. The move to mobile apps has further degraded the value of domain names because the app connects directly with the online service without using domain names at all.

As a result, domain names are waning in importance and influence. Still, domain names remain a critical part of any online endeavor. New start-up companies, or existing companies seeking to launch a new brand, face a very crowded domain name space. Even if the company gets a relatively clean trademark search, it can be hard to find a desirable domain name for a new brand that is not already registered. Often, companies must purchase their desired domain name from a domain-name speculator.

Occasionally, domain-name speculators will figure out a new company's intended domain name before it has been registered. Either there will be a public announcement of a new product launch before the domain name is secured, or speculators will make guesses (such as when a sports franchise considers moving to a new city or a corporate merger is imminent). In any of these cases, the domain name will be snatched up quickly by speculators if it is not secured before the publicity. The clear lesson: Register or purchase any desired domain names before making any public announcements.

Some of the major legal regulations of domain names include the following:

Trademark Infringement

Merely registering a domain name containing a third-party trademark is usually not trademark infringement because the defendant hasn't made a use in commerce. Doing anything else with the domain name, such as publishing a website using the domain name or offering the domain name for sale, might infringe.

Courts carefully scrutinize the exact domain name and how the defendant uses it. [Trademark].com often infringes the trademark owner's rights, but [trademark]sucks.com frequently does not. *See* Toyota Motor Sales, U.S.A., Inc. v. Tabari, 610 F.3d 1171 (9th Cir. 2010) (offering a taxonomy of presumptively legitimate and illegitimate domain names). The better-reasoned cases also will consider if the associated website contains a disclaimer or otherwise instantly clarifies the relationship between the domain name registrant and the trademark owner. However, other cases have found that the domain name standing alone creates "initial interest confusion" (discussed in more detail later) by including a third-party trademark, irrespective of the associated website's content.

Trademark Dilution

As mentioned, in the 1990s, courts expanded dilution law to cover cybersquatting and other domain name misuses.

Anti-Cybersquatting Consumer Protection Act (ACPA)

Passed in 1999 to curb cybersquatting, a successful ACPA claim requires the trademark owner to establish that the defendant:

> (1) registers, traffics in or uses a domain name that is identical or confusingly similar to a trademark or dilutive of a famous mark,* and

> (2) has a bad faith intent to profit from the trademark, which does not include situations where the registrant reasonably believed that it was making a fair or otherwise lawful use of the domain name.

These elements clearly ban 1990s-style cybersquatting registrations-for-ransom, and that activity has largely ceased. The elements also presumptively ban deliberate typosquatting on third-party trademarks. Although it was not clearly designed to do so, ACPA may apply to other speculative activity, such as registering trademarked domain names to put up ads on the pages. *See, e.g.,* Verizon Cal., Inc. v. Navigation Catalyst Sys., Inc., 2008 WL 2651163 (C.D. Cal. 2008); Tex. Int'l Prop. Assocs. v. Hoerbiger Holding AG, 2009 U.S. Dist. LEXIS 40409 (N.D. Tex. May 12, 2009).

A successful ACPA plaintiff can get statutory damages of up to $100,000 per domain name, attorneys' fees and the domain name transferred or canceled. (Cancelation is not a common remedy because any canceled domain name almost certainly will be reregistered by other domain name speculators). Alternatively, ACPA allows trademark owners to sue to recover the domain name (an "in rem" action) in certain cases, such as when the domain name registrant is in a foreign jurisdiction.

---

* ACPA also protects the Red Cross and Olympics (and related) trademarks.

ACPA also contains separate protection for domain names containing personal names that are registered for profitable resale (15 U.S.C. § 8131) and a safe harbor for domain name registrars.

Uniform Dispute Resolution Policy (UDRP) and Uniform Rapid Suspension (URS)

Before Congress passed ACPA, ICANN was working on a self-regulatory process to curb cybersquatting. Congress ultimately felt that ICANN was taking too long, so Congress enacted ACPA. A few months later, ICANN launched the Uniform Domain-Name Dispute-Resolution Policy (UDRP), an extra-judicial administrative proceeding to adjudicate domain name disputes. All domain name registrants in ICANN-operated TLDs (i.e., most major TLDs) agree to be bound to UDRP proceedings when they register the domain names.

Because they were designed to solve the same problem (cybersquatting) and were drafted around the same time (1999), the UDRP and ACPA have similar requirements. A UDRP complainant can succeed if it can show that the domain name registrant:

- has a domain name that "is identical or confusingly similar to a trademark or service mark in which the complainant has rights,"
- has "no rights or legitimate interests in respect of the domain name," and
- the "domain name has been registered and is being used in bad faith."

UDRP proceedings offer a number of advantages for trademark owners over judicial proceedings via ACPA or other legal doctrines. First, UDRP proceedings are fast and cheap; they can be done in a matter of months for typically fewer than $10,000, compared to judicial proceedings that take years and cost hundreds of thousands of dollars. Second, trademark owners win most UDRP proceedings. Trademark owners can select the UDRP vendor, so naturally they all select the vendors with the best batting average for complainants. Third, the UDRP's bad-faith standards ("being used in bad faith") is broader than the ACPA's parallel standard ("bad-faith intent to profit"), so it's possible to win UDRP proceedings where the registrant's motives are not clearly profit oriented. Finally, because all registrants agree to be bound by the UDRP procedures, there are no problems with jurisdiction, service of process, etc.

UDRP proceedings have one obvious disadvantage compared to ACPA claims: Because the UDRP is an extra-judicial administrative proceeding, the only remedy is to have the violating domain name transferred or canceled. Complainants cannot get damages or an injunction. Furthermore, a registrant can stop or overturn a UDRP proceeding by bringing a declaratory judgment action in court. As a result, trademark owners sometimes prefer to go to court for its finality and better remedies.

Nevertheless, the UDRP is more popular than the ACPA. More disputes are handled under the UDRP every year than in ten years of ACPA cases. Darryl C. Wilson, *Battle Galactica: Recent Advances and Retreats in the Struggle for the Preservation of Trademark Rights on the Internet*, 12 J. HIGH TECH. L. 1 (2011).

For a more-detailed comparison of ACPA and UDRP, see this comparison chart at INTA.

In addition to the UDRP, trademark owners have an even quicker dispute resolution option called the URS ("Uniform Rapid Suspension") System. The elements of a URS are similar to, but more stringent than, the elements of a UDRP. The URS process moves more quickly and has only a single remedy: suspension of the domain name for the remainder of its registration period.

ICANN has a variety of other dispute resolution procedures beyond UDRP and URS, especially with respect to new TLDs.

State Domain-Name Laws

State efforts to regulate Internet activities inherently raise dormant commerce clause issues, but a number of states have enacted domain name-specific laws nonetheless. A few examples include:

- Utah SB 26, codified at Utah Code § 70-3a-309, which is structurally similar to the ACPA but has some extra benefits for trademark owners.
- California Business & Professions Code §§ 17525–17528.5, which gives ACPA-like rights to personal names.
- California Election Code §§ 18320–18323, the "California Political Cyberfraud Abatement Act," which restricts "a knowing and willful act concerning a political Web site that is committed with the intent to deny a person access to a political Web site, deny a person the opportunity to register a domain name for a political Web site, or cause a person reasonably to believe that a political Web site has been posted by a person other than the person who posted the Web site, and would cause a reasonable person, after reading the Web site, to believe the site actually represents the views of the proponent or opponent of a ballot measure."

B.   Metatags

Every web page is built by code that instructs the user's web-browsing software how to display the web page. This code can also instruct search engine robots how they can gather information from the page. These instructions, sometimes called "metatags," are normally not visible to web users unless they look at the page's source code.

There are hundreds of different types of metatags that website operators can use to accomplish different purposes. The three best-known metatags:

- The "title tag" causes the user's web browser to display the page's title when users visit the page. Search engines often display the page title as part of their search results for the page.
- The "description metatag" allows the website operator to propose language for the search engines to display in search results. Google sometimes adopts the website's proposed language verbatim; other times, Google creates its own description for the website or uses a third party's description of the website.
- The "keyword metatag" allows the website operator to communicate index terms for the website. In theory, a website will pick some terms that summarize the website's

content, and the search engines can choose to give extra credit to those self-selected index terms when determining how to rank its search results. In the 1990s, some unscrupulous websites would "stuff" the keyword metatags with irrelevant or duplicative information to try to fool the search engines. As a result of these efforts to game the search engines' algorithms, search engines—including Google—routinely ignore the keyword metatags altogether. *See* Matt Cutts, *Google Doesn't Use the Keywords Meta Tag in Web Search*, GOOGLE WEBMASTER CENTRAL BLOG, Sept. 21, 2009. Nor do keyword metatags show up when users view the page.

Courts have struggled with the legal implications of metatags. First, courts do not understand the different types of metatags. Second, courts do not understand that search engines handle metatags in different ways. Third, and most crucially, courts incorrectly assume that including a third-party trademark in keyword metatags will cause the page to rank high in searches on that trademark, even though the keyword metatag almost certainly has no effect on search results.

Because of this misimpression, courts often apply a de facto rule that including a third-party trademark in keyword metatags is per se trademark infringement, as the following case illustrates:

VENTURE TAPE CORP. V. MCGILLS GLASS WAREHOUSE, 540 F.3D 56 (1ST CIR. 2008)

McGills Glass Warehouse ("McGills"), an Internet-based retailer of stained-glass supplies, and its owner Donald Gallagher, appeal from a district court judgment finding them liable for infringement of the registered trademarks "Venture Tape" and "Venture Foil," and awarding the marks' owner, Venture Tape Corporation ("Venture"), an equitable share of McGills' profits, as well as costs and attorney's fees. We affirm.

I.

In 1990, Venture, a manufacturer of specialty adhesive tapes and foils used in the stained-glass industry, procured two federal trademark registrations (Nos. 1,579,001 and 1,583,644) for products called "Venture Tape" and "Venture Foil," respectively. Over the next fifteen years, Venture expended hundreds of thousands of dollars to promote the two marks in both print and Internet advertising. Consequently, its products gained considerable popularity, prestige, and good will in the world-wide stained glass market.

Through its Internet website, McGills also sells adhesive tapes and foils which directly compete with "Venture Tape" and "Venture Foil." Beginning in 2000, and without obtaining Venture's permission or paying it any compensation, McGills' owner Donald Gallagher intentionally "embedded" the Venture marks in the McGills website, both by including the marks in the website's metatags—a component of a webpage's programming that contains descriptive information about the webpage which is typically not observed when the webpage is displayed in a web browser—and in white lettering on a white background screen, similarly invisible to persons viewing the webpage. Gallagher, fully aware that the McGills website did not sell these two Venture products, admittedly took these actions because he had heard that Venture's marks would attract people using Internet search engines to the McGills website.

Because the marks were hidden from view, Venture did not discover McGills' unauthorized use of its marks until 2003. . . .

Although Venture adduced evidence that McGills generated almost $1.9 million in gross sales during the period of its infringement from 2000–2003, Venture eventually requested only $230,339.17, the amount that it estimated to be McGills' net profits. Citing McGills' willful infringement and alleging McGills engaged in obstructionist discovery tactics, Venture sought $188,583.06 in attorney's fees and $7,564.75 in costs. After a hearing on Venture's motion, the district court granted Venture's requested recovery. . . .

II.

A. Lanham Act Liability . . .

"The purpose of a trademark is to identify and distinguish the goods of one party from those of another. To the purchasing public, a trademark 'signi[fies] that all goods bearing the trademark' originated from the same source and that 'all goods bearing the trademark are of an equal level of quality.' " To establish trademark infringement under the Lanham Act, Venture was required to prove that: (1) it owns and uses the "Venture Tape" and "Venture Foil" marks; (2) McGills used the same or similar marks without Venture's permission; and (3) McGills' use of the Venture marks likely confused Internet consumers, thereby causing Venture harm (e.g., lost sales). The parties agree that no genuine factual dispute exists concerning the first two elements of proof.[5]

Our focus then becomes the "likelihood of confusion" among Internet consumers. This inquiry requires us to assess eight criteria: (1) the similarity of Venture's and McGills' marks; (2) the similarity of their goods; (3) the relationship between their channels of trade (e.g., Internet-based commerce); (4) the relationship between their advertising; (5) the classes of their prospective purchasers; (6) any evidence of actual confusion of Internet consumers; (7) McGills' subjective intent in using Venture's marks; and (8) the overall strength of Venture's marks [hereinafter "*Pignons* factors" or "*Pignons* analysis"]. No single criterion is necessarily dispositive in this circumstantial inquiry.

By the conduct of its case below, McGills effectively admitted seven of the eight elements of the *Pignons* analysis. The record contains numerous admissions that meta tags and invisible background text on McGills' website incorporated Venture's exact marks. In his deposition, Gallagher admitted that the parties are direct competitors in the stained glass industry and that both companies use websites to promote and market their products. Gallagher even admitted that he intentionally used Venture Tape's marks on McGills' website for the express purpose of attracting customers to McGills' website and that he chose "Venture Tape" because of its strong reputation in the stained glass industry. These admissions

---

[5] Venture's registration of the two marks, when coupled with its continuous use of them from 1990 to 1995, is incontestible evidence of Venture's exclusive right to use the marks. Further, McGills concedes that, without Venture's permission, Gallagher embedded the marks verbatim on the McGills website.

illustrate the similarity (indeed, identity) of the marks used, the similarity of the goods, the close relationship between the channels of trade and advertising, and the similarity in the classes of prospective purchasers. They also support the conclusions that McGills acted with a subjective intent to trade on Venture's reputation and that Venture's mark is strong. Accordingly, only the sixth factor—evidence of actual consumer confusion—is potentially in dispute.

On appeal, McGills argues that Gallagher had no way of knowing whether or not his use of the Venture marks on the McGills website had been successful, i.e., whether the marks actually lured any Internet consumer to the website. Thus, the company contends that summary judgment in Venture's favor was improper because there was no evidence of actual confusion. However, McGills' various protestations below and on appeal that there is no direct evidence of actual consumer confusion, even if accepted as true, are ultimately beside the point.

Although Venture might have attempted to adduce evidence of actual consumer confusion (e.g., Internet user market surveys) in support of a favorable *Pignons* determination, the absence of such proof is not dispositive of the *Pignons* analysis. "[A] trademark holder's burden is to show likelihood of confusion, not actual confusion. While evidence of actual confusion is 'often deemed the best evidence of possible future confusion, proof of actual confusion is not essential to finding likelihood of confusion.'"

McGills' admissions regarding the other seven *Pignons* factors, particularly Gallagher's admission that his purpose in using the Venture marks was to lure customers to his site, permit us to conclude that no genuine dispute exists regarding the likelihood of confusion. As a result, Venture was entitled to summary judgment on the liability issue.

B. Award of Profits under the Lanham Act

[The court upheld an award of $230,339.17, McGills' net profits for the three-and-a-half-year period of infringement, holding that the district court's finding of willfulness was not clearly erroneous. Gallagher's "admittedly intentional use" was enough even though he didn't know this use was illegal. His "intentional concealment" of the marks by displaying them in the same color as the webpage background provided strong circumstantial evidence of "willfulness." Venture didn't have to show any harm to its own business. The court also upheld an attorney's fee award of $188,583.06, for similar reasons.]

NOTES AND QUESTIONS

White-on-White Text. White-on-white text was a trick that some website operators used around 2000 to include third-party trademarks into their website without showing those trademarks to users. Because it was an effort to game the search engine algorithms, many search engines reconfigured their algorithms to ignore white-on-white text. As a result, McGills' white-on-white text was probably as ineffective as the keyword metatags. It's also not a good idea from a legal standpoint. *See* Agdia, Inc. v. Xia, 2017 WL 3438174 (N.D. Ind. 2017).

Willfulness and Diversion. McGills admitted that it was trying to get its web pages to show up when users searched for Venture Tape's trademarks. It seems clear that the court morally objected to McGills' behavior. But why?

Assume McGills succeeded in getting the search engines to index it for Venture Tape's trademarks. McGills apparently is a legitimate competitor of Venture Tape, and McGills's goal is to let Venture Tape's potential buyers of stained-glass adhesive tape know that McGills can fulfill their needs as well, perhaps at a lower cost or with better quality. Are such efforts to educate potential consumers about competitive alternatives a good thing or a bad thing? What use was McGills entitled to make of Venture Tape's mark in order to inform consumers that McGills offered an alternative?

Were any consumers likely to be confused about the relationship between McGills and Venture Tape? Before any user clicks through to visit McGills, the user will see a search results page that contains a title, description and URL for each search result. As a result, users get a preview of what they are likely to find when they click on a link before they click, which informs their clicking decisions. *See* Eric Goldman, *Deregulating Relevancy in Internet Trademark Law*, 54 EMORY L.J. 507 (2005). If consumers thought it was worth checking out McGills' website after seeing the search results preview, isn't that a good thing? Or does the possibility that they might have thought McGills was a Venture Tape reseller still leave room for confusion?

Remedies. The court's damage award disgorged all of McGills' profits for over three years. Why did the court impose such a harsh remedy?

Keyword Metatags and Nominative Use. Playboy Enterprises, Inc. v. Welles, 279 F.3d 796 (9th Cir. 2002), involved Terri Welles, who was *Playboy* magazine's Playmate of the Year 1981. She referenced this title in several ways in her website, including putting the words "Playboy" and "Playmate" in the keyword metatags of her website. The court rejected Playboy's trademark claims over the keyword metatags, concluding that Welles's references to "Playboy" and "Playmate" qualified as a protected nominative use because she had, in fact, been *Playboy*'s Playmate of the Year 1981 and was entitled to use that title in her self-promotion. In contrast, Welles's inclusion of the term "PMOY '81" as the web page's background (its "wallpaper") was not nominative use because such references were more than necessary to identify Welles.

If a company references its competitor's trademark in a factually true statement (i.e., "our products compete with [third-party trademark]") in the keyword metatags, would that similarly qualify as nominative use?

The Law Lags the Technology. Courts properly educated about the demise of keyword metatags should find them legally immaterial. *See, e.g.,* Sazerac Brands LLC v. Peristyle LLC, 2017 WL 4558022 (E.D. Ky. 2017) ("Sazerac fails to explain why metatags should still form the basis for Lanham Act liability in light of major search engines' change in policy.").

Description Metatags. Because search engines might publish the contents of description metatags verbatim, courts will treat a description metatag's content as ad copy and apply the associated legal standards. *See* North American Medical Corp. v. Axiom Worldwide, Inc., 522 F.3d 1211 (11th Cir. 2008).

C.   Keyword Advertising

Keyword advertising has exploded into a $50+ billion/year industry. Google is by far the market leader, so we will focus on Google's practices. You are surely familiar with keyword advertisements on Google. They are presently displayed in the area labeled "ad" at the top of the search results page.

Google's main keyword advertising program is called AdWords. Generally, advertisers submit to Google a list of desired keywords, the associated ad copy and an auction bid price for each keyword. When consumers enter a search query at Google, Google looks to see which advertisers have placed auction bids for the keywords in that query. If more than one advertiser has submitted a bid, Google conducts an auction to determine the display order for advertisers. When a person clicks on an ad, the advertiser pays Google for the click.

However, the auction is not based solely on the advertisers' submitted bids. Google's revenue depends on click price multiplied by click quantity, so Google tries to estimate which ad ranking will maximize revenue. Google uses an "ad quality score" that acts as a proxy for consumers' propensity to click on a particular ad. Google displays keyword ads in an order determined by blending bid prices with ad quality scores.

Google runs another program called AdSense. AdSense allows third-party online publishers to display keyword advertising sourced by Google on their websites. Google then shares the revenues generated from this advertising with the publisher. When ads are displayed through AdSense, Google automatically analyzes the publisher's web page to isolate some keywords that describe the page's content. Google then auctions the keywords it has distilled from each page.

Some bids placed by advertisers are for keywords that contain third-party trademarks. For example, Volvo might place a bid to have its ad copy displayed when users search for the term "Mercedes." Some trademark owners have objected to third-party advertisers appearing in response to "their" trademarks, especially competitors. This has led to numerous legal disputes.

In response to these disputes, and in an effort to reduce their own liability, the major search engines have voluntarily adopted policies about when they will permit advertising on keywords that contain third-party trademarks.

Google's *U.S. Trademark Policy* for AdWords does not restrict the bidding on any keywords due to trademark owner complaints, but it will restrict the appearance of the trademark in ad copy if requested by a trademark owner. However, even when requested, Google will not restrict the trademark in ad copy by "resellers," "informational sites," "authorized advertisers" and other specified situations. It will restrict "Acme is better than Bigco" at Bigco's request.

Trademark owners routinely invoke search-engine policies to limit third-party advertisers. Often, the search engine's remedies eliminate the need for further legal proceedings.

Still, keyword advertising has spurred a substantial amount of litigation. Google and other search engines have been sued dozens of times for *selling* trademarked keywords, but no court has definitively concluded that keyword sellers are liable for trademark infringement. Given that in-court challenges to keyword selling have largely dried up, the practice appears de facto to be permitted.

Buying third-party trademarks for keyword advertising has also been the subject of countless lawsuits, but trademark owners rarely win those lawsuits. "[C]ourts have repeatedly found that the purchase of a competitor's marks as keywords alone, without additional behavior that confuses consumers, is not actionable." Alzheimer's Disease and Related Disorders Ass'n, Inc. v. Alzheimer's Found. of Am., Inc., 2018 WL 1918618 (S.D.N.Y. 2018).

Advertisers may be more legally vulnerable when they include the third-party trademark in the keyword ad copy, but even in that case, advertisers routinely win. *See, e.g.*, Infostream Grp. Inc. v. Avid Life Media Inc., 2013 WL 6018030 (C.D. Cal. 2013) (granting motion to dismiss); Gen. Steel Domestic Sales, LLC v. Chumley, 2013 WL 1900562 (D. Colo. 2013) (defense won despite trademark use in ad copy).

The advertiser-favorable results can be substantially attributed to the following case, which wasn't a complete defense win but nevertheless eliminated a lot of doctrinal ambiguity that was giving hope to plaintiffs. The case illustrates the kinds of questions a court should ask in evaluating alleged consumer confusion from keyword advertising, and it shows a healthy skepticism towards the typical anti-technology and anti-consumer arguments advanced by trademark owners.

NETWORK AUTOMATION, INC. V. ADVANCED SYSTEM CONCEPTS, INC., 638 F.3D 1137 (9TH CIR. 2011)

> "We must be acutely aware of excessive rigidity when applying the law in the Internet context; emerging technologies require a flexible approach."

Brookfield Commc'ns, Inc. v. West Coast Entm't Corp., 174 F.3d 1036, 1054 (9th Cir. 1999).

Network Automation ("Network") and Advanced Systems Concepts ("Systems") are both in the business of selling job scheduling and management software, and both advertise on the Internet. Network sells its software under the mark AutoMate, while Systems' product is sold under the registered trademark ActiveBatch. Network decided to advertise its product by purchasing certain keywords, such as "ActiveBatch," which when keyed into various search engines, most prominently Google and Microsoft Bing, produce a results page showing "www.NetworkAutomation.com" as a sponsored link. Systems' objection to Network's use of its trademark to interest viewers in Network's website gave rise to this trademark infringement action.

The district court was confronted with the question whether Network's use of ActiveBatch to advertise its products was a clever and legitimate use of readily available technology, such as Google's AdWords, or a likely violation of the Lanham Act, 15 U.S.C. § 1114. The court found a likelihood of initial interest confusion by applying the eight factors we established more than three decades ago in *AMF Inc. v. Sleekcraft Boats*, 599 F.2d 341 (9th Cir. 1979), and reasoning that the three most important factors in "cases involving the Internet" are (1) the similarity of the marks; (2) the relatedness of the goods; and (3) the marketing channel used. The court therefore issued a preliminary injunction against Network's use of the mark ActiveBatch.

Mindful that the sine qua non of trademark infringement is consumer confusion, and that the *Sleekcraft* factors are but a nonexhaustive list of factors relevant to determining the likelihood of consumer confusion, we conclude that Systems' showing of a likelihood of confusion was insufficient to support injunctive relief. Therefore, we vacate the injunction and reverse and remand.

I. Factual and Procedural Background

Systems is a software engineering and consulting firm founded in 1981. It has used the ActiveBatch trademark since 2000, and it procured federal registration of the mark in 2001. Systems markets ActiveBatch software to businesses, which use the product to centralize and manage disparate tasks. Network is a software company founded in 1997 under the name Unisyn. Its signature product, AutoMate, also provides businesses with job scheduling, event monitoring, and related services. Network has approximately 15,000 total customers, and between 4,000 and 5,000 active customers, including Fortune 500 companies and mid-sized and small firms. The cost of a license to use AutoMate typically ranges from $995 to $10,995. There is no dispute that Network and Systems are direct competitors, or that ActiveBatch and AutoMate are directly competing products.

. . . Network purchased "ActiveBatch" as a keyword from Google AdWords and a comparable program offered by Microsoft's Bing search engine.

As a result, consumers searching for business software who enter "ActiveBatch" as a search term would locate a results page where the top objective results are links to Systems' own website and various articles about the product. In the "Sponsored Links" or "Sponsored Sites" section of the page, above or to the right of the regular results, users see Network's advertisement, either alone or alongside Systems' own sponsored link. The text of Network's advertisements begin with phrases such as "Job Scheduler," "Intuitive Job Scheduler," or "Batch Job Scheduling," and end with the company's web site address, www.NetworkAutomation.com. The middle line reads: "Windows Job Scheduling + Much More. Easy to Deploy, Scalable. D/L Trial." . . .

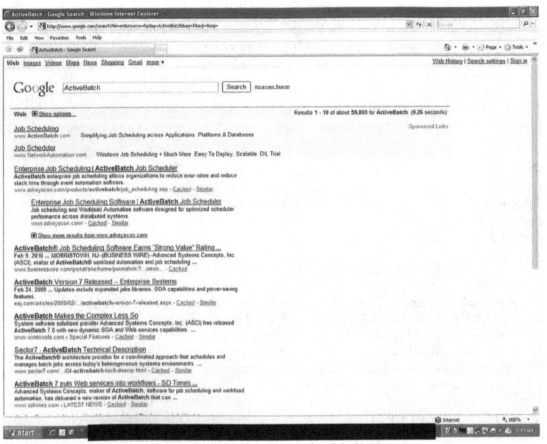

[Screenshot from the court's opinion]

507

[Screenshot taken March 17, 2011]

III. DISCUSSION . . .

To prevail on a claim of trademark infringement under the Lanham Act, 15 U.S.C. § 1114, a party "must prove: (1) that it has a protectible ownership interest in the mark; and (2) that the defendant's use of the mark is likely to cause consumer confusion."

Network does not contest the ownership or its use of the mark. . . .

This case, therefore, turns on whether Network's use of Systems' trademark is likely to cause consumer confusion. Network argues that its use of Systems' mark is legitimate "comparative, contextual advertising" which presents sophisticated consumers with clear choices. Systems characterizes Network's behavior differently, accusing it of misleading consumers by hijacking their attention with intentionally unclear advertisements. . . .

B. Here we consider whether the use of another's trademark as a search engine keyword to trigger one's own product advertisement violates the Lanham Act. We begin by examining the *Sleekcraft* factors that are most relevant to the determination whether the use is likely to cause initial interest confusion.[4] While the district court analyzed each of the *Sleekcraft* factors, it identified the three most important factors as (1) the similarity of the marks, (2) the relatedness of the goods or services, and (3) the simultaneous use of the Web as a marketing channel, for any case addressing trademark infringement on the Internet. . . .

However, we did not intend *Brookfield* to be read so expansively as to forever enshrine these three factors—now often referred to as the "Internet trinity" or "Internet troika"—as the test for trademark infringement on the Internet. *Brookfield* was the first to present a claim of initial interest confusion on the Internet; we recognized at the time it would not be the last, and so emphasized flexibility over rigidity. Depending on the facts of each specific case arising on the Internet, other factors may emerge as more illuminating on the question of consumer confusion. . .

The "troika" is a particularly poor fit for the question presented here. The potential infringement in this context arises from the risk that while using Systems' mark to search for information about its product, a consumer might be confused by a results page that shows a competitor's advertisement on the same screen, when that advertisement does not clearly identify the source or its product.

. . . [B]ecause the sine qua non of trademark infringement is consumer confusion, when we examine initial interest confusion, the owner of the mark must demonstrate likely confusion, not mere diversion. . . .

1. Strength of the Mark

"The stronger a mark—meaning the more likely it is to be remembered and associated in the public mind with the mark's owner—the greater the protection it is accorded by the trademark laws." . . .

This factor is probative of confusion here because a consumer searching for a generic term is more likely to be searching for a product category. *See* [*Brookfield*] at 1058 n. 19 ("Generic terms are those used by the public to refer generally to the product rather than a particular brand of the product."). That consumer is more likely to expect to encounter links and advertisements from a variety of sources. By contrast, a user searching for a distinctive term is more likely to be looking for a particular product, and therefore could be more susceptible to confusion when sponsored links appear that advertise a similar product from a different source. On the other hand, if the ordinary consumers of this particular product are particularly sophisticated and knowledgeable, they might also be aware that Systems is the source of ActiveBatch software and not be confused at all.

The district court acknowledged that the parties failed to address the strength of the mark, but it concluded that the factor favors Systems. It reasoned that ActiveBatch is a suggestive mark because it "requires a mental leap from the mark to the product," and as a registered

---

[4] Systems' argument rests only on the theory of initial interest confusion. It does not argue source confusion.

509

trademark it is "inherently distinctive." We agree.[†] Because the mark is both Systems' product name and a suggestive federally registered trademark, consumers searching for the term are presumably looking for its specific product, and not a category of goods. Nonetheless, that may not be the end of the inquiry about this factor, as the sophistication of the consumers of the product may also play a role. . . .

2. Proximity of the Goods

"Related goods are generally more likely than unrelated goods to confuse the public as to the producers of the goods." "[T]he danger presented is that the public will mistakenly assume there is an association between the producers of the related goods, though no such association exists."

. . . However, the proximity of the goods would become less important if advertisements are clearly labeled or consumers exercise a high degree of care, because rather than being misled, the consumer would merely be confronted with choices among similar products. [*Playboy*] at 1035 (Berzon, J., concurring) ("[S]uch choices do not constitute trademark infringement off the internet, and I cannot understand why they should on the Internet.").

Because the products at issue here are virtually interchangeable, this factor may be helpful, but it must be considered in conjunction with the labeling and appearance of the advertisements and the degree of care exercised by the consumers of the ActiveBatch software. By weighing this factor in isolation and failing to consider whether the parties' status as direct competitors would actually lead to a likelihood of confusion, the district court allowed this factor to weigh too heavily in the analysis.

3. Similarity of the Marks

"[T]he more similar the marks in terms of appearance, sound, and meaning, the greater the likelihood of confusion." . . . "Similarity of the marks is tested on three levels: sight, sound, and meaning. Each must be considered as they are encountered in the marketplace."

In *Sleekcraft*, we concluded that the marks "Sleekcraft" and "Slickcraft" were similar in terms of sight, sound, and meaning by examining the actual situations in which consumers were likely to read, hear, and consider the meaning of the terms. Such an inquiry is impossible here where the consumer does not confront two distinct trademarks. . . . Again, however, because the consumer keys in Systems' trademark, which results in Network's sponsored link, depending on the labeling and appearance of the advertisement, including whether it identifies Network's own mark, and the degree of care and sophistication of the consumer, it could be helpful in determining initial interest confusion.

[†] [Editor's note: Unfortunately, the district court and the appeals court are wrong. A registered mark is presumed *distinctive*, that is, presumed to identify the source of a product or service; it is not necessarily *inherently* distinctive, automatically telling consumers that it identifies source. A court might grant weight to the PTO's decision to register the trademark without requiring the applicant to show secondary meaning, thus reflecting an administrative judgment that the term is inherently distinctive. But a trademark, including a registered trademark, need not be inherently distinctive; it might have *acquired* distinctiveness over time, so consumers learned that it identifies source, as with AMERICAN AIRLINES® or the shape of the Coca-Cola bottle. While this is not dispositive here, the error demonstrates some of the challenges courts face in applying trademark law.]

4. Evidence of Actual Confusion

"[A] showing of actual confusion among significant numbers of consumers provides strong support for the likelihood of confusion." However, "actual confusion is not necessary to a finding of likelihood of confusion under the Lanham Act." Indeed, "[p]roving actual confusion is difficult . . . and the courts have often discounted such evidence because it was unclear or insubstantial."

. . . As the district court noted, neither Network nor Systems provided evidence regarding actual confusion, which is not surprising given the procedural posture. Therefore, while this is a relevant factor for determining the likelihood of confusion in keyword advertising cases, its importance is diminished at the preliminary injunction stage of the proceedings. The district court correctly concluded that this factor should be accorded no weight.

5. Marketing Channels

"Convergent marketing channels increase the likelihood of confusion." In *Sleekcraft*, the two products were sold in niche marketplaces, including boat shows, specialty retail outlets, and trade magazines. However, this factor becomes less important when the marketing channel is less obscure. Today, it would be the rare commercial retailer that did not advertise online, and the shared use of a ubiquitous marketing channel does not shed much light on the likelihood of consumer confusion. *See Playboy*, 354 F.3d at 1028 ("Given the broad use of the Internet today, the same could be said for countless companies. Thus, this factor merits little weight.").

Therefore, the district court's determination that because both parties advertise on the Internet this factor weighed in favor of Systems was incorrect.

6. Type of Goods and Degree of Care

"Low consumer care . . . increases the likelihood of confusion." "In assessing the likelihood of confusion to the public, the standard used by the courts is the typical buyer exercising ordinary caution. . . . When the buyer has expertise in the field, a higher standard is proper though it will not preclude a finding that confusion is likely. Similarly, when the goods are expensive, the buyer can be expected to exercise greater care in his purchases; again, though, confusion may still be likely."

The nature of the goods and the type of consumer is highly relevant to determining the likelihood of confusion in the keyword advertising context. A sophisticated consumer of business software exercising a high degree of care is more likely to understand the mechanics of Internet search engines and the nature of sponsored links, whereas an un-savvy consumer exercising less care is more likely to be confused. The district court determined that this factor weighed in Systems' favor because "there is generally a low degree of care exercised by Internet consumers." However, the degree of care analysis cannot begin and end at the marketing channel. We still must consider the nature and cost of the goods, and whether "the products being sold are marketed primarily to expert buyers." . . .

We have recently acknowledged that the default degree of consumer care is becoming more heightened as the novelty of the Internet evaporates and online commerce becomes commonplace. In *Toyota Motor Sales v. Tabari*, 610 F.3d 1171 (9th Cir. 2010), we vacated a preliminary injunction that prohibited a pair of automobile brokers from using Toyota's "Lexus" mark in their domain names. We determined that it was unlikely that a reasonably prudent consumer would be confused into believing that a domain name that included a product name would necessarily have a formal affiliation with the maker of the product, as "[c]onsumers who use the Internet for shopping are generally quite sophisticated about such matters." The *Tabari* panel reasoned,

> [I]n the age of FIOS, cable modems, DSL and T1 lines, reasonable, prudent and experienced internet consumers are accustomed to such exploration by trial and error. They skip from site to site, ready to hit the back button whenever they're not satisfied with a site's contents. They fully expect to find some sites that aren't what they imagine based on a glance at the domain name or search engine summary. Outside the special case of . . . domains that actively claim affiliation with the trademark holder, consumers don't form any firm expectations about the sponsorship of a website until they've seen the landing page—if then.

We further explained that we expect consumers searching for expensive products online to be even more sophisticated.

Therefore the district court improperly concluded that this factor weighed in Systems' favor based on a conclusion reached by our court more than a decade ago . . . that Internet users on the whole exercise a low degree of care. While the statement may have been accurate then, we suspect that there are many contexts in which it no longer holds true.

7. Defendant's Intent

"When the alleged infringer knowingly adopts a mark similar to another's, reviewing courts presume that the defendant can accomplish his purpose: that is, that the public will be deceived." Nevertheless, we have also "recognized that liability for infringement may not be imposed for using a registered trademark in connection with truthful comparative advertising."

Therefore, much like the proximity of the goods, the defendant's intent may be relevant here, but only insofar as it bolsters a finding that the use of the trademark serves to mislead consumers rather than truthfully inform them of their choice of products. The district court incorrectly considered the intent factor in isolation, and concluded that it weighed in Systems' favor without first determining that Network intended to deceive consumers rather than compare its product to ActiveBatch.

8. Likelihood of Expansion of the Product Lines

. . . Where two companies are direct competitors, this factor is unimportant. Therefore, the district court correctly declined to consider the likelihood of expansion.

9. Other Relevant Factors

The eight Sleekcraft factors are "not exhaustive. Other variables may come into play depending on the particular facts presented." In the keyword advertising context the "likelihood of confusion will ultimately turn on what the consumer saw on the screen and reasonably believed, given the context." Hearts on Fire Co. v. Blue Nile, Inc., 603 F. Supp. 2d 274, 289 (D. Mass. 2009).[6] In *Playboy*, we found it important that the consumers saw banner advertisements that were "confusingly labeled or not labeled at all." We noted that clear labeling "might eliminate the likelihood of initial interest confusion that exists in this case."

The appearance of the advertisements and their surrounding context on the user's screen are similarly important here. The district court correctly examined the text of Network's sponsored links, concluding that the advertisements did not clearly identify their source. However, the district court did not consider the surrounding context. In *Playboy*, we also found it important that Netscape's search engine did not clearly segregate the sponsored advertisements from the objective results. Here, even if Network has not clearly identified itself in the text of its ads, Google and Bing have partitioned their search results pages so that the advertisements appear in separately labeled sections for "sponsored" links. The labeling and appearance of the advertisements as they appear on the results page includes more than the text of the advertisement, and must be considered as a whole.

C. Given the nature of the alleged infringement here, the most relevant factors to the analysis of the likelihood of confusion are: (1) the strength of the mark; (2) the evidence of actual confusion; (3) the type of goods and degree of care likely to be exercised by the purchaser; and (4) the labeling and appearance of the advertisements and the surrounding context on the screen displaying the results page.

The district court did not weigh the *Sleekcraft* factors flexibly to match the specific facts of this case. It relied on the Internet "troika," which is highly illuminating in the context of domain names, but which fails to discern whether there is a likelihood of confusion in a keywords case. Because the linchpin of trademark infringement is consumer confusion, the district court abused its discretion in issuing the injunction. . . .

NOTES AND QUESTIONS

The Initial Interest Confusion Doctrine. What is "initial interest confusion," and how does the doctrine enhance the court's analysis? If you did not fully understand the court's references to the doctrine, you are not alone. Courts have articulated dozens of different formulations of the doctrine; each circuit has its own articulation of the doctrine; and not infrequently, there are *intra*-circuit inconsistencies in the doctrine's articulation. *See* Eric Goldman, *Deregulating Relevancy in Internet Trademark Law*, 54 EMORY L.J. 507 (2005).

---

[6] The *Hearts on Fire* court identified a new seven-factor test to determine whether there is a likelihood of consumer confusion arising from a firm's use of a competitor's trademark as a search engine keyword triggering its own sponsored links. Network urges us to adopt the *Hearts on Fire* factors. While we agree that the decision's reasoning is useful, we decline to add another multi-factor test to the extant eight-factor *Sleekcraft* test.

Although initial interest confusion cases date back to the early 1970s, the most-famous statement of the initial interest confusion doctrine comes from the Ninth Circuit's *Brookfield* case: "use of another's trademark in a manner reasonably calculated to capture initial consumer attention, even though no actual sale is finally completed as a result of the confusion." However, as you saw in *Network Automation*, the Ninth Circuit does not apply the doctrine as broadly as that definition might imply.

Although trademark owners routinely claim initial interest confusion, and although it used to be a serious threat to the defense even when point-of-sale confusion was obviously unlikely, the doctrine almost never helps the trademark owner win its case anymore.

In one striking case, *1-800 Contacts, Inc. v. Lens.com, Inc.*, 722 F.3d 1229 (10th Cir. 2013), the court articulated a broad definition of initial interest confusion but then imposed an almost impossibly high evidentiary standard for proving it. The appeals court treated an ad's clickthrough rate as a dispositive proxy for a survey measuring consumer confusion. Since a 3% clickthrough rate for an online ad would be an astonishing success—while a plaintiff typically needs well over 10% confusion to prevail—an ad's low clickthrough rates will almost always indicate a *lack* of initial interest confusion. *But see* SanMedica Int'l, LLC v. Amazon.com, Inc., 2016 WL 527055 (D. Utah Jan. 16, 2016) (Amazon's remarkable clickthrough rate of 11% for one product was high enough to defeat summary judgment). So while trademark owners will continue to assert initial interest confusion, their success rate with the doctrine will likely be trivial for keyword advertising.

Inferring Searcher Intent from Their Keywords. The *Network Automation* court says:

> Because the mark is both Systems' product name and a suggestive federally registered trademark, consumers searching for the term are presumably looking for its specific product, and not a category of goods.

There are at least two problems with this statement. First, this is an appellate court making an empirical presumption about consumer behavior. Notice that the court did not cite any research or provide any other support for this presumption. How does this court know this to be true? Why is an appellate court making this categorical statement without any support? What if the court is actually wrong about consumer behavior?

Second, the court's presumption *is* almost certainly wrong. Can you think of circumstances where consumers might use a trademark to search for a category of goods? One circumstance: a category of goods where there is a strong market leader and few well-accepted synonyms to describe the category. Consider, for example, the "Clapper" (some of you may remember the advertisements "Clap On! Clap Off! The CLAPPER!!!" *See* http://www.youtube.com/watch?v=cfgN5tUgjb8). How would you describe that category of goods? If you can't think of a succinct but accurate term for the product category, you might consider doing a keyword search for "the Clapper" and be delighted to find other vendors in the niche.

Even if consumers aren't seeking a category of goods when they use a trademark, they still might be looking for something other than the trademarked product. *See* Stefan Bechtold &

Catherine Tucker, *Trademarks, Triggers, and Online Search*, 11 J. EMPIRICAL L. STUD. 718 (2014) (concluding, from a European dataset of Google searches, that consumers' use of trademarks as search terms does not consistently represent an attempt only to reach the trademark owner's website); Jeffrey P. Dotson et al, *Brand Attitudes and Search Engine Queries*, 37 J. INTERACTIVE MKTG. 105 (2016) (using actual Google search queries; suggesting diverse motivations for brand search); David J. Franklyn & David A. Hyman, *Trademarks As Keywords: Much Ado About Something?*, 26 HARV. J.L. & TECH. 481 (2013) (using consumer surveys to ask consumers what they expected when they searched for specific trademarks; finding that many consumers would find advertisements from competitors highly relevant); Goldman, *Deregulating Relevancy*, *supra* (giving examples of many possible searcher intents from a single trademark used as a search term).

The empirical evidence from these studies suggests that most consumers aren't confused, and many consumers are actively helped, by competitive keyword advertising. Franklyn and Hyman do find, however, that many consumers have trouble telling the difference between "organic" and paid links shown by search engines, despite the "ad" label on the latter. While this confusion about why different results are shown may appropriately be addressed by general consumer-protection law, it isn't a trademark concern.

What If the Advertiser Never Buys the Trademark at All? Assume that BlueJet, an airline, buys the keyword "airlines" and enables "broad matching," which causes the ad to appear for any search query that contains the keyword, even if the query contains other words. For example, a search for "United Airlines" or "Delta Airlines" may return ads for BlueJet because of the word "airlines," not "united" or "delta." Is there a claim for trademark infringement even though BlueJet never purchased the trademarks as keywords? *See, e.g.,* Rhino Sports, Inc. v. Sport Court, Inc., 2007 WL 1302745 (D. Ariz. 2007).

Publicity Rights Analogue. Habush v. Cannon, 346 Wis.2d 709 (Wis. App. Ct. 2013), held that buying a person's name (in that case, a rival lawyer) as a keyword for competitive advertising didn't violate the person's publicity rights. *See generally* Eric Goldman & Angel Reyes III, *Regulation of Lawyers' Use of Competitive Keyword Advertising*, 2016 U. ILL. L. REV. 103. Chapter 14 revisits the issue.

Other Countries' Rules May Be Stricter. In the United States, if an ad on Google led to a page of results on Amazon that included the trademark owner's products as well as other, clearly labeled alternatives, that would pose no problem. In Germany, by contrast, such an ad will infringe the trademark owner's rights. *Decision of the Federal Supreme Court of 25 July 2019 in Case I ZR 29/18.* Likewise, E.U. courts may require "negative matching" to prevent ads like BlueJet's from showing up when a searcher inputs a different airline's name, although the European Union has also approved non-confusing keyword advertising. *Compare* Interflora Inc. v. Marks and Spencer Plc, [2013] EWHC 1484 (Ch)), *with* DealDash OYJ v. ContextLogic, Inc., 2018 WL 3820654 (N.D. Cal. Aug. 10, 2018).

As the last two chapters illustrated, copyright and trademark law can restrict advertiser behavior. This chapter looks at three other ways—trade secrets, patents and idea-submission principles—that competitors and others can use intangible rights to limit advertiser behavior. This chapter concludes with a brief look at antitrust as another limit on competitor behavior.

1.   Trade Secrets

A.   An Overview of Trade Secret Law

A "trade secret" is information that derives value because it is secret. Think of a trade secret as information only one business knows that provides it some competitive advantage. So long as the business derives that advantage by keeping the information secret, the business can prevent others from misappropriating the information, which in turn helps preserve that competitive advantage.

Trade secrets last as long as the information is valuable and secret. As a result, it is possible for a trade secret to be protected perpetually. For example, the formula for making Coca-Cola soda has been protected as a trade secret since 1886, with no end in sight.[*] In contrast, patents have a finite life of fewer than twenty years, after which everyone is free to replicate the invention and compete directly with the inventor. By keeping the formula a trade secret instead of patenting it, Coca-Cola has obtained 110+ extra years of protection (so far) from direct competition.

Although trade secrets are protected from misappropriation by corporate espionage or misuse by former employees, they are not protected from independent invention or reverse engineering. So if a competitor can figure out the trade secret independently or through reverse engineering, the trade secret "owner" can do nothing to stop the competitor from using that information to compete more effectively. No one has independently derived the exact recipe for Coca-Cola, but if someone did, trade-secret law would be powerless to stop them from making soda tasting exactly like Coca-Cola.

In general, a trade secret loses its protection when it is no longer a secret. For example, published information is no longer a trade secret. A trade secret can also lose protection when the owner does not take reasonable efforts to ensure its secrecy. However, if a secret is inadvertently disclosed, or disseminated after being misappropriated despite the owner's reasonable efforts, the courts will often protect the information due to the owner's diligence.

---

[*] This idea was disputed in *Original Recipe*, THIS AMERICAN LIFE (Feb. 11, 2011), suggesting that the original Coca-Cola formula has been publicly disclosed for a while, though no one has been able to replicate the taste (yet).

Frequently, a trade secret owner wants or needs to share the trade secret with certain business partners, such as vendors or customers. To avoid losing trade secret status, the owner can share the information under a trade secret license that restricts the recipients' use and disclosure of the information. These trade-secret licenses can take many forms, but usually the licenses are characterized as a non-disclosure agreements (NDAs) or confidentiality clauses in the parties' contracts. These confidentiality restrictions can extend to non-trade secret information (i.e., information that the discloser provides to the recipient even if the information does not qualify as a trade secret), although non-secret information is usually excluded from the license. Trade-secret licenses are ubiquitous throughout the business world.

Trade secrets are protected by both state and federal law. Almost all states have adopted some version of the "Uniform Trade Secret Act," but adoptions are not entirely uniform. In partial response to this lack of uniformity, Congress enacted the Defend Trade Secrets Act (DTSA) in 2016. The DTSA does not preempt state laws, and trade-secret owners routinely bring both state and DTSA claims simultaneously.

To illustrate the opportunities and challenges of trade secrets, the book takes a closer look at two categories of trade secrets that advertising professionals routinely encounter: marketing plans and customer lists. Over the course of your career, you will encounter many other categories of trade secrets, but we expect these two categories will come up early and often in your career.

B.   Future Marketing Plans as a Trade Secret

Future marketing plans—such as new products being developed and launched—frequently qualify as a trade secret. Premature disclosure of this information can tip off competitors about a company's plans, allowing the competitors to quickly mimic the plans (and thereby reduce or eliminate any first-mover advantage) or make countermoves. It can also spoil coordinated efforts to publicize a launch. Therefore, trade-secret protection for future marketing plans can have significant value to marketers.

The following case involves an employee leaving one company to work for a competitor. The former employer fights back to protect the employee's knowledge of future marketing plans. Pay close attention to exactly what information the court thinks is protectable as a trade secret (and when it qualifies for or loses that protection), and the court's steps to protect that information. Also, how does this employee's transition to a competitor differ from the ordinary movement of employees within an industry?

PEPSICO, INC. V. REDMOND, 54 F.3D 1262 (7TH CIR. 1995)

. . . I.

The facts of this case lay [*sic*] against a backdrop of fierce beverage-industry competition between Quaker and PepsiCo, especially in "sports drinks" and "new age drinks." Quaker's sports drink, "Gatorade," is the dominant brand in its market niche. PepsiCo introduced its

Gatorade rival, "All Sport," in March and April of 1994, but sales of All Sport lag far behind those of Gatorade. Quaker also has the lead in the new-age-drink category. Although PepsiCo has entered the market through joint ventures with the Thomas J. Lipton Company and Ocean Spray Cranberries, Inc., Quaker purchased Snapple Beverage Corp., a large new-age-drink maker, in late 1994. PepsiCo's products have about half of Snapple's market share. Both companies see 1995 as an important year for their products: PepsiCo has developed extensive plans to increase its market presence, while Quaker is trying to solidify its lead by integrating Gatorade and Snapple distribution. Meanwhile, PepsiCo and Quaker each face strong competition from Coca Cola Co., which has its own sports drink, "PowerAde," and which introduced its own Snapple-rival, "Fruitopia," in 1994, as well as from independent beverage producers.

William Redmond, Jr., worked for PepsiCo in its Pepsi-Cola North America division ("PCNA") from 1984 to 1994. Redmond became the General Manager of the Northern California Business Unit in June, 1993, and was promoted one year later to General Manager of the business unit covering all of California, a unit having annual revenues of more than 500 million dollars and representing twenty percent of PCNA's profit for all of the United States.

Redmond's relatively high-level position at PCNA gave him access to inside information and trade secrets. Redmond, like other PepsiCo management employees, had signed a confidentiality agreement with PepsiCo. That agreement stated in relevant part that he

> w[ould] not disclose at any time, to anyone other than officers or employees of [PepsiCo], or make use of, confidential information relating to the business of [PepsiCo] . . . obtained while in the employ of [PepsiCo], which shall not be generally known or available to the public or recognized as standard practices.

Donald Uzzi, who had left PepsiCo in the beginning of 1994 to become the head of Quaker's Gatorade division, began courting Redmond for Quaker in May, 1994. Redmond met in Chicago with Quaker officers in August, 1994, and on October 20, 1994, Quaker, through Uzzi, offered Redmond the position of Vice President-On Premise Sales for Gatorade. Redmond did not then accept the offer but continued to negotiate for more money. Throughout this time, Redmond kept his dealings with Quaker secret from his employers at PCNA.

On November 8, 1994, Uzzi extended Redmond a written offer for the position of Vice President-Field Operations for Gatorade and Redmond accepted. . . .

On November 10, 1994, Redmond met with Barnes and told her that he had decided to accept the Quaker offer and was resigning from PCNA.

. . . PepsiCo filed this diversity suit on November 16, 1994, seeking a temporary restraining order to enjoin Redmond from assuming his duties at Quaker and to prevent him from disclosing trade secrets or confidential information to his new employer. The district court granted PepsiCo's request that same day but dissolved the order sua sponte two days later, after determining that PepsiCo had failed to meet its burden of establishing that it would suffer irreparable harm. The court found that PepsiCo's fears about Redmond were based upon a mistaken understanding of his new position at Quaker and that the likelihood that Redmond would improperly reveal any confidential information did not "rise above mere speculation."

From November 23, 1994, to December 1, 1994, the district court conducted a preliminary injunction hearing on the same matter. At the hearing, PepsiCo offered evidence of a number of trade secrets and confidential information it desired protected and to which Redmond was privy. First, it identified PCNA's "Strategic Plan," an annually revised document that contains PCNA's plans to compete, its financial goals, and its strategies for manufacturing, production, marketing, packaging, and distribution for the coming three years. Strategic Plans are developed by Weatherup and his staff with input from PCNA's general managers, including Redmond, and are considered highly confidential. The Strategic Plan derives much of its value from the fact that it is secret and competitors cannot anticipate PCNA's next moves. PCNA managers received the most recent Strategic Plan at a meeting in July, 1994, a meeting Redmond attended. PCNA also presented information at the meeting regarding its plans for Lipton ready-to-drink teas and for All Sport for 1995 and beyond, including new flavors and package sizes.

Second, PepsiCo pointed to PCNA's Annual Operating Plan ("AOP") as a trade secret. The AOP is a national plan for a given year and guides PCNA's financial goals, marketing plans, promotional event calendars, growth expectations, and operational changes in that year. The AOP, which is implemented by PCNA unit General Managers, including Redmond, contains specific information regarding all PCNA initiatives for the forthcoming year. The AOP bears a label that reads "Private and Confidential—Do Not Reproduce" and is considered highly confidential by PCNA managers.

In particular, the AOP contains important and sensitive information about "pricing architecture"—how PCNA prices its products in the marketplace. Pricing architecture covers both a national pricing approach and specific price points for given areas. Pricing architecture also encompasses PCNA's objectives for All Sport and its new age drinks with reference to trade channels, package sizes and other characteristics of both the products and the customers at which the products are aimed. Additionally, PCNA's pricing architecture outlines PCNA's customer development agreements. These agreements between PCNA and retailers provide for the retailer's participation in certain merchandising activities for PCNA products. As with other information contained in the AOP, pricing architecture is highly confidential and would be extremely valuable to a competitor. Knowing PCNA's pricing architecture would allow a competitor to anticipate PCNA's pricing moves and underbid PCNA strategically whenever and wherever the competitor so desired. PepsiCo introduced evidence that Redmond had detailed knowledge of PCNA's pricing architecture and that he was aware of and had been involved in preparing PCNA's customer development agreements with PCNA's California and California-based national customers. Indeed, PepsiCo showed that Redmond, as the General Manager for California, would have been responsible for implementing the pricing architecture guidelines for his business unit.

PepsiCo also showed that Redmond had intimate knowledge of PCNA "attack plans" for specific markets. Pursuant to these plans, PCNA dedicates extra funds to supporting its brands against other brands in selected markets. To use a hypothetical example, PCNA might budget an additional $500,000 to spend in Chicago at a particular time to help All Sport close its market gap with Gatorade. Testimony and documents demonstrated Redmond's awareness of these plans and his participation in drafting some of them.

Finally, PepsiCo offered evidence of PCNA trade secrets regarding innovations in its selling and delivery systems. Under this plan, PCNA is testing a new delivery system that could give PCNA an advantage over its competitors in negotiations with retailers over shelf space and merchandising. Redmond has knowledge of this secret because PCNA, which has invested over a million dollars in developing the system during the past two years, is testing the pilot program in California.

Having shown Redmond's intimate knowledge of PCNA's plans for 1995, PepsiCo argued that Redmond would inevitably disclose that information to Quaker in his new position, at which he would have substantial input as to Gatorade and Snapple pricing, costs, margins, distribution systems, products, packaging and marketing, and could give Quaker an unfair advantage in its upcoming skirmishes with PepsiCo. Redmond and Quaker countered that Redmond's primary initial duties at Quaker as Vice President-Field Operations would be to integrate Gatorade and Snapple distribution and then to manage that distribution as well as the promotion, marketing and sales of these products. Redmond asserted that the integration would be conducted according to a pre-existing plan and that his special knowledge of PCNA strategies would be irrelevant. This irrelevance would derive not only from the fact that Redmond would be implementing pre-existing plans but also from the fact that PCNA and Quaker distribute their products in entirely different ways: PCNA's distribution system is vertically integrated (i.e., PCNA owns the system) and delivers its product directly to retailers, while Quaker ships its product to wholesalers and customer warehouses and relies on independent distributors. The defendants also pointed out that Redmond had signed a confidentiality agreement with Quaker preventing him from disclosing "any confidential information belonging to others," as well as the Quaker Code of Ethics, which prohibits employees from engaging in "illegal or improper acts to acquire a competitor's trade secrets." Redmond additionally promised at the hearing that should he be faced with a situation at Quaker that might involve the use or disclosure of PCNA information, he would seek advice from Quaker's in-house counsel and would refrain from making the decision.

PepsiCo responded to the defendants' representations by pointing out that the evidence did not show that Redmond would simply be implementing a business plan already in place. On the contrary, as of November, 1994, the plan to integrate Gatorade and Snapple distribution consisted of a single distributorship agreement and a two-page "contract terms summary." Such a basic plan would not lend itself to widespread application among the over 300 independent Snapple distributors. Since the integration process would likely face resistance from Snapple distributors and Quaker had no scheme to deal with this probability, Redmond, as the person in charge of the integration, would likely have a great deal of influence on the process. PepsiCo further argued that Snapple's 1995 marketing and promotion plans had not necessarily been completed prior to Redmond's joining Quaker, that Uzzi disagreed with portions of the Snapple plans, and that the plans were open to re-evaluation. Uzzi testified that the plan for integrating Gatorade and Snapple distribution is something that would happen in the future. Redmond would therefore likely have input in remaking these plans, and if he did, he would inevitably be making decisions with PCNA's strategic plans and 1995 AOP in mind. Moreover, PepsiCo continued, diverging testimony made it difficult to know exactly what Redmond would be doing at Quaker. Redmond described his job as "managing the entire sales effort of Gatorade at the field level, possibly including strategic planning," and at least at one point considered his job to be equivalent to that of a Chief Operating Officer. Uzzi, on the other hand, characterized Redmond's position as "primarily and initially to restructure and integrate our—the distribution systems for Snapple and for Gatorade, as per our distribution plan" and then to "execute marketing, promotion and sales plans in the marketplace." Uzzi also denied having given Redmond detailed information about any business plans, while Redmond described such a plan in depth in an affidavit and said that he received the information from Uzzi. Thus, PepsiCo asserted, Redmond would have a high position in the Gatorade hierarchy, and PCNA trade secrets and confidential information would necessarily influence his decisions. Even if Redmond could somehow refrain from relying on this information, as he promised he would, his actions in leaving PCNA, Uzzi's actions in hiring Redmond, and the varying testimony regarding Redmond's new responsibilities, made Redmond's assurances to PepsiCo less than comforting.

On December 15, 1994, the district court issued an order enjoining Redmond from assuming his position at Quaker through May, 1995, and permanently from using or disclosing any PCNA trade secrets or confidential information....

II. . . .

A. The Illinois Trade Secrets Act ("ITSA"), which governs the trade secret issues in this case, provides that a court may enjoin the "actual or threatened misappropriation" of a trade secret. A party seeking an injunction must therefore prove both the existence of a trade secret and the misappropriation. The defendants' appeal focuses solely on misappropriation; although the defendants only reluctantly refer to PepsiCo's marketing and distribution plans as trade secrets, they do not seriously contest that this information falls under the ITSA.[5]

The question of threatened or inevitable misappropriation in this case lies at the heart of a basic tension in trade secret law. Trade secret law serves to protect "standards of commercial morality" and "encourage [ ] invention and innovation" while maintaining "the public interest in having free and open competition in the manufacture and sale of unpatented goods." Yet that same law should not prevent workers from pursuing their livelihoods when they leave their current positions. . . .

This tension is particularly exacerbated when a plaintiff sues to prevent not the actual misappropriation of trade secrets but the mere threat that it will occur. While the ITSA plainly permits a court to enjoin the threat of misappropriation of trade secrets, there is little

---

[5] Under the ITSA, trade secret "means information, including but not limited to, technical or non-technical data, a formula, pattern, compilation, program, device, method, technique, drawing, process, financial data, or list of actual or potential customers that:

(1) is sufficiently secret to derive economic value, actual or potential, from not generally being known to other persons who can obtain economic value from its disclosure or use; and

(2) is the subject of efforts that are reasonable under the circumstances to maintain its secrecy or confidentiality." . . .

law in Illinois or in this circuit establishing what constitutes threatened or inevitable misappropriation. . . .

PepsiCo presented substantial evidence at the preliminary injunction hearing that Redmond possessed extensive and intimate knowledge about PCNA's strategic goals for 1995 in sports drinks and new age drinks. The district court concluded on the basis of that presentation that unless Redmond possessed an uncanny ability to compartmentalize information, he would necessarily be making decisions about Gatorade and Snapple by relying on his knowledge of PCNA trade secrets. It is not the "general skills and knowledge acquired during his tenure with" PepsiCo that PepsiCo seeks to keep from falling into Quaker's hands, but rather "the particularized plans or processes developed by [PCNA] and disclosed to him while the employer-employee relationship existed, which are unknown to others in the industry and which give the employer an advantage over his competitors.". . .

Admittedly, PepsiCo has not brought a traditional trade secret case, in which a former employee has knowledge of a special manufacturing process or customer list and can give a competitor an unfair advantage by transferring the technology or customers to that competitor. PepsiCo has not contended that Quaker has stolen the All Sport formula or its list of distributors. Rather PepsiCo has asserted that Redmond cannot help but rely on PCNA trade secrets as he helps plot Gatorade and Snapple's new course, and that these secrets will enable Quaker to achieve a substantial advantage by knowing exactly how PCNA will price, distribute, and market its sports drinks and new age drinks and being able to respond strategically. This type of trade secret problem may arise less often, but it nevertheless falls within the realm of trade secret protection under the present circumstances.

Quaker and Redmond assert that they have not and do not intend to use whatever confidential information Redmond has by virtue of his former employment. They point out that Redmond has already signed an agreement with Quaker not to disclose any trade secrets or confidential information gleaned from his earlier employment. They also note with regard to distribution systems that even if Quaker wanted to steal information about PCNA's distribution plans, they would be completely useless in attempting to integrate the Gatorade and Snapple beverage lines.

The defendants' arguments fall somewhat short of the mark. Again, the danger of misappropriation in the present case is not that Quaker threatens to use PCNA's secrets to create distribution systems or co-opt PCNA's advertising and marketing ideas. Rather, PepsiCo believes that Quaker, unfairly armed with knowledge of PCNA's plans, will be able to anticipate its distribution, packaging, pricing, and marketing moves. Redmond and Quaker even concede that Redmond might be faced with a decision that could be influenced by certain confidential information that he obtained while at PepsiCo. In other words, PepsiCo finds itself in the position of a coach, one of whose players has left, playbook in hand, to join the opposing team before the big game. Quaker and Redmond's protestations that their distribution systems and plans are entirely different from PCNA's are thus not really responsive. . . .

For the foregoing reasons, we affirm the district court's order enjoining Redmond from assuming his responsibilities at Quaker through May, 1995, and preventing him forever from disclosing PCNA trade secrets and confidential information.

NOTES AND QUESTIONS

The Inevitable Disclosure Doctrine. The court defines the "inevitable disclosure" doctrine as occurring when "defendant's new employment will inevitably lead him to rely on the plaintiff's trade secrets." This case is a flagship example of the doctrine.

PepsiCo could always sue Redmond and Quaker for using any PepsiCo proprietary information if that actually happened. But, rather than enforcement after a violation, the inevitable disclosure doctrine assumes that Redmond cannot avoid spilling the beans. An injunction keeps him from being put in a position where trade secrets will inevitably be disclosed.

By making a categorical assumption that trade secrets will be leaked regardless of the employee's and employer's efforts not to do so, the inevitable disclosure doctrine has significant effects on the labor market, both for employee mobility and for competitors recruiting experts from other industry players.

As a result, courts rarely accept inevitable-disclosure arguments pursuant to state trade-secret laws and usually only do so in situations involving high-level executives. The Defend Trade Secrets Act (DTSA) makes the inevitable-disclosure doctrine unlikely under federal law. The DTSA says: "a court may grant an injunction to prevent any. . . .threatened misappropriation . . . provided the order does not prevent a person from entering into an employment relationship, and that conditions placed on such employment shall be based on evidence of threatened misappropriation and not merely on the information the person knows."

Scope of Injunctive Relief. Because Redmond's knowledge about PepsiCo's 1995 marketing plans would become public information in relatively short order, the court upheld a six-month restriction on Redmond taking the Quaker job. What is Redmond supposed to do with his time in the interim?

Marketing Plans as a Trade Secret. What exactly did Redmond know that was verboten?

Employee Raids. An omitted part of the opinion said:

> The court also pointed out that Quaker, through Uzzi, seemed to express an unnatural interest in hiring PCNA employees: all three of the people interviewed for the position Redmond ultimately accepted worked at PCNA. Uzzi may well have focused on recruiting PCNA employees because he knew they were good and not because of their confidential knowledge.

This type of hiring pattern, sometimes called an "employee raid," is fairly common. A manager switches jobs and then cherry-picks his or her top-performing subordinates.

PepsiCo's lawsuit against Redmond surely signaled PepsiCo's feelings about any future Quaker efforts to raid more PepsiCo employees.

Denouement of the PepsiCo v. Redmond *Lawsuit.* PepsiCo's All Sport drink never gained huge success. PepsiCo finally gave up trying to build its own product and in 2001 bought the entire Quaker company for over $13 billion. PepsiCo subsequently divested the All Sport brand, which still exists as an independent brand.

PepsiCo's acquisition of Quaker came despite Quaker's colossal mismanagement of Snapple. After buying the Snapple brand for $1.7 billion in 1994, Quaker resold it twenty-seven months later for $300 million—a staggering loss of $1.4 billion. James F. Peltz, *Quaker-Snapple: $1.4 Billion Is Down the Drain*, L.A. TIMES, Mar. 28, 1997. As a result, the Quaker-Snapple acquisition is often ranked as one of the biggest M&A flops of all time.

William Redmond left Quaker in 1996 and has since become a serial CEO, mostly in the consume- products space. *See* his *BusinessWeek biography*.

Donald R. Uzzi also left Quaker in 1996 and has gone on to various high-level corporate leadership roles. In 2003, he settled charges with the Securities & Exchange Commission regarding allegedly false financial statements made at his post-Quaker employer, Sunbeam. *See* SEC v. Albert Dunlap, No. 01-8437-CIV (Jan. 27, 2003).

C.   Customer Lists as a Trade Secret

Lists of actual or prospective customers are another critical category of trade secrets. The conventional wisdom is that it's easier and cheaper to make a new sale to an existing customer than to procure a new customer. After all, an existing customer already knows the company, has already chosen it and is more likely to have a favorable firsthand experience. Therefore, companies derive significant value from their customer lists.

Meanwhile, a company's list of existing customers would be a very useful list of prospective customers for a competitor that would simultaneously help build the rival's business and take away that business from the company.

Like the *Pepsico* case, the following case involves a former employer lawsuit against a departing employee. In *Pepsico*, Redmond did not bring over Pepsi's customer list to his new employer. This time, the employee did. What parts, if any, of the customer list qualify as a trade secret? How much of the list's value resides in the customers' identities (without any contact info), the salesperson's knowledge of the customer's unique preferences, or any personal relationship that the salesperson may have developed over the years with the customer? Does (and should) trade secret protection extend to all three of these attributes?

GARY VAN ZEELAND TALENT, INC. V. SANDAS, 84 WIS. 2D 202 (1978)

The appeal is from a summary judgment which dismissed the complaint of Gary Van Zeeland Talent, Inc., against its former employee, Edwin J. Sandas. Van Zeeland is a talent booking agency. Its principal business is placing musical groups in nightclubs and other places of entertainment.

Sandas, who had no previous experience in talent agency work, became an employee of Van Zeeland in 1972. Van Zeeland trained him in the methods of working with musical groups and clubs and the importance of matching musical talent to the needs of a club. Sandas was, however, a former band musician, and he was familiar with the procedures of booking bands through agents.

Sandas left the employment of Van Zeeland in 1975. Prior to the time he did so, he made copies of his employer's club or "customer" list. He admitted that he took the list because he was planning to start his own business in competition with Van Zeeland Talent, Inc. Shortly after termination of his employment, he commenced his own talent agency. . . .

We conclude that the customer list was not a trade secret. The list which Sandas took was prepared for the sole purpose of assuring that Christmas cards were sent to all Van Zeeland's customers. Because it did not contain street addresses, it was not used for actual mailing purposes, but only for the purpose of determining that Christmas cards had been sent to the customers on the list. It contained no street addresses, no telephone numbers, no business information in respect to the type of music preferred by the customer, no names of managers or owners, and no other information of any kind other than the club name, the city, and the state.

Van Zeeland kept far more extensive information about its customers than was contained in the list taken by Sandas. It kept billing records, the names of bands placed with various clubs, the dates of engagements, the individuals with whom the placements were made, the club name, the prices, the commissions, and credit information.

The defendant's affidavit in support of the motion for summary judgment established that it would be possible to compile or prepare a list like the one taken by Sandas from other sources. It was equally undisputed that it would take time and effort to prepare such a list.

Van Zeeland acknowledged that it would be relatively simple to prepare a customer list—the names of the clubs—in comparison to the more difficult task of matching appropriate talent with those clubs. There is no assertion that any list which matched bands with customers was taken. Van Zeeland admitted that a list of customers without detailed information about club preferences would be relatively useless.

Immediately after Sandas left Van Zeeland, he commenced a competing talent agency business. It is undisputed that, during the second month following the commencement of his own businesses, 80 percent of the telephone calls made by Sandas in placing bands were to clubs listed on the document taken from Van Zeeland.

Additionally, it is undisputed that, at the time that Sandas joined Van Zeeland, he signed an employment agreement which, among other provisions, contained the following:

7. Disclosure of information. The Employee recognizes and acknowledges that the list of the Employer's customers, as it may exist from time to time, is a valuable, special, and unique asset of the Employer's business. The Employee will not, during or after the term of his employment, disclose the list of the Employer's customers or any part thereof to any person, firm, corporation, association, or other entity for any reason or purpose whatsoever. In the event of a breach or threatened breach by the Employee of the provisions of this paragraph, the Employer shall be entitled to an injunction restraining the Employee from disclosing, in whole or in part, the list of the Employer's customers, or from rendering any services to any person, firm, corporation, association, or other entity to whom such list, in whole or in part, has been disclosed or is threatened to be disclosed. Nothing herein shall be construed as prohibiting the Employer from pursuing any other remedies available to the Employer for such breach or threatened breach, including the recovery of damages from the Employee.

Under these undisputed facts, then, the initial question is whether the customer list taken by Sandas was a trade secret entitled to legal protection.

Customer lists, in some circumstances, may be protected as trade secrets. Restatement of Torts, sec. 757, comment b at 5 (1939), defines a trade secret:

A trade secret may consist of any formula, pattern, device or compilation of information which is used in one's business, and which gives him an opportunity to obtain an advantage over competitors who do not know or use it.

. . . [T]he general rule is that customer lists are not protected, and it is in the unusual case that such lists will be afforded the status of a trade secret. The difficulty in making this determination is capsulized in Alexander, *Commercial Torts*, sec. 3.4, p. 216 (1973), when he states:

Perhaps more than any other area of trade-secret law, customer lists present problems of extreme commercial importance and of a close balancing of the interest of the employer and employee.

. . . It is apparent that what Van Zeeland seeks in this action is the restraint of competition, and it seeks to prevent Sandas from offering similar services to customers on the list which have previously been afforded musical booking services by Van Zeeland. The question basically, then, is whether such special protection contrary to the old and well established concepts of the common law should be afforded to Van Zeeland under the circumstances of this case.

A general statement of the relevant balancing factors which may be applied in determining whether a customer list should be protected under the trade secrets concept is contained in *Developments in the Law—Competitive Torts*, 77 Harv. L. Rev. 888, 955-56 (1964):

The use of customer lists and contacts by ex-employees stands on the periphery of trade secret law. Written customer lists generally have been regarded as trade secrets when the nature of the industry permits the list to be kept secret and the list cannot readily be duplicated by independent means. The size of the list and the type of information it contains about the customers may be relevant to the latter determination, as may the amount of time and effort which went into its composition.

Some economic considerations militate against protecting customer lists. Most are developed in the normal course of business and probably would be produced whether or not protected. The customer benefits from their promulgation, for more firms then compete for his order. Also, once someone has discovered a customer with particular preferences, it is wasted effort for other firms to have to discover him again. Incentive to compile lists may be strengthened by legal protection in a few cases; and without protection businesses will guard lists more closely, with resulting inefficiency and diversion of resources into industrial security. However, economic arguments for protecting customer lists are at best marginal and the case for protection rests almost entirely on the need to deter employee disloyalty. (footnotes omitted)

The philosophical position of this court has been set forth in two recent cases, *Abbott Laboratories v. Norse Chemical Corp.*, 33 Wis. 2d 445 (1967), and *American Welding & Engineering Co., Inc., v. Luebke*, 37 Wis. 2d 697 (1968). In both *Abbott* and *American Welding*, we considered the six factors mentioned in Restatement of Torts, sec. 757, comment b at 6 (1939), as being relevant in determining whether the material sought to be protected is a trade secret. That comment states:

Some factors to be considered in determining whether given information is one's trade secret are: (1) the extent to which the information is known outside of his business; (2) the extent to which it is known by employees and others involved in his business; (3) the extent of measures taken by him to guard the secrecy of the information; (4) the value of the information to him and to his competitors; (5) the amount of effort or money expended by him in developing the information; (6) the ease or difficulty with which the information could be properly acquired or duplicated by others.

. . . The Van Zeeland list was completely silent in respect to key personnel to be contacted and failed even to include street addresses. There was, indeed, complicated marketing data which was compiled by Van Zeeland which was included in its ordinary business records, which reflected the musical placements with individual customers, the individual dealt with, and the credit record of the customer. There is nothing in the record, however, to show that any attempt was made to keep this information secret, and such information was not taken by Sandas.

In *Abbott*, we pointed out that a customer list for artificial sweeteners was a matter of common knowledge and was available through trade journals throughout the industry. In the instant case, the evidence revealed that the customers for musical entertainment could be located easily through telephone directories, calls to chambers of commerce, and newspaper advertising. It is quite apparent then that the information contained on the list was readily available to anyone within or without the Van Zeeland business who wished to go through the routine of making inquiries from established sources. No special knowledge or expertise was required to gather this information. Moreover, the information on the list was only of marginal value to anyone. Van Zeeland's own testimony acknowledged that information merely in respect to the names and locations of the clubs was insufficient. Van Zeeland's testimony was capsulized in the plaintiff counsel's synopsis of testimony, "One must know the nature of each particular club with whom one deals. I procure this information by calling clubs."

It is apparent that the type of information which Van Zeeland considered important could not be contained in any listing or summary of club names and state and city addresses. . . .

The tenor of the Van Zeeland brief on this appeal reveals that much of Van Zeeland's concern is not over the utility of the customer list to Sandas or over the deprivation of the exclusive use of that list by Van Zeeland, but rather the concern that Sandas, in the course of his employment, had acquired such expertise and know-how in the placement of musical groups as to make him a significant competitor. Much of the Van Zeeland brief is concerned with the fact that Sandas came to Van Zeeland as a twenty-one-year-old impoverished cookware salesman but has now left the organization after having been trained by Van Zeeland to such an extent that he is an expert in talent placement. The law, however, does not protect against that type of unfairness, if unfairness it be. Rather, it encourages the mobility of workers; and so long as a departing employee takes with him no more than his experience and intellectual development that has ensued while being trained by another, and no trade secrets or processes are wrongfully appropriated, the law affords no recourse. . . .

We accordingly conclude, applying the general standards developed in *Abbott* and *American Welding* and the basic considerations of the Restatement of Torts, sec. 757, that the Van Zeeland customer list did not constitute a trade secret. . . .

Van Zeeland's customer list was at best of only transitory value. Like the customer list in *American Welding*, it was probably partially obsolete at the time it came into Sandas' possession. The information contained in the Van Zeeland customer list is now, less than three years after Sandas left the employment, already of greatly diminished value. Exhibit 3, incorporated in the record, lists 1200 clubs. Of the 30 clubs listed in Milwaukee, only 16 are currently listed in the Milwaukee telephone directory, and of the 23 listed in Madison, only 11 are currently listed in the Madison telephone directory. It is apparent that this information was of only transitory significance . . .

NOTES AND QUESTIONS

Was Sandas' Behavior Ethical? The talent agency hired a youthful Sandas and taught him the business. Sandas contractually agreed not to take customer lists or to compete with the talent agency, and Sandas admitted that he could have recreated this list without taking it. Why did Sandas take the list instead of recreating it? Irrespective of the legal conclusion, was it right for him to do so? How would you counsel a new client who revealed that he had taken information from a previous employer to start his own business?

Even if you support Sandas' choices, you might nevertheless sympathize with the talent agency. What could the talent agency have done differently to successfully restrict Sandas' ability to leave the agency and go into competition with it after teaching him everything?

Customer Lists vs. Customer Relationships. In many sales-driven organizations, the customer list is not really valuable by itself. Instead, the real value lies in the personal relationships the salesperson forms with the customer contacts. Employers can have a difficult time maintaining these personal relationships when the salesperson leaves. Without an enforceable non-compete agreement from the salesperson (no easy feat), customers are likely to follow the salesperson to his or her new home.

Customer Lists in an Internet Era. Given how the Internet has made it so much easier to compile factual information, including research on prospective customers, should we be less concerned about the taking of customer lists, especially if they do not contain any enhanced information uniquely added by the employer?

2.   Patents

Overview of Patents

The patent system is complex and full of arcane nuances, so this overview is necessarily simplified. Novel, useful and non-obvious ideas are eligible for patent protection.[*] To obtain a patent, the inventor (or the inventor's assignee) submits an application to the U.S. Patent & Trademark Office. Between filing fees and legal bills, a typical patent application costs more than $10,000 just to file with the government (in some cases substantially more). A patent examiner reviews the application, provides comments to the applicant and ultimately decides whether or not the patent should issue. It typically takes several years and at least $50,000 to get an issued patent.

An issued patent provides the owner with the exclusive right to make, use, sell, offer for sale or import the invention for the patent's duration, which is typically twenty years from the filing date for the patent application. The patent does not grant the affirmative right to commercialize the invention. For example, biotech-related patents still require FDA approval before the invention can be commercialized. A patent owner also can decide not to exploit or license the patented idea at all.

Patent litigation is a high-stakes affair. Because patents effectively allow the patent owner to control a product market, alleged patent infringers are often fighting for the ability to continue their commercial activity—and they are willing to reinvest some of their expected profits to do so. Meanwhile, patent damages can be large—awards of hundreds of millions of dollars (or more) are possible—and sometimes a patent owner is trying to exclude other companies from a market to keep competition from degrading prices and profits. Due to the high stakes and arcane nature of both patent law and patented technology, both litigants

---

[*] There are three types of patents: utility, design and plant patents. We will address only utility patents.

often spend a lot of money. Many law firms quote a patent litigant (plaintiff or defendant) an anticipated price tag of $5+ million to reach a trial.

To get a patent, the applicant must describe the patented invention well enough that other industry players could replicate the invention. This means that when a patent application becomes public (typically, eighteen months after filing), competitors can review the patent, learn from it, and use the patent application's ideas to spur new ones outside the patent's scope. Further, when the patent expires, everyone is free to use the invention with the help of the public disclosures made in the patent process. As discussed earlier, Coca-Cola has been able to get over a century of extra protection for its distinctive soda formula by relying on trade secret protection instead of patents.

Meanwhile, once the application is published, a patent applicant cannot claim the information disclosed in the application as a trade secret—even if the application eventually is not granted.

Finally, in industries with rapidly evolving technologies, lengthy time periods for getting issued patents (the four+ year application period) degrades the patents' usefulness. In those cases, by the time the patent has issued, the industry has cycled to the next generation of technology.

Patents and the Advertising Industry

Historically, most advertising lawyers spent very little time thinking about patents. However, that may be changing, and patents play an increasingly important role in the advertising industry. There are now patents on just about every corner of the advertising business, such as *Patent #6757661* (issued June 29, 2004) for "high-volume targeting of advertisements to user of online service," or *Patent #4024660* (issued May 24, 1977) for an "advertising pocket for shopping carts."

Many patents in the advertising industry protect a method of advertising (a "business method"); and many of those methods are performed by encoding the method in software. The Supreme Court has repeatedly cast doubt on the validity of business-method and software patents, though its opinions have not quite rejected them outright. *See, e.g.*, Alice Corp. Pty. Ltd v. CLS Bank Int'l, 134 S. Ct. 2347 (2014); Bilski v. Kappos, 561 U.S. 593 (2010). This leaves business-method and software patents, including those related to advertising, in an uncertain but precarious position. *See, e.g.*, Customedia Tech. v. DISH Network, 951 F.3d 1359 (Fed. Cir. 2020) (patent claiming a way of facilitating targeted advertising via a multimedia system was invalid; "do[ing] a known thing on a computer" is not patent-eligible).

Advertising lawyers should be aware of statutory time limits for filing patent applications. In the United States, patent applicants have a one-year grace period after they "offer" the invention for sale to file a patent application. Any subsequently filed patent application for that invention will be time-barred. Advertising a patentable invention (even in a one-to-one sales pitch) often qualifies as an "offer" for sale. In foreign countries, there is no one-year grace period; an offer for sale in the United States may immediately and permanently forego the ability to file any further foreign patent applications on the advertised product. Therefore, when an advertiser initially begins advertising a new product, advertising counsel should double-check that the client has filed all desired patent applications on the advertised product or is prepared to forego some or all patent protection for the product.

3.   Idea Submissions

There are a surprisingly large number of lawsuits—including advertising-related cases—over a company benefiting from a commercially valuable idea submitted by a third party. We refer to these cases as "idea-submission" cases. Ideas can be submitted in a variety of ways, ranging from an oral "elevator pitch" to submission through postal mail or email.

Idea-submission cases can implicate multiple legal doctrines. An idea might be protectable under patent or trade secret law; a written submission might be protectable under copyright law, although copyright does not protect the ideas as such; and there could be an express, implied-in-fact or quasi- contract between the discloser and the recipient governing the idea transmission. Occasionally, courts will find protection for a submitted idea even if none of these legal doctrines apply.

Although most idea-submission lawsuits fail eventually, companies usually try to reduce their exposure to idea-submission cases, such as refusing to open any unsolicited postal mail and putting legends on web feedback forms indicating that the feedback submitter waives any claims for the company's subsequent use of the feedback.

Try to figure out why the next two cases reach divergent conclusions. Pay attention to the specific role of contracts in each.

BURGESS V. COCA-COLA CO., 245 GA. APP. 206 (GA. APP. CT. 2000)

Robert L. Burgess sued The Coca-Cola Company ("Coca-Cola") for allegedly taking his creative ideas and using them in a commercial that featured anthropomorphic polar bears drinking Coca-Cola. Burgess sought recovery under theories of misappropriation of ideas, breach of express and implied contract, breach of a confidential relationship, unjust enrichment, quantum meruit, and promissory estoppel. After two years of discovery during which over thirty-five people were deposed, Coca-Cola moved for summary judgment. Following a lengthy hearing, the trial court granted Coca-Cola's motion. For the following reasons, we affirm. . . .

. . . Burgess approached Coca-Cola in January 1989 to pitch a creative concept he referred to as "The Fantastic World of Coca-Cola." There is no evidence that Coca-Cola agreed to compensate Burgess for the disclosure of his idea prior to his pitching it for the first time to Coca-Cola executive John B. White. The presentation included seven storyboards which depicted various aspects of the concept. This "Fantastic World," as Burgess explained, was an imaginary world located inside a Coca-Cola vending machine and populated with a wide variety of Coca-Cola characters, including, as shown by one of the storyboards, a family of white teddy bear-like "cola bears" making ice to cool the Coca-Cola. Burgess also provided

White with a written narrative of his concept. This first narrative did not mention bears. White told Burgess he was not in a position to help him. However, believing the concept might be suitable for a toy line, White introduced Burgess to Bruce Gilbert and Mike Ellison with Coca-Cola's Merchandise Licensing Division.

After hearing the "Fantastic World" pitch, Gilbert told Burgess he was intrigued by the idea of doing a line of Coca-Cola toys. However, Gilbert explained to Burgess that Coca-Cola was not in the business of manufacturing toys; rather, it licensed its trademark to companies for use on merchandise. Therefore, both Gilbert and Ellison told Burgess that before Coca-Cola could proceed any further, Burgess would have to interest a major toy company in his idea. Gilbert and Ellison informed Burgess orally and by letter dated January 12, 1989, that any compensation for the use of his idea would come only from the toy manufacturer. Coca-Cola then introduced Burgess to executives with Kenner Toys in Cincinnati, Ohio.

Burgess pitched his same "Fantastic World" idea to Kenner representatives in February 1989. Initially, they were impressed. The representatives were especially pleased with the cola bears and asked Burgess to develop his ideas further. On March 14, 1989, Kenner made a presentation to Coca-Cola using storyboards developed by Kenner and by Burgess. Coca-Cola liked the presentation, which focused on a line of plush toy teddy bears to be marketed to children between two and ten years of age. On June 14, 1989, the toy idea was again pitched to senior Coca-Cola executives who agreed that Kenner could move forward with its development of the toy line. However, because its products had never been marketed to such young children, Coca-Cola asked Kenner in a letter dated August 18, 1989, to obtain a "seal of approval" from a reputable organization as well as a safety endorsement from an independent company before Coca-Cola would agree to licensing its trademark.

While it worked to satisfy Coca-Cola's conditions, Kenner began negotiations regarding the payment of royalties to Coca-Cola for use of its trademark and to Burgess for his creative efforts. While in the process of finalizing the deal, Kenner began test-marketing the sale of Coca-Cola plush toys, including a teddy bear. The results were surprisingly negative. Consequently, Kenner decided to abandon the project and to release Burgess to pitch his "Fantastic World" idea to other companies. Kenner paid Burgess $25,000 for his efforts on their behalf. There is no evidence that Burgess performed any consulting services for Coca-Cola. Further, Burgess admits that Coca-Cola never reached any agreement with him or with Kenner regarding the payment of royalties.

Burgess presented his "Fantastic World" toy idea to other companies, but they were not interested. From 1989 to 1992, Burgess also continued to contact different Coca-Cola executives, attempting to generate interest in various aspects of his idea, for example, a commercial about an evil character who steals the Coca-Cola recipe. The ideas were all related to the overall "Fantastic World" theme and involved many different characters, including "space aliens" and "cola kids." The evidence is undisputed that Coca-Cola never implemented, nor contracted with any licensee to implement, Burgess' "Fantastic World" concept.

In July 1991, Coca-Cola hired Creative Artists Agency ("CAA") of Hollywood, California, to develop new advertising. CAA was responsible for generating fresh advertising ideas for

Coca-Cola's consideration. Coca-Cola executives did not participate in any aspect of CAA's creative process; they only reviewed the final submissions. One of the many concepts approved and ultimately made into a commercial was "Bears at the Theater." This commercial featured a family of anthropomorphic polar bears who were drinking Coca-Cola while they watched the aurora borealis. The commercial was the idea of Ken Stewart, the husband of a CAA executive. The evidence shows that Stewart came up with the idea on his own, free from any input from Coca-Cola personnel. He was unaware of any of Burgess' ideas. In fact, Stewart was inspired by his Labrador Retriever puppy, who apparently looked like a polar bear. Burgess presented no evidence from which a jury could reasonably infer that Stewart's idea for the "Bears at the Theater" commercial was created using Burgess' "Fantastic World" concept or any of its parts, including the cola bears.

The "Bears in the Theater" commercial, first broadcast in 1993, was one of twenty-seven commercial spots aired as part of Coca-Cola's "Always" campaign. Because "Bears in the Theater" was so well received by the public, Coca-Cola produced several more commercials focusing on the polar bear family. The success of these commercials prompted several companies to contact Coca-Cola for the rights to market plush and plastic Coca-Cola CAA polar bear figurines. Coca-Cola eventually agreed to license the CAA polar bear to several different companies.

Burgess claimed that the CAA polar bear, with its human attributes and family values, was taken from the cola bears he had envisioned in his Fantastic World. Not only did Coca-Cola adduce evidence showing that the CAA polar bear was independently created by Stewart, it introduced evidence showing that the use of a polar bear "spokescharacter" was not novel. First, Coca-Cola demonstrated a long history of various companies using animated anthropomorphic animals as product spokescharacters, including Kellogg's Tony the Tiger, Star Kist's Charlie the Tuna, and Nine Lives' Morris the Cat. Walter Maes, an advertising executive with 27 years of experience, explained that anthropomorphic characters have been used in the industry for decades and that there is nothing novel about such spokescharacters generally. Second, Robert Vianello, a professor of film and television, pointed out that anthropomorphic bears have been put to a number of commercial uses predating Burgess' disclosure of his idea to Coca-Cola. For example, the Icee Company has had an animated polar bear representing its frozen drink products since the 1960s. Such widespread use of anthropomorphic bears was further evidenced by the book, *Teddy Bears in Advertising Art.* Third and finally, Coca-Cola has used anthropomorphic bears, including polar bears, in its own advertising on many occasions since 1923. Coca-Cola used an anthropomorphic white bear called "Teddy Snow Crop" to market its Minute Maid frozen orange juice in 1961. It has also licensed the use of its "Enjoy Coke" logo on a variety of plush animals, including bears.

1.

(a) To survive summary judgment on a claim for wrongful appropriation of or for conversion of an unpatented or unpatentable idea or product, a plaintiff must adduce some evidence from which a jury may infer the existence of each of these essential elements: "1) the idea must be novel; 2) the disclosure of the idea must be made in confidence; 3) the idea must be adopted and made use of by the defendant; and 4) the idea must be sufficiently concrete in its development to be usable." Burgess argues that the CAA anthropomorphic polar bear featured in Coca-Cola's "Always" campaign was an unauthorized use of the cola bears element of his "Fantastic World of Coca-Cola" concept. However, even if Coca-Cola had made use of Burgess' cola bears idea, which the evidence does not support, Burgess' claim fails because using an anthropomorphic polar bear to sell a soft drink is not a novel idea.

As we have held:

> To be novel the concept must be peculiar and not generally available or known to others in the trade. To be protected, an idea must possess genuine novelty and invention, which it cannot have if it merely is an adaptation of existing knowledge, albeit a clever, useful, or sensible adaptation.

Coca-Cola demonstrated that anthropomorphic bears, including polar bears, had been used to sell a number of products, including its own, decades before Burgess ever pitched his "Fantastic World" concept. In short, it was simply a variation on an existing theme. That Burgess' cola bears were presented in a fresh or different setting does not constitute novelty because "creating a new and better way of doing something" already existent is not sufficient. "Without the element of novelty [Burgess] was deprived of an essential element entitling [him] to recover."

(b) Further, even if Burgess' concept was novel, he is not entitled to recover when the unrebutted evidence shows that Stewart and CAA created "Bears at the Theater" on their own initiative, by wholly independent means, and without any input or information from Coca-Cola or Burgess. Because Coca-Cola is entitled to the complete defense of "independent creation," the trial court properly granted summary judgment on this claim.

2.

Each of Burgess' remaining claims depends upon his nonnovel idea acting either as consideration for a promise between Coca-Cola and himself or as a benefit conferred upon Coca-Cola. As we have held, however, under these circumstances, nonnovel ideas are insufficient "to serve as consideration for a promise of confidentiality[2] or as a basis for asserting unjust enrichment." Burgess' remaining claims fail as a matter of law because nonnovel ideas do not constitute protected property interests under Georgia law. Therefore, nonnovel ideas are inadequate as consideration, and "when one submits [such] an idea to another, no promise to pay for its use may be implied, and no asserted agreement enforced." Similarly, because a nonnovel idea confers no benefit upon the defendant, claims based upon quantum meruit and unjust enrichment for a defendant's alleged use of the idea must fail. And, because nonnovel ideas lack value sufficient to create a property interest, the unauthorized use of another's nonnovel idea would not result in an injustice, a necessary element in a promissory estoppel claim. Therefore, Burgess' claim for promissory estoppel must also fail. In fact, under these circumstances, "[l]ack of novelty in an idea is fatal to any cause of action for its unlawful use." Consequently, we find no error in the trial court's grant of summary judgment to Coca-Cola on Burgess' remaining claims.

TACO BELL CORP. V. TBWA CHIAT/DAY INC., 552 F.3D 1137 (9TH CIR. 2009)

Taco Bell Corp. ("Taco Bell") appeals the district court's summary judgment in favor of its former advertising agency, TBWA Worldwide, Inc. ("TBWA"), in Taco Bell's lawsuit seeking indemnification. This case follows a judgment issued against Taco Bell in the federal district court for the Western District of Michigan for breach by Taco Bell of an implied contract for using a third party's Chihuahua character in its advertising developed by TBWA. Taco Bell sought indemnification from TBWA on the ground that the liability Taco Bell incurred in favor of the third party was caused by TBWA. . . .

I. Background

In June 1996, Ed Alfaro, a licensing manager at Taco Bell, attended a trade show in New York where he first discovered a cartoon depiction of a Chihuahua dog character ("Psycho Chihuahua") being marketed by its creators, Tom Rinks and Joe Shields of Wrench LLC, a Michigan corporation (collectively, "Wrench"). Alfaro told Rinks and Shields that he wanted to explore the use of Psycho Chihuahua by Taco Bell.

During the Summer and Fall of 1996, Wrench provided Taco Bell with goods bearing Psycho Chihuahua's image. From that time through June 1997, Alfaro tried to build support within Taco Bell for its use of Psycho Chihuahua in its advertising. He showed the goods to Taco Bell's senior managers and advertising agency at that time, Bozell Worldwide ("Bozell"). Taco Bell conducted a focus group study which included Psycho Chihuahua and several other designs. Alfaro reported to a senior Taco Bell executive that Psycho Chihuahua was the most popular out of all the designs.

In November 1996, Taco Bell and Wrench's licensing agent, Strategy Licensing, discussed the possible use of Psycho Chihuahua as Taco Bell's mascot and Taco Bell requested that

---

[2] There is no evidence that a confidential relationship as defined in OCGA § 23-2-58 existed between Coca-Cola and Burgess prior to his disclosing his "Fantastic World" concept. As we have held, the mere fact that two persons have transacted business in the past based on oral commitments or understandings and that they have come to repose trust and confidence in each other as the result of such dealings is not sufficient, in and of itself, to warrant a finding that a confidential relationship exists between them within the contemplation of the Code section.

Strategy Licensing submit a proposal on financial terms for the use of Psycho Chihuahua. On November 18, 1996, Strategy Licensing submitted a proposal but Taco Bell did not accept it. Discussions continued about Taco Bell's possible use of Psycho Chihuahua and Taco Bell understood that if it decided to use that character, Taco Bell would have to pay Wrench for such use.

In February 1997, Taco Bell's then-parent company, Pepsi Co., made a presentation to Taco Bell's marketing department regarding the possibility of using Psycho Chihuahua in a Taco Bell "Cinco de Mayo" promotion. Taco Bell then conducted additional focus group studies on Psycho Chihuahua which resulted in positive consumer response.

In March 1997, Taco Bell changed advertising agencies from Bozell to TBWA. Taco Bell commissioned TBWA to create a new advertising campaign for 1998.

Between February and April 1997, Alfaro continued to work with Wrench to develop possibilities for Taco Bell's use of Psycho Chihuahua.

In May 1997, TBWA presented approximately thirty advertising ideas to Taco Bell for its new campaign. One of the ideas involved a male Chihuahua dog passing a female Chihuahua dog to get to Taco Bell food. The executives to which the ideas were presented included Taco Bell's president, Peter Waller, and its chief marketing officer, Vada Hill. Waller and Hill selected TBWA's Chihuahua idea as one of the five advertisements that would be test-marketed during the Summer of 1997. Months later, market research demonstrated favorable results for the TBWA Chihuahua test advertisement and Waller and Hill chose that character as the center of its new advertising campaign starting in January 1998.

Meanwhile, Alfaro believed the character Wrench had created from the original Psycho Chihuahua closely resembled the TBWA Chihuahua to be used in Taco Bell commercials. He alerted Taco Bell's in-house counsel that Wrench would likely sue because of the similarities between the characters. Taco Bell sent a box of Psycho Chihuahua materials to TBWA at some point between June 27, 1997 and July 26, 1997. Alfaro drafted a memorandum that accompanied the materials, describing the parallel path he had taken with Wrench and their idea of using a Chihuahua to advertise Taco Bell food.

By January 1998, Taco Bell began using a Chihuahua to advertise its food. Wrench then sued Taco Bell, claiming that Taco Bell was using Psycho Chihuahua in its advertising without providing compensation to Wrench. Wrench LLC v. Taco Bell Corp., 51 F. Supp. 2d 840 (W.D. Mich. 1999).

In February 1998, Taco Bell and TBWA entered into a joint defense and confidentiality agreement ("Joint Defense Agreement"). They also executed a contract controlling their business relationship ("Agency Agreement"). The Agency Agreement was executed January 19, 1999 but the parties agreed to make the effective date retroactive to April 1, 1997 to include all of TBWA's services to Taco Bell from the beginning of their business relationship.

In its defense in *Wrench*, Taco Bell alleged there was no contract with Wrench because Alfaro had no authority to bind the company, the Chihuahua character used by Taco Bell was not Psycho Chihuahua, and the Chihuahua character used by Taco Bell was independently created by TBWA.

TBWA created and broadcast over forty more Chihuahua commercials between January 1998 and June 2000. In June 2003, the *Wrench* jury determined that Taco Bell had breached an implied contract by using Psycho Chihuahua without compensating Wrench. All copyright claims were disposed of prior to trial. A judgment was entered against Taco Bell in the amount of $30,174,031.00, and the court subsequently amended the judgment to account for pre-judgment and post-judgment interest, bringing the total to over $42,000,000.00.

Taco Bell requested full indemnification from TBWA for its liability to Wrench. Within weeks of the *Wrench* trial, Taco Bell filed this lawsuit against TBWA, suing it for breach of the Agency Agreement, express indemnification, and declaratory relief. Both sides moved for summary judgment. The district court denied Taco Bell's motion and granted TBWA's cross-motion. Summary judgment was entered in favor of TBWA, and this appeal followed.

II. Discussion . . .

A. *Wrench* Verdict

The first issue we consider is whether the *Wrench* jury findings are proof of TBWA's fault, obligating it to indemnify Taco Bell for the liability Taco Bell incurred.

A verdict sheet that was provided to the *Wrench* jury reflects what that jury found:

> Question Number 1: Did Wrench prove by a preponderance of the evidence that Wrench and Taco Bell had a mutual understanding that if Taco Bell used the Psycho Chihuahua character in its advertising and on products, Taco Bell would pay Wrench for this use?

> Question Number 2: Did Wrench prove by a preponderance of the evidence that Taco Bell used the Psycho Chihuahua character in its advertising from 1997 to 2000 and that the character used by Taco Bell was not independently created by [TWBA]?

> Question Number 3: Did Wrench prove by a preponderance of the evidence that it suffered damages because Taco Bell did not pay for its use of the Psycho Chihuahua character?

The *Wrench* jury answered all three questions affirmatively.

According to Taco Bell, these findings are proof of TBWA's fault. Because TBWA was involved in the creation of the TBWA Chihuahua character and TBWA had possession of the Psycho Chihuahua materials, Taco Bell argues the jury's findings that Psycho Chihuahua was used by Taco Bell and the character used was not independently created by TBWA confirms wrongdoing by TBWA. Taco Bell relies heavily on the second question in the verdict sheet submitted to the *Wrench* jury, but as to that question, the court in the *Wrench* trial instructed the jury:

> Let me give you some things to consider in determining whether the Taco Bell Chihuahua is the same character as the Psycho Chihuahua character. . . .

> If you find that the Taco Bell Chihuahua is the same character as the Psycho Chihuahua character, then you must still consider whether, on the one hand, Taco Bell used Wrench's creation of the Psycho Chihuahua character or, on the other hand, whether Taco Bell and [TBWA] created the Taco Bell Chihuahua on an independent creative, but parallel path.

> In answering this question, in addition to considering the differences and similarities—differences between and similarities of the two dogs, as I pointed out in the preceding paragraph, you should consider . . . the access or lack thereof to the Psycho Chihuahua character by people at Taco Bell and [TBWA].

Considering these instructions to the *Wrench* jury, no inference of fault by TBWA can be drawn from the jury's verdict. The instructions leave unclear what the *Wrench* jury determined on the issue of independent creation of the Chihuahua character. The jury was told to consider "whether Taco Bell and [TBWA] created the Taco Bell Chihuahua on an independent creative, but parallel path." The court also asked the jury to consider "the access or lack thereof to the Psycho Chihuahua character by people at Taco Bell and [TBWA]." The *Wrench* jury was never instructed to differentiate between Taco Bell and TBWA or determine which party was at fault for the liability to Wrench.

The undisputed facts do not support a finding of fault or negligence on the part of TBWA. TBWA was not a party to the implied contract between Taco Bell and Wrench and was unaware of its existence. TBWA had no knowledge of Psycho Chihuahua nor Taco Bell's contact with Wrench before proposing a Chihuahua character for Taco Bell advertising on June 2, 1997. The facts that Taco Bell did not have input on TBWA's creation of its advertising character and that a box of Psycho Chihuahua materials was sent to TBWA are of no consequence not only because TBWA created its own Chihuahua character before it received the Psycho Chihuahua materials, but also because Taco Bell was found liable for the use of Psycho Chihuahua without compensating Wrench, not copyright infringement. Taco Bell's arguments speak to copyright issues not pertinent to this case because those claims were disposed of before trial.

The Agency Agreement's indemnification provisions require TBWA to indemnify Taco Bell for liability incurred as a result of "(i) any materials created, produced, and/or furnished by [TBWA] for [Taco Bell] . . . (ii) [TBWA's] fault or negligence in the performance of its obligations hereunder; or (iii) [TBWA's] breach of its obligations under this Agreement." Even if liability arose from "materials created, produced, and/or furnished by [TBWA] for [Taco Bell]," Paragraph 7.1 includes an exception for claims covered by Paragraph 7.2, claims resulting from Taco Bell's fault. Although Taco Bell argues the *Wrench* jury finding warrants an inference that TBWA misappropriated Wrench's material, neither the verdict nor the undisputed facts allow a finding of TBWA's fault, but only Taco Bell's breach of a contract. The district court properly determined no obligation for TBWA to indemnify Taco Bell under the Agency Agreement arose from the verdict.

Furthermore, as properly decided by the district court, TBWA cannot be held at fault under the Agency Agreement which allows it to rely on the approval of Taco Bell. Taco Bell approved the Chihuahua character proposed by TBWA and continued to approve the Chihuahua advertisements for broadcasting after the *Wrench* lawsuit was initiated, despite the existence of its implied contractual commitment to Wrench. . . .

Taco Bell argues that its approval of advertising created by TBWA was only an approval of costs as provided for in Paragraph 4.1[2] of the Agency Agreement. This argument contradicts the statement of Taco Bell's counsel at oral argument of the summary judgment motions in the district court:

> So I would dispute strongly that there was an approval of the ads in the form of agreeing that they go forward and shifting the risk. I wouldn't dispute that there was approval in the sense of, Yes, let's run them. I think we'll sell some more tacos. That, I think there was an approval of.

---

[2] 4. Approvals and Billing Procedures.
4.1 Approvals. [TBWA] will obtain [Taco Bell's] prior approval for all work [TBWA] does on [Taco Bell's] behalf. If [TBWA] believes actual costs for production projects, subject to an estimate, will vary by more than 10%, [TBWA] will send [Taco Bell] a revised estimate for [Taco Bell's] approval. Variances under 10% will be deemed approved by [Taco Bell]. After a project is completed, [TBWA] will reconcile actual costs against the estimates and an appropriate adjustment will be made.

In addition to the fact that the commercials were broadcast, the admission of Taco Bell's counsel confirmed that Taco Bell approved the Chihuahua commercials for airing. The district court correctly considered Taco Bell's approval to broadcast the Chihuahua commercials after Wrench filed its lawsuit a dispositive factor in Taco Bell's fault-based indemnification claim against TBWA. The admission confirmed that there was approval pursuant to the Agency Agreement's authorization section.

Paragraph 6.4 of the Agency Agreement states:

> 6.4 Authorization. [TBWA] will be entitled to rely and act upon any instruction, approval or authorization given by [Taco Bell] or by any of [Taco Bell's] representatives.

Under this paragraph, TBWA was permitted to rely on Taco Bell's approval of advertising TBWA created. The district court properly relied on the fact that Taco Bell approved for airing the Chihuahua commercials between January 1998 and June 2000 while denying the existence of its contractual obligation to Wrench. Under the Agency Agreement, TBWA cannot be found at fault for liability arising from advertisements approved by Taco Bell.

B. Agency Agreement

The next issue we consider is whether TBWA is at fault for breach of the Agency Agreement, leading to Taco Bell's liability in *Wrench*. Subparagraph 7.2(iii) provides that Taco Bell will indemnify TBWA for any liability resulting from "risks which have been brought to the attention of and discussed with [Taco Bell] and [Taco Bell] has nevertheless elected to proceed as evidenced in writing and signed by either the Vice President of Advertising or Senior Vice President-Marketing of [Taco Bell]."

Taco Bell argues that the district court ignored material evidence of TBWA's breach of its obligations under Paragraph 7 to "exercise its best judgment in the preparation and placing of [Taco Bell's] advertising and publicity with a view to avoiding any claims, proceedings, or suits being made or instituted against Taco Bell." It is Taco Bell's position that it was TBWA's responsibility to make sure Taco Bell's advertising campaign did not misuse Psycho Chihuahua and TBWA breached its duty when it failed to do advertising copy clearance, uncover an application for a trademark, and bring risks of using a Chihuahua in advertising to Taco Bell's attention. Subparagraph 7.2(iii), speaking to Taco Bell's indemnification obligations to TBWA, does not require any copy clearance, trademark searches, or risk reporting by TBWA, but obligates Taco Bell to indemnify TBWA when Taco Bell elects to proceed in the event that risks are brought to its attention. Additionally, Taco Bell was the party aware of the potential risks of using a Chihuahua character in its advertising. It was Taco Bell that had an undisclosed contract with Wrench and denied the existence of that contract. Taco Bell's argument that TBWA failed to meet an obligation under the Agency Agreement by failing to do copyright and trademark searches is meritless not only because it is not supported by the language in the Agency Agreement, but also because the *Wrench* liability included neither copyright nor trademark damages. As discussed, the entire judgment was based on Taco Bell's breach of an implied contract to pay Wrench for use of Psycho Chihuahua. . . .

III. Conclusion

The district court properly concluded there is evidence only of Taco Bell's fault in its liability to Wrench. As a result, no indemnification obligation from TBWA to Taco Bell arose.

NOTES AND QUESTIONS

Idea Submission Protection and Copyright Preemption. In the related ruling of *Wrench LLC v. Taco Bell Corp.*, 256 F.3d 446 (6th Cir. 2001), the court held that copyright law didn't preempt Wrench's implied contract claim. However, in other cases, copyright preemption can narrow or eliminate an idea submission claim. Courts sometimes (but inconsistently) find contract breach claims preempted by copyright law when the contract restrictions overlap with the exclusive rights of copyright owners. Some causes of action (such as conversion or unjust enrichment) are regularly preempted by copyright law when the subject material is a copyrighted work.

Anthropomorphic Animals in Ads. The *Burgess* case indicated that using anthropomorphic animals (in that case, polar bears) lacked sufficient novelty to satisfy the claim. The *Taco Bell* litigation also involved an anthropomorphic animal (in that case, a talking Chihuahua) but reached a contrary result. Why the difference?

One possibility is that jurisdictions are split on idea novelty as a prerequisite to the plaintiff's cause of action. Some jurisdictions, such as New York, typically require novelty for an idea submission case; other jurisdictions, such as California, take a more-relaxed approach.

Reliance on Ad Agency's Independent Development. In both the *Burgess* and *Taco Bell* cases, the advertisers relied on independently created suggestions from their ad agencies. In the *Burgess* case, this independent development was sufficient to excuse the advertiser; in the *Taco Bell* case, it wasn't. Why the difference?

Coca-Cola's successful defense of independent development is actually quite remarkable. If you represented Coca-Cola or CAA, what kind of evidence would you try to present to demonstrate independent development?

Notice also the finger-pointing between the advertiser and the ad agency. Given the collaborative and iterative nature of developing an ad from concept to execution, such finger-pointing among the various players is fairly typical. We will revisit the interactions between advertisers and ad agencies in Chapter 17.

Damage Award. The *Taco Bell* jury awarded the plaintiffs over $30 million, which with interest grew to $42 million. If Taco Bell had struck a deal with the plaintiffs before the ad campaign, how much do you think Taco Bell would have paid them? Why do you think Taco Bell decided not to pay? Did Taco Bell make a bad decision, or did they make a good decision with a bad outcome?

4.   Antitrust

Like patent law, antitrust law is another complex corner of the law that warrants more in-depth coverage than this book can provide. In broad strokes, antitrust law seeks to promote competition. (A corollary: Antitrust laws protect *competition*, not *competitors*.) A competitive market maximizes "consumer welfare." Operationalizing this, antitrust targets conduct that reduces competition and harms consumer welfare by increasing price, reducing output or offering consumers inferior options. In some cases, antitrust violations can be criminal. Antitrust violations can also trigger treble damages, attorneys' fees and costs.

The use of advertising usually does not raise specific antitrust concerns. For example, although monopolies often raise antitrust scrutiny, "monopolistic competition"—the process of developing consumer brand loyalty sufficient to allow commodity manufacturers to charge supra-competitive prices—does not inherently implicate antitrust law. In part, this reflects the prevailing views of economists (discussed in Chapter 2) that advertising is pro-competitive.

Many antitrust cases involve a battle over the applicable standard of legal review. The two main ones are "rule of reason" and "per se," although numerous variations exist. The "rule of reason" standard evaluates the reasonableness of the anticompetitive behavior based on a consideration of all facts and circumstances. Because of its inclusive review process, "rule of reason" inquiry makes it hard to determine the legitimacy of a company's choices ex ante. The "per se" standard means the choice is presumptively illegal unless rebutted by a satisfactorily legitimate explanation. Examples of "per se" illegal activities include agreements among competitors to fix prices or restrict production—in such cases, the law prohibits the behavior whether or not the defendants constitute a "monopoly" in the ordinary sense, because price-fixing and coordinated-output restrictions are considered to be inherently detrimental to the proper functioning of markets.

Antitrust also restricts industry-dominant companies from taking advantage of their "market power." This often prompts a debate about what constitutes the "relevant market" to determine if the company in fact has market power in that market. For example: Is Amazon an "Internet retailer" or a "retailer"? Antitrust plaintiffs in monopolization cases favor defining the relevant market more narrowly, while antitrust defendants favor defining the relevant market more broadly. To resolve which market is the relevant market (and thus what share of the market the defendant has), economists are often used to argue about what prospective customers view as viable substitute offerings.

A.   Competitive Harm from False Advertising

One central element of a competitive market is advertising. Thus, as discussed in the next section, courts in antitrust cases and the FTC in its role as antitrust enforcer have often looked askance at coordinated attempts by competitors to restrict truthful advertising.

But what of *false* advertising? As the Supreme Court has "long established, . . . false or misleading advertising has an anticompetitive effect." California Dental Ass'n v. Federal Trade Comm'n, 526 U.S. 756 (1999). In one important sense, false advertising clearly harms the market as a whole: It erects barriers to the success of truthfully advertising competitors, making even truthful claims less believable and encouraging a "market for lemons," as discussed in Chapter 4. But antitrust and false advertising law, as distinct branches of "unfair competition" law, have diverged doctrinally in their treatment of false advertising. For an argument that this divergence has harmed consumers, *see* Michael A. Carrier & Rebecca Tushnet, *An Antitrust Framework for False Advertising* (forthcoming, IOWA L. REV. 2021).

On the most-general level, there is a higher bar to the application of antitrust law, as harm is required to the market as a whole before there can be an antitrust violation. False advertising, in contrast, can occur even if just an individual competitor is injured (along with the deceived consumers who are both the mechanisms by which harm is inflicted on a competitor and victims in their own right). Reciprocally, there are significant barriers to proving a monopolization claim. Demonstrating monopoly power involves the challenges of defining a market and showing power within that market; even if the defendant is a monopolist, it is not liable for causing harm to competition unless it has engaged in "exclusionary conduct."

Antitrust cases have developed three approaches to false advertising that allegedly constitutes exclusionary conduct, with no governing standard yet provided by the Supreme Court. The first approach completely absolves false advertisers of antitrust liability. The second assumes that false advertising causes de minimis harm. The third offers a case-by-case approach.

No Liability

In the Fifth and Seventh Circuits, courts have reasoned that false statements enhance competition in advertising markets and that antitrust claims based on disparaging rivals are not actionable. For example, *Sanderson v. Culligan*, 415 F.3d 620 (7th Cir. 2005), stated that "[c]ommercial speech is not actionable under the antitrust laws." The court asserted that "[a]ntitrust law condemns practices that drive up prices by curtailing output" but that "[f]alse statements about a rival's goods . . . do not curtail output in either the short or long run," but instead "just set the stage for competition in a different venue: the advertising market."

Similarly, the Fifth Circuit in *Retractable Technologies v. Becton Dickinson*, 842 F.3d 883 (5th Cir. 2016), drew a distinction between "business torts, which harm competitors, and truly anticompetitive activities, which harm the market," and stated that "absent a demonstration that a competitor's false advertisements had the potential to eliminate, or did in fact eliminate, competition, an antitrust lawsuit will not lie." The court found that the plaintiff "may have lost some sales or market share" because of the defendant's false advertising, "but it remains a vigorous competitor" and did not face "barriers to entry" from the conduct.

Carrier & Tushnet criticize the premise that misleading advertising "generally sets competition into motion." Just as arson generates economic activity without being economically productive, false advertising forces competitors to fight back on unfair ground, expending resources defending truth against falsehood instead of investing them elsewhere, harming their overall ability to compete.

De Minimis Approach

The Second, Sixth, Ninth, Tenth and Eleventh Circuits apply a presumption that the exclusionary effects of false advertising are de minimis. This framework originated in the leading antitrust treatise, An Analysis of Antitrust Principles and Their Application, which is now authored by Philip Areeda and Herbert Hovenkamp. The 1978 version of the treatise introduced the de minimis approach. It posits that the "more typical deception defendant is the smaller firm or recent entrant that makes its false claims, collects the payments from deceived consumers, and then disappears or becomes judgment-proof." In contrast, the "false claim leading to or perpetuating durable market power by a firm capable of being sued is much less likely." Relying on these claims, the treatise then concludes that "[b]ecause the likelihood of significant creation of durable market power is so small in most observed instances—and because the prevalence of arguably improper misrepresentation is so great—the courts would be wise to regard misrepresentations as presumptively de minimis." (Carrier & Tushnet suggest that the treatise's description of the "typical deception defendant" is not reflected in the case law. For example, false advertising of prices by AT&T allowed it to extend its market dominance among iPhone users and extract millions of dollars in extra fees from its customers. *See* Statement of Commissioner Rohit Chopra, In the Matter of AT&T Mobility, LLC, Commission File No. X150009, Nov. 5, 2019.)

The treatise suggests that a plaintiff can rebut the de minimis presumption by showing that the alleged anticompetitive conduct is (1) clearly false, (2) clearly material, (3) clearly likely to induce reasonable reliance, (4) made to buyers without knowledge of subject matter, (5) continued for prolonged periods and (6) not readily susceptible of neutralization or other offsets by rivals. How do these factors compare with your understanding of Lanham Act false advertising?

Case by Case Approach

The Third, Eighth and D.C. Circuits take a case-by-case approach. *See, e.g.*, W. Pa. Allegheny Health Sys. v. UPMC, 627 F.3d 85 (3d Cir. 2010) ("anticompetitive conduct can include . . . making false statements about a rival to potential investors and customers" and "defamation, which plainly is not competition on the merits, can give rise to antitrust liability, especially when it is combined with other anticompetitive acts."). In those circuits, false advertising often is recognized as part of an overall anticompetitive strategy. For example, the D.C. Circuit found that Microsoft's deceptive statements to Java-based software developers about the interoperability of Windows-based systems with other platforms resulted in developers' inadvertently producing software compatible only with Windows, which was one of the many kinds of anticompetitive conduct in which Microsoft engaged. U.S. v. Microsoft, 253 F.3d 34 (D.C. Cir. 2001).

NOTES AND QUESTIONS

Is there any need for antitrust liability for false advertising given the availability of false advertising law? Carrier & Tushnet suggest that stronger remedies may be appropriate for false advertising by a monopolist, given the damage a monopolist can do to competition in general. They also argue that federal standing for the monopolist's customers—not available under the Lanham Act—is an additional benefit of antitrust analysis, as is the ability to analyze false advertising and other anticompetitive behavior together to consider their overall effects, which false advertising law alone cannot do.

European authorities have proven more welcoming to arguments that false advertising by a dominant competitor is an abuse of its market position. *See* Morten Nissen & Frederik Haugsted, *Badmouthing Your Competitor's Products: When Does Denigration Become an Antitrust Issue?*, ANTITRUST SOURCE, Feb. 2020 (discussing European cases).

B.   Competitor Agreements to Restrict Advertising

Especially because false advertising is already illegal, advertising professionals should pay special attention to antitrust concerns that arise when competitors agree to restrict advertising. The "Three Tenors" case illustrates how things can go wrong.

Some factual background: The case involved two media conglomerates, PolyGram and Warner, and three operatic superstars called the Three Tenors, José Carreras, Plácido Domingo and Luciano Pavarotti.

The Three Tenors created three recordings in association with the World Cup. A PolyGram subsidiary owned the first recording ("3T1"), created in 1990. Warner owned the second recording ("3T2"), created in 1994. Both recordings were very successful. 3T1 and 3T2 were both among the best-selling classical recordings in the United States in 1994, 1995, 1996 and 1997, and 3T1 became the best-selling classical record of all time. Nevertheless, as business rivals, PolyGram and Warner competed with each other in selling 3T1 and 3T2.

In 1998, the Three Tenors performed a third World Cup concert ("3T3"). PolyGram and Warner agreed that Warner would distribute 3T3 in the United States and PolyGram would distribute it in the rest of the world.

Subsequently, PolyGram and Warner worried that 3T1 and 3T2 would compete with 3T3 and thereby undercut their ability to recoup their substantial investments in 3T3, especially after they learned the Three Tenors' 1998 set list largely overlapped previous recordings. As a result, executives of PolyGram and Warner agreed to refrain from advertising or reducing prices of 3T1 or 3T2 audio or video products in all markets in the weeks surrounding the release of 3T3 (the "moratorium agreement"). PolyGram and Warner subsequently issued written instructions to their operating companies worldwide that forbade price discounting and advertising of 3T1 and 3T2 from August 1, 1998 through October 15, 1998. When the parties' legal departments learned of the moratorium agreement, they sent pretextual letters disavowing the agreement, but both parties nevertheless adhered to its terms.

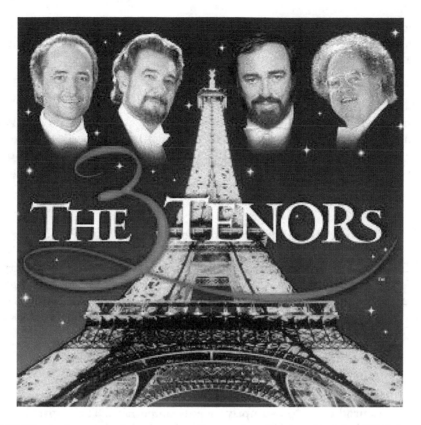

In 2001, the FTC brought an enforcement action under Section 5 of the FTC Act, which proceeded through the FTC's administrative adjudication process. For this purpose, the FTC Act Section 5 legal analysis effectively mirrors Section 1 of the Sherman Act.

IN THE MATTER OF POLYGRAM HOLDING, INC., FTC DOCKET #9298 (2003)

MURIS, Chairman.

INTRODUCTION . . .

Our story takes place not on the opera stage, but in the business world of operatic recordings. The drama is not so stirring, and no one loses his head, at least not literally. The story is troubling, nonetheless. Two recording companies agree to form a joint venture to market a new recording, by three of the world's foremost singers, and to split the costs and profits. By itself, such an agreement, even by competitors, is often beneficial, because it helps bring a new product to market. Here, however, the story turns dark when it becomes apparent that the new recording will repeat much of the repertoire of existing recordings, diminishing its marketing potential and worrying the recording companies. While other businesses might have worked harder to develop an improved or more distinctive product to attract greater consumer interest, our protagonists chose another route. They agreed to restrict their marketing of competing products that they respectively controlled—products that were clearly outside the joint venture they had formed. They imposed a moratorium on discounting and promotion of those recordings that might otherwise siphon off sales of the new product. We now consider whether such an agreement unreasonably restrains trade in violation of the antitrust laws. We conclude that it does. . . .

III. ANALYSIS OF THE CHALLENGED RESTRAINTS

. . . [W]e first must determine whether the agreement between PolyGram and Warner to forgo discounting and advertising of 3T1 and 3T2 falls within the category of restraints that are likely, absent countervailing procompetitive justifications, to have anticompetitive effects—i.e., to lead to higher prices or reduced output. In making this assessment, we consider what judicial experience and economic learning tell us about the likely competitive effects of such restrictions.

A. The Likely Anticompetitive Effects of the Moratorium

In keeping with the analytical structure detailed above, we start with an inquiry into whether the restraints at issue here—the agreement not to discount and the agreement not to advertise—are inherently suspect under the antitrust laws, in that they fall within a category of restraints that warrant summary condemnation because of their likely harm to competition. We find ample basis for concluding that they are. . . .

2. The Agreement Not To Advertise

We also find that the agreement between PolyGram and Warner not to advertise their earlier Three Tenors products is presumptively anticompetitive. The Supreme Court in *CDA* [California Dental Ass'n. v. Federal Trade Commission, 526 U.S. 756 (1999)] indicated that, in ordinary commercial markets—like the one at issue here—complete bans on truthful advertising normally are likely to cause competitive harm. Indeed, the Court repeatedly has recognized that advertising facilitates competition. By informing consumers of the nature and prices of the goods or services available in a market, and thus creating an incentive for suppliers of the products and services to compete along these dimensions, advertising "performs an indispensable role in the allocation of resources in a free enterprise system." Restrictions on truthful and nondeceptive advertising harm competition, because they make it more difficult for consumers to discover information about the price and quality of goods or services, thereby reducing competitors' incentives to compete with each other with respect to such features. These principles apply not just to price advertising, but also to information about qualitative aspects of goods and services. "[A]ll elements of a bargain—quality, service, safety, and durability—and not just the immediate cost, are favorably affected by the free opportunity to select among alternative offers."

Complaint Counsel's economic expert testified that an agreement among competitors not to advertise is likely to harm consumers and competition by raising consumers' search costs and reducing sellers' incentives to lower prices. One reason a restriction on advertising may reduce a seller's incentives to lower prices is that, absent an ability to advertise, lower per-unit prices may not be sufficiently offset by higher volume. Dr. Stockum relied on several empirical studies that have found that advertising restrictions result in consumers' paying higher prices.[52] One of these studies, for example, showed that even a short-lived restraint on advertising can lead to higher prices. On the basis of economic theory and empirical studies, Dr. Stockum concluded that, absent an efficiency justification, Respondents' agreement not to advertise or promote the catalog Three Tenors albums is very likely to be anticompetitive. Dr. Ordover, Respondents' economic expert, agreed in his deposition that a naked agreement among competitors not to advertise is likely to cause consumer harm. This testimony reinforces the general proposition that restrictions on advertising, such as those imposed here, are likely to reduce competition and harm consumers.

B. Respondents' Justifications

Having concluded that both elements of Respondents' moratorium agreement were indeed inherently suspect restraints of trade because of their likely harm to competition, we turn to Respondents' proffered justifications. Respondents' sole argument in this regard is that the moratorium served a plausible procompetitive interest by preventing the PolyGram and Warner operating companies from using the promotional opportunity created by the 1998 Paris concert and the release of the new album to "free ride" on the joint venture. In

---

[52] .... *See* Lee Benham, *The Effect of Advertising on the Price of Eyeglasses*, 15 J.L. & ECON. 337 (1972) (restricting the advertising of eyeglasses raised the average retail price by $7.48); Lee Benham & Alexandra Benham, *Regulating Through the Professions: A Perspective on Information Control*, 18 J.L. & ECON. 421 (1975) (prices were 25-40% higher in markets with greater professional information controls, including advertising restrictions); Ronald S. Bond et al., Staff Report on Effects of Restrictions on Advertising and Commercial Practice in the Professions: The Case of Optometry (Executive Summary), Bureau of Economics, Federal Trade Commission (Sept. 1980) (price for combined eye exam and glasses was $29 less in cities with least restrictive advertising regimes); John F. Cady, *An Estimate of the Price Effects of Restrictions on Drug Price Advertising*, 14 ECON. INQUIRY 493 (1976) (states restricting the advertising of prescription drugs have prices that are 2.9% higher than states that do not restrict advertising); Steven R. Cox et al., *Consumer Information and the Pricing of Legal Services*, 30 J. INDUS. ECON. 305 (1982) (attorneys who advertised had lower fees than those who did not advertise); Roger Feldman & James W. Begun, *The Welfare Cost of Quality Changes Due to Professional Regulation*, 34 J. INDUS. ECON. 17 (1985) (total loss of consumer welfare from state regulations governing optometrists that, inter alia, banned price advertising was $156 million); Roger Feldman & James W. Begun, *Does Advertising of Prices Reduce the Mean and Variance of Prices?*, 18 ECON. INQUIRY 487 (1980) (ban on advertising by optometrists and opticians increased prices by 11%); Roger Feldman & James W. Begun, The Effects of Advertising: Lessons from Optometry, 13 J. Hum. Resources 247 (1978) (price is 16% higher in states that ban optometric and optician price advertising); Amihai Glazer, *Advertising, Information and Prices—A Case Study*, 19 ECON. INQUIRY 661 (1981) (grocery prices rose because of newspaper strike in Queens County, NY, that eliminated large amounts of supermarket advertising, and fell after the strike ended); Deborah Haas-Wilson, *The Effect of Commercial Practice Restrictions: The Case of Optometry*, 29 J.L. & ECON. 165 (1986) (prices were 26–33% lower in markets in which price and non-price media advertising by optometrists occurred); William W. Jacobs et al., Staff Report on Improving Consumer Access to Legal Services: The Case for Removing Restrictions on Truthful Advertising (Executive Summary), Bureau of Economics, Federal Trade Commission (Nov. 1984) (restrictions on attorney advertising resulted in prices that were 5–10% higher); John E. Kwoka, Jr., *Advertising and the Price and Quality of Optometric Services*, 74 AM. ECON. REV. 211 (Mar. 1984) (prices of eye exams were $11–$12 lower in markets with advertising than in markets with advertising restrictions); James H. Love & Frank H. Stephen, *Advertising, Price and Quality in Self-Regulating Professions: A Survey*, 3 INT'L. J. ECON. BUS. 227 (1996) (reviewed 17 studies and found that restrictions on advertising generally have the effect of raising prices paid by consumers); Alex R. Maurizi et al., *Competing for Professional Control: Professional Mix in the Eyeglasses Industry*, 24 J.L. & ECON. 351 (1981) (advertisers charged approximately $7 less than non-advertisers); Robert H. Porter, *The Impact of Government Policy on the U.S. Cigarette Industry*, in EMPIRICAL APPROACHES TO CONSUMER PROTECTION ECONOMICS 446 (Pauline M. Ippolito & David T. Scheffman eds., 1986) (demand fell by 7.5% as result of 1971 ban on television and radio advertising in the cigarette industry; during the ban, prices increased from 3–6%); John R. Schroeter et al., *Advertising and Competition in Routine Legal Service Markets: An Empirical Investigation*, 36 J. INDUS. ECON. 49 (1987) (advertising made demand more elastic, meaning that consumers were more responsive to price differences); Robert L. Steiner, *Does Advertising Lower Consumer Prices?*, 37 J. MARKETING 19 (Oct. 1973) (advertising resulted in lower toy prices to the consumer).

particular, Respondents assert that PolyGram and Warner were concerned that aggressive promotion of 3T1 or 3T2 during the 3T3 release period would divert sales from 3T3, and that the prospect of such diversion could induce them to withhold promotional efforts in support of 3T3. They further assert that lack of success with 3T3 could have undermined the success of subsequent joint venture products—i.e., a proposed "Greatest Hits" album and a Boxed Set.

We reject these arguments as a matter of law because they go far beyond the range of justifications that are cognizable under the antitrust laws. Respondents are not asserting that restraints on the joint venture activities are reasonably necessary to achieve efficiencies in its operations, nor even that expansion of the joint venture is reasonably necessary to achieve such efficiencies. Rather, they are arguing that competitors may agree to restrict competition by products wholly outside a joint venture, to increase profits for the products of the joint venture itself. Such a claim is "nothing less than a frontal assault on the basic policy of the Sherman Act," for it displaces market-based outcomes regarding the mix of products to be offered with collusive determinations that certain new products will be offered under a shield from direct competition.

Preventing free-riding can be a legitimate efficiency. The most widely recognized application in antitrust of this efficiency is, as Respondents suggest, limiting intrabrand competition to improve interbrand competition. In such cases, the scope of the restraint is necessarily limited to products that are within the control (at least initially) of the entity that owns the restricted brand. Here, despite Respondents' invocation of a Three Tenors "brand," there is obviously no such thing, because one entity did not legally control all Three Tenors products. The marketing rights to 3T1 and 3T2 were held not by the joint venture but, rather, independently by the parties to the venture. . . .

The sort of behavior that Respondents disparage as "free-riding"—i.e., taking advantage of the interest in competing products that promotional efforts for one product may induce—is an essential part of the process of competition that occurs daily throughout our economy. For example, when General Motors ("GM") creates a new sport utility vehicle ("SUV") and promotes it, through price discounts, advertising, or both, other SUVs can "free ride" on the fact that GM's promotion inevitably stimulates consumer interest, not just in GM's SUV, but in the SUV category itself. Our antitrust laws exist to protect this response, because it is in reality the competition that drives a market economy to benefit consumers. There is no doubt that GM's SUV will likely be more profitable if its competitors do not respond. Promoting profitability, however, is not now, nor has it ever been, recognized as a basis to restrain interbrand competition under the antitrust laws . . .

Thus, we hold that the Respondents' "free-riding" argument is simply an attempt to shield themselves from legitimate interbrand competition. As such, the proffered justification is not cognizable under antitrust law. This conclusion, together with our previous conclusion that the restraints at issue are of the sort that are likely to harm competition, provides us with ample ground to condemn Respondents' actions as unlawful under Section 1, without further analysis. . . .

C. A More Detailed Factual Analysis...

2. Competitive Effect of Respondents' Advertising Restrictions

. . . Complaint Counsel's music industry marketing expert, Dr. Moore, explained that a record company's decisions regarding advertising and wholesale price are linked, and if there is no advertising, there is less incentive for the company to offer the recording at a significantly reduced price. Dr. Moore further testified—and Respondents' executives confirmed—that record companies advertise to increase their sales, and that such advertising generally results in lower retail prices for consumers.

Furthermore, before the moratorium, advertising was an important part of competition between 3T1 and 3T2. In 1994, when 3T2 was released, PolyGram advertised to inform consumers that 3T1 was the "original" Three Tenors recording, was still widely available, and indeed was often available at a discounted price. Largely as a result of its marketing campaign, PolyGram sold almost one million audio and video recordings of 3T1 in the second half of 1994, as compared with 377,000 in the same period in 1993. In turn, Warner used advertising to create a distinct identity for 3T2, suggesting to consumers that the newer release was the superior product. PolyGram and Warner again used advertising to highlight the advantages of their respective Three Tenors products during the Three Tenors' world concert tours in 1996 and 1997.

. . . The ban on advertising was intended to protect sales of 3T3 by withholding information from consumers about the nature and price of competing products. As one Warner executive explained at trial, the companies did not want consumers to "start comparing the repertoire along with the price and make a determination that, you know, the '94 concert is just fine for a few dollars less." We agree with the ALJ that the anticompetitive effect of this strategy is obvious....

NOTES AND QUESTIONS

Subsequent Proceeding. Polygram appealed the FTC Commissioners' decision to the D.C. Circuit, which upheld the FTC's ruling. Polygram Holding Inc v. Federal Trade Commission, 416 F. 3d 29 (D.C. Cir. 2005).

Advertising as Pro-Competitive. Notice how much of the antitrust analysis mirrors the debates about the social benefits and costs of advertising we discussed in Chapter 2. In this case, the FTC decidedly viewed advertising as a pro-competition tool.

Spillover Effects. PolyGram and Warner defended their actions, in part, based on worries that promotion of 3T3 would stimulate demand for other works by the same artists. The FTC rejected that argument, saying that these spillover effects are part of ordinary economic activity. *See generally* Brett M. Frischmann & Mark A. Lemley, *Spillovers*, 107 COLUM. L. REV. 257 (2007); Eric Goldman, *Brand Spillovers*, 22 HARV. J. L. & TECH. 381 (2009).

"Intrabrand" Competition. To what extent do you think that different albums in a musical group's catalog compete with each other? Does a live album compete with a studio album? If

this case were heard today, would the widespread availability of digital downloads and streaming of individual album tracks change the analysis?

Keyword Advertising Restrictions. Trademark owners sometimes contractually restrict third parties—including vendors, customers and even competitors—from bidding on their trademarks as online advertising keywords. These restrictions are essentially agreements to reduce advertising. By contract, they mean that the trademark owner can bid on certain keywords and the other parties cannot. Trademark owners might feel justified in imposing these restrictions as a way of protecting their trademark interests; and in the case of *1-800 Contacts*, they routinely inserted keyword bidding restrictions in settlement agreements after suing their competitors for purported trademark infringement. Without legitimate justifications, however, they can be anti-competitive.

The FTC did not approve of 1-800 Contacts' practices, even when the parties agreed to the provisions in agreements to settle litigation. In the Matter of 1-800 Contacts, Inc., 2018 WL 6078349 (FTC Docket #9372, Nov. 7, 2018). (As of May 2020, this ruling is on appeal to the Second Circuit). The FTC, sitting as a commission to review the FTC Administrative Law Judge's decision, held (on a 4-1 vote) that 1-800 Contacts engaged in anti-competitive practices by restricting its competitors' truthful advertising.

The majority rejected that 1-800 Contacts' trademark claims were legitimate, which in turn undermined the legitimacy of the settlement agreements:

> [A]part from a single district court summary judgment decision from over ten years ago, no court has found bidding on trademark keywords to constitute trademark infringement, absent some additional factor, such as a misleading use of the trademark in the ad text that confuses consumers as to the advertisement's source, sponsorship, or affiliation. Rather, "[c]ourts have consistently rejected the notion that buying or creating internet search terms, alone, is enough to raise a claim of trademark infringement."

The keyword bidding restrictions created a number of competition problems:

> [T]he Challenged Agreements cut off advertising in a way that interfered with the operation of competitive forces in the online sale of contact lenses and disrupted consumers' mechanisms for comparing and selecting between alternative online sources. . . .

> [T]he Challenged Agreements reduced the number of competitor ads, and increased sales for 1-800 Contacts while reducing the sales for its rivals. . . .

> [T]he Challenged Agreements insulate 1-800 Contacts from normal competitive forces and divert sales from low-priced sellers to a high-priced seller is direct evidence of an increase in price. The higher prices that consumers are paying do not reflect a producer selling a differentiated product, such as a product with new technology or additional features that offer more than the products of low-priced sellers. Instead, the higher prices are a consequence of 1-800 Contacts shielding itself

from competitive pressure by preventing consumers from obtaining information that would enable comparison shopping. . . .Restricting the advertising presented to such consumers at the critical time when they are about to make a purchase impedes their ability to compare prices, which leaves them unaware of alternatives to 1-800 Contacts' higher-priced products.

The majority also noted how the restrictions reduced the revenue of keyword sellers like Google and Bing. Thus, without sufficient justification for restrictions from trademark law, the keyword advertising restrictions violated antitrust law.

Separately, a consumer class-action antitrust lawsuit led to a series of settlements from 1-800 Contacts and the competitors who agreed to the keyword-bidding restrictions. The total settlement fund is $40 million, of which 1-800 Contacts paid $15 million. Thus, superficially innocuous provisions of settlement agreements turned into extremely expensive legal entanglements for 1-800 Contacts and its acquiescing competitors. It's a reminder that any efforts to restrict third-party advertising should be run by antitrust lawyers.

Price Setting as a Regulated Activity. A company's price-setting decisions can raise antitrust issues in multiple ways. Agreeing on prices with competitors—effectively what PolyGram and Warner did by agreeing not to discount prices—typically violates antitrust laws (and can be criminal), but even independent pricing decisions can run into trouble. Setting prices too low can violate minimum pricing laws; and it may be considered predatory pricing and seen as an effort to drive out competitors. Setting prices too high can constitute price-gouging in emergency situations. Further, charging customers different prices can be regulated by the Robinson-Patman Act, a Depression-era federal statute which prohibits certain types of price discrimination, and potentially by other laws. Nevertheless, vendors are routinely attracted to price discrimination because it can help increase profits.

Collusion on Advertising Restrictions. If businesses collude to reduce advertising costs without restricting advertising quantity, antitrust law is still implicated.

In *Marker Völkl (International) GmbH & Tecnica Group S.p.A.*, F.T.C. File No. 1210004, 79 Fed. Reg. 30143 (May 27, 2014), the FTC alleged that well-known endorsers are the most-effective (and costly) marketing tools in selling ski equipment. Ski-equipment manufacturers usually compete for endorsers, and manufacturers may offer endorsers extra money to switch endorsements when their contracts end.

However, two manufacturers agreed not to recruit any skiers who'd previously endorsed the other or was otherwise "claimed" by the other, and they ultimately expanded that agreement to cover all their employees. The aim, naturally, was to avoid paying endorsers and employees more money. According to the FTC, "[a]greements between competitors not to compete for professional services, for employees, or for other inputs, are presumptively anticompetitive or inherently suspect, if not per se unlawful." The parties agreed to a consent order barring such conduct.

Antitrust Scrutiny of Advertising Intermediaries. Antitrust law typically focuses on manufacturers and retailers, including, in some cases, how they use advertising to advance their position. The *Polygram* case involves manufacturers who impermissibly coordinated their actions. Sometimes, antitrust scrutiny can attach to other players in the advertising industry, such as publishers. For example, many major metropolitan newspapers benefited from the Newspaper Preservation Act of 1970, a statutory exception to antitrust law that allowed local competitors to work together. More recently, Google and Facebook have received considerable antitrust speculation for their roles as advertising intermediaries due to their significant share of the online advertising market, and Amazon has attracted attention both for its advertising and its other functions as market-maker and market-shaper. Lina M. Khan, *Amazon's Antitrust Paradox*, 126 YALE L.J. 710 (2016).

Advertisements routinely depict people—their images, names, voices and other aspects of their personalities. This chapter looks at the special legal issues that arise from depicting people in ads.

1.   Overview of Publicity Rights

Publicity rights generally protect the use of people's names, images, voices or other personality attributes from unconsented commercialization.

Publicity rights evolved out of a person's privacy rights. In the United States, privacy rights generally trace back to the immensely influential privacy article by Samuel D. Warren and Louis D. Brandeis, *The Right to Privacy*, 4 HARV. L. REV. 193 (1890). Both Warren and Brandeis were lawyers at the time; Brandeis went on to become a celebrated U.S. Supreme Court justice.

The article reacted to improvements in camera technology. Initially, camera shutter speeds were so slow that people had to pose (i.e., stand still) for photographs. However, technological evolutions reduced shutter speeds, which allowed photographers to take photos of people without their consent. Warren and Brandeis argued that "the existing law affords a principle from which may be invoked to protect the privacy of the individual from invasion either by the too enterprising press, the photographer, or the possessor of any other modern device for rewording or reproducing scenes or sounds."

Recapping privacy law in the early 1960s, Dean William Prosser classified privacy legal claims over the intervening seventy years into four categories. *See* William L. Prosser, *Privacy*, 48 CAL. L. REV. 383 (1960) and RESTATEMENT (SECOND) OF TORTS (for which Prosser was the reporter). This included a category for "[a]ppropriation, for the defendant's advantage, of the plaintiff's name or likeness," which has evolved into the modern "publicity right."

Although the publicity rights doctrine is well-recognized, its legal implementation is a little chaotic. There is no federal publicity right. Currently, about half the states statutorily codify publicity rights, and some statutes explicitly provide that publicity rights survive beyond a person's death.* *See, e.g.*, CAL. CIVIL CODE § 3344.1 (surviving rights for seventy years post-mortem); INDIANA CODE 32–36 (surviving rights for 100 years post-mortem). In some states, publicity rights are protected by common-law doctrines. In a few states, publicity rights are protected by both statute and common law.

---

* However, some statutes require pre-death commercialization as a precondition of publicity rights' descendibility.

Because many celebrities reside there, California and New York play particularly important roles in the development of publicity rights laws. However, publicity rights are not limited to celebrities, and they often protect both famous and non-famous individuals.

Publicity rights generally govern two discrete activities: (1) "merchandising" by selling an item that incorporates some identifiable part of the person, such as the incorporation of a celebrity's image on a t-shirt or a videogame containing a character that resembles an actual person and (2) the depiction of a person in ad copy.

This chapter focuses almost exclusively on the ad copy cases. Typically, ad-copy publicity-rights cases are doctrinally easier than merchandising cases, but both types of cases can create difficult line-drawing situations. In addition, the publicity-rights doctrines have an uneasy fit with the First Amendment, especially in the merchandising context.

Publicity rights only protect individuals. Trademark law and related doctrines provide analogous protection for businesses' brand names and other identifiers. If a person's name develops secondary meaning in association with commercial offerings, people can develop trademark rights in their name or other attributes to complement their publicity rights (which exist automatically). When enforcing those rights, trademark law requires that the defendant's usage creates a likelihood of consumer confusion. In contrast, consumer confusion is not a prerequisite of a publicity-rights claim.

2.   Publicity Rights and Ad Copy

With very limited exceptions, depicting a person in ad copy requires the person's consent. Even with this fairly clear rule, plenty of ambiguity remains. This part looks at the depiction of various personality attributes to explore the boundaries of the publicity rights doctrine.

A.   A Person's Name

In reading this opinion, it may be helpful to know that a "Henley shirt" is a collarless polo shirt. It is named after Henley-on-Thames, England, whose rowers wore uniforms in this style.

HENLEY V. DILLARD DEPARTMENT STORES, 46 F. SUPP. 2D 587 (N.D. TEX. 1999)

. . . FACTS. . .

Plaintiff Donald Hugh Henley ("Henley" or "Plaintiff"), is a popular and critically acclaimed rock and roll musician. He began his music career in the 1970s as the founder and member of the band The Eagles. In the 1980s and 1990s, Henley maintained a successful solo career by continuing to produce platinum albums and perform on tour in concerts around the world.

On September 3 and 4, 1997, Defendant Dillard Department Stores ("Dillard" or "Defendant") ran a newspaper advertisement for a shirt known as a "henley." The ad features a photograph of a man wearing a henley shirt with the words, "This is Don" in large print, beside the picture, and an arrow pointing toward the man's head from the words. Underneath the words is the statement, "This is Don's henley" in the same size print, with a second arrow pointing to the shirt. The advertisement also included the name of the retailer, "Dillard's", general information about the sale price of the shirts, the name of the shirt's manufacturer, the available sizes and the following: "Sometimes Don tucks it in; other times he wears it loose—it looks great either way. Don loves his henley; you will too." The ad ran in newspapers throughout Texas and in Mexico.

DISCUSSION . . .

B. Right to Publicity

The right of publicity is often described as the "inherent right of every human being to control the commercial use of his or her identity." The right to publicity is considered an intellectual property right. It is a more expansive right than any common law or statutory trademark infringement right because it does not require a showing of likelihood of confusion.

The tort of misappropriation of one's name or likeness is generally referred to as the "Right of Publicity" and is based on section 652C of the Restatement of Torts which reads, "One who appropriates to his own use or benefit the name or likeness of another is subject to liability to the other for invasion of his privacy." The Fifth Circuit has specifically identified three elements a plaintiff must prove to recover for the tort of misappropriation of name and likeness in Texas: (1) the defendant appropriated the plaintiff's name or likeness for the value associated with it, and not in an incidental manner or for a newsworthy purpose; (2) the plaintiff can be identified from the publication; and (3) there was some advantage or benefit to the defendant.

The right of publicity is designed to protect the commercial interests of celebrities in their identities. It is intended to protect the value of a celebrity's notoriety or skill. Because a celebrity's identity can be valuable in the promotion of products, "the celebrity has an interest that may be protected from the unauthorized commercial exploitation of that identity." Such celebrities have an exclusive legal right to control and profit from the commercial use of their name, personality and identity. "If the celebrity's identity is commercially exploited, there has been an invasion of his right whether or not his 'name or likeness' is used." The tort does not protect the use of the celebrity's name per se, but rather the value associated with that name. . . .

1. Did Defendant Appropriate the Plaintiff's Name or Likeness for the Value Associated with it, and not in an Incidental Manner or for a Newsworthy Purpose?

The threshold issue to determine in analyzing this element is whether Defendant actually appropriated Defendant's name or likeness. . . .

While use of the expression "Don's henley" is arguably the use of Plaintiff's name, a genuine issue of fact exists as to whether that expression is, indeed, Plaintiff's name. However, Courts have recognized that a defendant may be held liable for using a phrase or image that clearly identifies the celebrity, in addition to finding liability for using a plaintiff's precise name. Because the use of the expression "Don's henley" is so clearly recognizable as a likeness of Plaintiff, the Court finds that no reasonable juror could conclude that the phrase "Don's henley" does not clearly identify the Plaintiff, Don Henley. . . .

The second issue the Court must resolve is whether Defendant appropriated Plaintiff's name or likeness for the value associated with it, and not in an incidental manner. Defendant argues that "there has been no evidence presented that Dillard chose to use the wording 'Don's henley' in order to capitalize on the alleged value of the name Don Henley." The Court disagrees, and in fact, finds that Defendant has presented no reasonable evidence to defeat Plaintiff's summary judgment motion. Plaintiff presents uncontroverted deposition testimony from Lisa M. Robertson, the creator of the print advertisement, admitting that use of Don Henley's 'name' was intended to make the ad more interesting. She . . . intended to use the expression as a "play on words" and intended consumers to recognize this advertisement as a "wordplay" on the name "Don Henley."[2] In other words, Defendant admitted that she did not intend potential consumers to perceive the ad as depicting an anonymous man named "Don." She intended for them to associate the expression "Don's henley" with the Plaintiff Don

---

[2] Q: Well, what prompted you to come up with the idea "This is Don. This is Don's Henley"?
A: Well, I was trying to find a play on words to use for the ad.
Q: And there's no doubt that when you were using the words "This is Don. This is Don's henley," the Don Henley wordplay meant Don Henley the recording artist, not some other person named Don Henley?
A: Well, obviously the name—yes, I mean I knew it was Don Henley; that was where it came from. But it wasn't, you know, to imply that he was a part of it.
Q: I think you said earlier that by using the word—by using the headline "This is Don. This is Don's henley," you intended a wordplay, correct?
A: Yes.
Q: And so it was your intention for consumers to recognize this advertisement as a wordplay.
A: Yes.
Q: And for the wordplay to work, the consumer had to recognize the name Don Henley, right?
A: Well, you'd have to know who he was to get it, yes.
Q: So for it to work or for them to get it, they must recognize the similarity between the words "This is Don. This is Don's henley" and the name of the recording artist Don Henley, correct?
A: Yes.

Henley. Furthermore, Debra L. Green, the ad's designer, admitted that she believed the expression "Don's henley" would catch the consumers' eye because of its similarity to the name "Don Henley." Therefore, Defendant admits Dillard used the play on words, "Don's henley" to attract consumers as they associated the expression and the ad with Plaintiff Don Henley. In other words, they used the value associated with Don Henley's identity and personality in order to attract consumers' attention.

Defendant presents testimony from Dillard's Vice President of Sales Promotion, William B. Warner, suggesting that the use of the words "Don's henley" adds no value to the advertisement. Warner testified that he believes there is no value associated with the expression "Don's henley," and that the singular and sole purpose of choosing and printing that phrase was "fun." In fact, Defendant argues, the use of the expression, "Don's henley" was incidental to the primary focus of the advertisement. The portions of the ad that were of "chief importance" were the "handwritten text and arrows . . . the visual presentation of information." . . .

. . . The Court finds it unreasonable to draw the inference Defendant requests. Defendant's evidence could not lead a reasonable jury to conclude that the use of the words "Don's henley" was for any purpose other than to attract the attention of consumers.

. . . Defendant's use of the message "This is Don. This is Don's henley." in large letters, centered in the print ad was clearly and admittedly intended to attract the consumers' attention. The Court is hard pressed to believe that a reasonable jury could conclude that the size and style of the letters, rather than the message created with those letters, are the focus of the ad. No reasonable jury could conclude that the use of the word play was merely incidental to the advertisement.

2. Can the Plaintiff be Identified from the Publication?

The second element Plaintiff must satisfy to prove an infringement of the Right of Publicity, is that "plaintiff as a human being must be 'identifiable' from the total context of the defendant's use." While there are many ways a plaintiff can be identified in a defendant's use, the most obvious is use of a name that distinguishes the plaintiff. "Identifiability of plaintiff will probably not be a disputable issue in the majority of meritorious Right of Publicity cases." This is due to the fact that defendants will usually make the plaintiff's identity as identifiable as possible so as to draw the maximum amount of attention to the defendant's product. "The intent, state of mind and degree of knowledge of a defendant may shed light on the identifiability issue." "To establish liability, plaintiff need prove no more than that he or she is reasonably identifiable in defendant's use to more than a de [minimis] number of persons." . . .

The Court finds that the issue of identifiability is indisputable in this case because Defendant has offered no evidence to suggest that Plaintiff is not identifiable from the ad. Plaintiff's survey evidence indicates that sixty-five percent of survey respondents believed there was a spokesperson or endorser in the ad. Of those who said there was a spokesperson or endorser, twenty-three percent said the spokesperson or endorser was Don Henley.[8] In other words, fifteen percent of those asked believed Don Henley was a spokesman for or endorser of the ad, and thus, necessarily identified him from the ad. The results of this survey clearly prove that Don Henley was reasonably identifiable in Defendant's ad to more than a de minimis number of persons.

Further, in evaluating the intent and state of mind of Defendant, the evidence is undisputed that Defendant intended to appropriate Don Henley's identity and intended that consumers associate the ad with Don Henley. First, as stated *supra*, the creators of the ad admitted they intended consumers to associate Don Henley with the ad. Second, the Defendant intended to appropriate the image of performing artist Don Henley, not some other, anonymous person by that same name. This is proven by Plaintiff's evidence that the ad creators drafted an earlier version of the ad that added quotes or paraphrases from eight Don Henley song titles to the ad at issue.[9] The Court concludes that there is no fact issue from which a reasonable jury could conclude that Plaintiff was not identifiable from the ad.

3. Was there an Advantage or Benefit to Defendant?

Defendant insists that Plaintiff cannot prove a benefit inured to Dillard because the sales generated by the ad were not sufficient to cover the costs of running the ad. Plaintiff argues that the Court need consider no more than the fact that the ad was created with the belief that the use of the words "Don's henley" would help sell its product.

. . . Comment d [of the Restatement (Second) of Torts § 652C] reads: "It is only when the publicity is given for the purpose of appropriating to the defendant's benefit the commercial or other values associated with the name or likeness that the right of privacy is invaded." Comment d further suggests that the notion that a benefit must inure to the defendant is intertwined with the factor requiring that the plaintiff prove the defendant appropriated the plaintiff's name or likeness for its value and not for an incidental use. The "benefit" element requires Plaintiff to prove that Defendant derived some commercial benefit from the use of plaintiff's name or likeness as opposed to deriving no commercial benefit due to the fact that the use was incidental. . . .

The plaintiff in a right to publicity action is not required to show that the defendant made money off the commercial use of the name or likeness, as Defendant suggests. It is immaterial that Defendant made little profit after the ad ran, only ran the advertisement once, and received no feedback on the ad. What Plaintiff must prove is that Defendant

---

[8] It is arguable that, had the respondents been shown Defendant's ad and been asked "Who do you think is identified in this ad?" a different result would have occurred. In order to name Don Henley as the spokesperson or endorser of the ad (as the question was asked by the surveyor), the surveyees were required to believe the ad was, in fact, endorsed by Henley. Had the surveyees been asked the question "Who do you think is identified in this ad?" it is likely that the number responding "Don Henley" would have increased due to the fact that they would not have been required to believe he endorsed the product or gave his permission to have his name or likeness used in the ad. They would only have been required to believe he was identifiable from the ad.

[9] The ad, in draft form read, "If <u>all you want to do is dance</u> / pick up your <u>witchy woman</u> / <u>take it to the limit</u> in our cotton henley. We promise, you've spent <u>your last worthless evening</u>! Give her <u>the best of your love</u>, and when the party's over, toss our machine washable henley right in the <u>dirty laundry</u>. <u>In the long run</u>, you'll love the great colors and the super-sturdy construction. But hurry in, they may be <u>already gone</u>." [Editor's note: we underlined the song titles, which are a mixture of Eagles songs and Don Henley solo songs.]

received a commercial benefit from use of Plaintiff's name or likeness that, without Plaintiff's image, he would not otherwise have received. Defendant's sophisticated and experienced ad creators described the benefit they received as being able to catch the eye of the consumer and make the ad more interesting. By appropriating Plaintiff's name or likeness, Defendant received the benefit of a celebrity endorsement without asking permission or paying a fee.

To reiterate an earlier point, the Right of Publicity cause of action exists to protect a celebrity's identity, which can be valuable in the promotion of products. Such celebrities have an exclusive legal right to control and profit from the commercial use of their name, personality and identity. . . . The Court, thus, refuses to require a plaintiff to prove that a defendant made a profit or secured a tangible benefit from use of the plaintiff's name or likeness.

. . . Defendant should not be shielded from liability because "the product promoted is undesirable, the ad [is] clumsy or somehow ineffective, or sales slump[ed] during the relevant time period." Rather, Dillard should be held liable because it received a benefit by getting to use a celebrity's name for free in its advertising. Whether or not the advertising worked for Dillard is wholly irrelevant. The Court concludes that there is no fact issue from which a reasonable jury could conclude that Defendant did not receive a benefit from its use of Plaintiff's likeness. . . .

NOTES AND QUESTIONS

Celebrities v. Ordinary People. This case emphasizes Don Henley's celebrity status. However, as illustrated by cases such as *Cohen* (discussed later), celebrity status is not required for a valid publicity rights claim.

How Far Does a Name's Protection Extend? Would the case's result have changed if Dillard had referenced "Donald's henley?" "Dawn's henley?" "Donny's henley?" "Dom's henley?" Once the court believed that Dillard was intentionally trying to evoke Don Henley, was Dillard liable no matter what variation of "Don Henley" they used? The ad derives value from the pun on Henley's name, but the court doesn't acknowledge that consumers had to expend some mental effort to decode the pun.

Consumer Surveys. The case says "fifteen percent of those asked believed Don Henley was a spokesman for or endorser of the ad." But what if the other 85% clearly understood that the ad was a joke? Should a small minority of consumers suppress advertisements where the vast majority got the joke?

Consumer surveys are common in trademark and false advertising cases, but they are relatively rare in publicity rights cases.

Celebrities on a First-Name Basis. During the 2010 Super Bowl, the online brokerage E*Trade ran one of its "talking baby" commercials. In the commercial, the protagonist is explaining to his "girlfriend" (a baby girl) that he didn't call because he was taking advantage of E*Trade's services. The girlfriend accusatorily asks, "And that milkaholic Lindsay wasn't over?" After an awkward pause, the protagonist then replies "Lindsay?" in an

560

unsure voice while a previously unseen baby girl in the protagonist's room—presumably, the "Lindsay" both babies are referencing—reveals herself to the camera and says "Milk-a-what?"

This ad prompted a $50 million lawsuit from Lindsay Lohan, a successful teen actress who battled highly publicized substance-addiction issues. Lohan v. E*Trade Secs. LLC, No. 10-004579 (N.Y. Sup. Ct. complaint filed March 8, 2010). Lohan claimed that the ad's "Lindsay" references were meant to be her. Among other things, she claimed that her first name is so well-known that ad viewers would have assumed it was her. Lohan and E*Trade subsequently settled the lawsuit on confidential terms.[*]

Lohan was born in 1986. In the 1980s, "Lindsay" was the forty-fourth most-popular girl name according to the Baby NameVoyager website (and the homophone "Lindsey" was the forty-second most popular). In 2010, "Lindsay" was the 596th most popular girl's name. Is either fact relevant?

No matter what first name E*Trade chose for the milkaholic character, does E*Trade face an unavoidable risk that some celebrity who shares the name and has a substance abuse problem will claim the ad refers to him or her?

Does the following billboard, promoting tourism with the slogan "MORE RUSH THAN YOU GET FROM TALK RADIO," misappropriate anyone's personality rights? Does the capitalization matter?

---

[*] Lindsay Lohan has an expansive view of her publicity rights, and that has not fared well in court. *See, e.g.,* Lohan v. Take-Two Interactive Software, Inc., 31 N.Y.3d 111 (N.Y. Ct. App. 2018).

Nicknames. Elroy Hirsch was a University of Wisconsin athlete who went on to become a successful and well-known professional football player. Hirsch received the nickname "Crazylegs" as described in *Hirsch v. S.C. Johnson & Son. Inc.*, 280 N.W.2d 129 (Wis. 1979):

> In the fourth game of his first season of play at Wisconsin, he acquired the name, "Crazylegs." In that game, Hirsch ran 62 yards for a touchdown, wobbling down the sideline looking as though he might step out of bounds at any moment. Hirsch's unique running style, which looked something like a whirling eggbeater, drew the attention of a sportswriter for the Chicago Daily News who tagged Hirsch with the nickname, "Crazylegs." It is undisputed that the name stuck, and Hirsch has been known as "Crazylegs" ever since.

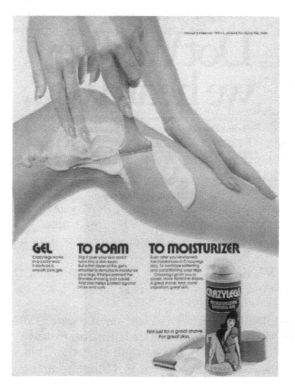

The court upheld Hirsch's claim against the product name. Does that surprise you?

Using a Celebrity's "Abandoned" Name. In *Abdul-Jabbar v. General Motors Corp.*, 85 F.3d 407 (9th Cir. 1996), the former basketball star Kareem Abdul-Jabbar alleged that the car manufacturer GMC violated the Lanham Act and California's statutory and commo- law right of publicity by using his former name, Lew Alcindor, without his consent, in a television ad aired during the 1993 NCAA men's basketball tournament. The court of appeals agreed that a jury could find GMC liable.

The ad involved a voiceover that asked, "Who holds the record for being voted the most outstanding player of this tournament?" The screen then displayed, "Lew Alcindor, UCLA, '67, '68, '69." The voiceover then asked, "Has any car made the 'Consumer Digest's Best Buy' list more than once? [and responds:] The Oldsmobile Eighty-Eight has." The ad also called the car "A Definite First Round Pick."

Abdul-Jabbar adopted his present name in 1971 and hadn't used "Lew Alcindor" for commercial purposes in over ten years at the time of decision. The court of appeals reasoned that, under California common law, the key issue was whether his "identity" had been appropriated; California statutory law protected "name, voice, signature, photograph, or likeness." Using the former name could constitute use of his "identity," and the statute wasn't limited to presently used names. "To the extent GMC's use of the plaintiff's birth name attracted television viewers' attention, GMC gained a commercial advantage." Whether the name Lew Alcindor "equalled" Kareem Abdul-Jabbar in consumers' minds was a question for the jury.

In addition, Abdul-Jabbar provided sufficient evidence for a jury to find that he was injured "economically because the ad will make it difficult for him to endorse other automobiles and emotionally because people may be led to believe he has abandoned his current name and assume he has renounced his religion." (Abdul-Jabbar changed his name as a result of his religious conversion to Islam).

While Lew Alcindor's "abandoned" name was arguably well-known, the more likely scenario is a celebrity's new stage name becomes more well-known than his or her birth name. For example, the real name of 50 Cent is Curtis Jackson. If ad copy referenced Curtis Jackson, would that violate his publicity rights if few consumers would realize that is the same person as 50 Cent?

References to True Facts About Celebrities in Ad Copy. Why can't GM's ad copy recite the true fact that Alcindor was the NCAA tournament MVP three times? What changes, if any, could GM make to its ad copy to reference Lew Alcindor and not violate his publicity rights?

In the discussion about GM's liability for false endorsement under the Lanham Act and the possibility of a nominative use defense, the court says:

> Had GMC limited itself to the "trivia" portion of its ad, GMC could likely defend the reference to Lew Alcindor as a nominative fair use. But by using Alcindor's record to make a claim for its car—like the basketball star, the Olds 88 won an "award" three years in a row, and like the star, the car is a "champ" and a "first round pick"—GMC

has arguably attempted to "appropriate the cachet of one product for another," if not also to "capitalize on consumer confusion." We therefore hold that there is a question of fact as to whether GMC is entitled to a fair use defense.

This suggests GMC could have referenced Alcindor if it did not connect Alcindor's accomplishments to its product claims. But if GMC doesn't make that cognitive connection for the viewer, why would GMC invoke Alcindor's accomplishments? Worse, it might be even more suspicious if GMC invoked Alcindor's accomplishments without tying them to product claims; otherwise, it might look even more like an implied endorsement from Alcindor/Abdul-Jabbar. Given that GMC faces trouble either way, how could GMC revamp the ad copy?

The Boundaries of Commercial Speech. Jordan v. Jewel Food Stores, Inc., 743 F.3d 509 (7th Cir. 2014), held that an ad congratulating basketball legend Michael Jordan, run in a special issue of *Sports Illustrated* celebrating Jordan's career, was commercial speech, so the Lanham Act and right of publicity apply to it. Why did Jewel run this ad and use this particular ad copy?

Tweeting About Celebrities. A paparazzi photographed actress Katherine Heigl exiting a Duane Reade drugstore carrying two Duane Reade shopping bags. Duane Reade then tweeted the photo with the text "Love a quick #DuaneReade run? Even @KatieHeigl can't resist shopping #NYC's favorite drugstore."

Duane Reade
@DuaneReade ⟋ Follow

Love a quick #DuaneReade run? Even @KatieHeigl can't resist shopping #NYC's favorite drugstore bit.ly/1gLHctl pic.twitter.com/uGTc3k1Mii

⟋ Reply ⟳ Retweet ⋆ Favorite ⋯ More

RETWEETS   FAVORITES
74   181

Assume that the tweet is factually correct, and assume Duane Reade properly procured any required copyright licenses to the photo. Does Katherine Heigl have a valid right of publicity claim against Duane Reade? She sued, and Duane Reade removed the tweet. The case settled with Duane Reade making an unspecified payment to a charity associated with Heigl.

Is there any way Duane Reed could share this photo with their audiences without Heigl's permission? Is there any caption that would be allowable? *See generally* Ashley Messenger, *Rethinking the Right of Publicity in the Context of Social Media*, 24 WIDENER L. REV. 259 (2018).

Test Yourself. In July 2014, NBA basketball player LeBron James, often nicknamed "King James," announced that he was re-signing with the Cleveland Cavaliers. This announcement sparked a flurry of tweets on Twitter. Which, if any, of the following would escape liability under the standard applied in *Henley*?

DiGiorno Pizza ✔
@DiGiornoPizza

🐦 Follow

lot of pizza getting eaten in Cleveland rn
#WelcomeHomeLebron □□□

9:39 AM - 11 Jul 2014

40 RETWEETS 65 FAVORITES

Denny's ✔
@DennysDiner

🐦 Follow

if only you would have signed with *us*, king james, if
only. we coulda been a contender, we coulda been
somebody...

9:45 AM - 11 Jul 2014

198 RETWEETS 297 FAVORITES

Applebee's ✔
@Applebees

🐦 Follow

We are melting in anticipation @KingJames!!
#TheKingisBack

10:29 AM - 11 Jul 2014

26 RETWEETS 52 FAVORITES

Cottonelle ✔
@cottonelle

🐦 Follow

LeBron James is returning to Cleveland. Lesson: Stick with
what works, like Cottonelle TP and Flushable Wipes

9:33 AM - 11 Jul 2014

318 RETWEETS 141 FAVORITES

Charmin ✔ 🐦 Follow
@Charmin

Looks like the king is returning his "throne" back to Cleveland. The internet is officially in meltdown & blowout mode. #tweetfromtheseat

9:56 AM - 11 Jul 2014

24 RETWEETS 13 FAVORITES   ↩ ⇄ ★

Product Reviews. Later in this chapter, we'll discuss the special rules applicable to endorsements and testimonials. For now, let's just consider the publicity-rights angle. Can an advertiser quote a favorable Yelp review or newspaper review in its ads and reference the author's name? If a celebrity mentions in an interview that she regularly uses the advertiser's product, can the advertiser mention this fact in future ads?

Although it seems like quoting or referencing truthful published endorsements or testimonials in ads (without the person's permission) should be permissible, publicity rights make it a legally uncertain practice. Most advertisers take the conservative route and obtain permission before including these quotes or references with attribution. However, when it comes to Yelp reviews, sometimes advertisers include the quote without attributing it to the reviewer's name. And if a celebrity gives a shout-out to an advertiser, it may be too hard to obtain the celebrity's consent and yet too tempting not to spread the news.

Press Releases. Recall *Yeager v. Cingular Wireless LLC* from Chapter 2. The case found a publicity-rights violation when a Cingular press release touting its disaster preparedness equipment—called MACH 1 and MACH 2—invoked legendary pilot Chuck Yeager's accomplishment of flying at Mach 1 speed.

Ad Agency Liability. In *Abdul-Jabbar,* the court treated the advertiser (GM) and its ad agency (Leo Burnett) as equally liable for the publicity rights violation. We'll revisit ad agency liability in Chapter 17.

Personality Trademarks and Publicity Rights Compared. Recall that getting a trademark requires making a "use in commerce" of the term, such as by affixing a person's name or likeness as the source identifier for goods or services available in the marketplace. Furthermore, to get a trademark in a personal name, the individual must show that his or her name has achieved secondary meaning, i.e., that when consumers see the name, they think of a single source of marketplace goods or services (e.g., Sears' Kardashian Kollection).

As a result of the "use in commerce" and secondary-meaning requirements, non-celebrities rarely will have trademark rights protecting some aspect of their personality. Indeed, many celebrities will not have protectable trademark rights, either because they have not commodified their personality or have not achieved the requisite secondary meaning.

Even when celebrities have trademark rights in their personalities, publicity rights claims are usually easier to win (in jurisdictions that have recognized publicity rights). Unlike trademark law, publicity rights do not require showing a likelihood of consumer confusion about product source. Also, as the *Henley* and *Abdul-Jabbar* cases indicate, courts will often apply publicity rights doctrines broadly, while they may not apply trademark doctrine so expansively.

Nevertheless, if their names or other personality attributes are eligible for trademark protection, celebrities may find value in securing federaltrademark registration to complement their publicity rights. For example, federal-trademark registration provides presumptively valid rights and ensures access to federal courts, without the state-by-state coverage of publicity rights.

Keyword Advertising on Names. Assume that an advertiser purchases a person's name as the trigger for its keyword advertising, i.e., when searchers use the search query "Joe Smith," a competitor's advertisement appears. Assume the plaintiff does not have any trademark rights in his or her name. Does the purchase of the keyword-advertising trigger violate the person's publicity or privacy rights? Does it matter if the ad copy references the name? *See* Habush v. Cannon, 346 Wis. 2d 709 (Wis. App. Ct. 2013) (dismissing a Wisconsin publicity rights claim for one lawyer purchasing keyword ads on another lawyer's name); Eric Goldman & Angel Reyes III, *Regulation of Lawyers' Use of Competitive Keyword Advertising*, 2016 U. ILL. L. REV. 103.

Incidental Uses. In general, a product that is fully protected by the First Amendment—such a book, movie or play—extends that constitutional protection to advertising for it, potentially overriding publicity-rights claims that might otherwise apply to the advertising. This principle is confusingly called "incidental" use because the advertising is "incidental" to the protected speech. *See, e.g.,* Lerman v. Flynt Distrib. Co., 745 F.2d 123 (2d Cir. 1984); Namath v. Sports Illustrated, 48 A.D.2d 487, 371 N.Y.S.2d 10, (1st Dep't 1975), *aff'd*, 352 N.E.2d 584 (N.Y. 1976). This exception may apply even where the advertisement does not conform precisely to the content of the underlying publication. *See, e.g.,* Velez v. VV Publ'g Corp., 135 A.D.2d 47, 524 N.Y.S.2d 186 (1st Dep't 1988) (rejecting right of publicity claim where photo of plaintiff in magazine was used in subsequent advertisement which added cartoon bubble containing text to photo). Indeed, one court found that the incidental-use (and related public-interest) exception covered an ad using the then-Mayor of New York's first name because the advertised magazine occasionally reported on the Mayor:

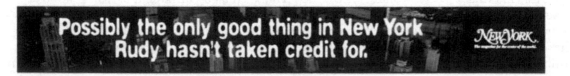

N.Y. Magazine v. Metropo. Transp. Auth., 987 F. Supp. 254 (S.D.N.Y. 1997), *aff'd on other grounds*, 136 F.3d 123 (2d Cir. 1998).

B.   A Person's Voice

California's publicity rights statute expressly protects the use of a person's voice in ad copy. Does this extend to "sound-alike" voices?

MIDLER V. FORD MOTOR CO., 849 F.2D 460 (9TH CIR. 1988)

This case centers on the protectability of the voice of a celebrated chanteuse from commercial exploitation without her consent. Ford Motor Company and its advertising agency, Young & Rubicam, Inc., in 1985 advertised the Ford Lincoln Mercury with a series of nineteen 30 or 60 second television commercials in what the agency called "The Yuppie Campaign." The aim was to make an emotional connection with Yuppies,* bringing back memories of when they were in college. Different popular songs of the seventies were sung on each commercial. The agency tried to get "the original people," that is, the singers who had popularized the songs, to sing them. Failing in that endeavor in ten cases the agency had the songs sung by "sound-alikes." Bette Midler, the plaintiff and appellant here, was done by a sound-alike.

Midler is a nationally known actress and singer. She won a Grammy as early as 1973 as the Best New Artist of that year. Records made by her since then have gone Platinum and Gold. She was nominated in 1979 for an Academy award for Best Female Actress in *The Rose*, in which she portrayed a pop singer. Newsweek in its June 30, 1986 issue described her as an "outrageously original singer/comedian." Time hailed her in its March 2, 1987 issue as "a legend" and "the most dynamic and poignant singer-actress of her time."

When Young & Rubicam was preparing the Yuppie Campaign it presented the commercial to its client by playing an edited version of Midler singing "Do You Want To Dance," taken from the 1973 Midler album, "The Divine Miss M." After the client accepted the idea and form of the commercial, the agency contacted Midler's manager, Jerry Edelstein. The conversation went as follows: "Hello, I am Craig Hazen from Young and Rubicam. I am calling you to find out if Bette Midler would be interested in doing . . . ?" Edelstein: "Is it a commercial?" "Yes." "We are not interested."

Undeterred, Young & Rubicam sought out Ula Hedwig whom it knew to have been one of "the Harlettes," a backup singer for Midler for ten years. Hedwig was told by Young & Rubicam that "they wanted someone who could sound like Bette Midler's recording of [Do You Want To Dance]." She was asked to make a "demo" tape of the song if she was interested. She made an a capella demo and got the job.

At the direction of Young & Rubicam, Hedwig then made a record for the commercial. The Midler record of "Do You Want To Dance" was first played to her. She was told to "sound as much as possible like the Bette Midler record," leaving out only a few "aahs" unsuitable for the commercial. Hedwig imitated Midler to the best of her ability.

After the commercial was aired Midler was told by "a number of people" that it "sounded exactly" like her record of "Do You Want To Dance." Hedwig was told by "many personal

---

* [Editor's note: "Yuppie" is an acronym for "Young Urban Professional," an affluent segment of the Baby Boomer generation.]

friends" that they thought it was Midler singing the commercial. Ken Fritz, a personal manager in the entertainment business not associated with Midler, declares by affidavit that he heard the commercial on more than one occasion and thought Midler was doing the singing.

Neither the name nor the picture of Midler was used in the commercial; Young & Rubicam had a license from the copyright holder to use the song. At issue in this case is only the protection of Midler's voice. The district court described the defendants' conduct as that "of the average thief." They decided, "If we can't buy it, we'll take it." The court nonetheless believed there was no legal principle preventing imitation of Midler's voice and so gave summary judgment for the defendants. Midler appeals. . . .

California Civil Code section 3344 is ... of no aid to Midler. The statute affords damages to a person injured by another who uses the person's "name, voice, signature, photograph or likeness, in any manner." The defendants did not use Midler's name or anything else whose use is prohibited by the statute. The voice they used was Hedwig's, not hers. The term "likeness" refers to a visual image not a vocal imitation. The statute, however, does not preclude Midler from pursuing any cause of action she may have at common law; the statute itself implies that such common law causes of action do exist because it says its remedies are merely "cumulative."

The companion statute protecting the use of a deceased person's name, voice, signature, photograph or likeness states that the rights it recognizes are "property rights." By analogy the common law rights are also property rights. Appropriation of such common law rights is a tort in California. . . .

Why did the defendants ask Midler to sing if her voice was not of value to them? Why did they studiously acquire the services of a sound-alike and instruct her to imitate Midler if Midler's voice was not of value to them? What they sought was an attribute of Midler's identity. Its value was what the market would have paid for Midler to have sung the commercial in person.

. . . A voice is as distinctive and personal as a face. The human voice is one of the most palpable ways identity is manifested. We are all aware that a friend is at once known by a few words on the phone. At a philosophical level it has been observed that with the sound of a voice, "the other stands before me." A fortiori, these observations hold true of singing, especially singing by a singer of renown. The singer manifests herself in the song. To impersonate her voice is to pirate her identity.

We need not and do not go so far as to hold that every imitation of a voice to advertise merchandise is actionable. We hold only that when a distinctive voice of a professional singer is widely known and is deliberately imitated in order to sell a product, the sellers have appropriated what is not theirs and have committed a tort in California. Midler has made a showing, sufficient to defeat summary judgment, that the defendants here for their own profit in selling their product did appropriate part of her identity.

NOTES AND QUESTIONS

Why Copyright Wasn't an Issue. Bobby Freeman wrote the song "Do You Wanna Dance?" and recorded it in 1958. A 1965 cover version by the Beach Boys is perhaps the best-known version. Midler herself covered the song, with a jazzier and much slower arrangement, under the title "Do You Want To Dance?" in 1973. Midler did not own the copyright to the song's music and lyrics, so Ford didn't need her permission to perform the copyrighted music and lyrics in the advertisement. Because Ford did not use Midler's 1973 sound recording either, it did not need a copyright license for that recording.

Damages. On remand, a jury awarded Midler $400,000 from Ford's ad agency Young & Rubicam (Ford had already exited the case). Midler had asked for damages of $10 million.

How should damages be computed in a sound-alike case? *Waits v. Frito Lay, Inc.*, 978 F.2d 1093 (9th Cir. 1992), a sound-alike case involving raspy-voiced singer Tom Waits and a radio advertisement for "SalsaRio Doritos," explores that question. The jury awarded $2.6 million in compensatory and punitive damages and attorneys' fees against the manufacturer Frito-Lay and its advertising agency Tracy-Locke. The defendants appealed to the Ninth Circuit. That court upheld the award in its entirety, ruling that damages were not limited to economic injury (though the economic *value* of the use to the advertiser is important for liability). Injury to Waits' peace, happiness and feelings was also compensable.

He was particularly embarrassed by the ad because it seemed to contradict his anti-commercial stance: "[B]ecause of his outspoken public stance against doing commercial endorsements, the Doritos commercial humiliated Waits by making him an apparent hypocrite."

In addition, the jury could award him damages for injury to goodwill (his artistic reputation and reputation for refusing to endorse products). Further, the court upheld an award based on lost future publicity value. If Waits *did* do a commercial in the future, his asking price would be lowered because of the Doritos ad.

Moreover, the court upheld the punitive damages award, holding that the jury could have found the defendants' conduct "despicable because they knowingly impugned Waits' integrity in the public eye," and that defendants acted in conscious disregard of Waits' right of publicity.

Asking Permission. Businesspeople frequently believe that "it's better to ask for forgiveness than permission." Do the *Midler* and *Waits* cases provide supporting evidence for this maxim? When you are a practicing lawyer, will you prospectively ask publicity rightsholders for their consent in ambiguous situations?

Singers Closely Identified with Famous Songs. Assume that ad copy includes a performance of a properly licensed song sung by a non-sound-alike. On publicity rights grounds, can a singer of that song nevertheless object to use of that song because the song is so closely identified with him or her? The answer appears to be no.

Sinatra v. Goodyear Tire & Rubber Co., 435 F.2d 711 (9th Cir. 1970), involved Goodyear's radio and television ads promoting its "wide boots" tires. The ad copy included portions of the song "These Boots Are Made For Walkin'," a 1966 #1 hit for Nancy Sinatra (the daughter of Frank Sinatra). The ad agency properly secured licenses to the song's musical work copyright, owned by Criterion Music (not Sinatra). Sinatra alleged, among other things, "that the song has been so popularized by the plaintiff that her name is identified with it; [and] that she is best known by her connection with the song." Nevertheless, the Ninth Circuit concluded that her lawsuit was preempted by copyright law.

Oliveria v. Frito-Lay, Inc., 251 F.3d 56 (2d Cir. 2001), addresses a slightly different situation. Oliveria, who performs under the name "Astrud Gilberto," sang the well-known 1964 recording of the song "The Girl from Ipanema." Frito-Lay obtained the proper copyright licenses to use that recording in a television ad for its baked potato chips. Nevertheless, Oliveria claimed she had become known as the eponymous Girl from Ipanema due to the recording's success and her many subsequent performances of the song. The court rejected Oliveria's trademark claim because she did not cite "a single precedent throughout the history of trademark supporting the notion that a performing artist acquires a trademark or service mark signifying herself in a recording of her own famous performance." The court said that Oliveria's state-law claims could be refiled in state court, but Oliveria never did so.

C.   A Person's Visual Depiction

Visually depicting a person in ad copy is usually squarely covered by the person's publicity/privacy rights. It might also constitute an endorsement or testimonial, which is discussed later in this chapter. Just to make sure nothing visual is missed, along with specific references to pictures and portraits, many state laws also protect against the unauthorized use of "likenesses," which probably refers to drawings of people instead of photos or videos of them.

Lookalikes

To get around this general rule, some advertisers have hired look-alike actors to portray famous celebrities. As with sound-alikes, courts generally have rejected this workaround.

For example, *Allen v. National Video, Inc.*, 610 F. Supp. 612 (S.D.N.Y. 1985), involved an ad depicting a look-alike of the famous director and actor Woody Allen:

> The present action arises from an advertisement, placed by National to promote its nationally franchised video rental chain, containing a photograph of defendant Boroff taken on September 2, 1983. The photograph portrays a customer in a National Video store, an individual in his forties, with a high forehead, tousled hair, and heavy black glasses. The customer's elbow is on the counter, and his face, bearing an expression at once quizzical and somewhat smug, is leaning on his hand. It is not disputed that, in general, the physical features and pose are characteristic of plaintiff.

The staging of the photograph also evokes associations with plaintiff. Sitting on the counter are videotape cassettes of "Annie Hall" and "Bananas," two of plaintiff's best known films, as well as "Casablanca" and "The Maltese Falcon." The latter two are Humphrey Bogart films of the 1940's associated with plaintiff primarily because of his play and film "Play It Again, Sam," in which the spirit of Bogart appears to the character played by Allen and offers him romantic advice. In addition, the title "Play It Again, Sam" is a famous, although inaccurate, quotation from "Casablanca."

The individual in the advertisement is holding up a National Video V.I.P. Card, which apparently entitles the bearer to favorable terms on movie rentals. The woman behind the counter is smiling at the customer and appears to be gasping in exaggerated excitement at the presence of a celebrity.

The photograph was used in an advertisement which appeared in the March 1984 issue of "Video Review," a magazine published in New York and distributed in the Southern District, and in the April 1984 issue of "Take One," an in-house publication which National distributes to its franchisees across the country. The headline on the advertisement reads "Become a V.I.P. at National Video. We'll Make You Feel Like a Star." The copy goes on to explain that holders of the V.I.P. card receive "hassle-free movie renting" and "special savings" and concludes that "you don't need a famous face to be treated to some pretty famous service."

The same photograph and headline were also used on countercards distributed to National's franchisees. Although the advertisement that ran in "Video Review" contained a disclaimer in small print reading "Celebrity double provided by Ron

574

Smith's Celebrity Look-Alike's, Los Angeles, Calif.," no such disclaimer appeared in the other versions of the advertisement.

The defendants explained the look-alike's appearance in the ad copy this way:

> Although defendants concede that they sought to evoke by reference plaintiff's general persona, they strenuously deny that they intended to imply that the person in the photograph was actually plaintiff or that plaintiff endorsed National. ... According to defendants, the idea of the advertisement is that even people who are not stars are treated like stars at National Video. They insist that the advertisement depicts a "Woody Allen fan," so dedicated that he has adopted his idol's appearance and mannerisms, who is able to live out his fantasy by receiving star treatment at National Video. The knowing viewer is supposed to be amused that the counter person actually believes that the customer is Woody Allen.

Do you find that explanation credible?

Allen ultimately succeeded on his trademark claim of likely confusion over his endorsement, and the court did not definitively resolve his publicity/privacy rights claims because the New York statute covered only a portrait or picture, and the court was unsure that a look-alike could count as a portrait or picture. However, the court's discussion of those claims is nevertheless useful:

> . . . New York has never recognized the right to privacy as part of its common law.

> . . . [T]he New York legislature passed sections 50 and 51 of the Civil Rights Law in 1903. In its present form the statute provides that

>> A person, firm or corporation that uses for advertising purposes, or for purposes of trade, the name, portrait or picture* of any living person without having first obtained the written consent of such person, is guilty of a misdemeanor.

> Section 51 provides in addition that

>> Any person whose name, portrait or picture is used within the state for advertising purposes or for purposes of trade without the written consent first obtained as above provided may maintain an equitable action in the supreme court of this state against the person, firm or corporation so using his name, portrait or picture, to prevent and restrain the use thereof; and may also sue and recover damages for any injuries sustained by reason of such use and if defendant shall have knowingly used such person's name, portrait or picture in such a manner as is forbidden or declared to be unlawful by the last section, the jury, in its discretion, may award exemplary damages. . . .

---

* [Editor's note: The New York statute now covers voice as well.]

The right to privacy recognized by the Civil Rights law has been strictly construed, both because it is in derogation of New York common law and because of potential conflict with the First Amendment, particularly where public figures are involved. To make out a violation, a plaintiff must satisfy three distinct elements: 1) use of his or her name, portrait, or picture, 2) for commercial or trade purposes, 3) without written permission. Merely suggesting certain characteristics of the plaintiff, without literally using his or her name, portrait, or picture, is not actionable under the statute. Plaintiff here must therefore demonstrate, inter alia, that the advertisement in question appropriates his "portrait or picture."

In addition to the statutory right to privacy, plaintiff in this case argues that defendants have violated his "right of publicity," an analogous right recognized in the common law of many jurisdictions. ... Unlike the Civil Rights Law provision, which is primarily designed to compensate for the hurt feelings of private people who find their identities usurped for another's commercial gain, the right of publicity protects this property interest of the celebrity in his or her public identity. It is primarily this interest which Woody Allen seeks to vindicate in the case at bar.

The New York Court of Appeals, however, recently has held that no separate common law cause of action to vindicate the right of publicity exists in New York. Stephano v. News Grp. Publ'ns, Inc., 64 N.Y.2d 174 (1984). . . .

In examining the undisputed facts of this case with reference to plaintiff's summary judgment motion, it is immediately clear that two of the three prongs of the Civil Rights Law are satisfied. First, there is no question that the photograph said to be of plaintiff was used for commercial purposes, since it appeared in a magazine advertisement soliciting business for National Video franchisees. Second, defendants do not dispute that plaintiff never gave his consent to the use of the photograph, either orally or in writing. It therefore appears that the only element of plaintiff's case over which there is any serious dispute is whether the photograph is a "portrait or picture" of plaintiff.

Plaintiff argues that Boroff's physical resemblance to him, when viewed in conjunction with the undeniable attempt to evoke plaintiff's image through the selection of props and poses, makes the photograph in question a "portrait or picture" of plaintiff as a matter of law. Plaintiff notes that it is not necessary that all persons seeing the photograph actually identify him, only that he be identifiable from the photograph. . . .

More helpful are a line of cases holding that any recognizable likeness, not just an actual photograph, may qualify as a "portrait or picture." . . .

Therefore, if defendants had used, for example, a clearly recognizable painting or cartoon of plaintiff, it would certainly constitute a "portrait or picture" within the meaning of the statute. The case of a look-alike, however, is more problematic. A painting, drawing or manikin has no existence other than as a representation of something or someone; if the subject is recognizable, then the work is a "portrait." Defendant Boroff, however, is not a manikin. He is a person with a right to his own identity and his own face. Plaintiff's privacy claim therefore requires the court to answer the almost metaphysical question of when one person's face, presented in a certain context, becomes, as a matter of law, the face of another.

This question is not merely theoretical. The use in an advertisement of a drawing, which has no other purpose than to represent its subject, must give rise to a cause of action under the Civil Rights Law, because it raises the obvious implication that its subject has endorsed or is otherwise involved with the product being advertised. There is no question that this amounts to an appropriation of another's likeness for commercial advantage.

A living and breathing actor, however, has the right to exploit his or her own face for commercial gain. This right is itself protected by the Civil Rights Law. The privacy law does not prohibit one from evoking certain aspects of another's personality, but it does prohibit one from actually representing oneself as another person. The look-alike situation falls somewhere in between and therefore presents a difficult question.

As you can see, New York's approaches to publicity and privacy rights are different than California's. California has overlapping statutory and common-law publicity rights, while New York has only statutory privacy rights.

A more decisive New York look-alike case is *Onassis v. Christian Dior*, 472 N.Y.S.2d 254 (N.Y. Sup. Ct. 1984), which involved ad copy that included a look-alike of former First Lady Jacqueline Kennedy Onassis. The court harshly condemned the defendants:

> Is the illusionist to be free to step aside, having reaped the benefits of his creation, and permitted to disclaim the very impression he sought to create? If we were to permit it, we would be sanctioning an obvious loophole to evade the statute. If a person is unwilling to give his or her endorsement to help sell a product, either at an offered price or at any price, no matter—hire a double and the same effect is achieved. The essential purpose of the statute must be carried out by giving it a common sense reading which bars easy evasion. ... Let the word go forth—there is no free ride. The commercial hitchhiker seeking to travel on the fame of another will have to learn to pay the fare or stand on his own two feet.

The wedding of the Diors was everything a wedding should be: no tears, no rice, no in-laws, no smarmy toasts, for once no Mendelssohn. Just a legendary private affair.

The Boundaries of Identifiability

In theory, advertisers can avoid publicity rights entanglements by showing only a seemingly unidentifiable portion of the person. This is trickier than it sounds.

COHEN V. HERBAL CONCEPTS, 63 N.Y.2D 379 (N.Y. 1984)

Plaintiffs bring this action pursuant to section 51 of the Civil Rights Law seeking damages from defendants for publishing photographs of them for advertising purposes. It is conceded for purposes of this appeal that plaintiffs are the persons shown in the photographs and that defendants used the photographs as claimed without their consent. The legal issue submitted is whether a photograph of the nude plaintiffs, mother and child, which shows their bodies full length as viewed from a position behind and to the right of them, and which does not show their faces, reveals sufficiently identifiable likenesses to withstand defendants' motions for summary judgment. We hold that it does.

The action arises from these facts.

On the July 4th weekend in 1977, plaintiffs were visiting friends in Woodstock, New York, and Susan Cohen and her four-year-old daughter, Samantha, went bathing in a stream located on their friends' private property. Without their consent, defendant James Krieger took photographs of plaintiffs and subsequently sold them to defendant Herbal Concepts, Inc., a seller and advertiser of consumer products. Herbal Concepts used one of the photographs in an advertisement for Au Naturel, a product designed to help women eliminate body cellulite, those "fatty lumps and bumps that won't go away." The advertisement appeared in two editions of *House and Garden*, which is published by defendant Condé Nast Publications, Inc., and in single editions of *House Beautiful* and *Cosmopolitan*, which are published by defendant Hearst Corporation. Ira Cohen subsequently recognized his wife and daughter in the advertisements while reading one of the magazines and this action followed. . . .

. . . [I]n New York privacy claims are founded solely upon sections 50 and 51 of the Civil Rights Law. The statute protects against the appropriation of a plaintiff's name or likeness for defendants' benefit. Thus, it creates a cause of action in favor of "[a]ny person whose name, portrait or picture is used within this state for advertising purposes or for the purposes of trade without . . . written consent." The action may be brought to enjoin the prohibited use and may also seek damages for any injuries sustained including exemplary damages for a knowing violation of the statute. We are concerned in this case with the appropriation of plaintiffs' likenesses. Defendants claim that there has been no wrong because even if the photograph depicts plaintiffs, they are not identifiable from it.

The statute is designed to protect a person's identity, not merely a property interest in his or her "name", "portrait" or "picture", and thus it implicitly requires that plaintiff be capable of identification from the objectionable material itself. That is not to say that the action may only be maintained when plaintiff's face is visible in the advertising copy. Presumably, by using the term "portrait" the Legislature intended a representation which includes a facial reproduction, either artistically or by photograph, but if we are to give effect to all parts of the statute, it applies also to the improper use of a "picture" of plaintiff which does not show the face. Manifestly, there can be no appropriation of plaintiff's identity for commercial purposes if he or she is not recognizable from the picture and a privacy action could not be sustained, for example, because of the nonconsensual use of a photograph of a hand or a foot without identifying features. But assuming that the photograph depicts plaintiff, whether it presents a recognizable likeness is generally a jury question unless plaintiff cannot be identified because of the limited subject matter revealed in the photograph or the quality of the image. Before a jury may be permitted to decide the issue, to survive a motion for summary judgment, plaintiff must satisfy the court that the person in the photograph is capable of being identified from the advertisement alone and that plaintiff has been so identified.

The sufficiency of plaintiff's evidence for purposes of the motion will necessarily depend upon the court's determination of the quality and quantity of the identifiable characteristics displayed in the advertisement and this will require an assessment of the clarity of the photograph, the extent to which identifying features are visible, and the distinctiveness of those features. This picture depicts two nude persons, a woman and a child, standing in water a few inches deep. The picture quality is good and there are no obstructions to block the view of the subjects. The woman is carrying a small unidentified object in her left hand and is leading the child with her right hand. Neither person's face is visible but the backs and right sides of both mother and child are clearly presented and the mother's right breast can be seen. The identifying features of the subjects include their hair, bone structure, body contours and stature and their posture. Considering these factors, we conclude that a jury could find that someone familiar with the persons in the photograph could identify them by looking at the advertisement. Although we do not rely on the fact, it is also reasonable to assume that just as something in the advertising copy may aid recognition, identifiability may be enhanced also in photograph depicting two persons because observers may associate the two and thus more easily identify them when they are seen together.

The plaintiffs also submitted evidence that they were identified as the persons in defendants' advertisement by Ira Cohen's affidavit in which he stated that while leafing through one of defendants' magazines he "recognized [his] wife and daughter immediately." That was prima facie sufficient.

Defendants contend Mr. Cohen's affidavit is not probative on the issue of identification because he was present when the photograph was taken, as indeed he was. He was not only present, he was incensed by the photographer's intrusion and chased him away. Essentially, defendants' contention is that Mr. Cohen's identification is tainted by this independent knowledge that plaintiffs were photographed by defendant Krieger while bathing. Although Mr. Cohen's presence when the photograph was taken may have increased his ability to identify his wife and child, the motion court or the jury at trial could conclude that he also recognized them from the photograph and his presence when it was taken, standing alone, does not disqualify him from offering evidence that he did so. . . .

NOTES AND QUESTIONS

Other Causes of Action? Could the Cohens have sued the photographer for harassment or public disclosure of private facts (discussed in Chapter 15)? Would the property owner have a claim against the photographer for trespass? Could the advertisers be secondarily liable for that trespass? See the California Civil Code Section 1708.08 (California's "anti-paparazzi" statute), which says in part:

> (a) A person is liable for physical invasion of privacy when the defendant knowingly enters onto the land of another person without permission or otherwise committed a trespass in order to physically invade the privacy of the plaintiff with the intent to capture any type of visual image, sound recording, or other physical impression of the plaintiff engaging in a personal or familial activity and the physical invasion occurs in a manner that is offensive to a reasonable person . . .

> (f) (1) The transmission, publication, broadcast, sale, offer for sale, or other use of any visual image, sound recording, or other physical impression that was taken or captured in violation of subdivision (a) . . . shall not constitute a violation of this section unless the person, in the first transaction following the taking or capture of the visual image, sound recording, or other physical impression, publicly transmitted, published, broadcast, sold or offered for sale, the visual image, sound recording, or other physical impression with actual knowledge that it was taken or captured in violation of subdivision (a) . . . and provide[s] compensation, consideration, or remuneration, monetary or otherwise, for the rights to the unlawfully obtained visual image, sound recording, or other physical impression.

Under a statute like this, could Herbal Concepts have been liable for buying the photos from Krieger? How would this statute fare in a constitutional challenge?

Recreating the Cohen Photo. If the advertiser and photographer liked the scene so much, could they have freely recreated the scene with paid models and avoided all liability risks?

Other Partial Depictions. California's statutory right of publicity expressly provides that liability based on a photograph requires that the plaintiff be "readily identifiable." Cal. Civ.

Code § 3344(a). Does this legal standard differ from the legal standard applied by the *Cohen* court, which required that "the person in the photograph is capable of being identified from the advertisement alone and that plaintiff has been so identified"?

Test Yourself (#1). Look at the photo in the upper right of the following ad. Assume the woman on the left did not sign a proper publicity release. Does the photo violate her publicity rights?

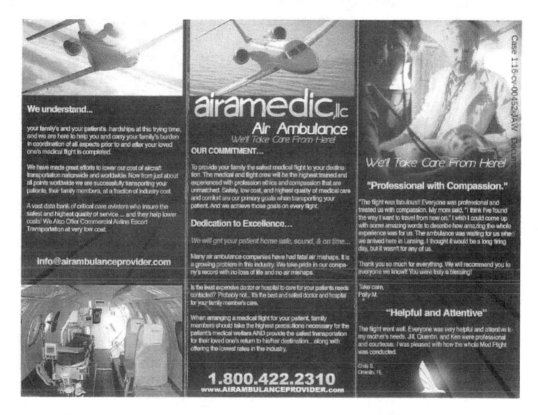

The court said:

> Ms. Rosecrans' face is not visible in the photograph and the brochure does not identify her by name. To know that the person in the photograph is Ms. Rosecrans, the person would have to recognize Lisa Weeks (whose face is visible) as Ms. Rosecrans' daughter and extrapolate that the figure in the photograph must have been Ms. Weeks' mother, perhaps because the person knew that Ms. Rosecrans once worked as a flight nurse. For a person to arrive at these conclusions, he or she would have to have known Ms. Rosecrans extremely well and, given their familiarity with Ms. Rosecrans, would likely discount any negative implications from the photograph. By contrast, the average person would not be able to identify Ms. Rosecrans as the person in the photograph. Nor is there anything remotely pejorative or scandalous about the photograph and its context. To the contrary, in the brochure, Airamedic is praising the professionalism and dedication of its staff, including by implication Ms. Rosecrans.

As a result, the court awarded Rosecrans damages of only one dollar. Rosecrans v. Airamedic, LLC, 2017 U.S. Dist. LEXIS 47719 (D. Me. 2017).

Test Yourself (#2). Is the person in this image identifiable?

The court said no, because "the only visible facial characteristic is a small, shadowy sliver of the individual's chin; the "remaining viewable aspects" were "common, plain, and non-identifying"; "the photograph could be of any countless number of white males" and tagging the plaintiff's Instagram account @dumb_and_dunder didn't use his "name" or make him readily identifiable as the person in the photo. Young v. Greystar Real Estate Partners, LLC, 2019 U.S. Dist. LEXIS 149731 (S.D. Cal. 2019). Do you agree with this analysis? Should an Instagram handle be distinguished from a nickname or abandoned legal name?

Are people becoming increasingly identifiable over time? Technology continues to improve, such as automatic facial recognition. People also wear distinctive clothing or have unique body art and tattoos. *See* Yolanda M. King, *The Right-of-Publicity Challenges for Tattoo Copyrights*, 16 NEV. L.J. 441 (2016). Plus, as photos and videos reach larger audiences, the odds increase that someone will know the person and recognize something unique about them. *See, e.g.*, Jonathan Krim, *Subway Fracas Escalates into Test of the Internet's Power to Shame*, WASH. POST, July 7, 2005 (discussing the naming and shaming of the South Korean "dog poop girl"). Due to these converging factors, perhaps it is becoming impossible to use an unconsented photograph of a person in ad copy, irrespective of whether the person's face is shown.

Identifiability When a Person Isn't Shown at All. Because the photos depicted the individuals' backside, the *Cohen* case and the note examples following it all involved low degrees of identifiability, but at least a person was depicted. Can publicity rights apply even if you can't see a person at all? Surprisingly, the answer might be "yes" in some circumstances.

Motschenbacher v. R.J. Reynolds Tobacco Co., 498 F.2d 821 (9th Cir. 1974), involved the following facts:

> Plaintiff Motschenbacher is a professional driver of racing cars, internationally known and recognized in racing circles and by racing fans. He derives part of his income from manufacturers of commercial products who pay him for endorsing their products.
>
> During the relevant time span, plaintiff has consistently "individualized" his cars to set them apart from those of other drivers and to make them more readily identifiable as his own. Since 1966, each of his cars has displayed a distinctive narrow white pinstripe appearing on no other car. This decoration has adorned the leading edges of the cars' bodies, which have uniformly been solid red. In addition, the white background for his racing number "11" has always been oval, in contrast to the circular backgrounds of all other cars.
>
> In 1970, defendants, R. J. Reynolds Tobacco Company and William Esty Company, produced and caused to be televised a commercial which utilized a "stock" color photograph depicting several racing cars on a racetrack. Plaintiff's car appears in the foreground, and although plaintiff is the driver, his facial features are not visible.
>
> In producing the commercial, defendants altered the photograph: they changed the numbers on all racing cars depicted, transforming plaintiff's number "11" into "71";

they "attached" a wing-like device known as a "spoiler" to plaintiff's car; they added the word "Winston," the name of their product, to that spoiler and removed advertisements for other products from the spoilers of other cars. However, they made no other changes, and the white pinstriping, the oval medallion, and the red color of plaintiff's car were retained. They then made a motion picture from the altered photograph, adding a series of comic strip-type "balloons" containing written messages of an advertising nature; one such balloon message, appearing to emanate from plaintiff, was: "Did you know that Winston tastes good, like a cigarette should?" They also added a sound track consisting in part of voices coordinated with, and echoing, the written messages. The commercial was subsequently broadcast nationally on network television and in color.

[screenshot from the ad.
Altered Motschenbacher car depicted in the lower left]

Several of plaintiff's affiants who had seen the commercial on television had immediately recognized plaintiff's car and had inferred that it was sponsored by Winston cigarettes.

On the question of identifiability, the court concluded:

[T]he "likeness" of plaintiff is itself unrecognizable; however, the [district] court's further conclusion of law to the effect that the driver is not identifiable as plaintiff is erroneous in that it wholly fails to attribute proper significance to the distinctive decorations appearing on the car. As pointed out earlier, these markings were not only peculiar to the plaintiff's cars but they caused some persons to think the car in question was plaintiff's and to infer that the person driving the car was the plaintiff.

As a result, the court said that Motschenbacher stated a cause of action for a publicity/privacy rights violation. In other words, the advertiser may have violated Motschenbacher's publicity/privacy rights by depicting a modified version of his car.

Compare this analysis to *Roberts v. Bliss*, 229 F. Supp. 3d 240 (S.D.N.Y. 2017). Bliss produced a video called "10 Hours," showing Roberts walking around New York City and being subjected to repeated catcalls and sexual innuendo by strangers. Bliss retained the video's copyright. The video went viral and was viewed over forty million times. Bliss licensed the video to TGI Friday's, which made advertisements where it completely replaced all depictions of Roberts with images of some of its appetizers, thus making it look like the strangers were directing the catcalls and innuendo to the food:

Anyone who saw the original video would get TGI Friday's "joke," but you are not alone if you don't find this very funny.

Because the food replaced Roberts' image entirely, she had little chance with a publicity rights claim. (What about the other people depicted who didn't get replaced?) Instead, Roberts sued for Lanham Act false endorsement. The court still rejected the claim:

> Although the ad may well call to a viewer's mind the 10 Hours video, and perhaps even Roberts because of her role in it, the ad does not use Roberts' image or persona, nor suggest in any way that Roberts herself endorsed the product advertised....
>
> While the advertisement does "call to mind" 10 Hours, the supplantation of Roberts with large gimmicky images of appetizers is an "obvious[] modification" of, and a "conscious departure" from, the original work. This modification, moreover, is outlandish, not subtle.... The ad replaces Roberts—the object of the harassing men's attention in the 10 Hours video—with the appetizers. They are now the subject of the men's desire. That, together with the play on words between "appcalling" and "catcalling," is what makes it a parody. And because the parody is obvious, the "risk of consumer confusion is at its lowest." ... That Roberts, of course, looks nothing like the overblown images of walking food, and that an online video designed to highlight

a societal ill and a chain restaurant attempting to promote its appetizers occupy distinct merchandising markets, reinforces the conclusion that it is implausible that a viewer of the ad would be confused about whether Roberts endorsed it.

D.   Evoking a Persona

As we've seen, courts apply the publicity/privacy rights doctrines expansively when ad copy includes any potentially identifiable attribute of a person. But what if ad copy incorporates none of these personal attributes, and no one would think that a celebrity actually appeared in the ad (as viewers might have in *Motsenbacher*), and yet a celebrity persona is still recognizable? As the next case indicates, publicity rights can be stretched to cover that situation, too.

WHITE V. SAMSUNG ELECTRONICS AMERICA, INC., 989 F.2D 1512 (9TH CIR. 1993)

KOZINSKI, Circuit Judge, dissenting from a request for an en banc rehearing.

. . . Concerned about what it sees as a wrong done to Vanna White, the panel majority erects a property right of remarkable and dangerous breadth: Under the majority's opinion, it's now a tort for advertisers to remind the public of a celebrity. Not to use a celebrity's name, voice, signature or likeness; not to imply the celebrity endorses a product; but simply to evoke the celebrity's image in the public's mind. This Orwellian notion withdraws far more from the public domain than prudence and common sense allow. . . .

. . . II.

Samsung ran an ad campaign promoting its consumer electronics. Each ad depicted a Samsung product and a humorous prediction: One showed a raw steak with the caption "Revealed to be health food. 2010 A.D." Another showed Morton Downey, Jr. in front of an American flag with the caption "Presidential candidate. 2008 A.D." The ads were meant to convey—humorously—that Samsung products would still be in use twenty years from now.

The ad that spawned this litigation starred a robot dressed in a wig, gown and jewelry reminiscent of Vanna White's hair and dress; the robot was posed next to a Wheel-of-Fortune-like game board. The caption read "Longest-running game show. 2012 A.D." The gag here, I take it, was that Samsung would still be around when White had been replaced by a robot.*

---

* [Editor's note: As of 2020, Vanna White still works on *Wheel of Fortune*, a position she has held since 1982, though she stopped physically turning letters in 1997. Steak became a central part of the Atkins Diet fad in the early 2000s. Morton Downey Jr. did not run for president in 2008, but actor Fred Thompson did, and many other actors and television personalities have won high office since the Samsung ad, including Donald Trump (president), Al Franken (U.S. Senator from Massachusetts), Jesse Ventura (Minnesota governor) and Arnold Schwarzenegger (California governor).]

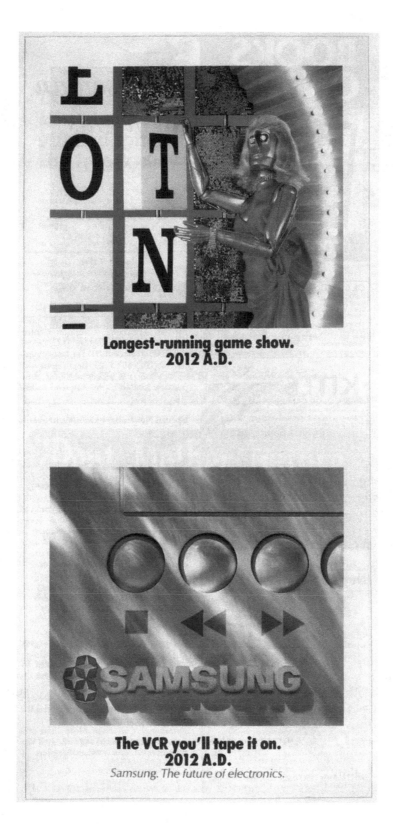

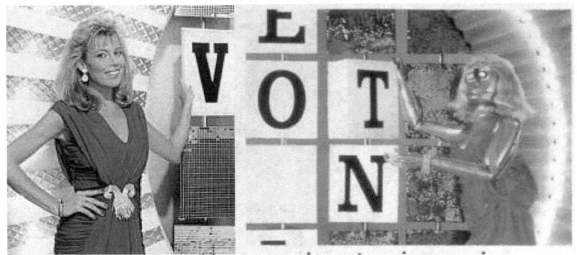

[photo of Vanna White (left) compared to close-up of Samsung ad (right)]

Perhaps failing to see the humor, White sued, alleging Samsung infringed her right of publicity by "appropriating" her "identity." Under California law, White has the exclusive right to use her name, likeness, signature and voice for commercial purposes. But Samsung didn't use her name, voice or signature, and it certainly didn't use her likeness. The ad just wouldn't have been funny had it depicted White or someone who resembled her—the whole joke was that the game show host(ess) was a robot, not a real person. No one seeing the ad could have thought this was supposed to be White in 2012.

The district judge quite reasonably held that, because Samsung didn't use White's name, likeness, voice or signature, it didn't violate her right of publicity. Not so, says the panel majority: The California right of publicity can't possibly be limited to name and likeness. If it were, the majority reasons, a "clever advertising strategist" could avoid using White's name or likeness but nevertheless remind people of her with impunity, "effectively eviscerat[ing]" her rights. To prevent this "evisceration," the panel majority holds that the right of publicity must extend beyond name and likeness, to any "appropriation" of White's "identity"— anything that "evoke[s]" her personality.

III.

But what does "evisceration" mean in intellectual property law? Intellectual property rights aren't like some constitutional rights, absolute guarantees protected against all kinds of interference, subtle as well as blatant. They cast no penumbras, emit no emanations: The very point of intellectual property laws is that they protect only against certain specific kinds of appropriation. I can't publish unauthorized copies of, say, *Presumed Innocent*; I can't make a movie out of it. But I'm perfectly free to write a book about an idealistic young prosecutor on trial for a crime he didn't commit. So what if I got the idea from *Presumed Innocent*? So what if it reminds readers of the original? Have I "eviscerated" Scott Turow's intellectual property rights? Certainly not. All creators draw in part on the work of those who came before, referring to it, building on it, poking fun at it; we call this creativity, not piracy.

The majority isn't, in fact, preventing the "evisceration" of Vanna White's existing rights; it's creating a new and much broader property right, a right unknown in California law. It's replacing the existing balance between the interests of the celebrity and those of the public by a different balance, one substantially more favorable to the celebrity. Instead of having an exclusive right in her name, likeness, signature or voice, every famous person now has an exclusive right to anything that reminds the viewer of her. After all, that's all Samsung did: It used an inanimate object to remind people of White, to "evoke [her identity]."

Consider how sweeping this new right is. What is it about the ad that makes people think of White? It's not the robot's wig, clothes or jewelry; there must be ten million blond women (many of them quasi-famous) who wear dresses and jewelry like White's. It's that the robot is posed near the "Wheel of Fortune" game board. Remove the game board from the ad, and no one would think of Vanna White. But once you include the game board, anybody standing beside it—a brunette woman, a man wearing women's clothes, a monkey in a wig and gown—would evoke White's image, precisely the way the robot did. It's the "Wheel of Fortune" set, not the robot's face or dress or jewelry that evokes White's image. The panel is giving White an exclusive right not in what she looks like or who she is, but in what she does for a living . . .

The intellectual property right created by the panel here has [no] essential limitations: No fair use exception; no right to parody; no idea-expression dichotomy. It impoverishes the public domain, to the detriment of future creators and the public at large. Instead of well-defined, limited characteristics such as name, likeness or voice, advertisers will now have to cope with vague claims of "appropriation of identity," claims often made by people with a wholly exaggerated sense of their own fame and significance. Future Vanna Whites might not get the chance to create their personae, because their employers may fear some celebrity will claim the persona is too similar to her own. The public will be robbed of parodies of celebrities, and our culture will be deprived of the valuable safety valve that parody and mockery create.

Moreover, consider the moral dimension, about which the panel majority seems to have gotten so exercised. Saying Samsung "appropriated" something of White's begs the question: Should White have the exclusive right to something as broad and amorphous as her "identity"? Samsung's ad didn't simply copy White's schtick—like all parody, it created something new. True, Samsung did it to make money, but White does whatever she does to make money, too; the majority talks of "the difference between fun and profit," but in the entertainment industry fun is profit. Why is Vanna White's right to exclusive for-profit use of her persona—a persona that might not even be her own creation, but that of a writer, director or producer—superior to Samsung's right to profit by creating its own inventions? Why should she have such absolute rights to control the conduct of others, unlimited by the idea-expression dichotomy or by the fair use doctrine? . . .

. . .VI.

Finally, I can't see how giving White the power to keep others from evoking her image in the public's mind can be squared with the First Amendment. Where does White get this right to control our thoughts? The majority's creation goes way beyond the protection given a trademark or a copyrighted work, or a person's name or likeness. All those things control one particular way of expressing an idea, one way of referring to an object or a person. But not allowing any means of reminding people of someone? That's a speech restriction unparalleled in First Amendment law. . . .

The majority dismisses the First Amendment issue out of hand because Samsung's ad was commercial speech. So what? Commercial speech may be less protected by the First Amendment than noncommercial speech, but less protected means protected nonetheless. And there are very good reasons for this. Commercial speech has a profound effect on our culture and our attitudes. Neutral-seeming ads influence people's social and political attitudes, and themselves arouse political controversy. "Where's the Beef?" turned from an advertising catchphrase into the only really memorable thing about the 1984 presidential campaign. Four years later, Michael Dukakis called George Bush "the Joe Isuzu of American politics."[8]

In our pop culture, where salesmanship must be entertaining and entertainment must sell, the line between the commercial and noncommercial has not merely blurred; it has disappeared. Is the Samsung parody any different from a parody on *Saturday Night Live* or in *Spy Magazine*? Both are equally profit-motivated. Both use a celebrity's identity to sell things—one to sell VCRs, the other to sell advertising. Both mock their subjects. Both try to make people laugh. Both add something, perhaps something worthwhile and memorable, perhaps not, to our culture. Both are things that the people being portrayed might dearly want to suppress.

Commercial speech is a significant, valuable part of our national discourse. The Supreme Court has recognized as much, and has insisted that lower courts carefully scrutinize commercial speech restrictions, but the panel totally fails to do this. . . .

VII.

. . . In the name of fostering creativity, the majority suppresses it. Vanna White and those like her have been given something they never had before, and they've been given it at our expense. I cannot agree.

NOTES AND QUESTIONS

Denouement. White ultimately won $403,000 in damages in the case.

Who Owns the Right? Let's assume that Samsung did, in fact, tortiously evoke White's role in its ads. Who is the proper plaintiff—White, the *Wheel of Fortune* producers, both or neither?

In *Wendt v. Host International, Inc.*, 197 F.3d 1284 (9th Cir. 1999), Judge Kozinski again dissented from the denial of an en banc hearing, after a panel held that two actors who had

---

[88] [Editor's note: Joe Isuzu was a fictional car salesman who starred in a series of 1980s television advertisements for Isuzu cars and trucks. He was an inveterate liar who made incredible claims about Isuzu's cars, and the ads themselves acknowledged his lies.]

portrayed characters on the TV show *Cheers* had publicity rights against the use of robots that vaguely resembled them in bars licensed by the copyright owner.[*]

The district court granted summary judgment for the defendants because it found that the robots didn't look like the plaintiffs: "[T]here is [no] similarity at all . . . except that one of the robots, like one of the plaintiffs, is heavier than the other. . . . The facial features are totally different." Nevertheless, the appeals court concluded that "material facts exist that might cause a reasonable jury to find [the robots] sufficiently 'like' [Wendt and Ratzenberger] to violate" their right of publicity.

After the case was remanded to the district court, the parties settled.

While *Wendt* is not an advertising-law case per se, it does indicate that obtaining a copyright license to fictional characters may not be enough to use the fictional characters in ad copy. Where an actor may be publicly associated with the character, the actor's publicity rights mean consent may also be necessary. Ideally, the producers of the fictional work obtain permission from the actor to relicense his or her publicity rights as part of a copyright license. Otherwise, separate permissions from both the copyright holder and the actor may be required.

For more on the *White* case and its implications for the boundaries of publicity rights, *see* Stacey L. Dogan, *An Exclusive Right to Evoke*, 44 B.C. L. REV. 291 (2003).

Under this precedent, if ad copy depicts an empty Cleveland Cavaliers jersey with the number "23," has the advertiser violated LeBron James's publicity rights? (Does it matter whether this is during a time when LeBron James was a member of the Cavaliers' team?)

Specificity. In the *White* case, it was clear that the robot evoked Vanna White. In other cases, it may be less clear who is being evoked. If the evoking isn't clearly specific to the plaintiff, then that will give courts another reason to reject the expansion of publicity rights coverage.

For example, 5-Hour ENERGY drink ran a television ad in which an actor claims to have accomplished a series of seemingly impossible feats, including mastering origami "while beating the record for Hacky Sack," with the help of the drink. See the ad at https://www.youtube.com/watch?v=aro0aTGBPUE.

---

[*] Host changed the robots' names to "Hank" and "Bob," though the characters on the TV show were Norm and Cliff.

Johannes "Ted" Martin "holds the world record for most consecutive kicks (no knees) in the footbag (i.e., hacky sack) singles category and has held that record since 1988 (with the exception of a brief period of fifty days in 1997)." Martin sued Living Essentials, makers of 5-Hour ENERGY. The courts rejected his claims. Martin v. Living Essentials, LLC, 160 F. Supp. 3d 1042 (N.D. Ill. 2016), *aff'd*, 653 Fed. Appx. 482 (7th Cir. 2016).

The appeals court explained: "[W]e agree with the district court that the phrase 'the record for Hacky Sack' is too ambiguous to call an 'attribute' of Martin. . . . [N]o reasonable viewer would interpret the commercial for 5–hour ENERGY as referring to Martin, and because he does not plausibly allege that Living Essentials invoked his 'identity' through the actor's statement, Martin fails to state a claim" per Illinois' publicity rights statute.

In rejecting Martin's Lanham Act false endorsement claim, the appeals court amplified on Martin's non-identifiability:

> [W]e cannot imagine how this ad would confuse anyone into thinking that Martin himself endorses 5–hour ENERGY or that his use of the caffeinated drink explains a record set before the product came to market. The mention of Hacky Sack, after all, is sandwiched between obviously absurd achievements (which fine print in the 30–second commercial disclaims as "not actual results," although who possibly would believe that the actor, with or without an energy shot, had disproved the theory of relativity or found the elusive Bigfoot?). And Martin's personal endorsement of 5–hour ENERGY cannot logically be inferred from the actor's claim that he "mastered origami while beating the record for Hacky Sack"; the actor cannot be accused of impersonating Martin, since he brags of besting, not holding for years, a footbag record. To eclipse Martin's record in five hours would require a superhuman effort of three to four kicks per second, but, that aside, why would a viewer assume that it was Martin's footbag record which had fallen? The actor is shown kicking two footbags, and Guinness World Records credits Finnish footbagger Juha–Matti Rytilahti, not Martin, with the most consecutive kicks of two footbags.

The district court reinforced the latter point, noting that there were fourteen different hacky sack world records, so it's not clear to which record (and record holder) the ad referred.

A related case is *Martin v. Wendy's International, Inc.*, 2017 WL 1545684 (N.D. Ill. April 28, 2017). Wendy's included a Guinness-branded footbag in its Kid's Meal along with various statements about footbag-related world records. The footbag instructions said that "Back in 1997, Ted Martin made his world record of 63,326 kicks in a little less than nine hours!" and encouraged customers to try to beat it. Echoing the "incidental use" doctrine discussed *supra*, the court held that Wendy's did not violate Martin's publicity rights because "it would be nonsensical to hold that the law prohibits Guinness from reciting that bare fact in a promotional item but permits it to include the fact in the books it sells." It also held that Wendy's did not violate the Lanham Act prohibition on false endorsement because "mentioning plaintiff's record on the instructional card served only to offer a sample of the sort of world records Guinness publishes." Compare the *Abdul-Jabbar v. General Motors* ruling discussed at the chapter's beginning, as well as the *Jewel* case involving a tribute to Michael Jordan. Whether a celebrity mention is in something courts understand as "commercial speech" can thus be very important.

Also consider *Daniels v. FanDuels, Inc.*, No. 18S-CQ-00134 (Ind. Sup. Ct. 2018), concluding that "when informational and statistical data of college athletes is presented on a fantasy sports website[,] it would be difficult to draw the conclusion that the athletes are endorsing any particular product such that there has been a violation of the right of publicity."

E.   Logistical Considerations

Obtaining Consent. Getting consent is essential to avoiding a publicity rights claim, but the advertiser must draft the consent properly and respect any limitations on the consent. *See, e.g.*, Sahoury v. Meredith Corp., 2012 WL 3185964 (D. N.J. Aug. 2, 2012) (breastfeeding mom had viable contract breach claims when she signed broad publicity consent but was orally told that the video footage would only appear in limited outlets and wouldn't use her or the baby's full name and those restrictions weren't followed).

Consider the following ad for a law firm:

The depicted firefighter, Robert Keiley, joined the FDNY in 2004—three years after 9/11. Therefore, he was not "there." Keiley signed a broad publicity consent, but he says he thought that his depiction would be used in a fire-prevention ad and the 9/11 picture was photoshopped into his hands. *See* Reuven Fenton & Jennifer Fermino, *Law Firm's Ad Trick a 9/11 'Insult,'* N.Y. POST, March 28, 2011. Did the law firm or its ad agency do anything wrong?

To state the obvious, it is even less advisable to tell a factual story using photos without the depicted individuals' consent at all. *See* Nolan v. State of N.Y., 2018 NY Slip Op 51789(U) (N.Y. Ct. Claims 2018) (advertiser committed defamation when it featured, without her consent, a photo of the plaintiff in an HIV-related ad saying "I am positive" and "I have rights," leading to a $125,000 damages award).

Labor Union Relations. Many advertising agencies and some large advertisers have signed agreements with actors' labor unions, such as the Screen Actors Guild (SAG) and the American Federation of Television and Radio Artists (AFTRA). Each agreement should be reviewed carefully, but in general they (1) require that advertisers use only union members as actors in advertisements (with some exceptions, such as showing a company employee doing his or her normal job) and (2) specify minimum payments to actors, including payments for pensions and health benefits as well as "residuals" (ongoing payments for continued use of the ad copy).

Damages and Attorneys' Fees. We previously discussed publicity rights damages in connection with the sound-alike cases, which showed that damages available for publicity rights violations are wide-ranging. Some publicity rights statutes provide statutory damages provisions that plaintiffs can elect to receive instead of actual damages. California's statutory damages amount is $750, which can create a large number of class-action lawsuits. California's statute also requires the losing party to pay the winning party's attorneys' fees—a further incentive for plaintiffs to bring cases, but it creates the risk that a plaintiff will pay a lot of money to the defendant for picking the fight.

The following case, *Olive v. General Nutrition Centers, Inc.*, 30 Cal.App.5th 804 (Cal. App. Ct. 2018), illustrates the difficulties of setting damages in publicity rights cases and the interplay with attorneys' fees.

Jason Olive and about fifteen other models appeared in a GNC ad campaign pursuant to licenses. GNC wanted to continue using those ads beyond the license scope while they transitioned to a new ad campaign. The other models consented to the extension for additional license fees, but Olive refused. He turned down a $150,000 offer, an amount which clearly included a premium for Olive being the last holdout. GNC then spent $350,000 to remove Olive from the deprecated ad campaign.

All told, GNC used Olive's image for about a year beyond the license. GNC was prepared to pay damages for this usage, but the parties deeply disagreed on the amount.

GNC proposed $4,800 for the year, a number based on what the other models actually accepted as license fees.

Olive wanted more. A lot more. The opinion says Olive asked for:

> actual damages of $1.5 million for the licensing fee to use his likeness in 2012-2013; past and future emotional distress damages of $2 million; restitution for GNC's profits based on the unlicensed use of his likeness in a range that went from approximately $54 million to as high as $175.9 million; and punitive damages of at least five times the amount of the jury's damage award. During argument, Olive asked the jury to award restitution in amounts ranging from $11.7 to $35.2 million.

Elsewhere, the court says Olive's "bottom-range" restitution damage was $11 million, and his "mid-point" restitution damage was $20 million plus punitive damages of five times that amount. The trial court says Olive "recommended" damages of $23.5 million. These lofty restitution numbers reflect that California's publicity rights statute awards the net revenue attributable to a violation. Because the ad depicting Olive (and other models) promoted GNC, he wanted a piece of GNC's entire corporate revenues for the year.

The jury awarded Olive $213,000 in actual damages and $910,000 in emotional distress damages. The jury did not award any share of GNC's revenues or punitive damages.

The damages award of $1.1 million was more than 200 times what GNC proposed and less than 5% of what Olive proposed. "The trial court noted that both parties were visibly disappointed after the jury rendered its verdict. . . . The court emphasized counsel's facial reactions, stating '[t]his . . . mutually transparent display was unprecedented in the court's experience.'"

With respect to California's mandatory attorneys' fee-shifting provision, the court concluded that neither party won because the jury award diverged so greatly from both parties' proposed amounts. If Olive's damages requests had been more reasonable, he surely would have received his attorneys' fees as the prevailing party; but his inflated damages requests probably helped increase the jury's damages award.

Meanwhile, GNC made a more-than-million-dollar mistake—and that's after GNC incurred $350,000 of avoidable removal costs. Ideally, GNC would sign mistake-proof license agreements with models, but union rules may prevent that. Otherwise, GNC needed to manage its licenses better. Had GNC approached Olive before the license's expiration, it could have surely obtained his consent for a few thousand dollars.

3. Endorsements and Testimonials

In addition to the publicity rights and related doctrines that govern depicting people in ads, those ads must comply with the rules governing endorsements and testimonials. We discussed this issue a bit in Chapter 6 regarding distinguishing ads from editorial content, and you may wish to refamiliarize yourself with the discussion there.

The leading source of such rules is the FTC's Guides Concerning Use of Endorsements and Testimonials in Advertising.* *See* 16 C.F.R. §§ 255.0-255.5. The FTC defines an "endorsement" and "testimonial" (the FTC equates the two) as:

> any advertising message (including verbal statements, demonstrations, or depictions of the name, signature, likeness or other identifying personal characteristics of an individual or the name or seal of an organization) that consumers are likely to believe reflects the opinions, beliefs, findings, or experiences of a party other than the sponsoring advertiser, even if the views expressed by that party are identical to those of the sponsoring advertiser.

While this definition is not especially clear, it is intended to exclude the statements of people that consumers are likely to recognize as actors hired by the advertiser. A paradigmatic endorsement is when a celebrity personally vouches for the product's quality; a paradigmatic testimonial is when a person describes his or her experiences with the product (such as the amount of weight lost using a diet aid) or is depicted in before/after pictures. Actors playing out an obviously fictional or hypothetical scripted scene in an advertisement aren't making endorsements or testimonials.

Some of the key requirements of the Endorsement and Testimonials Guidelines:

- Endorsements must reflect the endorser's actual beliefs or experiences
- Endorsers may not make representations that would be deceptive if made by the advertiser
- If the ad copy says an endorser uses the product, that must be true
- If the ad copy represents that the endorser is an expert, the endorser must have the requisite qualifications
- The advertiser must disclose any connections with the endorser that would affect the endorsement's credibility

Many of these guidelines are logical extensions of general false advertising principles and thus not controversial in the abstract. However, specific contexts can raise tricky issues. The FTC has released numerous guidance documents, including Disclosures 11 for Social Media Influencers, designed to inform endorsers and those who work with them.

Example: Online Product Reviews. In 2009, the FTC said the guidelines cover online product reviews. The FTC expressed concern about situations where an advertiser provides a financial benefit—including free product samples—to a blogger to write a blog post. Due to the benefit, the FTC believes the blog post becomes a paid endorsement or testimonial. As a

---

* Other countries' regulators are expressing similar interest in these situations. The Canadian Code of Advertising Standards, for example, requires that any "material connection" between an influencer and a brand be "clearly and prominently disclosed in close proximity to the representation about the product or service," and also refers advertisers to the FTC Guidelines for examples to assist them in conforming to Canadian law. *See also* Influencer Marketing Steering Committee, Disclosure Guidelines, Apr. 19, 2018 (further Canadian guidance).

result, the FTC expects the blogger to prominently disclose the benefit to avoid misleading the readers about the putative authenticity of the blogger's views.

The FTC's position treats traditional journalists, who the FTC thinks do not need to disclose receiving free product samples if they do so as part of their jobs, differently than identically situated bloggers, who should make such disclosures. The FTC has offered dubious justifications for this Internet exceptionalism. Furthermore, the FTC's guidelines regulate what many people would consider "editorial content" (the blog post), not obvious commercial speech or advertising.

Example: Celebrity Interviews. Consumers will recognize a celebrity touting a product in a traditional thirty-second ad as a paid endorser. But what if the celebrity appears on a nighttime talk show and casually mentions how much better she's doing now that she's using a particular weight loss program?

If it would not be obvious to most consumers that she was being paid as a spokesperson by the weight-loss program, the FTC views her casual reference to the weight loss program as a paid endorsement/testimonial—meaning she would need to disclose that fact when she drops the casual reference. And, because she is a spokesperson, what she says on the talk show is subject to the same substantiation requirements as an ordinary ad would be. As a reminder, the FTC interprets its substantiation obligation assuming that consumers usually understand a testimonial to reflect typical results—so the advertiser would need to substantiate typical results like those the celebrity achieved or instruct the celebrity to disclose enough qualifiers so consumers wouldn't be misled about typicality. If you were writing a contract with an endorser who might appear on talk shows, how would you deal with this issue?

What about non-celebrities? Does it matter whether or not they are presented as experts? In one case, the security company ADT paid three people over $300,000 to appear on television shows, including the *Today Show* and local newscasts, and post content online, including on blogs. These endorsers were touted as "The Safety Mom," a home-security expert and a tech expert. They described ADT's security system as "amazing" or "incredible" and touted its capabilities, safety benefits and cost. ADT set up these interviews through its PR firms and booking agents, providing reporters and anchors with suggested interview questions and background video. The experts never disclosed their payments from ADT.

The FTC brought an enforcement action against ADT. The resulting consent order prohibited ADT from misrepresenting that any discussion or demonstration of its products or services was an independent review by an impartial expert, required ADT to clearly and prominently disclose any material connections with the experts and required ADT to remove existing reviews and endorsements that had been misrepresented as independent or that failed to disclose a material connection. *See In re* ADT LLC, F.T.C. File No. 122 3121 (Mar. 11, 2014). A connection is material, according to the FTC, when the connection might materially affect the weight or credibility a consumer gives the endorsement.

Why do you think the FTC is concerned with such situations? Without this rule, would advertisers be able to disseminate unsubstantiated claims by using paid endorsers, or are there other constraints on advertisers that might block abuse of this loophole? What do reasonable consumers expect when they see a celebrity or "expert" touting some product or service in an "interview" by a reporter associated with a TV station? If the interviewee makes only vague, general statements, would that be puffery? Even if consumers don't understand that she's a paid spokesperson, are they harmed if all she does is puff?

Example: Celebrity Instagramming. Kim Kardashian endorsed a prescription pharmaceutical on Instagram without disclosing her financial connection to the drugmaker:

Note the first substantive comment from "flawlessfashionstore": "[I don't know] if she's getting paid for this and do not care. But it is safe for mom & baby. I called my doctor because I couldn't even keep water down." Assume this comment is both true and being proffered by an ordinary consumer. If this speaker can make this statement without extensive disclosures, why can't Kardashian? Does Kardashian's celebrity status make her claims more believable? Does the fact that Kardashian is using her real name make her claims more believable?

The FDA issued a warning to the drugmaker, resulting in the following message, which required scrolling twice on an ordinary mobile device:

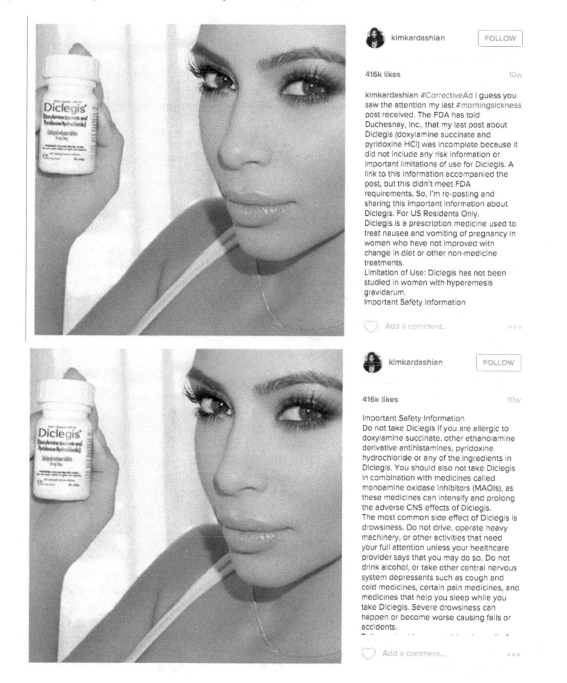

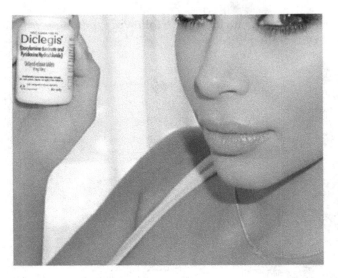

Tell your healthcare provider about all of your medical conditions, including if you are breastfeeding or plan to breastfeed. Diclegis can pass into your breast milk and may harm your baby. You should not breastfeed while using Diclegis. Additional safety information can be found at www.DiclegisImportantSafetyInfo.com or www.Diclegis.com. Duchesnay USA encourages you to report negative side effects of prescription drugs to the FDA. Visit www.fda.gov/medwatch or call 1-800-FDA-1088.

view all 8,058 comments

reneerowe_ @sandyrowe21

sithembil3_muluba How much are they paying you to promote this @kimkardashian

sweetpotatogirl @seeleyavenue you know it's legit

seeleyavenue @sarahfurnishricchio

♡ Add a comment...   o o o

Was this an appropriate remedial action? Reportedly, Kardashian was paid nearly half a million dollars for the initial post, which contributed to a 500%increase in social mentions of the drug within the following weeks; sales increased 21%, despite the limited evidence that it is any better than the far-cheaper vitamin B6 (one of the ingredients in Diclegis). Amil Niazi, *Why Instagram Influencers Shouldn't Be Shilling For Big Pharma*, CHATELAINE, Feb. 24, 2020. Does the difficulty of after-the-fact corrective disclosure help justify the FTC's arguably expansive rules?

The FTC also secured a $15.2 million judgment against a tea seller that made unsubstantiated claims about weight loss, migraine treatment and cancer treatment and who paid influencers to tout the products without proper disclosure. The seller claimed it required proper disclosure from its endorsers (who included Kylie Jenner and Demi Lovato), but it tolerated numerous violations without taking action. Federal Trade Comm'n v. Teami, LLC, No. 20-cv-00518-VMC-TGW (M.D. Fla. filed Mar. 17, 2020) (stipulated judgment). Going forward, the company must communicate disclosure obligations to influencers and obtain signed acknowledgements from them, and it must monitor their compliance and take real actions to address violations.

Example: Pinterest. The FTC issued a "closing letter" to Cole Haan, a shoe seller, indicating that it would take no further action based on the following situation. Cole Haan conducted a "Wandering Sole" contest on Pinterest, a social media site where users can save and organize images known as "pins" in collections called "boards." The contest rules instructed contestants to create Pinterest boards titled "Wandering Sole," which had to include five shoe images from Cole Haan's Wandering Sole Pinterest Board as well as five images of the contestants' "favorite places to wander." Contestants were told to use "#WanderingSole" in each pin description, and Cole Haan promised to award a $1,000 shopping spree to the contestant with the most creative entry.

Were contestants "endorsers" in the ordinary sense? The FTC stated that the pins featuring Cole Haan products were endorsements, and that the fact that the pins were incentivized by the contest "would not reasonably be expected by consumers who saw the pins." The FTC faulted Cole Haan for failing to instruct contestants to label their pins and Pinterest boards to make it clear that they had pinned Cole Haan products as part of a contest. The "#WanderingSole" hashtag was inadequate to disclose the financial incentive at issue. The FTC didn't take further action because it hadn't previously addressed whether contest entry was a material connection between advertiser and content disseminator that required disclosure and because the contest was short and attracted few entrants. *Letter from Mary Engle*, Mar. 20, 2014.

What connections, if any, between advertiser and social media influencer would the FTC consider too trivial to merit disclosure? How can the advertiser know for sure?

Endorsers' Individual Liability. The FTC initially indicated that it would enforce the Endorsement and Testimonials Guidelines principally against advertisers, not individual bloggers or endorsers. The FTC also indicated that an advertiser can satisfy the guidelines by (1) prospectively telling endorsers to make the proper sponsorship disclosures and (2) retrospectively monitoring the resulting online posts to ensure compliance (and taking corrective action where necessary). Still, the FTC reserves its right to pursue endorsers individually. For example, in the Teami enforcement (discussed *supra*), the FTC sent warnings to some of the influencers. This isn't a new position for the FTC; they sent warning letters in 2017 to twenty-one social media influencers regarding their obligations to comply with the Endorsements & Testimonials Guidelines. Among other things, the FTC took the position that "tagging a brand in an Instagram picture is an endorsement of the brand and requires an appropriate disclosure." The FTC has occasionally carried out its threat. *See CSGO Lotto Owners Settle FTC's First-Ever Complaint Against Individual Social Media Influencers*, Federal Trade Commission, Sept. 7, 2017.

Should endorsers face individual liability for violating these guidelines? China's 2015 *Advertising Law* provides that anyone who endorses a product may be jointly liable for any violation of the advertising law if he or she ought to have known of the violation and may be banned from endorsing other products or services for a period of three years. Under this provision, basketball player Yao Ming was sued for endorsing fish oil pills that were less effective than claimed in the advertisement. Would such a rule be appropriate in the United States? Would such a rule be constitutional? *Cf.* Luman v. Theismann, 647 Fed. Appx. 804 (9th Cir. 2016) (celebrity spokesperson wasn't liable for false advertising under California law because he was not the "seller" of the product); Ramson v. Layne, 668 F.Supp. 1162 (N.D. Ill. 1987) (celebrity spokesperson could be liable for endorsing product with misleading representations in script he agreed to read).

Showcasing Celebrity Activity. In one NAD proceeding, eSalon had a Pinterest page called "Hair Colors We Love" with pictures of celebrities. The NAD found that the photos implied that the celebrities endorsed eSalon products and recommended that eSalon only pin photos of celebrities who used eSalon. eSalon, NAD Case No. 5645 (Oct. 17, 2013).

Do you agree that pinning photos with the caption "Hair Colors We Love" implies endorsement by the celebrities? Separately, when a custom hair-color producer pins photos with the caption "Hair Colors We Love," does that implicitly represent that the producer can replicate those hair colors on request? What sort of substantiation would you have asked eSalon for, as their counsel?

Fabricated Endorsements. Sometimes, advertisers simply fabricate endorsements, such as fake online consumer reviews touting the advertiser's offerings or bashing rivals' offerings. *See, e.g.*, Press Release, New York Office of the Attorney General, *A.G. Schneiderman Announces Agreement With 19 Companies To Stop Writing Fake Online Reviews And Pay More Than $350,000 In Fines*, Sept. 23, 2013 (announcing settlements with numerous companies that had written fake consumer reviews for themselves on websites such as Yelp, Google Local and CitySearch).

Fake endorsements are not unique to the Internet. Sony's David Manning incident provides a useful case study. For about a year starting in 2000, Sony's Columbia Pictures ran advertisements for several movies containing laudatory comments from "David Manning," identified as a movie reviewer for the *Ridgefield (Conn.) Press*. While the *Ridgefield Press* is a real newspaper, David Manning was a fictitious person, and the quotes attributed to Manning were all fabricated. Why a Sony employee chose to engage in this artifice is baffling; as one journalist wrote, "[t]he shocking part is that practically every movie these days, good or bad, garners [a] poster-friendly blurb from some critic—even no-name hacks toiling for virtually unknown publications." Josh Grossberg, *Sony's Fake Critic Fallout*, E! ONLINE, June 6, 2001.

A *Newsweek* article on June 2, 2001, exposed Sony's ruse. Legal proceedings ensued.

Several private consumer class-action lawsuits were brought against Sony for false advertising, unfair competition and related claims. Sony tried to dismiss one such lawsuit on the grounds that its advertisements were protected by California's anti-SLAPP statute, which applies to certain types of speech. In *Rezec v. Sony Pictures Entertainment*, 116 Cal. App. 4th 135 (Cal. App. Ct. 2004), a divided California appellate court rejected Sony's dismissal attempt because the ads were commercial speech, which the court said is not protected by anti-SLAPP laws.

Sony subsequently settled the class-action lawsuit for an announced value of $1.5 million, including $500,000 allocated to consumers who saw some of the movies advertised using the fake quotes. Perhaps not surprisingly, only 170 consumers' claims—totaling fewer than $5,100—were tendered. *See* William Booth, *Big Payday for Lawyers In Sony Fake-Blurb Deal*, WASH. POST, Sept. 10, 2005. Sony gave the remaining amount to charity.

Several attorneys general also explored actions against Sony. Sony settled with Connecticut's attorney general for $325,000, plus the promise to stop using fake quotes and showing ads depicting employees giving enthusiastic fake testimonials (a common practice among movie studios at the time).

Are Celebrity Endorsements a Good Investment? The evidence is mixed about whether celebrity endorsements are a good deal for advertisers. *Compare* Peter Dabol, *Celebrities in Advertising Are Almost Always a Big Waste of Money*, AD. AGE, Jan. 12, 2011 ("[A] celebrity has little to no impact on an ad's effectiveness. In fact, regardless of gender or age, ads without celebrities out-performed ads with them"), *with* Anita Elberse & Jeroen Verleun, *The Economic Value of Celebrity Endorsements*, 52 J. ADVERT. RES. 149 (2012) (signing a celebrity athletic endorser was associated with a 4% increase in sales and higher stockholder returns, but the sales benefits leveled off over time).

In contrast, there is general consensus that consumer "word-of-mouth" recommendations, also at issue in many modern endorsement cases, have substantial selling power. *See, e.g.*, Jack Neff, *GE Study Proves Consumers Respond More to Shared Content Than to Paid Placements*, AD. AGE, Jan. 25, 2012; *cf.* Natasha T. Brison et al., *Facebook Likes and Sport Brand Image: An Empirical Examination of the National Advertising Division's Coastal Contacts' Decision*, 25 J. LEGAL ASPECTS SPORT 104 (2015) (Facebook "likes" increased favorable consumer perceptions of brands and likely purchase intentions). Many consumers report that influencer recommendations have spurred them to make a purchase. Do these results suggest that the FTC is correct to be concerned about new media endorsement situations?

Celebrity endorsers routinely make poor choices that degrade their reputation with consumers. *See, e.g.*, Alissa Fleck, *8 High-Profile Celebrity Endorsements That Backfired*, ADWEEK, Aug, 23, 2018. To protect advertisers' "investment" in the endorser relationship, endorsement contracts commonly include a "morals clause" allowing the advertiser to exit the relationship for the endorser's bad conduct. What constitutes verboten conduct is highly negotiated; it can range from serious criminal convictions to an advertiser's concern that the relationship is harming its reputation. The #MeToo era has highlighted the potential importance of morals clauses, as advertisers have sought to disassociate from alleged sexual harassers and abusers, whether or not their behavior is proven in a court of law. *See, e.g.*, Eriq Gardner, *PBS Scores $1.5 Million Win at Tavis Smiley Trial*, HOLLYWOOD REP., Mar. 4, 2020. For more thoughts on negotiating morals clauses, see https://www.ericgoldman.org/Courses/contracts/draftingexercise2writeup.pdf.

If an advertising law course were taught fifty years ago, it almost certainly would not have discussed privacy issues. For decades, most members of the advertising community have been in denial about consumer privacy concerns. Many advertising professionals treat consumer data the way that journalists treat story tips: Once they get the information—by whatever provenance—they feel it's fair game to use it without restriction.

This *laissez faire* attitude among advertising professionals is grossly out of sync with anti-advertising sentiments among consumers and regulators. To many consumers, ads feel intrusive. Ads that target us based on sensitive information (e.g., a recent bankruptcy or hospital stay) feel even more intrusive.

As a result, the advertising community routinely clashes with those who seek to regulate its privacy practices. Typically, regulators give advertisers a chance to self-regulate by developing industry standards that provide minimum levels of consumer protection. If a self-regulatory effort fails or takes too long, the regulators come in, crack down and shake up the industry. This chapter will explore the consequences of several such crackdowns.

This chapter will first look at privacy conceptually, identifying the ways in which various privacy claims/harms might intersect with advertising. Then we will take a look at a few specific privacy regimes, although we are not trying to make you experts in any one law. Instead, you should look for patterns and traps for the unwary. Finally, we present case studies so you can see how "privacy" in the abstract operationalizes in practice.

1.   What Does "Privacy" Mean?

Despite its ubiquity, the word "privacy" is semantically ambiguous. Because the word "privacy" means many different things, people often talk past each other in discussions about privacy. Privacy scholar Dan Solove notes:

> Lillian BeVier writes: "Privacy is a chameleon-like word, used denotatively to designate a wide range of wildly disparate interests—from confidentiality of personal information to reproductive autonomy—and connotatively to generate goodwill on behalf of whatever interest is being asserted in its name." Other commentators have lamented that privacy is "vague and evanescent," "protean," and suffering from "an embarrassment of meanings." "Perhaps the most striking thing about the right to privacy," philosopher Judith Jarvis Thomson has observed, "is that nobody seems to have any very clear idea what it is."
>
> Often, privacy problems are merely stated in knee-jerk form: "That violates my privacy!" When we contemplate an invasion of privacy—such as having our personal

information gathered by companies in databases—we instinctively recoil. Many discussions of privacy appeal to people's fears and anxieties. What commentators often fail to do, however, is translate those instincts into a reasoned, well-articulated account of why privacy problems are harmful. When people claim that privacy should be protected, it is unclear precisely what they mean.

Daniel J. Solove, *A Taxonomy of Privacy*, 154 U. PENN. L. REV. 477 (2006). "Nearly every attempt to define privacy winds up being too specific to apply generally or too general to be useful." WOODROW HARTZOG, PRIVACY'S BLUEPRINT: THE BATTLE TO CONTROL THE DESIGN OF NEW TECHNOLOGIES (2018). Due to the semantic ambiguity and the potential to talk past each other, conversations about advertising and privacy often can be frustrating for all involved.

In terms of the law, "privacy" frequently has been equated with Prosser's privacy torts. As discussed in Chapter 14, Dean William Prosser taxonomized privacy legal claims into four types. *See* William L. Prosser, *Privacy*, 48 CAL. L. REV. 383 (1960); RESTATEMENTS (SECOND) OF TORTS (for which Prosser was the reporter). Prosser's four privacy torts are:

1) Intrusion upon the plaintiff's seclusion or solitude or into his private affairs;
2) Public disclosure of embarrassing private facts about the plaintiff;
3) Publicity that places the plaintiff in a false light in the public eye; and
4) Appropriation, for the defendant's advantage, of the plaintiff's name or likeness.

We discussed the fourth tort, commercial appropriation, in Chapter 14 in our discussion about publicity rights. A few words about the other three:

Intrusion into Seclusion occurs when there is an offensive intrusion into a private place. For example, a homeowner enjoys nude sunbathing in his backyard, which is well screened by hedges to prevent people from ordinarily being able to see him. An intrusion into seclusion might occur if a photographer uses an unusually high-powered zoom lens to take photos of the nude sunbather from a distant skyscraper or hill.

Public Disclosure of Private Facts occurs when someone publicizes a true but private fact without a sufficient public interest. For example, publishing photos of an injured person as she is being wheeled from an ambulance into the hospital's emergency room can constitute a public disclosure of private facts. The facts are true (the accurate depiction of the victim's injuries) and they were visible in a public place (the ER), but there may be weak justifications for publishing the photos of a person in a medically vulnerable condition.

False Light occurs when someone offensively publishes a true fact that recklessly places someone else in a false light. For example, false light might occur if a newspaper publishes an article about sexually transmitted diseases in the pornography industry and includes a stock photo of a pornography actress with the story, even though the article does not state or imply the actress has an STD and she does not, in fact, have an STD. *Cf.* Manzari v. Associated Newspapers Ltd., 830 F.3d 881 (9th Cir. 2016). The relationship between defamation and false light is like the relationship between literal falsity and falsity by necessary implication. Defamation applies to false assertions of fact, while false light applies when everything said is true but the combination nevertheless creates a false impression.

The above examples are illustrative but not conclusive. Privacy plaintiffs have stretched these doctrines to cover a myriad of other circumstances. Plaintiffs frequently allege Prosser's privacy torts in advertising-related cases, though the claims routinely meet with little or no success. Instead, statutory or contract claims are more likely to succeed.

2.   Privacy Harms

A.   What Counts as a Harm?

Because privacy has so many definitions, it's hard to pin down exactly how and why advertising causes privacy harms for consumers. After all, if consumers don't like the ads, they can just disregard them, right?

With the renewed legislative attention to advertising and privacy, this thinking is, at best, incomplete. Advertisers have to be sensitive to all the possible privacy-related harms they may cause or contribute to, such as:

- *Unwanted Intrusion.* Some consumers feel like telemarketing, door-to-door sales and junk mail are an invasion of their home. Some consumers feel that interruptive broadcast ads, such as TV and radio, and online ads like pop-ups or interstitial ads are also intrusive.
- *Out-of-Pocket Receiving Costs.* Consumers may incur out-of-pocket costs from ads they receive. For example, text messages may impose per-message costs; and junk mail or newspaper advertising inserts may have disposal costs.
- *Overly Personal Targeting.* Consumers can feel uncomfortable when an advertiser targets advertising based on "private" or sensitive personal characteristics, such as ads for baby-related items targeted to women who have miscarried or hair restoration services targeted at middle-aged men.
- *Price/Service Discrimination.* When advertisers know their consumers better, they may try to ascertain the consumers' maximum willingness to pay and adjust pricing accordingly. Advertisers may also make distinctions between consumers, rewarding (or sometimes overcharging) more-loyal consumers compared to less-loyal consumers. Price discrimination among ordinary consumers often strikes those consumers—and their elected representatives—as extremely unfair. To the extent that loyalty (or lack of access to alternatives) can be expected to correlate with other socially relevant classifications, such as age, race, gender or income, the resistance to ad targeting may be even greater. *See* Jennifer Valentino-DeVries et al., *Websites Vary Prices, Deals Based on Users' Information*, WALL ST. J., Dec. 24, 2012 ("In what appears to be an unintended side effect of Staples' pricing methods—likely a function of retail competition with its rivals—the Journal's testing also showed that areas that tended to see the discounted prices had a higher average income than areas that tended to see higher prices.").

- *Unwanted Disclosures to the Government.* Advertisers who maintain databases containing personal information about consumers may be targeted by government entities seeking to learn more about consumers and their activities.
- *Unwanted Disclosures to Other Parties.* A personal information database also can result in unwanted data disclosures to various third parties, such as responses to litigants' discovery requests and unintentional disclosures to third parties, including acquisition by hackers. As just one example, Eli Lilly once sent an email regarding the antidepressant Prozac but made all of the recipients' email addresses visible to each other, thus inadvertently disclosing highly sensitive medical information. Federal Trade Comm'n, *Eli Lilly Settles FTC Charges Concerning Security Breach* (Jan. 18, 2002). As another example, ads can sometimes reveal personal or confidential information when seen by a family member. *See e.g., How to Stop Facebook from Ruining Your Holiday Gift Surprises*, MONEY, Dec. 4, 2014. In the worst case, unintentional disclosures can lead to identity theft or physical or financial harm.

For more examples of privacy-related harms, *see* Daniel J. Solove, *A Taxonomy of Privacy*, 154 U. PENN. L. REV. 477 (2006); *see also* M. Ryan Calo, *The Boundaries of Privacy Harm*, 86 IND. L.J. 1131 (2011); Ryan Calo, *Privacy Harm Exceptionalism*, 12 COLO. TECH. L.J. 361 (2014).

Privacy harms can be difficult to measure because they may not occur immediately (or be recognized). For example, assume a hacker obtains a database of private consumer information. Some or all of the people in the database may experience identity theft, but it could take months or years for them to realize they are victims. Or it's possible that the stolen data is never used (or, in fact, was never actually stolen, or was never decrypted), in which case the purported victims will never actually suffer any actual losses at all. *See In re* Zappos.com, Inc., Customer Data Security Breach Litigation, MDL No. 2357 (D. Nev. June 1, 2015) ("Even if Plaintiffs' risk of identity theft and fraud was substantial and immediate in 2012, the passage of [3.5 years of litigation] without a single report from Plaintiffs that they in fact suffered the harm they fear must mean something.").

Privacy harms also could be so trivial that they may not warrant the heavy costs of judicial administration. For example, in *Harris v. Time*, 191 Cal. App. 3d 449 (1987), a junk-mail recipient claimed that the mailer induced him to open the envelope on false pretenses. The court rejected the claim, harshly, on the grounds of "de minimis non curat lex"—the law disregards trifles. Unfortunately for advertisers, there is no categorical "de minimis non curat lex" legal defense to privacy-related lawsuits, even if consumers in fact only suffered trifling harms.

B.   How Courts Treat Privacy Harms

Courts consider the plaintiff's alleged harms in privacy cases in two different places. First, to access the federal court system, plaintiffs must demonstrate "Article III standing," which requires that plaintiffs show they "(1) suffered an injury in fact, (2) that is fairly traceable to the challenged conduct of the defendant, and (3) that is likely to be redressed by a favorable judicial decision." An injury-in-fact requires the plaintiff to show they "suffered an invasion of a legally protected interest that is concrete and particularized and actual or imminent, not conjectural or hypothetical."

In the absence of Article III standing, the court must dismiss the case. Defendants routinely challenge plaintiffs' Article III standing as an opening move in litigation. State courts aren't bound by Article III standing requirements, though they may have similar doctrines.

Second, plaintiffs who want cash payments need to establish their damages from the defendant's alleged legal violation. Without showing damages, the plaintiff might not get any payments; and sometimes, the absence of damages will be fatal to the plaintiff's case entirely. Courts do not always carefully distinguish Article III standing from the claim's substantive prima facie elements.

In a key 2016 case, the Supreme Court addressed whether an alleged statutory violation (in the case, violation of the Fair Credit Reporting Act) constituted a per se injury for Article III standing purposes, even if the plaintiff didn't allege any further injury. Spokeo, Inc. v. Robins, 136 S. Ct. 1540 (2016).

Such a rule would susbtantially help privacy plaintiffs. By claiming a statutory violation, their case automatically could advance to the next step in litigation. In contrast, if statutory violations don't automatically confer an injury for Article III purposes, more privacy cases will fail—even where the defendant may have, in fact, violated the statute.

The Court's opinion contained apparently conflicting statements, so subsequent courts have interpreted the opinion in multiple and inconsistent ways. Nevertheless, courts applying *Spokeo* have become increasingly willing to find Article III standing in privacy cases.

Two 2020 Ninth Circuit cases involving Facebook show how abstract privacy harms can satisfy Article III standing. *Campbell v. Facebook*, 951 F.3d 1106 (9th Cir. 2020), held that most alleged violations of a privacy statute satisfy Article III standing without any further showing of an "injury-in-fact." The Ninth Circuit then followed this ruling with *In re Facebook, Inc., Internet Tracking Litigation*, 956 F.3d 589 (9th Cir. 2020), which extended *Campbell* in two important ways.

First, a consumer's potential loss of control over his or her personal data can satisfy Article III standing. The court said: "Plaintiffs have adequately alleged that Facebook's tracking and collection practices would cause harm or a material risk of harm to their interest in controlling their personal information."

Second, commercialization of personal data, without authorization, can also satisfy Article III standing. The court noted:

> Plaintiffs allege that their browsing histories carry financial value. They point to the existence of a study that values users' browsing histories at $52 per year, as well as research panels that pay participants for access to their browsing histories. Plaintiffs also sufficiently allege that Facebook profited from this valuable data...Plaintiffs allegedly did not provide authorization for the use of their personal information, nor

did they have any control over its use to produce revenue. This unauthorized use of their information for profit would entitle Plaintiffs to profits unjustly earned.

This is a potentially seismic ruling because plaintiffs can always show that their personal data had some value whenever the defendant uses it commercially, even if the consumers couldn't actually sell their data in the open market. *See, e.g.*, Chris J. Hoofnagle & Jay Whittington, *Free: Accounting for the Costs of the Internet's Most Popular Price*, 61 UCLA L. REV. 606 (2014).

Collectively, the Ninth Circuit's rulings seemingly ensure that privacy plaintiffs should always have Article III standing because these two "harms" will occur in virtually every alleged privacy violation. If so, relatively few privacy cases will fail for lack of Article III standing, though the plaintiffs may still have to show damage as part of their prima facie case.

Another way plaintiffs have successfully established Article III standing is by claiming that the defendant consumed some of a mobile device's battery life. Yet power consumption, as a harm, does not create an injury-in-fact with respect to a desktop or laptop computer that's plugged into a charging source. Does this special treatment of mobile devices, compared to other computing devices, make sense?

3. The Law of Advertising and Privacy

A. Who Enforces Privacy Violations?

For the most part, the regulatory institutions for false advertising discussed in Chapter 3 also regulate privacy concerns, including federal government agencies (especially the Federal Trade Commission), state attorneys general and consumer class-action lawyers. During President Obama's administration, the Federal Trade Commission played an unusually prominent role in the privacy-enforcement community, repeatedly describing itself as "the nation's leading privacy enforcement agency." The California Attorney General's office also has a high profile due to its role enforcing the California Consumer Privacy Act (CCPA) (of which we will say more below), and class-action law firms specializing in plaintiffs' privacy work have emerged. There are some industry standards, such as the Network Advertising Initiative's (NAI) Code of Conduct, but state-level regulation is making it harder to develop national standards.

Unlike some other areas of false advertising, competitors rarely sue each other over consumer privacy issues because competitors often engage in dicey practices and don't wish to indirectly implicate their own practices. For that reason, and also because privacy issues generally don't involve ad content, the National Advertising Division (NAD) also does not play a major role.

B.   Spotlight on the FTC Act

The FTC Act Section 5 authorizes the FTC to enforce against "unfair or deceptive acts or practices in or affecting commerce." The FTC (like most serial plaintiffs) defines consumer deception broadly. For example, the FTC has brought numerous deception-based enforcement actions against companies based on language in their privacy policies that many advertising lawyers would have considered puffery.

Sometimes, the FTC relies only on Section 5's "unfairness" prong, defined as acts that "cause or are likely to cause substantial injury to consumers that consumers themselves cannot reasonably avoid and that is not outweighed by countervailing benefits to consumers or competition." The FTC has used its unfairness authority to pursue dozens of enforcement actions against companies that suffered data security breaches, claiming lax security practices constitute an unfair trade practice. However, the FTC's unfairness authority has limits, often related to the tangibility (or lack thereof) of the harms at issue. LabMD, Inc. v. Fed. Trade Comm'n, 894 F.3d 1221 (11th Cir. 2018).

C.   Regulating the Lifecycle of Data

Each privacy law has its own unique elements and jurisprudence, but it would be impossible for this book to cover the vast spectrum of privacy laws (take a privacy law course if you can). Therefore, the book presents the topic in a more conceptual way, from an advertiser's perspective. As usual, this discussion focuses on U.S. law, but we'll discuss the implications of European privacy law later in the chapter.

Retailing pioneer John Wanamaker reportedly said: "Half the money I spend on advertising is wasted; the trouble is I don't know which half." Advertisers want to figure out which of their ad dollars are being wasted and stop wasting them. By doing so, advertisers could improve the economic return from their advertising by getting their ads in front of the right consumers (and, naturally, not advertising to the wrong consumers) and delivering the right message for the audience.

Consumer data—both personally identifiable and aggregate data—might help achieve these goals. Some marketers maintain that targeting specific consumers based on their data increases sales. *Compare* Leslie K. John et al, *Ads That Don't Overstep*, HARV. BUS. REV., Jan-Feb. 2018 ("Research has shown that digital targeting meaningfully improves the response to advertisements and that ad performance declines when marketers' access to consumer data is reduced. . . . [W]hen a law that required websites to inform visitors of covert tracking started to be enforced in the Netherlands, in 2013, advertisement click-through rates dropped. Controlled experiments have found similar results."), *with*Veronica Marotta et al, *Online Tracking and Publishers' Revenues: An Empirical Analysis*, May 2019 (personalized ads increase publishers' revenues only a little).

An advertiser seeking to improve advertising efficacy can adopt the following three-step process for consumer data, either directly or with the assistance of proxies such as publishers (Chapter 17 looks more closely at the interactions between advertisers and publishers):

First, advertisers/publishers aggregate consumer data. Second, advertisers/publishers sort through the consumer data to determine or improve ad targeting. Third, advertisers/publishers use the consumer data to deliver their ads to the targeted consumers. The following parts will look at each of these three stages in turn.

D. Step 1: Aggregate Consumer Data

There are three main ways an advertiser can acquire possession of consumer data. First, the advertiser can obtain the data directly from consumers themselves. Second, the advertiser can license data about consumers from third-party databases. Third, the advertiser can aggregate data from other publicly available sources, ranging from government records (such as real property titles) to automatically gathering data posted on websites ("scraping" data). We start with a brief technical note about cookie and tracking technologies, then look more closely at each of these three methods.

Collecting Data from Users

Advertisers can collect data from users simply by asking them for it. Consumers will often freely self-report data when asked.

Advertisers can also collect data passively by watching consumer behavior. For example, retail stores in physical space can monitor their shoppers moving around the store by seeing where their mobile device tries to establish a connection.

Advertisers and publishers also passively collect consumer information via the Internet. The use of "cookies" is one common method. Cookies are small datastrings that are stored on a user's computer and uniquely identify an individual or computer. Sometimes, the cookies themselves do not contain any information supplied by the user. Instead, they act as a "key" to a database of profiles where the website stores information it wants to associate with the cookie. Thus, when a web user has a cookie on his or her computer, the website can check the cookie's unique identifier against its profile database, pull the information from the database and proceed accordingly.

Cookies can help ad networks uniquely identify individuals as they travel across the Internet. The cookie's unique identifier tells the ad network it has seen the user before. This can help the ad network customize the ad shown to the user. Customization may be as targeted as an ad optimized for the user's apparent interest or as generic as imposing a "frequency cap" that prevents a specific ad from being shown too many times to the same person.

Advertisers and ad networks do not rely solely on the traditional "HTTP cookie" to uniquely identify a user's computer. For example, "browser fingerprints" let advertisers or ad networks uniquely identify users or computers without telling consumers at all. *See, e.g.,*

Web Browsers Leave 'Fingerprints' Behind as You Surf the Net, EFF Press Release (May 17, 2010). Consumers may be frustrated by these alternative tracking methods if they have undertaken technological efforts to manage their HTTP cookies (using tools available through their web browser or browser plug-ins), and those efforts are thwarted by bypassing HTTP cookies. At minimum, this suggests an ongoing cat-and-mouse game between users and advertisers: Users undertake more efforts to suppress cookies, and advertisers use technological tricks to get around these suppression efforts.

Laws Restricting Data Collection

Data collection from users is subject to a wide variety of statutory restrictions under U.S. law. Some examples include:

The Electronic Communications Privacy Act (the "ECPA") strongly protects private electronic communications such as telephone calls and email from real-time third-party interception, and it less strongly protects those communications (such as voicemails or emails sitting in an in-box) while in storage. When advertisers or their proxies (such as ad networks) try to gather information from users' online activities, the ECPA can come into play, and the ECPA is frequently alleged in Internet privacy lawsuits.

Another generally applicable statute is the Computer Fraud & Abuse Act (the "CFAA"), which (among other things) restricts accessing a networked computer without proper authorization and obtaining information from that computer. 18 U.S.C. § 1030(a)(2). Among other things, this prohibits surreptitious monitoring devices installed on computers or cellphones. While that may sound like common sense, common Internet technologies such as cookies or unique IDs in URLs can look like surreptitious monitoring devices to plaintiffs' lawyers.

When collecting information from users, the ECPA and CFAA can be negated by getting informed user consent through a properly formed privacy policy. This sounds easy enough in theory, but it raises plenty of challenges in practice. We discuss privacy policies later in this chapter.

Other statutory restrictions on data collection from users restrict particular industries or classes of users. For example, the Children's Online Privacy Protection Act ("COPPA") restricts online data collection from children under thirteen years of age without verifiable parental consent.

The following case involves a state statute that restricts businesses from asking users to voluntarily share their data. If you think you have a good idea of what the term "personal identification information" means, the court's conclusion probably will surprise you.

PINEDA V. WILLIAMS-SONOMA STORES, INC., 51 CAL. 4TH 524 (CAL. 2011)

The Song-Beverly Credit Card Act of 1971 (Credit Card Act) is "designed to promote consumer protection." One of its provisions, section 1747.08, prohibits businesses from requesting that cardholders provide "personal identification information" during credit card transactions, and then recording that information. . . .

FACTS AND PROCEDURAL HISTORY . . .

The complaint alleged the following:

Plaintiff visited one of defendant's California stores and selected an item for purchase. She then went to the cashier to pay for the item with her credit card.

The cashier asked plaintiff for her ZIP code and, believing she was required to provide the requested information to complete the transaction, plaintiff provided it. The cashier entered plaintiff's ZIP code into the electronic cash register and then completed the transaction. At the end of the transaction, defendant had plaintiff's credit card number, name, and ZIP code recorded in its database.

Defendant subsequently used customized computer software to perform reverse searches from databases that contain millions of names, e-mail addresses, telephone numbers, and street addresses, and that are indexed in a manner resembling a reverse telephone book. The software matched plaintiff's name and ZIP code with plaintiff's previously undisclosed address, giving defendant the information, which it now maintains in its own database. Defendant uses its database to market products to customers and may also sell the information it has compiled to other businesses. . . .

DISCUSSION . . .

Section 1747.08, subdivision (a) provides, in pertinent part, "[N]o person, firm, partnership, association, or corporation that accepts credit cards for the transaction of business shall . . . : [¶] . . . [¶] (2) Request, or require as a condition to accepting the credit card as payment in full or in part for goods or services, the cardholder to provide *personal identification information*, which the person, firm, partnership, association, or corporation accepting the credit card writes, causes to be written, or otherwise records upon the credit card transaction form or otherwise." (italics added.)[6] Subdivision (b) defines personal identification information as "information concerning the cardholder, other than information set forth on the credit card, and including, but not limited to, the cardholder's address and telephone number." Because we must accept as true plaintiff's allegation that defendant requested and then recorded her ZIP code, the outcome of this case hinges on whether a cardholder's ZIP code, without more, constitutes personal identification information within the meaning of section 1747.08. We hold that it does.

Subdivision (b) defines personal identification information as "information *concerning* the cardholder . . . including, but not limited to, the cardholder's address and telephone number."

---

[6] Section 1747.08 contains some exceptions, including when a credit card is being used as a deposit or for cash advances, when the entity accepting the card is contractually required to provide the information to complete the transaction or is obligated to record the information under federal law or regulation, or when the information is required for a purpose incidental to but related to the transaction, such as for shipping, delivery, servicing, or installation.

614

(italics added.) "Concerning" is a broad term meaning "pertaining to; regarding; having relation to; [or] respecting . . . ." A cardholder's ZIP code, which refers to the area where a cardholder works or lives, is certainly information that pertains to or regards the cardholder.

In nonetheless concluding the Legislature did not intend for a ZIP code, without more, to constitute personal identification information, the Court of Appeal pointed to the enumerated examples of such information in subdivision (b), i.e., "the cardholder's address and telephone number." Invoking the doctrine *ejusdem generis*, whereby a "general term ordinarily is understood as being 'restricted to those things that are similar to those which are enumerated specifically'", the Court of Appeal reasoned that an address and telephone number are "specific in nature regarding an individual." By contrast, the court continued, a ZIP code pertains to the *group* of individuals who live within the ZIP code. Thus, the Court of Appeal concluded, a ZIP code, without more, is unlike the other terms specifically identified in subdivision (b).

There are several problems with this reasoning. First, a ZIP code is readily understood to be part of an address; when one addresses a letter to another person, a ZIP code is always included. The question then is whether the Legislature, by providing that "personal identification information" includes "the cardholder's address", intended to include components of the address. The answer must be yes. Otherwise, a business could ask not just for a cardholder's ZIP code, but also for the cardholder's street and city in addition to the ZIP code, so long as it did not also ask for the house number. Such a construction would render the statute's protections hollow. Thus, the word "address" in the statute should be construed as encompassing not only a complete address, but also its components.

Second, the court's conclusion rests upon the assumption that a complete address and telephone number, unlike a ZIP code, are specific to an individual. That this assumption holds true in all, or even most, instances is doubtful. In the case of a cardholder's home address, for example, the information may pertain to a group of individuals living in the same household. Similarly, a home telephone number might well refer to more than one individual. The problem is even more evident in the case of a cardholder's *work* address or telephone number—such information could easily pertain to tens, hundreds, or even thousands of individuals. Of course, section 1747.08 explicitly provides that a cardholder's address and telephone number constitute personal identification information; that such information *might also* pertain to individuals other than the cardholder is immaterial. Similarly, that a cardholder's ZIP code pertains to individuals in addition to the cardholder does not render it dissimilar to an address or telephone number.

More significantly, the Court of Appeal ignores another reasonable interpretation of what the enumerated terms in section 1747.08, subdivision (b) have in common, that is, they both constitute information unnecessary to the sales transaction that, alone or together with other data such as a cardholder's name or credit card number, can be used for the retailer's business purposes. Under this reading, a cardholder's ZIP code is similar to his or her address or telephone number, in that a ZIP code is both unnecessary to the transaction and can be used, together with the cardholder's name, to locate his or her full address. The retailer can then, as plaintiff alleges defendant has done here, use the accumulated information for its own purposes or sell the information to other businesses.

There are several reasons to prefer this latter, broader interpretation over the one adopted by the Court of Appeal. First, the interpretation is more consistent with the rule that courts should liberally construe remedial statutes in favor of their protective purpose, which, in the case of section 1747.08, includes addressing "the misuse of personal identification information for, inter alia, marketing purposes." The Court of Appeal's interpretation, by contrast, would permit retailers to obtain indirectly what they are clearly prohibited from obtaining directly, "end-running" the statute's clear purpose. This is so because information that can be permissibly obtained under the Court of Appeal's construction could easily be used to locate the cardholder's complete address or telephone number. Such an interpretation would vitiate the statute's effectiveness. Moreover, that the Legislature intended a broad reading of section 1747.08 can be inferred from the expansive language it employed, e.g., "concerning" in subdivision (b) and "*any* personal identification information" in subdivision (a)(1). (Italics added.) The use of the broad word "any" suggests the Legislature did not want the category of information protected under the statute to be narrowly construed. . . .

Thus, in light of the statutory language, as well as the legislative history and evident purpose of the statute, we hold that personal identification information, as that term is used in section 1747.08, includes a cardholder's ZIP code. . . .

NOTES AND QUESTIONS

Exceptions. In *Apple v. Superior Court ex rel Krescent*, 56 Cal. 4th 128 (2013), the California Supreme Court said the Song-Beverly requirements didn't apply to electronic downloads such as MP3 files from the iTunes store. Also, based on statutory exclusions, online retailers can ask for buyers' addresses (including zip codes), and gas stations may ask customers for their zip codes as part of authenticating the credit cards.

Zip Codes as "Personal Identification Information." On average, a zip code has over 7,000 people living in it. How does the court reach the counterintuitive result that a zip code is "personal identification information?" Following the court's logic, would a person's state or country also be "personal identification information?" After all, that is part of a person's address too.

Taxonomy of Personal Data. Data is sometimes taxonomized based on:

- *"Sensitive" vs. "non-sensitive" data.* Sensitive data can include personal health or financial information. People are more reluctant to share these types of information and are more easily embarrassed or harmed when others learn it.
- *"Personally identifiable" vs. "non-personally identifiable" information.* "Personally identifiable information" is typically referred to by the acronym "PII." PII can be used to uniquely identify a person. Unfortunately, there is no consensus about what constitutes PII. Older privacy statutes define PII using a laundry list of data items, but there is little analytical rigor to what specific data items are included or excluded in those definitions. More-recent privacy statutes, like the California Consumer Privacy Act, treat virtually all information about consumers as personal information, subject to limited exclusions.

Re-identification. Re-identification is a variant of a problem we discussed in Chapter 14: People might be identifiable even when their faces aren't shown. In this case, Williams-Sonoma could "re-identify" their customers by combining two pieces of information (name and zip code) with information from third-party databases. Merging these two databases allowed Williams-Sonoma to uniquely identify their customers and determine their customers' addresses even though the customers never told them this information. These types of re-identifications are common. Unfortunately, the court's holding ("personal identification information, as that term is used in Section 1747.08, includes a cardholder's ZIP code") doesn't reference or depend on Williams-Sonoma's re-identification, even though the issue was on the judges' minds.

As this case illustrates, bits of data, in combination, may uniquely identify a person, even if each bit (such as a zip code) standing alone is not very unique to a consumer. As a result, it's incoherent to regulate PII more heavily than non-PII because individual bits of non-PII can become PII when combined. *See* Paul Ohm, *Broken Promises of Privacy: Responding to the Surprising Failure of Anonymization*, 57 UCLA L. REV. 1701 (2010). If so, this helps explain why more recent privacy statutes start with the presumption that PII includes every bit of consumer data, no matter how seemingly "anonymous."

Offline Marketing. The media tends to focus on online data collection, but offline data gathering practices for marketing purposes are pervasive and potentially legally problematic. *See, e.g.*, Kashmir Hill, *How Target Figured Out A Teen Girl Was Pregnant Before Her Father Did*, FORBES, Feb. 16, 2012.

Privacy Policies

Some statutes require companies to publish a privacy policy but don't dictate its substantive terms. *See, e.g.*, CAL. CIVIL CODE § 1798.83; CAL. BUS. & PROF. CODE §§ 22575–79. Other statutes require companies to publish a privacy policy and specify its contents. *See, e.g.*, Gramm-Leach-Bliley Act (financial industry); Health Insurance Portability & Accountability Act (HIPAA) (healthcare industry); COPPA (with specific requirements for a privacy policy for preteen website users); California Consumer Privacy Act. Historically, privacy policies sought consumers' consent to the companies' practices—which may not be very protective of consumers' privacy interests at all.

To prove that consumers agreed to a privacy policy's provisions, consumers should affirmatively assent to its terms. Online users can be required to "click through" the privacy policy—though many companies still only present privacy policies as a link in their website's footer (to dubious legal effect). Offline, it can be harder to obtain customer consent to a privacy policy when the company doesn't otherwise have a written contract with the customer.

Acquiring Data from Third-Party Databases

Once a company acquires consumer data, it can usually be licensed to other entities without any restrictions (other than those voluntarily imposed through a privacy policy during the data collection). Indeed, many companies license consumer data to third parties, some as their core business and others as a complement.

There are a few statutory limits on consumer data licensing. For example, the Fair Credit Reporting Act restricts the licensing of consumer credit data for use in making credit decisions.

Acquiring Data from Public Sources

Advertisers can acquire data from public records generally without restriction. For example, advertisers can obtain real property titles, including mortgage information, from county records offices; and many state bars publish directories containing the names and addresses of licensed lawyers. The government sometimes charges a fee to provide the information in a more advertiser-friendly format, but the underlying data is in the public domain. The government also may choose to withhold selected information for good reason, such as privacy concerns, but those decisions are subject to First Amendment scrutiny and must be narrow in nature. *See, e.g.*, L.A. Police Dep't. v. United Reporting Publ'g Corp., 528 U.S. 32 (1999) (upholding a regulation preventing the release of arrestee mailing addresses from a facial challenge).

Scraping

In the Internet era, advertisers try to mine any available online sources of consumer data. If the database publisher doesn't make the dataset available for downloading in a convenient way, advertisers or independent services may engage in a process sometimes called "scraping." Advertisers configure an automated tool (sometimes called a scraper, a robot or a spider) to access the database and automatically download its contents.

Although scraping may sound sinister, it is widely practiced on the Internet. For example, Google's main search index is the product of scraping. However, just because scraping is common doesn't mean it's legal. While scraping lawsuits are rare, they pose significant legal risk to the scraper. *See* Register.com, Inc. v. Verio, Inc., 356 F.3d 393 (2d Cir. 2004); Facebook Inc. v. Power Ventures, Inc., 844 F.3d 1058 (9th Cir. 2016). *But see* hiQ Labs, Inc. v. LinkedIn Corp., 938 F.3d 985 (9th Cir. 2019).

E.   Step 2: Ad Sorting and Targeting

The prior part looked at the legal restrictions on the acquisition of consumer data. This part looks at the legal restrictions on the advertiser's ability to use data to estimate consumer interest and target its advertising accordingly.

There are two primary ways to target ads: contextually and behaviorally.

In contextual targeting, a publisher publishes editorial content that attracts consumers and creates advertising inventory adjacent to the editorial content. For example, a print newspaper may contain several topically distinct sections—local news, sports, business, entertainment—and show different ads in the sections that might appeal to readers of that editorial content, i.e., tire ads in the sports section, insurance ads in the business section, movie ads in the entertainment section, etc. Online, Google is the paradigmatic contextual targeter: It provides results keyed to particular search terms; and when it serves ads to other publishers, it targets the ads through contextual analysis of the surrounding material. Online contextual targeting does not require tracking the user's browsing history; the targeting reflects the user's online location at that moment.

While contextual targeting isn't targeted on a per-person basis, it can be highly targeted. For example, highly specialized niche magazines—say, *Golf Magazine*—have such tightly focused audiences that advertisers have a pretty good idea of the type of consumer they are reaching. Although the publisher may not care about the personal information of any specific reader, it needs enough aggregate information about readers to convince advertisers that its readers are worth reaching.

In contrast, behavioral targeting develops targeting criteria based on a consumer's actions. So, for example, if a consumer searches for a flight to Hawaii, advertisers might develop a list of possible targetable criteria implicit in this search—the consumer may be looking for flights, but also hotels, rental cars, recreational activities in Hawaii, travel guides and travel gear like luggage. The holy grail of behavioral advertising is to combine this piece of data (potential trip to Hawaii) with other facts gleaned from the consumer's prior behavior. So if the consumer visited vegetarian websites and booked a horseback riding tour on a previous vacation, advertisers could refine their pitches even more granularly to reflect those manifested interests. The search the consumer did three days ago on one website could then affect the results he or she would see on another, separately owned site.

The whole reason advertisers engage in ad targeting is to make more money. Otherwise, why would advertisers spend the time and money to aggregate the consumer data and determine targeting criteria? However, behavioral ad targeting does not guarantee an increase in advertiser profits. *See* Tanya Irwin, *MIT: Personalized Ads Don't Always Work*, MEDIAPOST MARKETINGDAILY, June 1, 2011 (ad targeting may work better as consumers get closer to transacting).

Although most people associate ad targeting with the Internet and other direct marketing media such as direct mail or telemarketing, advertisers routinely try to personalize ad targeting to the maximum extent permitted by a medium's technology.

Regulation of Behavioral Advertising

Most browser software now lets users indicate that they do not want to be tracked, called a "Do-Not-Track" setting. Websites can choose to honor or ignore the signal. California law requires many websites to disclose in their privacy policy if they honor a browser's Do-Not-Track signal. CAL. BUS. & PROFS. CODE § 22575(b)(5). Most websites ignore it.

Efforts to prevent consumer tracking can baffle advertisers because its consequences apparently contravene its purported objectives. If advertisers can't deliver personally targeted ads, then advertisers will, at the margins, reduce their total ad spend because some previously profitable ads will no longer be feasible—presumably a good outcome from some consumer advocates' perspectives. On the other hand, untracked consumers will still see ads, but they won't be targeted. In this situation, the ads will be less relevant to consumers and therefore less likely to actually help consumers. Thus, from the advertisers' perspective, "Do Not Track" efforts make things worse for consumers, not better.

Despite this, surveys routinely indicate that consumers strongly favor "Do Not Track" regulation. Why? One possibility: Advertising can change consumer preferences—and the more targeted the ad, the more effective it may be at doing so. Consumers also may be concerned that ad targeting will lead to price discrimination, costing them money. Consumers may fear they will be subject to illegal discrimination such as redlining (basing the price of marketplace goods/services on the buyer's race).

Most frequently, consumers feel that ad targeting is "creepy." *See, e.g.,* Omer Tene & Jules Polonetsky, *A Theory of Creepy: Technology, Privacy and Shifting Social Norms,* 16 YALE J.L. & TECH. 59 (2013). It is easy to dismiss this sentiment as perhaps irrational—at most, the machines are watching, not individuals. *See* Eric Goldman, *Data Mining and Attention Consumption,* PRIVACY AND TECHNOLOGIES OF IDENTITY: A CROSS-DISCIPLINARY CONVERSATION 225 (Katherine Strandburg & Daniela Raicu, eds. 2006). Nevertheless, consumers are typically uncomfortable with anything that feels like surreptitious monitoring.

First-party targeting—targeting consumers based on their behavior on a website, e.g., "because you searched for X, you may also be interested in Y"—is more acceptable to consumers than third-party targeting, which involves acquiring and using data about the consumer from third parties, and explaining first-party targeting can even increase consumers' interest in the advertised products. Leslie K. John et al, *Ads That Don't Overstep,* HARV. BUS. REV., Jan-Feb. 2018; Tami Kim et al, *Why Am I Seeing This Ad? The Effect of Ad Transparency on Ad Effectiveness,* 45 J. CONSUMER RESEARCH 906 (2019).

Other Targeting Restrictions

There are numerous other laws restricting the criteria that marketers use for targeting, especially when it involves potential discrimination (e.g., redlining) or sensitive personal information like health or financial information, such as the Fair Credit Reporting Act's strict limits on using credit ratings for ad targeting. Chapter 19 discusses some of these limits.

F.   Step 3: Ad Delivery

The prior part reviewed the legal restrictions on using data already in a database for ad targeting purposes. This part reviews the legal restrictions on delivering ads once the advertiser has determined who it would like to get them.

In general, advertisers have First Amendment-protected rights to disseminate their messages to consumers. As we discussed in Chapter 2, the First Amendment protections are partially diluted because advertisers' messages are commercial speech, which receives only a medium level of protection. And while consumers have limited rights to control what content they consume, the First Amendment necessitates that listeners' rights have to give way sometimes.

A variety of legislative solutions try to balance these conflicting interests. Eric Goldman's *A Coasean Analysis of Marketing*, 2006 WIS. L. REV. 1151, offers a spectrum of consumers' rights to control their exposure and advertisers' rights to reach consumers:

Entitlement Spectrum

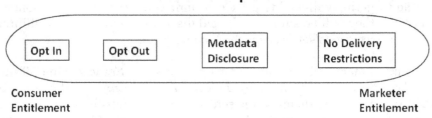

An *opt-in scheme* requires marketers to obtain consumer consent before disseminating marketing to them. Currently, the only marketing delivery media governed on an opt-in basis are fax marketing and certain text messages.

An *opt-out scheme* allows consumers to prevent future marketing exposures, on a medium-specific basis, across all marketers (such as a do-not-call registry) or from only particular marketers (such as marketer-specific opt-outs from future email marketing or telemarketing). Several direct marketing media, such as email marketing, telemarketing and (to a lesser extent) direct mail, are governed by opt-out regulatory schemes.

A *mandatory metadata* disclosure scheme requires marketers to make specified disclosures that help the consumer sort the marketing or assess its trustworthiness. Metadata can provide consumers with more information about the marketer, such as requiring telemarketers to display their phone numbers readable by Caller ID or requiring that marketing display the marketer's physical address. Metadata can also provide a summary or description of the marketing contents, such as a summary label that marketing is "advertising."

Some media have *no delivery restrictions* on marketing at all. In these situations, a consumer cannot avoid unwanted exposures to marketing in that medium (except, of course, by avoiding the medium altogether). Unrestricted media include most broadcasting (television, radio and cable) and print periodical marketing, as well as billboards and other physical signs.

Opt-ins represent one end of the allocative spectrum—the consumer has an entitlement to be free from marketing. At the other end of the spectrum, a marketer has an entitlement to disseminate marketing to consumers in those media where the marketer's rights are unrestricted. In between these two end points are opt-outs and mandatory metadata schemes, where the entitlement is not absolute. Instead, each party shoulders some burden and, in effect, "shares" the entitlement. For example, with opt-outs, the marketer initially has the entitlement, but consumers can obtain the entitlement for themselves by communicating their preferences.

In general, to the extent statutes preference consumers over advertisers, the First Amendment imposes greater limits on the statute. Restrictions on marketing delivery methods regularly get challenged under the First Amendment. Because typically those restrictions are subject to intermediate scrutiny, marketers win some cases; the government wins others.

Example #1: Statutory Opt-out of Yellow Pages Distribution

Dex Media West, Inc. v. City of Seattle, 793 F. Supp. 2d 1213 (W.D. Wash. 2011), *rev'd,* 696 F.3d 952 (9th Cir. 2012), involved a Seattle ordinance allowing consumers to opt out of yellow pages delivery and imposing certain licensing restrictions and fees on yellow pages publishers, along with a requirement that they prominently inform consumers of the opt-out option. As of May 12, 2011, city residents had made 136,651 opt-out requests through the city's opt-out system—averaging 17,081 new opt-outs per day—out of a total population of roughly 600,000.

The district court concluded that the yellow page directories constituted "commercial speech" because they contained ads for many different products, the ads referenced specific products and the publisher had an economic interest to deliver the directories. The court distinguished yellow pages from ad-supported newspapers: "[A]ny noncommercial aspects of the speech at issue in yellow pages directories are merely tangential to Plaintiffs' predominantly commercial purpose. While the noncommercial aspects of the directories may render their receipt more welcome by some residents, these aspects of the directories are not at the core of their purpose."

The district court concluded that the ordinance satisfied *Central Hudson* (for review, see Chapter 2). In support of that conclusion, the court cited the city's "substantial" interests in (1) waste reduction, (2) resident privacy and (3) recovery of the costs of running the opt-out system. How does delivery of a yellow pages directory to a consumer constitute a "privacy invasion?"

The Ninth Circuit reversed. The court of appeals identified several components to the yellow pages: (1) business "white pages" sections, which provide names, addresses, and phone numbers of local businesses and professionals in alphabetical order; (2) traditional yellow pages, which list businesses by category of product or service; and (3) public interest material, which includes community information, maps and government listings. Paid ads were mixed in with the listings, typically containing less than half of the content. "Display advertising comprised about 35% of the 2010 Dex Seattle Metro yellow pages."

Though many of the ads in the directories were commercial speech, the ordinance regulated the directories as a whole, and the directories weren't commercial speech. The directory did more than propose a commercial transaction, and "[t]here is no evidence that the editorial content is added as a mere sham to convert a pure advertising leaflet into noncommercial speech." The fact that the phonebook companies depended on ads to pay for the directories didn't make them any different from the *New York Times* or broadcast television, which are also ad-dependent. Because the directories weren't commercial speech, strict scrutiny applied, and the ordinance failed.

Example #2: Content Delivery to Private Property

Seattle failed to suppress yellow pages distribution, but maybe it would have done better positioning the law as an anti-trespass measure. The next case shows how "privacy" interests at home can trump other First Amendment considerations.

TILLMAN V. DISTRIBUTION SYSTEMS OF AMERICA, INC., 224 A.D.2D 79 (N.Y. APP. DIV. 1996)

We hold that neither a publisher nor a distributor has any constitutional right to continue to throw a newspaper onto the property of an unwilling recipient after having been notified not to do so. "Traditionally the American law punishes persons who enter onto the property of another after having been warned by the owner to keep off . . . . [The State may leave] the decision as to whether distributers [*sic*] of literature may lawfully call at a home where it belongs—with the homeowner himself. [The State] can punish those who call at a home in defiance of the previously expressed will of the occupant." "[W]e perceive of no reason crucial to defendant's First Amendment rights that would require a householder to retrieve an unwanted paper from his lawn."

The plaintiffs reside in Jericho, New York. The defendant Distribution Systems of America, Inc., (hereinafter DSA) is a domestic corporation which is in the business of distributing newspapers and other publications. The defendant Newsday, Inc., (hereinafter Newsday) is a domestic corporation which is the parent of DSA and which is itself a wholly-owned subsidiary of the Times Mirror Company. Newsday admittedly avails itself of DSA's services in the making of deliveries. DSA is engaged in the distribution, on a saturation basis, of a publication known as "This Week."

According to the plaintiff Kenneth Tillman, the unsolicited newspapers, together with pull-out advertisements, were typically enclosed in a plastic bag and placed on Mr. Tillman's driveway; on other occasions, they were left on the front lawn or jammed in between the storm door and the front door of the house.

Beginning in 1990, Mr. and Mrs. Tillman made repeated requests to DSA, seeking to have these unwanted deliveries discontinued. According to Mr. Tillman, agents of DSA repeatedly promised to stop the deliveries. The Tillmans were eventually forced to resort to a lawyer, and the lawyer's requests were likewise met with assertions that the deliveries had been or would be stopped. Notwithstanding these assertions, it eventually became clear that DSA was either unwilling, as a matter of principle, or unable, as a matter of internal mismanagement, to comply with the Tillmans' request. . . .

"The ancient concept that 'a man's home is his castle' into which 'not even the king may enter' has lost none of its vitality, and none of the recognized exceptions includes any right to communicate offensively with another." "An individual's right to communicate must be balanced against the recipient's right 'to be let alone' in places in which the latter possesses a right of privacy." In accordance with this general principle, it has been held that a vendor has no right under the Constitution or otherwise to send unwanted material into the home of another, even if the flow of valid ideas is impeded by such prohibition. In *Rowan v. U.S. Post Office Dep't.*, 90 S.Ct. at 1490-91 (emphasis added) the court upheld a statute pursuant to which a person could require the removal of his name from a mailing list stating in relevant part:

> In today's complex society we are inescapably captive audiences for many purposes, but a sufficient measure of individual autonomy must survive to permit every householder to exercise control over unwanted mail. To make the householder the exclusive and final judge of what will cross his threshold undoubtedly has the effect of impeding the flow of ideas, information, and arguments that, ideally, he should receive and consider. Today's merchandising methods, the plethora of mass mailings subsidized by low postal rates, and the growth of the sale of large mailing lists as an industry in itself have changed the mailman from a carrier of primarily private communications, as he was in a more leisurely day, and have made him an adjunct of the mass mailer who sends unsolicited and often unwanted mail into every home. It places no strain on the doctrine of judicial notice to observe that whether measured by pieces or pounds, Everyman's mail today is made up overwhelmingly of material he did not seek from persons he does not know. And all too often it is matter he finds offensive. . . .

> The Court has traditionally respected the right of a householder to bar, by order or notice, solicitors, hawkers, and peddlers from his property. In this case the mailer's right to communicate is circumscribed only by an affirmative act of the addressee giving notice that he wishes no further mailings from that mailer.

> To hold less would tend to license a form of trespass and would make hardly more sense than to say that a radio or television viewer may not twist the dial to cut off an offensive or boring communication and thus bar its entering his home. Nothing in the Constitution compels us to listen to or view any unwanted communication, whatever its merit; we see no basis for according the printed word or pictures a different or more preferred status because they are sent by mail. . . .

[L]ocal governments have, on several occasions, attempted to come to the aid of those homeowners who find it increasingly difficult to hold out, as their "castles" are besieged by mail, by phone, or, as in this case, by paper bombardment. Several ordinances, which to some extent regulate unsolicited distribution of written material, unsolicited mailings, unsolicited phone calls, or unsolicited commercial visits, have been challenged in the courts on First Amendment grounds. In general, the ordinances challenged have proved susceptible to constitutional attack, often because of the overbreadth of the particular ordinance's reach, or because a classification contained in the ordinance violates the equal protection clause. . . .

[W]e do not believe that, in extending constitutional protection to commercial speech, in general, the Supreme Court necessarily eroded the privacy protection afforded to a landowner who, as an individual, has knowingly decided to bar a certain type of speech, commercial or otherwise, from his or her property.

The most critical and fundamental distinction between the cases cited above, on the one hand, and the present case, on the other, is based on the fact that here we are not dealing with a government agency which seeks to preempt in some way the ability of a publisher to contact a potential reader; rather, we are dealing with a reader who is familiar with a publisher's product, and who is attempting to prevent the unwanted dumping of this product on his property. None of the cases cited by the defendants stands for the proposition that the Free Speech Clause prohibits such a landowner from resorting to his common-law remedies in order to prevent such unwanted dumping. There is, in our view, nothing in either the Federal or State Constitutions which requires a landowner to tolerate a trespass whenever the trespasser is a speaker, or the distributor of written speech, who is unsatisfied with the fora which may be available on public property, and who thus attempts to carry his message to private property against the will of the owner. . . .

The constitutional right of free speech does not correspond to the "right" to force others to listen to whatever one has to say. By the same token, the right to publish, distribute, and sell a newspaper does not correspond to the "right" to force others to buy or to read whatever one has written, or to spend their own time or money unwillingly participating in the distribution process by which a newspaper travels from the printing press to its ultimate destination, i.e., disposal. The state does all that it needs to do in order to protect the constitutional rights of a newspaper publisher when it refrains from censorship, and when it allows the distribution of the newspaper into the hands of the ultimate reader to proceed in accordance with the natural economic laws of a free market. The state need not, and in our opinion, should not, compel anyone to read, to buy, or even to touch, pick up, or handle a newspaper of which the individual in question wants to have no part. For these essential reasons, we affirm the order and judgment appealed from, which enjoined the defendants from continuing to deposit their newspaper on the plaintiffs' property.

NOTES AND QUESTIONS

As you can see, this court had a very strong view about the sanctity of one's home. In contrast, in *Miller v. Distribution Systems of America, Inc.*, 175 Misc.2d 513 (N.Y. Sup. Ct. 1997), a court awarded nominal damages of $1 in a trespass case involving the same defendant.

If consumers could have claimed a trespass to real property claim for the unwanted deposit of yellow pages, did the Seattle ordinance simply protect a property owner's already-existing right to be free from trespass? The Seattle ordinance went beyond giving homeowners the right to opt out of delivery.

Isn't Opting Out Helpful to Advertisers? In theory, opt-out notifications help advertisers and publishers. An opt-out tells the advertiser that the consumer isn't interested in hearing the pitch, so the advertiser can save the time and cost of trying to reach an uninterested prospect. In the case of the yellow pages, a consumer opt-out lets the publisher save the costs of manufacturing and delivering a directory that the consumer will likely toss in the recycle bin. Indeed, the *Dex* plaintiffs purportedly weren't opposed to an opt-out scheme; they told the courts they were developing their own nationwide opt-out system for their companies (making city-by-city opt-out regulations annoying to the extent the procedures conflicted with their national solution).

Despite this attractive theoretical argument, opt-out systems create several problems in practice. First, opt-out systems are often not granular enough to depict a consumer's actual preferences. Take the Do-Not-Call registry as an example. Some consumers object to all telemarketing calls on principle, and other consumers might want to categorically block telemarketing calls to avoid the risk of making impulse decisions they might regret. However, some people argue that many consumers would tolerate (or even welcome) a beneficial telemarketing call—say, a substantial discount offer on a product the consumer wants to buy. (Those same consumers would probably prefer the same offer to be delivered via a less-intrusive medium than telemarketing, but the advertiser may have cost or efficacy reasons to use telemarketing as the offer delivery medium). Nevertheless, registering for the Do-Not-Call registry would block the beneficial calls along with the unwanted calls—a missed opportunity for both advertisers and consumers. *See* Ian Ayres & Matthew Funk, *Marketing Privacy*, 20 YALE J. ON REG. 77 (2003). As Ayres and Funk explain, the opt-out system could be designed more granularly to screen out the unwanted calls but facilitate calls that consumers want. However, a more granular system is more complicated and costly for everyone—consumers, advertisers and the government operating the system—and therefore it's rarely pursued as a policy option.

Second, the operators of opt-out registries charge advertisers to check the registry. For example, a nationwide license to access the FTC's Do-Not-Call registry costs over $16,000 a year. Advertisers also incur internal costs checking the registry. Effectively, these costs act like a tax to advertisers to communicating via media governed by opt-out schemes. In some cases, the costs overwhelm the advertisers' expected profits, making the ad campaign unprofitable to pursue.

4.   Privacy in the European Union (E.U.)

Thus far, we've discussed U.S. privacy law. The approaches to privacy regulation vary widely across the globe, and most developed countries have more stringent privacy laws than the United States. For a deeper dive, see the book by Global Advertising Lawyers Alliance (GALA), PRIVACY LAW: A GLOBAL LEGAL PERSPECTIVE ON DATA PROTECTION RELATING TO ADVERTISING AND MARKETING (2020).

This part focuses on the European Union's General Data Protection Regulation, or GDPR, which came into effect in May 2018. The GDPR has many implications for advertising law both in Europe and internationally. The GDPR will affect the advertising community for the foreseeable future, so odds are high that you will have to navigate the GDPR—whether you want to or not.

This section gives you just a broad sketch of the GDPR. The actual text (https://eur-lex.europa.eu/legal-content/EN/TXT/PDF/?uri=CELEX:32016R0679&from=EN) is eighty-eight pages of dense and impenetrable legalese (much of it in the passive voice). Each E.U. country is required to implement the GDPR in its own laws, which creates country-by-country variations in implementation, and the GDPR is supplemented by rulings from the European Court of Justice, official and unofficial guidance from the European Data Protection Board, national Supervisory Authorities and others. If you're actually making a business decision governed by the GDPR, you'll need to consult with an expert in E.U. data-protection law. For more on why Americans struggle to understand the GDPR, *see* Meg Leta Jones & Margot E. Kaminski, *An American's Guide to the GDPR*, 98 DENV. L. REV. __ (2020).

European advertisers must also comply with the ePrivacy Directive (Directive 2002/58/EC, as modified by Directive 2009/136/EC), sometimes called the "Cookie Directive." The ePrivacy Directive regulates communication privacy in numerous ways, including requiring consent for:

- Any direct marketing by phone, fax, email, text, or other electronic message. Individuals must affirmatively opt-in—i.e., the checkbox must be presented as unchecked—to receive these marketing materials (with limited exceptions).
- Placing or reading cookies or other client-side persistent identifiers. Individual consent usually is sought in a web banner. This is why you often see websites asking for permission to place cookies.

When the laws overlap, advertisers must comply with both.

Who Must Comply with the GDPR?

The GDPR applies to anyone who "processes" personal data, defined as "any operation or set of operations which is performed on personal data or on sets of personal data, whether or not by automated means."

The GDPR defines two roles: data "controllers" and "processors." The GDPR places a heavier compliance burden on controllers, so the distinction between the two is critical.

A controller "determines the purposes and means of processing personal data." A processor "processes personal data on behalf of a controller." In some cases, this will be fairly clear. An example:

> A brewery has many employees. It signs a contract with a payroll company to pay the wages. The brewery tells the payroll company when the wages should be paid and when an employee leaves or has a pay rise. The brewery alsoprovides all other details for the salary slip and payment. The payroll company provides the IT system and stores the employees' data. The brewery is the data controller and the payroll company is the data processor.

In some cases, an advertiser that collects information directly from consumers would be the controller; and third-party vendors that help the advertiser communicate with those consumers would be processors. (The GDPR applies to all individuals, not just consumers, but this note focuses on the consumer context).

However, because the GDRP's definitions are flexible, it will not always be clear who is a controller and who is a processor. The GDPR also contemplates that entities working together can be "joint controllers," making the classification decision even more difficult. As one commentator wrote, "deciding who is a data controller and who a data processor in complicated areas like modern targeted advertising is maddeningly difficult." Lilian Edwards, *Data Protection: Enter the General Data Protection Regulation, in* LAW, POLICY AND THE INTERNET (2018).

What Data Does the GDPR Cover?

The GDPR defines "personal data" as "any information relating to an identified or identifiable natural person ('data subject'); an identifiable natural person is one who can be identified, directly or indirectly, in particular by reference to an identifier such as a name, an identification number, location data, an online identifier or to one or more factors specific to the physical, physiological, genetic, mental, economic, cultural or social identity of that natural person."

Like most privacy laws, this definition attempts to distinguish personal data from non-personal data; but as we discussed earlier in this chapter, even very general data about a person can become identifiable when combined with enough other data. Some items are categorically personal data, like names, telephone numbers and email addresses, and other items—like IP addresses or a unique identifier in a browser cookie—likely qualify as well.

However, the definition could be read much more broadly to cover virtually every scrap of data about any person. The GDPR only excludes truly "anonymous" data, if such a thing even exists.

The GDPR has extra protections for "sensitive" personal data. The GDPR prohibits processing data "revealing racial or ethnic origin, political opinions, religious or philosophical beliefs, or trade union membership, and the processing of genetic data, biometric data for the purpose of uniquely identifying a natural person, data concerning health or data concerning a natural person's sex life or sexual orientation," subject to many exclusions. There are also extra protections for information about criminal convictions and offenses.

GDPR's Rights and Obligations

The GDPR creates a wide range of rights for consumers and requirements on controllers and processors.

GDPR Article 5 enumerates six "principles" that apply to all processing of personal data:

- *Lawfulness, Fairness and Transparency*. Personal data shall be "processed lawfully, fairly and in a transparent manner."
- *Purpose Limitation*. Personal data shall be "collected for specified, explicit and legitimate purposes and not further processed in a manner that is incompatible with those purposes" (subject to some public interest exceptions).

- *Data Minimization.* Personal data shall be "adequate, relevant and limited to what is necessary in relation to the purposes for which they are processed."
- *Accuracy.* Personal data shall be "accurate and, where necessary, kept up to date."
- *Storage Limitation.* Personal data shall be "kept in a form which permits identification of data subjects for no longer than is necessary for the purposes for which the personal data are processed" (subject to some public-interest exceptions).
- *Integrity and Confidentiality (a/k/a Security).* Personal data shall be "processed in a manner that ensures appropriate security of the personal data."

As you can see, these vaguely worded principles are more aspirational than prescriptive. This reflects the GDPR's general regulatory approach. The GDPR wants companies to comply both with the letter and the spirit of the lawt, and it creates the possibility of enforcement when the spirit of the law isn't honored. As Jones and Kaminski explain, "The GDPR is often vague because it tasks companies with figuring out how to best implement its aspirations." The GDPR's aspirational approach to regulation conflicts with American jurisprudential norms that favor bright-line rules that provide more legal certainty.

The GDPR prohibits the processing of personal data unless permitted under one of six "lawful" bases, which include consumer consent. However, the GDPR substantially raises the bar on when consent is properly given. The GDPR requires that consumers opt in, with granular consent options, for different processing operations. Consent cannot be obtained via pre-checked boxes or in the terms of service, and consent generally shouldn't be a precondition of registration. Because of the complexities associated with obtaining proper consent from consumers, controllers will often will it more expedient or less risky to try to rely on one of the five other lawful bases for processing. As Jones and Kaminski state bluntly: "The GDPR is not primarily based on consent."

In addition to the Article 5 principles, Chapter III of the GDPR describes eight consumer rights:

- *Right to Be Informed.* Consumers have the right to know when their data is being collected and why. Articles 13 and 14 enumerate minimum requirements of privacy disclosures.
- *Right of Access.* Consumers have the right to see their data.
- *Right to Rectification.* Consumers have the right to correct erroneous information about them.
- *Right of Erasure (also called the "right to be forgotten").* Consumers have the right to delete personal data about them in many circumstances.
- *Right to Restrict Processing.* Consumers have the right to restrict processing of their personal data in many circumstances.
- *Right to Data Portability.* Consumers have the right to obtain and reuse personal data about them for their own purposes across different services in certain cases.
- *Right to Object.* Consumers have the right to object to and prevent their data from being used for specified purposes, including an absolute right to stop their data being used for direct-marketing purposes.
- *Rights Related to Automated Decision Making.* A decision with legal effects may be made solely by a machine, and consumers may be profiled, only with consumers'

explicit consent, or where necessary for the contract, or as otherwise legally authorized.

The GDPR also requires various operational procedures that make companies more proactive about data protection and to treat it less like a "check-the-box" compliance function. For example, it expects companies to implement "data protection by design and by default," companies are required to conduct "data protection impact assessments" before undertaking significant actions, and some companies must designate a "Data Protection Officer." The GDPR also requires companies to report data breaches to government regulators and, in some cases, directly to consumers.

As mentioned earlier, data processors have fewer obligations than data controllers. A data processor must comply with its contracts with data controllers and:

- not use a sub-processor without the controller's permission;
- cooperate with regulators;
- ensure the security of its processing;
- keep records of processing activities;
- notify the data controller of any personal data breaches;
- employ a Data Protection Officer (in some cases); and
- appoint a representative within the European Union (if the processor isn't established in the E.).

Remedies

The GDPR authorizes direct consumer lawsuits for violations, either individually or through public interest organizations. Violations also can be enforced by government agencies, which can seek fines of up to €20M or 4% of a company's global annual revenue (and, in the case of a group of companies, 4% of the group's global annual revenue), whichever is greater.

Jurisdictional Reach

The GDPR applies to:

(1) Companies established in the E.U., regardless of whether data processing takes place inside or outside the E.U. or the data relates to E.U. residents. Thus, a U.S. company with a physical presence in the E.U. may be subject to GDPR both for E.U. consumer data and non-E.U. consumer data.

(2) Companies not established in the E.U. that process E.U. residents' data where the processing is (a) related to offering goods or services to individuals in the E.U. or (b) related to monitoring behavior by individuals in the E.U. These companies must appoint a representative in the E.U.

Thus, the GDPR purports to govern the processing of E.U. consumer data by companies that have no physical presence in the E.U. at all. So, a Silicon Valley-based Internet startup with a globally available website might need to comply with the GDPR from day one. However, the GDPR's potentially global reach raises many complex issues about transborder conflicts-of-laws and enforcements, so the GDPR's actual application to non-E.U. companies may not be as broad as the GDPR claims. As a practical matter, E.U.-based regulators will prioritize their enforcement efforts and, for the foreseeable future, the regulators are likely to have higher-value targets than small U.S. start-up companies with offices exclusively in the U.S. Still, E.U. regulators will inevitably bring cases that test this geographic issue.

So the legally conservative approach would be for everyone in the U.S. advertising community to comply with the GDPR unless they have no E.U. offices and never touch E.U. consumer data. Indeed, many U.S.-only companies have chosen to do just that. This is a reason why every advertising law professional must be familiar with the GDPR. However, compliance with the GDPR is quite expensive, and it goes far beyond what's required under U.S. law. Therefore, many other participants in the U.S. advertising industry will choose to ignore the GDPR unless/until they have physical offices in the E.U. *See* Kurt Wimmer, *Free Expression and EU Privacy Regulation: Can the GDPR Reach U.S. Publishers?*, 68 SYR. L. REV. 547 (2018).

Even if a U.S. company never directly collects E.U. consumer data, it might still encounter the GDPR if it receives transborder data transfers of E.U. consumer data from its business partners. For example, the GDPR regulates when a European company hires a U.S.-based advertising agency to help with ad buys, and the company wants to share consumer data with the agency. In this situation, the company is the data controller and the ad agency is a data processor; and the company must legally impose GDPR-based restrictions on the agency to satisfy its own GDPR obligations.* Thus, a U.S.-only company might still need to comply with the GDPR, at least in part, to facilitate such business arrangements.

Implications for Advertising

Historically, American advertisers have earnestly swept up as much consumer data as possible, remixed it in infinite ways looking to optimize yields and kept it forever. Also, data brokers buy and sell consumer data without any notice to consumers or ability to opt-out. All of these activities run directly contrary to both the letter and the spirit of the GDPR. Something will have to give.

Some of the changes we've already seen due to the GDPR:

- Immediately after the GDPR came into effect, online "programmatic" ads in Europe dropped 25-40%. Jessica Davies, *GDPR Mayhem: Programmatic Ad Buying Plummets in Europe*, DIGIDAY, May 25, 2018.
- A number of key U.S. publications, including the *Los Angeles Times* and the *Chicago Tribune*, blocked European readers from accessing their online editions, Adam Satariano, *U.S. News Outlets Block European Readers Over New Privacy Rules*, N.Y. TIMES, May 25, 2018, and the *Washington Post* launched a new ad-free online

---

* There is a separate issue about whether E.U. data can be transferred to the United States at all. Such transborder movements of data to non-E.U. countries are permitted only when adequate/appropriate safeguards are in place to protect consumer privacy. The United States as a country has not received an adequacy determination, but the self-certification mechanism known as "Privacy Shield" has. The Privacy Shield adequacy determination is currently being litigated in E.U. courts.

subscription for European readers that costs 50% more than online subscriptions that include ads. Melynda Fuller, *'Washington Post' Introduces Premium EU Subscription Following GDPR*, MEDIAPOST, May 18, 2018.

- There is growing evidence that the GDPR benefits incumbents over start-ups. In particular, Google and Facebook have done better, or fared less badly, after the GDPR than their competitors. *See, e.g.*, Damien Geradin et al, *GDPR Myopia: How a Well-Intended Regulation ended up Favoring Google in Ad Tech*, May 11, 2020.

5.   California's Consumer Privacy Act

Important caveat: This note is current as of July 1, 2020, but things are still changing constantly.

By spending about $3 million of his personal fortune, a California real estate developer with a yen for privacy and money to burn qualified a privacy initiative for the November 2018 California statewide ballot. If passed by voters, the initiative's language—which contained numerous provisions that were toxic to the business community—would have been exceptionally difficult to amend.

Following the ballot certification, the developer offered the California legislature a deal: If it immediately passed a law substantially similar to the initiative, he would withdraw the initiative from the ballot. This deal was attractive to all sides. The developer would get his desired policy outcome without spending millions more to sway voters. Meanwhile, for opponents and the legislature, passing a bill would retain the legislature's power to improve and superintend the law over time, plus the opponents would avoid spending an estimated $100 million to fight the initiative.

In a chaotic seven-day period in June 2018, the California legislature introduced, amended and enacted AB 375, the California Consumer Privacy Act ("CCPA"). The legislature didn't hold any hearings on the law, and it got minimal input from affected stakeholders.

Following passage of the CCPA, the California legislature made numerous, but mostly cleanup or minor, amendments in 2019. The legislature will likely adopt a few more (mostly minor) amendments in 2020.

In parallel, the law required the California Attorney General's Office (the "DOJ") to develop regulations, a process that took two years. The DOJ issued its final regulations in June 2020, just a few weeks before the DOJ could start enforcing the law.

Collectively, the CCPA and regulations create what one of your casebook authors has described as "a 21,000+ word unreadable mess." Still, we provide you a roadmap to the law so you can think about the relevant questions to research and discuss with a client.

A.   Who Has to Comply with the Law?

The law applies to any business that "collects consumers' personal information, or on the behalf of which such information is collected and that alone, or jointly with others, determines the purposes and means of the processing of consumers' personal information, that does business in the State of California" and satisfies one of these three requirements:

1) has at least $25 million in annual revenues (from anywhere, not just California), or
2) derives 50%+ of its revenues from selling consumer data, or
3) "annually buys, receives for the business' commercial purposes, sells, or shares for commercial purposes, alone or in combination, the personal information of 50,000 or more consumers, households, or devices" (1798.140(c)).

The law excludes the collection or sale of "a consumer's personal information if every aspect of that commercial conduct takes place wholly outside of California[, i.e.,] if the business collected that information while the consumer was outside of California, no part of the sale of the consumer's personal information occurred in California, and no personal information collected while the consumer was in California is sold" (1798.145(a)(6)). Due to the ambiguity of what qualifies as "doing business" in a state, many out-of-state businesses have felt compelled to comply with the law despite not having any employees or property in California.

The law expressly says it is "not limited to information collected electronically or over the Internet[; the law applies] to the collection and sale of all personal information collected by a business from consumers" (1798.175). The DOJ estimated that the CCPA applies to up to 400,000 businesses in California, including many small- and medium-sized businesses. *See* STATE OF CALIFORNIA- DEPARTMENT OF FINANCE, ECONOMIC AND FISCAL IMPACT STATEMENT, CALIFORNIA CONSUMER PRIVACY ACT (CCPA) REGULATIONS (Aug. 14, 2019).

The law reaches so many small businesses because it covers any business that "receives . . . the personal information of" 50k+ consumers, including the "receipt" of credit cards and IP addresses. A business can clear that threshold with an average of 137 unique credit card sales per day (fourteen sales/hour over a ten-hour business day), or, for a website, an average of 137 unique IP addresses per day, a tiny amount of traffic.

B.   What is "Personal Information?"

The law applies to consumers' "personal information." "Consumers" are natural persons who are California residents (1798.140(g)), including customers, prospective customers, employees/contractors and business contacts (like vendor salespeople). In 2019, the California legislature excluded employees/business contacts from the law for a year; it may temporarily renew this extension in 2020.

The law defines "personal information" as information that "identifies, relates to, describes, is reasonably capable of being associated with, or could reasonably be linked, directly or indirectly, with a particular consumer or household" (1798.140(o)). The statute specifies many examples of personal information, including geolocation data, biometric information and olfactory information. The reference to "household," an undefined term not in the GDPR, creates numerous potential problems, but the regulations mostly ameliorated those concerns. Given the ability to reidentify information discussed earlier in this chapter, *all* data about individuals possessed by a business may qualify as "personal information."

"Personal information" excludes "information that is lawfully made available from federal, state, or local government records" (1798.140(o)(2)) and "consumer information that is deidentified or in the aggregate consumer information" (1798.145(a)(5)).

The CCPA categorically does not apply when other specified privacy laws apply, such as information covered by Health Insurance Portability and Accountability Act of 1996 (1798.145(c)(1)), Fair Credit Reporting Act (1798.145(d)), Gramm-Leach-Bliley Act (1798.145(e)), Driver's Privacy Protection Act of 1994 (1798.145(f)) and more.

C.   Consumer Rights Created by the Law

The CCPA provides six consumer rights:

1) and 2) "Right to Know" and Right of Data Portability

Businesses are required to make disclosures about their generic collection practices (1798.100) and their data sales or transfers (1798.115). Upon request, businesses must also disclose the specific categories of personal information they have collected from the consumer and the "specific pieces of personal information it has collected about that consumer," in a portable format (1798.110). The CCPA has detailed requirements for privacy policies (especially 1798.130(a)(5)), and the regulations add many more requirements.

These rights create pathways for malefactors to illegitimately obtain highly valuable consumer data. To prevent this outcome, the CCPA required the DOJ to define what constitutes a "verifiable consumer request." (1798.140(y)). The DOJ mostly punted, saying that "determining the appropriate verification standard is fact- and scenario-specific" and providing a multi-factor test for businesses to consider, as well as some general rules such as that password-protected accounts will often qualify as reliable verifiers.

3) Erasure Right (1798.105)

Upon a consumer's request, a business shall delete any personal information about the consumer that the business collected from the consumer.

Businesses can refuse deletion requests when it "is necessary for the business or service provider to maintain the consumer's personal information" to do various enumerated things, including completing a transaction or a reasonably anticipated transaction.

4) Right to Say "No" to Data Sales

Consumers can opt out of sales of their personal information, and the business can't ask them to reconsider for at least twelve months (1798.135(a)(5)) with limited exceptions specified in the regulations. There are special provisions for consumers under sixteen

(1798.120(d)) and a special opt-out for third-party data resales (1798.115(d)). If a business sells personal information, then it must "[p]rovide a clear and conspicuous link on the business' Internet homepage, titled 'Do Not Sell My Personal Information,' to an Internet Web page that enables a consumer, or a person authorized by the consumer, to opt out of the sale of the consumer's personal information."

The CCPA defines "sale" broadly to include any disclosure from one business to another "for monetary or other valuable consideration" (1798.140(t)(1)). Due to the ambiguous meaning of "other valuable consideration," the law potentially applies to many activities and data transfers that are not straight cash-for-data.

5) Non-Discrimination Provisions (1798.125)

"A business shall not discriminate against a consumer because the consumer exercised any of the consumer's rights under this title," though a business may charge "a consumer a different price or rate, or [provide] a different level or quality of goods or services to the consumer, if that difference is reasonably related to the value provided to the consumer by the consumer's data." Businesses may offer "financial incentives" (circularly defined as "a program, benefit, or other offering, including payments to consumers, related to the collection, retention, or sale of personal information") to compensate for the collection, sale or deletion of data, but not if the financial incentives are "unjust, unreasonable, coercive, or usurious in nature." The regulations provide numerous formulas to value data for justifying any price or service discrimination.

6) Private Right of Action for Data Breaches

The law creates a private cause of action when "nonencrypted or nonredacted personal information . . . is subject to an unauthorized access and exfiltration, theft, or disclosure as a result of the business' violation of the duty to implement and maintain reasonable security procedures and practices appropriate to the nature of the information to protect the personal information" (1798.150). In those cases, consumers may obtain the greater of actual damages or statutory damages within a range of $100 to $750 "per consumer per incident." To proceed with this private cause of action, consumers must first give the defendant a thirty-day cure period; and if the business is able to cure the problem (whatever "cure" means in the context of a data theft), statutory damages become unavailable.

D.   "User-Enabled Global Privacy Controls"

The regulations added a provision (not in the statute) requiring businesses to honor "user-enabled global privacy controls," defined as signals communicated through browser software or plug-ins indicating that consumers want to opt-out of data sales. This technology does not exist today, so this provision is unlikely to prove practically significant in the near term.

E.   Transparency Reports

In another provision added in the regulations, a business that "buys, receives for the business's commercial purposes, sells, or shares for commercial purposes" personal information for at least ten million California consumers in a calendar year must publish a transparency report about certain types of consumer requests and their processing times and decisions. The DOJ claimed that these transparency reports will help it with enforcement priorities and provide valuable data to researchers.

F.   Who Can Enforce the CCPA?

Other than consumers' private right of action for data breaches, the law does not allow for private causes of action (1798.150(c)), either directly or through indirect means like California Business & Professions Code § 17200, which ordinarily creates a civil claim for legal violations. Plaintiffs are testing this restriction in court.

Except for data breaches, the law can be enforced only by the California Attorney General's office (1798.155) and only after giving businesses a thirty-day cure period (1798.155(b)). Civil penalties can run up to $2,500 "per violation," though if violations are intentional, the cap increases to $7,500 per violation (1798.155(b)).

G.   The Future

The CCPA continues to evolve dynamically. The California legislature will likely enact additional amendments in 2020. The DOJ will begin enforcing the law, which will signal its enforcement priorities. Some of those enforcements may spill over into court, though contested enforcements will be rare because most businesses will correct violations in the thirty-day cure period or strike a deal with the DOJ. There could also be prospective challenges to the law, but that seems unlikely.

The November 2020 ballot will include a new ballot initiative, the California Privacy Rights Act of 2020 (CPRA), from the same team that funded the CCPA ballot initiative.

6.   Case Studies for Review

A.   Practice Problem: Asylum626

Asylum626 was a Doritos promotion targeted at young people in which they were inserted into a horror-movie plot. As the ad agency explained, "The more information you gave us at registration, the creepier the experience." Users could provide their names, email addresses, Twitter addresses and Facebook accounts, which would allow Asylum626 to publish posts via their accounts (something disclosed at signup):

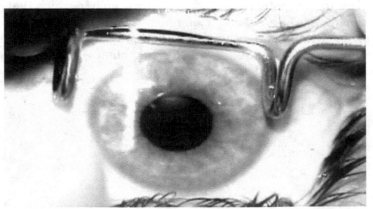

The campaign used Facebook Connect to choose two of the users' friends and "put" them in the asylum. The user could pick which friend to save; then the campaign invited the teens' entire social networks to try and "save" them, posting on their Facebook pages and Twitter feeds. Doritos promised to "use your webcam to bring you into the asylum in real time."

[A still from Asylum626]

Users also had to take the position of torturer in order to finish the experience. In addition, they needed to buy Doritos to get special codes that unlocked the final level. The result was one-to-one tailoring of the campaign and intense engagement with the brand: Users took responsibility for the ad content they were showing to others, using it as part of their social relationships.

One consumer group complained that the immersive, cross-platform nature of this game/ad was likely to put users in an accepting state of "flow," making them more inclined to accept the underlying brand message. *See* Supplemental materials to *Complaint and Request for Investigation of PepsiCo's Deceptive Practices in Marketing Doritos to Adolescents* filed with the Federal Trade Commission on Oct. 19, 2011, available at DigitalAds.org.

What concerns would you have as a lawyer asked to clear this campaign? As a parent who discovered (or failed to discover) that your child was participating? Are the privacy concerns here inherently entangled with other issues (promoting junk food, manipulating people who aren't adults), or can they be separately addressed?

How (if at all) would you conform this promotion to the requirements of the GDPR and/or CCPA?

B. More Examples to Test Yourself

The Burger King "Whopper Detour" Promotion

In 2018, Burger King ran the "Whopper Detour" promotion. Customers who installed Burger King's mobile app could unlock a coupon to purchase a Whopper burger for only one cent—but only if they were within 600 feet of a McDonald's location (the app recognized a Burger King-established "geofence" around each location). What privacy issues does this promotion raise? What other legal and business concerns do you have about this promotion?

AeroMexico's "DNA Discounts" Promotion

In response to the U.S. federal government's repeated denigration of Mexico and Mexicans, the airline AeroMexico posted a YouTube video claiming that it would provide discounts on airfare equivalent to the percentage of passengers' Mexican ancestry. This promotion may have been apocryphal, but assume for a moment that AeroMexico indeed rolled it out. What privacy issues would this promotion raise? What other legal and business concerns would you have about this promotion?

C. FTC Enforcement Against Snapchat

This part takes a close look at an FTC enforcement action for deceptive marketing by an Internet service. The FTC's enforcement target in this enforcement action is Snapchat, a service that allows users to send photos and videos to each other. (The service has since rebranded as "Snap," but we've retained the Snapchat moniker).

Historically, Snapchat's main point of competitive differentiation has been letting a photo sender "expire" the photo or video after a few seconds, which (in theory) lets the sender retain control over the photo's or video's future distribution. Despite the common assertions that younger generations don't value privacy, Snapchat usage exploded, especially among millennials, because it seemingly allowed young adults to express their true selves without risking lifetime consequences.

Unfortunately, as you'll see below, Snapchat did not deliver on its basic promise of letting photo senders prevent photo or video recipients from keeping or republishing the materials.

This led to an FTC enforcement action. The following process is fairly typical for the FTC and investigated companies. The FTC notified Snapchat that it was launching an investigation, probably accompanied by requests for additional information. At that point, Snapchat could have dug in its heels for a fight. Instead, like most targets of an FTC investigation, Snapchat apparently chose to cooperate with the FTC investigation and explore settlement options.

When the parties reached a settlement, the matter was publicly announced by posting a draft complaint against Snapchat simultaneously with the settlement agreement. You will read both documents momentarily. Both documents are drafted under the threat of the FTC actually pursuing an expensive and debilitating enforcement case, so you shouldn't assume a judge would agree with the statements of either fact or law.

As part of the public announcement, the FTC also posted an "Analysis of Proposed Consent Order to Aid Public Comment" and a press release. The FTC then allowed public comment on the settlement for thirty days before submitting the settlement to a final approval. The commission received forty public comments on the settlement, most of them trivial or nonsensical. The FTC Commissioners granted final approval of the settlement in December 2014.

As you read the complaint and settlement agreement, think about which of the FTC's legal positions are straightforward and which represent an aggressive or possibly overreaching interpretation of the law. It is not uncommon for the FTC to interpret its governing laws expansively, especially in a settlement where the enforcement target is cooperating rather than fighting.

What are the pros and cons of the FTC taking aggressive legal positions? Arguably, if regulators only pursue guaranteed victories, they tacitly encourage regulated entities to flirt with or go over the legal line. However, when regulators overzealously pursue cases where the defendant actually engaged in legally permissible behavior, they impose substantial costs on the defendant and make other industry participants fear that their legitimate behavior will be similarly targeted. Do you feel any differently about what constitutes the right enforcement balance in emerging technology fields? How should regulators handle innovative, but potentially risky to consumers, services such as Snapchat?

Why do you think the FTC chose to pursue the enforcement action against Snapchat as opposed to the thousands of other important enforcement targets? Were there viable alternatives to FTC enforcement? Would those alternatives have resolved the issue as effectively as the FTC's action did?

IN THE MATTER OF SNAPCHAT, INC., DOCKET NO. C-4501 (COMPLAINT)
December 23, 2014

. . . RESPONDENT'S BUSINESS PRACTICES

3. Snapchat provides a mobile application that allows consumers to send and receive photo and video messages known as "snaps." Before sending a snap, the application requires the sender to designate a period of time that the recipient will be allowed to view the snap. Snapchat markets the application as an "ephemeral" messaging application, having claimed that once the timer expires, the snap "disappears forever."

4. Snapchat launched its mobile application on Apple Inc.'s iOS operating system in September 2011 and on Google Inc.'s Android operating system in October 2012. Snapchat added video messaging to the iOS version of its application in December 2012 and to the Android version of its application in February 2013.

5. Both the iTunes App Store and the Google Play store list Snapchat among the top 15 free applications. As of September 2013, users transmit more than 350 million snaps daily.

SNAPCHAT'S "DISAPPEARING" MESSAGES (COUNTS 1 AND 2)

6. Snapchat marketed its application as a service for sending "disappearing" photo and video messages, declaring that the message sender "control[s] how long your friends can view your message." Before sending a snap, the application requires the sender to designate a period of time – with the default set to a maximum of 10 seconds – that the recipient will be allowed to view the snap, as depicted below:

7. Since the application's launch on iOS until May 2013, and since the application's launch on Android until June 2013, Snapchat disseminated, or caused to be disseminated, to consumers the following statements on its product description page on the iTunes App Store and Google Play:

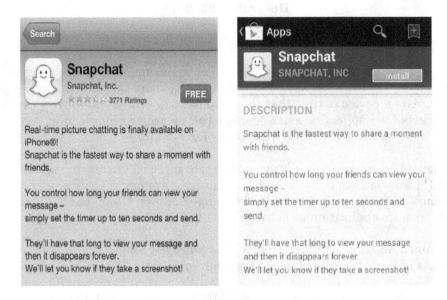

8. From October 2012 to October 2013, Snapchat disseminated, or caused to be disseminated, to consumers the following statement on the "FAQ" page on its website:

Is there any way to view an image after the time has expired?
No, snaps disappear after the timer runs out. . . .

9. Despite these claims, several methods exist by which a recipient can use tools outside of the application to save both photo and video messages, allowing the recipient to access and view the photos or videos indefinitely.

10. For example, when a recipient receives a video message, the application stores the video file in a location outside of the application's "sandbox" (i.e., the application's private storage area on the device that other applications cannot access). Because the file is stored in this unrestricted area, until October 2013, a recipient could connect his or her mobile device to a computer and use simple file browsing tools to locate and save the video file. This method for saving video files sent through the application was widely publicized as early as December 2012. Snapchat did not mitigate this flaw until October 2013, when it began encrypting video files sent through the application.

11. Furthermore, third-party developers have built applications that can connect to Snapchat's application programming interface ("API"), thereby allowing recipients to log into the Snapchat service without using the official Snapchat application. Because the timer and related "deletion" functionality is dependent on the recipient's use of the official Snapchat application, recipients can instead simply use a third-party application to download and save

both photo and video messages. As early as June 2012, a security researcher warned Snapchat that it would be "pretty easy to write a tool to download and save the images a user receives" due to the way the API functions. Indeed, beginning in spring 2013, third-party developers released several applications on the iTunes App Store and Google Play that recipients can use to save and view photo or video messages indefinitely. On Google Play alone, ten of these applications have been downloaded as many as 1.7 million times.

12. The file browsing tools and third-party applications described in paragraphs 10 and 11 are free or low cost and publicly available on the Internet. In order to download, install, and use these tools, a recipient need not make any modifications to the iOS or Android operating systems and would need little technical knowledge.

13. In addition to the methods described in paragraphs 10-12, a recipient can use the mobile device's screenshot capability to capture an image of a snap while it appears on the device screen.

14. Snapchat claimed that if a recipient took a screenshot of a snap, the sender would be notified. On its product description pages, as described in paragraph 7, Snapchat stated: "We'll let you know if [recipients] take a screenshot!" In addition, from October 2012 to February 2013, Snapchat disseminated, or caused to be disseminated, to consumers the following statement on the "FAQ" page on its website:

> **What if I take a screenshot?**
> Screenshots can be captured if you're quick. The sender will be notified immediately.

15. However, recipients can easily circumvent Snapchat's screenshot detection mechanism. For example, on versions of iOS prior to iOS 7, the recipient need only double press the device's Home button in rapid succession to evade the detection mechanism and take a screenshot of any snap without the sender being notified. This method was widely publicized.

Count 1

16. As described in Paragraphs 6, 7, and 8, Snapchat has represented, expressly or by implication, that when sending a message through its application, the message will disappear forever after the user-set time period expires.

17. In truth and in fact, as described in Paragraph 9-12, when sending a message through its application, the message may not disappear forever after the user-set time period expires. Therefore, the representation set forth in Paragraph 16 is false or misleading.

Count 2

18. As described in Paragraphs 7 and 14, Snapchat has represented, expressly or by implication, that the sender will be notified if the recipient takes a screenshot of a snap.

19. In truth and in fact, as described in Paragraph 15, the sender may not be notified if the recipient takes a screenshot of a snap. Therefore, the representation set forth in Paragraph 18 is false or misleading.

SNAPCHAT'S COLLECTION OF GEOLOCATION INFORMATION
(Count 3)

20. From June 2011 to February 2013, Snapchat disseminated or caused to be disseminated to consumers the following statements in its privacy policy:

> We do not ask for, track, or access any location-specific information from your device at any time while you are using the Snapchat application.

21. In October 2012, Snapchat integrated an analytics tracking service in the Android version of its application that acted as its service provider. While the Android operating system provided notice to consumers that the application may access location information, Snapchat did not disclose that it would, in fact, access location information, and continued to represent that Snapchat did "not ask for, track, or access any location-specific information . . ."

22. Contrary to the representation in Snapchat's privacy policy, from October 2012 to February 2013, the Snapchat application on Android transmitted Wi-Fi-based and cell-based location information from users' mobile devices to its analytics tracking service provider.

Count 3

23. As described in Paragraph 21, Snapchat has represented, expressly or by implication, that it does not collect users' location information.

24. In truth and in fact, as described in Paragraph 22, Snapchat did collect users' location information. Therefore, the representation set forth in Paragraph 23 is false or misleading.

SNAPCHAT'S COLLECTION OF CONTACTS INFORMATION
(Counts 4 and 5)

Snapchat's Deceptive Find Friends User Interface

25. Snapchat provides its users with a feature to find friends on the service. During registration, the application prompts the user to "Enter your mobile number to find your friends on Snapchat!," implying – prior to September 2012 – through its user interface that the mobile phone number was the only information Snapchat collected to find the user's friends, as depicted below:

Users can also access this "Find Friends" feature at any time through the application's menu options.

26. However, when the user chooses to Find Friends, Snapchat collects not only the phone number a user enters, but also, without informing the user, the names and phone numbers of all the contacts in the user's mobile device address book.

27. Snapchat did not provide notice of, or receive user consent for, this collection until September 2012, at which time the iOS operating system was updated to provide a notification when an application accessed the user's address book.

Count 4

28. As described in Paragraphs 25, through its user interface, Snapchat represented, expressly or by implication, that the only personal information Snapchat collected when the user chose to Find Friends was the mobile number that the user entered.

29. In truth and in fact, as described in Paragraph 26, the mobile number that the user entered was not the only personal information that Snapchat collected. Snapchat also collected the names and phone numbers of all contacts in the user's mobile device address book. Therefore, the representation set forth in Paragraph 28 is false or misleading.

Snapchat's Deceptive Privacy Policy Statement Regarding the Find Friends Feature

30. From June 2011 to February 2013, Snapchat disseminated or caused to be disseminated to consumers the following statements, or similar statements, in its privacy policy regarding its Find Friends feature:

> Optional to the user, we also collect an email, *phone* number, and facebook id for purpose of finding friends on the service. (Emphasis in original).

31. As explained in Paragraph 26, the Snapchat application collected more than email, phone number, and Facebook ID for purpose of finding friends on the service. The application collected the names and phone numbers of all contacts in the user's mobile device address book.

Count 5

32. As described in Paragraph 30, Snapchat, through its privacy policy, represented, expressly or by implication, that the only personal information Snapchat collected from a user for the purpose of finding friends on the service was email, phone number, and Facebook ID.

33. In truth and in fact, as described in Paragraph 31, email, phone number, and Facebook ID was not the only personal information that Snapchat collected for the purpose of finding friends on the service. Snapchat collected the names and phone numbers of all contacts in the user's mobile device address book when the user chose to Find Friends. Therefore, the representation set forth in Paragraph 32 is false or misleading.

SNAPCHAT'S FAILURE TO SECURE ITS FIND FRIENDS FEATURE
(Count 6)

34. Snapchat failed to securely design its Find Friends feature. As described in paragraph 25, Snapchat prompts the user to enter a mobile phone number that will be associated with the user's account. In addition, as described in paragraph 26, Snapchat collects the names and phone numbers of all the contacts in the user's address book. Snapchat's API uses this information to locate the user's friends on the service.

35. From September 2011 to December 2012, Snapchat failed to verify that the phone number that an iOS user entered into the application did, in fact, belong to the mobile device being used by that individual. Due to this failure, an individual could create an account using a phone number that belonged to another consumer, enabling the individual to send and receive snaps associated with another consumer's phone number.

36. Numerous consumers complained to Snapchat that individuals had created Snapchat accounts with phone numbers belonging to other consumers, leading to the misuse and unintentional disclosure of consumers' personal information. For example, consumers complained that they had sent snaps to accounts under the belief that they were communicating with a friend, when in fact they were not, resulting in the unintentional disclosure of photos containing personal information. In addition, consumers complained that accounts associated with their phone numbers had been used to send inappropriate or offensive snaps.

37. Snapchat could have prevented the misuse and unintentional disclosure of consumers' personal information by verifying phone numbers using common and readily available methods.

38. Indeed, in December 2012, Snapchat began performing short message-service ("SMS") verification to confirm that the entered phone number did in fact belong to the mobile device being used by that individual.

39. In addition, from September 2011 to December 2013, Snapchat failed to implement effective restrictions on the number of Find Friend requests that any one account could make to its API. Furthermore, Snapchat failed to implement any restrictions on serial and automated account creation. As a result of these failures, in December 2013, attackers were able to use multiple accounts to send millions of Find Friend requests using randomly generated phone numbers. The attackers were able to compile a database of 4.6 million Snapchat usernames and the associated mobile phone numbers. The exposure of usernames and mobile phone numbers could lead to costly spam, phishing, and other unsolicited communications.

40. From June 2011 to May 2012, Snapchat disseminated or caused to be disseminated to consumers the following statement in its privacy policy:

> The Toyopa Group, LLC is dedicated to securing customer data and, to that end, employs the best security practices to keep your data protected.

41. From May 2012 to February 2013, Snapchat disseminated or caused to be disseminated to consumers the following statement in its privacy policy:

> Snapchat takes reasonable steps to help protect your personal information in an effort to prevent loss, misuse, and unauthorized access, disclosure, alteration, and destruction.

42. From February 2013 to the present, Snapchat disseminated or caused to be disseminated to consumers the following statement in its privacy policy:

> We take reasonable measures to help protect information about you from loss, theft, misuse and unauthorized access, disclosure, alteration and destruction.

Count 6

43. As described in Paragraphs 40-42, Snapchat has represented, expressly or by implication, that it employs reasonable security measures to protect personal information from misuse and unauthorized disclosure.

44. In truth and in fact, as described in Paragraphs 34-39, in many instances, Snapchat did not employ reasonable security measures to protect personal information from misuse and unauthorized disclosure. Therefore, the representation set forth in Paragraph 43 is false or misleading.

45. The acts and practices of respondent as alleged in this complaint constitute deceptive acts or practices in or affecting commerce in violation of Section 5(a) of the Federal Trade Commission Act, 15 U.S.C. § 45(a).

IN THE MATTER OF SNAPCHAT, INC., DOCKET NO. C-4501 (DECISION AND ORDER)
DECEMBER 23, 2014

. . . DEFINITIONS

For purposes of this Order, the following definitions shall apply: . . .

3. "Covered information" shall mean information from or about an individual consumer, including but not limited to (a) a first and last name; (b) a home or other physical address, including street name and name of city or town; (c) an email address or other online contact information, such as an instant messaging user identifier or a screen name; (d) a telephone number; (e) a persistent identifier, such as a customer number held in a "cookie," a static Internet Protocol ("IP") address, a mobile device ID, or processor serial number; (f) precise geo-location data of an individual or mobile device, including GPS-based, Wi-Fi-based, or cell-based location information; (g) an authentication credential, such as a username or password; or (h) any communications or content that is transmitted or stored through respondent's products or services.

4. "Computer" shall mean any desktop, laptop computer, tablet, handheld device, telephone, or other electronic product or device that has a platform on which to download, install, or run any software program, code, script, or other content and to play any digital audio, visual, or audiovisual content.

I.

IT IS ORDERED that respondent and its officers, agents, representatives, and employees, directly or indirectly, shall not misrepresent in any manner, expressly or by implication, in or affecting commerce, the extent to which respondent or its products or services maintain and protect the privacy, security, or confidentiality of any covered information, including but not limited to: (1) the extent to which a message is deleted after being viewed by the recipient; (2) the extent to which respondent or its products or services are capable of detecting or notifying the sender when a recipient has captured a screenshot of, or otherwise saved, a message; (3) the categories of covered information collected; or (4) the steps taken to protect against misuse or unauthorized disclosure of covered information.

II.

IT IS FURTHER ORDERED that respondent, in or affecting commerce, shall, no later than the date of service of this order, establish and implement, and thereafter maintain, a comprehensive privacy program that is reasonably designed to: (1) address privacy risks related to the development and management of new and existing products and services for consumers, and (2) protect the privacy and confidentiality of covered information, whether collected by respondent or input into, stored on, captured with, or accessed through a computer using respondent's products or services. Such program, the content and implementation of which must be fully documented in writing, shall contain privacy controls and procedures appropriate to respondent's size and complexity, the nature and scope of respondent's activities, and the sensitivity of the covered information, including:

A. the designation of an employee or employees to coordinate and be accountable for the privacy program;

B. the identification of reasonably foreseeable, material risks, both internal and external, that could result in the respondent's unauthorized collection, use, or disclosure of covered information, and assessment of the sufficiency of any safeguards in place to control these risks. At a minimum, this privacy risk assessment should include consideration of risks in each area of relevant operation, including, but not limited to: (1) employee training and management, including training on the requirements of this order; and (2) product design, development and research;

C. the design and implementation of reasonable privacy controls and procedures to address the risks identified through the privacy risk assessment, and regular testing or monitoring of the effectiveness of the privacy controls and procedures;

D. the development and use of reasonable steps to select and retain service providers capable of maintaining security practices consistent with this order, and requiring service providers by contract to implement and maintain appropriate safeguards;

E. the evaluation and adjustment of respondent's privacy program in light of the results of the testing and monitoring required by subpart C, any material changes to respondent's operations or business arrangements, or any other circumstances that respondent knows, or has reason to know, may have a material impact on the effectiveness of its privacy program.

III.

IT IS FURTHER ORDERED that, in connection with its compliance with Part II of this order, respondent shall obtain initial and biennial assessments and reports ("Assessments") from a qualified, objective, independent third-party professional, who uses procedures and standards generally accepted in the profession. A person qualified to prepare such Assessments shall have a minimum of three (3) years of experience in the field of privacy and data protection. . . . The reporting period for the Assessments shall cover: (1) the first one hundred eighty (180) days after service of the order for the initial Assessment; and (2) each two (2) year period thereafter for twenty (20) years after service of the order for the biennial Assessments. Each Assessment shall:

A. set forth the specific privacy controls that respondent has implemented and maintained during the reporting period;

B. explain how such privacy controls are appropriate to respondent's size and complexity, the nature and scope of respondent's activities, and the sensitivity of the covered information;

C. explain how the safeguards that have been implemented meet or exceed the protections required by Part II of this order; and

D. certify that the privacy controls are operating with sufficient effectiveness to provide reasonable assurance to protect the privacy of covered information and that the controls have so operated throughout the reporting period.

Each Assessment shall be prepared and completed within sixty (60) days after the end of the reporting period to which the Assessment applies. . . .

IV.

IT IS FURTHER ORDERED that respondent shall maintain and upon request make available to the Federal Trade Commission for inspection and copying, unless respondent asserts a valid legal privilege, a print or electronic copy of:

A. for a period of five (5) years from the date of preparation or dissemination, whichever is later, statements disseminated to consumers that describe the extent to which respondent maintains and protects the privacy, security and confidentiality of any covered information, including, but not limited to, any statement related to a change in any website or service controlled by respondent that relates to the privacy, security, and confidentiality of covered information, with all materials relied upon in making or disseminating such statements;

B. for a period of five (5) years from the date received, all consumer complaints directed at respondent, or forwarded to respondent by a third party, that relate to the conduct prohibited by this order and any responses to such complaints;

C. for a period of five (5) years from the date received, any documents, whether prepared by or on behalf of respondent that contradict, qualify, or call into question respondent's compliance with this order; and

D. for a period of five (5) years after the date of preparation of each Assessment required under Part III of this order, all materials relied upon to prepare the Assessment, whether prepared by or on behalf of respondent including but not limited to all plans, reports, studies, reviews, audits, audit trails, policies, training materials, and assessments, for the compliance period covered by such Assessment...

VIII.

This order will terminate on December 23, 2034, or twenty (20) years from the most recent date that the United States or the Commission files a complaint (with or without an accompanying consent decree) in federal court alleging any violation of the order, whichever comes later. . . .

NOTES AND QUESTIONS

The settlement terms are consistent with the FTC's typical terms in privacy cases, including "a comprehensive privacy program," biennial privacy audits, and recordkeeping—for twenty years.

The FTC alleged six counts against Snapchat. Do you think it would it have pursued the enforcement action if Snapchat had only committed one of the violations? Or was Snapchat's overall cluster of problems a key part of the FTC's decision to pursue the matter? Do you think it made a difference that Snapchat's defects affected the principal product feature it marketed to consumers?

Assume you are Snapchat's counsel when it is first developing its service, and you expect Snapchat will draw close attention from the FTC given the FTC's general interest in Internet services that advertise privacy features for their users. Anticipating the possibility of an FTC enforcement action, what would you tell Snapchat to do differently from the beginning to avoid the FTC's enforcement? Think about which problems relate to Snapchat's design from the outset.

Which, if any, of its problems could Snapchat have avoided through better disclosures to consumers? How exactly do you concisely explain to consumers that the product makes photos quickly disappear . . . except for the numerous ways that it doesn't?

The FTC's screenshots are often drawn from screens that consumers saw while using the product, not from advertising trying to persuade consumers to choose or download the product. Is the FTC taking the position that any improperly documented software constitutes a consumer deception? As a comparison example, if Microsoft Word's tutorial improperly described a feature of the software, would the FTC say that Microsoft engaged in a deceptive trade practice?

Is it fair to say that the FTC cracked down on Snapchat because Snapchat's software was buggy? All software programs have bugs of some sort.

If you represented Snapchat and the FTC notified you that it was investigating the facts enumerated in the complaint, would you choose to fight against the FTC? Why or why not? Does it affect your decision that the FTC's settlement included no cash payment from Snapchat?

Even though Snapchat didn't pay any money to the FTC as part of its settlement, how would you value the costs to Snapchat of this settlement? How much do you think the "comprehensive privacy program" and biennial audits cost? Consider the consent agreement's length (twenty years, when Snapchat had been in existence for only two years before the investigation started) and the "nuisance" factor as Snapchat tries to innovate with new services and compete against companies not similarly encumbered with FTC oversight. What do you think Snapchat will look like in 2034?

Think back to our discussion about "personal information" and the unexpected breadth of that concept in the *Pineda* case. Do you understand this definition from the FTC?

> "Covered information" shall mean information from or about an individual consumer, including but not limited to (a) a first and last name; (b) a home or other physical address, including street name and name of city or town; (c) an email address or other online contact information, such as an instant messaging user identifier or a screen name; (d) a telephone number; (e) a persistent identifier, such as a customer number held in a "cookie," a static Internet Protocol ("IP") address, a mobile device ID, or processor serial number; (f) precise geo-location data of an individual or mobile device, including GPS-based, Wi-Fi-based, or cell-based location information; (g) an authentication credential, such as a username or password; or (h) any communications or content that is transmitted or stored through respondent's products or services.

In particular, what pieces of data about consumers, no matter how obscure or minor, are clearly *excluded* from this definition?

In Paragraph 11 of the complaint, the FTC notes the findings of a security researcher. This is not unusual. Privacy plaintiffs regularly keep up with technical discussions about security holes or bugs in software. These security researcher findings often become the foundation for an enforcement action.

Paragraph 37 of the complaint says "Snapchat could have prevented the misuse and unintentional disclosure of consumers' personal information by verifying phone numbers using common and readily available methods." Do you think Snapchat had failed to take adequate precautionary measures? Perhaps this reminds you of Judge Hand's negligence formula from *The T.J. Hooper* and *United States v. Carroll Towing*, both of which dealt with the adoption curves of new technological developments. In those cases, the "Hand Formula" defines negligence using the formula "B > PxL," where B = cost of preventing the injury and PxL is the cost of injury times the probability of injury occurring. Under that formula, was Snapchat "negligent?" What information would you need to know to make that determination?

In Paragraph 39 of the complaint, the FTC recounts how "attackers" hacked Snapchat's database. Is this evidence that Snapchat committed deceptive practices on its consumers by promising more than it was prepared to deliver, or does it show Snapchat was a victim of possibly criminal behavior that deserved prosecutorial help from law enforcement? (Or both simultaneously?)

In Paragraphs 40–42, the FTC cites the following language in Snapchat's privacy policy:

- The Toyopa Group, LLC is dedicated to securing customer data and, to that end, employs the best security practices to keep your data protected.
- Snapchat takes reasonable steps to help protect your personal information in an effort to prevent loss, misuse, and unauthorized access, disclosure, alteration, and destruction.
- We take reasonable measures to help protect information about you from loss, theft, misuse and unauthorized access, disclosure, alteration and destruction.

Do provisions of a privacy policy qualify as marketing claims? Do you think many consumers relied upon these statements when deciding to transact with Snapchat? What, if any, of these statements might be puffery? Did Snapchat actually fail to honor the statements? What evidence demonstrates that failing?

In Paragraph 44, the FTC says Snapchat did not use "reasonable security procedures." What steps did Snapchat need to take to satisfy the FTC that it had reasonable security procedures? Or is the FTC's position that any corporation that suffers any security breach has per se demonstrated that it lacked reasonable security procedures?

The Snappening. In October 2014—after the settlement was announced but before the FTC finally approved it—hackers released tens of thousands of private photos that had been shared between individual Snapchat users. Mike Isaac, *A Look Behind the Snapchat Photo Leak Claims*, N.Y. TIMES, Oct. 17, 2014. (The release was colloquially referred to as the "Snappening," a portmanteau of "Snapchat" and a "happening"). Snapchat users had stored photos on an independent service called Snapsaved, which had been designed to demonstrate that Snapchat's disappearing-content claims were bogus. When Snapsaved was hacked, its photo archives were released to the wild. If a Snapchat user sent a photo to another Snapchat user who was also using Snapsaved, then the sender's photo may have been released even though the sender had never interacted with Snapsaved.

Should Snapchat be responsible for the hack of a third-party service's database? Should Snapchat have done more to prevent Snapsaved from being able to obtain and save users' photos? Should the revelation of the hack-and-release have affected (or even scuttled) the in-process FTC settlement?

In 2015, Snapchat took several steps to block the possibility of third-party services like Snapsaved. Stephen Levy, *Snapchat's Non-Vanishing Message: You Can Trust Us*, BACKCHANNEL.COM, Apr. 2, 2015.

This chapter addresses several types of promotional campaigns, including coupons, giveaways, sweepstakes and contests. Marketing people love these types of promotions because they pique consumer interest and get them to try new products or switch brands. Because of the extra consumer appeal of promotions, they are subject to special regulatory treatment.

1. Coupons

In general, coupons must comply with the ordinary rules requiring ads to be truthful and non-misleading, with specific attention to price claims and, where necessary, to the regulation of the use of "free" by the FTC and state laws.*

In addition to heightened restrictions in certain industries, general false advertising law constrains coupon offers, and the advertiser must disclose material conditions. In *Martin v. Coca-Cola Co.*, 785 F. Supp. 3 (D.D.C. 1992), Coca-Cola put an ad on bottles of Diet Coke: "Save 25 cents on your next purchase of a 2 or 3 liter bottle or multi-pack of Coca-Cola products with coupon on back of label." But the coupon was only good for twenty-five cents off Diet Sprite or Diet Minute Maid soda. The court deemed the plaintiff's argument that this was deceptive "preposterous." Do you agree? Would a reasonable consumer expect that "Coca-Cola products," without qualification, included Coke or Diet Coke—the very product on which the coupon appeared?

A more-likely legal issue, however, is a coupon offer inadvertently gone wrong. Here's an example:

IN RE KENTUCKY GRILLED CHICKEN COUPON MARKETING & SALES PRACTICES LITIGATION, 2010 WL 2742310 (N.D. ILL. 2010)

On February 4, 2010, plaintiffs Christine Doering, James Asanuma, Veronica Mora, Kay Ready, and Daleen Brown (together "Plaintiffs"), on behalf of themselves and a purported class of over five million other people, filed a "Master Consolidated Class Action Complaint" in this multidistrict class action lawsuit. Plaintiffs allege claims for breach of contract (Count

---

* Some specially regulated industries have extra constraints on marketing techniques, including coupons. *Coldwell Banker Residential Real Estate Services, Inc. v. New Jersey Real Estate Commission*, 576 A.2d 938 (N.J. App. Div. 1990), upheld a ban on the use of coupons for furniture by real estate brokers against First Amendment and due process challenges. The targeted evil was "the capacity of extraneous inducements to distract the residential buyer and seller from the material elements of their decisions to list, sell and buy their homes. To many buyers and sellers, these are among the mostsignificant financial decisions they face. Distracting gimmickry creates dangers which are the legitimate concern of the [regulators]." Indeed, the psychological/marketing literature generally agrees that coupons and similar offers may create a sense of obligation or otherwise undermine consumers' sales resistance. But is that a problem?

I), common law fraud (Count VI), and violations of the consumer protection statutes of Illinois, Michigan, and California (Counts II–V & VII) in relation to a free product giveaway in May 2009. Pending before the court is defendant Yum! Brands, Inc. ("Yum!") and defendant KFC Corporation's ("KFC") (together "Defendants") motion to dismiss. For the reasons stated below, Defendants' motion is denied.

BACKGROUND . . .

Defendant KFC is the world's most popular chicken restaurant chain, and is a subsidiary of defendant Yum!. In April 2009, Defendants introduced a new product called "Kentucky Grilled Chicken." Defendants promoted "Kentucky Grilled Chicken" as a healthy fast-food menu option and incorporated the new menu item as part of their overall campaign to improve KFC's reputation for healthiness. Defendants' campaign included a "Kentucky Grilled Chicken" giveaway, which was announced by Oprah Winfrey on May 5, 2009, on her television talk show. Pursuant to the terms of the giveaway, any individual could obtain a free meal at KFC by first downloading a coupon from either unthinkfc.com or from Oprah Winfrey's website and then redeeming the coupon at a participating KFC franchise between May 5, 2009 and May 19, 2009, with the exception of May 10, 2009 (Mother's Day). When presented at a KFC restaurant, the coupon entitled the bearer to a free two-piece "Kentucky Grilled Chicken" meal, with two sides and a biscuit.

Defendants "began almost immediately to refuse to honor the coupons." At first they did so by "limit[ing] the promotion to the first 100 coupons presented at each KFC restaurant, per day." On May 7, 2009, Defendants "stopped the promotion altogether . . . [and] instructed franchises to stop honoring the coupons." Many of the KFC locations that refused to honor the coupon continued to offer "Kentucky Grilled Chicken" for purchase. From May 5 to May 7, 2009, at least 10.2 million coupons were downloaded from unthinkfc.com. Only 4.5 million coupons were actually redeemed at KFC franchises.

After stopping the coupon promotion, Defendants offered consumers the option of applying for a "rain check" for the promised free "Kentucky Grilled Chicken" meal. To apply for a "rain check," the consumer was required to fill out a form with the consumer's name and address, attach his or her coupon to the form, and mail the form to KFC or give it to a KFC team member. Defendants told consumers these procedures were necessary "so that KFC could verify the coupons' validity." Following receipt of the "rain check" application, KFC would then send the consumer a new coupon for a free meal at a later date, as well as an additional complimentary Pepsi product. . . .

ANALYSIS

. . .II. Count VI—Common Law Fraud

. . . Defendants argue that Plaintiffs' common law fraud claim must be dismissed because Plaintiffs have failed to allege facts "that plausibly give rise to an inference that KFC 'never intended to honor' the coupons."

Plaintiffs allege in their Master Complaint that "Defendants, in fact, never intended to honor the Coupons as represented." While Plaintiffs, of course, cannot know Defendants' state of mind, they have supported this general allegation with additional facts alleged in the Master Complaint. For example, Plaintiffs allege that, "[o]n information and belief, many of the KFC locations that refused to redeem the coupons had ample supplies of Kentucky Grilled Chicken on hand, and continued to make those supplies available for purchase." The "information and belief" on which this allegation rests includes the experiences of plaintiff Veronica Mora on May 5, 2009, who allegedly visited a KFC restaurant in Sylmar, California, where employees refused to honor the coupon while continuing to sell "Kentucky Grilled Chicken" to customers. It is also alleged that none of the four named plaintiffs who attempted to redeem the coupons in person were told that the specific KFC restaurant they visited had actually run out of "Kentucky Grilled Chicken."

Defendants argue that they could not have plausibly harbored an intention not to honor the coupons, when it is undisputed that Defendants honored 4.5 million coupons in the first two days of the promotion. However, Plaintiffs have also alleged that Defendants "began almost immediately to refuse to honor the coupons" and "stopped the promotion altogether on May 7, 2009—two days after it was announced," which left 5.7 million coupons unredeemed.

Based on the allegations of the Master Complaint, the court finds it plausible that Defendants never intended to honor the coupon as represented. It can be reasonably inferred from Defendants' choice to publicize their offer "on the highly popular 'Oprah' show" that Defendants hoped their promotion would reach millions of consumers. It is also reasonable to assume that Defendants contemplated the possibility that millions of consumers would seize the opportunity to obtain a free "Kentucky Grilled Chicken" meal, and that Defendants considered what would happen if individual KFC restaurants ran out of the advertised product. With these considerations in mind, the court finds that it is plausible Defendants intended all along to offer a "rain check" in place of the coupon, or otherwise limit redemption of the coupon beyond the terms stated on its face. Plaintiffs have alleged sufficient facts to comport with the pleading requirements of Rule 8 and state a plausible claim for common law fraud.

III. Counts II, III, IV, V, & VII—Consumer Protection Statutes

. . . Plaintiffs contend that the Master Complaint's allegations are sufficient to support their statutory claims under the relevant state consumer protection statutes, because the allegations go beyond breach of contract to "implicate [ ] consumer protection concerns."

As discussed above, Plaintiffs have adequately alleged that Defendants "never intended to honor the Coupons." Based on this allegation, Plaintiffs characterize Defendants' actions as "a classic 'bait and switch' " and note that this type of conduct is actionable under the relevant state consumer protection statutes. . . .

Because Plaintiffs have alleged that Defendants never intended to honor their promotion from the outset, Plaintiffs' allegations "involve [ ] more than the mere fact that a defendant promised something and then failed to do it." Additionally, this court finds that the contract at issue in this litigation implicates an "inherent consumer interest" on its face, insofar as

Defendants' offer was allegedly accepted by millions of consumers across the nation. For these reasons, the court declines to dismiss Plaintiffs' statutory claims as being redundant to the claim for breach of contract.

A. Count II—Illinois

In Count II of their Master Complaint, Plaintiffs allege that Defendants' actions violate Section 2 and Section 2P of the Illinois Consumer Fraud and Deceptive Business Practices Act ("ICFA"), 815 ILCS 505/1, et seq. Relying on the language of the statute, Defendants argue that Plaintiffs' claims under the ICFA should be dismissed because "the offering of a free meal does not fall within the scope of the ICFA."

1. Section 2

Section 2 of the ICFA declares that it is unlawful to engage in:

> Unfair methods of competition and unfair or deceptive acts or practices, including but not limited to the use or employment of any deception, fraud, false pretense, false promise, misrepresentation or the concealment, suppression or omission of any material fact, with intent that others rely upon the concealment, suppression or omission of such material fact . . . in the conduct of any trade or commerce . . . whether any person has in fact been misled, deceived or damaged thereby.

815 ILCS 505/2. Defendants argue that Plaintiffs cannot state a cause of action under Section 2, because Defendants' alleged actions as set forth in the Master Complaint do not describe an act or practice that has taken place "in the conduct of any trade or commerce."

The ICFA defines the terms "trade" and "commerce" as "the advertising, offering for sale, sale, or distribution of any services and any property, . . . commodity, or thing of value." 815 ILCS 505/1(f). Defendants note that this definition "describe[s] four steps of a typical commercial sale" and argue that, because "the coupon did not involve any sale or offer of sale," the statute is inapplicable to the facts of this case. Defendants' interpretation ignores the plain language of the statute. This language is unambiguous, insofar as the use of the disjunctive "or" clearly signifies that allegations of unfair or deceptive acts or practices occurring at any one of the four stages in the life cycle of a typical consumer transaction ("advertising, offering for sale, sale, or distribution") will suffice to state a claim under Section 2. The court declines Defendant's invitation to read the disjunctive term "or" as though it means the conjunctive term "and" in this context.

The court further disagrees with Defendants' argument that the coupon did not constitute an "advertisement" because it was not "disseminated in connection with a 'commercial transaction.'" Plaintiffs have alleged that Defendants offered the coupon as part of their advertising campaign for their new line of chicken. . . . The allegations of the Master Complaint support the reasonable inference that the goal of Defendants' advertising campaign was to promote future sales of "Kentucky Grilled Chicken" and other KFC products, especially in light of the fact that the coupons were only redeemable in person at participating KFC restaurants. Because the "Kentucky Grilled Chicken" giveaway can reasonably be considered an attempt "to induce directly or indirectly any person to enter into any obligation or acquire any title or interest in any merchandise," the "Kentucky Grilled Chicken" giveaway can be considered an "advertisement" for purposes of the ICFA.

2. Section 2P

Plaintiffs also allege that Defendants violated Section 2P of the ICFA, which states:

> It is an unlawful practice for any person to promote or advertise any business, product, utility service . . . or interest in property, by means of offering free prizes, gifts, or gratuities *to any consumer*, unless all material terms and conditions relating to the offer are clearly and conspicuously disclosed at the outset of the offer so as to leave no reasonable probability that the offering might be misunderstood.

815 ILCS 505/2P (emphasis added). Defendants argue that Plaintiffs' claims under Section 2P necessarily fail because (1) Plaintiffs are not "consumers" under the ICFA's definition of this term, and (2) Plaintiffs have not alleged any "unclear or inconspicuous disclosure."

The ICFA defines "consumer" as "any person who purchases or contracts for the purchase of merchandise not for resale in the ordinary course of his trade or business but for his use or that of a member of his household." Because "[n]one of the plaintiffs was required to purchase anything to receive a free meal," Defendants assert that Plaintiffs cannot state a claim for relief under Section 2P. The statutory definition of "consumer" is not as limited as Defendants contend. On its face, the ICFA definition does not require a "consumer" to have purchased merchandise from a named defendant. Nor does this reading make sense in the context of Section 2P. Section 2P applies to situations in which businesses promote their products by offering "free prizes, gifts, or gratuities to any consumer." Section 2P would be rendered meaningless if an individual must first purchase the "free" product to be considered a "consumer" for purposes of the protections set forth therein.

Defendants also argue that "[t]his case has nothing to do with the failure to clearly and conspicuously disclose the terms of the promotion." In response, Plaintiffs contend that the Master Complaint is "rife with allegations of after-the-fact conditions placed on the offer by Defendants and their employees." The conditions cited by Plaintiffs include (1) that redemption of the coupons would be limited "to the first 100 coupons presented at each KFC restaurant, per day, regardless of the supplies of 'Kentucky Grilled Chicken' on hand" and (2) that consumers would not be able to redeem the coupon after a certain date, at which point consumers would be required to provide their names and addresses before receiving a "rain check" good for a free meal at a later date. Section 2P requires disclosure of "all material terms and conditions relating to the offer . . . at the outset of the offer," for purposes of ensuring that the there is "no reasonable probability that the offering might be misunderstood." . . . Plaintiffs have set forth sufficient allegations in the Master Complaint to plausibly suggest that Defendants at some point made a decision to revise the terms of the offer and did not "clearly and conspicuously" disclose the new contract terms to Plaintiffs before Plaintiffs accepted the offer. . . .

[The court made similar rulings about plaintiffs' Michigan and California law claims, as well as defendants' contentions that they offered "rain checks" sufficient to satisfy relevant statutory safe harbors for sellers who run out of a product but offer consumers the same terms within a reasonable time once they've restocked. Given the allegations that, among other things, the supposed "rain checks" imposed additional requirements to provide personal information and that restaurants actually had the chicken in stock but still refused to honor the coupons, defendants hadn't shown that the complaint should be dismissed.]
NOTES AND QUESTIONS

How should Yum! have worded the coupon so that it clearly and conspicuously disclosed the limits on the offer? In response to surprisingly high demand for an offer, what should an advertiser do? Statutory safe harbors for rain checks do exist. However, as this case indicates, the rain checks must be as nearly equivalent to the initial offer as possible (other than the unavoidable delay in honoring the offer).

Reese Witherspoon's fashion label had related problems when it offered a free dress giveaway to teachers "while supplies last," when it actually meant only to distribute 250 free dresses.

draperjames ✔
771.6k followers

DRAPER JAMES ☺
♡
Teachers

View More on Instagram

♡ ◯ ⬆   🔖

59,306 likes

draperjames

Dear Teachers: We want to say thank you. During quarantine, we see you working harder than ever to educate our children. To show our gratitude, Draper James would like to give teachers a free dress. To apply, complete the form at the link in bio before this Sunday, April 5th, 11:59 PM ET. (Offer valid while supplies last - winners will be notified on Tuesday, April 7th.) ✏️🖼️ 👗 x The Draper James Team

Know a teacher who deserves a pick-me-up? Forward this post or tag your favorite educator in comments. 📣 #DJLovesTeachers

view all 41,041 comments

Although Draper James quickly clarified its intent, it was too late: "By the close of the application period, Draper James had almost one million applications —which was approximately seven times the total number of dresses they had sold in 2019." Vanessa Friedman, *Reese Witherspoon's Fashion Line Offered Free Dresses to Teachers. They Didn't Mean Every Teacher*, N.Y. TIMES, Mar. 15, 2020. And the "applicants" who didn't get dresses did end up on Draper James' mailing list—creating additional problems with whether this promotion was an illegal lottery, as you will see in the next section.

Digital Distribution. Distributing coupons electronically can cost less than other distribution methods, but electronic coupons may be harder to control. Among other things, coupon issuers should consider the possibility that a coupon will go viral and plan accordingly.

For example, in 2006, a Starbucks in Atlanta emailed a coupon for a free "iced grande beverage" to a relatively small number of employees and business partners and encouraged them to forward the email coupon to friends and family. The email got forwarded to millions of people nationwide, resulting in such large demand that Starbucks canceled the promotion (otherwise, Starbucks's losses could have been millions of dollars). What should Starbucks have done differently?

There are several types of coupon problems:

- *Redistributed Coupons.* Often, coupons are meant to induce consumers to switch brands. If too many coupons end up in the hands of existing brand loyalists, their redemptions allow the loyalists to make their already-planned purchases at a lower cost. Thus, the advertiser may want to restrict coupon transferability to keep existing consumers from getting too many coupons.
- *Violation of Redemption Restrictions.* Coupons often restrict who can redeem them and how and when they can be redeemed. Redemptions in violation of those terms— whether due to fraud or ignorance by the consumer or sloppy oversight by the person accepting the redeemed coupon—can undermine the coupon issuer's economic expectations.

- *Fraudulent Coupons.* Some fraudsters make and redeem fake coupons. The person accepting redemption may not recognize the fake. Coupon counterfeiting may sound like a nickel-and-dime problem, but it can be a lucrative and sizable business. *See, e.g.*, Brad Tuttle, *The $40 Million Counterfeit Coupon Caper*, TIME.COM, July 19, 2012. An industry organization, the Coupon Information Center, attempts to combat fake coupons.

Because managing coupon redemptions can be complicated, advertisers and retailers often rely on third-party service providers to help with various administrative aspects.

Counter-Measures. Some retailers combat competitors' offers with price or coupon matches. By allowing a consumer who proves the existence of a cheaper price elsewhere to get the same deal at her usual store, the retailer, in theory, avoids losing a customer.

Price-match offers must be carefully drafted and enforced, as Wal-Mart discovered to its sorrow in 2014. Competitor Dollar General offered a $9.50 sale price for "all counts and sizes" of Pampers Swaddlers diapers, and $6.50 for packs of lower-end Luvs diapers. Because Dollar General typically stocks smaller packages, this equated to a discount of about fifty cents per pack. But Wal-Mart and other competitors stock much bigger packages with retail prices of up to $38. Relying on price match promises, consumers clogged understaffed Wal-Mart checkout lines, and some consumers received discounts of up to 75% until Wal-Mart stopped honoring the Dollar General offer. Wal-Mart now instructs cashiers that a price match requires that the item's size, quantity, brand, flavor and color are identical to the product carried by Wal-Mart. (Note that Wal-Mart often commissions manufacturers, even national brands, to supply unique product variants that are unavailable elsewhere). A Wal-Mart spokesperson ultimately said that the Dollar General offer was ineligible for the price match because it didn't specify "like-for -ike item." One consumer's reaction to being denied a match was: "It said, 'any count, any size.' How much more specific do you have to get?" Serena Ng & Kelly Banjo, *Volatile Brew: Price-Matching and Social Media*, WALL ST. J., July 23, 2014.

If you were Wal-Mart's counsel, how would you draft the price-match policy to avoid this problem in the future? How would you succinctly communicate it to consumers? Do the consumers who were refused a match have any potential legal claims? If Wal-Mart deliberately stocks "unmatchable" products, is the price match claim misleading?

Retailer Issues. What happens if the retailer misunderstands the manufacturer's coupon offer? *Renner v. Procter & Gamble Co.*, 54 Ohio App.3d 79, 561 N.E.2d 959 (1988), involved a coupon offering a free box of basic-size Luvs diapers "or equivalent off any larger size (up to $3.75)." "FREE" was the most prominent part of the coupon.

[coupon reproduced by court]

Renner took the coupon to a store where the basic size was priced at more than $3.75, and the cashier refused to give him the box for free, though he was able to redeem the coupon for a free box at a different store. Procter & Gamble ultimately explained to the first store that its intent was to provide a coupon for a free box of basic-size diapers *or* $3.75 off any larger size. Renner sued for violation of Ohio Administrative Code 109:4-3-02(A)(1), which provided that:

> It is a deceptive act or practice in connection with a consumer transaction for a supplier, in the sale or offering for sale of goods or services, to make any offer in written or printed advertising or promotional literature without stating clearly and conspicuously in close proximity to the words stating the offer any material exclusions, reservations, limitations, modifications, or conditions. Disclosure shall be easily legible to anyone reading the advertising or promotional literature and shall be sufficiently specific so as to leave no reasonable probability that the terms of the offer might be misunderstood.

The court of appeals found in P&G's favor: Given that P&G intended to give consumers a free basic-size box, there were arguably no "material exclusions, reservations, limitations, modifications, or conditions" attached to the offer in the first place. "More importantly, however, we agree with the trial court that the $3.75 limitation was of sufficient clarity and conspicuousness so that it left 'no reasonable probability' that its terms would be misunderstood to apply such limitation to the free basic size disposable diaper offer, rather than merely to the alternative offer." The court suggested that the first store's misunderstanding didn't benefit P&G (since it was trying to get consumers to try the product) and, that out of 2.5 billion similar coupons mailed, there had been very few complaints. Was there anything more that P&G could reasonably have done?

Other Giveaways. Perhaps even more than coupons, free samples or other "free" offers have excellent selling power, engendering warm feelings toward the "giver" and triggering reciprocity norms in consumers that may induce them to make a purchase. Gifts may also induce consumers to focus on the short term—the immediate enjoyment of the gift—instead of the long-term consequences of a purchase decision.

But "free" gifts have implicit strings attached. Therefore, the 2009 CARD Act bars credit card issuers from offering "any tangible item," such as t-shirts or pizza, to students who sign up for a credit card. Issuers also can't offer any gifts "near the campus" or at an "event sponsored by or related to an institution of higher learning."

Do such prohibitions reflect unjustified paternalism or reasonable regulation? These tactics are certainly promotional from the perspective of marketers; they build brand loyalty and generate consumer demand. Can you imagine any First Amendment argument against regulating the provision of free samples or gifts? *See* Discount Tobacco City & Lottery, Inc. v. U.S., 674 F.3d 509 (6th Cir. 2012) (holding that free tobacco samples and gifts with purchase of tobacco were protected by the First Amendment as "promotional methods that convey the twin messages of reinforcing brand loyalty and encouraging switching from competitors' brands"). *But see* Nicopure Labs, LLC v. Food & Drug Admin., 944 F.3d 267 (D.C. Cir. 2019) (rejecting *Discount Tobacco*'s reasoning; zero is a price and regulating price constitutes economic, not speech, regulation). There are multiple ways to generate sales, and they may be subject to different forms of regulation and different levels of First Amendment scrutiny.

Pure giveaways, like unrestricted coupon offers, can go very badly. In 2008, when the popular band Guns N' Roses had already delayed the release of its next album, *Chinese Democracy*, for a decade, Dr. Pepper offered to give every American a free can of Dr. Pepper soda if the album were released in the next year. Unfortunately for Dr. Pepper, Guns N' Roses did release the album that year. Dr. Pepper quickly set up a website allowing consumers to redeem their free can, but that website quickly crashed. In the end, very few consumers received their free cans, and Guns N' Roses lawyers threatened Dr. Pepper with a lawsuit. Dr. Pepper publicly claimed that it was just responding to an invitation from the band's managers. What sort of documentation would you want for such a promotion if you were Dr. Pepper's lawyers? How would you tell your clients to plan to implement a possible redemption?

2.   Sweepstakes and Contests

Sweepstakes and contests are common: Marketers and non-profit organizations of every size run them, and many are offered in good faith, with valuable prizes awarded.

Nonetheless, advertisers have a checkered history with sweepstakes and prizes. Certain advertisers engaged in repeated abuses, in which consumers—particularly elderly consumers—were induced to buy hundreds and even thousands of dollars' worth of magazine subscriptions, for example, in the mistaken belief that purchasing subscriptions would increase their chances of winning large prizes. Misleading sweepstakes advertising thus led to numerous lawsuits and legislative and regulatory responses. *See, e.g.*, FTC, *FTC Sues to Stop Massive Sweepstakes Scam*, Sept. 23, 2013 (lawsuit alleging consumers were defrauded of more than $11 million by mass mailings that they'd "won" $2 million, which could be claimed by sending in a fee of $20 or $30; small print indicated that the fee was only paying for a list of others' sweepstakes). These sorts of practices, lacking the clear and conspicuous disclosure of the relevant terms, are unfair and deceptive and likely to bring significant trouble to advertisers who try them.

Because the rules governing sweepstakes and contests are so detailed and differ substantially from state to state, no lawyer should approve either without doing a careful review of all the relevant rules and regulations in all fifty states, plus U.S. territories. One multistate checklist may be found in DAVID H. BERNSTEIN & BRUCE P. KELLER, THE LAW OF ADVERTISING, MARKETING AND PROMOTIONS § 7 (2017). By way of warning, it has thirty-two items on the basic checklist, and four more for Internet promotions. The Global Advertising Lawyers Alliance, an industry organization, also puts out a guide to sweepstakes regulations around the world. Often, sweepstakes and contest clearance is best handled by a lawyer who specializes in the field.

However, sweepstakes are also extremely popular with clients, because clients expect substantial exposure from them. Even small-scale Instagram influencers may run such contests—and risk running afoul of the law. *See* Taylor Lorenz, *Everyone Is Giving Away Cash on Instagram*, N.Y. TIMES, Apr. 27, 2020 (explaining that influencers promise a chance at cash for people who follow a list of the influencer's recommended accounts).

A. How Can a Contest or Sweepstakes Avoid Being an Illegal Lottery?

An illegal lottery has three components: (1) a prize, which can be anything of tangible value, (2) determined on the basis of chance, (3) where consideration is paid to participate.

A sweepstakes eliminates the third factor (consideration) so that it involves a prize based on chance, but people may participate without payment.

A contest eliminates the second factor (chance) so that people are eligible for the prize if they provide the specified consideration, but there is no element of chance in the prize allocation. An example is a talent contest where the prize goes to the person who experts judge as the most talented (though, as we will discuss below, states have different standards for determining when a contest has an element of chance).

Advertisers need to be very careful about avoiding illegal lotteries (which can constitute crimes). Chance and consideration have a frustrating habit of creeping back into well-designed efforts to eliminate them.

Why are prizes such an attractive technique for advertisers? Psychologists suggest that the apparent "gift," whether from a coupon, a free sample or a "free" chance to win something, triggers reciprocity norms among consumers, making them feel grateful and even creating a sense of obligation or debt to the advertiser. For extensive evidence on this point, *see* Robert Cialdini, *Influence: The Psychology of Persuasion* (rev. ed. 1998). Another possibility is that consumers overvalue the prize or overestimate their chance of winning, so consumers feel like they are getting more value from the advertiser than the advertiser is actually paying. Also, from an advertiser's standpoint, it's a way of providing a price discount or extra benefit to consumers without explicitly lowering prices, which the advertiser might want to avoid.

Element One: Prize

The Court of Appeals for the Seventh Circuit, in *George v. National Collegiate Athletic Association*, 613 F.3d 658 (7th Cir. 2010), initially allowed a class action to proceed over the distribution of tickets to the popular NCAA Basketball Tournament. The complaint alleged this was an illegal lottery because it required applicants to submit a $6–$10 handling fee along with the face value of the tickets to get a chance to win tickets. If the applicants weren't selected, they would be reimbursed for the face value of the tickets but not for the handling fee. Even though an applicant could only win one pair of tickets, many applicants bought multiple entries to maximize their chances of getting that pair, so both successful and unsuccessful applicants could incur multiple handling fees.

The Court of Appeals initially determined that plaintiffs sufficiently pled the elements of (1) prize, (2) chance, and (3) consideration, concluding that if the NCAA had set up its ticket distribution process so that the handling fee was refunded to non-winners, the process would have been legal. This opinion was then vacated, 623 F.3d 1135 (7th Cir. 2010), and the panel certified to the Indiana Supreme Court the state-law questions.

In *George v. National Collegiate Athletic Association*, 945 N.E.2d 150 (Ind. 2011), the Indiana Supreme Court concluded that the NCAA's ticket-allocation process was not an illegal lottery under Indiana law because winners (those who got tickets) received no "prize"—they got nothing more than losers did. Both winners and losers were out-of-pocket for the handling fee, and "[t]hose applicants whose offers to purchase tickets are accepted receive tickets for $150 per ticket, whereas those applicants whose offers are rejected receive $150 in cash per ticket." Did the NCAA successfully evade the prohibition on lotteries? Could other advertisers do the same thing, making their profits on "handling fees?" Would it matter if, at the time of allocation, the "street value" of the tickets was more than the face value?

Another issue about prizes does not relate to illegal lotteries, but to trademark owners' possible objection to the use of their marks in describing prizes. Apple issued guidelines stating its opposition to using iPads and other Apple products as prizes without Apple's authorization. Given the trademark doctrine of nominative use, does Apple have that right? Arguably, merely giving away an iTunes gift card shouldn't suggest a connection with Apple. What would you tell a client who wants to offer an Apple product as a prize?

Element Two: Chance

If the element of chance is absent, then the promotion is a contest of skill and not a game of chance. This is important because, in most states, it is legally permissible for contests of skill to require an entry fee or proof of purchase, though some states—including Arizona, Connecticut, Florida, Illinois, New Jersey and Vermont—prohibit skill contests that require consideration.

The game contains elements of chance when the outcome depends on future events, such as the predicted winners of sports competitions—that is, even an educated guess may turn the contest into illegal gambling in some states, if consideration is required to enter. Fantasy sports leagues have generated substantial controversy on this point, though they are now generally tolerated. Most states allow consideration-based contests of skill as long as skill is the dominant factor in determining who wins, though a minority will allow such contests as long as winning isn't *purely* the result of chance.

Courts that apply the "dominant factor" test ask: (1) whether the contest is impossible to win without skill, and whether there is enough opportunity for entrants to make informed decisions; (2) whether the average player has enough skill to participate; (3) whether skill determines the actual result of the game, not just some element of the promotion; and (4) whether participants are aware of the skill and criteria that will be used to determine the winner.

However, courts that use this test still differ in results. Some courts have found Three Card Monte and word puzzle games to be games of skill, whereas shell games, dice games and bingo are games of chance. There's a split on whether pinball and poker are games of chance or skill. Is a hole-in-one golf contest skill-based? Florida's attorney general determined that it was skill, but South Carolina's attorney general believed that making a hole in one is so dependent on luck that the contest was fairly described as predominantly chance-based. For an online contest, the participant's speed of response to a problem or puzzle might not be skill-based given that response times may depend on devices and services outside the entrant's control.

Contests of skill have to be judged based on specific, objective criteria by competent judges. Using random luck such as a coin flip to break ties isn't allowed, since it reintroduces chance. For trivia contests and the like, the correct answer must be ascertainable from authoritative reference works; the rules must clearly and conspicuously disclose this, and questions and answers with supporting data and judging procedures must be on file with an independent organization prior to the contest. F.T.C. Modifying Order, No. 8824, 52 F.R. 3221 (1987). Various states, including Connecticut and Florida, have other specific requirements for skill-based promotions.

What if chance is eliminated because "everyone wins?" Many states, including California, have special requirements when every participant is a winner or when everyone who makes a purchase or a visit to a location wins. There's an obvious interaction here with the rules on "free" offers—among other things, the price of the underlying good must not be raised to account for the cost of the prize.

Element Three: Consideration

Be aware: The cases on this element vary a lot from state to state. A national advertiser should be very conservative; a local advertiser should be very precise.

Currently, all states permit sweepstakes in connection with advertising products and services as long as no consideration is required. In this context, consideration often means something different than its definition in the contract formation sense. Consideration includes buying a product, even when the price is the standard price. If the prize is merely a discount coupon, some states will view that as a consideration issue because a winner must spend some of her own money to obtain the prize.

The majority view is that any substantial expenditure of effort, such as taking a long survey or making multiple visits to a store, constitutes consideration. In the minority view, any effort that provides commercial value to the advertiser, such as "refer a friend" promotions, will be consideration.

In some states, requiring the consumer to visit a store constitutes consideration. *State ex rel. Schillberg v. Safeway Stores*, 450 P.2d 949 (Wash. 1969), held that consideration sufficient to support a contract is enough to constitute consideration for a lottery. "[O]ne need not part with something of value, tangible or intangible, to supply the essential consideration for a lottery." According to the Washington Supreme Court, the time, thought, attention and energy expended by members of the public in studying Safeway's advertising and journeying to a Safeway store to procure a prize slip, as well as the actual increase in patronage that resulted from the contest, amounted to consideration. Other states have disagreed.

In most states, filling out an entry form, taking a short survey or mailing or phoning in an entry don't qualify as consideration. However, the more effort is required, the more likely it is to constitute consideration. Would giving your name and address to the advertiser and consenting to receive further targeted promotions count as consideration? What about giving your friends' names? What about "liking" the advertiser's Facebook page? Consider the Instagram giveaways mentioned above: One business model is that an intermediary provides the cash and pays the influencer to promote the giveaway on her feed; entry requires following the accounts of dozens of "sponsors." The intermediary charges the sponsors to be on the list, and the sponsors can expect to gain thousands of followers. Is following a list of Instagram accounts consideration? Would your answer be the same if the influencer simply agreed with a number of other influencers to give away cash to people who followed all the influencers on their list? Does it matter if "following" (and unfollowing) is technically very simple—just a matter of pressing a button next to each account on the list, which can be done in about a minute?

"Post consideration"—some type of payment before the winner can claim the prize—is also illegal in many states. Thus, some states specifically ban "notifying" people that they've won a prize if they have to buy something, pay money or submit to a sales presentation to claim the prize. Other states allow certain conditions, such as attending a sales presentation or paying shipping and handling fees, provided that all the advertising clearly and conspicuously discloses these limits.

B.   Alternate Means of Entry

Sweepstakes usually provide at least two different methods of entering the sweepstakes. The first entry method requires the consumer to do something valuable for the advertiser, such as buying something from the advertiser. That entry method will qualify as consideration, creating an apparent illegal lottery.

To avoid an illegal lottery, the advertiser must provide a second entry method that doesn't require any consideration. This is typically called an "alternate means of entry" or "AMOE." The chances of winning through the alternate means of entry must be equal to the chances of winning through purchase. Advertisers inexperienced with promotions can easily neglect this essential step—Google, for example, when it launched its new Google Home Max speaker, started a contest that required a purchase from the Google Store for entry. Edgar, *Google Ran An Illegal Lottery — And We Got Them to Stop*, MOUSE PRINT, May 27, 2019.

Because the alternate means of entry is the key to negating any consideration in the sweepstakes and avoiding an illegal lottery, advertisers relying on it must structure it properly. A sweepstakes can provide multiple alternate entry methods, even if some methods create consideration, so long as there always remains one consideration-free entry method.

A typical alternate means of entry is to let the consumer enter the sweepstakes by mailing in a postcard. Although the postcard imposes some costs on consumers—postage, the costs of the postcard and the time required to fill it out—typically those costs aren't treated as "consideration" (but check relevant state laws).

This was how Google fixed its promotion:

> **5. HOW TO ENTER:** NO PURCHASE NECESSARY TO ENTER OR WIN. To enter the Sweepstakes, you must meet one of the following criteria:
>
> - You receive and click on the custom URL via email from Google; or
>
> - You mail a 3.5" x 5" postcard to Google, postmarked by no later than June 15, 2019. Your postcard must include your name, phone number, home address, and a written statement that you would like to be entered into the Sweepstakes. The postcard must also be addressed to:
>
>   Lesya Pishchevskaya
>   lesyap
>   1600 Amphitheatre Parkway
>   Mountain View, CA 94043.

In order to ensure that consumers understand that no consideration is required, a sweepstakes must prominently disclose that no purchase is necessary and explain the alternate means of entry. One implication of this rule is that, if a product contains a sweepstakes piece, the package must disclose the alternate means of entry—that information can't just be confined to ads or displays.

Some states enforce these requirements vigorously. In 2013, A&P Supermarkets paid $102,000 to settle the New York Attorney General's charge that A&P violated state law with its "Frozen Food Month Sweepstakes," in which any customer who purchased more than $50 in frozen-food products at an A&P store was automatically entered in a sweepstakes. Though the official rules disclosed a free alternate method of entry, the attorney general considered this insufficient. Along with the monetary payment, A&P promised to advertise the free method of entry with larger signs, to include copies of the official rules in the stores and to advertise the free method with "equal prominence" to the paid entry. Seth Heyman, *Recent Sweepstakes Enforcement Actions Illustrate Legal Pitfalls*, THE BUS. LAW CENTER, Oct. 18, 2013.

Online-only alternate means of entry may not be sufficient because some states believe that not all eligible potential participants have free access to the Internet. It's true that not everyone has easy Internet access, but not everyone has easy access to a stamped postcard either. New York does not allow online-only alternate means of entry for store-based contests on a theory that the elderly may be excluded, but this discomfort may change with time.

For those advertisers committed to running an online contest, one solution is to limit eligibility to those United States residents who already have Internet access to avoid consideration problems. Rules should also cover Internet-security issues, such as hacking and technical glitches, and the Internet-only nature of the contest should be prominently disclosed. Asking entrants for personal information or to watch an online ad raises consideration issues, which in turn may be averted by providing an offline alternate means of entry or at least some way to avoid submitting the information or watching the ad.

What about other new methods of communication? The following case involves the use of text messages, which are faster than traditional mail, but raise special questions because carriers charge extra fees for messages to particular numbers. If the advertiser gets a cut of those fees, consideration problems arise.

COUCH V. TELESCOPE INC., 2007 U.S. DIST. LEXIS 104142 (C.D. CAL. 2007), APPEAL DISMISSED, COUCH V. TELESCOPE INC., 611 F.3D 629 (9TH CIR. 2010)

. . . These four cases all involve games conducted in conjunction with four popular television programs: *American Idol*, *Deal or No Deal*, *1 vs. 100*, and *The Apprentice*. The Defendants in all four cases have brought motions to dismiss. As these motions present identical legal issues and involve similar facts, the goal of judicial economy warrants their joint resolution. Except as noted, this Order applies equally to all parties in each of the four presented cases.

    A.   Couch v. Telescope: The *American Idol* Challenge

American Idol is a televised singing competition that has been broadcast by Defendant Fox Broadcasting Company since 2002. During airings of the program, promotions invite viewers to participate in the "American Idol Challenge," a trivia game. A trivia question is posed, along with three possible answers. Viewers then have 24 hours to answer the question, either by sending a text message to 51555 or by registering on the program's website. Although entering online is free, viewers who enter by sending text messages incur a 99 cent fee, in addition to standard text messaging rates charged by their wireless carriers. Each week, winners are selected at random from among those entries with correct answers. There is a $10,000 weekly prize and $100,000 grand prize. . . . Plaintiff Darlene Couch, a Georgia resident, has entered the American Idol Challenge via text message, paid the 99 cent fee, and has not won a prize. She alleges that the American Idol Challenge is an illegal lottery. She now seeks relief under California Business and Professions Code § 17200 (the Unfair Competition Law, or "UCL") and Connecticut General Statute § 52-554. Defendants move to dismiss both claims for relief. . . .

[The other TV shows involved essentially the same setup for prizes.]

III. Discussion

    A.   Plaintiffs' First Claims for Relief: Unfair Competition

. . . Here, Plaintiffs allege that Defendants violated California Penal Code § 319 by running an illegal lottery; this is the "unlawful practice" for which they seek remedy under § 17200.

Defendants argue that Plaintiffs fail to state a claim for three reasons: first, American Idol Challenge, the Lucky Case Game, [1] vs. 100, and Get Rich with Trump (collectively, "the Games") are not illegal lotteries under California Penal Code § 319; second, Plaintiffs lack standing to pursue relief under the UCL, and; third, the doctrine of in pari delicto bars their claims. The Court considers each of these arguments in turn.

1. Illegal Lottery

Defendants first argue that [the promotions] are not illegal lotteries under California law because they provide free alternative methods of entry. Consequently, Defendants argue that Plaintiffs' UCL claims, predicated on violation of the lottery law, must fail as a matter of law. The Court disagrees. Article IV § 19 of the California Constitution prohibits lotteries (with the notable exception of the official state lottery). This reflects a long-standing public policy against lotteries. *See, e.g.*, Phalen v. Virginia, 49 U.S. 163, 168 (1850) (describing lotteries as a "wide-spread pestilence" that "infests the whole community: it enters every dwelling; it reaches every class; it preys upon the hard earnings of the poor; it plunders the ignorant and simple."). The chief evil to be remedied by anti-lottery laws is "to prevent people from giving up money or money's worth in the hope that chance will make their investment profitable."

State law defines a lottery as: any scheme for the disposal of property by chance, among persons who have paid or promised to pay any valuable consideration for the chance of obtaining such property . . . upon any agreement, understanding or expectation that it is to be distributed or disposed of by lot or chance. CAL. PEN. CODE § 319. The essential elements of a lottery, therefore, are chance, consideration, and the prize.[4] If any one of the three elements is missing, the game or scheme at issue is not a lottery. Conducting a lottery or selling lottery tickets is a misdemeanor under state law.

Defendants concede that the elements of chance and prize are met. They argue instead that there is an absence of consideration: because they offer viewers a free alternative method of entry (that is, because viewers can enter online for free, rather than pay 99 cents per text message), there is no consideration and thus no lottery. Plaintiffs counter that because some viewers paid for the privilege of entering, the game is a lottery as to them, notwithstanding that other viewers entered for free.

Summarizing the "implicit holdings" of the leading lottery cases specifically on the question of consideration, the court in *People v. Shira* explained, in order for a promotional giveaway scheme to be legal any and all persons must be given a ticket free of charge and without any of them paying for the opportunity of a chance to win a prize. Conversely, a promotional scheme is illegal where any and all persons cannot participate in a chance for the prize and some of the participants who want a chance to win must pay for it. 62 Cal. App. 3d 442, 459 (1976). The critical factual distinction between cases in which a lottery was not found and those in which a lottery was found is that the former "involved promotional schemes by using

---

[4] The three-element definition of lotteries is firmly established. Notwithstanding this well-worn definition, the Court is mindful of Chief Justice Warren's pertinent admonition: "So varied have been the techniques used by promoters to conceal the joint factors of prize, chance, and consideration, and so clever have they been in applying these techniques to feigned as well as legitimate business activities, that it has often been difficult to apply the decision of one case to the facts of another."

prize tickets to increase the purchases of legitimate goods and services in the free market place" whereas in the latter "the game itself is the product being merchandized." *Id*; *see also* Haskell, 965 F. Supp at 1404 (stating the broad principle that "business promotions are not lotteries so long as tickets to enter are not conditioned upon a purchase."). The presence of a free alternative method of entry in the leading cases made it clear that the money customers paid was for the products purchased (gasoline or movie tickets), and not for the chance of winning a prize. The relevant question here, therefore, is whether the Games were nothing more than "organized scheme[s] of chance," in which payment was induced by the chance of winning a prize.

The relevant question is not, as Defendants contend, whether some people could enter for free. In [other cases], the courts concluded that those who made payments purchased something of equivalent value. The indiscriminate distribution of tickets to purchasers and non-purchasers alike was evidence thereof. Here, however, Defendants' offers of free alternative methods of entry do not alter the basic fact that viewers who sent in text messages paid only for the privilege of entering the Games. They received nothing of equivalent economic value in return. Accordingly, the Court finds that Plaintiffs have sufficiently alleged that Defendants conducted illegal lotteries as defined by California law.

2. Standing

[The court found that plaintiffs sufficiently alleged that the wrongful conduct took place in California.]

3. In Pari Delicto

Finally, Defendants argue that Plaintiffs' cases must be dismissed because of the doctrine of in pari delicto, which holds that "a plaintiff who has participated in wrongdoing may not recover damages from the wrongdoing." California courts, citing the long-standing public policy against gambling, have thus refused to adjudicate disputes arising out of "gambling contracts or transactions." In the instant case, however, Defendants and Plaintiffs are not in pari delicto, or "equally at fault."

Defendants are alleged to have violated the UCL by conducting lotteries, an activity expressly forbidden by California law. There is no equivalent legal wrong under California law of playing a lottery. Under state law, and as alleged in the Complaints, Defendants may be in delicto but there is no pari: Plaintiffs have committed no legal wrong by sending in their text message entries. Nor is this a case, like the long line of California cases establishing the doctrine, in which a wronged player seeks to recover a gaming debt. Instead, Plaintiffs seek declaratory judgments that the Games are illegal lotteries, injunctive relief against the continued operation of the Games, and restitution for amounts unlawfully collected. Rather than asking the Court to accept the legitimacy of a gaming activity by deciding a dispute arising out of the activity, Plaintiffs seek to stop the Games themselves. Accordingly, the Court finds that the doctrine of in pari delicto does not bar Plaintiffs' claims.
. . .

[Claims under other states' consumer-protection laws also survived.]

NOTES AND QUESTIONS

The problem here is that the producers added the ninety-nine cent fee to the text messages and pocketed that cash. If viewers' text message entries had only incurred whatever fees were charged by the consumer's wireless carrier, and not also fees that went to the TV show's producers, then the defendants would have been in the clear because that would be analogous to requiring a self-addressed stamped envelope (which, after all, involves a payment to the U.S. Postal Service). Is this result consistent with the Indiana case earlier in this chapter absolving the NCAA of running an illegal lottery? The Indiana Supreme Court found that there were no real "winners" of the ticket distribution system, just some people who got tickets and other people who were refunded an equivalent amount of cash. Here, however, there were winners and losers—is that enough of a difference?

Do you agree with the court's reasoning that as long as some consumers are paying just for the chance to win, it is an illegal lottery, even though they could have avoided paying by going online? *See* Hardin v. NBC Universal, 283 Ga. 477 (2008) (text-messaging fee was not consideration when there was an online alternate method of entry, and the evidence was that most people entered online). Note that in *Couch*, the court didn't discuss how the TV shows disclosed the various means of entry and their disparate costs. Would disclosure alone be enough to protect consumers?

The parties ultimately settled the case. Consumers could obtain a refund of their text-messaging fees, and the defendants agreed for five years not to "create, sponsor or operate any contest or sweepstakes, for which entrants are offered the possibility of winning a prize, in which people who enter via premium text message do not receive something of comparable value to the premium text message charge in addition to the entry." The class lawyers received over $5 million.

Loot Boxes. Many video games offer "loot boxes," where players pay real-world money (directly, or through the purchase of in-game virtual currency) to buy a randomized package of virtual items that may help with gameplay. The loot box purchase contains an element of surprise: Some loot boxes will contain rare and valuable items, but others will contain items of lesser value. Players and regulators have claimed that such loot boxes constitute a "game of chance," while game-makers have tried to sidestep such allegations by enhancing their disclosures and analogizing to other variable-value purchases like baseball trading cards.

What if an AMOE is Impossible? In *Levin v. Jordan's Furniture, Inc.*, 944 N.E.2d 1096 (Table), 2011 WL 1450357 (Mass. App. Ct. 2011), Jordan's promised that customers who bought certain items of furniture during the promotional period would get those items free if the Boston Red Sox swept the 2008 World Series. In 2007, Jordan's had run a similar promotion, and an estimated 30,000 customers received free furniture after the Red Sox won the 2007 World Series. (Note that Jordan's changed the terms a bit the second time around!) In 2008, however, the Phillies won the World Series. A disappointed customer sued. Massachusetts law bars illegal lotteries, which as noted above require (1) a prize, (2) some element of chance and (3) consideration or the payment of a price. Because of the structure of the promotion, there was no AMOE.

It was undisputed that the free furniture was a prize and that there was an element of chance. However, the plaintiff failed to plead that any part of the purchase price of the furniture was paid for the chance to win the prize, and the court concluded that there was therefore no illegal lottery. Thus, the chance of winning may be conditioned on purchase, so long as no part of the price is paid for the chance to win.

What would you advise a business that wants to run such a promotion? What sort of evidence would you keep on hand to substantiate that no part of the price covered the chance to win? What happens if a consumer does properly allege that the price reflects the cost of the prize, as, in a profit-seeking business, one might imagine it did?

C.   Other Rules about Sweepstakes and Contests

Figure Out the Prizes First

The IRS requires sponsors to report prizes worth a fair market value of $600 or more. 26 U.S.C. § 6041. Anti-gambling statutes may make a sweepstakes illegal if the number of prizes depends the number of entrants, so the prizes should be fixed before the promotion begins. Florida, New York and Rhode Island (the latter only if local retail stores are involved) require advertisers to register the sweepstakes and submit the rules to the state in advance and to post security when the total prize exceeds a low dollar value threshold. A list of winners must be filed to release the security. Many other states also require lists of winners to be published and made available on request. Other states may require registration depending on the circumstances; for example, Arizona mandates it when proof of purchase is required for a skill contest. Several states have record-retention requirements, and some treat the failure to award prizes—even if unclaimed—as unlawful. Some states allow the rules to state that "unclaimed prizes will not be awarded," but others explicitly require "second chance" random drawings. These are easy rules for marketers to miss!

How to Formulate and Communicate the Sweepstakes or Contest Rules

Advertising that allows consumers to enter a sweepstakes or contest must include the material terms or a cost-free means of obtaining the rules. Those rules must be fairly detailed: They should specify the entry method; the free AMOE and that payment will not increase the chance of winning; how the winner will be selected; who is eligible (which should exclude those connected to the sponsor) and what they must do to claim prizes; key dates, including the dates for using an AMOE; limits on entry (e.g., one per household, five entries per day); odds of winning (it's acceptable to say that those depend on the number of eligible entries, as long as that's true); other conditions ("while supplies last," "void where prohibited by law," and so on, including anything required by state law); total value of prizes; the sponsor's name and address; and the availability of a list of winners.

Though abbreviated disclosures are allowed in certain forms of advertising as long as the full rules are readily available, the short-form description of the contest can't be materially misleading. For example, the Federal Communications Commission fined a Boston radio station $4,000 for promoting a contest as a chance to win a choice of one of three cars. The on-air announcements didn't explain that the winner only won a two-year lease, not full

674

ownership. Moreover, the "winner" only got the lease if she passed a credit check. The fact that the official rules on the promotion's website disclosed all these terms was insufficient because these serious limits weren't broadcast. *In re* Greater Boston Radio, Inc., FCC File No.: EB-08-IH-5305 (Feb. 28, 2013). However, in general, broadcasters can disclose material contest terms online rather than in their broadcasts, as long as the terms don't differ substantively from what's announced. *See* Amendment of Section 73.1216 of the Commission's Rules Related to Broadcast Licensee-Conducted Contests, 80 Fed. Reg. 64354 (2015).

Is this Twitter disclosure successful? What other information, if any, would you need to evaluate it?

Similar to other disclosures, less-significant matters can wait for disclosure in the full rules. Among other things, the rules should specify what happens if something goes wrong—for example, if more prizes are won than the specified odds (which might happen if a printer makes an error in printing game pieces). The rules should also contemplate what happens if the promised prize isn't available, although advertisers typically procure the prize before the sweepstakes or contest starts to ensure its availability to the winner.

Even if people exploit gaps in the official rules, the advertiser must honor its own rules. Food company Beatrice ran a sweepstakes that was "cracked" by one player who submitted 4,018 winning entries worth more than $16 million. Beatrice ended the sweepstakes early when the player informed it of the vulnerability. The company ended up paying a settlement totaling $2 million to 2,400 sweepstakes players, plus an additional sum to the individual player, after a lawsuit for breach of contract. *Beatrice Mails First Checks from Game-Contest Lawsuit*, ASSOC. PRESS, Apr. 28, 1988.

If the advertiser plans to publicize the winners, then it should specify that entry constitutes consent to such publicity (see the section on the right of publicity in Chapter 14 for discussion of when written consent is required). It's fairly typical for advertisers to require a winner to sign documentation—including a publicity consent—after being chosen but before the prize is awarded, but such additional hurdles to receiving the prize should be disclosed in the rules. Some states also specifically regulate contests in which the winner's name or likeness will be publicized, and Tennessee expressly bans prizes contingent on publicity releases.

States (including Florida, Massachusetts, New York and Texas) may have particular requirements for what must be disclosed in the rules and how the rules must be displayed. Checking to ensure compliance with every state in which the contest is valid is therefore vital. Rules may need to be posted in retail outlets, or specific elements such as a description or value of the prizes or the geographic area of the contest must be posted. In order to make nationally acceptable materials, the advertiser may simply create point-of-sale displays with the full rules including every piece of information required anywhere. But there are still risks: Washington limits how often and for how long grocery stores may use sweepstakes, and Connecticut bans sweepstakes in certain stores.

Broadcast ads should include "no purchase necessary," information on where to obtain the full rules and an alternate means of entry, end date, any eligibility restrictions, and the ubiquitous "void where prohibited."

Subject-Matter Specific Restrictions. There are often restrictions for sweepstakes tied to specific products or services such as 900 numbers (see the FTC publication Complying with the 900 Number Rule), alcoholic beverages, banking, dairy products, food retailers, insurance, gasoline and tobacco. Why do you think regulators targeted banking for specific restrictions? Perhaps it's reasonable to be concerned about encouraging consumers to use irrelevant reasons to choose financial products, but why worry about dairy products?

Many states also have extremely detailed regulations for promotions that require consumers to sit through a sales presentation to win or to have a chance to win. *See, e.g.*, TEX. BUS. & COMMERCE CODE, Title 13, ch. 621. Why might states conclude that consumers are particularly vulnerable in these circumstances?

Moreover, many states regulate specific types of prizes, such as live animals and lottery tickets, or promotions in which all prizes might not be won.

Sweepstakes targeted at children raise additional issues. CARU, the children's arm of the Better Business Bureau that reviews children's advertising (performing the same function for such advertising as its sister the NAD does for general advertising), told Discovery Girls Magazine to change its advertising for a sweepstakes. The magazine, which is directed to children ages eight and up, required entrants to provide an email address and complete a survey with over fifty questions, many "personal in nature," in exchange for a chance to win an iPod Nano. The sweepstakes therefore collected personally identifiable information from children without first obtaining prior verifiable parental consent, in violation of COPPA (the Children's Online Privacy Protection Act) and of CARU's guidelines. In addition, the sweepstakes didn't clearly disclose the odds of winning. ASRC Press Release, *CARU Recommends Discovery Girls Magazine Modify Sweepstakes Advertising; Company Agrees to Do So*, Sept. 18, 2013.

Likewise, CARU acted against the Boy Scouts of America (now "Scouts BSA") when its Boy's Life Magazine failed to include its "Many Will Enter, Five Will Win" odds statement in the magazine's ad announcing the contest. Even though the odds were disclosed prominently on the magazine's website, which was the only method of entry, CARU was concerned that a child looking at the magazine ad could develop an unrealistic expectation of winning the sweepstakes. Since the ad is usually the child's first contact with the sweepstakes, it was not sufficient to clear up confusion later on. As advertising lawyers commenting on the case observed, this result "emphasizes the importance for marketers and advertisers of properly drafting an abbreviated rules statement and including it in the promotional materials for the sweepstakes. Many companies fail to put an odds statement in abbreviated rules targeting child and adult audiences, even though many state laws (not just the CARU guidelines) specifically require the disclosure of this information in advertising." Maura Marcheski & Melissa Landau Steinman, *The Sweepstakes Games You Can't Afford to Lose*, ALL ABOUT ADVERT. L., Oct. 16, 2013.

Note that so far we've only discussed U.S. rules—an international contest requires compliance with still more rules. Canada, for example, technically prohibits sweepstakes but allows promotions in which the winner is chosen at random but then required to demonstrate a skill. Thus, American sweepstakes that extend to Canada often impose an extra requirement that Canadian winners correctly answer a simple math question. Quebec requires the rules to be in French and that the sponsor have a local presence; many contests exclude Quebecois residents.

Other countries, such as India and Sweden, consider sweepstakes to be the same as lotteries and ban them unconditionally. A number of countries, including Argentina, France, Mexico and Poland, require translation into a local language—even if the contest is run online from the United States. Many countries specify the form and content of required disclosures, and may additionally regulate what kinds of personal information the marketer can ask for or what uses may be made of that information. Some common U.S. provisions—including publicity or liability releases, limitations on liability and forum selection clauses—may be unenforceable. Even including them in the rules may give rise to liability for unfair practices. Some countries (including the United States) tax prizes, while other countries, including Brazil, Mexico and Spain, impose the taxes on the promoters themselves. Some require preregistration with local authorities, a local drawing and posting of security.

Illegal sweepstakes can subject marketers to civil and criminal liability, so it is worth taking the time to get this right. A lawyer should consider the countries important to the advertiser's strategy, as well as its appetite for risk.

After the Contest Ends

When the contest ends, the legal work is not yet over. The sponsor must give away all the prizes. Ideally, every winner should sign an affirmation of eligibility, publicity release and release of liability before receiving a prize, a requirement which of course should previously have been disclosed in the official rules. The sponsor must file a 1099-MISC tax form for anyone receiving prizes worth at least $600. The sponsor should publish a winners list on its website and send the list to any states in which it was registered. The winners list and related records should be retained for at least ninety days, though two years is advisable.

D. Direct Mail Advertising of Sweepstakes and Contests

The law is often most specific with respect to past practices that have generated substantial consumer harm. The Deceptive Mail Prevention and Enforcement Act of 1999 governs solicitations sent through the mail. 39 U.S.C. 3001 et seq. It requires numerous disclosures to be sent for any sweepstakes. Some of Congress's concerns can be seen in specific prohibitions, such as bars on: claims that people are winners unless they've actually won prizes; purchase requirements; the use of fake checks that don't clearly state that they are non-negotiable and have no cash value; and seals, names or terms that imply an affiliation with or endorsement by the federal government. The Deceptive Mail Prevention and Enforcement Act does not apply to sweepstakes and skill contests that are not directed to a specific named individual or that do not include an opportunity to order a product or service (e.g., magazine subscriptions).

Numerous states also regulate sweepstakes and contest disclosures, in much the same vein.

Consider the following ad:

Does it adequately disclose that the recipient is not yet a winner? The FTC considered that the small print disclaimers about the odds were irrelevant because the larger print was a message that person actually won. Indeed, many consumers sought to claim their prize at Fowlerville Ford, only to be met with a sales pitch. In re Fowlerville Ford, FTC Docket No. C-4433 (2014). You might wonder: Would reasonable consumers really think they'd won? As Roger Ford has explained, "[d]ealers use this form of ex post targeting or filtering to bring especially gullible customers into the business so they can sell them new cars. Savvy consumers, sensing an implausible offer, throw the flyers away; ones who are more likely to overpay for a car come in to see if they've won something." Roger Allan Ford, *Data Scams*, 57 HOUS. L. REV. 111 (2019). These dynamics help explain the extreme suspicion regulators often apply to sweepstakes.

Similarly, the Telemarketing Sales Rule covers prize promotions made on the phone, requiring disclosure of the odds, the fact that purchase is not required, and other conditions on receiving the prize.

Despite the extensive, contest-specific regulation, general consumer-protection laws still apply. In *Haskell v. Time, Inc.*, 965 F. Supp. 1398 (E.D. Cal. 1997), the plaintiff sued under California's consumer-protection laws. The defendants sold magazine and book subscriptions but extensively promoted them with millions of sweepstakes mailings. As a result of past disputes, the mailings focused on the tautological claim that "the recipient is the winner, if the recipient has and returns the winning entry." Most people didn't respond to the mailings, and most of the people who responded only entered the sweepstakes, without buying products. Eighteen of twenty-three $1 million prizes had been awarded to people whose entries were not accompanied by a purchase.

Mailings said "that because mailing costs are high, a failure to enter the sweepstakes or purchase products may result in the customer's name being dropped from the mailing list," and that failure to enter meant losing the opportunity to win, e.g.:

> . . . As you can see from the enclosed NOTICE OF FORFEITURE made out to [recipient's name], if your entry doesn't make it on time we'll have no choice but to void the assigned numbers—and that means you'll automatically forfeit all prize money any of your Guaranteed Finalist numbers may have won. And as much as we'd like to, we can't make any exceptions even for folks like you who enter regularly. . . .

As for dropping customers, the solicitations said things like:

> We really regret it but we simply cannot afford to keep on writing to groups of people who never buy magazines. If you do not order now, or write to stay on our list, you may be among the first to go. Those who are dropped now will miss out—there's no guarantee of another chance for them.

> Mailing costs have skyrocketed. . . . Names must be cut from our regular mailing list. Groups of people who do not order will be the first to go.

> With costs rising as they are we must restrict our best offerings to groups of people who buy magazines. We're sorry to have to say so, but—if you do not order this time or write to stay on our list, you may find yourself excluded from the most rewarding opportunities in our history. Don't let your name be dropped. An order right now will keep your name on our regular mailing list.

The court largely rejected the plaintiff's claims. The plaintiff failed to show that a substantial number of consumers were likely to be deceived, even if a few on occasion were. None of the mailings conditioned sweepstakes entry on a purchase, and they clearly disclosed that recipients could write to stay on the list instead of making a purchase. Even if customers came to believe that purchases would get them more entries, based on defendants' past practices of sending more solicitations to previous purchasers, that implicit expectation wasn't consideration for purposes of the lottery statute. The rules were clear that no purchase was required to win; defendants also continued mailing to people who entered without ordering anything; and the fact that most entrants didn't buy anything showed that consumers understood that no purchase was required.

However, small aspects of defendants' practices could violate the law. For example, one defendant's "Prompt-Pay" sweepstakes might be an illegal lottery, if it rewarded existing customers with sweepstakes entries for paying before they were legally obligated to pay. Even after years of lawsuits and regulations, which shaped every nuance of the mailings, this experienced advertiser didn't necessarily get it right.

State attorneys general in recent years have reached some major settlements, including with the successful defendants above. In 2000, Time settled lawsuits by the attorneys general of forty-eight states and the District of Columbia, agreeing to pay over $4.9 million for past conduct and to include clear and conspicuous disclosures of the odds of winning its contests, the fact that no purchase is necessary, and the fact that purchase will not improve the odds of winning. A year later, Publishers Clearinghouse agreed to a $34 million multistate settlement incorporating similar provisions and, in addition, requiring it to create safeguards to protect especially vulnerable consumers. Publishers Clearinghouse was required to review the accounts of consumers who made frequent purchases and eliminate from its mailing list those who were determined to be confused or disoriented or to make excessive purchases. *See* State of Connecticut Attorney General's Office, *Ct. Reaches Unprecedented $34 Million Settlement with Publishers Clearinghouse*. Why might the attorneys general have brought the suits if the disclosures were already in the form described above? Who has the right idea about what a "reasonable consumer" would be thinking?

Consider also the following case, where the advertiser relied on the inattention and inaction of consumers and the state stepped in.

STATE V. IMPERIAL MARKETING, 203 W.VA. 203 (1998)

. . . I. PROCEDURAL HISTORY

Suarez Corporation Industries, located in Canton, Ohio, and its affiliated enterprises are in the business of selling consumer goods, such as simulated jewelry, through the use of direct mail marketing solicitations. Many solicitations were sent by Suarez to West Virginia residents prior to the institution of this action in 1994. . . .

Specifically, the Attorney General instituted this action in the Circuit Court of Kanawha County against numerous defendants, including Suarez, alleging that the solicitation activities of the defendants constituted multiple transgressions of the West Virginia Consumer Credit and Protection Act and, particularly, the Prizes and Gifts Act contained therein. . . . Ultimately, the litigation focused upon three specific marketing efforts of Suarez involving several thousand West Virginia consumers. [Editor's note: We omit discussion of two of the promotions.]

. . . With regard to the second solicitation, consumers were notified that they had been awarded a cash prize of "as much as $1,000." The consumers were also told, however, that the prize had been placed in a five-piece clutch purse ensemble which could be purchased for $12, plus $2 for special packaging and insurance. The solicitation indicated that "priority handling" would be afforded to consumers purchasing the purse ensemble. If consumers desired the cash prize without purchasing the purse ensemble, consumers were required to follow a [convoluted] claim procedure . . . .[6]

. . . Subsequently, on April 25, 1997, the circuit court entered the final order permanently enjoining Suarez from violating the West Virginia Consumer Credit and Protection Act and the Prizes and Gifts Act. . . . As the final order stated, the evidence established that the solicitations "were actually misleading by virtue of material misrepresentations made, and that they exceed acceptable standards and practices allowing a certain degree of puffing in respect to sales transactions." . . .

This appeal followed. . . .

III. THE PERMANENT INJUNCTION

. . . "The West Virginia Prizes and Gifts Act, was designed by the West Virginia Legislature to assist in protecting West Virginia citizens from being victimized by misleading and deceptive practices when a seller is attempting to market a product using a prize or gift as an inducement."

. . . As W. Va. Code, 46A-6D-3(a) [1992], concerning having won a prize or gift, provides in part:

> [A] person may not, in connection with the sale or lease or solicitation for the sale or lease of goods, property or service, represent that another person has won anything of value or is the winner of a contest, unless all of the following conditions are met:
>
> (1) The recipient of the prize, gift or item of value is given the prize, gift or item of value without obligation; and
>
> (2) The prize, gift or item of value is delivered to the recipient at no expense to him or her, within ten days of the representation.

---

[6] The record contains the following instructions for claiming the cash prize without purchasing the five-piece clutch purse ensemble:

If not ordering and to claim your cash prize only, cut out and affix the prize confirmation code located on the front [of] the Declaration of Cash Prize form to a 3-1/2 x 5-1/2 inch index card with your name, address and phone number and insert all into your own # 10 white envelope. Failure to follow these instructions will cause forfeiture of your cash prize. Mail to Bulk-Sort Center . . . to claim your cash prize. Do not use the enclosed envelope that is for ordering only, or your cash prize and status as an eligible finalist will be waived. Since we will be required to remove your check from the purse if not ordering, we are required to give priority handling to those who accept the purse. The record indicates that in almost no circumstances did the cash prize exceed a nominal amount.

Moreover, as W. Va. Code, 46A-6D-4(a) [1992], concerning eligibility to receive a prize or gift, provides:

> A person may not represent that another person is eligible or has a chance to win or to receive a prize, gift or item of value without clearly and conspicuously disclosing on whose behalf the contest or promotion is conducted, as well as all material conditions which a participant must satisfy. In an oral solicitation all material conditions shall be disclosed prior to requesting the consumer to enter into the sale or lease. Additionally, in any written material covered by this section, each of the following shall be clearly and prominently disclosed:
>
> (1) Immediately adjacent to the first identification of the prize, gift or item of value to which it relates; or
>
> (2) In a separate section entitled "Consumer Disclosure" which title shall be printed in no less than ten-point bold-face type and which section shall contain only a description of the prize, gift or item of value and the disclosures outlined in paragraphs (i), (ii) and (iii) of this subdivision:
>
> (i) The true retail value of each item or prize;
>
> (ii) The actual number of each item, gift or prize to be awarded; and
>
> (iii) The odds of receiving each item, gift or prize.

. . . Although ostensibly requiring no purchase or obligation, the solicitations under consideration, while suggesting a certain mutability on the surface, possess a persistent deceptive quality beneath. . . .

[C]onsumers were notified that they had been awarded a cash prize of "as much as $1,000." The consumers were also told, however, that the prize had been placed in a five-piece clutch purse ensemble which could be purchased for $12, plus $2 for special packaging and insurance. The solicitation indicated that "priority handling" would be afforded to consumers purchasing the purse ensemble. If consumers desired the cash prize without purchasing the purse ensemble, consumers were required to follow a [convoluted] claim procedure . . . . Thus, the violation of W. Va. Code, 46A-6D-3(a) [1992], i.e., that the recipient of a prize or gift must be given the prize or gift "without obligation" and that it be delivered to the recipient "at no expense," is evidenced by the following language of the clutch purse solicitation:

> As a guaranteed cash prize winner, the 5 piece Givone Clutch Purse Ensemble holding your check will be transferred to you when you cover the sponsor's special publicity discount fee of just $12, plus $2 for special packaging and insurance. * * * Remember, since the checks will already be in the purses, we are required by the sponsor's rules to give priority handling to those who are able to accept entitlement to their purse by submitting the minimum fee.

. . . During the course of this litigation, both the Attorney General and Suarez elicited the testimony of various consumers before the circuit court concerning the solicitations. Whereas the witnesses for the State indicated that the true import of the solicitations was difficult to grasp and that they had experienced a certain degree of bureaucratic hubris in their communications with Suarez, the witnesses called by Suarez suggested that the solicitations were quite clear and that their dealings with Suarez were satisfactory. The futility of that type of extrinsic evidence in cases of this nature, however, is evidenced by the fact that, during a one year period only, more than 17,000 West Virginia consumers received solicitations from Suarez or its affiliated enterprises. Rather, under the circumstances of this action, and in view of the solicitations described above, this Court is of the opinion that the testimony of the consumers failed to establish a genuine issue of material fact within the meaning of Rule 56. As the final order of April 25, 1997, stated: "It is irrelevant, however, that there are some West Virginia consumers who are satisfied with their merchandise. The issue is: whether defendant, in its solicitation efforts in West Virginia . . . engaged in conduct which is calculated to or likely to, deceive and misrepresent the offer, and thereby violate [West Virginia law]." . . .

[The court upheld a requirement that defendant offer refunds to customers without requiring them to return the merchandise they had received but set aside a $500,000 penalty that would be imposed if defendants didn't comply. The concurring opinion, directly below, suggested that given the facts it recited, such a penalty would be appropriate if the district court explained its award more clearly.]

STARCHER, Justice, concurring:

. . . I write to make clear that the permanent injunction against Suarez and the award of relief to West Virginia consumers is warranted, not only because of these three solicitations, but also because of the dozens of other solicitations entered into the record by the Attorney General. Seventeen Suarez solicitations were attached to one pleading alone.

Simply put, each of these solicitations contains language clearly violating the Consumer Credit and Protection Act and the Prizes and Gifts Act. I was unable to count the number of times the phrases "Official Prize Claim Notice," "Winners Certification Claim Form," or "Cash Prize Release Document" were used. Each solicitation began by telling the consumer that he or she was a winner—but buried in the fine print, or on another letter in the envelope, was the hint they really weren't a big winner after all. Therefore, many of the solicitations violate W. Va. Code, 46A-6D-3 [1992], which prohibits persons from making representations that someone has won a prize unless that prize is awarded to the consumer without obligation and delivered within 10 days of the representation.

Another problem with the solicitations in the record is that, while every solicitation carried the disclaimer "no purchase necessary," every solicitation also carried the suggestion the recipient was more likely to be a winner or would get their prize faster if they first bought some merchandise. W. Va. Code, 46A-6D-4(c) [1992] prohibits persons from making representations that as a condition of receiving a prize, the consumer must pay money or purchase, lease or rent goods or services.

Another example is a solicitation that tells the consumer that they have won a "4-Door Chevrolet Caprice, Model Year 1995 if your Vehicle Award Claim is confirmed as a winning claim"—and attached is a note entitling the consumer to three "Bonus Awards" "worth up to $300." As discussed in the majority opinion, the use of the vague language "worth up to" is a clear violation of the Consumer Credit and Protection Act. *See* W. Va. Code, 46A-6D-4(a)(2)(i) [1992] (written sweepstakes materials must contain "[t]he true retail value of each item or prize").

The record also contains a solicitation from the "tie-breaker supervisor" of the "Payables Desk, Department of Sweepstakes Administration" which tells the recipient that he or she is "tied" with other individuals to win a cash prize—without telling the reader the odds of winning, that is, how many other people the reader was "tied" with. This solicitation was likely drafted by someone who full-well knew the language was misleading, but thought it could later be argued that it "technically" was within the bounds of every consumer protection statute in the country. On the contrary, because the solicitation is misleading on its face, and because it fails to state the odds the consumer has of winning the sweepstakes, it violates West Virginia's consumer protection laws. *See* W. Va. Code, 46A-6D-4(a)(2)(iii) [1992] (written sweepstakes materials must contain "[t]he odds of receiving each item, gift or prize"). . . .

NOTES AND QUESTIONS

Among other problems with the advertiser's conduct, the Federal Trade Commission has done some research indicating that consumers generally ignore the "up to" part of an "up to X" claim. *See FTC Report: Many Consumers Believe "Up To" Claims Promise Maximum Results*, June 29, 2012.

Go back and review the quotes from the *Haskell* case, in which the court found that no reasonable consumer would misunderstand the defendants' solicitations. What are the key differences between the solicitations in this case and those found acceptable in *Haskell*? *See also* Freeman v. Time, Inc., 68 F.3d 285 (9th Cir. 1995) (finding no violation of law where mailers used statements in large type that Freeman had won a sweepstakes, qualified by language in smaller type indicating that he had not yet won, for example: "If you return the grand prize winning number, we'll officially announce that MICHAEL FREEMAN HAS WON $1,666,675.00 AND PAYMENT IS SCHEDULED TO BEGIN"). The acceptable solicitations used all-caps and other attention-getting mechanisms to suggest that recipients were already winners or would get more chances to win by buying—how much more did they do to correct any potential misunderstandings than the defendants in the West Virginia case?

Note also the multiple provisions of the West Virginia laws at issue, which are not unique to West Virginia. Each type of offer triggers specific disclosure requirements, and as the concurrence emphasizes, conduct that pushes multiple legal boundaries can collectively add up to convince a court of an advertiser's deceptive intent.

E. Externalities of Contests

Promotions can occasionally run the risk of generating claims for ordinary negligence. In *Weirum v. RKO General, Inc.*, 539 P.2d 36 (Cal. 1975), a radio station "with an extensive teenage audience" held a contest where prizes went to the first person to locate a mobile disc jockey driving a conspicuous car and then fulfill another condition such as answering a question. The radio station periodically broadcast information about his location and intended destination. Two minors in separate cars failed to win the prize in one location and then tried to follow the DJ's car to the next location, jockeying for position at speeds up to eighty miles per hour. One of them (it wasn't clear which one) negligently forced a car off the highway, killing the driver. While one stopped to report the accident, the other stopped only momentarily, kept up the pursuit and collected a cash prize from the DJ.

The jury found that the radio station was liable for the death, and the California Supreme Court affirmed the verdict. The court emphasized the excitement the station tried to generate with announcements such as "9:30 and The Real Don Steele is back on his feet again with some money and he is headed for the Valley. Thought I would give you a warning so that you can get your kids out of the street." The key question was whether the station owed any duty to the driver from broadcasting the contest, and the answer was found in the principle that people must use ordinary care to prevent others from being injured as a result of their conduct. Foreseeability was the essential factual question, and the record supported the jury's finding:

> These tragic events unfolded in the middle of a Los Angeles summer, a time when young people were free from the constraints of school and responsive to relief from vacation tedium. Seeking to attract new listeners, [the station] devised an "exciting" promotion. Money and a small measure of momentary notoriety awaited the swiftest response. It was foreseeable that defendant's youthful listeners, finding the prize had eluded them at one location, would race to arrive first at the next site and in their haste would disregard the demands of highway safety.

> Indeed, [the DJ] testified that he had in the past noticed vehicles following him from location to location. He was further aware that the same contestants sometimes appeared at consecutive stops.

The intervening negligence of the contestants didn't preclude liability for the station: The likelihood that contestants would react in this way was exactly what made the station's actions negligent. The court rejected the argument that imposing liability on the station would lead to advertisers' liability to people who were trampled in a rush to get to a sale (something that has, more recently, occurred numerous times at post-Thanksgiving Black Friday sales). The court said that:

> The giveaway contest was no commonplace invitation to an attraction available on a limited basis. It was a competitive scramble in which the thrill of the chase to be the one and only victor was intensified by the live broadcasts which accompanied the pursuit. In the assertedly analogous situations described by defendant, any haste involved in the purchase of the commodity is an incidental and unavoidable result of

the scarcity of the commodity itself. In such situations there is no attempt, as here, to generate a competitive pursuit on public streets, accelerated by repeated importuning by radio to be the very first to arrive at a particular destination. Manifestly the "spectacular" bears little resemblance to daily commercial activities.

The court further commented that the station "could have accomplished its objectives of entertaining its listeners and increasing advertising revenues by adopting a contest format which would have avoided danger to the motoring public."

NOTES AND QUESTIONS

What kinds of contest formats would generate similar excitement and entertainment without creating the same risks?

Suppose your client wants to hold a Black Friday sale that includes live tweeting by salespeople and a Twitter hashtag for shoppers to use as well in order to generate "buzz" for the sale. In the past, some Black Friday sales have led to people getting trampled or engaging in fisticuffs. Would this be the kind of "live broadcast" that risked liability under *Weirum*? In an age in which it seems that almost everyone records themselves and reports their activities in real time, is it foreseeable that people will behave badly in pursuit of *any* highly desirable good that's only available in limited quantities and for a short time?

Although rare, similar negligence-type arguments can sometimes be made against non-time-limited promotions. *Njewadda v. Showtime Networks, Inc.*, 2019 NY Slip Op 29031, (N.Y. Sup. Ct. Jan. 29, 2019), involved an oversized "shocking" and "menacing" ad for the serial killer TV show *Dexter* that, placed at the entrance of a subway, allegedly startled and overwhelmed the plaintiff so much that she fell down the subway stairs, resulting in injury. The court held that "[a] cause of action arising solely out of the placement of an advertisement is not a cognizable cause of action in New York."

Publishers' House Rules. In addition to complying with the law, promotions must also satisfy any house rules set by publishers. For example, all the major television networks have their own disclosure policies, though these house rules largely track the legal requirements for contests. Facebook has a well-known restriction that "Personal Timelines and friend connections must not be used to administer promotions (e.g., 'share on your Timeline to enter' or 'share on your friend's Timeline to get additional entries' and 'tag your friends in this post to enter' are not permitted)."

How do contests differ from other forms of promotion using social media? Consider the following picture, showing an offer of free food for various social media–related activities:

[photo by Will Bachman, 2012]

Does the advertiser need to disclose anything else? (If you think the answer is "no," do two separate tweets using the hashtag #seoulfoodnyc from the same account earn the account holder two free orders of fries?). How would the FTC analyze this under the endorsement guidelines discussed in Chapter 14? What about trademark law: Suppose Twitter wants to charge a licensing fee for the use of its name in this way and claims that unauthorized uses cause confusion?

Most discussions about the advertising industry focus on the interplay between advertisers and consumers. After all, the whole point of advertising is for advertisers to change consumer behavior. However, many other players in the advertising ecosystem play essential roles. This chapter looks at them.

Consider how a broadcast advertisement reaches a consumer:

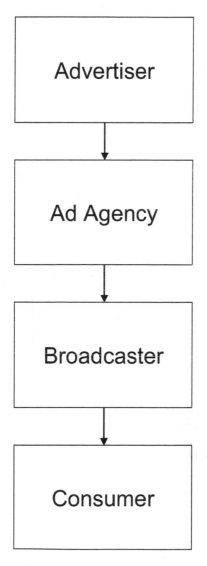

In this diagram, an advertiser retains an advertising agency to help the advertiser prepare the advertisement. On the advertiser's behalf, the advertising agency then enters into contracts with broadcasters (such as TV or radio stations) to run the ad. After delivering the ad to the broadcaster, the broadcaster airs the ad to its audience.

An ad campaign can involve many intermediaries. Consider, for example, a newspaper coupon distribution:

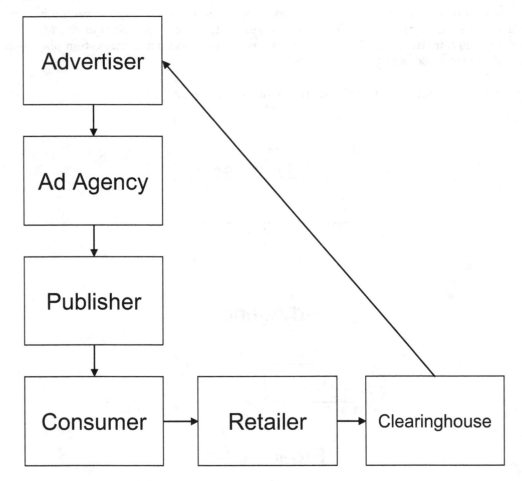

The advertiser and ad agency prepare the ad copy, place it with a newspaper or other coupon distributor, and then a consumer will clip it. A consumer redeems the coupon at a retailer, which typically tenders the coupon to a clearinghouse that will verify the coupon's authenticity (and police for coupon fraud) and pay retailers on behalf of the advertiser. The advertiser then settles up with the clearinghouse.

An email campaign might look like this:

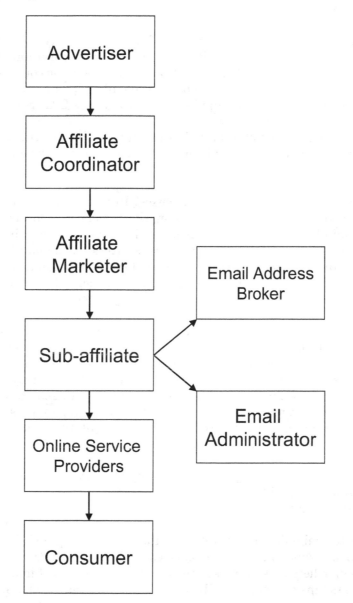

Assume the advertiser seeks new registrants for its website. The advertiser may approach a vendor that coordinates promotional opportunities for affiliate marketers seeking payment opportunities. The vendor can notify these affiliate marketers of the advertiser's opportunity. Participating affiliate marketers may send emails to promote the advertiser or run ads through different websites. The ads may be using copy supplied by the advertiser, or the copy may be prepared by the affiliate marketer. The affiliate marketers may have their own service providers, such as vendors who sell lists of email addresses or who help send large volumes of email. The affiliate marketers may also solicit the help of "sub-affiliates"—other marketers who would be willing to help out (for a cut of the action), such as websites that host ad-supported content.

Due to the multiple layers, the advertiser may not know the identity of the affiliate marketer or the identity or presence of any sub-affiliates because the advertiser only has a relationship with the coordinating vendor. The advertiser also may not know the contents of the emails used to promote it; who received the emails; how the email recipients were identified and selected; or if the sender complied with applicable laws (such as CAN-SPAM).

As you can imagine, the presence of intermediaries between the advertiser and consumer increases the costs of advertising. After all, each player wants to make a profit, and each profit margin adds to the advertiser's overall cost.

So why would advertisers incur these extra expenses? In theory, each intermediary brings specialized expertise to the process. An affiliate marketer may have low-cost ways to access a community of like-minded individuals. For example, imagine someone who knows how to communicate and sell to a community of very active knitters—a community that most outsiders don't fully understand. It may be too costly for any individual advertiser or ad agency to learn how to reach and effectively persuade that niche. Therefore, it may be cheaper to outsource the outreach to experts who already know that audience.

At the same time, a complex web of outsourced relationships can diffuse responsibility for any problems. If the ultimate ad is illegal, who bears responsibility? Often, each participant can point the finger at the others, effectively saying that legal compliance was someone else's responsibility. For example, when "kid-tracking" apps touted their ability to track possibly cheating spouses—a feature that can also be used by abusers,can enable stalking and can be illegal if the user installs an app surreptitiously—some of the app makers blamed affiliates for the relevant ads. Jennifer Valentino-DeVries, *Hundreds of Apps Can Empower Stalkers to Track Their Victims*, N.Y. TIMES, May 19, 2018.

This chapter explores some of the legal and regulatory issues various parties face. In many situations, the well-known problems of aligning principals' and agents' incentives structure or at least inform the legal rules.

After discussing potential officer and employee liability for a company's false advertising, this chapter will look at when advertising agencies are liable for their advertisers' ads (answer: sometimes), when advertisers are responsible for the acts of individual distributors or affiliate marketers (answer: occasionally) and when publishers are liable for the third-party ads they run (answer: possibly for offline publishers, usually not for online publishers). The chapter also looks at when publishers can be forced to run third-party ads (answer: never). The chapter will conclude with some discussion about payment disputes between publishers and advertisers.

1.   Officers and Employees

Proper defendants can sometimes include the advertiser's officers. Donsco, Inc. v. Casper Corp., 587 F.2d 602 (3d Cir. 1978). The FTC is more likely to pursue related parties, particularly corporate officers, than private litigants are, for general deterrence purposes and to force them to disgorge unjustly acquired consumer monies. For employees, directors and the like, the FTC considers liability appropriate "when the defendant participated directly in the violative conduct or had authority to control it" and had or should have had knowledge of it.

"Authority to control can be evidenced by active involvement in business affairs and the making of corporate policy," and such active involvement may also establish the requisite knowledge. FTC v. Lights of Am., Inc., 2013 WL 5230681 (C.D. Cal. Sept. 17, 2013). The knowledge standard includes people who intentionally avoid or are recklessly indifferent to the truth. Thus, even if an individual personally doesn't perceive or believe that ads are deceptive, her knowledge of multiple complaints about those ads can satisfy the knowledge requirement. FTC v. Ross, 743 F.3d 886 (4th Cir. 2014).

In addition, final yes-or-no authority over advertising isn't required for liability. A person who participated directly in meetings about advertising concepts and content, reviewed and edited ad copy, managed the day-to-day affairs of the marketing team and possessed hiring and firing authority over the head of the marketing department was held individually liable for false advertising. POM Wonderful, LLC v. FTC, 777 F.3d 478 (D.C. Cir. 2015).

The standard under the Lanham Act is slightly more limited: Individual liability can be appropriate for an officer or director who personally takes part in the unlawful activities or specifically directs employees to do so. *See, e.g.*, Donsco, Inc. v. Casper Corp., 587 F.2d 602 (3d Cir. 1978) ("A corporate officer is individually liable for the torts he personally commits and cannot shield himself behind a corporation when he is an actual participant in the tort. . . . This principle applies where the conduct constitutes unfair competition."); Polo Fashions, Inc. v. Craftex, Inc., 816 F.2d 145 (4th Cir. 1987) ("A corporate official may be held personally liable for tortious conduct committed by him, though committed primarily for the benefit of the corporation. This is true in trademark infringement and unfair trade practices cases."). Managing employees can also be held personally liable if they are the "moving, active, conscious forces behind" the corporation. Bambu Sales, Inc. v. Sultana Crackers, Inc., 683 F. Supp. 899 (E.D.N.Y. 1988).

Some states' consumer-protection laws also penalize anyone who aids and abets a violation. For example, a corporate officer or employee who knows that conduct is wrongful and provides substantial assistance or encouragement to it may be liable under state law. See People v. Sarpas, 225 Cal. App. 4th 1539 (Cal. Ct. App. 2014) (discussed in Chapter 9).

2.   Advertising Agencies

Typically, agents and principals are equally liable for any tortious behavior by the agent within the agency's scope. Therefore, advertisers are generally responsible for the acts of their advertising agencies.

Agencies also may be liable for the ad copy they help prepare and disseminate, as the following case illustrates.

DOHERTY, CLIFFORD, STEERS & SHENFIELD, INC. V. FEDERAL TRADE COMMISSION, 392 F.2D 921 (6TH CIR. 1968)

[The FTC determined that certain ads for Sucrets and Children's Sucrets cough medicine, manufactured by Merck, constituted false advertising. The FTC issued a cease-and-desist order against both Merck and its advertising agency, Doherty. The court discussed the order against Doherty:]

The Commission held that the advertising agency was an active participant in the preparation of the advertisements and that the agency knew or had reason to know that Merck's claims were false or deceptive.

Doherty urges that it acted only as agent for its client, relying in good faith on the information furnished by Merck. Doherty asserts that having used every available source to assure itself of the accuracy of Merck's claims, there was nothing else the advertising agency could have done. In substance, Doherty contends that there is no substantial evidence from which the Commission could have found that the agency knew or should have known that Merck's claims were false or deceptive. For these reasons Doherty seeks to have the Commission's order set aside and the complaint dismissed as to the agency.

The proper criterion in deciding in a case of this kind as to whether a cease and desist order should issue against the advertising agency is "the extent to which the advertising agency actually participated in the deception. This is essentially a problem of fact for the Commission." In order to be held to be a participant in such deception, the agency must know or have reason to know of the falsity of the advertising. Carter Products, Inc. v. F. T. C., 323 F.2d 523, 534 (5th Cir.).

The Commission held that among the obligations of Doherty as an advertising agency under its agreement with Merck, Doherty was to "offer general marketing consultation for both new and existing products," "formulate advertising Plans" and "prepare layouts and copy for advertisements;" that Doherty's function was to "originate advertising ideas;" that "the advertising at issue, therefore, is the product of both respondents jointly"; that the advertising agency "developed and put into final form the commercials involved in this proceeding"; and that "it is the final form of these commercials from which the falsity of the advertising may reasonably be imputed." We hold that the record in this case demonstrates that the advertising agency participated actively in the deception; and the Commission's findings of fact to this effect are supported by substantial evidence.

To be aware of the true extent of the therapeutic qualities of Sucrets and Children's Sucrets, the advertising agency needed to do nothing more than to read the packaging labels and instructions for use. . . . The advertising prepared by Doherty went far beyond the more modest claim appearing on the labels and instructions.

The protestations of innocence on the part of the advertising agency are refuted convincingly by a document in the record described as "Proposed 1962 Marketing Plan Sucrets Antiseptic Lozenges" prepared by Doherty. This document outlines an ambitious advertising program aimed at selling Sucrets directly to the "self-medicating" market, described as "the middle-lower socio-economic group," and designed to encourage mothers to buy Children's Sucrets for their children. . . . [T]he advertising agency [had an affirmative role] in promoting a program to create in the minds of the "self-medicating" consumer the impression that Sucrets will kill germs, cure sore throat, including "strep" throat, and alleviate "fiery" throat pain.

We find substantial evidence in the record to support the Commission's conclusion that the advertising agency knew or should have known the falsity of these claims. . . .

NOTES AND QUESTIONS

Agencies' Liability Under the FTC Act. The FTC has held numerous ad agencies liable for FTC Act violations. *See, e.g.,* Federal Trade Comm'n v. Mktg. Architects, Inc., No. 18-cv-00050 (D. Me. filed Feb. 5, 2018) (ad agency paid $2 million to settle charges stemming from its creation and dissemination of radio ads, and assistance with telemarketing, for deceptive weight-loss products and "free" offers). However, the agency will be liable only if it committed a knowing violation, while the advertiser may be liable with less scienter.

If you worked at an ad agency, what steps would you take to satisfy the FTC requirements? Must the agency get substantiation from the advertiser where the information is not on the product label? How many questions should the agency ask? Can the agency satisfy its obligations simply by reciting in its form contract that the advertiser must provide it with truthful information and must correct anything untrue or misleading in the ads the advertiser approves? Could the agency simply accept an advertiser's word that the advertiser has substantiation? Does it matter whether the substantiation is so technical that a layperson may have difficulty interpreting it? (To take one example, the FTC takes the position that certain *"gut check"* claims about weight loss should inherently raise suspicions requiring clear substantiation.)

Agencies' Liability Under the Lanham Act. The limited case law suggests that agencies may be held jointly liable with their clients under the Lanham Act. In *Nestlé Purina Petcare Co. v. Blue Buffalo Co.*, 2015 WL 1782661 (E.D. Mo. Apr. 20, 2015), the court allowed counterclaims against agencies to proceed when (1) one agency allegedly "designed and built" the website focused on the allegedly false claims, and (2) another agency allegedly "developed the content" of allegedly false ads on the advertiser's Facebook and Twitter accounts and "arranged for these links to [the challenged website] to appear when Google.com users search for terms related to Blue Buffalo."); *cf.* Duty Free Americas, Inc. v. Estee Lauder Companies, Inc., 797 F.3d 1248 (11th Cir. 2015) (recognizing the existence of contributory liability under the Lanham Act's false advertising provision; liability requires material contribution to the false advertising "either by knowingly inducing or causing the conduct, or by materially participating in it."). Research agencies assisting the advertiser with deceptive studies may also be held liable. Grant Airmass Corp. v. Gaymar Indus., Inc., 645 F. Supp. 1507 (S.D.N.Y. 1986) (applying contributory liability).

Agencies' Liability Under Other Legal Doctrines. Courts routinely treat advertising agencies as jointly and severally liable for other types of claims. For example, in *Waits v. Frito Lay*, 978 F.2d 1093 (9th Cir. 1992), Frito Lay's advertising agency helped recruit a Tom Waits sound-alike singer for an ad it produced for Frito Lay. The agency was jointly liable for the $2.6 million jury verdict.

Statutes may also expressly make advertising agencies liable for legal violations. For example, D.C. Code Section 22-1511 (a criminal false advertising statute) expressly references advertising agencies as one of the regulated entities.

Interagency Conflicts. In re Diamond Mortg. Corp. of Illinois, 118 B.R. 583 (Bkrtcy. N.D. Ill. 1989), involved a financial Ponzi scheme. The first ad agency (Molner) helped the advertiser prepare fraudulent ad copy; a second ad agency (Yaffe) helped place the ads with television broadcasters. The court had no sympathy for the second ad agency's lack of involvement in developing the ad copy:

> [L]ogic dictates that neither the producer of the commercial nor the agency responsible for airing it should be able to escape liability by blaming the other. The fact that these plaintiffs did not sue Molner is irrelevant. When Yaffe chose to put Molner's product on the air, it in effect adopted it as its own. It was the airing of those commercials that arguably led to these plaintiffs' losses. It follows that if Yaffe was going to air Molner's product, it acquired Molner's duty to ascertain that they were accurate. Molner may have written the [fraudulent] ads, but if Yaffe hadn't put them on the air, this lawsuit would not now be pending.

What to Do in Practice? Concerned about the risks of false advertising or other claims, advertising agencies routinely have their lawyers review the ad copy they produce for their advertisers. Whom do these lawyers represent? If the lawyer, ad agency and advertiser have a three-way conference call to discuss the lawyer's liability concerns, is that conversation subject to the attorney-client evidentiary privilege? (With respect to an advertiser's disclosure of potentially privileged information to an ad agency, *compare In re* Jenny Craig, Inc., 1994 WL 16774903 (F.T.C. 1994), *with* LG Elec. U.S.A., Inc. v. Whirlpool Corp., 661 F. Supp. 2d 958 (N.D. Ill. 2009)). If the lawyer represents only the ad agency, should the advertiser pay for its own independent counsel to review the ads as well?

Often, the agency will bill the full costs of this lawyer to the advertiser, plus any expense mark-up. Does this change your analysis about who the lawyer represents? If you are a lawyer retained by an advertising agency in this circumstance, consider what (if any) duties you have under the Model Rules of Professional Conduct Rule 1.8(f), which says: "A lawyer shall not accept compensation for representing a client from one other than the client unless: (1) the client gives informed consent; (2) there is no interference with the lawyer's independence of professional judgment or with the client–lawyer relationship; and (3) information relating to representation of a client is protected as required by Rule 1.6."

A contract between the advertising agency and advertiser typically has an indemnity clause requiring one party to defend the other against certain types of claims and pay any losses caused by those claims. Even if a court awards damages jointly and severally, the indemnity allows the parties to shift the financial exposure between each other. With respect to liability for false advertising, how would you draft the indemnity clause if you represented the ad agency? The advertiser? *See* Richard Pollet, *The Agency–Client Contract and Ethical Considerations in the Agency–Client Relationship*, PLI Advertising Law in the New Media Age 2000, 808 PLI/Comm 405 (Oct. 2000). Both sides can ameliorate their financial risk through insurance.

Other Vendors. In *FTC v. Chapman*, 714 F.3d 1211 (10th Cir. 2013), the court upheld an FTC judgment against a grant writer whose materials were sold through a grant-related telemarketing program. She was found to have violated a portion of the Telemarketing Sales Rule which provides that "[i]t is a deceptive telemarketing act or practice and a violation of this Rule for a person to provide substantial assistance or support to any seller or telemarketer when that person knows or consciously avoids knowing that the seller or telemarketer is engaged in any act or practice that violates [other portions] of this Rule." 16 C.F.R. § 310.3(b).

Though she claimed that she had no role in the misleading marketing, she was aware the state attorney general had investigated the business and requested that it change its marketing, but she never asked to see the marketing materials; she knew that a success-rate claim for one of her products was not substantiated; and she'd been advised by a former employee of the telemarketing company to be vigilant about monitoring its marketing. This was enough to establish her actual or constructive knowledge. As for "substantial assistance," it was "sufficient that Ms. Chapman played an integral part in the . . . scheme by providing the services and products they marketed to consumers" even if she was uninvolved in the marketing itself.

The FTC also pursues payment processors—entities that process credit card transactions for individual merchants—for knowingly, or with willful blindness, assisting violations of the FTCA and of its rules. *See, e.g.*, Federal Trade Comm'n v. Qualpay, Inc., No. 20-cv-00945 (M.D. Fla., proposed consent judgment filed Jun. 1, 2020). The FTC takes the position that telemarketing in general—and certain high-risk services such as debt relief, weight loss and business opportunities in particular—are well known for fraudulent seller conduct. Thus, the FTC believes there is a duty of inquiry for those providing substantial assistance to anyone engaging in telemarketing.

Is liability for content developers and payment processors justified for the same reasons as liability for ad agencies? Or is the FTC overreaching?

Trademark Licensors. Perhaps oddly, it is very difficult, if not impossible, to hold a trademark licensor liable for false advertising by a licensee, even if the trademark is a big part of the selling power of the licensee's product. Troncoso v. TGI Friday's Inc., 2020 WL

3051020 (S.D.N.Y. Jun. 8, 2020) (TGI Friday's, as licensor, was not responsible for the allegedly misleading name "TGI Fridays Potato Skins Snacks); Hilsley v. General Mills, Inc., 376 F. Supp. 3d 1043 (S.D. Cal. 2019) (licensor of cartoon characters on fruit-snack packaging was not responsible for allegedly misleading labeling); Parent v. Millercoors LLC, 2016 WL 3348818 (S.D. Cal. June 16, 2016) ("use of a trademark does not constitute an endorsement" where defendant licensed its mark to appear on allegedly misleading third-party ads)

3.   Distributors and Affiliates

As illustrated in the chapter's introduction, advertising campaigns often involve multiple intermediaries between the advertiser and consumer, including distributors, marketing affiliates or sub-affiliates.

Distributors in Multi-Level Marketing

In some cases, plaintiffs may allege that the main advertiser is vicariously liable—liable even in the absence of knowledge or fault—based on the falsehoods of distributors. *Proctor & Gamble Co. v. Haugen*, 222 F. 3d 1262 (10th Cir. 2000), concerned Amway's liability for false statements disseminated by its distributors:

> Vicarious liability may arise either from an employment or agency relationship. In the present case, the district court found P & G had failed to show that either kind of relationship existed between Amway and its distributors so as to give rise to a genuine issue of material fact regarding vicarious liability.
>
> With regard to the distributors' employment status vis-à-vis Amway, the Utah Supreme Court has drawn a distinction between an employee and an independent contractor. In general,
>
>> [a]n employee is one who is hired and paid a salary, a wage, or at a fixed rate, to perform the employer's work as directed by the employer and who is subject to a comparatively high degree of control in performing those duties. In contrast, an independent contractor is one who is engaged to do some particular project or piece of work, usually for a set total sum, who may do the job in his own way, subject to only minimal restrictions or controls and is responsible only for its satisfactory completion.
>
> Factors a court may consider in determining the nature of the relationship include: "(1) whatever covenants or agreements exist concerning the right of direction and control over the employee, whether express or implied; (2) the right to hire and fire; (3) the method of payment, i.e., whether in wages or fees, as compared to payment for a complete job or project; and (4) the furnishing of the equipment."
>
> In the present case, although Amway sets parameters within which its distributors function, those distributors and Amway stand in relation to one another essentially

as wholesaler and retailer and at the same time retailer and consumer. The record indicates that Amway sets certain rules, and provides certain resources like the AmVox voice message system (in the same way a wholesaler might provide factory warranty service and require a certain standard of behavior from its distributors), but Amway distributors, like retailers, act virtually autonomously in determining in what manner to sell (or consume) Amway products. Based on the undisputed evidence in the record before us, we conclude Amway does not exercise a "comparatively high degree of control" over them. Therefore, the distributors are more analogous to independent contractors than to employees under Utah law.

The evidence also fails to create a genuine issue of material fact as to whether the distributors were Amway's agents. An agent is "a person authorized by another to act on his behalf and under his control." "The existence of an agency relationship is determined from all the facts and circumstances in the case."

> Under agency law, an agent cannot make its principal responsible for the agent's actions unless the agent is acting pursuant to either actual or apparent authority. Actual authority incorporates the concepts of express and implied authority. Express authority exists whenever the principal directly states that its agent has the authority to perform a particular act on the principal's behalf. Implied authority, on the other hand, embraces authority to do those acts which are incidental to, or are necessary, usual, and proper to accomplish or perform, the main authority expressly delegated to the agent. Implied authority is actual authority based upon the premise that whenever the performance of certain business is confided to an agent, such authority carries with it by implication authority to do collateral acts which are the natural and ordinary incidents of the main act or business authorized. This authority may be implied from the words and conduct of the parties and the facts and circumstances attending the transaction in question.

In the present case, P & G cites no facts to show that Amway told the distributors to spread the subject message. The distributors' authority is therefore not "express" . . . . Nor did the distributors who spread the subject message act with implicit authority. Nothing in the record supports the conclusion that spreading the subject message, and indeed satanic rumors regarding P & G generally, was "natural[ly] and ordinar[ily]" incident to Amway's business.

For a contrasting result, *see* Youngevity Int'l v. Smith, 2019 WL 2918161 (S.D. Cal. Jul. 5, 2019) (multilevel marketing company could be held vicariously liable for statements made by distributors; despite their classification as independent contractors, there was a material issue of fact on agency, given that distributors "engaged in the allegedly false advertising for the purpose of attracting distributors and increasing sales," squarely within the scope of their roles, and distributors could be terminated for misbehavior).

Affiliate Marketing and Spam

The federal anti-spam law, CAN-SPAM, holds advertisers liable for illegal spam sent by marketing affiliates—entities with whom the advertisers contract to spread their messages—in certain circumstances. *See* 15 U.S.C. § 7705. Some state anti-spam laws have analogous advertiser liability provisions. However, with respect to non-spam marketing, advertiser liability for affiliate marketing typically isn't addressed by statute and thus exists, if at all, in the common law.

In all circumstances, plaintiffs have not found it easy to hold advertisers accountable for their affiliates' illegal activities. For example, in Fenn v. Redmond Venture, Inc., 2004 UT App 355 (Utah Ct. App. 2004), the advertiser defeated state anti-spam statutory liability for affiliate spam because its advertising contract banned spam. This feels disingenuous because the advertiser probably didn't care if downstream affiliates violated the contract clause so long as they were generating profitable sales. In other words, it's easy enough for advertisers to include an anti-spam clause in their contracts, but then take no effort to enforce it. Still, can you think of reasons why advertisers would want to police the activities of their downstream affiliates?

Other cases have held advertisers not liable for the spam sent by affiliates, such as *Hypertouch, Inc. v. Kennedy-Western University*, 2006 WL 648688 (N.D. Cal. 2006) (advertiser isn't responsible for affiliates' alleged violation of CAN-SPAM when plaintiff "failed to provide any evidence that [advertiser] had actual knowledge or consciously avoided knowledge of a current or future violation of the CAN-SPAM Act by anyone who sent the e-mails at issue"), and *United States v. Impulse Media*, 2008 WL 1968307 (W.D. Wash. 2008) (jury rejected CAN-SPAM claim that advertiser caused its affiliates to send spam).

Courts have also absolved affiliates for email sent by downstream sub-affiliates. *See* Ferron v. Echostar Satellite LLC, 2008 WL 4377309 (S.D. Ohio 2008) (no liability under state consumer protection law for spam sent by sub-affiliates); ASIS Internet Servs., v. Optin Glob., Inc., 2008 WL 1902217 (N.D. Cal. 2008) (no CAN-SPAM liability).

For more on this topic, see Jean Noonan & Michael Goodman, *Third-Party Liability for Federal Law Violations in Direct-to-Consumer Marketing: Telemarketing, Fax, and E-mail*, 63 BUS. LAW. 585 (2008).

Affiliate Liability Beyond Spam

Other areas where plaintiffs seek to hold companies responsible for the acts of their affiliates:

- *Collection of Sales Taxes*. Some states have passed laws to treat online affiliates as the equivalent of traveling salespeople, thus giving states the requisite physical nexus to impose sales tax collection obligations on those companies. *See* Overstock.com, Inc. v N.Y. State Dep't. of Tax. & Fin., 20 N.Y.3d 586 (N.Y. Ct. App. 2013) (upholding the tax).

- *Trademarks.* Trademark owners occasionally sue companies when affiliates bid on the trademark owner's trademark as keywords for search-engine advertising. Most courts, but not all, have rejected these arguments. *Compare* Sellify Inc. v. Amazon.com, Inc., 2010 WL 4455830 (S.D.N.Y. 2010), *with* 1-800 Contacts, Inc. v. Lens.com, Inc., 722 F.3d 1229 (10th Cir. 2013).
- *FTC Act.* The FTC takes the position that advertisers can be responsible if their affiliates write fake reviews. *See* FTC v. LeadClick Media, LLC, 838 F.3d 158 (2d Cir. 2016) (affiliate coordinator was liable for fake "news" written by affiliates; affiliate coordinator knew about fake sites and had authority to control the affiliates, and also participated in the deception by buying ad space on genuine news sites and selling the space to affiliates who advertised with fake news); *In re* Legacy Learning Sys., Inc., F.T.C. File No. 102 3055 (2011) ($250,000 settlement because affiliates wrote fake reviews that pretended to be the authentic views of consumers); .
- *Affiliate Links in Editorial Content.* BuzzFeed published product review guides written by its editorial department; a separate department subsequently added affiliate links to the guides and disclosed their presence. The NAD concluded that the affiliate links did not turn the guides into "national advertising" sufficient to require BuzzFeed to substantiate the claims in its guides. NAD 6210: Shopping Guides – St. Ives Renewing Collagen & Elastin Moisturizer, Sept. 18, 2018.
- *The Telephone Consumer Protection Act (TCPA).* The TCPA restricts telemarketing, including unsolicited text messages. In *Chutich v. Papa John's International, Inc.*, No. C10-1139 (W.D. Wash. 2012), a court certified a class action against Papa John's for the marketing practices of an affiliate hired by some of Papa John's franchisees (note the layering of potential liability given the franchising arrangement). Papa John's eventually settled the case for $16.5 million.

Franchisors/Dealers

In *City of New York v. T-Mobile USA, Inc.*, 67 Misc.3d 1203(A) (N.Y. Sup. Ct. 2020), the court held that T-Mobile could be liable for practices of stores run by a subsidiary because those stores create the impression of agency based on the relationship between the parties. This raised the doctrine of apparent authority for the conduct of the dealers who were labeled "authorized" in their signs, on T-Mobile's website and in stores).

4. Publishers

A. Publisher Liability for Advertisements (Offline)

Subject to some exceptions, publishers generally are liable for the contents of ads they publish. In other words, the law generally does not distinguish between advertisers who developed ad copy and the publishers who disseminate the ad copy, although in some cases the scienter prerequisite for liability is higher for publishers than advertisers. In a sense, the legal rules deputize publishers to act as gatekeepers and "police" the ads they publish—at peril of assuming liability for the ads they accept.

The following case is a landmark Supreme Court case on defamation liability, but many people overlook that the allegedly defamatory content was in a third-party ad provided to the publisher. Pay close attention to how the Court analyzes the newspaper's liability for publishing third-party ads.

NEW YORK TIMES V. SULLIVAN, 376 U.S. 254 (1964)

. . . Respondent L. B. Sullivan is one of the three elected Commissioners of the City of Montgomery, Alabama. He testified that he was

> Commissioner of Public Affairs, and the duties are supervision of the Police Department, Fire Department, Department of Cemetery and Department of Scales.

He brought this civil libel action against the four individual petitioners, who are Negroes and Alabama clergymen, and against petitioner the New York Times Company, a New York corporation which publishes the *New York Times*, a daily newspaper. A jury in the Circuit Court of Montgomery County awarded him damages of $500,000, the full amount claimed, against all the petitioners, and the Supreme Court of Alabama affirmed.

Respondent's complaint alleged that he had been libeled by statements in a full-page advertisement that was carried in the *New York Times* on March 29, 1960. Entitled "Heed Their Rising Voices," the advertisement began by stating that,

> As the whole world knows by now, thousands of Southern Negro students are engaged in widespread nonviolent demonstrations in positive affirmation of the right to live in human dignity as guaranteed by the U.S. Constitution and the Bill of Rights.

It went on to charge that,

> in their efforts to uphold these guarantees, they are being met by an unprecedented wave of terror by those who would deny and negate that document which the whole world looks upon as setting the pattern for modern freedom. . . .

Succeeding paragraphs purported to illustrate the "wave of terror" by describing certain alleged events. The text concluded with an appeal for funds for three purposes: support of the student movement, "the struggle for the right to vote," and the legal defense of Dr. Martin Luther King, Jr., leader of the movement, against a perjury indictment then pending in Montgomery.

The text appeared over the names of 64 persons, many widely known for their activities in public affairs, religion, trade unions, and the performing arts. Below these names, and under a line reading "We in the south who are struggling daily for dignity and freedom warmly endorse this appeal," appeared the names of the four individual petitioners and of 16 other persons, all but two of whom were identified as clergymen in various Southern cities. The advertisement was signed at the bottom of the page by the "Committee to Defend Martin

Luther King and the Struggle for Freedom in the South," and the officers of the Committee were listed.

Of the 10 paragraphs of text in the advertisement, the third and a portion of the sixth were the basis of respondent's claim of libel. They read as follows:

Third paragraph:

> In Montgomery, Alabama, after students sang "My Country, 'Tis of Thee" on the State Capitol steps, their leaders were expelled from school, and truckloads of police armed with shotguns and tear-gas ringed the Alabama State College Campus. When the entire student body protested to state authorities by refusing to reregister, their dining hall was padlocked in an attempt to starve them into submission.

Sixth paragraph:

> Again and again, the Southern violators have answered Dr. King's peaceful protests with intimidation and violence. They have bombed his home, almost killing his wife and child. They have assaulted his person. They have arrested him seven times—for "speeding," "loitering" and similar "offenses." And now they have charged him with "perjury"—a felony under which they could imprison him for ten years. . . .

> *"The growing movement of peaceful mass demonstrations by Negroes is something new in the South, something understandable.... Let Congress heed their rising voices, for they will be heard."*
>
> —*New York Times editorial*
> *Saturday, March 19, 1960*

Heed Their Rising Voices

As the whole world knows by now, thousands of Southern Negro students are engaged in widespread non-violent demonstrations in positive affirmation of the right to live in human dignity as guaranteed by the U. S. Constitution and the Bill of Rights. In their efforts to uphold these guarantees, they are being met by an unprecedented wave of terror by those who would deny and negate that document which the whole world looks upon as setting the pattern for modern freedom. ...

In Orangeburg, South Carolina, when 400 students peacefully sought to buy doughnuts and coffee at lunch counters in the business district, they were forcibly ejected, tear-gassed, soaked to the skin in freezing weather with fire hoses, arrested en masse and herded into an open barbed-wire stockade to stand for hours in the bitter cold.

In Montgomery, Alabama, after students sang "My Country, 'Tis of Thee" on the State Capitol steps, their leaders were expelled from school, and truckloads of police armed with shotguns and tear-gas ringed the Alabama State College Campus. When the entire student body protested to state authorities by refusing to re-register, their dining hall was padlocked in an attempt to starve them into submission.

In Tallahassee, Atlanta, Nashville, Savannah, Greensboro, Memphis, Richmond, Charlotte, and a host of other cities in the South, young American teen-agers, in face of the entire weight of official state apparatus and police power, have boldly stepped forth as protagonists of democracy. Their courage and amazing restraint have inspired millions and given a new dignity to the cause of freedom.

Small wonder that the Southern violators of the Constitution fear this new, non-violent brand of freedom fighter ... even as they fear the upswelling right-to-vote movement. Small wonder that they are determined to destroy the one man who, more than any other, symbolizes the new spirit now sweeping the South—the Rev. Dr. Martin Luther King, Jr., world-famous leader of the Montgomery Bus Protest. For it is his doctrine of non-violence which has inspired and guided the students in their widening wave of sit-ins; and it this same Dr. King who founded and is president of the Southern Christian Leadership Conference—the organization which is spearheading the surging right-to-vote movement. Under Dr. King's direction the Leadership Conference conducts Student Workshops and Seminars in the philosophy and technique of non-violent resistance.

Again and again the Southern violators have answered Dr. King's peaceful protests with intimidation and violence. They have bombed his home almost killing his wife and child. They have assaulted his person. They have arrested him seven times—for "speeding," "loitering" and similar "offenses." And now they have charged him with "perjury"—a felony under which they could imprison him for ten years. Obviously, their real purpose is to remove him physically as the leader to whom the students and millions of others—look for guidance and support, and thereby to intimidate all leaders who may rise in the South. Their strategy is to behead this affirmative movement, and thus to demoralize Negro Americans and weaken their will to struggle. The defense of Martin Luther King, spiritual leader of the student sit-in movement, clearly, therefore, is an integral part of the total struggle for freedom in the South.

Decent-minded Americans cannot help but applaud the creative daring of the students and the quiet heroism of Dr. King. But this is one of those moments in the stormy history of Freedom when men and women of good will must do more than applaud the rising-to-glory of others. The America whose good name hangs in the balance before a watchful world, the America whose heritage of Liberty these Southern Upholders of the Constitution are defending, is our America as well as theirs ...

We must heed their rising voices—yes—but we must add our own.

We must extend ourselves above and beyond moral support and render the material help so urgently needed by those who are taking the risks, facing jail, and even death in a glorious re-affirmation of our Constitution and its Bill of Rights.

We urge you to join hands with our fellow Americans in the South by supporting, with your dollars, this Combined Appeal for all three needs—the defense of Martin Luther King—the support of the embattled students—and the struggle for the right-to-vote.

Your Help Is Urgently Needed .... NOW!!

Stella Adler
Raymond Pace Alexander
Harry Van Arsdale
Harry Belafonte
Julie Belafonte
Dr. Algernon Black
Marc Blitzstein
William Branch
Marlon Brando
Mrs. Ralph Bunche
Diahann Carroll

Dr. Alan Knight Chalmers
Richard Coe
Nat King Cole
Cheryl Crawford
Dorothy Dandridge
Ossie Davis
Sammy Davis, Jr.
Ruby Dee
Dr. Philip Elliott
Dr. Harry Emerson Fosdick

Anthony Franciosa
Lorraine Hansbury
Rev. Donald Harrington
Nat Hentoff
James Hicks
Mary Hinkson
Van Heflin
Langston Hughes
Morris Iushewitz
Mahalia Jackson
Mordecai Johnson

John Killens
Eartha Kitt
Rabbi Edward Klein
Hope Lange
John Lewis
Viveca Lindfors
Carl Murphy
Don Murray
John Murray
A. J. Muste
Frederick O'Neal

L. Joseph Overton
Clarence Pickett
Shad Polier
Sidney Poitier
A. Philip Randolph
John Raitt
Elmer Rice
Jackie Robinson
Mrs. Eleanor Roosevelt
Bayard Rustin
Robert Ryan

Maureen Stapleton
Frank Silvera
Hope Stevens
George Tabori
Rev. Gardner C. Taylor
Norman Thomas
Kenneth Tynan
Charles White
Shelley Winters
Max Youngstein

We in the south who are struggling daily for dignity and freedom warmly endorse this appeal

Rev. Ralph D. Abernathy
(Montgomery, Ala.)

Rev. Fred L. Shuttlesworth
(Birmingham, Ala.)

Rev. Kelley Miller Smith
(Nashville, Tenn.)

Rev. W. A. Dennis
(Chattanooga, Tenn.)

Rev. C. K. Steele
(Tallahassee, Fla.)

Rev. Matthew D. McCollom
(Orangeburg, S. C.)

Rev. William Holmes Borders
(Atlanta, Ga.)

Rev. Douglas Moore
(Durham, N. C.)

Rev. Wyatt Tee Walker
(Petersburg, Va.)

Rev. Walter L. Hamilton
(Norfolk, Va.)

I. S. Levy
(Columbia, S. C.)

Rev. Martin Luther King, Sr.
(Atlanta, Ga.)

Rev. Henry C. Bunton
(Memphis, Tenn.)

Rev. S. S. Seay, Sr.
(Montgomery, Ala.)

Rev. Samuel W. Williams
(Atlanta, Ga.)

Rev. A. L. Davis
(New Orleans, La.)

Mrs. Katie E. Whickham
(New Orleans, La.)

Rev. W. H. Hall
(Hattiesburg, Miss.)

Rev. J. E. Lowery
(Mobile, Ala.)

Rev. T. J. Jemison
(Baton Rouge, La.)

COMMITTEE TO DEFEND MARTIN LUTHER KING AND THE STRUGGLE FOR FREEDOM IN THE SOUTH

312 West 125th Street, New York 27, N. Y. UNiversity 6-1700

Chairmen: A. Philip Randolph, Dr. Gardner C. Taylor; *Chairmen of Cultural Division:* Harry Belafonte, Sidney Poitier; *Treasurer:* Nat King Cole; *Executive Director:* Bayard Rustin; *Chairmen of Church Division:* Father George B. Ford, Rev. Harry Emerson Fosdick, Rev. Thomas Kilgore, Jr., Rabbi Edward E. Klein; *Chairman of Labor Division:* Morris Iushewitz

Please mail this coupon TODAY:

Committee To Defend Martin Luther King
and
The Struggle For Freedom In The South
312 West 125th Street, New York 27, N. Y.
UNiversity 6-1700

I am enclosing my contribution of $_____
for the work of the Committee.

Name _____ (PLEASE PRINT)

Address _____

City _____ Zone __ State __

☐ I want to help   ☐ Please send further information

Please make checks payable to:
Committee To Defend Martin Luther King

703

. . . It is uncontroverted that some of the statements contained in the two paragraphs were not accurate descriptions of events which occurred in Montgomery. [The court then described the various errors.]

. . . [The advertisement] was published by the Times upon an order from a New York advertising agency acting for the signatory Committee. The agency submitted the advertisement with a letter from A. Philip Randolph, Chairman of the Committee, certifying that the persons whose names appeared on the advertisement had given their permission. Mr. Randolph was known to the Times' Advertising Acceptability Department as a responsible person, and, in accepting the letter as sufficient proof of authorization, it followed its established practice. . . . The manager of the Advertising Acceptability Department testified that he had approved the advertisement for publication because he knew nothing to cause him to believe that anything in it was false, and because it bore the endorsement of "a number of people who are well known and whose reputation" he "had no reason to question." Neither he nor anyone else at the Times made an effort to confirm the accuracy of the advertisement, either by checking it against recent Times news stories relating to some of the described events or by any other means.

Alabama law denies a public officer recovery of punitive damages in a libel action brought on account of a publication concerning his official conduct unless he first makes a written demand for a public retraction and the defendant fails or refuses to comply. Respondent served such a demand upon each of the petitioners. . . . The Times did not publish a retraction in response to the demand, but wrote respondent a letter stating, among other things, that "we . . . are somewhat puzzled as to how you think the statements in any way reflect on you," and "you might, if you desire, let us know in what respect you claim that the statements in the advertisement reflect on you." Respondent filed this suit a few days later without answering the letter. The Times did, however, subsequently publish a retraction of the advertisement upon the demand of Governor John Patterson of Alabama, who asserted that the publication charged him with

> grave misconduct and . . . improper actions and omissions as Governor of Alabama and Ex-Officio Chairman of the State Board of Education of Alabama.

When asked to explain why there had been a retraction for the Governor but not for respondent, the Secretary of the Times testified:

> We did that because we didn't want anything that was published by The Times to be a reflection on the State of Alabama, and the Governor was, as far as we could see, the embodiment of the State of Alabama and the proper representative of the State, and, furthermore, we had by that time learned more of the actual facts which the and [sic] purported to recite and, finally, the ad did refer to the action of the State authorities and the Board of Education, presumably of which the Governor is the ex-officio chairman. . . .

On the other hand, he testified that he did not think that "any of the language in there referred to Mr. Sullivan." . . .

I.

We may dispose at the outset of two grounds asserted to insulate the judgment of the Alabama courts from constitutional scrutiny. . . . [Editor's note: The first was lack of state action.]

The second contention is that the constitutional guarantees of freedom of speech and of the press are inapplicable here, at least so far as the Times is concerned, because the allegedly libelous statements were published as part of a paid, "commercial" advertisement. The argument relies on *Valentine v. Chrestensen*, 316 U.S. 52, where the Court held that a city ordinance forbidding street distribution of commercial and business advertising matter did not abridge the First Amendment freedoms, even as applied to a handbill having a commercial message on one side but a protest against certain official action, on the other. The reliance is wholly misplaced. The Court in *Chrestensen* reaffirmed the constitutional protection for "the freedom of communicating information and disseminating opinion"; its holding was based upon the factual conclusions that the handbill was "purely commercial advertising" and that the protest against official action had been added only to evade the ordinance.

The publication here was not a "commercial" advertisement in the sense in which the word was used in *Chrestensen*. It communicated information, expressed opinion, recited grievances, protested claimed abuses, and sought financial support on behalf of a movement whose existence and objectives are matters of the highest public interest and concern. That the Times was paid for publishing the advertisement is as immaterial in this connection as is the fact that newspapers and books are sold. Any other conclusion would discourage newspapers from carrying "editorial advertisements" of this type, and so might shut off an important outlet for the promulgation of information and ideas by persons who do not themselves have access to publishing facilities—who wish to exercise their freedom of speech even though they are not members of the press. The effect would be to shackle the First Amendment in its attempt to secure "the widest possible dissemination of information from diverse and antagonistic sources." To avoid placing such a handicap upon the freedoms of expression, we hold that, if the allegedly libelous statements would otherwise be constitutionally protected from the present judgment, they do not forfeit that protection because they were published in the form of a paid advertisement. . . .

III.

. . . As to the Times, we similarly conclude that the facts do not support a finding of actual malice. The statement by the Times' Secretary that, apart from the padlocking allegation, he thought the advertisement was "substantially correct," affords no constitutional warrant for the Alabama Supreme Court's conclusion that it was a

> cavalier ignoring of the falsity of the advertisement [from which] the jury could not have but been impressed with the bad faith of The Times, and its maliciousness inferable therefrom.

The statement does not indicate malice at the time of the publication; even if the advertisement was not "substantially correct"—although respondent's own proofs tend to show that it was—that opinion was at least a reasonable one, and there was no evidence to impeach the witness' good faith in holding it. The Times' failure to retract upon respondent's demand, although it later retracted upon the demand of Governor Patterson, is likewise not adequate evidence of malice for constitutional purposes. . . .

Finally, there is evidence that the Times published the advertisement without checking its accuracy against the news stories in the Times' own files. The mere presence of the stories in the files does not, of course, establish that the Times "knew" the advertisement was false, since the state of mind required for actual malice would have to be brought home to the persons in the Times' organization having responsibility for the publication of the advertisement. With respect to the failure of those persons to make the check, the record shows that they relied upon their knowledge of the good reputation of many of those whose names were listed as sponsors of the advertisement, and upon the letter from A. Philip Randolph, known to them as a responsible individual, certifying that the use of the names was authorized. There was testimony that the persons handling the advertisement saw nothing in it that would render it unacceptable under the Times' policy of rejecting advertisements containing "attacks of a personal character"; their failure to reject it on this ground was not unreasonable. We think the evidence against the Times supports, at most, a finding of negligence in failing to discover the misstatements, and is constitutionally insufficient to show the recklessness that is required for a finding of actual malice. . . .

[JUSTICES BLACK and GOLDBERG filed concurrences, omitted.]

NOTES AND QUESTIONS

Newspaper Responsibility for Ads. Notice that the Court treats *The New York Times* as legally responsible for the third-party ad copy without discussing that treatment. This is consistent with general tort doctrines. By making the editorial decision to publish the ad, *The New York Times* took equal responsibility for the ad's legality along with the advertiser.

Publisher Standards. Many publishers voluntarily adopt internal guidelines about the ads they will accept for publication. These standards vary widely and are often vague and highly subjective. For example, *The New York Times*' Advertising Acceptability Manual (revised January 2015) says:

> Advertisements that are, in the opinion of The Times, indecent, vulgar, suggestive or otherwise offensive to good taste are unacceptable. Taste is judgment in which time, place and context make vital differences. Each advertisement must, therefore, be judged on its own merits.

The *Times'* standards enumerate its prevailing policy about the ads at issue in the *Sullivan* case:

> We believe that the broad principles of freedom of the press confer on us an obligation to keep our advertising columns open to all points of view. Therefore, The

New York Times accepts advertisements in which groups or individuals comment on public or controversial issues. We make no judgments on an advertiser's arguments, factual assertions or conclusions. We accept advocacy/opinion advertisements regardless of our editorial position on any given subject.

We do not, however, accept advocacy advertisements that are attacks of a personal nature, that seek to comment on private disputes or that contain vulgar or indecent language.

We do not accept advertisements that are gratuitously offensive on racial, religious or ethnic grounds or that are considered to be in poor taste. We do not verify, nor do we vouch for, statements of purported fact in advocacy/opinion advertisements. We reserve the right, however, to require documentation of factual claims when it is deemed necessary.

In addition, we do not accept advocacy advertisements that promote illegal activities or actions. We do not accept ads that are libelous or might be legally actionable. We also do not accept an advocacy ad that accused an entire country, race or religion as being guilty of a crime. And conversely we will not accept advertising that denies or trivializes great human tragedies such as the Armenian Genocide or World Trade Center bombing.

Advertisements that include photographs of individuals or the names of individuals as signatories, or which state or imply that named individuals support or endorse the messages, must be accompanied by a signed release wherein the sponsors certify that no one's name or photograph has been used in the advertisements without his or her consent. If affiliations of signatories are included in the opinion advertisement, then a line of copy which reads "Affiliations listed for identification purposes only" must appear in the advertisement.

The sponsor's name must be in the advertisement. If the advertiser is not known to our readers, the sponsor's mailing address or telephone number, email address or Web site address (that leads to direct contact with the advertiser) must appear in the advertisement.

Some publisher standards are driven by liability concerns (i.e., no defamatory ads); some are designed to prevent advertisers from making their ads appear like editorial content; and others may reflect idiosyncratic normative decisions. *See, e.g.*, Sarah Kershaw, *Google Tells Sites for 'Cougars' to Go Prowl Elsewhere*, N.Y. TIMES, May 14, 2010 (Google banned ads promoting "cougar sites," i.e., sites for older women seeking to date younger men, though Google accepted similar ads for other dating sites).

There are good reasons why publishers might reject ads that are legal. In some cases, the publisher is worried that its audience will think less of the publication based on the ads it runs. Think of the times you've changed the television or radio station because the content of an advertisement annoyed you, or you left a website because of some irritatingly animated or flashing ad. Or sometimes the publisher is making a bona fide effort to protect readers/viewers from scams or other harms.

Do these voluntary standards reduce or increase a publisher's liability exposure? On the one hand, by preemptively screening out risky ads, the publisher publishes fewer legally risky ads. On the other hand, plaintiffs may cite the standards against the publisher in a variety of ways, such as by arguing that the publisher's exercise of control over the ads should increase its liability for the ads it accepts. *See* the *Goddard* and *Langdon* cases, *infra*.

Publisher Investigation. Why didn't *The New York Times* undertake any effort to verify the ad's assertions? How much investigation of ads should publishers do?

Discrimination. In *Pittsburgh Press Co. v. Pittsburgh Commission on Human Relations*, 413 U.S. 376 (1973), the Supreme Court held that the First Amendment did not protect a newspaper's classified ad headings titled "help wanted—male" and "help wanted—female" because the headings facilitated illegal sex-based job discrimination. For more on discrimination in housing ads, see Chapter 19.

Publisher Liability for Personal Injuries. The following case shows how a publisher can become responsible for advertisers' misconduct.

KNEPPER V. BROWN, 345 OR. 320 (2008)

In this common-law fraud action, plaintiffs obtained a $1.5 million jury verdict against Dex Media, Inc. (Dex), based on Dex's involvement in creating and publishing a Yellow Pages advertisement that misrepresented a doctor's qualifications. On appeal, Dex argued that plaintiffs presented no evidence that the misrepresentation caused the injuries that plaintiffs claimed (pain and physical deformities resulting from a botched liposuction procedure) and that it therefore was entitled to a directed verdict or to a judgment notwithstanding the jury's verdict. The Court of Appeals disagreed and affirmed the judgment for plaintiffs. We allowed Dex's petition for review and, for the reasons that follow, now affirm the decision of the Court of Appeals and the judgment of the trial court. . . .

Dr. Timothy Brown is a licensed medical doctor who holds certifications from the American Board of Medical Specialties in dermatology and anatomic and clinical pathology. Brown started a dermatology practice in Oregon in 1985 and thereafter maintained an advertisement in Dex's Yellow Pages directory, under the heading "Physicians and Surgeons" and the subheading "Dermatology (skin)." The advertisement listed various services and prominently noted that Brown was "Certified by the American Board of Dermatology."

In 1993, Brown began to offer "tumescent" liposuction in his office, after receiving some limited informal training in how to perform that procedure. He mentioned the new service in his 1993/94 Yellow Pages advertisement, which still appeared under the "Dermatology" subheading and which still referred to his board certification in dermatology.

In 1996, Brown placed a second advertisement in Dex's Yellow Pages—this time under the subheading "Surgery, Plastic and Reconstructive." The new advertisement stated that Brown performed liposuction, wrinkle treatments, and sclerotherapy. It also stated that Brown was "Board Certified"—without specifying any area of certification.

The new advertisements were added at the urging of a Dex sales representative, Mueller. Brown's office manager, Newman, told Mueller that Brown was interested in attracting more liposuction patients. Mueller met with Newman to help her "mock up" a new advertisement. Mueller told Newman that the "plastic and reconstruction surgery" subheading in the Yellow Pages would be the best place to reach that target market. Mueller also told Newman that the advertisement should identify Brown as "board certified," because "patients were expecting a [board certified] plastic surgeon to do these techniques." Newman repeatedly told Mueller that she was concerned that such an advertisement would be misleading, because Brown's board certification was in dermatology, not plastic and reconstructive surgery. Mueller continued to push for a nonspecific "board certified" designation under the "Surgery, Plastic and Reconstructive" subheading, and Brown, who had the final say, acceded to Mueller's advice.

Early in 1997, plaintiff M. M. Knepper was considering cosmetic liposuction surgery. She knew that she wanted to be treated by a plastic surgeon. She consulted the "Surgery, Plastic and Reconstructive" subheading in the Yellow Pages and compiled a list of doctors and medical facilities that performed liposuction. Knepper saw Brown's advertisement and included his name and telephone number on her list, believing him to be a plastic surgeon because of the location of his ad and the "board certified" designation that appeared after his name. Knepper did not call Brown's office at the time, however.

Some months later, Knepper attended a Women's Show and stopped at a booth offering information about Brown's cosmetic surgery practice. Knepper recognized Brown's name from her list of potential plastic surgeons. She picked up a brochure, which stated that Brown was board certified in, among other things, "Dermatologic Surgery." One of Brown's employees, who was manning the booth, told Knepper that Brown was a board-certified plastic surgeon. Knepper thereafter made an appointment to discuss liposuction with Brown. At the consultation, Brown also told Knepper that he was board certified in plastic surgery.

Knepper decided to retain Brown, and he performed a liposuction procedure on her in December 1997. After the procedure, Knepper contacted Brown's office to report continuing pain and "misshapenness," and Brown performed two more liposuction procedures in an unsuccessful attempt to repair the damage. Plaintiffs eventually filed the present action against Brown and Dex, alleging claims of medical malpractice, fraud, conspiracy to commit fraud, and loss of consortium. Brown later settled with plaintiffs, leaving plaintiffs' fraud claim (and the derivative conspiracy and loss of consortium claims) against Dex to be decided at trial. Plaintiffs' fraud claim alleged that (1) Dex knew that Brown was not board certified in plastic and reconstructive surgery; (2) Dex and Brown together designed and developed an advertisement that falsely implied that Brown was a board-certified plastic surgeon; (3) Knepper wanted a board-certified plastic surgeon to perform liposuction surgery on her; (4) Knepper relied in part on the misleading Dex advertisement and retained Brown to perform liposuction surgery; (5) if Knepper had known the truth about Brown's credentials, she would not have consented to surgery by him; and (6) Brown performed the liposuction negligently, causing injury to plaintiffs. . . .

. . . Plaintiffs also presented the testimony of Dr. Lloyd Hale, a plastic surgeon, regarding the nature and extent of Knepper's injuries and whether Knepper's three liposuction procedures were performed in a manner that met the applicable standard of care. Hale also testified about the qualifications of dermatologists, as opposed to those of plastic surgeons, to perform surgical procedures. He observed that dermatologists usually do not receive formalized surgical training, while plastic surgeons receive extensive surgical training over a period of many years. Hale further observed that surgical knowledge, training, and experience are important for obtaining good results from liposuction. Hale acknowledged that plastic surgeons do not always meet the standard of care for liposuction or other surgical procedures, but he stated that he had never seen an injury like Knepper's—which he described as an "uncorrectable disaster"—at the hands of a doctor who had gone through formalized surgical training. . . .

Dex's initial argument is that, to hold Dex liable for fraud, plaintiffs were required, but failed, to present evidence establishing that Brown's negligent treatment of Knepper was a reasonably foreseeable consequence of Dex's publication of Brown's advertisement. . . . Dex argues that plaintiffs were required to prove that the particular type of injury that Knepper suffered—a botched medical procedure at the hands of a third party (Brown)—was a reasonably foreseeable consequence of Dex's publication of Brown's misleading advertisement. . . .

Courts have noted that, when an intentional tort is involved, the range of legal causation can be quite broad: "'For an intended injury, the law is astute to discover even very remote causation.'" W. Page Keeton, Prosser and Keeton on Torts § 43, 293 n.6 (5th ed. 1984). Still, the historical references to "proximate injury" as an element of fraud indicates that courts also recognize that there is some limitation on the consequences for which a perpetrator of an intentional fraud may be held liable. A requirement that any claimed damages be foreseeable appropriately recognizes that the scope of liability for an intentional, fraudulent misrepresentation depends on the nature of the misrepresentation, the audience to whom the misrepresentation was directed, and the nature of the action or forbearance, intended or negligent, that the misrepresentation justifiably induced. Restatement (Second) of Torts § 548A (1977) incorporates that requirement:

> "A fraudulent misrepresentation is a legal cause of a pecuniary loss resulting from action or inaction in reliance upon it if, but only if, the loss might reasonably be expected to result from the reliance." . . .

When we apply that foreseeability principle in the present case, it is clear that plaintiffs' damages reasonably might be expected to result from their reliance on Dex's misrepresentation. An advertisement that misrepresents a medical provider's qualifications self-evidently creates a risk that a consumer who seeks treatment from the provider in reliance on that misrepresentation will suffer an adverse result that would not have occurred if the provider's qualifications had been as represented. The testimony at trial showed that Knepper's injuries fell precisely within the foreseeable risk of harm that the misrepresentation created: Knepper testified that she wanted to have a board-certified plastic surgeon perform the liposuction, and a juror could infer from that testimony that Knepper believed that she was more likely to suffer an adverse result from being treated by a medical provider who was not board certified in plastic surgery. Further, plaintiffs' medical expert testified that he had never seen adverse results like the ones that Knepper experienced from a medical provider who was certified in plastic surgery. A juror could infer from that testimony that plaintiffs' injuries probably would not have occurred if Knepper had received treatment from a board-certified plastic surgeon (as she believed Brown to be). Stated in terms of the applicable legal standard, Dex had reason to expect that Knepper would act in justifiable reliance on Dex's misrepresentation by retaining Brown for the surgery, and that an adverse result was more likely if Brown, rather than a board-certified plastic surgeon, performed liposuction surgery. There is no additional requirement that plaintiffs also prove that Dex in fact did foresee that Knepper would suffer the particular adverse results of the medical services that Brown performed. It follows that plaintiffs' injuries were foreseeable as a result of Dex's intentional misrepresentation, and that is all that plaintiffs had to show. Dex must respond in damages accordingly.

We turn to Dex's next argument . . . Dex contends that, to prevent an unconstitutional chilling effect on the free flow of information, Oregon courts must recognize that publishers require some additional protection from claims arising out of false or misleading advertisements, and cannot be held liable for the publication of such advertisements unless the publication is done maliciously or with intent to harm another or in reckless disregard of that possibility.

We think that Dex's argument demands too much. This is not a case of the unwitting publication of an advertisement that turns out to be false. It is, instead, a case in which the publisher took a knowing and active part in the perpetration of the fraud. Punishing fraud has no impermissible "chilling" effect on the right to express views on "any subject whatever." *See* Article I, section 8, of the Oregon Constitution (protecting such a right of expression). Fraud is excepted from that constitutional protection. What Dex argues would extend constitutional protection to fraud, and we reject that argument.

As we have explained, plaintiffs' evidence permitted the jury to infer that the fraudulent misrepresentation by Dex and Brown was designed to mislead potential patients into believing that Brown was a board-certified plastic surgeon, thereby luring them into accepting surgery by Brown that he was not specially trained to perform. The misrepresentation created the risk that those who relied on it would be harmed as a particular result of Brown's lack of expertise as a plastic surgeon, and that is what happened to plaintiffs. The trial judge did not err in refusing to grant Dex's motions for directed verdict and judgment notwithstanding the jury's verdict. . . .

NOTES AND QUESTIONS

Advertiser Misconduct Doesn't Necessarily Relieve Publishers. According to the court, Dr. Brown made several misrepresentations directly to Mrs. Knepper after she saw the ad, and Dr. Brown's negligence in surgery is the most-direct cause of Mrs. Knepper's injuries. Why didn't Dr. Brown's subsequent misconduct cut off Dex's liability?

The "Empty Chair" Problem. Dr. Brown settled before trial, leaving Dex as the only defendant in front of the jury. This created a situation sometimes called the "empty chair" phenomenon. The jury may have had sympathy toward Mrs. Knepper and ire toward Dr.

Brown, but Dr. Brown wasn't around to punish. The jury could only direct that ire toward the remaining defendant, Dex. At minimum, it was a risky decision for Dex to proceed to a jury as the only defendant.

We might criticize Dex's decision to proceed to trial rather than settle after Dr. Brown settled. However, defendants' desire to avoid being the only defendant in front of a jury can set up a "race" among defendants to settle, which can allow the plaintiff to conduct an auction where the settlement price for each remaining defendant goes up as prior defendants settle.

Commissions and Rogue Salespeople. Often, advertising salespeople are paid on commission. In theory, commission compensation aligns the salesperson's interests with the company's interests of maximizing revenue. In practice, salespeople may be willing to stretch the truth to generate a sale, knowing that any repercussions from their misstatements will come long after they have spent their commission check. For example, it took a dozen years to get a final determination that Dex salesperson Mueller's sale was illegitimate. For this reason and others, commission compensation may not ensure salespeople act in the publisher's best interest. What could/should Dex have done differently to dissuade Mueller from overselling Dr. Brown?

B.   Publisher Liability for Advertisements (Online)

The general rule, exemplified by *New York Times v. Sullivan*, is that publishers are liable for the ads they disseminate. However, this rule does not apply to online publishers. In 1996, Congress enacted 47 U.S.C. § 230 (as part of the Communications Decency Act, or CDA), which in turn was part of the Telecommunications Act of 1996. 230(c)(1) says:

> No provider or user of an interactive computer service shall be treated as the publisher or speaker of any information provided by another information content provider.

A successful 230(c)(1) defense has three elements:

1) It applies to "providers or users of interactive computer services." All online publishers are presumptively covered by this term.

2) The plaintiff's claims must try to treat the defendant as a "publisher or speaker" of content. Courts have interpreted this language to apply to virtually all types of claims. However, the statute (230(e)) expressly excludes four types of claims from 230(c)'s coverage:

   o Prosecutions of federal crimes, although prosecutions of state crimes are preempted.
   o "Intellectual property claims." This clearly means that federal copyright and federal trademark claims are not preempted by Section 230. In most jurisdictions, state law IP claims, such as state trade-secret or publicity-rights claims, also are not preempted by Section 230. *See* Doe v.

> Friendfinder Network, Inc., 540 F. Supp. 2d 288 (D.N.H. 2008); Atlantic Recording Corp. v. Project Playlist, Inc., 603 F. Supp. 2d 690 (S.D.N.Y. 2009). However, in the Ninth Circuit, state IP claims *are* preempted by Section 230. Perfect 10 v. ccBill, 488 F.3d 1102 (9th Cir 2007); *see also* Hepp v. Facebook, Inc., 19-cv-04034-JMY (E.D. Pa. Jun. 5, 2020) (adopting *Perfect 10*). Furthermore, federal trade-secret claims pursuant to the Defend Trade Secrets Act *are* covered by Section 230.
>   o Claims under the federal Electronic Communications Privacy Act (an anti-wiretapping law) or analogous state laws.
>   o Certain claims related to the promotion of sex trafficking (the "FOSTA" exception).

If the plaintiff's claim does not fit in one of these statutory exclusions, Section 230 presumptively characterizes the claim as a "publisher or speaker" claim even if the term "publisher" or "speaker" isn't in the claim elements.

3) The claim must be based on "information provided by another information content provider." In general, this requirement distinguishes between first-party content (content originated by the publisher) and third-party content (someone else's content). If the plaintiff's claim relates to third-party content, as opposed to first-party content, Section 230 applies. The division between first-party content and third-party content is not always crystal clear, however. As a result, Section 230 litigation often explores this ambiguous division.

In effect, Section 230(c)(1) says that online publishers are categorically not liable for claims based on third-party content unless the claims are federal criminal prosecutions, IP claims (but only federal IP claims in the Ninth Circuit), sex-trafficking promotions or the Electronic Communications Privacy Act. The United States is the only country that has adopted such an intermediary-favorable rule.

Case law interpreting Section 230(c)(1) has virtually uniformly held that online publishers can claim Section 230(c)(1) protection for claims related to third-party advertisements. It does not matter that the publisher profits from the advertisement, even if its profits vary with user activity such as clicks or purchases. *See, e.g.*, Cisneros v. Yahoo!, Inc., CGC-04-433518 (Cal. Superior Ct. 2008) (addressing a case over search engines' display of gambling ads paid on a CPC basis: "the fact that defendants made money from selling IInternet access to sponsored sites [is] irrelevant to the application of Section 230."); Inventel Prods., LLC v. Li, 2019 U.S. Dist. LEXIS 175943 (D.N.J. Oct. 10, 2019) (Section 230 preempts application of New Jersey Consumer Fraud Act against Google for publishing deceptive materials created by others).

This next case illustrates a sophisticated but unsuccessful effort to undermine Section 230(c)(1)'s protection of a publisher (Google) for allegedly tortious third-party ads (mobile services). Why did Google accept these ads, and does it strike you as fair that Google has no responsibility for them? And does it make sense that the same ads might have generated liability for offline publishers?

GODDARD V. GOOGLE, INC., 640 F. SUPP. 2D 1193 (N. D. CAL. 2009)

I. BACKGROUND

Plaintiff Jenna Goddard ("Plaintiff") alleges that she and a class of similarly situated individuals were harmed as a result of clicking on allegedly fraudulent web-based advertisements for mobile subscription services.[*] She alleges that Defendant Google, Inc. ("Google") illegally furthered this scheme. . . . Google asserted that each of Plaintiff's claims was barred by § 230(c)(1) of the Communications Decency Act ("CDA"), which prevents a website from being treated as the "publisher or speaker" of third-party content, and thus typically immunizes website operators from liability arising from the transmission of such content. As Google argued, claims that seek to impose liability on a website operator as the speaker or publisher of third-party content—or to impose liability that is "merely a rephrasing of" such speaker or publisher liability, Barnes v. Yahoo!, Inc., 570 F.3d 1096, 1106 (9th Cir. 2009)—are barred by the CDA unless the website also is an "information content provider," meaning that it "is 'responsible, in whole or in part, for the creation or development of' the offending content." Fair Housing Council of San Fernando Valley v. Roommates.Com, LLC (Roommates), 521 F.3d 1157, 1162 (9th Cir. 2008) (en banc) (quoting 47 U.S.C. § 230(f)(3)).

Faced with the implications of this clear analytic framework, which was articulated in the Ninth Circuit's 2008 en banc decision in *Roommates*, Plaintiff resorted to creative argument in an attempt to show that her claims did not seek to hold Google liable for the dissemination of online content at all. The Court rejected Plaintiff's artful pleading and dismissed the complaint. Plaintiff was granted leave to amend, with express instructions that she attempt to "establish Google's involvement in 'creating or developing' the AdWords, either 'in whole or in part,'" so as to avoid CDA immunity.

In her amended complaint, Plaintiff now alleges that "Google's involvement [in creating the allegedly fraudulent advertisements] was so pervasive that the company controlled much of the underlying commercial activity engaged in by the third-party advertisers." Plaintiff alleges that Google "not only encourages illegal conduct, [but] collaborates in the development of the illegal content and, effectively, requires its advertiser customers to engage in it." These allegations, if supported by other specific allegations of fact, clearly would remove Plaintiff's action from the scope of CDA immunity. The quoted allegations, however, are mere "labels and conclusions" amounting to a "formulaic recitation of the elements" of CDA developer liability, and as such, they "will not do." Bell Atl. Corp. v. Twombly, 550 U.S. 544, 555 (2007). Rather, the Court must examine the pleading to determine whether Plaintiff alleges mechanisms that plausibly suggest the collaboration, control, or compulsion that she ascribes to Google's role in the creation of the offending AdWords. Having undertaken such an examination, the Court concludes that Plaintiff has not come close to substantiating the "labels and conclusions" by which she attempts to evade the reach of the CDA. Accordingly, her complaint once again must be dismissed. . . .

---

[*] [Editor's note: among other things at issue, the case involved advertisements for "free" ringtones that unexpectedly subscribed downloaders to subscription services charged through their cellphone bills.]

III. DISCUSSION

As explained at length in this Court's earlier order, the CDA has been interpreted to provide a "robust" immunity for Internet service providers and websites, with courts "adopting a relatively expansive definition of 'interactive computer service' and a relatively restrictive definition of 'information content provider.'" Carafano v. Metrosplash.com, Inc., 339 F.3d 1119, 1123 (9th Cir. 2003). Thus, a website operator does not become liable as an "information content provider" merely by "augmenting the content [of online material] generally." *Roommates*, 521 F.3d at 1167–68. Rather, the website must contribute "materially . . . to its alleged unlawfulness." *Id.* at 1167–68. A website does not so "contribute" when it merely provides third parties with neutral tools to create web content, even if the website knows that the third parties are using such tools to create illegal content. *See, e.g., id.* at 1169 & n. 24 (noting that where a plaintiff brings a claim "based on a website operator's passive acquiescence in the misconduct of its users," the website operator generally will be immune "even if the users committed their misconduct using tools of general availability provided by the website operator"); *see also* Zeran v. Am. Online, Inc., 129 F.3d 327, 333 (4th Cir. 1997) (holding that provider is shielded from liability despite receiving notification of objectionable content on its website and failing to remove it).

A. Developer liability

Plaintiff identifies several mechanisms by which Google allegedly contributes to the illegality of the offending advertisements, or even "requires" the inclusion of illegal content in such advertisements. Each of these mechanisms involves Google's "Keyword Tool," which Plaintiff describes as a "suggestion tool" employing an algorithm to suggest specific keywords to advertisers.[3] To demonstrate that the Keyword Tool is not a "neutral tool" of the kind uniformly permitted within the scope of CDA immunity, Plaintiff alleges that when a potential advertiser enters the word "ringtone" into Google's Keyword Tool, the tool suggests the phrase "free ringtone," and that this suggestion is more prevalent than others that may appear. Plaintiff contends that the suggestion of the word "free," when combined with Google's knowledge "of the mobile content industry's unauthorized charge problems," makes the Keyword Tool "neither innocuous nor neutral." Plaintiff also alleges that Google disproportionately suggests the use of the term "free ringtone" to ordinary users of Google's web search function, causing them to view the allegedly fraudulent MSSPs' [Editor's note: this is an acronym for "mobile subscription service provider"] AdWords with greater frequency.

Even assuming that Google is aware of fraud in the mobile subscription service industry and yet disproportionately suggests the term "free ringtone" in response to an advertiser's entry of the term "ringtone," Plaintiff's argument that the Keyword Tool "materially contributes" to the alleged illegality does not establish developer liability. The argument is nearly identical to that rejected by the Ninth Circuit in *Carafano v. Metrosplash*, 339 F.3d 1119 (9th Cir. 2003). There, the defendant website provided its users with a "detailed questionnaire" that included multiple-choice questions wherein "members select[ed] answers . . . from menus

---

[3] Plaintiff also alleges that Google representatives meet with certain advertisers in order to assist them with the creation of AdWords, but she does not allege that these representatives have contributed in any way to the allegedly illegal MSSP AdWords that give rise to this action.

providing between four and nineteen options." Although they included sexually suggestive phrases that might facilitate the development of libelous profiles, the menus of pre-prepared responses were considered neutral tools because "the selection of the content was left exclusively to the user."

Under *Carafano*, even if a particular tool "facilitate[s] the expression of information," it generally will be considered "neutral" so long as users ultimately determine what content to post, such that the tool merely provides "a framework that could be utilized for proper or improper purposes." Indeed, as already noted, the provision of neutral tools generally will not affect the availability of CDA immunity "even if a service provider knows that third parties are using such tools to create illegal content." As a result, a plaintiff may not establish developer liability merely by alleging that the operator of a website should have known that the availability of certain tools might facilitate the posting of improper content. Substantially greater involvement is required, such as the situation in which the website "elicits the allegedly illegal content and makes aggressive use of it in conducting its business."

Like the menus in *Carafano*, Google's Keyword Tool is a neutral tool. It does nothing more than provide options that advertisers may adopt or reject at their discretion. "[T]he selection of the content [is] left exclusively to the user." While a website clearly will not "automatically [enjoy] immun[ity] so long as the content originated with another information content provider," Plaintiff's allegations, if true, would not establish that Google did anything to encourage the posting of false or misleading AdWords, much less that Google "elicit[ed] . . . [or] ma[de] aggressive use of [them] in conducting its business." As in *Carafano*, where the dating website easily could have been expected to know that the inclusion of sexually suggestive options in its "pre-prepared" user profile responses might well encourage libelous impersonations or pranks, Plaintiff's suggestion that Google should have been aware of the danger of combining the words "free" and "ringtone" does not make Google a co-developer of the offending AdWords. Indeed, "the [allegedly misleading] posting[s] w[ere] contrary to [Google's] express polic[y]," which warns advertisers that they "are responsible for the keywords [they] select and for ensuring that [their] use of the keywords does not violate any applicable laws." . . .

. . . Plaintiff alleges that Google effectively "requires" advertisers to engage in illegal conduct. Yet Plaintiff's use of the word "requires" is inconsistent with the facts that Plaintiff herself alleges. The purported "requirement" flows from Google's alleged "suggestion" of the phrase "free ringtone" through its Keyword Tool, and from the MSSPs' purported knowledge that only "free ringtones" generate substantial revenue-producing Internet traffic. According to Plaintiff, MSSPs "[f]acing the Hobson's choice of accepting either Google's 'suggestions' or drastically reduced revenue . . . have accepted Google's 'suggestions' to include the keyword 'free' along with the keyword 'ringtone' in order to advertise to the majority of 'ringtone' searches, whether their products are free or not."

In Google's apt paraphrase, Plaintiff is alleging "that Google's mathematical algorithm 'suggests' the use of the word 'free' in relation to 'ringtone' as a means of attracting more visitors to [the MSSPs'] sites, and that MSSPs whose offerings are not actually free are literally powerless to resist." This reasoning fails to disclose a "requirement" of any kind, nor does it suggest the type of "direct and palpable" involvement that otherwise is required to avoid CDA immunity. Such involvement might occur where a website "remov[es] the word 'not' from a user's message reading '[Name] did not steal the artwork' in order to transform an innocent message into a libelous one." Even accepting Plaintiff's factual allegations as true, the allegations do not come close to suggesting involvement at such a level, or, indeed, that Google's AdWords program was anything other than "a framework that could be utilized for proper or improper purposes."

B. Contract claims in light of *Barnes v. Yahoo!*

As in her original complaint, Plaintiff alleges that she and similarly situated individuals were intended third-party beneficiaries of Google's Advertising Terms, which in turn incorporate a Content Policy requiring that mobile subscription service advertisers display certain information about their products, including whether downloading the products will result in charges to the consumer. Plaintiff alleges that Google "breached" its Content Policy. . . .

Read as broadly as possible, [the 2009 Ninth Circuit opinion in *Barnes v. Yahoo!*] stands for the proposition that when a party engages in conduct giving rise to an independent and enforceable contractual obligation, that party may be "h[eld] . . . liable [not] as a publisher or speaker of third-party content, but rather as a counter-party to a contract, as a promisor who has breached." Theoretically, intended third-party beneficiaries—whose rights under a contract are different from those of the contracting parties but still are legally cognizable— could invoke the distinction drawn in *Barnes* between liability for acts that are coextensive with publishing or speaking and liability for breach of an independent contractual duty. In a third-party-beneficiary case, "as in any other contract case, the duty the defendant allegedly violated [would] spring [ ] from a contract—an enforceable promise—not from any non-contractual conduct or capacity of the defendant." A court thus would be able to infer that the defendant had "implicitly agreed to an alteration" in the baseline rule that there is "no liability for publishing or speaking the content of other information service providers."

In the instant case, there is no allegation that Google ever promised Plaintiff or anyone else, in any form or manner, that it would enforce its Content Policy. Under California law, "[i]f a contract is to be a basis of liability for the [defendant's] violation of [its own terms and conditions] . . . [,] it must be a contract in which the [defendant] promises to abide by [these terms]." Google's Advertising Terms and incorporated Content Policy constituted a promise by Google's advertising customers to Google in exchange for participation in Google's advertising service. Neither agreement contains any promise by Google to enforce its terms of use or otherwise to remove noncompliant advertisements. *Cf.* Green v. America Online, 318 F.3d 465, 472 (3d Cir. 2003) (holding that "Green failed to state a claim for breach of contract because . . . by their terms, the Member Agreement and Community Guidelines were not intended to confer any rights on Green and AOL did not promise to protect Green from the acts of other subscribers").

Moreover, even if Google had promised to enforce its Advertising Terms and incorporated Content Policy—and it did not—Plaintiff would not be a third-party beneficiary of that promise. In that scenario, Google would be the promisor under the agreement and each allegedly fraudulent MSSP would be a promisee. But a third party is not an intended beneficiary of an agreement unless the promisee intends the agreement to benefit the third party. For Plaintiff to be an intended third-party beneficiary of Google's alleged promise, the Advertising Terms would have to reflect an intent by each allegedly fraudulent MSSP to benefit Plaintiff. That proposition simply is illogical, and this Court . . . is "aware of no case in which a third-party-beneficiary contract was formed when a promisee bargained for and obtained a promisor's engagement to force the promisee to satisfy its own obligation to the third party."

Undoubtedly, the allegedly fraudulent MSSPs did promise to abide by the Content Policy, and Plaintiff might well sue them as an intended third-party beneficiary of their contract with Google. But Plaintiff's claim against Google rests not on any promise, but on a "general [content] policy . . . on the part of [Google]," a theory of liability that *Barnes* expressly precludes. Plaintiff's inability to point to any promise by Google, and her ultimate reliance on Google's Content Policy, reveals that unlike the claim in *Barnes*, which rested on a promise that scarcely could have been clearer or more direct, Plaintiff's contract claim alleges liability that "is [not] different from, and [is] merely a rephrasing of, liability for negligent undertaking." This Court already has rejected Plaintiff's contract claim on that very ground . . . and now does so again.

IV. CONCLUSION

As in the original complaint, each of Plaintiff's claims would treat Google as the publisher or speaker of third-party content. Yet Plaintiff has failed to allege facts that plausibly would support a conclusion that Google created or developed, in whole or in part, any of the allegedly fraudulent AdWords advertisements. Plaintiff offers numerous theories of such involvement, but these theories merely lend truth to the Ninth Circuit's observation that there almost always will be some "argu[ment] that something the website operator did encouraged the illegality." As the en banc court cautioned in *Roommates*, only

> [w]here it is *very clear* that the website directly participates in developing the alleged illegality . . . [will] immunity . . . be lost. . . . [I]n cases of enhancement by implication or development by inference[,] . . . section 230 must be interpreted to protect websites not merely from ultimate liability, but from having to fight costly and protracted legal battles.

(emphasis added). Here, Plaintiff's theory is at best one of "enhancement by implication or development by inference." These "implications" and "inferences" fall well short of making it "very clear" that Google contributed to any alleged illegality, and Plaintiff's complaint clearly must be dismissed. . . .

[The court then declined to give the plaintiff a chance to file another amended complaint:] [T]he Ninth Circuit implicitly has identified a special form of "prejudice" to defendants who improperly are denied early dismissal of claims falling within the zone of CDA immunity. As the court stated in *Roommates*, "close cases . . . . must be resolved in favor of immunity, lest we cut the heart out of section 230 by forcing websites to . . . fight[ ] off claims that they promoted or encouraged—or at least tacitly assented to—the illegality of third parties." Because the CDA "must be interpreted to protect websites not merely from ultimate liability, but from having to fight costly and protracted legal battles," this Court's conclusion that Plaintiff almost certainly will be unable to state a claim compels the additional conclusion that Google must be extricated from this lawsuit now lest the CDA's "robust" protections be eroded by further litigation. For these reasons, Plaintiff's complaint will be dismissed without leave to amend.

NOTES AND QUESTIONS

Internet Exceptionalism. Section 230(c)(1) strikes many people as counterintuitive because it makes legal distinctions between the online and offline worlds. It exposes online publishers to far less liability for third-party ads than offline publishers face because offline publishers can be held liable for editorial decisions such as the decision to publish a particular ad, while the online publisher can't be.

For example, assume an advertiser runs the same ad in both an offline newspaper and a website. If the ad copy is defamatory, the offline newspaper shares equal liability for the ad, while the website would be immune—even though advertiser's identity and the content of the ad copy is identical! The medium of publication determines the liability result.

Would Section 230(c)(1) change the results in the *Sullivan* or *Knepper* cases if its legal principle applied to offline advertising?

Dismissal on a Motion to Dismiss. The court granted Google's 12(b)(6) motion to dismiss. This means that Google never had to answer the complaint, respond to discovery requests, file a summary judgment motion or convince a jury. If Section 230(c)(1) applies to a case, usually the result is a fairly cheap and early end to the lawsuit. As the opinion indicated, quick resolution of Section 230(c)(1)–immunized lawsuits advances the immunity's underlying policy.

How Far Can a Publisher Go in Helping an Advertiser Prepare Ad Copy and Still Remain Eligible for Section 230 Protection? The line between first-party content and third-party content can be ambiguous when online publishers help advertisers prepare ad copy. In the *Goddard* case, for example, Google suggested that advertisers buy certain terms as keyword ad triggers. The ultimate decision of which terms to purchase might ultimately rest with the advertiser, but Google's involvement could be influential. Does Google's persuasion differ from Mueller's influence of Dr. Brown's choices in the *Knepper* case? If Google's keyword-suggestion tool recommended that Dr. Brown purchase the keyword phrase "board-certified plastic and reconstructive surgery" for his advertisements, should Google be liable for any resulting personal injury?

While it's not clear just how much a publisher can help advertisers structure illegal ads, Section 230 definitely has limits. In *FTC v. LeadClick Media, LLC*, 838 F.3d 158 (2d Cir. 2016), LeadClick ran an affiliate network that provided ads to third-party websites, including fake-news websites, i.e., the articles about the advertiser's products looked like legitimate news articles and had consumer comments providing (also fake) testimonials. The Second Circuit held LeadClick had directly violated the FTC Act by committing deceptive acts, which the court tautologically said was "allowing" third parties to commit wrongful acts. Furthermore, LeadClick partially helped the websites develop their wrongful content by, for example, occasionally suggesting edits to the fake news websites.

Illegal Ads and the Federal Criminal Prosecution Exception. By its terms, Section 230 does not apply to federal criminal prosecutions. Google found out the hard way what happens when Section 230 isn't available. In 2011, the Department of Justice and Google settled allegations that Google had illegally accepted third-party advertisements for illicit pharmaceuticals (such as cheap Canadian pharmaceuticals). Google paid a civil forfeiture of $500 million, an amount comprising both Google's ad revenues from the illegal ads *plus* the profits made by the pharmaceutical retailers running those ads.

Liability for Linking. Some government agencies believe that a company is liable for third-party content it links to, as if the linked third-party content were the company's own advertising. *See, e.g.,* SEC Release Nos. 34-58288, IC-28351; File No. S7-23-08 (Aug. 7, 2008).

The SEC proposed that a securities issuer is responsible under securities laws for third-party web content it links to if "the context of the hyperlink and the hyperlinked information together create a reasonable inference that the company has approved or endorsed the hyperlinked information." Thus, if the linked content makes factual claims the issuer itself couldn't lawfully make, the guidance says linking to the content would violate the securities laws. But this would make the issuer (the company establishing the link) liable for third-party content on a remote website—exactly what Section 230 seems to prevent. See also the discussion in Chapter 18 about the FDA's policy on the need to submit third-party content for pre-review.

For a different result, *see In re* Gemtronics, Inc., Docket No. 9330, Initial Decision (F.T.C. A.L.J. Sept. 16, 2009) (a dietary supplement seller was not liable for comments on a website that it did not own or control but (among other things) it had linked to). When *should* an advertiser's attempts to increase the reach of existing content justify imposing responsibility for that content on the advertiser?

C.   Publisher "Must Carry" Obligations

With limited exceptions, publishers may freely refuse to publish ads for any reason. Stated differently, publishers cannot be required to publish ads against their will; such requirements violate the First Amendment's Freedom of Speech and Press clauses. The following Supreme Court case reinforced that expansive First Amendment interpretation.

MIAMI HERALD PUBLISHING CO. V. TORNILLO, 418 U.S. 241 (1974)

The issue in this case is whether a state statute granting a political candidate a right to equal space to reply to criticism and attacks on his record by a newspaper violates the guarantees of a free press.

I.

In the fall of 1972, appellee, Executive Director of the Classroom Teachers Association, apparently a teachers' collective bargaining agent, was a candidate for the Florida House of Representatives. On September 20, 1972, and again on September 29, 1972, appellant printed editorials critical of appellee's candidacy. In response to these editorials, appellee demanded that appellant print verbatim his replies, defending the role of the Classroom Teachers Association and the organization's accomplishments for the citizens of Dade County. Appellant declined to print the appellee's replies, and appellee brought suit in Circuit Court, Dade County, seeking declaratory and injunctive relief and actual and punitive damages in excess of $5,000. The action was premised on Florida Statute § 104.38 (1973), a "right of reply" statute which provides that, if a candidate for nomination or election is assailed regarding his personal character or official record by any newspaper, the candidate has the right to demand that the newspaper print, free of cost to the candidate, any reply the candidate may make to the newspaper's charges. The reply must appear in as conspicuous a place and in the same kind of type as the charges which prompted the reply, provided it does not take up more space than the charges. Failure to comply with the statute constitutes a first-degree misdemeanor. . . .

III.

A.

The challenged statute creates a right to reply to press criticism of a candidate for nomination or election. The statute was enacted in 1913, and this is only the second recorded case decided under its provisions.

Appellant contends the statute is void on its face because it purports to regulate the content of a newspaper in violation of the First Amendment. Alternatively it is urged that the statute is void for vagueness, since no editor could know exactly what words would call the statute into operation. It is also contended that the statute fails to distinguish between critical comment which is, and which is not, defamatory.

B.

The appellee and supporting advocates of an enforceable right of access to the press vigorously argue that government has an obligation to ensure that a wide variety of views reach the public. The contentions of access proponents will be set out in some detail. It is urged that, at the time the First Amendment to the Constitution was ratified in 1791 as part of our Bill of Rights, the press was broadly representative of the people it was serving. While many of the newspapers were intensely partisan and narrow in their views, the press collectively presented a broad range of opinions to readers. Entry into publishing was inexpensive; pamphlets and books provided meaningful alternatives to the organized press for the expression of unpopular ideas, and often treated events and expressed views not covered by conventional newspapers. A true marketplace of ideas existed in which there was relatively easy access to the channels of communication.

Access advocates submit that, although newspapers of the present are superficially similar to those of 1791, the press of today is in reality very different from that known in the early years of our national existence. In the past half century, a communications revolution has seen the introduction of radio and television into our lives, the promise of a global community through the use of communications satellites, and the specter of a "wired" nation by means of an expanding cable television network with two-way capabilities. The printed press, it is said, has not escaped the effects of this revolution. Newspapers have become big business, and there are far fewer of them to serve a larger literate population. Chains of newspapers, national newspapers, national wire and news services, and one-newspaper towns[13] are the dominant features of a press that has become noncompetitive and enormously powerful and influential in its capacity to manipulate popular opinion and change the course of events. Major metropolitan newspapers have collaborated to establish news services national in scope. Such national news organizations provide syndicated "interpretive reporting" as well as syndicated features and commentary, all of which can serve as part of the new school of "advocacy journalism."

The elimination of competing newspapers in most of our large cities, and the concentration of control of media that results from the only newspaper's [sic] being owned by the same interests which own a television station and a radio station, are important components of this trend toward concentration of control of outlets to inform the public. The result of these vast changes has been to place in a few hands the power to inform the American people and shape public opinion.[15] Much of the editorial opinion and commentary that is printed is that of syndicated columnists distributed nationwide and, as a result, we are told, on national and world issues there tends to be a homogeneity of editorial opinion, commentary, and interpretive analysis. The abuses of bias and manipulative reportage are, likewise, said to be the result of the vast accumulations of unreviewable power in the modern media empires. In effect, it is claimed, the public has lost any ability to respond or to contribute in a meaningful way to the debate on issues. The monopoly of the means of communication allows for little or no critical analysis of the media except in professional journals of very limited readership.

> This concentration of nationwide news organizations—like other large institutions—has grown increasingly remote from and unresponsive to the popular constituencies on which they depend and which depend on them.

Report of the Task Force in Twentieth Century Fund Task Force Report for a National News Council, A Free and Responsive Press 4 (1973). Appellee cites the report of the Commission on Freedom of the Press, chaired by Robert M. Hutchins, in which it was stated, as long ago as 1947, that "[t]he right of free public expression has . . . lost its earlier reality."

---

[13] "Nearly half of U.S. daily newspapers, representing some three-fifths of daily and Sunday circulation, are owned by newspaper groups and chains, including diversified business conglomerates. One-newspaper towns have become the rule, with effective competition operating in only 4 percent of our large cities." Background Paper by Alfred Balk in Twentieth Century Fund Task Force Report for a National News Council, A Free and Responsive Press 18 (1973).

[15] "Local monopoly in printed news raises serious questions of diversity of information and opinion. What a local newspaper does not print about local affairs does not see general print at all. And, having the power to take initiative in reporting and enunciation of opinions, it has extraordinary power to set the atmosphere and determine the terms of local consideration of public issues." B. Bagdikian, The Information Machines 127 (1971).

The obvious solution, which was available to dissidents at an earlier time when entry into publishing was relatively inexpensive, today would be to have additional newspapers. But the same economic factors which have caused the disappearance of vast numbers of metropolitan newspapers, have made entry into the marketplace of ideas served by the print media almost impossible. It is urged that the claim of newspapers to be "surrogates for the public" carries with it a concomitant fiduciary obligation to account for that stewardship. From this premise, it is reasoned that the only effective way to insure fairness and accuracy and to provide for some accountability is for government to take affirmative action. The First Amendment interest of the public in being informed is said to be in peril because the "marketplace of ideas" is today a monopoly controlled by the owners of the market. . . .

IV.

However much validity may be found in these arguments, at each point the implementation of a remedy such as an enforceable right of access necessarily calls for some mechanism, either governmental or consensual. If it is governmental coercion, this at once brings about a confrontation with the express provisions of the First Amendment and the judicial gloss on that Amendment developed over the years. . . .

We see that . . . the Court has expressed sensitivity as to whether a restriction or requirement constituted the compulsion exerted by government on a newspaper to print that which it would not otherwise print. The clear implication has been that any such a compulsion to publish that which "'reason' tells them should not be published" is unconstitutional. A responsible press is an undoubtedly desirable goal, but press responsibility is not mandated by the Constitution, and, like many other virtues, it cannot be legislated.

Appellee's argument that the Florida statute does not amount to a restriction of appellant's right to speak, because "the statute in question here has not prevented the Miami Herald from saying anything it wished," begs the core question. Compelling editors or publishers to publish that which "'reason' tells them should not be published" is what is at issue in this case. The Florida statute operates as a command in the same sense as a statute or regulation forbidding appellant to publish specified matter. Governmental restraint on publishing need not fall into familiar or traditional patterns to be subject to constitutional limitations on governmental powers. The Florida statute exacts a penalty on the basis of the content of a newspaper. The first phase of the penalty resulting from the compelled printing of a reply is exacted in terms of the cost in printing and composing time and materials and in taking up space that could be devoted to other material the newspaper may have preferred to print. It is correct, as appellee contends, that a newspaper is not subject to the finite technological limitations of time that confront a broadcaster, but it is not correct to say that, as an economic reality, a newspaper can proceed to infinite expansion of its column space to accommodate the replies that a government agency determines or a statute commands the readers should have available.

Faced with the penalties that would accrue to any newspaper that published news or commentary arguably within the reach of the right-of-access statute, editors might well conclude that the safe course is to avoid controversy. Therefore, under the operation of the Florida statute, political and electoral coverage would be blunted or reduced. . . .

Even if a newspaper would face no additional costs to comply with a compulsory access law and would not be forced to forgo publication of news or opinion by the inclusion of a reply, the Florida statute fails to clear the barriers of the First Amendment because of its intrusion into the function of editors. A newspaper is more than a passive receptacle or conduit for news, comment, and advertising. The choice of material to go into a new paper, and the decisions made as to limitations on the size and content of the paper, and treatment of public issues and public official—whether fair or unfair—constitute the exercise of editorial control and judgment. It has yet to be demonstrated how governmental regulation of this crucial process can be exercised consistent with First Amendment guarantees of a free press as they have evolved to this time. . . .

[JUSTICES BRENNAN and WHITE filed concurrences. Justice White's concurrence observed that Florida's "law runs afoul of the elementary First Amendment proposition that government may not force a newspaper to print copy which, in its journalistic discretion, it chooses to leave on the newsroom floor."]

NOTES AND QUESTIONS

The 1970s Media Industry. As the case indicates, the 1970s saw a lot of media-industry consolidation. At the time of the case, many communities had a small number of publishers who could reach an appreciable percentage of the local community—one daily newspaper, up to three broadcast television stations and some radio stations. If, for whatever reason, one of those publishers exhibited bias or made an error and wasn't willing to correct it, there were not many alternative ways in the local community to advance a counter-narrative.

Today's media industry is very different. Concentration has accelerated further: Sinclair Broadcast Group, for example, owns hundreds of television stations across the country and mandates that they all share the same conservative programming with their viewers, and newspaper consolidation is much more advanced than it was in the 1970s. Yet it can still be hard to find a single publisher who can reach large percentages of a given local community. Anyone who has a problem with a publisher's bias or errors can self-publish through websites, blogs, message boards or email lists but may not be able to find the same audience that the original publisher reached. Facebook and Google offer new points of concentration, spurring objections when Google removes a website from its search index or restricts a search advertiser. We will revisit objections to Google's marketplace power in the *Langdon* case below.

The 1970s media consolidation makes the *Miami Herald* case even more remarkable. The Court effectively says that, even if a single publisher has a de facto monopoly on the ability to reach the local community, it still cannot be forced to carry unwanted content. Presumably, in the modern media ecosystem with multitudinous publication alternatives, must-carry obligations on publishers would be even less justified.

Exception: Broadcasting. Unlike other publishers, broadcasters licensed by the Federal Communications Commission (FCC) can be subject to must-carry obligations. Consider the "Equal Time Rule," 47 U.S.C. § 315. The rule requires broadcasters to provide political candidates with equal broadcasting opportunities. As a result, if a broadcaster sells a one-minute ad to one candidate, it must allow that candidate's opponents to buy a one-minute ad at favorable prices. Broadcaster must-carry obligations are premised, in part, on the perception that broadcast spectrum is scarce, which necessitates regulatory restriction on entry to the broadcast market. Other media do not have the same legal restrictions on marketplace entry, which reduces the importance of must-carry obligations for those media.

Exception: Government as Advertising Venue Provider. When the government is the "publisher" or otherwise sells advertising inventory, must-carry rules take on a different perspective. Because the government's rejection of advertisements constitutes state action restricting the advertiser's speech, the advertiser can challenge the rejection as a Constitutional violation.

In *Perry Education Association v. Perry Local Educators' Association*, 460 U.S. 37 (1983), a school district gave the teachers' union a preferential right to distribute materials through the interschool mail system. A rival union complained that this preferential distribution right violated its First Amendment rights. The U.S. Supreme Court ultimately rejected the complaint, saying that the mail system did not qualify as a "public forum" or "limited public forum," in which the government would not be allowed to discriminate on the basis of content or viewpoint. The Court then determined that the school district's restrictions were reasonable:

> [W]hen government property is not dedicated to open communication, the government may—without further justification—restrict use to those who participate in the forum's official business. Finally, the reasonableness of the limitations on PLEA's access to the school mail system is also supported by the substantial alternative channels that remain open for union-teacher communication to take place. These means range from bulletin boards to meeting facilities to the United States mail. . . . There is no showing here that PLEA's ability to communicate with teachers is seriously impinged by the restricted access to the internal mail system. The variety and type of alternative modes of access present here compare favorably with those in other nonpublic forum cases where we have upheld restrictions on access.

Courts have divided on how to treat advertising allowed by public authorities on property open to the public. *Compare, e.g.,* Seattle Mideast Awareness Campaign v. King County, 781 F. 3d 489 (9th Cir. 2015) (finding public-transit advertising to be a limited public forum and that transit authorities could impose restrictions on false or misleading speech), *with, e.g.,* AFDI v. Suburban Mobility Auth. for Reg'l Transp., 698 F. 3d 885 (6th Cir. 2012) (finding that, by allowing political advertising, transit authority created a designated public forum and could not further restrict content without satisfying strict scrutiny) *and* Christ's Bride Ministries, Inc. v. Se. Pa. Transp. Auth., 148 F.3d 242 (3d Cir. 1998) (transit authority's decision to remove anti-abortion ads would not have satisfied rational basis review).

Statutory Protection for Refusing Ads. In addition to the First Amendment, 47 U.S.C. § 230(c)(2)—another part of the Communications Decency Act that supplements Section 230(c)(1) discussed above—provides online publishers with a statutory safe harbor for refusing ads. It states:

> No provider or user of an interactive computer service shall be held liable on account of (A) any action voluntarily taken in good faith to restrict access to or availability of material that the provider or user considers to be obscene, lewd, lascivious, filthy, excessively violent, harassing, or otherwise objectionable, whether or not such material is constitutionally protected. . . .

The next case shows how Section 230 supplements the First Amendment to give publishers the discretion to reject unwanted ads.

LANGDON V. GOOGLE, INC., 474 F. SUPP. 2D 622 (D. DEL. 2007)

. . . Plaintiff has two IInternet websites; www.NCJusticeFraud.com ("NCJustice") and www.ChinaIsEvil.com ("China"). The Amended Complaint alleges that the NCJustice website exposes fraud perpetrated by various North Carolina government officials and employees, including Roy Cooper ("Cooper"), the North Carolina Attorney General, and that the China website delineates atrocities committed by the Chinese government. The Amended Complaint alleges that Defendants refused to run ads on the two websites, specifically two Cooper ads on the NCJustice website and one ad on the China website.

More particularly, Plaintiff alleges that Google gave a fraudulent excuse for not running the Cooper ads, that the reasons for refusal do not appear in its website or in its ad content policy, and that Google gave no reason for not running the China ad. . . .

Plaintiff's allegations against Microsoft are that he applied for and was accepted into Microsoft's pilot ad program, submitted his China ad, but never received a response. Plaintiff alleges that ignoring him resulted in a de facto refusal to run his ad. He alleges that Microsoft is using fraud to breach its contract.

Plaintiff's allegations against Yahoo are that he attempted to advertise on Yahoo's search engine, but was told by a Yahoo representative that it does not accept advertising for websites it does not host. Plaintiff alleges he wrote to Yahoo regarding the matter but received no response. . . .

Plaintiff alleges that he has no viable alternative other than to advertise on Defendants' search engines. He seeks declaratory and injunctive relief and compensatory and punitive damages. . . .

3. Defendants' First Amendment Rights

Google and Microsoft argue that Plaintiff's claims are barred as a matter of law, and that the relief sought by him is precluded by their First Amendment Rights. Google points to the relief sought by Plaintiff that Google, Yahoo, and Microsoft place Plaintiff's ads for his websites in prominent places on their search engine results and that Defendants "honestly" rank Plaintiff's websites.

Google argues that such relief would compel it to speak in a manner deemed appropriate by Plaintiff and would prevent Google from speaking in ways that Plaintiff dislikes. It contends such relief contravenes the First Amendment. Plaintiff did not respond to this issue.

The First Amendment guarantees an individual the right to free speech, "a term necessarily comprising the decision of both what to say and what not to say." Defendants are correct in their position that the injunctive relief sought by Plaintiff contravenes Defendants' First Amendment rights. *See* Miami Herald Publ'g Co. v. Tornillo, 418 U.S. 241 (1974) (forcing newspapers to print candidates' replies to editorials is an impermissible burden on editorial control and judgment); Sinn v. The Daily Nebraskan, 829 F.2d 662 (8th Cir. 1987) (University newspaper's rejection of roommate advertisements in which advertisers stated their gay or lesbian orientation was a constitutionally protected editorial decision); Associates & Aldrich Co. v. Times Mirror Co., 440 F.2d 133 (9th Cir. 1971) (Court cannot compel the publisher of a private daily newspaper to accept and print advertising in the exact form submitted based upon the freedom to exercise subjective editorial discretion in rejecting a proffered article). Accordingly, the Court will grant Google's and Microsoft's Motion To Dismiss the Amended Complaint on the basis that Plaintiff seeks relief precluded by their First Amendment rights.

4. Communications Decency Act

Google and Microsoft argue that the Communications Decency Act, 47 U.S.C. § 230(c)(2)(A), provides them immunity from suit from claims grounded upon their exercise of editorial discretion over Internet content and editorial decisions regarding screening and deletion of content from their services. . . .

Plaintiff argues that § 230 is inapplicable because none of the Defendants refused to run the Cooper ads because they were obscene or that the websites were harassing. He also argues that neither Google nor Microsoft offered a reason for not running the China ads and that Yahoo provided a false reason for not running the ads. Plaintiff argues that Defendants cannot create "purported reasons" for not running the ads. . . .

It is evident from the allegations in the Amended Complaint that Plaintiff attempts to hold Defendants liable for decisions relating to the monitoring, screening, and deletion of content from their network. As noted by the *Green* Court, these actions are "quintessentially related to a publisher's role" and "§ 230 'specifically proscribes liability' in such circumstances."

Plaintiff's position that § 230 is inapplicable is not well-taken. Plaintiff argues there was no refusal to run his ads on the basis they were obscene or harassing, and that Defendants cannot create "purported reasons for not running his ads." He omits, however, reference to that portion of § 230 which provides immunity from suit for restricting material that is "otherwise objectionable."

Section 230 provides Google, Yahoo, and Microsoft immunity for their editorial decisions regarding screening and deletion from their network. Therefore, the Court will grant the Motions To Dismiss all such claims as raised by Plaintiff.

5. Plaintiff's First Amendment Rights

Defendants argue that Plaintiff cannot state a claim for violation of his right to free speech under either the United States or Delaware Constitution because they are not state actors. Particularly, Google contends that the Amended Complaint makes clear that it is a for-profit company as it is identified as a corporation and there are allegations of Google's for-profit AdWords program.

Plaintiff alleges that Internet search engines are public forums, and that private property opened to the public may be subject to the First Amendment. Plaintiff compares Internet search engines to malls and/or shopping centers and contends that Google has dedicated its private property as a public forum. Plaintiff relies upon several U.S. Supreme Court cases to support his position. He also posits that Google works with private and public universities and that this government entwinement with a private entity results in state action as required by 42 U.S.C. § 1983.

When bringing a § 1983 claim, a plaintiff must allege that some person has deprived him of a federal right, and that the person who caused the deprivation acted under color of state law. To act under "color of state law" a defendant must be "clothed with the authority of state law."

Plaintiff has failed to state a claim that Defendants violated his First Amendment right to free speech. Defendants are private, for profit companies, not subject to constitutional free speech guarantees. They are Internet search engines that use the Internet as a medium to conduct business. . . .

Plaintiff's analogy of Defendants' private networks to shopping centers and his position that since they are open to the public they become public forums is not supported by case law. The Supreme Court has consistently held that a private shopping center is not a public forum for speech purposes. The Court has routinely rejected the assumption that people who want to express their views in a private facility, such as a shopping center, have a constitutional right to do so. Private property does not "lose its private character merely because the public is generally invited to use it for designated purposes." Similarly, the Court finds unavailing Plaintiff's argument that he has no reasonable alternative to advertising on Defendants' search engines. *See* Cyber Promotions, Inc. v. American Online, Inc., 948 F.Supp. 436, 443 (E.D. Pa. 1996) (private company had numerous alternatives for reaching customers including mail, television, cable, newspapers, magazines, and competing commercial online services).

Defendants are not state actors. Plaintiff has failed to state a § 1983 claim, and therefore, the Court will grant the Motions To Dismiss the First Amendment Claims. . . .

NOTES AND QUESTIONS

Courts routinely conclude that search engines have virtually unrestricted discretion to decide what content to carry and how to order it, relying on First Amendment and Section 230 grounds. *See, e.g.*, O'Kroley v. Fastcase, Inc., 831 F.3d 352 (6th Cir. 2016); Zhang v. Baidu.com, Inc., 10 F. Supp. 3d 433 (S.D.N.Y. 2014); *see also* Prager Univ. v. Google LLC, 951 F.3d 991 (N.D. Cal. 2020) (YouTube isn't a "company town" and therefore is not obligated to follow the First Amendment for its users).

If all of the major search engines independently decide not to carry Langdon's search ads, what cost-effective advertising alternatives does Langdon have in practice? Note that search advertising is usually charged on a cost-per-click basis, meaning that Langdon does not have to pay for running the ads unless someone clicks on them. Therefore, unlike many forms of advertising which require an upfront payment, search advertising can be extremely low-cost for highly targeted, lightly clicked ads. Then again, due to Google's ad quality score, Langdon's ads will not necessarily show to consumers regardless of what bids Langdon placed for his ads.

5.   Advertisers' Payments to Publishers

This subpart looks at some common issues with payments between advertisers and publishers.

Payment Methods for Advertising

Publishers typically charge advertisers using one of the following methods:

- *Fixed Fee.* The advertiser pays a fixed amount for the advertising services, such as a set monthly fee, regardless of how many people actually see the ad copy. Roadside billboards and consumer-classified advertisements in print periodicals are typically charged on this basis.

- *Per Impression.* The advertiser pays based on the number of consumers who are exposed to the ad copy, typically priced in blocks of 1,000 consumers. As a result, it is often called "CPM" advertising (cost per thousand impressions, where "M" is the Roman numeral for 1,000). Broadcast advertising and online-display advertising is often sold on a CPM basis.

- *Per Click/Per Call.* The advertiser pays based on the number of consumers who directly respond to the advertiser. For example, online keyword advertising is typically charged on a cost-per-click ("CPC") basis. Each time a consumer clicks on the link in the keyword ad, the advertiser pays the agreed-upon CPC amount. A variation is to charge per-call for the number of phone calls to a unique telephone number in the ad copy (*see, e.g.*, Google AdWords' bid-per-call option).

- *Per Action.* Sometimes, the advertiser wants consumers to take a specified action beyond just clicking or calling, such as filling out an online form or creating an online account. An ad may be charged on a cost-per-action ("CPA") basis when consumers take the desired action. A variation is when advertisers pay for every new customer attributable to the publisher, regardless of how much the customer spends with the advertiser. These ads may be described as cost-per-acquisition (also "CPA").

- *Revenue Share.* An advertiser can pay the publisher by sharing incremental revenues generated by ads disseminated by the publisher. For example, many online retailers pay independent contractors ("affiliates") a percentage of all new sales directly attributable to the affiliate's promotional efforts. *Note:* In some industries, such as real estate, travel, medical and legal services, getting paid a commission may require the publisher to have the requisite state-issued license or may be an illegal referral scheme.

How do publishers and advertisers decide which payment method is best? In a perfectly efficient market, it shouldn't matter. Assume that an advertiser is running a direct-response advertisement for a widget it makes that will generate $1.00 of gross profit per unit, and the advertiser is willing to share half of that profit ($0.50 per unit) with the publisher. Assume a print publisher has an audience of 1,000,000 readers, 1% of the readers will contact the advertiser in response to the ad (10,000 readers), and 2.5% of those will actually buy an average of one widget (resulting in 250 buyers and 250 widgets sold). In this case, the advertisement will generate $250 of gross profit for the advertiser. The advertiser should be willing to pay:

- On a fixed-fee basis: $125 (50% of the advertiser's expected profits)
- On a CPM basis: 12.5 cents CPM (1 million, or 1,000 M, readers x $0.125 CPM = $125)
- On a CPC basis: 1.25 cents (10,000 reader contacts x $0.0125 = $125)
- Using a revenue share: if the product price is $10, then gross revenue would be $2,500 (gross profit, as noted above, is $250), and the revenue share would be 5%.

In reality, the parties often won't know how well the ad will actually perform. Unless the publisher and advertiser have a solid track record of experience with each other, neither party may know how the publisher's audience will respond to the advertiser's offering.

As a result, the different pricing options effectively shift risk between the advertiser and the publisher. With the fixed-fee option, the publisher knows exactly how much it will be paid, and the advertiser assumes all of the risk about the audience's propensity to buy its offering.

In contrast, with a revenue share, the advertiser takes no risk—it only pays if it gets new incremental sales—while the publisher assumes all of the risk of performance. Thus, with the revenue share, the publisher might get paid zero dollars for its advertising services, even if the poor performance is due solely to how the advertiser handles interested consumers and not due to the publisher's failure to deliver interested consumers.

Ad pricing options can be placed on a risk continuum:

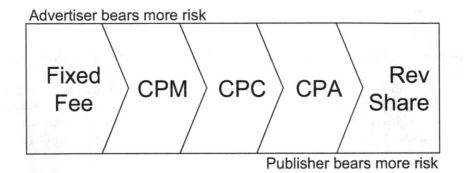

As you can see, CPC advertising fits in the middle of the risk continuum. The publisher takes some risk that it can deliver consumers to the advertiser's doorstep, but once there, the advertiser has the onus to convert those consumers into buyers. Meanwhile, the advertiser does not pay the publisher anything until the publisher delivers a consumer to the advertiser's doorstep. This compromise in risk sharing may help explain the massive success of CPC pricing for online-keyword advertising. At minimum, it gives one good explanation for why many advertisers prefer CPC keyword advertising over fixed-fee ads like Yellow Pages, where advertisers bear all of the performance risk.

The risk continuum is less relevant to brand advertising, which does not seek to generate immediate sales anyway but aims to increase consumer familiarity with and trust for the brand. Instead, for mass-market consumer goods, brand advertisers often want widespread exposure to as many consumers as possible. This partially explains why brand advertisers frequently accept CPM advertising for broadcast ads—broadcasters can deliver big audiences, and the risks to advertisers inherent in CPM advertising matter less. (Also, broadcast may be more effective at communicating brand messages to consumers than print or text.)

Tracking and Measuring Activity

With CPM, CPC and CPA advertising, the compensated activity must be tracked by someone. For, example, who determines how many ad impressions were delivered? Advertisers are reluctant to rely on publisher self-reporting of impressions. After all, publishers—and their commissioned salespeople—have financial incentives to lie.

As a result, in some sectors of the advertising industry, third-party service providers measure publisher activity. For example, the Nielsen service measures the number of TV broadcast viewers and radio listeners. Its measurement methodologies can vary, but often the measurement vendors use population sampling to measure the media consumption of a small but statistically significant subgroup. Vendors can then extrapolate those numbers to the larger community.

In the print-publishing business, the Alliance for Audited Media (AAM), formerly known as the Audit Bureau of Circulations (ABC), is a leading service provider. The AAM promulgates general rules for counting the number of copies circulated by publishers (such as how to count paid subscriptions and freely distributed copies) and audits individual publishers to verify their counts.

The Prevalence of Fraud

Despite the AAM, print publishers have been caught overstating their circulation numbers to advertisers with disquieting frequency. For example, in the early 2000s, major newspapers such as *Newsday*, the *Chicago Sun-Times* and the *Dallas Morning News* were all embroiled in circulation inflation scandals. *See, e.g.*, Frank Ahrens, *Circulation Fraud Contained, Audit Group Says*, WASH. POST, Nov. 12, 2004.

In re Newsday Litigation, 2008 WL 2884784 (E.D.N.Y. 2008), gives some perspective of the financial and criminal repercussions of circulation measurement fraud. The court says:

> The fraud was massive, resulting in losses affecting tens of thousands of victim advertisers in an amount originally estimated by Tribune itself as exceeding eighty million dollars. The charging documents generally allege that the fraud continued for almost four years, from January of 2000 through July of 2004.

Nine individuals were prosecuted as part of the fraud. In addition, *Newsday* and its sibling publication *Hoy* entered into an agreement with the federal government. According to the court:

> In the agreement, Newsday and Hoy each admit that they
>
>> violated federal criminal law by engaging in schemes that defrauded their advertisers, by systematically inflating paid circulation numbers reported in their books and records and falsely representing the accuracy of the inflated numbers to the Audit Bureau of Circulations ("ABC"), an industry organization.
>
> Newsday and Hoy further acknowledge in the agreement that they have made payments "of approximately $83 million, to date, to entities that placed ads in Newsday and Hoy in settlement of pending or potential claims" related to the circulation fraud. In addition, both Newsday and Hoy have agreed to pay $15 million to settle a civil forfeiture action commenced by the United States....

Measurement service providers for online activities generally have not yet gained the degree of recognition that providers like Nielsen and AAM have garnered offline. Accordingly, it is still fairly common for online publishers to self-report the number of ad impressions or clicks they deliver to advertisers. When online advertisers pay on a "cost-pe- action" or "revenue-share" basis, the advertisers measure the actions or revenues and report back to publishers. Reports of online activities are not easily verified by third parties, so online publishers and advertisers often disagree with each other about the measurements.

One "marketer turned ad fraud researcher" says that the rate of fraud in any digital ad campaign is "[b]etween 1 percent and 100 percent. There are no 0 percent fraud campaigns, that just means you're not seeing it." George P. Slefo, *Ad Fraud Fighter Augustine Fou*, ADAGE, Oct. 15, 2019.

His examples include mobile apps that load ads in background even when humans aren't using them. He blames intermediary companies who maximize their own profit when they maximize ad volume, but he also suggests that people in charge of digital marketing have incentives to spend all the budget allocated to them, and so they may not want to know about fraud. Double-digit click-through rates look attractive and successful, so it's hard to admit that they might signal fraud, not profit.

Disagreements About Numbers

The parties may also dispute the definition of the measured activity in the advertising contract. For example, in *Go2Net, Inc. v. C.I. Host, Inc.*, 60 P.3d 1245 (Wash. Ct. App. 2003), the advertiser agreed to pay for ad "impressions" but claimed that the online publisher Go2Net was overstating the number. The advertising agreements did not define the term "impressions." However, the agreements provided that the publisher's equipment would count the number of impressions:

> All impressions billed are based on Go2Net's ad engine count of impressions. In the event of a conflict between the number of impressions reported by Go2Net, Inc. and any remote server, the Go2Net, Inc. count stands. All payments will be based on Go2Net, Inc. ad server counts.

The contract added:

> Go2Net makes no representations or warranties relating to the results of Advertiser's advertising by means of the Internet, including without limitation, the number of page views or click-thrus such advertising will receive and any promotional effect thereof.

This set up an easy win for the publisher:

> Go2Net did exactly what the agreement said it could do: it billed C I Host based on Go2Net's ad engine count of impressions. Had C I Host wished to ensure that Go2Net's ad engine was counting only the number of times a human actually viewed the ad, it should have contracted to count the number of impressions itself, or specified its own definition of "impressions" in the agreements.

NOTES AND QUESTIONS

Non-Performance as a Defense to a Collections Action. Frequently, when a publisher sues an advertiser for non-payment, the advertiser will disparage the publisher's performance as a defense or counterclaim. By getting advertisers to prepay for advertising, publishers can avoid having to sue their customers for non-payment and avoid the associated risk of non-performance counterclaims.

Counting Robotic Activity. In the *Go2Net* case, the publisher was in the uncomfortable position of arguing that the advertiser should pay for impressions generated automatically by third-party activity. In many situations, publishers would automatically screen out those impressions and not attempt to charge for them. Some disputes arise when the publisher is less conservative about discounting automated activity than the advertiser would like the publisher to be.

Performance Assumptions. In *Go2Net*, the advertiser made certain assumptions about the number of clicks the advertisements would generate, and the advertiser canceled the ad campaign when the publisher failed to meet those assumptions. If the advertiser really cared about click-throughs, why did the parties agree to measure the publisher's performance based on impressions?

"Bad traffic" (i.e., poorly performing referrals from a publisher) is a common complaint by advertisers. To overcome this advertiser fear, Meredith, a major print publisher that charged for ads per impression, contractually promised to deliver a minimum sales "lift" (i.e., new incremental sales) for its largest advertisers. *See* Nat Ives, *Meredith Guarantees Top Advertisers Sales Gains*, AD. AGE, July 25, 2011.

Industry Standards. An industry group, the Internet Advertising Bureau (IAB), has developed guidelines for defining impressions that many publishers and advertisers now refer to. IAB, *Ad Impression Measurement Guidelines*, https://www.iab.com/guidelines/iab-measurement-guidelines/.

Under-Delivery. When publishers fail to deliver a promised number of impressions, they often fix this problem by giving the advertiser "make-goods," which are subsequent additional ads provided at no additional cost to reach the contracted quantity. For example, if a TV broadcaster promises that an upcoming TV series episode will deliver 5,000,000 viewers but the episode actually only attracts 3,000,000 viewers, the broadcaster may promise to "make good" the unrealized 2,000,000 viewers through subsequent additional advertising. A make-good remedy means the publisher doesn't have to refund money to advertisers for underperformance.

What is a "Click"? A lot of the online advertising in the 1990s was sold on a per-impression basis. Although some online advertising is still sold per-impression, CPC advertising has eclipsed it in importance.

However, measuring activity on a "per-click" basis does not eliminate definitional ambiguity. In the mid-2000s, advertisers brought class-action lawsuits against both Google and Yahoo claiming that the search engines charged for illegitimate clicks on the advertisers' CPC ads—a phenomenon called "click fraud," although the "fraud" reference may be a misnomer (or at least overly dramatic). Click fraud can occur in a variety of ways, including:

- Outright overstatement of activity.
- Charging for clicks produced by automated behavior, such as by robots automatically following online links.

- Charging for clicks that are made for illegitimate purposes. For example, competitor A may click on competitor B's ads to drain competitor B's advertising budget; or if the search engine "syndicates" the ad to a third-party website and shares some of the revenue with the website, the website operator has a financial incentive to click on the ad.

Both search engines ultimately entered into multi-million-dollar settlements with advertisers over these claims.

What is a "Visitor"? In *WebMD, LLC v. RDA International, Inc.*, 22 Misc. 3d 1114 (N.Y. Sup. Ct. 2009), the parties contracted for the publisher to deliver "36,000 visitors" to a specified website. The advertiser subsequently contended that the contract meant 36,000 *unique* visitors. The difference could be substantial; visitors who visited the specified website more than once would be counted as one unique visitor, under the advertiser's interpretation, and as a visitor each time they arrived at the specified website, under the publisher's interpretation. Like the advertiser's arguments in *Go2Net*, the advertiser's argument went nowhere:

> [A]lthough undefined, the term "visitors" is unambiguous. The definitions advanced by the organizations quoted by [advertiser] refer to "unique visitors," and do not define the term "visitor" to mean "unique visitor." If [advertiser] wished to be guaranteed "unique visitors" to the site, it should have specified such in the agreement.

Contract-Drafting Tips. Publishers should be very precise in their contracts about what they are delivering to advertisers. They should also include, as the publisher in *Go2Net* did, a provision saying that their measurements are determinative.

Advertisers also should precisely define what they are buying. If the advertiser wants *unique* visitors, it should say so. Or, if impressions are just a proxy for some other desired behavior (like clicks), the advertiser should make its performance assumptions explicit in the contract. Of course, this may be easier said than done. For example, unless you are a major advertiser, good luck negotiating with Google over its AdWords contract.

This chapter covers two major areas in which unique regulatory concerns are at issue. First, we examine food, drug and supplement regulation—each of which alone could justify a separate course. Second, we examine "organic" and other environmental or "green" claims, which implicate profound questions of scientific and agricultural policy, highlighting the ways in which regulators themselves can affect whether a word is truthful or meaningful as used in advertising.

1. The Food and Drug Administration (FDA)

Food, drugs, supplements and cosmetics (which we will not mention further in this section) are regulated by the FTC and the FDA, and they have overlapping jurisdiction. In 1971, the agencies issued a memorandum of understanding under which the FDA assumed primary responsibility for drug labeling and the FTC assumed primary responsibility for the advertising of food, medical devices and cosmetics. The FDA is responsible for ads for prescription drugs, and the FTC covers ads for over-the-counter drugs.

A. Prescription Drugs and Medical Devices

The FDA's authority to regulate prescription drug and medical device advertising arises from the 1938 Federal Food, Drug, and Cosmetic Act (FDCA), which authorizes the agency to comprehensively regulate drugs and medical devices in the United States.

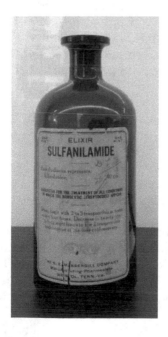

This photo from the FDA's Maryland headquarters shows a bottle of sulfanilamide elixir, which killed over 100 people in 1937, when the FDA lacked any substantial regulatory authority. The product was released even though the deadly ingredient, diethylene glycol, was known to be poisonous and even though simple animal tests would have revealed the danger. This incident led directly to the 1938 enactment of the FDCA, which, at first, limited the FDA's authority to safety regulation. Later, the FDA gained authority over drug efficacy (as it became clear that whether a drug is "safe" often depends on what condition it is supposed to treat).

As part of its mandate, the FDA regulates all forms of prescription drug advertising, including direct-to-consumer advertising. It generally defines advertising expansively to include any information, other than labeling, that promotes a drug product and is sponsored by a manufacturer.

Labeling, which is subject to more stringent regulations, includes "brochures, booklets, mailing pieces, detailing pieces, file cards, bulletins, calendars, price lists, catalogs, house organs, letters, motion picture films, film strips, lantern slides, sound recordings, exhibits, literature," and other matter directed toward medical professionals. *See* 21 C.F.R. 202.1(1)(2) (2000). Pharmaceutical companies are not allowed to market drugs for "off-label," non-approved uses. However, doctors may prescribe drugs off-label, and billions of dollars of revenue come from such use. In the past decade, numerous companies paid multi-million-dollar fines for unlawful off-label marketing to doctors.

More recently still, pharmaceutical companies have increasingly succeeded in arguing that restrictions on truthful, non-misleading marketing of off-label uses to doctors violate the First Amendment.

In *United States v. Caronia*, 703 F.3d 149 (2d Cir. 2012), the court of appeals vacated a pharmaceutical sales representative's conviction for conspiring to introduce a misbranded drug into interstate commerce. The conviction was based on Caronia's promotion of a drug for "off-label use," i.e., a use other than the one approved by the FDA. The court held that, to survive the First Amendment, the misbranding provisions of the FDCA must be construed "as not prohibiting and criminalizing the truthful off-label promotion of FDA-approved prescription drugs."

Amarin Pharma, Inc. v. U.S. Food & Drug Admin., 119 F. Supp. 3d 196 (S.D.N.Y. 2015), held that the drug company could make statements to doctors about off-label uses to promote prescriptions for those unapproved uses, so long as the statements were truthful and non-misleading. Because off-label use of drugs is lawful, penalizing truthful statements promoting an off-label use "'paternalistically' interferes with the ability of physicians and patients to receive potentially relevant treatment information."

Is there a constitutionally relevant difference between marketing off-label uses to doctors and marketing off-label uses to patients? Any assumption that physicians are particularly able to understand research results may be unwarranted. One study reported that, among teaching faculty, medical residents and medical students, "only 9% felt that they have had adequate training in biostatistics, and only 23% believed that they could identify whether the correct statistical methods have been applied in a study." In terms of actual statistical understanding, a review of multiple studies found that physicians' knowledge varies, but the average tended to be "in the middle of the possible score range, at levels below what would likely be considered mastery." Leila Kahwati et al., *Prescribers' Knowledge and Skills for Interpreting Research Results: A Systematic Review*, 37 J. CONTINUING EDUC. HEALTH PROF. 129 (2017); *see also* Caitlin K. Moynihan et al., *Physicians' Understanding of Clinical Trial Data in Professional Prescription Drug Promotion*, 31 J. AM. BOARD FAM. MED. 645 (2018) (finding "low to moderate" physician understanding of clinical trial-related terms used in pharmaceutical marketing materials).

The healthcare industry spent $14 billion on advertising in 2014, an increase of nearly 20% since 2011; much of that is direct-to-consumer (DTC) prescription drug advertising.

There is a vigorous debate about whether DTC advertising benefits consumers more than it harms them. Opponents argue that allowing such advertising, which many other countries ban, inevitably leads to drug makers promoting the creation and/or overdiagnosis of various conditions, pathologizing everyday life (the advent of "restless leg syndrome" is a typical example) and leading consumers to spend billions on treatments that tend to have significant side effects and risks . *Cf., e.g.*, L.B. Vater et al., *What Are Cancer Centers Advertising to the Public? A Content Analysis*, 160 ANNALS INTERNAL MED. 813 (2014) (finding that cancer center ads generally appeal to emotion rather than presenting data on treatment response, side effects, costs and alternatives). Proponents argue that consumers who identify problems that can be treated are better off, even if previous generations accepted conditions such as erectile dysfunction as inevitable.

Research suggests that drug ads do communicate important information about benefits and risks to the public, but imperfectly so. Ads for Lipitor, for example, didn't tell many consumers more than they already knew about the existence of cholesterol-lowering medicines, but they did inform 34% of ad viewers that Lipitor hasn't been shown to prevent heart attacks, compared to 5% who knew that without seeing the ad. On the other hand, that percentage demonstrates that most people who saw the Lipitor ad didn't understand the limitation.

Ads were best at communicating basic information such as the medicine's name and what it treats, with mixed effectiveness communicating about side effects and where to get more information. Viewers were more likely than non-viewers to perceive side effects as serious, but viewers were also not very good at remembering which side effects were mentioned; they often focused on just one out of a list. Over 60% of viewers said they trusted the information they'd seen in a specific ad shown to them, while a substantially lower percentage of those who weren't shown a specific ad but were asked about ads in general said so. Ads do lead many people to talk to their doctors, and a "small but significant minority" said they received prescriptions for the drugs as a result. *See* Henry J. Kaiser Family Foundation, *Understanding the Effects of Direct-to-Consumer Prescription Drug Advertising*, Nov. 2001.

The FDA mandates that advertisements for prescription drugs must include a true statement of: (1) the drug's generic name, in letters at least half as large as the letters in the brand name and as prominently placed as the brand name; (2) the drug's formula (for drugs with a single active ingredient, this means the generic name and quantity of that ingredient); and (3) a brief true summary of the drug's side-effects, contraindications, warnings and precautions, as well as the indications for use, providing a "fair balance" of the risks and effectiveness of the drug such that side effects and contraindications are featured with comparable prominence to the benefits. Consumer-directed ads must have fair balance information in language that consumers can understand. *See* F.D.A. Notice, *Direct to Consumer Promotion*, 60 F.R. 42,581, 42,583 (Aug. 16, 1995).

A prescription drug advertisement that violates the FDCA or an FDA regulation is considered "misbranded" and may lead to seizure, an injunction and criminal penalties. *See* 21 U.S.C. §§ 331, 332, 334.

Because it may be impractical to include all the "brief summary" information in very short ads, there is an exception to the brief summary requirement if "adequate provision" is made for distribution of the approved product labeling to as many people as possible. Adequate provision might include: (1) a toll free number in the ad; (2) print advertisements appearing contemporaneously in publications directed at the same audience, where the broadcast ad refers to at least one publication; (3) a URL in the ad; *and* (4) disclosure in the ad that healthcare providers may have more information. *See* FDA, *Guidance for Industry, Consumer-Directed Broadcast Advertisements*.

The most commonly used exception to the "brief summary" requirement is for "reminder advertisements," which highlight the name of the drug and drug company but don't communicate anything about the drug's indication or dosage recommendations. Even implicit representations about the drug's effects will remove the ad from the reminder category. Thus, when a Celebrex TV ad depicted a woman playing a guitar accompanied by the statement "With Celebrex, I will play the longer version," the FDA concluded that this was a full product ad because the statement made representations about the drug's indication and benefits, and so the company violated the rules by failing to include risk, side effect and contraindication information. The FDA also asked Pfizer to pull several ads for Viagra because they "ma[d]e clear that Viagra is intended for sex" but did not make the required disclosures.

MUSIC UP
SFX: Bag swoosh
VO: Remember

that guy

who used to

be called

"Wild Thing"?

MUSIC: Guitar riff

The guy who wanted to spend

the entire honeymoon indoors?

Remember

the one who

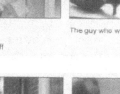
couldn't resist

a little mischief?

Yeah, that guy.

SFX: trumpet blasts

He's back!

VO: Viagra. Not all medications are for everyone.
SUPER: VIAGRA
(sildenafil citrate) tablets

VO: Ask your doctor if Viagra is right for you.
SUPER: Pfizer logo
blue.viagra.com 1-888-4VIAGRA

What would an acceptable ad for Viagra look like? Is the "brief summary" requirement consistent with the First Amendment?

Help-seeking or "see your doctor" ads describe the symptoms of a disease or condition and encourage consumers to consult their physicians to discuss treatment options, but the ads do not mention the drug's name. Because no drug is mentioned, the FDA doesn't consider these to be drug ads at all. *See* 21 C.F.R. § 202.1(e)(1).

Because "brief summaries" are often too lengthy and technical to effectively communicate risk information to consumers, and exhaustive lists of minor risks can distract and confuse consumers about the most-important risks, in 2004 the FDA issued a draft guidance—which does not have the force of law but describes the FDA's current thinking—allowing more consumer-friendly presentation of information. *See* FDA, *Draft Guidance for Industry, Brief Summary: Disclosing Risk Information in Consumer-Directed Print Advertisements* (revised Aug. 2015). Under this draft guidance, which is still the most recent statement from the FDA, advertisers have the option of using the "Highlights of Prescribing Information" category from the label, which includes only the most common and most serious risks.

As consumers and drug companies embraced the Internet for disseminating health information and drug advertising, the FDA did not issue Internet-specific guidance, preferring instead to use warning letters to indicate when a drug company had gone too far. In the fall of 2009, the FDA sent fourteen warning letters over sponsored links, stating that the links were misleading because they made representations about the efficacy of the named drugs but failed to communicate risk information or inadequately communicated the drugs' proper indication. Online, ads don't *need* to be short; they could in theory include full prescribing information—but then companies couldn't use short messaging services like Twitter, and in any event consumers are unlikely to read all that information. The FDA has so far focused on ensuring that risk communication occurs in the consumer's initial encounter with a benefit claim, but how that will work is up for debate.

The FDA has issued three additional draft guidance documents. The first focused on "interactive promotional media," including "blogs, microblogs, social networking sites, online communities, and live podcasts." *See* FDA, *Guidance for Industry Fulfilling Regulatory Requirements for Postmarketing Submissions of Interactive Promotional Media for Prescription Human and Animal Drugs and Biologics* (Jan. 2014). This guidance addresses the requirement that drug-making firms must submit all promotional labeling and advertising at the time of initial dissemination or publication, and indicates that the FDA will exercise enforcement discretion—not claim that a company has violated this requirement of the FDCA—in certain circumstances, "due to the high volume of information that may be posted within short periods of time using interactive promotional media that allow for real-time communication."

In other respects, the FDA intends to hold companies responsible for promotional communications on "sites that are owned, controlled, created, influenced, or operated by, or on behalf of, the firm. . . . Thus, a firm is responsible if it exerts influence over a site in any particular, even if the influence is limited in scope. For example, if the firm collaborates on or has editorial, preview, or review privilege over the content provided, then it is responsible for that content." The FDA also considers a firm responsible for content on third-party sites "if the firm has any control or influence on the third-party site, even if that influence is limited in scope." When a firm does control the placement of its promotional content on a site, it will have to submit both its content and the surrounding pages to the FDA to give context to its marketing. Finally, a company is responsible for content generated by an employee or agent acting on its behalf.

In addition, if access is restricted (e.g., members only), the company must submit all its content for the FDA's review; for unrestricted sites such as public Twitter feeds, more limited submissions are sufficient.

By contrast, "a firm generally is not responsible for UGC [user-generated content] that is truly independent of the firm (i.e., is not produced by, or on behalf of, or prompted by the firm in any particular). FDA will not ordinarily view UGC on firm-owned or firm-controlled venues such as blogs, message boards, and chat rooms as promotional content on behalf of the firm as long as the user has no affiliation with the firm and the firm had no influence on the UGC."

Consider whether the FTC's guidance is consistent with 47 U.S.C. § 230, discussed in Chapter 17, section 3(B). Does Section 230 render some cases non-actionable even where the drug maker has "influence" over third-party content?

The second draft document, "Guidance for Industry: Internet/Social Media Platforms with Character Space Limitations—Presenting Risk and Benefit Information for Prescription Drugs and Medical Devices" (June 2014), gives short shrift to character limits on Twitter and similar services. Important risk information is required within the same tweet as promotion of a drug's indication, plus a link to more information. If it won't fit, the FDA doesn't want the tweet to exist. Should drugs be promoted on Twitter?

The third draft document, "Guidance for Industry: Internet/Social Media Platforms: Correcting Independent Third-Party Misinformation About Prescription Drugs and Medical Devices" (June 2014), provides some leeway for manufacturers to act swiftly to correct misinformation disseminated by unrelated sources. If a company voluntarily corrects such misinformation in a truthful and non-misleading manner, disclosing that the correction comes from the company and linking to more information, the FDA won't object even if the corrective information does not satisfy other regulations of labeling and advertising.

Devices

The regulatory regime for medical devices is substantially different in some ways from that of regulating drugs. Where advertising is concerned, however, the issues are often similar. In 2013, the FDA sent a warning letter to genetic testing company 23andMe, informing the company that it was violating the FDCA by marketing its testing kit in ways that made it an unapproved device (an article intended for "the diagnosis of disease or other conditions, or in the cure, mitigation, treatment, or prevention of disease" or "intended to affect the structure or any function of the body," 21 U.S.C. §321(h)). 23andMe claimed that its test would provide "health reports on 254 diseases and conditions," including categories such as "carrier status," "health risks" and "drug response," and also that its test provided a "first step in prevention" that enabled users to "take steps toward mitigating serious diseases" such as diabetes, coronary heart disease and breast cancer. While 23andMe garnered substantial press attention for its contention that it was being unfairly targeted by the FDA, the company's claims illustrate why the FDCA provides for extensive regulation of medical devices. As the FDA pointed out, the results of the test could have serious health implications—a false positive for a breast cancer-associated gene, for example, could lead to prophylactic surgery, while a false negative could lead a consumer to ignore a real risk. Self-diagnosing drug response, likewise, presents real dangers.

Despite numerous opportunities, 23andMe failed to submit data showing its efficacy for the claimed purposes. "[T]he main purpose of compliance with FDA's regulatory requirements is to ensure that the tests work," but the company had apparently not conducted the studies that it had long promised the FDA. Instead, it launched new marketing campaigns, including TV ads. Thus, the FDA ordered the company to immediately discontinue marketing the test. As you should see, advertising regulation and substantive regulation of safety and efficacy go hand in hand: The advertising often determines what it is that must be proved safe and effective.

Enforcement

During the George W. Bush administration, the FDA's chief counsel believed that the First Amendment precluded many of the FDA's traditional regulatory measures and required top-level approval before issuing any warning letter (the first step in enforcement). In 2003, the FDA initiated only twenty-four enforcement actions in response to false or misleading advertisements from drug manufacturers. This was a 75% drop from the number of actions in 1999–2000. In addition, the FDA's responses to false and misleading advertisements slowed, with the average delay between ad placement and FDA action reaching almost six months. Under the Obama administration, the FDA returned to a somewhat more active role. In 2017, the Division of Drug Marketing, Advertising and Communications (DDMAC), which oversees prescription drug advertising, issued five warning letters—so the pace has slowed again.

The FDA did issue a spate of warning letters in 2020 related to the coronavirus pandemic. *See, e.g., Warning Letter,* Prefense LLC, MARCS-CMS 605488, Apr. 23, 2020 (identifying as misleading claims that "Prefense . . . protects you from germs with just one application per day! It's like wearing an invisible glove" and that Prefense could "protect you from pathogens up to 24 hours or for 10 hand washes").

Although the FDA does not require pre-clearance of promotional pieces except in "extraordinary circumstances," manufacturers are required to submit a copy of their advertising to the FDA at the time of its initial dissemination and may also submit it for subsequent disseminations. There has historically been a high rate of prepublication submission due in significant part to the high cost of developing corrective materials or campaigns, should the advertisement later be found objectionable.

Failure to submit advertising, however, takes a back seat to more substantive concerns in DDMAC warning letters. DDMAC targets minimization, omission or inappropriate display of risk information and unsubstantiated efficacy and safety claims. (See the Seasonale example in the section on disclosures in Chapter 6.)

B.   Food Advertising

The FTC regulates food advertising under its statutory authority to prohibit deceptive acts or practices under Sections 5 and 12 of the Federal Trade Commission Act (FTC Act). Section 5 of the FTC Act prohibits "unfair or deceptive acts or practices," and, in the case of food products, Sections 12 and 15 prohibit "any false advertisement" that is "misleading in a material respect."

To ensure consistency in the treatment of nutritional and health claims in food advertising and labeling, the FTC has taken steps to harmonize its enforcement with the FDA's food labeling regulations. The FTC would be unlikely to question a company's use of a health claim or a nutrient-content claim if the FDA explicitly has approved the claim. *See* 59 Fed. Reg. 28,388, 28,390–96 (June 1, 1994). In addition, the FDA's imprimatur will generally be sufficient to satisfy the FTC substantiation requirements.

Food advertising was significantly affected by the Nutrition Labeling and Education Act of 1990 (NLEA). *See* Pub. L. No. 101-535, 104 Stat. 2353 (codified in part at 21 U.S.C. § 343(i), (q) and (r)). In addition to requiring nutrition information on virtually all food products, the NLEA directed the FDA to standardize and limit the terms permitted on labels, and allowed only FDA-approved nutrient-content claims and health claims to appear on food labels.

The NLEA defines a health claim as "any claim that characterizes the relationship of any nutrient to a disease or health-related condition." *See* 21 C.F.R. § 101.14(a)(1). Current health claims recognized by the FDA include: calcium for osteoporosis; sodium for hypertension; fat and cholesterol for coronary disease; dietary fat for cancer; fiber and antioxidants found in fruits, vegetables and grains for cancer and heart disease; and soluble fiber for heart disease.

A nutrient claim, on the other hand, is one that expressly or by implication "characterizes the level of any nutrient." 21 U.S.C. 343 (r)(1)(A). As mandated by the NLEA, the FDA's regulations define certain absolute and comparative terms that can be used to characterize the level of a nutrient in a food. Absolute terms (*e.g.*, "low," "high," "lean") describe the amount of nutrient in one serving of a food. Relative or comparative terms (*e.g.*, "less," "reduced," "more") compare the amount of a nutrient in one food with the amount of the same nutrient in another food. Examples of approved "low" claims include "low cholesterol;" "low sodium;" "low fat;" and "low calorie." For "less" or "reduced" claims, the product must show 25% less caloric content, total fat, saturated fat, cholesterol, sodium or sugar than the comparative product.

The European Union's Approach

Regulation (EC) No 1924/2006 of the European Parliament and of the Council of 20 December, 2006, governs nutrition and health claims made on foods. Whereas the U.S. approach generally allows sellers to make non-disease claims such as "supports healthy liver function" without preapproval as long as they are properly substantiated, the EU does not distinguish between disease and function claims.

Health claims are only allowed "after a scientific assessment of the highest possible standard" carried out by the European Food Safety Authority (EFSA). Nutrition and health claims are not allowed to, among other things, "give rise to doubt about the safety and/or the nutritional adequacy of other foods," imply "that a balanced and varied diet cannot provide appropriate quantities of nutrients in general, or "refer to changes in bodily functions

[that]could give rise to or exploit fear in the consumer, either textually or through pictorial, graphic or symbolic representations." Claims are only permitted if "the average consumer can be expected to understand the beneficial effects as expressed in the claim"; there are other disclosure requirements as well, along with bans on references to rate or amount of weight loss or use of recommendations of individual doctors.

Most notably from an American perspective, health and nutrition claims in the EU are only permitted if they are specifically contained on lists developed pursuant to the regulation. In addition, "[r]eference to general, non-specific benefits of the nutrient or food for overall good health or health-related well-being may only be made if accompanied by a specific health claim included in the lists provided for [by the regulation]." Advertisers can reword authorized claims as long as the rewording is likely to have the same meaning for consumers and the rewording is designed to increase the understanding of the targeted consumers. "Vitamin A contributes to the maintenance of normal vision" could therefore not be rephrased as "Vitamin A . . . helps keep your vision in tip-top condition"; "helps keep" was fine, but "tip-top" would be understood to mean "very best" or "optimum," rather than as "normal" as in the authorized claim. ASA Adjudication on GlaxoSmithKline UK Ltd., Complaint No. A13-242431 (May 7, 2014).

Producers can apply to member states to authorize their health claims; member states then forward appropriate claims to the EFSA, which has five months to give its opinion. Member states submitted an unexpectedly high number of 44,000 health claims by the initial deadline of January 31, 2008. The EFSA submits claims it deems potentially acceptable to the European Commission, which then may ask the EFSA to evaluate those claims. This ultimately results in a list of approved or rejected health claims, with conditions of use or reasons for rejection. As of May 2020, the EFSA had ruled on *2,338 health claims*, 261 of which were authorized (exclusive of claims allowed to only one seller based on proprietary data). As this experience indicates, the U.S. model leads to many more health claims on the market. What are the costs and benefits of the two approaches?

China's Approach

China's 2015 Food Safety Law regulates labels and advertising, including nutrition claims, in ways somewhat similar to the U.S. system. For example, food must generally be labeled with its name, contact details for the food producer and other details, including ingredients and amounts of calories, protein, fat, carbohydrates and sodium. However, only ads for (much more stringently regulated, regionally approved) "health foods" may make health claims. Even health foods may not make disease-prevention or treatment claims; they also may not suggest that the food is necessary to maintain health or use any recommendation or certification by an endorser.

Unlike the FDCA, violation of China's FSL provides standing for consumers who purchase mislabeled products, allowing them to claim up to ten times the purchase price, or three times the losses suffered. This provision triggered a spate of "professional" consumer cases, and initially courts held that purchase with knowledge of the mislabeling was no barrier to recovery. However, this may be changing in some cases (China does not have a system of judicial precedent in the way that Western systems do). Jasmin Buijs, Bernd van der Meulen & Li Jiao, *Food Information In Chinese Food Law* (2018).

C.   Nutritional Supplement Advertising

The FTC regulates advertising claims for dietary and nutritional supplements using the same general principles it uses to regulate all other advertising: 1) whether the advertisement is truthful and not misleading; and 2) whether the advertiser has adequate substantiation for all objective product claims. As with food advertising, the FTC attempts to harmonize its advertising enforcement program with the FDA's labeling regulations and gives great deference to FDA scientific determinations.

The Dietary Supplement Health and Education Act (DSHEA) of 1994 requires that supplement labeling containing certain health claims must bear the mandatory disclaimer, "this statement has not been evaluated by the Food and Drug Administration. This product is not intended to diagnose, treat, cure or prevent any disease." 21 U.S.C. §§ 343(r)(6)(C). If products bear the disclaimer, they are exempt from FDA pre-authorization of "structure/function" claims (such as "Calcium builds strong bones"). DSHEA allows supplements to (1) "claim[ ] a benefit related to a classical nutrient deficiency disease and disclose[ ] the prevalence of such disease in the United States"; (2) "describe[ ] the role of a nutrient or dietary ingredient intended to affect the structure or function in humans"; (3) "characterize[ ] the documented mechanism by which a nutrient or dietary ingredient acts to maintain such structure or function"; and (4) "describe[ ] general well-being from consumption of a nutrient or dietary ingredient." 21 U.S.C. § 343(r)(6). Whereas prescription drugs can only make claims supported by at least two adequate and well-controlled studies, supplements can make claims that the FDA has not determined to be false or misleading: the default is reversed. Consumers decidedly do not understand the different regulatory regimes at work. *See* Arthur P. Goldman, *Unregulated Herbal Remedies—an Accident Waiting to Happen*, CHI. TRIB., Dec. 24, 2002, at C19 (most Americans are unaware that dietary supplements do not receive premarket testing).

DSHEA made it difficult for the FDA to regulate supplement claims, but both the FDA and the FTC continue to monitor the market. The FTC has devoted considerable attention to false and misleading supplement claims, which remain an important part of its docket, since the attraction of making such claims apparently outweighs fear of the FTC's enforcement authority. *See, e.g.*, Debra D. Burke & Anderson P. Page, *Regulating the Dietary Supplements Industry: Something Still Needs to Change*, 1 HASTINGS BUS. L.J. 121 (2005). Consumers who are hopeful, or desperate (or lack access to medical care), are willing to believe unsubstantiated claims, and advertisers are willing to make unproven claims supposedly based on science. The combination leads to great deception and inefficiency, with concomitant risks to consumers who see supplements as cheaper than expensive doctor visits and prescription drugs. *See, e.g.*, Michael A. McCann, *Dietary Supplement Labeling: Cognitive Biases, Market Manipulation & Consumer Choice*, 31 AM. J.L. & MED. 215 (2005).

In one study, DNA tests revealed that many herbal supplements, including popular supplements such as echinacea and St. John's wort, did not contain the advertised ingredients (one third of the forty-four tested), or contained far less than advertised; some also contained undisclosed glutens and undisclosed allergens such as black walnut, soy and rice . Steven G. Newmaster et al., *DNA Barcoding Detects Contamination and Substitution in North American Herbal Products*, 11 BMC MED. 222 (2013). "This suggests that the problems are widespread and that quality control for many companies, whether through ignorance, incompetence or dishonesty, is unacceptable," said David Schardt, a senior nutritionist at the Center for Science in the Public Interest, an advocacy group. "Given these results, it's hard to recommend any herbal supplements to consumers." Do you agree? A professor who'd conducted a similar study called the state of supplement regulation "the Wild West," and said most consumers had no idea how few safeguards were in place. "If you had a child who was sick and 3 out of 10 penicillin pills were fake, everybody would be up in arms," he said. "But it's O.K. to buy a supplement where 3 out of 10 pills are fake." Anahad O'Connor, *Herbal Supplements Are Often Not What They Seem*, N.Y. TIMES, Nov. 3, 2013.

In contrast to pharmaceutical companies, supplement manufacturers have been extremely active in resisting remaining FDA regulation of advertising claims on First Amendment grounds. Consider why supplement manufacturers, that face relatively limited regulation compared to pharmaceutical companies, have been so willing to litigate to get to say even more. (The pharmaceutical companies have resisted certain limits on pharmaco-sponsored continuing medical education and the distribution of studies that discuss off-label uses of drugs on First Amendment grounds, but they have not challenged the basic standards the FDA uses to determine what claims a drug may make on its label.) Industry size, industry structure and federal preemption of state-law torts when the FDA has formally approved a claim all play a role.

We will therefore spend most of the balance of this section on preemption or preclusion of private causes of action in areas regulated by the FDA and on First Amendment issues.

D. The FDCA's Interaction with Consumer Protection/Unfair Competition Laws

The Supreme Court has addressed the relationship between the Lanham Act and the FDCA/FDA regulations. While it seems to articulate a broad rule, there are many remaining questions. As you read the following case, keep in mind the differences between food regulation and drug/supplement regulation.

POM WONDERFUL LLC v. COCA-COLA CO., 573 U.S. 102 (2014)

KENNEDY, J.

POM Wonderful LLC makes and sells pomegranate juice products, including a pomegranate-blueberry juice blend. One of POM's competitors is the CocaCola Company. Coca-Cola's Minute Maid Division makes a juice blend sold with a label that, in describing the contents, displays the words "pomegranate blueberry" with far more prominence than other words on the label that show the juice to be a blend of five juices. In truth, the Coca-Cola product contains but 0.3% pomegranate juice and 0.2% blueberry juice.

Alleging that the use of that label is deceptive and misleading, POM sued Coca-Cola under § 43 of the Lanham Act. That provision allows one competitor to sue another if it alleges unfair competition arising from false or misleading product descriptions. The Court of Appeals for the Ninth Circuit held that, in the realm of labeling for food and beverages, a Lanham Act claim like POM's is precluded by a second federal statute. The second statute is the Federal Food, Drug, and Cosmetic Act (FDCA), which forbids the misbranding of food, including by means of false or misleading labeling. The ruling that POM's Lanham Act cause of action is precluded by the FDCA was incorrect. There is no statutory text or established interpretive principle to support the contention that the FDCA precludes Lanham Act suits like the one brought by POM in this case. Nothing in the text, history, or structure of the FDCA or the Lanham Act shows the congressional purpose or design to forbid these suits. Quite to the contrary, the FDCA and the Lanham Act complement each other in the federal regulation of misleading food and beverage labels. Competitors, in their own interest, may bring Lanham Act claims like POM's that challenge food and beverage labels that are regulated by the FDCA.

I. A.

This case concerns the intersection and complementarity of these two federal laws. A proper beginning point is a description of the statutes.

. . . Section 45 of the Lanham Act provides:

> The intent of this chapter is to regulate commerce within the control of Congress by making actionable the deceptive and misleading use of marks in such commerce; to protect registered marks used in such commerce from interference by State, or territorial legislation; to protect persons engaged in such commerce against unfair competition; to prevent fraud and deception in such commerce by the use of reproductions, copies, counterfeits, or colorable imitations of registered marks; and to provide rights and remedies stipulated by treaties and conventions respecting trademarks, trade names, and unfair competition entered into between the United States and foreign nations.

15 U. S. C. § 1127.

. . . The Lanham Act creates a cause of action for unfair competition through misleading advertising or labeling. Though in the end consumers also benefit from the Act's proper enforcement, the cause of action is for competitors, not consumers.

The term "competitor" is used in this opinion to indicate all those within the class of persons and entities protected by the Lanham Act. Competitors are within the class that may invoke the Lanham Act because they may suffer "an injury to a commercial interest in sales or business reputation proximately caused by [a] defendant's misrepresentations." The petitioner here asserts injury as a competitor.

The cause of action the Act creates imposes civil liability on any person who "uses in commerce any word, term, name, symbol, or device, or any combination thereof, or any false designation of origin, false or misleading description of fact, or false or misleading representation of fact, which . . . misrepresents the nature, characteristics, qualities, or geographic origin of his or her or another person's goods, services, or commercial activities.". . . This principle reflects the Lanham Act's purpose of "'protect[ing] persons engaged in [commerce within the control of Congress] against unfair competition.'" POM's cause of action would be straightforward enough but for Coca-Cola's contention that a separate federal statutory regime, the FDCA, allows it to use the label in question and in fact precludes the Lanham Act claim.

So the FDCA is the second statute to be discussed. The FDCA statutory regime is designed primarily to protect the health and safety of the public at large. The FDCA prohibits the misbranding of food and drink. A food or drink is deemed misbranded if, inter alia, "its labeling is false or misleading," information required to appear on its label "is not prominently placed thereon," or a label does not bear "the common or usual name of the food, if any there be." To implement these provisions, the Food and Drug Administration (FDA) promulgated regulations regarding food and beverage labeling, including the labeling of mixes of different types of juice into one juice blend. One provision of those regulations is particularly relevant to this case: If a juice blend does not name all the juices it contains and mentions only juices that are not predominant in the blend, then it must either declare the percentage content of the named juice or "[i]ndicate that the named juice is present as a flavor or flavoring," e.g., "raspberry and cranberry flavored juice drink." The Government represents that the FDA does not preapprove juice labels under these regulations. That contrasts with the FDA's regulation of other types of labels, such as drug labels, and is consistent with the less extensive role the FDA plays in the regulation of food than in the regulation of drugs.

Unlike the Lanham Act, which relies in substantial part for its enforcement on private suits brought by injured competitors, the FDCA and its regulations provide the United States with nearly exclusive enforcement authority, including the authority to seek criminal sanctions in some circumstances. Private parties may not bring enforcement suits. Also unlike the Lanham Act, the FDCA contains a provision pre-empting certain state laws on misbranding. That provision, which Congress added to the FDCA in the Nutrition Labeling and Education Act of 1990, forecloses a "State or political subdivision of a State" from establishing requirements that are of the type but "not identical to" the requirements in some of the misbranding provisions of the FDCA. It does not address, or refer to, other federal statutes or the preclusion thereof.

I. B.

POM Wonderful LLC is a grower of pomegranates and a distributor of pomegranate juices. Through its POM Wonderful brand, POM produces, markets, and sells a variety of pomegranate products, including a pomegranate blueberry juice blend.

POM competes in the pomegranate-blueberry juice market with the Coca-Cola Company. Coca-Cola, under its Minute Maid brand, created a juice blend containing 99.4% apple and grape juices, 0.3% pomegranate juice, 0.2% blueberry juice, and 0.1% raspberry juice. Despite the minuscule amount of pomegranate and blueberry juices in the blend, the front label of the Coca-Cola product displays the words "pomegranate blueberry" in all capital letters, on two separate lines. Below those words, Coca-Cola placed the phrase "flavored blend of 5 juices" in much smaller type. And below that phrase, in still smaller type, were the words "from concentrate with added ingredients"—and, with a line break before the final phrase— "and other natural flavors." The product's front label also displays a vignette of blueberries, grapes, and raspberries in front of a halved pomegranate and a halved apple.

Claiming that Coca-Cola's label tricks and deceives consumers, all to POM's injury as a competitor, POM brought suit under the Lanham Act. POM alleged that the name, label, marketing, and advertising of Coca-Cola's juice blend mislead consumers into believing the product consists predominantly of pomegranate and blueberry juice when it in fact consists predominantly of less expensive apple and grape juices. That confusion, POM complained, causes it to lose sales. POM sought damages and injunctive relief.

The District Court granted partial summary judgment to Coca-Cola on POM's Lanham Act claim, ruling that the FDCA and its regulations preclude challenges to the name and label of Coca-Cola's juice blend. . . .

The Court of Appeals for the Ninth Circuit affirmed in relevant part. Like the District Court, the Court of Appeals reasoned that Congress decided "to entrust matters of juice beverage labeling to the FDA"; the FDA has promulgated "comprehensive regulation of that labeling"; and the FDA "apparently" has not imposed the requirements on Coca-Cola's label that are sought by POM. "[U]nder [Circuit] precedent," the Court of Appeals explained, "for a court to act when the FDA has not—despite regulating extensively in this area— would risk undercutting the FDA's expert judgments and authority." For these reasons, and "[o]ut of respect for the statutory and regulatory scheme," the Court of Appeals barred POM's Lanham Act claim.

II. A.

... First, this is not a pre-emption case. In pre-emption cases, the question is whether state law is pre-empted by a federal statute, or in some instances, a federal agency action. This case, however, concerns the alleged preclusion of a cause of action under one federal statute by the provisions of another federal statute. So the state–federal balance does not frame the inquiry. Because this is a preclusion case, any "presumption against pre-emption," has no force. In addition, the preclusion analysis is not governed by the Court's complex categorization of the types of pre-emption. Although the Court's pre-emption precedent does not govern preclusion analysis in this case, its principles are instructive insofar as they are designed to assess the interaction of laws that bear on the same subject.

Second, this is a statutory interpretation case, and the Court relies on traditional rules of statutory interpretation. That does not change because the case involves multiple federal statutes. Nor does it change because an agency is involved. Analysis of the statutory text, aided by established principles of interpretation, controls.

... POM argues that this case concerns whether one statute, the FDCA as amended, is an "implied repeal" in part of another statute, i.e., the Lanham Act. POM contends that in such cases courts must give full effect to both statutes unless they are in "irreconcilable conflict," and that this high standard is not satisfied here. Coca-Cola resists this canon and its high standard. Coca-Cola argues that the case concerns whether a more specific law, the FDCA, clarifies or narrows the scope of a more general law, the Lanham Act. The Court's task, it claims, is to "reconcil[e]" the laws, and it says the best reconciliation is that the more specific provisions of the FDCA bar certain causes of action authorized in a general manner by the Lanham Act.

The Court does not need to resolve this dispute. Even assuming that Coca-Cola is correct that the Court's task is to reconcile or harmonize the statutes and not, as POM urges, to enforce both statutes in full unless there is a genuinely irreconcilable conflict, Coca-Cola is incorrect that the best way to harmonize the statutes is to bar POM's Lanham Act claim.

II. B.

Beginning with the text of the two statutes, it must be observed that neither the Lanham Act nor the FDCA, in express terms, forbids or limits Lanham Act claims challenging labels that are regulated by the FDCA. By its terms, the Lanham Act subjects to suit any person who "misrepresents the nature, characteristics, qualities, or geographic origin" of goods or services. This comprehensive imposition of liability extends, by its own terms, to misrepresentations on labels, including food and beverage labels. No other provision in the Lanham Act limits that understanding or purports to govern the relevant interaction between the Lanham Act and the FDCA. And the FDCA, by its terms, does not preclude Lanham Act suits. In consequence, food and beverage labels regulated by the FDCA are not, under the terms of either statute, off limits to Lanham Act claims. No textual provision in either statute discloses a purpose to bar unfair competition claims like POM's.

This absence is of special significance because the Lanham Act and the FDCA have coexisted since the passage of the Lanham Act in 1946. If Congress had concluded, in light of experience, that Lanham Act suits could interfere with the FDCA, it might well have enacted a provision addressing the issue during these 70 years. Congress enacted amendments to the FDCA and the Lanham Act, *see, e.g.*, Nutrition Labeling and Education Act of 1990; Trademark Law Revision Act of 1988, including an amendment that added to the FDCA an express pre-emption provision with respect to state laws addressing food and beverage misbranding. Yet Congress did not enact a provision addressing the preclusion of other federal laws that might bear on food and beverage labeling. This is "powerful evidence that Congress did not intend FDA oversight to be the exclusive means" of ensuring proper food and beverage labeling. Perhaps the closest the statutes come to addressing the preclusion of the Lanham Act claim at issue here is the pre-emption provision added to the FDCA in 1990 as part of the Nutrition Labeling and Education Act. But, far from expressly precluding suits arising under other federal laws, the provision if anything suggests that Lanham Act suits are not precluded.

This pre-emption provision forbids a "State or political subdivision of a State" from imposing requirements that are of the type but "not identical to" corresponding FDCA requirements for food and beverage labeling. It is significant that the complex pre-emption provision distinguishes among different FDCA requirements. It forbids state-law requirements that are of the type but not identical to only certain FDCA provisions with respect to food and beverage labeling. Just as significant, the provision does not refer to requirements imposed by other sources of law, such as federal statutes. For purposes of deciding whether the FDCA displaces a regulatory or liability scheme in another statute, it makes a substantial difference whether that other statute is state or federal. By taking care to mandate express pre-emption of some state laws, Congress if anything indicated it did not intend the FDCA to preclude requirements arising from other sources. Pre-emption of some state requirements does not suggest an intent to preclude federal claims.

The structures of the FDCA and the Lanham Act reinforce the conclusion drawn from the text. When two statutes complement each other, it would show disregard for the congressional design to hold that Congress nonetheless intended one federal statute to preclude the operation of the other. The Lanham Act and the FDCA complement each other in major respects, for each has its own scope and purpose. Although both statutes touch on food and beverage labeling, the Lanham Act protects commercial interests against unfair competition, while the FDCA protects public health and safety. The two statutes impose "different requirements and protections."

The two statutes complement each other with respect to remedies in a more fundamental respect. Enforcement of the FDCA and the detailed prescriptions of its implementing regulations is largely committed to the FDA. The FDA, however, does not have the same perspective or expertise in assessing market dynamics that day-to-day competitors possess. Competitors who manufacture or distribute products have detailed knowledge regarding how consumers rely upon certain sales and marketing strategies. Their awareness of unfair competition practices may be far more immediate and accurate than that of agency rulemakers and regulators. Lanham Act suits draw upon this market expertise by empowering private parties to sue competitors to protect their interests on a case-by-case basis. By "serv[ing] a distinct compensatory function that may motivate injured persons to come forward," Lanham Act suits, to the extent they touch on the same subject matter as the FDCA, "provide incentives" for manufacturers to behave well. Allowing Lanham Act suits takes advantage of synergies among multiple methods of regulation. This is quite consistent with the congressional design to enact two different statutes, each with its own mechanisms to enhance the protection of competitors and consumers.

A holding that the FDCA precludes Lanham Act claims challenging food and beverage labels would not only ignore the distinct functional aspects of the FDCA and the Lanham Act but also would lead to a result that Congress likely did not intend. Unlike other types of labels regulated by the FDA, such as drug labels, it would appear the FDA does not preapprove food and beverage labels under its regulations and instead relies on enforcement actions, warning letters, and other measures. Because the FDA acknowledges that it does not necessarily pursue enforcement measures regarding all objectionable labels, if Lanham Act claims were to be precluded then commercial interests—and indirectly the public at large— could be left with less effective protection in the food and beverage labeling realm than in many other, less regulated industries. It is unlikely that Congress intended the FDCA's protection of health and safety to result in less policing of misleading food and beverage labels than in competitive markets for other products.

II. C.

Coca-Cola argues the FDCA precludes POM's Lanham Act claim because Congress intended national uniformity in food and beverage labeling. Coca-Cola notes three aspects of the FDCA to support that position: delegation of enforcement authority to the Federal Government rather than private parties; express pre-emption with respect to state laws; and the specificity of the FDCA and its implementing regulations. But these details of the FDCA do not establish an intent or design to preclude Lanham Act claims.

Coca-Cola says that the FDCA's delegation of enforcement authority to the Federal Government shows Congress' intent to achieve national uniformity in labeling. But POM seeks to enforce the Lanham Act, not the FDCA or its regulations. The centralization of

FDCA enforcement authority in the Federal Government does not indicate that Congress intended to foreclose private enforcement of other federal statutes.

. . . Although the application of a federal statute such as the Lanham Act by judges and juries in courts throughout the country may give rise to some variation in outcome, this is the means Congress chose to enforce a national policy to ensure fair competition. It is quite different from the disuniformity that would arise from the multitude of state laws, state regulations, state administrative agency rulings, and state-court decisions that are partially forbidden by the FDCA's pre-emption provision. Congress not infrequently permits a certain amount of variability by authorizing a federal cause of action even in areas of law where national uniformity is important. The Lanham Act itself is an example of this design: Despite Coca-Cola's protestations, the Act is uniform in extending its protection against unfair competition to the whole class it describes. It is variable only to the extent that those rights are enforced on a case-by-case basis. The variability about which Coca-Cola complains is no different than the variability that any industry covered by the Lanham Act faces. And, as noted, Lanham Act actions are a means to implement a uniform policy to prohibit unfair competition in all covered markets.

Finally, Coca-Cola urges that the FDCA, and particularly its implementing regulations, addresses food and beverage labeling with much more specificity than is found in the provisions of the Lanham Act. That is true. The pages of FDA rulemakings devoted only to juice-blend labeling attest to the level of detail with which the FDA has examined the subject. *E.g.*, Food Labeling; Declaration of Ingredients; Common or Usual Name for Nonstandardized Foods; Diluted Juice Beverages, 58 Fed. Reg. 2897–2926 (1993). Because, as we have explained, the FDCA and the Lanham Act are complementary and have separate scopes and purposes, this greater specificity would matter only if the Lanham Act and the FDCA cannot be implemented in full at the same time. But neither the statutory structure nor the empirical evidence of which the Court is aware indicates there will be any difficulty in fully enforcing each statute according to its terms. . . .

* * *

Coca-Cola and the United States ask the Court to elevate the FDCA and the FDA's regulations over the private cause of action authorized by the Lanham Act. But the FDCA and the Lanham Act complement each other in the federal regulation of misleading labels. Congress did not intend the FDCA to preclude Lanham Act suits like POM's. The position Coca-Cola takes in this Court that because food and beverage labeling is involved it has no Lanham Act liability here for practices that allegedly mislead and trick consumers, all to the injury of competitors, finds no support in precedent or the statutes. The judgment of the Court of Appeals for the Ninth Circuit is reversed, and the case is remanded for further proceedings consistent with this opinion.

NOTES AND QUESTIONS

In early 2016, a jury found against POM on its false advertising claims against Coca-Cola.

After *POM Wonderful*, what should happen when private litigants argue that the defendant has engaged in false or misleading advertising that also violates the FDCA or FDA regulations? Before *POM Wonderful*, courts had attempted to draw a line between cases that required the *interpretation* of the FDCA or of FDA regulations—these were the sole province of the FDA—and cases that involved alleged falsity independent of the FDA. In the latter set of cases, courts could evaluate falsity, a traditional area of judicial competence, and could even use FDA rules as evidence of the meaning of certain terms, but the theory was that the cause of action would exist even in the absence of the FDCA. These cases seem relatively unaffected by *POM Wonderful*.

Consider, for example, the following highly influential case.

SANDOZ PHARMACEUTICALS CORPORATION V. RICHARDSON-VICKS, INC., 902 F.2D 222 (3D CIR. 1990)

. . . Sandoz alleges that Vicks's representations about its product, Vicks Pediatric Formula 44 ("Pediatric 44") [cough syrup], constituted false and deceptive advertising in violation of section 43(a) of the Lanham Act.

At the nub of the controversy is Vicks's assertion that Pediatric 44 starts to work the instant it is swallowed. Sandoz alleges that the representations about the instant action of the product are false. It also alleges that such representations constitute per se violations of the Lanham Act, given Vicks's failure to disclose, on Pediatric 44's label, that the demulcents which theoretically effectuate the immediate relief are intended to be active[1] yet are not approved by the Food and Drug Administration ("FDA"). . . .

Vicks's advertising claims with regard to Pediatric 44 are based on the effect of certain locally acting, inert sugary liquids known as "demulcents," which operate directly on cough receptors in the recipient's throat and respiratory passages. Demulcents are topically acting antitussives, in contrast to centrally acting antitussives, which are the traditional cough antidotes. Because these demulcents work on contact, Vicks claims that Pediatric 44 begins to reduce coughs as soon as it is swallowed.

Vicks performed various tests to support this conclusion. The record contains test results [that] support, if only marginally, Vicks's arguments that Pediatric 44 starts to work right away, that there is a scientific basis for this claim, and that Pediatrics 44 is superior to its competitors. However, the FDA has never approved any "demulcents" as effective for the relief of coughs, and whether Vicks's level of testing could meet the high standards for drug approval set by the FDA is far from certain. . . . [The court explained that if the demulcent was "active" according to the FDA, it would require extensive testing.]

Sandoz has presented no evidence showing that Pediatric 44's "inactive" label is misleading to the consuming public, and Sandoz did not actively pursue the argument, either here or in

---

[1] Demulcents have not been classified as inactive or active by the Food and Drug Administration, *see* 41 Fed.Reg. 38,354 (1976) (panel report listing demulcents in FDA category III, which covers ingredients for which "the available data are insufficient to classify" the ingredient, 21 C.F.R. § 330.10(a)(5)(iii) (1988)), but Sandoz argues that they are clearly active ingredients insofar as Vicks claims that they make its product effective.

the district court, that the "inactive" label in question was deceptive. Instead, it alleges that the label contains a literally false description of the product. In essence, Sandoz states that if Vicks claims that its demulcents enable Pediatric 44 to begin to work as soon as it is swallowed, then these demulcents are "active" ingredients within the meaning of 21 C.F.R. § 210.3(b)(7). . . .

The Lanham Act is primarily intended to protect commercial interests. . . . The FD & C Act, in contrast, is not focused on the truth or falsity of advertising claims. It requires the FDA to protect the public interest by "pass[ing] on the safety and efficacy of all new drugs and . . . promulgat[ing] regulations concerning the conditions under which various categories of OTC drugs . . . are safe, effective and not misbranded."

. . . . Sandoz's counsel argued to the district court that "[i]f [the demulcents] relieve coughs[,] they're active. That's true as a matter of common sense and normal English." Such an interpretation of FDA regulations, absent direct guidance from the promulgating agency, is not as simple as Sandoz proposes.

The FDA has not found conclusively that demulcents must be labelled as active or inactive ingredients within the meaning of 21 C.F.R. § 210.3(b)(7).[10] We decline to find and do not believe that the district court had to find, either "as a matter of common sense" or "normal English," that which the FDA, with all of its scientific expertise, has yet to determine. Because "agency decisions are frequently of a discretionary nature or frequently require expertise, the agency should be given the first chance to exercise that discretion or to apply that expertise." Thus, we are unable to conclude that Vicks's labeling of Pediatric 44's demulcents as inactive is literally false, even if Vicks concurrently claims that these ingredients enable its medicine to work the instant it is swallowed.

Sandoz's position would require us to usurp administrative agencies' responsibility for interpreting and enforcing potentially ambiguous regulations. Jurisdiction for the regulation of OTC drug marketing is vested jointly and exhaustively in the FDA and the FTC, and is divided between them by agreement. Neither of these agencies' constituent statutes creates an express or implied private right of action, and what the FD & C Act and the FTC Act do not create directly, the Lanham Act does not create indirectly, at least not in cases requiring original interpretation of these Acts or their accompanying regulations. . . .

NOTES AND QUESTIONS

If the FDA didn't exist, could the plaintiff have claimed that the defendant's label was false or misleading? On the other hand, given that the FDA does exist, if everyone else follows the FDA's rules for labeling active ingredients, isn't the defendant's use "false" according to the definition used by the market? Isn't the real problem here materiality?

Now examine another influential pre-*POM Wonderful* case, this one allowing a claim to proceed. Does *POM Wonderful* affect the court's reasoning?

---

[10] Sandoz is free to petition the FDA to investigate these alleged labeling violations. Sandoz represents that it has embarked upon this path already. The fact that it has been unable to get a quick response from the FDA, however, does not create a claim for Sandoz under the Lanham Act.

SOLVAY PHARMACEUTICALS, INC. V. ETHEX CORP., 2004 WL 742033 (D. MINN. 2004)

. . . Both Solvay and Ethex produce and market competing prescription pancreatic enzyme supplements used in the treatment of cystic fibrosis. Solvay's products are marketed under the trademark Creon, while Ethex's products are marketed under the trademark Pangestyme. Specifically at issue in this case are Creon 10 and 20 and Pagnestyme CN-10 and CN-20.

Solvay contends that Ethex has falsely and misleadingly promoted and advertised Pangestyme CN-10 and CN-20 as substitutes for Creon 10 and 20. According to Solvay, Ethex markets the Pangestyme products either expressly or by implication as "equivalent," "comparable," and "generic" versions of Creon, despite the fact that the two products are not, in fact, equivalent. Such false and misleading advertising and promotion has allegedly harmed Creon's sales and reputation, and puts cystic fibrosis patients at risk of receiving different treatment than that prescribed by their doctors.

[Solvay alleged violation of the Lanham Act and state unfair and deceptive trade practices laws.] . . .

Ethex objects that counts one through six are impermissible attempts to enforce the Federal Drug and Cosmetic Act ("FDCA"), which is only enforceable by the federal government. . . .

Solvay maintains that it is alleging in this case that Creon and Pangestyme are factually not "equivalent," "substitutable," "generic," "comparable," and "alternative," and that Ethex's representations are therefore factually false. Solvay has specifically disclaimed any FDA related allegation.

A. The FDCA and FDA

The primary regulatory system covering prescription drugs was created by the Food, Drug and Cosmetic Act ("FDCA"). The FDCA requires FDA approval, through a "new drug application" ("NDA"), before a new drug may be put on the market. A product similar to an NDA approved drug may be approved and marketed based on an "abbreviated new drug application" ("ANDA"). An ANDA requires the manufacturer of the similar drug to demonstrate that the two drugs are therapeutically equivalent, that is pharmaceutically equivalent[3] and bioequivalent.[4] Each year the FDA publishes Approved Drug Products with Therapeutic Equivalence Evaluations, commonly known as the "Orange Book," listing all NDA approved drugs along with therapeutic equivalence determinations. Enforcement of the FDCA is permitted exclusively "by and in the name of the United States" or, in certain circumstances, by a state.

Prescription pancreatic enzyme supplements are, like any other drug, subject to FDA regulation. In 1995 the FDA declared that all pancreatic enzyme drugs would require NDA

---

[3] Two drugs sharing the same active ingredients, strength, and dosage are considered "pharmaceutically equivalent."

[4] Two drugs that do not have significantly different rates and extent of absorption in the body are considered "bioequivalent."

or ANDA approval, but permitted such drugs to remain on the market while the FDA fleshed out the approval process. Thus, neither Creon nor Pangestyme has been tested, approved, compared or otherwise passed on by the FDA, and neither is listed in the Orange Book.

. . . Courts have come to the general conclusion that the FDA's enforcement of the FDCA is primarily concerned with the safety and efficacy of new drugs, while the Lanham Act is focused on the truth or falsity of advertising claims. More specifically, where a claim requires interpretation of a matter that is exclusively within the jurisdiction and expertise of the FDA and FDCA, plaintiffs cannot use the Lanham Act as a backdoor to private enforcement. However, "false statements are actionable under the Lanham Act, even if their truth may be generally within the purview of the FDA," where the truth or falsity of the statements in question can be resolved through reference to standards other than those of the FDA.

. . . Solvay is not relying on either explicit or implicit FDA endorsement or terms that only the FDA can define. Solvay alleges that any statement or representation that Pangestyme is "equivalent," "substitutable," "generic," "comparable," and "alternative" to Creon is literally false. Similar to the plaintiff in *Grove Fresh,* Solvay may use the FDA regulations listing definitions of bioequivalence, pharmaceutical equivalence, and therapeutic equivalence to establish the appropriate standard by which to judge the literal falsity of Ethex's advertisements. However, "[e]ven without the FDA regulation . . . [plaintiff] could attempt to establish a violation of section 43(a) . . . . [by] provid[ing] other evidence establishing the proper market definition" of generic, equivalent, comparable, or substitutable. As Ethex acknowledges, an FDA determination is not necessarily required in order for two drugs to be properly considered equivalent.

The Court is thus satisfied that Solvay could, based on the allegations in the complaint, prove that Pangestyme and Creon are not substitutable, alternatives, equivalent, or comparable, and that any advertisement to the contrary is literally false. Such a claim does not require the Court to determine anything within the particular jurisdiction of the FDA and is within the purview of the Lanham Act. Plaintiff's claims will therefore not be dismissed on this basis. . . .

NOTES AND QUESTIONS

Consumer Confusion Over FDA Approval. Suppose a plaintiff submits credible evidence that a substantial number of the relevant consumers believe that the mere presence on the market of a drug implies FDA approval of that drug, even though in that particular instance the FDA has not approved the drug (this is the case for a number of drugs that were grandfathered into the current scheme). Should the plaintiff's implied falsity claim survive? *See* Mutual Pharmaceutical Company, Inc. v. Watson Pharmaceuticals, Inc., 2010 WL 446132 (D.N.J. 2010) (allegations that inclusion of drug on price lists and wholesaler ordering systems constituted implicit misrepresentation of FDA approval stated claim against grandfathered drug).

State Law Claims. As *POM Wonderful* mentioned, the FDCA preempts certain state law claims, but does preserve some in the area of food and supplement labeling where the state law is "identical" to the rules adopted by the FDA. Preemption is broader with respect to pharmaceuticals—perhaps justified by the extensive and individualized approval process for pharmaceuticals and the generally tighter rules on their advertising.

Compliance with FDA regulations will insulate a defendant from state-law claims regarding prescription drug labels. *See* Pa. Emp. Benefit Tr. Fund v. Zeneca, Inc., 2005 WL 2993937 (D. Del. 2005) ("By approving information to be included in the drug labeling, the FDA has determined that the information complies with its rules and regulations. Therefore, if the FDA labeling supports the statements made in advertising for an FDA-approved drug, the statements are not actionable under [Delaware law.]"). In addition, even after *POM Wonderful*, some courts find that statements specifically approved by the FDA can't be the basis of Lanham Act claims. *See* Apotex Inc. v. Acorda Therapeutics, Inc., 823 F.3d 51 (2nd Cir. 2016) ("[R]epresentations that are wholly consistent with an FDA label" aren't subject to Lanham Act liability, though "Lanham Act liability might arise if an advertisement uses information contained in an FDA-approved label that does not correspond substantially to the label, or otherwise renders the advertisement literally or implicitly false. . . . [I]n order to avoid chilling speech that ought to be protected, Acorda's advertisements cannot form the basis for Apotex's claims to the extent they were in line with the FDA-approved label.").

How do we know that the defendant is in compliance with the FDA's rules? The FDA rarely issues pronouncements that a specific advertiser is doing something correctly. If a court evaluates compliance, then might it risk disagreement with the FDA itself were the FDA to examine the ad at issue, since after all there is often room for judgment calls in applying regulations. On the other hand, the FDA is as resource-constrained and short-staffed as any federal agency, and it doesn't go after every violation of its regulations itself, so additional help from plaintiffs and courts might further the purposes of the statutory scheme.

For supplements, the statutory scheme is importantly different. Based on the FDCA's explicit preemption provision, which preempts non-identical state requirements, courts generally allow consumer claims to proceed when they enforce state standards for foods or supplements "identical" to those set out in the FDCA and FDA regulations. *See, e.g.,* Consumer Justice Ctr. v. Olympian Labs, Inc., 121 Cal. Rptr. 2d 749 (Cal. App. Ct. 2002). Thus, the states can create a privately enforceable cause of action identical to the FDCA, even though the FDCA itself expressly rejects a private cause of action based on violation of the FDCA. California in particular has taken up this invitation, as has its plaintiff's bar. Why would Congress do this?

Are there any reasons to treat consumer lawsuits differently from competitor lawsuits when it comes to preemption by the FDCA and FDA regulations? *POM Wonderful* didn't apply the "identical" standard because in the Court's analysis, it just didn't matter whether the Lanham Act imposed "identical" requirements on Coca-Cola to the FDA's rules, as long as there was no conflict with a label the FDA had *mandated*. After *POM Wonderful*, it may thus be easier for competitors to sue for false advertising than for directly deceived consumers who can't take advantage of the Lanham Act. Is this the right balance?

Consider the popular food labeling term "natural." "Natural" is a useful selling term for many producers, but it lacks a coherent definition. The FDA has sought comments on whether it ought to formulate a definition of "natural." Its existing policy is that "natural" means that "nothing artificial or synthetic (including all color additives regardless of source) has been included in, or has been added to, a food that would not normally be expected to be in the food." 58 Fed. Reg. 2302, 2407 (1993). Although it sought comment on whether it should define "natural" with respect to bioengineering, the comment period closed years ago and nothing further has happened. The First Circuit has held that it is plausible that "100% Natural" on cooking oil deceives consumers where the oil is produced from bioengineered ingredients. Lee v. Conagra Brands, Inc., --- F.3d ----, 2020 WL 2201949 (1st Cir. May 7, 2020).

Given the FDA's position, should consumer protection litigation be allowed to fill the regulatory gap if consumers do have expectations about what "natural" means? Or should courts refuse to decide such cases because the FDA has declined to act? Courts have split on the issue, though as the FDA's inaction stretches to decades, more of them have allowed consumer lawsuits to proceed.

Does it matter if consumers' expectations are incoherent or unreasonable? Fifty percent of consumers surveyed in 2009 said the "natural" label was important or very important to them, while only 35% said the same of "organic," even though only the latter has a clear regulatory definition and is held to much more stringent standards than the FDA concept of "natural." CONTEXT MARKETING, BEYOND ORGANIC: HOW EVOLVING CONSUMER CONCERNS INFLUENCE FOOD PURCHASES 4 (2009).

For comparison purposes, USDA's Food Safety and Inspection Service says all fresh meat qualifies as "natural," but meat that carries a "natural" label cannot contain any artificial flavors or flavorings, coloring ingredients, chemical preservatives or other artificial or synthetic ingredients and must not be more than "minimally processed." In one study, consumers who were unfamiliar with USDA natural labels were willing to pay $1.26 per pound more for steaks labeled natural, but those provided the definition of natural were unwilling to pay more for those steaks; they were willing to pay $3.07 per pound more for steak labeled natural *and* no growth hormones. Konstantinos G. Syrengelas et al, 40 APPLIED ECON. PERSP. & POL'Y 445 (2018). Does this suggest anything about whether "natural" is misleading for other foods?

The NAD and the FDA. The NAD distinguishes between general labeling requirements and certain specific FDA decisions. If a government agency mandates, or even approves for use, general language for all industry participants to use, the NAD will not contradict that. But the NAD will exercise its own judgment about specific claims.

In one case, Novartis claimed that its transdermal patch is "clinically proven more effective than Dramamine." The NARB upheld an NAD finding that this claim was not substantiated when used in ads, despite the fact that in 1979 the FDA approved labeling that supported this claim. The NARB was influenced by several factors: (1) a subsequent 1985 study cast doubt on the superiority claim, and the NAD was not confident that the FDA would reach the same result if it reevaluated the issue; (2) in 1979, there was no direct-to-consumer advertising, and in general the NAD was not confident that "the same rigor and review that would likely be afforded today was present;" (3) the support relied on pooling study results rather than a true head-to-head comparison, and it was not clear why the FDA (unusually) had allowed a comparative claim under these circumstances. The NAD panel was also "troubled by the fact that 183 of the 194 study participants in the three studies were employees of the advertiser, an unorthodox procedure at best."

The NARB noted that "there are many sound reasons for giving great, perhaps under appropriate circumstances even decisive, weight to federal agency decisions regarding advertising claims. However, such deference is not automatic, and it never completely replaces the obligation of the self-regulation system to exercise its own sound discretion." *See* Novartis Consumer Health, Report of NARB Panel 110 (NARB July 25, 2000). How does this compare to how the courts in the previous cases treated FDA decisions?

Novartis agreed to modify the ads but not to change the labeling (which would have required FDA approval).

E.   The First Amendment

In recent years, the FDA has faced significant First Amendment constraints on its ability to regulate as the courts give more weight to commercial speakers' interests in disseminating the information of their choice. The following case is of interest because of the scrutiny it gives to the FDA's evaluation of the clinical evidence, where one might think the FDA had a comparative advantage over a generalist judge.

ALLIANCE FOR NATURAL HEALTH U.S. V. SEBELIUS, 714 F. SUPP. 2D 48 (D.D.C. 2010)

Plaintiffs Alliance for Natural Health U.S., Durk Pearson, Sandy Shaw, and Coalition to End FDA and FTC Censorship have sued the Food and Drug Administration ("FDA" or "Agency") and other defendants, seeking review of the Agency's decision to deny plaintiffs' petition for authorization of qualified health claims regarding selenium-containing dietary supplements. Invoking both circuit and district court opinions that have addressed similar claims, plaintiffs seek a declaratory judgment that the FDA's final order denying plaintiffs' petition is invalid and a permanent injunction enjoining the Agency from "taking any action that would preclude [plaintiffs] from placing [their proposed selenium] health claims on [dietary supplement] labels." . . .

BACKGROUND

I. STATUTORY AND REGULATORY FRAMEWORK

A "dietary supplement" is a "product (other than tobacco) intended to supplement the diet that bears or contains" one or more of certain dietary ingredients, including vitamins, minerals, herbs or botanicals, amino acids, concentrates, metabolites, constituents, or extracts. A dietary supplement is deemed to be "food," which is defined in part as "articles used for food or drink for man or other animals," except when it meets the definition of a "drug," which is defined in part as "articles intended for use in the diagnosis, cure, mitigation, treatment, or prevention of disease in man or other animals." A "health claim" is "any claim made on the label or in labeling of a food, including a dietary supplement, that expressly or by implication . . . characterizes the relationship of any substance to a disease or health-related condition."

Under the Federal Food, Drug, and Cosmetic Act ("FFDCA"), manufacturers wishing to market a new drug must undergo a "strict and demanding" process designed to ensure consumer safety and product efficacy in order to obtain FDA approval before introducing the product into interstate commerce. "Prior to 1984, the FDA took the position that a statement that consumption of a food could prevent a particular disease was 'tantamount to a claim that the food was a drug . . . and therefore that its sale was prohibited until a new drug application had been approved.'" But in the mid-1980s, companies began making health claims on foods without seeking new drug approval, a practice the FDA supported. Congress subsequently enacted the Nutrition Labeling and Education Act of 1990 ("NLEA"), amending the FFDCA to provide the FDA with authority to regulate health claims on food.

The NLEA created a "safe harbor" from the "drug" designation for foods and dietary supplements labeled with health claims. Under the Act, a manufacturer may make a health claim on a food without FDA new drug approval if the FDA determines that "significant scientific agreement," based on the "totality of publicly available scientific evidence," supports the claim. For dietary supplement health claims, however, Congress declined to establish an authorization process and instead left the creation of an approval "procedure and standard" to the FDA. The FDA subsequently promulgated a regulation adopting the NLEA's standard for food health claims (i.e., "significant scientific agreement") for dietary supplement health claims. The FDA may consider a dietary supplement labeled with an unauthorized health claim to be a misbranded food; a misbranded drug; and/or an unapproved new drug. A dietary supplement labeled with such a claim, or a claim that is false or misleading, is subject to seizure, and the Agency may enjoin the product's distribution or seek criminal penalties against its manufacturer.

II. *PEARSON V. SHALALA* AND SUBSEQUENT CASE LAW

A. Introduction

Plaintiffs' lawsuit is the latest in a series of disputes between dietary supplement designers and the FDA regarding the Agency's regulation of health claims regarding dietary supplements after the passage of the NLEA. . . . The first of these lawsuits, challenging the FDA's rejection of the plaintiffs' proposed claims on First Amendment grounds, resulted in an invalidation of the Agency's regulations regarding health claim review by the D.C. Circuit. Since then, the FDA has struggled to balance its concerns for consumer protection and dietary supplement manufacturers' First Amendment commercial speech rights as defined by *Pearson I.* An abbreviated summary of these cases follows.

B. *Pearson I*

In 1995, a group of dietary supplement manufacturers filed suit against the FDA and other defendants under the First Amendment, challenging the FDA's rejection of four health claims that the manufacturers sought to include on certain dietary supplements. The claims characterized a relationship between dietary supplements and the risk of particular diseases.

The Agency, applying the "significant scientific agreement" standard set forth in 21 C.F.R. § 101.14, determined that the evidence concerning the supplements "was inconclusive . . . and thus failed to give rise to 'significant scientific agreement.'" The Agency therefore declined to authorize the claims, finding them to be "inherently misleading and thus entirely outside the protection of the First Amendment" as commercial speech. The FDA also declined to consider the proposed alternative of "permitting the claim[s] while requiring . . . corrective disclaimer[s]," arguing that even if the proposed claims were only "potentially misleading," it had no obligation under the First Amendment to consider a "disclaimer approach," as opposed to suppression, where the claims at issue lacked significant scientific agreement. . . .

[The court of appeals], applying the commercial speech test set forth in *Central Hudson Gas & Electric Corporation v. Public Service Commission of New York*, 447 U.S. 557 (1980),[5] held that there was not a "reasonable fit between the government's goals" of protecting public health and preventing consumer fraud and "the means chosen to advance those goals," namely, the rejection of plaintiffs' proposed health claims without consideration of disclaimers. Specifically, the [c]ourt held that under the First Amendment commercial speech doctrine, there is a "preference for disclosure over outright suppression" and for "less restrictive and more precise means" of regulating commercial speech. The Agency's rejection of disclaimers without a showing that they were insufficient to meet the government's goal of avoiding consumer confusion demonstrated a disregard for "less restrictive" means of speech regulation that violated the First Amendment. . . .

In requiring the Agency to consider the adequacy of possible disclaimers accompanying the manufacturers' proposed health claims, the [c]ourt recognized that "where evidence in support of a claim is outweighed by evidence against the claim, the FDA could deem it incurable by a disclaimer and ban it outright." Similarly, the [c]ourt "s[aw] no problem with the FDA imposing an outright ban on a claim where evidence in support of the claim is qualitatively weaker than evidence against the claim." However, the Court stated that the Agency "must still meet its burden of justifying a restriction on speech," and a "conclusory assertion" as to misleadingness is inadequate.

C. *Pearson II*

In late 2000, several of the plaintiffs from *Pearson I* and other dietary supplement designers, sellers, and manufacturers filed a second lawsuit to challenge the Agency's decision prohibiting plaintiffs from including on their dietary supplements' labels a health claim concerning folic acid.[7] After the decision in *Pearson I*, the FDA published a notice requesting submission of scientific data concerning the four health claims at issue in that case,

---

[5] The *Central Hudson* analysis, as clarified by the Supreme Court in *Thompson v. Western States Medical Center*, 535 U.S. 357 (2002), consists of four parts: 1) "whether 'the speech concerns lawful activity and is not misleading;' " 2) if the speech is protected, "whether the asserted government interest [in regulation] is substantial;" 3) "whether the regulation directly advances the governmental interest asserted;" and 4) "whether [the regulation] is not more extensive than is necessary to serve that interest."

[7] The folic acid health claim at issue in *Pearson II* was the same folic acid claim at issue in *Pearson I*, which stated that ".8 mg of folic acid in a dietary supplement is more effective in reducing the risk of neural tube defects than a lower amount in foods in common form." . . . *[S]ee also* Pearson I, 164 F.3d at 659 ("[I]t appears that credible evidence did support [the folic acid claim], and we suspect that a clarifying disclaimer could be added to the effect that 'The evidence in support of this claim is inconclusive.' ").

including the folic acid claim. . . . [T]he Agency issued a decision stating that it would not authorize the manufacturers' folic acid claim, even with clarifying disclaimers, because it found the claim to be inherently misleading. . . .

The district court agreed with the plaintiffs, finding that the FDA "failed to comply with the constitutional guidelines outlined in *Pearson [I]* " when it concluded, without explanation, that the "weight of the evidence is against . . . the proposed [folic acid] claim" and that the claim was therefore "inherently misleading" and not susceptible to correction by disclaimer. . . . [The court] disagreed with the FDA's weighing of the scientific data and found "as a matter of law that [the folic acid claim] is not 'inherently misleading.'" In coming to this conclusion, the court analyzed the scientific data regarding folic acid and concluded that "[t]he mere absence of significant affirmative evidence in support of a particular claim . . . does not translate into negative evidence 'against' it.'" Moreover, the court held that the "question which must be answered under *Pearson [I]* is whether there is any 'credible evidence'" in support of the claim. If so, unless that evidence is "outweighed by evidence against the claim" or is "qualitatively weaker" than evidence against the claim, the claim "may not be absolutely prohibited."

Because the court found that there was credible evidence to support the folic acid claim, it held that the FDA's determination that the folic acid claim was "inherently misleading" and could not be cured by disclaimers was "arbitrary and capricious" under the APA and that the FDA had not "undertake[n] the necessary analysis required by *Pearson [I]*." The court granted the plaintiffs' motion for a preliminary injunction and remanded the case to the FDA to "draft one or more appropriately short, succinct, and accurate disclaimers."

D. *Pearson III*

After the preliminary injunction was entered in *Pearson II*, the FDA filed a motion for reconsideration . . . . The district court . . . restated the holdings in *Pearson I*, which included 1) the obligation of the Agency to "demonstrate with empirical evidence that disclaimers . . . would bewilder consumers and fail to correct for deceptiveness," and 2) the establishment of "a very heavy burden which Defendants must satisfy if they wish to totally suppress a particular health claim."

E. *Whitaker v. Thompson*

In June 2001, the plaintiffs filed another lawsuit to challenge the Agency's decision not to authorize the antioxidant claim at issue in *Pearson I*.[12]

. . . [T]he court reviewed the Agency's analysis of the claim in light of *Pearson I*, noting that "[t]he deference due to an agency's expert evaluation of scientific data does not negate 'the duty of the court to ensure that an agency . . . conduct a process of reasoned decision-making." As such, the court reviewed over 150 intervention and observational studies regarding the relationship between antioxidant vitamins and cancer relied upon by the FDA in reaching its conclusions and found that nearly one-third of the studies "supported" the

---

[12] The claim at issue was that "Consumption of antioxidant vitamins may reduce the risk of certain kinds of cancers."

antioxidant/cancer relationship. The court determined that the FDA had "failed to follow its own [Guidance] Report and give appropriate weight" to these studies. . . . The court then found that the circumstances under which the Agency might ban a claim as misleading, described in *Pearson I*, were not present because 1) one-third of the evidence examined supported the claim; and 2) the FDA failed to provide "empirical evidence that an appropriate disclaimer would confuse customers and fail to correct for deceptiveness." As a result, the court granted a preliminary injunction after concluding that the Agency's decision to suppress the claim did not "comport with the First Amendment's clear preference for disclosure over suppression of commercial speech."

III. FACTUAL AND PROCEDURAL HISTORY

[The FDA previously exercised enforcement discretion with respect to two "qualified" versions of selenium health claims. "Qualified health claims" are health claims that include one or more disclaimers designed to eliminate potentially misleading assertions. The FDA created this category in response to *Pearson I*. The FDA accepted: 1) "Selenium may reduce the risk of certain cancers. Some scientific evidence suggests that consumption of selenium may reduce the risk of certain forms of cancer. However, FDA has determined that this evidence is limited and not conclusive;" and 2) "Selenium may produce anticarcinogenic effects in the body. Some scientific evidence suggests that consumption of selenium may produce anticarcinogenic effects in the body. However, [the] FDA has determined that this evidence is limited and not conclusive." The FDA then announced a plan to reevaluate the scientific evidence.]

In addition to opposing the FDA's planned re-evaluation of the qualified selenium health claims, plaintiffs submitted a health claim petition seeking authorization of ten new qualified health claims (collectively, "qualified selenium health claims")[16] concerning the purported relationship between selenium and cancer. Plaintiffs' submission included over 150 scientific articles purporting to examine one or more aspects of the relationship between selenium and cancer, which supplemented the 17 articles previously submitted to the FDA during the public comment period.

. . . The FDA concluded that while scientific evidence supports qualified health claims concerning the relationship between selenium intake and a reduced risk of bladder, prostate, and thyroid cancer, no such evidence exists to support a relationship between selenium intake and a reduced risk of urinary tract (other than bladder), lung and other respiratory tract, colon and other digestive tract, brain, liver, and breast cancers. The Agency also concluded that proposed Claims 1 and 2, regarding selenium intake and certain cancers and anticarcinogenic effects, "are misleading because they are overbroad, fail to disclose material information, and are not supported by the scientific evidence the agency reviewed. . . . " [The

---

[16] Plaintiffs proposed the following claims:

 1. Selenium may reduce the risk of certain cancers. Scientific evidence supporting this claim is convincing but not yet conclusive.

 2. Selenium may produce anticarcinogenic effects in the body. Scientific evidence supporting this claim is convincing but not yet conclusive.

[Plaintiffs proposed identical claims for specific forms of cancer.] . . . .

FDA denied most claims and said it would not take action against certain modified claims. Plaintiffs sued.][19] . . .

ANALYSIS

I. LEGAL STANDARD

A. Scope of Review

Plaintiffs raise their claims under the First Amendment to the United States Constitution. "[A c]ourt's review of 'constitutional challenges to agency actions . . . is de novo.'" The [c]ourt shall make "an independent assessment of [the plaintiffs'] claim of constitutional right when reviewing agency decision-making," and it need not accord deference to the agency's "pronouncement on a constitutional question."

. . . The [c]ourt concludes that it is obligated to conduct an independent review of the record and must do so without reliance on the Agency's determinations as to constitutional questions. But it would be inconsistent with binding precedent and wholly inappropriate to evaluate the voluminous scientific studies at issue in this case without some deference to the FDA's assessment of that technical data. Moreover, deference to the Agency's interpretation of scientific information, provided such interpretation is reasoned and not arbitrary or capricious, is consistent with the test set forth in *Pearson I*. By instructing the FDA to employ less restrictive means of regulating speech and to provide greater empirical support for its regulatory decisions, the D.C. Circuit did not purport to tell the Agency how to assess scientific data. Rather, it provided the Agency with guidelines for developing regulations once it had evaluated the evidence before it. . . .

B. Regulation of Commercial Speech

. . . The Supreme Court has "rejected the 'highly paternalistic' view that government has complete power to suppress or regulate commercial speech." Moreover, it has distinguished between "inherently misleading" speech and "potentially misleading" speech. "[Actually or inherently m]isleading advertising may be prohibited entirely. . . .But the States may not place an absolute prohibition on certain types of potentially misleading information . . . if the information also may be presented in a way that is not deceptive." Moreover, "[t]he First Amendment does not allow the FDA to simply assert that [a plaintiff's c]laim is misleading in order to 'supplant its burden to demonstrate that the harms it recites are real and that its restriction will in fact alleviate them to a material degree.'" Indeed, in *Pearson I*, the D.C. Circuit rejected the FDA's contention that health claims lacking "significant scientific

---

[19] The Agency stated that it would consider the exercise of its enforcement discretion for the following qualified health claims: 1) "One study suggests that selenium intake may reduce the risk of bladder cancer in women. However, one smaller study showed no reduction in risk. Based on these studies, FDA concludes that it is highly uncertain that selenium supplements reduce the risk of bladder cancer in women;" 2) "Two weak studies suggest that selenium intake may reduce the risk of prostate cancer. However, four stronger studies and three weak studies showed no reduction in risk. Based on these studies, FDA concludes that it is highly unlikely that selenium supplements reduce the risk of prostate cancer;" and 3) "One weak, small study suggests that selenium intake may reduce the risk of thyroid cancer. Based on this study, FDA concludes that it is highly uncertain that selenium supplements reduce the risk of thyroid cancer."

agreement" are inherently misleading as "almost frivolous." Even when it finds "that speech is misleading, the government must consider that 'people will perceive their own best interests if only they are well enough informed, and . . . the best means to that end is to open the channels of communication rather than to close them.'"

. . . The government has the burden of showing that the regulations on speech that it seeks to impose are "not more extensive than is necessary to serve" the interests it attempts to advance. Therefore, the Court in *Pearson I* noted that disclaimers are "constitutionally preferable to outright suppression," and that generally, "the preferred remedy is more disclosure, rather than less." For this reason, the [c]ourt in *Pearson I* concluded that "when government chooses a policy of suppression over disclosure—at least where there is no showing that disclosure would not suffice to cure misleadingness—the government disregards a far less restrictive means."

II. FDA'S COMPLETE BAN OF PLAINTIFFS' CLAIMS

In its response to plaintiffs' petition, the Agency denied four of the proffered claims outright. Under *Central Hudson* and *Pearson I*, the FDA may refuse to consider disclaimers for health claims (i.e., prohibit their use completely) only if such health claims are inherently misleading, or are potentially misleading but the Agency has deemed the claim "incurable by disclaimer." The court in *Whitaker* arguably went even further than *Pearson I*, holding that "any complete ban of a claim would be approved only under narrow circumstances, i.e., when there was almost no qualitative evidence in support of the claim and where the government provided empirical evidence proving that the public would still be deceived even if the claim was qualified by a disclaimer." The [c]ourt considers each of plaintiffs' claims to determine whether the FDA has met its burden with respect to those claims it has banned outright.[22]

A. Plaintiffs' "Certain Cancers" and "Anticarcinogenic Effects" Claims

The FDA asserts that claims that selenium may reduce the risk of certain cancers and may produce anticarcinogenic effects are "misleading on their face," "independent of the proffered scientific evidence." Specifically, the Agency concluded that the certain cancers claim "is incomplete and misleading because it fails to reveal the individual cancer(s) that selenium may have an effect on," thus leading a consumer to purchase selenium in hopes of preventing a cancer for which there is no evidence of risk reduction from selenium intake. The FDA also argues that by "referring in general terms to 'certain cancers,' the requested claim language . . . suggests that cancers at different sites are essentially the same disease and that it is not important to distinguish between them." Similarly, the anticarcinogenic effects claim "falsely implies that [selenium] can protect against all cancers," when in fact cancer "is not a single disease" but a "collective term for a large number of individual diseases that differ with respect to risk factors, etiology, methods of diagnosis and treatment, and mortality risk."

---

[22] The Court considers only the first sentence of each of plaintiffs' proposed claims, not the suggested disclaimer in the second sentence (i.e., that the "[s]cientific evidence supporting this claim is convincing but not yet conclusive"). To the extent the FDA denied these claims outright, it did so on the basis of the claimed relationship between selenium dietary supplements and various cancers, not because of the disclaimer. . . . To the extent the Court overturns the Agency's findings as to the substance of the health claims, it must allow the FDA to consider plaintiffs' proposed disclaimer and/or alternate disclaimers in the first instance.

Moreover, the Agency argues that the phrase "anticarcinogenic effects" is ambiguous because "anticarcinogenic" might mean both the "treatment and mitigation of existing cancer as well as the reduction of risk of getting cancer in the first place." Since "[c]laims about treatment or mitigation of disease are classified as drug claims, not health claims," the FDA "believes that no qualified claim based on that phrase would be truthful and non-misleading."

The Court concludes that the FDA's position fails under *Pearson I*. The Agency has not provided any empirical evidence, such as "studies" or "anecdotal evidence," that consumers would be misled by either of plaintiffs' claims were they accompanied by qualifications. Moreover, the explanation the FDA offers to demonstrate that plaintiffs' claims are misleading—that the claims leave out pertinent information—is not support for banning the claims entirely, but rather favors the approach of remedying any potential misleadingness by the disclosure of additional information.

The FDA's position is particularly troubling in light of its admission that plaintiffs' certain cancers claim "is literally true . . . in that there is credible evidence that selenium may reduce the risk of at least three cancers" and that the anticarcinogenic effects claim "is true to the extent that it refers to reducing the risk of . . . three cancers[.]" As the [D.C.] Circuit Court in *Pearson I* made clear, "the government's interest in preventing the use of labels that are true but do not mention [material information] would seem to be satisfied—at least ordinarily—by inclusion of a prominent disclaimer setting forth [that information]." Here, the FDA has not provided any evidence that completing plaintiffs' certain cancers claim by "reveal[ing] the individual cancer(s) that selenium may have an effect on" and explaining that cancers at different sites are different diseases and respond differently to treatments would not eliminate the consumer confusion it fears. And, the FDA's argument that "disclaimer language defining 'anticarcinogenic' as reducing the risk of, rather than treating or mitigating, cancer would not cure the misleading nature" of the claim because it "would still fail to specify the disease at issue" begs the question why an additional disclaimer, specifying the disease[s], would not remedy the purported problem.

Supreme Court precedent and *Pearson I* obligate the FDA to, at a minimum, consider "less restrictive" means of correcting that misleadingness before it turns to suppression. Because the Agency has not done so here, the [c]ourt will remand the claims relating to certain cancers and anticarcinogenic effects to the FDA for the purpose of drafting one or more disclaimers or, alternatively, setting forth empirical evidence that any disclaimer would fail to correct the claims' purported misleadingness.

B. Plaintiffs' Lung and Respiratory Tract Claim

In contrast to the certain cancers and anticarcinogenic effects claims, the FDA considered the scientific evidence proffered by plaintiffs and concluded that it could draw scientific conclusions from only four of those studies concerning plaintiffs' lung/respiratory tract claim. Because all of those studies reported "no significant difference in mean serum levels" between control cases and lung cancer cases, the Agency concluded that "there is no credible evidence for a claim about selenium supplements and reduced risk of lung cancer or other respiratory tract cancers." Plaintiffs contend that a number of the studies discounted by the

FDA provide sufficient credible evidence of a positive relationship between selenium intake and a lowered risk of lung and respiratory tract cancers.

As an initial matter, the FDA's determination regarding the lung and respiratory tract claim is not inconsistent with *Pearson I*, in which the [c]ourt allowed for the possibility that "where evidence in support of a claim is outweighed by evidence against the claim, the FDA could deem it incurable by a disclaimer and ban it outright." Here, the Agency claims that there is no evidence in support of the proposed claim and cites studies suggesting that there is no relationship between selenium intake and reduced lung cancer risk. However, the [c]ourt in *Pearson I* also suggested that when " 'credible evidence' supports a claim, that claim may not be absolutely prohibited." Therefore, the proper inquiry is what qualifies as "credible evidence" and is there any such evidence to support the lung and respiratory tract claim?

In its latest Guidance Document, the FDA states that it uses an "evidence-based review system" to evaluate the strength of the evidence in support of a statement. . . .

For example, it states that "[r]andomized, controlled trials offer the best assessment of a causal relationship between a substance and a disease." In contrast, "research synthesis studies" and "review articles" "do not provide sufficient information on the individual studies reviewed" to determine critical elements of the studies and/or whether those elements were flawed. The FDA also explains the questions it considers in determining whether scientific conclusions can be drawn from an intervention or observational study, such as where the studies were conducted (i.e., on what type of population); what type of information was collected; and what type of biomarker of disease risk was measured. If the FDA concludes that the elements of a study are flawed such that it is impossible to draw scientific conclusions from the study, it eliminates that study from further review.

Using the above procedure, the FDA disregarded the studies plaintiffs cite as "credible evidence" in support of their proposed lung/respiratory tract claim . . . . The Agency states that it eliminated the van den Brandt and Knekt studies because they were conducted on Dutch and Finnish populations whose average baseline selenium levels . . . are significantly lower than the levels observed in the "vast majority of the U.S. population." . . . As such, the FDA's decision not to extrapolate from these studies to the U.S. population is both rational based on the studies' conclusions and consistent with the Agency's evaluation criteria. . . .

Finally, the Agency rejected the SU.VI.MAX study because the study "did not confirm that all subjects were free of the cancers of interest prior to the intervention" and therefore may have involved subjects who already had cancer at the time the study began. Because of this omission, the FDA stated that it could not draw scientific conclusions from the study. However, the SU.VI.MAX study states that one of the criteria for participation in the study was "lack of disease likely to hinder active participation or threatened [*sic*] 5-year survival." . . .

To the extent that the FDA is concerned about possible limitations of the SU.VI.MAX study protocol and/or results, it must remedy such limitations with disclaimers. Accordingly, the Court remands the lung/respiratory tract claim to the Agency to determine an appropriate disclaimer in light of the SU.VI.MAX study.

C. Plaintiffs' Colon and Digestive Tract Claim

[The court reached similar conclusions with respect to the FDA's exclusion of certain studies from its analysis.]

III. FDA's QUALIFICATION OF PLAINTIFFS' PROSTATE CLAIM

After reviewing the scientific literature submitted with plaintiffs' petition, the FDA concluded that it could draw scientific conclusions regarding plaintiffs' prostate claim from eight observational studies and one intervention study. Of these, the Agency determined that two nested case-control studies suggested that selenium may reduce the risk of prostate cancer. However, the FDA rejected plaintiffs' proposed claim because it found the characterization of the evidence in support of the claim as "convincing but not yet conclusive" to be false and misleading. Instead, the Agency stated that it would exercise enforcement discretion with respect to the following qualified health claim: "Two weak studies suggest that selenium intake may reduce the risk of prostate cancer. However, four stronger studies and three weak studies showed no reduction in risk. Based on these studies, FDA concludes that it is highly unlikely that selenium supplements reduce the risk of prostate cancer."

The [c]ourt agrees with plaintiffs' contention that the FDA's proposed claim is at odds with the Supreme Court's mandate that there be a "reasonable fit" between the government's goal and the restrictions it imposes on commercial speech. The Agency has not drafted a "precise disclaimer" designed to qualify plaintiffs' claim while adhering to the "First Amendment preference for disclosure over suppression," as mandated. Rather, it has replaced plaintiffs' claim entirely. And the Agency's "qualification" effectively negates any relationship between prostate cancer risk and selenium intake. Indeed, the FDA's language is an example of a "disclaimer" that "contradict[s] the claim and defeats the purpose of making [it] in the first place." While such language might be appropriate were there no credible evidence in support of a positive relationship between prostate cancer risk and selenium intake, the Agency concedes that there is such evidence. As such, the FDA is obligated to at least consider the possibility of approving plaintiffs' proposed language with the addition of "short, succinct, and accurate disclaimers." Here, the FDA has completely eviscerated plaintiffs' claim, with no explanation as to why a less restrictive approach would not be effective. For instance, to the extent that the FDA takes issue with the proposed "convincing but not yet conclusive" claim, the Agency makes no attempt to demonstrate that this concern would not be accommodated by altering this portion of the claim with language that more accurately reflects the strength of the scientific evidence at issue. Such qualification would be a "far less restrictive means" than negation of plaintiffs' claim.

Moreover, in light of its review of the scientific literature, the [c]ourt finds that the Agency's "disclaimer" is inaccurate. . . . Even if the FDA determines the study evidences only a limited reduction in risk in certain subgroups, the [c]ourt concludes that the Agency erred in finding that the study "show[s] no reduction in [prostate cancer] risk."

. . . [T]he [c]ourt will remand plaintiffs' prostate claim to the FDA for the purpose of reconsidering the scientific literature and drafting one or more short, succinct, and accurate disclaimers in light of that review. . . .

NOTES AND QUESTIONS

Resolution. In October 2010, the FDA revised the qualified health claims at issue. The prostate claim can now read: "Selenium may reduce the risk of prostate cancer. Scientific evidence concerning this claim is inconclusive. Based on its review, FDA does not agree that selenium may reduce the risk of prostate cancer." From the advertiser's perspective, is this a better disclaimer? Are consumers likely to understand it?

Affirmative Efficacy Claims vs. Claims of Uncertain Efficacy. Pearson I resolved an important predicate question against the FDA. Before allowing a claim, the FDA wanted significant scientific agreement as to the ultimate conclusion: "this product reduces the risk of heart disease." The *Pearson I* court was concerned that the FDA therefore banned some truthful claims that could meet the "significant scientific agreement" standard in another way: claims for which it was true to say that "there is inconclusive evidence that this product may reduce the risk of heart disease" or that "this product may improve heart health, but there is no significant scientific agreement that this is true." The standard for testing the statements is formally the same, but the substance of the claim is very different—"it is true that this product works" as opposed to "it is true that this product might work, and it is also true that we don't really know." The FDA did not want to allow this kind of regression, but the court agreed that it was truthful and non-misleading to say, in appropriate cases, that preliminary results suggest a nutrient/disease relationship and that further studies are needed. Which position on the appropriate application of "significant scientific agreement" is more convincing, the FDA's or the court's?

Consider the district court's description of *Pearson II*, in which the district court "disagreed with the FDA's weighing of the scientific data." Is this an appropriate job for a court? Can it be avoided if the First Amendment is to have any force in the FDA context? Later, the court states that "it would be inconsistent with binding precedent and wholly inappropriate to evaluate the voluminous scientific studies at issue in this case without *some* deference to the FDA's assessment of that technical data" (emphasis added) (citing, among others, *Serono Labs., Inc. v. Shalala*, 158 F.3d 1313, 1320 (D.C.Cir.1998) (agency "evaluations of scientific data within its area of expertise" are "entitled to a *high* level of deference") (emphasis added)). Should the court have deferred further, or do the First Amendment interests at stake justify a higher level of judicial review?

Consider next the court's statement: "The mere absence of significant affirmative evidence in support of a particular claim . . . does not translate into negative evidence 'against' it." How seriously should we take this claim? Does this mean that an advertiser can claim "selenium protects against Alzheimer's" until the FDA produces convincing evidence to disprove the claim? Is this statement consistent with the FTC's substantiation requirement?

Now turn to the lung and respiratory tract claim. The existence of one positive study apparently means that plaintiffs can make their claims, no matter how many other studies produce negative results. Many statisticians would identify this conclusion as erroneous: If we were 95% certain that selenium does not protect against lung cancer, we would not be surprised if five out of 100 studies found a protective effect. In fact, we would *expect* 5% of trials, or one in twenty, to produce false positives.

The following cartoon shows this feature of scientific studies, as well as popular misunderstandings thereof:

9 "Significant," https://www.xkcd.com/882/ (alternative text reads: "'So, uh, we did the green study again and got no link. It was probably a—' 'RESEARCH CONFLICTED ON GREEN JELLY BEAN/ACNE LINK; MORE STUDY RECOMMENDED!'").

Under the standard set forth by the district court, how many negative studies would be required before the FDA could conclude that the single positive study reflected random variation rather than an actual protective effect? (Recall that in the *Whitaker* case discussed by the court, nearly one-third of the studies supported the claim that the advertiser wanted to make—which is to say that over two-thirds of the studies did not—and the advertiser got to make the claim.)

Finally, consider the disclaimer issue in light of what you have learned about disclosures and disclaimers. Are disclaimers likely to effectively qualify the claims at issue? If the FDA determines that disclaimers won't work, what sort of empirical evidence will it have to submit to satisfy a reviewing court of this conclusion? Would general evidence that consumers simply don't process technical disclaimers suffice?

Here are some examples of the disclaimers approved by the *Pearson* court:

> 0.8 mg folic acid in a dietary supplement is more effective in reducing the risk of neural tube defects than a lower amount in foods in common form. FDA does not endorse this claim. Public health authorities recommend that women consume 0.4 mg folic [acid] daily from fortified foods or dietary supplements or both to reduce the risk of neural tube defects.

> As part of a well-balanced diet that is low in saturated fat and cholesterol, Folic Acid, Vitamin B6 and Vitamin B-12 may reduce the risk of vascular disease. FDA evaluated the above claim and found that, while it is known that diets low in saturated fat and cholesterol reduce the risk of heart disease and other vascular diseases, the evidence in support of the above claim is inconclusive.

How well will these work? A study evaluating the DSHEA disclaimer and the *Pearson* disclaimer ("the scientific evidence is suggestive, but not conclusive") showed that they did not affect consumers' beliefs. Their presence on a supplement label had *no* significant effect on consumer reactions. Notably, the disclaimers were worthless at decreasing consumers' confidence in the health benefit claim, and worthless at decreasing consumers' belief that the FDA evaluated and approved that claim. Instead, consumers' level of trust in the government determined whether they believed that the government was evaluating dietary supplements, regardless of disclaimers. As for the specific health claims made by supplements, only consumers' preexisting level of education mattered: Higher education led to greater skepticism about supplement claims. *See* Paula Fitzgerald Bone & Karen Russo France, *Assessing Consumer Perceptions of Health Claims*, Nov. 17, 2005.

Could the FDA rely on the Bone and France study to argue that the same or similar disclaimers applied to different health claims would be just as ineffective? That is, the court's dissection of specific studies about selenium was quite particularized, but consumer perception of the disclaimer might be a separate issue, since it is not about the science but about how consumers interpret claims about science. Under the First Amendment, how specific does the FDA's evidence about the effectiveness of disclaimers have to be?

The FTC weighed in on this issue in response to the FDA's request for comments. Comments of the Staff of the Bureau of Economics, the Bureau of Consumer Protection, and the Office of Policy Planning of the Federal Trade Commission, *In the Matter of Assessing Consumer Perceptions of Health Claims*, Docket No. 2005N-0413 (Jan. 17, 2006). The FTC staff concluded, based on consumer testing, that current FDA language for qualified and unqualified claims didn't communicate the intended levels of scientific certainty to consumers. Indeed, consumers routinely perceived statements intended to indicate uncertainty as indicating more scientific consensus than statements that were supposed to indicate consensus. On the flip side, and to advertisers' detriment, the current language used to communicate that there was significant scientific agreement on a claim didn't actually indicate strong scientific certainty to consumers.

One worrying feature of the current language was the wide range of interpretations consumers gave it—"a qualified claim that, on average, communicates the correct level of scientific certainty may still mislead a substantial number of consumers." However, other language did exist that could communicate levels of certainty; "report card" formats showing where a particular claim fell on a spectrum consistently performed well in testing. Would a report card or similar ranking system (for example, one to five stars indicating the level of scientific consensus about a claim) satisfy the *Pearson* court?

Is Tobacco Different? Nicopure Labs, LLC v. Food & Drug Admin., 944 F.3d 267 (D.C. Cir. 2019), upheld a requirement that a tobacco product may be marketed as presenting a lower risk only if "the applicant has demonstrated that such product, as it is actually used by consumers," will both significantly reduce harm or risk to individual tobacco users and benefit the health of the population as a whole, taking into account current users and current non-users. Thus, it is not enough for the producer to show that the product is safer for an individual compared to smoking tobacco. Is this result consistent with *Pearson* and *Sebelius*? If the government can't decide whether certain studies should be disregarded in formulating a supplement claim, why can it decide that the meaning of "safer" is "safer for the population as a whole," rather than "safer for you than smoking tobacco would be, holding constant your likelihood of doing that instead"?

The *Nicopure* court relied on specific congressional findings that "modified risk tobacco products may encourage new users to take up tobacco products, rather than simply reduce risk to those who already use them." Congress cited an FTC study and found that advertisements that claim one tobacco product is less harmful than another mislead consumers, even when the putatively less risky products contain "disclosures and advisories intended to provide clarification." It specifically found that disclaimers and other "[l]ess restrictive and less comprehensive approaches [than FDA preapproval] have not and will not be effective" in communicating risks associated with tobacco products sold as safer.

In upholding a related regulation about advertising lower levels of or the absence of specific ingredients, the court pointed out that, in the context of tobacco, there was an extensive history showing that "[c]onsumers have frequently and erroneously read narrow safety statements about an identified substance as materially complete claims that the product is safe overall." Thus, the government could require the "testing of actual consumer perception" to show that "consumers will not be misled into believing that the product . . . is or has been demonstrated to be less harmful" more broadly before allowing a narrow "safer" claim.

2. "Organic" Claims: From the Wild West to the Walled Garden?

In the 1970s and 1980s, growing interest in traditional and less-chemically dependent methods of cultivation led to a rise in "organic" agriculture and "organic" claims on food. Unfortunately, the meaning of "organic" was unclear. Dozens of private and state organic certification bodies provided varying third-party organic certifications, and not all "organic" foods were certified. The 1990 Organic Foods Production Act (OFPA) established a national organic standard, rather than waiting to see if the market would ever converge on a definition.

Under OFPA, the U.S. Department of Agriculture (USDA) is responsible for regulating the use of "organic" on agricultural products. Only agricultural products that meet USDA standards can be labeled "organic" and use the USDA Organic seal. Under OFPA, the National Organic Standards Board (NOSB), which includes representatives from famers, retailers, consumers, environmental groups and food processors, makes recommendations to the USDA to define and regulate the organic label. In 1997, the USDA released the first proposed national organic standard, but did not follow NOSB recommendations in that its standard would have allowed food to be labeled organic even if it had undergone genetic modification or irradiation, had been fertilized with processed sewage sludge or (for livestock) had been treated with antibiotics. After significant consumer protest, a more-stringent revised standard was finalized in 2001. *See* ELAINE MARIE LIPSON, ONE NATION, ORGANICALLY GROWN (2001).

The "organic" label does not have any relationship to the producer's size. In fact, small farmers may find it harder to comply with the certification and recordkeeping requirements. Nor does organic mean local. Many organic foods are imported from other countries.

Among other things, the organic standard prohibits synthetic pesticides; prohibits genetic modification; prohibits irradiation; requires livestock to be given access to pasture; bans giving livestock growth hormones or antibiotics (sick animals are to be treated, but removed from the herd and not sold as organic); requires livestock to get organically grown feed; requires land to be free of chemical applications for three years before its crops can be considered organic; and requires written farm plans and audit trails. All growers and food processors who label their food organic, except those who make $5,000 or less per year from an organic enterprise, must be certified by an USDA-accredited, independent third-party agent. Knowingly misusing the organic label violates the law and may incur a civil penalty.

Under the rules, there are four categories for organic labeling: "100% organic" is just that. "Organic" requires 95% of the ingredients to be certified organic. Only these two categories can use the USDA Organic seal.

"Made with organic" requires 70% of the non-water, non-salt ingredients to be certified organic, and there are other requirements, including a rule that including "made with organic ingredients" is not allowed. Instead, the claim must specify the organic ingredients or food categories, i.e., "Made with Organic [specify ingredients and or food categories]," but it may not list more than three ingredients or food categories. *See* United States Dep't of Agriculture, *Guidance: Products in the "Made with Organic ***" Labeling Category* (Sept. 5, 2018); *see also* United States Dep't of Agriculture, *"Made with" Organic Labeling Examples* (Apr. 2014) (offering examples of allowed and non-allowed claims).

When the product is made with less than 70% organic ingredients, "organic" can be listed on the side panel only. The law also specifies display of the certifier's name and address and certain restrictions on permissible non-organic ingredients.

Is this scheme consistent with the First Amendment?

The Standard's History. Maine organic blueberry farmer and National Organic Program inspector Arthur Harvey successfully challenged several aspects of the rule initially adopted by the USDA. *See* Harvey v. Veneman, 396 F. 3d 28 (1st Cir. 2005). The rule initially could be read to allow the use of any non-organic ingredients "not commercially available in organic form" for multi-ingredient products labeled "organic." The court of appeals held that the OPFA didn't authorize a blanket exemption, but ingredients such as corn starch could be reviewed individually and allowed onto a list of acceptable nonorganic ingredients. Likewise, the rule improperly allowed the use of synthetic substances such as ascorbic acid and potassium hydroxide in processing organic-labeled items (though allowing this for "made with organic"-labeled items was acceptable), and improperly permitted the use of up to 20% conventional feed in the first nine months of a dairy herd's yearlong conversion to organic.

Proponents of the rule's initial version argued that these three provisions made producing organic products economically feasible, especially for smaller family farms. According to the CEO of Organic Valley Family of Farms, for example, "we realize, after this many years of experience, that synthetics are pretty necessary for a lot of different processes." Dan Sullivan, *Organics in the News*, March 31, 2005. Without synthetics, he argued, producers would abandon the "organic" label and move to the "made with organic" category, thus decreasing the amount of organic food available. By some estimates, more than 90% of multi-ingredient organic foods on the market, including many dairy products, would be disqualified from "organic" status under *Harvey*.

Congress responded to *Harvey* by amending OPFA to restore most of the initial rule. The Secretary of Agriculture could designate agricultural products that are commercially unavailable in organic form for short-term placement on a list of approved ingredients for organic-labeled products. For example, organic vanilla is grown in Madagascar, which is subject to major storms that interrupt supply. Processed organic products could be allowed to substitute small amounts of conventional vanilla when organic vanilla is commercially unavailable. Reversing the First Circuit, synthetic substances on the approved list may also be used in handling or processing an organic product. The law also allows more flexibility in the last year of transition of dairy herds to organic.

What Do Consumers Think "Organic" Means? Consumers Union surveyed consumers around the time of *Harvey* and found that 74% did not expect food labeled "made with organic" to contain artificial ingredients, despite the fact that synthetic ingredients are allowed in the

30% non-organic portion of the product. Eighty-five percent didn't expect food labeled "organic" to contain artificial ingredients (recall that the law requires only 95% organic content). The USDA does not have standards for "organic" fish; a rule was proposed in 2016, but one observer expects no action "indefinitely" or at least until there is a new administration. Amanda Nichols, *The State of Organic Aquaculture in the United States* (2019). Currently, importers can often use foreign standards to label their fish as organic even though they would not meet U.S. standards, although California bars the use of "organic" on the products of aquaculture until the United States develops a standard therefor. Cal. Health & Safety Code § 110827 (2017). Consumers Union found 93% agreement that organic fish should be produced with 100% organic feed like all other animals. *See* Urvashi Rangan, *Comment to National Organic Standards Board on Aquaculture Recommendations*, November 18, 2008.

To what extent should consumer perception control the regulatory definition of "organic"? If consumers knew more about the difficulties of producing 100% organic multi-ingredient/processed foods, would they be more forgiving, and should that make a difference?

REBECCA TUSHNET, IT DEPENDS ON WHAT THE MEANING OF "FALSE" IS: FALSITY AND MISLEADINGNESS IN COMMERCIAL SPEECH DOCTRINE, 41 LOYOLA L.A. L. REV. 101 (2008) (EXCERPT)

The overall effects of the organic regulations are hard to predict. One effect is to decrease producers' incentives to make processed food with organic content below the threshold, because they can't truthfully advertise the organic content and organic food is more expensive. At the same time, the "made with organic" rules may also encourage producers to make more products with 70 percent or greater organic content, even if they cost more than a 60 percent organic product, and discourage them from adding a tiny bit of organic material to a conventional product. Consumers may well benefit from a fairly high threshold, since a 10 percent organic product may not satisfy consumer expectations for "organic." Moreover, in the absence of a uniform definition, many people would find it too difficult to sort through varying claims and would either mistakenly discount all such claims or mistakenly accept them. In other words, the "market for lemons" problem can be avoided in the market for organic lemons, but only if each consumer doesn't have to parse the definition of organic.

Separately, the ability to use a small percentage of non-organic ingredients may encourage more makers of multi-ingredient, processed food to enter the organic market. However, it also risks confusing consumers who, for example, expect that their organic sausages will be made entirely from organic meat and not include inorganic casings. Another specific example from the USDA's proposed list of exempt ingredients is hops. Exempting hops may make it more difficult for small producers of fully organic beer to compete against large firms that use the maximum amount of nonorganic hops, which cost half as much as organic hops, even as it encourages the production of more "organic" beers. Because both sets of producers can advertise "organic" beer, the regulation may either aid consumers or deceive them, depending on what they think organic means.

The issue of consumer response to standard-setting is worth further discussion to show just how hard the problem is. By setting a standard, the government establishes what "organic" means. If people misunderstand the term—in other words, if they continue to give a different meaning to it—there is an information problem that leads to inefficient results. If people do not understand the term but nonetheless rely on it, then a key question is whether the government has gotten the social policy producing the underlying definition right. Moreover, the correctness of the government's definition has to be compared to the situation without regulation, in which producers could give the term multiple meanings as long as they were not intentionally fraudulent. If consumers still relied on the term without understanding it or understanding that different producers were using different definitions, the welfare effects would change, but not obviously in any particular direction. To this must be added the likelihood that consumers would discount the term "organic" if they believed it to be self-defined, moderating both the harms and benefits of varying definitions. Only if consumers carefully research multiple meanings of unregulated terms—and only if they do this again and again, for each term that makes a difference to them—can we expect the unregulated market to beat the government systematically in shaping meaning.

FTC, GREEN GUIDES STATEMENT OF BASIS AND PURPOSE (2012)

. . . The final [Green] Guides do not include a section on organic claims for two reasons. First, the USDA's NOP already addresses organic claims for agricultural products. Second, the Commission continues to lack sufficient evidence upon which to base generally applicable guidance for organic claims.

. . . [The] Commission also declines to issue general guidance on claims for products outside the NOP's jurisdiction. The record is simply too thin to support general guidance. Moreover, any advice the Commission promulgated for non-agricultural products could lead to general confusion or a perceived conflict with current or future NOP guidelines. In response to commenters concerned that the absence of guidance may result in fraud, the Commission reminds marketers they remain subject to the FTC Act's general proscriptions against unfair or deceptive marketing. As with any deceptive marketing claim, the Commission may bring an enforcement action against a marketer for deceptive organic claims.

Finally, some commenters requested a definition for "organic." The Commission, however, does not define terms. Instead, it examines how consumers interpret claims. At this time, the Commission lacks sufficient evidence regarding how consumers perceive organic claims to provide generally applicable advice.

LETTER FROM CONSUMERS UNION TO DAVID VLADECK, DIRECTOR, FTC BUREAU OF CONSUMER PROTECTION, MAR. 12, 2010

. . . We would like to take this opportunity to request that the Commission investigate the widespread, misleading use of "organic" claims on personal care products.

In particular, we have repeatedly asked the USDA to require that "organic" personal care products meet the same standards as "organic" food and to prohibit any use of the organic claim on products that don't meet the requirements of the NOP, such as seafood, fish and the subject of this particular complaint, personal care products. The USDA is superimposing a different labeling structure for "organic" personal care products and one that deviates from that required by the NOP. As a result, an extremely confusing marketplace exists for consumers shopping for "organic" personal care products. . . . [The] USDA is not requiring that all "organic" claims on personal care products, including those that do not bear the "USDA-organic" seal, be NOP compliant, which is required for food. . . .

Personal care products tend to contain many synthetic ingredients, and many consumers are willing to pay more to buy "organic" personal care products in order to avoid these synthetic ingredients. . . .

Organic personal care products that are not compliant with the NOP can contain many petroleum-derived ingredients, conventional agricultural ingredients (those that have been treated with pesticides, etc.), preservatives, colorings and fragrances which may use or contain chemicals of concern in the production or final product. For example, phthalates, some of which have been banned by the Consumer Product Safety Commission in children's products for reproductive health effect concerns, may be lurking in many of the fragrances that could be used in organic personal care products. Parabens, EDTA, PEGs, coal tar colors (FD&C), ethanolamines—are just a few examples of synthetic materials that should certainly be reviewed and approved before being used in an organic personal care product. We believe many of those materials would not be approved after review by the NOSB. Finally, water and salt are required to be exempt from organic certification and the final calculation of organic content in a given product. However, we have noted several cases where "organic waters" are listed on ingredient panels. This would not be allowed for "organic" food and should not be allowed for "organic" personal care products. These so-called "organic" products can mislead and deceive consumers into paying more for something they did not expect.

. . . [Consumers Union also highlighted that there was no percentage requirement for "made with organic" claims on personal care products, as there is for food. As a result, personal products with minimal organic content can make "organic" label claims with apparent impunity.]

In the absence of USDA enforcement against unsubstantiated organic claims, the cosmetics industry has launched competing "organic" certifications. There are several different industry-based organic certification programs including Organic and Sustainable Industry Standards (OASIS), National Sanitation Foundation (NSF) International certification, and another mark called ECOCERT, which only add to the marketplace confusion. . . .

For example, OASIS claims to be "the first organic standard for the U.S. beauty and personal care market, bringing clarity to consumer confusion around organic product claims—with a certification seal that will become the internationally accepted seal representing verified Organic standards for personal care. The only 'industry consensus' standard with the support of 30 founding members." Even though there are many certified USDA Organic personal care brands and products, OASIS tells consumers: "Until today, the USA has not had a dedicated organic standard for the beauty and personal care industry. In absence of a true industry standard, companies attempted to apply the USDA NOP (National Organic Program) Organic food standard for beauty and personal care ingredients and products. But the USDA's food standards were never designed for this industry, and limit certain types of 'green chemistry' posing significant challenges for those seeking to create certified organic products."

. . . In response to the question, "What is the difference between ECOCERT® and the USDA?" Organic wear® tells consumers: "ECOCERT® is the only organic certification for color cosmetics. USDA guidelines are for food products and they have no jurisdiction over color cosmetics." . . .

NOTES AND QUESTIONS

Is the Consumers Union position persuasive? Are the competing certifications evidence that the market is correcting the problem?

The FTC has taken some actions on "organic" claims. In 2017, it entered into a consent judgment against unsubstantiated claims that mattresses were "organic," when they were made of a majority of non-organic materials, mainly polyurethane, a plastic produced almost entirely from petroleum-based raw materials. *In re* Moonlight Slumber, LLC, FTC Docket No. C-4634 (2017). In 2019, another company agreed to a $1.76 million fine for falsely advertising its body washes, lotions, baby, hair care, bath and cleaning products as "certified organic," "USDA certified organic," and "Truly Organic," when the products either contained ingredients that were not certified under the National Organic Program or contained ingredients that were not organically sourced. Fed. Trade Comm'n v. Truly Organic, Inc., No. 19-23832-Civ-Scola (S.D. Fla. Sept. 18, 2019).

A Remaining Role for State Law? In re Aurora Dairy Corp. Organic Milk Marketing and Sales Practices Litigation, 621 F.3d 781 (8th Cir. 2010), considered whether the OFPA preempted state consumer protection law. As noted above, the OFPA creates a certification program through which agricultural producers may become certified to produce organic products. The OFPA also provides for the accreditation of certification agents, who inspect producers and make recommendations to the USDA regarding certification. Pursuant to the OFPA, the USDA-promulgated regulations, known as the National Organic Program (NOP), 7 C.F.R. pt. 205, defining which agricultural products qualify as organic.

One certifying agent, QAI, Inc., certified Aurora Dairy Corporation's dairy farm to produce organic milk. Aurora was never decertified, though the USDA proposed revoking its certification in 2007 due to willful violations of the OFPA, including multiple cases of using nonorganic cows to produce "organic" milk, failure to produce and handle milk in accordance with regulations, and recordkeeping failures. Aurora and the USDA eventually entered into a consent agreement pursuant to which Aurora agreed to improve its practices and submit to further review.

Aurora sold its milk to the retailer defendants. Class plaintiffs sued Aurora, the retailers, and QAI, alleging that the defendants failed to comply with the OFPA and NOP and that Aurora's milk violated the law by claiming to be organic when it wasn't. In addition, plaintiffs alleged that Aurora and the retailers made other false statements:

> [S]everal of the cartons featured depictions of pastoral scenes with cows grazing in pastures, and advertised the idyllic conditions under which the dairy cows lived.

Aurora advertised, "As producers of organic milk, our motto is 'Cows First,'" and, "We believe that animal welfare and cow comfort are the most important measures in organic dairy." Wal-Mart represented its milk was produced without the use of antibiotics or pesticides, and [that] organic farmers are committed to the humane treatment of animals. Safeway asserted its dairy cows "enjoy a healthy mix of fresh air, plenty of exercise, clean drinking water and a wholesome, 100% certified organic diet." Target declared, "Our milk comes from healthy cows that graze in organic pastures and eat wholesome organic feed."

The plaintiffs also alleged false advertising off the carton, such as Costco's *Costco Connection* magazine, which contained an article about Costco's house brand (for which Aurora was a supplier) claiming that "[t]he cows on the farm have quite the life. They feed on a balanced organic vegan diet and have access to organic pastures for grazing." The cases around the nation were consolidated, and the district court granted the motion to dismiss.

The court of appeals affirmed the dismissal of all claims against QAI. Congress meant to replace the "patchwork" of existing state regulations with a national standard defining organic food, which included the certification scheme under which QAI is an accredited certifying agent. Thus, all claims against QAI were preempted. Aurora's certification also allows it to sell or label products using the OFPA-regulated terms without penalty. There is an administrative procedure for appeals of a certification agent's decisions. "[T]o the extent state law permits outside parties, including consumers, to interfere with or second guess the certification process, the state law is an 'obstacle to the accomplishment of congressional objectives' of the OFPA" and was preempted. QAI couldn't comply with the OFPA and its regulations detailing the process for revoking certifications and also comply with any additional state law duty to revoke certifications.

For the same reasons, claims attacking Aurora's certification were preempted. Class plaintiffs argued that defendants must be both certified and compliant with the underlying requirements to comply with the OFPA, but in light of the statute's structure and purpose, compliance and certification couldn't be viewed separately. The goal of establishing national standards would be undermined by an inevitable divergence in application by numerous court systems. Not only different legal interpretations, but also "different enforcement strategies and priorities" could fragment uniformity. (Note the difference in this analysis from other courts which find that state enforcement of a federal scheme such as the FDCA does not conflict with the scheme, just increases the incentives to comply.) "[A]ny attempt to hold Aurora or the retailers liable under state law based upon its products supposedly not being organic directly conflicts with the role of the certifying agent . . . ." Thus, claims based on Aurora's and the retailers' selling milk as organic when it was not were preempted.

Other claims, however, remained. State-law challenges to the certification determination were preempted, but not state-law challenges to the "facts underlying certification." The defendants argued that, if OFPA certification is to mean anything, it must mean the certified products have met all the statutory and regulatory requirements. The court of appeals disagreed. Certification requires, among other things, preventive livestock healthcare practices, including sufficiently nutritional feed. Congress, the court felt confident, didn't intend to prevent states from enforcing animal cruelty laws, especially given the states' historic roles in the area of consumer protection, fraudand tort claims. Notably, "[c]ertification relies upon inspection and observation of only a portion of a producer's operations, and thus, the evidence which supported certification could, and very likely would, be different from the evidence which supports a state cause of action."

Preempting state-law claims unrelated to certification and certification compliance doesn't advance the purpose of establishing national standards for organic foods. In fact, preemption of consumer protection law might diminish consumer confidence if consumers become aware that the certifying agent didn't suspend certification in spite of clear facts to the contrary and that there wasn't anything that anyone else could do. Furthermore, "although broad factual preemption may increase organic production in the short term, consumers may well elect to avoid paying the premium for organic products upon realizing preemption grants organic producers a de facto license to violate state fraud, consumer protection, and false advertising laws with relative impunity . . . ." *See also* Quesada v. Herb Thyme Farms, 323 P.3d 1 (Cal. 2014) (claim that a grower intentionally mislabeled conventionally grown produce as organic wasn't preempted; reasoning similarly).

A Role for the Lanham Act? In *All One God Faith, Inc. v. The Hain Celestial Group, Inc.*, 2010 WL 2133209 (N.D. Cal. 2010), the plaintiff sued multiple defendants for falsely advertising their cosmetics as organic, alleging that consumers expect that personal-care products labeled as organic won't contain synthetic compounds such as preservatives, cleansing agents or moisturizing agents derived from conventionally produced agricultural materials, or petrochemicals. These expectations may well be causally connected to the federal "organic" standards for food, to which they conform, though plaintiff's amended complaint alleged that consumer research surveys established their existence.

In such cases, should the Lanham Act apply, which might functionally expand the scope of USDA regulation beyond what Congress or the USDA intended?

The court dismissed the complaint based on the primary jurisdiction doctrine, which allocates matters to relevant agencies first where Congress has given the agency comprehensive authority that requires expertise or uniformity. Defendants argued that deciding the case would force the court to evaluate how consumer understandings line up with existing regulations and potentially impose standards in conflict with those Congress mandated (for example, statutes and regulations arguably allow some use of synthetic ingredients in products labeled "organic," while the complaint alleged that reasonable consumers expect that organic products have no synthetic ingredients). The court agreed that it would have to interpret and apply USDA regulations to determine what "organically produced," "nonagricultural" and "synthetic" mean. The court stayed the case pending further USDA action.

Was this the right result? Compare it to the FDA preemption cases in section 1. Does the logic of the case survive *POM Wonderful*?

The Halo Effect. In a study, participants were asked to sample pairs of identical foods. One was labeled "organic" and the other "regular," though they were actually both organic. Participants estimated the "organic" foods to be lower in calories, higher in nutritional value and worth paying more for than the "regular" foods, though people who typically read nutrition labels and who often bought organic foods did somewhat better at estimating calories. Wan-chen Jenny Lee et al., *You Taste What You See: Do Organic Labels Bias Taste Perceptions?*, 29 FOOD QUALITY & PREFERENCE 33 (2013). Does "organic" mislead calorie-conscious consumers? Is that misleadingness justified by the other (truthful) information conveyed by the term?

3.   Green Marketing

"Green" marketing often covers the same types of goods that the FDA and USDA regulate, although it can be used far more broadly. The regulations, such as they are, on "green" claims provide a contrast to the more rule-based regulations covered in the first parts of this chapter. Think about whether the essentially reactive approach of "green" marketing regulation would be more appropriate for these other fields; whether "green" claims ought to get the same kind of detailed instructions as drugs or "organic" foods; or whether these differing types of regulation have been implemented appropriately given the different topics.

In 1992, in response to growing consumer interest in the environment, growing advertiser response to this interest and growing confusion about what environmental-type claims meant, the FTC issued its first Green Guides, providing specific criteria for using terms such as biodegradable, recyclable and recycled, as well as more general guidance. The Guides have been revised three times as environmental concerns changed and experience with green marketing claims improved. We will examine portions of the 2012 revisions, and the FTC's commentary on them.

FTC, STATEMENT OF BASIS AND PURPOSE (2012) (OPENING COMMENTARY)

The Commission issued the Green Guides, 16 CFR Part 260, to help marketers avoid deceptive environmental claims under Section 5 of the FTC Act, 15 U.S.C. 45.

Industry guides, such as these, are administrative interpretations of the law. Therefore, they do not have the force and effect of law and are not independently enforceable. The Commission, however, can take action under the FTC Act if a marketer makes an environmental claim inconsistent with the Guides. In any such enforcement action, the Commission must prove that the challenged act or practice is unfair or deceptive.

The Green Guides outline general principles that apply to all environmental marketing claims and provide guidance regarding many specific environmental benefit claims. The Guides explain how reasonable consumers likely interpret each such claim, describe the basic elements necessary to substantiate it and present options for qualifying it to avoid deception.[10]

Illustrative qualifications provide guidance for marketers who want assurance about how to make non-deceptive environmental claims, but [they] are not the only permissible

---

[10] The Guides, however, neither establish standards for environmental performance nor prescribe testing protocols.

approaches to qualifying a claim. As discussed below, although the Guides assist marketers in making non-deceptive environmental claims, the Guides cannot always anticipate which specific claims will, or will not, be deceptive because of incomplete consumerperception evidence and because perception often depends on context. . . .

[B]ecause the Guides are based on consumer understanding of environmental claims, consumer perception research provides the best evidence upon which to formulate guidance. The Commission therefore conducted its own study in July and August of 2009.

The study presented 3,777 participants with questions calculated to determine how they understood certain environmental claims. The first portion of the study examined general environmental benefit claims ("green" and "eco-friendly"), as well as "sustainable," "made with renewable materials," "made with renewable energy," and "made with recycled materials" claims. To examine whether consumers' understanding of these claims differed depending on the product being advertised, the study tested the claims as they appeared on three different products: wrapping paper, a laundry basket, and kitchen flooring.[11]

I.   General Issues

. . . . [T]he Commission agrees that enforcement is a key component of greater compliance. Therefore, in recent years it has stepped up enforcement against companies making deceptive environmental claims. For example, the Commission sued a company for providing environmental certifications to any businesses willing to pay a fee without considering their products' environmental attributes. Additionally, the Commission announced three actions charging marketers with making false and unsubstantiated claims that their products were biodegradable. The Commission also charged four sellers of clothing and other textile products with deceptively labeling and advertising these items as made of bamboo fiber, manufactured using an environmentally friendly process, and/or biodegradable. . . .

16 CFR PART 260: GUIDES FOR THE USE OF ENVIRONMENTAL MARKETING CLAIMS

§ 260.1 Purpose, Scope, and Structure of the Guides.

. . . (d) The guides consist of general principles, specific guidance on the use of particular environmental claims, and examples. . . . The examples provide the Commission's views on how reasonable consumers likely interpret certain claims. . . . [The examples don't] illustrate the only ways to comply with the guides. Marketers can use an alternative approach if the approach satisfies the requirements of Section 5 of the FTC Act. . . .

§ 260.3 General Principles.

. . . (b) Distinction between benefits of product, package, and service: Unless it is clear from the context, an environmental marketing claim should specify whether it refers to the product, the product's packaging, a service, or just to a portion of the product, package, or service. In general, if the environmental attribute applies to all but minor, incidental

---

[11] The study results support the 1998 Guides' approach of providing general, rather than product-specific, guidance because consumers generally viewed the tested claims similarly for the three tested products. . . .

components of a product or package, the marketer need not qualify the claim to identify that fact. However, there may be exceptions to this general principle. For example, if a marketer makes an unqualified recyclable claim, and the presence of the incidental component significantly limits the ability to recycle the product, the claim would be deceptive.

Example 1: A plastic package containing a new shower curtain is labeled "recyclable" without further elaboration. Because the context of the claim does not make clear whether it refers to the plastic package or the shower curtain, the claim is deceptive if any part of either the package or the curtain, other than minor, incidental components, cannot be recycled.

Example 2: A soft drink bottle is labeled "recycled." The bottle is made entirely from recycled materials, but the bottle cap is not. Because the bottle cap is a minor, incidental component of the package, the claim is not deceptive.

(c) Overstatement of environmental attribute: An environmental marketing claim should not overstate, directly or by implication, an environmental attribute or benefit. Marketers should not state or imply environmental benefits if the benefits are negligible.

Example 1: An area rug is labeled "50% more recycled content than before." The manufacturer increased the recycled content of its rug from 2% recycled fiber to 3%. Although the claim is technically true, it likely conveys the false impression that the manufacturer has increased significantly the use of recycled fiber.

Example 2: A trash bag is labeled "recyclable" without qualification. Because trash bags ordinarily are not separated from other trash at the landfill or incinerator for recycling, they are highly unlikely to be used again for any purpose. Even if the bag is technically capable of being recycled, the claim is deceptive since it asserts an environmental benefit where no meaningful benefit exists.

(d) Comparative claims: Comparative environmental marketing claims should be clear to avoid consumer confusion about the comparison. Marketers should have substantiation for the comparison.

Example 1: An advertiser notes that its glass bathroom tiles contain "20% more recycled content." Depending on the context, the claim could be a comparison either to the advertiser's immediately preceding product or to its competitors' products. The advertiser should have substantiation for both interpretations. Otherwise, the advertiser should make the basis for comparison clear, for example, by saying "20% more recycled content than our previous bathroom tiles." . . .

§ 260.4 General Environmental Benefit Claims.

(a) It is deceptive to misrepresent, directly or by implication, that a product, package, or service offers a general environmental benefit.

(b) Unqualified general environmental benefit claims are difficult to interpret and likely convey a wide range of meanings. In many cases, such claims likely convey that the product, package, or service has specific and far-reaching environmental benefits and may convey that the item or service has no negative environmental impact. Because it is highly unlikely that marketers can substantiate all reasonable interpretations of these claims, marketers should not make unqualified general environmental benefit claims.

(c) Marketers can qualify general environmental benefit claims to prevent deception about the nature of the environmental benefit being asserted. To avoid deception, marketers should use clear and prominent qualifying language that limits the claim to a specific benefit or benefits. Marketers should not imply that any specific benefit is significant if it is, in fact, negligible. If a qualified general claim conveys that a product is more environmentally beneficial overall because of the particular touted benefit(s), marketers should analyze trade-offs resulting from the benefit(s) to determine if they can substantiate this claim.[12] . . .

Example 1: The brand name "Eco-friendly" likely conveys that the product has far-reaching environmental benefits and may convey that the product has no negative environmental impact. Because it is highly unlikely that the marketer can substantiate these claims, the use of such a brand name is deceptive. A claim, such as "Eco-friendly: made with recycled materials," would not be deceptive if: (1) the statement "made with recycled materials" is clear and prominent; (2) the marketer can substantiate that the entire product or package, excluding minor, incidental components, is made from recycled material; (3) making the product with recycled materials makes the product more environmentally beneficial overall; and (4) the advertisement's context does not imply other deceptive claims.

Example 2: A marketer states that its packaging is now "Greener than our previous packaging." The packaging weighs 15% less than previous packaging, but it is not recyclable nor has it been improved in any other material respect. The claim is deceptive because reasonable consumers likely would interpret "Greener" in this context to mean that other significant environmental aspects of the packaging also are improved over previous packaging. A claim stating "Greener than our previous packaging" accompanied by clear and prominent language such as, "We've reduced the weight of our packaging by 15%," would not be deceptive, provided that reducing the packaging's weight makes the product more environmentally beneficial overall and the advertisement's context does not imply other deceptive claims.

Example 3: A marketer's advertisement features a picture of a laser printer in a bird's nest balancing on a tree branch, surrounded by a dense forest. In green type, the marketer states, "Buy our printer. Make a change." Although the advertisement does not expressly claim that the product has environmental benefits, the featured images, in combination with the text, likely convey that the product has far-reaching environmental benefits and may convey that the product has no negative environmental impact. Because it is highly unlikely that the marketer can substantiate these claims, this advertisement is deceptive. . . .

---

[12] [Editor's note: Some have contended that this statement requires companies to engage in "life-cycle analysis," a complicated and often hotly contested effort to measure the total environmental impact of a product from cradle to tomb. The FTC declined to explicitly require life-cycle analysis as a precondition for making an environmental benefit claim. As you read the examples, consider whether you agree that the FTC's reasoning covertly requires a life-cycle analysis.]

Example 5: A marketer reduces the weight of its plastic beverage bottles. The bottles' labels state: "Environmentally friendly improvement. 25% less plastic than our previous packaging." The plastic bottles are 25 percent lighter but otherwise are no different. The advertisement conveys that the bottles are more environmentally beneficial overall because of the source reduction. To substantiate this claim, the marketer likely can analyze the impacts of the source reduction without evaluating environmental impacts throughout the packaging's life cycle. If, however, manufacturing the new bottles significantly alters environmental attributes earlier or later in the bottles' life cycle, i.e., manufacturing the bottles requires more energy or a different kind of plastic, then a more comprehensive analysis may be appropriate.

[The FTC found that its consumer studies supported its recommendation against making general, unqualified environmental benefit claims. From its Statement of Basis and Purpose:] Specifically, on average, approximately half of the respondents viewing general, unqualified "green" and "eco-friendly" claims inferred specific, unstated environmental benefits. Moreover, 27 percent of respondents interpreted the unqualified claims "green" and "eco-friendly" as suggesting the product has no negative environmental impact.

. . . The Commission designed its questionnaire to be as non-suggestive and non-leading as possible. Thus, before asking any closed-ended questions about specific environmental attributes, the study asked open-ended questions about what, if anything, a claim suggested or implied about a product. The responses to these non-suggestive, open-ended questions show that a large percentage of the participants took particular environmental attribute claims from an unqualified claim. Fifty-three percent of respondents indicated, in this unprompted format, that the product had one or more implied specific environmental characteristics. For example, of those who were told that the product was "Green" or "Eco-Friendly," 33 percent indicated that the claim suggested that the product was made with recycled materials. . . .

As administrative interpretations of Section 5, the Guides do not create an obligation that does not already exist under Section 5. Rather, they clarify this obligation, cautioning marketers that unqualified general environmental benefit claims are difficult, if not impossible, to substantiate and reminding marketers not to make claims they cannot substantiate. . . .

Finally, although some commenters asked the Commission to include an example illustrating a non-deceptive, unqualified general environmental benefit claim, the Commission declines to do so. As discussed above, it is highly unlikely that marketers can substantiate all reasonable interpretations of such a claim. In fact, even the scenarios commenters described as meriting unqualified general environmental benefit claims illustrate the difficulty in substantiating such claims. For instance, one commenter suggested including an example about a local nursery selling organically grown, indigenous species of trees for local planting. Here, however, there may be negative environmental impacts depending on, among other things, the nursery's irrigation systems, waste disposal practices, and vehicle and machinery use. It also is highly unlikely that the nursery could substantiate all the specific claims reasonable consumers take away from a general "green" claim. For example, consumers may incorrectly assume that the nursery uses only renewable energy. Moreover, even if one could postulate an example where a product has no negative impact and has every implied environmental benefit, similar factual scenarios would be so rare that the example would have limited applicability and may lead to more confusion than benefit. Nevertheless, because the Guides are simply guidance, they do not foreclose the possibility that a marketer could create an advertisement for a particular product with general environmental claims that only implies claims the marketer can substantiate. . . .

§ 260.6 Certifications and Seals of Approval.

(a) It is deceptive to misrepresent, directly or by implication, that a product, package, or service has been endorsed or certified by an independent third-party.

(b) A marketer's use of the name, logo, or seal of approval of a third-party certifier or organization may be an endorsement, which should meet the criteria for endorsements provided in the FTC's Endorsement Guides, 16 C.F.R. Part 255 . . . .

(c) Third-party certification does not eliminate a marketer's obligation to ensure that it has substantiation for all claims reasonably communicated by the certification.

(d) A marketer's use of an environmental certification or seal of approval likely conveys that the product offers a general environmental benefit (see § 260.4) if the certification or seal does not convey the basis for the certification or seal, either through the name or some other means. Because it is highly unlikely that marketers can substantiate general environmental benefit claims, marketers should not use environmental certifications or seals that do not convey the basis for the certification. . . .

Example 1: An advertisement for paint features a "GreenLogo" seal and the statement "GreenLogo for Environmental Excellence." This advertisement likely conveys that: (1) the GreenLogo seal is awarded by an independent, third-party certifier with appropriate expertise in evaluating the environmental attributes of paint; and (2) the product has far-reaching environmental benefits. If the paint manufacturer awarded the seal to its own product, and no independent, third-party certifier objectively evaluated the paint using independent standards, the claim would be deceptive. The claim would not be deceptive if the marketer accompanied the seal with clear and prominent language: (1) indicating that the marketer awarded the GreenLogo seal to its own product; and (2) clearly conveying that the award refers only to specific and limited benefits. . . .

Example 4: A marketer's package features a seal of approval with the text "Certified Non-Toxic." The seal is awarded by a certifier with appropriate expertise in evaluating ingredient safety and potential toxicity. It applies standards developed by a voluntary consensus standard body. Although non-industry members comprise a majority of the certifier's board, an industry veto could override any proposed changes to the standards. This certification likely conveys that the product is certified by an independent organization. This claim would be deceptive because industry members can veto any proposed changes to the standards.

Example 5: A marketer's industry sales brochure for overhead lighting features a seal with the text "EcoFriendly Building Association" to show that the marketer is a member of that organization. Although the lighting manufacturer is, in fact, a member, this association has not evaluated the environmental attributes of the marketer's product. This advertisement would be deceptive because it likely conveys that the EcoFriendly Building Association evaluated the product through testing or other objective standards. It also is likely to convey that the lighting has far-reaching environmental benefits. The use of the seal would not be deceptive if the manufacturer accompanies it with clear and prominent qualifying language: (1) indicating that the seal refers to the company's membership only and that the association did not evaluate the product's environmental attributes; and (2) limiting the general environmental benefit representations, both express and implied, to the particular product attributes for which the marketer has substantiation. For example, the marketer could state: "Although we are a member of the EcoFriendly Building Association, it has not evaluated this product. Our lighting is made from 100 percent recycled metal and uses energy efficient LED technology."

Example 6: A product label contains an environmental seal, either in the form of a globe icon or a globe icon with the text "EarthSmart." EarthSmart is an independent, third-party certifier with appropriate expertise in evaluating chemical emissions of products. While the marketer meets EarthSmart's standards for reduced chemical emissions during product usage, the product has no other specific environmental benefits. Either seal likely conveys that the product has far-reaching environmental benefits, and that EarthSmart certified the product for all of these benefits. If the marketer cannot substantiate these claims, the use of the seal would be deceptive. The seal would not be deceptive if the marketer accompanied it with clear and prominent language clearly conveying that the certification refers only to specific and limited benefits. For example, the marketer could state next to the globe icon: "EarthSmart certifies that this product meets EarthSmart standards for reduced chemical emissions during product usage." Alternatively, the claim would not be deceptive if the EarthSmart environmental seal itself stated: "EarthSmart Certified for reduced chemical emissions during product usage." . . .

§ 260.7 Compostable Claims.

(a) It is deceptive to misrepresent, directly or by implication, that a product or package is compostable. [Editor's note: For this, as with degradability and recyclability claims, the FTC takes the position that a scientific definition of "compostable" is not controlling. Rather, the question is whether consumers will get what they expect, and if a theoretically compostable/biodegradable/recyclable product is not practically so in the consumer's area, the FTC will consider the claim deceptive unless it is sufficiently qualified to make the risks clear. So, for example, if recycling facilities are available to at least 60% of consumers or communities where products are sold, marketers can make unqualified recyclability claims. But below that, the lower the level of access to appropriate facilities, the more a marketer should emphasize the limited availability of recycling for the product.]

Example 1: A manufacturer indicates that its unbleached coffee filter is compostable. The unqualified claim is not deceptive, provided the manufacturer has substantiation that the filter can be converted safely to usable compost in a timely manner in a home compost pile or device. If so, the extent of local municipal or institutional composting facilities is irrelevant. . . .

Example 4: Nationally marketed lawn and leaf bags state "compostable" on each bag. The bags also feature text disclosing that the bag is not designed for use in home compost piles. Yard trimmings programs in many communities compost these bags, but such programs are not available to a substantial majority of consumers or communities where the bag is sold. The claim is deceptive because it likely conveys that composting facilities are available to a substantial majority of consumers or communities. To avoid deception, the marketer should clearly and prominently indicate the limited availability of such programs. A marketer could state "Appropriate facilities may not exist in your area," or provide the approximate percentage of communities or consumers for which such programs are available. . . .

§ 260.8 Degradable Claims.

. . . (c) It is deceptive to make an unqualified degradable claim for items entering the solid waste stream if the items do not completely decompose within one year after customary disposal. Unqualified degradable claims for items that are customarily disposed in landfills, incinerators, and recycling facilities are deceptive because these locations do not present conditions in which complete decomposition will occur within one year . . .

NOTES AND QUESTIONS

Are the Guides specific enough to provide useful rules for marketers? Are they consistent with the First Amendment? (Compare the limits on the FDA imposed by *Pearson* and subsequent cases.)

The FTC continues to engage in enforcement actions related to the Green Guides. Problematic claims often travel together. For example, *In re Down to Earth Designs, Inc.*, FTC File No. 122 3268 (settlement order, Jan. 17, 2014), involved biodegradability, compostability and other environmental claims.

Among the problems: The biodegradability claims violated the FTC Act because the advertiser couldn't substantiate that the products would completely break down and decompose into elements found in nature within one year after customary disposal in the trash; it was misleading to claim products would offer an environmental benefit when flushed; it was misleading to claim that diaper liners and wipes were compostable when they couldn't be composted if they were soiled with solid human waste; and it was misleading to advertise the diapers as plastic-free because one component of the system included plastic.

However, an ALJ rejected the FTC's position on "biodegradable" claims in the Guides. The ALJ found that the consumer meaning survey relied on by the FTC was too poorly designed to support the FTC's interpretation that an unqualified "biodegradable" claim meant that the product would "completely decompose within one year after customary disposal," which in most cases meant landfill disposal. Nonetheless, even the more reasonable interpretation that the products would biodegrade in a period between nine months and five years after customary disposal was unsubstantiated. FTC v. ECM BioFilms, No. 9358 (Jan. 28, 2015).

How should advertisers proceed when the truth of the matter is uncertain? In 1988, the National Association of Diaper Services ("NADS") commissioned a study that concluded that disposable diapers significantly contribute to America's solid waste output, which some called a crisis. The disposable diaper industry responded with its own life-cycle analyses concluding that the effects were mixed, but that the evidence arguably favored disposable diapers, given factors such as the energy required to heat water to clean cloth diapers. NADS then commissioned another study, which found that cloth diapers, when laundered by a diaper service, were better for the environment than disposables, though that study omitted the energy use and environmental impact of transporting the diapers to consumers. The different studies used completely incompatible assumptions about how many diaper users of each kind flushed fecal matter before disposal, so that the disposable-funded study concluded that cloth services used more than four times as much water as the NADS study concluded they did. One disposable maker's study found that cloth diaper usage consumed three times more energy than disposable usage, while the NADS study found that disposables used 70% more energy than cloth. The divergence came in part from the disposable-funded study counting co-generation (simultaneously generating electricity and usable heat) as an environmental benefit, while the cloth-funded study assumed that co-generation caused pollution.

What kind of claims could cloth diaper services make under the Green Guides? What kind of claims could disposable diaper manufacturers make? If they should both be allowed to make environmental claims, is that a strength or a weakness of the Guides? *See* John M. Church, *A Market Solution to Green Marketing: Some Lessons from the Economics of Information*, 79 MINN. L. REV. 245 (1994) (arguing that, in the absence of scientific consensus on measuring environmental impacts, consumer confusion and distrust of marketers' environmental claims indicates that the market for information is functioning efficiently).

Remaining State Regulations. Because the FTC took a while to act, states enacted a patchwork of regulations. California, New York and Rhode Island defined many terms also covered by the Green Guides. California enacted a qualified ban on generic terms such as "ecologically safe," "earth friendly" and "green," while Rhode Island banned certain terms such as "biodegradable" and "environmentally safe" outright. California prohibits representing a product as recyclable unless it can be "conveniently recycled" in every county with a population over 300,000. Some states, including California, make compliance with FTC rules a defense, but not all do (and the Green Guides might not count as "rules"). In states that adopted the FTC Guides as state law, such as Indiana and Wisconsin, the Guides have independent force, which they do not under federal law because they are merely interpretations of Section 5 of the FTCA. *See* E. Howard Barnett, *Green with Envy: The FTC, the EPA, the States, and the Regulation of Environmental Marketing*, 1 ENVTL. LAW. 491 (1995).

International Trade Barriers to Regulation of Green Marketing. NAFTA and GATT prohibit "technical barriers to trade." Labeling requirements and other regulations that make it difficult or impossible for importers to market their products may be invalidated by WTO panels if insufficiently justified. In a potentially unsettling development for those in favor of greener production processes, the U.S. ban on importing tuna whose producers engaged in processes deemed unsafe for dolphins was found to violate GATT. *See* United States—Restrictions on Import of Tuna, GATT DOC. DS21/R (Sept. 1991); *see generally* Douglas A. Kysar, *Preferences for Processes: The Process–Product Distinction and the Regulation of Consumer Choice*, 118 HARV. L. REV. 525 (2004). In what circumstances are U.S. advertising regulations justified, even if that keeps certain products out of the country?

The NAD and Environmental Claims. The NAD has devoted substantial attention to green claims. It has followed the lead of the FTC in disapproving general environmental benefit claims. In *Panasonic Corporation of North America*, NAD Case #4697 (7/16/2007), for example, claims for large-screen plasma televisions included: "Panasonic Plasmas are environmentally friendly. No lead. No mercury. No worries. Most LCD TVs have mercury." The NAD recommended discontinuing the general "environmentally friendly" claim, because large-screen plasma TVs consume large amounts of power, more than comparably sized LCDs, though the advertiser remained free to tout the absence of lead or mercury.

In *Seventh Generation, Inc.*, NAD Case #4488 (5/8/2006), by contrast, the NAD held that the claim that Seventh Generation cleaning products are "as gentle on the planet as they are on people" was puffery.

In *Tom's of Maine*, NAD Case # 3470 (6/1/1998), the label of Tom's of Maine Natural Mouthwash stated that it was "pure and natural" and contained "pure, simple ingredients from nature." But the product contained a polymer not sourced from nature, and thus the NAD held the advertising needed to be modified to avoid any claim, direct or by implication, that the product was 100% natural.

The Lanham Act and Environmental Claims. Static Control Components, Inc. v. Lexmark International, Inc., 487 F. Supp. 2d 861 (E.D. Ky. 2007), concerned Lexmark's sale of refillable printer toner cartridges. Lexmark didn't remanufacture all the cartridges or parts it collected. Hundreds of thousands of cartridges were incinerated, with their ash going to a landfill, which Lexmark called "thermally recycling."

Lexmark's prebate cartridges had a label about Lexmark's "Environmental Program:" "We manage resources today to ensure a beautiful tomorrow. Small steps can have big rewards. Thank you for your ongoing support, together we have recycled millions of toner cartridges, one cartridge at a time. See details inside about how you can continue to participate in this important environmental initiative." Lexmark's website claimed, "Return Prebate cartridges are a great choice for the environment." It further stated: "Lexmark Return Prebate Program Cartridges are sold at a discount in exchange for the customer's agreement to use the cartridge only once and return it only to Lexmark for remanufacturing or recycling," and that "Lexmark recycles Return Program Cartridges, keeping them out of the waste stream."

Lexmark conducted market research among people responsible for purchasing printers and physically replacing used cartridges with new or remanufactured cartridges. Responses to the "environmentally friendly message" included:

> The green environmental label gives you a better conscience.

> You want it to be green. You don't want this stuff out in the street. You want it to be recycled; you want it to be treated properly.

Focus groups asked to create their own names for the prebate program suggested names such as "Save the Toner Tree," "Responsible Use of Resources," "Environmental Express (so that people get the impression that it speeds up the process)," "Envirosave," and "Save $ and the Environment."

The court denied summary judgment on a competitor's false advertising claims. Statements such as "Lexmark recycles Return Program Cartridges, keeping them out of the waste stream" were unambiguous, but the court found that there were significant disputed facts about whether "thermal recycling" could count as recycling under certain definitions.

What would have been the result under the Green Guides as set forth above? Who should have the burden of showing whether consumers subscribe to the definitions Lexmark wanted to use?

CPSIA information can be obtained
at www.ICGtesting.com
Printed in the USA
LVHW021747200122
708924LV00006B/511